Support the **student workflow**

With its engaging learning and assessment tools, including an enhanced MindTap Reader, CengageNOW for *Quantitative Methods for Business* helps you take students from motivation to mastery. For instructors, CengageNOW provides control and customization with the opportunity to tailor the learning experience to improve outcomes.

Elevate thinking

Relevant exercises, multimedia study tools --including enhanced highlighting, note taking, and flashcards in the MindTap Reader-- and unique assessment tools promote higher levels of thinking by taking students from basic knowledge and understanding, to evaluate, assess, and analyze.

Promote better outcomes

A variety of assignable content and an engaging reader experience couple to empower students to master concepts, prepare for exams, and get a better grade. Students have access to videos that walk them through select homework problems, encouraging persistence in problem solving. Instructor gradebook and reporting options allow you to keep a pulse on where your students are struggling most.

Easily set your course

Craft your course and assignment setup to meet your desired outcomes. Flexible course organization and assignment options allow you to design your course to follow your teaching pedagogy and track student progress all from one intuitive program, while students can easily set study habits that work for them with enhancements to their reader experience.

Quantitative Methods
for Business 13e

David R. Anderson
University of Cincinnati

Dennis J. Sweeney
University of Cincinnati

Thomas A. Williams
**Rochester Institute
of Technology**

Jeffrey D. Camm
University of Cincinnati

James J. Cochran
University of Alabama

Michael J. Fry
University of Cincinnati

Jeffrey W. Ohlmann
University of Iowa

CENGAGE
Learning

Australia • Brazil • Japan • Korea • Mexico • Singapore • Spain • United Kingdom • United States

Quantitative Methods for Business,
Thirteenth Edition

David R. Anderson, Dennis J. Sweeney,
Thomas A. Williams, Jeffrey D. Camm,
James J. Cochran, Michael J. Fry, Jeffrey
W. Ohlmann

Vice President, General Manager,
  Science, Math, & Quantitative
  Business: Balraj Kalsi

Product Director: Joe Sabatino

Sr. Product Manager: Aaron Arnsparger

Sr. Content Developer: Maggie Kubale

Sr. Product Assistant: Brad Sullender

Marketing Manager: Heather Mooney

Sr. Marketing Coordinator: Eileen
  Corcoran

Content Project Manager: Jana Lewis

Media Developer: Chris Valentine

Manufacturing Planner: Ron Montgomery

Production Service: MPS Limited

Sr. Art Director: Stacy Shirley

Internal Designer: Michael Stratton/
  cmiller design

Cover Designer: Beckmeyer Design

Cover Image: iStockphoto.com/alienforce

Intellectual Property

  Analyst: Christina Ciaramella

  Project Manager: Betsy Hathaway

For product information and technology assistance, contact us at
Cengage Learning Customer & Sales Support, 1-800-354-9706

For permission to use material from this text or product,
submit all requests online at **www.cengage.com/permissions**
Further permissions questions can be emailed to
permissionrequest@cengage.com

Unless otherwise noted, figures and tables © Cengage Learning.

Library of Congress Control Number: 2014957045

ISBN: 978-1-285-86631-4

Cengage Learning
20 Channel Center Street
Boston, MA 02210
USA

Cengage Learning is a leading provider of customized learning
solutions with office locations around the globe, including
Singapore, the United Kingdom, Australia, Mexico, Brazil, and
Japan. Locate your local office at: **www.cengage.com/global**

Cengage Learning products are represented in Canada by
Nelson Education, Ltd.

To learn more about Cengage Learning Solutions, visit
www.cengage.com

Purchase any of our products at your local college store or at our
preferred online store **www.cengagebrain.com**

Printed in the United States of America
Print Number: 01   Print Year: 2015

To My Children
Krista, Justin, Mark, and Colleen
DRA

To My Children
Mark, Linda, Brad, Tim, Scott, and Lisa
DJS

To My Children
Cathy, David, and Kristin
TAW

To My Family
Karen, Jennifer, Stephanie, and Allison
JDC

To My Wife
Teresa
JJC

To My Family
Nicole and Ian
MJF

To My Family
Amie and Willa
JWO

Brief Contents

Contents

Chapter 15 Waiting Line Models 680

Preface

The purpose of this thirteenth edition, as with previous editions, is to provide undergraduate and graduate students with a conceptual understanding of the role that quantitative methods play in the decision-making process. The text describes the many quantitative methods developed over the years, explains how they work, and shows how the decision maker can apply and interpret them.

This book is applications-oriented and uses our problem scenario approach to gently introduce quantitative material. In each chapter, a problem is described in conjunction with the quantitative procedure being introduced. Development of the quantitative technique or model includes applying it to the problem to generate a solution or recommendation. This approach can help to motivate the student by demonstrating not only how the procedure works, but also how it contributes to the decision-making process.

The mathematical prerequisite for this text is an algebra course. The two chapters on probability and probability distributions will provide the necessary background for the use of probability in subsequent chapters. Throughout the text we use generally accepted notation for the topic being covered. As a result, students who pursue study beyond the level of this text will generally experience little difficulty reading more advanced material. To also assist in further study, a bibliography is included at the end of this book.

CHANGES IN THE THIRTEENTH EDITION

We are very excited about the changes in the thirteenth edition of *Quantitative Methods for Business*, and want to tell you about some of the changes we have made and why.

Updated Chapter 16: Simulation

The most substantial content change in this latest edition involves the coverage of simulation. We maintain an intuitive introduction by continuing to use the concepts of best-, worst-, and base-case scenarios, but we have added a more elaborate treatment of uncertainty by using Microsoft Excel to develop spreadsheet simulation models. Within the chapter, we explain how to construct a spreadsheet simulation model using only native Excel functionality. In the chapter appendix, we describe how an Excel add-in, Analytic Solver Platform, facilitates more sophisticated simulation analyses. This new appendix on Analytic Solver Platform replaces the previous edition's coverage of Crystal Ball, which we no longer pair with our textbook. Nine new problems are introduced, and several others have been updated to reflect the new simulation coverage.

Other Content Changes

A variety of other changes have been made throughout the text in response to user suggestions. The most prominent of these include a new section on variability in project management in Chapter 13, new Appendix A coverage of data tables and Goal Seek functionality in Excel 2013, and adjustment of forecasting notation in Chapter 6. The software previously used to create decision trees in the Chapter 4 appendix, TreePlan, has now been incorporated into the Excel add-in Analytic Solver Platform, and we have updated Chapter 4 accordingly.

New Q.M. in Action, Cases, and Problems

Q.M. in Action is the name of the short summaries that describe how the quantitative methods being covered in the chapter have been used in practice. In this edition, you will find numerous Q.M. in Action vignettes, cases, and homework problems. We have updated many of these Q.M. in Actions to provide more recent examples. In all, we have added 15 new Q.M. in Actions.

The end of each chapter of this book contains cases for students. The cases are more in-depth and often more open-ended than the end-of-chapter homework problems. We have added three new cases to this edition: one on linear programming applications in Chapter 9, one on distribution and network models in Chapter 10, and one on integer programming in Chapter 11. Solutions to all cases are available to instructors.

We have added more than 35 new homework problems to this edition. Many other homework problems have been updated to provide more timely references.

FEATURES AND PEDAGOGY

We continued many of the features that appeared in previous editions. Some of the important ones are noted here.

- Annotations: Annotations that highlight key points and provide additional insights for the student are a continuing feature of this edition. These annotations, which appear in the margins, are designed to provide emphasis and enhance understanding of the terms and concepts presented in the text.
- Notes and Comments: We provide Notes and Comments at the end of many sections to give the student additional insights about the methodology being discussed and its application. These insights include warnings about or limitations of the methodology, recommendations for application, brief descriptions of additional technical considerations, and other matters.
- Self-Test Exercises: Certain exercises are identified as self-test exercises. Completely worked-out solutions for these exercises are provided in Appendix G, entitled Self-Test Solutions and Answers to Even-Numbered Problems, located at the end of the book. Students can attempt the self-test problems and immediately check the solutions to evaluate their understanding of the concepts presented in the chapter. At the request of professors using our textbooks, we now provide the answers to even-numbered problems in this same appendix.
- Q.M. in Action: These articles are presented throughout the text and provide a summary of an application of quantitative methods found in business today. Adaptations of materials from the popular press, academic journals such as *Interfaces*, and write-ups provided by practitioners provide the basis for the applications in this feature.

ANCILLARY LEARNING AND TEACHING MATERIALS

For Students

Print and online resources are available to help the student work more efficiently as well as learn how to use Excel.

- LINGO: The student version of LINGO 14.0 software is available for download at no additional cost to students who purchase a new text, through a link on the student companion site.

- Analytic Solver Platform: An educational version of the latest version of the Analytic Solver Platform software is available at no cost with a new text.

For Instructors

Instructor ancillaries are now provided on the website. Included in this convenient format are the following:

- Solutions Manual: The Solutions Manual, prepared by the authors, includes solutions for all problems in the text.
- Solutions to Case Problems: Also prepared by the authors, it contains solutions to all case problems presented in the text.
- PowerPoint Presentation Slides: Prepared by John Loucks of St. Edwards University, the presentation slides contain a teaching outline that incorporates graphics to help instructors create even more stimulating lectures. The slides may be adapted using PowerPoint software to facilitate classroom use.
- Test Bank: Also prepared by John Loucks, the Test Bank in Microsoft Word files includes multiple choice, true/false, short-answer questions, and problems for each chapter.

Cengage Learning Testing Powered by Cognero is a flexible, online system that allows you to:

- author, edit, and manage test bank content from multiple Cengage Learning solutions
- create multiple test versions in an instant
- deliver tests from your LMS, your classroom, or wherever you want

COURSE OUTLINE FLEXIBILITY

The text provides instructors with substantial flexibility in selecting topics to meet specific course needs. Although many variations are possible, the single-semester and single-quarter outlines that follow are illustrative of the options available.

Suggested One-Semester Course Outline
> Introduction (Chapter 1)
> Probability Concepts (Chapters 2 and 3)
> Decision Analysis (Chapters 4 and 5)
> Forecasting (Chapter 6)
> Linear Programming (Chapters 7, 8, and 9)
> Distribution and Network Models (Chapter 10)
> Integer Linear Programming (Chapter 11)
> Advanced Optimization Applications (Chapter 12)
> Project Scheduling: PERT/CPM (Chapter 13)
> Simulation (Chapter 15)

Suggested One-Quarter Course Outline
> Introduction (Chapter 1)
> Decision Analysis (Chapters 4 and 5)
> Linear Programming (Chapters 7, 8, and 9)
> Distribution and Network Models (Chapter 10)
> Integer Linear Programming (Chapter 11)

> Advanced Optimization Applications (Chapter 12)
> Project Scheduling: PERT/CPM (Chapter 13)
> Simulation (Chapter 15)

Many other possibilities exist for one-term courses, depending on the time available, course objectives, and backgrounds of the students.

ACKNOWLEDGMENTS

We were fortunate in having the thoughts and comments of a number of colleagues as we began work on this thirteenth edition of *Quantitative Methods for Business*. Our appreciation and thanks go to:

Larry Barchett
Ohio Valley University

Stacie A. Bosley
Hamline University

Gregory Chase
West Liberty University

Ali A. Choudry
Embry-Riddle University

Mary Fletcher
Mount Mary University

Edward Gordhammer
Embry-Riddle Aeronautical University

Wendy Keyes
California Baptist University

Kenneth Lawrence
New Jersey Institute of Technology

Holly S. Lutze
Texas Lutheran University

Penina Orenstein
Seton Hall University

Edward R. Sim
Hardin-Simmons University

Rahmat Tavallali
Walsh University

John S. Watters
McKendree University

Susan M. L. Zee
Southeastern Louisiana University

Writing and revising a textbook is a continuing process. We owe a debt to many of our colleagues and friends for their helpful comments and suggestions during the development of earlier editions. Among these are the following:

Ellen Parker Allen
Southern Methodist University

Gopesh Anand
The Ohio State University

Robert L. Armacost
University of Central Florida

Daniel Asera
University of Nevada, Las Vegas

Uttarayan Bagchi
University of Texas at Austin

Stephen Baglione
Saint Leo University

Ardith Baker
Oral Roberts University

Edward Baker
University of Miami

Norman Baker
University of Cincinnati

David Bakuli
Westfield State College

Robert T. Barrett
Francis Marion University

Oded Berman
University of Toronto

Gary Blau
Purdue University

William Bleuel
Pepperdine University

Richard G. Bradford
Avila University

Thomas Bundt
Hillsdale College

Heidi Burgiel
Bridgewater State College

Rodger D. Carlson
Morehead State University

Ying Chien
University of Scranton

Renato Clavijo
Robert Morris University

Ron Craig
Wilfrid Laurier University

Mary M. Danaher
Florida Atlantic University

Stanley Dick
Babson College

Swarna D. Dutt
State University of West Georgia

John Eatman
University of North
Carolina–Greensboro

Ronald Ebert
University of Missouri–
Columbia

Charlie Edmonson
University of Dayton

Don Edwards
University of South
Carolina

Ronald Ehresman
Baldwin-Wallace College

Peter Ellis
Utah State University

Lawrence Ettkin
University of Tennessee
at Chattanooga

James Evans
University of Cincinnati

Paul Ewell,
Bridgewater College

Ephrem Eyob
Virginia State University

Michael Ford
Rochester Institute of
Technology

Terri Friel
Eastern Kentucky
University

Phil Fry
Boise State University

Christian V. Fugar
Dillard University

Robert Garfinkel
University of Connecticut

Alfredo Gomez,
Florida Atlantic University

Bob Gregory
Bellevue University

Leland Gustafson
State University of
West Georgia

Joseph Haimowitz
Avila University

Nicholas G. Hall
The Ohio State University

Michael E. Hanna
University of Houston–
Clear Lake

John Hanson
University of San Diego

William V. Harper
Otterbein College

Melanie Hatch
Miami University

Harry G. Henderson
Davis & Elkins College

Carl H. Hess
Marymount University

Daniel G. Hotard
Southeastern Louisiana
University

David Hott
Florida Institute of
Technology

Woodrow W. Hughes
Jr., Converse College

Christine Irujo
Westfield State College

Barry Kadets
Bryant College

Birsen Karpak
Youngstown State
University

William C. Keller
Webb Institute of the
University of Phoenix

Christos Koulamas
Florida International
University

M. S. Krishnamoorthy
Alliant International
University

Melvin H. Kuhbander
Sullivan University

Anil Kukreja
Xavier University of
Louisiana

Alireza Lari
Fayetteville State
University

John Lawrence, Jr.
California State
University–Fullerton

Jodey Lingg
City University

John S. Loucks
St. Edwards University

Constantine Loucopoulos
Emporia State University

Donald R. MacRitchie
Framingham State College

Larry Maes
Davenport University

Ka-sing Man
Georgetown University

William G. Marchal
University of Toledo

Barbara J. Mardis
University of Northern Iowa

Kamlesh Mathur
Case Western Reserve
University

Joseph Mazzola
Duke University

Timothy McDaniel
Buena Vista University

Patrick McKeown
University of Georgia

Constance McLaren
Indiana State University

Mohammad Meybodi
Indiana University–
Kokomo

John R. Miller
Mercer University

Mario Miranda
The Ohio State University

Joe Moffitt
University of Massachusetts

Saeed Mohaghegh
Assumption College

Herbert Moskowitz
Purdue University

Shahriar Mostashari
Campbell University–
School of Business

Alan Neebe
University of North Carolina

V. R. Nemani
Trinity College

William C. O'Connor
University of Montana–
Western

Donald A. Ostasiewski
Thomas More College

David Pentico
Duquesne University

John E. Powell
University of South Dakota

B. Madhusudan Rao
Bowling Green State University

Handanhal V. Ravinder
University of New Mexico

Avuthu Rami Reddy
University of Wisconsin

Donna Retzlaff-Roberts
University of Memphis

Don R. Robinson
Illinois State University

Richard Rosenthal
Naval Postgraduate School

Kazim Ruhi
University of Maryland

Susan D. Sandblom
Scottsdale Community College

Tom Schmidt
Simpson College

Antoinette Somers
Wayne State University

Rajesh Srivastava
Florida Gulf Coast University

Donald E. Stout, Jr.
Saint Martin's College

Minghe Sun
University of Texas at San Antonio

Christopher S. Tang
University of California–
Los Angeles

Giri Kumar Tayi
State University of New York–Albany

Willban Terpening
Gonzaga University

Dothang Truong
Fayetteville State University

Vicente A. Vargas
University of San Diego

William Vasbinder
Becker College

Emre Veral
City University of New York–Baruch

Elizabeth J. Wark
Springfield College

John F. Wellington
Indiana University–Purdue University, Fort Wayne

Robert P. Wells
Becker College

Laura J. White
University of West Florida

Edward P. Winkofsky
University of Cincinnati

Cynthia Woodburn
Pittsburg State University

Neba L J Wu
Eastern Michigan University

Kefeng Xu
University of Texas at San Antonio

Mari Yetimyan
San Jose State University

Our associates from organizations who provided application write-ups made a major contribution to the text. These individuals are cited in a credit line on the associated Q.M. in Action.

We are also indebted to our product manager, Aaron Arnsparger; our marketing manager, Heather Mooney; our senior content developer, Maggie Kubale; our content project manager, Jana Lewis; our media editor, Chris Valentine; and others at Cengage Learning for their counsel and support during the preparation of this text.

David R. Anderson
Dennis J. Sweeney
Thomas A. Williams
Jeffrey D. Camm
James J. Cochran
Michael J. Fry
Jeffrey W. Ohlmann

CHAPTER 1

Introduction

CONTENTS

This book is concerned with the use of quantitative methods to assist in decision making. It emphasizes not the methods themselves, but rather how they can contribute to better decisions. A variety of names exists for the body of knowledge involving quantitative approaches to decision making. Today, the terms most commonly used—*management science* (MS), *operations research* (OR), *decision science*, and *business analytics*—are often used interchangeably.

The scientific management revolution of the early 1900s, initiated by Frederic W. Taylor, provided the foundation for the use of quantitative methods in management. However, modern research in the use of quantitative methods in decision making, for the most part, originated during the World War II period. At that time, teams of people with diverse specialties (e.g., mathematicians, engineers, and behavioral scientists) were formed to deal with strategic and tactical problems faced by the military. After the war, many of these team members continued their research into quantitative approaches to decision making.

Two developments that occurred during the post–World War II period led to the growth and use of quantitative methods in nonmilitary applications. First, continued research resulted in numerous methodological developments. Arguably the most notable of these developments was the discovery by George Dantzig, in 1947, of the simplex method for solving linear programming problems. At the same time these methodological developments were taking place, digital computers prompted a virtual explosion in computing power. Computers enabled practitioners to use the methodological advances to solve a large variety of problems. The computer technology explosion continues, and personal computers can now be used to solve problems larger than those solved on mainframe computers in the 1990s.

To reinforce the applied nature of the text and to provide a better understanding of the variety of applications in which *quantitative methods* (Q.M.) have been used successfully, Q.M. in Action articles are presented throughout the text. Each Q.M. in Action article summarizes an application of quantitative methods in practice. The first Q.M. in Action, Revenue Management at AT&T Park, describes one of the most important applications of quantitative methods in the sports and entertainment industry.

Q.M. *in* ACTION

REVENUE MANAGEMENT AT AT&T PARK*

Imagine the difficult position Russ Stanley, Vice President of Ticket Services for the San Francisco Giants, found himself facing late in the 2010 baseball season. Prior to the season, his organization had adopted a dynamic approach to pricing its tickets similar to the model successfully pioneered by Thomas M. Cook and his operations research group at American Airlines. Stanley desparately wanted the Giants to clinch a playoff birth, but he didn't want the team to do so *too quickly*.

When dynamically pricing a good or service, an organization regularly reviews supply and demand of the

*Based on Peter Horner, "The Sabre Story," *OR/MS Today* (June 2000); Ken Belson, "Baseball Tickets Too Much? Check Back Tomorrow," *New York Times.com* (May 18, 2009); and Rob Gloster, "Giants Quadruple Price of Cheap Seats as Playoffs Drive Demand," *Bloomberg Businessweek* (September 30, 2010).

product and uses operations research to determine if the price should be changed to reflect these conditions. As the scheduled takeoff date for a flight nears, the cost of a ticket increases if seats for the flight are relatively scarce. On the other hand, the airline discounts tickets for an approaching flight with relatively few ticketed passengers. Through the use of optimization to dynamically set ticket prices, American Airlines generates nearly $1 billion annually in incremental revenue.

The management team of the San Francisco Giants recognized similarities between their primary product (tickets to home games) and the primary product sold by airlines (tickets for flights) and adopted a similar revenue management system. If a particular Giants' game is appealing to fans, tickets sell quickly and demand far

(*continued*)

exceeds supply as the date of the game approaches; under these conditions fans will be willing to pay more and the Giants charge a premium for the ticket. Similarly, tickets for less attractive games are discounted to reflect relatively low demand by fans. This is why Stanley found himself in a quandary at the end of the 2010 baseball season. The Giants were in the middle of a tight pennant race with the San Diego Padres that effectively increased demand for tickets to Giants' games, and the team was actually scheduled to play the Padres in San Fransisco for the last three games of the season. While Stanley certainly wanted his club to win its division and reach the Major League Baseball playoffs, he also recognized that his team's revenues would be greatly enhanced if it didn't qualify for the playoffs until the last day of the season. "I guess financially it is better to go all the way down to the last game," Stanley said in a late season interview. "Our hearts are in our stomachs; we're pacing watching these games."

Does revenue management and operations research work? Today, virtually every airline uses some sort of revenue-management system, and the cruise, hotel, and car rental industries also now apply revenue-management methods. As for the Giants, Stanley said dynamic pricing provided a 7 to 8% increase in revenue per seat for Giants' home games during the 2010 season. Coincidentally, the Giants did win the National League West division on the last day of the season and ultimately won the World Series. Several professional sports franchises are now looking to the Giants' example and considering implementation of similar dynamic ticket-pricing systems.

1.1 Problem Solving and Decision Making

Problem solving can be defined as the process of identifying a difference between the actual and the desired state of affairs and then taking action to resolve this difference. For problems important enough to justify the time and effort of careful analysis, the problem-solving process involves the following seven steps:

1. Identify and define the problem.
2. Determine the set of alternative solutions.
3. Determine the criterion or criteria that will be used to evaluate the alternatives.
4. Evaluate the alternatives.
5. Choose an alternative.
6. Implement the selected alternative.
7. Evaluate the results to determine whether a satisfactory solution has been obtained.

Decision making is the term generally associated with the first five steps of the problem-solving process. Thus, the first step of decision making is to identify and define the problem. Decision making ends with the choosing of an alternative, which is the act of making the decision.

Let us consider the following example of the decision-making process. For the moment, assume you are currently unemployed and that you would like a position that will lead to a satisfying career. Suppose your job search results in offers from companies in Rochester, New York; Dallas, Texas; Greensboro, North Carolina; and Pittsburgh, Pennsylvania. Further suppose that it is unrealistic for you to decline all of these offers. Thus, the alternatives for your decision problem can be stated as follows:

1. Accept the position in Rochester.
2. Accept the position in Dallas.
3. Accept the position in Greensboro.
4. Accept the position in Pittsburgh.

The next step of the problem-solving process involves determining the criteria that will be used to evaluate the four alternatives. Obviously, the starting salary is a factor of some importance. If salary were the only criterion important to you, the alternative selected as "best" would be the one with the highest starting salary. Problems in which the objective is to find the best solution with respect to one criterion are referred to as **single-criterion decision problems**.

Suppose that you also conclude that the potential for advancement and the location of the job are two other criteria of major importance. Thus, the three criteria in your decision problem are starting salary, potential for advancement, and location. Problems that involve more than one criterion are referred to as **multicriteria decision problems**.

The next step of the decision-making process is to evaluate each of the alternatives with respect to each criterion. For example, evaluating each alternative relative to the starting salary criterion is done simply by recording the starting salary for each job alternative. However, evaluating each alternative with respect to the potential for advancement and the location of the job is more difficult because these evaluations are based primarily on subjective factors that are often difficult to quantify. Suppose for now that you decide to measure potential for advancement and job location by rating each of these criteria as poor, fair, average, good, or excellent. The data you compile are shown in Table 1.1.

You are now ready to make a choice from the available alternatives. What makes this choice phase so difficult is that the criteria are probably not all equally important, and no one alternative is "best" with regard to all criteria. When faced with a multicriteria decision problem, the third step in the decision-making process often includes an assessment of the relative importance of the criteria. Although we will present a method for dealing with situations like this one later in the text, for now let us suppose that after a careful evaluation of the data in Table 1.1, you decide to select alternative 3. Alternative 3 is thus referred to as the **decision**.

At this point in time, the decision-making process is complete. In summary, we see that this process involves five steps:

1. Define the problem.
2. Identify the alternatives.
3. Determine the criteria.
4. Evaluate the alternatives.
5. Choose an alternative.

Note that missing from this list are the last two steps in the problem-solving process: implementing the selected alternative and evaluating the results to determine whether a satisfactory solution has been obtained. This omission is not meant to diminish the importance

TABLE 1.1   DATA FOR THE JOB EVALUATION DECISION-MAKING PROBLEM

Alternative	Starting Salary	Potential for Advancement	Job Location
1. Rochester	$48,500	Average	Average
2. Dallas	$46,000	Excellent	Good
3. Greensboro	$46,000	Good	Excellent
4. Pittsburgh	$47,000	Average	Good

FIGURE 1.1   THE RELATIONSHIP BETWEEN PROBLEM SOLVING AND DECISION
MAKING

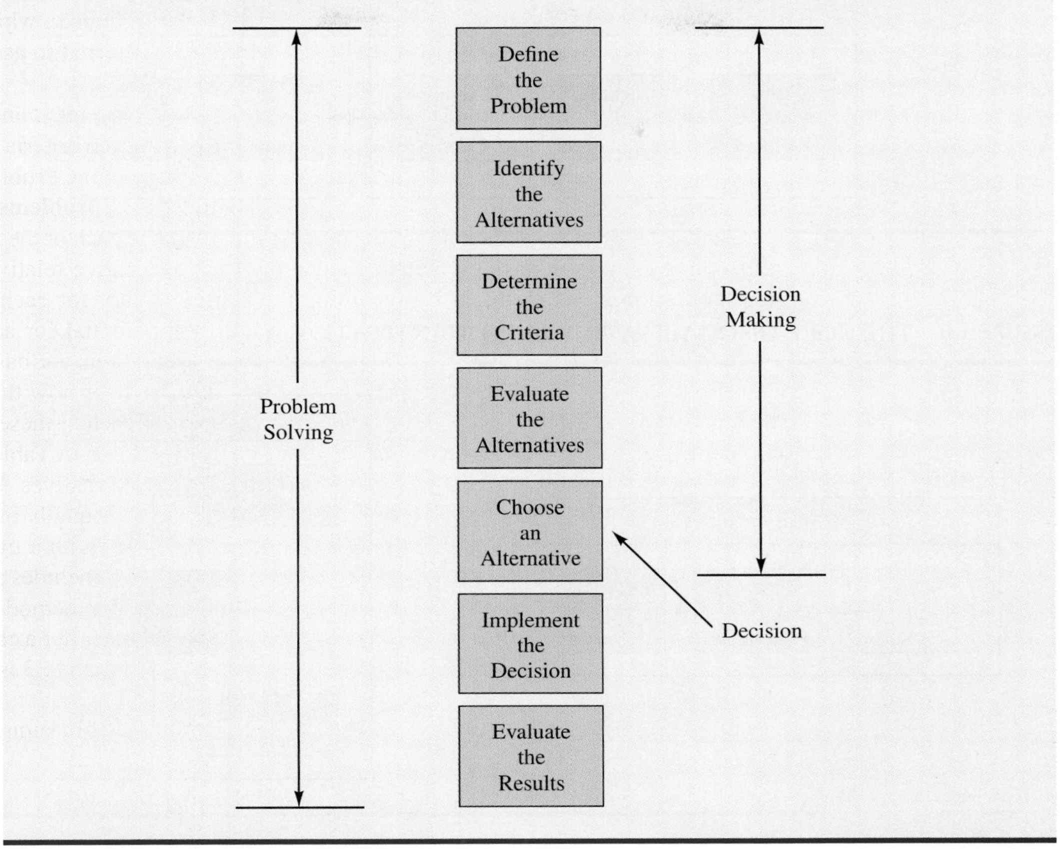

of each of these activities, but to emphasize the more limited scope of the term *decision
making* as compared to the term *problem solving*. Figure 1.1 summarizes the relationship
between these two concepts.

1.2 Quantitative Analysis and Decision Making

Consider the flowchart presented in Figure 1.2. Note that we combined the first three steps
of the decision-making process under the heading of "Structuring the Problem" and the
latter two steps under the heading "Analyzing the Problem." Let us now consider in greater
detail how to carry out the activities that make up the decision-making process.

Figure 1.3 shows that the analysis phase of the decision-making process may take two
basic forms: qualitative and quantitative. Qualitative analysis is based primarily on the manager's judgment and experience; it includes the manager's intuitive "feel" for the problem and
is more an art than a science. If the manager has had experience with similar problems, or
if the problem is relatively simple, heavy emphasis may be placed upon a qualitative analysis.
However, if the manager has had little experience with similar problems, or if the problem

FIGURE 1.2   A SUBCLASSIFICATION OF THE DECISION-MAKING PROCESS

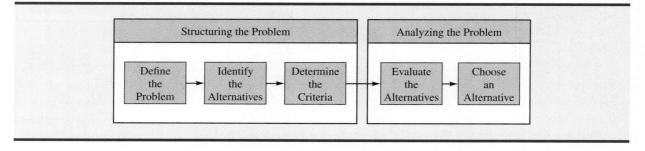

FIGURE 1.3   THE ROLE OF QUALITATIVE AND QUANTITATIVE ANALYSIS

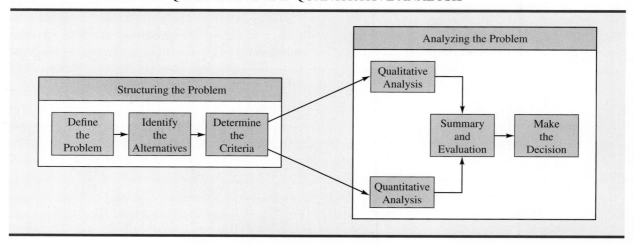

Quantitative methods are especially helpful with large, complex problems. For example, in the coordination of the thousands of tasks associated with landing the Apollo 11 safely on the moon, quantitative techniques helped to ensure that more than 300,000 pieces of work performed by more than 400,000 people were integrated smoothly.

is sufficiently complex, then a quantitative analysis of the problem can be an especially important consideration in the manager's final decision.

When using a quantitative approach, an analyst will concentrate on the quantitative facts or data associated with the problem and develop mathematical expressions that describe the objectives, constraints, and other relationships that exist in the problem. Then, by using one or more mathematical methods, the analyst will make a recommendation based on the quantitative aspects of the problem.

Although skills in the qualitative approach are inherent in the manager and usually increase with experience, the skills of the quantitative approach can be learned only by studying the assumptions and methods of management science. A manager can increase decision-making effectiveness by learning more about quantitative methodology and by better understanding its contribution to the decision-making process. A manager who is knowledgeable in quantitative decision-making procedures is in a much better position to compare and evaluate the qualitative and quantitative sources of recommendations and ultimately to combine the two sources to make the best possible decision.

The box in Figure 1.3 entitled "Quantitative Analysis" encompasses most of the subject matter of this text. We will consider a managerial problem, introduce the appropriate quantitative methodology, and then develop the recommended decision.

Some of the reasons why a quantitative approach might be used in the decision-making process include the following:

1. The problem is complex, and the manager cannot develop a good solution without the aid of quantitative analysis.
2. The problem is critical (e.g., a great deal of money is involved), and the manager desires a thorough analysis before making a decision.
3. The problem is new, and the manager has no previous experience from which to draw.
4. The problem is repetitive, and the manager saves time and effort by relying on quantitative procedures to automate routine decision recommendations.

(1.3) Quantitative Analysis

From Figure 1.3 we see that quantitative analysis begins once the problem has been structured. It usually takes imagination, teamwork, and considerable effort to transform a rather general problem description into a well-defined problem that can be approached via quantitative analysis. It is important to involve the stakeholders (the decision maker, users of results, etc.) in the process of structuring the problem to improve the likelihood that the ensuing quantitative analysis will make an important contribution to the decision-making process. When those familiar with the problem agree that it has been adequately structured, work can begin on developing a model to represent the problem mathematically. Solution procedures can then be employed to find the best solution for the model. This best solution for the model then becomes a recommendation to the decision maker. The process of developing and solving models is the essence of the quantitative analysis process.

Model Development

Models are representations of real objects or situations and can be presented in various forms. For example, a scale model of an airplane is a representation of a real airplane. Similarly, a child's toy truck is a model of a real truck. The model airplane and toy truck are examples of models that are physical replicas of real objects. In modeling terminology, physical replicas are referred to as **iconic models**.

A second classification includes models that are physical in form but do not have the same physical appearance as the object being modeled. Such models are referred to as **analog models**. The speedometer of an automobile is an analog model; the position of the needle on the dial represents the speed of the automobile. A thermometer is another analog model representing temperature.

A third classification of models—the type we will primarily be studying—includes representations of a problem by a system of symbols and mathematical relationships or expressions. Such models are referred to as **mathematical models** and are a critical part of any quantitative approach to decision making. For example, the total profit from the sale of a product can be determined by multiplying the profit per unit by the quantity sold. Let x represent the number of units produced and sold, and let P represent the total profit. With a profit of $10 per unit, the following mathematical model defines the total profit earned by producing and selling x units:

$$P = 10x \qquad \textbf{(1.1)}$$

The purpose, or value, of any model is that it enables us to make inferences about the real situation by studying and analyzing the model. For example, an airplane designer might test an iconic model of a new airplane in a wind tunnel to learn about the potential flying characteristics of the full-size airplane. Similarly, a mathematical model may be used to make inferences about how much profit will be earned if a specified quantity of a particular product is sold. According to the mathematical model of equation (1.1), we would expect that selling three units of the product ($x = 3$) would provide a profit of $P = 10(3) = \$30$.

In general, experimenting with models requires less time and is less expensive than experimenting with the real object or situation. One can certainly build and study a model airplane in less time and for less money than it would take to build and study the full-size airplane. Similarly, the mathematical model in equation (1.1) allows a quick identification of profit expectations without requiring the manager to actually produce and sell x units. Models also reduce the risks associated with experimenting with the real situation. In particular, bad designs or bad decisions that cause the model airplane to crash or the mathematical model to project a $\$10,000$ loss can be avoided in the real situation.

Herbert A. Simon, a Nobel Prize winner in economics and an expert in decision making, said that a mathematical model does not have to be exact; it just has to be close enough to provide better results than can be obtained by common sense.

The value of model-based conclusions and decisions depends on how well the model represents the real situation. The more closely the model airplane represents the real airplane, the more accurate will be the conclusions and predictions. Similarly, the more closely the mathematical model represents the company's true profit–volume relationship, the more accurate will be the profit projections.

Because this text deals with quantitative analysis based on mathematical models, let us look more closely at the mathematical modeling process. When initially considering a managerial problem, we usually find that the problem definition phase leads to a specific objective, such as maximization of profit or minimization of cost, and possibly a set of restrictions or **constraints**, which express limitations on resources. The success of the mathematical model and quantitative approach will depend heavily on how accurately the objective and constraints can be expressed in mathematical equations or relationships.

The mathematical expression that defines the quantity to be maximized or minimized is referred to as the **objective function**. For example, suppose x denotes the number of units produced and sold each week, and the firm's objective is to maximize total weekly profit. With a profit of $\$10$ per unit, the objective function is $10x$. A production capacity constraint would be necessary if, for instance, 5 hours are required to produce each unit and only 40 hours are available per week. The production capacity constraint is given by

$$5x \le 40 \qquad\qquad \textbf{(1.2)}$$

The value of $5x$ is the total time required to produce x units; the symbol $\le$ indicates that the production time required must be less than or equal to the 40 hours available.

The decision problem or question is the following: How many units of the product should be produced each week to maximize profit? A complete mathematical model for this simple production problem is

$$\text{Maximize} \quad 10x \quad \text{objective function}$$
$$\text{subject to (s.t.)}$$
$$\left.\begin{array}{l} 5x \le 40 \\ x \ge 0 \end{array}\right\} \text{constraints}$$

The $x \ge 0$ constraint requires the production quantity x to be greater than or equal to zero, which simply recognizes the fact that it is not possible to manufacture a negative number

FIGURE 1.4 FLOWCHART OF THE PROCESS OF TRANSFORMING MODEL INPUTS INTO OUTPUT

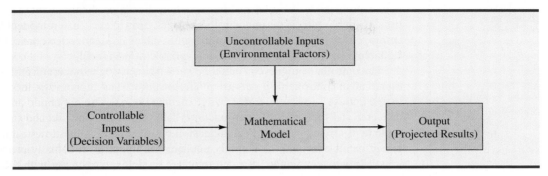

of units. The optimal solution to this simple model can be easily calculated and is given by $x = 8$, with an associated profit of $80. This model is an example of a linear programming model. In subsequent chapters we will discuss more complicated mathematical models and learn how to solve them in situations for which the answers are not nearly so obvious.

In the preceding mathematical model, the profit per unit ($10), the production time per unit (5 hours), and the production capacity (40 hours) are factors not under the control of the manager or decision maker. Such factors, which can affect both the objective function and the constraints, are referred to as **uncontrollable inputs** to the model. Inputs that are controlled or determined by the decision maker are referred to as **controllable inputs** to the model. In the example given, the production quantity x is the controllable input to the model. Controllable inputs are the decision alternatives specified by the manager and thus are also referred to as the **decision variables** of the model.

Once all controllable and uncontrollable inputs are specified, the objective function and constraints can be evaluated and the output of the model determined. In this sense, the output of the model is simply the projection of what would happen if those particular factors and decisions occurred in the real situation. A flowchart of how controllable and uncontrollable inputs are transformed by the mathematical model into output is shown in Figure 1.4. A similar flowchart showing the specific details for the production model is shown in Figure 1.5. Note that we have used "Max" as an abbreviation for maximize.

FIGURE 1.5 FLOWCHART FOR THE PRODUCTION MODEL

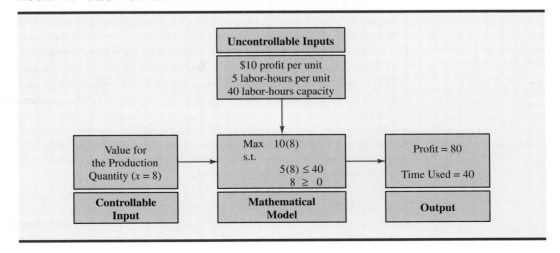

As stated earlier, the uncontrollable inputs are those the decision maker cannot influence. The specific controllable and uncontrollable inputs of a model depend on the particular problem or decision-making situation. In the production problem, the production time available (40) is an uncontrollable input. However, if it were possible to hire more employees or use overtime, the number of hours of production time would become a controllable input and therefore a decision variable in the model.

Uncontrollable inputs can either be known exactly or be uncertain and subject to variation. If all uncontrollable inputs to a model are known and cannot vary, the model is referred to as a **deterministic model**. Corporate income tax rates are not under the influence of the manager and thus constitute an uncontrollable input in many decision models. Because these rates are known and fixed (at least in the short run), a mathematical model with corporate income tax rates as the only uncontrollable input would be a deterministic model. The distinguishing feature of a deterministic model is that the uncontrollable input values are known in advance.

If any of the uncontrollable inputs are uncertain and subject to variation, the model is referred to as a **stochastic** or **probabilistic model**. An uncontrollable input in many production planning models is demand for the product. Because future demand may be any of a range of values, a mathematical model that treats demand with uncertainty would be considered a stochastic model. In the production model, the number of hours of production time required per unit, the total hours available, and the unit profit were all uncontrollable inputs. Because the uncontrollable inputs were all known to take on fixed values, the model was deterministic. If, however, the number of hours of production time per unit could vary from 3 to 6 hours depending on the quality of the raw material, the model would be stochastic. The distinguishing feature of a stochastic model is that the value of the output cannot be determined even if the value of the controllable input is known because the specific values of the uncontrollable inputs are unknown. In this respect, stochastic models are often more difficult to analyze.

Data Preparation

Another step in the quantitative analysis of a problem is the preparation of the data required by the model. Data in this sense refer to the values of the uncontrollable inputs to the model. All uncontrollable inputs or data must be specified before we can analyze the model and recommend a decision or solution for the problem.

In the production model, the values of the uncontrollable inputs or data were $10 per unit for profit, 5 hours per unit for production time, and 40 hours for production capacity. In the development of the model, these data values were known and incorporated into the model as it was being developed. If the model is relatively small with respect to the number of the uncontrollable input values, the quantitative analyst will probably combine model development and data preparation into one step. In these situations the data values are inserted as the equations of the mathematical model are developed.

However, in many mathematical modeling situations, the data or uncontrollable input values are not readily available. In these situations, the analyst may know that the model will require profit per unit, production time, and production capacity data, but the values will not be known until the accounting, production, and engineering departments can be consulted. Rather than attempting to collect the required data as the model is being developed, the analyst will usually adopt a general notation for the model development step, and a separate data preparation step will then be performed to obtain the uncontrollable input values required by the model.

Using the general notation

$$c = \text{profit per unit}$$
$$a = \text{production time in hours per unit}$$
$$b = \text{production capacity in hours}$$

the model development step for the production problem would result in the following general model (recall x = the number of units to produce and sell):

$$\text{Max } cx$$

s.t.

$$ax \leq b$$
$$x \geq 0$$

A separate data preparation step to identify the values for c, a, and b would then be necessary to complete the model.

Many inexperienced quantitative analysts assume that once the problem is defined and a general model developed, the problem is essentially solved. These individuals tend to believe that data preparation is a trivial step in the process and can be easily handled by clerical staff. Actually, this is a potentially dangerous assumption that could not be further from the truth, especially with large-scale models that have numerous data input values. For example, a moderate-sized linear programming model with 50 decision variables and 25 constraints could have more than 1300 data elements that must be identified in the data preparation step. The time required to collect and prepare these data and the possibility of data collection errors will make the data preparation step a critical part of the quantitative analysis process. Often, a fairly large database is needed to support a mathematical model, and information systems specialists also become involved in the data preparation step.

Model Solution

Once the model development and data preparation steps are completed, we proceed to the model solution step. In this step, the analyst attempts to identify the values of the decision variables that provide the "best" output for the model. The specific decision-variable value or values providing the "best" output are referred to as the **optimal solution** for the model. For the production problem, the model solution step involves finding the value of the production quantity decision variable x that maximizes profit while not causing a violation of the production capacity constraint.

One procedure that might be used in the model solution step involves a trial-and-error approach in which the model is used to test and evaluate various decision alternatives. In the production model, this procedure would mean testing and evaluating the model using various production quantities or values of x. As noted in Figure 1.5, we could input trial values for x and check the corresponding output for projected profit and satisfaction of the production capacity constraint. If a particular decision alternative does not satisfy one or more of the model constraints, the decision alternative is rejected as being **infeasible**, regardless of the corresponding objective function value. If all constraints are satisfied, the decision alternative is **feasible** and is a candidate for the "best" solution or recommended decision. Through this trial-and-error process of evaluating selected decision alternatives, a decision maker can identify a good—and possibly the best—feasible solution to the problem. This solution would then be the recommended decision for the problem.

TABLE 1.2 TRIAL-AND-ERROR SOLUTION FOR THE PRODUCTION MODEL OF FIGURE 1.5

Decision Alternative (Production Quantity) x	Projected Profit	Total Hours of Production	Feasible Solution? (Hours Used $\leq$ 40)
0	0	0	Yes
2	20	10	Yes
4	40	20	Yes
6	60	30	Yes
8	80	40	Yes
10	100	50	No
12	120	60	No

Table 1.2 shows the results of a trial-and-error approach to solving the production model of Figure 1.5. The recommended decision is a production quantity of 8 because the feasible solution with the highest projected profit occurs at $x = 8$.

Although the trial-and-error solution process is often acceptable and can provide valuable information for the manager, it has the drawbacks of not necessarily providing the best solution and of being inefficient in terms of requiring numerous calculations if many decision alternatives are considered. Thus, quantitative analysts have developed special solution procedures for many models that are much more efficient than the trial-and-error approach. Throughout this text, you will be introduced to solution procedures that are applicable to the specific mathematical models. Some relatively small models or problems can be solved by hand computations, but most practical applications require the use of a computer.

The model development and model solution steps are not completely separable. An analyst will want both to develop an accurate model or representation of the actual problem situation and to be able to find a solution to the model. If we approach the model development step by attempting to find the most accurate and realistic mathematical model, we may find the model so large and complex that it is impossible to obtain a solution. In this case, a simpler and perhaps more easily understood model with a readily available solution procedure is preferred even though the recommended solution may be only a rough approximation of the best decision. As you learn more about quantitative solution procedures, you will form a better understanding of the types of mathematical models that can be developed and solved.

Try Problem 8 to test your understanding of the concept of a mathematical model and what is referred to as the optimal solution to the model.

After obtaining a model solution, the quantitative analyst will be interested in determining the quality of the solution. Even though the analyst has undoubtedly taken many precautions to develop a realistic model, often the usefulness or accuracy of the model cannot be assessed until model solutions are generated. Model testing and validation are frequently conducted with relatively small "test" problems with known or at least expected solutions. If the model generates the expected solutions, and if other output information appears correct or reasonable, the go-ahead may be given to use the model on the full-scale problem. However, if the model test and validation identify potential problems or inaccuracies inherent in the model, corrective action, such as model modification or collection of more accurate input data, may be taken. Whatever the corrective action, the model solution will not be used in practice until the model satisfactorily passes testing and validation.

Report Generation

An important part of the quantitative analysis process is the preparation of managerial reports based on the model's solution. As indicated in Figure 1.3, the solution based on the quantitative analysis of a problem is one of the inputs the manager considers before making a final decision. Thus, the results of the model must appear in a managerial report that can be easily understood by the decision maker. The report includes the recommended decision and other pertinent information about the results that may be useful to the decision maker.

A Note Regarding Implementation

As discussed in Section 1.2, the manager is responsible for integrating the quantitative solution with qualitative considerations to determine the best possible decision. After completing the decision-making process, the manager must oversee the implementation and follow-up evaluation of the decision. During the implementation and follow-up, the manager should continue to monitor the performance of the model. At times, this process may lead to requests for model expansion or refinement that will require the quantitative analyst to return to an earlier step of the process.

Successful implementation of results is critical to any application of quantitative analysis. If the results of the quantitative analysis are not correctly implemented, the entire effort may be of no value. Because implementation often requires people to change the way they do things, it often meets with resistance. People may want to know, "What's wrong with the way we've been doing it?" One of the most effective ways to ensure successful implementation is to include users throughout the modeling process. A user who feels a part of identifying the problem and developing the solution is much more likely to enthusiastically implement the results, and the input the quantitative analyst receives from these users can substantially enhance the models being developed. The success rate for implementing the results of a quantitative analysis project is much greater for those projects characterized by extensive user involvement. The Q.M. in Action, Quantitative Analysis at Merrill Lynch, discusses some of the reasons for the success of quantitative analysis at Merrill Lynch.

Q.M. *in* ACTION

QUANTITATIVE ANALYSIS AT MERRILL LYNCH*

For over 25 years, the Management Science Group at Merrill Lynch has successfully implemented quantitative models for a wide variety of decision problems. The group has applied quantitative methods for portfolio optimization, asset allocation, financial planning, marketing analysis, credit and liquidity assessment, as well as developing pricing and compensation structures. Although technical expertise and objectivity are clearly important factors in any analytical group, the management science group attributes much of its success to communications skills, teamwork, professional development for its members, and consulting skills.

From the earliest discussion of a potential project, the group focuses on fully understanding the problem and its business impact. Each client is asked, "Whose life will this change?" and "By how much?" The answers to these questions help the group understand who really has responsibility for the project, the processes involved, and how recommendations will be implemented. Analysts assigned to a project are fully engaged from start to finish. They are involved in project scope definition, data collection, analysis, development of recommendations,

*Based on R. Nigam, "Structuring and Sustaining Excellence in Management Science at Merrill Lynch," *Interfaces* 38, no. 3 (May/June 2008): 202–209.

(continued)

and marketing those recommendations to the client. The group prides itself on technology transfer; that is, it gives any models it develops to the clients with assistance and training on the use of the models. This leads to longer-term impact through ongoing use of the model. Finally, like any good organization focused on improvement, the Management Science Group seeks feedback from clients after every project it completes.

This approach to problem solving and the implementation of quantitative analysis has been a hallmark of the Management Science Group. The impact and success of the group translates into hard dollars, repeat business, and recognition through a number of prestigious professional awards. The group received the annual Edelman Award given by the Institute for Operations Research and the Management Sciences (INFORMS) for effective use of management science for organizational success as well as the INFORMS Prize, given for long-term and high-impact use of quantitative methods within an organization.

NOTES AND COMMENTS

1. Developments in computer technology have increased the availability of quantitative methods to decision makers. A variety of software packages is now available for personal computers. Versions of Microsoft Excel and LINGO are widely used to apply quantitative methods to business problems. Various chapter appendixes provide step-by-step instructions for using Excel and LINGO to solve problems in the text.

1.4 Models of Cost, Revenue, and Profit

Some of the most basic quantitative models arising in business and economic applications involve the relationships among a volume variable—such as production volume or sales volume—and cost, revenue, and profit. Through the use of these models, a manager can determine the projected cost, revenue, or profit associated with a planned production quantity or a forecasted sales volume. Financial planning, production planning, sales quotas, and other areas of decision making can benefit from such cost, revenue, and profit models.

Cost and Volume Models

The cost of manufacturing or producing a product is a function of the volume produced. This cost can usually be defined as a sum of two costs: fixed cost and variable cost. **Fixed cost** is the portion of the total cost that does not depend on the production volume; this cost remains the same no matter how much is produced. **Variable cost**, on the other hand, is the portion of the total cost that depends on and varies with the production volume. To illustrate how cost and volume models can be developed, we will consider a manufacturing problem faced by Nowlin Plastics.

Nowlin Plastics produces a line of cell phone covers. Nowlin's best-selling cover is its Viper model, a slim but very durable black and gray plastic cover. Several products are produced on the same manufacturing line, and a setup cost is incurred each time a changeover is made for a new product. Suppose the setup cost for the Viper is $3000; this setup cost is a fixed cost and is incurred regardless of the number of units eventually produced. In addition, suppose that variable labor and material costs are $2 for each unit produced. The cost–volume model for producing x units of the Viper can be written as

$$C(x) = 3000 + 2x \qquad \textbf{(1.3)}$$

where

> x = production volume in units
>
> $C(x)$ = total cost of producing x units

Once a production volume is established, the model in equation (1.3) can be used to compute the total production cost. For example, the decision to produce x = 1200 units would result in a total cost of $C(1200) = 3000 + 2(1200) = \$5400$.

Marginal cost is defined as the rate of change of the total cost with respect to production volume; that is, the cost increase associated with a one-unit increase in the production volume. In the cost model of equation (1.3), we see that the total cost $C(x)$ will increase by \$2 for each unit increase in the production volume. Thus, the marginal cost is \$2. With more complex total cost models, marginal cost may depend on the production volume. In such cases, we could have marginal cost increasing or decreasing with the production volume x.

Revenue and Volume Models

Management of Nowlin Plastics will also want information about projected revenue associated with selling a specified number of units. Thus, a model of the relationship between revenue and volume is also needed. Suppose that each Viper cover sells for \$5. The model for total revenue can be written as

$$R(x) = 5x \qquad \textbf{(1.4)}$$

where

> x = sales volume in units
>
> $R(x)$ = total revenue associated with selling x units

Marginal revenue is defined as the rate of change of total revenue with respect to sales volume, that is, the increase in total revenue resulting from a one-unit increase in sales volume. In the model of equation (1.4), we see that the marginal revenue is \$5. In this case, marginal revenue is constant and does not vary with the sales volume. With more complex models, we may find that marginal revenue increases or decreases as the sales volume x increases.

Profit and Volume Models

One of the most important criteria for management decision making is profit. Managers need to know the profit implications of their decisions. If we assume that we will only produce what can be sold, the production volume and sales volume will be equal. We can then combine equations (1.3) and (1.4) to develop a profit–volume model that determines profit associated with a specified production-sales volume. Total profit is total revenue minus total cost; therefore, the following model provides the profit associated with producing and selling x units:

$$\begin{aligned} P(x) &= R(x) - C(x) \\ &= 5x - (3000 + 2x) = -3000 + 3x \end{aligned} \qquad \textbf{(1.5)}$$

Thus, the model for profit $P(x)$ can be derived from the models of the revenue–volume and cost–volume relationships.

Breakeven Analysis

Using equation (1.5), we can now determine the profit associated with any production volume x. For example, suppose that a demand forecast indicates that 500 units of the product can be sold. The decision to produce and sell the 500 units results in a projected profit of

$$P(500) = -3000 + 3(500) = -1500$$

In other words, a loss of $1500 is predicted. If sales are expected to be 500 units, the manager may decide against producing the product. However, a demand forecast of 1800 units would show a projected profit of

$$P(1800) = -3000 + 3(1800) = 2400$$

This profit may be sufficient to justify proceeding with the production and sale of the product.

We see that a volume of 500 units will yield a loss, whereas a volume of 1800 provides a profit. The volume that results in total revenue equaling total cost (providing $0 profit) is called the **breakeven point**. If the breakeven point is known, a manager can quickly infer that a volume above the breakeven point will generate a profit, whereas a volume below the breakeven point will result in a loss. Thus, the breakeven point for a product provides valuable information for a manager who must make a yes/no decision concerning production of the product.

Let us now return to the Nowlin Plastics example and show how the profit model in equation (1.5) can be used to compute the breakeven point. The breakeven point can be found by setting the profit expression equal to zero and solving for the production volume. Using equation (1.5), we have

$$P(x) = -3000 + 3x = 0$$
$$3x = 3000$$
$$x = 1000$$

Try Problem 12 to test your ability to determine the breakeven point for a quantitative model.

With this information, we know that production and sales of the product must exceed 1000 units before a profit can be expected. The graphs of the total cost model, the total revenue model, and the location of the breakeven point are shown in Figure 1.6. In Appendix A we discuss how Excel can be used to perform a breakeven analysis for the Nowlin Plastics production example.

FIGURE 1.6   GRAPH OF THE BREAKEVEN ANALYSIS FOR NOWLIN PLASTICS

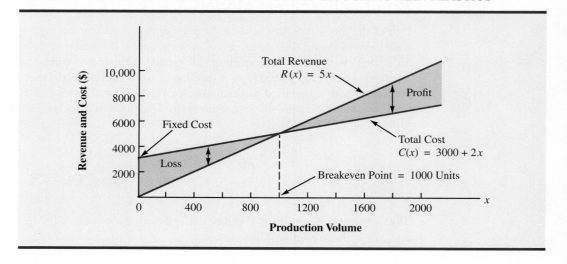

1.5 Quantitative Methods in Practice

In this section we present a brief overview of the quantitative methods covered in this text. There are numerous applications for each of the following methods.

Linear Programming Linear programming is a problem-solving approach developed for situations involving maximizing or minimizing a linear function subject to linear constraints that limit the degree to which the objective can be pursued. The production model developed in Section 1.3 (see Figure 1.5) is an example of a simple linear programming model.

Integer Linear Programming Integer linear programming is an approach used for problems that can be set up as linear programs with the additional requirement that some or all of the decision recommendations be integer values.

Project Scheduling: PERT/CPM In many situations managers are responsible for planning, scheduling, and controlling projects that consist of numerous separate jobs or tasks performed by a variety of departments, individuals, and so forth. PERT (Program Evaluation and Review Technique) and CPM (Critical Path Method) help managers carry out their project scheduling and tracking responsibilities.

Inventory Models Inventory models are used by managers faced with the problem of maintaining sufficient inventories to meet demand for goods while incurring the lowest possible inventory holding costs.

Waiting Line or Queueing Models Waiting line or queueing models help managers understand and make better decisions concerning the operation of systems involving waiting lines.

Simulation Simulation is a technique used to model the operation of a complex system. This technique employs a computer program to model the operation and perform simulation computations.

Decision Analysis Decision analysis can be used to determine optimal strategies in situations involving several decision alternatives and an uncertain or risk-filled pattern of future events.

Forecasting Forecasting methods are techniques that can be used to predict future aspects of a business operation.

Markov-Process Models Markov-process models are useful in studying the evolution of certain systems over repeated trials. For example, Markov processes have been used to describe the probability that a machine, functioning in one period, will function or break down in some future period.

We believe barriers to the use of quantitative methods can best be removed by increasing the manager's understanding of how quantitative analysis can be applied. The text will help you develop an understanding of which quantitative methods are most useful, how they are used, and, most importantly, how they can assist managers in making better decisions.

The Q.M. in Action, Impact of Operations Research on Everyday Living, describes some of the many ways quantitative analysis affects our everyday lives.

Q.M. *in* ACTION

IMPACT OF OPERATIONS RESEARCH ON EVERYDAY LIVING*

Mark Eisner, Communications Associate of the School of Operations Research and Information Engineering at Cornell University, once said that operations research "is probably the most important field nobody has ever heard of." The impact of operations research on everyday living over the past 20 years is substantial.

Suppose you schedule a vacation to Florida and use the Orbitz website to book your flights. An algorithm developed by operations researchers will search among millions of options to find the cheapest fare. Another algorithm will schedule the flight crews and aircraft used by the airline. If you rent a car in Florida, the price you pay for the car is determined by a mathematical model that seeks to maximize revenue for the car rental firm. If you do some shopping on your trip and decide to ship your purchases home using UPS, another algorithm

determines the truck on which your packages are loaded, which route the truck should follow, and where your packages should be placed on the truck to minimize loading and unloading time.

If you enjoy watching college basketball, operations research plays a role in what games you see. Michael Trick, a professor at the Tepper School of Business at Carnegie Mellon, designed a system for scheduling each year's Atlantic Coast Conference men's and women's basketball games. Even though it might initially appear that scheduling 16 games among the nine men's teams would be easy, it requires sorting through hundreds of millions of possible combinations of possible schedules. Each of those possibilities entails some desirable and some undesirable characteristics. For example, you do not want to schedule too many consecutive home games for any team, and you want to ensure that each team plays the same number of weekend games.

*Based on Virginia Postrel, "Operations Everything," The Boston Globe, June 27, 2004.

NOTES AND COMMENTS

1. In the United States, the Institute for Operations Research and the Management Sciences (INFORMS) and the Decision Sciences Institute (DSI) are two flagship professional societies that publish journals and newsletters dealing with current research and applications of operations research and management science techniques. In Canada, the Canadian Operational Research Society (CORS) provides similar services.

2. Several European countries, including (but not limited to) Great Britain, France, Italy, Germany, Austria, and the Czech Republic, have their own professional operations research and management science societies, and these societies belong to the Association of European Operational Research Societies (EURO). Professional operations research and management science societies from Latin American and Iberian peninsula countries, including (but not limited to) Chile, Brazil, Argentina, Colombia, Spain, Uruguay, Portugal, and Mexico, all belong to the Asociación Latino-Iberoamericana de Investigación Operativa (ALIO). Professional operations research and management science societies from Australia, Japan, China, India, Malaysia, Thailand, New Zealand, and other countries from Asia and the Pacific Rim belong to the Association of Asian Pacific Operational Research Societies (APORS). African operations research societies include the Operations Research Society of South Africa (ORSSA) and the Operations Research Society of Eastern Africa (ORSEA). The International Federation of Operational Research Societies (IFORS) is the global organization to which most of these (and other) professional operations research and management science societies belong.

Summary

This text focuses on the use of quantitative methods to help managers make better decisions. The discussion in this chapter centered on the problem orientation of the decision-making process and an overview of how mathematical models can be used in this type of analysis.

The difference between the model and the situation or managerial problem it represents is an important consideration. Mathematical models are abstractions of real-world situations and, as such, cannot capture all the aspects of the real situation. However, if a model can capture the major relevant aspects of the problem and can then provide a meaningful solution recommendation, it can be a valuable aid to decision making.

One of the characteristics of quantitative analysis that will become increasingly apparent as we proceed through the text is the search for a best solution to the problem. In carrying out the quantitative analysis, we attempt to develop procedures for finding the "best" or optimal solution.

Glossary

Analog model Although physical in form, an analog model does not have a physical appearance similar to the real object or situation it represents.

Breakeven point The volume at which total revenue equals total cost.

Constraint A restriction or limitation imposed on a problem.

Controllable input The decision alternatives that can be specified by the decision maker.

Decision The alternative selected.

Decision making The process of defining the problem, identifying the alternatives, determining the criteria, evaluating the alternatives, and choosing an alternative.

Decision variable Another term for controllable input.

Deterministic model A model in which all uncontrollable inputs are known and cannot vary.

Feasible solution A decision alternative or solution that satisfies all constraints.

Fixed cost The portion of the total cost that does not depend on the volume; this cost remains the same no matter how much is produced.

Iconic model A physical replica, or representation, of a real object.

Infeasible solution A decision alternative or solution that violates one or more constraints.

Marginal cost The rate of change of the total cost with respect to volume.

Marginal revenue The rate of change of total revenue with respect to volume.

Mathematical model Mathematical symbols and expressions used to represent a real situation.

Model A representation of a real object or situation.

Multicriteria decision problem A problem that involves more than one criterion; the objective is to find the "best" solution, taking into account all the criteria.

Objective function The mathematical expression that defines the quantity to be maximized or minimized.

Optimal solution The specific decision variable value or values that provide the "best" output for the model.

Problem solving The process of identifying a difference between the actual and the desired state of affairs and then taking action to resolve the difference.

Single-criterion decision problem A problem in which the objective is to find the "best" solution with respect to just one criterion.

Stochastic model A model in which at least one uncontrollable input is uncertain and subject to variation; stochastic models are also referred to as probabilistic models.

Uncontrollable input The factors that cannot be controlled by the decision maker.
Variable cost The portion of the total cost that is dependent on and varies with the volume.

Problems

1. Define the terms *management science* and *operations research*.

2. List and discuss the steps of the decision-making process.

3. Discuss the different roles played by the qualitative and quantitative approaches to managerial decision making. Why is it important for a manager or decision maker to have a good understanding of both of these approaches to decision making?

4. A firm recently built a new plant that will use more than 50 production lines and machines to produce over 500 different products. The production scheduling decisions are critical because sales will be lost if customer demand is not met on time. If no individual in the firm has had experience with this production operation, and if new production schedules must be generated each week, why should the firm consider a quantitative approach to the production scheduling problem?

5. What are the advantages of analyzing and experimenting with a model as opposed to a real object or situation?

6. Suppose a manager must choose between the following two mathematical models of a given situation: (a) a relatively simple model that is a reasonable approximation of the real situation and (b) a thorough and complex model that is the most accurate mathematical representation of the real situation possible. Why might the model described in part (a) be preferred by the manager?

7. Suppose you are going on a weekend trip to a city that is d miles away. Develop a model that determines your round-trip gasoline costs. What assumptions or approximations are necessary to treat this model as a deterministic model? Are these assumptions or approximations acceptable to you?

8. Recall the production model from Section 1.3:

$$\text{Max} \quad 10x$$
$$\text{s.t.}$$
$$5x \le 40$$
$$x \ge 0$$

Suppose the firm in this example considers a second product that has a unit profit of $5 and requires 2 hours for each unit produced. Assume total production capacity remains 40 units. Use y as the number of units of product 2 produced.
   a. Show the mathematical model when both products are considered simultaneously.
   b. Identify the controllable and uncontrollable inputs for this model.
   c. Draw the flowchart of the input–output process for this model (see Figure 1.5).
   d. What are the optimal solution values of x and y?
   e. Is this model a deterministic or a stochastic model? Explain.

9. Suppose we modify the production model from Section 1.3 to obtain the following mathematical model:

$$\text{Max} \quad 10x$$
$$\text{s.t.}$$
$$ax \le 40$$
$$x \ge 0$$

where a is the number of hours required for each unit produced. With $a = 5$, the optimal solution is $x = 8$. If we have a stochastic model in which the value of a varies between 3 and 6 (i.e., $a = 3$, $a = 4$, $a = 5$, or $a = 6$) as the possible values for the number of hours required per unit, what is the optimal value for x? What problems does this stochastic model cause?

10. A retail store in Des Moines, Iowa, receives shipments of a particular product from Kansas City and Minneapolis. Let

$$x = \text{units of product received from Kansas City}$$
$$y = \text{units of product received from Minneapolis}$$

   a. Write an expression for the total units of product received by the retail store in Des Moines.
   b. Shipments from Kansas City cost $0.20 per unit, and shipments from Minneapolis cost $0.25 per unit. Develop an objective function representing the total cost of shipments to Des Moines.
   c. Assuming the monthly demand at the retail store is 5000 units, develop a constraint that requires 5000 units to be shipped to Des Moines.
   d. No more than 4000 units can be shipped from Kansas City and no more than 3000 units can be shipped from Minneapolis in a month. Develop constraints to model this situation.
   e. Of course, negative amounts cannot be shipped. Combine the objective function and constraints developed to state a mathematical model for satisfying the demand at the Des Moines retail store at minimum cost.

11. For most products, higher prices result in a decreased demand, whereas lower prices result in an increased demand (economists refer to such products as *normal goods*). Let

$$d = \text{annual demand for a product in units}$$
$$p = \text{price per unit}$$

Assume that a firm accepts the following price–demand relationship as being a realistic representation of its market:

$$d = 800 - 10p$$

where p must be between $20 and $70.

   a. How many units can the firm sell at the $20 per-unit price? At the $70 per-unit price?
   b. What happens to annual units demanded for the product if the firm increases the per-unit price from $26 to $27? From $42 to $43? From $68 to $69? What is the suggested relationship between per-unit price and annual demand for the product in units?
   c. Show the mathematical model for the total revenue (TR), which is the annual demand multiplied by the unit price.
   d. Based on other considerations, the firm's management will only consider price alternatives of $30, $40, and $50. Use your model from part (b) to determine the price alternative that will maximize the total revenue.
   e. What are the expected annual demand and the total revenue according to your recommended price?

12. The O'Neill Shoe Manufacturing Company will produce a special-style shoe if the order size is large enough to provide a reasonable profit. For each special-style order, the company incurs a fixed cost of $2000 for the production setup. The variable cost is $60 per pair, and each pair sells for $80.

   a. Let x indicate the number of pairs of shoes produced. Develop a mathematical model for the total cost of producing x pairs of shoes.

b.   Let P indicate the total profit. Develop a mathematical model for the total profit realized from an order for x pairs of shoes.

c.   What is the breakeven point?

13.   Micromedia offers computer training seminars on a variety of topics. In the seminars each student works at a personal computer, practicing the particular activity that the instructor is presenting. Micromedia is currently planning a two-day seminar on the use of Microsoft Excel in statistical analysis. The projected fee for the seminar is $600 per student. The cost for the conference room, instructor compensation, lab assistants, and promotion is $9600. Micromedia rents computers for its seminars at a cost of $60 per computer per day.

a.   Develop a model for the total cost to put on the seminar. Let x represent the number of students who enroll in the seminar.

b.   Develop a model for the total profit if x students enroll in the seminar.

c.   Micromedia has forecasted an enrollment of 30 students for the seminar. How much profit will be earned if its forecast is accurate?

d.   Compute the breakeven point.

14.   Eastman Publishing Company is considering publishing a paperback textbook on spreadsheet applications for business. The fixed cost of manuscript preparation, textbook design, and production setup is estimated to be $160,000. Variable production and material costs are estimated to be $6 per book. Demand over the life of the book is estimated to be 4000 copies. The publisher plans to sell the text to college and university bookstores for $46 each.

a.   What is the breakeven point?

b.   What profit or loss can be anticipated with a demand of 3800 copies?

c.   With a demand of 3800 copies, what is the minimum price per copy that the publisher must charge to break even?

d.   If the publisher believes that the price per copy could be increased to $50.95 and not affect the anticipated demand of 4000 copies, what action would you recommend? What profit or loss can be anticipated?

15.   Preliminary plans are underway for construction of a new stadium for a major league baseball team. City officials question the number and profitability of the luxury corporate boxes planned for the upper deck of the stadium. Corporations and selected individuals may purchase a box for $300,000. The fixed construction cost for the upper-deck area is estimated to be $4,500,000, with a variable cost of $150,000 for each box constructed.

a.   What is the breakeven point for the number of luxury boxes in the new stadium?

b.   Preliminary drawings for the stadium show that space is available for the construction of up to 50 luxury boxes. Promoters indicate that buyers are available and that all 50 could be sold if constructed. What is your recommendation concerning the construction of luxury boxes? What profit is anticipated?

16.   Financial Analysts, Inc., is an investment firm that manages stock portfolios for a number of clients. A new client has requested that the firm handle an $800,000 portfolio. As an initial investment strategy, the client would like to restrict the portfolio to a mix of the following two stocks:

Stock	Price/ Share	Estimated Annual Return/Share
Oil Alaska	$50	$6
Southwest Petroleum	$30	$4

Let

$$x = \text{number of shares of Oil Alaska}$$
$$y = \text{number of shares of Southwest Petroleum}$$

a. Develop the objective function, assuming that the client desires to maximize the total annual return.
b. Show the mathematical expression for each of the following three constraints:
    (1) Total investment funds available are $800,000.
    (2) Maximum Oil Alaska investment is $500,000.
    (3) Maximum Southwest Petroleum investment is $450,000.

Note: Adding the $x \geq 0$ and $y \geq 0$ constraints provides a linear programming model for the investment problem. A solution procedure for this model will be discussed in Chapter 7.

17. Models of inventory systems frequently consider the relationships among a beginning inventory, a production quantity, a demand or sales, and an ending inventory. For a given production period j, let

s_{j-1} = beginning inventory for period j (ending inventory from period $j - 1$, the previous period)
x_j = production quantity in period j
d_j = demand in period j
s_j = ending inventory for period j

a. Write the mathematical relationship or model that shows ending inventory as a function of beginning inventory, production, and demand.
b. What constraint should be added if production capacity for period j is given by C_j?
c. What constraint should be added if inventory requirements for period j mandate an ending inventory of at least I_j?

Case Problem   Scheduling a Golf League

Chris Lane, the head professional at Royal Oak Country Club, must develop a schedule of matches for the couples' golf league that begins its season at 4:00 P.M. tomorrow. Eighteen couples signed up for the league, and each couple must play every other couple over the course of the 17-week season. Chris thought it would be fairly easy to develop a schedule, but after working on it for a couple of hours, he has been unable to come up with a schedule. Because Chris must have a schedule ready by tomorrow afternoon, he has asked you to help him. A possible complication is that one of the couples told Chris that they may have to cancel for the season. They told Chris they would let him know by 1:00 P.M. tomorrow whether they will be able to play this season.

Managerial Report

Prepare a report for Chris Lane. Your report should include, at a minimum, the following items:

1. A schedule that will enable each of the 18 couples to play every other couple over the 17-week season.
2. A contingency schedule that can be used if the couple that contacted Chris decides to cancel for the season.

CHAPTER 2

Introduction to Probability

Business decisions are often based on an analysis of uncertainties such as the following:

1. What are the "chances" that sales will decrease if we increase prices?
2. What is the "likelihood" that a new assembly method will increase productivity?
3. How "likely" is it that the project will be completed on time?
4. What are the "odds" that a new investment will be profitable?

Probability provides a more precise description of uncertainty than expressions such as chances are "pretty good," chances are "fair," and so on.

Probability is a numeric measure of the likelihood that an event will occur. Thus, probabilities could be used as measures of the degree of uncertainty associated with the four events previously listed. If probabilities were available, we could determine the likelihood of each event occurring.

Probability values are always assigned on a scale from 0 to 1. A probability of 0 indicates that an event will not occur (is an **impossible event**); a probability of 1 indicates that an event is certain to occur (is a **certain event**). Other probabilities between 0 and 1 represent varying degrees of likelihood that an event will occur. The closer a probability is to 0, the less likely the associated event is to occur; the closer a probability is to 1, the more likely the associated event is to occur. Figure 2.1 depicts this view of probability.

Probability is important in decision making because it provides a way to measure, express, and analyze the uncertainties associated with future events. The Q.M. in Action, Probability to the Rescue, describes the role that probability played in the efforts to rescue 33 Chilean miners.

FIGURE 2.1   PROBABILITY AS A NUMERIC MEASURE OF THE LIKELIHOOD OF AN EVENT OCCURRING

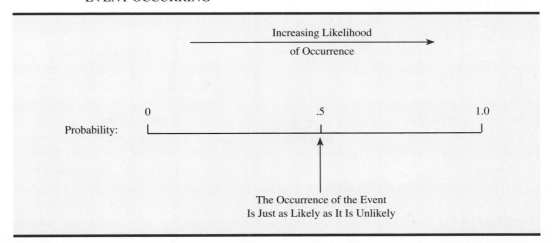

Q.M. *in* ACTION

PROBABILITY TO THE RESCUE*

On August 5, 2010, the San José copper and gold mine suffered a cave-in. Thirty-three men were trapped over 2000 feet underground in the Atacama Desert near Copiapó, Chile. While most feared that these men's prospects were grim, several attempts were made to locate the miners and determine if they were still alive. Seventeen days later, rescuers reached the men with a 5½-inch borehole and ascertained that they were still alive.

*The authors are indebted to Dr. Michael Duncan and Clinton Cragg of NASA for providing input for this Q.M. in Action.

(continued)

After locating the men and establishing the means to communicate and deliver food, water, and medical supplies to them, the rescue effort could proceed in earnest. While it was important to bring these men safely to the surface as quickly as possible, it was imperative that the rescue effort also proceed cautiously. "The mine is old and there is concern of further collapses," Murray & Roberts Cementation Managing Director Henry Laas said in an interview with the *Santiago Times*. "The rescue methodology therefore has to be carefully designed and implemented."

The Chilean government asked NASA to consult on the rescue operation. In response, NASA sent a four-person team consisting of an engineer (Clinton Cragg), two physicians (Michael Duncan and J. D. Polk), and a psychologist (Al Holland). When asked why a space agency was brought in to consult on the rescue of trapped miners, Duncan stated, "We brought our experience in vehicle design and long duration confinement to our Chilean counterparts."

The probability of failure was prominent in the thoughts of everyone involved. "We were thinking that the rescue vehicle would have to make over forty round trips, so in consideration of the probability of part failures we suggested the rescue team have three rigs and several sets of replacement parts available." said Cragg. "We also tried to increase the probability of success by placing spring loaded rollers on the sides of the cage so the cage itself would not be damaged through direct contact with the rock wall as it moved through the rescue portal."

Duncan added, "While we and the Chileans would have preferred to have precise estimates of various probabilities based on historical data, the uniqueness of the situation made this infeasible. For example, a miner had to stand virtually straight up in the cage on an ascent that was originally estimated to last two to four hours per miner, so we had to be concerned about fainting. All we could do was consider what we thought to be the facts and apply what we had learned from astronauts' experiences in their returns from short and long duration space missions." Duncan continued, "We recommended the miners wear compression hosiery on lower extremities to prevent blood pooling, and that they load up on salty solutions such as chicken consommé prior to their ascents. We used all of this information to develop a subjective estimate of the probability a miner would faint on ascent," Duncan then concluded. "It actually took fifteen minutes to bring the cage up from the bottom of the mine, so our estimates in this case were very conservative. Considering the risk involved, that is exactly what we wanted."

Ultimately the rescue approach designed by the Chileans in consultation with the NASA team was successful. On October 13, 2010, the last of the 33 miners emerged; the 13-foot-long, 924-pound steel Fénix 2 rescue capsule withstood over 40 trips into and out of the mine, and no miner suffered from syncope (i.e., fainting) on his ascent.

The use of subjective probabilities in unique situations is common for NASA. How else could NASA estimate the probability that micrometeoroids or space debris will damage a space vehicle? With the limited space available on a space vehicle, assessing probability of failure for various components and the risks associated with these potential failures becomes critical to how NASA decides which spare components will be included on a space flight. NASA also employs probability to estimate the likelihood of crew health and performance issues arising on space exploration missions. Risk assessment teams then use these estimates in their mission design.

2.1 Experiments and the Sample Space

In discussing probability, we define an **experiment** to be any process that generates well-defined outcomes. On any single repetition of an experiment, *one and only one* of the possible experimental outcomes will occur. Several examples of experiments and their associated outcomes follow.

Experiment	Experimental Outcomes
Toss a coin	Head, tail
Select a part for inspection	Defective, nondefective
Conduct a sales call	Purchase, no purchase
Roll a standard die	1, 2, 3, 4, 5, 6
Play a football game	Win, lose, tie

The first step in analyzing a particular experiment is to carefully define the experimental outcomes. When we define *all* possible experimental outcomes, we identify the **sample space** for the experiment; that is, the set of all possible experimental outcomes. Any one particular experimental outcome is also referred to as a **sample point** and is an element of the sample space.

Consider the experiment of tossing a coin. The experimental outcomes are defined by the upward face of the coin—a head or a tail. If we let S denote the sample space, we can use the following notation to describe the sample space and sample points for the coin-tossing experiment:

$$S = \{\text{Head, Tail}\}$$

Using this notation for the second experiment in the preceding table, selecting a part for inspection, provides a sample space with sample points as follows:

$$S = \{\text{Defective, Nondefective}\}$$

Try Problem 1, parts (a) and (b), for practice in listing the experimental outcomes (sample points) for an experiment.

Finally, suppose that we consider the fourth experiment in the table, rolling a standard die. The experimental outcomes are defined as the number of dots appearing on the upward face of the die. In this experiment, the numeric values 1, 2, 3, 4, 5, and 6 represent the possible experimental outcomes or sample points. Thus the sample space is denoted

$$S = \{1, 2, 3, 4, 5, 6\}$$

NOTES AND COMMENTS

1. In probability, the notion of an experiment is somewhat different from the laboratory sciences. In the laboratory sciences, the researcher assumes that each time an experiment is repeated in exactly the same way, the same outcome will occur. For the type of experiment we study in probability, the outcome is determined by chance. Even though the experiment might be repeated in exactly the same way, a different outcome may occur. Because of this difference, the experiments we study in probability are sometimes called random experiments.

2.2 Assigning Probabilities to Experimental Outcomes

With an understanding of an experiment and the sample space, let us now see how prob-abilities for the experimental outcomes can be determined. The probability of an experi-mental outcome is a numeric measure of the likelihood that the experimental outcome will occur on a single repetition of the experiment. In assigning probabilities to experimental outcomes, two **basic requirements of probability** must be satisfied:

1. The probability values assigned to each experimental outcome (sample point) must be between 0 and 1. If we let E_i indicate the ith experimental outcome and $P(E_i)$ indicate the probability of this experimental outcome, we must have

$$0 \leq P(E_i) \leq 1 \text{ (for all } i) \tag{2.1}$$

2. The sum of *all* of the experimental outcome probabilities must be 1. For example, if a sample space has k experimental outcomes, we must have

$$P(E_1) + P(E_2) + \cdots + P(E_k) = 1 \tag{2.2}$$

Any method of assigning probability values to the experimental outcomes that satisfies these two requirements and results in reasonable numeric measures of the likelihood of the outcomes is acceptable. In practice, the classical method, the relative frequency method, or the subjective method is often used.

Classical Method

To illustrate the classical method of assigning probabilities, let us again consider the ex-periment of flipping a coin. On any one flip, we will observe one of two experimental outcomes: head or tail. It is reasonable to assume the two possible outcomes are equally likely. Therefore, as one of the two equally likely outcomes is a head, we logically should conclude that the probability of observing a head is $1/2$, or 0.50. Similarly, the probability of observing a tail is 0.50. When the assumption of equally likely outcomes is used as a basis for assigning probabilities, the approach is referred to as the **classical method**. If an experiment has n possible outcomes, application of the classical method would lead us to assign a probability of $1/n$ to each experimental outcome.

As another illustration of the classical method, consider again the experiment of roll-ing a standard die. In Section 2.1 we described the sample space and sample points for this experiment with the notation

$$S = \{1, 2, 3, 4, 5, 6\}$$

A standard die is designed so that the six experimental outcomes are equally likely, and hence each outcome is assigned a probability of $1/6$. Thus, if $P(1)$ denotes the probability that one dot appears on the upward face of the die, then $P(1) = 1/6$. Similarly, $P(2) = 1/6$, $P(3) = 1/6$, $P(4) = 1/6$, $P(5) = 1/6$, and $P(6) = 1/6$. Note that this probability assignment satisfies the two basic requirements for assigning probabilities. In fact, requirements (2.1) and (2.2) are automatically satisfied when the classical method is used, because each of the n sample points is assigned a probability of $1/n$.

Try Problem 2, part (b), for practice with the classical method.

The classical method was developed originally to analyze gambling probabilities for which the assumption of equally likely outcomes often is reasonable. In many business problems, however, this assumption is not valid. Hence, alternative methods of assigning probabilities are required.

Relative Frequency Method

Consider a firm that is preparing to market a new product. In order to estimate the probability that a customer will purchase the product, a test market evaluation has been set up wherein salespeople call on potential customers. Each sales call conducted has two possible outcomes: The customer purchases the product, or the customer does not purchase the product. With no reason to assume that the two experimental outcomes are equally likely, the classical method of assigning probabilities is inappropriate.

Try Problem 2, part (c), for practice in assigning probabilities to experimental outcomes using the relative frequency approach.

Suppose that in the test market evaluation of the product, 400 potential customers were contacted; 100 purchased the product, but 300 did not. In effect, we have repeated the experiment of contacting a customer 400 times and have found that the product was purchased 100 times. Thus, we might decide to use the relative frequency of the number of customers that purchased the product as an estimate of the probability of a customer making a purchase. We could assign a probability of $100/400 = 0.25$ to the experimental outcome of purchasing the product. Similarly, $300/400 = 0.75$ could be assigned to the experimental outcome of not purchasing the product. This approach to assigning probabilities is referred to as the **relative frequency method**. It is important to note that if we repeated this experiment 400 additional times, we may not obtain exactly the same probability estimate that we obtained from the first 400 trials of the experiment. The relative frequency approach only generates an empirical estimate of the actual probability of an experimental outcome, and different executions of the relative frequency approach can yield differing estimates of the probability of the same experimental outcome.

Subjective Method

The **subjective method** of assigning probabilities is most appropriate when we cannot realistically assume that the experimental outcomes are equally likely and when little relevant data are available. When the subjective method is used to assign probabilities to the experimental outcomes, we may use any information available, such as our experience or intuition. After considering all available information, a probability value that expresses our *degree of belief* (on a scale from 0 to 1) that the experimental outcome will occur is specified. Because subjective probability expresses a person's degree of belief, it is personal. Using the subjective method, different people may assign different probabilities to the same experimental outcome.

The subjective method requires extra care to ensure that the two basic requirements of equations (2.1) and (2.2) are satisfied. Regardless of a person's degree of belief, the probability value assigned to each experimental outcome must be between 0 and 1, inclusive, and the sum of all the probabilities for the experimental outcomes must equal 1.

Consider the case in which Tom and Judy Elsbernd just made an offer to purchase a house. Two outcomes are possible:

$$E_1 = \text{their offer is accepted}$$
$$E_2 = \text{their offer is rejected}$$

Judy believes that the probability that their offer will be accepted is 0.8; thus, Judy would set $P(E_1) = 0.8$ and $P(E_2) = 0.2$. Tom, however, believes that the probability that their offer will be accepted is 0.6; hence, Tom would set $P(E_1) = 0.6$ and $P(E_2) = 0.4$. Note that Tom's probability estimate for E_1 reflects a greater pessimism that their offer will be accepted.

Bayes' theorem (see Section 2.5) provides a means for combining subjectively determined prior probabilities with probabilities obtained by other means to obtain revised, or posterior, probabilities.

Both Judy and Tom assigned probabilities that satisfy the two basic requirements. The fact that their probability estimates differ reflects the personal nature of the subjective method.

These three approaches for assigning probabilities to experimental outcomes are often used in various combinations. For example, in some business situations managers may combine estimates from the classical or relative frequency approach with subjective probability estimates to obtain improved probability estimates.

2.3 Events and Their Probabilities

An **event** is a collection of sample points (experimental outcomes). For example, in the experiment of rolling a standard die, the sample space has six sample points and is denoted $S = \{1, 2, 3, 4, 5, 6\}$. Now consider the event that the number of dots shown on the upward face of the die is an even number. The three sample points in this event are 2, 4, and 6. Using the letter A to denote this event, we write A as a collection of sample points:

$$A = \{2, 4, 6\}$$

Thus, if the experimental outcome or sample point were 2, 4, or 6, we would say that the event A has occurred.

Much of the focus of probability analysis is involved with computing probabilities for various events that are of interest to a decision maker. If the probabilities of the sample points are defined, the *probability of an event* is equal to the sum of the probabilities of the sample points in the event.

Returning to the experiment of rolling a standard die, we used the classical method to conclude that the probability associated with each sample point is $1/6$. Thus, the probability of rolling a 2 is $1/6$, the probability of rolling a 4 is $1/6$, and the probability of rolling a 6 is $1/6$. The probability of event A—an even number of dots on the upward face of the die—is

$$P(A) = P(2) + P(4) + P(6)$$
$$= \frac{1}{6} + \frac{1}{6} + \frac{1}{6} = \frac{3}{6} = \frac{1}{2}$$

Try Problem 6 for practice in assigning probabilities to events.

Any time that we can identify all the sample points of an experiment and assign the corresponding sample point probabilities, we can use the preceding approach to compute the probability of an event. However, in many experiments the number of sample points is large, and the identification of the sample points, as well as determining their associated probabilities, becomes extremely cumbersome if not impossible. In the remainder of this chapter we present some basic probability relationships that can be used to compute the probability of an event without knowing all the individual sample point probabilities. These probability relationships require a knowledge of the probabilities for some events in the experiment. Probabilities of other events are then computed from these known probabilities using one or more of the probability relationships.

NOTES AND COMMENTS

1. The sample space, S, is itself an event. It contains all the experimental outcomes, so it has a probability of 1; that is, $P(S) = 1$.
2. When the classical method is used to assign probabilities, the assumption is that the experimental outcomes are equally likely. In such cases, the probability of an event can be computed by counting the number of experimental outcomes in the event and dividing the result by the total number of experimental outcomes.

 # Some Basic Relationships of Probability

In this section we present several relationships that will be helpful in computing probabilities. The relationships are the complement of an event, the addition law, conditional probability, and the multiplication law.

Complement of an Event

For an event A, the **complement of event** A is the event consisting of all sample points in sample space S that are *not* in A. The complement of A is denoted by A^c. Figure 2.2 provides a diagram, known as a **Venn diagram**, that illustrates the concept of a complement. The rectangular area represents the sample space for the experiment and as such contains all possible sample points. The circle represents event A and contains only the sample points that belong to A. The remainder of the rectangle contains all sample points not in event A, which by definition is the complement of A.

In any probability application, event A and its complement A^c must satisfy the condition

$$P(A) + P(A^c) = 1$$

Solving for $P(A)$, we have

$$P(A) = 1 - P(A^c) \tag{2.3}$$

FIGURE 2.2 COMPLEMENT OF EVENT A

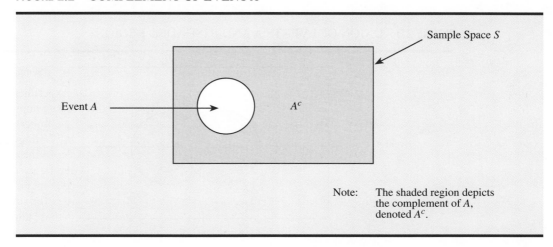

Note: The shaded region depicts the complement of A, denoted A^c.

Equation (2.3) shows that the probability of an event A can be computed by subtraction if the probability of its complement, $P(A^c)$, is known. Similarly, subtraction can be used to compute the probability of the compliment A^c of an event A if the probability of the event $P(A)$, is known.

Consider the case of a sales manager who, after reviewing sales reports, states that 80% of new customer contacts result in no sale. By letting A denote the event of a sale and A^c denote the event of no sale, the manager is stating that $P(A^c) = 0.80$. Using equation (2.3), we see that

$$P(A) = 1 - P(A^c) = 1 - 0.80 = 0.20$$

which shows that there is a 0.20 probability that a sale will be made on a new customer contact.

In another case, a purchasing agent states a 0.90 probability that a supplier will send a shipment that is free of defective parts. Using the complement, we can conclude a $1 - 0.90 = 0.10$ probability that the shipment will contain some defective parts.

Addition Law

The addition law is a useful relationship when we have two events and are interested in knowing the probability that at least one of the events occurs. That is, with events A and B, we are interested in knowing the probability that event A or event B or both will occur. Before we present the addition law, we need to discuss two concepts concerning combinations of events: the *union* of events and the *intersection* of events.

Key words for the union of events ($A \cup B$) are "either A or B occurs" or "at least one of the two events occurs." Note that the conjunction "or" commonly indicates a union of events.

For two events A and B, the **union of events A and B** is the event containing all sample points belonging to A *or B or both*. The union is denoted $A \cup B$. The Venn diagram shown in Figure 2.3 depicts the union of events A and B; the shaded region contains all the sample points in event A, as well as all the sample points in event B. The fact that the circles overlap (or intersect) indicates that some sample points are contained in both A and B.

Key words for the intersection of events ($A \cap B$) are "both A and B occur." Note that the conjunction "and" commonly indicates an intersection of events.

For two events A and B, the **intersection of events A and B** is the event containing the sample points belonging to *both A and B*. The intersection is denoted by $A \cap B$. The Venn diagram depicting the intersection of the two events is shown in Figure 2.4. The area where the two circles overlap is the intersection; it contains the sample points that are in both A and B.

FIGURE 2.3   UNION OF EVENTS A AND B (SHADED REGION)

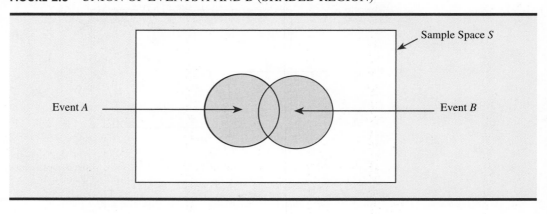

FIGURE 2.4   INTERSECTION OF EVENTS *A* AND *B* (SHADED REGION)

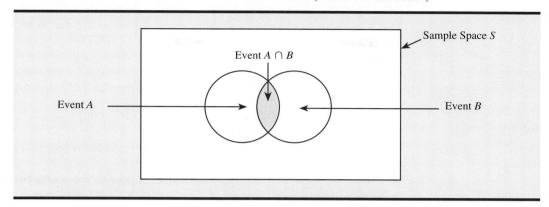

The addition law provides a way to compute the probability of event *A* or *B* or both occurring. In other words, the addition law is used to compute the probability of the union of two events, $A \cup B$. The **addition law** is formally stated as follows:

$$P(A \cup B) = P(A) + P(B) - P(A \cap B) \qquad \textbf{(2.4)}$$

To obtain an intuitive understanding of the addition law, note that the first two terms in the addition law, $P(A) + P(B)$, account for all the sample points in $A \cup B$. However, as the sample points in the intersection $A \cap B$ are in both *A* and *B*, when we compute $P(A) + P(B)$, we in effect are counting each of the sample points in $A \cap B$ twice. We correct for this double counting by subtracting $P(A \cap B)$.

To apply the addition law, let us consider the following situations in a college course in quantitative methods for decision making. Of 200 students taking the course, 160 passed the midterm examination and 140 passed the final examination; 124 students passed both exams. Let

$$A = \text{event of passing the midterm exam}$$
$$B = \text{event of passing the final exam}$$

This relative frequency information leads to the following probabilities:

$$P(A) = \frac{160}{200} = 0.80$$

$$P(B) = \frac{140}{200} = 0.70$$

$$P(A \cap B) = \frac{124}{200} = 0.62$$

After reviewing the grades, the instructor decided to give a passing grade to any student who passed at least one of the two exams; note that this implies the instructor will give a passing grade to any student who passed the midterm exam *or* passed the final exam. That is, any student who passed the midterm, any student who passed the final, and any student who passed both exams would receive a passing grade. What is the probability of a student receiving a passing grade in this course?

Your first reaction may be to try to count how many of the 200 students passed at least one exam, but note that the probability question is about the union of the events A and B. That is, we want to know the probability that a student passed the midterm (A), passed the final (B), or passed both. Thus we want to know $P(A \cup B)$. Using the addition law (2.4) for the events A and B, we have

$$P(A \cup B) = P(A) + P(B) - P(A \cap B)$$

Knowing the three probabilities on the right-hand side of this equation, we obtain

$$P(A \cup B) = 0.80 + 0.70 - 0.62 = 0.88$$

This result indicates an 88% chance of a student passing the course because of the 0.88 probability of passing at least one of the exams.

Now consider a study involving the television-viewing habits of married couples. It was reported that 30% of the husbands and 20% of the wives were regular viewers of a particular Friday evening program. For 12% of the couples in the study, both husband and wife were regular viewers of the program. What is the probability that at least one member of a married couple is a regular viewer of the program?

Let

$$H = \text{husband is a regular viewer}$$
$$W = \text{wife is a regular viewer}$$

We have $P(H) = 0.30$, $P(W) = 0.20$, and $P(H \cap W) = 0.12$; thus, the addition law yields

$$P(H \cup W) = P(H) + P(W) - P(H \cap W) = 0.30 + 0.20 - 0.12 = 0.38$$

An event and its complement are mutually exclusive and their union is the entire sample space.

This result shows a 0.38 probability that at least one member of a married couple is a regular viewer of the program.

Before proceeding, let us consider how the addition law is applied to **mutually exclusive events**. Two or more events are said to be mutually exclusive if the events do not have any sample points in common—that is, there are no sample points in the intersection of the events. For two events A and B to be mutually exclusive, $P(A \cap B) = 0$. Figure 2.5 provides

FIGURE 2.5   MUTUALLY EXCLUSIVE EVENTS

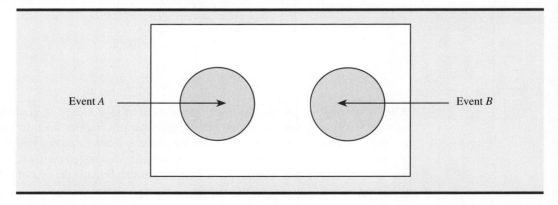

Event A Event B

a Venn diagram depicting two mutually exclusive events. Because $P(A \cap B) = 0$ for the *special case of mutually exclusive events,* the addition law becomes

$$P(A \cup B) = P(A) + P(B) \qquad \textbf{(2.5)}$$

To compute the probability of the union of two mutually exclusive events, we simply add the corresponding probabilities.

Conditional Probability

In many probability situations, being able to determine the probability of one event when another related event is known to have occurred is important. Suppose that we have an event A with probability $P(A)$ and that we obtain new information or learn that another event, denoted B, has occurred. If A is related to B, we will want to take advantage of this information in computing a new or revised probability for event A.

This new probability of event A is written $P(A \mid B)$. The "|" denotes the fact that we are considering the probability of event A *given the condition that event B has occurred.* Thus, the notation $P(A \mid B)$ is read "the probability of A given B."

With two events A and B, the general definitions of **conditional probability** for A given B and for B given A are as follows:

For a conditional probability such as $P(A \mid B) = 0.25$, the probability value of 0.25 refers only to the probability of event A. No information is provided about the probability of event B.

$$P(A \mid B) = \frac{P(A \cap B)}{P(B)} \qquad \textbf{(2.6)}$$

$$P(B \mid A) = \frac{P(A \cap B)}{P(A)} \qquad \textbf{(2.7)}$$

Note that for these expressions to have meaning, $P(B)$ cannot equal 0 in equation (2.6) and $P(A)$ cannot equal 0 in equation (2.7). *Also note that $P(A \mid B) \neq P(B \mid A)$, unless $P(A) = P(B)$.*

To obtain an intuitive understanding of the use of equation (2.6), consider the Venn diagram in Figure 2.6. The shaded region (both light gray and dark gray) denotes that

FIGURE 2.6   CONDITIONAL PROBABILITY $P(A \mid B) = P(A \cap B)/P(B)$

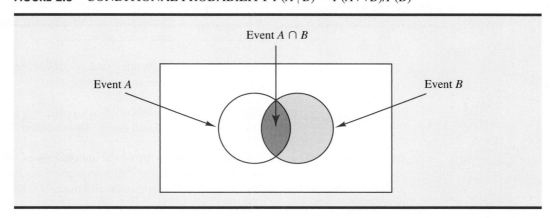

Event $A \cap B$

Event A Event B

TABLE 2.1   CONTINGENCY TABLE FOR PROMOTIONAL STATUS OF POLICE OFFICERS DURING THE PAST TWO YEARS

	Promoted	Not Promoted	Total
Men	288	672	960
Women	36	204	240
Total	324	876	1200

Try Problem 12 for practice computing conditional probabilities.

event B has occurred; the dark gray shaded region denotes the event $(A \cap B)$. We know that once B has occurred, the only way that we can also observe event A is for event $(A \cap B)$ to occur. Thus, the ratio $P(A \cap B)/P(B)$ provides the probability that we will observe event A when event B has already occurred.

We can apply conditional probability to the promotional status of male and female officers of a major metropolitan police force. The force consists of 1200 officers: 960 men and 240 women. Over the past two years, 324 officers have been promoted. Table 2.1 shows the specific breakdown of promotions for male and female officers. Such a table is often called a *contingency table* or a *crosstabulation*.

After reviewing the promotional record, a committee of female officers filed a discrimination case on the basis that only 36 female officers had received promotions during the past two years. The police administration argued that the relatively low number of promotions for female officers is due not to discrimination but to the fact that few female officers are on the force. We use conditional probability to evaluate the discrimination charge.

Let

$$M = \text{event an officer is a man}$$
$$W = \text{event an officer is a woman}$$
$$B = \text{event an officer is promoted}$$

Dividing the data values in Table 2.1 by the total of 1200 officers permits us to summarize the available information as follows:

$$P(M \cap B) = \frac{288}{1200} = 0.24 \qquad \text{probability that an officer is a man } and \text{ is promoted}$$

$$P(M \cap B^c) = \frac{672}{1200} = 0.56 \qquad \text{probability that an officer is a man } and \text{ is not promoted}$$

$$P(W \cap B) = \frac{36}{1200} = 0.03 \qquad \text{probability that an officer is a woman } and \text{ is promoted}$$

$$P(W \cap B^c) = \frac{204}{1200} = 0.17 \qquad \text{probability that an officer is a woman } and \text{ is not promoted}$$

Because each of these values gives the probability of the intersection of two events, these probabilities are called **joint probabilities**. Table 2.2, which provides a summary of the probability information for the police officer promotion situation, is referred to as a **joint probability table**.

TABLE 2.2   JOINT PROBABILITY TABLE FOR POLICE OFFICER PROMOTIONS

	Promoted	Not Promoted	Total
Men	0.24	0.56	0.80
Women	0.03	0.17	0.20
Total	0.27	0.73	1.00

Joint probabilities appear in the body of the table.

Marginal probabilities appear in the margins of the table.

The values in the margins of the joint probability table provide the probabilities of each single event separately: $P(M) = 0.80$, $P(W) = 0.20$, $P(B) = 0.27$, and $P(B^c) = 0.73$, which indicate that 80% of the force is male, 20% of the force is female, 27% of all officers received promotions, and 73% were not promoted. These probabilities are referred to as **marginal probabilities** because of their location in the margins of the joint probability table. Returning to the issue of discrimination against the female officers, we see that the probability of promotion of an officer is $P(B) = 0.27$ (regardless of whether that officer is male or female). However, the critical issue in the discrimination case involves the two conditional probabilities $P(B \mid M)$ and $P(B \mid W)$; that is, what is the probability of a promotion *given* that the officer is a man and what is the probability of a promotion *given* that the officer is a woman? If these two probabilities are equal, the discrimination case has no basis because the chances of a promotion are the same for male and female officers. However, different conditional probabilities will support the position that male and female officers are treated differently in terms of promotion.

Using equation (2.7), the conditional probability relationship, we obtain

$$P(B \mid M) = \frac{P(B \cap M)}{P(M)} = \frac{0.24}{0.80} = 0.30 \left(= \frac{288/1200}{960/1200} = \frac{288}{960} \right)$$

$$P(B \mid W) = \frac{P(B \cap W)}{P(W)} = \frac{0.03}{0.20} = 0.15 \left(= \frac{36/1200}{240/1200} = \frac{36}{240} \right)$$

What conclusions do you draw? The probability of a promotion for a male officer is 0.30, which is twice the 0.15 probability of a promotion for a female officer. Although the use of conditional probability does not in itself prove that discrimination exists in this case, the conditional probability values strongly support the argument presented by the female officers.

In this illustration, $P(B) = 0.27$, $P(B \mid M) = 0.30$, and $P(B \mid W) = 0.15$. Clearly, the probability of promotion (event B) differs by gender. In particular, as $P(B \mid M) \neq P(B)$, events B and M are **dependent events**. The probability of event B (promotion) is higher when M (the officer is male) occurs. Similarly, with $P(B \mid W) \neq P(B)$, events B and W are dependent events. But, if the probability of event B was not changed by the existence of event M—that is, $P(B \mid M) = P(B)$—events B and M would be **independent events**. Two events A and B are *independent* if

$$P(B \mid A) = P(B)$$

or

$$P(A \mid B) = P(A)$$

Otherwise, the events are *dependent*.

The Q.M. in Action, Product Testing for Quality Control at Morton International, describes how a subsidiary of Morton International used conditional probability to help decide to implement a quality control test.

Q.M. *in* ACTION

PRODUCT TESTING FOR QUALITY CONTROL AT MORTON INTERNATIONAL*

Morton International is a company with businesses in salt, household products, rocket motors, and specialty chemicals. Carstab Corporation, a subsidiary of Morton, produces a variety of specialty chemical products designed to meet the unique specifications of its customers. For one particular customer, Carstab produced an expensive catalyst used in chemical processing. Some, but not all, of the product produced by Carstab met the customer's specifications.

Carstab's customer agreed to test each lot after receiving it to determine whether the catalyst would perform the desired function. Lots that did not pass the customer's test would be returned to Carstab. Over time, Carstab found that the customer was accepting 60% of the lots and returning 40%. In probability terms, each Carstab shipment to the customer had a 0.60 probability of being accepted and a 0.40 probability of being returned.

Neither Carstab nor its customer was pleased with these results. In an effort to improve service, Carstab explored the possibility of duplicating the customer's test prior to shipment. However, the high cost of the special testing equipment made that alternative infeasible. Carstab's chemists then proposed a new, relatively low-cost test designed to indicate whether a lot would pass the customer's test. The probability question of interest was: What is the probability that a lot will pass the customer's test given that it passed the new Carstab test?

A sample of lots was tested under both the customer's procedure and Carstab's proposed procedure. Results were that 55% of the lots passed Carstab's test, and 50% of the lots passed both the customer's and Carstab's test. In probability notation, we have

A = the event the lot passes the customer's test
B = the event the lot passes Carstab's test

where

$$P(B) = 0.55 \text{ and } P(A \cap B) = 0.50$$

The probability information sought was the conditional probability $P(A \mid B)$ given by

$$P(A \mid B) = \frac{P(A \cap B)}{P(B)} = \frac{0.50}{0.55} = 0.909$$

Prior to Carstab's new test, the probability that a lot would pass the customer's test was 0.60. However, the new results showed that given that a lot passed Carstab's new test, it had a 0.909 probability of passing the customer's test. This result was good supporting evidence for the use of the test prior to shipment. Based on this probability analysis, the preshipment testing procedure was implemented at the company. Immediate results showed an improved level of customer service. A few lots were still being returned; however, the percentage was greatly reduced. The customer was more satisfied and return shipping costs were reduced.

*Based on information provided by Michael Haskell of Morton International.

Multiplication Law

The **multiplication law** can be used to find the probability of an intersection of two events. The multiplication law is derived from the definition of conditional probability. Using equations (2.6) and (2.7) and solving for $P(A \cap B)$, we obtain the multiplication law:

$$P(A \cap B) = P(A \mid B)P(B) \tag{2.8}$$

$$P(A \cap B) = P(B \mid A)P(A) \tag{2.9}$$

The multiplication law is useful in situations for which probabilities such as $P(A)$, $P(B)$, $P(A \mid B)$, and/or $P(B \mid A)$ are known but $P(A \cap B)$ is not. For example, suppose that a newspaper circulation department knows that 84% of its customers subscribe to the daily edition of the paper. Let D denote the event that a customer subscribes to the daily edition; hence, $P(D) = 0.84$. In addition, the department knows that the conditional probability that a customer who already holds a daily subscription also subscribes to the Sunday edition (event S) is 0.75; that is, $P(S \mid D) = 0.75$. What is the probability that a customer subscribes to both the daily and Sunday editions of the newspaper? Using equation (2.9), we compute $P(D \cap S)$:

$$P(D \cap S) = P(S \mid D)P(D) = 0.75(0.84) = 0.63$$

This result tells us that 63% of the newspaper's customers subscribe to both the daily and Sunday editions.

Before concluding this section, let us consider the special case of the multiplication law when the events involved are independent. Recall that independent events exist whenever $P(B \mid A) = P(B)$ or $P(A \mid B) = P(A)$. Returning to the multiplication law, equations (2.8) and (2.9), we can substitute $P(A)$ for $P(A \mid B)$ and $P(B)$ for $P(B \mid A)$. Hence, for the *special case of independent events,* the multiplication law becomes

$$P(A \cap B) = P(A)P(B) \tag{2.10}$$

Thus, to compute the probability of the intersection of two independent events, we simply multiply the corresponding probabilities. For example, a service station manager knows from past experience that 40% of her customers use a credit card when purchasing gasoline. What is the probability that the next two customers purchasing gasoline will both use a credit card? If we let

A = the event that the first customer uses a credit card

B = the event that the second customer uses a credit card

the event of interest is $A \cap B$. With no other information, it is reasonable to assume A and B are independent events. Thus,

$$P(A \cap B) = P(A)P(B) = (.40)(.40) = 0.16$$

NOTES AND COMMENTS

1. Do not confuse mutually exclusive events with independent events. Two events with nonzero probabilities cannot be both mutually exclusive and independent. If one mutually exclusive event is known to occur, the probability of the other occurring is reduced to zero. Thus, they cannot be independent.

2.5 Bayes' Theorem

In the discussion of conditional probability, we indicated that revising probabilities when new information is obtained is an important phase of probability analysis. Often, we begin an analysis with initial or **prior probability** estimates for specific events of interest; these initial estimates are generally developed using either the relative frequency approach (applied to historical data) or the subjective approach. Then, from sources such as a sample, a special report, or a product test, we obtain some additional information about the events. With this new information, we update the prior probability values by calculating revised probabilities, referred to as **posterior probabilities**. **Bayes' theorem** provides a means for making these probability revisions. The steps in this probability revision process are shown in Figure 2.7.

We can apply Bayes' theorem to a manufacturing firm that receives shipments of parts from two different suppliers. Let A_1 denote the event that a part is from supplier 1 and A_2 denote the event that a part is from supplier 2. Currently, 65% of the parts purchased by the company are from supplier 1, and the remaining 35% are from supplier 2. Thus, if a part is selected at random, we would assign the prior probabilities $P(A_1) = 0.65$ and $P(A_2) = 0.35$.

The quality of the purchased parts varies with the source of supply. Based on historical data, the conditional probabilities of receiving good and bad parts from the two suppliers are shown in Table 2.3. Thus, if we let G denote the event that a part is good and B denote the event that a part is bad, the information in Table 2.3 provides the following conditional probability values:

$$P(G \mid A_1) = 0.98 \quad P(B \mid A_1) = 0.02$$
$$P(G \mid A_2) = 0.95 \quad P(B \mid A_2) = 0.05$$

The tree diagram shown in Figure 2.8 depicts the process of the firm receiving a part from one of the two suppliers and then discovering that the part is good or bad as a two-step experiment. Of the four possible experimental outcomes, two correspond to the part being good, and two correspond to the part being bad.

Each of the experimental outcomes is the intersection of two events, so we can use the multiplication rule to compute the probabilities. For instance,

$$P(A_1 \cap G) = P(A_1)P(G \mid A_1)$$

FIGURE 2.7   PROBABILITY REVISION USING BAYES' THEOREM

Prior Probabilities	New Information	Application of Bayes' Theorem	Posterior Probabilities

TABLE 2.3   CONDITIONAL PROBABILITIES OF RECEIVING GOOD AND BAD PARTS FROM TWO SUPPLIERS

	Good Parts	Bad Parts	
Supplier 1	0.98	0.02	$P(B \mid A_1)$
Supplier 2	0.95	0.05	

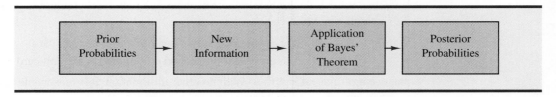

FIGURE 2.8 TWO-STEP TREE DIAGRAM

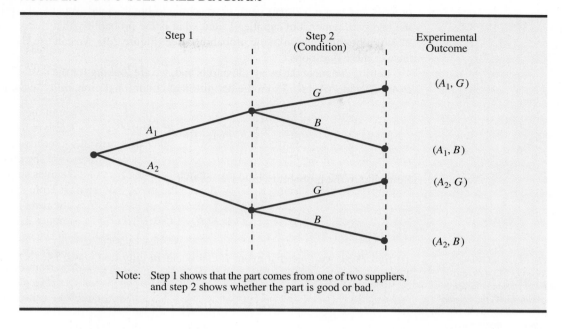

Note: Step 1 shows that the part comes from one of two suppliers, and step 2 shows whether the part is good or bad.

The process of computing these joint probabilities can be depicted in what is sometimes called a *probability tree,* as shown in Figure 2.9. From left to right in the tree, the probabilities for each of the branches at step 1 are the prior probabilities, and the probabilities for each branch at step 2 are conditional probabilities. To find the probabilities of each experimental outcome, we simply multiply the probabilities on the branches leading to the outcome. Each of these joint probabilities is shown in Figure 2.9, along with the known probabilities for each branch. Note that the probabilities of the four experimental outcomes sum to 1.

FIGURE 2.9 PROBABILITY TREE FOR TWO-SUPPLIER EXAMPLE

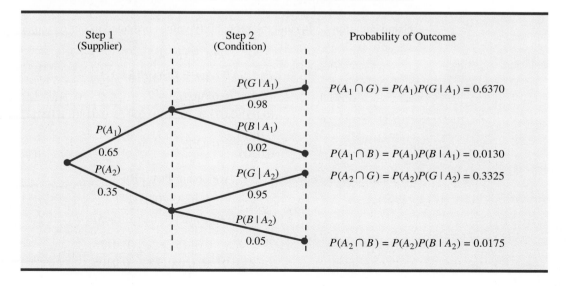

Now suppose that the parts from the two suppliers are used in the firm's manufacturing process and that a bad part causes a machine to break down. What is the probability that the bad part came from supplier 1, and what is the probability that it came from supplier 2? With the information in the probability tree (Figure 2.9), we can use Bayes' theorem to answer these questions.

Letting B denote the event the part is bad, we are looking for the posterior probabilities $P(A_1 \mid B)$ and $P(A_2 \mid B)$. From the definition of conditional probability, we know that

$$P(A_1 \mid B) = \frac{P(A_1 \cap B)}{P(B)} \tag{2.11}$$

Referring to the probability tree, we see that

$$P(A_1 \cap B) = P(A_1)P(B \mid A_1) \tag{2.12}$$

The Reverend Thomas Bayes (1702–1761), a Presbyterian minister, is credited with the original work leading to the version of Bayes' theorem in use today.

To find $P(B)$, we note that event B can occur in only two ways: $(A_1 \cap B)$ and $(A_2 \cap B)$. Therefore, we have

$$\begin{aligned} P(B) &= P(A_1 \cap B) + P(A_2 \cap B) \\ &= P(A_1)P(B \mid A_1) + P(A_2)P(B \mid A_2) \end{aligned} \tag{2.13}$$

Substituting from equations (2.12) and (2.13) into equation (2.11) and writing a similar result for $P(A_2 \mid B)$, we obtain Bayes' theorem for the case of two events.

$$P(A_1 \mid B) = \frac{P(A_1)P(B \mid A_1)}{P(A_1)P(B \mid A_1) + P(A_2)P(B \mid A_2)} \tag{2.14}$$

$$P(A_2 \mid B) = \frac{P(A_2)P(B \mid A_2)}{P(A_1)P(B \mid A_1) + P(A_2)P(B \mid A_2)} \tag{2.15}$$

Using equation (2.14) and the probability values provided in our example, we have

$$\begin{aligned} P(A_1 \mid B) &= \frac{P(A_1)P(B \mid A_1)}{P(A_1)P(B \mid A_1) + P(A_2)P(B \mid A_2)} \\[2mm] &= \frac{(0.65)(0.02)}{(0.65)(0.02) + (0.35)(0.05)} = \frac{0.0130}{0.0130 + 0.0175} \\[2mm] &= \frac{0.0130}{0.0305} = 0.4262 \end{aligned}$$

In addition, using equation (2.15), we obtain $P(A_2 \mid B)$:

$$\begin{aligned} P(A_2 \mid B) &= \frac{(0.35)(0.05)}{(0.65)(0.02) + (0.35)(0.05)} \\[2mm] &= \frac{0.0175}{0.0130 + 0.0175} = \frac{0.0175}{0.0305} = 0.5738 \end{aligned}$$

TABLE 2.4 SUMMARY OF BAYES' THEOREM CALCULATIONS FOR THE TWO-SUPPLIER PROBLEM

(1) Events A_i	(2) Prior Probabilities $P(A_i)$	(3) Conditional Probabilities $P(B \mid A_i)$	(4) Joint Probabilities $P(A_i \cap B)$	(5) Posterior Probabilities $P(A_i \mid B)$
A_1	0.65	0.02	0.0130	0.0130/0.0305 = 0.4262
A_2	0.35	0.05	0.0175	0.0175/0.0305 = 0.5738
	1.00		$P(B) = 0.0305$	1.0000

Note that in this application we initially started with a probability of 0.65 that a part selected at random was from supplier 1. However, given information that the part is bad, we determine the probability that the part is from supplier 1 drops to 0.4262. If the part is bad, the probability that the part was from supplier 2 increases from 0.35 to 0.5738; that is, $P(A_2 \mid B) = 0.5738$.

Bayes' theorem is applicable when the events for which we want to compute posterior probabilities are mutually exclusive and their union is the entire sample space.[1] Bayes' theorem can be extended to the case of n mutually exclusive events $A_1, A_2, \ldots, A_n$, whose union is the entire sample space. In such a case Bayes' theorem for the computation of any posterior probability $P(A_i \mid B)$ becomes

$$P(A_i \mid B) = \frac{P(A_i)P(B \mid A_i)}{P(A_1)P(B \mid A_1) + P(A_2)P(B \mid A_2) + \cdots + P(A_n)P(B \mid A_n)} \quad \textbf{(2.16)}$$

Try Problem 20 for practice using Bayes' theorem to compute posterior probabilities.

With prior probabilities $P(A_1), P(A_2), \ldots, P(A_n)$ and the appropriate conditional probabilities $P(B \mid A_1), P(B \mid A_2), \ldots, P(B \mid A_n)$, equation (2.16) can be used to compute the posterior probability of the events $A_1, A_2, \ldots, A_n$.

The Tabular Approach

The tabular approach is helpful in conducting the Bayes' theorem calculations simultaneously for all events A_i. Such an approach is shown in Table 2.4. The computations shown there involve the following steps.

Step 1. Prepare three columns:
Column 1—The mutually exclusive events for which posterior probabilities are desired
Column 2—The prior probabilities for the events
Column 3—The conditional probabilities of the new information given each event

Step 2. In column 4, compute the joint probabilities for each event and the new information B by using the multiplication law. To get these joint probabilities, multiply the prior probabilities in column 2 by the corresponding conditional probabilities in column 3—that is, $P(A_i \cap B) = P(A_i)P(B \mid A_i)$.

Step 3. Sum the joint probabilities in column 4 to obtain the probability of the new information, $P(B)$. In the example there is a 0.0130 probability that a part is

---

[1]If the union of events is the entire sample space, the events are often called *collectively exhausted*.

from supplier 1 and is bad and a 0.0175 probability that a part is from supplier 2 and is bad. These are the only two ways by which a bad part can be obtained, so the sum 0.0130 + 0.0175 shows an overall probability of 0.0305 of finding a bad part from the combined shipments of both suppliers.

Step 4. In column 5, compute the posterior probabilities by using the basic relationship of conditional probability:

$$P(A_i \mid B) = \frac{P(A_i \cap B)}{P(B)}$$

Try Problem 25 for an application of Bayes' theorem involving the tabular approach.

Note that the joint probabilities $P(A_i \cap B)$ appear in column 4, whereas $P(B)$ is the sum of the column 4 values.

Q.M. *in* ACTION

USING BAYES' THEOREM TO DEFEAT COMMENT SPAM*

In an article published in the *International Journal of Network Security & Its Applications*, an algorithm for detecting spam in blogs (which is often called comment spam or blog spam) is outlined. The content available in blogs, forums, and email archives is a rich source for search engines, making these environments attractive targets for comment spammers. Some comment spammers use the information culled from these environments to identify and reach potential customers, others place trackbacks or ping pongs that are designed to attract traffic to the spammer's website or blog, while still others launch man-in-the-middle attacks to cripple network servers or to phish for information on potential victims. Comment spam also wastes a user's time with unwanted comments and consumes bandwidth, and it ultimately can have a deleterious impact on the traffic and success of

the spammed forum. Therefore, the identification of comment spammers is critical.

The comment spam detection algorithm is based on Bayes' theorem. First, the probability that a word is found in a blog comment spam post is determined. For example, if a post is comment spam, the word "free" has a relatively high probability of occurring in the post. Then the overall probability that any post is comment spam is established. Bayes' theorem is applied to these two probabilities to derive the probability that a post containing the word in question is comment spam. If this probability exceeds some threshold, the potential post is not allowed. The individual responsible for maintaining the blog can set the threshold probability to reflect her or his tolerance for comment spam.

A spam attacker using automated tools such as xRumer can send millions of spam mails and cause many problems with little effort, so blogs need a sound defense against comment spammers. Bayes' theorem can help organizations to quickly and accurately distinguish comment spam from legitimate posts and avoid the deleterious effects of comment spam.

*Dhinaharan Nagamalai, Beatrice Cynthia Dhinakaran, and Jae Kwang Lee (2010). "Bayesian Based Comment Spam Defending Tool." *International Journal of Network Security & Its Applications*, 2(4): 267–280.

NOTES AND COMMENTS

1. Bayes' theorem is used in decision analysis (see Chapter 4). The prior probabilities often are subjective estimates provided by a decision maker. Sample information is obtained and posterior probabilities are computed for use in developing a decision strategy.

2. An event and its complement are mutually exclusive, and their union is the entire sample space. Thus, Bayes' theorem is always applicable for computing posterior probabilities of an event and its complement.

Simpson's Paradox

As we have discussed in Sections 2.4 and 2.5, the concept of conditional probability quantifies the effect of an event B on the likelihood of another event A. It is possible for the apparent association between two events to be reversed upon considering a third event; this phenomenon is referred to as **Simpson's paradox**. Simpson's paradox often occurs when data from two or more subsets of a population are combined or aggregated to produce a summary crosstabulation in an attempt to show how two events are related. In such cases, we must be careful in drawing conclusions from the aggregated data about the relationship between the two events because the conclusions based upon the aggregated data can be completely reversed if we look at the disaggregated data. To provide an illustration of Simpson's paradox, we consider an example involving the analysis of verdicts for two judges.

Judges Ron Luckett and Dennis Kendall presided over cases in Common Pleas Court and Municipal Court during the past three years. Some of the verdicts they rendered were appealed. In most of these cases the appeals court upheld the original verdicts, but in some cases those verdicts were reversed. Table 2.5 illustrates the crosstabulation of cases broken down by verdict (upheld or reversed) and judge (Luckett or Kendall). This crosstabulation shows the number of appeals for which the verdict was upheld and the number of appeals for which the verdict was reversed for each judge (the column percentages in parentheses next to each value).

A review of the column percentages shows that 14% of the verdicts were reversed for Judge Luckett, but only 12% of the verdicts were reversed for Judge Kendall. That is, $P(\text{reversed} \mid \text{Luckett}) = 0.14$ and $P(\text{reversed} \mid \text{Kendall}) = 0.12$. Based on this data, we might conclude that Judge Kendall is doing a better job because a lower percentage of his verdicts are being reversed upon appeal.

A closer look at the data, however, suggests there may be a problem with the conclusion that Judge Kendall's verdicts are reversed less often. If we further break down the verdict data by the type of court (Common Pleas or Municipal) in which the cases were heard, we obtain the crosstabulations in Table 2.6; column percentages are also shown in parentheses next to each value.

From the crosstabulation and column percentages for Luckett, we see that his verdicts were reversed in 9% of the Common Pleas Court cases and in 15% of the Municipal Court cases. That is, $P(\text{reversed} \mid \text{Luckett and Common Pleas Court}) = 0.09$ and $P(\text{reversed} \mid \text{Luckett and Municipal Court}) = 0.15$. From the crosstabulation and column percentages for Kendall, we see that his verdicts were reversed in 10% of the Common Pleas Court cases and in 20% of the Municipal Court cases. That is, $P(\text{reversed} \mid \text{Kendall and Common Pleas Court}) = 0.10$ and $P(\text{reversed} \mid \text{Kendall and Municipal Court}) = 0.20$. Since $P(\text{reversed} \mid \text{Luckett and Common Pleas Court}) < P(\text{reversed} \mid \text{Kendall and Common Pleas Court})$ and

TABLE 2.5   SUMMARY OF VERDICTS UPHELD AND REVERSED FOR JUDGES
LUCKETT AND KENDALL

Verdict	Judge		Total
	Luckett	Kendall	
Upheld	129 (86%)	110 (88%)	239
Reversed	21 (14%)	15 (12%)	36
Total (%)	150 (100%)	125 (100%)	275

TABLE 2.6   SUMMARY OF VERDICTS UPHELD AND REVERSED IN COMMON PLEAS AND MUNICIPAL COURT FOR JUDGES LUCKETT AND KENDALL

	Judge Luckett		
Verdict	**Common Pleas**	**Municipal Court**	**Total**
Upheld	29 (91%)	100 (85%)	129
Reversed	3 (9%)	18 (15%)	21
Total (%)	32 (100%)	118 (100%)	150
	Judge Kendall		
Verdict	**Common Pleas**	**Municipal Court**	**Total**
Upheld	90 (90%)	20 (80%)	110
Reversed	10 (10%)	5 (20%)	15
Total (%)	100 (100%)	25 (100%)	125

P(reversed | Luckett and Municipal Court) $<$ P(reversed | Kendall and Municipal Court), we see that Judge Luckett demonstrates a better record than Judge Kendall in each court. This result contradicts the conclusion we reached when we aggregated the data across both courts for the original crosstabulation. It appeared then that Judge Kendall had the better record. This example illustrates Simpson's paradox.

The original crosstabulation was obtained by aggregating the data in the separate crosstabulations for the two courts. Note that for both judges the percentage of appeals that resulted in reversals was much higher in Municipal Court than in Common Pleas Court. Because Judge Luckett tried a much higher percentage of his cases in Municipal Court, the aggregated data favored Judge Kendall. When we look at the crosstabulations for the two courts separately, however, Judge Luckett clearly shows the better record. Thus, for the original crosstabulation, we see that the *type of court* is a hidden variable that cannot be ignored when evaluating the records of the two judges.

Because of Simpson's paradox, we need to be particularly careful when drawing conclusions using aggregated data. Before drawing any conclusions about the relationship between two events shown for a crosstabulation involving aggregated data, you should investigate whether any hidden variables could affect the results. The QM in Action, Accurate Comparison of Unemployment Rates, provides an interesting and real example of Simpson's paradox.

NOTES AND COMMENTS

1. While Simpson's paradox is named for Edward Simpson (who described the paradox in 1951), the phenomenon was previously documented in papers by Pearson, Lee, and Bramley-Moore in 1899 and again by Yule in 1903. For this reason some refer to Simpson's paradox as the reversal paradox, the amalgamation paradox, or the Yule–Simpson effect.

Q.M. *in* ACTION

*ACCURATE COMPARISON OF UNEMPLOYMENT RATES—WHICH RECESSION WAS MORE SEVERE?**

In a December 2009 article in *The Wall Street Journal*, Cari Tuna asked, "Is the current economic slump worse than the recession of the early 1980s?" Tuna observed that if one uses the unemployment rate as the standard, on the surface the answer to this question appears to be no; the jobless rate was 10.2% in October of 2009, which is substantially below the peak of 10.8% in November and December of 1982.

Tuna then considers the question seperately for each of several education groups. Surprisingly, the unemployment rate among workers in each education group (*high-school dropouts*, *high-school graduates*, *some college*, and *college graduates*) was higher in October of 2009 than it was during the 1980s recession.

How can this be? How could the overall unemployment rate be lower in 2009 than it was during the recession of the early 1980s, while the unemployment rate for each of these groups was higher in 2009 than it was during the early 1980s recession? The anomaly is an example of Simpson's paradox—the phenomenon by which the

─────────

*Based on C. Tuna, "When Combined Data Reveal the Flaw of Averages in a Statistical Anomaly Dubbed Simpson's Paradox: Aggregated Numbers Obscure Trends in Job Market, Medicine and Baseball," *The Wall Street Journal*, December 2, 2009 (http://online.wsj.com/article /SB125970744553071829.html).

apparent association between two events is reversed upon consideration of a third event.

As Tuna explains, the 2009 overall unemployment rate appears to be lower because college graduates (who have the lowest unemployment rate among education groups) were a larger proportion of the workforce in 2009 than they were in the early 1980s (they were approximately one-third of the 2009 workforce and 25% in the early 1980s). At the same time, the proportion of high-school dropouts fell from almost 20% in the early 1980s to approximately 10% in 2009. Even though the 2009 unemployment rate was higher among both groups than it was during the recession of the early 1980s, the discrepancies in contributions to the composition of the labor force by these two groups reverses the result when data from the two groups are aggregated.

In this case the data aggregated across education groups suggests the opposite of what the disaggregated data imply, and consideration of the aggregated data leads to an erroneous conclusion. Examples of Simpson's paradox are common across industries; Tuna cites examples from medicine, sports, education, and air travel. If we are not careful in our analyses, we can draw incorrect conclusions from aggregate data and as a result make poor decisions.

Summary

In this chapter we introduced basic probability concepts and illustrated how probability analysis can provide helpful decision-making information. We described how probability can be interpreted as a numeric measure of the likelihood that an event will occur, and discussed various ways that probabilities can be assigned to events. In addition, we showed that the probability of an event can be computed either by summing the probabilities of the experimental outcomes (sample points) comprising the event or by using the basic relationships of probability. When additional information becomes available, we showed how conditional probability and Bayes' theorem can be used to obtain revised or posterior probabilities. We also demonstrated how an apparent association between two events can be reversed upon consideration of a third event through the phenomenon of Simpson's paradox.

The probability concepts covered will be helpful in future chapters when we describe quantitative methods based on the use of probability information. Specific chapters and quantitative methods that make use of probability are as follows:

- Chapter 3   Probability distributions
- Chapter 4   Decision analysis
- Chapter 5   Utility and game theory
- Chapter 13   Project scheduling: PERT/CPM
- Chapter 14   Inventory models
- Chapter 15   Waiting line models
- Chapter 16   Simulation
- Chapter 17   Markov processes

Glossary

Addition law A probability law used to compute the probability of a union: $P(A \cup B) = P(A) + P(B) - P(A \cap B)$. For mutually exclusive events, $P(A \cap B) = 0$, and the addition law simplifies to $P(A \cup B) = P(A) + P(B)$.

Basic requirements of probability Two requirements that restrict the manner in which probability assignments can be made:

1. For each experimental outcome E_i, $0 \leq P(E_i) \leq 1$.
2. $P(E_1) + P(E_2) + \cdots + P(E_k) = 1$.

Bayes' theorem A method used to compute posterior probabilities.

Certain event An event that is certain to occur. The probability of a certain event is 1.

Classical method A method of assigning probabilities that is based on the assumption that the experimental outcomes are equally likely.

Complement of event A The event containing all sample points that are not in A.

Conditional probability The probability of an event given another event has occurred. The conditional probability of A given B is $P(A \mid B) = P(A \cap B)/P(B)$.

Dependent events Two events A and B for which $P(A \mid B) \neq P(A)$ or $P(B \mid A) \neq P(B)$; that is, the probability of one event is altered or affected by knowing whether the other event occurs.

Event A collection of sample points or experimental outcomes.

Experiment Any process that generates well-defined outcomes.

Impossible event An event that is certain not to occur. The probability of an uncertain event is 0.

Independent events Two events A and B for which $P(A \mid B) = P(A)$ and $P(B \mid A) = P(B)$; that is, the events have no influence on each other.

Intersection of events A and B The event containing all sample points that are in both A and B.

Joint probability The probability of the intersection of two events.

Joint probability table A table used to display joint and marginal probabilities.

Marginal probabilities The values in the margins of the joint probability table, which provide the probability of each event separately.

Multiplication law A probability law used to compute the probability of an intersection: $P(A \cap B) = P(A \mid B)P(B)$ or $P(A \cap B) = P(B \mid A)P(A)$. For independent events, this simplifies to $P(A \cap B) = P(A)P(B)$.

Mutually exclusive events Events that have no sample points in common; that is, $A \cap B$ is empty and $P(A \cap B) = 0$.

Posterior probabilities Revised probabilities of events based on additional information.

Prior probabilities Initial probabilities of events.

Probability A numeric measure of the likelihood that an event will occur.

Relative frequency method A method of assigning probabilities based on experimentation or historical data.

Sample point An experimental outcome and an element of the sample space.

Sample space The set of all sample points (experimental outcomes).

Simpson's paradox The phenomenon by which the apparent association between two events is reversed upon consideration of a third event.

Subjective method A method of assigning probabilities based on judgment.

Union of events A and B The event containing all sample points that are in A, in B, or in both.

Venn diagram A graphical device for representing the sample space and operations involving events.

Problems

1. A study examined waiting times in the X-ray department for a hospital in Jacksonville, Florida. A clerk recorded the number of patients waiting for service at 9:00 A.M. on 20 consecutive days and obtained the following results.

Number Waiting	Number of Days Outcome Occurred
0	2
1	5
2	6
3	4
4	3
	Total 20

   a. Define the experiment the clerk conducted.
   b. List the experimental outcomes.
   c. Assign probabilities to the experimental outcomes.
   d. What method did you use?

2. A company that franchises coffee houses conducted taste tests for a new coffee product. The company prepared four blends and randomly chose individuals to do a taste test and state which of the four blends they liked best. Results of the taste test for 100 individuals are given.

Blend	Taste-Testers' Preference
1	20
2	30
3	35
4	15

   a. Define the experiment being conducted. How many times was it repeated?
   b. Prior to conducting the experiment, it is reasonable to assume preferences for the four blends are equal. What probabilities would you assign to the experimental outcomes prior to conducting the taste test? What method did you use?
   c. After conducting the taste test, what probabilities would you assign to the experimental outcomes? What method did you use?

3. A company that manufactures toothpaste is studying five different package designs. Assuming that one design is just as likely to be selected by a consumer as any other design, what selection probability would you assign to each of the package designs? In an actual experiment, 100 consumers were asked to pick the design they preferred. The following data were obtained. Do the data confirm the belief that one design is just as likely to be selected as another? Explain.

Design	Number of Times Preferred
1	5
2	15
3	30
4	40
5	10

4. In a recent year the U.S. Internal Revenue Service (IRS) received 132,275,830 individual tax returns. The actual number of each type of individual return received by the IRS during the year is given below:

Type of Return	Total Returns Filed
1040A, Income Under $25,000	31,675,935
Non 1040A, Income Under $25,000	20,295,694
Income $25,000–$50,000	30,828,932
Income $50,000–$100,000	26,463,973
Income $100,000 & Over	12,893,802
Schedule C, Receipts Under $25,000	3,376,943
Schedule C, Receipts $25,000–$100,000	3,867,743
Schedule C, Receipts $100,000 & Over	2,288,550
Schedule F, Receipts Under $100,000	318,646
Schedule F, Receipts $100,000 & Over	265,612

Suppose an IRS auditor must randomly select and examine an individual return.
   a. What is the probability that the auditor will select an individual return from the 1040A, Income Under $25,000 category?
   b. What is the probability that the selected return did *not* use Schedule C?
   c. What is the probability that the selected return reported income or reciepts of $100,000 & Over?
   d. In 2006 the IRS examined 1% of all individual returns. Assuming the examined returns were evenly distributed across the ten categories in the above table, how many returns from the Non 1040A, Income $50,000–$100,000 category were examined?
   e. When examining 2006 individual income tax returns, IRS auditors found that individual taxpayers still owed $13,045,221,000 in income taxes due to errors the individual taxpayers had made on this year's individual income tax returns (this is referred to by the IRS as *recommended individual taxes*). Use this information to estimate the recommended additional taxes for the Schedule C, Receipts $100,000 & Over category.

5. Strom Construction made a bid on two contracts. The owner identified the possible outcomes and subjectively assigned the following probabilities.

Experimental Outcome	Obtain Contract 1	Obtain Contract 2	Probability
1	Yes	Yes	0.15
2	Yes	No	0.15
3	No	Yes	0.30
4	No	No	0.25

    a. Are these valid probability assignments? Why or why not?

    b. If not, what would have to be done to make the probability assignments valid?

6. A sample of 100 customers of Montana Gas and Electric resulted in the following frequency distribution of monthly charges.

Amount ($)	Number
0–49	13
50–99	22
100–149	34
150–199	26
200–249	5

    a. Let A be the event that monthly charges are $150 or more. Find $P(A)$.

    b. Let B be the event that monthly charges are less than $150. Find $P(B)$.

7. Suppose that a sample space has five equally likely experimental outcomes: $E_1, E_2, E_3, E_4,$ E_5. Let

$$A = \{E_1, E_2\}$$
$$B = \{E_3, E_4\}$$
$$C = \{E_2, E_3, E_5\}$$

    a. Find $P(A)$, $P(B)$, and $P(C)$.

    b. Find $P(A \cup B)$. Are A and B mutually exclusive?

    c. Find A^c, C^c, $P(A^c)$, and $P(C^c)$.

    d. Find $A \cup B^c$ and $P(A \cup B^c)$.

    e. Find $P(B \cup C)$.

8. In a recent article *U.S. News and World Report* rated pediatric hospitals and provided data on several characteristics, including daily inpatient volume and nurse-to-patient ratio, for the top 30 hospitals on its list. Suppose we consider a daily inpatient volume of at least 200 to be high and a nurse-to-patient ratio of at least 3.0 to be high. Sixteen hospitals had a daily inpatient volume of at least 200, one-third of the hospitals had a nurse-to-patient ratio of at least 3.0, and seven of the hospitals had both a daily inpatient volume of at least 200 and a nurse-to-patient ratio of at least 3.0.

    a. Find the probability of a hospital having a daily inpatient volume of at least 200, the probability of a hospital having a nurse-to-patient ratio of at least 3.0, and the probability of a hospital having both a daily inpatient volume of at least 200 and a nurse-to-patient ratio of at least 3.0.

    b. What is the probability that a hospital had a daily inpatient volume of at least 200 or a nurse-to-patient ratio of at least 3.0 or both?

    c. What is the probability that a hospital had neither a daily inpatient volume of at least 200 nor a nurse-to-patient ratio of at least 3.0?

9. A pharmaceutical company conducted a study to evaluate the effect of an allergy relief medicine; 250 patients with symptoms that included itchy eyes and a skin rash received the new drug. The results of the study are as follows: 90 of the patients treated experienced eye relief, 135 had their skin rash clear up, and 45 experienced relief of both itchy eyes and the skin rash. What is the probability that a patient who takes the drug will experience relief of at least one of the two symptoms?

10. A quality control specialist has sampled 25 widgets from the production line. A widget can have minor or major defects. Of the 25 sampled widgets, 4 have minor defects and 2 have major defects. What is the probability that a widget has a major defect, given that it has a defect?

11. Let A be an event that a person's primary method of transportation to and from work is an automobile and B be an event that a person's primary method of transportation to and from work is a bus. Suppose that in a large city $P(A) = 0.45$ and $P(B) = 0.35$.
   a. Are events A and B mutually exclusive? What is the probability that a person uses an automobile or a bus in going to and from work?
   b. Find the probability that a person's primary method of transportation is some means other than a bus.

12. For two events A and B, $P(A) = 0.5$, $P(B) = 0.60$, and $P(A \cap B) = 0.40$.
   a. Find $P(A \mid B)$.
   b. Find $P(B \mid A)$.
   c. Are A and B independent? Why or why not?

13. A survey of MBA students obtained the following data on "Students' first reason for application to the school in which they matriculated."

		Reason for Application			
		School Quality	School Cost or Convenience	Other	Totals
Enrollment Status	Full Time	421	393	76	890
	Part Time	400	593	46	1039
	Totals	821	986	122	1929

   a. Develop a joint probability table using these data.
   b. Use the marginal probabilities of school quality, school cost or convenience, and other to comment on the most important reason for choosing a school.
   c. If a student goes full time, what is the probability that school quality will be the first reason for choosing a school?
   d. If a student goes part time, what is the probability that school quality will be the first reason for choosing a school?
   e. Let A be the event that a student is full time and let B be the event that the student lists school quality as the first reason for applying. Are events A and B independent? Justify your answer.

14. The checking accounts of Sun Bank are categorized by the age of account and the account balance. Auditors will select accounts at random from the following 1000 accounts (numbers in the table are the number of accounts in each category):

	Account Balance		
Age of the Account	**0–$499**	**$500–$999**	**$1000 or More**
Less than 2 years	120	240	90
2 years or more	75	275	200

a. What is the probability that an account is less than 2 years old?
b. What is the probability that an account has a balance of $1000 or more?
c. What is the probability that two accounts will both have a balance of $1000 or more?
d. What is the probability that an account has a balance of $500–$999 given that its age is 2 years or more?
e. What is the probability that an account is less than 2 years old and has a balance of $1000 or more?
f. What is the probability that an account is at least 2 years old given that the balance is $500–$999?

15. During a recent period of high unemployment, hundreds of thousands of drivers dropped their automobile insurance. Sample data representative of the national automobile insurance coverage for individuals 18 years of age and older are shown here.

		Automobile Insurance	
		Yes	**No**
Age	**18 to 34**	1500	340
	35 and over	1900	260

a. Develop a joint probability table for these data and use the table to answer the remaining questions.
b. What do the marginal probabilities tell you about the age of the U.S. population?
c. What is the probability that a randomly selected individual does not have automobile insurance coverage?
d. If the individual is between the ages of 18 and 34, what is the probability that the individual does not have automobile insurance coverage?
e. If the individual is age 35 or over, what is the probability that the individual does not have automobile insurance coverage?
f. If the individual does not have automobile insurance, what is the probability that the individual is in the 18–34 age group?
g. What does the probability information tell you about automobile insurance coverage in the United States?

16. A purchasing agent placed a rush order for a particular raw material with two different suppliers, A and B. If neither order arrives in four days, the production process must be shut down until at least one of the orders arrives. The probability that supplier A can deliver the material in four days is 0.55. The probability that supplier B can deliver the material in four days is 0.35.
a. What is the probability that both suppliers deliver the material in four days? Because two separate suppliers are involved, assume independence.
b. What is the probability that at least one supplier delivers the material in four days?
c. What is the probability that the production process is shut down in four days because of a shortage of raw material (that is, both orders are late)?

17. Interested in learning more about its fans, the marketing office of the Arena Football League (AFL) conducted a survey at one of its games. The survey had 989 respondents: 759 males and 230 females. Out of the 989 total respondents, 196 stated that they had attended multiple AFL games. Of these 196 fans that had attended multiple games, 177 were male. Using this survey information, answer the following questions.
    a. What is the probability that a randomly selected fan has attended multiple games?
    b. Given that a randomly selected fan has attended multiple games, what is the probability of this person being male?
    c. What is the probability of a randomly selected fan being male and having attended multiple games?
    d. Given that a randomly selected fan is male, what is the probability that this person has attended multiple games?
    e. What is the probability that a randomly selected fan is male or has attended multiple games?

18. In the evaluation of a sales training program, a firm discovered that of 50 salespeople receiving a bonus last year, 20 had attended a special sales training program. The firm employs 200 salespeople. Let B = the event that a salesperson makes a bonus and S = the event that a salesperson attends the sales training program.
    a. Find $P(B)$, $P(S \mid B)$, and $P(S \cap B)$.
    b. Assume that 40% of the salespeople attended the training program. What is the probability that a salesperson makes a bonus given that the salesperson attended the sales training program, $P(B \mid S)$?
    c. If the firm evaluates the training program in terms of its effect on the probability of a salesperson's receiving a bonus, what is your evaluation of the training program? Comment on whether B and S are dependent or independent events.

19. A company studied the number of lost-time accidents occurring at its Brownsville, Texas, plant. Historical records show that 6% of the employees had lost-time accidents last year. Management believes that a special safety program will reduce the accidents to 5% during the current year. In addition, it estimates that 15% of those employees having had lost-time accidents last year will have a lost-time accident during the current year.
    a. What percentage of the employees will have lost-time accidents in both years?
    b. What percentage of the employees will have at least one lost-time accident over the two-year period?

20. The prior probabilities for events A_1, A_2, and A_3 are $P(A_1) = 0.20$, $P(A_2) = 0.50$, and $P(A_3) = 0.30$. The conditional probabilities of event B given A_1, A_2, and A_3 are $P(B \mid A_1) = 0.50$, $P(B \mid A_2) = 0.40$, and $P(B \mid A_3) = 0.30$.
    a. Compute $P(B \cap A_1)$, $P(B \cap A_2)$, and $P(B \cap A_3)$.
    b. Apply Bayes' theorem, equation (2.16), to compute the posterior probability $P(A_2 \mid B)$.
    c. Use the tabular approach to applying Bayes' theorem to compute $P(A_1 \mid B)$, $P(A_2 \mid B)$, and $P(A_3 \mid B)$.

21. A consulting firm submitted a bid for a large research project. The firm's management initially felt there was a 50/50 chance of getting the bid. However, the agency to which the bid was submitted subsequently requested additional information on the bid. Experience indicates that on 75% of the successful bids and 40% of the unsuccessful bids the agency requested additional information.
    a. What is the prior probability that the bid will be successful (i.e., prior to receiving the request for additional information)?
    b. What is the conditional probability of a request for additional information given that the bid will ultimately be successful?

c. Compute a posterior probability that the bid will be successful given that a request for additional information has been received.

22. Companies that do business over the Internet can often obtain probability information about website visitors from previous websites visited. For instance, Par Fore created a website to market golf equipment and apparel, and the organization has collected data from its website visitors. Management would like a certain offer to appear for female visitors and a different offer to appear for male visitors. A sample of past website visits indicates that 60% of the visitors to *ParFore.com* are male and 40% are female.
    a. What is your prior probability that the next visitor to the Par Fore website will be female?
    b. Suppose you know that the current visitor at the Par Fore website previously visited the Dillard's website and that women are three times as likely to visit this website as men. What is your revised probability that the visitor is female? Should you display the offer that has more appeal to female visitors or the one that has more appeal to male visitors?

23. An oil company purchased an option on land in Alaska. Preliminary geologic studies assigned the following prior probabilities.

$$P(\text{high quality oil}) = 0.50$$
$$P(\text{medium quality oil}) = 0.20$$
$$P(\text{no oil}) = 0.30$$

    a. What is the probability of finding oil?
    b. After 200 feet of drilling on the first well, a soil test is made. The probabilities of finding the particular type of soil identified by the test are

$$P(\text{soil} \mid \text{high quality oil}) = 0.20$$
$$P(\text{soil} \mid \text{medium quality oil}) = 0.20$$
$$P(\text{soil} \mid \text{no oil}) = 0.30$$

How should the firm interpret the soil test? What are the revised probabilities, and what is the new probability of finding oil?

24. During a recent year, speeding was reported in 12.9% of all automobile accidents in the United States. Assume the probability that speeding is reported in an accident is 0.129, the probability of an accident in which speeding is reported leading to a fatality is 0.196, and the probability of an accident in which speeding is not reported leading to a fatality is 0.05. Suppose you learn of an accident involving a fatality. What is the probability that speeding was reported?

25. The Wayne Manufacturing Company purchases a certain part from suppliers A, B, and C. Supplier A supplies 60% of the parts, B 30%, and C 10%. The quality of parts varies among the suppliers, with A, B, and C parts having 0.25%, 1%, and 2% defective rates, respectively. The parts are used in one of the company's major products.
    a. What is the probability that the company's major product is assembled with a defective part? Use the tabular approach to Bayes' theorem to solve.
    b. When a defective part is found, which supplier is the likely source?

26. Bayes' theorem and conditional probability can be used in medical diagnosis. Prior probabilities of diseases are based on the physician's assessment of factors such as geographic location, seasonal influence, and occurrence of epidemics. Assume that a patient is believed to have one of two diseases, denoted D_1 and D_2, with $P(D_1) = 0.60$ and $P(D_2) = 0.40$,

and that medical research shows a probability associated with each symptom that may accompany the diseases. Suppose that, given diseases D_1 and D_2, the probabilities that a patient will have symptoms S_1, S_2, or S_3 are as follows:

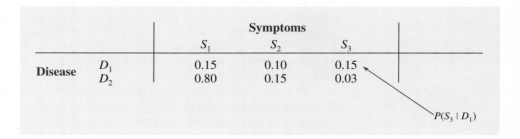

		Symptoms		
		S_1	S_2	S_3
Disease	D_1	0.15	0.10	0.15
	D_2	0.80	0.15	0.03

$P(S_3 \mid D_1)$

After finding that a certain symptom is present, the medical diagnosis may be aided by finding the revised probabilities that the patient has each particular disease. Compute the posterior probabilities of each disease for the following medical findings.

a.   The patient has symptom S_1.
b.   The patient has symptom S_2.
c.   The patient has symptom S_3.
d.   For the patient with symptom S_1 in part (a), suppose that symptom S_2 also is present. What are the revised probabilities of D_1 and D_2?

27.   In an article about investment alternatives, *Money* magazine reported that drug stocks provide a potential for long-term growth, with over 50% of the adult population of the United States taking prescription drugs on a regular basis. For adults age 65 and older, 82% take prescription drugs regularly. For adults age 18 to 64, 49% take prescription drugs regularly. The 18–64 age group accounts for 83.5% of the adult population (*Statistical Abstract of the United States*, 2008).

a.   What is the probability that a randomly selected adult is 65 or older?
b.   Given that an adult takes prescription drugs regularly, what is the probability that the adult is age 65 or older?

28.   According to the Open Doors 2011 Report, 9.5% of all full-time U.S. undergraduate students studied abroad during the 2009–2010 academic year (Institute of International Education, November 14, 2011). Assume that participation records show women make up 60% of the students who studied abroad during the 2009–2010 academic year, but women make up only 49% of the students who didn't participate.

a.   Let A_1 = the student studied abroad during the 2009–2010 academic year
        A_2 = the student did not study abroad during the 2009–2010 academic year
        W = the student is a female student
      Using the given information, what are the values for $P(A_1)$, $P(A_2)$, $P(W \mid A_1)$, and $P(W \mid A_2)$?
b.   What is the probability that a female student studied abroad during the 2009–2010 academic year?
c.   What is the probability that a male student studied abroad during the 2009–2010 academic year?
d.   Given the preceding results, what were the percentage of women and the percentage of men studying full-time during the 2009–2010 academic year?

29.   Recently, management at Oak Tree Golf Course received a few complaints about the condition of the greens. Several players complained that the greens are too fast. Rather than react to the comments of just a few, the Golf Association conducted a survey of 100 male and 100 female golfers. The survey results are summarized here.

	Male Golfers			Female Golfers	
	Greens Condition			**Greens Condition**	
Handicap	**Too Fast**	**Acceptable**	**Handicap**	**Too Fast**	**Acceptable**
Under 15	10	40	**Under 15**	1	9
15 or more	25	25	**15 or more**	39	51

a. Combine these two crosstabulations into a single crosstabulation, with Male and Female as the row labels and Too Fast and Acceptable as the column labels. Which group shows the highest proportion saying that the greens are too fast?

b. Refer to the initial crosstabulations. For those players with low handicaps (better players), which group (male or female) shows the highest proportion saying the greens are too fast?

c. Refer to the initial crosstabulations. For those players with higher handicaps, which group (male or female) shows the highest proportion saying the greens are too fast?

d. What conclusions can you draw about the preferences of men and women concerning the speed of the greens? Are the conclusions you draw from part (a) as compared with parts (b) and (c) consistent? Explain any apparent inconsistencies.

30. A small private midwestern university has been accused of favoring male applicants in its admissions process. Prior to the current academic year, 44% of male applicants were admitted by the university while only 33% of female applicants were admitted. The numbers of applicants accepted and denied for each gender are provided in the following table for the College of Engineering and the College of Business.

	College of Engineering		College of Business	
	Male Applicants	**Female Applicants**	**Male Applicants**	**Female Applicants**
Accept	60	20	10	20
Deny	60	20	30	60

a. Combine these two crosstabulations into a single crosstabulation, with Accept and Deny as the row labels and Male and Female as the column labels. Use these data to confirm the reported rates of acceptance across the university by gender (44% of male applicants were admitted and 33% of female applicants were admitted).

b. Refer to the initial crosstabulations. What are your conclusions about the possible gender bias in the admission process? Is this consistent with the conclusions you reach when assessing the aggregated data in part (a) of this question?

Case Problem   Hamilton County Judges

Hamilton County judges try thousands of cases per year. In an overwhelming majority of the cases disposed, the verdict stands as rendered. However, some cases are appealed, and of those appealed, some of the cases are reversed. Kristen DelGuzzi of the *Cincinnati Enquirer* conducted a study of cases handled by Hamilton County judges over a three-year period. Shown in Table 2.7 are the results for 182,908 cases handled (disposed) by 38 judges in Common Pleas Court, Domestic Relations Court, and Municipal Court. Two of the judges (Dinkelacker and Hogan) did not serve in the same court for the entire three-year period.

TABLE 2.7 CASES DISPOSED, APPEALED, AND REVERSED IN HAMILTON COUNTY COURTS

Common Pleas Court

Judge	Total Cases Disposed	Appealed Cases	Reversed Cases
Fred Cartolano	3037	137	12
Thomas Crush	3372	119	10
Patrick Dinkelacker	1258	44	8
Timothy Hogan	1954	60	7
Robert Kraft	3138	127	7
William Mathews	2264	91	18
William Morrissey	3032	121	22
Norbert Nadel	2959	131	20
Arthur Ney, Jr.	3219	125	14
Richard Niehaus	3353	137	16
Thomas Nurre	3000	121	6
John O'Connor	2969	129	12
Robert Ruehlman	3205	145	18
J. Howard Sundermann	955	60	10
Ann Marie Tracey	3141	127	13
Ralph Winkler	3089	88	6
Total	43,945	1762	199

Domestic Relations Court

Judge	Total Cases Disposed	Appealed Cases	Reversed Cases
Penelope Cunningham	2729	7	1
Patrick Dinkelacker	6001	19	4
Deborah Gaines	8799	48	9
Ronald Panioto	12,970	32	3
Total	30,499	106	17

Municipal Court

Judge	Total Cases Disposed	Appealed Cases	Reversed Cases
Mike Allen	6149	43	4
Nadine Allen	7812	34	6
Timothy Black	7954	41	6
David Davis	7736	43	5
Leslie Isaiah Gaines	5282	35	13
Karla Grady	5253	6	0
Deidra Hair	2532	5	0
Dennis Helmick	7900	29	5
Timothy Hogan	2308	13	2
James Patrick Kenney	2798	6	1
Joseph Luebbers	4698	25	8
William Mallory	8277	38	9
Melba Marsh	8219	34	7
Beth Mattingly	2971	13	1
Albert Mestemaker	4975	28	9
Mark Painter	2239	7	3
Jack Rosen	7790	41	13
Mark Schweikert	5403	33	6
David Stockdale	5371	22	4
John A. West	2797	4	2
Total	108,464	500	104

The purpose of the newspaper's study was to evaluate the performance of the judges. Appeals are often the result of mistakes made by judges, and the newspaper wanted to know which judges were doing a good job and which were making too many mistakes. You have been called in to assist in the data analysis. Use your knowledge of probability and conditional probability to help with the ranking of the judges. You also may be able to analyze the likelihood of cases handled by the different courts being appealed and reversed.

Managerial Report

Prepare a report with your rankings of the judges. Also include an analysis of the likelihood of appeal and case reversal in the three courts. At a minimum, your report should include the following:

1. The probability of cases being appealed and reversed in the three different courts.
2. The probability of a case being appealed for each judge.
3. The probability of a case being reversed for each judge.
4. The probability of reversal given an appeal for each judge.
5. Rank the judges within each court. State the criteria you used and provide a rationale for your choice.

Case Problem ## College Softball Recruiting

College softball programs have a limited number of scholarships to offer promising high school seniors, so the programs invest a great deal of effort in evaluating these players. One measure of performance the programs commonly use to evaluate recruits is the *batting average*—the proportion of at-bats (excluding times when the player is walked or hit by a pitch) in which the player gets a hit. For example, a player who gets 50 hits in 150 at-bats has a batting average of

$$\frac{50}{150} = 0.333$$

A college softball program is considering two players, Fran Hayes and Millie Marshall, who have recently completed their senior years of high school. Their respective statistics for their junior and senior years are as shown in Table 2.8.

TABLE 2.8   SUMMARY OF BATTING PERFORMANCES IN JUNIOR AND SENIOR YEARS BY HAYES AND MARSHALL

	Junior Year		Senior Year	
	At-Bats	**Hits**	**At-Bats**	**Hits**
Fran Hayes	200	70	40	15
Millie Marshall	196	67	205	76

Managerial Report

The Athletic Director and Coach of the women's softball team at a large public university are trying to decide to which of these two players they will offer an athletic scholarship (i.e., an opportunity to attend the university for free in exchange for playing on the university's softball team). Take the following steps to determine which player had the better batting average over the two-year period provided in the table, and use your results to advise the Athletic Director and Coach on their decision.

1. Calculate the batting average of each player for her junior year; then also calculate the batting average of each player for her senior year. Which player would this analysis lead you to choose?
2. Calculate the batting average of each player for her combined junior and senior years. Which player would this analysis lead you to choose?
3. After considering both of your analyses, which player would you choose? Why?
4. Prepare a report on your findings for the atheletic director and coach of the college program. Focus on clearly explaining the discrepancy in your two analyses.

CHAPTER 3

Probability Distributions

In this chapter we continue the study of probability by introducing the concepts of random variables and probability distributions. We consider the probability distributions of both discrete and continuous random variables. Of particular interest are the binomial, Poisson, uniform, normal, and exponential probability distributions. These probability distributions are of great interest because they are used extensively in practice. The Q.M. in Action, ESPN and Probability, describes how the development and use of a probability distribution helped the organization enhance its audience's enjoyment and understanding of sports.

Q.M. *in* ACTION

ESPN AND PROBABILITY*

The Entertainment and Sports Programming Network, known as ESPN since 1985, was originally established as a nationwide cable-television network dedicated to broadcasting and producing sports-related programming. The Bristol, Connecticut–based network, which provides programming 24 hours a day throughout the year, has grown rapidly since its debut on September 7, 1979. At various times its programming has included Major League Baseball, the National Football League (NFL), the National Basketball Association (NBA), the National Hockey League (NHL), NASCAR, NCAA Football and Basketball, Major League Soccer (MLS), the Men's and Women's professional golf associations (PGA and LPGA), and Men's and Women's professional tennis (ATP and WTA). ESPN is now in over 100 million homes in the United States, and ESPN International spans over 200 countries and territories on all seven continents and includes 46 television networks reaching over 350 million subscribers in 16 languages, plus wireless, interactive, print, radio, broadband, event management, and consumer products.

ESPN's rapid growth has coincided with a dramatic increase in sports fans' desire for more sophisticated analyses. The organization responded to this trend by establishing its Production Analytics department, a group of analysts who provide all of ESPN's media platforms with statistical analyses for a wide variety of sports problems. Senior Director of the Production Analytics department Jeff Bennett explains that "ESPN appreciates the sports fan's passion for meaningful analytics, and we are dedicated to creating and providing this content.

Basic probability and statistics are critical tools in our analytic arsenal."

Alok Pattani, who is an Analytics Specialist in the Production Analytics department, further describes the department's uses of some specific probability concepts. "For example, we use very basic probability to determine the likelihood an NBA team will win one of the first three picks in the NBA draft. The league holds a Draft Lottery to determine which of its fourteen teams that didn't qualify for the playoffs during the most recent season will receive each of the first three picks, which are considered to be extremely valuable. The lottery is weighted so that teams with worse records have better chances of obtaining early picks, and we use information on how many chances each team is allocated to calculate the probability that any of these fourteen teams will win one of those top picks.

"Conditional probability is also very important; when we look at the probability a team will win a home game or a player will get a hit when playing at night, we are using conditional probability." Alok continues, "We use probability distributions extensively in our work, especially the binomial and normal distributions. We apply the binomial distribution to all kinds of success and failure situations such as wins and losses, field goals and missed shots in basketball, complete and incomplete passes in football, and hits and outs in baseball. The binomial distribution is also useful when estimating the probability of a hitting streak in baseball or a winning streak in any sport."

Bennett adds, "The results of these types of analyses are of great interest to ESPN's base. They enhance the fan's enjoyment and understanding of his or her favorite sports, and that is good business for ESPN."

*The authors are indebted to Jeff Bennett and Alok Pattani of ESPN Inc. for providing input for this Q.M. in Action.

3.1 Random Variables

Recall that in Chapter 2 we defined an experiment as any process that generates well-defined outcomes. We now want to concentrate on the process of assigning *numeric values* to experimental outcomes. To do so we introduce the notion of a random variable.

For any particular experiment a random variable can be defined so that each possible experimental outcome generates exactly one numeric value for the random variable. For example, if we consider the experiment of selling automobiles for one day at a particular dealership, we could describe the experimental outcomes in terms of the *number* of cars sold. In this case, if x = number of cars sold, x is called a random variable. The particular numeric value that the random variable assumes depends on the outcome of the experiment; that is, we will not know the specific value of the random variable until we have observed the experimental outcome. For example, if on a given day three cars are sold, the value of the random variable is 3; if on another day (a repeat of the experiment) four cars are sold, the value is 4. We define a random variable as follows:

Random variables must assume numeric values.

A **random variable** is a numeric description of the outcome of an experiment.

Some additional examples of experiments and their associated random variables are given in Table 3.1. Although many experiments have experimental outcomes that lend themselves quite naturally to numeric values, others do not. For example, for the experiment of tossing a coin one time, the experimental outcome will be either a head or a tail, neither of which has a natural numeric value. However, we still may want to express the outcomes in terms of a random variable. Thus, we need a rule that can be used to assign a numeric value to each of the experimental outcomes. One possibility is to let the random variable $x = 1$ if the experimental outcome is a head and $x = 0$ if the experimental outcome is a tail. Although the numeric values for x are arbitrary, x is a random variable because it describes the experimental outcomes numerically.

A random variable may be classified as either discrete or continuous, depending on the numeric values it may assume. A random variable that may assume only a finite or an infinite sequence (e.g., 1, 2, 3, . . .) of values is a **discrete random variable**. The number of units sold, the number of defects observed, the number of customers that enter a bank during one day of operation, and so on are examples of discrete random variables. The first two and the last random variables in Table 3.1 are discrete. Random variables such as weight, time, and temperature that may assume any value in a certain interval or collection of intervals are **continuous random variables**. For instance, the third random variable in Table 3.1 is a continuous random variable because it may assume any value in the interval from 0 to 100 (for example, 56.33 or 64.223).

Try Problem 1 for practice in identifying discrete and continuous random variables.

TABLE 3.1 EXAMPLES OF RANDOM VARIABLES

Experiment	Random Variable (x)	Possible Values for the Random Variable
Make 100 sales calls	Total number of sales	0, 1, 2, . . . , 100
Inspect a shipment of 70 radios	Number of defective radios	0, 1, 2, . . . , 70
Build a new library	Percentage of project completed after 6 months	$0 \leq x \leq 100$
Operate a restaurant	Number of customers entering in one day	0, 1, 2, . . .

NOTES AND COMMENTS

1. One way to determine whether a random variable is discrete or continuous is to think of the values of the random variable as points on a line. Choose two points representing values the random variable might assume. If the entire line segment between the two points also represents possible values for the random variable, the random variable is continuous. An alternative (but equivalent) way of determining whether a random variable is discrete or continuous is to choose two points that represent values the random variable might assume. If, no matter what two points you initially chose, you can always find a third point between your initial two points that also represents a value of the random variable, the random variable is continuous. For example, if your random variable is the exact weight of a bag of potato chips and you choose 16.0005 ounces and 16.0006 ounces as your original two points, the point 16.00051 (or 16.00052 or 16.00053, etc.) ounces represents a possible value of the exact weight of the bag of potato chips and lies between your intial two points. No matter what two values you initially select, you can find another value that represents a value of the random variable and lies between your initial two points. On the other hand, if your random variable is the number of customers who enter a restaurant in a day and you choose 109 customers and 110 customers as your initial two points, there is no point that represents a value of the random variable and lies between your initial two points (i.e., you cannot have 109.7 customers enter a restaurant on a particular day). This indicates that the random variable is discrete.

3.2 Discrete Random Variables

We can demonstrate the use of a discrete random variable by considering the sales of automobiles at DiCarlo Motors, Inc., in Saratoga, New York. The owner of DiCarlo Motors is interested in the daily sales volume for automobiles. Suppose that we let x be a random variable denoting the number of cars sold on a given day. Sales records show that 5 is the maximum number of cars that DiCarlo has ever sold during one day. The owner believes that the previous history of sales adequately represents what will occur in the future, so we would expect the random variable x to assume one of the numeric values 0, 1, 2, 3, 4, or 5. The possible values of the random variable are finite; thus we would classify x as a discrete random variable.

Probability Distribution of a Discrete Random Variable

Suppose that in checking DiCarlo's sales records we find that over the past year the firm was open for business 300 days. The sales volumes generated and the frequency of their occurrence are summarized in Table 3.2. With these historical data available, the owner of

TABLE 3.2 CARS SOLD PER DAY AT DICARLO MOTORS

Sales Volume	Number of Days
No sales	54
One car	117
Two cars	72
Three cars	42
Four cars	12
Five cars	3
Total	300

TABLE 3.3   PROBABILITY DISTRIBUTION FOR THE NUMBER OF CARS SOLD PER DAY

x	$f(x)$
0	0.18
1	0.39
2	0.24
3	0.14
4	0.04
5	0.01
Total	1.00

DiCarlo Motors believes that the relative frequency method will provide a reasonable means of assessing the probabilities for the random variable x. The **probability function**, denoted $f(x)$, provides the probability that the random variable x takes on a specific value. Because on 54 of the 300 days of historical data DiCarlo Motors did not sell any cars and because no sales corresponds to $x = 0$, we assign to $f(0)$ the value $^{54}/_{300} = 0.18$. Similarly, $f(1)$ denotes the probability that x takes on the value 1, so we assign to $f(1)$ the value $^{117}/_{300} = 0.39$. After computing the relative frequencies for the other possible values of x, we can develop a table of x and $f(x)$ values. Table 3.3 shows a tabular presentation of the probability distribution of the random variable x.

We can also represent the probability distribution of x graphically. In Figure 3.1 the values of the random variable x are shown on the horizontal axis. The probability that x takes on each of these values is shown on the vertical axis. For many discrete random variables the probability distribution also can be represented as a formula that provides $f(x)$ for every possible value of x. We illustrate this approach in the next section.

FIGURE 3.1   PROBABILITY DISTRIBUTION FOR THE NUMBER OF CARS SOLD PER DAY

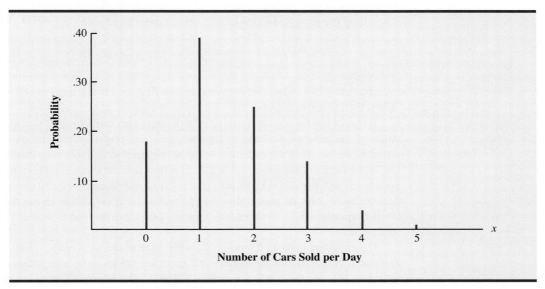

In Section 2.2 we defined the two basic requirements of all probability assignments as $0 \leq P(E_i) \leq 1$ and $\Sigma P(E_i) = 1$. Equations (3.1) and (3.2) are the analogs of these basic requirements.

In the development of a **discrete probability distribution**, two requirements must always be satisfied:

$$f(x) \geq 0 \tag{3.1}$$

$$\Sigma f(x) = 1 \tag{3.2}$$

Equation (3.1) specifies that the probabilities associated with each value of x must be greater than or equal to zero, whereas equation (3.2) indicates that the sum of the probabilities for all values of the random variable x must be equal to 1. Table 3.3 shows that equations (3.1) and (3.2) are satisfied. Thus, the probability distribution developed for DiCarlo Motors is a valid discrete probability distribution.

After establishing a random variable and its probability distribution, we can develop a variety of additional probability information, depending on the needs and interests of the decision maker. For example, in the DiCarlo Motors problem the probability distribution shown in Table 3.3 can be used to provide the following information:

1. There is a 0.18 probability that no cars will be sold during a day.
2. The most probable sales volume is 1, with $f(1) = 0.39$.
3. There is a 0.05 probability of an outstanding sales day with four or five cars being sold.

Try Problem 3 for practice in constructing a discrete probability distribution.

Using probability information such as that just given, DiCarlo's management can understand better the uncertainties associated with the car sales operation. Perhaps this improved understanding can serve as the basis for a new policy or decision that will increase the effectiveness of the firm.

Expected Value

After constructing the probability distribution for a random variable, we often want to compute the mean or expected value of the random variable. The **expected value** of a discrete random variable is a weighted average of all possible values of the random variable, where the weights are the probabilities associated with the values. The mathematical formula for computing the expected value of a discrete random variable x is

$$E(x) = \mu = \Sigma x f(x) \tag{3.3}$$

As equation (3.3) shows, both the notations $E(x)$ and μ are used to refer to the expected value of a random variable.

To compute the expected value of a discrete random variable, we must multiply each value of the random variable by its corresponding probability and then add the resulting terms. Calculation of the expected value of the random variable (number of daily sales) for DiCarlo Motors is shown in Table 3.4. The first column contains the values of the random variable x, and the second column contains their associated probabilities $f(x)$. Multiplying each value of x by its probability $f(x)$ provides the $xf(x)$ values in the third column. Following equation (3.3), we sum this column, $\Sigma x f(x)$, to find the expected value of 1.50 cars sold per day.

The expected value of a random variable is the mean, or average, value. For experiments that can be repeated numerous times, the expected value can be interpreted as the "long-run" average value for the random variable. However, the expected value is not necessarily the

TABLE 3.4   EXPECTED VALUE CALCULATION

x	$f(x)$	$xf(x)$
0	0.18	$0(0.18) = 0.00$
1	0.39	$1(0.39) = 0.39$
2	0.24	$2(0.24) = 0.48$
3	0.14	$3(0.14) = 0.42$
4	0.04	$4(0.04) = 0.16$
5	0.01	$5(0.01) = \underline{0.05}$
		$E(x) = 1.50$

number that we think the random variable will assume the next time the experiment is conducted. In fact, it is impossible for DiCarlo to sell exactly 1.50 cars on any day. However, if we envision selling cars at DiCarlo Motors for many days into the future, the expected value of 1.50 cars provides the mean, or average, daily sales volume.

The expected value can be important to a manager from both the planning and decision-making points of view. For example, suppose that DiCarlo Motors will be open 60 days during the next three months. How many cars will be sold during this time? Although we can't specify the exact sales for any given day, the expected value of 1.50 cars per day provides an expected or average sales estimate of $60(1.50) = 90$ cars for the next three-month period. In terms of setting sales quotas and/or planning orders, the expected value may provide helpful decision-making information.

Variance

The expected value gives us an idea of the average or central value for the random variable, but we often want a measure of the dispersion, or variability, of the possible values of the random variable. For example, if the values of the random variable range from quite large to quite small, we would expect a large value for the measure of variability. If the values of the random variable show only modest variation, we would expect a relatively small value for the measure of variability. The variance is a measure commonly used to summarize the variability in the values of a random variable. The mathematical expression for the *variance* of a discrete random variable is

An alternative formula for the variance of a discrete random variable is $Var(x) = \Sigma x^2 f(x) - \mu^2$.

$$\text{Var}(x) = \sigma^2 = \Sigma(x - \mu)^2 f(x) \qquad \textbf{(3.4)}$$

As equation (3.4) shows, an essential part of the variance formula is a *deviation, $x - \mu$*, which measures how far a particular value of the random variable is from the expected value or mean, μ. In computing the variance of a discrete random variable, we square the deviations and then weight them by the corresponding probability. The sum of these weighted squared deviations for all values of the random variable is the **variance**. In other words, the variance is a weighted average of the squared deviations.

The calculation of the variance for the number of daily sales in the DiCarlo Motors problem is summarized in Table 3.5. We see that the variance for the number of cars sold per day is 1.25. A related measure of variability is the **standard deviation**, σ, which is

TABLE 3.5   VARIANCE CALCULATION

x	$x - \mu$	$(x - \mu)^2$	$f(x)$	$(x - \mu)^2 f(x)$
0	$0 - 1.50 = -1.50$	2.25	0.18	$2.25(0.18) = 0.4050$
1	$1 - 1.50 = -0.50$	0.25	0.39	$0.25(0.39) = 0.0975$
2	$2 - 1.50 = 0.50$	0.25	0.24	$0.25(0.24) = 0.0600$
3	$3 - 1.50 = 1.50$	2.25	0.14	$2.25(0.14) = 0.3150$
4	$4 - 1.50 = 2.50$	6.25	0.04	$6.25(0.04) = 0.2500$
5	$5 - 1.50 = 3.50$	12.25	0.01	$12.25(0.01) = \underline{0.1225}$
				$\sigma^2 = 1.2500$

defined as the positive square root of the variance. For DiCarlo Motors, the standard deviation of the number of cars sold per day is

$$\sigma = \sqrt{1.25} = 1.118$$

For the purpose of easier managerial interpretation, the standard deviation may be preferred over the variance because it is measured in the same units as the random variable ($\sigma = 1.118$ cars sold per day). The variance (σ^2) is measured in squared units and is thus more difficult for a manager to interpret.

Try Problem 4 to be sure you can compute the expected value, variance, and standard deviation.

At this point our interpretation of the variance and the standard deviation is limited to comparisons of the variability of different random variables. For example, if the daily sales data from a second DiCarlo dealership in Albany, New York, provided $\sigma^2 = 2.56$ and $\sigma = 1.6$, we can conclude that the number of cars sold per day at this dealership exhibits more variability than at the first DiCarlo dealership, where $\sigma^2 = 1.25$ and $\sigma = 1.118$. Later in this chapter we discuss the normal distribution. For that probability distribution, we show that the variance and the standard deviation of the random variable are essential for making probability calculations.

The Q.M. in Action, Long Island City, New York, describes how Citbank models the length of waiting lines at its ATMs as discrete random variables in order to provide better service to its customers.

Q.M. *in* ACTION

CITIBANK*
LONG ISLAND CITY, NEW YORK

Citibank, the retail banking division of Citigroup, offers a wide range of financial services, including checking and saving accounts, loans and mortgages, insurance, and investment services. It delivers these services through a unique system referred to as Citibanking.

Citibank was one of the first banks in the United States to introduce automatic teller machines (ATMs). Citibank's ATMs, located in Citicard Banking Centers (CBCs), let customers do all of their banking in one place with the touch of a finger, 24 hours a day, 7 days a week. More than 150 different banking functions—from deposits to managing investments—can be performed with ease. Citibank customers use ATMs for 80% of their transactions.

Each Citibank CBC operates as a waiting line system with randomly arriving customers seeking service

---

*The authors are indebted to Ms. Stacey Karter, Citibank, for providing this Q.M. in Action.

(continued)

at one of the ATMs. If all ATMs are busy, the arriving customers wait in line. Periodic CBC capacity studies are used to analyze customer waiting times and to determine whether additional ATMs are needed.

Data collected by Citibank showed that the random customer arrivals followed a probability distribution known as the Poisson distribution. Using the Poisson distribution, Citibank can compute probabilities for the number of customers arriving at a CBC during any time period and make decisions concerning the number of ATMs needed. For example, let x = the number of customers arriving during a one-minute period. Assuming that a particular CBC has a mean arrival rate of two customers per minute, the following table shows the prob-abilities for the number of customers arriving during a one-minute period.

x	Probability
0	.1353
1	.2707
2	.2707
3	.1804
4	.0902
5 or more	.0527

Discrete probability distributions, such as the one used by Citibank, are the topic of this chapter. In addition to the Poisson distribution, you will learn about the binomial and hypergeometric distributions and how they can be used to provide helpful probability information.

3.3 Binomial Probability Distribution

In this section we consider a class of experiments that meet the following conditions:

1. The experiment consists of a sequence of n identical *trials*.
2. Two outcomes are possible on each trial. We refer to one outcome as a *success* and the other as a *failure*.
3. The probabilities of the two outcomes do not change from one trial to the next.
4. The trials are independent (i.e., the outcome of one trial does not affect the outcome of any other trial).

Experiments that satisfy conditions 2, 3, and 4 are said to be generated by a *Bernoulli process*. In addition, if condition 1 is satisfied (there are n identical trials), we have a *binomial experiment*. An important discrete random variable associated with the binomial experiment is the number of outcomes labeled success in the n trials. If we let x denote the value of this random variable, then x can have a value of 0, 1, 2, 3, . . . , n, depending on the number of successes observed in the n trials. The probability distribution associated with this random variable is called the **binomial probability distribution**.

Try Problem 9, parts (a–d), for practice computing binomial probabilities.

In cases where the binomial distribution is applicable, the mathematical formula for computing the probability of any value for the random variable is the binomial probability function

$$f(x) = \frac{n!}{x!(n-x)!}p^x(1-p)^{n-x} \qquad x = 0, 1, \ldots, n \qquad \textbf{(3.5)}$$

where

$$n = \text{number of trials}$$
$$p = \text{probability of success on one trial}$$
$$x = \text{number of successes in } n \text{ trials}$$
$$f(x) = \text{probability of } x \text{ successes in } n \text{ trials}$$

The term $n!$ in the preceding expression is referred to as *n factorial* and is defined as

$$n! = n(n - 1)(n - 2) \cdots (2)(1)$$

For example, $4! = (4)(3)(2)(1) = 24$. Also, by definition, the special case of zero factorial is $0! = 1$.

Nastke Clothing Store Problem

To illustrate the binomial probability distribution, let us consider the experiment of customers entering the Nastke Clothing Store. To keep the problem relatively small, we restrict the experiment to the next three customers. If, based on experience, the store manager estimates that the probability of a customer making a purchase is 0.30, what is the probability that exactly two of the next three customers make a purchase?

We first want to demonstrate that three customers entering the clothing store and deciding whether to make a purchase can be viewed as a binomial experiment. Checking the four requirements for a binomial experiment, we note the following:

1. The experiment can be described as a sequence of three identical trials, one trial for each of the three customers who will enter the store.
2. Two outcomes—the customer makes a purchase (success) or the customer does not make a purchase (failure)—are possible for each trial.
3. The probabilities of the purchase (0.30) and no purchase (0.70) outcomes are assumed to be the same for all customers.
4. The purchase decision of each customer is independent of the purchase decision of the other customers.

Thus, if we define the random variable x as the number of customers making a purchase (i.e., the number of successes in the three trials), we satisfy the requirements of the binomial probability distribution.

With $n = 3$ trials and the probability of a purchase $p = 0.30$ for each customer, we use equation (3.5) to compute the probability of two customers making a purchase. This probability, denoted $f(2)$, is

$$f(2) = \frac{3!}{2!1!} (0.30)^2 (0.70)^1$$

$$= \frac{3 \times 2 \times 1}{2 \times 1 \times 1} (0.30)^2 (0.70)^1 = 0.189$$

Try Problem 12 for an application of the binomial distribution.

Similarly, the probability of no customers making a purchase, denoted $f(0)$, is

$$f(0) = \frac{3!}{0!3!} (0.30)^0 (0.70)^3$$

$$= \frac{3 \times 2 \times 1}{1 \times 3 \times 2 \times 1} (0.30)^0 (0.70)^3 = 0.343$$

TABLE 3.6 PROBABILITY DISTRIBUTION FOR THE NUMBER OF CUSTOMERS MAKING A PURCHASE

x	$f(x)$
0	0.343
1	0.441
2	0.189
3	0.027
Total	1.000

Equation (3.5) can be used in a similar manner to show that the probabilities of one and three purchases are $f(1) = 0.441$ and $f(3) = 0.027$. Table 3.6 and Figure 3.2 summarize the binomial probability distribution for the Nastke Clothing Store problem.

If we consider any variation of the Nastke problem, such as 10 customers rather than 3 customers entering the store, the binomial probability function given by equation (3.5) still applies. For example, the probability that 4 of the 10 customers make a purchase is

$$f(4) = \frac{10!}{4!6!} (0.30)^4 (0.70)^6 = 0.2001$$

In this binomial experiment, $n = 10$, $x = 4$, and $p = 0.30$.

FIGURE 3.2 PROBABILITY DISTRIBUTION FOR THE NASTKE CLOTHING STORE PROBLEM

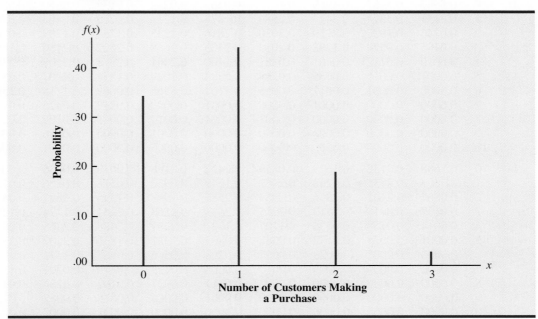

With modern computers and calculators, these tables are almost unnecessary. It is easy to evaluate equation (3.5) directly.

With the use of equation (3.5), tables have been developed that provide the probability of x successes in n trials for a binomial experiment. Such a table of binomial probability values is provided in Appendix B. We include a partial binomial table in Table 3.7. In order to use this table, specify the values of n, p, and x for the binomial experiment of interest. Check the use of this table by employing it to verify the probability of four successes in 10 trials for the Nastke Clothing Store problem. Note that the value of $f(4) = 0.2001$ can be read directly from the table of binomial probabilities, making it unnecessary to perform the calculations required by equation (3.5).

TABLE 3.7   SELECTED VALUES FROM THE BINOMIAL PROBABILITY TABLE. EXAMPLE: $n = 10, x = 4,$ $p = 0.30; f(4) = 0.2001$

n	x	p									
		0.05	0.10	0.15	0.20	0.25	0.30	0.35	0.40	0.45	0.50
9	0	0.6302	0.3874	0.2316	0.1342	0.0751	0.0404	0.0207	0.0101	0.0046	0.0020
	1	0.2985	0.3874	0.3679	0.3020	0.2253	0.1556	0.1004	0.0605	0.0339	0.0176
	2	0.0629	0.1722	0.2597	0.3020	0.3003	0.2668	0.2162	0.1612	0.1110	0.0703
	3	0.0077	0.0446	0.1069	0.1762	0.2336	0.2668	0.2716	0.2508	0.2119	0.1641
	4	0.0006	0.0074	0.0283	0.0661	0.1168	0.1715	0.2194	0.2508	0.2600	0.2461
	5	0.0000	0.0008	0.0050	0.0165	0.0389	0.0735	0.1181	0.1672	0.2128	0.2461
	6	0.0000	0.0001	0.0006	0.0028	0.0087	0.0210	0.0424	0.0743	0.1160	0.1641
	7	0.0000	0.0000	0.0000	0.0003	0.0012	0.0039	0.0098	0.0212	0.0407	0.0703
	8	0.0000	0.0000	0.0000	0.0000	0.0001	0.0004	0.0013	0.0035	0.0083	0.0176
	9	0.0000	0.0000	0.0000	0.0000	0.0000	0.0000	0.0001	0.0003	0.0008	0.0020
10	0	0.5987	0.3487	0.1969	0.1074	0.0563	0.0282	0.0135	0.0060	0.0025	0.0010
	1	0.3151	0.3874	0.3474	0.2684	0.1877	0.1211	0.0725	0.0403	0.0207	0.0098
	2	0.0746	0.1937	0.2759	0.3020	0.2816	0.2335	0.1757	0.1209	0.0763	0.0439
	3	0.0105	0.0574	0.1298	0.2013	0.2503	0.2668	0.2522	0.2150	0.1665	0.1172
	4	0.0010	0.0112	0.0401	0.0881	0.1460	**0.2001**	0.2377	0.2508	0.2384	0.2051
	5	0.0001	0.0015	0.0085	0.0264	0.0584	0.1029	0.1536	0.2007	0.2340	0.2461
	6	0.0000	0.0001	0.0012	0.0055	0.0162	0.0368	0.0689	0.1115	0.1596	0.2051
	7	0.0000	0.0000	0.0001	0.0008	0.0031	0.0090	0.0212	0.0425	0.0746	0.1172
	8	0.0000	0.0000	0.0000	0.0001	0.0004	0.0014	0.0043	0.0106	0.0229	0.0439
	9	0.0000	0.0000	0.0000	0.0000	0.0000	0.0001	0.0005	0.0016	0.0042	0.0098
	10	0.0000	0.0000	0.0000	0.0000	0.0000	0.0000	0.0000	0.0001	0.0003	0.0010
11	0	0.5688	0.3138	0.1673	0.0859	0.0422	0.0198	0.0088	0.0036	0.0014	0.0005
	1	0.3293	0.3835	0.3248	0.2362	0.1549	0.0932	0.0518	0.0266	0.0125	0.0054
	2	0.0867	0.2131	0.2866	0.2953	0.2581	0.1998	0.1395	0.0887	0.0531	0.0269
	3	0.0137	0.0710	0.1517	0.2215	0.2581	0.2568	0.2254	0.1774	0.1259	0.0806
	4	0.0014	0.0158	0.0536	0.1107	0.1721	0.2201	0.2428	0.2365	0.2060	0.1611
	5	0.0001	0.0025	0.0132	0.0388	0.0803	0.1321	0.1830	0.2207	0.2360	0.2256
	6	0.0000	0.0003	0.0023	0.0097	0.0268	0.0566	0.0985	0.1471	0.1931	0.2256
	7	0.0000	0.0000	0.0003	0.0017	0.0064	0.0173	0.0379	0.0701	0.1128	0.1611
	8	0.0000	0.0000	0.0000	0.0002	0.0011	0.0037	0.0102	0.0234	0.0462	0.0806
	9	0.0000	0.0000	0.0000	0.0000	0.0001	0.0005	0.0018	0.0052	0.0126	0.0269
	10	0.0000	0.0000	0.0000	0.0000	0.0000	0.0000	0.0002	0.0007	0.0021	0.0054
	11	0.0000	0.0000	0.0000	0.0000	0.0000	0.0000	0.0000	0.0000	0.0002	0.0005

Expected Value and Variance for the Binomial Distribution

From the probability distribution in Table 3.6, we can use equation (3.3) to compute the expected value or expected number of customers making a purchase:

$$\mu = \Sigma\, xf(x) = 0(0.343) + 1(0.441) + 2(0.189) + 3(0.027) = 0.9$$

Note that we could have obtained this same expected value simply by multiplying n (the number of trials) by p (the probability of success on any one trial):

$$np = 3(0.30) = 0.9$$

For the special case of a binomial probability distribution, the expected value of the random variable is given by

$$\mu = np \qquad\qquad \textbf{(3.6)}$$

Thus, if you know that the probability distribution is binomial, you do not have to make the detailed calculations required by equation (3.3) to compute the expected value.

Suppose that during the next month Nastke's Clothing Store expects 1000 customers to enter the store. What is the expected number of customers who will make a purchase? Using equation (3.6), the answer is $\mu = np = (1000)(0.3) = 300$. To increase the expected number of sales, Nastke's must induce more customers to enter the store and/or somehow increase the probability that any individual customer will make a purchase after entering.

For the special case of a binomial distribution, the variance of the random variable is

*Try Problem 9, part (e),
for practice computing the
expected value, variance,
and standard deviation of a
binomial random variable.*

$$\sigma^2 = np(1 - p) \qquad\qquad \textbf{(3.7)}$$

For the Nastke Clothing Store problem with three customers, the variance and standard deviation for the number of customers making a purchase are

$$\sigma^2 = np(1 - p) = 3(0.3)(0.7) = 0.63$$
$$\sigma = \sqrt{0.63} = 0.79$$

(3.4) Poisson Probability Distribution

In this section we will consider a discrete random variable that often is useful when we are dealing with the number of occurrences of an event over a specified interval of time or space. For example, the random variable of interest might be the number of arrivals at a car wash in 1 hour, the number of repairs needed in 10 miles of highway, or the number of leaks in 100 miles of pipeline. If the following two assumptions are satisfied, the **Poisson probability distribution** is applicable:

1. The probability of an occurrence of the event is the same for any two intervals of equal length.
2. The occurrence or nonoccurrence of the event in any interval is independent of the occurrence or nonoccurrence in any other interval.

The probability function of the Poisson random variable is given by equation (3.8):

$$f(x) = \frac{\lambda^x e^{-\lambda}}{x!} \qquad \text{for } x = 0, 1, 2, \ldots \qquad\qquad \textbf{(3.8)}$$

where

$$\lambda = \text{mean or average number of occurrences in an interval}$$
$$e = 2.71828$$
$$x = \text{number of occurrences in the interval}$$
$$f(x) = \text{probability of } x \text{ occurrences in the interval}$$

Note that equation (3.8) shows no upper limit to the number of possible values that a Poisson random variable can realize. That is, x is a discrete random variable with an infinite sequence of values ($x = 0, 1, 2, \ldots$); the Poisson random variable has no set upper limit.

An Example Involving Time Intervals

Suppose that we are interested in the number of arrivals at the drive-in teller window of a bank during a 15-minute period on weekday mornings. If we assume that the probability of a car arriving is the same for any two time periods of equal length and that the arrival or nonarrival of a car in any time period is independent of the arrival or nonarrival in any other time period, the Poisson probability function is applicable. Then if we assume that an analysis of historical data shows that the average number of cars arriving during a 15-minute interval of time is 10, the Poisson probability function with $\lambda = 10$ applies:

$$f(x) = \frac{\lambda^x e^{-\lambda}}{x!} = \frac{10^x e^{-10}}{x!} \qquad \text{for } x = 0, 1, 2, \ldots$$

Bell Labs used the Poisson distribution in modeling the arrival of phone calls.

If we wanted to know the probability of five arrivals in 15 minutes, we would set $x = 5$ and obtain[1]

$$f(5) = \frac{10^5 e^{-10}}{5!} = 0.0378$$

Although we determined this probability by evaluating the probability function with $\lambda = 10$ and $x = 5$, the use of Poisson probability distribution tables often is easier. These tables provide probabilities for specific values of x and λ. We included such a table as Appendix C. For convenience we reproduce a portion of it as Table 3.8. To use the table of Poisson probabilities, you need know only the values of x and λ. Thus, from Table 3.8, the probability of five arrivals in a 15-minute period is the value in the row corresponding to $x = 5$ and the column corresponding to $\lambda = 10$. Hence, $f(5) = 0.0378$.

Try Problem 14 for practice computing Poisson probabilities.

An Example Involving Length or Distance Intervals

Suppose that we are concerned with the occurrence of major defects in a section of highway one month after resurfacing. We assume that the probability of a defect is the same for any two intervals of equal length and that the occurrence or nonoccurrence of a defect in any one interval is independent of the occurrence or nonoccurrence in any other interval. Thus, the Poisson probability distribution applies.

Suppose that major defects occur at the average rate of two per mile. We want to find the probability that no major defects will occur in a particular 3-mile section of the

---

[1] Values of $e^{-\lambda}$ are available in Appendix E and can be easily computed with most modern calculators.

TABLE 3.8 SELECTED VALUES FROM THE POISSON PROBABILITY TABLE. EXAMPLE: $\lambda = 10, x = 5$; $f(5) = 0.0378$

					λ					
x	9.1	9.2	9.3	9.4	9.5	9.6	9.7	9.8	9.9	10
0	0.0001	0.0001	0.0001	0.0001	0.0001	0.0001	0.0001	0.0001	0.0001	0.0000
1	0.0010	0.0009	0.0009	0.0008	0.0007	0.0007	0.0006	0.0005	0.0005	0.0005
2	0.0046	0.0043	0.0040	0.0037	0.0034	0.0031	0.0029	0.0027	0.0025	0.0023
3	0.0140	0.0131	0.0123	0.0115	0.0107	0.0100	0.0093	0.0087	0.0081	0.0076
4	0.0319	0.0302	0.0285	0.0269	0.0254	0.0240	0.0226	0.0213	0.0201	0.0189
5	0.0581	0.0555	0.0530	0.0506	0.0483	0.0460	0.0439	0.0418	0.0398	**0.0378**
6	0.0881	0.0851	0.0822	0.0793	0.0764	0.0736	0.0709	0.0682	0.0656	0.0631
7	0.1145	0.1118	0.1091	0.1064	0.1037	0.1010	0.0982	0.0955	0.0928	0.0901
8	0.1302	0.1286	0.1269	0.1251	0.1232	0.1212	0.1191	0.1170	0.1148	0.1126
9	0.1317	0.1315	0.1311	0.1306	0.1300	0.1293	0.1284	0.1274	0.1263	0.1251
10	0.1198	0.1210	0.1219	0.1228	0.1235	0.1241	0.1245	0.1249	0.1250	0.1251
11	0.0991	0.1012	0.1031	0.1049	0.1067	0.1083	0.1098	0.1112	0.1125	0.1137
12	0.0752	0.0776	0.0799	0.0822	0.0844	0.0866	0.0888	0.0908	0.0928	0.0948
13	0.0526	0.0549	0.0572	0.0594	0.0617	0.0640	0.0662	0.0685	0.0707	0.0729
14	0.0342	0.0361	0.0380	0.0399	0.0419	0.0439	0.0459	0.0479	0.0500	0.0521
15	0.0208	0.0221	0.0235	0.0250	0.0265	0.0281	0.0297	0.0313	0.0330	0.0347
16	0.0118	0.0127	0.0137	0.0147	0.0157	0.0168	0.0180	0.0192	0.0204	0.0217
17	0.0063	0.0069	0.0075	0.0081	0.0088	0.0095	0.0103	0.0111	0.0119	0.0128
18	0.0032	0.0035	0.0039	0.0042	0.0046	0.0051	0.0055	0.0060	0.0065	0.0071
19	0.0015	0.0017	0.0019	0.0021	0.0023	0.0026	0.0028	0.0031	0.0034	0.0037
20	0.0007	0.0008	0.0009	0.0010	0.0011	0.0012	0.0014	0.0015	0.0017	0.0019
21	0.0003	0.0003	0.0004	0.0004	0.0005	0.0006	0.0006	0.0007	0.0008	0.0009
22	0.0001	0.0001	0.0002	0.0002	0.0002	0.0002	0.0003	0.0003	0.0004	0.0004
23	0.0000	0.0001	0.0001	0.0001	0.0001	0.0001	0.0001	0.0001	0.0002	0.0002
24	0.0000	0.0000	0.0000	0.0000	0.0000	0.0000	0.0000	0.0001	0.0001	0.0001

highway. The interval length is 3 miles, so $\lambda = (2 \text{ defects/mile})(3 \text{ miles}) = 6$ represents the expected number of major defects over the 3-mile section of highway. Thus, by using equation (3.8) or Appendix C with $\lambda = 6$ and $x = 0$, we obtain the probability of no major defects of 0.0025. Thus, finding no major defects in the 3-mile section is very unlikely. In fact, there is a $1 - 0.0025 = 0.9975$ probability of at least one major defect in that section of highway.

NOTES AND COMMENTS

1. When working with the Poisson probability distribution, you need to be sure that λ is the mean number of occurrences for the desired interval. For instance, suppose that you know that 30 calls come into a switchboard every 15 minutes. To compute Poisson probabilities for the number of calls coming in over a 5-minute period, you would use $\lambda = 10$; to compute probabilities for the number of calls coming in over a 1-minute period, you would use $\lambda = 2$.

Continuous Random Variables

In this section we introduce probability distributions for continuous random variables. Recall from Section 3.1 that random variables that may assume any value in a certain interval or collection of intervals are said to be *continuous*. Examples of continuous random variables include the following:

1. The *number of ounces* of soup placed in a can labeled "8 ounces"
2. The *flight time* of an airplane traveling from Chicago to New York
3. The *lifetime* of the monitor of a new laptop computer
4. The *drilling depth* required to reach oil in an offshore drilling operation

To understand the nature of continuous random variables more fully, suppose that, in the first example, one can of soup has 8.2 ounces and another 8.3 ounces. Other cans could weigh 8.25 ounces, 8.225 ounces, and so on. In fact, the actual weight can be any numeric value from 0 ounces for an empty can to, say, 8.5 ounces for a can filled to capacity. Because this interval contains infinitely many values, we can no longer list each value of the random variable and then identify its associated probability. In fact, for continuous random variables we need a new method for computing the probabilities associated with the values of the random variable.

Applying the Uniform Distribution

Let x denote the flight time of an airplane traveling from Chicago to New York. Assume that the minimum time is 2 hours and that the maximum time is 2 hours 20 minutes. Thus, in terms of minutes, the flight time can be any value in the interval from 120 minutes to 140 minutes (e.g., 124 minutes, 125.48 minutes, etc.). As the random variable x can take on any value from 120 to 140 minutes, x is a continuous rather than a discrete random variable. Assume that sufficient actual flight data are available to conclude that the probability of a flight time between 120 and 121 minutes is the same as the probability of a flight time within any other 1-minute interval up to and including 140 minutes. With every 1-minute interval being equally likely, the random variable x has a **uniform probability distribution**. The following **probability density function** describes the uniform probability distribution for the flight time random variable:

$$f(x) = \begin{cases} \dfrac{1}{20} & \text{for } 120 \leq x \leq 140 \\ 0 & \text{elsewhere} \end{cases} \qquad (3.9)$$

Figure 3.3 shows a graph of this probability density function. In general, the uniform probability density function for a random variable x is

$$f(x) = \begin{cases} \dfrac{1}{b-a} & \text{for } a \leq x \leq b \\ 0 & \text{elsewhere} \end{cases} \qquad (3.10)$$

FIGURE 3.3   UNIFORM PROBABILITY DENSITY FUNCTION FOR FLIGHT TIME

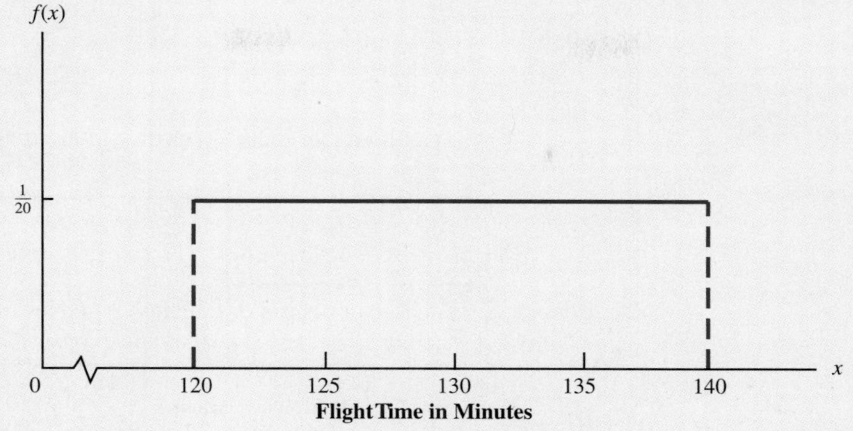

In the flight time example, $a = 120$ and $b = 140$.

In the graph of a probability density function, $f(x)$ shows the height or value of the function at any particular value of x. Because the probability density function for flight time is *uniform*, the height or value of the function is the same for each value of x between 120 and 140. That is, $f(x) = {}^1/_{20}$ for all values of x between 120 and 140. The probability density function $f(x)$, unlike the probability function for a discrete random variable, represents the height of the function at any particular value of x and *not* probability. Recall that, for each value of a discrete random variable (say, $x = 2$), the probability function yielded the probability of x having *exactly* that value [that is, $f(2)$]. However, a continuous random variable has infinitely many values, so we can no longer identify the probability for each specific value of x. Rather, we must consider probability in terms of the likelihood that a random variable takes on a value within a *specified interval*. For instance, in the flight time example an acceptable probability question is: What is the probability that the flight time is between 120 and 130 minutes? That is, what is $P(120 \leq x \leq 130)$? As the flight time must be between 120 and 140 minutes and as the probability is uniformly distributed over this interval, we feel comfortable saying that $P(120 \leq x \leq 130) = 0.50$. Indeed, as we will show, this is correct.

Area as a Measure of Probability

Refer to Figure 3.4 and consider the *area under the graph of $f(x)$* over the interval from 120 to 130. Note that the region is rectangular in shape and that the area of a rectangle is simply the width times the height. With the width of the interval equal to $130 - 120 = 10$ and the height of the graph $f(x) = {}^1/_{20}$, the area = width × height = $10({}^1/_{20}) = {}^{10}/_{20} = 0.50$.

FIGURE 3.4   AREA PROVIDES PROBABILITY OF FLIGHT TIME

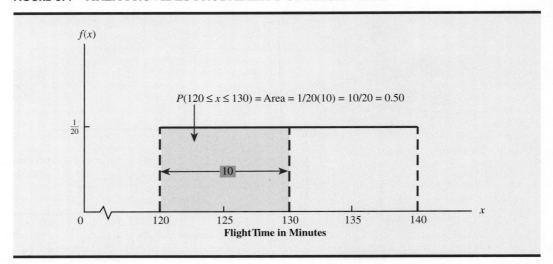

What observation can you make about the area under the graph of $f(x)$ and probability? They are identical! Indeed, that is true for all continuous random variables. In other words, once you have identified a probability density function $f(x)$ for a continuous random variable, you can obtain the probability that x takes on a value between some lower value a and some higher value b by computing the *area* under the graph of $f(x)$ over the interval a to b.

With the appropriate probability distribution and the interpretation of area as probability, we can answer any number of probability questions. For example, what is the probability of a flight time between 128 and 136 minutes? The width of the interval is $136 - 128 = 8$. With the uniform height of $1/20$, $P(128 \leq x \leq 136) = {}^8/_{20} = 0.40$.

Note that $P(120 \leq x \leq 140) = 20(1/20) = 1$; the total area under the $f(x)$ graph is equal to 1. This property holds for all continuous probability distributions and is the analog of the requirement that the sum of the probabilities must equal 1 for a discrete probability distribution. A continuous probability distribution also requires that $f(x) \geq 0$ for all values of x. It is the analog of the requirement that $f(x) \geq 0$ for discrete probability distributions.

Two principal differences between continuous random variables and probability distributions and their discrete counterparts stand out.

1. We no longer talk about the probability of the random variable taking on a particular value. Instead we talk about the probability of the random variable taking on a value within some given interval.

2. The probability of the random variable taking on a value within some given interval is defined to be the area under the graph of the probability density function over the interval. This definition implies that the probability that a continuous random variable takes on any particular value is zero because the area under the graph of $f(x)$ at a single point is zero.

Try Problem 18 to practice computing probabilities using the uniform probability distribution.

The Q.M. in Action, Procter & Gamble, describes how a large manufacturer of consumer goods used a model of random variables to assist in deciding whether to expand one of its production facilities.

PROCTER & GAMBLE*
CINCINNATI, OHIO

Procter & Gamble (P&G) produces and markets such products as detergents, disposable diapers, over-the-counter pharmaceuticals, dentifrices, bar soaps, mouthwashes, and paper towels. Worldwide, it has the leading brand in more categories than any other consumer products company. Since its merger with Gillette, P&G also produces and markets razors, blades, and many other personal care products.

As a leader in the application of statistical methods in decision making, P&G employs people with diverse academic backgrounds: engineering, statistics, operations research, and business. The major quantitative technologies for which these people provide support are probabilistic decision and risk analysis, advanced simulation, quality improvement, and quantitative methods (e.g., linear programming, regression analysis, probability analysis).

The Industrial Chemicals Division of P&G is a major supplier of fatty alcohols derived from natural substances such as coconut oil and from petroleum-based derivatives. The division wanted to know the economic risks and opportunities of expanding its fatty-alcohol production facilities, so it called in P&G's experts in probabilistic decision and risk analysis to help. After structuring and modeling the problem, they determined that the key to profitability was the cost difference between the petroleum- and coconut-based raw materials. Future costs were unknown, but the analysts were able to approximate them with the following continuous random variables.

x = the coconut oil price per pound of fatty alcohol

and

y = the petroleum raw material price per pound of fatty alcohol

Because the key to profitability was the difference between these two random variables, a third random variable, $d = x - y$, was used in the analysis. Experts were interviewed to determine the probability distributions for x and y. In turn, this information was used to develop a probability distribution for the difference in prices d. This continuous probability distribution showed a .90 probability that the price difference would be $.0655 or less and a .50 probability that the price difference would be $.035 or less. In addition, there was only a .10 probability that the price difference would be $.0045 or less.[†]

The Industrial Chemicals Division thought that being able to quantify the impact of raw material price differences was key to reaching a consensus. The probabilities obtained were used in a sensitivity analysis of the raw material price difference. The analysis yielded sufficient insight to form the basis for a recommendation to management.

The use of continuous random variables and their probability distributions was helpful to P&G in analyzing the economic risks associated with its fatty-alcohol production. In this chapter, you will gain an understanding of continuous random variables and their probability distributions, including one of the most important probability distributions in statistics, the normal distribution.

---

*The authors are indebted to Joel Kahn of Procter & Gamble for providing this Q.M. in Action.

†The price differences stated here have been modified to protect proprietary data.

NOTES AND COMMENTS

1. For any continuous random variable the probability of any particular value is zero, so $P(a \leq x \leq b) = P(a < x < b)$. Thus, the probability of a random variable assuming a value in any interval is the same whether the endpoints are included or not.

2. To see more clearly why the height of a probability density function is not a probability, think about a random variable with a uniform probability distribution of

$$f(x) = \begin{cases} 2 & \text{for } 0 \leq x \leq 0.5 \\ 0 & \text{elsewhere} \end{cases}$$

The height of the probability density function is 2 for values of x between 0 and 0.5. But we know that probabilities can never be greater than 1.

 3.6 # Normal Probability Distribution

Perhaps the most important probability distribution used to describe a continuous random variable is the **normal probability distribution**. It is applicable in a great many practical problem situations, and its probability density function has the form of the bell-shaped curve shown in Figure 3.5. The mathematical function that provides the bell-shaped curve of the normal probability density function follows:

The normal distribution was first observed by Abraham de Moivre, a French mathematician, in the early 1700s. De Moivre's work was motivated by the study of probability associated with gambling and games of chance.

$$f(x) = \frac{1}{\sigma \sqrt{2\pi}} e^{-(x - \mu)^2/2\sigma^2} \qquad \text{for } -\infty < x < \infty \qquad \textbf{(3.11)}$$

where

μ = mean or expected value of the random variable x

σ^2 = variance of the random variable x

σ = standard deviation of the random variable x

$\pi = 3.14159$

$e = 2.71828$

FIGURE 3.5   NORMAL PROBABILITY DISTRIBUTION

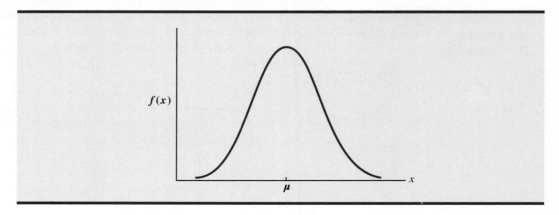

FIGURE 3.6 TWO NORMAL DISTRIBUTIONS WITH $\mu = 50$

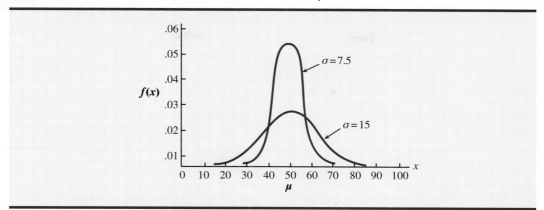

Recall from the previous discussion of continuous random variables that $f(x)$ is the height of the curve at a particular value of x. Thus, once we specify the mean (μ) and either the standard deviation (σ) or variance (σ^2), we can use equation (3.11) to determine the graph for the corresponding normal distribution. Figure 3.6 shows two normal distributions, one with $\mu = 50$ and $\sigma = 15$ and another with $\mu = 50$ and $\sigma = 7.5$. Note in particular the effect that the standard deviation σ has on the general shape of the normal curve. A larger standard deviation tends to flatten and broaden the curve because larger values of σ indicate greater variability in the values of the random variable.

Fortunately, whenever we use the normal distribution to answer probability questions, we do not have to use the probability density function of equation (3.11). In fact, when we use the normal distribution, we will have tables of probability values [areas under the $f(x)$ curve] that can provide the desired probability information. To show how to use the tables of areas or probabilities for the normal distribution, we must first introduce the standard normal distribution.

Standard Normal Distribution

A random variable that has a normal distribution with a mean of 0 and a standard deviation of 1 is said to have a **standard normal distribution**. We use the letter z to designate this particular normal random variable. Figure 3.7 shows the graph of the standard normal distribution. Note that it has the same general appearance as other normal distributions, but with the special properties of $\mu = 0$ and $\sigma = 1$. The units on the horizontal axis (z) measure the number of standard deviations from the mean.

Recall the procedure for finding probabilities associated with a continuous random variable. We want to determine the probability of the random variable having a value in a specified interval from a to b. Thus we have to find the area under the curve in the interval from a to b. In the preceding section we showed that finding probabilities, or areas under the curve, for a uniform distribution was relatively easy. All we had to do was multiply the width of the interval by the height of the graph. However, finding areas under the normal distribution curve appears at first glance to be much more difficult because the height of the curve varies. The mathematical technique for obtaining these areas is beyond the scope of the text, but fortunately tables are available that provide the areas or probability values

FIGURE 3.7   STANDARD NORMAL DISTRIBUTION

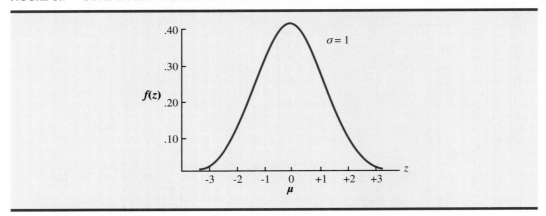

for the standard normal distribution. Table 3.9 is such a table of areas. This table is also available as Appendix D.

The graphs at the top of Table 3.9 show that the area in the table is the probability of a standard normal random variable being less than or equal to a specific value of z. Such probabilities are referred to as **cumulative probabilities**. In using Table 3.9 to determine a cumulative probability, note that the value of z with one decimal appears in the left-hand column of the table, with the second decimal appearing in the top row. Negative values of z are provided on the first page of the table, whereas positive values of z are provided on the second page. For example, for $z = -0.85$, we find -0.8 in the left-hand column and the second decimal 0.05 in the top row of the first page of the table. Then, by looking in the body of the table, we find an area or probability of 0.1977. This is the cumulative probability that the standard normal random variable is less than or equal to $z = -0.85$. This area is shown graphically at the top of Table 3.9. As another example, we can use the second page of the table to determine that the cumulative probability that the standard normal random variable is less than or equal to $z = 1.25$. We find 1.2 in the left-hand column and the second decimal 0.05 in the top row of the second page of the table. In the body of the table we find an area or probability of 0.8944. This is the cumulative probability that the standard normal random variable is less than or equal to $z = 1.25$. This area is also shown graphically at the top of Table 3.9.

Suppose that we wanted to use the cumulative standard normal distribution table to determine the probability that the standard normal random variable z will be between -1.00 and $+1.00$. Table 3.9 shows the cumulative probability that z is less than or equal to $+1.00$ is 0.8413 and the cumulative probability that z is less than or equal to -1.00 is 0.1587. Thus, the probability that z will be between -1.00 and $+1.00$ must be the difference between these two cumulative probabilities: $0.8413 - 0.1587 = 0.6826$. This is shown graphically in Figure 3.8.

The probability that a standard normal random variable z is between a and b is always the difference between two cumulative probabilities: one for z = b and one for z = a.

Similarly, we can find the probability that the standard normal random variable z will be between -2.00 and $+2.00$. Using the cumulative probabilities at $z = +2.00$ and $z = -2.00$, the probability that z will be between -2.00 and $+2.00$ is $0.9772 - 0.0228 = 0.9544$. In addition, we can use the cumulative probabilities at $z = +3.00$ and $z = -3.00$ to conclude that the probability z will be between -3.00 and $+3.00$ is $0.9986 - 0.0013 = 0.9973$. Since the total probability or total area under the curve is equal to 1.0000, the probability of 0.9973 tells us that z will almost always fall between -3.00 and $+3.00$.

TABLE 3.9 CUMULATIVE PROBABILITIES FOR THE STANDARD NORMAL DISTRIBUTION

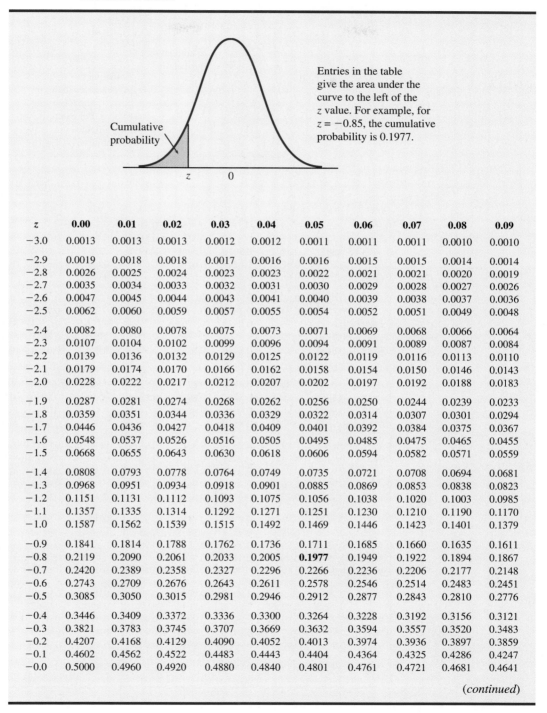

Entries in the table give the area under the curve to the left of the z value. For example, for $z = -0.85$, the cumulative probability is 0.1977.

Cumulative probability

z	0.00	0.01	0.02	0.03	0.04	0.05	0.06	0.07	0.08	0.09
−3.0	0.0013	0.0013	0.0013	0.0012	0.0012	0.0011	0.0011	0.0011	0.0010	0.0010
−2.9	0.0019	0.0018	0.0018	0.0017	0.0016	0.0016	0.0015	0.0015	0.0014	0.0014
−2.8	0.0026	0.0025	0.0024	0.0023	0.0023	0.0022	0.0021	0.0021	0.0020	0.0019
−2.7	0.0035	0.0034	0.0033	0.0032	0.0031	0.0030	0.0029	0.0028	0.0027	0.0026
−2.6	0.0047	0.0045	0.0044	0.0043	0.0041	0.0040	0.0039	0.0038	0.0037	0.0036
−2.5	0.0062	0.0060	0.0059	0.0057	0.0055	0.0054	0.0052	0.0051	0.0049	0.0048
−2.4	0.0082	0.0080	0.0078	0.0075	0.0073	0.0071	0.0069	0.0068	0.0066	0.0064
−2.3	0.0107	0.0104	0.0102	0.0099	0.0096	0.0094	0.0091	0.0089	0.0087	0.0084
−2.2	0.0139	0.0136	0.0132	0.0129	0.0125	0.0122	0.0119	0.0116	0.0113	0.0110
−2.1	0.0179	0.0174	0.0170	0.0166	0.0162	0.0158	0.0154	0.0150	0.0146	0.0143
−2.0	0.0228	0.0222	0.0217	0.0212	0.0207	0.0202	0.0197	0.0192	0.0188	0.0183
−1.9	0.0287	0.0281	0.0274	0.0268	0.0262	0.0256	0.0250	0.0244	0.0239	0.0233
−1.8	0.0359	0.0351	0.0344	0.0336	0.0329	0.0322	0.0314	0.0307	0.0301	0.0294
−1.7	0.0446	0.0436	0.0427	0.0418	0.0409	0.0401	0.0392	0.0384	0.0375	0.0367
−1.6	0.0548	0.0537	0.0526	0.0516	0.0505	0.0495	0.0485	0.0475	0.0465	0.0455
−1.5	0.0668	0.0655	0.0643	0.0630	0.0618	0.0606	0.0594	0.0582	0.0571	0.0559
−1.4	0.0808	0.0793	0.0778	0.0764	0.0749	0.0735	0.0721	0.0708	0.0694	0.0681
−1.3	0.0968	0.0951	0.0934	0.0918	0.0901	0.0885	0.0869	0.0853	0.0838	0.0823
−1.2	0.1151	0.1131	0.1112	0.1093	0.1075	0.1056	0.1038	0.1020	0.1003	0.0985
−1.1	0.1357	0.1335	0.1314	0.1292	0.1271	0.1251	0.1230	0.1210	0.1190	0.1170
−1.0	0.1587	0.1562	0.1539	0.1515	0.1492	0.1469	0.1446	0.1423	0.1401	0.1379
−0.9	0.1841	0.1814	0.1788	0.1762	0.1736	0.1711	0.1685	0.1660	0.1635	0.1611
−0.8	0.2119	0.2090	0.2061	0.2033	0.2005	**0.1977**	0.1949	0.1922	0.1894	0.1867
−0.7	0.2420	0.2389	0.2358	0.2327	0.2296	0.2266	0.2236	0.2206	0.2177	0.2148
−0.6	0.2743	0.2709	0.2676	0.2643	0.2611	0.2578	0.2546	0.2514	0.2483	0.2451
−0.5	0.3085	0.3050	0.3015	0.2981	0.2946	0.2912	0.2877	0.2843	0.2810	0.2776
−0.4	0.3446	0.3409	0.3372	0.3336	0.3300	0.3264	0.3228	0.3192	0.3156	0.3121
−0.3	0.3821	0.3783	0.3745	0.3707	0.3669	0.3632	0.3594	0.3557	0.3520	0.3483
−0.2	0.4207	0.4168	0.4129	0.4090	0.4052	0.4013	0.3974	0.3936	0.3897	0.3859
−0.1	0.4602	0.4562	0.4522	0.4483	0.4443	0.4404	0.4364	0.4325	0.4286	0.4247
−0.0	0.5000	0.4960	0.4920	0.4880	0.4840	0.4801	0.4761	0.4721	0.4681	0.4641

(continued)

TABLE 3.9   CUMULATIVE PROBABILITIES FOR THE STANDARD NORMAL
DISTRIBUTION *(Continued)*

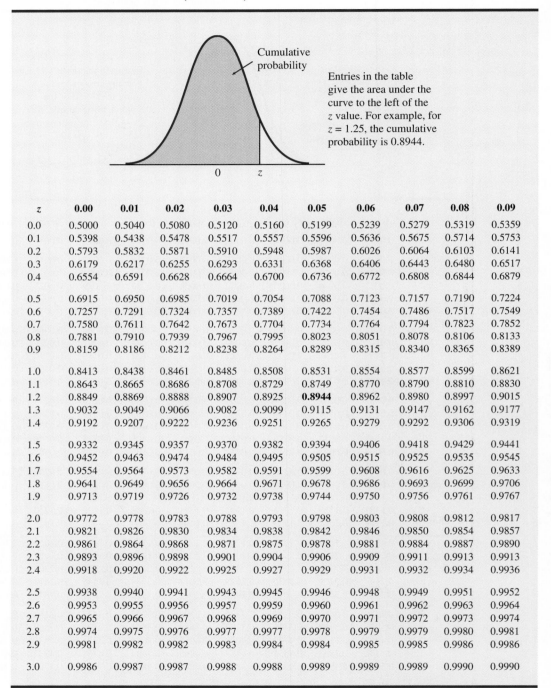

Cumulative probability

Entries in the table give the area under the curve to the left of the z value. For example, for $z = 1.25$, the cumulative probability is 0.8944.

z	0.00	0.01	0.02	0.03	0.04	0.05	0.06	0.07	0.08	0.09
0.0	0.5000	0.5040	0.5080	0.5120	0.5160	0.5199	0.5239	0.5279	0.5319	0.5359
0.1	0.5398	0.5438	0.5478	0.5517	0.5557	0.5596	0.5636	0.5675	0.5714	0.5753
0.2	0.5793	0.5832	0.5871	0.5910	0.5948	0.5987	0.6026	0.6064	0.6103	0.6141
0.3	0.6179	0.6217	0.6255	0.6293	0.6331	0.6368	0.6406	0.6443	0.6480	0.6517
0.4	0.6554	0.6591	0.6628	0.6664	0.6700	0.6736	0.6772	0.6808	0.6844	0.6879
0.5	0.6915	0.6950	0.6985	0.7019	0.7054	0.7088	0.7123	0.7157	0.7190	0.7224
0.6	0.7257	0.7291	0.7324	0.7357	0.7389	0.7422	0.7454	0.7486	0.7517	0.7549
0.7	0.7580	0.7611	0.7642	0.7673	0.7704	0.7734	0.7764	0.7794	0.7823	0.7852
0.8	0.7881	0.7910	0.7939	0.7967	0.7995	0.8023	0.8051	0.8078	0.8106	0.8133
0.9	0.8159	0.8186	0.8212	0.8238	0.8264	0.8289	0.8315	0.8340	0.8365	0.8389
1.0	0.8413	0.8438	0.8461	0.8485	0.8508	0.8531	0.8554	0.8577	0.8599	0.8621
1.1	0.8643	0.8665	0.8686	0.8708	0.8729	0.8749	0.8770	0.8790	0.8810	0.8830
1.2	0.8849	0.8869	0.8888	0.8907	0.8925	**0.8944**	0.8962	0.8980	0.8997	0.9015
1.3	0.9032	0.9049	0.9066	0.9082	0.9099	0.9115	0.9131	0.9147	0.9162	0.9177
1.4	0.9192	0.9207	0.9222	0.9236	0.9251	0.9265	0.9279	0.9292	0.9306	0.9319
1.5	0.9332	0.9345	0.9357	0.9370	0.9382	0.9394	0.9406	0.9418	0.9429	0.9441
1.6	0.9452	0.9463	0.9474	0.9484	0.9495	0.9505	0.9515	0.9525	0.9535	0.9545
1.7	0.9554	0.9564	0.9573	0.9582	0.9591	0.9599	0.9608	0.9616	0.9625	0.9633
1.8	0.9641	0.9649	0.9656	0.9664	0.9671	0.9678	0.9686	0.9693	0.9699	0.9706
1.9	0.9713	0.9719	0.9726	0.9732	0.9738	0.9744	0.9750	0.9756	0.9761	0.9767
2.0	0.9772	0.9778	0.9783	0.9788	0.9793	0.9798	0.9803	0.9808	0.9812	0.9817
2.1	0.9821	0.9826	0.9830	0.9834	0.9838	0.9842	0.9846	0.9850	0.9854	0.9857
2.2	0.9861	0.9864	0.9868	0.9871	0.9875	0.9878	0.9881	0.9884	0.9887	0.9890
2.3	0.9893	0.9896	0.9898	0.9901	0.9904	0.9906	0.9909	0.9911	0.9913	0.9913
2.4	0.9918	0.9920	0.9922	0.9925	0.9927	0.9929	0.9931	0.9932	0.9934	0.9936
2.5	0.9938	0.9940	0.9941	0.9943	0.9945	0.9946	0.9948	0.9949	0.9951	0.9952
2.6	0.9953	0.9955	0.9956	0.9957	0.9959	0.9960	0.9961	0.9962	0.9963	0.9964
2.7	0.9965	0.9966	0.9967	0.9968	0.9969	0.9970	0.9971	0.9972	0.9973	0.9974
2.8	0.9974	0.9975	0.9976	0.9977	0.9977	0.9978	0.9979	0.9979	0.9980	0.9981
2.9	0.9981	0.9982	0.9982	0.9983	0.9984	0.9984	0.9985	0.9985	0.9986	0.9986
3.0	0.9986	0.9987	0.9987	0.9988	0.9988	0.9989	0.9989	0.9989	0.9990	0.9990

FIGURE 3.8 PROBABILITY OF z BETWEEN -1.00 AND $+1.00$

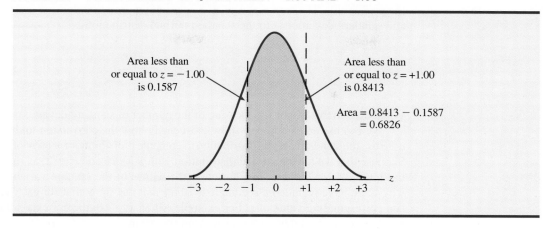

As a final example, what is the probability that the normal random variable z is greater than 2.00? From Table 3.9, we find that the cumulative probability that z is less than or equal to 2.00 is 0.9772. Since the total area under the curve is equal to 1.0000, the probability that z will be greater than 2.00 must be $1.0000 - 0.9772 = 0.0228$. This is shown graphically in Figure 3.9. As the examples in this section have shown, you should be able to use the cumulative probabilities in Table 3.9 to answer a variety of probability questions about the standard normal random variable z.

Computing Probabilities for Any Normal Distribution

The reason we discuss the standard normal distribution so extensively is that we can compute probabilities for any normal distribution by first converting to the standard normal distribution. Thus, when we have a normal distribution with any mean μ and any standard deviation σ, we can answer probability questions about this distribution by converting to

FIGURE 3.9 PROBABILITY OF z GREATER THAN 2.00

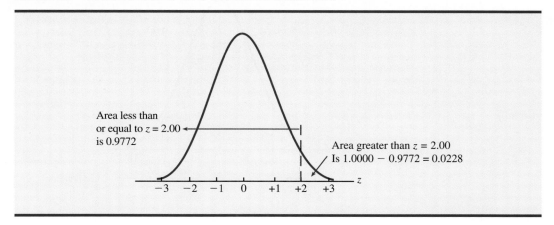

the standard normal distribution. We then use Table 3.9 and the appropriate z values to find the probability. The formula used to convert any normal random variable x with mean μ and standard deviation σ to the standard normal distribution is

$$z = \frac{x - \mu}{\sigma} \qquad\qquad \textbf{(3.12)}$$

When used in this way, z is a measure of the number of standard deviations that x is from μ.

We can use an example to show most easily how the conversion to the z value allows us to use the standard normal distribution to compute probabilities for any normal distribution. Suppose that we have a normal distribution with $\mu = 10$ and $\sigma = 2$, as shown graphically in Figure 3.10. Note that, in addition to the values of the random variable shown on the x axis, we have included a second axis (the z axis) to show that for each value of x there is a corresponding value of z. For example, when $x = 10$, the corresponding z value (the number of standard deviations away from the mean) is $z = (x - \mu)/\sigma = (10 - 10)/2 = 0$. Similarly, for $x = 14$ we have $z = (x - \mu)/\sigma = (14 - 10)/2 = 2$.

Now suppose that we want to know the probability that the random variable x is between 10 and 14; that is, $P(10 \leq x \leq 14)$. We do not have tables that provide this probability directly. However, note that in Figure 3.10 the area under the curve (probability) for x between 10 and 14 is the same as the area under the curve for z between 0 and 2. Using $z = 2.00$ and Table 3.9, we find that the cumulative probability of z being less than or equal to 2.00 is 0.9772. Similarly, Table 3.9 shows that the cumulative probability of z being less than or equal to 0.00 is 0.5000. Thus, the probability that the standard normal random variable z is between 0.00 and 2.00 is $0.9772 - 0.5000 = 0.4772$. Thus, we conclude that the probability of x being between 10 and 14 is also 0.4772.

This procedure applies to any normal distribution problem. That is, for any x value a corresponding z value is given by equation (3.12). To find the probability that x is in a specified interval, simply convert the x interval to its corresponding z interval. Then use the table for the standard normal distribution to answer the probability question.

FIGURE 3.10   NORMAL DISTRIBUTION WITH $\mu = 10$ AND $\sigma = 2$

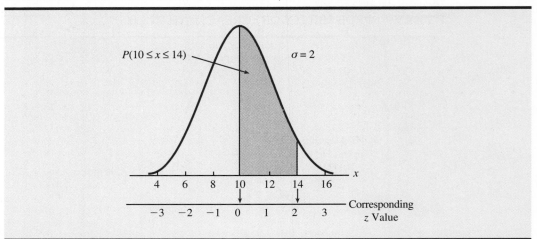

Grear Tire Company Problem

Suppose that Grear Tire Company just developed a new steel-belted radial tire that will be sold through a national chain of discount stores. Because the tire is a new product, Grear's management believes that the mileage guarantee offered with the tire will be an important factor in consumer acceptance of the product. Before finalizing the tire mileage guarantee policy, Grear's management wants some probability information concerning the number of miles the tires will last.

From actual road tests with the tires, Grear's engineering group estimates the mean tire mileage at $\mu = 36{,}500$ miles and the standard deviation at $\sigma = 5000$ miles. In addition, the data collected indicate that a normal distribution is a reasonable assumption.

What percentage of the tires, then, can be expected to last more than 40,000 miles? In other words, what is the probability that the tire mileage will exceed 40,000? To compute this probability, we need to find the area of the shaded region in Figure 3.11.

At $x = 40{,}000$ we have

$$z = \frac{x - \mu}{\sigma} = \frac{40{,}000 - 36{,}500}{5000} = \frac{3500}{5000} = 0.70$$

Thus the probability that the normal distribution for tire mileage will have an x value greater than 40,000 is the same as the probability that the standard normal distribution will have a z value greater than 0.70. Using Table 3.9, we find that the cumulative probability that z is less than or equal to 0.70 is 0.7580. Thus, the probability that z will be greater than 0.70 must be $1.0000 - 0.7580 = 0.2420$. In terms of the tire mileage x, we can conclude that there is a 0.2420 probability that x will be greater than 40,000 miles. Thus, we can anticipate about 24.2% of the tires manufactured by Grear will last more than 40,000 miles.

Let us now assume that Grear is considering a guarantee that will provide a discount on a new set of tires if the mileage on the original tires doesn't exceed the mileage stated on the guarantee. What should the guarantee mileage be if Grear wants no more than 10% of the tires to be eligible for the discount? This question is interpreted graphically in Figure 3.12. Note that 10% of the area is below the unknown guarantee mileage. Because this 10% is the lower tail of the normal probability distribution, 0.1000 is the cumulative probability that the tire mileage will be less than or equal to the unknown guarantee

FIGURE 3.11 GREAR TIRE COMPANY TIRE MILEAGE

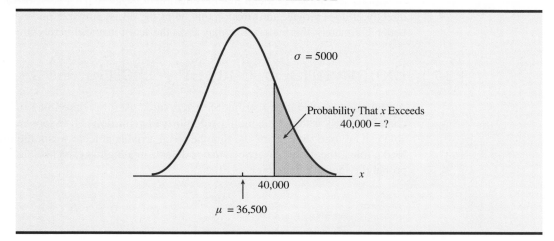

FIGURE 3.12   GREAR'S DISCOUNT GUARANTEE

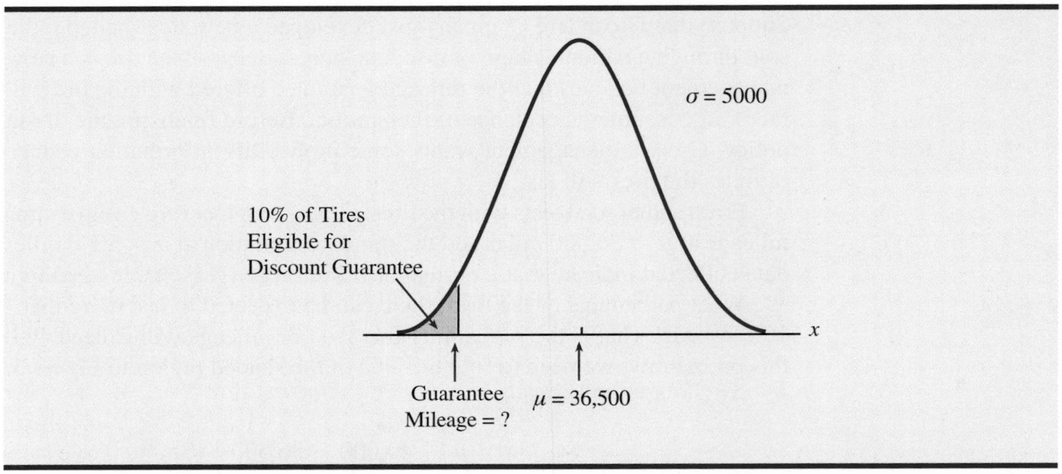

mileage. The question is now, How many standard deviations (z value) do we have to be below the mean to a achieve a 0.1000 cumulative probability? This time we will look into the body of Table 3.9 and try to find the cumulative probability 0.1000. We cannot find 0.1000 exactly, but a cumulative probability 0.1003 is close. Here we find the corresponding $z = -1.28$. This tells us that we must be 1.28 below the mean to find the desired tire guarantee mileage. This mileage is

$$\text{Guarantee mileage} = \mu - 1.28\sigma$$
$$= 36{,}500 - 1.28(5000) = 30{,}100$$

Therefore, a guarantee of 30,100 miles will meet the requirement that approximately 10% of the tires will be eligible for the discount. With this information the firm might confidently set its tire mileage guarantee at 30,000 miles.

Try Problem 23 for practice finding a z value that cuts off a particular probability.   Again we see the important role that probability distributions play in providing decision-making information. Once a probability distribution is established for a particular problem, it can be used rather quickly and easily to provide information about the likelihood of various scenarios. Although this information does not make a decision recommendation directly, it does provide information that helps the decision maker understand the problem better. Ultimately, this information may assist the decision maker in reaching a good decision.

3.7 Exponential Probability Distribution

A continuous probability distribution that is often useful in describing the time needed to complete a task is the **exponential probability distribution**. The exponential random variable can be used to describe the time between arrivals at a car wash, the time required to load a truck, the distance between major defects in a highway, and so on. The exponential probability density function is

$$f(x) = \frac{1}{\mu} e^{-x/\mu} \qquad \text{for } x \geq 0,\, \mu > 0 \qquad \textbf{(3.13)}$$

To provide an example of the exponential probability distribution, suppose that the loading time for a truck at a factory dock follows an exponential probability distribution. If the mean, or average, loading time is 15 minutes ($\mu = 15$), the appropriate probability density function is

$$f(x) = \frac{1}{15} e^{-x/15}$$

Figure 3.13 shows the graph of this density function.

Computing Probabilities for the Exponential Distribution

As with any continuous probability distribution, the area under the curve corresponding to some interval provides the probability that the random variable takes on a value in that interval. For instance, for the factory loading dock example, the probability that 6 minutes or less ($x \leq 6$) are needed to load a truck is defined to be the area under the curve from $x = 0$ to $x = 6$. Similarly, the probability that a loading time is 18 minutes or less ($x \leq 18$) is the area under the curve from $x = 0$ to $x = 18$. Note also that the probability of loading a truck in between 6 and 18 minutes ($6 \leq x \leq 18$) is the area under the curve from $x = 6$ to $x = 18$.

To compute exponential probabilities such as those previously described, the following formula provides the probability of obtaining a value for the exponential random variable of less than or equal to some specific value of x, denoted by x_0:

$$P(x \leq x_0) = 1 - e^{-x_0/\mu} \tag{3.14}$$

FIGURE 3.13 EXPONENTIAL DISTRIBUTION FOR LOADING TIME AT THE LOADING DOCK WITH $\mu = 15$

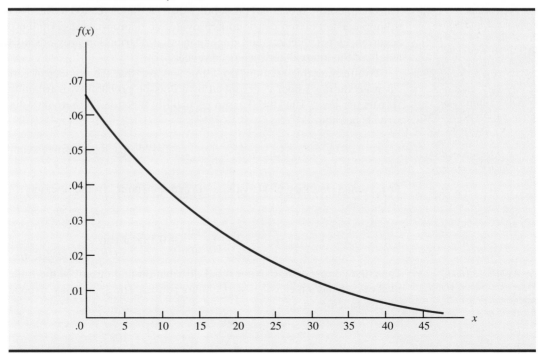

Thus, for the factory loading dock example, equation (3.14) becomes

$$P(\text{loading time} \le x_0) = 1 - e^{-x_0/15}$$

Hence, the probability that 6 minutes or less ($x \le 6$) are needed to load a truck is

$$P(\text{loading time} \le 6) = 1 - e^{-6/15} = 0.3297$$

Note also that the probability that 18 minutes or less ($x \le 18$) are needed to load a truck is

$$P(\text{loading time} \le 18) = 1 - e^{-18/15} = 0.6988$$

Try Problem 29 for practice finding probabilities with the exponential probability distribution.

Thus, the probability that 6 to 18 minutes are required to load a truck is $0.6988 - 0.3297 = 0.3691$. Probabilities for any other interval can be computed in a similar manner.

Relationship Between the Poisson and Exponential Distributions

In Section 3.4 we introduced the Poisson distribution as a discrete probability distribution that often is useful when we are dealing with the number of occurrences over a specified interval of time or space. Recall that the Poisson probability function is

$$f(x) = \frac{\lambda^x e^{-\lambda}}{x!}$$

where

$$\lambda = \text{expected value or mean number of occurrences in an interval}$$

The Poisson and exponential probability distributions are used in the chapter on waiting line models (Chapter 15). In these models the Poisson distribution is used as the probability distribution for the number of arrivals, while the exponential probability distribution is used as the probability distribution for the service time.

The continuous exponential probability distribution is related to the discrete Poisson distribution. The Poisson distribution provides an appropriate description of the number of occurrences per interval, and the exponential distribution provides a description of the length of the interval between occurrences.

To illustrate this relationship, let us suppose that the number of cars that arrive at a car wash during 1 hour is described by a Poisson probability distribution with a mean of 10 cars per hour. Thus the Poisson probability function that provides the probability of x arrivals per hour is

$$f(x) = \frac{10^x e^{-10}}{x!}$$

The average number of arrivals is 10 cars per hour, so the average time between cars arriving is

$$\frac{1 \text{ hour}}{10 \text{ cars}} = 0.1 \text{ hour/car}$$

Try Problems 30 and 31 for applications of the exponential probability distribution.

Thus, the corresponding exponential distribution that describes the time between the arrival of cars has a mean of $\mu = 0.1$ hours per car. The appropriate exponential probability density function is

$$f(x) = \frac{1}{0.1} e^{-x/0.1} = 10e^{-10x}$$

Summary

In this chapter we continued the discussion of probability by introducing the important concepts of random variables and probability distributions. Random variables provide numeric descriptions of the outcomes of experiments. When random variables are used, computations of the expected value, variance, and standard deviation can help the decision maker understand characteristics of the problem under study. We discussed the probability distributions for both discrete and continuous random variables.

Of particular interest are special probability distributions such as the binomial, Poisson, uniform, normal, and exponential distributions. These distributions provide wide applicability, and special formulas and/or tables make the probability information easily available.

Through a variety of problems and applications, we illustrated the role that probability distributions play in providing decision-making information. Although the probability values generated by the techniques and methods of this chapter do not by themselves make decision recommendations, they do provide assistance to the decision maker in terms of understanding the uncertainties inherent in the problem. Ultimately, this better understanding may lead to new and better decisions.

Glossary

Binomial probability distribution The probability distribution for a discrete random variable, used to compute the probability of x successes in n trials.

Continuous random variable A random variable that may assume any value in an interval or collection of intervals.

Cumulative probability The probability that a random variable takes on a value less than or equal to stated value.

Discrete probability distribution A table, graph, or equation describing the values of the random variable and the associated probabilities.

Discrete random variable A random variable that may assume only a finite or infinite sequence of values.

Expected value A weighted average of the values of the random variable, for which the probability function provides the weights. If an experiment can be repeated a large number of times, the expected value can be interpreted as the "long-run average."

Exponential probability distribution A continuous probability distribution that is useful in describing the time to complete a task or the time between occurrences of an event.

Normal probability distribution A continuous probability distribution whose probability density function is bell shaped and determined by the mean, μ, and standard deviation, σ.

Poisson probability distribution The probability distribution for a discrete random variable, used to compute the probability of x occurrences over a specified interval.

Probability density function The function that describes the probability distribution of a continuous random variable.

Probability function A function, denoted $f(x)$, that provides the probability that a discrete random variable x takes on some specific value.

Random variable A numeric description of the outcome of an experiment.

Standard deviation The positive square root of the variance.

Standard normal distribution A normal distribution with a mean of 0 and a standard deviation of 1.

Uniform probability distribution A continuous probability distribution in which the probability that the random variable will assume a value in any interval of equal length is the same for each interval.

Variance A measure of the dispersion or variability in the random variable. It is a weighted average of the squared deviations from the mean, μ.

Problems

1. The following examples are experiments and their associated random variables. In each case identify the values the random variable can assume and state whether the random variable is discrete or continuous:

Experiment	Random Variable (x)
a. Take a 20-question examination	Number of questions answered correctly
b. Observe cars arriving at a tollbooth	Number of cars arriving at the tollbooth for 1 hour
c. Audit 50 tax returns	Number of returns containing errors
d. Observe an employee's work for 8 hours	Number of nonproductive hours
e. Weigh a shipment of goods	Number of pounds

2. The following table shows a partial probability distribution for the MRA Company's projected profits (in thousands of dollars) for the first year of operation (the negative value denotes a loss):

x	$f(x)$
-100	0.10
0	0.20
50	0.30
100	0.25
150	0.10
200	

a. Find the missing value of $f(200)$. What is your interpretation of this value?
b. What is the probability that MRA will be profitable?
c. What is the probability that MRA will make at least $100,000?

3. Data were collected on the number of operating rooms in use at Tampa General Hospital over a 20-day period. On 3 of the days only one operating room was used; on 5 days, two were used; on 8 days, three were used; and on 4 days all four rooms were used.
a. Use the relative frequency approach to construct a probability distribution for the number of operating rooms in use on any given day.
b. Draw a graph of the probability distribution.
c. Show that your probability distribution satisfies the requirements for a valid discrete probability distribution.

4. Shown is a probability distribution for the random variable x.

x	$f(x)$
3	0.25
6	0.50
9	0.25
Total	1.00

    a.   Compute $E(x)$, the expected value of x.
    b.   Compute σ^2, the variance of x.
    c.   Compute σ, the standard deviation of x.

5. Brandon Lang is a creative entrepreneur who has developed a novelty soap item called Jack-pot to target consumers with a gambling habit. Inside each bar of Jackpot shower soap is a single rolled-up bill of U.S. currency. The currency (rolled up and sealed in shrink-wrap) is appropriately inserted into the soap mixture prior to the cutting and stamping procedure. The distribution of paper currency (per 1000 bars of soap) is given in the following table.

Distribution of Paper Currency Prizes	
Bill Denomination	**Number of Bills**
$1	520
$5	260
$10	120
$20	70
$50	29
$100	1
Total	1000

    a.   What is the expected amount of money in a single bar of Jackpot soap?
    b.   What is the standard deviation of the money in a single bar of Jackpot soap?
    c.   How many bars of soap would a customer have to buy so that, on average, he or she has purchased three bars containing a $50 or $100 bill?
    d.   If a customer buys 8 bars of soap, what is the probability that at least one of these bars contains a bill of $20 or larger?

6   The National Center for Health Statistics reported the following data on the number of children born in individual pregnancies in 1996 and 2006 (*The World Almanac*, 2010):

Number of Children	1996 Frequency	2006 Frequency
one child	3,671,455	3,971,276
twins	100,750	137,085
triplets	5,298	6,118
quadruplets	560	355
quintuplets or more	81	67

    a.   Define a random variable x = number of children born in a single pregnancy in 1996 and develop a probability distribution for the random variable. Let x = 5 represent quintuplets or more.

b. Compute the expected value and variance for the number of children born in a single pregnancy in 1996.

c. Define a random variable y = number of children born in a single pregnancy in 2006 and develop a probability distribution for the random variable. Let $y = 5$ represent quintuplets or more.

d. Compute the expected value and variance for the number of children born in a single pregnancy in 2006.

e. Do these data support the conclusion that the increased use of fertility drugs by older women has generated an upward trend in multiple births?

7. The demand for Carolina Industries' product varies greatly from month to month. Based on the past two years of data, the following probability distribution shows the company's monthly demand:

Unit Demand	Probability
300	0.20
400	0.30
500	0.35
600	0.15

a. If the company places monthly orders equal to the expected value of the monthly demand, what should Carolina's monthly order quantity be for this product?

b. Assume that each unit demanded generates $70 in revenue and that each unit ordered costs $50. How much will the company gain or lose in a month if it places an order based on your answer to part (a) and the actual demand for the item is 300 units?

c. What are the variance and standard deviation for the number of units demanded?

8. The J. R. Ryland Computer Company is considering a plant expansion that will enable the company to begin production of a new computer product. The company's president must determine whether to make the expansion a medium- or large-scale project. The demand for the new product involves an uncertainty, which for planning purposes may be low demand, medium demand, or high demand. The probability estimates for the demands are 0.20, 0.50, and 0.30, respectively. Letting x indicate the annual profit in $1000s, the firm's planners developed profit forecasts for the medium- and large-scale expansion projects.

		Medium-Scale Expansion Profits		Large-Scale Expansion Profits	
		x	$f(x)$	y	$f(y)$
	Low	50	0.20	0	0.20
Demand	Medium	150	0.50	100	0.50
	High	200	0.30	300	0.30

a. Compute the expected value for the profit associated with the two expansion alternatives. Which decision is preferred for the objective of maximizing the expected profit?

b. Compute the variance for the profit associated with the two expansion alternatives. Which decision is preferred for the objective of minimizing the risk or uncertainty?

9. Consider a binomial experiment with 2 trials and $p = 0.4$.
   a. Compute the probability of 1 success, $f(1)$.
   b. Compute $f(0)$.
   c. Compute $f(2)$.
   d. Find the probability of at least one success.
   e. Find the expected value, variance, and standard deviation.

10. Consider a binomial experiment with $n = 10$ and $p = 0.10$. Use the binomial tables (Appendix B) to answer parts (a) through (d).
   a. Find $f(0)$.
   b. Find $f(2)$.
   c. Find $P(x \leq 2)$.
   d. Find $P(x \geq 1)$.
   e. Find $E(x)$.
   f. Find $\text{Var}(x)$ and σ.

11. A recent survey by the *New Statesman* on British social attitudes asked respondents if they believe that inequality is too large. The survey found that 74% of the respondents do believe inequality is too large.
   a. In a sample of six British citizens, what is the probability that two believe inequality is too large?
   b. In a sample of six British citizens, what is the probability that at least two respondents believe that inequality is too large?
   c. In a sample of four British citizens, what is the probability that none believe inequality is too large?

12. When a new machine is functioning properly, only 3% of the items produced are defective. Assume that we will randomly select two parts produced on the machine and that we are interested in the number of defective parts found.
   a. Describe the conditions under which this situation would be a binomial experiment.
   b. How many experimental outcomes yield one defect?
   c. Compute the probabilities associated with finding no defects, one defect, and two defects.

13. Military radar and missile detection systems are designed to warn a country of enemy attacks. A reliability question deals with the ability of the detection system to identify an attack and issue the warning. Assume that a particular detection system has a 0.90 probability of detecting a missile attack. Answer the following questions using the binomial probability distribution:
   a. What is the probability that one detection system will detect an attack?
   b. If two detection systems are installed in the same area and operate independently, what is the probability that at least one of the systems will detect the attack?
   c. If three systems are installed, what is the probability that at least one of the systems will detect the attack?
   d. Would you recommend that multiple detection systems be operated? Explain.

14. Consider a Poisson probability distribution with 2 as the average number of occurrences per time period.
   a. Write the appropriate Poisson probability function.
   b. What is the average number of occurrences in three time periods?
   c. Write the appropriate Poisson probability function to determine the probability of x occurrences in three time periods.
   d. Find the probability of two occurrences in one time period.
   e. Find the probability of six occurrences in three time periods.
   f. Find the probability of five occurrences in two time periods.

15. Telephone calls arrive at the rate of 48 per hour at the reservation desk for Regional Airways.
    a. Find the probability of receiving 3 calls in a 5-minute interval.
    b. Find the probability of receiving 10 calls in 15 minutes.
    c. Suppose that no calls are currently on hold. If the agent takes 5 minutes to complete processing the current call, how many callers do you expect to be waiting by that time? What is the probability that no one will be waiting?
    d. If no calls are currently being processed, what is the probability that the agent can take 3 minutes for personal time without being interrupted?

16. More than 50 million guests stayed at bed and breakfasts (B&Bs) last year. The website for the Bed and Breakfast Inns of North America, which averages approximately seven visitors per minute, enables many B&Bs to attract guests without waiting years to be mentioned in guidebooks.
    a. What is the probability of no website visitors in a 1-minute period?
    b. What is the probability of two or more website visitors in a 1-minute period?
    c. What is the probability of one or more website visitors in a 30-second period?
    d. What is the probability of five or more website visitors in a 1-minute period?

17. Airline passengers arrive randomly and independently at the passenger screening facility at a major international airport. The mean arrival rate is 10 passengers per minute.
    a. What is the probability of no arrivals in a 1-minute period?
    b. What is the probability of 3 or fewer arrivals in a 1-minute period?
    c. What is the probability of no arrivals in a 15-second period?
    d. What is the probability of at least 1 arrival in a 15-second period?

18. A random variable x is uniformly distributed between 1.0 and 1.5.
    a. Show the graph of the probability density function.
    b. Find $P(x = 1.25)$.
    c. Find $P(1.00 \leq x \leq 1.25)$.
    d. Find $P(1.20 < x < 1.50)$.

19. Delta Airlines quotes a flight time of 2 hours, 5 minutes for its flights from Cincinnati to Tampa. Suppose we believe that actual flight times are uniformly distributed between 2 hours and 2 hours, 20 minutes.
    a. Show the graph of the probability density function for flight times.
    b. What is the probability that the flight will be no more than 5 minutes late?
    c. What is the probability that the flight will be more than 10 minutes late?
    d. What is the expected flight time?

20. Most computer languages have a function that can be used to generate random numbers. In Microsoft's Excel, the RAND function can be used to generate random numbers between 0 and 1. If we let x denote the random number generated, then x is a continuous random variable with the probability density function:

$$f(x) = \begin{cases} 1 & \text{for } 0 \leq x \leq 1 \\ 0 & \text{elsewhere} \end{cases}$$

    a. Graph the probability density function.
    b. What is the probability of generating a random number between 0.25 and 0.75?
    c. What is the probability of generating a random number with a value less than or equal to 0.30?
    d. What is the probability of generating a random number with a value greater than 0.60?

21. For the standard normal random variable z, compute the following probabilities:
    a. $P(0 \leq z \leq 0.83)$
    b. $P(-1.57 \leq z \leq 0)$
    c. $P(z > 0.44)$
    d. $P(z \geq 20.23)$
    e. $P(z < 1.20)$
    f. $P(z \leq 20.71)$

22. For the standard normal random variable z, find z for each situation.
    a. The area to the left of z is 0.9750.
    b. The area between 0 and z is 0.4750.
    c. The area to the left of z is 0.7291.
    d. The area to the right of z is 0.1314.
    e. The area to the left of z is 0.6700.
    f. The area to the right of z is 0.3300.

23. For the standard normal random variable z, find z for each situation.
    a. The area to the left of z is 0.2119.
    b. The area between $-z$ and z is 0.9030.
    c. The area between $-z$ and z is 0.2052.
    d. The area to the left of z is 0.9948.
    e. The area to the right of z is 0.6915.

24. The demand for a new product is estimated to be normally distributed with $\mu = 200$ and $\sigma = 40$. Let x be the number of units demanded, and find the following probabilities:
    a. $P(180 \leq x \leq 220)$
    b. $P(x \geq 250)$
    c. $P(x \leq 100)$
    d. $P(225 \leq x \leq 250)$

25. The College Board National Office recently reported that in 2011–2012, the 547,038 high school juniors who took the ACT achieved a mean score of 530 with a standard deviation of 123 on the mathematics portion of the test (http://media.collegeboard.com/digitalServices/pdf /research/2013/TotalGroup-2013.pdf). Assume these test scores are normally distributed.
    a. What is the probability that a high school junior who takes the test will score at least 610 on the mathematics portion of the test?
    b. What is the probability that a high school junior who takes the test will score no higher than 460 on the mathematics portion of the test?
    c. What is the probability that a high school junior who takes the test will score between 460 and 550 on the mathematics portion of the test?
    d. How high does a student have to score to be in the top 10% of high school juniors on the mathematics portion of the test?

26. General Hospital's patient account division has compiled data on the age of accounts receivable. The data collected indicate that the age of the accounts follows a normal distribution with $\mu = 28$ days and $\sigma = 8$ days.
    a. What portion of the accounts is between 20 and 40 days old—that is, $P(20 \leq x \leq 40)$?
    b. The hospital administrator is interested in sending reminder letters to the oldest 15% of accounts. How many days old should an account be before a reminder letter is sent?
    c. The hospital administrator wants to give a discount to those accounts that pay their balance by the twenty-first day. What percentage of the accounts will receive the discount?

27. To boost holiday sales, a jewelry store in Bismarck, North Dakota, is advertising the following promotion: "If more than seven inches of cumulative snow fall on December 24, 25, 26, 27, and 28, you get your money back on all purchase made on December 17." To analyze this promotion, the store manager has collected data and determined that

snowfall over this 5-day period in December is normally distributed with an average of 6 inches and standard deviation of 0.559 inches. What is the probability that the store will have to refund the money to its December 17 customers?

28. A machine fills containers with a particular product. The standard deviation of filling weights computed from past data is 0.6 ounces. If only 2% of the containers hold less than 18 ounces, what is the mean filling weight for the machine? That is, what must μ equal? Assume that the filling weights have a normal distribution.

29. Consider the exponential probability density function:

$$f(x) = \frac{1}{3} e^{-x/3} \qquad \text{for } x \geq 0$$

   a. Write the formula for $P(x \leq x_0)$.
   b. Find $P(x \leq 2)$.
   c. Find $P(x \geq 3)$.
   d. Find $P(x \leq 5)$.
   e. Find $P(2 \leq x \leq 5)$.

30. CopRadar.com reports that the average time for an average driver to react to a red traffic light (which includes recognizing that the light has changed, deciding to stop or to continue, and engaging the brake if stopping) is 2.3 seconds. Assume the time to react to a red traffic light follows an exponential distribution.
   a. What is the probability that it will take less than 2 seconds for a driver to react to a red traffic light?
   b. What is the probability that it will take more than 3 seconds for a driver to react to a red traffic light?
   c. What is the probability that it will take between 2 and 3 seconds for a driver to react to a red traffic light?

31. The time between arrivals of vehicles at a particular intersection follows an exponential probability distribution with a mean of 12 seconds.
   a. Sketch this exponential probability distribution.
   b. What is the probability that the time between vehicle arrivals is 12 seconds or less?
   c. What is the probability that the time between vehicle arrivals is 6 seconds or less?
   d. What is the probability that there will be 30 or more seconds between arriving vehicles?

32. The lifetime (hours) of an electronic device is a random variable with the exponential probability density function:

$$f(x) = \frac{1}{50} e^{-x/50} \qquad \text{for } x \geq 0$$

   a. What is the mean lifetime of the device?
   b. What is the probability that the device fails in the first 25 hours of operation?
   c. What is the probability that the device operates 100 or more hours before failure?

33. The time (in minutes) between telephone calls at an insurance claims office has the exponential probability distribution:

$$f(x) = 0.50e^{-0.50x} \qquad \text{for } x \geq 0$$

   a. What is the mean time between telephone calls?
   b. What is the probability of 30 seconds or less between telephone calls?
   c. What is the probability of 1 minute or less between telephone calls?
   d. What is the probability of 5 or more minutes without a telephone call?

34. Sparagowski & Associates conducted a study of service times at the drive-up window of fast-food restaurants. The average time between placing an order and receiving the order at McDonald's restaurants was 2.78 minutes. Waiting times, such as these, frequently follow an exponential distribution.
    a. What is the probability that a customer's service time is less than 2 minutes?
    b. What is the probability that a customer's service time is more than 5 minutes?
    c. What is the probability that a customer's service time is more than 2.78 minutes?

Case Problem   Specialty Toys

Specialty Toys, Inc., sells a variety of new and innovative children's toys and believes that the preholiday season is the best time to introduce a new toy. Many families use this time to look for new ideas for December holiday gifts. When Specialty has a new toy with good market potential, it chooses an October market entry date.

In order to get toys in its stores by October, Specialty places one-time orders with its manufacturers in June or July of each year. Demand for children's toys can be highly volatile. If a new toy catches on, a sense of shortage in the marketplace often increases the demand to very high levels and large profits can be realized. On the other hand, new toys can also flop, leaving Specialty stuck with high levels of inventory that must be sold at reduced prices. The most important question the company faces is deciding how many units of a new toy should be purchased to meet expected sales demand. If too few are purchased, sales will be lost; if too many are purchased, profits will be reduced because of low prices realized in clearance sales.

For the coming season, Specialty plans to introduce a new product called Weather Teddy. This variation of a talking teddy bear is made by a company in Taiwan. When a child presses Teddy's hand, the bear begins to talk. With the aid of a built-in barometer, Teddy says one of five responses that predict the weather conditions. The responses range from "It looks to be a very nice day! Have fun" to "I think it may rain today. Don't forget your umbrella." Tests with the product show that even though it is not a perfect weather predictor, its predictions are surprisingly good. Several of Specialty's managers claimed Teddy gave predictions of the weather that were as good as the local television weather forecasters.

Specialty faces the decision of how many Weather Teddy units to order for the coming holiday season. Members of the management team recommended order quantities of 15,000, 18,000, 24,000, and 28,000. Considerable disagreement concerning the market potential is evidenced by the different order quantities suggested. The product management team has asked you for an analysis of the stock-out probabilities for various order quantities, an estimate of the profit potential, and help in making an order quantity recommendation. Specialty expects to sell Weather Teddy for $24, and the cost is $16 per unit. If inventory remains after the holiday season, Specialty will sell all surplus inventory for $5 per unit. After reviewing the sales history of similar products, Specialty's senior sales forecaster predicted an expected demand of 20,000 units with a 0.95 probability that demand would be between 10,000 units and 30,000 units.

Managerial Report

Prepare a managerial report that addresses the following issues and recommends an order quantity for the Weather Teddy product:

1. Use the sales forecaster's prediction to describe a normal probability distribution that can be used to approximate the demand distribution. Sketch the distribution and show its mean and standard deviation.

2. Compute the probability of a stock-out for the order quantities suggested by members of the management team.
3. Compute the projected profit for the order quantities suggested by the management team under three scenarios. Worst case: sales = 10,000 units; most likely case: sales = 20,000 units; and best case: sales = 30,000 units.
4. One of Specialty's managers felt that the profit potential was so great that the order quantity should have a 70% chance of meeting demand and only a 30% chance of any stock-outs. What quantity would be ordered under this policy, and what is the projected profit under the three scenarios in part 3?
5. Provide your own recommendation for an order quantity and note the associated profit projections. Provide a rationale for your recommendation.

Appendix 3.1   Computing Discrete Probabilities with Excel

Excel has the capability of computing probabilities for several discrete probability distributions including the binomial and Poisson. In this appendix, we describe how Excel can be used to compute the probabilities for any binomial probability distribution. The procedures for the Poisson probability distributions are similar to the one we describe for the binomial probability distribution.

Let us return to the Nastke Clothing Store problem, where the binomial probabilities of interest are based on a binomial experiment with $n = 10$ and $p = 0.30$. We assume that the user is interested in the probability of $x = 4$ successes in the 10 trials. The following steps describe how to use Excel to produce the desired binomial probability:

Step 1. Select a cell in the worksheet where you want the binomial probability to appear
Step 2. Select the **Formulas** tab (see Appendix A)
Step 3. Choose the **Insert Function** option
Step 4. When the **Insert Function** dialog box appears:
Choose **Statistical** from the **Or select a category** box
Choose **BINOM.DIST** from the **Select a function** box
Click **OK**
Step 5. When the **Function Arguments** dialog box appears:
Enter 4 in the **Number_s** box (the value of x)
Enter 10 in the **Trials** box (the value of n)
Enter 0.30 in the **Probability_s** box (the value of p)
Enter false in the **Cumulative** box[2]
  Note: At this point the desired binomial probability of 0.2001 is automatically computed and appears near the bottom of the dialog box.
Click **OK** and the binomial probability will appear in the worksheet cell requested in Step 1.

A user who wants other binomial probabilities may obtain the information without repeating the steps for each probability desired. Perhaps the easiest alternative is to stay in step 5. After the four entries have been made and the first probability appears, simply return to the **Number_s** box and insert a new value of x. The new probability will appear. Repeated changes can be made in the dialog box, including changes to the trials, probability,

---

[2]Placing false in the cumulative box provides the probability of exactly four successes. Placing true in this box provides the cumulative probability of four or fewer successes.

and/or cumulative boxes. For each change, the desired probability will appear. When **OK** is selected, only the last binomial probability will be placed in the worksheet.

The Excel functions BINOM.DIST and POISSON.DIST are only recognized by Excel 2010. Earlier versions of Excel will use the function names BINOMDIST and POISSON, respectively, to compute the same values using the same steps.

If the user wants to insert multiple binomial probabilities into the worksheet, the desired values of x are entered into the worksheet first. Then, in step 5, the user enters the cell location of one of the values of x in the numbers box. After completing the steps for one binomial probability, individuals experienced with Excel can use Excel's Copy command to copy the binomial function into the cells where the other binomial probabilities are to appear.

The Excel procedure for generating Poisson probabilities is similar to the procedure just described. Step 4 can be used to select the **POISSON.DIST** function name. The dialog box in step 5 will guide the user through the input values required to compute the desired probabilities.

Appendix 3.2   Computing Probabilities for Continuous Distributions with Excel

Excel has the capability of computing probabilities for several continuous probability distributions, including the normal and exponential probability distributions. In this appendix, we describe how Excel can be used to compute probabilities for any normal probability distribution. The procedures for the exponential and other continuous probability distributions are similar to the one we describe for the normal probability distribution.

Let us return to the Grear Tire Company problem, where the tire mileage was described by a normal probability distribution with $\mu = 36{,}500$ and $\sigma = 5000$. Assume we are interested in the probability that tire mileage will exceed 40,000 miles. The following steps describe how to use Excel to compute the desired normal probability:

Step 1. Select a cell in the worksheet where you want the normal probability to appear
Step 2. Select the **Formulas** tab (see Appendix A)
Step 3. Choose the **Insert Function** option
Step 4. When the **Insert Function** dialog box appears:
    Choose **Statistical** from the **Or select a category** box
    Choose **NORM.DIST** from the **Select a function** box
    Click **OK**
Step 5. When the **Function Arguments** dialog box appears:
    Enter 40000 in the **X** box
    Enter 36500 in the **Mean** box
    Enter 5000 in the **Standard_dev** box
    Enter true in the **Cumulative** box
    Click **OK**

The Excel functions NORM.DIST, NORM.INV, and EXPON.DIST are only recognized by Excel 2010. Earlier versions of Excel will use the function names NORMDIST, NORM-INV, and EXPONDIST, respectively, to compute the same values using the same steps.

At this point, 0.7580 will appear in the cell selected in step 1, indicating that the cumulative probability that the tire mileage is less than or equal to 40,000 miles is 0.7580. Therefore, the probability that tire mileage will exceed 40,000 miles is $1 - 0.7580 = 0.2420$.

Excel uses an inverse computation to convert a given cumulative normal probability into a value for the random variable. For example, what mileage guarantee should Grear offer if the company wants no more than 10% of the tires to be eligible for the guarantee? To compute the mileage guarantee by using Excel, follow the procedure just described. However, two changes are necessary: In step 4, choose **NORM.INV** from the **Select a function** box; in step 5, enter the cumulative probability of 0.10 in the **Probability** box and then enter the mean and the standard deviation. When **OK** is selected in step 5, the tire mileage guarantee of 30,092, or approximately 30,100, miles appears in the worksheet.

The Excel procedure for generating exponential probabilities is similar to the procedure just described. Step 4 can be used to choose the **EXPON.DIST** function name. The dialog box in step 5 will guide the user through the input values required to compute the desired probability. Note that the value entered in the **Lambda** box is $1/\mu$. When **OK** is selected in step 5, the cumulative exponential probability appears in the worksheet.

CHAPTER 4

Decision Analysis

CONTENTS

Decision analysis can be used to develop an optimal strategy when a decision maker is faced with several decision alternatives and an uncertain or risk-filled pattern of future events. For example, Ohio Edison used decision analysis to choose the best type of particulate control equipment for coal-fired generating units when it faced future uncertainties concerning sulfur content restrictions, construction costs, and so on. The State of North Carolina used decision analysis in evaluating whether to implement a medical screening test to detect metabolic disorders in newborns. The Q.M. in Action, Natural Resource Management, discusses the use of decision analysis to evaluate alternative actions to protect endangered species.

Even when a careful decision analysis has been conducted, the uncertain future events make the final consequence uncertain. In some cases, the selected decision alternative may provide good or excellent results. In other cases, a relatively unlikely future event may occur, causing the selected decision alternative to provide only fair or even poor results. The risk associated with any decision alternative is a direct result of the uncertainty associated with the final consequence. A good decision analysis includes careful consideration of risk. Through risk analysis the decision maker is provided with probability information about the favorable as well as the unfavorable consequences that may occur.

We begin the study of decision analysis by considering problems that involve reasonably few decision alternatives and reasonably few possible future events. Influence diagrams and payoff tables are introduced to provide a structure for the decision problem and

---

Q.M. *in* ACTION

NATURAL RESOURCE MANAGEMENT*

Caution must be exercised when making decisions on what protective measures are taken to protect an endangered or threatened species. A conservative action may not be sufficient to save the species, while an aggressive action may have serious economic consequences— decision analysis has long been used to strike a balance between these two concerns. However, in recent years policy analysts have been giving increasing consideration to another issue: the potential deleterious long-run effects the decision ultimately may have on the endangered or threatened species' ecosystem. Conservationists and policy analysts are now recognizing that the resilience of an ecological system, or the degree of disturbance that an ecological system can absorb without changing substantially, must be an important consideration when making these decisions.

In research funded by the U.S. Geological Survey and the U.S. Fish and Wildlife Service, B. Ken Williams of the Wildlife Society and Fred A. Johnson and James D. Nichols of the U.S. Geological Survey have developed a means for using decision analysis that considers resilience of an ecological system when assessing alternative strategies for protecting an endangered or threatened species. Another strategy, transplanting members of an endangered or threatened species to areas outside the species' established habitat, is assessed with decision analysis by Tracy Rout of the Quantitative and Applied Ecology Group at the University of Melbourne.

Although the resilience of the ecological system and the intended ecological and social benefits of various strategies for protecting a species are difficult to measure, this approach strives to consider them when selecting from various alternative strategies. Incorporating the resilience of the ecological system into decision analysis of alternative strategies for protecting endangered and threatened species promises to lead to actions that simultaneously enhance the probability of the species' survival and reduce the risk to the ecological system.

---

*Based on Fred A. Johnson, B. Ken Williams, and James D. Nichols, "Resilience Thinking and a Decision-Analytic Approach to Conservation: Strange Bedfellows or Essential Partners?" *Ecology and Society* 17(4): 28 and Tracy M. Rout, Eve McDonald-Madden, Tara G. Martin, Nicola J. Mitchell, Hugh P. Possingham, and Doug P. Armstrong, "How to Decide Whether to Move Species Threatened by Climate Change." *PLoS ONE* 8(10).

to illustrate the fundamentals of decision analysis. We then introduce decision trees to show the sequential nature of decision problems. Decision trees are used to analyze more complex problems and to identify an optimal sequence of decisions, referred to as an optimal decision strategy. Sensitivity analysis shows how changes in various aspects of the problem affect the recommended decision alternative.

4.1 Problem Formulation

The first step in the decision analysis process is problem formulation. We begin with a verbal statement of the problem. We then identify the **decision alternatives**; the uncertain future events, referred to as **chance events**; and the **consequences** associated with each combination of decision alternative and chance event outcome. Let us begin by considering a construction project of the Pittsburgh Development Corporation.

Pittsburgh Development Corporation (PDC) purchased land that will be the site of a new luxury condominium complex. The location provides a spectacular view of downtown Pittsburgh and the Golden Triangle, where the Allegheny and Monongahela Rivers meet to form the Ohio River. PDC plans to price the individual condominium units between $300,000 and $1,400,000.

PDC commissioned preliminary architectural drawings for three different projects: one with 30 condominiums, one with 60 condominiums, and one with 90 condominiums. The financial success of the project depends upon the size of the condominium complex and the chance event concerning the demand for the condominiums. The statement of the PDC decision problem is to select the size of the new luxury condominium project that will lead to the largest profit given the uncertainty concerning the demand for the condominiums.

Given the statement of the problem, it is clear that the decision is to select the best size for the condominium complex. PDC has the following three decision alternatives:

$$d_1 = \text{a small complex with 30 condominiums}$$
$$d_2 = \text{a medium complex with 60 condominiums}$$
$$d_3 = \text{a large complex with 90 condominiums}$$

A factor in selecting the best decision alternative is the uncertainty associated with the chance event concerning the demand for the condominiums. When asked about the possible demand for the condominiums, PDC's president acknowledged a wide range of possibilities but decided that it would be adequate to consider two possible chance event outcomes: a strong demand and a weak demand.

In decision analysis, the possible outcomes for a chance event are referred to as the **states of nature**. The states of nature are defined so they are mutually exclusive (no more than one can occur) and collectively exhaustive (at least one must occur); thus one and only one of the possible states of nature will occur. For the PDC problem, the chance event concerning the demand for the condominiums has two states of nature:

$$s_1 = \text{strong demand for the condominiums}$$
$$s_2 = \text{weak demand for the condominiums}$$

Management must first select a decision alternative (complex size); then a state of nature follows (demand for the condominiums) and finally a consequence will occur. In this case, the consequence is PDC's profit.

Influence Diagrams

An **influence diagram** is a graphical device that shows the relationships among the decisions, the chance events, and the consequences for a decision problem. The **nodes** in an influence diagram represent the decisions, chance events, and consequences. Rectangles or squares depict **decision nodes**, circles or ovals depict **chance nodes**, and diamonds depict **consequence nodes**. The lines connecting the nodes, referred to as *arcs,* show the direction of influence that the nodes have on one another. Figure 4.1 shows the influence diagram for the PDC problem. The complex size is the decision node, demand is the chance node, and profit is the consequence node. The arcs connecting the nodes show that both the complex size and the demand influence PDC's profit.

Payoff Tables

Given the three decision alternatives and the two states of nature, which complex size should PDC choose? To answer this question, PDC will need to know the consequence associated with each decision alternative and each state of nature. In decision analysis, we refer to the consequence resulting from a specific combination of a decision alternative and a state of nature as a **payoff**. A table showing payoffs for all combinations of decision alternatives and states of nature is a **payoff table**.

Payoffs can be expressed in terms of profit, cost, time, distance, or any other measure appropriate for the decision problem being analyzed.

Because PDC wants to select the complex size that provides the largest profit, profit is used as the consequence. The payoff table with profits expressed in millions of dollars is shown in Table 4.1. Note, for example, that if a medium complex is built and demand turns out to be strong, a profit of $14 million will be realized. We will use the notation V_{ij} to denote the payoff associated with decision alternative i and state of nature j. Using Table 4.1, $V_{31} = 20$ indicates a payoff of $20 million occurs if the decision is to build a large complex (d_3) and the strong demand state of nature (s_1) occurs. Similarly, $V_{32} = -9$ indicates a loss of $9 million if the decision is to build a large complex (d_3) and the weak demand state of nature (s_2) occurs.

FIGURE 4.1   INFLUENCE DIAGRAM FOR THE PDC PROJECT

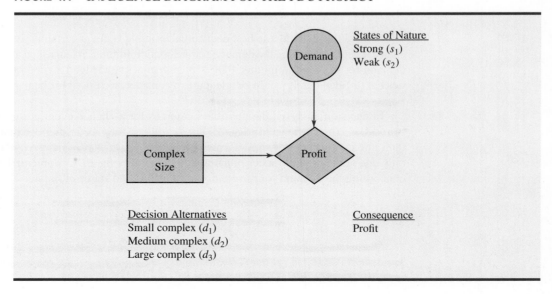

TABLE 4.1 PAYOFF TABLE FOR THE PDC CONDOMINIUM PROJECT
(PAYOFFS IN $ MILLIONS)

	State of Nature	
Decision Alternative	**Strong Demand s_1**	**Weak Demand s_2**
Small complex, d_1	8	7
Medium complex, d_2	14	5
Large complex, d_3	20	−9

Decision Trees

A decision tree provides a graphical representation of the decision-making process. Figure 4.2 presents a decision tree for the PDC problem. Note that the decision tree shows the natural or logical progression that will occur over time. First, PDC must make a decision regarding the size of the condominium complex (d_1, d_2, or d_3). Then, after the decision is implemented, either state of nature s_1 or s_2 will occur. The number at each endpoint of the tree indicates the payoff associated with a particular sequence. For example, the topmost payoff of 8 indicates that an $8 million profit is anticipated if PDC constructs a small condominium complex (d_1) and demand turns out to be strong (s_1). The next payoff of 7 indicates an anticipated profit of $7 million if PDC constructs a small condominium complex (d_1) and demand turns out to be weak (s_2). Thus, the decision tree provides a graphical depiction of the sequences of decision alternatives and states of nature that provide the six possible payoffs for PDC.

If you have a payoff table, you can develop a decision tree. Try Problem 1, part (a).

The decision tree in Figure 4.2 shows four nodes, numbered 1−4. Squares are used to depict decision nodes and circles are used to depict chance nodes. Thus, node 1 is a decision node, and nodes 2, 3, and 4 are chance nodes. The **branches** connect the nodes; those

FIGURE 4.2 DECISION TREE FOR THE PDC CONDOMINIUM PROJECT
(PAYOFFS IN $ MILLIONS)

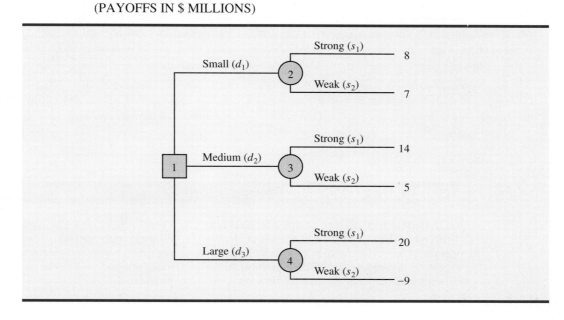

leaving the decision node correspond to the decision alternatives. The branches leaving each chance node correspond to the states of nature. The payoffs are shown at the end of the states-of-nature branches. We now turn to the question: How can the decision maker use the information in the payoff table or the decision tree to select the best decision alternative? Several approaches may be used.

The Q.M. in Action, Using Decision Analysis to Decide Whether to Transplant Endangered or Threatened Species, describes how decision analysis is used to assess whether it is advisable to transplant members of an endangered or threatened species into a new habitat.

Q.M. *in* ACTION

USING DECISION ANALYSIS TO DECIDE WHETHER TO TRANSPLANT ENDANGERED OR THREATENED SPECIES*

One strategy for attempting to prevent the extinction of an endangered or threatened species is to transplant members of the species to areas outside the species' established habitat. This strategy, which is often referred to as assisted migration, is controversial not only because it is difficult to assess the likelihood that the transplanted species will survive in new habitats, but also because it is difficult to anticipate the impact transplanted species will have on other species in its new habitat if it survives. Ecosystems are extremely complex, and a species that is not native to a particular habitat can potentially devastate the species that are native to the habitat.

Tracy Rout, a post-doctoral research fellow in the Quantitative and Applied Ecology Group at the University of Melbourne, uses decision analysis to address this issue. In order to make an informed decision on whether to transplant a particular endangered or threatened species to a new habitat, she considers the likelihood the transplanted species will survive in the new habitat, the impact the transplanted species will have on its new habitat if it survives, the probability the endangered or threatened species will become extinct if not transplanted, and the costs associated with the extinction of this species. Her decision tree features a single decision node for whether to transplant the endangered or threatened species. If the species is not transplanted, two states of nature can occur: the species becomes extinct or the species survives. If the species is transplanted, the first ensuing state of nature is whether the species survives in its new habitat. If the species does survive its introduction into the new habitat, the next state of nature is the impact the introduction of the new species has on its new habitat.

It is difficult to determine the values of inputs into this decision tree, but once reliable estimates of these values are developed, the decision tree provides important information that can be used to make better decisions about whether to transplant an endangered or threatened species into a new habitat. If there are several new habitats under consideration, the decision tree can be applied to each to help decision makers understand which of these new habitats is most promising.

NOTES AND COMMENTS

1. The first step in solving a complex problem is to decompose the problem into a series of smaller subproblems. Decision trees provide a useful way to decompose a problem and illustrate the sequential nature of the decision process.

2. People often view the same problem from different perspectives. Thus, the discussion regarding the development of a decision tree may provide additional insight about the problem.

4.2 Decision Making Without Probabilities

In this section we consider approaches to decision making that do not require knowledge of the probabilities of the states of nature. These approaches are appropriate in situations in which the decision maker has little confidence in his or her ability to assess the probabilities, or in which a simple best-case and worst-case analysis is desirable. Because different approaches sometimes lead to different decision recommendations, the decision maker must understand the approaches available and then select the specific approach that, according to the judgment of the decision maker, is the most appropriate.

Optimistic Approach

The **optimistic approach** evaluates each decision alternative in terms of the *best* payoff that can occur. The decision alternative that is recommended is the one that provides the best possible payoff. For a problem in which maximum profit is desired, as in the PDC problem, the optimistic approach would lead the decision maker to choose the alternative corresponding to the largest profit. For problems involving minimization, this approach leads to choosing the alternative with the smallest payoff.

To illustrate the optimistic approach, we use it to develop a recommendation for the PDC problem. First, we determine the maximum payoff for each decision alternative; then we select the decision alternative that provides the overall maximum payoff. These steps systematically identify the decision alternative that provides the largest possible profit. Table 4.2 illustrates these steps.

Because 20, corresponding to d_3, is the largest payoff, the decision to construct the large condominium complex is the recommended decision alternative using the optimistic approach.

Conservative Approach

The **conservative approach** evaluates each decision alternative in terms of the *worst* payoff that can occur. The decision alternative recommended is the one that provides the best of the worst possible payoffs. For a problem in which the output measure is profit, as in the PDC problem, the conservative approach would lead the decision maker to choose the alternative that maximizes the minimum possible profit that could be obtained. For problems involving minimization, this approach identifies the alternative that will minimize the maximum payoff.

To illustrate the conservative approach, we use it to develop a recommendation for the PDC problem. First, we identify the minimum payoff for each of the decision alternatives; then we select the decision alternative that maximizes the minimum payoff. Table 4.3 illustrates these steps for the PDC problem.

Many people think of a good decision as one in which the consequence is good. However, in some instances, a good, well-thought-out decision may still lead to a bad or undesirable consequence while a poor, ill-conceived decision may still lead to a good or desirable consequence.

For a maximization problem, the optimistic approach often is referred to as the maximax approach; for a minimization problem, the corresponding terminology is minimin.

For a maximization problem, the conservative approach is often referred to as the maximin approach; for a minimization problem, the corresponding terminology is minimax.

TABLE 4.2 MAXIMUM PAYOFF FOR EACH PDC DECISION ALTERNATIVE

Decision Alternative	Maximum Payoff	
Small complex, d_1	8	
Medium complex, d_2	14	
Large complex, d_3	20	← Maximum of the maximum payoff values

TABLE 4.3   MINIMUM PAYOFF FOR EACH PDC DECISION ALTERNATIVE

Decision Alternative	Minimum Payoff	
Small complex, d_1	7	← Maximum of the mini-mum payoff values
Medium complex, d_2	5	
Large complex, d_3	−9	

Because 7, corresponding to d_1, yields the maximum of the minimum payoffs, the decision alternative of a small condominium complex is recommended. This decision approach is considered conservative because it identifies the worst possible payoffs and then recommends the decision alternative that avoids the possibility of extremely "bad" payoffs. In the conservative approach, PDC is guaranteed a profit of at least $7 million. Although PDC may make more, it *cannot* make less than $7 million.

Minimax Regret Approach

In decision analysis, **regret** is the difference between the payoff associated with a particular decision alternative and the payoff associated with the decision that would yield the most desirable payoff for a given state of nature. Thus, regret represents how much potential payoff one would forgo by selecting a particular decision alternative given that a specific state of nature will occur. This is why regret is often referred to as **opportunity loss**.

As its name implies, under the **minimax regret approach** to decision making one would choose the decision alternative that minimizes the maximum state of regret that could occur over all possible states of nature. This approach is neither purely optimistic nor purely conservative. Let us illustrate the minimax regret approach by showing how it can be used to select a decision alternative for the PDC problem.

Suppose that PDC constructs a small condominium complex (d_1) and demand turns out to be strong (s_1). Table 4.1 showed that the resulting profit for PDC would be $8 million. However, given that the strong demand state of nature (s_1) has occurred, we realize that the decision to construct a large condominium complex (d_3), yielding a profit of $20 million, would have been the best decision. The difference between the payoff for the best decision alternative ($20 million) and the payoff for the decision to construct a small condominium complex ($8 million) is the regret or opportunity loss associated with decision alternative d_1 when state of nature s_1 occurs; thus, for this case, the opportunity loss or regret is $20 million − $8 million = $12 million. Similarly, if PDC makes the decision to construct a medium condominium complex (d_2) and the strong demand state of nature (s_1) occurs, the opportunity loss, or regret, associated with d_2 would be $20 million − $14 million = $6 million.

In general, the following expression represents the opportunity loss, or regret:

$$R_{ij} = |V_j^* - V_{ij}| \tag{4.1}$$

where

R_{ij} = the regret associated with decision alternative d_i and state of nature s_j

V_j^* = the payoff value[1] corresponding to the best decision for the state of nature s_j

V_{ij} = the payoff corresponding to decision alternative d_i and state of nature s_j

---

[1]In maximization problems, V_j^* will be the largest entry in column j of the payoff table. In minimization problems, V_j^* will be the smallest entry in column j of the payoff table.

TABLE 4.4 OPPORTUNITY LOSS, OR REGRET, TABLE FOR THE PDC CONDOMINIUM PROJECT ($ MILLIONS)

	State of Nature	
Decision Alternative	**Strong Demand s_1**	**Weak Demand s_2**
Small complex, d_1	12	0
Medium complex, d_2	6	2
Large complex, d_3	0	16

Note the role of the absolute value in equation (4.1). For minimization problems, the best payoff, V_j^*, is the smallest entry in column j. Because this value always is less than or equal to V_{ij}, the absolute value of the difference between V_j^* and V_{ij} ensures that the regret is always the magnitude of the difference.

Using equation (4.1) and the payoffs in Table 4.1, we can compute the regret associated with each combination of decision alternative d_i and state of nature s_j. Because the PDC problem is a maximization problem, V_j^* will be the largest entry in column j of the payoff table. Thus, to compute the regret, we simply subtract each entry in a column from the largest entry in the column. Table 4.4 shows the opportunity loss, or regret, table for the PDC problem.

The next step in applying the minimax regret approach is to list the maximum regret for each decision alternative; Table 4.5 shows the results for the PDC problem. Selecting the decision alternative with the *minimum* of the *maximum* regret values—hence, the name *minimax regret*—yields the minimax regret decision. For the PDC problem, the alternative to construct the medium condominium complex, with a corresponding maximum regret of $6 million, is the recommended minimax regret decision.

For practice in developing a decision recommendation using the optimistic, conservative, and minimax regret approaches, try Problem 1, part (b).

Note that the three approaches discussed in this section provide different recommendations, which in itself isn't bad. It simply reflects the difference in decision-making philosophies that underlie the various approaches. Ultimately, the decision maker will have to choose the most appropriate approach and then make the final decision accordingly. The main criticism of the approaches discussed in this section is that they do not consider any information about the probabilities of the various states of nature. In the next section we discuss an approach that utilizes probability information in selecting a decision alternative.

TABLE 4.5 MAXIMUM REGRET FOR EACH PDC DECISION ALTERNATIVE

Decision Alternative	**Maximum Regret**	
Small complex, d_1	12	
Medium complex, d_2	6	← Minimum of the maximum regret
Large complex, d_3	16	

Decision Making with Probabilities

In many decision-making situations, we can obtain probability assessments for the states of nature. When such probabilities are available, we can use the **expected value approach** to identify the best decision alternative. Let us first define the expected value of a decision alternative and then apply it to the PDC problem.

    Let

$$N = \text{the number of states of nature}$$
$$P(s_j) = \text{the probability of state of nature } s_j$$

Because one and only one of the N states of nature can occur, the probabilities must satisfy two conditions:

$$P(s_j) \geq 0 \qquad \text{for all states of nature} \tag{4.2}$$

$$\sum_{j=1}^{N} P(s_j) = P(s_1) + P(s_2) + \cdots + P(s_N) = 1 \tag{4.3}$$

The **expected value (EV)** of decision alternative d_i is defined as follows:

$$EV(d_i) = \sum_{j=1}^{N} P(s_j) V_{ij} \tag{4.4}$$

In words, the expected value of a decision alternative is the sum of weighted payoffs for the decision alternative. The weight for a payoff is the probability of the associated state of nature and therefore the probability that the payoff will occur. Let us return to the PDC problem to see how the expected value approach can be applied.

    PDC is optimistic about the potential for the luxury high-rise condominium complex. Suppose that this optimism leads to an initial subjective probability assessment of 0.8 that demand will be strong (s_1) and a corresponding probability of 0.2 that demand will be weak (s_2). Thus, $P(s_1) = 0.8$ and $P(s_2) = 0.2$. Using the payoff values in Table 4.1 and equation (4.4), we compute the expected value for each of the three decision alternatives as follows:

$$EV(d_1) = 0.8(8) + 0.2(7) \quad\; = 7.8$$
$$EV(d_2) = 0.8(14) + 0.2(5) \quad = 12.2$$
$$EV(d_3) = 0.8(20) + 0.2(-9) = 14.2$$

Thus, using the expected value approach, we find that the large condominium complex, with an expected value of \$14.2 million, is the recommended decision.

    The calculations required to identify the decision alternative with the best expected value can be conveniently carried out on a decision tree. Figure 4.3 shows the decision tree for the PDC problem with state-of-nature branch probabilities. Working backward through the decision tree, we first compute the expected value at each chance node. That is, at each chance node, we weight each possible payoff by its probability of occurrence. By doing so, we obtain the expected values for nodes 2, 3, and 4, as shown in Figure 4.4.

    Because the decision maker controls the branch leaving decision node 1 and because we are trying to maximize the expected profit, the best decision alternative at node 1 is d_3. Thus, the decision tree analysis leads to a recommendation of d_3, with an expected value

Computer packages are available to help in constructing more complex decision trees. See Appendix 4.1.

FIGURE 4.3   PDC DECISION TREE WITH STATE-OF-NATURE BRANCH PROBABILITIES

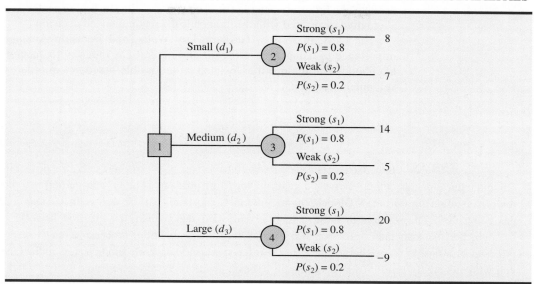

FIGURE 4.4   APPLYING THE EXPECTED VALUE APPROACH USING A DECISION TREE

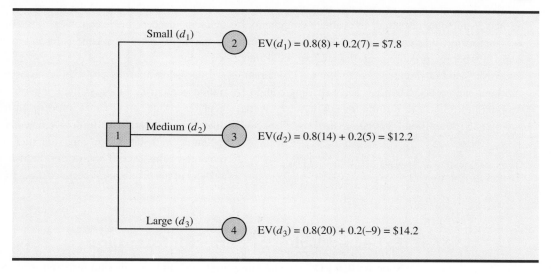

of \$14.2 million. Note that this recommendation is also obtained with the expected value approach in conjunction with the payoff table.

Other decision problems may be substantially more complex than the PDC problem, but if a reasonable number of decision alternatives and states of nature are present, you can use the decision tree approach outlined here. First, draw a decision tree consisting of decision nodes, chance nodes, and branches that describe the sequential nature of the problem. If you use the expected value approach, the next step is to determine the probabilities for each of the states of nature and compute the expected value at each chance node. Then select the decision branch leading to the chance node with the best expected value. The decision alternative associated with this branch is the recommended decision.

The Q.M. in Action, Gushers, Dry Wells, and Decision Analysis, describes the importance of using data in the oil and natural gas industry to accurately estimate the likelihoods and the profit associated with possible outcomes in order to make wise development decisions.

Q.M. *in* ACTION

GUSHERS, DRY WELLS, AND DECISION ANALYSIS*

Oil and natural gas are big businesses: nine of the top ten organizations in Fortune's Global 500 are oil and gas companies. The rewards in these industries can be high, but the associated risks are also great. Oil prices at or above $100 per barrel make an oil reservoir with potentially 1 million barrels of supply appear to be an enticing development venture. But as Adam Farris, senior vice president of business development for Drillinginfo, explains, realizing this potential $100 million stream of revenue is not simple. He points out that the acquisition, processing, and interpretation of the seismic data necessary to evaluate the potential well before drilling could cost $30 million. Typical deals involve the procurement of access to thousands of acres of land (a single well may require 120 acres), and land can cost $30,000 per acre. Drilling can cost from $5 million to $10 million for U.S. onshore wells and up to $100 million for offshore drilling. The costs

of producing the oil and getting it to market are also substantial. If the well is drilled and does not produce oil, the company has incurred the costs associated with the acquisition, processing, and interpretation of the seismic data, obtaining access to the land, and drilling with no resulting revenue.

"If you are a major integrated oil and gas company, your profit on $100 million will be $1 million to $12 million (a bit higher for independent operators)," states Farris. "Many will lose money overall. Analytical approaches that impact the success rate of finding or reducing the cost to develop and produce oil and gas can make energy more affordable, safer and environmentally conscious."

Decision analysis provides a means for oil exploration companies to assess the complex data in a systematic manner and extract information from the data that ultimately are used to decide whether to drill in a potential well site. Identifying well sites for which the potential gains exceed and justify the risk of drilling is critical to the economic success of these firms.

*Based on Adam Farris, "How Big Data is Changing the Oil & Gas Industry." *Analytics* (November/December 2012).

Expected Value of Perfect Information

Suppose that PDC has the opportunity to conduct a market research study that would help evaluate buyer interest in the condominium project and provide information that management could use to improve the probability assessments for the states of nature. To determine the potential value of this information, we begin by supposing that the study could provide *perfect information* regarding the states of nature; that is, we assume for the moment that PDC could determine with certainty, prior to making a decision, which state of nature is going to occur. To make use of this perfect information, we will develop a decision strategy that PDC should follow once it knows which state of nature will occur. A decision strategy is simply a decision rule that specifies the decision alternative to be selected after new information becomes available.

TABLE 4.6   PAYOFF TABLE FOR THE PDC CONDOMINIUM PROJECT ($ MILLIONS)

	State of Nature	
Decision Alternative	**Strong Demand s_1**	**Weak Demand s_2**
Small complex, d_1	8	7
Medium complex, d_2	14	5
Large complex, d_3	20	−9

To help determine the decision strategy for PDC, we reproduced PDC's payoff table as Table 4.6. Note that, if PDC knew for sure that state of nature s_1 would occur, the best decision alternative would be d_3, with a payoff of $20 million. Similarly, if PDC knew for sure that state of nature s_2 would occur, the best decision alternative would be d_1, with a payoff of $7 million. Thus, we can state PDC's optimal decision strategy when the perfect information becomes available as follows:

If s_1, select d_3 and receive a payoff of $20 million.

If s_2, select d_1 and receive a payoff of $7 million.

What is the expected value for this decision strategy? To compute the expected value with perfect information, we return to the original probabilities for the states of nature: $P(s_1) =$ 0.8 and $P(s_2) = 0.2$. Thus, there is a 0.8 probability that the perfect information will indicate state of nature s_1, and the resulting decision alternative d_3 will provide a $20 million profit. Similarly, with a 0.2 probability for state of nature s_2, the optimal decision alternative d_1 will provide a $7 million profit. Thus, from equation (4.4) the expected value of the decision strategy that uses perfect information is $0.8(20) + 0.2(7) = 17.4$.

We refer to the expected value of $17.4 million as the *expected value with perfect information* (EVwPI).

Earlier in this section we showed that the recommended decision using the expected value approach is decision alternative d_3, with an expected value of $14.2 million. Because this decision recommendation and expected value computation were made without the benefit of perfect information, $14.2 million is referred to as the *expected value without perfect information* (EVwoPI).

The expected value with perfect information is $17.4 million, and the expected value without perfect information is $14.2; therefore, the expected value of the perfect information (EVPI) is $17.4 − $14.2 = $3.2 million. In other words, $3.2 million represents the additional expected value that can be obtained if perfect information were available about the states of nature.

It would be worth $3.2 million for PDC to learn the level of market acceptance before selecting a decision alternative.

Generally speaking, a market research study will not provide "perfect" information; however, if the market research study is a good one, the information gathered might be worth a sizable portion of the $3.2 million. Given the EVPI of $3.2 million, PDC might seriously consider a market survey as a way to obtain more information about the states of nature.

In general, the **expected value of perfect information (EVPI)** is computed as follows:

$$\text{EVPI} = |\text{EVwPI} - \text{EVwoPI}| \qquad \textbf{(4.5)}$$

where

$$\text{EVPI} = \text{expected value of perfect information}$$
$$\text{EVwPI} = \text{expected value } \textit{with} \text{ perfect information about the states of nature}$$
$$\text{EVwoPI} = \text{expected value } \textit{without} \text{ perfect information about the states of nature}$$

For practice in determining the expected value of perfect information, try Problem 14.

Note the role of the absolute value in equation (4.5). For minimization problems, the expected value with perfect information is always less than or equal to the expected value without perfect information. In this case, EVPI is the magnitude of the difference between EVwPI and EVwoPI, or the absolute value of the difference as shown in equation (4.5).

NOTES AND COMMENTS

1. We restate the *opportunity loss,* or *regret,* table for the PDC problem (see Table 4.4) as follows:

	State of Nature	
	Strong Demand	Weak Demand
Decision	s_1	s_2
Small complex, d_1	12	0
Medium complex, d_2	6	2
Large complex, d_3	0	16

Using $P(s_1)$, $P(s_2)$, and the opportunity loss values, we can compute the *expected opportunity loss* (EOL) for each decision alternative. With $P(s_1) = 0.8$ and $P(s_2) = 0.2$, the expected

opportunity loss for each of the three decision alternatives is

$$\text{EOL}(d_1) = 0.8(12) + 0.2(0) = 9.6$$
$$\text{EOL}(d_2) = 0.8(6) + 0.2(2) = 5.2$$
$$\text{EOL}(d_3) = 0.8(0) + 0.2(16) = 3.2$$

Regardless of whether the decision analysis involves maximization or minimization, the *minimum* expected opportunity loss always provides the best decision alternative. Thus, with $\text{EOL}(d_3) = 3.2$, d_3 is the recommended decision. In addition, the minimum expected opportunity loss always is *equal to the expected value of perfect information.* That is, EOL(best decision) = EVPI; for the PDC problem, this value is $3.2 million.

4.4   Risk Analysis and Sensitivity Analysis

Risk analysis helps the decision maker recognize the difference between the expected value of a decision alternative and the payoff that may actually occur. **Sensitivity analysis** also helps the decision maker by describing how changes in the state-of-nature probabilities and/or changes in the payoffs affect the recommended decision alternative.

Risk Analysis

A decision alternative and a state of nature combine to generate the payoff associated with a decision. The **risk profile** for a decision alternative shows the possible payoffs along with their associated probabilities.

Let us demonstrate risk analysis and the construction of a risk profile by returning to the PDC condominium construction project. Using the expected value approach, we identified the large condominium complex (d_3) as the best decision alternative. The expected value of $14.2 million for d_3 is based on a 0.8 probability of obtaining a $20 million

FIGURE 4.5   RISK PROFILE FOR THE LARGE COMPLEX DECISION ALTERNATIVE FOR THE PDC CONDOMINIUM PROJECT

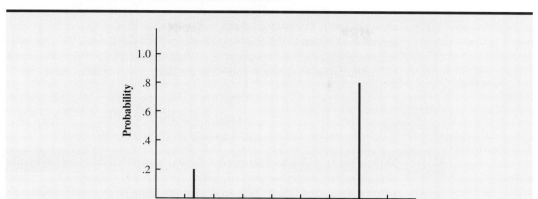

profit and a 0.2 probability of obtaining a $9 million loss. The 0.8 probability for the $20 million payoff and the 0.2 probability for the −$9 million payoff provide the risk profile for the large complex decision alternative. This risk profile is shown graphically in Figure 4.5.

Sometimes a review of the risk profile associated with an optimal decision alternative may cause the decision maker to choose another decision alternative even though the expected value of the other decision alternative is not as good. For example, the risk profile for the medium complex decision alternative (d_2) shows a 0.8 probability for a $14 million payoff and a 0.2 probability for a $5 million payoff. Because no probability of a loss is associated with decision alternative d_2, the medium complex decision alternative would be judged less risky than the large complex decision alternative. As a result, a decision maker might prefer the less risky medium complex decision alternative even though it has an expected value of $2 million less than the large complex decision alternative.

Sensitivity Analysis

Sensitivity analysis can be used to determine how changes in the probabilities for the states of nature or changes in the payoffs affect the recommended decision alternative. In many cases, the probabilities for the states of nature and the payoffs are based on subjective assessments. Sensitivity analysis helps the decision maker understand which of these inputs are critical to the choice of the best decision alternative. If a small change in the value of one of the inputs causes a change in the recommended decision alternative, the solution to the decision analysis problem is sensitive to that particular input. Extra effort and care should be taken to make sure the input value is as accurate as possible. On the other hand, if a modest-to-large change in the value of one of the inputs does not cause a change in the recommended decision alternative, the solution to the decision analysis problem is not sensitive to that particular input. No extra time or effort would be needed to refine the estimated input value.

One approach to sensitivity analysis is to select different values for the probabilities of the states of nature and the payoffs and then resolve the decision analysis problem. If the recommended decision alternative changes, we know that the solution is sensitive to the changes made. For example, suppose that in the PDC problem the probability for a strong demand is revised to 0.2 and the probability for a weak demand is revised to 0.8. Would the recommended decision alternative change? Using $P(s_1) = 0.2$, $P(s_2) = 0.8$, and equation (4.4), the revised expected values for the three decision alternatives are

$$\text{EV}(d_1) = 0.2(8) \ \ + 0.8(7) \ \ = \ \ 7.2$$
$$\text{EV}(d_2) = 0.2(14) + 0.8(5) \ \ = \ \ 6.8$$
$$\text{EV}(d_3) = 0.2(20) + 0.8(-9) = -3.2$$

With these probability assessments, the recommended decision alternative is to construct a small condominium complex (d_1), with an expected value of \$7.2 million. The probability of strong demand is only 0.2, so constructing the large condominium complex (d_3) is the least preferred alternative, with an expected value of $-\$3.2$ million (a loss).

Thus, when the probability of strong demand is large, PDC should build the large complex; when the probability of strong demand is small, PDC should build the small complex. Obviously, we could continue to modify the probabilities of the states of nature and learn even more about how changes in the probabilities affect the recommended decision alternative. The drawback to this approach is the numerous calculations required to evaluate the effect of several possible changes in the state-of-nature probabilities.

Computer software packages for decision analysis make it easy to calculate these revised scenarios.

For the special case of two states of nature, a graphical procedure can be used to determine how changes for the probabilities of the states of nature affect the recommended decision alternative. To demonstrate this procedure, we let p denote the probability of state of nature s_1; that is, $P(s_1) = p$. With only two states of nature in the PDC problem, the probability of state of nature s_2 is

$$P(s_2) = 1 - P(s_1) = 1 - p$$

Using equation (4.4) and the payoff values in Table 4.1, we determine the expected value for decision alternative d_1 as follows:

$$\begin{aligned} \text{EV}(d_1) &= P(s_1)(8) + P(s_2)(7) \\ &= p(8) + (1 - p)(7) \\ &= 8p + 7 - 7p = p + 7 \end{aligned} \quad \textbf{(4.6)}$$

Repeating the expected value computations for decision alternatives d_2 and d_3, we obtain expressions for the expected value of each decision alternative as a function of p:

$$\text{EV}(d_2) = 9p + 5 \qquad \textbf{(4.7)}$$

$$\text{EV}(d_3) = 29p - 9 \qquad \textbf{(4.8)}$$

Thus, we have developed three equations that show the expected value of the three decision alternatives as a function of the probability of state of nature s_1.

We continue by developing a graph with values of p on the horizontal axis and the associated EVs on the vertical axis. Because equations (4.6), (4.7), and (4.8) are linear equations, the graph of each equation is a straight line. For each equation, we can obtain the line

FIGURE 4.6 EXPECTED VALUE FOR THE PDC DECISION ALTERNATIVES
AS A FUNCTION OF p

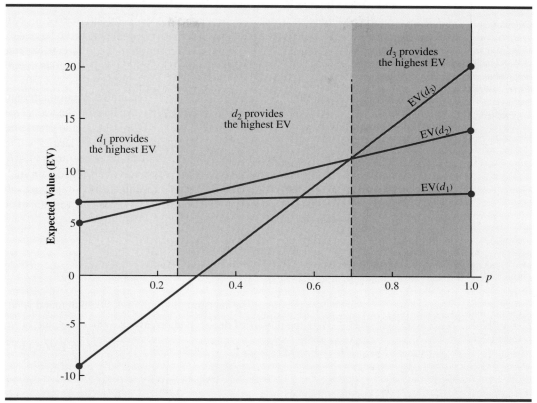

by identifying two points that satisfy the equation and drawing a line through the points. For instance, if we let $p = 0$ in equation (4.6), $EV(d_1) = 7$. Then, letting $p = 1$, $EV(d_1) = 8$. Connecting these two points, (0,7) and (1,8), provides the line labeled $EV(d_1)$ in Figure 4.6. Similarly, we obtain the lines labeled $EV(d_2)$ and $EV(d_3)$; these lines are the graphs of equations (4.7) and (4.8), respectively.

Figure 4.6 shows how the recommended decision changes as p, the probability of the strong demand state of nature (s_1), changes. Note that for small values of p, decision alternative d_1 (small complex) provides the largest expected value and is thus the recommended decision. When the value of p increases to a certain point, decision alternative d_2 (medium complex) provides the largest expected value and is the recommended decision. Finally, for large values of p, decision alternative d_3 (large complex) becomes the recommended decision.

The value of p for which the expected values of d_1 and d_2 are equal is the value of p corresponding to the intersection of the $EV(d_1)$ and the $EV(d_2)$ lines. To determine this value, we set $EV(d_1) = EV(d_2)$ and solve for the value of p:

$$p + 7 = 9p + 5$$
$$8p = 2$$
$$p = \frac{2}{8} = 0.25$$

Hence, when $p = 0.25$, decision alternatives d_1 and d_2 provide the same expected value. Repeating this calculation for the value of p corresponding to the intersection of the $EV(d_2)$ and $EV(d_3)$ lines, we obtain $p = 0.70$.

Graphical sensitivity analysis shows how changes in the probabilities for the states of nature affect the recommended decision alternative. Try Problem 8.

Using Figure 4.6, we can conclude that decision alternative d_1 provides the largest expected value for $p \leq 0.25$, decision alternative d_2 provides the largest expected value for $0.25 \leq p \leq 0.70$, and decision alternative d_3 provides the largest expected value for $p \geq 0.70$. Because p is the probability of state of nature s_1 and $(1 - p)$ is the probability of state of nature s_2, we now have the sensitivity analysis information that tells us how changes in the state-of-nature probabilities affect the recommended decision alternative.

Sensitivity analysis calculations can also be made for the values of the payoffs. In the original PDC problem, the expected values for the three decision alternatives were as follows: $EV(d_1) = 7.8$, $EV(d_2) = 12.2$, and $EV(d_3) = 14.2$. Decision alternative d_3 (large complex) was recommended. Note that decision alternative d_2 with $EV(d_2) = 12.2$ was the second best decision alternative. Decision alternative d_3 will remain the optimal decision alternative as long as $EV(d_3)$ is greater than or equal to the expected value of the second best decision alternative. Thus, decision alternative d_3 will remain the optimal decision alternative as long as

$$EV(d_3) \geq 12.2 \tag{4.9}$$

Let

$$S = \text{the payoff of decision alternative } d_3 \text{ when demand is strong}$$
$$W = \text{the payoff of decision alternative } d_3 \text{ when demand is weak}$$

Using $P(s_1) = 0.8$ and $P(s_2) = 0.2$, the general expression for $EV(d_3)$ is

$$EV(d_3) = 0.8S + 0.2W \tag{4.10}$$

Assuming that the payoff for d_3 stays at its original value of $-\$9$ million when demand is weak, the large complex decision alternative will remain optimal as long as

$$EV(d_3) = 0.8S + 0.2(-9) \geq 12.2 \tag{4.11}$$

Solving for S, we have

$$0.8S - 1.8 \geq 12.2$$
$$0.8S \geq 14$$
$$S \geq 17.5$$

Recall that when demand is strong, decision alternative d_3 has an estimated payoff of $\$20$ million. The preceding calculation shows that decision alternative d_3 will remain optimal as long as the payoff for d_3 when demand is strong is at least $\$17.5$ million.

Assuming that the payoff for d_3 when demand is strong stays at its original value of $\$20$ million, we can make a similar calculation to learn how sensitive the optimal solution is with regard to the payoff for d_3 when demand is weak. Returning to the expected value calculation of equation (4.10), we know that the large complex decision alternative will remain optimal as long as

$$EV(d_3) = 0.8(20) + 0.2W \geq 12.2 \tag{4.12}$$

Solving for W, we have

$$16 + 0.2 \geq 12.2$$
$$0.2W \geq -3.8$$
$$W \geq -19$$

Recall that when demand is weak, decision alternative d_3 has an estimated payoff of $-\$9$ million. The preceding calculation shows that decision alternative d_3 will remain optimal as long as the payoff for d_3 when demand is weak is at least $-\$19$ million.

Sensitivity analysis can assist management in deciding whether more time and effort should be spent obtaining better estimates of payoffs and probabilities.

Based on this sensitivity analysis, we conclude that the payoffs for the large complex decision alternative (d_3) could vary considerably, and d_3 would remain the recommended decision alternative. Thus, we conclude that the optimal solution for the PDC decision problem is not particularly sensitive to the payoffs for the large complex decision alternative. We note, however, that this sensitivity analysis has been conducted based on only one change at a time. That is, only one payoff was changed and the probabilities for the states of nature remained $P(s_1) = 0.8$ and $P(s_2) = 0.2$. Note that similar sensitivity analysis calculations can be made for the payoffs associated with the small complex decision alternative d_1 and the medium complex decision alternative d_2. However, in these cases, decision alternative d_3 remains optimal only if the changes in the payoffs for decision alternatives d_1 and d_2 meet the requirements that $EV(d_1) \leq 14.2$ and $EV(d_2) \leq 14.2$.

The Q.M. in Action, Reducing the Threat of Terrorism Through Decision Analysis, describes how U.S. Customs and Border Protection uses decision analysis to reduce the risk of terrorism in commercial truck crossings at land ports of entry in the southwestern United States.

Q.M. *in* ACTION

REDUCING THE THREAT OF TERRORISM THROUGH DECISION ANALYSIS*

Border security is a critical component of a nation's security. For a country the size of the United States, border crossings are particularly difficult to patrol, monitor, and control. The U.S. Customs and Border Protection (CBP), the federal government agency responsible for border management and control, is one of the world's largest law enforcement organizations. CBP has over 60,000 employees who routinely receive approximately 1 million visitors, screen almost 70,000 cargo containers, and seize approximately six tons of illicit drugs daily. Making this many decisions every day necessitates that CBT agents quickly and efficiently evaluate the information available on each individual, vehicle, boat, plane, or helicopter that is attempting to cross a border and enter the United States.

*Based on Niyazi Onur Bakır, "A Decision Tree Model for Evaluating Countermeasures to Secure Cargo at United States Southwestern Ports of Entry." *Decision Analysis* 5(4): 230–248.

Niyazi Onur Bakır of the National Center for Risk and Economic Analysis of Terrorism Events (CREATE) at the University of Southern California has developed a decision tree approach to reduce vulnerabilities to terrorism in commercial truck crossings at land ports of entry in the southwestern United States. The model takes into consideration potential costs and benefits associated with improving transportation security, inspections at Mexican land ports, and inspections at U.S. land ports. Costs that are considered include not only the actual costs of making these improvements but also the costs associated with security breaches and false alarms.

Ultimately, the model provides guidelines for conditions under which the various improvements under consideration should be undertaken. Results demonstrate that through the use of decision analysis, CBP can provide increased security at a decreased cost.

NOTES AND COMMENTS

1. Some decision analysis software automatically provides the risk profiles for the optimal decision alternative. These packages also allow the user to obtain the risk profiles for other decision alternatives. After comparing the risk profiles, a decision maker may decide to select a decision alternative with a good risk profile even though the expected value of the decision alternative is not as good as the optimal decision alternative.

2. A *tornado diagram,* a graphical display, is particularly helpful when several inputs combine to determine the value of the optimal solution. By varying each input over its range of values, we obtain information about how each input affects the value of the optimal solution. To display this information, a bar is constructed for the input, with the width of the bar showing how the input affects the value of the optimal solution. The widest bar corresponds to the input that is most sensitive. The bars are arranged in a graph with the widest bar at the top, resulting in a graph that has the appearance of a tornado.

4.5 Decision Analysis with Sample Information

In applying the expected value approach, we showed how probability information about the states of nature affects the expected value calculations and thus the decision recommendation. Frequently, decision makers have preliminary or **prior probability** assessments for the states of nature that are the best probability values available at that time. However, to make the best possible decision, the decision maker may want to seek additional information about the states of nature. This new information can be used to revise or update the prior probabilities so that the final decision is based on more accurate probabilities for the states of nature. Most often, additional information is obtained through experiments designed to provide **sample information** about the states of nature. Raw material sampling, product testing, and market research studies are examples of experiments (or studies) that may enable management to revise or update the state-of-nature probabilities. These revised probabilities are called **posterior probabilities**.

Let us return to the PDC problem and assume that management is considering a 6-month market research study designed to learn more about potential market acceptance of the PDC condominium project. Management anticipates that the market research study will provide one of the following two results:

1. Favorable report: A substantial number of the individuals contacted express interest in purchasing a PDC condominium.
2. Unfavorable report: Very few of the individuals contacted express interest in purchasing a PDC condominium.

Influence Diagram

By introducing the possibility of conducting a market research study, the PDC problem becomes more complex. The influence diagram for the expanded PDC problem is shown in Figure 4.7. Note that the two decision nodes correspond to the research study and the complex-size decisions. The two chance nodes correspond to the research study results and demand for the condominiums. Finally, the consequence node is the profit. From the arcs of the influence diagram, we see that demand influences both the research study results and profit. Although demand is currently unknown to PDC, some level of demand for the condominiums already exists in the Pittsburgh area. If existing demand is strong, the research study is likely to find a substantial number of individuals who express an interest in purchasing a condominium.

FIGURE 4.7   INFLUENCE DIAGRAM FOR THE PDC PROBLEM WITH SAMPLE
INFORMATION

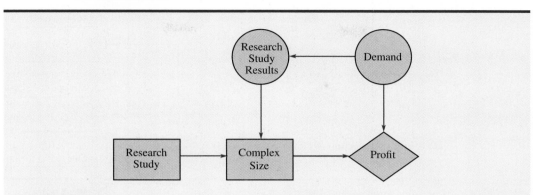

However, if the existing demand is weak, the research study is more likely to find a substantial
number of individuals who express little interest in purchasing a condominium. In this sense,
existing demand for the condominiums will influence the research study results, and clearly,
demand will have an influence upon PDC's profit.

The arc from the research study decision node to the complex-size decision node indicates that the research study decision precedes the complex-size decision. No arc spans
from the research study decision node to the research study results node because the decision to conduct the research study does not actually influence the research study results.
The decision to conduct the research study makes the research study results available, but it
does not influence the results of the research study. Finally, the complex-size node and the
demand node both influence profit. Note that if a stated cost to conduct the research study
were given, the decision to conduct the research study would also influence profit. In such a
case, we would need to add an arc from the research study decision node to the profit node
to show the influence that the research study cost would have on profit.

Decision Tree

The decision tree for the PDC problem with sample information shows the logical sequence
for the decisions and the chance events in Figure 4.8.

First, PDC's management must decide whether the market research should be conducted.
If it is conducted, PDC's management must be prepared to make a decision about the size of
the condominium project if the market research report is favorable and, possibly, a different
decision about the size of the condominium project if the market research report is unfavorable.
In Figure 4.8, the squares are decision nodes and the circles are chance nodes. At each decision
node, the branch of the tree that is taken is based on the decision made. At each chance node,
the branch of the tree that is taken is based on probability or chance. For example, decision
node 1 shows that PDC must first make the decision of whether to conduct the market research
study. If the market research study is undertaken, chance node 2 indicates that both the favorable report branch and the unfavorable report branch are not under PDC's control and will be
determined by chance. Node 3 is a decision node, indicating that PDC must make the decision
to construct the small, medium, or large complex if the market research report is favorable.
Node 4 is a decision node showing that PDC must make the decision to construct the small,
medium, or large complex if the market research report is unfavorable. Node 5 is a decision

FIGURE 4.8 THE PDC DECISION TREE INCLUDING THE MARKET RESEARCH STUDY

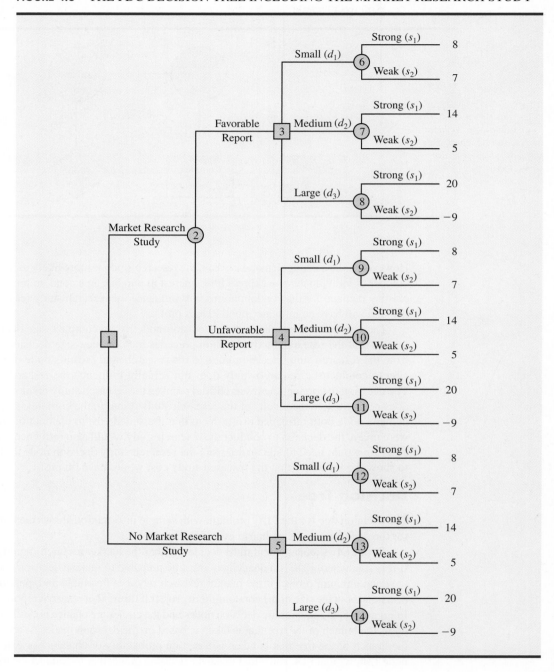

node indicating that PDC must make the decision to construct the small, medium, or large complex if the market research is not undertaken. Nodes 6 to 14 are chance nodes indicating that the strong demand or weak demand state-of-nature branches will be determined by chance.

Analysis of the decision tree and the choice of an optimal strategy require that we know the branch probabilities corresponding to all chance nodes. PDC has developed the following branch probabilities:

If the market research study is undertaken

We explain in Section 4.6 how the branch probabilities for P(Favorable report) and P(Unfavorable report) can be developed.

$$P(\text{Favorable report}) = 0.77$$
$$P(\text{Unfavorable report}) = 0.23$$

If the market research report is favorable

$$P(\text{Strong demand given a favorable report}) = 0.94$$
$$P(\text{Weak demand given a favorable report}) = 0.06$$

If the market research report is unfavorable

$$P(\text{Strong demand given an unfavorable report}) = 0.35$$
$$P(\text{Weak demand given an unfavorable report}) = 0.65$$

If the market research report is not undertaken, the prior probabilities are applicable.

$$P(\text{Strong demand}) = 0.80$$
$$P(\text{Weak demand}) = 0.20$$

The branch probabilities are shown on the decision tree in Figure 4.9.

Decision Strategy

A **decision strategy** is a sequence of decisions and chance outcomes where the decisions chosen depend on the yet-to-be-determined outcomes of chance events.

The approach used to determine the optimal decision strategy is based on a backward pass through the decision tree using the following steps:

1. At chance nodes, compute the expected value by multiplying the payoff at the end of each branch by the corresponding branch probabilities.
2. At decision nodes, select the decision branch that leads to the best expected value. This expected value becomes the expected value at the decision node.

Starting the backward pass calculations by computing the expected values at chance nodes 6 to 14 provides the following results:

$$
\begin{aligned}
\text{EV(Node 6)} &= 0.94(8) + 0.06(7) &&= 7.94 \\
\text{EV(Node 7)} &= 0.94(14) + 0.06(5) &&= 13.46 \\
\text{EV(Node 8)} &= 0.94(20) + 0.06(-9) &&= 18.26 \\
\text{EV(Node 9)} &= 0.35(8) + 0.65(7) &&= 7.35 \\
\text{EV(Node 10)} &= 0.35(14) + 0.65(5) &&= 8.15 \\
\text{EV(Node 11)} &= 0.35(20) + 0.65(-9) &&= 1.15 \\
\text{EV(Node 12)} &= 0.80(8) + 0.20(7) &&= 7.80 \\
\text{EV(Node 13)} &= 0.80(14) + 0.20(5) &&= 12.20 \\
\text{EV(Node 14)} &= 0.80(20) + 0.20(-9) &&= 14.20 \\
\end{aligned}
$$

FIGURE 4.9   THE PDC DECISION TREE WITH BRANCH PROBABILITIES

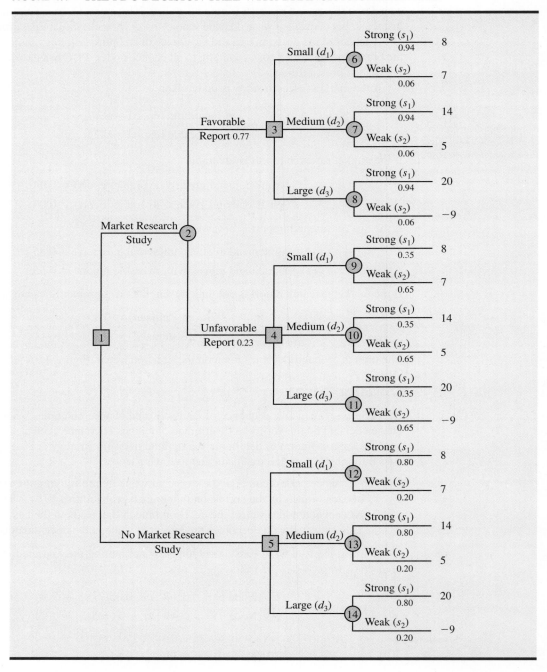

FIGURE 4.10 PDC DECISION TREE AFTER COMPUTING EXPECTED VALUES AT
CHANCE NODES 6 TO 14

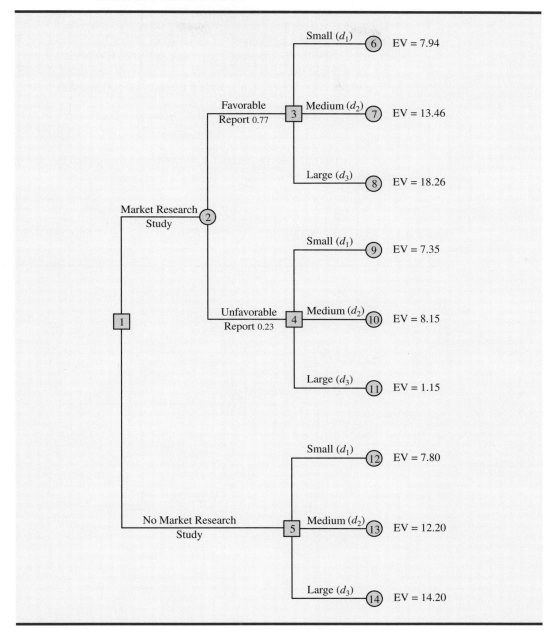

Figure 4.10 shows the reduced decision tree after computing expected values at these chance nodes.

Next, move to decision nodes 3, 4, and 5. For each of these nodes, we select the decision alternative branch that leads to the best expected value. For example, at node 3 we have the choice of the small complex branch with EV(Node 6) = 7.94, the medium complex branch with EV(Node 7) = 13.46, and the large complex branch with EV(Node 8) = 18.26. Thus, we select the large complex decision alternative branch and the expected value at node 3 becomes EV(Node 3) = 18.26.

For node 4, we select the best expected value from nodes 9, 10, and 11. The best decision alternative is the medium complex branch that provides EV(Node 4) = 8.15. For node 5, we select the best expected value from nodes 12, 13, and 14. The best decision alternative is the large complex branch that provides EV(Node 5) = 14.20. Figure 4.11 shows the reduced decision tree after choosing the best decisions at nodes 3, 4, and 5.

The expected value at chance node 2 can now be computed as follows:

$$EV(\text{Node 2}) = 0.77EV(\text{Node 3}) + 0.23EV(\text{Node 4})$$
$$= 0.77(18.26) + 0.23(8.15) = 15.93$$

This calculation reduces the decision tree to one involving only the two decision branches from node 1 (see Figure 4.12).

FIGURE 4.11 PDC DECISION TREE AFTER CHOOSING BEST DECISIONS AT NODES 3, 4, AND 5

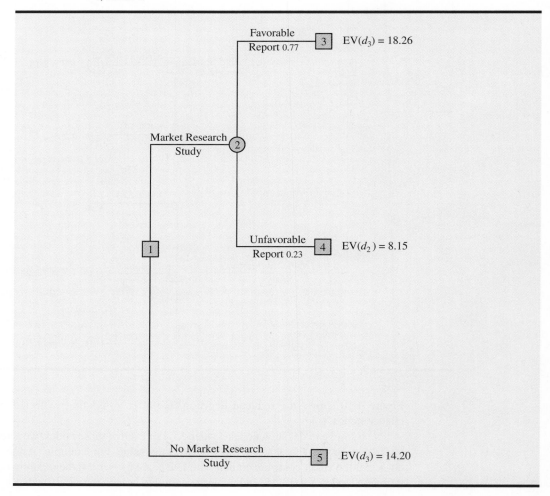

FIGURE 4.12 PDC DECISION TREE REDUCED TO TWO DECISION BRANCHES

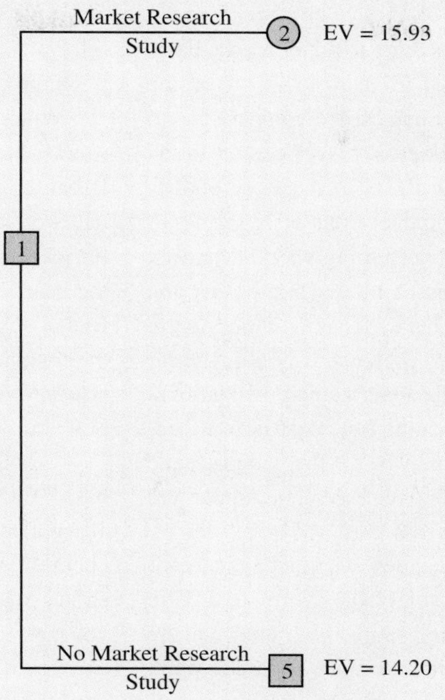

Finally, the decision can be made at decision node 1 by selecting the best expected values from nodes 2 and 5. This action leads to the decision alternative to conduct the market research study, which provides an overall expected value of 15.93.

Problem 16 will test your ability to develop an optimal decision strategy.

The optimal decision for PDC is to conduct the market research study and then carry out the following decision strategy:

If the market research is favorable, construct the large condominium complex.

If the market research is unfavorable, construct the medium condominium complex.

The analysis of the PDC decision tree describes the methods that can be used to analyze more complex sequential decision problems. First, draw a decision tree consisting of decision and chance nodes and branches that describe the sequential nature of the problem. Determine the probabilities for all chance outcomes. Then, by working backward through the tree, compute expected values at all chance nodes and select the best decision branch at all decision nodes. The sequence of optimal decision branches determines the optimal decision strategy for the problem.

The Q.M. in Action, Decision Analysis At Bat, describes the application of decision analysis to guide a batter's strategy during an at-bat in a baseball game.

Q.M. *(in)* ACTION

DECISION ANALYSIS AT BAT*

Evan Gattis took a circuitous route to major league base-ball. His path to becoming a 26-year-old rookie on the 2013 Atlanta Braves' roster has earned comparisons to Roy Hobbs, the mythical baseball player central to the novel and movie *The Natural*. As in the story of Roy Hobbs, Gattis dropped completely out of baseball for several years before returning in a big way. In his first month in the major leagues, he hit six home runs and was named the National League's Rookie of the Month. He duplicated both feats in his second month—he hit six more home runs and was again named the National League's Rookie of the Month. But what is most un-usual about Gattis is that he may be the first major league baseball player to give credit to management science and decision analysis for his success.

While in the minor leagues, Gattis began read-ing the work of University of Texas Professor J. Eric Bickel, who has used decision analysis to determine the optimal decisions for a hitter to make in each count. "One paper I wrote was how to act on different pitch counts," Bickel said. "Sometimes the batter will just let a pitch go by on purpose. If it's three balls, no strikes,

a lot of times the coach will say, 'Don't swing at the pitch, no matter what.'"

What Bickel said is that most people don't under-stand why a batter would take a pitch on a 3–0 count. Because one more ball will result in a walk and put the batter on first base, under these circumstances the oppos-ing pitcher will usually put a very hittable fastball through the heart of the strike zone on the next pitch. However, Bickel's research demonstrates why taking a pitch when the count is three balls and no strikes rather than swinging at what will likely be a very hittable pitch increases the probability the batter will ultimately get on base.

"About 38 percent of all batters eventually get on base," Bickel said. "At 3–0, 77 percent of batters eventu-ally get on base. Suppose you're sitting there with a 3–0 count. If you let the pitch go by, and the pitcher throws a strike, you're down to a 63 percent chance of getting on. If you instead put that ball in play, you only have a one-third chance of getting on base. Your choice is to put the ball in play and have a one-third chance of getting on base, or take a strike and still have a 63 percent chance of getting on base. That's why you take it."

Bickel has used decision analysis to determine a batter's optimal strategies for all ball/strike counts. His decision analysis and his lucid explanation of the result-ing optimal strategies for various ball/strike counts have helped shape the way Gattis approaches each pitch when he is at bat.

---

*Based on Joe Lemire, "This Photo Is Just One Good Reason You Need to Know the Story of Evan Gattis," Sports Illustrated (June 10, 2013) and "Mastering the Numbers Game—Sports Illustrated Coverage." Petroleum and Geosystems Engineering News, University of Texas at Austin, http://www.pge.utexas.edu/news/136-eric-bickel.

Risk Profile

Figure 4.13 provides a reduced decision tree showing only the sequence of decision al-ternatives and chance events for the PDC optimal decision strategy. By implementing the optimal decision strategy, PDC will obtain one of the four payoffs shown at the terminal branches of the decision tree. Recall that a risk profile shows the possible payoffs with their associated probabilities. Thus, in order to construct a risk profile for the optimal decision strategy, we will need to compute the probability for each of the four payoffs.

Note that each payoff results from a sequence of branches leading from node 1 to the payoff. For instance, the payoff of $20 million is obtained by following the upper branch from node 1, the upper branch from node 2, the lower branch from node 3, and the upper branch from node 8. The probability of following that sequence of branches can be found by multiplying the probabilities for the branches from the chance nodes in the sequence. Thus, the probability of the $20 million payoff is $(0.77)(0.94) = 0.72$. Similarly, the probabilities

FIGURE 4.13   PDC DECISION TREE SHOWING ONLY BRANCHES ASSOCIATED WITH OPTIMAL DECISION STRATEGY

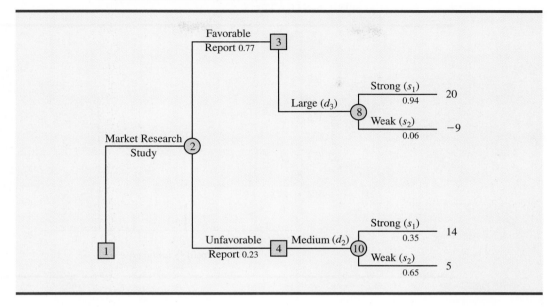

for each of the other payoffs are obtained by multiplying the probabilities for the branches from the chance nodes leading to the payoffs. By doing so, we find the probability of the $-\$9$ million payoff is $(0.77)(0.06) = 0.05$; the probability of the \$14 million payoff is (0.23) $(0.35) = 0.08$; and the probability of the \$5 million payoff is $(0.23)(0.65) = 0.15$. The following table showing the probability distribution for the payoffs for the PDC optimal decision strategy is the tabular representation of the risk profile for the optimal decision strategy.

Payoff (\$ millions)	Probability
−9	0.05
5	0.15
14	0.08
20	0.72
	1.00

Figure 4.14 provides a graphical representation of the risk profile. Comparing Figures 4.5 and 4.14, we see that the PDC risk profile is changed by the strategy to conduct the market research study. In fact, the use of the market research study lowered the probability of the \$9 million loss from 0.20 to 0.05. PDC's management would most likely view that change as a considerable reduction in the risk associated with the condominium project.

Expected Value of Sample Information

In the PDC problem, the market research study is the sample information used to determine the optimal decision strategy. The expected value associated with the market research study is \$15.93. In Section 4.3 we showed that the best expected value if the market research study

FIGURE 4.14   RISK PROFILE FOR PDC CONDOMINIUM PROJECT WITH SAMPLE
INFORMATION SHOWING PAYOFFS ASSOCIATED WITH OPTIMAL
DECISION STRATEGY

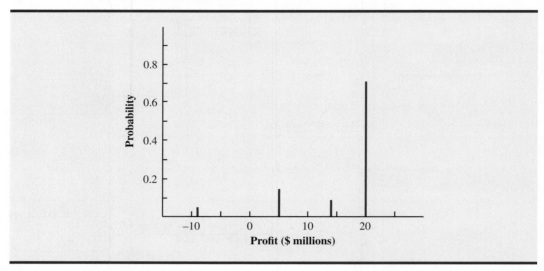

is *not* undertaken is $14.20. Thus, we can conclude that the difference, $15.93 − $14.20 = $1.73, is the **expected value of sample information (EVSI)**. In other words, conducting the market research study adds $1.73 million to the PDC expected value. In general, the expected value of sample information is as follows:

$$EVSI = |EVwSI − EVwoSI| \qquad \textbf{(4.13)}$$

where

$$EVSI = \text{expected value of sample information}$$
$$EVwSI = \text{expected value } \textit{with} \text{ sample information about the states of nature}$$
$$EVwoSI = \text{expected value } \textit{without} \text{ sample information about the states of nature}$$

The EVSI = $1.73 million suggests PDC should be willing to pay up to $1.73 million to conduct the market research study.

Note the role of the absolute value in equation (4.13). For minimization problems, the expected value with sample information is always less than or equal to the expected value without sample information. In this case, EVSI is the magnitude of the difference between EVwSI and EVwoSI; thus, by taking the absolute value of the difference as shown in equation (4.13), we can handle both the maximization and minimization cases with one equation.

Efficiency of Sample Information

In Section 4.3 we showed that the expected value of perfect information (EVPI) for the PDC problem is $3.2 million. We never anticipated that the market research report would obtain perfect information, but we can use an **efficiency** measure to express the value of the market research information. With perfect information having an efficiency rating of 100%, the efficiency rating E for sample information is computed as follows:

$$E = \frac{\text{EVSI}}{\text{EVPI}} \times 100 \qquad\qquad \textbf{(4.14)}$$

For the PDC problem,

$$E = \frac{1.73}{3.2} \times 100 = 54.1\%$$

In other words, the information from the market research study is 54.1% as efficient as perfect information.

Low efficiency ratings for sample information might lead the decision maker to look for other types of information. However, high efficiency ratings indicate that the sample information is almost as good as perfect information and that additional sources of information would not yield substantially better results.

4.6 Computing Branch Probabilities with Bayes' Theorem

In Section 4.5 the branch probabilities for the PDC decision tree chance nodes were specified in the problem description. No computations were required to determine these probabilities. In this section we show how **Bayes' theorem** can be used to compute branch probabilities for decision trees.

The PDC decision tree is shown again in Figure 4.15. Let

$$F = \text{Favorable market research report}$$
$$U = \text{Unfavorable market research report}$$
$$s_1 = \text{Strong demand (state of nature 1)}$$
$$s_2 = \text{Weak demand (state of nature 2)}$$

At chance node 2, we need to know the branch probabilities $P(F)$ and $P(U)$. At chance nodes 6, 7, and 8, we need to know the branch probabilities $P(s_1 \mid F)$, the probability of state of nature 1 given a favorable market research report, and $P(s_2 \mid F)$, the probability of state of nature 2 given a favorable market research report. $P(s_1 \mid F)$ and $P(s_2 \mid F)$ are referred to as *posterior probabilities* because they are conditional probabilities based on the outcome of the sample information. At chance nodes 9, 10, and 11, we need to know the branch probabilities $P(s_1 \mid U)$ and $P(s_2 \mid U)$; note that these are also posterior probabilities, denoting the probabilities of the two states of nature *given* that the market research report is unfavorable. Finally, at chance nodes 12, 13, and 14, we need the probabilities for the states of nature, $P(s_1)$ and $P(s_2)$, if the market research study is not undertaken.

In performing the probability computations, we need to know PDC's assessment of the probabilities for the two states of nature, $P(s_1)$ and $P(s_2)$, which are the prior probabilities as discussed earlier. In addition, we must know the **conditional probability** of the market

FIGURE 4.15 THE PDC DECISION TREE

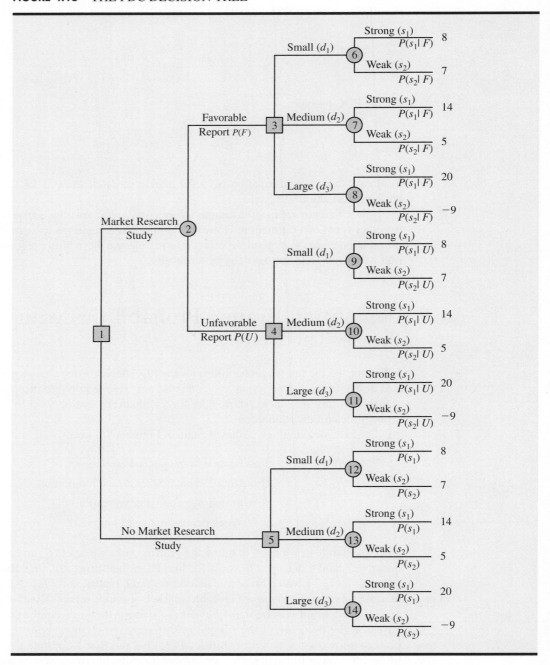

research outcomes (the sample information) *given* each state of nature. For example, we need to know the conditional probability of a favorable market research report given that the state of nature is strong demand for the PDC project; note that this conditional probability of F given state of nature s_1 is written $P(F \mid s_1)$. To carry out the probability calculations, we will need conditional probabilities for all sample outcomes given all states of nature, that is, $P(F \mid s_1)$, $P(F \mid s_2)$, $P(U \mid s_1)$, and $P(U \mid s_2)$. In the PDC problem we assume that the following assessments are available for these conditional probabilities:

	Market Research	
State of Nature	**Favorable, F**	**Unfavorable, U**
Strong demand, s_1	$P(F \mid s_1) = 0.90$	$P(U \mid s_1) = 0.10$
Weak demand, s_2	$P(F \mid s_2) = 0.25$	$P(U \mid s_2) = 0.75$

A favorable market research report given that the state of nature is weak demand is often referred to as a "false positive," while the converse (an unfavorable market research report given that the state of nature is strong demand) is referred to as a "false negative."

Note that the preceding probability assessments provide a reasonable degree of confidence in the market research study. If the true state of nature is s_1, the probability of a favorable market research report is 0.90, and the probability of an unfavorable market research report is 0.10. If the true state of nature is s_2, the probability of a favorable market research report is 0.25, and the probability of an unfavorable market research report is 0.75. The reason for a 0.25 probability of a potentially misleading favorable market research report for state of nature s_2 is that when some potential buyers first hear about the new condominium project, their enthusiasm may lead them to overstate their real interest in it. A potential buyer's initial favorable response can change quickly to a "no thank you" when later faced with the reality of signing a purchase contract and making a down payment.

In the following discussion we present a tabular approach as a convenient method for carrying out the probability computations. The computations for the PDC problem based on a favorable market research report (F) are summarized in Table 4.7. The steps used to develop this table are as follows:

Step 1. In column 1 enter the states of nature. In column 2 enter the *prior probabilities* for the states of nature. In column 3 enter the *conditional probabilities* of a favorable market research report (F) given each state of nature.

Step 2. In column 4 compute the **joint probabilities** by multiplying the prior probability values in column 2 by the corresponding conditional probability values in column 3.

Step 3. Sum the joint probabilities in column 4 to obtain the probability of a favorable market research report, $P(F)$.

Step 4. Divide each joint probability in column 4 by $P(F) = 0.77$ to obtain the revised or *posterior probabilities*, $P(s_1 \mid F)$ and $P(s_2 \mid F)$.

Table 4.7 shows that the probability of obtaining a favorable market research report is $P(F) = 0.77$. In addition, $P(s_1 \mid F) = 0.94$ and $P(s_2 \mid F) = 0.06$. In particular, note that a

TABLE 4.7 BRANCH PROBABILITIES FOR THE PDC CONDOMINIUM PROJECT BASED ON A FAVORABLE MARKET RESEARCH REPORT

States of Nature s_j	Prior Probabilities $P(s_j)$	Conditional Probabilities $P(F \mid s_j)$	Joint Probabilities $P(F \cap s_j)$	Posterior Probabilities $P(s_j \mid F)$
s_1	0.8	0.90	0.72	0.94
s_2	0.2	0.25	0.05	0.06
	1.0		$P(F) = 0.77$	1.00

TABLE 4.8   BRANCH PROBABILITIES FOR THE PDC CONDOMINIUM PROJECT BASED ON AN UNFAVORABLE MARKET RESEARCH REPORT

States of Nature s_j	Prior Probabilities $P(s_j)$	Conditional Probabilities $P(U \mid s_j)$	Joint Probabilities $P(U \cap s_j)$	Posterior Probabilities $P(s_j \mid U)$
s_1	0.8	0.10	0.08	0.35
s_2	0.2	0.75	0.15	0.65
	1.0		$P(U) = 0.23$	1.00

favorable market research report will prompt a revised or posterior probability of 0.94 that the market demand of the condominium will be strong, s_1.

The tabular probability computation procedure must be repeated for each possible sample information outcome. Table 4.8 shows the computations of the branch probabilities of the PDC problem based on an unfavorable market research report. Note that the probability of obtaining an unfavorable market research report is $P(U) = 0.23$. If an unfavorable report is obtained, the posterior probability of a strong market demand, s_1, is 0.35 and of a weak market demand, s_2, is 0.65. The branch probabilities from Tables 4.7 and 4.8 were shown on the PDC decision tree in Figure 4.9.

Problem 23 asks you to compute the posterior probabilities.

The tabular method can be used directly to compute the branch probabilities in the decision tree. Alternatively, equation (4.15) provides a general formula for Bayes' theorem for computing posterior probabilities.

BAYES' THEOREM

$$P(A_i \mid B) = \frac{P(B \mid A_i) \, P(A_i)}{\Sigma_j \, P(B \mid A_j) \, P(A_j)} \qquad \textbf{(4.15)}$$

To perform the Bayes' theorem calculations for $P(s_1 \mid U)$ with equation (4.15), we replace B with U (unfavorable report) and A_i with s_1 in (4.15) so that we have

$$P(s_1 \mid U) = \frac{P(U \mid s_1) \, P(s_1)}{\Sigma_j \, P(U \mid s_j) \, P(s_j)}$$

$$= \frac{0.10 \times 0.80}{(0.10 \times 0.80) + (0.20 \times 0.75)} = 0.35$$

which provides the same value as the tabular approach used to generate the values in Table 4.7.

The discussion in this section shows an underlying relationship between the probabilities on the various branches in a decision tree. It would be inappropriate to assume different prior probabilities, $P(s_1)$ and $P(s_2)$ without determining how these changes would alter $P(F)$ and $P(U)$, as well as the posterior probabilities $P(s_1 \mid F)$, $P(s_2 \mid F)$, $P(s_1 \mid U)$, and $P(s_2 \mid U)$.

The Q.M. in Action, Decision Analysis Helps Treat and Prevent Hepatitis B, discusses how medical researchers use posterior probability information and decision analysis to understand the risks and costs associated with treatment and screening procedures.

Q.M. *in* ACTION

DECISION ANALYSIS HELPS TREAT AND PREVENT HEPATITIS B*

Hepatitis B is a viral disease that left untreated can lead to fatal liver conditions such as cirrhosis and cancer. The hepatitis B virus can be treated, and there exists a vaccine to prevent it. However, in order to make economically prudent allocations of their limited health care budgets, public health officials require analysis on the cost effectiveness (health benefit per dollar investment) of any potential health program. Unfortunately, since hepatitis B is a slow-progressing condition whose victims are often unaware of their potentially fatal infection, gathering data on the benefits of any public health policy addressing hepatitis B would take decades.

A multidisciplinary team consisting of management science researchers and a liver transplant surgeon from Stanford University applied decision analysis techniques to determine which combination of hepatitis B screening, treatment, and vaccination would be appropriate in the United States. Their decision tree contained the

sequential decisions of: (1) whether or not to perform a blood test to screen an individual for a hepatitis B infection, (2) whether or not to treat infected individuals, and (3) whether or not to vaccinate a noninfected (or nonscreened) individual.

For each policy, composed of a sequence of screening, treatment, and vaccination decisions, the researchers utilized existing infection and treatment knowledge to model future disease progression. Implementing their decision model in an Excel spreadsheet, the researchers concluded that it is cost effective to screen adult Asian and Pacific Islanders so that infected individuals can be treated (these individuals are genetically at a high risk for hepatitis B infection). Although it is not cost effective to universally vaccinate all U.S. adult Asian and Pacific Islanders, it proves to be cost effective to vaccinate people in close contact with infected individuals. Influenced by these findings, the Centers for Disease Control updated its official policy in 2008 to recommend screening all adult Asian and Pacific Islanders and all adults in areas of intermediate (2 to 7%) hepatitis B prevalence.

---

*David W. Hutton, Margaret L. Brandeau, and Samuel K. So, "Doing Good with Good OR: Supporting Cost-Effective Hepatitis B Interventions." *Interfaces* 41 (May/June 2011): 289–300.

Summary

Decision analysis can be used to determine a recommended decision alternative or an optimal decision strategy when a decision maker is faced with an uncertain and risk-filled pattern of future events. The goal of decision analysis is to identify the best decision alternative or the optimal decision strategy given information about the uncertain events and the possible consequences or payoffs. The uncertain future events are called chance events, and the outcomes of the chance events are called states of nature.

We showed how influence diagrams, payoff tables, and decision trees could be used to structure a decision problem and describe the relationships among the decisions, the chance events, and the consequences. We presented three approaches to decision making without probabilities: the optimistic approach, the conservative approach, and the minimax regret approach. When probability assessments are provided for the states of nature, the expected value approach can be used to identify the recommended decision alternative or decision strategy.

In cases where sample information about the chance events is available, a sequence of decisions has to be made. First we must decide whether to obtain the sample information. If the answer to this decision is yes, an optimal decision strategy based on the specific sample information must be developed. In this situation, decision trees and the expected value approach can be used to determine the optimal decision strategy.

Even though the expected value approach can be used to obtain a recommended decision alternative or optimal decision strategy, the payoff that actually occurs will usually have a value different from the expected value. A risk profile provides a probability distribution for the possible payoffs and can assist the decision maker in assessing the risks associated with different decision alternatives. Finally, sensitivity analysis can be conducted to determine the effect changes in the probabilities for the states of nature and changes in the values of the payoffs have on the recommended decision alternative.

Glossary

Bayes' theorem A theorem that enables the use of sample information to revise prior probabilities.

Branch Lines showing the alternatives from decision nodes and the outcomes from chance nodes.

Chance event An uncertain future event affecting the consequence, or payoff, associated with a decision.

Chance nodes Nodes indicating points where an uncertain event will occur.

Conditional probabilities The probability of one event given the known outcome of a (possibly) related event.

Consequence The result obtained when a decision alternative is chosen and a chance event occurs. A measure of the consequence is often called a payoff.

Consequence nodes Nodes of an influence diagram indicating points where a payoff will occur.

Conservative approach An approach to choosing a decision alternative without using probabilities. For a maximization problem, it leads to choosing the decision alternative that maximizes the minimum payoff; for a minimization problem, it leads to choosing the decision alternative that minimizes the maximum payoff.

Decision alternatives Options available to the decision maker.

Decision nodes Nodes indicating points where a decision is made.

Decision strategy A strategy involving a sequence of decisions and chance outcomes to provide the optimal solution to a decision problem.

Decision tree A graphical representation of the decision problem that shows the sequential nature of the decision-making process.

Efficiency The ratio of EVSI to EVPI as a percentage; perfect information is 100% efficient.

Expected value (EV) For a chance node, it is the weighted average of the payoffs. The weights are the state-of-nature probabilities.

Expected value approach An approach to choosing a decision alternative based on the expected value of each decision alternative. The recommended decision alternative is the one that provides the best expected value.

Expected value of perfect information (EVPI) The expected value of information that would tell the decision maker exactly which state of nature is going to occur (i.e., perfect information).

Expected value of sample information (EVSI) The difference between the expected value of an optimal strategy based on sample information and the "best" expected value without any sample information.

Influence diagram A graphical device that shows the relationship among decisions, chance events, and consequences for a decision problem.

Joint probabilities The probabilities of both sample information and a particular state of nature occurring simultaneously.

Minimax regret approach An approach to choosing a decision alternative without using probabilities. For each alternative, the maximum regret is computed, which leads to choosing the decision alternative that minimizes the maximum regret.

Node An intersection or junction point of an influence diagram or a decision tree.

Opportunity loss, or regret The amount of loss (lower profit or higher cost) from not making the best decision for each state of nature.

Optimistic approach An approach to choosing a decision alternative without using probabilities. For a maximization problem, it leads to choosing the decision alternative corresponding to the largest payoff; for a minimization problem, it leads to choosing the decision alternative corresponding to the smallest payoff.

Payoff A measure of the consequence of a decision such as profit, cost, or time. Each combination of a decision alternative and a state of nature has an associated payoff (consequence).

Payoff table A tabular representation of the payoffs for a decision problem.

Posterior (revised) probabilities The probabilities of the states of nature after revising the prior probabilities based on sample information.

Prior probabilities The probabilities of the states of nature prior to obtaining sample information.

Risk analysis The study of the possible payoffs and probabilities associated with a decision alternative or a decision strategy.

Risk profile The probability distribution of the possible payoffs associated with a decision alternative or decision strategy.

Sample information New information obtained through research or experimentation that enables an updating or revision of the state-of-nature probabilities.

Sensitivity analysis The study of how changes in the probability assessments for the states of nature or changes in the payoffs affect the recommended decision alternative.

States of nature The possible outcomes for chance events that affect the payoff associated with a decision alternative.

Problems

1. The following payoff table shows profit for a decision analysis problem with two decision alternatives and three states of nature:

	State of Nature		
Decision Alternative	s_1	s_2	s_3
d_1	250	100	25
d_2	100	100	75

a. Construct a decision tree for this problem.
b. If the decision maker knows nothing about the probabilities of the three states of nature, what is the recommended decision using the optimistic, conservative, and minimax regret approaches?

2. Suppose that a decision maker faced with four decision alternatives and four states of nature develops the following profit payoff table:

| | State of Nature | | | |
Decision Alternative	s_1	s_2	s_3	s_4
d_1	14	9	10	5
d_2	11	10	8	7
d_3	9	10	10	11
d_4	8	10	11	13

a. If the decision maker knows nothing about the probabilities of the four states of nature, what is the recommended decision using the optimistic, conservative, and minimax regret approaches?
b. Which approach do you prefer? Explain. Is establishing the most appropriate approach before analyzing the problem important for the decision maker? Explain.
c. Assume that the payoff table provides *cost* rather than profit payoffs. What is the recommended decision using the optimistic, conservative, and minimax regret approaches?

3. Southland Corporation's decision to produce a new line of recreational products resulted in the need to construct either a small plant or a large plant. The best selection of plant size depends on how the marketplace reacts to the new product line. To conduct an analysis, marketing management has decided to view the possible long-run demand as low, medium, or high. The following payoff table shows the projected profit in millions of dollars:

| | Long-Run Demand | | |
Plant Size	Low	Medium	High
Small	150	200	200
Large	50	200	500

a. What is the decision to be made, and what is the chance event for Southland's problem?
b. Construct an influence diagram.
c. Construct a decision tree.
d. Recommend a decision based on the use of the optimistic, conservative, and minimax regret approaches.

4. Amy Lloyd is interested in leasing a new Honda and has contacted three automobile dealers for pricing information. Each dealer offered Amy a closed-end 36-month lease with no down payment due at the time of signing. Each lease includes a monthly charge and a mileage allowance. Additional miles receive a surcharge on a per-mile basis. The monthly lease cost, the mileage allowance, and the cost for additional miles follow:

Dealer	Monthly Cost	Mileage Allowance	Cost per Additional Mile
Hepburn Honda	$299	36,000	$0.15
Midtown Motors	$310	45,000	$0.20
Hopkins Automotive	$325	54,000	$0.15

Amy decided to choose the lease option that will minimize her total 36-month cost. The difficulty is that Amy is not sure how many miles she will drive over the next three years. For purposes of this decision, she believes it is reasonable to assume that she will drive 12,000 miles per year, 15,000 miles per year, or 18,000 miles per year. With this assumption Amy estimated her total costs for the three lease options. For example, she figures that the Hepburn Honda lease will cost her $10,764 if she drives 12,000 miles per year, $12,114 if she drives 15,000 miles per year, or $13,464 if she drives 18,000 miles per year.

a. What is the decision, and what is the chance event?

b. Construct a payoff table for Amy's problem.

c. If Amy has no idea which of the three mileage assumptions is most appropriate, what is the recommended decision (leasing option) using the optimistic, conservative, and minimax regret approaches?

d. Suppose that the probabilities that Amy drives 12,000, 15,000, and 18,000 miles per year are 0.5, 0.4, and 0.1, respectively. What option should Amy choose using the expected value approach?

e. Develop a risk profile for the decision selected in part (d). What is the most likely cost, and what is its probability?

f. Suppose that after further consideration Amy concludes that the probabilities that she will drive 12,000, 15,000, and 18,000 miles per year are 0.3, 0.4, and 0.3, respectively. What decision should Amy make using the expected value approach?

5. In American football, touchdowns are worth 6 points. After scoring a touchdown, the scoring team may subsequently attempt to score 1 or 2 additional points. Going for 1 point is virtually an assured success, while going for 2 points is successful only with probability p. Consider the following game situation. The Temple Wildcats are losing by 14 points to the Killeen Tigers near the end of regulation time. The only way for Temple to win (or tie) this game is to score two touchdowns while not allowing Killeen to score again. The Temple coach must decide whether to attempt a 1-point or 2-point conversion after each touchdown. If the score is tied at the end of regulation time, the game goes into overtime. The Temple coach believes that there is a 50% chance that Temple will win if the game goes into overtime. The probability of successfully converting a 1-point conversion is 1.0. The probability of successfully converting a 2-point conversion is p.

a. Assume Temple will score two touchdowns and Killeen will not score. Create a decision tree for the decision of whether Temple's coach should go for a 1-point conversion or a 2-point conversion after each touchdown. The terminal nodes in the decision tree should be either WIN or LOSE for Temple.

b. Assume that a WIN results in a value of 1.0 and LOSE results in a value of 0. Further, assume that the probability of converting a 2-point conversion is $p = 0.4$. Should Temple's coach go for a 1-point conversion or 2-point conversion after scoring the first touchdown?

6. Investment advisors estimated the stock market returns for four market segments: computers, financial, manufacturing, and pharmaceuticals. Annual return projections vary depending on whether the general economic conditions are improving, stable, or declining. The anticipated annual return percentages for each market segment under each economic condition are as follows:

	Economic Condition		
Market Segment	**Improving**	**Stable**	**Declining**
Computers	10	2	−4
Financial	8	5	−3
Manufacturing	6	4	−2
Pharmaceuticals	6	5	−1

a.   Assume that an individual investor wants to select one market segment for a new investment. A forecast shows stable to declining economic conditions with the following probabilities: improving (0.2), stable (0.5), and declining (0.3). What is the preferred market segment for the investor, and what is the expected return percentage?

b.   At a later date, a revised forecast shows a potential for an improvement in economic conditions. New probabilities are as follows: improving (0.4), stable (0.4), and declining (0.2). What is the preferred market segment for the investor based on these new probabilities? What is the expected return percentage?

7.   Hudson Corporation is considering three options for managing its data processing operation: continuing with its own staff, hiring an outside vendor to do the managing (referred to as *outsourcing*), or using a combination of its own staff and an outside vendor. The cost of the operation depends on future demand. The annual cost of each option (in thousands of dollars) depends on demand as follows:

	Demand		
Staffing Options	**High**	**Medium**	**Low**
Own staff	650	650	600
Outside vendor	900	600	300
Combination	800	650	500

a.   If the demand probabilities are 0.2, 0.5, and 0.3, which decision alternative will minimize the expected cost of the data processing operation? What is the expected annual cost associated with that recommendation?

b.   Construct a risk profile for the optimal decision in part (a). What is the probability of the cost exceeding $700,000?

8.   The following payoff table shows the profit for a decision problem with two states of nature and two decision alternatives:

	State of Nature	
Decision Alternative	s_1	s_2
d_1	10	1
d_2	4	3

a.   Use graphical sensitivity analysis to determine the range of probabilities of state of nature s_1 for which each of the decision alternatives has the largest expected value.

b.   Suppose $P(s_1) = 0.2$ and $P(s_2) = 0.8$. What is the best decision using the expected value approach?

c.   Perform sensitivity analysis on the payoffs for decision alternative d_1. Assume the probabilities are as given in part (b), and find the range of payoffs under states of nature s_1 and s_2 that will keep the solution found in part (b) optimal. Is the solution more sensitive to the payoff under state of nature s_1 or s_2?

9.   Myrtle Air Express decided to offer direct service from Cleveland to Myrtle Beach. Management must decide between a full-price service using the company's new fleet of jet aircraft and a discount service using smaller capacity commuter planes. It is clear that the best choice depends on the market reaction to the service Myrtle Air offers. Management developed estimates of the contribution to profit for each type of service based upon

two possible levels of demand for service to Myrtle Beach: strong and weak. The following table shows the estimated quarterly profits (in thousands of dollars):

	Demand for Service	
Service	Strong	Weak
Full price	$960	−$490
Discount	$670	$320

a. What is the decision to be made, what is the chance event, and what is the consequence for this problem? How many decision alternatives are there? How many outcomes are there for the chance event?
b. If nothing is known about the probabilities of the chance outcomes, what is the recommended decision using the optimistic, conservative, and minimax regret approaches?
c. Suppose that management of Myrtle Air Express believes that the probability of strong demand is 0.7 and the probability of weak demand is 0.3. Use the expected value approach to determine an optimal decision.
d. Suppose that the probability of strong demand is 0.8 and the probability of weak demand is 0.2. What is the optimal decision using the expected value approach?
e. Use graphical sensitivity analysis to determine the range of demand probabilities for which each of the decision alternatives has the largest expected value.

10. Video Tech is considering marketing one of two new video games for the coming holiday season: Battle Pacific or Space Pirates. Battle Pacific is a unique game and appears to have no competition. Estimated profits (in thousands of dollars) under high, medium, and low demand are as follows:

	Demand		
Battle Pacific	High	Medium	Low
Profit	$1000	$700	$300
Probability	0.2	0.5	0.3

Video Tech is optimistic about its Space Pirates game. However, the concern is that profitability will be affected by a competitor's introduction of a video game viewed as similar to Space Pirates. Estimated profits (in thousands of dollars) with and without competition are as follows:

Space Pirates with Competition	Demand		
	High	Medium	Low
Profit	$800	$400	$200
Probability	0.3	0.4	0.3

Space Pirates without Competition	Demand		
	High	Medium	Low
Profit	$1600	$800	$400
Probability	0.5	0.3	0.2

   a.   Develop a decision tree for the Video Tech problem.

   b.   For planning purposes, Video Tech believes there is a 0.6 probability that its competitor will produce a new game similar to Space Pirates. Given this probability of competition, the director of planning recommends marketing the Battle Pacific video game. Using expected value, what is your recommended decision?

   c.   Show a risk profile for your recommended decision.

   d.   Use sensitivity analysis to determine what the probability of competition for Space Pirates would have to be for you to change your recommended decision alternative.

11. For the Pittsburgh Development Corporation problem in Section 4.3, the decision alternative to build the large condominium complex was found to be optimal using the expected value approach. In Section 4.4 we conducted a sensitivity analysis for the payoffs associated with this decision alternative. We found that the large complex remained optimal as long as the payoff for the strong demand was greater than or equal to $17.5 million and as long as the payoff for the weak demand was greater than or equal to $-$19$ million.

   a.   Consider the medium complex decision. How much could the payoff under strong demand increase and still keep decision alternative d_3 the optimal solution?

   b.   Consider the small complex decision. How much could the payoff under strong demand increase and still keep decision alternative d_3 the optimal solution?

12. The distance from Potsdam to larger markets and limited air service have hindered the town in attracting new industry. Air Express, a major overnight delivery service, is considering establishing a regional distribution center in Potsdam. However, Air Express will not establish the center unless the length of the runway at the local airport is increased. Another candidate for new development is Diagnostic Research, Inc. (DRI), a leading producer of medical testing equipment. DRI is considering building a new manufacturing plant. Increasing the length of the runway is not a requirement for DRI, but the planning commission feels that doing so will help convince DRI to locate its new plant in Potsdam. Assuming that the town lengthens the runway, the Potsdam planning commission believes that the probabilities shown in the following table are applicable.

	DRI Plant	No DRI Plant
Air Express Center	0.30	0.10
No Air Express Center	0.40	0.20

For instance, the probability that Air Express will establish a distribution center and DRI will build a plant is 0.30.

    The estimated annual revenue to the town, after deducting the cost of lengthening the runway, is as follows:

	DRI Plant	No DRI Plant
Air Express Center	$600,000	$150,000
No Air Express Center	$250,000	-$200,000

If the runway expansion project is not conducted, the planning commission assesses the probability that DRI will locate its new plant in Potsdam at 0.6; in this case, the estimated annual revenue to the town will be $450,000. If the runway expansion project is not conducted and DRI does not locate in Potsdam, the annual revenue will be $0 because no cost will have been incurred and no revenues will be forthcoming.

a. What is the decision to be made, what is the chance event, and what is the consequence?

b. Compute the expected annual revenue associated with the decision alternative to lengthen the runway.

c. Compute the expected annual revenue associated with the decision alternative not to lengthen the runway.

d. Should the town elect to lengthen the runway? Explain.

e. Suppose that the probabilities associated with lengthening the runway were as follows:

	DRI Plant	**No DRI Plant**
Air Express Center	0.40	0.10
No Air Express Center	0.30	0.20

What effect, if any, would this change in the probabilities have on the recommended decision?

13. Seneca Hill Winery recently purchased land for the purpose of establishing a new vineyard. Management is considering two varieties of white grapes for the new vineyard: Chardonnay and Riesling. The Chardonnay grapes would be used to produce a dry Chardonnay wine, and the Riesling grapes would be used to produce a semidry Riesling wine. It takes approximately four years from the time of planting before new grapes can be harvested. This length of time creates a great deal of uncertainty concerning future demand and makes the decision about the type of grapes to plant difficult. Three possibilities are being considered: Chardonnay grapes only; Riesling grapes only; and both Chardonnay and Riesling grapes. Seneca management decided that for planning purposes it would be adequate to consider only two demand possibilities for each type of wine: strong or weak. With two possibilities for each type of wine, it was necessary to assess four probabilities. With the help of some forecasts in industry publications, management made the following probability assessments:

	Riesling Demand	
Chardonnay Demand	**Weak**	**Strong**
Weak	0.05	0.50
Strong	0.25	0.20

Revenue projections show an annual contribution to profit of $20,000 if Seneca Hill only plants Chardonnay grapes and demand is weak for Chardonnay wine, and $70,000 if Seneca only plants Chardonnay grapes and demand is strong for Chardonnay wine. If Seneca only plants Riesling grapes, the annual profit projection is $25,000 if demand is weak for Riesling grapes and $45,000 if demand is strong for Riesling grapes. If Seneca plants both types of grapes, the annual profit projections are shown in the following table:

	Riesling Demand	
Chardonnay Demand	**Weak**	**Strong**
Weak	$22,000	$40,000
Strong	$26,000	$60,000

a.   What is the decision to be made, what is the chance event, and what is the consequence? Identify the alternatives for the decisions and the possible outcomes for the chance events.
b.   Develop a decision tree.
c.   Use the expected value approach to recommend which alternative Seneca Hill Winery should follow in order to maximize expected annual profit.
d.   Suppose management is concerned about the probability assessments when demand for Chardonnay wine is strong. Some believe it is likely for Riesling demand to also be strong in this case. Suppose the probability of strong demand for Chardonnay and weak demand for Riesling is 0.05 and that the probability of strong demand for Chardonnay and strong demand for Riesling is 0.40. How does this change the recommended decision? Assume that the probabilities when Chardonnay demand is weak are still 0.05 and 0.50.
e.   Other members of the management team expect the Chardonnay market to become saturated at some point in the future, causing a fall in prices. Suppose that the annual profit projections fall to $50,000 when demand for Chardonnay is strong and Chardonnay grapes only are planted. Using the original probability assessments, determine how this change would affect the optimal decision.

14.   The following profit payoff table was presented in Problem 1:

	State of Nature		
Decision Alternative	s_1	s_2	s_3
d_1	250	100	25
d_2	100	100	75

The probabilities for the states of nature are $P(s_1) = 0.65$, $P(s_2) = 0.15$, and $P(s_3) = 0.20$.
a.   What is the optimal decision strategy if perfect information were available?
b.   What is the expected value for the decision strategy developed in part (a)?
c.   Using the expected value approach, what is the recommended decision without perfect information? What is its expected value?
d.   What is the expected value of perfect information?

15.   The Lake Placid Town Council decided to build a new community center to be used for conventions, concerts, and other public events, but considerable controversy surrounds the appropriate size. Many influential citizens want a large center that would be a showcase for the area. But the mayor feels that if demand does not support such a center, the community will lose a large amount of money. To provide structure for the decision process, the council narrowed the building alternatives to three sizes: small, medium, and large. Everybody agreed that the critical factor in choosing the best size is the number of people who will want to use the new facility. A regional planning consultant provided demand estimates under three scenarios: worst case, base case, and best case. The worst-case scenario corresponds to a situation in which tourism drops substantially; the base-case scenario corresponds to a situation in which Lake Placid continues to attract visitors at current levels; and the best-case scenario corresponds to a substantial increase in tourism. The consultant has provided probability assessments of 0.10, 0.60, and 0.30 for the worst-case, base-case, and best-case scenarios, respectively.

The town council suggested using net cash flow over a 5-year planning horizon as the criterion for deciding on the best size. The following projections of net cash flow (in thousands of dollars) for a 5-year planning horizon have been developed. All costs, including the consultant's fee, have been included.

	Demand Scenario		
Center Size	Worst Case	Base Case	Best Case
Small	400	500	660
Medium	−250	650	800
Large	−400	580	990

a. What decision should Lake Placid make using the expected value approach?

b. Construct risk profiles for the medium and large alternatives. Given the mayor's concern over the possibility of losing money and the result of part (a), which alternative would you recommend?

c. Compute the expected value of perfect information. Do you think it would be worth trying to obtain additional information concerning which scenario is likely to occur?

d. Suppose the probability of the worst-case scenario increases to 0.2, the probability of the base-case scenario decreases to 0.5, and the probability of the best-case scenario remains at 0.3. What effect, if any, would these changes have on the decision recommendation?

e. The consultant has suggested that an expenditure of $150,000 on a promotional campaign over the planning horizon will effectively reduce the probability of the worst-case scenario to zero. If the campaign can be expected to also increase the probability of the best-case scenario to 0.4, is it a good investment?

16. Consider a variation of the PDC decision tree shown in Figure 4.9. The company must first decide whether to undertake the market research study. If the market research study is conducted, the outcome will either be favorable (F) or unfavorable (U). Assume there are only two decision alternatives, d_1 and d_2, and two states of nature, s_1 and s_2. The payoff table showing profit is as follows:

	State of Nature	
Decision Alternative	s_1	s_2
d_1	100	300
d_2	400	200

a. Show the decision tree.

b. Using the following probabilities, what is the optimal decision strategy?

$P(F) = 0.56$ $P(s_1 \mid F) = 0.57$ $P(s_1 \mid U) = 0.18$ $P(s_1) = 0.40$

$P(U) = 0.44$ $P(s_2 \mid F) = 0.43$ $P(s_2 \mid U) = 0.82$ $P(s_2) = 0.60$

17. Hemmingway, Inc., is considering a $5 million research and development (R&D) project. Profit projections appear promising, but Hemmingway's president is concerned because the probability that the R&D project will be successful is only 0.50. Furthermore, the president knows that even if the project is successful, it will require that the company build a new production facility at a cost of $20 million in order to manufacture the product. If the facility is built, uncertainty remains about the demand and thus uncertainty about the profit that will be realized. Another option is that if the R&D project is successful, the company could sell the rights to the product for an estimated $25 million. Under this option, the company would not build the $20 million production facility.

The decision tree is shown in Figure 4.16. The profit projection for each outcome is shown at the end of the branches. For example, the revenue projection for the high demand outcome is $59 million. However, the cost of the R&D project ($5 million) and the cost

FIGURE 4.16   DECISION TREE FOR HEMMINGWAY, INC.

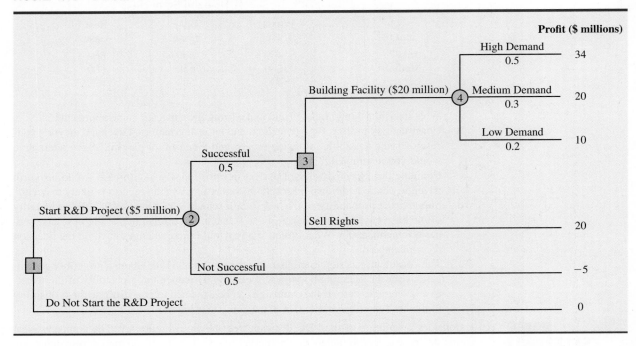

of the production facility ($20 million) show the profit of this outcome to be $59 − $5 − $20 = $34 million. Branch probabilities are also shown for the chance events.

a.   Analyze the decision tree to determine whether the company should undertake the R&D project. If it does, and if the R&D project is successful, what should the company do? What is the expected value of your strategy?

b.   What must the selling price be for the company to consider selling the rights to the product?

c.   Develop a risk profile for the optimal strategy.

18.   Dante Development Corporation is considering bidding on a contract for a new office building complex. Figure 4.17 shows the decision tree prepared by one of Dante's analysts. At node 1, the company must decide whether to bid on the contract. The cost of preparing the bid is $200,000. The upper branch from node 2 shows that the company has a 0.8 probability of winning the contract if it submits a bid. If the company wins the bid, it will have to pay $2,000,000 to become a partner in the project. Node 3 shows that the company will then consider doing a market research study to forecast demand for the office units prior to beginning construction. The cost of this study is $150,000. Node 4 is a chance node showing the possible outcomes of the market research study.

Nodes 5, 6, and 7 are similar in that they are the decision nodes for Dante to either build the office complex or sell the rights in the project to another developer. The decision to build the complex will result in an income of $5,000,000 if demand is high and $3,000,000 if demand is moderate. If Dante chooses to sell its rights in the project to another developer, income from the sale is estimated to be $3,500,000. The probabilities shown at nodes 4, 8, and 9 are based on the projected outcomes of the market research study.

a.   Verify Dante's profit projections shown at the ending branches of the decision tree by calculating the payoffs of $2,650,000 and $650,000 for first two outcomes.

b.   What is the optimal decision strategy for Dante, and what is the expected profit for this project?

FIGURE 4.17 DECISION TREE FOR THE DANTE DEVELOPMENT CORPORATION

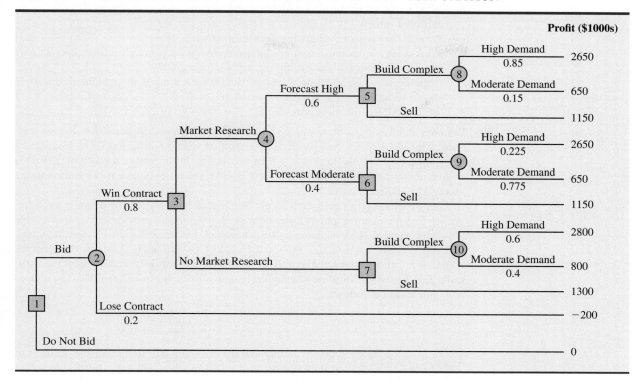

c. What would the cost of the market research study have to be before Dante would change its decision about the market research study?

d. Develop a risk profile for Dante.

19. Hale's TV Productions is considering producing a pilot for a comedy series in the hope of selling it to a major television network. The network may decide to reject the series, but it may also decide to purchase the rights to the series for either one or two years. At this point in time, Hale may either produce the pilot and wait for the network's decision or transfer the rights for the pilot and series to a competitor for $100,000. Hale's decision alternatives and profits (in thousands of dollars) are as follows:

Decision Alternative	State of Nature		
	Reject, s_1	1 Year, s_2	2 Years, s_3
Produce pilot, d_1	−100	50	150
Sell to competitor, d_2	100	100	100

The probabilities for the states of nature are $P(s_1) = 0.20$, $P(s_2) = 0.30$, and $P(s_3) = 0.50$. For a consulting fee of $5000, an agency will review the plans for the comedy series and indicate the overall chances of a favorable network reaction to the series. Assume that the agency review will result in a favorable (F) or an unfavorable (U) review and that the following probabilities are relevant:

$$P(F) = 0.69 \qquad P(s_1 \mid F) = 0.09 \qquad P(s_1 \mid U) = 0.45$$
$$P(U) = 0.31 \qquad P(s_2 \mid F) = 0.26 \qquad P(s_2 \mid U) = 0.39$$
$$P(s_3 \mid F) = 0.65 \qquad P(s_3 \mid U) = 0.16$$

a. Construct a decision tree for this problem.
b. What is the recommended decision if the agency opinion is not used? What is the expected value?
c. What is the expected value of perfect information?
d. What is Hale's optimal decision strategy assuming the agency's information is used?
e. What is the expected value of the agency's information?
f. Is the agency's information worth the $5000 fee? What is the maximum that Hale should be willing to pay for the information?
g. What is the recommended decision?

20. Embassy Publishing Company received a six-chapter manuscript for a new college textbook. The editor of the college division is familiar with the manuscript and estimated a 0.65 probability that the textbook will be successful. If successful, a profit of $750,000 will be realized. If the company decides to publish the textbook and it is unsuccessful, a loss of $250,000 will occur.

Before making the decision to accept or reject the manuscript, the editor is considering sending the manuscript out for review. A review process provides either a favorable (F) or unfavorable (U) evaluation of the manuscript. Past experience with the review process suggests that probabilities $P(F) = 0.7$ and $P(U) = 0.3$ apply. Let s_1 = the textbook is successful, and s_2 = the textbook is unsuccessful. The editor's initial probabilities of s_1 and s_2 will be revised based on whether the review is favorable or unfavorable. The revised probabilities are as follows:

$$P(s_1 \mid F) = 0.75 \qquad P(s_1 \mid U) = 0.417$$
$$P(s_2 \mid F) = 0.25 \qquad P(s_2 \mid U) = 0.583$$

a. Construct a decision tree assuming that the company will first make the decision of whether to send the manuscript out for review and then make the decision to accept or reject the manuscript.
b. Analyze the decision tree to determine the optimal decision strategy for the publishing company.
c. If the manuscript review costs $5000, what is your recommendation?
d. What is the expected value of perfect information? What does this EVPI suggest for the company?

21. A real estate investor has the opportunity to purchase land currently zoned residential. If the county board approves a request to rezone the property as commercial within the next year, the investor will be able to lease the land to a large discount firm that wants to open a new store on the property. However, if the zoning change is not approved, the investor will have to sell the property at a loss. Profits (in thousands of dollars) are shown in the following payoff table:

	State of Nature	
Decision Alternative	**Rezoning Approved** s_1	**Rezoning Not Approved** s_2
Purchase, d_1	600	−200
Do not purchase, d_2	0	0

a. If the probability that the rezoning will be approved is 0.5, what decision is recommended? What is the expected profit?
b. The investor can purchase an option to buy the land. Under the option, the investor maintains the rights to purchase the land anytime during the next three months while

learning more about possible resistance to the rezoning proposal from area residents. Probabilities are as follows:

$$\text{Let } H = \text{High resistance to rezoning}$$
$$L = \text{Low resistance to rezoning}$$

$P(H) = 0.55$	$P(s_1 \mid H) = 0.18$	$P(s_2 \mid H) = 0.82$
$P(L) = 0.45$	$P(s_1 \mid L) = 0.89$	$P(s_2 \mid L) = 0.11$

What is the optimal decision strategy if the investor uses the option period to learn more about the resistance from area residents before making the purchase decision?

c. If the option will cost the investor an additional \$10,000, should the investor purchase the option? Why or why not? What is the maximum that the investor should be willing to pay for the option?

22. Lawson's Department Store faces a buying decision for a seasonal product for which demand can be high, medium, or low. The purchaser for Lawson's can order one, two, or three lots of the product before the season begins but cannot reorder later. Profit projections (in thousands of dollars) are shown.

	State of Nature		
	High Demand	**Medium Demand**	**Low Demand**
Decision Alternative	s_1	s_2	s_3
Order 1 lot, d_1	60	60	50
Order 2 lots, d_2	80	80	30
Order 3 lots, d_3	100	70	10

a. If the prior probabilities for the three states of nature are 0.3, 0.3, and 0.4, respectively, what is the recommended order quantity?

b. At each preseason sales meeting, the vice president of sales provides a personal opinion regarding potential demand for this product. Because of the vice president's enthusiasm and optimistic nature, the predictions of market conditions have always been either "excellent" (E) or "very good" (V). Probabilities are as follows:

$P(E) = 0.70$	$P(s_1 \mid E) = 0.34$	$P(s_1 \mid V) = 0.20$
$P(V) = 0.30$	$P(s_2 \mid E) = 0.32$	$P(s_2 \mid V) = 0.26$
	$P(s_3 \mid E) = 0.34$	$P(s_3 \mid V) = 0.54$

What is the optimal decision strategy?

c. Use the efficiency of sample information and discuss whether the firm should consider a consulting expert who could provide independent forecasts of market conditions for the product.

23. Suppose that you are given a decision situation with three possible states of nature: s_1, s_2, and s_3. The prior probabilities are $P(s_1) = 0.2$, $P(s_2) = 0.5$, and $P(s_3) = 0.3$. With sample information I, $P(I \mid s_1) = 0.1$, $P(I \mid s_2) = 0.05$, and $P(I \mid s_3) = 0.2$. Compute the revised or posterior probabilities: $P(s_1 \mid I)$, $P(s_2 \mid I)$, and $P(s_3 \mid I)$.

24. To save on expenses, Rona and Jerry agreed to form a carpool for traveling to and from work. Rona preferred to use the somewhat longer but more consistent Queen City Avenue. Although Jerry preferred the quicker expressway, he agreed with Rona that they should

take Queen City Avenue if the expressway had a traffic jam. The following payoff table provides the one-way time estimate in minutes for traveling to or from work:

	State of Nature	
	Expressway Open	Expressway Jammed
Decision Alternative	s_1	s_2
Queen City Avenue, d_1	30	30
Expressway, d_2	25	45

Based on their experience with traffic problems, Rona and Jerry agreed on a 0.15 probability that the expressway would be jammed.

In addition, they agreed that weather seemed to affect the traffic conditions on the expressway. Let

$$C = \text{clear}$$
$$O = \text{overcast}$$
$$R = \text{rain}$$

The following conditional probabilities apply:

$$P(C \mid s_1) = 0.8 \qquad P(O \mid s_1) = 0.2 \qquad P(R \mid s_1) = 0.0$$
$$P(C \mid s_2) = 0.1 \qquad P(O \mid s_2) = 0.3 \qquad P(R \mid s_2) = 0.6$$

a. Use Bayes' theorem for probability revision to compute the probability of each weather condition and the conditional probability of the expressway open, s_1, or jammed, s_2, given each weather condition.
b. Show the decision tree for this problem.
c. What is the optimal decision strategy, and what is the expected travel time?

25. The Gorman Manufacturing Company must decide whether to manufacture a component part at its Milan, Michigan, plant or purchase the component part from a supplier. The resulting profit is dependent upon the demand for the product. The following payoff table shows the projected profit (in thousands of dollars):

	State of Nature		
	Low Demand	Medium Demand	High Demand
Decision Alternative	s_1	s_2	s_3
Manufacture, d_1	−20	40	100
Purchase, d_2	10	45	70

The state-of-nature probabilities are $P(s_1) = 0.35$, $P(s_2) = 0.35$, and $P(s_3) = 0.30$.
a. Use a decision tree to recommend a decision.
b. Use EVPI to determine whether Gorman should attempt to obtain a better estimate of demand.

c. A test market study of the potential demand for the product is expected to report either a favorable (F) or unfavorable (U) condition. The relevant conditional probabilities are as follows:

$$P(F \mid s_1) = 0.10 \qquad P(U \mid s_1) = 0.90$$
$$P(F \mid s_2) = 0.40 \qquad P(U \mid s_2) = 0.60$$
$$P(F \mid s_3) = 0.60 \qquad P(U \mid s_3) = 0.40$$

What is the probability that the market research report will be favorable?
d. What is Gorman's optimal decision strategy?
e. What is the expected value of the market research information?
f. What is the efficiency of the information?

Case Problem 1 Property Purchase Strategy

Glenn Foreman, president of Oceanview Development Corporation, is considering submitting a bid to purchase property that will be sold by sealed bid at a county tax foreclosure. Glenn's initial judgment is to submit a bid of $5 million. Based on his experience, Glenn estimates that a bid of $5 million will have a 0.2 probability of being the highest bid and securing the property for Oceanview. The current date is June 1. Sealed bids for the property must be submitted by August 15. The winning bid will be announced on September 1.

If Oceanview submits the highest bid and obtains the property, the firm plans to build and sell a complex of luxury condominiums. However, a complicating factor is that the property is currently zoned for single-family residences only. Glenn believes that a referendum could be placed on the voting ballot in time for the November election. Passage of the referendum would change the zoning of the property and permit construction of the condominiums.

The sealed-bid procedure requires the bid to be submitted with a certified check for 10% of the amount bid. If the bid is rejected, the deposit is refunded. If the bid is accepted, the deposit is the down payment for the property. However, if the bid is accepted and the bidder does not follow through with the purchase and meet the remainder of the financial obligation within six months, the deposit will be forfeited. In this case, the county will offer the property to the next highest bidder.

To determine whether Oceanview should submit the $5 million bid, Glenn conducted some preliminary analysis. This preliminary work provided an assessment of 0.3 for the probability that the referendum for a zoning change will be approved and resulted in the following estimates of the costs and revenues that will be incurred if the condominiums are built:

Cost and Revenue Estimates	
Revenue from condominium sales	$15,000,000
Cost	
Property	$5,000,000
Construction expenses	$8,000,000

If Oceanview obtains the property and the zoning change is rejected in November, Glenn believes that the best option would be for the firm not to complete the purchase of the property. In this case, Oceanview would forfeit the 10% deposit that accompanied the bid.

Because the likelihood that the zoning referendum will be approved is such an important factor in the decision process, Glenn suggested that the firm hire a market research service to conduct a survey of voters. The survey would provide a better estimate of the likelihood that the referendum for a zoning change would be approved. The market research firm that Oceanview Development has worked with in the past has agreed to do the study for $15,000. The results of the study will be available August 1, so that Oceanview will have this information before the August 15 bid deadline. The results of the survey will be either a prediction that the zoning change will be approved or a prediction that the zoning change will be rejected. After considering the record of the market research service in previous studies conducted for Oceanview, Glenn developed the following probability estimates concerning the accuracy of the market research information:

$$P(A \mid s_1) = 0.9 \qquad P(N \mid s_1) = 0.1$$
$$P(A \mid s_2) = 0.2 \qquad P(N \mid s_2) = 0.8$$

where

A = prediction of zoning change approval
N = prediction that zoning change will not be approved
s_1 = the zoning change is approved by the voters
s_2 = the zoning change is rejected by the voters

Managerial Report

Perform an analysis of the problem facing the Oceanview Development Corporation, and prepare a report that summarizes your findings and recommendations. Include the following items in your report:

1. A decision tree that shows the logical sequence of the decision problem
2. A recommendation regarding what Oceanview should do if the market research information is not available
3. A decision strategy that Oceanview should follow if the market research is conducted
4. A recommendation as to whether Oceanview should employ the market research firm, along with the value of the information provided by the market research firm

Include the details of your analysis as an appendix to your report.

Case Problem 2   Lawsuit Defense Strategy

John Campbell, an employee of Manhattan Construction Company, claims to have injured his back as a result of a fall while repairing the roof at one of the Eastview apartment buildings. He filed a lawsuit against Doug Reynolds, the owner of Eastview Apartments, asking for damages of $1,500,000. John claims that the roof had rotten sections and that his fall could have been prevented if Mr. Reynolds had told Manhattan Construction about the problem. Mr. Reynolds notified his insurance company, Allied Insurance, of the lawsuit. Allied must defend Mr. Reynolds and decide what action to take regarding the lawsuit.

Some depositions and a series of discussions took place between both sides. As a result, John Campbell offered to accept a settlement of $750,000. Thus, one option is for Allied to pay John $750,000 to settle the claim. Allied is also considering making John a counteroffer of $400,000 in the hope that he will accept a lesser amount to avoid the time and cost of going to trial. Allied's preliminary investigation shows that John's case is strong; Allied is concerned that John may reject its counteroffer and request a jury trial. Allied's lawyers spent some time exploring John's likely reaction if they make a counteroffer of $400,000.

The lawyers concluded that it is adequate to consider three possible outcomes to represent John's possible reaction to a counteroffer of $400,000: (1) John will accept the counteroffer and the case will be closed; (2) John will reject the counteroffer and elect to have a jury decide the settlement amount; or (3) John will make a counteroffer to Allied of $600,000. If John does make a counteroffer, Allied decided that it will not make additional counteroffers. It will either accept John's counteroffer of $600,000 or go to trial.

If the case goes to a jury trial, Allied considers three outcomes possible: (1) the jury may reject John's claim and Allied will not be required to pay any damages; (2) the jury will find in favor of John and award him $750,000 in damages; or (3) the jury will conclude that John has a strong case and award him the full amount of $1,500,000.

Key considerations as Allied develops its strategy for disposing of the case are the probabilities associated with John's response to an Allied counteroffer of $400,000 and the probabilities associated with the three possible trial outcomes. Allied's lawyers believe that the probability that John will accept a counteroffer of $400,000 is 0.10, the probability that John will reject a counteroffer of $400,000 is 0.40, and the probability that John will, himself, make a counteroffer to Allied of $600,000 is 0.50. If the case goes to court, they believe that the probability that the jury will award John damages of $1,500,000 is 0.30, the probability that the jury will award John damages of $750,000 is 0.50, and the probability that the jury will award John nothing is 0.20.

Managerial Report

Perform an analysis of the problem facing Allied Insurance and prepare a report that summarizes your findings and recommendations. Be sure to include the following items:

1. A decision tree
2. A recommendation regarding whether Allied should accept John's initial offer to settle the claim for $750,000
3. A decision strategy that Allied should follow if they decide to make John a counteroffer of $400,000
4. A risk profile for your recommended strategy

Appendix 4.1   Using Analytic Solver Platform to Create Decision Trees

In this appendix, we describe how Analytic Solver Platform can be used to develop a decision tree for the PDC problem presented in Section 4.3. The decision tree for the PDC problem is shown in Figure 4.18.

Getting Started: An Initial Decision Tree

To build a decision tree for the PDC problem using Analytic Solver Platform, follow these steps in a blank workbook in Excel:

Step 1. Select cell A1
Step 2. Click the **ANALYTIC SOLVER PLATFORM** tab on the Ribbon
Step 3. Click **Decision Tree** in the **Tools** group
        Select **Node**, and click **Add Node**

FIGURE 4.18   DECISION TREE FOR THE PDC CONDOMINIUM PROJECT (PAYOFFS IN MILLIONS $)

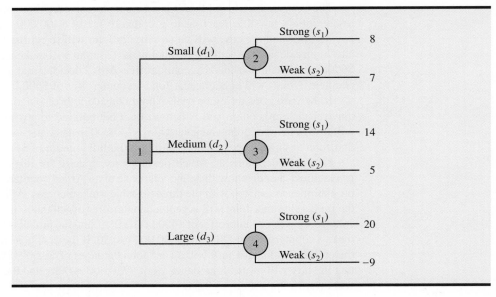

Step 4. When the **Decision Tree** dialog box appears, verify that **Decision** is selected for **Node Type**, and click **OK**

A decision tree with one decision node and two branches (initially labeled as "Decision 1" and "Decision 2") appears, as shown in Figure 4.19.

Adding a Branch

The PDC problem has three decision alternatives (small, medium, and large condominium complexes), so we must add another decision branch to the tree.

Step 1. Select cell B5
Step 2. Click the **ANALYTIC SOLVER PLATFORM** tab in the Ribbon

FIGURE 4.19   DECISION TREE WITH ONE DECISION NODE AND TWO BRANCHES CREATED WITH ANALYTIC SOLVER PLATFORM

	A	B	C	D	E	F	G	H
1								
2				Decision 1				
3							0	
4					0	0		
5			1					
6		0						
7				Decision 2				
8							0	
9					0	0		

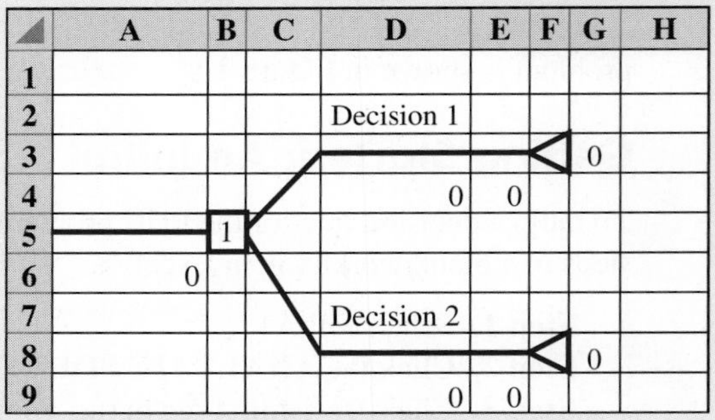

FIGURE 4.20   DECISION TREE FOR THE PDC PROBLEM WITH THREE
BRANCHES CREATED WITH ANALYTIC SOLVER PLATFORM

	A	B	C	D	E	F	G	H
1								
2				Decision 1				
3							0	
4					0	0		
5								
6								
7				Decision 2				
8		1					0	
9	0				0	0		
10								
11								
12				New Branch				
13							0	
14					0	0		

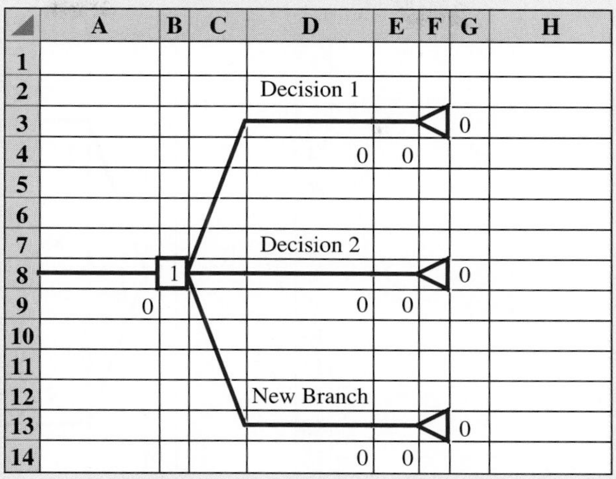

Step 3. Click **Decision Tree** in the **Tools** group
      Select **Branch**, and click **Add Branch**
Step 4. When the **Decision Tree** dialog box appears, verify that **Decision** is selected
      for **Node Type**, and click **OK**

A revised tree with three decision branches now appears in the Excel worksheet as shown
in Figure 4.20.

Naming the Decision Alternatives

The decision alternatives can be named by selecting the cells containing the labels "Decision 1," "Decision 2," and "New Branch," and then entering the corresponding PDC names
Small, *Medium*, and *Large* (cells D2, D7, and D12). After naming the alternatives, the PDC
tree with three decision branches appears as shown in Figure 4.21.

Adding Chance Nodes

The chance event for the PDC problem is the demand for the condominiums, which may
be either strong or weak. Thus, a chance node with two branches must be added at the end
of each decision alternative branch. To add a chance node with two branches to the top
decision alternative branch:

Step 1. Select cell F3
Step 2. Click the **ANALYTIC SOLVER PLATFORM** tab in the Ribbon
Step 3. Select **Decision Tree** from the **Tools** group
      Select **Node**, and click **Add Node**
Step 4. When the **Decision Tree** dialog box appears, select **Event/Chance** in the **Node
      Type** area
      Click **OK**

The tree now appears as shown in Figure 4.22.

FIGURE 4.21 DECISION TREE FOR THE PDC PROBLEM WITH RENAMED BRANCHES CREATED WITH ANALYTIC SOLVER PLATFORM

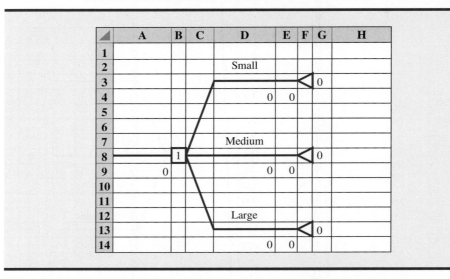

FIGURE 4.22 DECISION TREE FOR THE PDC PROBLEM WITH AN ADDED CHANCE NODE CREATED WITH ANALYTIC SOLVER PLATFORM

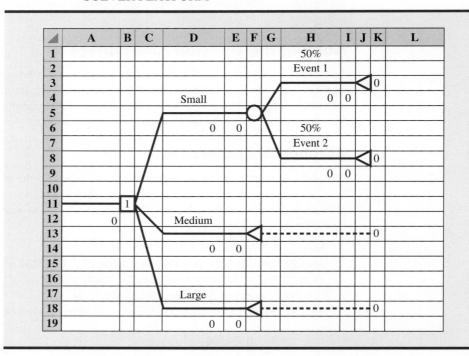

We next select the cells containing "Event 1" and "Event 2" (cells H2 and H7) and re-name them *Strong* and *Weak* to provide the proper names for the PDC states of nature. After doing so, we can copy the subtree for the chance node in cell F5 to the other two decision branches to complete the structure of the PDC decision tree as follows:

Step 1. Select cell F5
Step 2. Click the **ANALYTIC SOLVER PLATFORM** tab in the Ribbon
Step 3. Click **Decision Tree** in the **Tools** group
       Select **Node**, and click **Copy Node**
Step 4. Select cell F13
Step 5. Click the **ANALYTIC SOLVER PLATFORM** tab in the Ribbon
Step 6. Click **Decision Tree** in the **Tools** group
       Select **Node**, and click **Paste Node**

This copy-and-paste procedure places a chance node at the end of the Medium decision branch. Repeating the same copy-and-paste procedure for the Large decision branch completes the structure of the PDC decision tree, as shown in Figure 4.23.

FIGURE 4.23 PDC DECISION TREE CREATED WITH ANALYTIC SOLVER PLATFORM

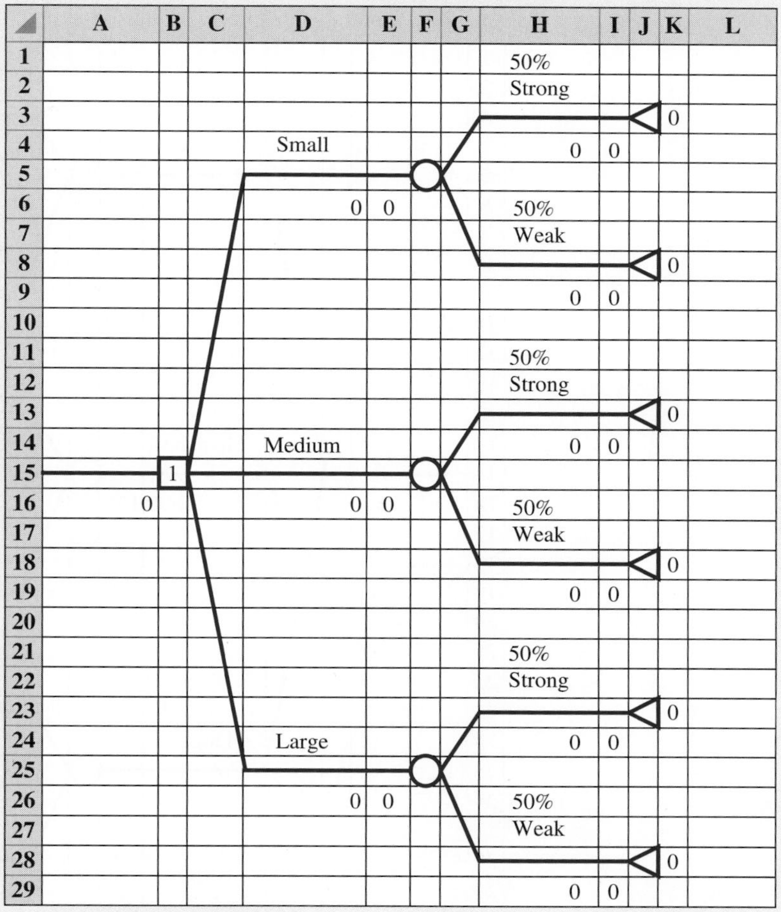

Inserting Probabilities and Payoffs

We now insert probabilities and payoffs into the decision tree. In Figure 4.23, we see that an equal probability of 0.5 is assigned automatically to each of the chance outcomes. For PDC, the probability of strong demand is 0.8 and the probability of weak demand is 1 minus the probability of strong demand, $= 1 - 0.8 = 0.2$. We can enter *0.8* into cell H1 and the formula $=1 - H1$ into cell H6. We enter the formula $=$H1 into cells H11 and H21, and we enter the formula $=$H6 into cells H16 and H26. In this way, all probabilities will be updated correctly if we change the value in cell H1.

To insert the payoffs, we enter *8* in H4, *7* in cell H9, *14* in cell H14, *5* in cell H19, *20* in cell H24, and −*9* in cell H29. Note in Figure 4.24 that the payoffs also appear in the right-hand margin of the decision tree. The payoffs in the right margin are computed by a formula that adds the payoffs on all of the branches leading to the associated terminal node. For the PDC problem, no payoffs are associated with the decision alternatives branches, so we leave the default values of zero in cells D6, D16, and D26. The PDC decision tree is now complete. After inserting the PDC probabilities and payoffs, the PDC decision tree appears as shown in Figure 4.24.

FIGURE 4.24   PDC DECISION TREE WITH BRANCH PROBABILITIES AND
PAYOFFS CREATED WITH ANALYTIC SOLVER PLATFORM

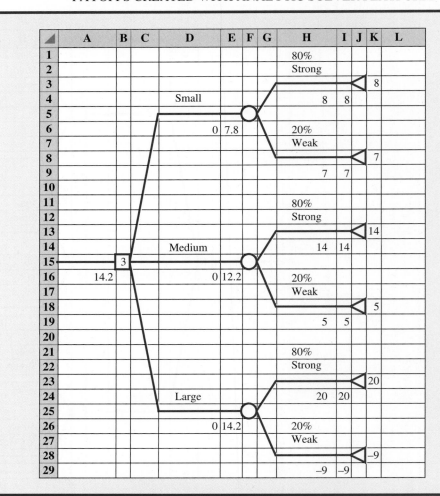

Interpreting the Result

When probabilities and payoffs are inserted, Analytic Solver Platform automatically makes the rollback computations necessary to determine the optimal solution. Optimal decisions are identified by the number in the corresponding decision node. In the PDC decision tree in Figure 4.24, cell B15 contains the decision node. Note that a "3" appears in this node, which tells us that decision alternative branch 3 provides the optimal decision. We can also easily identify the best decision using the Highlight function in Analytic Solver Platform. To highlight the best decision follow these steps:

> **Step 1.** Click the **ANALYTIC SOLVER PLATFORM** tab in the Ribbon
> **Step 2.** Click **Decision Tree** in the **Tools** group
> Select **Highlight**, and click **Highlight Best**

Analytic Solver Platform highlights the best decision for the PDC problem. From Figure 4.25, we see that decision analysis recommends that PDC construct the Large condominium complex. The expected value of this decision appears at the beginning of the tree

FIGURE 4.25   PDC DECISION TREE WITH BEST DECISION HIGHLIGHTED CREATED WITH ANALYTIC SOLVER PLATFORM

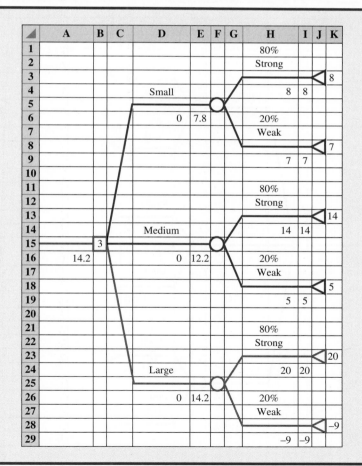

in cell A16. Thus, we see that the optimal expected value is \$14.2 million. The expected values of the other decision alternatives are displayed at the end of the corresponding decision branch. Thus, referring to cells E6 and E16, we see that the expected value of the Small complex is \$7.8 million and the expected value of the Medium complex is \$12.2 million.

Using software such as Analytic Solver Platform to develop decision trees allows for quick and easy sensitivity analysis. We can easily analyze the impact of changing branch probabilities and payoffs by simply changing these values in Excel and observing the impact on the optimal decision using Analytic Solver Platform. For instance, if we want to examine the impact of different values of Strong demand on our decision, we can change the value of cell H1 and see whether this changes the optimal decision.

A convenient way to summarize the sensitivity of a decision to a particular parameter is to combine the decision tree from XLMiner with a Data Table in Excel. Suppose we want to evaluate the impact of different probabilities of strong demand over a wide range of possibilities. The Excel worksheet shown in Figure 4.26 demonstrates the use of a Data Table to perform this sensitivity analysis. To create this Data Table, we follow these steps once we have created the decision tree for this problem in XLMiner:

FIGURE 4.26 PDC DECISION TREE AND DATA TABLE ILLUSTRATING SENSITIVITY ANALYSIS CREATED WITH ANALYTIC SOLVER PLATFORM

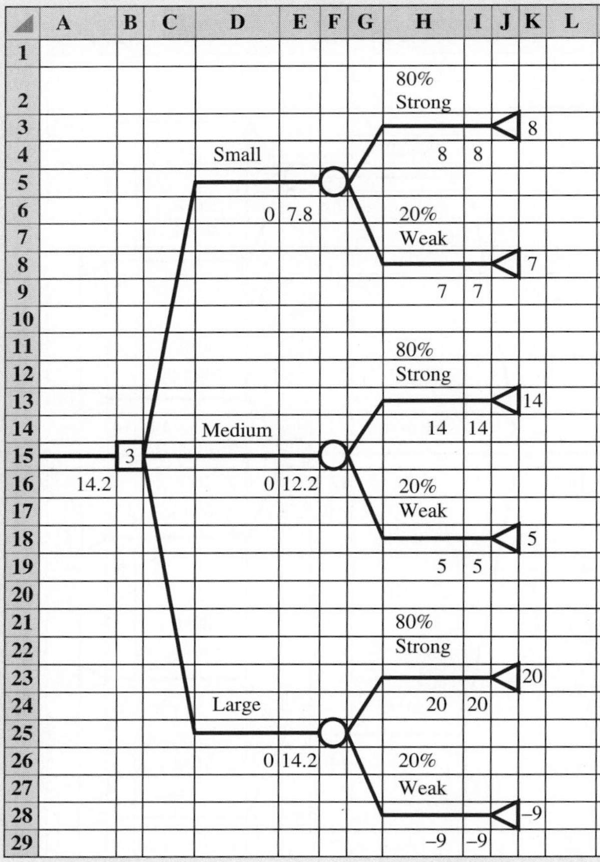

	Data Table	
Probability Strong Demand	**Expected Value**	**Best Decision**
	14.2	Large
0.0	7	Small
0.1	7.1	Small
0.2	7.2	Small
0.3	7.7	Medium
0.4	8.6	Medium
0.5	9.5	Medium
0.6	10.4	Medium
0.7	11.3	Medium
0.8	14.2	Large
0.9	17.1	Large
1.0	20	Large

The Excel function CHOOSE chooses a value from a list of possibilities based on the index in the referenced cell. Here, the CHOOSE function chooses "Small" in cell O3 if the value in cell B15 is 1; it enters "Medium" if the value in cell B15 is 2; it enters "Large" if the value in cell B15 is 3.

Step 1. Enter the values *0.0, 0.1, 0.2*, etc. into cells M4 to M14, as shown in Figure 4.25, to represent the different scenarios for the probability of Strong demand

Step 2. Enter =A16 into cell N3 to keep track of the optimal expected value in each scenario

Step 3. Enter the formula =CHOOSE(B15,"Small","Medium","Large") into cell O3. This will return the best decision in each scenario

Step 4. Select cells M3:O14

Step 5. Click the **DATA** tab in the Ribbon

Step 6. Click **What-If Analysis** from the **Data Tools** group
Select **Data Table…**

Step 7. When the **Data Table** dialog box opens, enter =H1 into the **Column input cell:** box
Click **OK**

By entering =H1 in Step 7, we tell Excel to substitute the values of 0, 0.1, 0.2, and so on for the probability of Strong demand and then return the related outputs.

Figure 4.26 shows the completed decision tree and Data Table. From Figure 4.26, we see that the best decision is to construct the Small complex if the probability of strong demand is 0, 0.1, or 0.2, the Medium complex if the probability is any value shown between 0.3 and 0.7, and the Large complex if the probability of strong demand is 0.8 or greater. The Data Table also provides the expected values for these decisions in each scenario. Such sensitivity analysis can be greatly beneficial in demonstrating which values should be clarified, if possible, by procuring additional information.

CHAPTER 5

Utility and Game Theory

CONTENTS

The decision analysis situations presented in Chapter 4 often expressed consequences or payoffs in terms of monetary values. With probability information available about the outcomes of the chance events, we defined the optimal decision alternative as the one that provided the best expected monetary value. However, in some situations the decision alternative with the best expected monetary value may not be the preferred alternative. A decision maker may also wish to consider intangible factors such as risk, image, or other nonmonetary criteria in order to evaluate the decision alternatives. When monetary value does not necessarily lead to the most preferred decision, expressing the value (or worth) of a consequence in terms of its utility will permit the use of expected utility to identify the most desirable decision alternative. The discussion of utility and its application in decision analysis is presented in the first part of this chapter.

In the last part of this chapter we introduce the topic of game theory. Game theory is the study of developing optimal strategies where two or more decision makers, usually called players, compete as adversaries. Game theory can be viewed as a relative of decision analysis. A key difference, however, is that each player selects a decision strategy not by considering the possible outcomes of a chance event, but by considering the possible strategies selected by one or more competing players.

We note here that utility and game theory are separable topics. Either or both may be studied, and it is not required that you cover one topic before the other. The Q.M. in Action, Game Theory Used in 700-MHz Auction, describes how participants in an FCC auction used game theory to develop bidding strategies.

 Q.M. *in* ACTION

GAME THEORY USED IN 700-MHz AUCTION*

On January 24, 2008, the Federal Communications Commission (FCC) auctioned the rights to operate the 700-MHz frequency band in the United States. This bandwidth became available due to the switch of over-the-air television broadcasts from analog to digital transmission. The 700-MHz frequency bandwidth is highly desirable to companies because the high frequency can penetrate walls and other obstacles. Companies including Google, AT&T, Verizon Wireless, and many others placed bids on the rights to operate in this frequency band.

Game theory was central to this auction, as it was used by the FCC to establish the overall rules and procedures for the auction. To promote competition, the FCC used a "blind auction" format in which each

bid was anonymous. A blind auction assures that each bidder does not know which competitor(s) they are bidding against. Thus, large firms could not use their market dominance and deep pockets to intimidate smaller firms from placing additional bids. Further, bidding was allowed to continue until no new bids were received in order to prevent last-second winning bids (a practice known as auction sniping).

Most participants hired game theorists to devise bid strategies. Economists, mathematicians, engineers, and many others assisted companies in developing optimal bid plans. The auction lasted 261 rounds over 38 days and resulted in 101 winning bidders. The auction generated over $19 billion in revenue for the FCC.

*From E. Woyke, "Peeking into the Spectrum Auction." Forbes, 2007.

(5.1) The Meaning of Utility

Utility is a measure of the total worth or relative desirability of a particular outcome; it reflects the decision maker's attitude toward a collection of factors such as profit, loss, and risk. Researchers have found that as long as the monetary value of payoffs stays within a range that the decision maker considers reasonable, selecting the decision alternative with the best expected monetary value usually leads to selection of the most preferred decision. However, when the payoffs are extreme, decision makers are often unsatisfied or uneasy with the decision that simply provides the best expected monetary value.

As an example of a situation in which utility can help in selecting the best decision alternative, let us consider the problem faced by Swofford, Inc., a relatively small real estate investment firm located in Atlanta, Georgia. Swofford currently has two investment opportunities that require approximately the same cash outlay. The cash requirements necessary prohibit Swofford from making more than one investment at this time. Consequently, three possible decision alternatives may be considered.

The three decision alternatives, denoted d_1, d_2, and d_3, are

$$d_1 = \text{make investment A}$$
$$d_2 = \text{make investment B}$$
$$d_3 = \text{do not invest}$$

The monetary payoffs associated with the investment opportunities depend on the investment decision and on the direction of the real estate market during the next six months (the chance event). Real estate prices will go up, remain stable, or go down. Thus the states of nature, denoted s_1, s_2, and s_3, are

$$s_1 = \text{real estate prices go up}$$
$$s_2 = \text{real estate prices remain stable}$$
$$s_3 = \text{real estate prices go down}$$

Using the best information available, Swofford has estimated the profits, or payoffs, associated with each decision alternative and state-of-nature combination. The resulting payoff table is shown in Table 5.1.

The best estimate of the probability that real estate prices will go up is 0.3; the best estimate of the probability that prices will remain stable is 0.5; and the best estimate of the probability that prices will go down is 0.2. Thus the expected values for the three decision alternatives are

$$EV(d_1) = 0.3(\$30,000) + 0.5(\$20,000) \quad + 0.2(-\$50,000) = \quad \$9000$$
$$EV(d_2) = 0.3(\$50,000) + 0.5(-\$20,000) + 0.2(-\$30,000) = -\$1000$$
$$EV(d_3) = 0.3(\$0) \qquad + 0.5(\$0) \qquad + 0.2(\$0) \qquad = \qquad \$0$$

Using the expected value approach, the optimal decision is to select investment A with an expected monetary value of $9000. Is it really the best decision alternative? Let us consider

TABLE 5.1   PAYOFF TABLE FOR SWOFFORD, INC.

Decision Alternative	State of Nature		
	Prices Up s_1	Prices Stable s_2	Prices Down s_3
Investment A, d_1	$30,000	$20,000	-$50,000
Investment B, d_2	$50,000	-$20,000	-$30,000
Do not invest, d_3	$0	$0	$0

some other factors that relate to Swofford's capability for absorbing the loss of $50,000 if investment A is made and prices actually go down.

Actually, Swofford's current financial position is weak. This condition is partly reflected in Swofford's ability to make only one investment. More important, however, the firm's president believes that, if the next investment results in a substantial loss, Swofford's future will be in jeopardy. Although the expected value approach leads to a recommendation for d_1, do you think the firm's president would prefer this decision? We suspect that the president would select d_2 or d_3 to avoid the possibility of incurring a $50,000 loss. In fact, a reasonable conclusion is that, if a loss of even $30,000 could drive Swofford out of business, the president would select d_3, believing that both investments A and B are too risky for Swofford's current financial position.

The way we resolve Swofford's dilemma is first to determine Swofford's utility for the various monetary outcomes. Recall that the utility of any outcome is the total worth of that outcome, taking into account all risks and consequences involved. If the utilities for the various consequences are assessed correctly, the decision alternative with the highest expected utility is the most preferred, or best, alternative. In the next section we show how to determine the utility of the monetary outcomes so that the alternative with the highest expected utility can be identified.

Utility and Decision Making

The procedure we use to establish utility values for the payoffs in Swofford's situation requires that we first assign a utility value to the best and worst possible payoffs. Any values will work as long as the utility assigned to the best payoff is greater than the utility assigned to the worst payoff. In this case, $50,000 is the best payoff and −$50,000 is the worst. Suppose, then, that we arbitrarily make assignments to these two payoffs as follows:

Utility values of 0 and 1 could have been selected here; we selected 0 and 10 in order to avoid any possible confusion between the utility value for a payoff and the probability p.

$$\text{Utility of } -\$50,000 = U(-\$50,000) = 0$$
$$\text{Utility of } \$50,000 = U(\$50,000) = 10$$

Let us now determine the utility associated with every other payoff.

Consider the process of establishing the utility of a payoff of $30,000. First we ask Swofford's president to state a preference between a guaranteed $30,000 payoff and an opportunity to engage in the following **lottery**, or bet, for some probability of p that we select:

Lottery: Swofford obtains a payoff of $50,000 with probability p
and a payoff of −$50,000 with probability $(1 − p)$

p is often referred to as the indifference probability.

If p is very close to 1, Swofford's president would obviously prefer the lottery to the guaranteed payoff of $30,000 because the firm would virtually ensure itself a payoff of $50,000. If p is very close to 0, Swofford's president would clearly prefer the guarantee of $30,000. In any event, as p increases continuously from 0 to 1, the preference for the guaranteed payoff of $30,000 decreases and at some point is equal to the preference for the lottery. At this value of p, Swofford's president would have equal preference for the guaranteed payoff of $30,000 and the lottery; at greater values of p, Swofford's president would prefer the lottery to the guaranteed $30,000 payoff. For example, let us assume that when $p = 0.95$, Swofford's president is indifferent between the guaranteed payoff of \$30,000 and the lottery. For this value of p, we can compute the utility of a \$30,000 payoff as follows:

$$U(\$30,000) = pU(\$50,000) + (1 - p)U(-\$50,000)$$
$$= 0.95(10) + (0.05)(0)$$
$$= 9.5$$

Obviously, if we had started with a different assignment of utilities for a payoff of \$50,000 and −\$50,000, the result would have been a different utility for \$30,000. For example, if we had started with an assignment of 100 for \$50,000 and 10 for −\$50,000, the utility of a \$30,000 payoff would be

$$U(\$30,000) = 0.95(100) + 0.05(10)$$
$$= 0.95 + 0.05$$
$$= 95.5$$

Hence, we must conclude that the utility assigned to each payoff is not unique but merely depends on the initial choice of utilities for the best and worst payoffs. We will discuss utility choice further at the end of the section. For now, however, we will continue to use a value of 10 for the utility of \$50,000 and a value of 0 for the utility of −\$50,000.

Before computing the utility for the other payoffs, let us consider the implication of Swofford's president assigning a utility of 9.5 to a payoff of \$30,000. Clearly, when $p = 0.95$, the expected value of the lottery is

$$EV(\text{lottery}) = 0.95(\$50,000) + 0.05(-\$50,000)$$
$$= \$47,500 - \$2,500$$
$$= \$45,000$$

Although the expected value of the lottery when $p = 0.95$ is \$45,000, Swofford's president is indifferent between the lottery (and its associated risk) and a guaranteed payoff of \$30,000. Thus, Swofford's president is taking a conservative, or risk-avoiding, viewpoint. A decision maker who would choose a guaranteed payoff over a lottery with a superior expected payoff is a risk avoider (or is said to be risk averse). The president would rather have \$30,000 for certain than risk anything greater than a 5% chance of incurring a loss of \$50,000. In other words, the difference between the EV of \$45,000 and the guaranteed payoff of \$30,000 is the risk premium that Swofford's president would be willing to pay to avoid the 5% chance of losing \$50,000.

The difference between the expected value of the lottery and the guaranteed payoff can be viewed as the risk premium the decision maker is willing to pay.

To compute the utility associated with a payoff of −\$20,000, we must ask Swofford's president to state a preference between a guaranteed −\$20,000 payoff and an opportunity to engage again in the following lottery:

> Lottery: Swofford obtains a payoff of \$50,000 with probability p
> and a payoff of −\$50,000 with probability $(1 - p)$

Note that this lottery is exactly the same as the one we used to establish the utility of a payoff of \$30,000 (in fact, we can use this lottery to establish the utility for any monetary value in the Swofford payoff table). We need to determine the value of p that would make the president indifferent between a guaranteed payoff of −\$20,000 and the lottery. For example, we might begin by asking the president to choose between a certain loss of $20,000 and the lottery with a payoff of $50,000 with probability $p = 0.90$ and a payoff of $-\$50,000$ with probability $(1 - p) = 0.10$. What answer do you think we would get? Surely, with this high probability of obtaining a payoff of $50,000, the president would elect the lottery. Next, we might ask whether $p = 0.85$ would result in indifference between the loss of $20,000 for certain and the lottery. Again the president might prefer the lottery. Suppose that we continue until we get to $p = 0.55$, at which point the president is indifferent between the payoff of $-\$20,000$ and the lottery. That is, for any value of p less than 0.55, the president would take a loss of $20,000 for certain rather than risk the potential loss of $50,000 with the lottery; and for any value of p above 0.55, the president would choose the lottery. Thus, the utility assigned to a payoff of $-\$20,000$ is

$$U(-\$20,000) = pU(\$50,000) + (1 - p)U(-\$50,000)$$
$$= 0.55(10) + 0.45(0)$$
$$= 5.5$$

Again let us assess the implication of this assignment by comparing it to the expected value approach. When $p = 0.55$, the expected value of the lottery is

$$EV(\text{lottery}) = 0.55(\$50,000) + 0.45(-\$50,000)$$
$$= \$27,500 - \$22,500$$
$$= \$5000$$

Thus, Swofford's president would just as soon absorb a certain loss of $20,000 as take the lottery and its associated risk, even though the expected value of the lottery is $5000. Once again this preference demonstrates the conservative, or risk-avoiding, point of view of Swofford's president.

In these two examples we computed the utility for the monetary payoffs of $30,000 and $-\$20,000$. We can determine the utility for any monetary payoff M in a similar fashion. First, we must find the probability p for which the decision maker is indifferent between a guaranteed payoff of M and a lottery with a payoff of $50,000 with probability p and $-\$50,000$ with probability $(1 - p)$. The utility of M is then computed as follows:

$$U(M) = pU(\$50,000) + (1 - p)U(-\$50,000)$$
$$= p(10) + (1 - p)0$$
$$= 10p$$

Using this procedure, we developed utility values for the rest of the payoffs in Swofford's problem. The results are presented in Table 5.2.

Now that we have determined the utility value of each of the possible monetary values, we can write the original payoff table in terms of utility values. Table 5.3 shows the utility for the various outcomes in the Swofford problem. The notation we use for the entries in the utility table is U_{ij}, which denotes the utility associated with decision alternative d_i and state of nature s_j. Using this notation, we see that $U_{23} = 4.0$.

The Expected Utility Approach

We can now apply the expected value computations introduced in Chapter 4 to the utilities in Table 5.3 in order to select an optimal decision alternative for Swofford, Inc. However, because utility values represent such a special case of expected value, we will refer to

TABLE 5.2   UTILITY OF MONETARY PAYOFFS FOR SWOFFORD, INC.

Monetary Value	Indifference Value of p	Utility Value
$50,000	Does not apply	10.0
$30,000	0.95	9.5
$20,000	0.90	9.0
$ 0	0.75	7.5
−$20,000	0.55	5.5
−$30,000	0.40	4.0
−$50,000	Does not apply	0.0

TABLE 5.3   UTILITY TABLE FOR SWOFFORD, INC.

| Decision Alternative | State of Nature | | |
	Prices Up s_1	Prices Stable s_2	Prices Down s_3
Investment A, d_1	9.5	9.0	0.0
Investment B, d_2	10.0	5.5	4.0
Do not invest, d_3	7.5	7.5	7.5

the expected value when applied to utility values as the **expected utility (EU)**. Thus, the expected utility approach requires the analyst to compute the expected utility for each decision alternative and then select the alternative yielding the highest expected utility. With N possible states of nature, the expected utility of a decision alternative d_i is given by

$$EU(d_i) = \sum_{j=1}^{N} P(s_j)U_{ij} \qquad (5.1)$$

The expected utility for each of the decision alternatives in the Swofford problem is

$$EU(d_1) = 0.3(9.5) + 0.5(9.0) + 0.2(0.0) = 7.35$$
$$EU(d_2) = 0.3(10.0) + 0.5(5.5) + 0.2(4.0) = 6.55$$
$$EU(d_3) = 0.3(7.5) + 0.5(7.5) + 0.2(7.5) = 7.50$$

Can you use the expected utility approach to determine the optimal decision? Try Problem 1.

Note that the optimal decision using the expected utility approach is d_3, do not invest. The ranking of alternatives according to the president's utility assignments and the associated monetary values is as follows:

Ranking of Decision Alternatives	Expected Utility	Expected Monetary Value
Do not invest	7.50	$ 0
Investment A	7.35	$9000
Investment B	6.55	−$1000

Note also that although investment A had the highest expected monetary value of $9000, the analysis indicates that Swofford should decline this investment. The rationale behind not selecting investment A is that the 0.20 probability of a $50,000 loss was considered to involve a serious risk by Swofford's president. The seriousness of this risk and its associated impact on the company were not adequately reflected by the expected monetary value of investment A. We assessed the utility for each payoff to assess this risk adequately.

Summary of Steps for Determining the Utility of Money

Before considering other aspects of utility, let us summarize the steps involved in determining the utility for a monetary value and using it within the decision analysis framework. The following steps state in general terms the procedure used to solve the Swofford, Inc., investment problem:

Step 1. Develop a payoff table using monetary values.

Step 2. Identify the best and worst payoff values in the table and assign each a utility value, with U(best payoff) > U(worst payoff).

Step 3. For every other monetary value M in the original payoff table, do the following to determine its utility value:

    a. Define the lottery: The best payoff is obtained with probability p and the worst payoff is obtained with probability $(1 - p)$.

    b. Determine the value of p such that the decision maker is indifferent between a guaranteed payoff of M and the lottery defined in step 3(a).

    c. Calculate the utility of M as follows:

$$U(M) = pU(\text{best payoff}) + (1 - p)U(\text{worst payoff})$$

Step 4. Convert the payoff table from monetary values to utility values.

Step 5. Apply the expected utility approach to the utility table developed in step 4 and select the decision alternative with the highest expected utility.

NOTES AND COMMENTS

1. In the Swofford problem we have been using a utility of 10 for the best payoff and 0 for the worst. We could have chosen any values so long as the utility associated with the best payoff exceeds the utility associated with the worst payoff. In practice, frequently a utility of 1 is associated with the best payoff and a utility of 0 is associated with the worst payoff. Had we made this choice, the utility for any monetary value M would have been the value of p at which the decision maker was indifferent between a guaranteed payoff of M and a lottery in which the best payoff is obtained with probability p and the worst payoff is obtained with probability $(1 - p)$. Thus, the utility for any monetary value would have been equal to the probability of earning the best payoff. Often this choice is made because of the ease in computation. We chose not to do so to emphasize the distinction between the utility values and the indifference probabilities for the lottery.

2. Other approaches to decision analysis, such as the optimistic, conservative, and minimax regret

(*continued*)

approaches covered in Chapter 4, can be applied to utilities.

3. The procedure we described for determining the utility of monetary consequences can also be used to develop a utility measure for non-monetary consequences. Assign the best consequence a utility of 10 and the worst a utility of 0. Then create a lottery with a probability of p for the best consequence and $(1 - p)$ for the worst consequence. For each of the other consequences, find the value of p that makes the decision maker indifferent between the lottery and the consequence. Then calculate the utility of the consequence in question as follows:

$$U(\text{consequence}) = pU(\text{best consequence}) + (1 - p)U(\text{worst consequence})$$

5.3 Utility: Other Considerations

In this section we describe how a risk-avoiding decision maker and a risk-taking decision maker differ in their assessment of utility. Expected utility is then used to show how a risk-avoiding decision maker and a risk-taking decision maker may prefer different decision alternatives for the same decision problem. We close this section by comparing expected monetary value and expected utility as criteria for decision making.

Risk Avoiders Versus Risk Takers

The financial position of Swofford, Inc., was such that the firm's president evaluated investment opportunities from a conservative, or risk-avoiding, point of view. However, if the firm had a surplus of cash and a stable future, Swofford's president might have been looking for investment alternatives that, although perhaps risky, contained a potential for substantial profit. That type of behavior would demonstrate that the president is a risk taker with respect to this decision.

A **risk taker** is a decision maker who would choose a lottery over a guaranteed payoff when the expected value of the lottery is inferior to the guaranteed payoff. In this section we analyze the decision problem faced by Swofford from the point of view of a decision maker who would be classified as a risk taker. We then compare the conservative, or risk-avoiding, point of view of Swofford's president with the behavior of a decision maker who is a risk taker.

For the decision problem facing Swofford, Inc., using the general procedure for developing utilities as discussed in Section 5.2, a risk taker might express the utility for the various payoffs shown in Table 5.4. As before, $U(\$50,000) = 10$ and $U(-\$50,000) = 0$. Note the difference in behavior reflected in Table 5.4 and Table 5.2. That is, in determining the value of p at which the decision maker is indifferent between a guaranteed payoff of M and a lottery in which $50,000 is obtained with probability p and $-\$50,000$ with probability $(1 - p)$, the risk taker is willing to accept a greater risk of incurring a loss of $50,000 in order to gain the opportunity to realize a profit of $50,000.

To help develop the utility table for the risk taker, we have reproduced the Swofford, Inc., payoff table in Table 5.5. Using these payoffs and the risk taker's utility values given in Table 5.4, we can write the risk taker's utility table as shown in Table 5.6.

TABLE 5.4 REVISED UTILITY VALUES FOR SWOFFORD, INC., ASSUMING A RISK TAKER

Monetary Value	Indifference Value of p	Utility Value
$50,000	Does not apply	10.0
$30,000	0.50	5.0
$20,000	0.40	4.0
$ 0	0.25	2.5
−$20,000	0.15	1.5
−$30,000	0.10	1.0
−$50,000	Does not apply	0.0

TABLE 5.5 PAYOFF TABLE FOR SWOFFORD, INC.

Decision Alternative	Prices Up s_1	State of Nature Prices Stable s_2	Prices Down s_3
Investment A, d_1	$30,000	$20,000	−$50,000
Investment B, d_2	$50,000	−$20,000	−$30,000
Do not invest, d_3	$0	$0	$0

Using the state-of-nature probabilities $P(s_1) = 0.3$, $P(s_2) = 0.5$, and $P(s_3) = 0.2$, the expected utility for each decision alternative is

$$EU(d_1) = 0.3(5.0) + 0.5(4.0) + 0.2(0.0) = 3.50$$
$$EU(d_2) = 0.3(10.0) + 0.5(1.5) + 0.2(1.0) = 3.95$$
$$EU(d_3) = 0.3(2.5) + 0.5(2.5) + 0.2(2.5) = 2.50$$

What is the recommended decision? Perhaps somewhat to your surprise, the analysis recommends investment B, with the highest expected utility of 3.95. Recall that this investment has a −$1000 expected monetary value. Why is it now the recommended decision? Remember that the decision maker in this revised problem is a risk taker. Thus, although the expected value of investment B is negative, utility analysis has shown that this decision maker is enough of a risk taker to prefer investment B and its potential for the $50,000 profit.

TABLE 5.6 UTILITY TABLE OF A RISK TAKER FOR SWOFFORD, INC.

Decision Alternative	Prices Up s_1	State of Nature Prices Stable s_2	Prices Down s_3
Investment A, d_1	5.0	4.0	0.0
Investment B, d_2	10.0	1.5	1.0
Do not invest, d_3	2.5	2.5	2.5

The expected utility values give the following order of preference of the decision alternatives for the risk taker and the associated expected monetary values:

Ranking of Decision Alternatives	Expected Utility	Expected Monetary Value
Investment B	3.95	−$1000
Investment A	3.50	$9000
Do not invest	2.50	$0

Comparing the utility analysis for a risk taker with the more conservative preferences of the president of Swofford, Inc., who is a risk avoider, we see that, even with the same decision problem, different attitudes toward risk can lead to different recommended decisions. The utility values established by Swofford's president indicated that the firm should not invest at this time, whereas the utilities established by the risk taker showed a preference for investment B. Note that both of these decisions differ from the best expected monetary value decision, which was investment A.

We can obtain another perspective of the difference between behaviors of a risk avoider and a risk taker by developing a graph that depicts the relationship between monetary value and utility. We use the horizontal axis of the graph to represent monetary values and the vertical axis to represent the utility associated with each monetary value. Now, consider the data in Table 5.2, with a utility value corresponding to each monetary value for the original Swofford, Inc., problem. These values can be plotted on a graph such as that in Figure 5.1, and a curve can be drawn through the observed points. The resulting curve is the **utility**

FIGURE 5.1 UTILITY FUNCTION FOR MONEY FOR THE RISK AVOIDER

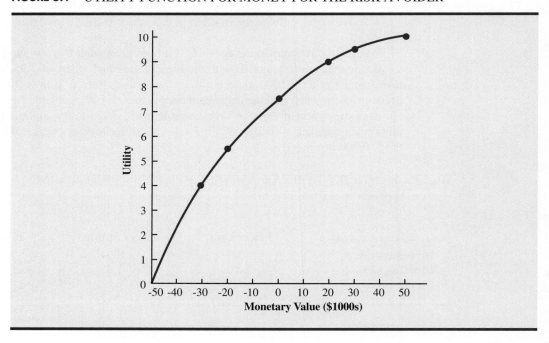

FIGURE 5.2   UTILITY FUNCTION FOR MONEY FOR THE RISK TAKER

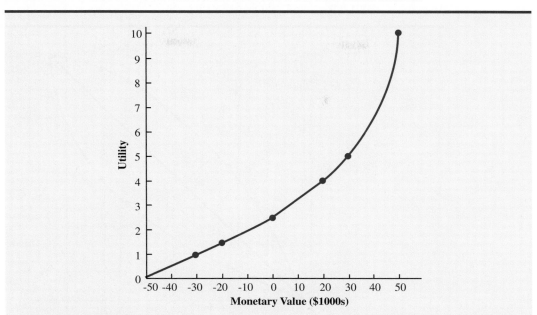

function for money for Swofford's president. Recall that these points reflected the conservative, or risk-avoiding, nature of Swofford's president. Hence, we refer to the curve in Figure 5.1 as a utility function for a risk avoider. Using the data in Table 5.4 developed for a risk taker, we can plot these points on a graph such as that in Figure 5.2. The resulting curve depicts the utility function for a risk taker.

By looking at the utility functions of Figures 5.1 and 5.2, we can begin to generalize about the utility functions for risk avoiders and risk takers. Although the exact shape of the utility function will vary from one decision maker to another, we can see the general shape of these two types of utility functions. The utility function for a risk avoider shows a diminishing marginal return for money. For example, the increase in utility going from a monetary value of −$30,000 to $0 is 7.5 − 4.0 = 3.5, whereas the increase in utility in going from $0 to $30,000 is only 9.5 − 7.5 = 2.0.

However, the utility function for a risk taker shows an increasing marginal return for money. For example, in Figure 5.2, the increase in utility in going from −$30,000 to $0 is 2.5 − 1.0 = 1.5, whereas the increase in utility in going from $0 to $30,000 is 5.0 − 2.5 = 2.5. Note also that in either case the utility function is always increasing; that is, more money leads to more utility. All utility functions possess this property.

Try Problem 5 for practice in plotting the utility function for risk-avoider, risk-taker, and risk-neutral decision makers.

We have concluded that the utility function for a risk avoider shows a diminishing marginal return for money and that the utility function for a risk taker shows an increasing marginal return. When the marginal return for money is neither decreasing nor increasing but remains constant, the corresponding utility function describes the behavior of a decision maker who is neutral to risk. The following characteristics are associated with a **risk-neutral decision maker**:

1. The utility function can be drawn as a straight line connecting the "best" and the "worst" points.

FIGURE 5.3   UTILITY FUNCTION FOR RISK-AVOIDER, RISK-TAKER, AND RISK-NEUTRAL DECISION MAKERS

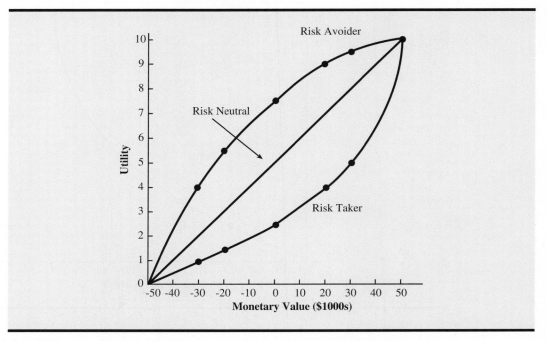

2. The expected utility approach and the expected value approach applied to monetary payoffs result in the same action.

Figure 5.3 depicts the utility function of a risk-neutral decision maker using the Swofford, Inc., problem data. For comparison purposes, we also show the utility functions for the cases where the decision maker is either a risk taker or a risk avoider.

Generally, when the payoffs for a particular decision-making problem fall into a reasonable range—the best is not too good and the worst is not too bad—decision makers tend to express preferences in agreement with the expected monetary value approach. Thus, we suggest asking the decision maker to consider the best and worst possible payoffs for a problem and assess their reasonableness. If the decision maker believes that they are in the reasonable range, the decision alternative with the best expected monetary value can be used. However, if the payoffs appear unreasonably large or unreasonably small (for example, a huge loss) and if the decision maker believes that monetary values do not adequately reflect her or his true preferences for the payoffs, a utility analysis of the problem should be considered.

Unfortunately, determination of the appropriate utilities is not a trivial task. As we have shown, measuring utility requires a degree of subjectivity on the part of the decision maker, and different decision makers will have different utility functions. This aspect of utility often causes decision makers to feel uncomfortable about using the expected utility approach. However, if you encounter a decision situation in which you are convinced that monetary value is not the sole measure of performance, and if you agree that a quantitative analysis of the decision problem is desirable, you should recommend that utility analysis be considered.

NOTES AND COMMENTS

1. Circumstances often dictate whether one acts as a risk avoider or a risk taker when making a decision. You may think of yourself as a risk avoider when faced with financial decisions, but if you have ever purchased a lottery ticket you have actually acted as a risk taker. For example, suppose you purchase a $1.00 lottery ticket for a simple lottery in which the object is to pick the six numbers that will be drawn from 50 potential numbers. Also suppose that if you win (correctly choose all six numbers that are drawn), you will receive $1,000,000. There are 15,890,700 possible winning combinations, so your probability of winning is $1/15,890,700 \approx 0.00000006293$ (i.e., *very low*) and the expected monetary value of your ticket is

$$\frac{1}{15,890,700}\,(\$1,000,000 - 1\$)$$

$$+\left(1 - \frac{1}{15,890,700}\right)(-\$1)$$

$$=\frac{1}{15,890,700}\,(\$1,000,000 - \$1)$$

$$+\frac{15,890,699}{15,890,700}\,(-\$1)$$

$$\approx -\$0.94$$

(Why is the payoff for winning equal to $1,000,000 − $1? You had to pay for your ticket!)

If a lottery ticket has a negative expected value, why does anyone play? The answer is in utility—most people who play lotteries associate great utility with the possiblity of winning the $1,000,000 prize and relatively little utility with the $1.00 cost for a ticket, and so the expected value of the utility of the lottery ticket is positive even though the expected monetary value of the ticket is negative.

2. In many decision-making problems, expected monetary value and expected utility will lead to identical recommendations. In fact, this result will always be true if the decision maker is risk neutral. In general, if the decision maker is almost risk neutral over the range of payoffs (from lowest to highest) for a particular decision problem, the decision alternative with the best expected monetary value leads to selection of the most preferred decision alternative. The trick lies in recognizing the range of monetary values over which a decision maker's utility function is risk neutral.

5.4 Introduction to Game Theory

In decision analysis, a single decision maker seeks to select an optimal decision alternative after considering the possible outcomes of one or more chance events. In **game theory**, two or more decision makers are called players, and they compete as adversaries against each other. Each player selects a strategy independently without knowing in advance the strategy of the other player or players. The combination of the competing strategies provides the value of the game to the players. Game theory applications have been developed for situations in which the competing players are teams, companies, political candidates, armies, and contract bidders.

Until 1944, when Von Neumann and Morgenstern published the book Theory of Games and Economic Behavior, *the literature on decisions involving risk consisted primarily of applications involving the use of probability in gambling.*

In this section we describe **two-person, zero-sum games**. *Two-person* means that two competing players take part in the game. *Zero-sum* means that the gain (or loss) for one player is equal to the corresponding loss (or gain) for the other player (what one player wins, the other player loses). As a result, the gain and loss balance out so that the game results in the sum of zero. Let us demonstrate a two-person, zero-sum game and its solution by considering two companies competing for market share.

Competing for Market Share

Suppose that two companies are the only manufacturers of a particular product; they compete against each other for market share. In planning a marketing strategy for the coming year, each company is considering three strategies designed to take market share from the other company. The three strategies, assumed to be the same for both companies, are as follows:

Strategy 1   Increase advertising
Strategy 2   Provide quantity discounts
Strategy 3   Extend product warranty

A payoff table showing the percentage gain in the market share for Company A expected for each combination of strategies follows. The notations a_1, a_2, and a_3 identify the three strategies for Company A; the notations b_1, b_2, and b_3 identify the three strategies for Company B. It is a zero-sum game because any gain in market share for Company A is a loss in market share for Company B.

		Company B		
		Increase Advertising b_1	Quantity Discounts b_2	Extend Warranty b_3
Company A	Increase Advertising, a_1	4	3	2
	Quantity Discounts, a_2	−1	4	1
	Extend Warranty, a_3	5	−2	0

In interpreting the entries in the table we see that if Company A increases advertising (a_1) and Company B increases advertising (b_1), Company A will come out ahead with an increase in market share of 4%; because this is a zero-sum game, Company B will suffer a corresponding 4% decrease in market share. On the other hand, if Company A provides quantity discounts (a_2) and Company B increases advertising (b_1), Company A is projected to lose 1% of market share to Company B. Company A is seeking payoff values that show relatively large increases in its market share. Company B is seeking payoff values that show decreases or small increases in Company A's market share, and thus better results for Company B.

This game involving market share meets the requirements of a two-person, zero-sum game. The two companies are the two players and the zero-sum occurs because the gain (or loss) in market share for Company A is the same as the loss (or gain) in market share for Company B. Due to the planning horizon, each company must select a strategy before knowing the other company's strategy. What are the optimal strategies for the two companies?

The logic of game theory assumes that each company or player has the same information and will select a strategy that provides the best possible outcome from its point of view. Suppose Company A selects strategy a_1. Market share increases of 4%, 3%, or 2% are possible depending upon Company B's strategy. If Company B believes that Company A will use strategy a_1, then Company B will employ strategy b_3. Under the assumption that Company B will select the strategy that is best for it, Company A analyzes the game by protecting itself against the actions of Company B. In doing so, Company A identifies the minimum possible payoff for each of its actions. This payoff is the minimum value in each row of the payoff matrix. These row minimums are computed in the payoff table as follows:

| | | **Company B** | | | |
		Increase Advertising b_1	**Quantity Discounts** b_2	**Extend Warranty** b_3	**Minimum**
Company A	**Increase Advertising,** a_1	4	3	2	②
	Quantity Discounts, a_2	−1	4	1	−1
	Extend Warranty, a_3	5	−2	0	−2

Maximum of
row minimums

Considering the entries in the Minimum column, we see that Company A can be guaranteed an increase in market share of at least 2% by selecting the strategy that provides the *maximum of the row minimums* (strategy a_1). Thus, Company A follows a *maximin* procedure and selects strategy a_1 as its best strategy.

Let us now look at the payoff table from the point of view of the other player, Company B. The entries in the payoff table represent losses in market share. Consider what happens to Company B if strategy b_1 is selected. Market share decreases of 4%, −1%, and 5% are possible. Under the assumption that Company A will select the strategy that is best for it, Company B knows that if it selects strategy b_1, a loss in market share of as much as 5% could be incurred. Thus, Company B analyzes the game by considering the maximum value in each column, which provides the maximum decrease in its market share for each Company A strategy. These column maximums are computed as follows:

| | | **Company B** | | | |
		Increase Advertising b_1	**Quantity Discounts** b_2	**Extend Warranty** b_3	**Minimum**
Company A	**Increase Advertising,** a_1	4	3	2	②
	Quantity Discounts a_2	−1	4	1	−1
	Extend Warranty, a_3	5	−2	0	−2
	Maximum	5	4	②	

Minimum of
column maximums

Maximum of
row minimums

By considering the entries in the Maximum row, Company B can be guaranteed a decrease in market share of no more than 2% by selecting the strategy that provides the *minimum of the column maximums* (strategy b_3). Thus, Company B follows a *minimax* procedure and selects strategy b_3 as its best strategy. Under strategy b_3, Company B knows that Company A cannot gain more than 2% in market share.

Identifying a Pure Strategy

Whenever the maximum of the row minimums *equals* the minimum of the column maximums, the players cannot improve their outcomes by changing strategies. The game is said to have a **saddle point**. With a saddle point, the optimal strategies and the value of the game cannot be improved by either player changing strategies. Thus, a **pure strategy** has been identified as being optimal for both players. The requirement for a pure strategy is as follows:

$$\text{Maximum(Row minimums)} = \text{Minimum(Column maximums)}$$

That is, the maximin value for Player A equals the minimax value for Player B, and so Player A would not alter his strategy even if he knew Player B's strategy and Player B would not alter her strategy even if she knew Player A's strategy. In our example, the solution to the game is a pure strategy. If Company A increases its advertising (strategy a_1), Company B's optimal strategy is to extend its product warranty (strategy b_3); if Company B chooses to extend its product warranty (strategy b_3), Company A's optimal strategy is to increase its advertising (strategy a_1). The value of the game shows that this optimal solution will increase Company A's market share by 2% and decrease Company B's market share by 2%.

With a pure strategy, neither player can improve its position by changing to a different strategy. In our marketing example, the pure strategy for Company A is a_1. When Company B selects its pure strategy b_3, the value of the game shows an increase in Company A's market share of 2%. Note that if Company B tries to change its pure strategy from b_3, Company A's market share will increase 4% if b_1 is selected or will increase 3% if b_2 is selected. Company B must stay with its pure strategy b_3 to obtain its best result. Similarly, note that if Company A tries to change its pure strategy from a_1, Company A's market share will increase only 1% if a_2 is selected or will not increase at all if a_3 is selected. Company A must stay with its pure strategy a_1 in order to keep its 2% increase in market share. Thus, even if one of the players discovered in advance the opponent's strategy, no advantage could be gained by switching to a different strategy.

If a pure strategy exists, it is the optimal solution for the game.

When a pure strategy is optimal for a two-person, zero-sum game, the following steps will find the optimal strategy for each player:

Step 1. Compute the minimum payoff for each row (Player A).
Step 2. For Player A, select the strategy that provides the *maximum* of the row minimums.
Step 3. Compute the maximum payoff for each column (Player B).
Step 4. For Player B, select the strategy that provides the *minimum* of the column maximums.
Step 5. If the maximin value (step 2) equals the minimax value (step 4), an optimal pure strategy exists for both players. The optimal strategy for Player A is identified in step 2, and the optimal strategy for Player B is identified in step 4. The value of the game is given by the value at the saddle point where the optimal strategies for both players intersect.

If in step 5 the maximin value for Player A does not equal the minimax value for Player B, a pure strategy is not optimal for the two-person, zero-sum game. In this case, a *mixed strategy* is best. In the next section we show when it is necessary to employ a mixed strategy.

Mixed Strategy Games

Consider the two-person, zero-sum game that occurs in a football game. The two competing players are the two football teams. On each play, the game is zero-sum because the yardage gained by one team is equal to the yardage lost by the other team. As usual in game theory, each team must select its strategy before knowing the strategy selected by the other team. In this example, let Team A be the team on offense trying to gain yardage and Team B be the team on defense trying to keep the yardage gained by Team A to a minimum. We define the offensive strategies for Team A as follows:

$$a_1 = \text{running play}$$
$$a_2 = \text{passing play}$$

The defensive strategies for Team B are as follows:

$$b_1 = \text{run defense}$$
$$b_2 = \text{pass defense}$$

The payoff table shows the yardage gained by Team A depending upon the strategies selected by the two teams.

		Team B	
		Run Defense b_1	**Pass Defense** b_2
Team A	**Run, a_1**	1	6
	Pass, a_2	15	0

Applying the five-step procedure used to identify a pure strategy, the row minimums and the column maximums are as follows:

		Team B		
		Run Defense b_1	**Pass Defense** b_2	**Minimum**
Team A	**Run, a_1**	1	6	①
	Pass, a_2	15	0	0
	Maximum	15	⑥	

The maximum of the row minimums is 1 and the minimum of the column maximums is 6. Because these values are not equal, the two-person, zero-sum game does not have an optimal pure strategy. In this case, a **mixed strategy** solution is best. With a mixed strategy the optimal solution for each player is to randomly select among the alternative strategies. In the football example, then, the offensive Team A will mix up or vary its selection of running (a_1) and passing (a_2) plays, while the defensive Team B will mix up or vary its selection of a run defense (b_1) and a pass defense (b_2).

When you think about a football game, it becomes clear that a pure strategy such as Team A always selecting a running play would not work. Team B would recognize Team

A's pure strategy and would always be prepared with a run defense. Thus, a Team A mixed strategy of sometimes running and sometimes passing would make sense. When a mixed strategy solution is needed, game theory will determine the optimal probabilities for each strategy for each player. That is, the game theory solution of the football example will tell the offensive team the optimal probabilities for a running play and a passing play. At the same time, the solution will tell the defensive team the optimal probabilities for a run defense and a pass defense. The following discussion shows how to calculate these mixed strategy probabilities.

Let

$$p = \text{the probability Team A selects a running play}$$
$$(1 - p) = \text{the probability Team A selects a passing play}$$

When a mixed strategy solution exists, we seek to determine the probability p for Team A such that Team B cannot improve its result by changing its defensive strategy. First assume that Team B selects a run defense as shown in column b_1. If Team A selects a running play with probability p and a passing play with probability $(1 - p)$, the expected value of the yardage gain for Team A is computed as follows:

If Team B selects b_1:

$$\text{EV(Yardage)} = 1p + 15(1 - p)$$

If Team B selects its pass defense as shown in column b_2, the expected value of the yardage gain for Team A will be as follows:

If Team B selects b_2:

$$\text{EV(Yardage)} = 6p + 0(1 - p) = 6p$$

To guarantee that Team B cannot change its strategy and decrease the expected value of the yardage gained by Team A, we set the two expected values equal and solve for the value of p.

$$1p + 15(1 - p) = 6p$$
$$1p + 15 - 15p = 6p$$
$$20p = 15$$
$$p = 15/20 = 0.75$$

With $p = 0.75, (1 - p) = 1 - 0.75 = 0.25$. This result tells Team A it should select a running play with a 0.75 probability and a passing play with a 0.25 probability. The expected value of the yardage gained, which is the *value of the game,* is

$$\text{EV(Yardage)} = 1p + 15(1 - p) = 1(0.75) + 15(0.25) = 4.5 \text{ yards per play}$$

Now let us consider the optimal probabilities for Team B. Let

$$q = \text{the probability Team B selects a run defense}$$
$$(1 - q) = \text{the probability Team B selects a pass defense}$$

Using the same logic we used for computing Team A's optimal probabilities, we want to determine the value of q such that Team A cannot increase the expected value of the yardage gained by changing its offensive strategy. We first compute the expected value of the yardage for Team B for the following two cases:

If Team A selects a_1:

$$EV(\text{Yardage}) = 1q + 6(1 - q)$$

If Team A selects a_2:

$$EV(\text{Yardage}) = 15q + 0(1 - q) = 15q$$

To guarantee that Team A cannot change its strategy and affect the expected value of the yardage for Team B, we set the two expected values equal and solve for the value of q as follows:

$$1q + 6(1 - q) = 15q$$
$$1q + 6 - 6q = 15q$$
$$20q = 6$$
$$q = 6/20 = 0.30$$

With $q = 0.30$, $(1 - q) = 1 - 0.30 = 0.70$. This result tells Team B that it should select a run defense with a 0.30 probability and a pass defense with a 0.70 probability. The expected yardage gained, which is the value of the game, will remain 4.5 yards per play.

Thus, we have the optimal mixed strategy solution for the football game example. Any 2×2 two-person, zero-sum mixed strategy game can be solved algebraically as shown in this example. If a larger two-person, zero-sum game involves a mixed strategy, solving it is a bit more complicated.

A Larger Mixed Strategy Game

Consider the following two-person, zero-sum game:

		Player B		
		b_1	b_2	b_3
Player A	a_1	0	−1	2
	a_2	5	4	−3
	a_3	2	3	−4

Following the usual procedure for identifying a pure strategy, we compute the row minimums and the column maximums:

		Player B			
		b_1	b_2	b_3	**Minimum**
Player A	a_1	0	−1	2	⊖1
	a_2	5	4	−3	−3
	a_3	2	3	−4	−4
Maximum		5	4	②	

The maximum of the row minimums is -1 and the minimum of the column maximums is 2. Because the maximin and minimax values are not equal, the two-person, zero-sum game does not have an optimal pure strategy. However, with a problem larger than 2×2, we cannot use the algebraic solution for the mixed strategy probabilities as we did in the previous example.

If a game larger than 2×2 requires a mixed strategy, we first look for dominated strategies in order to reduce the size of the game. A **dominated strategy** exists if another strategy *is at least as good* regardless of what the opponent does. For example, consider strategies a_2 and a_3. The payoff table shows that in column b_1, $5 > 2$; in column b_2, $4 > 3$; and in column b_3, $-3 > -4$. Thus, regardless of what Player B does, Player A will always prefer the higher values of strategy a_2 compared to strategy a_3. Thus, strategy a_3 is dominated by strategy a_2 and can be dropped from consideration by Player A. Eliminating dominated strategies from the game reduces its size. After eliminating a_3, the reduced game becomes

		\multicolumn{3}{c}{Player B}		
		b_1	b_2	b_3
Player A	a_1	0	-1	2
	a_2	5	4	-3

Next, we look for more dominated strategies. Player A finds no other dominated strategies. However, consider strategies b_1 and b_2 for Player B. Remember that Player B is interested in smaller values. The payoff table shows that in row a_1, $-1 < 0$, and in row a_2, $4 < 5$. Thus, regardless of what Player A does, Player B would always prefer the smaller values of strategy b_2 compared to strategy b_1. Thus, strategy b_1 is dominated by strategy b_2 and can be eliminated from the game. With this dominated strategy eliminated, the reduced game becomes

		\multicolumn{2}{c}{Player B}	
		b_1	b_3
Player A	a_1	-1	2
	a_2	4	-3

Problem 14 asks you to find the optimal probabilities for this example.

By successively eliminating dominated strategies, we reduce the game to a 2×2 game. The algebraic solution procedure described earlier in this section can now be used to identify the optimal probabilities for the mixed strategy solution.

Identifying and eliminating dominated strategies may reduce the game to a 2×2 game. If so, an algebraic procedure may be used to determine the mixed strategy solution.

Finally, it is important to realize that no hard-and-fast rule identifies dominated strategies. Basically, the analyst must make pairwise comparisons of the decision strategies in an attempt to identify dominated strategies. The goal is to identify and eliminate dominated strategies sequentially in order to reduce the game to a 2×2 game so that an algebraic solution procedure can be used to solve for the mixed strategy probabilities.

Summary of Steps for Solving Two-Person, Zero-Sum Games

The following summary shows the steps used to solve two-person, zero-sum games:

1. Use the maximin procedure for Player A and the minimax procedure for Player B to determine whether a pure strategy solution exists. (See previous steps for identifying a pure strategy.) If a pure strategy exists, it is the optimal solution.
2. If a pure strategy does not exist and the game is larger than 2×2, identify a dominated strategy to eliminate a row or column. Develop the reduced payoff table and continue to use dominance to eliminate as many additional rows and columns as possible.
3. If the reduced game is 2×2, solve for the optimal mixed strategy probabilities algebraically.

In 1994, John Harsanui. John Nash, and Reinhard Selten received the Nobel Prize in Economics for their work on noncooperative game theory.

If the game cannot be reduced to a 2×2 game, a linear programming model can be used to solve for the optimal mixed strategy probabilities. The formulation of a linear programming model to solve these larger game theory problems is beyond the scope of this text.

Extensions

Problem 17 demonstrates a simple constant-sum game theory problem.

We presented the basic model for two-person, zero-sum games. However, game theory models extend beyond two-person, zero-sum games. One extension is a two-person, constant-sum game that occurs when the payoffs for the strategies chosen sum to a constant other than zero. In addition, game theory can be extended to include more general n-person games. Cooperative games where players are allowed preplay communications are another variation. Finally, some game theory models allow an infinite number of strategies to be available for the players.

Summary

In this chapter we showed how utility could be used in decision-making situations in which monetary value did not provide an adequate measure of the payoffs. Utility is a measure of the total worth of a consequence. As such, utility takes into account the decision maker's assessment of all aspects of a consequence, including profit, loss, risk, and perhaps additional nonmonetary factors. The examples showed how the use of expected utility can lead to decision recommendations that differ from those based on expected monetary value.

A decision maker's judgment must be used to establish the utility for each consequence. We presented a step-by-step procedure to determine a decision maker's utility for monetary payoffs. We also discussed how conservative, risk-avoiding decision makers assess utility differently from more aggressive, risk-taking decision makers. If the decision maker is risk neutral, we showed that the solution using expected utility is identical to the solution using expected monetary value.

We presented an introduction to game theory by describing how to solve two-person, zero-sum games. In these games, the two players end up with the sum of the gain (loss) to one player and the loss (gain) to the other player always equal to zero. We described the steps that can be used to determine whether a two-person, zero-sum game results in an optimal pure strategy. If a pure strategy is optimal, a saddle point determines the value of the game. If an optimal pure strategy does not exist for a two-person, zero-sum 2×2 game, we showed how to identify an optimal mixed strategy. With a mixed strategy, each player uses probability to select a strategy for each play of the game. We showed how dominance could be used to reduce the size of mixed strategy games. If the elimination of dominated strategies can reduce a larger game to a 2×2 game, an algebraic solution procedure can be used to find a solution. If the game cannot be reduced to a 2×2 game, a linear programming model is needed to determine the optimal mixed strategy solution.

Glossary

Dominated strategy A strategy is dominated if another strategy is at least as good for every strategy that the opposing player may employ. A dominated strategy will never be selected by the player and as such can be eliminated in order to reduce the size of the game.

Expected utility (EU) The weighted average of the utilities associated with a decision alternative. The weights are the state-of-nature probabilities.

Game theory The study of decision situations in which two or more players compete as adversaries. The combination of strategies chosen by the players determines the value of the game to each player.

Lottery A hypothetical investment alternative with a probability p of obtaining the best payoff and a probability of $(1 - p)$ of obtaining the worst payoff.

Mixed strategy A game solution in which the player randomly selects the strategy to play from among several strategies with positive probabilities. The solution to the mixed strategy game identifies the probabilities that each player should use to randomly select the strategy to play.

Pure strategy A game solution that provides a single best strategy for each player.

Risk avoider A decision maker who would choose a guaranteed payoff over a lottery with a better expected payoff.

Risk taker A decision maker who would choose a lottery over a better guaranteed payoff.

Risk-neutral decision maker A decision maker who is neutral to risk. For this decision maker the decision alternative with the best expected monetary value is identical to the alternative with the highest expected utility.

Saddle point A condition that exists when pure strategies are optimal for both players in a two-person, zero-sum game. The saddle point occurs at the intersection of the optimal strategies for the players, and the value of the saddle point is the value of the game.

Two-person, zero-sum game A game with two players in which the gain to one player is equal to the loss to the other player.

Utility A measure of the total worth of a consequence reflecting a decision maker's attitude toward considerations such as profit, loss, and risk.

Utility function for money A curve that depicts the relationship between monetary value and utility.

Problems

1. A firm has three investment alternatives. Payoffs are in thousands of dollars.

| | Economic Conditions | | |
Decision Alternative	Up, s_1	Stable, s_2	Down, s_3
Investment A, d_1	100	25	0
Investment B, d_2	75	50	25
Investment C, d_3	50	50	50
Probabilities	0.40	0.30	0.30

a. Using the expected value approach, which decision is preferred?
b. For the lottery having a payoff of $100,000 with probability p and $0 with probability $(1 - p)$, two decision makers expressed the following indifference probabilities. Find the most preferred decision for each decision maker using the expected utility approach.

	Indifference Probability (p)	
Profit	**Decision Maker A**	**Decision Maker B**
$75,000	0.80	0.60
$50,000	0.60	0.30
$25,000	0.30	0.15

c. Why don't decision makers A and B select the same decision alternative?

2. Alexander Industries is considering purchasing an insurance policy for its new office building in St. Louis, Missouri. The policy has an annual cost of $10,000. If Alexander Industries doesn't purchase the insurance and minor fire damage occurs, a cost of $100,000 is anticipated; the cost if major or total destruction occurs is $200,000. The costs, including the state-of-nature probabilities, are as follows:

		Damage	
Decision Alternative	**None, s_1**	**Minor, s_2**	**Major, s_3**
Purchase insurance, d_1	10,000	10,000	10,000
Do not purchase insurance, d_2	0	100,000	200,000
Probabilities	0.96	0.03	0.01

a. Using the expected value approach, what decision do you recommend?
b. What lottery would you use to assess utilities? (*Note:* Because the data are costs, the best payoff is $0.)
c. Assume that you found the following indifference probabilities for the lottery defined in part (b). What decision would you recommend?

Cost	Indifference Probability
10,000	$p = 0.99$
100,000	$p = 0.60$

d. Do you favor using expected value or expected utility for this decision problem? Why?

3. In a certain state lottery, a lottery ticket costs $2. In terms of the decision to purchase or not to purchase a lottery ticket, suppose that the following payoff table applies:

	State of Nature	
Decision Alternatives	**Win, s_1**	**Lose, s_2**
Purchase lottery ticket, d_1	300,000	−2
Do not purchase lottery ticket, d_2	0	0

a. A realistic estimate of the chances of winning is 1 in 250,000. Use the expected value approach to recommend a decision.

b. If a particular decision maker assigns an indifference probability of 0.000001 to the $0 payoff, would this individual purchase a lottery ticket? Use expected utility to justify your answer.

4. Two different routes accommodate travel between two cities. Route A normally takes 60 minutes and route B normally takes 45 minutes. If traffic problems are encountered on route A, the travel time increases to 70 minutes; traffic problems on route B increase travel time to 90 minutes. The probability of a delay is 0.20 for route A and 0.30 for route B.

a. Using the expected value approach, what is the recommended route?

b. If utilities are to be assigned to the travel times, what is the appropriate lottery? (*Note:* The smaller times should reflect higher utilities.)

c. Use the lottery of part (b) and assume that the decision maker expresses indifference probabilities of

$$p = 0.80 \quad \text{for 60 minutes}$$
$$p = 0.60 \quad \text{for 70 minutes}$$

What route should this decision maker select? Is the decision maker a risk taker or a risk avoider?

5. Three decision makers have assessed utilities for the following decision problem (payoff in dollars):

		State of Nature	
Decision Alternative	s_1	s_2	s_3
d_1	20	50	−20
d_2	80	100	−100

The indifference probabilities are as follows:

	Indifference Probability (p)		
Payoff	**Decision Maker A**	**Decision Maker B**	**Decision Maker C**
100	1.00	1.00	1.00
80	0.95	0.70	0.90
50	0.90	0.60	0.75
20	0.70	0.45	0.60
−20	0.50	0.25	0.40
−100	0.00	0.00	0.00

a. Plot the utility function for money for each decision maker.

b. Classify each decision maker as a risk avoider, a risk taker, or risk neutral.

c. For the payoff of 20, what is the premium that the risk avoider will pay to avoid risk? What is the premium that the risk taker will pay to have the opportunity of the high payoff?

6. In Problem 5, if $P(s_1) = 0.25$, $P(s_2) = 0.50$, and $P(s_3) = 0.25$, find a recommended decision for each of the three decision makers. (*Note:* For the same decision problem, different utilities can lead to different decisions.)

7. Suppose that the point spread for a particular sporting event is 10 points and that with this spread you are convinced you would have a 0.60 probability of winning a bet on your team. However, the local bookie will accept only a $1000 bet. Assuming that such bets are legal, would you bet on your team? (Disregard any commission charged by the bookie.) Remember that *you* must pay losses out of your own pocket. Your payoff table is as follows:

	State of Nature	
Decision Alternatives	**You Win**	**You Lose**
Bet	$1000	−$1000
Don't bet	$0	$0

a. What decision does the expected value approach recommend?
b. What is *your* indifference probability for the $0 payoff? (Although this choice isn't easy, be as realistic as possible. It is required for an analysis that reflects your attitude toward risk.)
c. What decision would you make based on the expected utility approach? In this case are you a risk taker or a risk avoider?
d. Would other individuals assess the same utility values you do? Explain.
e. If your decision in part (c) was to place the bet, repeat the analysis assuming a minimum bet of $10,000.

8. A Las Vegas roulette wheel has 38 different numerical values. If an individual bets on one number and wins, the payoff is 35 to 1.
a. Show a payoff table for a $10 bet on one number for decision alternatives of bet and do not bet.
b. What is the recommended decision using the expected value approach?
c. Do the Las Vegas casinos want risk-taking or risk-avoiding customers? Explain.
d. What range of utility values would a decision maker have to assign to the $0 payoff in order to have expected utility justify a decision to place the $10 bet?

9. A new product has the following profit projections and associated probabilities:

Profit	Probability
$150,000	0.10
$100,000	0.25
$ 50,000	0.20
$0	0.15
−$ 50,000	0.20
−$100,000	0.10

a. Use the expected value approach to decide whether to market the new product.
b. Because of the high dollar values involved, especially the possibility of a $100,000 loss, the marketing vice president has expressed some concern about the use of the expected value approach. As a consequence, if a utility analysis is performed, what is the appropriate lottery?
c. Assume that the following indifference probabilities are assigned. Do the utilities reflect the behavior of a risk taker or a risk avoider?

Profit	Indifference Probability(p)
$100,000	0.95
$ 50,000	0.70
$0	0.50
−$ 50,000	0.25

    d.   Use expected utility to make a recommended decision.

    e.   Should the decision maker feel comfortable with the final decision recommended by the analysis?

10.   A television network has been receiving low ratings for its programs. Currently, management is considering two alternatives for the Monday night 8:00 P.M.–9:00 P.M. time slot: a comedy with a well-known star or a reality show. The percentages of viewing audience estimates depend on the degree of program acceptance. The relevant data are as follows:

	Percentage of Viewing Audience	
Program Acceptance	Comedy	Reality Show
High	30%	40%
Moderate	25%	20%
Poor	20%	15%

The probabilities associated with program acceptance levels are as follows:

	Probability	
Program Acceptance	Comedy	Reality Show
High	0.30	0.30
Moderate	0.60	0.40
Poor	0.10	0.30

    a.   Using the expected value approach, which program should the network choose?

    b.   For a utility analysis, what is the appropriate lottery?

    c.   Based on the lottery in part (b), assume that the network's program manager has assigned the following indifference probabilities. Based on the use of utility measures, which program would you recommend? Is the manager a risk taker or a risk avoider?

Percentage of Audience	Indifference Probability (p)
30%	0.40
25%	0.30
20%	0.10

11.   Consider the following two-person, zero-sum game. Identify the pure strategy. What is the value of the game?

		Player B		
		b_1	b_2	b_3
Player A	a_1	8	5	7
	a_2	2	4	10

12. Two opposing armies, Red and Blue, must each decide whether to attack or defend. These decisions are made without knowledge of the opposing army's decision. The payoff table, in terms of value of property gained or lost for the Red Army, appears below. Any gains for the Red Army are losses for the Blue Army.

		Blue Army	
		Attack	Defend
Red Army	Attack	30	50
	Defend	40	0

    a. What is the optimal mixed strategy for the Red Army?
    b. What is the optimal mixed strategy for the Blue Army?

13. Two Indiana state senate candidates must decide which city to visit the day before the November election. The same four cities—Indianapolis, Evansville, Fort Wayne, and South Bend—are available for both candidates. These cities are listed as strategies 1 to 4 for each candidate. Travel plans must be made in advance, so the candidates must decide which city to visit prior to knowing the other candidate's plans. Values in the following table show thousands of voters for the Republican candidate based on the strategies selected by the two candidates. Which city should each candidate visit, and what is the value of the game?

		Democrat Candidate			
		Indianapolis	Evansville	Fort Wayne	South Bend
		b_1	b_2	b_3	b_4
Republican Candidate	Indianapolis, a_1	0	−15	−8	20
	Evansville, a_2	30	−5	5	−10
	Fort Wayne, a_3	10	−25	0	20
	South Bend, a_4	20	20	10	15

14. In Section 5.5, we showed the following two-person, zero-sum game had a mixed strategy:

		Player B		
		b_1	b_2	b_3
Player A	a_1	0	−1	2
	a_2	5	4	−3
	a_3	2	3	−4

    a. Use dominance to reduce the game to a 2 × 2 game. Which strategies are dominated?
    b. Determine the optimal mixed strategy solution.
    c. What is the value of the game?

15. In a gambling game, Player A and Player B both have a $1 and a $5 bill. Each player selects one of the bills without the other player knowing the bill selected. Simultaneously they both reveal the bills selected. If the bills do not match, Player A wins Player B's bill. If the bills match, Player B wins Player A's bill.
     a. Develop the game theory table for this game. The values should be expressed as the gains (or losses) for Player A.
     b. Is there a pure strategy? Why or why not?
     c. Determine the optimal strategies and the value of this game. Does the game favor one player over the other?
     d. Suppose Player B decides to deviate from the optimal strategy and begins playing each bill 50% of the time. What should Player A do to improve Player A's winnings? Comment on why it is important to follow an optimal game theory strategy.

16. Two companies compete for a share of the soft drink market. Each worked with an advertising agency in order to develop alternative advertising strategies for the coming year. A variety of television advertisements, product promotions, in-store displays, and so on provides four different strategies for each company. The following table summarizes the projected change in market share for Company A once the two companies select their advertising strategy for the coming year. What is the optimal solution to this game for each of the players? What is the value of the game?

		Company B			
		b_1	b_2	b_3	b_4
	a_1	3	0	2	4
Company A	a_2	2	−2	1	0
	a_3	4	2	5	6
	a_4	−2	6	−1	0

17. If a soccer game ends in a tie, it goes into a penalty-kick shootout in which each team chooses five players to take penalty kicks. The team that makes the most subsequent penalty kicks wins the game. In a penalty-kick shootout, the shooter and the keeper each decide simultaneously on a direction to move. They can choose left, right, or middle. These strategies yield the following game theory table, where the first value is the shooter's probability of scoring and the second value is the keeper's probability of stopping the shot:

		Keeper		
		Left	Center	Right
	Left	0.35, 0.65	0.90, 0.10	0.85. 0.15
Shooter	Center	0.30, 0.70	0.25, 0.75	0.45, 0.55
	Right	0.95, 0.05	0.90, 0.10	0.30, 0.70

This is an example of a constant-sum game since each pair of entries in the game theory table sums to 1. This can be analyzed in the same manner as a zero-sum game.
     a. Use dominance to reduce the game to a 2 × 2 game. Which strategies are dominated?
     b. What is the solution to this game for the shooter and for the keeper?
     c. What is the shooter's expected probability of scoring?

Case Problem Utility, Game Theory, and Product Line Extension Decisions

ABC, Inc. and XYZ, Co. are the two dominant companies providing chargers, adapters, and other accessories for cell phones. Each of these Silicon Valley companies is developing a new line of smartphone accessories, and each has a choice of technologies to use for these accessories. Each company can choose to focus on older (cheaper) technology, recent (more expensive) technology, or cutting-edge (very expensive) technology. The share each company will gain or lose in the cell-phone accessories market depends on its technology choice and the technology choice of its competitor. The choice in technology investment must be made by each company before its competitor's choice is revealed.

ABC, Inc. and XYZ, Co. are both led by young, aggressive CEOs; ABC's CEO is Jack Webster and XYZ is run by Curtis Madsen. The CEOs of ABC and XYZ are each trying to determine the best technology in which to invest. The following tables provide market share values and indifference probability values, p, for both Jack Webster (ABC) and Curtis Madsen (XYZ). Jack and Curtis have identical indifference probability values.

Market Share Gain (Loss)	Indifference Probability, p
25	—
20	0.85
15	0.70
10	0.58
5	0.45
0	0.35
−5	0.27
−10	0.20
−15	0.12
−20	0.05
−25	—

The following table shows the three possible technology investments (old, recent, and cutting edge) for ABC and XYZ and the resulting market share gain (or loss) for ABC, Inc. Because ABC and XYZ are the dominant companies in this market, whatever market share is gained by ABC is lost by XYZ and vice versa.

		XYZ, Co.		
		Old	Recent	Cutting Edge
	Old	5	−10	−15
ABC, Inc.	**Recent**	10	−5	−10
	Cutting Edge	20	5	−20

Managerial Report

Perform an analysis of the best decision of technology investment for ABC Inc. Prepare a report you would provide to Jack Webster that summarizes your analysis and findings. Include the following:

1. A graph of the utility function for ABC, Inc. Explain whether you would characterize Jack Webster as a risk taker or a risk avoider and why.
2. Payoff tables for ABC, Inc. and XYZ, Co. using expected utilities for ABC and XYZ.
3. Recommendation for the best decision for ABC, Inc. and XYZ, Co. Is this a zero-sum game?
4. Detailed calculations and analysis to support your recommendation.
5. A discussion of how the expected utilities would change if ABC is taken over by a more conservative, risk-avoiding firm.

CHAPTER 6

Time Series Analysis and Forecasting

CONTENTS

The purpose of this chapter is to provide an introduction to time series analysis and forecasting. Suppose we are asked to provide quarterly forecasts of sales for one of our company's products over the coming one-year period. Production schedules, raw materials purchasing, inventory policies, and sales quotas will all be affected by the quarterly forecasts we provide. Consequently, poor forecasts may result in poor planning and increased costs for the company. How should we go about providing the quarterly sales forecasts? Good judgment, intuition, and an awareness of the state of the economy may give us a rough idea or "feeling" of what is likely to happen in the future, but converting that feeling into a number that can be used as next year's sales forecast is challenging. The Q.M. in Action, Forecasting Energy Needs in the Utility Industry, describes the role that forecasting plays in the utility industry.

A forecast is simply a prediction of what will happen in the future. Managers must accept that regardless of the technique used, they will not be able to develop perfect forecasts.

Forecasting methods can be classified as qualitative or quantitative. Qualitative methods generally involve the use of expert judgment to develop forecasts. Such methods are appropriate when historical data on the variable being forecast are either unavailable or not applicable. Quantitative forecasting methods can be used when (1) past information about the variable being forecast is available, (2) the information can be quantified, and (3) it is reasonable to assume that past is prologue (i.e., the pattern of the past will continue into the future). We will focus exclusively on quantitative forecasting methods in this chapter.

If the historical data are restricted to past values of the variable to be forecast, the forecasting procedure is called a *time series method* and the historical data are referred to as a

Q.M. *in* ACTION

FORECASTING ENERGY NEEDS IN THE UTILITY INDUSTRY*

Duke Energy is a diversified energy company with a portfolio of natural gas and electric businesses and an affiliated real estate company. In 2006, Duke Energy merged with Cinergy of Cincinnati, Ohio, to create one of North America's largest energy companies, with assets totaling more than $70 billion. As a result of this merger the Cincinnati Gas & Electric Company became part of Duke Energy. Today, Duke Energy services over 5.5 million retail electric and gas customers in North Carolina, South Carolina, Ohio, Kentucky, Indiana, and Ontario, Canada.

Forecasting in the utility industry offers some unique perspectives. Because energy is difficult to store, this product must be generated to meet the instantaneous requirements of the customers. Electrical shortages are not just lost sales, but "brownouts" or "blackouts." This situation places an unusual burden on the utility forecaster. On the positive side, the demand for energy and the sale of energy are more predictable than for many other products. Also, unlike the situation in a multiproduct firm, a great

amount of forecasting effort and expertise can be concentrated on the two products: gas and electricity.

The largest observed electric demand for any given period, such as an hour, a day, a month, or a year, is defined as the peak load. The forecast of the annual electric peak load guides the timing decision for constructing future generating units, and the financial impact of this decision is great. Obviously, a timing decision that leads to having the unit available no sooner than necessary is crucial.

The energy forecasts are important in other ways also. For example, purchases of coal as fuel for the generating units are based on the forecast levels of energy needed. The revenue from the electric operations of the company is determined from forecasted sales, which in turn enters into the planning of rate changes and external financing. These planning and decision-making processes are among the most important managerial activities in the company. It is imperative that the decision makers have the best forecast information available to assist them in arriving at these decisions.

---

*Based on information provided by Dr. Richard Evans of Duke Energy.

time series. The objective of time series analysis is to uncover a pattern in the historical data or time series and then extrapolate the pattern into the future; the forecast is based solely on past values of the variable and/or on past forecast errors.

In Section 6.1 we discuss the various kinds of time series that a forecaster might be faced with in practice. These include a constant or horizontal pattern, a trend, a seasonal pattern, both a trend and a seasonal pattern, and a cyclical pattern. In order to build a quantitative forecasting model it is also necessary to have a measurement of forecast accuracy. Different measurements of forecast accuracy, and their respective advantages and disadvantages, are discussed in Section 6.2. In Section 6.3 we consider the simplest case, which is a horizontal or constant pattern. For this pattern, we develop the classical moving average, weighted moving average, and exponential smoothing models. Many time series have a trend, and taking this trend into account is important; in Section 6.4 we provide regression models for finding the best model parameters when a linear trend is present. Finally, in Section 6.5 we show how to incorporate both a trend and seasonality into a forecasting model.

Time Series Patterns

A **time series** is a sequence of observations on a variable measured at successive points in time or over successive periods of time. The measurements may be taken every hour, day, week, month, or year, or at any other regular interval.[1] The pattern of the data is an important factor in understanding how the time series has behaved in the past. If such behavior can be expected to continue in the future, we can use it to guide us in selecting an appropriate forecasting method.

To identify the underlying pattern in the data, a useful first step is to construct a time series plot. A **time series plot** is a graphical presentation of the relationship between time and the time series variable; time is represented on the horizontal axis and values of the time series variable are shown on the vertical axis. Let us first review some of the common types of data patterns that can be identified when examining a time series plot.

Horizontal Pattern

A horizontal pattern exists when the data fluctuate randomly around a constant mean over time. To illustrate a time series with a horizontal pattern, consider the 12 weeks of data in Table 6.1. These data show the number of gallons of gasoline (in 1000s) sold by a gasoline distributor in Bennington, Vermont, over the past 12 weeks. The average value or mean for this time series is 19.25 or 19,250 gallons per week. Figure 6.1 shows a time series plot for these data. Note how the data fluctuate around the sample mean of 19,250 gallons. Although random variability is present, we would say that these data follow a horizontal pattern.

The term **stationary time series**[2] is used to denote a time series whose statistical properties are independent of time. In particular this means that

1. The process generating the data has a constant mean.
2. The variability of the time series is constant over time.

A time series plot for a stationary time series will always exhibit a horizontal pattern with random fluctuations. However, simply observing a horizontal pattern is not sufficient

---

[1]We limit our discussion to time series for which the values of the series are recorded at equal intervals. Cases in which the observations are made at unequal intervals are beyond the scope of this text.

[2]For a formal definition of stationarity, see K. Ord and R. Fildes (2012), *Principles of Business Forecasting*. Mason, OH: Cengage Learning, p. 155.

TABLE 6.1 GASOLINE SALES TIME SERIES

Gasoline

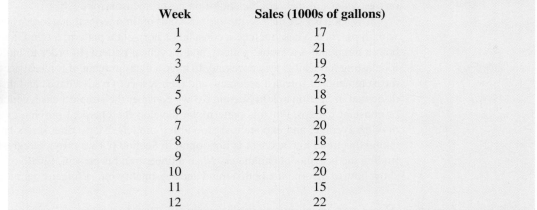

Week	Sales (1000s of gallons)
1	17
2	21
3	19
4	23
5	18
6	16
7	20
8	18
9	22
10	20
11	15
12	22

FIGURE 6.1 GASOLINE SALES TIME SERIES PLOT

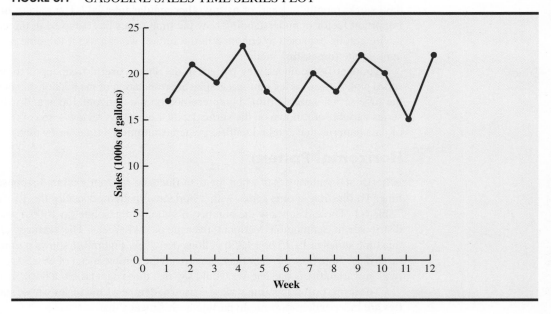

evidence to conclude that the time series is stationary. More advanced texts on forecasting discuss procedures for determining if a time series is stationary and provide methods for transforming a time series that is nonstationary into a stationary series.

Changes in business conditions often result in a time series with a horizontal pattern that shifts to a new level at some point in time. For instance, suppose the gasoline distributor signs a contract with the Vermont Sate Police to provide gasoline for state police cars located in southern Vermont beginning in week 13. With this new contract, the distributor naturally expects to see a substantial increase in weekly sales starting in week 13. Table 6.2 shows the number of gallons of gasoline sold for the original time series and the 10 weeks

TABLE 6.2 GASOLINE SALES TIME SERIES AFTER OBTAINING THE CONTRACT WITH THE VERMONT STATE POLICE

WEB file

GasolineRevised

Week	Sales (1000s of gallons)	Week	Sales (1000s of gallons)
1	17	12	22
2	21	13	31
3	19	14	34
4	23	15	31
5	18	16	33
6	16	17	28
7	20	18	32
8	18	19	30
9	22	20	29
10	20	21	34
11	15	22	33

after signing the new contract. Figure 6.2 shows the corresponding time series plot. Note the increased level of the time series beginning in week 13. This change in the level of the time series makes it more difficult to choose an appropriate forecasting method. Selecting a forecasting method that adapts well to changes in the level of a time series is an important consideration in many practical applications.

Trend Pattern

Although time series data generally exhibit random fluctuations, a time series may also show gradual shifts or movements to relatively higher or lower values over a longer period

FIGURE 6.2 GASOLINE SALES TIME SERIES PLOT AFTER OBTAINING THE CONTRACT WITH THE VERMONT STATE POLICE

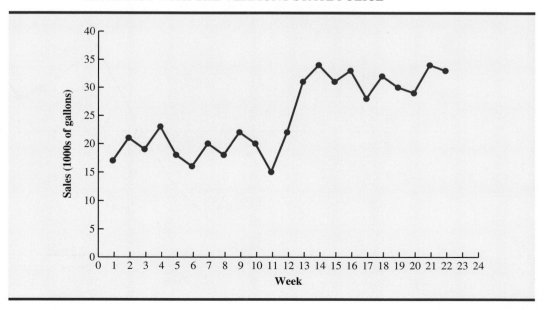

of time. If a time series plot exhibits this type of behavior, we say that a **trend pattern** exists. A trend is usually the result of long-term factors such as population increases or decreases, shifting demographic characteristics of the population, improving technology, and/or changes in consumer preferences.

To illustrate a time series with a linear trend pattern, consider the time series of bicycle sales for a particular manufacturer over the past 10 years, as shown in Table 6.3 and Figure 6.3. Note that 21,600 bicycles were sold in year 1, 22,900 were sold in year 2, and so on. In year 10, the most recent year, 31,400 bicycles were sold. Visual inspection of the time series plot shows some up and down movement over the past 10 years, but the time series seems also to have a systematically increasing or upward trend.

TABLE 6.3   BICYCLE SALES TIME SERIES

Bicycle

Year	Sales (1000s)
1	21.6
2	22.9
3	25.5
4	21.9
5	23.9
6	27.5
7	31.5
8	29.7
9	28.6
10	31.4

FIGURE 6.3   BICYCLE SALES TIME SERIES PLOT

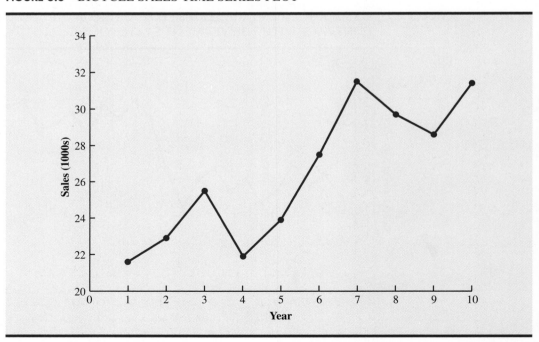

The trend for the bicycle sales time series appears to be linear and increasing over time, but sometimes a trend can be described better by other types of patterns. For instance, the data in Table 6.4 and the corresponding time series plot in Figure 6.4 show the sales revenue for a cholesterol drug since the company won FDA approval for the drug 10 years ago. The time series increases in a nonlinear fashion; that is, the rate of change of revenue does not increase by a constant amount from one year to the next. In fact, the revenue appears to be growing in an exponential fashion. Exponential relationships such as this are appropriate when the percentage change from one period to the next is relatively constant.

Seasonal Pattern

The trend of a time series can be identified by analyzing movements in historical data over multiple years. **Seasonal patterns** are recognized by observing recurring patterns

TABLE 6.4 CHOLESTEROL DRUG REVENUE TIME SERIES ($ MILLIONS)

WEB file

Cholesterol

Year	Revenue
1	23.1
2	21.3
3	27.4
4	34.6
5	33.8
6	43.2
7	59.5
8	64.4
9	74.2
10	99.3

FIGURE 6.4 CHOLESTEROL DRUG REVENUE TIMES SERIES PLOT ($ MILLIONS)

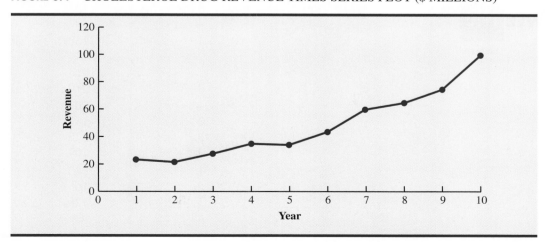

over successive periods of time. For example, a manufacturer of swimming pools expects low sales activity in the fall and winter months, with peak sales in the spring and summer months to occur each year. Manufacturers of snow removal equipment and heavy clothing, however, expect the opposite yearly pattern. Not surprisingly, the pattern for a time series plot that exhibits a recurring pattern over a one-year period due to seasonal influences is called a seasonal pattern. While we generally think of seasonal movement in a time series as occurring within one year, time series data can also exhibit seasonal patterns of less than one year in duration. For example, daily traffic volume shows within-the-day "seasonal" behavior, with peak levels occurring during rush hours, moderate flow during the rest of the day and early evening, and light flow from midnight to early morning. Another example of an industry with sales that exhibit easily discernible seasonal patterns within a day is the restaurant industry.

As an example of a seasonal pattern, consider the number of umbrellas sold at a clothing store over the past five years. Table 6.5 shows the time series and Figure 6.5 shows the corresponding time series plot. The time series plot does not indicate a long-term trend in sales. In fact, unless you look carefully at the data, you might conclude that the data follow a horizontal pattern with random fluctuation. However, closer inspection of the fluctuations in the time series plot reveals a systematic pattern in the data that occurs within each year. That is, the first and third quarters have moderate sales, the second quarter has the highest sales, and the fourth quarter tends to have the lowest sales volume. Thus, we would conclude that a quarterly seasonal pattern is present.

TABLE 6.5   UMBRELLA SALES TIME SERIES

Umbrella

Year	Quarter	Sales
1	1	125
	2	153
	3	106
	4	88
2	1	118
	2	161
	3	133
	4	102
3	1	138
	2	144
	3	113
	4	80
4	1	109
	2	137
	3	125
	4	109
5	1	130
	2	165
	3	128
	4	96

FIGURE 6.5 UMBRELLA SALES TIME SERIES PLOT

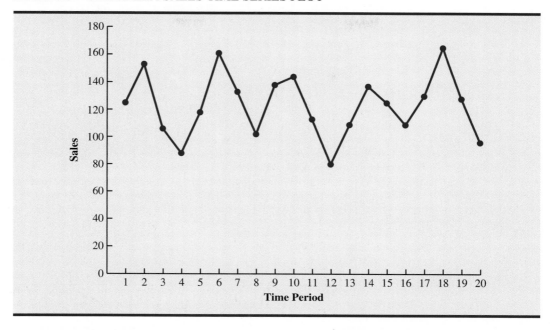

Trend and Seasonal Pattern

Some time series include both a trend and a seasonal pattern. For instance, the data in Table 6.6 and the corresponding time series plot in Figure 6.6 show quarterly television set sales for a particular manufacturer over the past four years. Clearly an increasing trend is

TABLE 6.6 QUARTERLY TELEVISION SET SALES TIME SERIES

TVSales

Year	Quarter	Sales (1000s)
1	1	4.8
	2	4.1
	3	6.0
	4	6.5
2	1	5.8
	2	5.2
	3	6.8
	4	7.4
3	1	6.0
	2	5.6
	3	7.5
	4	7.8
4	1	6.3
	2	5.9
	3	8.0
	4	8.4

FIGURE 6.6 QUARTERLY TELEVISION SET SALES TIME SERIES PLOT

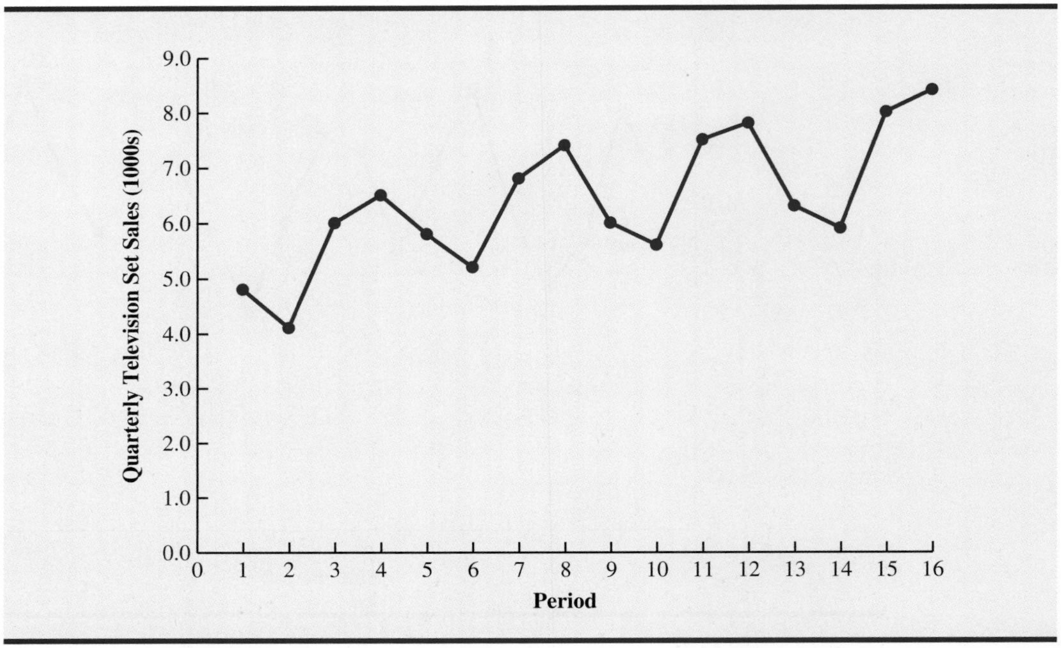

present. However, Figure 6.6 also indicates that sales are lowest in the second quarter of each year and highest in quarters 3 and 4. Thus, we conclude that a seasonal pattern also exists for television sales. In such cases we need to use a forecasting method that is capable of dealing with both trend and seasonality.

Cyclical Pattern

A **cyclical pattern** exists if the time series plot shows an alternating sequence of points below and above the trend line that lasts for more than one year. Many economic time series exhibit cyclical behavior with regular runs of observations below and above the trend line. Often the cyclical component of a time series is due to multiyear business cycles. For example, periods of moderate inflation followed by periods of rapid inflation can lead to a time series that alternates below and above a generally increasing trend line (e.g., a time series for housing costs). Business cycles are extremely difficult, if not impossible, to forecast. As a result, cyclical effects are often combined with long-term trend effects and referred to as trend-cycle effects. In this chapter we do not deal with cyclical effects that may be present in the time series.

Selecting a Forecasting Method

The underlying pattern in the time series is an important factor in selecting a forecasting method. Thus, a time series plot should be one of the first analytic tools employed when trying to determine which forecasting method to use. If we see a horizontal pattern, then we need to select a method appropriate for this type of pattern. Similarly, if we observe a trend in the data, then we need to use a forecasting method that is capable of handling a trend effectively. In the next two sections we illustrate methods for assessing forecast accuracy and consider forecasting models that can be used in situations for which the underlying pattern is horizontal; in other words, no trend or seasonal effects are present. We then consider methods appropriate when trend and/or seasonality are present in the data. The Q.M. in Action, Forecasting Demand for a Broad Product Line of Office Products, describes the considerations made by ACCO Brands when forecasting demand for its consumer and office products.

Q.M. *in* ACTION

FORECASTING DEMAND FOR A BROAD LINE OF OFFICE PRODUCTS*

ACCO Brands Corporation is one of the world's largest suppliers of branded office and consumer products and print finishing solutions. The company's widely recognized brands include AT-A-GLANCE®, Day-Timer®, Five Star®, GBC®, Hilroy®, Kensington®, Marbig®, Mead®, NOBO, Quartet®, Rexel, Swingline®, Tilibra®, Wilson Jones®, and many others.

Because it produces and markets a wide array of products with a myriad of demand characteristics, ACCO Brands relies heavily on sales forecasts in planning its manufacturing, distribution, and marketing activities. By viewing its relationship in terms of a supply chain, ACCO Brands and its customers (which are generally retail chains) establish close collaborative relationships and consider each other to be valued partners. As a result, ACCO Brands' customers share valuable information and data that serve as inputs into ACCO Brands' forecasting process.

In her role as a forecasting manager for ACCO Brands, Vanessa Baker appreciates the importance of this additional information. "We do separate forecasts of demand for each major customer," said Baker, "and we generally use twenty-four to thirty-six months of history to generate monthly forecasts twelve to eighteen months into the future. While trends are important, several of our major product lines, including school, planning and organizing, and decorative calendars, are heavily seasonal, and seasonal sales make up the bulk of our annual volume."

Daniel Marks, one of several account-level strategic forecast managers for ACCO Brands, adds,

The supply chain process includes the total lead time from identifying opportunities to making or procuring

the product to getting the product on the shelves to align with the forecasted demand; this can potentially take several months, so the accuracy of our forecasts is critical throughout each step of the supply chain. Adding to this challenge is the risk of obsolescence. We sell many dated items, such as planners and calendars, which have a natural, built-in obsolescence. In addition, many of our products feature designs that are fashion-conscious or contain pop culture images, and these products can also become obsolete very quickly as tastes and popularity change. An overly optimistic forecast for these products can be very costly, but an overly pessimistic forecast can result in lost sales potential and give our competitors an opportunity to take market share from us.

In addition to looking at trends, seasonal components, and cyclical patterns, Baker and Marks must contend with several other factors. Baker notes, "We have to adjust our forecasts for upcoming promotions by our customers." Marks agrees and adds:

We also have to go beyond just forecasting consumer demand; we must consider the retailer's specific needs in our order forecasts, such as what type of display will be used and how many units of a product must be on display to satisfy their presentation requirements. Current inventory is another factor—if a customer is carrying either too much or too little inventory, that will affect their future orders, and we need to reflect that in our forecasts. Will the product have a short life because it is tied to a cultural fad? What are the retailer's marketing and markdown strategies? Our knowledge of the environments in which our supply chain partners are competing helps us to forecast demand more accurately, and that reduces waste and makes our customers, as well as ACCO Brands, far more profitable.

---

*The authors are indebted to Vanessa Baker and Daniel Marks of ACCO Brands for providing input for this Q.M. in Action.

6.2 Forecast Accuracy

In this section we begin by developing forecasts for the gasoline time series shown in Table 6.1 using the simplest of all the forecasting methods, an approach that uses the most recent week's sales volume as the forecast for the next week. For instance, the distributor sold 17,000 gallons of gasoline in week 1; this value is used as the forecast for week 2. Next, we use 21, the actual value of sales in week 2, as the forecast for week 3, and so on. The forecasts obtained for the historical data using this method are shown in Table 6.7 in the column labeled Forecast. Because of its simplicity, this method is often referred to as a naïve forecasting method.

How accurate are the forecasts obtained using this naïve forecasting method? To answer this question we will introduce several measures of forecast accuracy. These measures are used to determine how well a particular forecasting method is able to reproduce the time series data that are already available. By selecting the method that is most accurate for the data already known, we hope to increase the likelihood that we will obtain more accurate forecasts for future time periods.

The key concept associated with measuring forecast accuracy is **forecast error**. If we denote Y_t and $\hat{Y}_t$ as the actual and forecasted values of the time series for period t, respectively, the forecasting error for period t is

$$e_t = Y_t - \hat{Y}_t \tag{6.1}$$

That is, the forecast error for time period t is the difference between the actual and the forecasted values for period t.

TABLE 6.7 COMPUTING FORECASTS AND MEASURES OF FORECAST ACCURACY USING THE MOST RECENT VALUE AS THE FORECAST FOR THE NEXT PERIOD

Week	Time Series Value	Forecast	Forecast Error	Absolute Value of Forecast Error	Squared Forecast Error	Percentage Error	Absolute Value of Percentage Error
1	17						
2	21	17	4	4	16	19.05	19.05
3	19	21	−2	2	4	−10.53	10.53
4	23	19	4	4	16	17.39	17.39
5	18	23	−5	5	25	−27.78	27.78
6	16	18	−2	2	4	−12.50	12.50
7	20	16	4	4	16	20.00	20.00
8	18	20	−2	2	4	−11.11	11.11
9	22	18	4	4	16	18.18	18.18
10	20	22	−2	2	4	−10.00	10.00
11	15	20	−5	5	25	−33.33	33.33
12	22	15	7	7	49	31.82	31.82
		Totals	5	41	179	1.19	211.69

For instance, because the distributor actually sold 21,000 gallons of gasoline in week 2 and the forecast, using the sales volume in week 1, was 17,000 gallons, the forecast error in week 2 is

$$\text{Forecast Error in week 2} = e_2 = Y_2 - \hat{Y}_2 = 21 - 17 = 4$$

The fact that the forecast error is positive indicates that in week 2 the forecasting method underestimated the actual value of sales. Next we use 21, the actual value of sales in week 2, as the forecast for week 3. Since the actual value of sales in week 3 is 19, the forecast error for week 3 is $e_3 = 19 - 21 = -2$. In this case, the negative forecast error indicates the forecast overestimated the actual value for week 3. Thus, the forecast error may be positive or negative, depending on whether the forecast is too low or too high. A complete summary of the forecast errors for this naïve forecasting method is shown in Table 6.7 in the column labeled Forecast Error. It is important to note that because we are using a past value of the time series to produce a forecast for period t, we do not have sufficient data to produce a naïve forecast for the first week of this time series.

A simple measure of forecast accuracy is the mean or average of the forecast errors. If we have n periods in our time series and k is the number of periods at the beginning of the time series for which we cannot produce a naïve forecast, the mean forecast error (MFE) is

$$\text{MFE} = \frac{\sum\limits_{t=k+1}^{n} e_t}{n - k} \qquad (6.2)$$

Table 6.7 shows that the sum of the forecast errors for the gasoline sales time series is 5; thus, the mean or average error is $5/11 = 0.45$. Because we do not have sufficient data to produce a naïve forecast for the first week of this time series, we must adjust our calculations in both the numerator and denominator accordingly. This is common in forecasting; we often use k past periods from the time series to produce forecasts, and so we frequently cannot produce forecasts for the first k periods. In those instances the summation in the numerator starts at the first value of t for which we have produced a forecast (so we begin the summation at $t = k + 1$), and the denominator (which is the number of periods in our time series for which we are able to produce a forecast) will also reflect these circumstances. In the gasoline example, although the time series consists of 12 values, to compute the mean error we divided the sum of the forecast errors by 11 because there are only 11 forecast errors (we cannot generate forecast sales for the first week using this naïve forecasting method).

Also note that in the gasoline time series, the mean forecast error is positive, which implies that the method is generally underforecasting; in other words, the observed values tend to be greater than the forecasted values. Because positive and negative forecast errors tend to offset one another, the mean error is likely to be small; thus, the mean error is not a very useful measure of forecast accuracy.

The **mean absolute error**, denoted MAE, is a measure of forecast accuracy that avoids the problem of positive and negative forecast errors offsetting one another. As you might expect given its name, MAE is the average of the absolute values of the forecast errors:

$$\text{MAE} = \frac{\sum\limits_{t=k+1}^{n} |e_t|}{n - k} \qquad (6.3)$$

This is also referred to as the mean absolute deviation or MAD. Table 6.7 shows that the sum of the absolute values of the forecast errors is 41; thus

$$\text{MAE} = \text{average of the absolute value of forecast errors} = \frac{41}{11} = 3.73$$

Another measure that avoids the problem of positive and negative errors offsetting each other is obtained by computing the average of the squared forecast errors. This measure of forecast accuracy, referred to as the **mean squared error**, is denoted MSE:

$$\text{MSE} = \frac{\sum_{t=k+1}^{n} e_t^2}{n - k} \qquad (6.4)$$

From Table 6.7, the sum of the squared errors is 179; hence,

$$\text{MSE} = \text{average of the sum of squared forecast errors} = \frac{179}{11} = 16.27$$

The size of MAE and MSE depends upon the scale of the data. As a result, it is difficult to make comparisons for different time intervals (such as comparing a method of forecasting monthly gasoline sales to a method of forecasting weekly sales) or to make comparisons across different time series (such as monthly sales of gasoline and monthly sales of oil filters). To make comparisons such as these we need to work with relative or percentage error measures. The **mean absolute percentage error**, denoted MAPE, is such a measure. To compute MAPE we must first compute the percentage error for each forecast:

$$\left(\frac{e_t}{Y_t}\right)100$$

For example, the percentage error corresponding to the forecast of 17 in week 2 is computed by dividing the forecast error in week 2 by the actual value in week 2 and multiplying the result by 100. For week 2 the percentage error is computed as follows:

$$\text{Percentage error for week 2} = \left(\frac{e_2}{Y_2}\right)100 = \left(\frac{4}{21}\right)100 = 19.05\%$$

Thus, the forecast error for week 2 is 19.05% of the observed value in week 2. A complete summary of the percentage errors is shown in Table 6.7 in the column labeled Percentage Error. In the next column, we show the absolute value of the percentage error. Finally, we find the MAPE, which is calculated as:

$$\text{MAPE} = \frac{\sum_{t=k+1}^{n} \left|\left(\frac{e_t}{Y_t}\right)100\right|}{n - k} \qquad (6.5)$$

Table 6.7 shows that the sum of the absolute values of the percentage errors is 211.69; thus

$$\text{MAPE} = \text{average of the absolute value of percentage forecast errors}$$

$$= \frac{211.69}{11} = 19.24\%$$

In summary, using the naïve (most recent observation) forecasting method, we obtained the following measures of forecast accuracy:

$$MAE = 3.73$$
$$MSE = 16.27$$
$$MAPE = 19.24\%$$

Try Problem 1 for practice in computing measures of forecast accuracy.

These measures of forecast accuracy simply measure how well the forecasting method is able to forecast historical values of the time series. Now, suppose we want to forecast sales for a future time period, such as week 13. In this case the forecast for week 13 is 22, the actual value of the time series in week 12. Is this an accurate estimate of sales for week 13? Unfortunately there is no way to address the issue of accuracy associated with forecasts for future time periods. However, if we select a forecasting method that works well for the historical data, and we have reason to believe the historical pattern will continue into the future, we should obtain forecasts that will ultimately be shown to be accurate.

Before closing this section, let us consider another method for forecasting the gasoline sales time series in Table 6.1. Suppose we use the average of all the historical data available as the forecast for the next period. We begin by developing a forecast for week 2. Since there is only one historical value available prior to week 2, the forecast for week 2 is just the time series value in week 1; thus, the forecast for week 2 is 17,000 gallons of gasoline. To compute the forecast for week 3, we take the average of the sales values in weeks 1 and 2. Thus,

$$\hat{Y}_3 = \frac{17 + 21}{2} = 19$$

Similarly, the forecast for week 4 is

$$\hat{Y}_4 = \frac{17 + 21 + 19}{3} = 19$$

The forecasts obtained using this method for the gasoline time series are shown in Table 6.8 in the column labeled Forecast. Using the results shown in Table 6.8, we obtained the following values of MAE, MSE, and MAPE:

$$MAE = \frac{26.81}{11} = 2.44$$

$$MSE = \frac{89.07}{11} = 8.10$$

$$MAPE = \frac{141.34}{11} = 12.85\%$$

We can now compare the accuracy of the two forecasting methods we have considered in this section by comparing the values of MAE, MSE, and MAPE for each method.

	Naïve Method	Average of Past Values
MAE	3.73	2.44
MSE	16.27	8.10
MAPE	19.24%	12.85%

TABLE 6.8   COMPUTING FORECASTS AND MEASURES OF FORECAST ACCURACY
USING THE AVERAGE OF ALL THE HISTORICAL DATA AS THE FORECAST
FOR THE NEXT PERIOD

Week	Time Series Value	Forecast	Forecast Error	Absolute Value of Forecast Error	Squared Forecast Error	Percentage Error	Absolute Value of Percentage Error
1	17						
2	21	17.00	4.00	4.00	16.00	19.05	19.05
3	19	19.00	0.00	0.00	0.00	0.00	0.00
4	23	19.00	4.00	4.00	16.00	17.39	17.39
5	18	20.00	−2.00	2.00	4.00	−11.11	11.11
6	16	19.60	−3.60	3.60	12.96	−22.50	22.50
7	20	19.00	1.00	1.00	1.00	5.00	5.00
8	18	19.14	−1.14	1.14	1.31	−6.35	6.35
9	22	19.00	3.00	3.00	9.00	13.64	13.64
10	20	19.33	0.67	0.67	0.44	3.33	3.33
11	15	19.40	−4.40	4.40	19.36	−29.33	29.33
12	22	19.00	3.00	3.00	9.00	13.64	13.64
		Totals	4.52	26.81	89.07	2.75	141.34

For each of these measures, the average of past values provides more accurate forecasts than using the most recent observation as the forecast for the next period. In general, if the underlying time series is stationary, the average of all the historical data will provide the most accurate forecasts.

Evaluating different forecasts based on historical accuracy is only helpful if historical patterns continue into the future. As we noted in Section 6.1, the 12 observations of Table 6.1 comprise a stationary time series. In Section 6.1 we mentioned that changes in business conditions often result in a time series that is not stationary. We discussed a situation in which the gasoline distributor signed a contract with the Vermont State Police to provide gasoline for state police cars located in southern Vermont. Table 6.2 shows the number of gallons of gasoline sold for the original time series and the 10 weeks after signing the new contract, and Figure 6.2 shows the corresponding time series plot. Note the change in level in week 13 for the resulting time series. When a shift to a new level such as this occurs, it takes several periods for the forecasting method that uses the average of all the historical data to adjust to the new level of the time series. However, in this case the simple naïve method adjusts very rapidly to the change in level because it uses only the most recent observation available as the forecast.

Measures of forecast accuracy are important factors in comparing different forecasting methods, but we have to be careful to not rely too heavily upon them. Good judgment and knowledge about business conditions that might affect the value of the variable to be forecast also have to be considered carefully when selecting a method. Historical forecast accuracy is not the sole consideration, especially if the pattern exhibited by the time series is likely to change in the future.

In the next section we will introduce more sophisticated methods for developing forecasts for a time series that exhibits a horizontal pattern. Using the measures of forecast accuracy developed here, we will be able to assess whether such methods provide more accurate forecasts than we obtained using the simple approaches illustrated in this section. The methods that we will introduce also have the advantage that they adapt well to situations in which the time series changes to a new level. The ability of a forecasting method to adapt quickly to changes in level is an important consideration, especially in short-term forecasting situations.

6.3 Moving Averages and Exponential Smoothing

In this section we discuss three forecasting methods that are appropriate for a time series with a horizontal pattern: moving averages, weighted moving averages, and exponential smoothing. These methods are also capable of adapting well to changes in the level of a horizontal pattern such as what we saw with the extended gasoline sales time series (Table 6.2 and Figure 6.2). However, without modification they are not appropriate when considerable trend, cyclical, or seasonal effects are present. Because the objective of each of these methods is to "smooth out" random fluctuations in the time series, they are referred to as smoothing methods. These methods are easy to use and generally provide a high level of accuracy for short-range forecasts, such as a forecast for the next time period.

Moving Averages

The moving averages method uses the average of the most recent k data values in the time series as the forecast for the next period. Mathematically, a **moving average** forecast of order k is as follows:

$$\hat{Y}_{t+1} = \frac{\Sigma(\text{most recent } k \text{ data values})}{k} = \frac{\displaystyle\sum_{i=t-k+1}^{t} Y_i}{k}$$

$$= \frac{Y_{t-k+1} + \cdots + Y_{t-1} + Y_t}{k} \tag{6.6}$$

where

$\hat{Y}_{t+1} =$ forecast of the time series for period $t + 1$

$Y_i =$ actual value of the time series in period i

$k =$ number of periods of time series data used to generate the forecast

The term *moving* is used because every time a new observation becomes available for the time series, it replaces the oldest observation in the equation and a new average is computed. Thus, the periods over which the average is calculated change, or move, with each ensuing period.

To illustrate the moving averages method, let us return to the original 12 weeks of gasoline sales data in Table 6.1 and Figure 6.1. The time series plot in Figure 6.1 indicates that the gasoline sales time series has a horizontal pattern. Thus, the smoothing methods of this section are applicable.

To use moving averages to forecast a time series, we must first select the order k, or number of time series values to be included in the moving average. If only the most recent values of the time series are considered relevant, a small value of k is preferred. If a greater number of past values are considered relevant, then we generally opt for a larger value of k. As mentioned earlier, a time series with a horizontal pattern can shift to a new level over time. A moving average will adapt to the new level of the series and resume providing good forecasts in k periods. Thus a smaller value of k will track shifts in a time series more quickly (the naïve approach discussed earlier is actually a moving average for $k = 1$). On the other hand, larger values of k will be more effective in smoothing out random fluctuations. Thus, managerial judgment based on an understanding of the behavior of a time series is helpful in choosing an appropriate value of k.

To illustrate how moving averages can be used to forecast gasoline sales, we will use a three-week moving average ($k = 3$). We begin by computing the forecast of sales in week 4 using the average of the time series values in weeks 1 to 3.

$$\hat{Y}_4 = \text{average of weeks 1 to 3} = \frac{17 + 21 + 19}{3} = 19$$

Thus, the moving average forecast of sales in week 4 is 19 or 19,000 gallons of gasoline. Because the actual value observed in week 4 is 23, the forecast error in week 4 is $e_4 = 23 - 19 = 4$.

We next compute the forecast of sales in week 5 by averaging the time series values in weeks 2–4.

$$\hat{Y}_5 = \text{average of weeks 2 to 4} = \frac{21 + 19 + 23}{3} = 21$$

Hence, the forecast of sales in week 5 is 21 and the error associated with this forecast is $e_5 = 18 - 21 = -3$. A complete summary of the three-week moving average forecasts for the gasoline sales time series is provided in Table 6.9. Figure 6.7 shows the original time series plot and the three-week moving average forecasts. Note how the graph of the moving average forecasts has tended to smooth out the random fluctuations in the time series.

TABLE 6.9   SUMMARY OF THREE-WEEK MOVING AVERAGE CALCULATIONS

Week	Time Series Value	Forecast	Forecast Error	Absolute Value of Forecast Error	Squared Forecast Error	Percentage Error	Absolute Value of Percentage Error
1	17						
2	21						
3	19						
4	23	19	4	4	16	17.39	17.39
5	18	21	−3	3	9	−16.67	16.67
6	16	20	−4	4	16	−25.00	25.00
7	20	19	1	1	1	5.00	5.00
8	18	18	0	0	0	0.00	0.00
9	22	18	4	4	16	18.18	18.18
10	20	20	0	0	0	0.00	0.00
11	15	20	−5	5	25	−33.33	33.33
12	22	19	3	3	9	13.64	13.64
		Totals	0	24	92	−20.79	129.21

FIGURE 6.7   GASOLINE SALES TIME SERIES PLOT AND THREE-WEEK MOVING
AERAGE FORECASTS

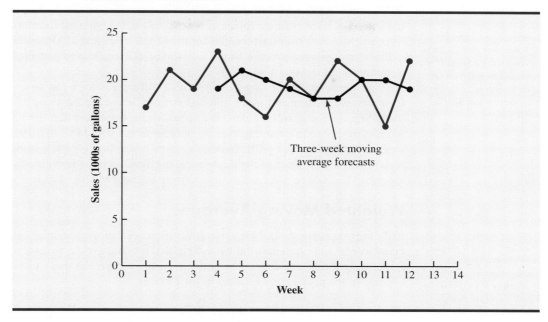

*Can you now use moving
averages to develop
forecasts? Try Problem 7.*

To forecast sales in week 13, the next time period in the future, we simply compute the
average of the time series values in weeks 10, 11, and 12.

$$\hat{Y}_{13} = \text{average of weeks 10 to 12} = \frac{20 + 15 + 22}{3} = 19$$

Thus, the forecast for week 13 is 19 or 19,000 gallons of gasoline.

Forecast Accuracy   In Section 6.2 we discussed three measures of forecast accuracy:
mean absolute error (MAE); mean squared error (MSE); and mean absolute percentage
error (MAPE). Using the three-week moving average calculations in Table 6.9, the values
for these three measures of forecast accuracy are

$$\text{MAE} = \frac{\sum_{t=4}^{12} |e_t|}{12 - 3} = \frac{24}{9} = 2.67$$

$$\text{MSE} = \frac{\sum_{t=4}^{12} e_t^2}{12 - 3} = \frac{92}{9} = 10.22$$

$$\text{MAPE} = \frac{\sum_{t=4}^{12} \left| \left(\frac{e_t}{Y_t} \right) 100 \right|}{12 - 3} = \frac{129.21}{9} = 14.36\%$$

In situations where you need to compare forecasting methods for different time periods, such as comparing a forecast of weekly sales to a forecast of monthly sales, relative measures such as MAPE are preferred.

In Section 6.2 we showed that using the most recent observation as the forecast for the next week (a moving average of order $k = 1$) resulted in values of MAE = 3.73, MSE = 16.27, and MAPE = 19.24%. Thus, in each case the three-week moving average approach has provided more accurate forecasts than simply using the most recent observation as the forecast. Also note how the formulas for the MAE, MSE, and MAPE reflect that our use of a three-week moving average leaves us with insufficient data to generate forecasts for the first three weeks of our time series.

To determine if a moving average with a different order k can provide more accurate forecasts, we recommend using trial and error to determine the value of k that minimizes the MSE. For the gasoline sales time series, it can be shown that the minimum value of MSE corresponds to a moving average of order $k = 6$ with MSE = 6.79. If we are willing to assume that the order of the moving average that is best for the historical data will also be best for future values of the time series, the most accurate moving average forecasts of gasoline sales can be obtained using a moving average of order $k = 6$.

Weighted Moving Averages

A moving average forecast of order k is just a special case of the weighted moving averages method in which each weight is equal to 1/k; for example, a moving average forecast of order k = 3 is just a special case of the weighted moving averages method in which each weight is equal to $\frac{1}{3}$.

In the moving averages method, each observation in the moving average calculation receives equal weight. One variation, known as **weighted moving averages**, involves selecting a different weight for each data value in the moving average and then computing a weighted average of the most recent k values as the forecast.

$$\hat{Y}_{t+1} = w_t Y_t + w_{t-1} Y_{t-1} + \cdots + w_{t-k+1} Y_{t-k+1} \qquad \textbf{(6.7)}$$

where

$\hat{Y}_{t+1}$ = forecast of the time series for period $t + 1$

Y_t = actual value of the time series in period t

w_t = weight applied to the actual time series value for period t

k = number of periods of time series data used to generate the forecast

Generally the most recent observation receives the largest weight, and the weight decreases with the relative age of the data values. Let us use the gasoline sales time series in Table 6.1 to illustrate the computation of a weighted three-week moving average. We will assign a weight of $w_t = \frac{3}{6}$ to the most recent observation, a weight of $w_{t-1} = \frac{2}{6}$ to the second most recent observation, and a weight of $w_{t-2} = \frac{1}{6}$ to the third most recent observation. Using this weighted average, our forecast for week 4 is computed as follows:

$$\text{Forecast for week 4} = \frac{1}{6}(17) + \frac{2}{6}(21) + \frac{3}{6}(19) = 19.33$$

Use Problem 8 to practice using weighted moving averages to produce forecasts.

Note that the sum of the weights is equal to 1 for the weighted moving average method.

Forecast Accuracy   To use the weighted moving averages method, we must first select the number of data values to be included in the weighted moving average and then choose weights for each of these data values. In general, if we believe that the recent past is a better predictor of the future than the distant past, larger weights should be given to the more recent observations. However, when the time series is highly variable, selecting approximately equal weights for the data values may be preferable. The only requirements in selecting the weights are that they be nonnegative and that their sum must equal 1. To determine whether one particular combination of number of data values and weights provides a more accurate forecast than another combination, we recommend using MSE as the measure of forecast accuracy. That is, if we assume that the combination that is best for the past will also be best for the future, we would use the combination of number of data values and weights that minimized MSE for the historical time series to forecast the next value in the time series.

Exponential Smoothing

Exponential smoothing also uses a weighted average of past time series values as a forecast; it is a special case of the weighted moving averages method in which we select only one weight—the weight for the most recent observation. The weights for the other data values are computed automatically and become smaller as the observations move farther into the past. The exponential smoothing model follows.

$$\hat{Y}_{t+1} = \alpha Y_t + (1 - \alpha)\hat{Y}_t \qquad \textbf{(6.8)}$$

where

$$\hat{Y}_{t+1} = \text{forecast of the time series for period } t + 1$$
$$Y_t = \text{actual value of the time series in period } t$$
$$\hat{Y}_t = \text{forecast of the time series for period } t$$
$$\alpha = \text{smoothing constant } (0 \le \alpha \le 1)$$

There are several exponential smoothing procedures. Because it has a single smoothing constant α, the method presented here is often referred to as single exponential smoothing.

Equation (6.8) shows that the forecast for period $t + 1$ is a weighted average of the actual value in period t and the forecast for period t. The weight given to the actual value in period t is the **smoothing constant** α and the weight given to the forecast in period t is $1 - \alpha$. It turns out that the exponential smoothing forecast for any period is actually a weighted average of *all the previous actual values* of the time series. Let us illustrate by working with a time series involving only three periods of data: Y_1, Y_2, and Y_3.

To initiate the calculations, we let $\hat{Y}_1$ equal the actual value of the time series in period 1; that is, $\hat{Y}_1 = Y_1$. Hence, the forecast for period 2 is

$$\hat{Y}_2 = \alpha Y_1 + (1 - \alpha)\hat{Y}_1$$
$$= \alpha Y_1 + (1 - \alpha)Y_1$$
$$= Y_1$$

We see that the exponential smoothing forecast for period 2 is equal to the actual value of the time series in period 1.

The forecast for period 3 is

$$\hat{Y}_3 = \alpha Y_2 + (1 - \alpha)\hat{Y}_2 = \alpha Y_2 + (1 - \alpha)Y_1$$

Finally, substituting this expression for $\hat{Y}_3$ into the expression for $\hat{Y}_4$, we obtain

$$\hat{Y}_4 = \alpha Y_3 + (1 - \alpha)\hat{Y}_3$$
$$= \alpha Y_3 + (1 - \alpha)[\alpha Y_2 + (1 - \alpha)Y_1]$$
$$= \alpha Y_3 + \alpha(1 - \alpha)Y_2 + (1 - \alpha)^2 Y_1$$

The term exponential smoothing *comes from the exponential nature of the weighting scheme for the historical values.*

We now see that $\hat{Y}_4$ is a weighted average of the first three time series values. The sum of the coefficients, or weights, for Y_1, Y_2, and Y_3 equals 1. A similar argument can be made to show that, in general, any forecast $\hat{Y}_{t+1}$ is a weighted average of all the t previous time series values.

Despite the fact that exponential smoothing provides a forecast that is a weighted average of all past observations, all past data do not need to be retained to compute the forecast for the next period. In fact, equation (6.8) shows that once the value for the smoothing constant α is selected, only two pieces of information are needed to compute the forecast for period $t + 1$: Y_t, the actual value of the time series in period t; and $\hat{Y}_t$, the forecast for period t.

To illustrate the exponential smoothing approach to forecasting, let us again consider the gasoline sales time series in Table 6.1 and Figure 6.1. As indicated previously, to initialize the calculations we set the exponential smoothing forecast for period 2 equal to the actual value of the time series in period 1. Thus, with $Y_1 = 17$, we set $\hat{Y}_2 = 17$ to initiate the computations. Referring to the time series data in Table 6.1, we find an actual time series value in period 2 of $Y_2 = 21$. Thus, in period 2 we have a forecast error of $e_2 = 21 - 17 = 4$.

Continuing with the exponential smoothing computations using a smoothing constant of $\alpha = 0.2$, we obtain the following forecast for period 3.

$$\hat{Y}_3 = 0.2Y_2 + 0.8\hat{Y}_2 = 0.2(21) + 0.8(17) = 17.8$$

Once the actual time series value in period 3, $Y_3 = 19$, is known, we can generate a forecast for period 4 as follows.

$$\hat{Y}_4 = 0.2Y_3 + 0.8\hat{Y}_3 = 0.2(19) + 0.8(17.8) = 18.04$$

Continuing the exponential smoothing calculations, we obtain the weekly forecast values shown in Table 6.10. Note that we have not shown an exponential smoothing forecast or a forecast error for week 1 because no forecast was made (we used actual sales for week 1 as the forecasted sales for week 2 to initialize the exponential smoothing process). For week 12, we have $Y_{12} = 22$ and $\hat{Y}_{12} = 18.48$. We can we use this information to generate a forecast for week 13.

$$\hat{Y}_{13} = 0.2Y_{12} + 0.8\hat{Y}_{12} = 0.2(22) + 0.8(18.48) = 19.18$$

TABLE 6.10 SUMMARY OF THE EXPONENTIAL SMOOTHING FORECASTS AND FORECAST ERRORS FOR THE GASOLINE SALES TIME SERIES WITH SMOOTHING CONSTANT $\alpha = 0.2$

Week	Time Series Value	Forecast	Forecast Error	Squared Forecast Error
1	17			
2	21	17.00	4.00	16.00
3	19	17.80	1.20	1.44
4	23	18.04	4.96	24.60
5	18	19.03	−1.03	1.06
6	16	18.83	−2.83	8.01
7	20	18.26	1.74	3.03
8	18	18.61	−0.61	0.37
9	22	18.49	3.51	12.32
10	20	19.19	0.81	0.66
11	15	19.35	−4.35	18.92
12	22	18.48	3.52	12.39
		Totals	10.92	98.80

FIGURE 6.8   ACTUAL AND FORECAST GASOLINE TIME SERIES WITH SMOOTHING
CONSTANT $\alpha = 0.2$

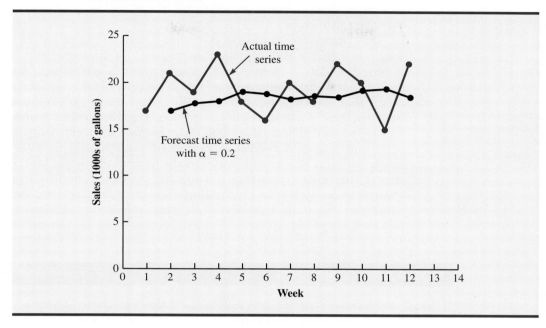

*Try Problem 9 for practice
using exponential
smoothing to produce
forecasts.*

Thus, the exponential smoothing forecast of the amount sold in week 13 is 19.18, or 19,180 gallons of gasoline. With this forecast, the firm can make plans and decisions accordingly.

Figure 6.8 shows the time series plot of the actual and forecast time series values. Note in particular how the forecasts "smooth out" the irregular or random fluctuations in the time series.

Forecast Accuracy   In the preceding exponential smoothing calculations, we used a smoothing constant of $\alpha = 0.2$. Although any value of α between 0 and 1 is acceptable, some values will yield more accurate forecasts than others. Insight into choosing a good value for α can be obtained by rewriting the basic exponential smoothing model as follows.

$$\hat{Y}_{t+1} = \alpha Y_t + (1 - \alpha)\hat{Y}_t$$
$$\hat{Y}_{t+1} = \alpha Y_t + \hat{Y}_t - \alpha \hat{Y}_t$$
$$\hat{Y}_{t+1} = \hat{Y}_t + \alpha(Y_t - \hat{Y}_t) = \hat{Y}_t + \alpha e_t$$

(6.9)

Thus, the new forecast $\hat{Y}_{t+1}$ is equal to the previous forecast $\hat{Y}_t$ plus an adjustment, which is the smoothing constant α times the most recent forecast error, $e_t = Y_t - \hat{Y}_t$. That is, the forecast in period $t + 1$ is obtained by adjusting the forecast in period t by a fraction of the forecast error from period t. If the time series contains substantial random variability, a small value of the smoothing constant is preferred. The reason for this choice is that if much of the forecast error is due to random variability, we do not want to overreact and adjust the forecasts too quickly. For a time series with relatively little random variability, a forecast error is more likely to represent a real change in the level of the series. Thus, larger values of the smoothing constant provide the advantage of quickly adjusting the forecasts to changes in the time series; this allows the forecasts to react more quickly to changing conditions.

The criterion we will use to determine a desirable value for the smoothing constant α is the same as the criterion we proposed for determining the order or number of periods of data to include in the moving averages calculation. That is, we choose the value of α that minimizes the MSE. A summary of the MSE calculations for the exponential smoothing forecast of gasoline sales with $\alpha = 0.2$ is shown in Table 6.10. Note that there is one less squared error term than the number of time periods; this is because we had no past values with which to make a forecast for period 1. The value of the sum of squared forecast errors is 98.80; hence MSE = 98.80/11 = 8.98. Would a different value of α provide better results in terms of a lower MSE value? Trial and error is often used to determine if a different smoothing constant α can provide more accurate forecasts, but we can avoid trial and error and determine the value of α that minimizes MSE through the use of nonlinear optimization as discussed in Chapter 12 (see Exercise 12.19).

NOTES AND COMMENTS

1. Spreadsheet packages are effective tools for implementing exponential smoothing. With the time series data and the forecasting formulas in a spreadsheet as shown in Table 6.10, you can use the MAE, MSE, and MAPE to evaluate different values of the smoothing constant α.

2. We presented the moving average, weighted moving average, and exponential smoothing methods in the context of a stationary time series. These methods can also be used to forecast a nonstationary time series that shifts in level but exhibits no trend or seasonality. Moving averages with small values of k adapt more quickly than moving averages with larger values of k. Weighted moving averages that place relatively large weights on the most recent values adapt more quickly than weighted moving averages that place relatively equal weights on the k time series values used in calculating the forecast. Exponential smoothing models with smoothing constants closer to 1 adapt more quickly than models with smaller values of the smoothing constant.

6.4 Linear Trend Projection

In this section we present forecasting methods that are appropriate for time series exhibiting trend patterns. Here we show how **regression analysis** may be used to forecast a time series with a linear trend. In Section 6.1 we used the bicycle sales time series in Table 6.3 and Figure 6.3 to illustrate a time series with a trend pattern. Let us now use this time series to illustrate how regression analysis can be used to forecast a time series with a linear trend. The data for the bicycle time series are repeated in Table 6.11 and Figure 6.9.

Although the time series plot in Figure 6.9 shows some up and down movement over the past 10 years, we might agree that the linear trend line shown in Figure 6.10 provides a reasonable approximation of the long-run movement in the series. We can use regression analysis to develop such a linear trend line for the bicycle sales time series.

In regression analysis we use known values of variables to estimate the relationship between one variable (called the **dependent variable**) and one or more other related

TABLE 6.11   BICYCLE SALES TIME SERIES

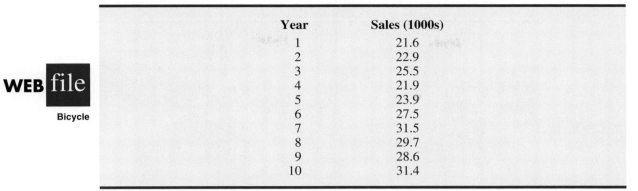

Year	Sales (1000s)
1	21.6
2	22.9
3	25.5
4	21.9
5	23.9
6	27.5
7	31.5
8	29.7
9	28.6
10	31.4

WEB file

Bicycle

FIGURE 6.9   BICYCLE SALES TIME SERIES PLOT

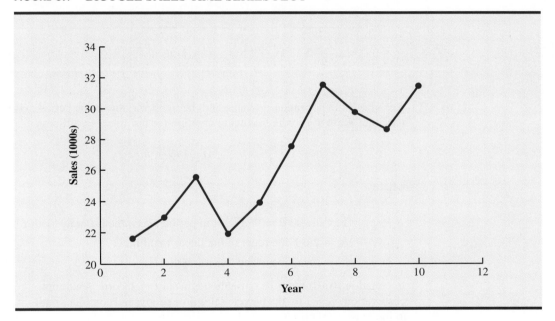

variables (called **independent variables**). This relationship is usually found in a manner that minimizes the sum of squared errors (and so also minimizes the MSE). With this relationship we can then use values of the independent variables to estimate the associated value of the dependent variable. When we estimate a linear relationship between the dependent variable (which is usually denoted as y) and a single independent variable (which is usually denoted as x), this is referred to as **simple linear regression**. Estimating the relationship between the dependent variable and a single independent variable requires that we find the values of parameters b_0 and b_1 for the straight line $y = b_0 + b_1 x$.

Because our use of simple linear regression analysis yields the linear relationship between the independent variable and the dependent variable that minimizes the MSE, we can use this approach to find a best-fitting line to a set of data that exhibits a linear trend. In finding a linear trend, the variable to be forecasted (Y_t, the actual value of the time series in

FIGURE 6.10   TREND REPRESENTED BY A LINEAR FUNCTION FOR THE BICYCLE
SALES TIME SERIES

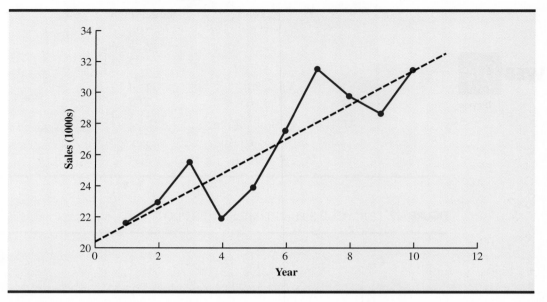

period t) is the dependent variable and the trend variable (time period t) is the independent
variable. We will use the following notation for our linear trendline.

$$\hat{Y}_t = b_0 + b_1 t \tag{6.10}$$

where

$t =$ the time period

$\hat{Y}_t =$ linear trend forecast in period t (i.e., the estimated value of Y_t in period t)

$b_0 =$ the Y-intercept of the linear trendline

$b_1 =$ the slope of the linear trendline

In equation (6.10) the time variable begins at $t = 1$ corresponding to the first time series
observation (year 1 for the bicycle sales time series) and continues until $t = n$ corresponding
to the most recent time series observation (year 10 for the bicycle sales time series). Thus,
for the bicycle sales time series $t = 1$ corresponds to the oldest time series value and $t = 10$
corresponds to the most recent year. Calculus may be used to show that the equations given
below for b_0 and b_1 yield the line that minimizes the MSE. The equations for computing
the values of b_0 and b_1 are

$$b_1 = \frac{\sum\limits_{t=1}^{n} t Y_t - \sum\limits_{t=1}^{n} t \sum\limits_{t=1}^{n} Y_t \bigg/ n}{\sum\limits_{t=1}^{n} t^2 - \left(\sum\limits_{t=1}^{n} t\right)^2 \bigg/ n} \tag{6.11}$$

$$b_0 = \bar{Y} - b_1 \bar{t} \tag{6.12}$$

where

$$t = \text{the time period}$$
$$Y_t = \text{actual value of the time series in period } t$$
$$n = \text{number of periods in the time series}$$
$$\overline{Y} = \text{average value of the time series; that is, } \overline{Y} = \sum_{t=1}^{n} Y_t \bigg/ n$$
$$\overline{t} = \text{mean value of } t; \text{ that is, } \overline{t} = \sum_{t=1}^{n} t \bigg/ n$$

Let us calculate b_0 and b_1 for the bicycle data in Table 6.11; the intermediate summary calculations necessary for computing the values of b_0 and b_1 are

t	Y_t	tY_t	t^2
1	21.6	21.6	1
2	22.9	45.8	4
3	25.5	76.5	9
4	21.9	87.6	16
5	23.9	119.5	25
6	27.5	165.0	36
7	31.5	220.5	49
8	29.7	237.6	64
9	28.6	257.4	81
10	31.4	314.0	100
Totals 55	264.5	1545.5	385

And the final calculations of the values of b_0 and b_1 are

$$\overline{t} = \frac{55}{10} = 5.5$$

$$\overline{Y} = \frac{264.5}{10} = 26.45$$

$$b_1 = \frac{1545.5 - (55)(264.5)/10}{385 - 55^2/10} = 1.10$$

$$b_0 = 26.45 - 1.10(5.5) = 20.40$$

Problem 20 provides additional practice in using regression analysis to estimate the linear trend in a time series data set.

Therefore,

$$\hat{Y}_t = 20.4 + 1.1t \tag{6.13}$$

is the regression equation for the linear trend component for the bicycle sales time series.

The slope of 1.1 in this trend equation indicates that over the past 10 years, the firm has experienced an average growth in sales of about 1100 units per year. If we assume that the past 10-year trend in sales is a good indicator for the future, we can use equation (6.13) to project the trend component of the time series. For example, substituting $t = 11$ into equation (6.13) yields next year's trend projection, $\hat{Y}_{11}$:

$$\hat{Y}_{11} = 20.4 + 1.1(11) = 32.5$$

Thus, the linear trend model yields a sales forecast of 32,500 bicycles for the next year.

TABLE 6.12   SUMMARY OF THE LINEAR TREND FORECASTS AND FORECAST
ERRORS FOR THE BICYCLE SALES TIME SERIES

Week	Sales (1000s) Y_t	Forecast $\hat{Y}_t$	Forecast Error	Squared Forecast Error
1	21.6	21.5	0.1	0.01
2	22.9	22.6	0.3	0.09
3	25.5	23.7	1.8	3.24
4	21.9	24.8	−2.9	8.41
5	23.9	25.9	−2.0	4.00
6	27.5	27.0	0.5	0.25
7	31.5	28.1	3.4	11.56
8	29.7	29.2	0.5	0.25
9	28.6	30.3	−1.7	2.89
10	31.4	31.4	0.0	0.00
			Total	30.70

Table 6.12 shows the computation of the minimized sum of squared errors for the bicycle sales time series. As previously noted, minimizing sum of squared errors also minimizes the commonly used measure of accuracy, MSE. For the bicycle sales time series,

$$\text{MSE} = \frac{\sum_{t=1}^{n} e_t^2}{n} = \frac{30.7}{10} = 3.07$$

Note that in this example we are not using past values of the time series to produce forecasts, and so $k = 0$; that is, we can produce a forecast for each period of the time series and so do not have to adjust our calculations of the MAE, MSE, or MAPE for k.

We can also use the trendline to forecast sales farther into the future. For instance, using Equation (6.13), we develop annual forecasts for two and three years into the future as follows:

$$\hat{Y}_{12} = 20.4 + 1.1(12) = 33.6$$
$$\hat{Y}_{13} = 20.4 + 1.1(13) = 34.7$$

Note that the forecasted value increases by 1100 bicycles in each year.

NOTES AND COMMENTS

1. Statistical packages such as Minitab and SAS, as well as Excel, have routines to perform regression analysis. Regression analysis minimizes the sum of squared error and under certain assumptions it also allows the analyst to make statistical statements about the parameters and the forecasts.

2. While the use of a linear function to model the trend is common, some time series exhibit a curvilinear (nonlinear) trend. More advanced texts discuss how to develop nonlinear models such as quadratic models and exponential models for these more complex relationships.

In this section we used simple linear regression to estimate the relationship between the dependent variable (Y_t, the actual value of the time series in period t) and a single independent variable (the trend variable t). However, some regression models include several independent variables. When we estimate a linear relationship between the dependent variable and more than one independent variable, this is referred to as multiple linear regression. In the next section we will apply multiple linear regression to time series that include seasonal effects and to time series that include both seasonal effects and a linear trend.

6.5 Seasonality

In this section we show how to develop forecasts for a time series that has a seasonal pattern. To the extent that seasonality exists, we need to incorporate it into our forecasting models to ensure accurate forecasts. We begin the section by considering a seasonal time series with no trend and then discuss how to model seasonality with a linear trend.

Seasonality Without Trend

Let us consider again the data from Table 6.5, the number of umbrellas sold at a clothing store over the past five years. We repeat the data here in Table 6.13, and Figure 6.11 again shows the corresponding time series plot. The time series plot does not indicate any long-term trend in sales. In fact, unless you look carefully at the data, you might conclude that the data follow a horizontal pattern with random fluctuation and that single exponential smoothing could be used to forecast sales. However, closer inspection of the time series plot reveals a pattern in the fluctuations. That is, the first and third quarters have moderate sales, the second quarter the highest sales, and the fourth quarter tends to be the lowest quarter in terms of sales volume. Thus, we conclude that a quarterly seasonal pattern is present.

We can model a time series with a seasonal pattern by treating the season as a categorical variable. **Categorical variables** are data used to categorize observations of data. When

TABLE 6.13   UMBRELLA SALES TIME SERIES

Umbrella

Year	Quarter	Sales
1	1	125
	2	153
	3	106
	4	88
2	1	118
	2	161
	3	133
	4	102
3	1	138
	2	144
	3	113
	4	80
4	1	109
	2	137
	3	125
	4	109
5	1	130
	2	165
	3	128
	4	96

FIGURE 6.11   UMBRELLA SALES TIME SERIES PLOT

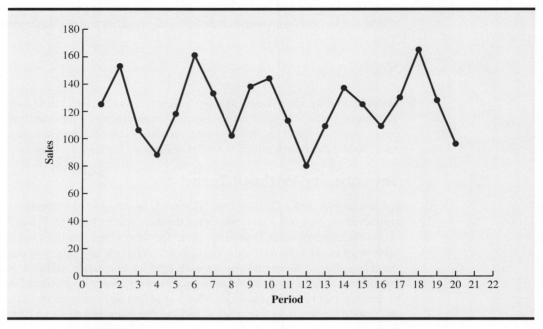

a categorical variable has k levels, $k - 1$ dummy variables (sometimes called 0-1 variables) are required. So if there are four seasons, we need three dummy variables. For instance, in the umbrella sales time series, the quarter to which each observation corresponds is treated as a season; it is a categorical variable with four levels: Quarter 1, Quarter 2, Quarter 3, and Quarter 4. Thus, to model the seasonal effects in the umbrella time series we need $4 - 1 = 3$ dummy variables. The three dummy variables can be coded as follows:

$$\text{Qtr1}_t = \begin{cases} 1 & \text{if period } t \text{ is a Quarter 1} \\ 0 & \text{otherwise} \end{cases}$$

$$\text{Qtr2}_t = \begin{cases} 1 & \text{if period } t \text{ is a Quarter 2} \\ 0 & \text{otherwise} \end{cases}$$

$$\text{Qtr3}_t = \begin{cases} 1 & \text{if period } t \text{ is a Quarter 3} \\ 0 & \text{otherwise} \end{cases}$$

Using F_t to denote the forecasted value of sales for period t, the general form of the equation relating the number of umbrellas sold to the quarter the sales take place follows.

$$\hat{Y}_t = b_0 + b_1 \text{ Qtr1}_t + b_2 \text{ Qtr2}_t + b_3 \text{ Qtr3}_t \qquad \textbf{(6.14)}$$

Note that we have numbered the observations in Table 6.14 as periods 1 to 20. For example, year 3, quarter 3 is observation 11.

Note that the fourth quarter will be denoted by a setting of all three dummy variables to 0. Table 6.14 shows the umbrella sales time series with the coded values of the dummy variables shown. We can use a multiple linear regression model to find the values of b_0, b_1, b_2, and b_3 that minimize the sum of squared errors. For this regression model Y_t is the dependent variable and the quarterly dummy variables Qtr1_t, Qtr2_t, and Qtr3_t are the independent variables.

TABLE 6.14 UMBRELLA SALES TIME SERIES WITH DUMMY VARIABLES

Period	Year	Quarter	Qtr1	Qtr2	Qtr3	Sales
1	1	1	1	0	0	125
2		2	0	1	0	153
3		3	0	0	1	106
4		4	0	0	0	88
5	2	1	1	0	0	118
6		2	0	1	0	161
7		3	0	0	1	133
8		4	0	0	0	102
9	3	1	1	0	0	138
10		2	0	1	0	144
11		3	0	0	1	113
12		4	0	0	0	80
13	4	1	1	0	0	109
14		2	0	1	0	137
15		3	0	0	1	125
16		4	0	0	0	109
17	5	1	1	0	0	130
18		2	0	1	0	165
19		3	0	0	1	128
20		4	0	0	0	96

Using the data in Table 6.14 and regression analysis, we obtain the following equation:

$$\hat{Y}_t = 95.0 + 29.0 \, \text{Qtr1}_t + 57.0 \, \text{Qtr2}_t + 26.0 \, \text{Qtr3}_t \qquad \textbf{(6.15)}$$

we can use Equation (6.15) to forecast quarterly sales for next year.

For practice using categorical variables to estimate seasonal effects, try Problem 24.

Quarter 1: Sales = 95.0 + 29.0(1) + 57.0(0) + 26.0(0) = 124
Quarter 2: Sales = 95.0 + 29.0(0) + 57.0(1) + 26.0(0) = 152
Quarter 3: Sales = 95.0 + 29.0(0) + 57.0(0) + 26.0(1) = 121
Quarter 4: Sales = 95.0 + 29.0(0) + 57.0(0) + 26.0(0) = 95

It is interesting to note that we could have obtained the quarterly forecasts for next year by simply computing the average number of umbrellas sold in each quarter, as shown in the following table.

Year	Quarter 1	Quarter 2	Quarter 3	Quarter 4
1	125	153	106	88
2	118	161	133	102
3	138	144	113	80
4	109	137	125	109
5	130	165	128	96
Average	124	152	121	95

Nonetheless, for more complex problem situations, such as dealing with a time series that has both trend and seasonal effects, this simple averaging approach will not work.

Seasonality with Trend

We now consider situations for which the time series contains both a seasonal effect and a linear trend by showing how to forecast the quarterly television set sales time series introduced in Section 6.1. The data for the television set time series are shown in Table 6.15. The time series plot in Figure 6.12 indicates that sales are lowest in the second quarter of each year and increase in quarters 3 and 4. Thus, we conclude that a seasonal pattern exists for television set sales. However, the time series also has an upward linear trend that will need to be accounted for in order to develop accurate forecasts of quarterly sales. This is easily done by combining the dummy variable approach for handling seasonality with the approach we discussed in Section 6.4 for handling a linear trend.

The general form of the regression equation for modeling both the quarterly seasonal effects and the linear trend in the television set time series is:

$$\hat{Y}_t = b_0 + b_1 \text{Qtr1}_t + b_2 \text{Qtr2}_t + b_3 \text{Qtr3}_t + b_4 t \qquad (6.16)$$

where

$\hat{Y}_t$ = forecast of sales in period t

Qtr1_t = 1 if time period t corresponds to the first quarter of the year; 0, otherwise

Qtr2_t = 1 if time period t corresponds to the second quarter of the year; 0, otherwise

Qtr3_t = 1 if time period t corresponds to the third quarter of the year; 0, otherwise

t = time period

TABLE 6.15   TELEVISION SET SALES TIME SERIES

Year	Quarter	Sales (1000s)
1	1	4.8
	2	4.1
	3	6.0
	4	6.5
2	1	5.8
	2	5.2
	3	6.8
	4	7.4
3	1	6.0
	2	5.6
	3	7.5
	4	7.8
4	1	6.3
	2	5.9
	3	8.0
	4	8.4

FIGURE 6.12   TELEVISION SET SALES TIME SERIES PLOT

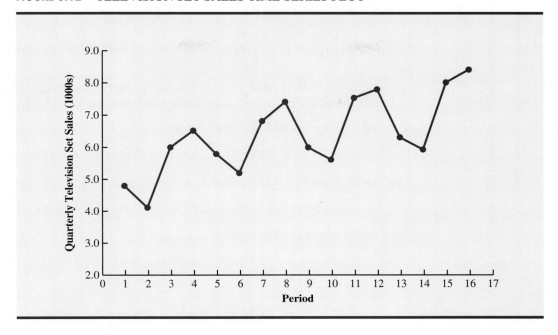

For this regression model Y_t is the dependent variable and the quarterly dummy variables $Qtr1_t$, $Qtr2_t$, and $Qtr3_t$ and the time period t are the independent variables.

Table 6.16 shows the revised television set sales time series that includes the coded values of the dummy variables and the time period t. Using the data in Table 6.16 with the

TABLE 6.16   TELEVISION SET SALES TIME SERIES WITH DUMMY VARIABLES AND TIME PERIOD

Period	Year	Quarter	Qtr1	Qtr2	Qtr3	Sales (1000s)
1	1	1	1	0	0	4.8
2		2	0	1	0	4.1
3		3	0	0	1	6.0
4		4	0	0	0	6.5
5	2	1	1	0	0	5.8
6		2	0	1	0	5.2
7		3	0	0	1	6.8
8		4	0	0	0	7.4
9	3	1	1	0	0	6.0
10		2	0	1	0	5.6
11		3	0	0	1	7.5
12		4	0	0	0	7.8
13	4	1	1	0	0	6.3
14		2	0	1	0	5.9
15		3	0	0	1	8.0
16		4	0	0	0	8.4

regression model that includes both the seasonal and trend components, we obtain the following equation that minimizes our sum of squared errors:

$$\hat{Y}_t = 6.07 - 1.36 \, \text{Qtr1}_t - 2.03 \, \text{Qtr2}_t - 0.304 \, \text{Qtr3}_t + 0.146t \qquad \textbf{(6.17)}$$

We can now use equation (6.17) to forecast quarterly sales for next year. Next year is year 5 for the television set sales time series; that is, time periods 17, 18, 19, and 20.

Forecast for Time Period 17 (Quarter 1 in Year 5)

$$\hat{Y}_{17} = 6.07 - 1.36(1) - 2.03(0) - 0.304(0) + 0.146(17) = 7.19$$

Forecast for Time Period 18 (Quarter 2 in Year 5)

$$\hat{Y}_{18} = 6.07 - 1.36(0) - 2.03(1) - 0.304(0) + 0.146(18) = 6.67$$

Forecast for Time Period 19 (Quarter 3 in Year 5)

$$\hat{Y}_{19} = 6.07 - 1.36(0) - 2.03(0) - 0.304(1) + 0.146(19) = 8.54$$

Forecast for Time Period 20 (Quarter 4 in Year 5)

$$\hat{Y}_{20} = 6.07 - 1.36(0) - 2.03(0) - 0.304(0) + 0.146(20) = 8.99$$

Thus, accounting for the seasonal effects and the linear trend in television set sales, the estimates of quarterly sales in year 5 are 7190, 6670, 8540, and 8990.

The dummy variables in the equation actually provide four equations, one for each quarter. For instance, if time period t corresponds to quarter 1, the estimate of quarterly sales is

Quarter 1: Sales $= 6.07 - 1.36(1) - 2.03(0) - 0.304(0) + 0.146t = 4.71 + 0.146t$

Similarly, if time period t corresponds to quarters 2, 3, and 4, the estimates of quarterly sales are:

Quarter 2: Sales $= 6.07 - 1.36(0) - 2.03(1) - 0.304(0) + 0.146t = 4.04 + 0.146t$
Quarter 3: Sales $= 6.07 - 1.36(0) - 2.03(0) - 0.304(1) + 0.146t = 5.77 + 0.146t$
Quarter 4: Sales $= 6.07 - 1.36(0) - 2.03(0) - 0.304(0) + 0.146t = 6.07 + 0.146t$

Problem 28 provides another example of using regression analysis to forecast time series data with both trend and seasonal effects.

The slope of the trend line for each quarterly forecast equation is 0.146, indicating a consistent growth in sales of about 146 sets per quarter. The only difference in the four equations is that they have different intercepts.

Models Based on Monthly Data

In the preceding television set sales example, we showed how dummy variables can be used to account for the quarterly seasonal effects in the time series. Because there were four levels for the categorical variable season, three dummy variables were required. However,

Whenever a categorical variable such as season has k levels, k − 1 dummy variables are required.

many businesses use monthly rather than quarterly forecasts. For monthly data, season is a categorical variable with 12 levels, and thus $12 - 1 = 11$ dummy variables are required. For example, the 11 dummy variables could be coded as follows:

$$\text{Month1} = \begin{cases} 1 & \text{if January} \\ 0 & \text{otherwise} \end{cases}$$

$$\text{Month2} = \begin{cases} 1 & \text{if February} \\ 0 & \text{otherwise} \end{cases}$$

$$\vdots$$

$$\text{Month1} = \begin{cases} 1 & \text{if November} \\ 0 & \text{otherwise} \end{cases}$$

Other than this change, the approach for handling seasonality remains the same.

Summary

This chapter provided an introduction to basic methods of time series analysis and forecasting. We first showed that the underlying pattern in the time series can often be identified by constructing a time series plot. Several types of data patterns can be distinguished, including a horizontal pattern, a trend pattern, and a seasonal pattern. The forecasting methods we have discussed are based on which of these patterns are present in the time series.

We also discussed that the accuracy of the method is an important factor in determining which forecasting method to use. We considered three measures of forecast accuracy: mean absolute error (MAE), mean squared error (MSE), and mean absolute percentage error (MAPE). Each of these measures is designed to determine how well a particular forecasting method is able to reproduce the time series data that are already available. By selecting the method that is most accurate for the data already known, we hope to increase the likelihood that we will obtain more accurate forecasts for future time periods.

For a time series with a horizontal pattern, we showed how moving averages, weighted moving averages, and exponential smoothing can be used to develop a forecast. The moving averages method consists of computing an average of past data values and then using that average as the forecast for the next period. In the weighted moving average and exponential smoothing methods, weighted averages of past time series values are used to compute forecasts. These methods also adapt well to a horizontal pattern that shifts to a different level and then resumes a horizontal pattern.

For time series that have only a long-term linear trend, we showed how regression analysis can be used to make trend projections. For a time series with a seasonal pattern, we showed how dummy variables and regression analysis can be used to develop an equation with seasonal effects. We then extended the approach to include situations where the time series contains both a seasonal and a linear trend effect by showing how to combine the dummy variable approach for handling seasonality with the approach for handling a linear trend.

Glossary

Categorical (dummy) variable A variable used to categorize observations of data. Used when modeling a time series with a seasonal pattern.

Cyclical pattern A cyclical pattern exists if the time series plot shows an alternating sequence of points below and above the trend line lasting more than one year.

Dependent variable The variable that is being predicted or explained in a regression analysis.

Exponential smoothing A forecasting method that uses a weighted average of past time series values as the forecast; it is a special case of the weighted moving averages method in which we select only one weight—the weight for the most recent observation.

Forecast error The difference between the actual time series value and the forecast.

Independent variable A variable used to predict or explain values of the dependent variable in regression analysis.

Mean absolute error (MAE) The average of the absolute values of the forecast errors.

Mean absolute percentage error (MAPE) The average of the absolute values of the percentage forecast errors.

Mean squared error (MSE) The average of the sum of squared forecast errors.

Moving averages A forecasting method that uses the average of the k most recent data values in the time series as the forecast for the next period.

Regression analysis A procedure for estimating values of a dependent variable given the values of one or more independent variables in a manner that minimizes the sum of the squared errors.

Seasonal pattern A seasonal pattern exists if the time series plot exhibits a repeating pattern over successive periods.

Smoothing constant A parameter of the exponential smoothing model that provides the weight given to the most recent time series value in the calculation of the forecast value.

Stationary time series A time series whose statistical properties are independent of time. For a stationary time series, the process generating the data has a constant mean and the variability of the time series is constant over time.

Time series A sequence of observations on a variable measured at successive points in time or over successive periods of time.

Time series plot A graphical presentation of the relationship between time and the time series variable. Time is shown on the horizontal axis and the time series values are shown on the verical axis.

Trend pattern A trend pattern exists if the time series plot shows gradual shifts or movements to relatively higher or lower values over a longer period of time.

Weighted moving averages A forecasting method that involves selecting a different weight for the k most recent data values values in the time series and then computing a weighted average of the of the values. The sum of the weights must equal one.

Problems

1. Consider the following time series data.

Week	1	2	3	4	5	6
Value	18	13	16	11	17	14

Using the naïve method (most recent value) as the forecast for the next week, compute the following measures of forecast accuracy.

a. Mean absolute error
b. Mean squared error
c. Mean absolute percentage error
d. What is the forecast for week 7?

2. Refer to the time series data in Exercise 1. Using the average of all the historical data as a forecast for the next period, compute the following measures of forecast accuracy:
a. Mean absolute error
b. Mean squared error
c. Mean absolute percentage error
d. What is the forecast for week 7?

3. Exercises 1 and 2 used different forecasting methods. Which method appears to provide the more accurate forecasts for the historical data? Explain.

4. Consider the following time series data.

Month	1	2	3	4	5	6	7
Value	24	13	20	12	19	23	15

a. Compute MSE using the most recent value as the forecast for the next period. What is the forecast for month 8?
b. Compute MSE using the average of all the data available as the forecast for the next period. What is the forecast for month 8?
c. Which method appears to provide the better forecast?

5. Consider the following time series data.

Week	1	2	3	4	5	6
Value	18	13	16	11	17	14

a. Construct a time series plot. What type of pattern exists in the data?
b. Develop a three-week moving average for this time series. Compute MSE and a forecast for week 7.
c. Use $\alpha = 0.2$ to compute the exponential smoothing values for the time series. Compute MSE and a forecast for week 7.
d. Compare the three-week moving average forecast with the exponential smoothing forecast using $\alpha = 0.2$. Which appears to provide the better forecast based on MSE? Explain.
e. Use trial and error to find a value of the exponential smoothing coefficient α that results in a smaller MSE than what you calculated for $\alpha = 0.2$.

6. Consider the following time series data.

Month	1	2	3	4	5	6	7
Value	24	13	20	12	19	23	15

a. Construct a time series plot. What type of pattern exists in the data?
b. Develop a three-week moving average for this time series. Compute MSE and a forecast for week 8.
c. Use $\alpha = 0.2$ to compute the exponential smoothing values for the time series. Compute MSE and a forecast for week 8.
d. Compare the three-week moving average forecast with the exponential smoothing forecast using $\alpha = 0.2$. Which appears to provide the better forecast based on MSE?
e. Use trial and error to find a value of the exponential smoothing coefficient α that results in a smaller MSE than what you calculated for $\alpha = 0.2$.

Gasoline

7. Refer to the gasoline sales time series data in Table 6.1.
    a. Compute four-week and five-week moving averages for the time series.
    b. Compute the MSE for the four-week and five-week moving average forecasts.
    c. What appears to be the best number of weeks of past data (three, four, or five) to use in the moving average computation? Recall that MSE for the three-week moving average is 10.22.

8. Refer again to the gasoline sales time series data in Table 6.1.
    a. Using a weight of 1/2 for the most recent observation, 1/3 for the second most recent, and 1/6 for third most recent, compute a three-week weighted moving average for the time series.
    b. Compute the MSE for the weighted moving average in part (a). Do you prefer this weighted moving average to the unweighted moving average? Remember that the MSE for the unweighted moving average is 10.22.
    c. Suppose you are allowed to choose any weights as long as they sum to 1. Could you always find a set of weights that would make the MSE smaller for a weighted moving average than for an unweighted moving average? Why or why not?

9. With the gasoline time series data from Table 6.1, show the exponential smoothing forecasts using $\alpha = 0.1$.
    a. Applying the MSE measure of forecast accuracy, would you prefer a smoothing constant of $\alpha = 0.1$ or $\alpha = 0.2$ for the gasoline sales time series?
    b. Are the results the same if you apply MAE as the measure of accuracy?
    c. What are the results if MAPE is used?

10. With a smoothing constant of $\alpha = 0.2$, equation (6.8) shows that the forecast for week 13 of the gasoline sales data from Table 6.1 is given by $\hat{Y}_{13} = 0.2Y_{12} + 0.8\hat{Y}_{12}$. However, the forecast for week 12 is given by $\hat{Y}_{12} = 0.2Y_{11} + 0.8\hat{Y}_{11}$. Thus, we could combine these two results to show that the forecast for week 13 can be written

$$\hat{Y}_{13} = 0.2Y_{12} + 0.8(0.2Y_{11} + 0.8\hat{Y}_{11}) = 0.2Y_{12} + 0.16Y_{11} + 0.64\hat{Y}_{11}$$

   a. Making use of the fact that $\hat{Y}_{11} = 0.2Y_{10} + 0.8\hat{Y}_{10}$ (and similarly for $\hat{Y}_{10}$ and $\hat{Y}_{9}$), continue to expand the expression for $\hat{Y}_{13}$ until it is written in terms of the past data values $Y_{12}, Y_{11}, Y_{10}, Y_{9}, Y_{8}$, and the forecast for period 8.
   b. Refer to the coefficients or weights for the past values $Y_{12}, Y_{11}, Y_{10}, Y_{9}$, and Y_{8}. What observation can you make about how exponential smoothing weights past data values in arriving at new forecasts? Compare this weighting pattern with the weighting pattern of the moving averages method.

11. For the Hawkins Company, the monthly percentages of all shipments received on time over the past 12 months are 80, 82, 84, 83, 83, 84, 85, 84, 82, 83, 84, and 83.
    a. Construct a time series plot. What type of pattern exists in the data?
    b. Compare a three-month moving average forecast with an exponential smoothing forecast for $\alpha = 0.2$. Which provides the better forecasts using MSE as the measure of model accuracy?
    c. What is the forecast for next month?

12. Corporate triple A bond interest rates for 12 consecutive months follow.

   9.5   9.3   9.4   9.6   9.8   9.7   9.8   10.5   9.9   9.7   9.6   9.6

   a. Construct a time series plot. What type of pattern exists in the data?
   b. Develop three-month and four-month moving averages for this time series. Does the three-month or four-month moving average provide the better forecasts based on MSE? Explain.
   c. What is the moving average forecast for the next month?

13. The values of Alabama building contracts (in millions of dollars) for a 12-month period follow.

240 350 230 260 280 320 220 310 240 310 240 230

   a. Construct a time series plot. What type of pattern exists in the data?
   b. Compare a three-month moving average forecast with an exponential smoothing forecast. Use $\alpha = 0.2$. Which provides the better forecasts based on MSE?
   c. What is the forecast for the next month?

14. The following time series shows the sales of a particular product over the past 12 months.

Month	Sales	Month	Sales
1	105	7	145
2	135	8	140
3	120	9	100
4	105	10	80
5	90	11	100
6	120	12	110

   a. Construct a time series plot. What type of pattern exists in the data?
   b. Use $\alpha = 0.3$ to compute the exponential smoothing values for the time series.
   c. Use trial and error to find a value of the exponential smoothing coefficient α that results in a relatively small MSE.

CFI

15. Ten weeks of data on the Commodity Futures Index are 7.35, 7.40, 7.55, 7.56, 7.60, 7.52, 7.52, 7.70, 7.62, and 7.55.
   a. Construct a time series plot. What type of pattern exists in the data?
   b. Use trial and error to find a value of the exponential smoothing coefficient α that results in a relatively small MSE.

SuperBowlRatings

16. Since its inception in 1967, the Super Bowl has been one of the most watched events on U.S. television every year. The number of U.S. households that tuned in for each Super Bowl, reported by Nielsen.com, is provided in the data set SuperBowlRatings.
   a. Construct a time series plot for the data. What type of pattern exists in the data? Discuss some of the patterns that may have resulted in the pattern exhibited in the time series plot of the data.
   b. Given the pattern of the time series plot developed in part (a), do you think the forecasting methods discussed in this chapter are appropriate to develop forecasts for this time series? Explain.
   c. Use simple linear regression analysis to find the parameters for the line that minimizes MSE for this time series.

17. Consider the following time series.

t	1	2	3	4	5
Y_t	6	11	9	14	15

   a. Construct a time series plot. What type of pattern exists in the data?
   b. Use simple linear regression analysis to find the parameters for the line that minimizes MSE for this time series.
   c. What is the forecast for $t = 6$?

18. The following table reports the percentage of stocks in a portfolio for the nine previous quarters.

Year	Quarter	Stock%
1	1	29.8
1	2	31.0
1	3	29.9
1	4	30.1
2	1	32.2
2	2	31.5
2	3	32.0
2	4	31.9
3	1	30.0

   a. Construct a time series plot. What type of pattern exists in the data?
   b. Use trial and error to find a value of the exponential smoothing coefficient α that results in a relatively small MSE.
   c. Using the exponential smoothing model you developed in part (b), what is the forecast of the percentage of stocks in a typical portfolio for the second quarter of year 3?

19. Consider the following time series.

t	1	2	3	4	5	6	7
Y_t	120	110	100	96	94	92	88

   a. Construct a time series plot. What type of pattern exists in the data?
   b. Use simple linear regression analysis to find the parameters for the line that minimizes MSE for this time series.
   c. What is the forecast for $t = 8$?

20. Because of high tuition costs at state and private universities, enrollments at community colleges have increased dramatically in recent years. The following data show the enrollment (in thousands) for Jefferson Community College for the nine most recent years.

Year	Enrollment (1000s)
1	6.5
2	8.1
3	8.4
4	10.2
5	12.5
6	13.3
7	13.7
8	17.2
9	18.1

   a. Construct a time series plot. What type of pattern exists in the data?
   b. Use simple linear regression analysis to find the parameters for the line that minimizes MSE for this time series.
   c. What is the forecast for next year?

21. The Centers for Disease Control and Prevention Office on Smoking and Health (OSH) is the lead federal agency responsible for comprehensive tobacco prevention and control. OSH was established in 1965 to reduce the death and disease caused by tobacco use and exposure to secondhand smoke. One of the many responsibilities of the OSH is to collect

data on tobacco use. The following data show the percentage of U.S. adults who were users of tobacco for a recent 11-year period (http://www.cdc.gov/tobacco/data_statistics/tables/trends/cig_smoking/index.htm).

Year	Percentage of Adults Who Smoke
1	22.8
2	22.5
3	21.6
4	20.9
5	20.9
6	20.8
7	19.8
8	20.6
9	20.6
10	19.3
11	18.9

a. Construct a time series plot. What type of pattern exists in the data?
b. Use simple linear regression to find the parameters for the line that minimizes MSE for this time series.
c. One of OSH's goals is to cut the percentage of U.S. adults who were users of tobacco to 12% or less within nine years of the last year of these data. Does your regression model from part (b) suggest that OSH is on target to meet this goal? If not, use your model from part (b) to estimate the number of years that must pass after these data have been collected before OSH will achieve this goal.

22. The president of a small manufacturing firm is concerned about the continual increase in manufacturing costs over the past several years. The following figures provide a time series of the cost per unit for the firm's leading product over the past eight years.

Year	Cost/Unit ($)	Year	Cost/Unit ($)
1	20.00	5	26.60
2	24.50	6	30.00
3	28.20	7	31.00
4	27.50	8	36.00

a. Construct a time series plot. What type of pattern exists in the data?
b. Use simple linear regression analysis to find the parameters for the line that minimizes MSE for this time series.
c. What is the average cost increase that the firm has been realizing per year?
d. Compute an estimate of the cost/unit for next year.

Exercise

23. The medical community unanimously agrees on the health benefits of regular exercise, but are adults listening? During each of the past 15 years, a polling organization has surveyed Americans about their exercise habits. In the most recent of these polls, slightly over half of all American adults reported that they exercise for 30 or more minutes at least three times per week. The following data show the percentages of adults who reported that they exercise for 30 or more minutes at least three times per week during each of the 15 years of this study.

Year	Percentage of Adults Who Reported That They Exercise for 30 or More Minutes at Least Three Times per Week
1	41.0
2	44.9
3	47.1
4	45.7
5	46.6
6	44.5
7	47.6
8	49.8
9	48.1
10	48.9
11	49.9
12	52.1
13	50.6
14	54.6
15	52.4

a. Construct a time series plot. Does a linear trend appear to be present?

b. Use simple linear regression to find the parameters for the line that minimizes MSE for this time series.

c. Use the trend equation from part (b) to forecast the percentage of adults next year (year 16 of the study) who will report that they exercise for 30 or more minutes at least three times per week.

d. Would you feel comfortable using the trend equation from part (b) to forecast the percentage of adults three years from now (year 18 of the study) who will report that they exercise for 30 or more minutes at least three times per week?

24. Consider the following time series.

SELF test

Quarter	Year 1	Year 2	Year 3
1	71	68	62
2	49	41	51
3	58	60	53
4	78	81	72

a. Construct a time series plot. What type of pattern exists in the data?

b. Use a multiple linear regression model with dummy variables as follows to develop an equation to account for seasonal effects in the data. Qtr1 = 1 if Quarter 1, 0 otherwise; Qtr2 = 1 if Quarter 2, 0 otherwise; Qtr3 = 1 if Quarter 3, 0 otherwise.

c. Compute the quarterly forecasts for next year.

25. Consider the following time series data.

Quarter	Year 1	Year 2	Year 3
1	4	6	7
2	2	3	6
3	3	5	6
4	5	7	8

a. Construct a time series plot. What type of pattern exists in the data?

b. Use a multiple regression model with dummy variables as follows to develop an equation to account for seasonal effects in the data. Qtr1 = 1 if Quarter 1, 0 otherwise; Qtr2 = 1 if Quarter 2, 0 otherwise; Qtr3 = 1 if Quarter 3, 0 otherwise.

c. Compute the quarterly forecasts for next year.

26. The quarterly sales data (number of copies sold) for a college textbook over the past three years follow.

TextbookSales

Quarter	Year 1	Year 2	Year 3
1	1690	1800	1850
2	940	900	1100
3	2625	2900	2930
4	2500	2360	2615

a. Construct a time series plot. What type of pattern exists in the data?

b. Use a regression model with dummy variables as follows to develop an equation to account for seasonal effects in the data. Qtr1 = 1 if Quarter 1, 0 otherwise; Qtr2 = 1 if Quarter 2, 0 otherwise; Qtr3 = 1 if Quarter 3, 0 otherwise.

c. Compute the quarterly forecasts for next year.

d. Let $t = 1$ to refer to the observation in quarter 1 of year 1; $t = 2$ to refer to the observation in quarter 2 of year 1; . . . ; and $t = 12$ to refer to the observation in quarter 4 of year 3. Using the dummy variables defined in part (b) and also using t, develop an equation to account for seasonal effects and any linear trend in the time series. Based upon the seasonal effects in the data and linear trend, compute the quarterly forecasts for next year.

27. Air pollution control specialists in southern California monitor the amount of ozone, carbon dioxide, and nitrogen dioxide in the air on an hourly basis. The hourly time series data exhibit seasonality, with the levels of pollutants showing patterns that vary over the hours in the day. On July 15, 16, and 17, the following levels of nitrogen dioxide were observed for the 12 hours from 6:00 A.M. to 6:00 P.M.

Pollution

July 15:	25	28	35	50	60	60	40	35	30	25	25	20
July 16:	28	30	35	48	60	65	50	40	35	25	20	20
July 17:	35	42	45	70	72	75	60	45	40	25	25	25

a. Construct a time series plot. What type of pattern exists in the data?

b. Use a multiple linear regression model with dummy variables as follows to develop an equation to account for seasonal effects in the data:

Hour1 = 1 if the reading was made between 6:00 A.M. and 7:00 A.M.; 0 otherwise

Hour2 = 1 if the reading was made between 7:00 A.M. and 8:00 A.M.; 0 otherwise

$$\vdots$$

Hour11 = 1 if the reading was made between 4:00 P.M. and 5:00 P.M.; 0 otherwise

Note that when the values of the 11 dummy variables are equal to 0, the observation corresponds to the 5:00 P.M. to 6:00 P.M. hour.

c. Using the equation developed in part (b), compute estimates of the levels of nitrogen dioxide for July 18.

d. Let $t = 1$ to refer to the observation in hour 1 on July 15; $t = 2$ to refer to the observation in hour 2 of July 15; . . . ; and $t = 36$ to refer to the observation in hour 12 of July 17. Using the dummy variables defined in part (b) and t, develop an equation to account for seasonal effects and any linear trend in the time series. Based upon the seasonal effects in the data and linear trend, compute estimates of the levels of nitrogen dioxide for July 18.

SouthShore

28. South Shore Construction builds permanent docks and seawalls along the southern shore of Long Island, New York. Although the firm has been in business only five years, revenue has increased from $308,000 in the first year of operation to $1,084,000 in the most recent year. The following data show the quarterly sales revenue in thousands of dollars.

Quarter	Year 1	Year 2	Year 3	Year 4	Year 5
1	20	37	75	92	176
2	100	136	155	202	282
3	175	245	326	384	445
4	13	26	48	82	181

a. Construct a time series plot. What type of pattern exists in the data?
b. Use a multiple regression model with dummy variables as follows to develop an equation to account for seasonal effects in the data. Qtr1 = 1 if Quarter 1, 0 otherwise; Qtr2 = 1 if Quarter 2, 0 otherwise; Qtr3 = 1 if Quarter 3, 0 otherwise.
c. Let Period = 1 to refer to the observation in quarter 1 of year 1; Period = 2 to refer to the observation in quarter 2 of year 1; . . . and Period = 20 to refer to the observation in quarter 4 of year 5. Using the dummy variables defined in part (b) and Period, develop an equation to account for seasonal effects and any linear trend in the time series. Based upon the seasonal effects in the data and linear trend, compute estimates of quarterly sales for year 6.

Case Problem 1   Forecasting Food and Beverage Sales

The Vintage Restaurant, on Captiva Island near Fort Myers, Florida, is owned and operated by Karen Payne. The restaurant just completed its third year of operation. During that time, Karen sought to establish a reputation for the restaurant as a high-quality dining establishment that specializes in fresh seafood. Through the efforts of Karen and her staff, her restaurant has become one of the best and fastest-growing restaurants on the island.

To better plan for future growth of the restaurant, Karen needs to develop a system that will enable her to forecast food and beverage sales by month for up to one year in advance. Table 6.17 shows the value of food and beverage sales ($1000s) for the first three years of operation.

Managerial Report

Perform an analysis of the sales data for the Vintage Restaurant. Prepare a report for Karen that summarizes your findings, forecasts, and recommendations. Include the following:

1. A time series plot. Comment on the underlying pattern in the time series.
2. Using the dummy variable approach, forecast sales for January through December of the fourth year.

Assume that January sales for the fourth year turn out to be $295,000. What was your forecast error? If this error is large, Karen may be puzzled about the difference between your forecast and the actual sales value. What can you do to resolve her uncertainty in the forecasting procedure?

TABLE 6.17   FOOD AND BEVERAGE SALES FOR THE VINTAGE RESTAURANT ($1000s)

Month	First Year	Second Year	Third Year
January	242	263	282
February	235	238	255
March	232	247	265
April	178	193	205
May	184	193	210
June	140	149	160
July	145	157	166
August	152	161	174
September	110	122	126
October	130	130	148
November	152	167	173
December	206	230	235

Vintage

Case Problem 2   Forecasting Lost Sales

The Carlson Department Store suffered heavy damage when a hurricane struck on August 31. The store was closed for four months (September through December), and Carlson is now involved in a dispute with its insurance company about the amount of lost sales during the time the store was closed. Two key issues must be resolved: (1) the amount of sales Carlson would have made if the hurricane had not struck and (2) whether Carlson is entitled to any compensation for excess sales due to increased business activity after the storm. More than $8 billion in federal disaster relief and insurance money came into the county, resulting in increased sales at department stores and numerous other businesses.

Table 6.18 gives Carlson's sales data for the 48 months preceding the storm. Table 6.19 reports total sales for the 48 months preceding the storm for all department stores in the county, as well as the total sales in the county for the four months the Carlson Department Store was closed. Carlson's managers asked you to analyze these data and develop

TABLE 6.18   SALES FOR CARLSON DEPARTMENT STORE ($ MILLIONS)

Month	Year 1	Year 2	Year 3	Year 4	Year 5
January		1.45	2.31	2.31	2.56
February		1.80	1.89	1.99	2.28
March		2.03	2.02	2.42	2.69
April		1.99	2.23	2.45	2.48
May		2.32	2.39	2.57	2.73
June		2.20	2.14	2.42	2.37
July		2.13	2.27	2.40	2.31
August		2.43	2.21	2.50	2.23
September	1.71	1.90	1.89	2.09	
October	1.90	2.13	2.29	2.54	
November	2.74	2.56	2.83	2.97	
December	4.20	4.16	4.04	4.35	

CarlsonSales

TABLE 6.19   DEPARTMENT STORE SALES FOR THE COUNTY ($ MILLIONS)

CountySales

Month	Year 1	Year 2	Year 3	Year 4	Year 5
January		46.80	46.80	43.80	48.00
February		48.00	48.60	45.60	51.60
March		60.00	59.40	57.60	57.60
April		57.60	58.20	53.40	58.20
May		61.80	60.60	56.40	60.00
June		58.20	55.20	52.80	57.00
July		56.40	51.00	54.00	57.60
August		63.00	58.80	60.60	61.80
September	55.80	57.60	49.80	47.40	69.00
October	56.40	53.40	54.60	54.60	75.00
November	71.40	71.40	65.40	67.80	85.20
December	117.60	114.00	102.00	100.20	121.80

estimates of the lost sales at the Carlson Department Store for the months of September through December. They also asked you to determine whether a case can be made for excess storm-related sales during the same period. If such a case can be made, Carlson is entitled to compensation for excess sales it would have earned in addition to ordinary sales.

Managerial Report

Prepare a report for the managers of the Carlson Department Store that summarizes your findings, forecasts, and recommendations. Include the following:

1. An estimate of sales for Carlson Department Store had there been no hurricane
2. An estimate of countywide department store sales had there been no hurricane
3. An estimate of lost sales for the Carlson Department Store for September through December

In addition, use the countywide actual department stores sales for September through December and the estimate in part (2) to make a case for or against excess storm-related sales.

Appendix 6.1   Forecasting with Excel Data Analysis Tools

In this appendix we show how Excel can be used to develop forecasts using three forecasting methods: moving averages, exponential smoothing, and trend projection. We also show how to use Excel Solver for least-squares fitting of models to data.

Moving Averages

To show how Excel can be used to develop forecasts using the moving averages method, we develop a forecast for the gasoline sales time series in Table 6.1 and Figure 6.1. We assume that the user has entered the week in rows 2 through 13 of column A and the sales data for the 12 weeks into worksheet rows 2 through 13 of column B (as in Figure 6.13).

FIGURE 6.13   GASOLINE SALES DATA IN EXCEL ARRANGED TO USE THE MOVING
AVERAGES FUNCTION TO DEVELOP FORECASTS

	A	B
1	Week	Sales (1000s of gallons)
2	1	17
3	2	21
4	3	19
5	4	23
6	5	18
7	6	16
8	7	20
9	8	18
10	9	22
11	10	20
12	11	15
13	12	22

The following steps can be used to produce a three-week moving average.

*If the **Data Analysis** option
does not appear in the
Analysis group, you will
have to include the Add-In in
Excel. To do so, click on the
File tab, then click **Options**,
and then **Add-Ins**. Click **Go**
next to the **Excel Add-Ins**
drop-down box. Click the
box next to **Analysis
ToolPak** and click **OK**.*

Step 1. Select the **Data** tab
Step 2. From the **Analysis** group select the **Data Analysis** option
Step 3. When the **Data Analysis** dialog box appears, choose **Moving Average** and
click **OK**
Step 4. When the **Moving Average** dialog box appears:
      Enter B2:B13 in the **Input Range** box
      Enter 3 in the **Interval** box
      Enter C2 in the **Output Range** box
      Click **OK**

Once you have completed this step (as shown in Figure 6.14), the three-week moving average
forecasts will appear in column C of the worksheet as in Figure 6.15. Note that forecasts for periods of other lengths can be computed easily by entering a different value in the **Interval** box.

FIGURE 6.14   EXCEL MOVING AVERAGE DIALOGUE BOX FOR A 3-PERIOD MOVING
AVERAGE

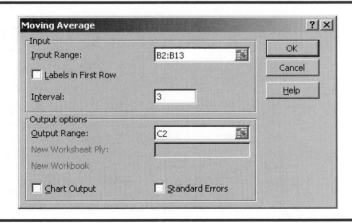

FIGURE 6.15   GASOLINE SALES DATA AND OUTPUT OF MOVING AVERAGES
FUNCTION IN EXCEL

	A	B	C
1	Week	Sales (1000s of gallons)	F_t
2	1	17	#N/A
3	2	21	#N/A
4	3	19	19
5	4	23	21
6	5	18	20
7	6	16	19
8	7	20	18
9	8	18	18
10	9	22	20
11	10	20	20
12	11	15	19
13	12	22	19

Exponential Smoothing

To show how Excel can be used for exponential smoothing, we again develop a forecast
for the gasoline sales time series in Table 6.1 and Figure 6.1. We assume that the user has
entered the week in rows 2 through 13 of column A and the sales data for the 12 weeks
into worksheet rows 2 through 13 of column B (as in Figure 6.13), and that the smoothing
constant is $\alpha = 0.2$. The following steps can be used to produce a forecast.

Step 1. Select the **Data** tab
Step 2. From the **Analysis** group select the **Data Analysis** option
Step 3. When the **Data Analysis** dialog box appears, choose **Exponential Smooth-
ing** and click **OK**
Step 4. When the **Exponential Smoothing** dialog box appears:
　　　　　Enter B2:B13 in the **Input Range** box
　　　　　Enter 0.8 in the **Damping factor** box
　　　　　Enter C2 in the **Output Range** box
　　　　　Click **OK**

Once you have completed this step (as shown in Figure 6.16), the exponential smoothing
forecasts will appear in column C of the worksheet (as in Figure 6.17). Note that the value
we entered in the **Damping factor** box is $1 - \alpha$; forecasts for other smoothing constants
can be computed easily by entering a different value for $1 - \alpha$ in the **Damping factor** box.

Trend Projection

To show how Excel can be used for trend projection, we develop a forecast for the bicycle
sales time series in Table 6.3 and Figure 6.3. We assume that the user has entered the year
(1–10) for each observation into worksheet rows 2 through 11 of column A and the sales
values into worksheet rows 2 through 11 of column B as shown in Figure 6.18. The following
steps can be used to produce a forecast for year 11 by trend projection.

Step 1. Select the **Formulas** tab
Step 2. Select two cells in the row where you want the regression coefficients b_1 and
b_0 to appear (for this example, choose D1 and E1)

FIGURE 6.16   EXCEL EXPONENTIAL SMOOTHING DIALOGUE BOX FOR $\alpha = 0.20$

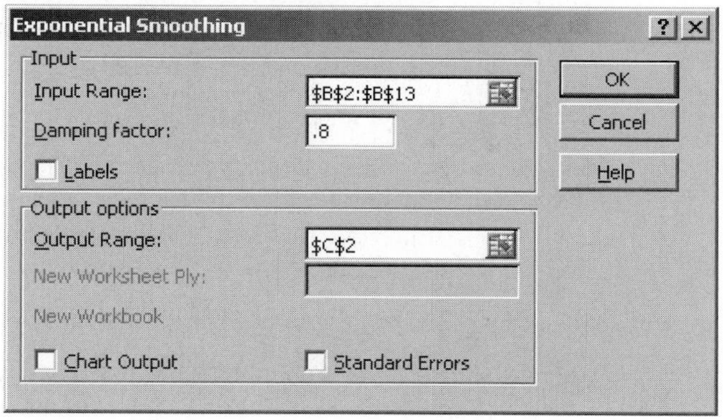

Exponential Smoothing	? X
Input	
Input Range:	$B$2:$B$13	OK
Damping factor:	.8	Cancel
☐ Labels		Help
Output options	
Output Range:	$C$2	
New Worksheet Ply:		
New Workbook		
☐ Chart Output	☐ Standard Errors	

FIGURE 6.17   GASOLINE SALES DATA AND OUTPUT OF EXPONENTIAL SMOOTHING FUNCTION IN EXCEL

	A	B	C
1	Week	Sales (1000s of gallons)	F_t
2	1	17	#N/A
3	2	21	17
4	3	19	17.8
5	4	23	18.04
6	5	18	19.032
7	6	16	18.8256
8	7	20	18.26048
9	8	18	18.60838
10	9	22	18.48671
11	10	20	19.18937
12	11	15	19.35149
13	12	22	18.48119

FIGURE 6.18   BICYCLE SALES DATA IN EXCEL ARRANGED TO USE THE LINEST FUNCTION TO FIND THE LINEAR TREND

	A	B
1	Year	Sales (1000s)
2	1	21.6
3	2	22.9
4	3	25.5
5	4	21.9
6	5	23.9
7	6	27.5
8	7	31.5
9	8	29.7
10	9	28.6
11	10	31.4

Step 3. Click on the **Insert Function** key

Step 4. When the **Insert Function** dialog box appears:
Choose **Statistical** in the **Or select a category** box
Choose **LINEST** in the **Select a function** box
Click **OK**

See Figure 6.19 for an example of this step.

Step 5. When the **Function Arguments** dialog box appears:
Enter B2:B11 in the **Known_y's** box
Enter A2:A11 in the **Known_x's** box
Click **OK**

See Figure 6.20 for an example of this step.

Step 6. Hit the F2 key and then simultaneously hit the Shift, Control, and Enter keys (Shift + Control + Enter) to create an array that contains the values of the regression coefficients b_1 and b_0

At this point you have generated the regression coefficients b_1 and b_0 in the two cells you originally selected in step 1. It is important to note that cell D1 contains b_1 and cell E1 contains b_0.

To generate a forecast, in a blank cell, multiply the value of the independent variable t by b_1 and add the value of b_0 to this product. For example, if you wish to use this linear trend model to generate a forecast for year 11 and the value of b_1 is in cell D1 and the value of b_0 is in cell E1, then enter $=11*D1+E1$ in a blank cell. The forecast for year 11, in this case 32.5, will appear in the blank cell in which you enter this formula.

FIGURE 6.19   EXCEL INSERT FUNCTION DIALOGUE BOX FOR THE FINDING THE TREND LINE USING THE LINEST FUNCTION IN EXCEL

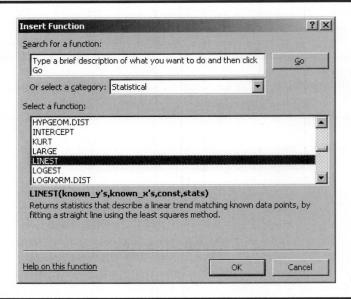

FIGURE 6.20   EXCEL FUNCTION ARGUMENTS DIALOGUE BOX FOR THE FINDING
THE TREND LINE USING THE LINEST FUNCTION IN EXCEL

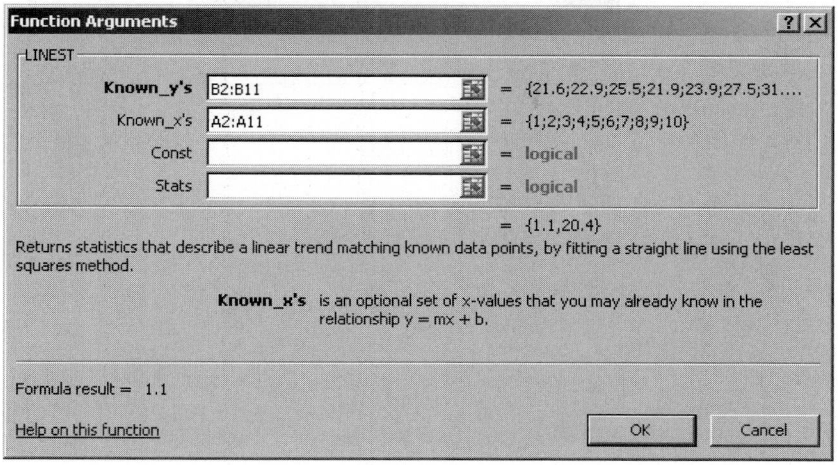

Models with Seasonality and No Trend

To show how Excel can be used to fit models with seasonality, we develop a forecast for
the umbrella sales time series in Table 6.13 and Figure 6.11. We assume that the user has
entered the year (1–5) for each observation into worksheet rows 3 through 22 of column
A; the values for the quarter in worksheet rows 3 through 22 of column B; the values for
the quarterly dummy variables $Qtr1_t$, $Qtr2_t$, and $Qtr3_t$ in worksheet rows 3 through 22 of
columns C, D, and E, respectively; and the sales values into worksheet rows 3 through 22
of column F. The following steps can be used to produce a forecast for year 11 by trend
projection as shown in Figure 6.21.

Step 1. Select the **Formulas** tab

Step 2. Select four cells in the row where you want the regression coefficients b_3, b_2,
b_1, and b_0 to appear (for this example, choose G1:J1)

Step 3. Click on the **Insert Function** key

Step 4. When the **Insert Function** dialog box appears:
Choose **Statistical** in the **Or select a category** box
Choose **LINEST** in the **Select a function** box
Click **OK**

Step 5. When the **Function Arguments** dialog box appears:
Enter F3:F22 in the **Known_y's** box
Enter C3:E22 in the **Known_x's** box
Click **OK**

See Figure 6.22 for an example of this step.

Step 6. Hit the F2 key and then simultaneously hit the Shift, Control, and Enter keys
(Shift + Control + Enter) to create an array that contains the values of the
regression coefficients b_3, b_2, b_1, and b_0

FIGURE 6.21   UMBRELLA SALES DATA IN EXCEL ARRANGED TO USE THE LINEST FUNCTION TO FIND THE SEASONAL COMPONENTS

	A	B	C	D	E	F
1				Dummy Variables		
2	Year	Quarter	Quarter 1	Quarter 2	Quarter 3	Y_t
3	1	1	1	0	0	125
4	1	2	0	1	0	153
5	1	3	0	0	1	106
6	1	4	0	0	0	88
7	2	1	1	0	0	118
8	2	2	0	1	0	161
9	2	3	0	0	1	133
10	2	4	0	0	0	102
11	3	1	1	0	0	138
12	3	2	0	1	0	144
13	3	3	0	0	1	113
14	3	4	0	0	0	80
15	4	1	1	0	0	109
16	4	2	0	1	0	137
17	4	3	0	0	1	125
18	4	4	0	0	0	109
19	5	1	1	0	0	130
20	5	2	0	1	0	165
21	5	3	0	0	1	128
22	5	4	0	0	0	96
23						

FIGURE 6.22   EXCEL FUNCTION ARGUMENTS DIALOGUE BOX FOR FINDING THE SEASONAL COMPONENTS USING THE LINEST FUNCTION IN EXCEL

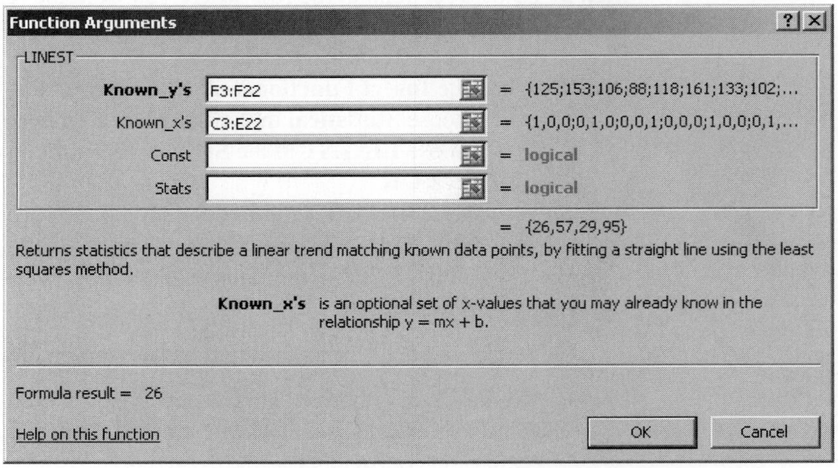

At this point you have generated the regression coefficients b_3, b_2, b_1, and b_0 in cells G1:J1 selected in step 1. It is important to note that the first cell you selected contains b_3, the second cell you selected contains b_2, the third cell you selected contains b_1, and the fourth cell you selected contains b_0 (i.e., if you selected cells G1:J1 in step 1, the value of b_1 will be in cell G1, the value of b_2 will be in H1, the value of b_1 will be in I1, and the value of b_0 will be in cell J1).

To generate a forecast, in a blank cell, add together b_0 and the product of b_1 and Qtr1$_t$, the product of b_2 and Qtr2$_t$, and the product of b_3 and Qtr3$_t$. For example, if you wish to use this linear trend model to generate a forecast for the first quarter of next year and the value of b_3 is in cell G1, the value of b_2 is in cell H1, the value of b_1 is in cell I1, and the value of b_0 is in cell J1, then enter $=1*G1+0*H1+0*I1+J1$ in a blank cell. The forecast for the first quarter of next year, in this case 124.0, will appear in the blank cell in which you enter this formula.

Models with Seasonality and Linear Trend

To show how Excel can be used to fit models with seasonality and a linear trend, we develop a forecast for the umbrella set time series in Table 6.13 and Figure 6.11. We assume that the user has entered the year (1–5) for each observation into worksheet rows 3 through 22 of column A; the values for the quarter in worksheet rows 3 through 22 of column B; the values for the quarterly dummy variables Qtr1$_t$, Qtr2$_t$, and Qtr3$_t$ into worksheet rows 3 through 22 of columns C, D, and E, respectively; the values of period t into worksheet rows 3 through 22 of column F; and the sales values into worksheet rows 3 through 22 of column G. The following steps can be used to produce a forecast for year 11 by trend projection as shown in Figure 6.23.

FIGURE 6.23   UMBRELLA TIME SERIES DATA IN EXCEL ARRANGED TO USE THE LINEST FUNCTION TO FIND BOTH THE SEASONAL COMPONENTS AND TREND COMPONENT

	A	B	C	D	E	F	G
1				Dummy Variables			
2	Year	Quarter	Quarter 1	Quarter 2	Quarter 3	t	Y_t
3	1	1	1	0	0	1	125
4	1	2	0	1	0	2	153
5	1	3	0	0	1	3	106
6	1	4	0	0	0	4	88
7	2	1	1	0	0	5	118
8	2	2	0	1	0	6	161
9	2	3	0	0	1	7	133
10	2	4	0	0	0	8	102
11	3	1	1	0	0	9	138
12	3	2	0	1	0	10	144
13	3	3	0	0	1	11	113
14	3	4	0	0	0	12	80
15	4	1	1	0	0	13	109
16	4	2	0	1	0	14	137
17	4	3	0	0	1	15	125
18	4	4	0	0	0	16	109
19	5	1	1	0	0	17	130
20	5	2	0	1	0	18	165
21	5	3	0	0	1	19	128
22	5	4	0	0	0	20	96
23							

Step 1. Select the **Formulas** tab

Step 2. Select five cells in the row where you want the regression coefficients b_4, b_3, b_2, b_1, and b_0 to appear for this example; choose H1:L1

Step 3. Click on the **Insert Function** key

Step 4. When the **Insert Function** dialog box appears:

Choose **Statistical** in the **Or select a category** box

Choose **LINEST** in the **Select a function** box

Click **OK**

Step 5. When the **Function Arguments** dialog box appears:

Enter G3:G22 in the **Known_y's** box

Enter C3:F22 in the **Known_x's** box

Click **OK**

Step 6. Hit the F2 key and then simultaneously hit the Shift, Control, and Enter keys (Shift + Control + Enter) to create an array that contains the values of the regression coefficients b_4, b_3, b_2, b_1, and b_0

At this point you have generated the regression coefficients b_4, b_3, b_2, b_1, and b_0 in cells H1:L1 selected in step 1. It is important to note that the first cell you selected contains b_4, the second cell you selected contains b_3, the third cell you selected contains b_2, the fourth cell you selected contains b_1, and the fifth cell you selected contains b_0 (i.e., if you selected cells H1:L1 in step 1, the value of b_4 will be in cell H1, the value of b_1 will be in cell I1, the value of b_2 will be in J1, the value of b_1 will be in K1, and the value of b_0 will be in cell L1).

To generate a forecast, in a blank cell, add together b_0 and the product of b_1 and $Qtr1_t$, the product of b_2 and $Qtr2_t$, the product of b_3 and $Qtr3_t$, and the product of b_4 and t. For example, if you wish to use this linear trend model to generate a forecast for the first quarter of year 5 and the value of b_4 is in cell H1, the value of b_3 is in cell I1, the value of b_2 is in cell J1, the value of b_1 is in cell K1, and the value of b_0 is in cell L1, then enter $=17*H1+1*I1+0*J1+0*K1+L1$ in a blank cell. The forecast for the first quarter of next year, in this case 7.19, will appear in the blank cell in which you enter this formula.

CHAPTER 7

Introduction to Linear Programming

CONTENTS

Linear programming is a problem-solving approach developed to help managers make decisions. Numerous applications of linear programming can be found in today's competitive business environment. For instance, IBM uses linear programming to perform capacity planning and to make capacity investment decisions for its semiconductor manufacturing operations. GE Capital uses linear programming to help determine optimal lease structuring. Marathon Oil Company uses linear programming for gasoline blending and to evaluate the economics of a new terminal or pipeline. The Q.M. in Action, Timber Harvesting Model at MeadWestvaco Corporation, provides another example of the use of linear programming. Later in the chapter another Q.M. in Action illustrates how IBM uses linear programming and other quantitative methods to plan and operate its semiconductor supply chain.

To illustrate some of the properties that all linear programming problems have in common, consider the following typical applications:

1. A manufacturer wants to develop a production schedule and an inventory policy that will satisfy sales demand in future periods. Ideally, the schedule and policy will enable the company to satisfy demand and at the same time *minimize* the total production and inventory costs.

2. A financial analyst must select an investment portfolio from a variety of stock and bond investment alternatives. The analyst would like to establish the portfolio that *maximizes* the return on investment.

3. A marketing manager wants to determine how best to allocate a fixed advertising budget among alternative advertising media such as radio, television, newspaper, and magazine. The manager would like to determine the media mix that *maximizes* advertising effectiveness.

4. A company has warehouses in a number of locations. Given specific customer demands, the company would like to determine how much each warehouse should ship to each customer so that total transportation costs are *minimized.*

These examples are only a few of the situations in which linear programming has been used successfully, but they illustrate the diversity of linear programming applications. A close scrutiny reveals one basic property they all have in common. In each example, we were concerned with *maximizing* or *minimizing* some quantity. In example 1, the manufacturer wanted to minimize costs; in example 2, the financial analyst wanted to maximize return on investment; in example 3, the marketing manager wanted to maximize advertising effectiveness; and in example 4, the company wanted to minimize total transportation costs. In all linear programming problems, the maximization or minimization of some quantity is the objective.

Q.M. *in* ACTION

TIMBER HARVESTING MODEL AT MEADWESTVACO CORPORATION*

MeadWestvaco Corporation is a major producer of premium papers for periodicals, books, commercial printing, and business forms. The company also produces pulp and lumber, designs and manufactures packaging systems for beverage and other consumables markets, and is a world leader in the production of coated board and shipping containers. Quantitative analyses at MeadWestvaco are developed and implemented by the company's Decision Analysis Department. The department assists decision makers by providing them with analytical tools of quantitative methods as well as personal analysis and recommendations.

*Based on information provided by Dr. Edward P. Winkofsky of MeadWestvaco Corporation.

(*continued*)

MeadWestvaco uses quantitative models to assist with the long-range management of the company's timberland. Through the use of large-scale linear programs, timber harvesting plans are developed to cover a substantial time horizon. These models consider wood market conditions, mill pulpwood requirements, harvesting capacities, and general forest management principles. Within these constraints, the model arrives at an optimal harvesting and purchasing schedule based on discounted cash flow. Alternative schedules reflect changes in the various assumptions concerning forest growth, wood availability, and general economic conditions.

Quantitative methods are also used in the development of the inputs for the linear programming models. Timber prices and supplies as well as mill requirements must be forecast over the time horizon, and advanced sampling techniques are used to evaluate land holdings and to project forest growth. The harvest schedule is then developed using quantitative methods.

Linear programming was initially referred to as "programming in a linear structure." In 1948, Tjalling Koopmans suggested to George Dantzig that the name was much too long: Koopman's suggestion was to shorten it to linear programming. George Dantzig agreed, and the field we now know as linear programming was named.

All linear programming problems also have a second property: restrictions or **constraints** that limit the degree to which the objective can be pursued. In the first example, the manufacturer is restricted by constraints requiring product demand to be satisfied and by the constraints limiting production capacity. The financial analyst's portfolio problem is constrained by the total amount of investment funds available and the maximum amounts that can be invested in each stock or bond. The marketing manager's media selection decision is constrained by a fixed advertising budget and the availability of the various media. In the transportation problem, the minimum-cost shipping schedule is constrained by the supply of product available at each warehouse. Thus, constraints are another general feature of every linear programming problem.

7.1 A Simple Maximization Problem

RMC, Inc., is a small firm that produces a variety of chemical-based products. In a particular production process, three raw materials are used to produce two products: a fuel additive and a solvent base. The fuel additive is sold to oil companies and is used in the production of gasoline and related fuels. The solvent base is sold to a variety of chemical firms and is used in both home and industrial cleaning products. The three raw materials are blended to form the fuel additive and solvent base as indicated in Table 7.1, which shows that a ton of fuel additive is a mixture of 0.4 tons of material 1 and 0.6 tons of material 3. A ton of solvent base is a mixture of 0.5 tons of material 1, 0.2 tons of material 2, and 0.3 tons of material 3.

TABLE 7.1   MATERIAL REQUIREMENTS PER TON FOR THE RMC PROBLEM

	Product	
	Fuel Additive	**Solvent Base**
Material 1	0.4	0.5
Material 2		0.2
Material 3	0.6	0.3

0.6 tons of material 3 is used
in each ton of fuel additive

RMC's production is constrained by a limited availability of the three raw materials. For the current production period, RMC has available the following quantities of each raw material:

Material	Amount Available for Production
Material 1	20 tons
Material 2	5 tons
Material 3	21 tons

It is important to understand that we are maximizing profit contribution, not profit. Overhead and other shared costs must be deducted before arriving at a profit figure.

Because of spoilage and the nature of the production process, any materials not used for current production are useless and must be discarded.

The accounting department analyzed the production figures, assigned all relevant costs, and arrived at prices for both products that will result in a profit contribution[1] of $40 for every ton of fuel additive produced and $30 for every ton of solvent base produced. Let us now use linear programming to determine the number of tons of fuel additive and the number of tons of solvent base to produce in order to maximize total profit contribution.

Problem Formulation

Problem formulation is the process of translating a verbal statement of a problem into a mathematical statement. The mathematical statement of the problem is referred to as a **mathematical model**. Developing an appropriate mathematical model is an art that can only be mastered with practice and experience. Even though every problem has at least some unique features, most problems also have many common or similar features. As a result, some general guidelines for developing a mathematical model can be helpful. We will illustrate these guidelines by developing a mathematical model for the RMC problem.

Understand the Problem Thoroughly The RMC problem is relatively easy to understand. RMC wants to determine how much of each product to produce in order to maximize the total contribution to profit. The number of tons available for the three materials that are required to produce the two products will limit the number of tons of each product that can be produced. More complex problems will require more work in order to understand the problem. However, understanding the problem thoroughly is the first step in developing any mathematical model.

Describe the Objective RMC's objective is to maximize the total contribution to profit.

Describe Each Constraint Three constraints limit the number of tons of fuel additive and the number of tons of solvent base that can be produced.

Constraint 1: The number of tons of material 1 used must be less than or equal to the 20 tons available.

Constraint 2: The number of tons of material 2 used must be less than or equal to the 5 tons available.

Constraint 3: The number of tons of material 3 used must be less than or equal to the 21 tons available.

---

[1]From an accounting perspective, profit contribution is more correctly described as the contribution margin per ton; overhead and other shared costs have not been allocated to the fuel additive and solvent base costs.

Define the Decision Variables The **decision variables** are the controllable inputs in the problem. For the RMC problem the two decision variables are (1) the number of tons of fuel additive produced, and (2) the number of tons of solvent base produced. In developing the mathematical model for the RMC problem, we will use the following notation for the decision variables:

$$F = \text{number of tons of fuel additive}$$
$$S = \text{number of tons of solvent base}$$

Write the Objective in Terms of the Decision Variables RMC's profit contribution comes from the production of F tons of fuel additive and S tons of solvent base. Because RMC makes $40 for every ton of fuel additive produced and $30 for every ton of solvent base produced, the company will make $40F$ from the production of the fuel additive and $30S$ from the production of the solvent base. Thus,

$$\text{Total profit contribution} = 40F + 30S$$

Because the objective—maximize total profit contribution—is a function of the decision variables F and S, we refer to $40F + 30S$ as the **objective function**. Using "Max" as an abbreviation for maximize, we can write RMC's objective as follows:

$$\text{Max } 40F + 30S \tag{7.1}$$

Write the Constraints in Terms of the Decision Variables
Constraint 1:

$$\text{Tons of material 1 used} \leq \text{Tons of material 1 available}$$

Every ton of fuel additive that RMC produces will use 0.4 tons of material 1. Thus, $0.4F$ tons of material 1 is used to produce F tons of fuel additive. Similarly, every ton of solvent base that RMC produces will use 0.5 tons of material 1. Thus, $0.5S$ tons of material 1 is used to produce S tons of solvent base. Therefore, the number of tons of material 1 used to produce F tons of fuel additive and S tons of solvent base is

$$\text{Tons of material 1 used} = 0.4F + 0.5S$$

Because 20 tons of material 1 are available for use in production, the mathematical statement of constraint 1 is

$$0.4F + 0.5S \leq 20 \tag{7.2}$$

Constraint 2:

$$\text{Tons of material 2 used} \leq \text{Tons of material 2 available}$$

Fuel additive does not use material 2. However, every ton of solvent base that RMC produces will use 0.2 tons of material 2. Thus, $0.2S$ tons of material 2 is used to produce S tons of solvent base. Therefore, the number of tons of material 2 used to produce F tons of fuel additive and S tons of solvent base is

$$\text{Tons of material 2 used} = 0.2S$$

Because 5 tons of material 2 are available for production, the mathematical statement of constraint 2 is

$$0.2S \leq 5 \qquad\qquad (7.3)$$

Constraint 3:

Tons of material 3 used $\leq$ Tons of material 3 available

Every ton of fuel additive RMC produces will use 0.6 tons of material 3. Thus, $0.6F$ tons of material 1 is used to produce F tons of fuel additive. Similarly, every ton of solvent base RMC produces will use 0.3 tons of material 3. Thus, $0.3S$ tons of material 1 is used to produce S tons of solvent base. Therefore, the number of tons of material 3 used to produce F tons of fuel additive and S tons of solvent base is

Tons of material 3 used $= 0.6F + 0.3S$

Because 21 tons of material 3 are available for production, the mathematical statement of constraint 3 is

$$0.6F + 0.3S \leq 21 \qquad\qquad (7.4)$$

Add the Nonnegativity Constraints RMC cannot produce a negative number of tons of fuel additive or a negative number of tons of solvent base. Therefore, **nonnegativity constraints** must be added to prevent the decision variables F and S from having negative values. These nonnegativity constraints are

$$F \geq 0 \text{ and } S \geq 0$$

Nonnegativity constraints are a general feature of many linear programming problems and may be written in the abbreviated form:

$$F, S \geq 0 \qquad\qquad (7.5)$$

Mathematical Model for the RMC Problem

Problem formulation is now complete. We have succeeded in translating the verbal statement of the RMC problem into the following mathematical model:

$$\text{Max } 40F + 30S$$

Subject to (s.t.)

$0.4F + 0.5S \leq 20$	Material 1
$0.2S \leq \;\;5$	Material 2
$0.6F + 0.3S \leq 21$	Material 3
$F, S \geq 0$	

Our job now is to find the product mix (i.e., the combination of F and S) that satisfies all the constraints and, at the same time, yields a maximum value for the objective function. Once these values of F and S are calculated, we will have found the optimal solution to the problem.

This mathematical model of the RMC problem is a **linear program**. The RMC problem has an objective and constraints that, as we said earlier, are common properties of all *linear* programs. But what is the special feature of this mathematical model that makes it a linear program? The special feature that makes it a linear program is that the objective function and all constraint functions (the left-hand sides of the constraint inequalities) are linear functions of the decision variables.

Mathematical functions in which each variable appears in a separate term and is raised to the first power are called **linear functions**. The objective function ($40F + 30S$) is linear because each decision variable appears in a separate term and has an exponent of 1. The amount of material 1 used ($0.4F + 0.5S$) is also a linear function of the decision variables for the same reason. Similarly, the functions on the left-hand side of the material 2 and material 3 constraint inequalities (the constraint functions) are also linear functions. Thus, the mathematical formulation is referred to as a linear program.

Try Problem 1 to test your ability to recognize the types of mathematical relationships that can be found in a linear program.

Linear *programming* has nothing to do with computer programming. The use of the word *programming* here means "choosing a course of action." Linear programming involves choosing a course of action when the mathematical model of the problem contains only linear functions.

NOTES AND COMMENTS

1. The three assumptions necessary for a linear programming model to be appropriate are proportionality, additivity, and divisibility. *Proportionality* means that the contribution to the objective function and the amount of resources used in each constraint are proportional to the value of each decision variable. *Additivity* means that the value of the objective function and the total resources used can be found by summing the objective function contribution and the resources used for all decision variables. *Divisibility* means that the decision variables are continuous. The divisibility assumption plus the nonnegativity constraints mean that decision variables can take on any value greater than or equal to zero.

2. Quantitative analysts formulate and solve a variety of mathematical models that contain an objective function and a set of constraints. Models of this type are referred to as *mathematical programming models*. Linear programming models are a special type of mathematical programming model in that the objective function and all constraint functions are linear.

 # 7.2 Graphical Solution Procedure

A linear programming problem involving only two decision variables can be solved using a graphical solution procedure. Let us begin the graphical solution procedure by developing a graph that displays the possible solutions (F and S values) for the RMC problem. The graph in Figure 7.1 has values of F on the horizontal axis and values of S on the vertical axis. Any point on the graph can be identified by its F and S values, which indicate the position of the point along the horizontal and vertical axes, respectively. Thus, every point on the graph corresponds to a possible solution. The solution of $F = 0$ and $S = 0$ is referred to as the origin. Because both F and S must be nonnegative, the graph in Figure 7.1 only displays solutions where $F \geq 0$ and $S \geq 0$.

Earlier we determined that the inequality representing the material 1 constraint was

$$0.4F + 0.5S \leq 20$$

To show all solutions that satisfy this relationship, we start by graphing the line corresponding to the equation

$$0.4F + 0.5S = 20$$

FIGURE 7.1   GRAPH SHOWING TWO SOLUTIONS FOR THE TWO-VARIABLE
RMC PROBLEM

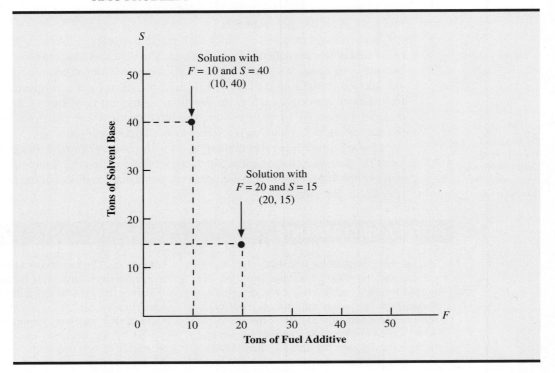

We graph this equation by identifying two points that satisfy this equation and then drawing a line through the points. Setting $F = 0$ and solving for S gives $0.5S = 20$, or $S = 40$;
hence the solution ($F = 0$, $S = 40$) satisfies the preceding equation. To find a second solution satisfying this equation, we set $S = 0$ and solve for F. Doing so, we obtain $0.4F = 20$,
or $F = 50$. Thus, a second solution satisfying the equation is ($F = 50$, $S = 0$). With these
two points, we can now graph the line. This line, called the *material 1 constraint line,* is
shown in Figure 7.2.

Recall that the inequality representing the material 1 constraint is

$$0.4F + 0.5S \leq 20$$

Can you identify all the solutions that satisfy this constraint? First, note that any point on
the line $0.4F + 0.5S = 20$ must satisfy the constraint. But where are the solutions satisfying $0.4F + 0.5S < 20$? Consider two solutions ($F = 10$, $S = 10$) and ($F = 40$, $S = 30$).
Figure 7.2 shows that the first solution is on the same side of the constraint line as the
origin while the second solution is on the side of the constraint line opposite of the origin.
Which of these solutions satisfies the material 1 constraint? For ($F = 10$, $S = 10$) we have

$$0.4F + 0.5S = 0.4(10) + 0.5(10) = 9$$

Because 9 tons is less than the 20 tons of material 1 available, the $F = 10$, $S = 10$ solution
satisfies the constraint. For $F = 40$ and $S = 30$ we have

$$0.4F + 0.5S = 0.4(40) + 0.5(30) = 31$$

FIGURE 7.2 MATERIAL 1 CONSTRAINT LINE

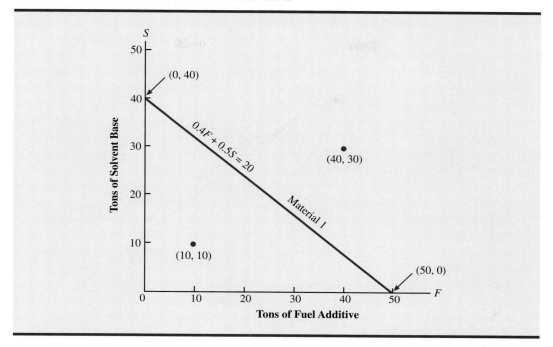

The 31 tons is greater than the 20 tons available, so the $F = 40$, $S = 30$ solution does not satisfy the constraint.

You should now be able to graph a constraint line and find the solution points that satisfy the constraint. Try Problem 2.

If a particular solution satisfies the constraint, all other solutions on the same side of the constraint line will also satisfy the constraint. If a particular solution does not satisfy the constraint, all other solutions on the same side of the constraint line will not satisfy the constraint. Thus, you need to evaluate only one solution to determine which side of a constraint line provides solutions that will satisfy the constraint. The shaded area in Figure 7.3 shows all the solutions that satisfy the material 1 constraint.

Next let us identify all solutions that satisfy the material 2 constraint:

$$0.2S \le 5$$

We start by drawing the constraint line corresponding to the equation $0.2S = 5$. Because this equation is equivalent to the equation $S = 25$, we simply draw a line whose S value is 25 for every value of F; this line is parallel to and 25 units above the horizontal axis. Figure 7.4 shows the line corresponding to the material 2 constraint. Following the approach we used for the material 1 constraint, we realize that only solutions on or below the line will satisfy the material 2 constraint. Thus, in Figure 7.4 the shaded area corresponds to the solutions that satisfy the material 2 constraint.

Similarly, we can determine the solutions that satisfy the material 3 constraint. Figure 7.5 shows the result. For practice, try to graph the feasible solutions that satisfy the material 3 constraint and determine whether your result agrees with that shown in Figure 7.5.

We now have three separate graphs showing the solutions that satisfy each of the three constraints. In a linear programming problem, we need to identify the solutions that satisfy

FIGURE 7.3   SOLUTIONS THAT SATISFY THE MATERIAL 1 CONSTRAINT

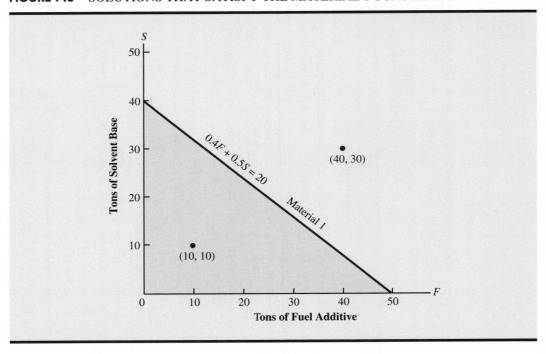

FIGURE 7.4   SOLUTIONS THAT SATISFY THE MATERIAL 2 CONSTRAINT

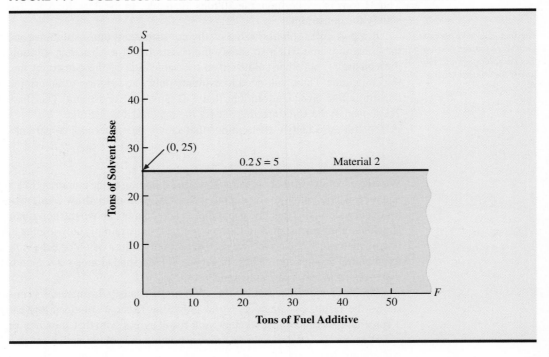

FIGURE 7.5   SOLUTIONS THAT SATISFY THE MATERIAL 3 CONSTRAINT

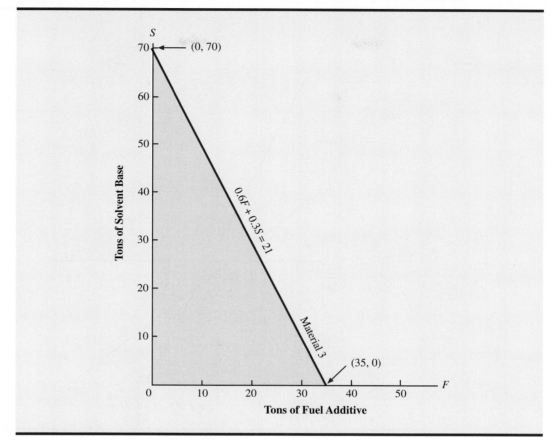

all the constraints *simultaneously.* To find these solutions, we can draw the three constraints on one graph and observe the region containing the points that do in fact satisfy all the constraints simultaneously.

The graphs in Figures 7.3, 7.4, and 7.5 can be superimposed to obtain one graph with all three constraints. Figure 7.6 shows this combined constraint graph. The shaded region in this figure includes every solution point that satisfies all the constraints simultaneously. Because solutions that satisfy all the constraints simultaneously are termed **feasible solutions**, the shaded region is called the *feasible solution region,* or simply the **feasible region**. Any point on the boundary of the feasible region, or within the feasible region, is a *feasible solution point* for the linear programming problem.

Can you now find the feasible region given several constraints? Try Problem 7.

Now that we have identified the feasible region, we are ready to proceed with the graphical solution method and find the optimal solution to the RMC problem. Recall that the optimal solution for a linear programming problem is the feasible solution that provides the best possible value of the objective function. Let us start the optimizing step of the graphical solution procedure by redrawing the feasible region on a separate graph. Figure 7.7 shows the graph.

One approach to finding the optimal solution would be to evaluate the objective function for each feasible solution; the optimal solution would then be the one yielding the

FIGURE 7.6   FEASIBLE REGION FOR THE RMC PROBLEM

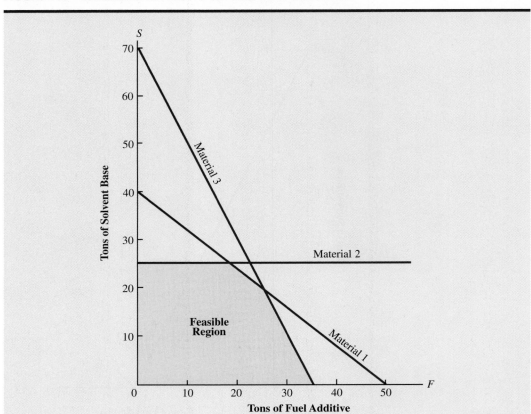

largest value. The difficulty with this approach is that the infinite number of feasible solutions makes evaluating all feasible solutions impossible. Hence, this trial-and-error procedure cannot be used to identify the optimal solution.

Rather than trying to compute the profit contribution for each feasible solution, we select an arbitrary value for profit contribution and identify all the feasible solutions that yield the selected value. For example, what feasible solutions provide a profit contribution of $240? These solutions are given by the values of F and S in the feasible region that will make the objective function

$$40F + 30S = 240$$

This expression is simply the equation of a line. Thus all feasible solutions (F, S) yielding a profit contribution of $240 must be on the line. We learned earlier in this section how to graph a constraint line. The procedure for graphing the profit or objective function line is the same. Letting $F = 0$, we see that S must be 8; thus the solution point $(F = 0, S = 8)$ is on the line. Similarly, by letting $S = 0$ we see that the solution point $(F = 6, S = 0)$ is also on the line. Drawing the line through these two points identifies all the solutions that have a profit contribution of $240. A graph of this profit line is presented in Figure 7.8. The graph shows that an infinite number of feasible production combinations will provide a $240 profit contribution.

FIGURE 7.7 FEASIBLE REGION FOR THE RMC PROBLEM

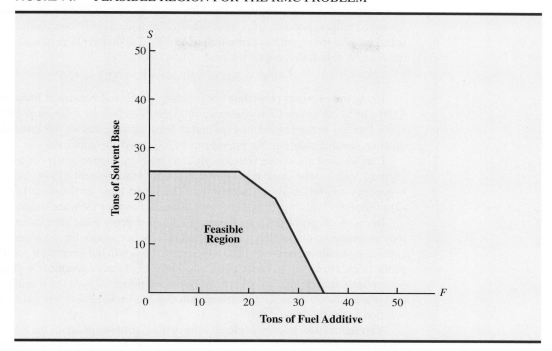

FIGURE 7.8 $240 PROFIT LINE FOR THE RMC PROBLEM

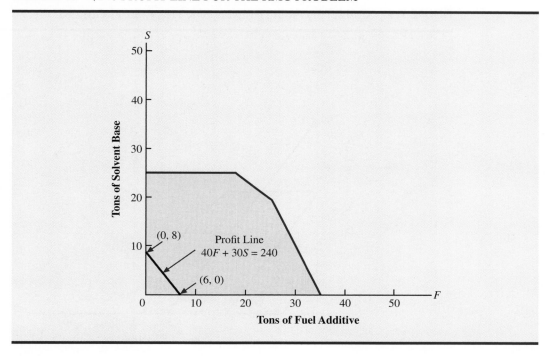

The objective is to find the feasible solution yielding the highest profit contribution, so we proceed by selecting higher profit contributions and finding the solutions that yield the stated values. For example, what solutions provide a profit contribution of $720? What solutions provide a profit contribution of $1200? To answer these questions, we must find the F and S values that are on the profit lines:

$$40F + 30S = 720 \text{ and } 40F + 30S = 1200$$

Using the previous procedure for graphing profit and constraint lines, we graphed the $720 and $1200 profit lines presented in Figure 7.9. Not all solution points on the $1200 profit line are in the feasible region, but at least some points on the line are; thus, we can obtain a feasible solution that provides a $1200 profit contribution.

Can we find a feasible solution yielding an even higher profit contribution? Look at Figure 7.9 and make some general observations about the profit lines. You should be able to identify the following properties: (1) The profit lines are *parallel* to each other, and (2) profit lines with higher profit contributions are farther from the origin.

Because the profit lines are parallel and higher profit lines are farther from the origin, we can obtain solutions that yield increasingly higher values for the objective function by continuing to move the profit line farther from the origin but keeping it parallel to the other profit lines. However, at some point any further outward movement will place the profit line entirely outside the feasible region. Because points outside the feasible region are unacceptable, the point in the feasible region that lies on the highest profit line is an optimal solution to the linear program.

You should now be able to identify the optimal solution point for the RMC problem. Use a ruler and move the profit line as far from the origin as you can. What is the last point in the feasible region? This point, which is the optimal solution, is shown graphically in Figure 7.10. The optimal values for the decision variables are the F and S values at this point.

FIGURE 7.9   SELECTED PROFIT LINES FOR THE RMC PROBLEM

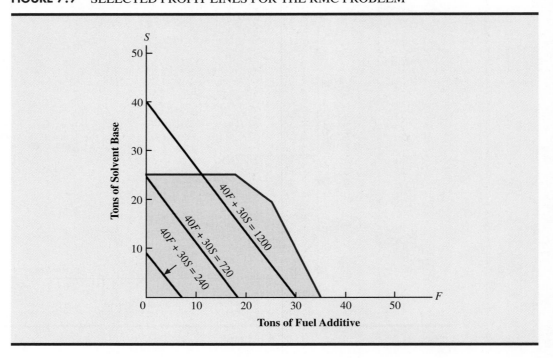

FIGURE 7.10 OPTIMAL SOLUTION FOR THE RMC PROBLEM

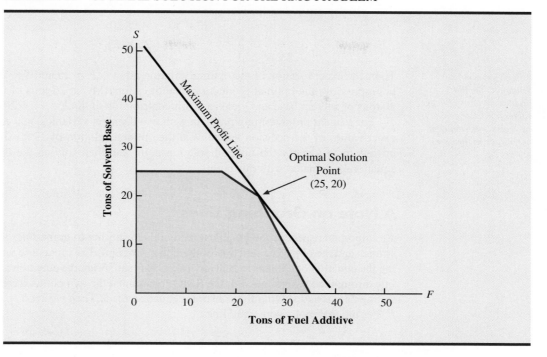

Depending on the accuracy of your graph, you may or may not be able to determine the exact optimal values of F and S directly from the graph. However, refer to Figure 7.6 and note that the optimal solution point for the RMC example is at the *intersection* of the material 1 and material 3 constraint lines. That is, the optimal solution is on both the material 1 constraint line,

$$0.4F + 0.5S = 20 \tag{7.6}$$

and the material 3 constraint line,

$$0.6F + 0.3S = 21 \tag{7.7}$$

Thus, the values of the decision variables F and S must satisfy both equations (7.6) and (7.7) simultaneously. Using (7.6) and solving for F gives

$$0.4F = 20 - 0.5S$$

or

$$F = 50 - 1.25S \tag{7.8}$$

Substituting this expression for F into equation (7.7) and solving for S yields

$$0.6(50 - 1.25S) + 0.3S = 21$$
$$30 - 0.75S + 0.3S = 21$$
$$-0.45S = -9$$
$$S = 20$$

Substituting $S = 20$ in equation (7.8) and solving for F provides

$$F = 50 - 1.25(20)$$
$$= 50 - 25 = 25$$

Although the optimal solution to the RMC problem consists of integer values for the decision variables, this result will not always be the case.

Thus, the exact location of the optimal solution point is $F = 25$ and $S = 20$. This solution point provides the optimal production quantities for RMC at 25 tons of fuel additive and 20 tons of solvent base and yields a profit contribution of $40(25) + 30(20) = \$1600$.

For a linear programming problem with two decision variables, you can determine the exact values of the decision variables at the optimal solution by first using the graphical procedure to identify the optimal solution point and then solving the two simultaneous equations associated with this point.

A Note on Graphing Lines

An important aspect of the graphical method is the ability to graph lines showing the constraints and the objective function of the linear program. The procedure we used for graphing the equation of a line is to find any two points satisfying the equation and then draw the line through the two points. For the RMC constraints, the two points were easily found by setting $F = 0$ and solving the constraint equation for S. Then we set $S = 0$ and solved for F. For the material 1 constraint line

$$0.4F + 0.5S = 20$$

Try Problem 10 to test your ability to use the graphical solution procedure to identify the optimal solution and find the exact values of the decision variables at the optimal solution.

this procedure identified the two points ($F = 0$, $S = 40$) and ($F = 50$, $S = 0$). The material 1 constraint line was then graphed by drawing a line through these two points.

All constraints and objective function lines in two-variable linear programs can be graphed if two points on the line can be identified. However, finding the two points on the line is not always as easy as shown in the RMC problem. For example, suppose a company manufactures two models of a tablet computer: the Professional (P) and the Assistant (A). Management needs 50 units of the Professional model for its own sales force and expects sales of the remaining Professionals to be less than or equal to 50% of the sales of the Assistant. A constraint enforcing this requirement is

$$P - 50 \leq 0.5A$$

or

$$P - 0.5A \leq 50$$

Using the equality form of the constraint and setting $P = 0$, we find that the point ($P = 0, A = -100$) is on the constraint line. Setting $A = 0$, we find a second point ($P = 50$, $A = 0$) on the constraint line. If we have drawn only the nonnegative ($P \geq 0, A \geq 0$) portion of the graph, the first point ($P = 0, A = -100$) cannot be plotted because $A = -100$ is not on the graph. Whenever we have two points on the line, but one or both of the points cannot be plotted in the nonnegative portion of the graph, the simplest approach is to enlarge the graph. In this example, the point ($P = 0, A = -100$) can be plotted by extending the graph to include the negative A axis. Once both points satisfying the constraint equation have been located, the line can be drawn. The constraint line and the solutions that satisfy the constraint $P - 0.5A \leq 50$ are shown in Figure 7.11.

FIGURE 7.11 SOLUTIONS THAT SATISFY THE CONSTRAINT $P - 0.5A \leq 50$

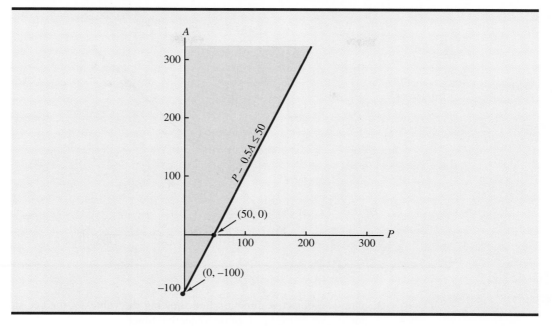

As another example, consider a problem involving two decision variables, R and T. Suppose that the number of units of R produced has to be at least equal to the number of units of T produced. A constraint enforcing this requirement is

$$R \geq T$$

or

$$R - T \geq 0$$

Can you graph a constraint line when the origin is on the constraint line? Try Problem 5.

To find all solutions satisfying the constraint as an equality, we first set $R = 0$ and solve for T. This result shows that the origin ($T = 0$, $R = 0$) is on the constraint line. Setting $T = 0$ and solving for R provides the same point. However, we can obtain a second point on the line by setting T equal to any value other than zero and then solving for R. For instance, setting $T = 100$ and solving for R, we find that the point ($T = 100$, $R = 100$) is on the line. With the two points ($R = 0$, $T = 0$) and ($R = 100$, $T = 100$), the constraint line $R - T = 0$ and the solutions that satisfy the constraint $R - T \geq 0$ can be plotted as shown in Figure 7.12.

Summary of the Graphical Solution Procedure for Maximization Problems

For additional practice in using the graphical solution procedure, try Problem 24.

As we have seen, the graphical solution procedure is a method for solving two-variable linear programming problems such as the RMC problem. The steps of the graphical solution procedure for a maximization problem are summarized here:

1. Prepare a graph for each constraint that shows the solutions that satisfy the constraint.
2. Determine the feasible region by identifying the solutions that satisfy all the constraints simultaneously.

FIGURE 7.12 FEASIBLE SOLUTIONS FOR THE CONSTRAINT $R - T \geq 0$

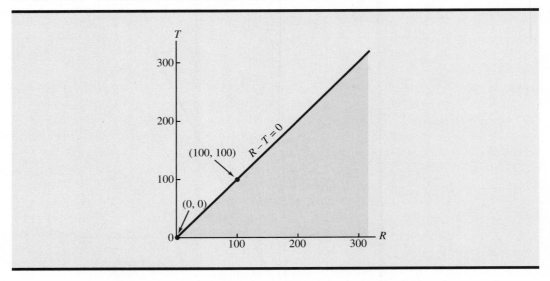

3. Draw an objective function line showing the values of the decision variables that yield a specified value of the objective function.
4. Move parallel objective function lines toward larger objective function values until further movement would take the line completely outside the feasible region.
5. Any feasible solution on the objective function line with the largest value is an optimal solution.

Slack Variables

In addition to the optimal solution and its associated profit contribution, the RMC managers will want information about the production requirements for the three materials. We can determine this information by substituting the optimal solution values ($F = 25$, $S = 20$) into the constraints of the linear program.

Constraint	Tons Required for $F = 25$, $S = 20$ Tons	Tons Available	Unused Tons
Material 1	$0.4(25) + 0.5(20) = 20$	20	0
Material 2	$0.2(20) = 4$	5	1
Material 3	$0.6(25) + 0.3(20) = 21$	21	0

Thus, the optimal solution tells management that the production of 25 tons of fuel additive and 20 tons of solvent base will require all available material 1 and material 3 but only 4 of the 5 tons of material 2. The 1 ton of unused material 2 is referred to as *slack*. In linear programming terminology, any unused or idle capacity for a $\leq$ constraint is referred to as the *slack associated with the constraint*. Thus, the material 2 constraint has a slack of 1 ton.

Can you identify the slack associated with a constraint? Try Problem 24, part (e).

Often variables, called **slack variables**, are added to the formulation of a linear programming problem to represent the slack, or unused capacity, associated with a constraint. Unused capacity makes no contribution to profit, so slack variables have coefficients of zero in the objective function. More generally, slack variables represent the difference between the right-hand side and the left-hand side of a $\leq$ constraint. After the addition of three slack variables, denoted S_1, S_2, and S_3, the mathematical model of the RMC problem becomes

$$\text{Max} \quad 40F + 30S + 0S_1 + 0S_2 + 0S_3$$

s.t.

$$
\begin{aligned}
0.4F + 0.5S + 1S_1 && = 20 \\
0.2S + 1S_2 && = 5 \\
0.6F + 0.3S + 1S_3 &= 21 \\
F, S, S_1, S_2, S_3 &\geq 0
\end{aligned}
$$

Can you write a linear program in standard form? Try Problem 18.

Whenever a linear program is written in a form with all the constraints expressed as equalities, it is said to be written in **standard form**.

Referring to the standard form of the RMC problem, we see that at the optimal solution ($F = 25$, $S = 20$) the values for the slack variables are

Constraint	Value of Slack Variable
Material 1	$S_1 = 0$
Material 2	$S_2 = 1$
Material 3	$S_3 = 0$

Could we have used the graphical analysis to provide some of the previous information? The answer is yes. By finding the optimal solution in Figure 7.6, we see that the material 1 constraint and the material 3 constraint restrict, or *bind*, the feasible region at this point. Thus, the optimal solution requires the use of all of these two resources. In other words, the graph shows that at the optimal solution material 1 and material 3 will have zero slack. But, because the material 2 constraint is not binding the feasible region at the optimal solution, we can expect some slack for this resource.

Finally, some linear programs may have one or more constraints that do not affect the feasible region; that is, the feasible region remains the same whether or not the constraint is included in the problem. Because such a constraint does not affect the feasible region, it is called a **redundant constraint**. Redundant constraints can be dropped from the problem without having any effect on the optimal solution. However, in most linear programming problems redundant constraints are not discarded because they are not immediately recognizable as being redundant. The RMC problem had no redundant constraints because each constraint had an effect on the feasible region.

NOTES AND COMMENTS

1. In the standard form representation of a linear program, the objective function coefficients for the slack variables are zero. This condition implies that slack variables, which represent unused resources, do not affect the value of the objective function. However, in some applications, some or all of the unused resources can be sold and contribute to profit. In such cases the corresponding slack variables become decision variables representing the amount of resources to be sold. For each of these variables, a nonzero coefficient in the objective function would reflect the profit associated with selling a unit of the corresponding resource.

2. Redundant constraints do not affect the feasible region; as a result they can be removed from a linear programming model without affecting the optimal solution. However, if the linear programming model is to be resolved later, changes in some of the data might change a previously redundant constraint into a binding constraint. Thus, we recommend keeping all constraints in the linear programming model even though one or more of the constraints may be redundant.

7.3 Extreme Points and the Optimal Solution

Suppose that the profit contribution for 1 ton of solvent base increases from $30 to $60 while the profit contribution for 1 ton of fuel additive and all the constraints remain unchanged. The complete linear programming model of this new problem is identical to the mathematical model in Section 7.2, except for the revised objective function:

$$\text{Max } 40F + 60S$$

How does this change in the objective function affect the optimal solution to the RMC problem? Figure 7.13 shows the graphical solution of the RMC problem with the revised objective function. Note that because the constraints do not change, the feasible region remains unchanged. However, the profit lines must be altered to reflect the new objective function.

By moving the profit line in a parallel manner away from the origin, we find the optimal solution as shown in Figure 7.13. The values of the decision variables at this point are $F = 18.75$ and $S = 25$. The increased profit for the solvent base caused a change in the optimal solution. In fact, as you might suspect, we cut back the production of the lower profit fuel additive and increase the production of the higher profit solvent base.

What do you notice about the location of the optimal solutions in the linear programming problems that we solved thus far? Look closely at the graphical solutions in Figures 7.10 and 7.13. An important observation that you should be able to make is that the optimal solutions occur at one of the vertices, or "corners," of the feasible region. In linear programming terminology these vertices are referred to as the **extreme points** of the feasible region.

FIGURE 7.13 OPTIMAL SOLUTION FOR THE RMC PROBLEM WITH AN OBJECTIVE FUNCTION OF $40F + 60S$

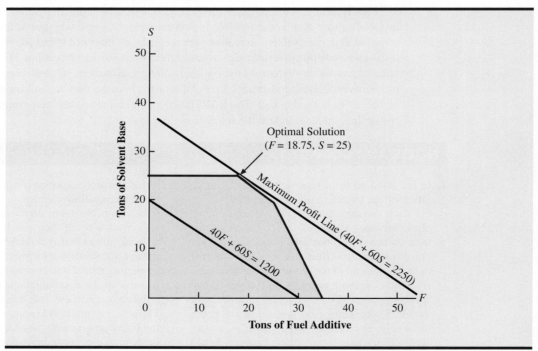

FIGURE 7.14 THE FIVE EXTREME POINTS OF THE FEASIBLE REGION FOR THE RMC PROBLEM

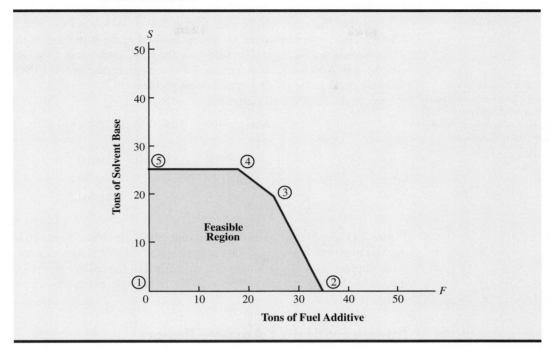

Thus, the RMC has five vertices or five extreme points (Figure 7.14). We can now state our observation about the location of optimal solutions:[2]

> The optimal solution to a linear programming problem can be found at an extreme point of the feasible region for the problem.

For additional practice in identifying the extreme points of the feasible region and determining the optimal solution by computing and comparing the objective function value at each extreme point, try Problem 13.

This property means that, if you are looking for the optimal solution to a linear programming problem, you do not have to evaluate all feasible solution points. In fact, you have to consider *only* the feasible solutions that occur at the extreme points of the feasible region. Thus, for the RMC problem, instead of computing and comparing the profit for all feasible solutions, we can find the optimal solution by evaluating the five extreme-point solutions and selecting the one that provides the highest profit. Actually, the graphical solution procedure is nothing more than a convenient way of identifying an optimal extreme point for two-variable problems.

Computer Solution of the RMC Problem

Computer programs designed to solve linear programming problems are widely available. After a short period of familiarization with the specific features of the program, most users can solve linear programming problems with few difficulties. Problems involving thousands of variables and thousands of constraints are now routinely solved with computer packages. Some of the leading commercial packages include CPLEX, LINGO, MOSEK, Gurobi,

---

[2]In Section 7.6 we show that two special cases (infeasibility and unboundedness) in linear programming have no optimal solution. The observation stated does not apply to these cases.

Excel Solver, and Analytic Solver Platform for Excel. Packages are also available for free download. A good example is Clp (COIN-OR linear programming) available from the COIN-OR organization at *http://www.coin-or.org*.

Probably the most widely used tool is Solver, which is built into Microsoft Excel. Therefore, the computer output we discuss is based on the output provided by Excel Solver. The complete details for how to formulate the RMC problem in Excel and use Solver are contained in Appendix 7.1. Appendix 7.2 demonstrates the use of LINGO, a stand-alone software package for solving optimization problems.

Instructions on how to solve linear programs using Excel and LINGO are provided in appendixes at the end of the chapter.

Recall the RMC linear program:

$$\text{Max} \quad 40F + 30S$$

s.t.

$$
\begin{aligned}
0.4F + 0.5S &\leq 20 \quad \text{Material 1} \\
0.2S &\leq 5 \quad \text{Material 2} \\
0.6F + 0.3S &\leq 21 \quad \text{Material 3} \\
F, S &\geq 0
\end{aligned}
$$

Figure 7.15 shows the optimal solution to the RMC problem. This output is based on the Answer Report from Excel Solver, but includes the variable names we have used in our linear programming model. This allows you to easily link the answer report to the model under discussion. We will use this style to show the solutions to optimization problems throughout Chapters 7–12.

Interpretation of Answer Report

Let us look more closely at the answer report in Figure 7.15 and interpret the computer solution provided for the RMC problem. First, note the number 1600.000 in the Objective Cells (Max) section, which appears in the Final Value column to the right of objective function value, Maximize Total Profit. This number indicates that the optimal solution to this problem will provide a profit of $1600. Directly below the objective function value are the values of

FIGURE 7.15   ANSWER REPORT FOR THE RMC PROBLEM

Objective Cells (Max)

Name	Original Value	Final Value
Maximize Total Profit	0.000	1600.000

Variable Cells

Model Variable	Name	Original Value	Final Value	Integer
F	Tons Produced Fuel Additive	0.000	25.000	Contin
S	Tons Produced Solvent Base	0.000	20.000	Contin

Constraints

Constraint Number	Name	Cell Value	Status	Slack
1	Material 1 Amount Used	20.000	Binding	0.000
2	Material 2 Amount Used	4.000	Not Binding	1.000
3	Material 3 Amount Used	21.000	Binding	0.000

the decision variables at the optimal solution. These are shown as the Final Value column of the Variable Cells section in the answer report. Thus, we have $F = 25$ tons of fuel additive and $S = 20$ tons of solvent base as the optimal production quantities. We will discuss the meaning of the Integer column in the Variable Cells section in Chapter 11.

The Constraints section of the answer report provides information about the status of the constraints. Recall that the RMC problem had three less-than-or-equal-to constraints corresponding to the tons available for each of the three raw materials. The information shown in the Slack column provides the value of the slack variable for each of the three constraints. This information is summarized as follows:

Constraint Number	Constraint Name	Value of Slack Variable
1	Material 1 Amount Used	0
2	Material 2 Amount Used	1
3	Material 3 Amount Used	0

Thus, we see that the binding constraints (the Material 1 Amount Used and Material 3 Amount Used constraints) have zero slack at the optimal solution. The Material 2 Amount Used constraint has 1 ton of slack, or unused capacity.

7.5 A Simple Minimization Problem

M&D Chemicals produces two products that are sold as raw materials to companies manufacturing bath soaps and laundry detergents. Based on an analysis of current inventory levels and potential demand for the coming month, M&D's management has specified that the combined production for products A and B must total at least 350 gallons. Separately, a major customer's order for 125 gallons of product A must also be satisfied. Product A requires 2 hours of processing time per gallon while product B requires 1 hour of processing time per gallon, and for the coming month, 600 hours of processing time are available. M&D's objective is to satisfy these requirements at a minimum total production cost. Production costs are $2 per gallon for product A and $3 per gallon for product B.

To find the minimum-cost production schedule, we will formulate the M&D Chemicals problem as a linear program. Following a procedure similar to the one used for the RMC problem, we first define the decision variables and the objective function for the problem. Let

$$A = \text{number of gallons of product A}$$
$$B = \text{number of gallons of product B}$$

Because the production costs are $2 per gallon for product A and $3 per gallon for product B, the objective function that corresponds to the minimization of the total production cost can be written as

$$\text{Min } 2A + 3B$$

Next, consider the constraints placed on the M&D Chemicals problem. To satisfy the major customer's demand for 125 gallons of product A, we know A must be at least 125. Thus, we write the constraint

$$1A \geq 125$$

Because the combined production for both products must total at least 350 gallons, we can write the constraint

$$1A + 1B \geq 350$$

Finally, the limitation on available processing time of 600 hours means that we need to add the constraint

$$2A + 1B \leq 600$$

After adding the nonnegativity constraints ($A, B \geq 0$), we have the following linear program for the M&D Chemicals problem:

Max $2A + 3B$

s.t.

$$1A \qquad\;\; \geq 125 \quad \text{Demand for product A}$$
$$1A + 1B \geq 350 \quad \text{Total production}$$
$$2A + 1B \leq 600 \quad \text{Processing time}$$
$$A, B \geq 0$$

Because the linear programming model has only two decision variables, the graphical solution procedure can be used to find the optimal production quantities. The graphical method for this problem, just as in the RMC problem, requires us to first graph the constraint lines to find the feasible region. By graphing each constraint line separately and then checking points on either side of the constraint line, the solutions that satisfy each constraint can be identified. By combining the solutions that satisfy each constraint on the same graph, we obtain the feasible region shown in Figure 7.16.

FIGURE 7.16   FEASIBLE REGION FOR THE M&D CHEMICALS PROBLEM

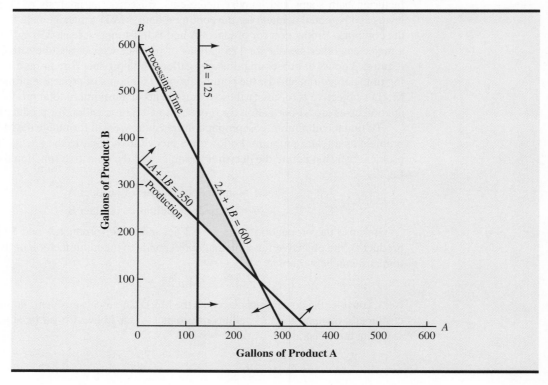

FIGURE 7.17 GRAPHICAL SOLUTION FOR THE M&D CHEMICALS PROBLEM

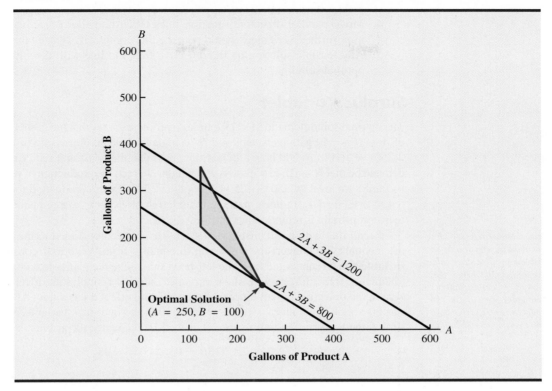

To find the minimum-cost solution, we now draw the objective function line corresponding to a particular total cost value. For example, we might start by drawing the line $2A + 3B = 1200$. This line is shown in Figure 7.17. Clearly some points in the feasible region would provide a total cost of $1200. To find the values of A and B that provide smaller total cost values, we move the objective function line in a lower left direction until, if we moved it any farther, it would be entirely outside the feasible region. Note that the objective function line $2A + 3B = 800$ intersects the feasible region at the extreme point $A = 250$ and $B = 100$. This extreme point provides the minimum-cost solution with an objective function value of 800. From Figures 7.16 and 7.17, we can see that the total production constraint and the processing time constraint are binding. Just as in every linear programming problem, the optimal solution occurs at an extreme point of the feasible region.

Summary of the Graphical Solution Procedure for Minimization Problems

Can you use the graphical solution procedure to determine the optimal solution for a minimization problem? Try Problem 31.

The steps of the graphical solution procedure for a minimization problem are summarized here:

1. Prepare a graph for each constraint that shows the solutions that satisfy the constraint.
2. Determine the feasible region by identifying the solutions that satisfy all the constraints simultaneously.

3. Draw an objective function line showing the values of the decision variables that yield a specified value of the objective function.

4. Move parallel objective function lines toward smaller objective function values until further movement would take the line completely outside the feasible region.

5. Any feasible solution on the objective function line with the smallest value is an optimal solution.

Surplus Variables

The optimal solution to the M&D Chemicals problem shows that the desired total production of $A + B = 350$ gallons is achieved by using all available processing time of $2A + 1B = 2(250) + 1(100) = 600$ hours. In addition, note that the constraint requiring that product A demand be met is satisfied with $A = 250$ gallons. In fact, the production of product A exceeds its minimum level by $250 - 125 = 125$ gallons. This excess production for product A is referred to as *surplus*. In linear programming terminology, any excess quantity corresponding to a $\geq$ constraint is referred to as surplus.

Excel Solver refers to all nonbinding constraints as having positive slack values regardless of whether they are $\geq$ or $\leq$ constraints. However, we will use "surplus" when referring to a nonbinding $\geq$ constraint.

Recall that with a $\leq$ constraint, a slack variable can be added to the left-hand side of the inequality to convert the constraint to equality form. With a $\geq$ constraint, a **surplus variable** can be subtracted from the left-hand side of the inequality to convert the constraint to equality form. Just as with slack variables, surplus variables are given a coefficient of zero in the objective function because they have no effect on its value. After including two surplus variables, S_1 and S_2, for the $\geq$ constraints and one slack variable, S_3, for the $\leq$ constraint, the linear programming model of the M&D Chemicals problem becomes

$$\text{Min} \quad 2A + 3B + 0S_1 + 0S_2 + 0S_3$$
$$\text{s.t.}$$
$$\begin{aligned}
1A \quad\quad - 1S_1 \quad\quad\quad\quad &= 125 \\
1A + 1B \quad\quad - 1S_2 \quad\quad &= 350 \\
2A + 1B \quad\quad\quad + 1S_3 &= 600 \\
A, B, S_1, S_2, S_3 &\geq 0
\end{aligned}$$

Try Problem 35 to test your ability to use slack and surplus variables to write a linear program in standard form.

All the constraints are now equalities. Hence, the preceding formulation is the standard form representation of the M&D Chemicals problem. At the optimal solution of $A = 250$ and $B = 100$, the values of the surplus and slack variables are as follows:

Constraint	Value of Surplus or Slack Variable
Demand for product A	$S_1 = 125$
Total production	$S_2 = 0$
Processing time	$S_3 = 0$

Refer to Figures 7.16 and 7.17. Note that the zero surplus and slack variables are associated with the constraints that are binding at the optimal solution—that is, the total production and processing time constraints. The surplus of 125 units is associated with the nonbinding constraint on the demand for product A.

In the RMC problem all the constraints were of the $\leq$ type, and in the M&D Chemicals problem the constraints were a mixture of $\geq$ and $\leq$ types. The number and types of constraints encountered in a particular linear programming problem depend on the specific conditions existing in the problem. Linear programming problems may have some $\leq$ constraints, some $\geq$ constraints, and some $=$ constraints. For an equality constraint, feasible solutions must lie directly on the constraint line.

Try Problem 34 to practice solving a linear program with all three constraint forms.

An example of a linear program with two decision variables, G and H, and all three constraint forms is given here:

$$\text{Min} \quad 2G + 2H$$
$$\text{s.t.}$$
$$1G + 3H \leq 12$$
$$3G + 1H \geq 13$$
$$1G - 1H = 3$$
$$G, H \geq 0$$

The standard-form representation of this problem is

$$\text{Min} \quad 2G + 2H + 0S_1 + 0S_2$$
$$\text{s.t.}$$
$$1G + 3H + 1S_1 \qquad\quad = 12$$
$$3G + 1H \qquad - 1S_2 = 13$$
$$1G - 1H \qquad\qquad\quad = 3$$
$$G, H, S_1, S_2 \geq 0$$

The standard form requires a slack variable for the $\leq$ constraint and a surplus variable for the $\geq$ constraint. However, neither a slack nor a surplus variable is required for the third constraint because it is already in equality form.

When solving linear programs graphically, it is not necessary to write the problem in its standard form. Nevertheless, it is helpful to be able to compute the values of the slack and surplus variables and understand what they mean. A final point: The standard form of the linear programming problem is equivalent to the original formulation of the problem. That is, the optimal solution to any linear programming problem is the same as the optimal solution to the standard form of the problem. The standard form does not change the basic problem; it only changes how we write the constraints for the problem.

Computer Solution of the M&D Chemicals Problem

The answer report for the M&D Chemicals Problem is presented in Figure 7.18. The answer report shows that the minimum-cost solution yields an objective function value of $800.

FIGURE 7.18   ANSWER REPORT FOR THE M&D CHEMICALS PROBLEM

Objective Cells (Min)

Name	Original Value	Final Value
Minimize Total Cost Product A	0.000	800.000

M&D   Variable Cells

Model Variable	Name	Original Value	Final Value	Integer
A	Gallons Produced Product A	0.000	250.000	Contin
B	Gallons Produced Product B	0.000	100.000	Contin

Constraints

Constraint Number	Name	Cell Value	Status	Slack
1	Demand for Product A	250.000	Not Binding	125.000
2	Total Production	350.000	Binding	0.000
3	Processing Time	600.000	Binding	0.000

The values of the decision variables show that 250 gallons of product A and 100 gallons of product B provide the minimum-cost solution.

The Slack column in the Constraints section of the answer report shows that the $\geq$ constraint corresponding to the demand for product A (see constraint 1) has a value of 125 units. Excel uses "slack" when referring to nonbinding $\geq$ or $\leq$ constraints. However, since this is a $\geq$ constraint, it tells us that production of product A in the optimal solution exceeds demand by 125 gallons. In other words, the demand for product A (constraint 1) has a surplus value of 125 units. The slack values are zero for the total production requirement (constraint 2) and the processing time limitation (constraint 3), which indicates that these constraints are binding at the optimal solution.

(7.6) Special Cases

In this section we discuss three special situations that can arise when we attempt to solve linear programming problems.

Alternative Optimal Solutions

From our discussion of the graphical solution procedure, we know that optimal solutions can be found at the extreme points of the feasible region. Now let us consider the special case where the optimal objective function line coincides with one of the binding constraint lines. It can lead to **alternative optimal solutions**, whereby more than one solution provides the optimal value for the objective function.

To illustrate the case of alternative optimal solutions, we return to the RMC problem. However, let us assume that the profit contribution for the solvent base (S) has increased to $50. The revised objective function is $40F + 50S$. Figure 7.19 shows the graphical solution to this problem. Note that the optimal solution still occurs at an extreme point. In fact, it occurs at two extreme points: extreme point ③ ($F = 25$, $S = 20$) and extreme point ④ ($F = 18.75$, $S = 25$).

The objective function values at these two extreme points are identical; that is,

$$40F + 50S = 40(25) + 50(20) = 2000$$

and

$$40F + 50S = 40(18.75) + 50(25) = 2000$$

Furthermore, any point on the line connecting the two optimal extreme points also provides an optimal solution. For example, the solution point ($F = 21.875$, $S = 22.5$), which is halfway between the two extreme points, also provides the optimal objective function value of

$$40F + 50S = 40(21.875) + 50(22.5) = 2000$$

A linear programming problem with alternative optimal solutions is generally a good situation for the manager or decision maker. It means that several combinations of the decision variables are optimal and that the manager can select the most desirable optimal solution. Unfortunately, determining whether a problem has alternative optimal solutions is not a simple matter.

Infeasibility

Infeasibility means that no solution to the linear programming problem satisfies all constraints, including the nonnegativity constraints. Graphically, infeasibility means that a feasible region does not exist; that is, no points satisfy all constraint equations and

FIGURE 7.19 OPTIMAL SOLUTIONS FOR THE RMC PROBLEM WITH AN OBJECTIVE FUNCTION OF $40F + 50S$

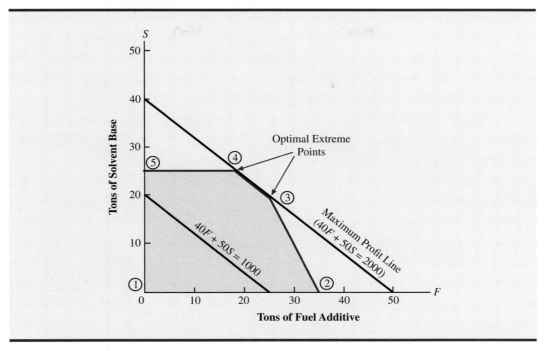

nonnegativity conditions simultaneously. To illustrate this situation, let us return to the problem facing RMC.

Problems with no feasible solution do arise in practice, most often because management's expectations are too high or because too many restrictions have been placed on the problem.

Suppose that management specified that at least 30 tons of fuel additive and at least 15 tons of solvent base must be produced. Figure 7.20 shows the graph of the solution region that reflects these requirements. The shaded area in the lower left-hand portion of the graph depicts those points satisfying the less-than-or-equal-to constraints on the amount of materials available. The shaded area in the upper right-hand portion depicts those points satisfying the minimum production requirements of 30 tons of fuel additive and 15 tons of solvent base. But none of the points satisfy both sets of constraints. Thus, if management imposes these minimum production requirements, no feasible solution to the linear programming problem is possible.

How should we interpret this infeasibility in terms of the current problem? First, we should tell management that, for the available amounts of the three materials, producing 30 tons of fuel additive and 15 tons of solvent base isn't possible. Moreover, we can tell management exactly how much more of each material is needed.

Material	Minimum Tons Required for $F = 30, S = 15$	Tons Available	Additional Tons Required
Material 1	$0.4(30) + 0.5(15) = 19.5$	20	—
Material 2	$0.2(15) = 3$	5	—
Material 3	$0.6(30) + 0.3(15) = 22.5$	21	1.5

FIGURE 7.20   NO FEASIBLE REGION FOR THE RMC PROBLEM WITH MINIMUM
PRODUCTION REQUIREMENTS

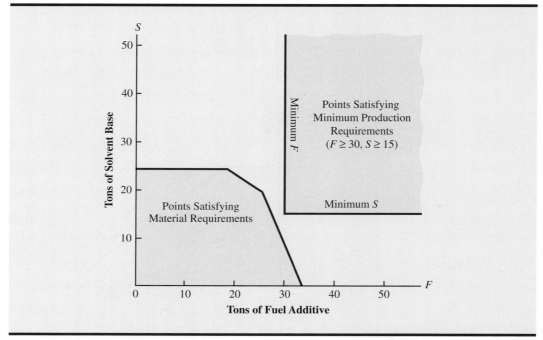

Thus, RMC has a sufficient supply of materials 1 and 2 but will need 1.5 additional tons of material 3 to meet management's production requirements of 30 tons of fuel additive and 15 tons of solvent base. If, after reviewing the preceding analysis, management still wants this level of production for the two products, RMC will have to obtain the additional 1.5 tons of material 3.

Often, many possibilities are available for corrective management action, once we discover the lack of a feasible solution. The important thing to realize is that linear programming analysis can help determine whether management's plans are feasible. By analyzing the problem using linear programming, we are often able to point out infeasible conditions and initiate corrective action.

Whenever you attempt to solve a problem that is infeasible using Excel Solver, you will obtain a message that says "Solver could not find a feasible solution." In this case, you know that no solution to the linear programming problem will satisfy all constraints. Careful inspection of your formulation is necessary to identify why the problem is infeasible. In some situations the only reasonable approach is to drop one or more constraints and resolve the problem. If you are able to find an optimal solution for this revised problem, you will know that the constraint(s) that were omitted are causing the problem to be infeasible.

Unbounded

The solution to a maximization linear programming problem is **unbounded** if the value of the solution may be made infinitely large without violating any of the constraints; for a minimization problem, the solution is unbounded if the value may be made infinitely small. This condition might be termed *managerial utopia*; for example, if this condition were to occur in a profit maximization problem, the manager could achieve an unlimited profit.

However, in linear programming models of real problems, the occurrence of an unbounded solution means that the problem has been improperly formulated. We know it is not possible to increase profits indefinitely. Therefore, we must conclude that if a profit maximization problem results in an unbounded solution, the mathematical model doesn't represent the real-world problem sufficiently. Usually, an unbounded problem results from the inadvertent omission of a constraint during problem formulation.

As an illustration, consider the following linear program with two decision variables, X and Y:

$$\text{Max} \quad 20X + 10Y$$
$$\text{s.t.}$$
$$1X \qquad \geq 2$$
$$1Y \leq 5$$
$$X, Y \geq 0$$

In Figure 7.21 we graphed the feasible region associated with this problem. Note that we can only indicate part of the feasible region because the feasible region extends indefinitely in the direction of the X-axis. Looking at the objective function lines in Figure 7.21, we see that the solution to this problem may be made as large as we desire. No matter what solution we pick, we will always be able to reach some feasible solution with a larger value. Thus, we say that the solution to this linear program is *unbounded*.

FIGURE 7.21 EXAMPLE OF AN UNBOUNDED PROBLEM

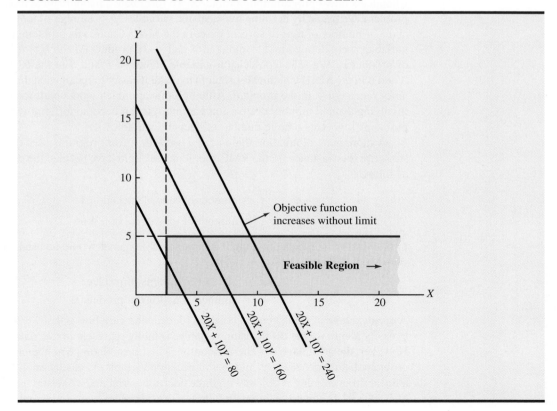

Can you recognize whether a linear program involves alternative optimal solutions, infeasibility, or is unbounded? Try Problems 42 and 43.

Whenever you attempt to solve a problem that is unbounded using Excel Solver, you will obtain a message that says, "The Objective Cell values do not converge." Because unbounded solutions cannot occur in real problems, the first thing you should do is to review your model to determine whether you have incorrectly formulated the problem.

NOTES AND COMMENTS

1. Infeasibility is independent of the objective function. It exists because the constraints are so restrictive that they allow no feasible region for the linear programming model. Thus, when you encounter infeasibility, making changes in the coefficients of the objective function will not help; the problem will remain infeasible.

2. The occurrence of an unbounded solution is often the result of a missing constraint. However, a change in the objective function may cause a previously unbounded problem to become bounded with an optimal solution. For example, the graph in Figure 7.21 shows an unbounded solution for the objective function Max $20X + 10Y$. However, changing the objective function to Max $-20X - 10Y$ will provide the optimal solution $X = 2$ and $Y = 0$ even though no changes have been made in the constraints.

7.7 General Linear Programming Notation

In this chapter we showed how to formulate mathematical models for the RMC and M&D Chemicals linear programming problems. To formulate a mathematical model of the RMC problem, we began by defining two decision variables: F = number of tons of fuel additive, and S = number of tons of solvent base. In the M&D Chemicals problem, the two decision variables were defined as A = number of gallons of product A, and B = number of gallons of product B. We selected decision variable names of F and S in the RMC problem and A and B in the M&D Chemicals problem to make it easier to recall what these decision variables represented in the problem. Although this approach works well for linear programs involving a small number of decision variables, it can become difficult when dealing with problems involving a large number of decision variables.

A more general notation that is often used for linear programs uses the letter x with a subscript. For instance, in the RMC problem, we could have defined the decision variables as follows:

$$x_1 = \text{number of tons of fuel additive}$$
$$x_2 = \text{number of tons of solvent base}$$

In the M&D Chemicals problem, the same variable names would be used, but their definitions would change:

$$x_1 = \text{number of gallons of product A}$$
$$x_2 = \text{number of gallons of product B}$$

A disadvantage of using general notation for decision variables is that we are no longer able to easily identify what the decision variables actually represent in the mathematical model. However, the advantage of general notation is that formulating a mathematical model for a problem that involves a large number of decision variables is much easier. For instance, for a linear programming problem with three decision variables, we would use variable names of $x_1, x_2,$ and x_3; for a problem with four decision variables, we would use variable names of

$x_1, x_2, x_3,$ and x_4; and so on. Clearly, if a problem involved 1000 decision variables, trying to identify 1000 unique names would be difficult. However, using the general linear programming notation, the decision variables would be defined as $x_1, x_2, x_3, \ldots, x_{1000}$.

To illustrate the graphical solution procedure for a linear program written using general linear programming notation, consider the following mathematical model for a maximization problem involving two decision variables:

$$\text{Max} \quad 3x_1 + 2x_2$$

s.t.

$$2x_1 + 2x_2 \leq 8$$
$$1x_1 + 0.5x_2 \leq 3$$
$$x_1, x_2 \geq 0$$

We must first develop a graph that displays the possible solutions (x_1 and x_2 values) for the problem. The usual convention is to plot values of x_1 along the horizontal axis and values of x_2 along the vertical axis. Figure 7.22 shows the graphical solution for this two-variable

FIGURE 7.22   GRAPHICAL SOLUTION OF A TWO-VARIABLE LINEAR PROGRAM WITH GENERAL NOTATION

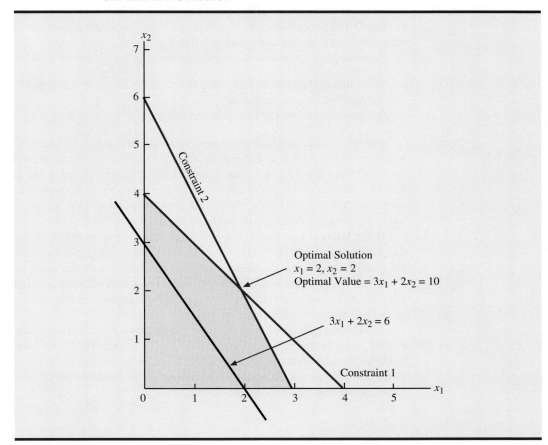

problem. Note that for this problem the optimal solution is $x_1 = 2$ and $x_2 = 2$, with an objective function value of 10.

Using general linear programming notation, we can write the standard form of the preceding problem as follows:

$$\text{Max} \quad 3x_1 + \quad 2x_2 + 0s_1 + 0s_2$$
$$\text{s.t.}$$
$$2x_1 + \quad 2x_2 + 1s_1 \qquad \quad = 8$$
$$1x_1 + 0.5x_2 + \qquad \quad 1s_2 = 3$$
$$x_1, x_2, s_1, s_2 \geq 0$$

Thus, at the optimal solution $x_1 = 2$ and $x_2 = 2$, the values of the slack variables are $s_1 = s_2 = 0$.

Summary

We formulated linear programming models for the RMC maximization problem and the M&D Chemicals minimization problem. For both problems we showed how a graphical solution procedure can be used to identify an optimal solution. To demonstrate how to interpret linear program solutions, we introduced answer reports similar to the output obtained from Excel Solver. In formulating a linear programming model of these problems, we developed a general definition of a linear program.

A linear program is a mathematical model with the following qualities:

1. A linear objective function that is to be maximized or minimized
2. A set of linear constraints
3. Variables restricted to nonnegative values

Slack variables may be used to write less-than-or-equal-to constraints in equality form, and surplus variables may be used to write greater-than-or-equal-to constraints in equality form. The value of a slack variable can usually be interpreted as the amount of unused resource, whereas the value of a surplus variable indicates the amount over and above some stated minimum requirement. When all constraints have been written as equalities, the linear program has been written in its standard form.

If the solution to a linear program is infeasible or unbounded, no optimal solution to the problem can be found. In the case of infeasibility, no feasible solutions are possible. In the case of an unbounded solution, the objective function can be made infinitely large for a maximization problem and infinitely small for a minimization problem. In the case of alternative optimal solutions, two or more optimal extreme points exist, and all the points on the line segment connecting them are also optimal.

The chapter concluded with a section showing how to write a mathematical model using general linear programming notation. The Q.M. in Action, IBM Uses Linear Programming to Help Plan and Execute Its Supply Chain Operations, provides just one of many examples of the widespread use of linear programming. In the next two chapters we will see many more applications of linear programming.

Q.M. *in* ACTION

IBM USES LINEAR PROGRAMMING TO HELP PLAN AND EXECUTE ITS SUPPLY CHAIN OPERATIONS*

A semiconductor technically refers to the material, usually silicon, used to build integrated circuits that become the main building components for electronic devices. But in casual usage, semiconductor manufacturing refers to the design and production of the actual integrated circuit that performs the calculations necessary to power your computers, smartphones, tablets, and virtually every other electronic device with which you are familiar.

Semiconductor supply chains are very complex because they typically stretch across the globe and include many different suppliers, manufacturers, distributors, and customers. Hundreds of operations are required to produce semiconductors, and lead times are often very long. To produce a finished semiconductor, the three-dimensional circuits must be deposited onto the base layer of semiconductive material through a process of deposition, photolithography, etching, and ion implantation. The circuits must then be thoroughly tested and packaged for shipment to customers. Small deviations in the manufacturing process result in different quality (speed) of devices. These different devices can sometimes be used as a substitute in times of shortages. For instance, if there are no medium-speed devices available for a certain manufacturing step, a high-speed device can be used instead, but a medium-speed device cannot be substituted for a high-speed device. This

creates a multitude of different possible flows through the supply chain that must be constantly managed.

IBM has been producing semiconductors for more than 50 years. IBM manufactures semiconductors in Asia and in North America, and they distribute them around the world. IBM has been using quantitative methods for many years to plan and execute its supply chain strategies. IBM's Central Planning Engine (CPE) is the set of tools the company uses to manage its supply chain activities for semiconductors. The CPE uses a combination of quantitative methods, including linear programming. The model constraints include limitations on production capacities, raw material availabilities, lead time delays, and demand requirements. There are also constraints to enforce the substitution possibilities for certain devices. While many different problem-solving methods are used in the CPE, linear programing is used in several different steps, including the allocation of production capacity to devices based on available capacities and materials.

IBM uses the CPE to perform both long-term strategic planning and short-term operational execution for its semiconductor supply chain. Because of the clever use of specific quantitative methods, these complex calculations can be completed in just a few hours. These fast solution times allow IBM to run several different possible scenarios in a single day and implement sensitivity analysis to understand possible risks in its supply chain. IBM credits the use of the CPE to increasing on-time deliveries by 15% and reducing inventory by 25 to 30%.

---

*Based on Alfred Degbotse, Brian T. Denton, Kenneth Fordyce, R. John Milne, Robert Orzell, Chi-Tai Wang, "IBM Blends Heuristics and Optimization to Plan Its Semiconductor Supply Chain," *Interfaces*, 2012, 1–12.

Glossary

Alternative optimal solutions The case in which more than one solution provides the optimal value for the objective function.

Constraint An equation or inequality that rules out certain combinations of decision variables as feasible solutions.

Decision variable A controllable input for a linear programming model.

Extreme point Graphically speaking, extreme points are the feasible solution points occurring at the vertices, or "corners," of the feasible region. With two-variable problems, extreme points are determined by the intersection of the constraint lines.

Feasible region The set of all feasible solutions.

Feasible solution A solution that satisfies all the constraints simultaneously.

Infeasibility The situation in which no solution to the linear programming problem satisfies all the constraints.

Linear functions Mathematical expressions in which the variables appear in separate terms and are raised to the first power.

Linear program A mathematical model with a linear objective function, a set of linear constraints, and nonnegative variables.

Mathematical model A representation of a problem where the objective and all constraint conditions are described by mathematical expressions.

Nonnegativity constraints A set of constraints that requires all variables to be nonnegative.

Objective function The expression that defines the quantity to be maximized or minimized in a linear programming model.

Problem formulation The process of translating a verbal statement of a problem into a mathematical statement called the *mathematical model.*

Redundant constraint A constraint that does not affect the feasible region. If a constraint is redundant, it can be removed from the problem without affecting the feasible region.

Slack variable A variable added to the left-hand side of a less-than-or-equal-to constraint to convert the constraint into an equality. The value of this variable can usually be interpreted as the amount of unused resource.

Standard form A linear program in which all the constraints are written as equalities. The optimal solution of the standard form of a linear program is the same as the optimal solution of the original formulation of the linear program.

Surplus variable A variable subtracted from the left-hand side of a greater-than-or-equal-to constraint to convert the constraint into an equality. The value of this variable can usually be interpreted as the amount over and above some required minimum level.

Unbounded The situation in which the value of the solution may be made infinitely large in a maximization linear programming problem or infinitely small in a minimization problem without violating any of the constraints.

Problems

1. Which of the following mathematical relationships could be found in a linear programming model, and which could not? For the relationships that are unacceptable for linear programs, state why.
    a. $-1A + 2B \leq 70$
    b. $2A - 2B = 50$
    c. $1A - 2B^2 \leq 10$
    d. $3\sqrt{A} + 2B \geq 15$
    e. $1A + 1B = 6$
    f. $2A + 5B + 1AB \leq 25$

2. Find the solutions that satisfy the following constraints:
    a. $4A + 2B \leq 16$
    b. $4A + 2B \geq 16$
    c. $4A + 2B = 16$

3. Show a separate graph of the constraint lines and the solutions that satisfy each of the
   following constraints:
   a. $3A + 2B \leq 18$
   b. $12A + 8B \geq 480$
   c. $5A + 10B = 200$

4. Show a separate graph of the constraint lines and the solutions that satisfy each of the
   following constraints:
   a. $3A - 4B \geq 60$
   b. $-6A + 5B \leq 60$
   c. $5A - 2B \leq 0$

5. Show a separate graph of the constraint lines and the solutions that satisfy each of the
   following constraints:
   a. $A \geq 0.25 (A + B)$
   b. $B \leq 0.10 (A + B)$
   c. $A \leq 0.50 (A + B)$

6. Three objective functions for linear programming problems are $7A + 10B$, $6A + 4B$,
   and $-4A + 7B$. Show the graph of each for objective function values equal to 420.

7. Identify the feasible region for the following set of constraints:

$$0.5A + 0.25B \geq 30$$
$$1A + 5B \geq 250$$
$$0.25A + 0.5B \leq 50$$
$$A, B \geq 0$$

8. Identify the feasible region for the following set of constraints:

$$2A - 1B \leq 0$$
$$-1A + 1.5B \leq 200$$
$$A, B \geq 0$$

9. Identify the feasible region for the following set of constraints:

$$3A - 2B \geq 0$$
$$2A - 1B \leq 200$$
$$1A \leq 150$$
$$A, B \geq 0$$

10. For the linear program

$$\text{Max} \quad 2A + 3B$$
$$\text{s.t.}$$
$$1A + 2B \leq 6$$
$$5A + 3B \leq 15$$
$$A, B \geq 0$$

   find the optimal solution using the graphical solution procedure. What is the value of the
   objective function at the optimal solution?

11. Solve the following linear program using the graphical solution procedure:

$$\text{Max} \quad 5A + 5B$$
$$\text{s.t.}$$
$$1A \leq 100$$
$$1B \leq 80$$
$$2A + 4B \leq 400$$
$$A, B \geq 0$$

12. Consider the following linear programming problem:

$$\text{Max} \quad 3A + 3B$$

s.t.

$$2A + 4B \leq 12$$
$$6A + 4B \leq 24$$
$$A, B \geq 0$$

a. Find the optimal solution using the graphical solution procedure.
b. If the objective function is changed to $2A + 6B$, what is the optimal solution?
c. How many extreme points are there? What are the values of A and B at each extreme point?

13. Consider the following linear program:

$$\text{Max} \quad 1A + 2B$$

s.t.

$$1A \qquad \leq 5$$
$$1B \leq 5$$
$$2A + 2B = 12$$
$$A, B \geq 0$$

a. Show the feasible region.
b. What are the extreme points of the feasible region?
c. Find the optimal solution using the graphical procedure.

14. Par, Inc., is a small manufacturer of golf equipment and supplies. Par's distributor believes a market exists for both a medium-priced golf bag, referred to as a standard model, and a high-priced golf bag, referred to as a deluxe model. The distributor is so confident of the market that, if Par can make the bags at a competitive price, the distributor will purchase all the bags that Par can manufacture over the next three months. A careful analysis of the manufacturing requirements resulted in the following table, which shows the production time requirements for the four required manufacturing operations and the accounting department's estimate of the profit contribution per bag:

| | Production Time (hours) | | | | |
Product	Cutting and Dyeing	Sewing	Finishing	Inspection and Packaging	Profit per Bag
Standard	$7/10$	$1/2$	1	$1/10$	$10
Deluxe	1	$5/6$	$2/3$	$1/4$	$ 9

The director of manufacturing estimates that 630 hours of cutting and dyeing time, 600 hours of sewing time, 708 hours of finishing time, and 135 hours of inspection and packaging time will be available for the production of golf bags during the next three months.

a. If the company wants to maximize total profit contribution, how many bags of each model should it manufacture?
b. What profit contribution can Par earn on those production quantities?
c. How many hours of production time will be scheduled for each operation?
d. What is the slack time in each operation?

15. Suppose that Par's management (Problem 14) encounters the following situations:
    a.   The accounting department revises its estimate of the profit contribution for the deluxe bag to $18 per bag.
    b.   A new low-cost material is available for the standard bag, and the profit contribution per standard bag can be increased to $20 per bag. (Assume that the profit contribution of the deluxe bag is the original $9 value.)
    c.   New sewing equipment is available that would increase the sewing operation capacity to 750 hours. (Assume that $10A + 9B$ is the appropriate objective function.)
    If each of these situations is encountered separately, what is the optimal solution and the total profit contribution?

16. Refer to the feasible region for Par, Inc., in Problem 14.
    a.   Develop an objective function that will make extreme point (0, 540) the optimal extreme point.
    b.   What is the optimal solution for the objective function you selected in part (a)?
    c.   What are the values of the slack variables associated with this solution?

17. Write the following linear program in standard form:

$$\text{Max} \quad 5A + 2B$$
$$\text{s.t.}$$
$$1A - 2B \leq 420$$
$$2A + 3B \leq 610$$
$$6A - 1B \leq 125$$
$$A, B \geq 0$$

18. For the linear program

$$\text{Max} \quad 4A + 1B$$
$$\text{s.t.}$$
$$10A + 2B \leq 30$$
$$3A + 2B \leq 12$$
$$2A + 2B \leq 10$$
$$A, B \geq 0$$

    a.   Write this problem in standard form.
    b.   Solve the problem using the graphical solution procedure.
    c.   What are the values of the three slack variables at the optimal solution?

19. Given the linear program

$$\text{Max} \quad 3A + 4B$$
$$\text{s.t.}$$
$$-1A + 2B \leq 8$$
$$1A + 2B \leq 12$$
$$2A + 1B \leq 16$$
$$A, B \geq 0$$

    a.   Write the problem in standard form.
    b.   Solve the problem using the graphical solution procedure.
    c.   What are the values of the three slack variables at the optimal solution?

20. For the linear program

$$\text{Max} \quad 3A + 2B$$

s.t.

$$
\begin{aligned}
A + B &\geq 4 \\
3A + 4B &\leq 24 \\
A &\geq 2 \\
A - B &\leq 0 \\
A, B &\geq 0
\end{aligned}
$$

   a. Write the problem in standard form.
   b. Solve the problem.
   c. What are the values of the slack and surplus variables at the optimal solution?

21. Consider the following linear program:

$$\text{Max} \quad 2A + 3B$$

s.t.

$$
\begin{aligned}
5A + 5B &\leq 400 \quad &\text{Constraint 1} \\
-1A + 1B &\leq 10 \quad &\text{Constraint 2} \\
1A + 3B &\geq 90 \quad &\text{Constraint 3} \\
A, B &\geq 0
\end{aligned}
$$

Figure 7.23 shows a graph of the constraint lines.

   a. Place a number (1, 2, or 3) next to each constraint line to identify which constraint it represents.
   b. Shade in the feasible region on the graph.
   c. Identify the optimal extreme point. What is the optimal solution?
   d. Which constraints are binding? Explain.
   e. How much slack or surplus is associated with the nonbinding constraint?

FIGURE 7.23   GRAPH OF THE CONSTRAINT LINES FOR EXERCISE 21

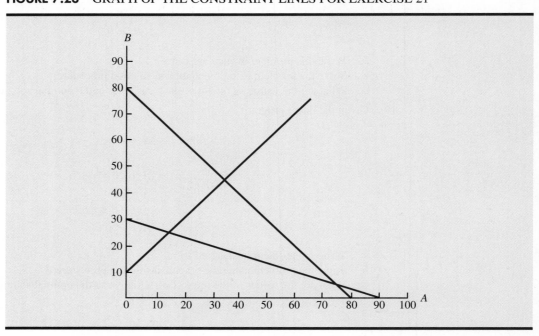

22. Reiser Sports Products wants to determine the number of All-Pro (*A*) and College (*C*) footballs to produce in order to maximize profit over the next four-week planning horizon. Constraints affecting the production quantities are the production capacities in three departments: cutting and dyeing; sewing; and inspection and packaging. For the four-week planning period, 340 hours of cutting and dyeing time, 420 hours of sewing time, and 200 hours of inspection and packaging time are available. All-Pro footballs provide a profit of $5 per unit and College footballs provide a profit of $4 per unit. The linear programming model with production times expressed in minutes is as follows:

$$\text{Max} \quad 5A + 4C$$
$$\text{s.t.}$$

$$12A + 6C \le 20{,}400 \quad \text{Cutting and dyeing}$$
$$9A + 15C \le 25{,}200 \quad \text{Sewing}$$
$$6A + 6C \le 12{,}000 \quad \text{Inspection and packaging}$$
$$A, C \ge 0$$

A portion of the graphical solution to the Reiser problem is shown in Figure 7.24.
a. Shade the feasible region for this problem.
b. Determine the coordinates of each extreme point and the corresponding profit. Which extreme point generates the highest profit?

FIGURE 7.24   PORTION OF THE GRAPHICAL SOLUTION FOR EXERCISE 22

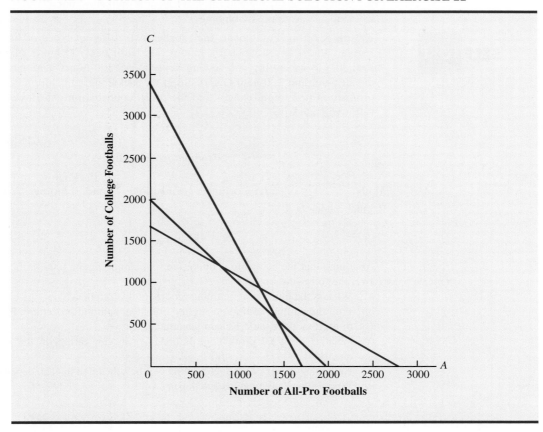

    c.   Draw the profit line corresponding to a profit of $4000. Move the profit line as far from the origin as you can in order to determine which extreme point will provide the optimal solution. Compare your answer with the approach you used in part (b).

    d.   Which constraints are binding? Explain.

    e.   Suppose that the values of the objective function coefficients are $4 for each All-Pro model produced and $5 for each College model. Use the graphical solution procedure to determine the new optimal solution and the corresponding value of profit.

23. Embassy Motorcycles (EM) manufacturers two lightweight motorcycles designed for easy handling and safety. The EZ-Rider model has a new engine and a low profile that make it easy to balance. The Lady-Sport model is slightly larger, uses a more traditional engine, and is specifically designed to appeal to women riders. Embassy produces the engines for both models at its Des Moines, Iowa, plant. Each EZ-Rider engine requires 6 hours of manufacturing time and each Lady-Sport engine requires 3 hours of manufacturing time. The Des Moines plant has 2100 hours of engine manufacturing time available for the next production period. Embassy's motorcycle frame supplier can supply as many EZ-Rider frames as needed. However, the Lady-Sport frame is more complex and the supplier can only provide up to 280 Lady-Sport frames for the next production period. Final assembly and testing requires 2 hours for each EZ-Rider model and 2.5 hours for each Lady-Sport model. A maximum of 1000 hours of assembly and testing time are available for the next production period. The company's accounting department projects a profit contribution of $2400 for each EZ-Rider produced and $1800 for each Lady-Sport produced.

    a.   Formulate a linear programming model that can be used to determine the number of units of each model that should be produced in order to maximize the total contribution to profit.

    b.   Solve the problem graphically. What is the optimal solution?

    c.   Which constraints are binding?

24. Kelson Sporting Equipment, Inc., makes two different types of baseball gloves: a regular model and a catcher's model. The firm has 900 hours of production time available in its cutting and sewing department, 300 hours available in its finishing department, and 100 hours available in its packaging and shipping department. The production time requirements and the profit contribution per glove are given in the following table:

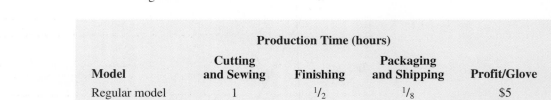

| Model | Production Time (hours) | | | |
	Cutting and Sewing	Finishing	Packaging and Shipping	Profit/Glove
Regular model	1	$1/2$	$1/8$	$5
Catcher's model	$3/2$	$1/3$	$1/4$	$8

Assuming that the company is interested in maximizing the total profit contribution, answer the following:

    a.   What is the linear programming model for this problem?

    b.   Find the optimal solution using the graphical solution procedure. How many gloves of each model should Kelson manufacture?

    c.   What is the total profit contribution Kelson can earn with the given production quantities?

    d.   How many hours of production time will be scheduled in each department?

    e.   What is the slack time in each department?

25. George Johnson recently inherited a large sum of money; he wants to use a portion of this money to set up a trust fund for his two children. The trust fund has two investment options: (1) a bond fund and (2) a stock fund. The projected returns over the life of the investments are 6% for the bond fund and 10% for the stock fund. Whatever portion of the inheritance George finally decides to commit to the trust fund, he wants to invest at least 30% of that amount in the bond fund. In addition, he wants to select a mix that will enable him to obtain a total return of at least 7.5%.
    a. Formulate a linear programming model that can be used to determine the percentage that should be allocated to each of the possible investment alternatives.
    b. Solve the problem using the graphical solution procedure.

26. The Sea Wharf Restaurant would like to determine the best way to allocate a monthly advertising budget of $1000 between newspaper advertising and radio advertising. Management decided that at least 25% of the budget must be spent on each type of media, and that the amount of money spent on local newspaper advertising must be at least twice the amount spent on radio advertising. A marketing consultant developed an index that measures audience exposure per dollar of advertising on a scale from 0 to 100, with higher values implying greater audience exposure. If the value of the index for local newspaper advertising is 50 and the value of the index for spot radio advertising is 80, how should the restaurant allocate its advertising budget in order to maximize the value of total audience exposure?
    a. Formulate a linear programming model that can be used to determine how the restaurant should allocate its advertising budget in order to maximize the value of total audience exposure.
    b. Solve the problem using the graphical solution procedure.

27. Blair & Rosen, Inc. (B&R) is a brokerage firm that specializes in investment portfolios designed to meet the specific risk tolerances of its clients. A client who contacted B&R this past week has a maximum of $50,000 to invest. B&R's investment advisor decides to recommend a portfolio consisting of two investment funds: an Internet fund and a Blue Chip fund. The Internet fund has a projected annual return of 12%, while the Blue Chip fund has a projected annual return of 9%. The investment advisor requires that at most $35,000 of the client's funds should be invested in the Internet fund. B&R services include a risk rating for each investment alternative. The Internet fund, which is the more risky of the two investment alternatives, has a risk rating of 6 per thousand dollars invested. The Blue Chip fund has a risk rating of 4 per thousand dollars invested. For example, if $10,000 is invested in each of the two investment funds, B&R's risk rating for the portfolio would be $6(10) + 4(10) = 100$. Finally, B&R developed a questionnaire to measure each client's risk tolerance. Based on the responses, each client is classified as a conservative, moderate, or aggressive investor. Suppose that the questionnaire results classified the current client as a moderate investor. B&R recommends that a client who is a moderate investor limit his or her portfolio to a maximum risk rating of 240.
    a. What is the recommended investment portfolio for this client? What is the annual return for the portfolio?
    b. Suppose that a second client with $50,000 to invest has been classified as an aggressive investor. B&R recommends that the maximum portfolio risk rating for an aggressive investor is 320. What is the recommended investment portfolio for this aggressive investor? Discuss what happens to the portfolio under the aggressive investor strategy.
    c. Suppose that a third client with $50,000 to invest has been classified as a conservative investor. B&R recommends that the maximum portfolio risk rating for a conservative investor is 160. Develop the recommended investment portfolio for the conservative investor. Discuss the interpretation of the slack variable for the total investment fund constraint.

28. Tom's, Inc., produces various Mexican food products and sells them to Western Foods, a chain of grocery stores located in Texas and New Mexico. Tom's, Inc., makes two salsa products: Western Foods Salsa and Mexico City Salsa. Essentially, the two products have different blends of whole tomatoes, tomato sauce, and tomato paste. The Western Foods Salsa is a blend of 50% whole tomatoes, 30% tomato sauce, and 20% tomato paste. The Mexico City Salsa, which has a thicker and chunkier consistency, consists of 70% whole tomatoes, 10% tomato sauce, and 20% tomato paste. Each jar of salsa produced weighs 10 ounces. For the current production period, Tom's, Inc., can purchase up to 280 pounds of whole tomatoes, 130 pounds of tomato sauce, and 100 pounds of tomato paste; the price per pound for these ingredients is $0.96, $0.64, and $0.56, respectively. The cost of the spices and the other ingredients is approximately $0.10 per jar. Tom's, Inc., buys empty glass jars for $0.02 each, and labeling and filling costs are estimated to be $0.03 for each jar of salsa produced. Tom's contract with Western Foods results in sales revenue of $1.64 for each jar of Western Foods Salsa and $1.93 for each jar of Mexico City Salsa.
    a. Develop a linear programming model that will enable Tom's to determine the mix of salsa products that will maximize the total profit contribution.
    b. Find the optimal solution.

29. AutoIgnite produces electronic ignition systems for automobiles at a plant in Cleveland, Ohio. Each ignition system is assembled from two components produced at AutoIgnite's plants in Buffalo, New York, and Dayton, Ohio. The Buffalo plant can produce 2000 units of component 1, 1000 units of component 2, or any combination of the two components each day. For instance, 60% of Buffalo's production time could be used to produce component 1 and 40% of Buffalo's production time could be used to produce component 2; in this case, the Buffalo plant would be able to produce 0.6(2000) = 1200 units of component 1 each day and 0.4(1000) = 400 units of component 2 each day. The Dayton plant can produce 600 units of component 1, 1400 units of component 2, or any combination of the two components each day. At the end of each day, the component production at Buffalo and Dayton is sent to Cleveland for assembly of the ignition systems on the following workday.
    a. Formulate a linear programming model that can be used to develop a daily production schedule for the Buffalo and Dayton plants that will maximize daily production of ignition systems at Cleveland.
    b. Find the optimal solution.

30. A financial advisor at Diehl Investments identified two companies that are likely candidates for a takeover in the near future. Eastern Cable is a leading manufacturer of flexible cable systems used in the construction industry, and ComSwitch is a new firm specializing in digital switching systems. Eastern Cable is currently trading for $40 per share, and ComSwitch is currently trading for $25 per share. If the takeovers occur, the financial advisor estimates that the price of Eastern Cable will go to $55 per share and ComSwitch will go to $43 per share. At this point in time, the financial advisor has identified ComSwitch as the higher-risk alternative. Assume that a client indicated a willingness to invest a maximum of $50,000 in the two companies. The client wants to invest at least $15,000 in Eastern Cable and at least $10,000 in ComSwitch. Because of the higher risk associated with ComSwitch, the financial advisor has recommended that at most $25,000 should be invested in ComSwitch.
    a. Formulate a linear programming model that can be used to determine the number of shares of Eastern Cable and the number of shares of ComSwitch that will meet the investment constraints and maximize the total return for the investment.
    b. Graph the feasible region.
    c. Determine the coordinates of each extreme point.
    d. Find the optimal solution.

31. Consider the following linear program:

$$\text{Min} \quad 3A + 4B$$
$$\text{s.t.}$$
$$1A + 3B \geq 6$$
$$1A + 1B \geq 4$$
$$A, B \geq 0$$

Identify the feasible region and find the optimal solution using the graphical solution procedure. What is the value of the objective function?

32. Identify the three extreme-point solutions for the M&D Chemicals problem (see Section 7.5). Identify the value of the objective function and the values of the slack and surplus variables at each extreme point.

33. Consider the following linear programming problem:

$$\text{Min} \quad A + 2B$$
$$\text{s.t.}$$
$$A + 4B \leq 21$$
$$2A + B \geq 7$$
$$3A + 1.5B \leq 21$$
$$-2A + 6B \geq 0$$
$$A, B \geq 0$$

a. Find the optimal solution using the graphical solution procedure and the value of the objective function.
b. Determine the amount of slack or surplus for each constraint.
c. Suppose the objective function is changed to max $5A + 2B$. Find the optimal solution and the value of the objective function.

34. Consider the following linear program:

$$\text{Min} \quad 2A + 2B$$
$$\text{s.t.}$$
$$1A + 3B \leq 12$$
$$3A + 1B \geq 13$$
$$1A - 1B = 3$$
$$A, B \geq 0$$

a. Show the feasible region.
b. What are the extreme points of the feasible region?
c. Find the optimal solution using the graphical solution procedure.

35. For the linear program

$$\text{Min} \quad 6A + 4B$$
$$\text{s.t.}$$
$$2A + 1B \geq 12$$
$$1A + 1B \geq 10$$
$$1B \leq 4$$
$$A, B \geq 0$$

  a. Write the problem in standard form.
  b. Solve the problem using the graphical solution procedure.
  c. What are the values of the slack and surplus variables?

36. As part of a quality improvement initiative, Consolidated Electronics employees complete a three-day training program on team building and a two-day training program on problem solving. The manager of quality improvement has requested that at least 8 training programs on team building and at least 10 training programs on problem solving be offered during the next six months. In addition, senior-level management has specified that at least 25 training programs must be offered during this period. Consolidated Electronics uses a consultant to teach the training programs. During the next quarter, the consultant has 84 days of training time available. Each training program on team building costs $10,000 and each training program on problem solving costs $8000.
  a. Formulate a linear programming model that can be used to determine the number of training programs on team building and the number of training programs on problem solving that should be offered in order to minimize total cost.
  b. Graph the feasible region.
  c. Determine the coordinates of each extreme point.
  d. Solve for the minimum-cost solution.

37. The New England Cheese Company produces two cheese spreads by blending mild cheddar cheese with extra sharp cheddar cheese. The cheese spreads are packaged in 12-ounce containers, which are then sold to distributors throughout the Northeast. The Regular blend contains 80% mild cheddar and 20% extra sharp, and the Zesty blend contains 60% mild cheddar and 40% extra sharp. This year, a local dairy cooperative offered to provide up to 8100 pounds of mild cheddar cheese for $1.20 per pound and up to 3000 pounds of extra sharp cheddar cheese for $1.40 per pound. The cost to blend and package the cheese spreads, excluding the cost of the cheese, is $0.20 per container. If each container of Regular is sold for $1.95 and each container of Zesty is sold for $2.20, how many containers of Regular and Zesty should New England Cheese produce?

38. Applied Technology, Inc. (ATI) produces bicycle frames using two fiberglass materials that improve the strength-to-weight ratio of the frames. The cost of the standard-grade material is $7.50 per yard and the cost of the professional-grade material is $9.00 per yard. The standard- and professional-grade materials contain different amounts of fiberglass, carbon fiber, and Kevlar, as shown in the following table:

	Standard Grade	**Professional Grade**
Fiberglass	84%	58%
Carbon fiber	10%	30%
Kevlar	6%	12%

  ATI signed a contract with a bicycle manufacturer to produce a new frame with a carbon fiber content of at least 20% and a Kevlar content of not greater than 10%. To meet the required weight specification, a total of 30 yards of material must be used for each frame.
  a. Formulate a linear program to determine the number of yards of each grade of fiberglass material that ATI should use in each frame in order to minimize total cost. Define the decision variables and indicate the purpose of each constraint.
  b. Use the graphical solution procedure to determine the feasible region. What are the coordinates of the extreme points?
  c. Compute the total cost at each extreme point. What is the optimal solution?

d. The distributor of the fiberglass material is currently overstocked with the professional-grade material. To reduce inventory, the distributor offered ATI the opportunity to purchase the professional-grade material for $8 per yard. Will the optimal solution change?

e. Suppose that the distributor further lowers the price of the professional-grade material to $7.40 per yard. Will the optimal solution change? What effect would an even lower price for the professional-grade material have on the optimal solution? Explain.

39. Innis Investments manages funds for a number of companies and wealthy clients. The investment strategy is tailored to each client's needs. For a new client, Innis has been authorized to invest up to $1.2 million in two investment funds: a stock fund and a money market fund. Each unit of the stock fund costs $50 and provides an annual rate of return of 10%; each unit of the money market fund costs $100 and provides an annual rate of return of 4%.

The client wants to minimize risk subject to the requirement that the annual income from the investment be at least $60,000. According to Innis's risk measurement system, each unit invested in the stock fund has a risk index of 8, and each unit invested in the money market fund has a risk index of 3; the higher risk index associated with the stock fund simply indicates that it is the riskier investment. Innis's client also specifies that at least $300,000 be invested in the money market fund.

a. Determine how many units of each fund Innis should purchase for the client to minimize the total risk index for the portfolio.

b. How much annual income will this investment strategy generate?

c. Suppose the client desires to maximize annual return. How should the funds be invested?

40. Eastern Chemicals produces two types of lubricating fluids used in industrial manufacturing. Both products cost Eastern Chemicals $1 per gallon to produce. Based on an analysis of current inventory levels and outstanding orders for the next month, Eastern Chemicals' management specified that at least 30 gallons of product 1 and at least 20 gallons of product 2 must be produced during the next two weeks. Management also stated that an existing inventory of highly perishable raw material required in the production of both fluids must be used within the next two weeks. The current inventory of the perishable raw material is 80 pounds. Although more of this raw material can be ordered if necessary, any of the current inventory that is not used within the next two weeks will spoil—hence, the management requirement that at least 80 pounds be used in the next two weeks. Furthermore, it is known that product 1 requires 1 pound of this perishable raw material per gallon and product 2 requires 2 pounds of the raw material per gallon. Because Eastern Chemicals' objective is to keep its production costs at the minimum possible level, the firm's management is looking for a minimum-cost production plan that uses all the 80 pounds of perishable raw material and provides at least 30 gallons of product 1 and at least 20 gallons of product 2. What is the minimum-cost solution?

41. Southern Oil Company produces two grades of gasoline: regular and premium. The profit contributions are $0.30 per gallon for regular gasoline and $0.50 per gallon for premium gasoline. Each gallon of regular gasoline contains 0.3 gallons of grade A crude oil and each gallon of premium gasoline contains 0.6 gallons of grade A crude oil. For the next production period, Southern has 18,000 gallons of grade A crude oil available. The refinery used to produce the gasolines has a production capacity of 50,000 gallons for the next production period. Southern Oil's distributors have indicated that demand for the premium gasoline for the next production period will be at most 20,000 gallons.

a. Formulate a linear programming model that can be used to determine the number of gallons of regular gasoline and the number of gallons of premium gasoline that should be produced in order to maximize total profit contribution.

b.   What is the optimal solution?
c.   What are the values and interpretations of the slack variables?
d.   What are the binding constraints?

42. Does the following linear program involve infeasibility, unbounded, and/or alternative optimal solutions? Explain.

$$\text{Max} \quad 4A + 8B$$
$$\text{s.t.}$$
$$2A + 2B \le 10$$
$$-1A + 1B \ge 8$$
$$A, B \ge 0$$

43. Does the following linear program involve infeasibility, unbounded, and/or alternative optimal solutions? Explain.

$$\text{Max} \quad 1A + 1B$$
$$\text{s.t.}$$
$$8A + 6B \ge 24$$
$$2B \ge 4$$
$$A, B \ge 0$$

44. Consider the following linear program:

$$\text{Max} \quad 1A + 1B$$
$$\text{s.t.}$$
$$5A + 3B \le 15$$
$$3A + 5B \le 15$$
$$A, B \ge 0$$

a.   What is the optimal solution for this problem?
b.   Suppose that the objective function is changed to $1A + 2B$. Find the new optimal solution.

45. Consider the following linear program:

$$\text{Max} \quad 1A - 2B$$
$$\text{s.t.}$$
$$-4A + 3B \le 3$$
$$1A - 1B \le 3$$
$$A, B \ge 0$$

a.   Graph the feasible region for the problem.
b.   Is the feasible region unbounded? Explain.
c.   Find the optimal solution.
d.   Does an unbounded feasible region imply that the optimal solution to the linear program will be unbounded?

46. The manager of a small independent grocery store is trying to determine the best use of her shelf space for soft drinks. The store carries national and generic brands and currently has 200 square feet of shelf space available. The manager wants to allocate at least 60% of the space to the national brands and, regardless of the profitability, allocate at least 10%

of the space to the generic brands. How many square feet of space should the manager allocate to the national brands and the generic brands under the following circumstances?

a. The national brands are more profitable than the generic brands.

b. Both brands are equally profitable.

c. The generic brand is more profitable than the national brand.

47. Discuss what happens to the M&D Chemicals problem (see Section 7.5) if the cost per gallon for product A is increased to $3.00 per gallon. What would you recommend? Explain.

48. For the M&D Chemicals problem in Section 7.5, discuss the effect of management's requiring total production of 500 gallons for the two products. List two or three actions M&D should consider to correct the situation you encounter.

49. PharmaPlus operates a chain of 30 pharmacies. The pharmacies are staffed by licensed pharmacists and pharmacy technicians. The company currently employs 85 full-time-equivalent pharmacists (combination of full time and part time) and 175 full-time-equivalent technicians. Each spring management reviews current staffing levels and makes hiring plans for the year. A recent forecast of the prescription load for the next year shows that at least 250 full-time-equivalent employees (pharmacists and technicians) will be required to staff the pharmacies. The personnel department expects 10 pharmacists and 30 technicians to leave over the next year. To accommodate the expected attrition and prepare for future growth, management states that at least 15 new pharmacists must be hired. In addition, PharmaPlus's new service quality guidelines specify no more than two technicians per licensed pharmacist. The average salary for licensed pharmacists is $40 per hour and the average salary for technicians is $10 per hour.

a. Determine a minimum-cost staffing plan for PharmaPlus. How many pharmacists and technicians are needed?

b. Given current staffing levels and expected attrition, how many new hires (if any) must be made to reach the level recommended in part (a)? What will be the impact on the payroll?

50. Expedition Outfitters manufactures a variety of specialty clothing for hiking, skiing, and mountain climbing. The company has decided to begin production on two new parkas designed for use in extremely cold weather: the Mount Everest Parka and the Rocky Mountain Parka. Expedition's manufacturing plant has 120 hours of cutting time and 120 hours of sewing time available for producing these two parkas. Each Mount Everest Parka requires 30 minutes of cutting time and 45 minutes of sewing time, and each Rocky Mountain Parka requires 20 minutes of cutting time and 15 minutes of sewing time. The labor and material cost is $150 for each Mount Everest Parka and $50 for each Rocky Mountain Parka, and the retail prices through the firm's mail order catalog are $250 for the Mount Everest Parka and $200 for the Rocky Mountain Parka. Because management believes that the Mount Everest Parka is a unique coat that will enhance the image of the firm, management specified that at least 20% of the total production must consist of this model. Assuming that Expedition Outfitters can sell as many coats of each type as it can produce, how many units of each model should it manufacture to maximize the total profit contribution?

51. English Motors, Ltd. (EML), developed a new four-wheel-drive sport utility vehicle. As part of the marketing campaign, EML produced a digitally recorded sales presentation to send to both owners of current EML four-wheel-drive vehicles as well as to owners of four-wheel-drive sport utility vehicles offered by competitors; EML refers to these two target markets as the current customer market and the new customer market. Individuals who receive the new promotion will also receive a coupon for a test drive of the new EML model for one weekend. A key factor in the success of the new promotion is the response rate, the percentage of individuals who receive the new promotion and test drive the new

model. EML estimates that the response rate for the current customer market is 25% and the response rate for the new customer market is 20%. For the customers who test drive the new model, the sales rate is the percentage of individuals who make a purchase. Marketing research studies indicate that the sales rate is 12% for the current customer market and 20% for the new customer market. The cost for each promotion, excluding the test drive costs, is $4 for each promotion sent to the current customer market and $6 for each promotion sent to the new customer market. Management also specified that a minimum of 30,000 current customers should test drive the new model and a minimum of 10,000 new customers should test drive the new model. In addition, the number of current customers who test drive the new vehicle must be at least twice the number of new customers who test drive the new vehicle. If the marketing budget, excluding test drive costs, is $1.2 million, how many promotions should be sent to each group of customers in order to maximize total sales?

52. Creative Sports Design (CSD) manufactures a standard-size tennis racquet and an oversize tennis racquet. The firm's racquets are extremely light due to the use of a magnesium-graphite alloy that was invented by the firm's founder. Each standard-size racquet uses 0.125 kilograms of the alloy and each oversize racquet uses 0.4 kilograms; over the next two-week production period, only 80 kilograms of the alloy are available. Each standard-size racquet uses 10 minutes of manufacturing time and each oversize racquet uses 12 minutes. The profit contributions are $10 for each standard-size racquet and $15 for each oversize racquet, and 40 hours of manufacturing time are available each week. Management specified that at least 20% of the total production must be the standard-size racquet. How many racquets of each type should CSD manufacture over the next two weeks to maximize the total profit contribution? Assume that because of the unique nature of its products, CSD can sell as many racquets as it can produce.

53. Management of High Tech Services (HTS) would like to develop a model that will help allocate its technicians' time between service calls to regular contract customers and new customers. A maximum of 80 hours of technician time is available over the two-week planning period. To satisfy cash flow requirements, at least $800 in revenue (per technician) must be generated during the two-week period. Technician time for regular customers generates $25 per hour. However, technician time for new customers only generates an average of $8 per hour because in many cases a new customer contact does not provide billable services. To ensure that new customer contacts are being maintained, the technician time spent on new customer contacts must be at least 60% of the time spent on regular customer contacts. Given these revenue and policy requirements, HTS would like to determine how to allocate technician time between regular customers and new customers so that the total number of customers contacted during the two-week period will be maximized. Technicians require an average of 50 minutes for each regular customer contact and 1 hour for each new customer contact.

    a. Develop a linear programming model that will enable HTS to allocate technician time between regular customers and new customers.
    b. Find the optimal solution.

54. Jackson Hole Manufacturing is a small manufacturer of plastic products used in the automotive and computer industries. One of its major contracts is with a large computer company and involves the production of plastic printer cases for the computer company's portable printers. The printer cases are produced on two injection molding machines. The M-100 machine has a production capacity of 25 printer cases per hour, and the M-200 machine has a production capacity of 40 cases per hour. Both machines use the same chemical material to produce the printer cases; the M-100 uses 40 pounds of the raw material per hour and the M-200 uses 50 pounds per hour. The computer company asked

Jackson Hole to produce as many of the cases during the upcoming week as possible; it will pay $18 for each case Jackson Hole can deliver. However, next week is a regularly scheduled vacation period for most of Jackson Hole's production employees; during this time, annual maintenance is performed for all equipment in the plant. Because of the downtime for maintenance, the M-100 will be available for no more than 15 hours, and the M-200 will be available for no more than 10 hours. However, because of the high set-up cost involved with both machines, management requires that, if production is scheduled on either machine, the machine must be operated for at least 5 hours. The supplier of the chemical material used in the production process informed Jackson Hole that a maximum of 1000 pounds of the chemical material will be available for next week's production; the cost for this raw material is $6 per pound. In addition to the raw material cost, Jackson Hole estimates that the hourly costs of operating the M-100 and the M-200 are $50 and $75, respectively.

a. Formulate a linear programming model that can be used to maximize the contribution to profit.

b. Find the optimal solution.

55. Xpress Technologies offers complete web design, programming, implementation, and hosting services for customers. Xpress prices their services by the project and categorizes each customer request into one of three possible project categories: simple HTML design, requires Java/Flash coding, requires secure transaction capabilities. Xpress charges $3000 for each simple HTML design project, $5000 for each Java/Flash coding project, and $8000 for each project requiring secure transaction capabilities. Xpress has two types of employees that it assigns to these projects: graphic designers who make $32/hour and programmers who make $36/hour. The company currently has two graphic designers and four programmers; each employee can work up to a total of 40 hours per week. Xpress estimates that a simple HTML project will require 2 hours from the graphic designers and 4 hours from the programmers; projects requiring Java/Flash coding require 5 hours from the graphic designers and 6 hours from the programmers; projects requiring secure transaction capabilities require 7 hours from the graphic designers and 12 hours from the programmers. Xpress currently has requests for eight simple HTML projects, six Java/Flash projects, and seven projects requiring secure transaction capabilities.

a. Develop a linear program that will help Xpress Technologies to choose which of the projects to accept for the coming week to maximize profits.

b. Find the optimal solution.

Case Problem 1   Workload Balancing

Digital Imaging (DI) produces color printers for both the professional and consumer markets. The DI consumer division recently introduced two new color printers. The DI-910 model can produce a 4″ × 6″ borderless color print in approximately 37 seconds. The more sophisticated and faster DI-950 can even produce a 13″ × 19″ borderless color print. Financial projections show profit contributions of $42 for each DI-910 and $87 for each DI-950.

The printers are assembled, tested, and packaged at DI's plant located in New Bern, North Carolina. This plant is highly automated and uses two manufacturing lines to produce the printers. Line 1 performs the assembly operation with times of 3 minutes per DI-910 printer and 6 minutes per DI-950 printer. Line 2 performs both the testing and packaging operations. Times are 4 minutes per DI-910 printer and 2 minutes per DI-950 printer. The shorter time for the DI-950 printer is a result of its faster print speed. Both manufacturing lines are in operation one 8-hour shift per day.

Managerial Report

Perform an analysis for Digital Imaging in order to determine how many units of each printer to produce. Prepare a report to DI's president presenting your findings and recommendations. Include (but do not limit your discussion to) a consideration of the following:

1. The recommended number of units of each printer to produce to maximize the total contribution to profit for an 8-hour shift. What reasons might management have for not implementing your recommendation?
2. Suppose that management also states that the number of DI-910 printers produced must be at least as great as the number of DI-950 units produced. Assuming that the objective is to maximize the total contribution to profit for an 8-hour shift, how many units of each printer should be produced?
3. Does the solution you developed in part (2) balance the total time spent on line 1 and the total time spent on line 2? Why might this balance or lack of it be a concern to management?
4. Management requested an expansion of the model in part (2) that would provide a better balance between the total time on line 1 and the total time on line 2. Management wants to limit the difference between the total time on line 1 and the total time on line 2 to 30 minutes or less. If the objective is still to maximize the total contribution to profit, how many units of each printer should be produced? What effect does this workload balancing have on total profit in part (2)?
5. Suppose that in part (1) management specified the objective of maximizing the total number of printers produced each shift rather than total profit contribution. With this objective, how many units of each printer should be produced per shift? What effect does this objective have on total profit and workload balancing?

For each solution that you develop, include a copy of your linear programming model and graphical solution in the appendix to your report.

Case Problem 2   Production Strategy

Better Fitness, Inc. (BFI), manufactures exercise equipment at its plant in Freeport, Long Island. It recently designed two universal weight machines for the home exercise market. Both machines use BFI-patented technology that provides the user with an extremely wide range of motion capability for each type of exercise performed. Until now, such capabilities have been available only on expensive weight machines used primarily by physical therapists.

At a recent trade show, demonstrations of the machines resulted in significant dealer interest. In fact, the number of orders that BFI received at the trade show far exceeded its manufacturing capabilities for the current production period. As a result, management decided to begin production of the two machines. The two machines, which BFI named the BodyPlus 100 and the BodyPlus 200, require different amounts of resources to produce.

The BodyPlus 100 consists of a frame unit, a press station, and a pec-dec station. Each frame produced uses 4 hours of machining and welding time and 2 hours of painting and finishing time. Each press station requires 2 hours of machining and welding time and 1 hour of painting and finishing time, and each pec-dec station uses 2 hours of machining and welding time and 2 hours of painting and finishing time. In addition, 2 hours are spent assembling, testing, and packaging each BodyPlus 100. The raw material costs are $450 for each frame, $300 for each press station, and $250 for each pec-dec station; packaging costs are estimated to be $50 per unit.

The BodyPlus 200 consists of a frame unit, a press station, a pec-dec station, and a leg-press station. Each frame produced uses 5 hours of machining and welding time and 4 hours of painting and finishing time. Each press station requires 3 hours of machining and welding time and 2 hours of painting and finishing time, each pec-dec station uses 2 hours of machining and welding time and 2 hours of painting and finishing time, and each leg-press station requires 2 hours of machining and welding time and 2 hours of painting and finishing time. In addition, 2 hours are spent assembling, testing, and packaging each BodyPlus 200. The raw material costs are $650 for each frame, $400 for each press station, $250 for each pec-dec station, and $200 for each leg-press station; packaging costs are estimated to be $75 per unit.

For the next production period, management estimates that 600 hours of machining and welding time; 450 hours of painting and finishing time; and 140 hours of assembly, testing, and packaging time will be available. Current labor costs are $20 per hour for machining and welding time; $15 per hour for painting and finishing time; and $12 per hour for assembly, testing, and packaging time. The market in which the two machines must compete suggests a retail price of $2400 for the BodyPlus 100 and $3500 for the BodyPlus 200, although some flexibility may be available to BFI because of the unique capabilities of the new machines. Authorized BFI dealers can purchase machines for 70% of the suggested retail price.

BFI's president believes that the unique capabilities of the BodyPlus 200 can help position BFI as one of the leaders in high-end exercise equipment. Consequently, she states that the number of units of the BodyPlus 200 produced must be at least 25% of the total production.

Managerial Report

Analyze the production problem at Better Fitness, Inc., and prepare a report for BFI's president presenting your findings and recommendations. Include (but do not limit your discussion to) a consideration of the following items:

1. The recommended number of BodyPlus 100 and BodyPlus 200 machines to produce
2. The effect on profits of the requirement that the number of units of the BodyPlus 200 produced must be at least 25% of the total production
3. Where efforts should be expended in order to increase contribution to profits

Include a copy of your linear programming model and graphical solution in an appendix to your report.

Case Problem 3 Hart Venture Capital

Hart Venture Capital (HVC) specializes in providing venture capital for software development and Internet applications. Currently HVC has two investment opportunities: (1) Security Systems, a firm that needs additional capital to develop an Internet security software package, and (2) Market Analysis, a market research company that needs additional capital to develop a software package for conducting customer satisfaction surveys. In exchange for Security Systems stock, the firm asked HVC to provide $600,000 in year 1, $600,000 in year 2, and $250,000 in year 3 over the coming three-year period. In exchange for Market Analysis stock, the firm asked HVC to provide $500,000 in year 1, $350,000 in year 2, and $400,000 in year 3 over the same three-year period. HVC believes that both investment opportunities are worth pursuing. However, because of other investments, HVC is willing to commit at most $800,000 for both projects in the first year, at most $700,000 in the second year, and $500,000 in the third year.

HVC's financial analysis team reviewed both projects and recommended that the company's objective should be to maximize the net present value of the total investment in Security Systems and Market Analysis. The net present value takes into account the estimated value of the stock at the end of the three-year period as well as the capital outflows that are necessary during each of the three years. Using an 8% rate of return, HVC's financial analysis team estimates that 100% funding of the Security Systems project has a net present value of $1,800,000, and 100% funding of the Market Analysis project has a net present value of $1,600,000.

HVC has the option to fund any percentage of the Security Systems and Market Analysis projects. For example, if HVC decides to fund 40% of the Security Systems project, investments of 0.40($600,000) = $240,000 would be required in year 1, 0.40($600,000) = $240,000 would be required in year 2, and 0.40($250,000) = $100,000 would be required in year 3. In this case, the net present value of the Security Systems project would be 0.40($1,800,000) = $720,000. The investment amounts and the net present value for partial funding of the Market Analysis project would be computed in the same manner.

Managerial Report

Perform an analysis of HVC's investment problem and prepare a report that presents your findings and recommendations. Be sure to include information on the following:

1. The recommended percentage of each project that HVC should fund and the net present value of the total investment
2. A capital allocation plan for Security Systems and Market Analysis for the coming three-year period and the total HVC investment each year
3. The effect, if any, on the recommended percentage of each project that HVC should fund if HVC is willing to commit an additional $100,000 during the first year
4. A capital allocation plan if an additional $100,000 is made available
5. Your recommendation as to whether HVC should commit the additional $100,000 in the first year

Provide model details and relevant computer output in a report appendix.

Appendix 7.1   Solving Linear Programs with Excel Solver

In this appendix we will use an Excel worksheet to solve the RMC linear programming problem. We will enter the problem data for the RMC problem in the top part of the worksheet and develop the linear programming model in the bottom part of the worksheet. Note that Appendix A contains much more detail on how to formulate models in Excel.

Formulation

Whenever we formulate a worksheet model of a linear program, we perform the following steps:

Step 1. Enter the problem data in the top part of the worksheet
Step 2. Specify cell locations for the decision variables
Step 3. Select a cell and enter a formula for computing the value of the objective function
Step 4. Select a cell and enter a formula for computing the left-hand side of each constraint
Step 5. Select a cell and enter a formula for computing the right-hand side of each constraint

The formula worksheet that we developed for the RMC problem using these five steps is shown in Figure 7.25. Let us review each of the preceding steps as they apply to the RMC problem.

Step 1. Enter the problem data in the top part of the worksheet
Cells B5 to C7 show the material requirements per ton of each product.
Cells B8 and C8 show the profit contribution per ton for the two products.
Cells D5 to D7 show the maximum amounts available for each of the three materials.

FIGURE 7.25   EXCEL FORMULA WORKSHEET FOR THE RMC PROBLEM

WEB file

RMC

	A	B	C	D
1	RMC			
2				
3			Material Requirements	
4	Material	Fuel Additive	Solvent Base	Amount Available
5	Material 1	0.4	0.5	20
6	Material 2	0	0.2	5
7	Material 3	0.6	0.3	21
8	Profit Per Ton	40	30	
9				
10				
11	Model			
12				
13		Decision Variables		
14		Fuel Additive	Solvent Base	
15	Tons Produced	25	20	
16				
17	Maximize Total Profit	=B8*B15+C8*C15		
18				
19	Constraints	Amount Used		Amount Available
20	Material 1	=B5*B15+C5*C15	<=	=D5
21	Material 2	=B6*B15+C6*C15	<=	=D6
22	Material 3	=B7*B15+C7*C15	<=	=D7
23				

Step 2. Specify cell locations for the decision variables
Cell B15 will contain the number of tons of fuel additive produced, and Cell C15 will contain the number of tons of solvent base produced.

Step 3. Select a cell and enter a formula for computing the value of the objective function
Cell B17: =B8*B15+C8*C15

Step 4. Select a cell and enter a formula for computing the left-hand side of each constraint. With three constraints, we have
Cell B20: =B5*B15+C5*C15
Cell B21: =C6*C15
Cell B22: =B7*B15+C7*C15

Step 5. Select a cell and enter a formula for computing the right-hand side of each constraint. With three constraints, we have
Cell D20: =D5
Cell D21: =D6
Cell D22: =D7

Note that descriptive labels make the model section of the worksheet easier to read and understand. For example, we added "Fuel Additive," "Solvent Base," and "Tons Produced" in rows 14 and 15 so that the values of the decision variables appearing in Cells B15 and C15 can be easily interpreted. In addition, we entered "Maximize Total Profit" in Cell A17 to indicate that the value of the objective function appearing in Cell B17 is the maximum profit contribution. In the constraint section of the worksheet we added the constraint names as well as the "<=" symbols to show the relationship that exists between the left-hand side and the right-hand side of each constraint. Although these descriptive labels are not necessary to use Excel Solver to find a solution to the RMC problem, the labels make it easier for the user to understand and interpret the optimal solution.

Excel Solver Solution

Excel contains an add-in known as Solver that can be used to solve many different types of optimization problems, including linear programs. Excel Solver, developed by Frontline Systems, can be used to solve all of the linear programming problems presented in this text.

The following steps describe how Excel Solver can be used to obtain the optimal solution to the RMC problem:

The Excel add-in Analytic Solver Platform (ASP), which is used in Chapter 16 of this textbook for simulation problems, can also be used to solve linear programs. ASP uses more sophisticated algorithms for solving optimization problems and can solve larger problems than Excel Solver. However, since all optimization problems in this textbook can be solved using Excel Solver, we do not specifically discuss the use of ASP for use in optimization.

Step 1. Select the **Data** tab from the Ribbon
Step 2. Select **Solver** from the **Analysis** Group (see Figure 7.25, where the Analysis Group and Data tab are displayed in the Ribbon)
Step 3. When the **Solver Parameters** dialog box appears (see Figure 7.26):
　　　Enter *B17* into the **Set Objective** box
　　　Select the **To: Max** option
　　　Enter *B15:C15* into the **By Changing Variable Cells** box
　　　Select **Add**
Step 4. When the **Add Constraint** dialog box appears:
　　　Enter *B20:B22* in the **Cell Reference** box
　　　Select **<=**
　　　Enter *D20:D22* in the **Constraint** box
　　　Click **OK**
Step 5. When the **Solver Parameters** dialog box reappears:
　　　Click the checkbox for **Make Unconstrained Variables Non-negative**
Step 6. In the **Select a Solving Method** dropdown menu
　　　Select **Simplex LP**

FIGURE 7.26　EXCEL SOLVER PARAMETERS DIALOG BOX FOR THE RMC PROBLEM

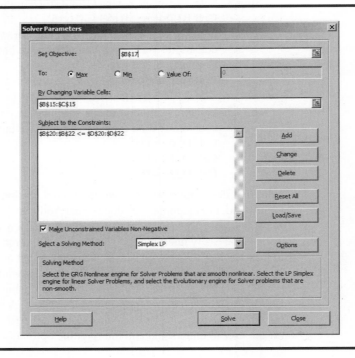

Step 7. Click **Solve**

Step 8. When the **Solver Results** dialog box appears:

Select **Keep Solver Solution**

Click **OK**

*The Excel Answer Report that is similar to Figure 7.15 is generated from the **Solver Results** dialog box. This is created by clicking on **Answer** in the **Reports** group before clicking **OK** in step 7. We will discuss the Sensitivity Report in Chapter 8.*

Figure 7.26 shows the completed Excel Solver Parameters dialog box, and Figure 7.27 shows the optimal solution in the worksheet. The optimal solution of 25 tons of fuel additive and 20 tons of solvent base is the same as we obtained using the graphical solution procedure. Solver also has an option to provide sensitivity analysis information. We discuss sensitivity analysis in Chapter 8.

In step 5 we selected the **Make Unconstrained Variables Non-negative** option in the **Solver Parameters** dialog box to avoid having to enter nonnegativity constraints for the decision variables. In general, whenever we want to solve a linear programming model in which the decision variables are all restricted to be nonnegative, we will select this option. In addition, in step 4 we entered all three less-than-or-equal-to constraints simultaneously by entering *B20:B22* into the **Cell Reference** box, selecting <=, and entering *D20:D22* into the **Constraint** box. Alternatively, we could have entered the three constraints one at a time.

The Solver Add-In should be found under the **Data** tab on the Excel Ribbon. If it does not appear here, you will have to add it by following the steps shown below.

Step 1. Select the **File** tab from the Ribbon

Step 2. Select **Options** from the **File** menu

Step 3. When the **Excel Options** dialog box appears, choose **Add-Ins**

Step 4. Click **Go** next to **Manage: Excel Add-ins**

Step 5. When the **Add-Ins** dialog box appears, select the checkbox for the **Solver Add-in**

FIGURE 7.27   EXCEL SOLVER SOLUTION FOR THE RMC PROBLEM

	A	B	C	D	E
1	**RMC**				
2					
3			**Material Requirements**		
4	**Material**	**Fuel Additive**	**Solvent Base**	**Amount Available**	
5	Material 1	0.4	0.5	20	
6	Material 2	0	0.2	5	
7	Material 3	0.6	0.3	21	
8	**Profit Per Ton**	40	30		
9					
10					
11	**Model**				
12					
13			**Decision Variables**		
14		**Fuel Additive**	**Solvent Base**		
15	**Tons Produced**	25	20		
16					
17	**Maximize Total Profit**	1600			
18					
19	**Constraints**	**Amount Used**		**Amount Available**	
20	Material 1	20	<=	20	
21	Material 2	4	<=	5	
22	Material 3	21	<=	21	
23					

Appendix 7.2 # Solving Linear Programs with LINGO

In this appendix we describe how to use LINGO to solve the RMC problem. When you start LINGO, two windows are immediately displayed. The outer, or mainframe, window contains all the command menus and the command toolbar. The smaller window is the model window; this window is used to enter and edit the linear programming model you want to solve.

As with any model, it is good to document your LINGO model with comments. A comment in a LINGO model begins with an exclamation point and ends with a semicolon. If desired, a comment can span multiple lines.

The first item we enter is a comment describing the objective function. Recall that the objective function for the RMC problem is to maximize profit. Hence we enter the following comment:

```
! MAXIMIZE PROFIT;
```

For the latest information on LINGO software see http://www.lindo.com.

Next we press the Enter key and then type the objective function. The objective function for the RMC problem is Max $40F + 30S$. Thus, in the second line of the LINGO model window, we enter the following expression:

```
MAX = 40*F + 30*S;
```

Note that in LINGO the symbol * is used to denote multiplication and that the objective function, like a comment, ends with a semicolon. In general, each mathematical expression (objective function and constraints) in LINGO is terminated with a semicolon.

Next, we press the Enter key to move to a new line. The first constraint in the RMC problem is $0.4F + 0.5S \leq 20$, for material 1. Thus, in the third and fourth lines of the LINGO model window, we enter the following expressions:

```
!MATERIAL 1 CONSTRAINT;
0.4*F + 0.5*S <= 20;
```

Note that LINGO interprets the <= symbol as $\leq$. Alternatively, we could enter < instead of <=. As was the case when entering the objective function, a semicolon is required at the end of the first constraint. Pressing the Enter key moves us to a new line, and we continue the process by entering the remaining comments and constraints as shown here:

```
!MATERIAL 2 CONSTRAINT;
0.2*S <= 5;
!MATERIAL 3 CONSTRAINT;
0.6*F + 0.3*S <= 21;
```

The model window will now appear as follows:

```
!MAXIMIZE PROFIT;
MAX = 40*F + 30*S;
!MATERIAL 1 CONSTRAINT;
0.4*F + 0.5*S <= 20;
!MATERIAL 2 CONSTRAINT;
0.2*S <= 5;
!MATERIAL 3 CONSTRAINT;
0.6*F + 0.3*S <= 21;
```

If you make an error in entering the model, you can correct it at any time by simply positioning the cursor where you made the error and entering the necessary correction.

FIGURE 7.28   SOLUTION TO THE RMC PROBLEM USING LINGO

```
Global optimal solution found.
Objective value:                              1600.000
Infeasibilities:                              0.000000
Total solver interations:                            2
Elapsed runtime seconds:                          0.04

Model Class:                                        LP

Total variables:            2
Nonlinear variables:        0
Integer variables:          0

Total constraints:          4
Nonlinear constraints:      0

Total nonzeros:             7
Nonlinear nonzeros:         0

               Variable            Value       Reduced Cost
                      F         25.00000           0.000000
                      S         20.00000           0.000000

                    Row  Slack or Surplus         Dual Price
                      1         1600.000           1.000000
                      2         0.000000          33.33333
                      3         1.000000           0.000000
                      4         0.000000          44.44444
```

To solve the model, select the **Solve** command from the **LINGO** menu or press the **Solve** button on the toolbar at the top of the mainframe window. LINGO will begin the solution process by determining whether the model conforms to all syntax requirements. If the LINGO model doesn't pass these tests, you will be informed by an error message. If LINGO does not find any errors in the model input, it will begin to solve the model. As part of the solution process, LINGO displays a **Solver Status** window that allows you to monitor the progress of the solver. LINGO displays the solution in a new window titled "Solution Report." The output that appears in the **Solution Report** window for the RMC problem is shown in Figure 7.28.

The first part of the output shown in Figure 7.28 indicates that an optimal solution has been found and that the value of the objective function is 1600. We see that the optimal solution is $F = 25$ and $S = 20$, and that the slack variables for the three constraints (rows 2–4) are 0, 1, and 0. We will discuss the use of the information in the Reduced Cost column and the Dual Price column in Chapter 8 where we discuss the topic of sensitivity analysis.

CHAPTER 8

Linear Programming: Sensitivity Analysis and Interpretation of Solution

Sensitivity analysis is the study of how changes in the coefficients of a linear programming problem affect the optimal solution. Using sensitivity analysis, we can answer questions such as the following:

1. How will a change in an *objective function coefficient* affect the optimal solution?
2. How will a change in a *right-hand-side value* for a constraint affect the optimal solution?

Because sensitivity analysis is concerned with how these changes affect the optimal solution, sensitivity analysis does not begin until the optimal solution to the original linear programming problem has been obtained. For this reason, sensitivity analysis is sometimes referred to as *postoptimality analysis*.

Our approach to sensitivity analysis parallels the approach used to introduce linear programming in Chapter 7. We introduce sensitivity analysis by using the graphical method for a linear programming problem with two decision variables. Then, we show how Excel Solver can be used to provide more complete sensitivity analysis information. Finally, we extend the discussion of problem formulation started in Chapter 7 by formulating and solving three larger linear programming problems. In discussing the solution for each of these problems, we focus on managerial interpretation of the optimal solution and sensitivity analysis information.

Sensitivity analysis and the interpretation of the optimal solution are important aspects of applying linear programming. The Q.M. in Action, Optimizing Refinery Operations at Chevron Using Linear Programming, explains how Chevron uses linear programing–based tools and sensitivity analysis to improve their oil refinery operations. Later in the chapter other Q.M. in Action features illustrate how Performance Analysis Corporation uses sensitivity analysis as part of an evaluation model for a chain of fast-food outlets, how GE Plastics (now part of the Saudi Basic Industries Corporation) uses a linear programming model involving thousands of variables and constraints to determine optimal production quantities, how Kimpton Hotels uses a linear program to set prices and room availability on Priceline, and how Duncan Industries Limited's linear programming model for tea distribution convinced management of the benefits of using quantitative analysis techniques to support the decision-making process.

Q.M. *in* ACTION

OPTIMIZING REFINERY OPERATIONS AT CHEVRON USING LINEAR PROGRAMMING

Chevron is a worldwide energy company with operations in more than 180 countries. Chevron has business units that operate in almost all aspects of energy exploration and production, including oil and gas, geothermal, solar, wind, and others. Chevron's oil and gas business requires refineries to take input crude oil and transform the crude oil into products such as gasoline and lubricants that are sold to downstream operations. The processes required to transform crude oil to useable products are complex

and involve many different decisions that impact the cost and overall quality of the output products.

Chevron has developed a linear programming–based tool to assist with many of its tactical and strategic decisions related to its refining operations. The decisions that are made based on the linear programming tool output include which crude oils to buy for input, which products to manufacture as output, and how to best operate the refinery. There are many complicating factors in these decisions, such as the fact that crude oils purchased from different areas all have slightly different characteristics

Based on T. Kutz, M. Davis, R. Creek, N. Kenaston, C. Stenstrom, and M. Connor, "Optimizing Chevron's Refineries," *Interfaces* 44, no. 1 (January/February 2014), 39–54.

(*continued*)

that require differing refining operations, which therefore makes them best suited for different output products. Further, prices for output products are often volatile and must be considered when deciding which products to refine.

Chevron first started using linear programs to assist with its decision making in refinery operations in the 1950s. Through the following decades, the company continued to update and expand its linear program–based tools to include additional complexities and exploit advances in computing power. Currently, Chevron uses a linear program–based tool at each of its seven refineries. The tool includes a spreadsheet interface to allow for ease of use in a familiar software environment.

One of the biggest benefits to the linear program–based tools is that they allow Chevron to consider a multitude of possible scenarios through sensitivity analysis. Because prices for gasoline, lubricants, and other output products change often, Chevron can use sensitivity analysis to evaluate the effects of changes on output product prices to its refinery decisions on which input crude oils to purchase and which output products to process.

Chevron believes that the results of its quantitative methods–based tools, including the linear program models, add more than $1 billion per year in overall benefits. In particular, Chevron estimates that using their tools to optimize their choice of crude oil inputs and choosing the best set of output products to refine generates more than $600 million per year in additional earnings and another $400 million per year of benefits through more efficient use of capital.

8.1   Introduction to Sensitivity Analysis

Sensitivity analysis is important to decision makers because real-world problems exist in a changing environment. Prices of raw materials change, product demands change, production capacities change, stock prices change, and so on. If a linear programming model has been used in such an environment, we can expect some of the coefficients in the model to change over time. As a result, we will want to determine how these changes affect the optimal solution. Sensitivity analysis provides information needed to respond to such changes without requiring a complete solution of a revised linear program.

Recall the RMC problem introduced in Chapter 7. RMC wanted to determine the number of tons of fuel additive (F) and the number of tons of solvent base (S) to produce in order to maximize the total profit contribution for the two products. Three raw material constraints limit the amounts of the two products that can be produced. The RMC linear programming model is restated here:

$$\text{Max} \quad 40F + 30S$$

s.t.

$$
\begin{array}{rcll}
0.4F + 0.5 & \leq & 20 & \text{Material 1} \\
0.2S & \leq & 5 & \text{Material 2} \\
0.6F + 0.3S & \leq & 21 & \text{Material 3} \\
F, S & \geq & 0 &
\end{array}
$$

The optimal solution, $F = 25$ tons and $S = 20$ tons, provided a maximum profit contribution of $1600.

The optimal solution was based on profit contributions of $40 per ton for the fuel additive and $30 per ton for the solvent base. However, suppose that we later learn that a price reduction causes the profit contribution for the fuel additive to fall from $40 to $30 per ton. Sensitivity analysis can be used to determine whether producing 25 tons of fuel additive and 20 tons of solvent base is still best. If it is, solving a modified linear programming problem with $30F + 30S$ as the new objective function is not necessary.

Sensitivity analysis can also be used to determine which coefficients in a linear programming model are crucial. For example, suppose that management believes that the $30 per ton profit contribution for the solvent base is only a rough estimate of the profit contribution that will actually be obtained. If sensitivity analysis shows that 25 tons of fuel additive and 20 tons of solvent base will be the optimal solution as long as the profit contribution for the solvent base is between $20 and $50, management should feel comfortable with the $30 per ton estimate and the recommended production quantities. However, if sensitivity analysis shows that 25 tons of fuel additive and 20 tons of solvent base will be the optimal solution only if the profit contribution for the solvent base is between $29.90 and $30.20 per ton, management may want to review the accuracy of the $30 per ton estimate.

Another aspect of sensitivity analysis concerns changes in the right-hand-side values of the constraints. Recall that in the RMC problem the optimal solution used all available material 1 and material 3. What would happen to the optimal solution and total profit contribution if RMC could obtain additional quantities of either of these resources? Sensitivity analysis can help determine how much each added ton of material is worth and how many tons can be added before diminishing returns set in.

8.2 Objective Function Coefficients

Let us begin sensitivity analysis by using the graphical solution procedure to demonstrate how a change in an objective function coefficient can affect the optimal solution to a linear programming problem. We begin with the graphical solution to the original RMC problem shown in Figure 8.1. The feasible region is shaded. The objective function $40F + 30S$ takes on its maximum value at the extreme point $F = 25$ and $S = 20$. Thus, $F = 25$ and $S = 20$ is the optimal solution and $40(25) + 30(20) = 1600$ is the value of the optimal solution.

FIGURE 8.1   OPTIMAL SOLUTION TO THE ORIGINAL RMC PROBLEM

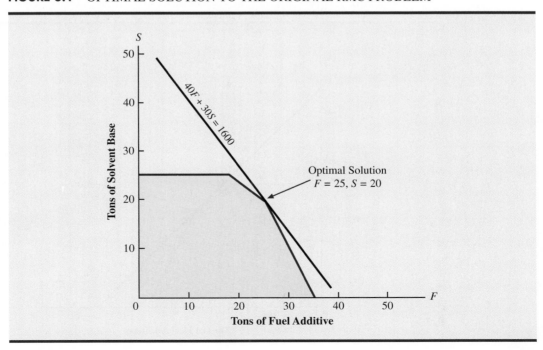

Now suppose RMC learns that a price reduction in the fuel additive has reduced its profit contribution to $30 per ton. With this reduction, RMC's management may question the desirability of maintaining the original optimal solution of $F = 25$ tons and $S = 20$ tons. Perhaps a different solution is now optimal. The RMC linear program with the revised objective function is as follows:

$$\text{Max} \quad 30F + 30S$$

s.t.

$$
\begin{aligned}
0.4F + 0.5S &\le 20 \quad \text{Material 1} \\
0.2S &\le 5 \quad \text{Material 2} \\
0.6F + 0.3S &\le 21 \quad \text{Material 3} \\
F, S &\ge 0
\end{aligned}
$$

Note that only the objective function has changed. Because the constraints have not changed, the feasible region for the revised RMC problem remains the same as the original problem. The graphical solution to the RMC problem with the objective function $30F + 30S$ is shown in Figure 8.2. Note that the extreme point providing the optimal solution is still $F = 25$ and $S = 20$. Thus, although the total profit contribution decreased to $30(25) + 30(20) = 1350$, the decrease in the profit contribution for the fuel additive from $40 per ton to $30 per ton does not change the optimal solution $F = 25$ and $S = 20$.

Now let us suppose that a further price reduction causes the profit contribution for the fuel additive to be reduced to $20 per ton. Is $F = 25$ and $S = 20$ still the optimal solution? Figure 8.3 shows the graphical solution to the RMC problem with the objective function revised to $20F + 30S$. The extreme point providing the optimal solution is now $F = 18.75$

FIGURE 8.2   REVISED OPTIMAL SOLUTION WITH THE RMC OBJECTIVE FUNCTION $30F + 30S$

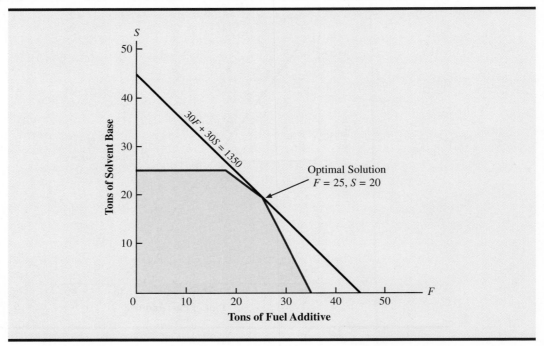

FIGURE 8.3 REVISED OPTIMAL SOLUTION WITH THE RMC OBJECTIVE FUNCTION
$20F + 30S$

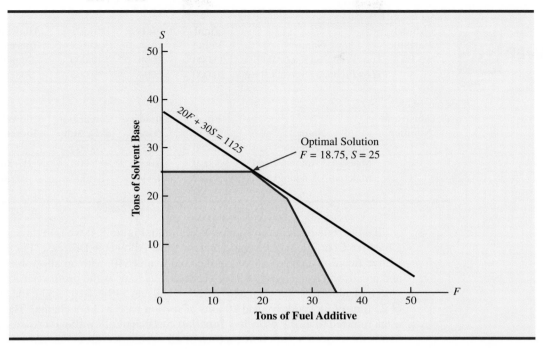

and $S = 25$. The total profit contribution decreased to $20(18.75) + 30(25) = 1125$. However, in this case, we see that decreasing the profit contribution for the fuel additive to $20 per ton changes the optimal solution. The solution $F = 25$ tons and $S = 20$ tons is no longer optimal. The solution $F = 18.75$ and $S = 25$ now provides the optimal production quantities for RMC.

The graphical solution is used here to help the reader visualize how changes to an objective function coefficient may or may not change the optimal solution.

What do we learn from the graphical solutions in Figures 8.1, 8.2, and 8.3? Changing one objective function coefficient changes the slope of the objective function line but leaves the feasible region unchanged. If the change in the objective function coefficient is small, the extreme point that provided the optimal solution to the original problem may still provide the optimal solution. However, if the change in the objective function coefficient is large enough, a different extreme point will provide a new optimal solution.

Computer solutions typically provide sensitivity analysis information.

Fortunately, computer packages such as Excel can easily provide sensitivity analysis information about the objective function coefficients for the original RMC linear programming problem. You do not have to reformulate and re-solve the linear programming problem to obtain the sensitivity analysis information. Appendix 8.1 explains how to generate a Sensitivity Report using Excel Solver. A sensitivity report similar to the output provided by Excel for the original RMC linear programming problem is shown in Figure 8.4. In addition to all of the Excel Solver Sensitivity Report information, the report in Figure 8.4 also shows the variables we used in our model. This allows you to easily link the sensitivity report to the model under discussion. We shall use this style of sensitivity report throughout this chapter.

In the Variable Cells section of the sensitivity report, the column labeled Final Value contains the optimal values of the decision variables. For the RMC problem the optimal solution is to produce 25 tons of fuel additive and 20 tons of solvent base. Associated with each decision variable is a reduced cost. We will discuss reduced costs in more detail after introducing the concept of shadow prices later in this chapter.

FIGURE 8.4   SENSITIVITY REPORT FOR THE RMC PROBLEM

Variable Cells

RMC

Model Variable	Name	Final Value	Reduced Cost	Objective Coefficient	Allowable Increase	Allowable Decrease
F	Tons Produced Fuel Additive	25.000	0.000	40.000	20.000	16.000
S	Tons Produced Solvent Base	20.000	0.000	30.000	20.000	10.000

Constraints

Constraint Number	Name	Final Value	Shadow Price	Constraint R.H. Side	Allowable Increase	Allowable Decrease
1	Material 1 Amount Used	20.000	33.333	20.000	1.500	6.000
2	Material 2 Amount Used	4.000	0.000	5.000	1E+30	1.000
3	Material 3 Amount Used	21.000	44.444	21.000	9.000	2.250

To the right of the Reduced Cost column in Figure 8.4, we find three columns labeled Objective Coefficient, Allowable Increase, and Allowable Decrease. For example, the objective function coefficient for the fuel additive is $40, with an allowable increase of $20 and an allowable decrease of $16. Therefore, as long as the profit contribution associated with fuel additive is between $40 + $20 = $60 and $40 − $16 = $24, the optimal solution of 25 tons of fuel additive and 20 tons of solvent base will not change. The value of $20 is often referred to as the **objective function coefficient allowable increase**, and the value of $16 is the **objective function coefficient allowable decrease**. The range between $24 and $60 is referred to as the **objective coefficient range** or **range of optimality** for the fuel additive variable. If the profit contribution for the fuel additive is outside this range, a different extreme point and a different solution will become optimal.

The objective function coefficient for the solvent base variable is $30. The allowable decrease of $10 and allowable increase of $20 for the solvent base variable show that the optimal solution will not change so long as the profit contribution for solvent base is between $30 + $20 = $50 and $30 − $10 = $20.

NOTES AND COMMENTS

1. The sensitivity analysis information provided for the objective function coefficients is based on the assumption that *only one objective function coefficient changes at a time* and that all other aspects of the original problem remain unchanged. Thus, an objective coefficient range is only applicable for changes to a single objective coefficient. We examine this issue in more depth in Section 8.4.

8.3 Right-Hand Sides

Let us expand the discussion of sensitivity analysis by considering how a change in the right-hand side of a constraint affects the feasible region and the optimal solution to a linear programming problem. As with sensitivity analysis for the objective function coefficients, we consider what happens when we make *one change at a time*. For example, suppose that in the RMC problem an additional 4.5 tons of material 3 becomes available. In this case, the right-hand side of the third constraint increases from 21 tons to 25.5 tons. The revised RMC linear programming model is as follows:

$$\text{Max} \quad 40F + 30S$$

s.t.

$$
\begin{aligned}
0.4F + 0.5S &\leq 20 &\quad \text{Material 1} \\
0.2S &\leq 5 &\quad \text{Material 2} \\
0.6F + 0.3S &\leq 25.5 &\quad \text{Material 3} \\
F, S &\geq 0
\end{aligned}
$$

Sensitivity analysis for right-hand sides is based on the assumption that only one right-hand side changes at a time. All other aspects of the problem are assumed to be as stated in the original problem.

The graphical solution to this problem is shown in Figure 8.5. Note how the feasible region expands because of the additional 4.5 tons of material 3. Application of the graphical solution procedure shows that the extreme point $F = 37.5$ tons and $S = 10$ tons is the new optimal solution. The value of the optimal solution is $40(37.5) + 30(10) = \$1800$. Recall that the optimal solution to the original RMC problem was $F = 25$ tons and $S = 20$ tons and the value of the optimal solution was $\$1600$. Thus, the additional 4.5 tons of material 3 in the revised problem provides a new optimal solution and increases the value of the optimal solution by $\$1800 - \$1600 = \$200$. On a per-ton basis, the additional 4.5 tons of material 3 increases the value of the optimal solution at the rate of $\$200/4.5 = \$44.44$ per ton.

Shadow prices often provide the economic information that helps make decisions about acquiring additional resources.

The **shadow price** is the change in the optimal objective function value per unit increase in the right-hand side of a constraint. Hence, the shadow price for the material 3 constraint is $\$44.44$ per ton. In other words, if we increase the right-hand side of the material 3 constraint by 1 ton, the value of the optimal solution will increase by $\$44.44$. Conversely, if we decrease the right-hand side of the material 3 constraint by 1 ton, the value of the optimal solution will decrease by $\$44.44$.

FIGURE 8.5   GRAPHICAL SOLUTION TO THE RMC PROBLEM WITH MATERIAL 3 CONSTRAINT $0.6F + 0.5S \leq 24.5$

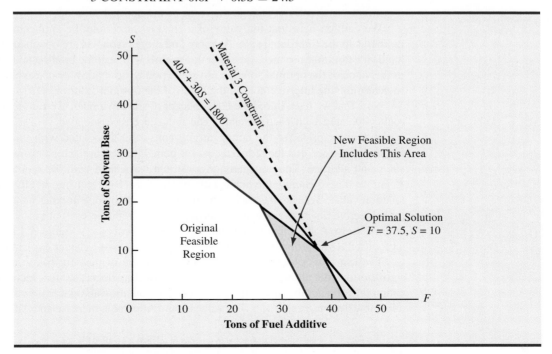

Fortunately, the sensitivity report for the original linear programming problem provides the shadow prices for all the constraints. *You do not have to reformulate and re-solve the linear programming problem to obtain the shadow price information.* The sensitivity report for the original RMC linear programming problem is shown in Figure 8.4.

Examine the Constraints section of the sensitivity report. The entries in the Final Value column indicate the number of tons of each material used in the optimal solution. Thus, RMC will use 20 tons of material 1, 4 tons of material 2, and 21 tons of material 3 in order to produce the optimal solution of 25 tons of fuel additive and 20 tons of solvent base.

The values in the Constraint R.H. Side column are the right-hand sides of the constraints for the RMC problem. The differences between the entries in the Constraint R.H. Side column and the Final Value column provide the values of the slack variables for the RMC problem. Thus, there are $20 - 20 = 0$ tons of slack for material 1, $5 - 4 = 1$ ton of slack for material 2, and $21 - 21 = 0$ tons of slack for material 3.

The column labeled Shadow Price provides the following information:

Computer solutions typically provide the shadow price for each constraint.

Constraint	Shadow Price
Material 1 Amount Used	$33.33
Material 2 Amount Used	$ 0.00
Material 3 Amount Used	$44.44

Note that the shadow price for material 3, $44.44 per ton, agrees with the calculations we made using the graphical solution procedure. We also observe that the shadow price for the material 1 constraint indicates that the value of the optimal solution will increase at the rate of $33.33 per ton of material 1. Finally, note that the shadow price for the material 2 constraint is $0.00. The optimal solution to the RMC problem shows that material 2 has a slack of 1 ton. Thus, at the optimal solution, 1 ton of material 2 is unused. The shadow price of $0.00 tells us that additional tons of material 2 will simply add to the amount of slack for constraint 2 and will not change the value of the optimal solution.

We caution here that the value of a shadow price may be applicable only for small increases in the right-hand side. As more and more resources are obtained and as the right-hand side continues to increase, other constraints will become binding and limit the change in the value of the optimal solution. At some point, the shadow price can no longer be used to determine the improvement in the value of the optimal solution.

Now that we have introduced the concept of shadow prices, we can define the **reduced cost** associated with each variable. The reduced cost associated with a variable is equal to the shadow price for the nonnegativity constraint associated with the variable.[1] From Figure 8.4 we see that the reduced cost for both variables are zero. This makes sense. Consider fuel additive. The nonegativity constraint associated with the fuel additive variable, F, is $F \geq 0$, so changing the nonnegativity constraint to $F \geq 1$ has no effect on the optimal solution value. Because increasing the right-hand side by one unit has no effect on the optimal objective function value, the shadow price (i.e., reduced cost) of this nonnegativity constraint is zero. A similar argument applies to the solvent base variable, S. Later we introduce a modified RMC problem that has a nonzero reduced cost to better explain this concept.

The last two columns in the Constraints section of the sensitivity report contain the **right-hand side allowable increase** and **allowable decrease** for each constraint. For example, consider the material 1 constraint with an allowable increase value of 1.5 and an allowable decrease value of 6. The values in the Allowable Increase and Allowable Decrease

---

[1]We also note that, if the value of a variable in an optimal solution is equal to the upper bound of the variable, then the reduced cost will be the shadow price of this upper-bound constraint.

The range of feasibility is also sometimes referred to as the right-hand-side range.

columns indicate that the shadow price of $33.33 is applicable for increases up to $20 + 1.5 = 21.5$ tons and decreases down to $20 - 6 = 14$ tons. The values between 14 tons and 21.5 tons are often referred to as the **range of feasibility** for the material 1 constraint.

Note that unlike the objective function coefficient ranges, it is not true that the optimal solution will not change if you stay within the range of feasibility. The range of feasibility only implies that the same set of binding constraints will remain binding and hence that the shadow price will accurately predict what will happen to the optimal objective function value as the right-hand side is changed.

Similar to sensitivity analysis for objective function coefficients, the sensitivity analysis for right-hand sides of constraints assumes that only one constraint right-hand side changes at a time.

In summary, the range of feasibility information provides the limits where the shadow prices are applicable. For changes outside the range, the problem must be re-solved to find the new shadow price. Note that the sensitivity analysis information for right-hand sides of constraints is only applicable for changes to a single right-hand side. If two or more right-hand sides of constraints change at the same time, it is easiest to re-solve the problem to see the effect of these changes. This issue is discussed in more detail in Section 8.4.

The Q.M. in Action, Evaluating Efficiency at Performance Analysis Corporation, illustrates the use of shadow prices as part of an evaluation model for a chain of fast-food outlets. This type of model will be studied in more detail in the next chapter when we discuss an application referred to as *data envelopment analysis*.

Q.M. *in* ACTION

EVALUATING EFFICIENCY AT PERFORMANCE ANALYSIS CORPORATION*

Performance Analysis Corporation specializes in the use of quantitative models to design more efficient and effective operations for a wide variety of chain stores. One such application uses linear programming methodology to provide an evaluation model for a chain of fast-food outlets.

According to the concept of Pareto optimality, a restaurant in a given chain is relatively inefficient if other restaurants in the same chain exhibit the following characteristics:

1. Operate in the same or worse environment
2. Produce at least the same level of *all* outputs
3. Utilize no more of *any* resource and *less* of at least one of the resources

To determine which of the restaurants are Pareto inefficient, Performance Analysis Corporation developed and solved a linear programming model. Model constraints involve requirements concerning the minimum acceptable levels of output and conditions imposed by uncontrollable elements in the environment, and the objective function calls for the minimization of the resources

necessary to produce the output. Solving the model produces the following output for each restaurant:

1. A score that assesses the level of so-called relative technical efficiency achieved by the particular restaurant over the time period in question.
2. The reduction in controllable resources or the increase of outputs over the time period in question needed for an inefficient restaurant to be rated as efficient.
3. A peer group of other restaurants with which each restaurant can be compared in the future.

Sensitivity analysis provides important managerial information. For example, for each constraint concerning a minimum acceptable output level, the shadow price tells the manager how much one more unit of output would increase the efficiency measure.

The analysis typically identifies 40% to 50% of the restaurants as underperforming, given the previously stated conditions concerning the inputs available and outputs produced. Performance Analysis Corporation finds that if all the relative inefficiencies identified are eliminated simultaneously, corporate profits typically increase approximately 5% to 10%. This increase is truly substantial given the large scale of operations involved.

*Based on information provided by Richard C. Morey of Performance Analysis Corporation.

1. Some texts and computer programs use the term *dual value* or *dual price* instead of *shadow price*. Often the meaning of these terms is identical to the definition given here for shadow price. However, you must be careful to understand exactly what is meant by the term being used.

Cautionary Note on the Interpretation of Shadow Prices

As stated previously, the shadow price is the change in the value of the optimal solution per unit increase in the right-hand side of a constraint. When the right-hand side of the constraint represents the amount of a resource available, the shadow price is often interpreted as the maximum amount one should be willing to pay for one additional unit of the resource. However, such an interpretation is not always correct. To see why, we need to understand the difference between sunk and relevant costs. A **sunk cost** is one that is not affected by the decision made. It will be incurred no matter what values the decision variables assume. A **relevant cost** is one that depends on the decision made. The amount of a relevant cost will vary depending on the values of the decision variables.

Let us reconsider the RMC problem. The amount of material 1 available is 20 tons. The cost of material 1 is a sunk cost if it must be paid regardless of the number of tons of fuel additive and solvent base produced. It would be a relevant cost if RMC only had to pay for the number of tons of material 1 actually used to produce fuel additive and solvent base. All relevant costs should be included in the objective function of a linear program. Sunk costs should not be included in the objective function. For RMC we have been assuming that the company has already paid for materials 1, 2, and 3. Therefore, the cost of the raw materials for RMC is a sunk cost and has not been included in the objective function.

Only relevant costs should be included in the objective function.

When the cost of a resource is *sunk*, the shadow price can be interpreted as the maximum amount the company should be willing to pay for one additional unit of the resource. When the cost of a resource used is relevant, the shadow price can be interpreted as the amount by which the value of the resource exceeds its cost. Thus, when the resource cost is relevant, the shadow price can be interpreted as the maximum premium over the normal cost that the company should be willing to pay for one unit of the resource.

1. Most computer software packages for solving linear programs provide the optimal solution, shadow price information, the objective coefficient ranges, and the ranges of feasibility. The labels used for these ranges may vary, but the meaning is usually the same as what we have described here.

2. We defined the shadow price as the change in the optimal objective function value per unit increase in a right-hand side of a constraint. The negative of the shadow price gives the change in the optimal objective function value per unit decrease in the right-hand side.

3. Whenever one of the right-hand sides is at an endpoint of its range, the shadow price only provides one-sided information. In this case, the shadow price only predicts the change in the optimal value of the objective function for changes toward the interior of the range.

4. A condition called *degeneracy* can cause a subtle difference in how we interpret changes in the objective function coefficients beyond the endpoints of the objective coefficient range. Degeneracy occurs when the shadow price equals zero for one of the binding constraints. Degeneracy does not affect the interpretation of changes toward the

interior of the objective coefficient range. However, when degeneracy is present, changes beyond the endpoints of the range do not necessarily mean a different solution will be optimal. From a practical point of view, changes beyond the endpoints of the range necessitate resolving the problem.

5. Managers are frequently called on to provide an economic justification for new technology. Often the new technology is developed, or purchased, in order to conserve resources. The shadow price can be helpful in such cases because it can be used to determine the savings attributable to the new technology by showing the savings per unit of resource conserved.

Limitations of Classical Sensitivity Analysis

As we have seen, classical sensitivity analysis can provide useful information on the sensitivity of the solution to changes in the model input data. However, classical sensitivity analysis does have its limitations. In this section we discuss three such limitations: simultaneous changes in input data, changes in constraint coefficients, and nonintuitive shadow prices. We give examples of these three cases and discuss how to deal effectively with these through re-solving the model with changes. In fact, in our experience, it is rarely the case that one solves a model once and makes a recommendation. More often than not, a series of models are solved using a variety of input data sets before a final plan is adopted. With improved algorithms and more powerful computers, solving multiple runs of a model is extremely cost- and time-effective.

Simultaneous Changes

Classical sensitivity analysis is based on the assumption that only one coefficient changes; it is assumed that all other coefficients will remain as stated in the original problem. Thus, the range analysis for the objective function coefficients and the constraint right-hand sides is only applicable for changes in a single coefficient. In many cases, however, we are interested in what would happen if two or more coefficients are changed simultaneously. The easiest way to examine the effect of simultaneous changes is to rerun the model. Computer solution methods such as Excel Solver make rerunning the model easy and fast for many applications.

Consider again the original RMC problem. Suppose RMC's accounting department reviews both the price and cost data for the two products. As a result, the profit contribution for the fuel additive is increased to $48 per ton and the profit contribution for the solvent base is decreased to $27 per ton. Figure 8.6 shows the answer report for this revised problem. The total profit has increased to $48(25) + $27(20) = $1740, but the optimal solution of 25 tons of fuel additive and 20 tons of solvent base has not changed.

Now suppose that the profit contribution for fuel additive is increased again to $55 per ton and the profit contribution for the solvent base remains at $27 per ton. If RMC produces 25 tons of fuel additive and 20 tons of solvent base, this will generate a profit of $55(25) + $27(20) = $1915. However, the answer report in Figure 8.7 shows that if we re-solve this problem with the new profit contribution values, the optimal solution changes. The optimal solution is to produce 35 tons of fuel additive and zero tons of solvent base. This optimal solution results in a profit of $55(35) + $27(0) = $1925.

Sensitivity analysis for the right-hand side of constraints has a similar limitation. The right-hand-side sensitivity analysis information is based on the assumption that only one right-hand side changes at a time. If two or more right-hand sides change simultaneously, the easiest way to observe the effect of these changes is to re-solve the model.

FIGURE 8.6 ANSWER REPORT FOR RMC PROBLEM WITH CHANGE IN PROFITS PER TON FOR FUEL ADDITIVE TO $48 AND SOLVENT BASE TO $27

Objective Cell (Max)

Name	Original Value	Final Value
Maximize Total Profit	0.000	1740.000

Variable Cells

Model Variable	Name	Original Value	Final Value	Integer
A	Tons Produced Fuel Additive	0.000	25.000	Contin
B	Tons Produced Solvent Base	0.000	20.000	Contin

Constraints

Constraint Number	Name	Cell Value	Status	Slack
1	Material 1 Amount Used	20.000	Binding	0.000
2	Material 2 Amount Used	4.000	Not Binding	1.000
3	Material 3 Amount Used	21.000	Binding	0.000

FIGURE 8.7 ANSWER REPORT FOR THE RMC PROBLEM WITH ADDITIONAL INCREASE IN PROFIT PER TON FOR FUEL ADDITIVE TO $55

Objective Cell (Max)

Name	Original Value	Final Value
Maximize Total Profit	0.000	1925.000

Variable Cells

Model Variable	Name	Original Value	Final Value	Integer
A	Tons Produced Fuel Additive	0.000	35.000	Contin
B	Tons Produced Solvent Base	0.000	0.000	Contin

Constraints

Constraint Number	Name	Cell Value	Status	Slack
1	Material 1 Amount Used	14.000	Not Binding	6.000
2	Material 2 Amount Used	0.000	Not Binding	5.000
3	Material 3 Amount Used	21.000	Binding	0.000

Changes in Constraint Coefficients

Classical sensitivity analysis provides no information about changes resulting from a change in the coefficient of a variable in a constraint. We return to the RMC problem to illustrate this idea.

Suppose RMC is considering a different blending formula such that a ton of fuel additive uses 0.5 tons of material 1 instead of 0.4 tons. The constraint for material 1 would then change to

$$0.5F + 0.5S \le 20$$

Even though this is a single change in a coefficient in the model, there is no way to tell from classical sensitivity analysis what impact the change in the coefficient of F will have on the

FIGURE 8.8   ANSWER REPORT FOR THE RMC PROBLEM WITH CHANGES TO CONSTRAINT
COEFFICIENTS

Objective Cell (Max)

Name	Original Value	Final Value
Maximize Total Profit	0.000	1500.000

Variable Cells

Model Variable	Name	Original Value	Final Value	Integer
A	Tons Produced Fuel Additive	0.000	30.000	Contin
B	Tons Produced Solvent Base	0.000	10.000	Contin

Constraints

Constraint Number	Name	Cell Value	Status	Slack
1	Material 1 Amount Used	20.000	Binding	0.000
2	Material 2 Amount Used	2.000	Not Binding	3.000
3	Material 3 Amount Used	21.000	Binding	0.000

solution. Instead, we must simply change the coefficient and rerun the model. The answer report appears in Figure 8.8. Note that it is optimal to produce 30 tons of fuel additive and 10 tons of solvent base. The optimal profit has also changed from $1600 to $40(30) + $30(10) = $1500. Changing to this new blending formula will cost RMC $1600 − $1500 = $100.

Nonintuitive Shadow Prices

Constraints with variables naturally on both the left-hand and right-hand sides often lead to shadow prices that have a nonintuitve explanation. To illustrate such a case and how we may deal with it, let us again reconsider the RMC problem.

Suppose that after reviewing the solution to the original RMC problem (sensitivity report shown in Figure 8.4), management decides that it is concerned with solutions requiring greater production of fuel additive than solvent base. Management believes that the profit generated per ton of fuel additive could decrease in the future, so it is more comfortable producing a greater amount of solvent base than fuel additive. If management wants to specify that RMC produces at least as much solvent base as fuel additive, then we must add the constraint

$$S \geq F$$

This new constraint will require RMC to produce at least as many tons of solvent base as fuel additive. The sensitivity report generated from resolving this problem with the new constraint is shown in Figure 8.9. This shows that it is optimal to produce 22.222 tons of fuel additive and 22.222 tons of solvent base. The total profit using this optimal solution is $40(22.222) + $30(22.222) = $1556.

Let us consider the shadow price for the Min Solvent Base Required constraint. The shadow price of −8.89 indicates that a one-unit increase in the right-hand side of the Min Solvent Base Required constraint will lower profits by $8.89. Thus, what the shadow price is really telling us is what will happen to the value of the optimal solution if the constraint is changed to

$$S \geq F + 1$$

FIGURE 8.9   SENSITIVITY REPORT FOR RMC PROBLEM WITH ADDITIONAL CONSTRAINT FOR
MINIMUM SOLVENT BASE PRODUCTION REQUIRED

Variable Cells

Model Variable	Name	Final Value	Reduced Cost	Objective Coefficient	Allowable Increase	Allowable Decrease
F	Tons Produced Fuel Additive	22.222	0.000	40.000	1E+30	16.000
S	Tons Produced Solvent Base	22.222	0.000	30.000	20.000	70.000

Constraints

Constraint Number	Name	Final Value	Shadow Price	Constraint R.H. Side	Allowable Increase	Allowable Decrease
1	Material 1 Amount Used	20.000	77.778	20.000	1.000	20.000
2	Material 2 Amount Used	4.444	0.000	5.000	1E+30	0.556
3	Material 3 Amount Used	20.000	0.000	21.000	1E+30	1.000
4	Min Solvent Base Required	22.222	−8.889	0.000	6.250	5.000

The interpretation for this shadow price of −8.89 is correctly stated as follows: If we are forced to produce 1 ton more of solvent base over and above the amount of fuel additive produced, total profits will decrease by $8.89. Conversely, if we relax the requirement by 1 ton ($S \geq F - 1$), total profits will increase by $8.89.

We might instead be more interested in what happens if we change the coefficient on F. For instance, what if management required RMC to produce an amount of solvent base that is at least 110% of the amount of fuel additive produce? In other words, the constraint would change to

$$S \geq 1.1F$$

The shadow price does *not* tell us what will happen in this case. Because we have changed the coefficient of F from 1.0 to 1.1, this is the same as the case discussed in the previous section: a change in the constraint coefficient. Since there is no way to get this information from classical sensitivity analysis, we need to re-solve the problem using the constraint $S \geq 1.1F$. To test the sensitivity of the solution to changes in the minimum required percentage of solvent base required, we can re-solve the model replacing the coefficient of F with any percentage of interest.

To get a feel for how the required percentage impacts total profit, we solved versions of this model varying the percentage from 100% to 200% in increments of 10%. In other words, we varied the coefficient of F from 1.0 to 2.0 in increments of 0.1. The impact of changing this percentage is shown in Figure 8.10, and the results are shown in Table 8.1.

What have we learned from this analysis? Notice from Figure 8.10 that the slope of the graph becomes steeper for values larger than 130%. This indicates that there is a shift in the rate of deterioration in profit starting at 130%. Table 8.1 shows why this is the case. For all percentages larger than 130%, we produce 25 tons of solvent base. We are unable to produce additional solvent base due to the material 2 constraint. This is because the left-hand side of the material 2 constraint 0.2(25) = 5, which is equal to the right-hand side. Thus, the material 2 constraint is binding whenever we produce 25 tons of material 2.

FIGURE 8.10 PROFIT FOR VARIOUS VALUES OF REQUIRED SOLVENT BASE AS A PERCENTAGE OF FUEL ADDITIVE PRODUCED

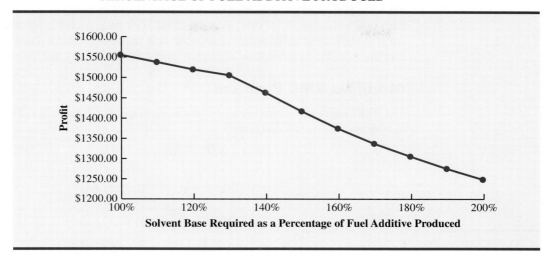

TABLE 8.1 SOLUTIONS FOR VARIOUS VALUES OF MINIMUM REQUIRED PRODUCTION OF SOLVENT BASE AS A PERCENTAGE OF FUEL ADDITIVE PRODUCED

Percent	Profit	Fuel Additive	Solvent Base
100%	$1556.00	22.222	22.222
110%	$1537.00	21.053	23.158
120%	$1520.00	20.000	24.000
130%	$1505.00	19.048	24.762
140%	$1464.00	17.857	25.000
150%	$1417.00	16.667	25.000
160%	$1375.00	15.625	25.000
170%	$1338.00	14.706	25.000
180%	$1306.00	13.889	25.000
190%	$1275.00	13.158	25.000
200%	$1250.00	12.500	25.000

Management now knows that minimum percentage requirements between 100% and 130% result in modest profit losses. Minimum percentage requirements greater than 130% result in greater profit losses. Greater minimum percentage requirements will result in more significant profit losses because we are unable to produce more than 25 tons of solvent base due to the material 2 constraint.

8.5 More Than Two Decision Variables

The graphical solution procedure is useful only for linear programs involving two decision variables. In practice, the problems solved using linear programming usually involve large numbers of variables and constraints. For instance, the Q.M. in Action, Determining

Optimal Production Quantities at GE Plastics, describes how a linear programming model with 3100 variables and 1100 constraints was solved in less than 10 seconds to determine the optimal production quantities at GE Plastics. In this section we discuss the formulation and computer solution for two linear programs with three decision variables. In doing so, we will show how to interpret the reduced-cost portion of the computer output and will also illustrate the interpretation of shadow prices for constraints that involve percentages.

Modified RMC Problem

The RMC linear programming problem was introduced in Section 7.1. The original problem formulation is restated here:

$$\text{Max} \quad 40F + 30S$$

s.t.

$$
\begin{array}{rl}
0.4F + 0.5S \le 20 & \text{Material 1} \\
0.2S \le 5 & \text{Material 2} \\
0.6F + 0.3S \le 21 & \text{Material 3} \\
F, S \ge 0
\end{array}
$$

Suppose that management also is considering producing a carpet cleaning fluid. Estimates are that each ton of carpet cleaning fluid will require 0.6 tons of material 1, 0.1 tons of material 2, and 0.3 tons of material 3. Because of the unique capabilities of the new product, RMC's management believes that the company will realize a profit contribution of $50 for each ton of carpet cleaning fluid produced during the current production period.

Let us consider the modifications in the original linear programming model that are needed to incorporate the effect of this additional decision variable. We let C denote the number of tons of carpet cleaning fluid produced. After adding C to the objective

DETERMINING OPTIMAL PRODUCTION QUANTITIES AT GE PLASTICS*

GE Plastics (GEP) is a $5 billion global materials supplier of plastics and raw materials to many industries (e.g., automotive, computer, and medical equipment). GEP has plants all over the globe. In the past, GEP followed a pole-centric manufacturing approach wherein each product was manufactured in the geographic area (Americas, Europe, or Pacific) where it was to be delivered. When many of GEP's customers started shifting their manufacturing operations to the Pacific, a geographic imbalance was created between GEP's capacity and demand in the form of overcapacity in the Americas and undercapacity in the Pacific.

Recognizing that a pole-centric approach was no longer effective, GEP adopted a global approach to its

manufacturing operations. Initial work focused on the high-performance polymers (HPP) division. Using a linear programming model, GEP was able to determine the optimal production quantities at each HPP plant to maximize the total contribution margin for the division. The model included demand constraints, manufacturing capacity constraints, and constraints that modeled the flow of materials produced at resin plants to the finishing plants and on to warehouses in three geographical regions (Americas, Europe, and Pacific). The mathematical model for a one-year problem has 3100 variables and 1100 constraints and can be solved in less than 10 seconds. The new system proved successful at the HPP division, and other GE Plastics divisions are adapting it for their supply chain planning.

In 2007, GEP was acquired by the Saudi Basic Industries Corporation (SABIC), the largest company in the Middle East and one of the largest companies in the world.

*Based on R. Tyagi, P. Kalish, and K. Akbay, "GE Plastics Optimizes the Two-Echelon Global Fulfillment Network at Its High-Performance Polymers Division," *Interfaces* (September/October 2004): 359–366.

FIGURE 8.11   SENSITIVITY REPORT FOR MODIFIED RMC PROBLEM

Variable Cells

Model Variable	Name	Final Value	Reduced Cost	Objective Coefficient	Allowable Increase	Allowable Decrease
F	Tons Produced Fuel Additive	27.500	0.000	40.000	60.000	6.667
S	Tons Produced Solvent Base	0.000	−12.500	30.000	12.500	1E+30
C	Tons Produced Carpet Cleaning Fluid	15.000	0.000	50.000	10.000	16.667

Constraints

Constraint Number	Name	Final Value	Shadow Price	Constraint R.H. Side	Allowable Increase	Allowable Decrease
1	Material 1 Amount Used	20.000	75.000	20.000	14.000	6.000
2	Material 2 Amount Used	1.500	0.000	5.000	1E+30	3.500
3	Material 3 Amount Used	21.000	16.667	21.000	9.000	11.000

function and to each of the three constraints, we obtain the linear program for the modified problem:

$$\text{Max} \quad 40F + 30S + 50C$$

$$\text{s.t.}$$

$$
\begin{aligned}
0.4F + 0.5S + 0.6C &\leq 20 \quad \text{Material 1} \\
0.2S + 0.1C &\leq 5 \quad \text{Material 2} \\
0.6F + 0.3S + 0.3C &\leq 21 \quad \text{Material 3} \\
F, S, C &\geq 0
\end{aligned}
$$

Figure 8.11 shows the sensitivity report for this solution to the modified RMC problem. The optimal solution calls for the production of 27.5 tons of fuel additive, 0 tons of solvent base, and 15 tons of carpet cleaning fluid. The value of the optimal solution is $40(27.5) + $30(0) + $50(15) = $1850.

Note the information contained in the Reduced Costs column of the Variable Cells section. Recall that reduced costs are the shadow prices of the corresponding nonnegativity constraints. As Figure 8.11 shows, the reduced costs for fuel additive and carpet cleaning fluid variables are zero because increasing the right-hand side of these nonnegativity constraints would not change the optimal objective function value. However, the reduced cost for the solvent base decision variable is −12.50. This means that the shadow price for the nonnegativity constraint associated with the solvent base decision variable is −12.50. The interpretation for this value is that if the nonnegativity constraint, $S \geq 0$, was changed to $S \geq 1$, the optimal objective function value would decrease by $12.50. In other words, if we forced the production of at least 1 ton of solvent base, the profit for the optimal solution would decrease by $12.50.[2]

Figure 8.11 also shows that the shadow prices for material 1 amount used and material 3 amount used are 75.000 and 16.667, respectively, indicating that these two constraints are binding in the optimal solution. Thus, each additional ton of material 1 would increase the value of the optimal solution by $75 and each additional ton of material 3 would increase the value of the optimal solution by $16.67.

---

[2]Another interpretation for this is that if we "reduce the cost" of the objective function coefficient for solvent base by −12.50 [i.e., change the profit contribution from solvent base to $30 − (−$12.50) = $42.50], then there is an optimal solution where we produce a nonzero amount of solvent base.

Bluegrass Farms Problem

To provide additional practice in formulating and interpreting the computer solution for linear programs involving more than two decision variables, we consider a minimization problem involving three decision variables. Bluegrass Farms, located in Lexington, Kentucky, has been experimenting with a special diet for its racehorses. The feed components available for the diet are a standard horse feed product, an enriched oat product, and a new vitamin and mineral feed additive. The nutritional values in units per pound and the costs for the three feed components are summarized in Table 8.2; for example, each pound of the standard feed component contains 0.8 units of ingredient A, 1 unit of ingredient B, and 0.1 units of ingredient C. The minimum daily diet requirements for each horse are 3 units of ingredient A, 6 units of ingredient B, and 4 units of ingredient C. In addition, to control the weight of the horses, the total daily feed for a horse should not exceed 6 pounds. Bluegrass Farms would like to determine the minimum-cost mix that will satisfy the daily diet requirements.

To formulate a linear programming model for the Bluegrass Farms problem, we introduce three decision variables:

S = number of pounds of the standard horse feed product

E = number of pounds of the enriched oat product

A = number of pounds of the vitamin and mineral feed additive

Using the data in Table 8.2, the objective function that will minimize the total cost associated with the daily feed can be written as follows:

$$\text{Min } 0.25S + 0.5E + 3A$$

Because the minimum daily requirement for ingredient A is 3 units, we obtain the constraint

$$0.8S + 0.2E \geq 3$$

The constraint for ingredient B is

$$1.0S + 1.5E + 3.0A \geq 6$$

and the constraint for ingredient C is

$$0.1S + 0.6E + 2.0A \geq 4$$

Finally, the constraint that restricts the mix to at most 6 pounds is

$$S + E + A \leq 6$$

TABLE 8.2   NUTRITIONAL VALUE AND COST DATA FOR THE BLUEGRASS FARMS PROBLEM

Feed Component	Standard	Enriched Oat	Additive
Ingredient A	0.8	0.2	0.0
Ingredient B	1.0	1.5	3.0
Ingredient C	0.1	0.6	2.0
Cost per pound	$0.25	$0.50	$3.00

Combining all the constraints with the nonnegativity requirements enables us to write the complete linear programming model for the Bluegrass Farms problem as follows:

$$\text{Min} \quad 0.25S + 0.50E + 3A$$

s.t.

$$
\begin{array}{rcll}
0.8S + 0.2E & \geq 3 & \text{Ingredient A} \\
1.0S + 1.5E + 3.0A & \geq 6 & \text{Ingredient B} \\
0.1S + 0.6E + 2.0A & \geq 4 & \text{Ingredient C} \\
S + E + A & \leq 6 & \text{Weight} \\
S, E, A & \geq 0 &
\end{array}
$$

The sensitivity report for the Bluegrass Farms problem is shown in Figure 8.12. After rounding, we see that the optimal solution calls for a daily diet consisting of 3.51 pounds of the standard horse feed product, 0.95 pounds of the enriched oat product, and 1.54 pounds of the vitamin and mineral feed additive. Thus, with feed component costs of $0.25, $0.50, and $3.00, the total cost of the optimal diet is

$$
\begin{array}{r}
3.51 \text{ pounds @ } \$0.25 \text{ per pound} = \$0.88 \\
0.95 \text{ pound @ } \$0.50 \text{ per pound} = \$0.47 \\
1.54 \text{ pounds @ } \$3.00 \text{ per pound} = \underline{\$4.62} \\
\text{Total cost} = \$5.97
\end{array}
$$

Looking at the Constraints section of the sensitivity report, we see that the final value for the Ingredient B LHS constraint is 9.554 and the right-hand side of this constraint is 6. Because this constraint is a greater-than-or-equal-to constraint, 3.554 is the surplus; the optimal solution exceeds the minimum daily diet requirement for ingredient B (6 units) by 3.554 units. Because the final values for the ingredient A and ingredient C constraints are

FIGURE 8.12   SENSITIVITY REPORT FOR THE BLUEGRASS FARMS PROBLEM

Variable Cells

Model Variable	Name	Final Value	Reduced Cost	Objective Coefficient	Allowable Increase	Allowable Decrease
S	Number of Pounds Standard	3.514	0.000	0.250	1E+30	0.643
E	Number of Pounds Enriched Oat	0.946	0.000	0.500	0.425	1E+30
A	Number of Pounds Additive	1.541	0.000	3.000	1E+30	1.478

WEB file

Bluegrass

Constraints

Constraint Number	Name	Final Value	Shadow Price	Constraint R.H. Side	Allowable Increase	Allowable Decrease
1	Ingredient A	3.000	1.216	3.000	0.368	1.857
2	Ingredient B	9.554	0.000	6.000	3.554	1E+30
3	Ingredient C	4.000	1.959	4.000	0.875	1.900
4	Weight	6.000	−0.919	6.000	2.478	0.437

equal to the right-hand sides for these constraints, we see that the optimal diet just meets the minimum requirements for ingredients A and C. The final value for the weight constraint is equal to the right-hand side (6 pounds). This tells us that this constraint has a slack value of zero, which means that the optimal solution provides a total daily feed weight of 6 pounds.

The shadow price (after rounding) for ingredient A is 1.22. Thus, increasing the right-hand side of the ingredient A constraint by one unit will cause the solution value to increase by $1.22. Conversely, it is also correct to conclude that a decrease of one unit in the right-hand side of the ingredient A constraint will decrease the total cost by $1.22. Looking at the Allowable Increase and Allowable Decrease columns in the Constraints section of the sensitivity report, we see that these interpretations are correct as long as the right-hand side of the ingredient A constraint is between $3 - 1.857 = 1.143$ and $3 + 0.368 = 3.368$.

Suppose that the Bluegrass management is willing to reconsider its position regarding the maximum weight of the daily diet. The shadow price of -0.92 (after rounding) for the weight constraint shows that a one-unit increase in the right-hand side of constraint 4 will reduce total cost by $0.92. The Allowable Increase column in the sensitivity report shows that this interpretation is correct for increases in the right-hand side up to a maximum of $6 + 2.478 = 8.478$ pounds. Thus, the effect of increasing the right-hand side of the weight constraint from 6 to 8 pounds is a decrease in the total daily cost of $2 \times \$0.92$, or $1.84. Keep in mind that if this change were made, the feasible region would change, and we would obtain a new optimal solution.

Next we look at the Variable Cells section of the sensitivity report. The Allowable Decrease column shows a lower limit of $0.25 - 0.643 = -0.393$ for the objective function coefficient associated with the standard horse feed product variable, S. Clearly, in a real problem, the objective function coefficient of S (the cost of the standard horse feed product) cannot take on a negative value. So, from a practical point of view, we can think of the lower limit for the objective function coefficient of S as being zero. We can thus conclude that no matter how much the cost of the standard mix were to decrease, the optimal solution would not change. Even if Bluegrass Farms could obtain the standard horse feed product for free, the optimal solution would still specify a daily diet of 3.51 pounds of the standard horse feed product, 0.95 pounds of the enriched oat product, and 1.54 pounds of the vitamin and mineral feed additive. However, any decrease in the per-unit cost of the standard feed would result in a decrease in the total cost for the optimal daily diet.

Note from Figure 8.12 that the allowable increases for the objective function coefficients associated with standard horse feed product and additive are shown as $1E+30$. This is the same notation as is used in Excel's Sensitivity Report; it means that these objective function coefficients have no upper limit. Even if the cost of additive were to increase, for example, from $3.00 to $13.00 per pound, the optimal solution would not change; the total cost of the solution, however, would increase by $10 (the amount of the increase) $\times 1.541$, or $15.41. You must always keep in mind that the interpretations we make using classical sensitivity analysis information are only appropriate if all other coefficients in the problem do not change. To consider simultaneous changes, we must re-solve the problem.

Linear programming has been successfully applied to a variety of applications. The Q.M. in Action, Kimpton Hotels Uses Optimization for Setting Prices on Priceline, provides an example from the hotel industry. The Q.M. in Action discusses how Kimpton Hotels uses linear programming and, specifically, the value of shadow prices, to set prices of rooms sold through Priceline.

KIMPTON HOTELS USES OPTIMIZATION FOR SETTING PRICES ON PRICELINE*

How to price rooms to maximize revenue is a problem faced by all hotels. If prices are set too low, demand will be higher, but total revenue may be lower than what would have been generated if the customer's willingness to pay was known. If the price is too high, demand may drop, resulting in empty rooms and lost revenue. Revenue management, sometimes called yield management, attempts to determine prices to charge and how many rooms to offer at each price so as to maximize revenue.

Kimpton Hotels owns over 50 boutique four-star hotels in the United States and Canada. Most of Kimpton's customers are business travelers who generally book later and are often willing to pay more than leisure travelers. The shorter lead time of business travelers presents a challenge for Kimpton, since it has less time to react by adjusting its prices when demand does not materialize.

Priceline.com is an Internet site that allows the user to specify the area he or she would like to visit, the dates of the visit, and the level of the hotel (three-star, four-

star, etc.) and to make a bid price for a room. Priceline searches a list of participating hotels for a hotel that matches the criteria specified by the user. This is known as opaque marketing because the hotel name is revealed to the user only when a match is found, at which point the user is committed. This opaqueness is important for the hotel, because it allows the hotel to segment the market and offer different prices without diluting its regularly posted prices.

Kimpton participates in the Priceline bidding process and has to submit prices and how many rooms are available at each price level over a specified set of dates. Using historical data, Kimpton predicts future demand and uses a technique known as dynamic programming to set prices. A linear program is then used to determine the number of rooms to offer at each price level. In particular, the shadow price on a room availability constraint is utilized to assess whether or not to offer another room at a given price in a given period. Since implementing this new optimization-based approach, rooms sold via Priceline have increased 11% and the average price for the rooms has increased by nearly 4%.

*Based on C. Anderson, "Setting Prices on Priceline," Interfaces 39, no. 4 (July/August 2009): 307–315.

8.6 Electronic Communications Problem

The Electronic Communications problem is a maximization problem involving four decision variables, two less-than-or-equal-to constraints, one equality constraint, and one greater-than-or-equal-to constraint. We will use this problem to provide a summary of the process of formulating a mathematical model, using Excel to obtain an optimal solution, and interpreting the solution and sensitivity report information. In the next chapter we will continue to illustrate how linear programming can be applied by showing additional examples from the areas of marketing, finance, and production management.

Electronic Communications manufactures portable radio systems that can be used for two-way communications. The company's new product, which has a range of up to 25 miles, is suitable for use in a variety of business and personal applications. The distribution channels for the new radio are as follows:

1. Marine equipment distributors
2. Business equipment distributors
3. National chain of retail stores
4. Direct mail

Because of differing distribution and promotional costs, the profitability of the product will vary with the distribution channel. In addition, the advertising cost and the personal sales

TABLE 8.3 PROFIT, ADVERTISING COST, AND PERSONAL SALES TIME DATA
FOR THE ELECTRONIC COMMUNICATIONS PROBLEM

Distribution Channel	Profit per Unit Sold	Advertising Cost per Unit Sold	Personal Sales Effort per Unit Sold
Marine distributors	$90	$10	2 hours
Business distributors	$84	$ 8	3 hours
National retail stores	$70	$ 9	3 hours
Direct mail	$60	$15	None

effort required will vary with the distribution channel. Table 8.3 summarizes the contribution to profit, advertising cost, and personal sales effort data for the Electronic Communications problem. The firm set the advertising budget at $5000. A maximum of 1800 hours of sales force time is available for allocation to the sales effort. Management also decided to produce exactly 600 units for the current production period. Finally, an ongoing contract with a national chain of retail stores requires that at least 150 units be distributed through this distribution channel.

Electronic Communications is now faced with the problem of determining the number of units that should be produced for each of the distribution channels in order to maximize the total contribution to profit. In addition to determining how many units should be allocated to each of the four distribution channels, Electronic Communications must also determine how to allocate the advertising budget and sales force effort to each of the four distribution channels.

Problem Formulation

We will now write the objective function and the constraints for the Electronic Communications problem. We begin with the objective function.

Objective function: Maximize profit

Four constraints are needed to account for the following restrictions: (1) a limited advertising budget, (2) limited sales force availability, (3) a production requirement, and (4) a retail stores distribution requirement.

Constraint 1 Advertising expenditure ≤ Budget

Constraint 2 Sales time used ≤ Time available

Constraint 3 Radios produced = Management requirement

Constraint 4 Retail distribution ≥ Contract requirement

These expressions provide descriptions of the objective function and the constraints. We are now ready to define the decision variables that will represent the decisions the manager must make. For the Electronic Communications problem, we introduce the following four decision variables:

M = the number of units produced for the marine equipment distribution channel

B = the number of units produced for the business equipment distribution channel

R = the number of units produced for the national retail chain distribution channel

D = the number of units produced for the direct mail distribution channel

Using the data in Table 8.3, we can write the objective function for maximizing the total contribution to profit associated with the radios as follows:

$$\text{Max } 90M + 84B + 70R + 60D$$

Let us now develop a mathematical statement of the constraints for the problem. For the advertising budget of $5000, the constraint that limits the amount of advertising expenditure can be written as follows:

$$10M + 8B + 9R + 15D \leq 5000$$

Similarly, with sales time limited to 1800 hours, we obtain the constraint

$$2M + 3B + 3R \leq 1800$$

Management's decision to produce exactly 600 units during the current production period is expressed as

$$M + B + R + D = 600$$

Finally, to account for the fact that the number of units distributed by the national chain of retail stores must be at least 150, we add the constraint

$$R \geq 150$$

Combining all of the constraints with the nonnegativity requirements enables us to write the complete linear programming model for the Electronic Communications problem as follows:

$$
\begin{array}{ll}
\text{Max} \quad 90M + 84B + 70R + 60D & \\
\text{s.t.} & \\
\quad 10M + 8B + 9R + 15D \leq 5000 & \text{Advertising budget} \\
\quad 2M + 3B + 3R \leq 1800 & \text{Sales force availability} \\
\quad M + B + R + D = 600 & \text{Production level} \\
\quad R \geq 150 & \text{Retail stores requirement} \\
\quad M, B, R, D \geq 0 &
\end{array}
$$

Solution and Interpretation

Figure 8.13 shows the sensitivity report for the Electronic Communications problem. The optimal decisions are to produce 25 units for the marine distribution channel ($M = 25$), 425 units for the business equipment distribution channel ($B = 425$), 150 units for the retail chain distribution channel ($R = 150$), and no units for the direct mail distribution channel ($D = 0$). The optimal solution to the problem will provide a profit of $90(25) + $84(425) + $70(150) + $60(0) = $48,450. Consider the information contained in the Reduced Cost

FIGURE 8.13   SENSITIVITY REPORT FOR THE ELECTRONIC COMMUNICATIONS PROBLEM

Variable Cells

Model Variable	Name	Final Value	Reduced Cost	Objective Coefficient	Allowable Increase	Allowable Decrease
M	Number of Units Produced Marine	25.000	0.000	90.000	1E+30	6.000
B	Number of Units Produced Business	425.000	0.000	84.000	6.000	34.000
R	Number of Units Produced Retail	150.000	0.000	70.000	17.000	1E+30
D	Number of Units Produced Direct Mail	0.000	−45.000	60.000	45.000	1E+30

WEB file

Electronic

Constraints

Constraint Number	Name	Final Value	Shadow Price	Constraint R.H. Side	Allowable Increase	Allowable Decrease
1	Advertising Budget	5000.000	3.000	5000.000	850.000	50.000
2	Sales Force Availability	1775.000	0.000	1800.000	1E+30	25.000
3	Production Level	600.000	60.000	600.000	3.571	85.000
4	Retail Stores Requirement	150.000	−17.000	150.000	50.000	150.000

column of the Variable Cells section of the sensitivity report in Figure 8.13. Recall that the reduced cost of a variable is the shadow price of the corresponding nonnegativity constraint. As the sensitivity analysis shows, the first three reduced costs are zero because the corresponding decision variables already have positive values in the optimal solution. However, the reduced cost of −45 for Number of Units Produced Direct Mail (D) tells us that profit will decrease by $45 for every unit produced for the direct mail channel. Stated another way, the objective function coefficient associated with D would have to be reduced by at least −$45 per unit [i.e., the profit contribution would have to be at least $60 − (−$45) = $105 per unit] before it would be profitable to use the direct mail distribution channel.

Next consider the Constraints section of the sensitivity report in Figure 8.13. The advertising budget constraint has a final value equal to the constraint right-hand side, indicating that the entire budget of $5000 has been used. The corresponding shadow price of 3 tells us that an additional dollar added to the advertising budget will increase the profit by $3. Thus, the possibility of increasing the advertising budget should be seriously considered by the firm. Comparing the final value to the right-hand-side value for the sales force availability, we see that this constraint has a slack value of 1800 − 1725 = 25 hours. In other words, the allocated 1800 hours of sales time are adequate to distribute the radios produced, and 25 hours of sales time will remain unused. Because the production level constraint is an equality constraint, it is expected that the final value will equal the right-hand side for this constraint. However, the shadow price of 60 associated with this constraint shows that if the firm were to consider increasing the production level for the radios, the value of the objective function, or profit, would increase at the rate of $60 per radio produced. Finally, the final value is equal to the right-hand side for the retail stores requirement constraint shows that this constraint is binding. The negative shadow price indicates that increasing the commitment from 150 to 151 units will actually decrease the profit by $17. Thus, Electronic Communications may want to consider reducing its commitment to the retail store distribution channel. A *decrease* in the commitment will actually increase profit at the rate of $17 per unit.

We now consider the Allowable Increase and Allowable Decrease columns from the Variable Cells section of the sensitivity report shown in Figure 8.13. The allowable increases and decreases for the objective function coefficients are

Name	Objective Coefficient	Allowable Increase	Allowable Decrease
Units Produced Marine	90.000	Infinite	6.000
Units Produced Business	84.000	6.000	34.000
Units Produced Retail	70.000	17.000	Infinite
Units Produced Direct Mail	60.000	45.000	Infinite

The current solution, or strategy, remains optimal, provided that the objective function coefficients do not increase or decrease by more than the allowed amounts. Note in particular the range associated with the direct mail distribution channel coefficient. This information is consistent with the earlier observation for the Reduced Cost portion of the output. In both instances, we see that the per-unit profit would have to increase to $60 + $45 = $105 before the direct mail distribution channel could be in the optimal solution with a positive value.

Finally, the sensitivity analysis for the allowable increases and decreases of the right-hand side of the constraints can be taken from Figure 8.13 as follows:

Name	Constraint R.H. Side	Allowable Increase	Allowable Decrease
Advertising Budget	5000.000	850.000	50.000
Sales Force Availability	1800.000	Infinite	25.000
Production Level	600.000	3.571	85.000
Retail Stores Requirement	150.000	50.000	150.000

Several interpretations of these right-hand-side ranges are possible. In particular, recall that the shadow price for the advertising budget enabled us to conclude that each $1 increase in the budget would improve the profit by $3. The current advertising budget is $5000. The allowable increase on the advertising budget is $850 and this implies that there is value in increasing the budget up to an advertising budget of $5850. Increases above this level would not necessarily be beneficial. Also note that the shadow price of -17 for the retail stores requirement suggested the desirability of reducing this commitment. The allowable decrease for this constraint is 150, and this implies that the commitment could be reduced to zero and the value of the reduction would be at the rate of $17 per unit.

Again, the *sensitivity analysis* provided by computer software packages for linear programming problems considers only *one change at a time*, with all other coefficients of the problem remaining as originally specified. As mentioned earlier, simultaneous changes are best handled by re-solving the problem.

Finally, recall that the complete solution to the Electronic Communications problem requested information not only on the number of units to be distributed over each channel, but also on the allocation of the advertising budget and the sales force effort to each distribution channel. Because the optimal solution is $M = 25$, $B = 425$, $R = 150$, and $D = 0$, we can simply evaluate each term in a given constraint to determine how much of the constraint

TABLE 8.4 PROFIT-MAXIMIZING STRATEGY FOR THE ELECTRONIC COMMUNICATIONS PROBLEM

Distribution Channel	Volume	Advertising Allocation	Sales Force Allocation (hours)
Marine distributors	25	$ 250	50
Business distributors	425	3400	1275
National retail stores	150	1350	450
Direct mail	0	0	0
Totals	600	$5000	1775
Projected total profit = $48,450			

resource is allocated to each distribution channel. For example, the advertising budget constraint of

$$10M + 8B + 9R + 15D \leq 5000$$

shows that $10M = 10(25) = \$250$, $8B = 8(425) = \$3400$, $9R = 9(150) = \$1350$, and $15D = 15(0) = \$0$. Thus, the advertising budget allocations are, respectively, $250, $3400, $1350, and $0 for each of the four distribution channels. Making similar calculations for the sales force constraint results in the managerial summary of the Electronic Communications optimal solution, as shown in Table 8.4.

Summary

We began the chapter with a discussion of sensitivity analysis, the study of how changes in the coefficients of a linear program affect the optimal solution. First, we showed how a graphical method can be used to determine how a change in one of the objective function coefficients or a change in the right-hand-side value for a constraint will affect the optimal solution to the problem. Because graphical sensitivity analysis is limited to linear programs with two decision variables, we showed how to use a computer software package such as Excel Solver to produce a sensitivity report containing the same information.

We continued our discussion of problem formulation, sensitivity analysis, and the interpretation of the solution by introducing modifications of the RMC problem. We also discussed several limitations of classical sensitivity analysis, including issues related to simultaneous changes, changes in constraint coefficients, and nonintuitive shadow prices. Then, in order to provide additional practice in formulating and interpreting the solution for linear programs involving more than two decision variables, we introduced the Bluegrass Farms problem, a minimization problem involving three decision variables. In the last section we summarized all the work to date using the Electronic Communications problem, a maximization problem with four decision variables: two less-than-or-equal-to constraints, one equality constraint, and one greater-than-or-equal-to constraint.

The Q.M. in Action, Tea Production and Distribution at Duncan Industries Limited, illustrates the diversity of problem situations in which linear programming can be applied and the importance of sensitivity analysis. In the next chapter we will see many more applications of linear programming.

Q.M. *in* ACTION

TEA PRODUCTION AND DISTRIBUTION AT DUNCAN INDUSTRIES LIMITED*

In India, one of the largest tea producers in the world, approximately $1 billion of tea packets and loose tea are sold. Duncan Industries Limited (DIL), the third largest producer of tea in the Indian tea market, sells about $37.5 million of tea, almost all of which is sold in packets.

DIL has 16 tea gardens, 3 blending units, 6 packing units, and 22 depots. Tea from the gardens is sent to blending units, which then mix various grades of tea to produce blends such as Sargam, Double Diamond, and Runglee Rungliot. The blended tea is transported to packing units, where it is placed in packets of different sizes and shapes to produce about 120 different product lines. For example, one line is Sargam tea packed in 500-gram cartons, another line is Double Diamond packed in 100-gram polythene pouches, and so on. The tea is then shipped to the depots that supply 11,500 distributors, through whom the needs of approximately 325,000 retailers are satisfied.

------
*Based on Nilotpal Chakravarti, "Tea Company Steeped in OR," *OR/MS Today* (April 2000).

For the coming month, sales managers provide estimates of the demand for each line of tea at each depot. Using these estimates, a team of senior managers would determine the amounts of loose tea of each blend to ship to each packing unit, the quantity of each line of tea to be packed at each packing unit, and the amounts of packed tea of each line to be transported from each packing unit to the various depots. This process requires two to three days each month and often results in stock-outs of lines in demand at specific depots.

Consequently, a linear programming model involving approximately 7000 decision variables and 1500 constraints was developed to minimize the company's freight cost while satisfying demand, supply, and all operational constraints. The model was tested on past data and showed that stock-outs could be prevented at little or no additional cost. Moreover, the model was able to provide management with the ability to perform various what-if types of exercises, convincing managers of the potential benefits of using management science techniques to support the decision-making process.

Glossary

Objective coefficient range (range of optimality) The range of values over which an objective function coefficient may vary without causing any change in the values of the decision variables in the optimal solution.

Objective function coefficient allowable increase (decrease) The allowable increase (decrease) of an objective function coefficient is the amount the coefficient may increase (decrease) without causing any change in the values of the decision variables in the optimal solution. The allowable increase/decrease for the objective function coefficients can be used to calculate the range of optimality.

Range of feasibility The range of values over which the shadow price is applicable.

Reduced cost If a variable is at its lower bound of zero, the reduced cost is equal to the shadow price of the nonnegativity constraint for that variable. In general, if a variable is at its lower or upper bound, the reduced cost is the shadow price for that simple lower or upper bound constraint.

Relevant cost A cost that depends upon the decision made. The amount of a relevant cost will vary depending on the values of the decision variables.

Right-hand-side allowable increase (decrease) The allowable increase (decrease) of the right-hand side of a constraint is the amount the right-hand side may increase (decrease) without causing any change in the shadow price for that constraint. The allowable increase and decrease for the right-hand side can be used to calculate the range of feasibility for that constraint.

Sensitivity analysis The study of how changes in the coefficients of a linear programming problem affect the optimal solution.

Shadow price The change in the optimal objective function value per unit increase in the right-hand side of a constraint.

Sunk cost A cost that is not affected by the decision made. It will be incurred no matter what values the decision variables assume.

Problems

1. Consider the following linear program:

$$\text{Max} \quad 3A + 2B$$
$$\text{s.t.}$$
$$1A + 1B \leq 10$$
$$3A + 1B \leq 24$$
$$1A + 2B \leq 16$$
$$A, B \geq 0$$

a. Use the graphical solution procedure to find the optimal solution.

b. Assume that the objective function coefficient for A changes from 3 to 5. Does the optimal solution change? Use the graphical solution procedure to find the new optimal solution.

c. Assume that the objective function coefficient for A remains 3, but the objective function coefficient for B changes from 2 to 4. Does the optimal solution change? Use the graphical solution procedure to find the new optimal solution.

d. The sensitivity report for the linear program in part (a) provides the following objective coefficient range information:

Variable	Objective Coefficient	Allowable Increase	Allowable Decrease
A	3.000	3.000	1.000
B	2.000	1.000	1.000

Use this objective coefficient range information to answer parts (b) and (c).

2. Consider the linear program in Problem 1. The value of the optimal solution is 27. Suppose that the right-hand side for constraint 1 is increased from 10 to 11.

a. Use the graphical solution procedure to find the new optimal solution.

b. Use the solution to part (a) to determine the shadow price for constraint 1.

c. The sensitivity report for the linear program in Problem 1 provides the following right-hand-side range information:

Constraint	Constraint R.H. Side	Allowable Increase	Allowable Decrease
1	10.000	1.200	2.000
2	24.000	6.000	6.000
3	16.000	Infinite	3.000

What does the right-hand-side range information for constraint 1 tell you about the shadow price for constraint 1?

    d.   The shadow price for constraint 2 is 0.5. Using this shadow price and the right-hand-side range information in part (c), what conclusion can you draw about the effect of changes to the right-hand side of constraint 2?

3.   Consider the following linear program:

$$\text{Min} \quad 8X + 12Y$$

s.t.

$$
\begin{aligned}
1X + 3Y &\geq 9 \\
2X + 2Y &\geq 10 \\
6X + 2Y &\geq 18 \\
X, Y &\geq 0
\end{aligned}
$$

    a.   Use the graphical solution procedure to find the optimal solution.

    b.   Assume that the objective function coefficient for X changes from 8 to 6. Does the optimal solution change? Use the graphical solution procedure to find the new optimal solution.

    c.   Assume that the objective function coefficient for X remains 8, but the objective function coefficient for Y changes from 12 to 6. Does the optimal solution change? Use the graphical solution procedure to find the new optimal solution.

    d.   The sensitivity report for the linear program in part (a) provides the following objective coefficient range information:

Variable	Objective Coefficient	Allowable Increase	Allowable Decrease
X	8.000	4.000	4.000
Y	12.000	12.000	4.000

How would this objective coefficient range information help you answer parts (b) and (c) prior to resolving the problem?

4.   Consider the linear program in Problem 3. The value of the optimal solution is 48. Suppose that the right-hand side for constraint 1 is increased from 9 to 10.

    a.   Use the graphical solution procedure to find the new optimal solution.

    b.   Use the solution to part (a) to determine the shadow price for constraint 1.

    c.   The sensitivity report for the linear program in Problem 3 provides the following right-hand-side range information:

Constraint	Constraint R.H. Side	Allowable Increase	Allowable Decrease
1	9.000	2.000	4.000
2	10.000	8.000	1.000
3	18.000	4.000	Infinite

What does the right-hand-side range information for constraint 1 tell you about the shadow price for constraint 1?

    d.   The shadow price for constraint 2 is 3. Using this shadow price and the right-hand-side range information in part (c), what conclusion can be drawn about the effect of changes to the right-hand side of constraint 2?

5. Refer to the Kelson Sporting Equipment problem (Chapter 7, Problem 24). Letting

$$R = \text{number of regular gloves}$$
$$C = \text{number of catcher's mitts}$$

leads to the following formulation:

$$
\begin{aligned}
\text{Max} \quad & 5R + 8C \\
\text{s.t.} \quad & \\
& R + \tfrac{3}{2}C \le 900 \quad \text{Cutting and sewing} \\
& \tfrac{1}{2}R + \tfrac{1}{3}C \le 300 \quad \text{Finishing} \\
& \tfrac{1}{8}R + \tfrac{1}{4}C \le 100 \quad \text{Packaging and shipping} \\
& R, C \ge 0
\end{aligned}
$$

The sensitivity report is shown in Figure 8.14.
a. What is the optimal solution, and what is the value of the total profit contribution?
b. Which constraints are binding?
c. What are the shadow prices for the resources? Interpret each.
d. If overtime can be scheduled in one of the departments, where would you recommend doing so?

6. Refer to the sensitivity information for the Kelson Sporting Equipment problem in Figure 8.14 (see Problem 5).
a. Determine the objective coefficient ranges.
b. Interpret the ranges in part (a).
c. Interpret the right-hand-side ranges.
d. How much will the value of the optimal solution improve if 20 extra hours of packaging and shipping time are made available?

7. Investment Advisors, Inc., is a brokerage firm that manages stock portfolios for a number of clients. A particular portfolio consists of U shares of U.S. Oil and H shares of Huber Steel. The annual return for U.S. Oil is $3 per share and the annual return for

---

FIGURE 8.14   SENSITIVITY REPORT FOR THE KELSON SPORTING EQUIPMENT PROBLEM

Variable Cells

Model Variable	Name	Final Value	Reduced Cost	Objective Coefficient	Allowable Increase	Allowable Decrease
R	Gloves Standard	500.000	0.000	5.000	7.000	1.000
C	Gloves Deluxe	150.000	0.000	8.000	2.000	4.667

Constraints

Constraint Number	Name	Final Value	Shadow Price	Constraint R.H. Side	Allowable Increase	Allowable Decrease
1	Cutting and Dyeing Hours Used	725.000	0.000	900.000	1E+30	175.000
2	Finishing Hours Used	300.000	3.000	300.000	100.000	166.667
3	Packaging and Shipping Hours Used	100.000	28.000	100.000	35.000	25.000

Huber Steel is $5 per share. U.S. Oil sells for $25 per share and Huber Steel sells for $50 per share. The portfolio has $80,000 to be invested. The portfolio risk index (0.50 per share of U.S. Oil and 0.25 per share for Huber Steel) has a maximum of 700. In addition, the portfolio is limited to a maximum of 1000 shares of U.S. Oil. The linear programming formulation that will maximize the total annual return of the portfolio is as follows:

$$\text{Max} \quad 3U + 5H \qquad \text{Maximize total annual return}$$

s.t.

$$25U + 50H \le 80{,}000 \quad \text{Funds available}$$
$$0.50U + 0.25H \le 700 \quad \text{Risk maximum}$$
$$1U \le 1000 \quad \text{U.S. Oil maximum}$$
$$U, H \ge 0$$

The sensitivity report for this problem is shown in Figure 8.15.
  a. What is the optimal solution, and what is the value of the total annual return?
  b. Which constraints are binding? What is your interpretation of these constraints in terms of the problem?
  c. What are the shadow prices for the constraints? Interpret each.
  d. Would it be beneficial to increase the maximum amount invested in U.S. Oil? Why or why not?

8. Refer to Figure 8.15, which shows the sensitivity report for Problem 7.
  a. How much would the return for U.S. Oil have to increase before it would be beneficial to increase the investment in this stock?
  b. How much would the return for Huber Steel have to decrease before it would be beneficial to reduce the investment in this stock?
  c. How much would the total annual return be reduced if the U.S. Oil maximum were reduced to 900 shares?

9. Recall the Tom's, Inc., problem (Chapter 7, Problem 28). Letting

$$W = \text{jars of Western Foods Salsa}$$
$$M = \text{jars of Mexico City Salsa}$$

FIGURE 8.15 SENSITIVITY REPORT FOR THE INVESTMENT ADVISORS PROBLEM

Variable Cells

Model Variable	Name	Final Value	Reduced Cost	Objective Coefficient	Allowable Increase	Allowable Decrease
U	U.S. Oil	800.000	0.000	3.000	7.000	0.500
H	Huber	1200.000	0.000	5.000	1.000	3.500

Constraints

Constraint Number	Name	Final Value	Shadow Price	Constraint R.H. Side	Allowable Increase	Allowable Decrease
1	Funds available	80000.000	0.093	80000.000	60000.000	15000.000
2	Risk maximum	700.000	1.333	700.000	75.000	300.000
3	U.S. Oil maximum	800.000	0.000	1000.000	1E+30	200.000

FIGURE 8.16 SENSITIVITY REPORT FOR THE TOM'S INC., PROBLEM

Variable Cells

Model Variable	Name	Final Value	Reduced Cost	Objective Coefficient	Allowable Increase	Allowable Decrease
W	Western Foods Salsa	560.000	0.000	1.000	0.250	0.107
M	Mexico City Salsa	240.000	0.000	1.250	0.150	0.250

Constraints

Constraint Number	Name	Final Value	Shadow Price	Constraint R.H. Side	Allowable Increase	Allowable Decrease
1	Whole tomatoes	4480.000	0.125	4480.000	1120.000	160.000
2	Tomato sauce	1920.000	0.000	2080.000	1E+30	160.000
3	Tomato paste	1600.000	0.188	1600.000	40.000	320.000

leads to the formulation:

$$\text{Max} \quad 1W + 1.25M$$

s.t.

$$
\begin{aligned}
5W + \quad 7M &\leq 4480 \quad \text{Whole tomatoes} \\
3W + \quad 1M &\leq 2080 \quad \text{Tomato sauce} \\
2W + \quad 2M &\leq 1600 \quad \text{Tomato paste} \\
W, M &\geq 0
\end{aligned}
$$

The sensitivity report is shown in Figure 8.16.
a. What is the optimal solution, and what are the optimal production quantities?
b. Specify the objective coefficient ranges.
c. What are the shadow prices for each constraint? Interpret each.
d. Identify each of the right-hand-side ranges.

10. Recall the Innis Investments problem (Chapter 7, Problem 39). Letting

$$S = \text{units purchased in the stock fund}$$

$$M = \text{units purchased in the money market fund}$$

leads to the following formulation:

$$\text{Min} \quad 8S + \quad 3M$$

s.t.

$$
\begin{aligned}
50S + 100M &\leq 1{,}200{,}000 \quad \text{Funds available} \\
5S + \quad 4M &\geq \quad 60{,}000 \quad \text{Annual income} \\
M &\geq \quad 3{,}000 \quad \text{Units in money market} \\
S, M &\geq 0
\end{aligned}
$$

The sensitivity report is shown in Figure 8.17.
a. What is the optimal solution, and what is the minimum total risk?
b. Specify the objective coefficient ranges.
c. How much annual income will be earned by the portfolio?
d. What is the rate of return for the portfolio?
e. What is the shadow price for the funds available constraint?
f. What is the marginal rate of return on extra funds added to the portfolio?

FIGURE 8.17 SENSITIVITY REPORT FOR THE INNIS INVESTMENTS PROBLEM

Variable Cells

Model Variable	Name	Final Value	Reduced Cost	Objective Coefficient	Allowable Increase	Allowable Decrease
S	Units in Stock Fund	4000.000	0.000	8.000	1E+30	4.250
M	Units in Money Market Fund	10000.000	0.000	3.000	3.400	1E+30

Constraints

Constraint Number	Name	Final Value	Shadow Price	Constraint R.H. Side	Allowable Increase	Allowable Decrease
1	Funds Available	1200000.000	−0.057	1200000.000	300000.000	420000.000
2	Annual Income	60000.000	2.167	60000.000	42000.000	12000.000
3	Units in Money Market	10000.000	0.000	3000.000	7000.000	1E+30

11. Refer to Problem 10 and the sensitivity report shown in Figure 8.17.
    a. Suppose the risk index for the stock fund (the objective function coefficient for S) increases from its current value of 8 to 12. How does the optimal solution change, if at all?
    b. Suppose the risk index for the money market fund (the objective function coefficient for M) increases from its current value of 3 to 3.5. How does the optimal solution change, if at all?
    c. Suppose the objective function coefficient for S increases to 12 and the objective function coefficient for M increases to 3.5. Can you determine how the optimal solution will change using the information in Figure 8.17?

12. Quality Air Conditioning manufactures three home air conditioners: an economy model, a standard model, and a deluxe model. The profits per unit are $63, $95, and $135, respectively. The production requirements per unit are as follows:

	Number of Fans	Number of Cooling Coils	Manufacturing Time (hours)
Economy	1	1	8
Standard	1	2	12
Deluxe	1	4	14

For the coming production period, the company has 200 fan motors, 320 cooling coils, and 2400 hours of manufacturing time available. How many economy models (E), standard models (S), and deluxe models (D) should the company produce in order to maximize profit? The linear programming model for the problem is as follows.

$$\text{Max} \quad 63E + 95S + 135D$$

s.t.

$$
\begin{aligned}
1E + 1S + 1D &\le 200 \quad \text{Fan motors} \\
1E + 2S + 4D &\le 320 \quad \text{Cooling coils} \\
8E + 12S + 14D &\le 2400 \quad \text{Manufacturing time} \\
E, S, D &\ge 0
\end{aligned}
$$

FIGURE 8.18   SENSITIVITY REPORT FOR THE QUALITY AIR CONDITIONING PROBLEM

Variable Cells

Model Variable	Name	Final Value	Reduced Cost	Objective Coefficient	Allowable Increase	Allowable Decrease
E	Economy Models	80.000	0.000	63.000	12.000	15.500
S	Standard Models	120.000	0.000	95.000	31.000	8.000
D	Deluxe Models	0.000	−24.000	135.000	24.000	1E+30

Constraints

Constraint Number	Name	Final Value	Shadow Price	Constraint R.H. Side	Allowable Increase	Allowable Decrease
1	Fan Motors	200.000	31.000	200.000	80.000	40.000
2	Cooling Coils	320.000	32.000	320.000	80.000	120.000
3	Manufacturing Time	2080.000	0.000	2400.000	1E+30	320.000

The sensitivity report is shown in Figure 8.18.
a.   What is the optimal solution, and what is the value of the objective function?
b.   Which constraints are binding?
c.   Which constraint shows extra capacity? How much?
d.   If the profit for the deluxe model were increased to $150 per unit, would the optimal solution change? Use the information in Figure 8.18 to answer this question.

13.   Refer to the sensitivity report in Figure 8.18.
a.   Identify the range of optimality for each objective function coefficient.
b.   Suppose the profit for the economy model is increased by $6 per unit, the profit for the standard model is decreased by $2 per unit, and the profit for the deluxe model is increased by $4 per unit. What will the new optimal solution be?
c.   Identify the range of feasibility for the right-hand-side values.
d.   If the number of fan motors available for production is increased by 100, will the shadow price for that constraint change? Explain.

14.   Digital Controls, Inc. (DCI) manufactures two models of a radar gun used by police to monitor the speed of automobiles. Model A has an accuracy of plus or minus 1 mile per hour, whereas the smaller model B has an accuracy of plus or minus 3 miles per hour. For the next week, the company has orders for 100 units of model A and 150 units of model B. Although DCI purchases all the electronic components used in both models, the plastic cases for both models are manufactured at a DCI plant in Newark, New Jersey. Each model A case requires 4 minutes of injection-molding time and 6 minutes of assembly time. Each model B case requires 3 minutes of injection-molding time and 8 minutes of assembly time. For next week the Newark plant has 600 minutes of injection-molding time available and 1080 minutes of assembly time available. The manufacturing cost is $10 per case for model A and $6 per case for model B. Depending upon demand and the time available at the Newark plant, DCI occasionally purchases cases for one or both models from an outside supplier in order to fill customer orders that could not be filled otherwise. The purchase cost is $14 for each model A case and $9 for each model B case. Management wants to develop a minimum cost plan that will determine how many cases of each model should be produced at the Newark plant and how many cases of each model should be purchased. The following decision variables were used to formulate a linear programming model for this problem:

$$AM = \text{number of cases of model A manufactured}$$
$$BM = \text{number of cases of model B manufactured}$$
$$AP = \text{number of cases of model A purchased}$$
$$BP = \text{number of cases of model B purchased}$$

The linear programming model that can be used to solve this problem is as follows:

$$\text{Min}\quad 10AM + 6BM + 14AP + 9BP$$

s.t.

$1AM +$		$+\ 1AP +$		$=\ 100$	Demand for model A
	$1BM +$		$1BP =$	150	Demand for model B
$4AM + 3BM$				$\le\ 600$	Injection molding time
$6AM + 8BM$				≤ 1080	Assembly time

$$AM, BM, AP, BP \ge 0$$

The sensitivity report is shown in Figure 8.19.

   a. What is the optimal solution and what is the optimal value of the objective function?
   b. Which constraints are binding?
   c. What are the shadow prices? Interpret each.
   d. If you could change the right-hand side of one constraint by one unit, which one would you choose? Why?

15. Refer to the sensitivity report for Problem 14 in Figure 8.19.
   a. Interpret the ranges of optimality for the objective function coefficients.
   b. Suppose that the manufacturing cost increases to $11.20 per case for model A. What is the new optimal solution?
   c. Suppose that the manufacturing cost increases to $11.20 per case for model A and the manufacturing cost for model B decreases to $5 per unit. Would the optimal solution change?

FIGURE 8.19 SENSITIVITY REPORT FOR THE DIGITAL CONTROLS, INC., PROBLEM

Variable Cells

Model Variable	Name	Final Value	Reduced Cost	Objective Coefficient	Allowable Increase	Allowable Decrease
AM	Models A Manufactured	100.000	0.000	10.000	1.750	1E+30
BM	Models B Manufactured	60.000	0.000	6.000	3.000	2.333
AP	Models A Purchased	0.000	1.750	14.000	1E+30	1.750
BP	Models B Purchased	90.000	0.000	9.000	2.333	3.000

Constraints

Constraint Number	Name	Final Value	Shadow Price	Constraint R.H. Side	Allowable Increase	Allowable Decrease
1	Demand for model A	100.000	12.250	100.000	11.429	100.000
2	Demand for model B	150.000	9.000	150.000	1E+30	90.000
3	Injection molding time	580.000	0.000	600.000	1E+30	20.000
4	Assembly time	1080.000	-0.375	1080.000	53.333	480.000

16. Tucker Inc. produces high-quality suits and sport coats for men. Each suit requires 1.2 hours of cutting time and 0.7 hours of sewing time, uses 6 yards of material, and provides a profit contribution of $190. Each sport coat requires 0.8 hours of cutting time and 0.6 hours of sewing time, uses 4 yards of material, and provides a profit contribution of $150. For the coming week, 200 hours of cutting time, 180 hours of sewing time, and 1200 yards of fabric material are available. Additional cutting and sewing time can be obtained by scheduling overtime for these operations. Each hour of overtime for the cutting operation increases the hourly cost by $15, and each hour of overtime for the sewing operation increases the hourly cost by $10. A maximum of 100 hours of overtime can be scheduled. Marketing requirements specify a minimum production of 100 suits and 75 sport coats. Let

$$S = \text{number of suits produced}$$
$$SC = \text{number of sport coats produced}$$
$$D1 = \text{hours of overtime for the cutting operation}$$
$$D2 = \text{hours of overtime for the sewing operation}$$

The sensitivity report is shown in Figure 8.20.

a. What is the optimal solution, and what is the total profit? What is the plan for the use of overtime?

b. A price increase for suits is being considered that would result in a profit contribution of $210 per suit. If this price increase is undertaken, how will the optimal solution change?

c. Discuss the need for additional material during the coming week. If a rush order for material can be placed at the usual price plus an extra $8 per yard for handling, would you recommend that the company consider placing a rush order for material? What is the maximum price Tucker would be willing to pay for an additional yard of material? How many additional yards of material should Tucker consider ordering?

d. Suppose the minimum production requirement for suits is lowered to 75. Would this change help or hurt profit? Explain.

FIGURE 8.20   SENSITIVITY REPORT FOR THE TUCKER INC. PROBLEM

Variable Cells

Model Variable	Name	Final Value	Reduced Cost	Objective Coefficient	Allowable Increase	Allowable Decrease
S	Suits Produced	100.000	0.000	190.000	35.000	1E+30
SC	Coats Produced	150.000	0.000	150.000	1E+30	23.333
D1	Overtime for Cutting	40.000	0.000	−15.000	15.000	172.500
D2	Overtime for Sewing	0.000	−10.000	−10.000	10.000	1E+30

Constraints

Constraint Number	Name	Final Value	Shadow Price	Constraint R.H. Side	Allowable Increase	Allowable Decrease
1	Cutting time	200.000	15.000	200.000	40.000	60.000
2	Sewing time	160.000	0.000	180.000	1E+30	20.000
3	Material	1200.000	34.500	1200.000	133.333	200.000
4	Overtime	40.000	0.000	100.000	1E+30	60.000
5	Suit minimum	100.000	−35.000	100.000	50.000	100.000
6	Sport coat minimum	150.000	0.000	75.000	75.000	1E+30

17. The Porsche Club of America sponsors driver education events that provide high-performance driving instruction on actual racetracks. Because safety is a primary consideration at such events, many owners elect to install roll bars in their cars. Deegan Industries manufactures two types of roll bars for Porsches. Model DRB is bolted to the car using existing holes in the car's frame. Model DRW is a heavier roll bar that must be welded to the car's frame. Model DRB requires 20 pounds of a special high-alloy steel, 40 minutes of manufacturing time, and 60 minutes of assembly time. Model DRW requires 25 pounds of the special high-alloy steel, 100 minutes of manufacturing time, and 40 minutes of assembly time. Deegan's steel supplier indicated that at most 40,000 pounds of the high-alloy steel will be available next quarter. In addition, Deegan estimates that 2000 hours of manufacturing time and 1600 hours of assembly time will be available next quarter. The profit contributions are $200 per unit for model DRB and $280 per unit for model DRW. The linear programming model for this problem is as follows:

$$\text{Max} \quad 200DRB + 280DRW$$
$$\text{s.t.}$$
$$20DRB + 25DRW \leq 40{,}000 \quad \text{Steel available}$$
$$40DRB + 100DRW \leq 120{,}000 \quad \text{Manufacturing minutes}$$
$$60DRB + 40DRW \leq 96{,}000 \quad \text{Assembly minutes}$$
$$DRB, DRW \geq 0$$

The sensitivity report is shown in Figure 8.21.
a. What are the optimal solution and the total profit contribution?
b. Another supplier offered to provide Deegan Industries with an additional 500 pounds of the steel alloy at $2 per pound. Should Deegan purchase the additional pounds of the steel alloy? Explain.
c. Deegan is considering using overtime to increase the available assembly time. What would you advise Deegan to do regarding this option? Explain.
d. Because of increased competition, Deegan is considering reducing the price of model DRB such that the new contribution to profit is $175 per unit. How would this change in price affect the optimal solution? Explain.
e. If the available manufacturing time is increased by 500 hours, will the shadow price for the manufacturing time constraint change? Explain.

FIGURE 8.21 SENSITIVITY REPORT FOR THE DEEGAN INDUSTRIES PROBLEM

Variable Cells

Model Variable	Name	Final Value	Reduced Cost	Objective Coefficient	Allowable Increase	Allowable Decrease
DRB	Model DRB	1000.000	0.000	200.000	24.000	88.000
DRW	Model DRW	800.000	0.000	280.000	220.000	30.000

Constraints

Constraint Number	Name	Final Value	Shadow Price	Constraint R.H. Side	Allowable Increase	Allowable Decrease
1	Steel available	40000.000	8.800	40000.000	909.091	10000.000
2	Manufacturing minutes	120000.000	0.600	120000.000	40000.000	5714.286
3	Assembly minutes	92000.000	0.000	96000.000	1E+30	4000.000

18. Davison Electronics manufactures two models of LCD televisions, identified as model A and model B. Each model has its lowest possible production cost when produced on Davison's new production line. However, the new production line does not have the capacity to handle the total production of both models. As a result, at least some of the production must be routed to a higher-cost, old production line. The following table shows the minimum production requirements for next month, the production line capacities in units per month, and the production cost per unit for each production line:

Model	Production Cost per Unit		Minimum Production Requirements
	New Line	Old Line	
A	$30	$50	50,000
B	$25	$40	70,000
Production Line Capacity	80,000	60,000	

Let

$$AN = \text{Units of model A produced on the new production line}$$
$$AO = \text{Units of model A produced on the old production line}$$
$$BN = \text{Units of model B produced on the new production line}$$
$$BO = \text{Units of model B produced on the old production line}$$

Davison's objective is to determine the minimum cost production plan. The sensitivity report is shown in Figure 8.22.

a. Formulate the linear programming model for this problem using the following four constraints:

Constraint 1: Minimum production for model A
Constraint 2: Minimum production for model B

FIGURE 8.22 SENSITIVITY REPORT FOR THE DAVISON ELECTRONICS PROBLEM

Variable Cells

Model Variable	Name	Final Value	Reduced Cost	Objective Coefficient	Allowable Increase	Allowable Decrease
AN	Model A Produced on New Line	50000.000	0.000	30.000	5.000	1E+30
AO	Model A Produced on Old Line	0.000	5.000	50.000	1E+30	5.000
BN	Model B Produced on New Line	30000.000	0.000	25.000	15.000	5.000
BO	Model B Produced on Old Line	40000.000	0.000	40.000	5.000	15.000

Constraints

Constraint Number	Name	Final Value	Shadow Price	Constraint R.H. Side	Allowable Increase	Allowable Decrease
1	Min production for A	50000.000	45.000	50000.000	20000.000	40000.000
2	Min production for B	70000.000	40.000	70000.000	20000.000	40000.000
3	Capacity of new production line	80000.000	−15.000	80000.000	40000.000	20000.000
4	Capacity of old production line	40000.000	0.000	60000.000	1E+30	20000.000

Constraint 3: Capacity of the new production line
Constraint 4: Capacity of the old production line

b. Using the sensitivity analysis information in Figure 8.22, what is the optimal solution and what is the total production cost associated with this solution?
c. Which constraints are binding? Explain.
d. The production manager noted that the only constraint with a negative shadow price is the constraint on the capacity of the new production line. The manager's interpretation of the shadow price was that a one-unit increase in the right-hand side of this constraint would actually increase the total production cost by $15 per unit. Do you agree with this interpretation? Would an increase in capacity for the new production line be desirable? Explain.
e. Would you recommend increasing the capacity of the old production line? Explain.
f. The production cost for model A on the old production line is $50 per unit. How much would this cost have to change to make it worthwhile to produce model A on the old production line? Explain.
g. Suppose that the minimum production requirement for model B is reduced from 70,000 units to 60,000 units. What effect would this change have on the total production cost? Explain.

19. Better Products, Inc., manufactures three products on two machines. In a typical week, 40 hours are available on each machine. The profit contribution and production time in hours per unit are as follows:

Category	Product 1	Product 2	Product 3
Profit/unit	$30	$50	$20
Machine 1 time/unit	0.5	2.0	0.75
Machine 2 time/unit	1.0	1.0	0.5

Two operators are required for machine 1; thus, 2 hours of labor must be scheduled for each hour of machine 1 time. Only one operator is required for machine 2. A maximum of 100 labor-hours is available for assignment to the machines during the coming week. Other production requirements are that product 1 cannot account for more than 50% of the units produced and that product 3 must account for at least 20% of the units produced.
a. How many units of each product should be produced to maximize the total profit contribution? What is the projected weekly profit associated with your solution?
b. How many hours of production time will be scheduled on each machine?
c. What is the value of an additional hour of labor?
d. Assume that labor capacity can be increased to 120 hours. Would you be interested in using the additional 20 hours available for this resource? Develop the optimal product mix, assuming that the extra hours are made available.

20. Adirondack Savings Bank (ASB) has $1 million in new funds that must be allocated to home loans, personal loans, and automobile loans. The annual rates of return for the three types of loans are 7% for home loans, 12% for personal loans, and 9% for automobile loans. The bank's planning committee has decided that at least 40% of the new funds must be allocated to home loans. In addition, the planning committee has specified that the amount allocated to personal loans cannot exceed 60% of the amount allocated to automobile loans.
a. Formulate a linear programming model that can be used to determine the amount of funds ASB should allocate to each type of loan in order to maximize the total annual return for the new funds.

b.   How much should be allocated to each type of loan? What is the total annual return? What is the annual percentage return?

c.   If the interest rate on home loans increased to 9%, would the amount allocated to each type of loan change? Explain.

d.   Suppose the total amount of new funds available was increased by $10,000. What effect would this have on the total annual return? Explain.

e.   Assume that ASB has the original $1 million in new funds available and that the planning committee has agreed to relax the requirement that at least 40% of the new funds must be allocated to home loans by 1%. How much would the annual return change? How much would the annual percentage return change?

21.   Round Tree Manor is a hotel that provides two types of rooms with three rental classes: Super Saver, Deluxe, and Business. The profit per night for each type of room and rental class is as follows:

		Rental Class		
		Super Saver	**Deluxe**	**Business**
Room	Type I	$30	$35	—
	Type II	$20	$30	$40

Type I rooms do not have dedicated work desks and are not available for the Business rental class.

Round Tree's management makes a forecast of the demand by rental class for each night in the future. A linear programming model developed to maximize profit is used to determine how many reservations to accept for each rental class. The demand forecast for a particular night is 130 rentals in the Super Saver class, 60 rentals in the Deluxe class, and 50 rentals in the Business class. Round Tree has 100 Type I rooms and 120 Type II rooms.

a.   Use linear programming to determine how many reservations to accept in each rental class and how the reservations should be allocated to room types. Is the demand by any rental class not satisfied? Explain.

b.   How many reservations can be accommodated in each rental class?

c.   Management is considering offering a free breakfast to anyone upgrading from a Super Saver reservation to Deluxe class. If the cost of the breakfast to Round Tree is $5, should this incentive be offered?

d.   With a little work, an unused office area could be converted to a rental room. If the conversion cost is the same for both types of rooms, would you recommend converting the office to a Type I or a Type II room? Why?

e.   Could the linear programming model be modified to plan for the allocation of rental demand for the next night? What information would be needed and how would the model change?

22.   Industrial Designs has been awarded a contract to design a label for a new wine produced by Lake View Winery. The company estimates that 150 hours will be required to complete the project. The firm's three graphic designers available for assignment to this project are Lisa, a senior designer and team leader; David, a senior designer; and Sarah, a junior designer. Because Lisa has worked on several projects for Lake View Winery, management specified that Lisa must be assigned at least 40% of the total number of hours assigned to the two senior designers. To provide label-designing experience for Sarah, Sarah must be assigned at least 15% of the total project time. However, the number of hours assigned to Sarah must not exceed 25% of the total number of hours assigned to the two senior

designers. Due to other project commitments, Lisa has a maximum of 50 hours available to work on this project. Hourly wage rates are $30 for Lisa, $25 for David, and $18 for Sarah.

    a.   Formulate a linear program that can be used to determine the number of hours each graphic designer should be assigned to the project in order to minimize total cost.

    b.   How many hours should each graphic designer be assigned to the project? What is the total cost?

    c.   Suppose Lisa could be assigned more than 50 hours. What effect would this have on the optimal solution? Explain.

    d.   If Sarah were not required to work a minimum number of hours on this project, would the optimal solution change? Explain.

23. Vollmer Manufacturing makes three components for sale to refrigeration companies. The components are processed on two machines: a shaper and a grinder. The times (in minutes) required on each machine are as follows:

	Machine	
Component	**Shaper**	**Grinder**
1	6	4
2	4	5
3	4	2

The shaper is available for 120 hours, and the grinder is available for 110 hours. No more than 200 units of component 3 can be sold, but up to 1000 units of each of the other components can be sold. In fact, the company already has orders for 600 units of component 1 that must be satisfied. The profit contributions for components 1, 2, and 3 are $8, $6, and $9, respectively.

    a.   Formulate and solve for the recommended production quantities.

    b.   What are the objective coefficient ranges for the three components? Interpret these ranges for company management.

    c.   What are the right-hand-side ranges? Interpret these ranges for company management.

    d.   If more time could be made available on the grinder, how much would it be worth?

    e.   If more units of component 3 can be sold by reducing the sales price by $4, should the company reduce the price?

24. National Insurance Associates carries an investment portfolio of stocks, bonds, and other investment alternatives. Currently $200,000 of funds are available and must be considered for new investment opportunities. The four stock options National is considering and the relevant financial data are as follows:

	Stock			
	A	**B**	**C**	**D**
Price per share	$100	$50	$80	$40
Annual rate of return	0.12	0.08	0.06	0.10
Risk measure per dollar invested	0.10	0.07	0.05	0.08

The risk measure indicates the relative uncertainty associated with the stock in terms of its realizing the projected annual return; higher values indicate greater risk. The risk measures are provided by the firm's top financial advisor.

National's top management has stipulated the following investment guidelines: The annual rate of return for the portfolio must be at least 9%, and no one stock can account for more than 50% of the total dollar investment.

a. Use linear programming to develop an investment portfolio that minimizes risk.

b. What are the objective coefficient ranges for the four variables? Interpret these ranges.

c. Suppose that the firm decides that the annual rate of return must be at least 10%. What does the shadow price associated with this constraint indicate about the change in risk that would occur from this increased rate of return?

25. Georgia Cabinets manufactures kitchen cabinets that are sold to local dealers throughout the Southeast. Because of a large backlog of orders for oak and cherry cabinets, the company decided to contract with three smaller cabinetmakers to do the final finishing operation. For the three cabinetmakers, the number of hours required to complete all the oak cabinets, the number of hours required to complete all the cherry cabinets, the number of hours available for the final finishing operation, and the cost per hour to perform the work are shown here:

	Cabinetmaker 1	Cabinetmaker 2	Cabinetmaker 3
Hours required to complete all the oak cabinets	50	42	30
Hours required to complete all the cherry cabinets	60	48	35
Hours available	40	30	35
Cost per hour	$36	$42	$55

For example, Cabinetmaker 1 estimates that it will take 50 hours to complete all the oak cabinets and 60 hours to complete all the cherry cabinets. However, Cabinetmaker 1 only has 40 hours available for the final finishing operation. Thus, Cabinetmaker 1 can only complete $40/50 = 0.80$, or 80%, of the oak cabinets if it worked only on oak cabinets. Similarly, Cabinetmaker 1 can only complete $40/60 = 0.67$, or 67%, of the cherry cabinets if it worked only on cherry cabinets.

a. Formulate a linear programming model that can be used to determine the percentage of the oak cabinets and the percentage of the cherry cabinets that should be given to each of the three cabinetmakers in order to minimize the total cost of completing both projects.

b. Solve the model formulated in part (a). What percentage of the oak cabinets and what percentage of the cherry cabinets should be assigned to each cabinetmaker? What is the total cost of completing both projects?

c. If Cabinetmaker 1 has additional hours available, would the optimal solution change? Explain.

d. If Cabinetmaker 2 has additional hours available, would the optimal solution change? Explain.

e. Suppose Cabinetmaker 2 reduced its cost to $38 per hour. What effect would this change have on the optimal solution? Explain.

26. Benson Electronics manufactures three components used to produce cell phones and other communication devices. In a given production period, demand for the three components may exceed Benson's manufacturing capacity. In this case, the company meets demand by purchasing the components from another manufacturer at an increased cost per unit.

Benson's manufacturing cost per unit and purchasing cost per unit for the three components are as follows:

Source	Component 1	Component 2	Component 3
Manufacture	$4.50	$5.00	$2.75
Purchase	$6.50	$8.80	$7.00

Manufacturing times in minutes per unit for Benson's three departments are as follows:

Department	Component 1	Component 2	Component 3
Production	2	3	4
Assembly	1	1.5	3
Testing & Packaging	1.5	2	5

For instance, each unit of component 1 that Benson manufactures requires 2 minutes of production time, 1 minute of assembly time, and 1.5 minutes of testing and packaging time. For the next production period, Benson has capacities of 360 hours in the production department, 250 hours in the assembly department, and 300 hours in the testing and packaging department.

a. Formulate a linear programming model that can be used to determine how many units of each component to manufacture and how many units of each component to purchase. Assume that component demands that must be satisfied are 6000 units for component 1, 4000 units for component 2, and 3500 units for component 3. The objective is to minimize the total manufacturing and purchasing costs.

b. What is the optimal solution? How many units of each component should be manufactured and how many units of each component should be purchased?

c. Which departments are limiting Benson's manufacturing quantities? Use the shadow price to determine the value of an *extra hour* in each of these departments.

d. Suppose that Benson had to obtain one additional unit of component 2. Discuss what the shadow price for the component 2 constraint tells us about the cost to obtain the additional unit.

27. Cranberries can be harvested using either a "wet" method or a "dry" method. Dry-harvested cranberries can be sold at a premium, while wet-harvested cranberries are used mainly for cranberry juice and bring in less revenue. Fresh Made Cranberry Cooperative must decide how much of its cranberry crop should be harvested wet and how much should be dry harvested. Fresh Made has 5000 barrels of cranberries that can be harvested using either the wet or dry method. Dry cranberries are sold for $32.50 per barrel and wet cranberries are sold for $17.50 per barrel. Once harvested, cranberries must be processed through several operations before they can be sold. Both wet and dry cranberries must go through dechaffing and cleaning operations. The dechaffing and the cleaning operations can each be run 24 hours per day for the 6-week season (for a total of 1008 hours). Each barrel of dry cranberries requires 0.18 hours in the dechaffing operation and 0.32 hours in the cleaning operation. Wet cranberries require 0.04 hours in the dechaffing operation and 0.10 hours in the cleaning operation. Wet cranberries must also go through a drying process. The drying process can also be operated 24 hours per day for the 6-week season, and each barrel of wet cranberries must be dried for 0.22 hours.

a. Develop a linear program that Fresh Made can use to determine the optimal amount of cranberries to dry harvest and wet harvest.

b. Solve the linear program in part (a). How many barrels should be dry harvested? How many barrels should be wet harvested?

c. Suppose that Fresh Made can increase its dechaffing capacity by using an outside firm for this operation. Fresh Made will still use its own dechaffing operation as much as possible, but it can purchase additional capacity from this outside firm for $500 per hour. Should Fresh Made purchase additional dechaffing capacity? Why or why not?

d. Interpret the shadow price for the constraint corresponding to the cleaning operation. How would you explain the meaning of this shadow price to management?

28. The Pfeiffer Company manages approximately $15 million for clients. For each client, Pfeiffer chooses a mix of three investment vehicles: a growth stock fund, an income fund, and a money market fund. Each client has different investment objectives and different tolerances for risk. To accommodate these differences, Pfeiffer places limits on the percentage of each portfolio that may be invested in the three funds and assigns a portfolio risk index to each client.

Here's how the system works for Dennis Hartmann, one of Pfeiffer's clients. Based on an evaluation of Hartmann's risk tolerance, Pfeiffer has assigned Hartmann's portfolio a risk index of 0.05. Furthermore, to maintain diversity, the fraction of Hartmann's portfolio invested in the growth and income funds must be at least 10% for each, and at least 20% must be in the money market fund.

The risk ratings for the growth, income, and money market funds are 0.10, 0.05, and 0.01, respectively. A portfolio risk index is computed as a weighted average of the risk ratings for the three funds, where the weights are the fraction of the portfolio invested in each of the funds. Hartmann has given Pfeiffer $300,000 to manage. Pfeiffer is currently forecasting a yield of 20% on the growth fund, 10% on the income fund, and 6% on the money market fund.

a. Develop a linear programming model to select the best mix of investments for Hartmann's portfolio.

b. Solve the model you developed in part (a).

c. How much may the yields on the three funds vary before it will be necessary for Pfeiffer to modify Hartmann's portfolio?

d. If Hartmann were more risk tolerant, how much of a yield increase could he expect? For instance, what if his portfolio risk index is increased to 0.06?

e. If Pfeiffer revised the yield estimate for the growth fund downward to 0.10, how would you recommend modifying Hartmann's portfolio?

f. What information must Pfeiffer maintain on each client in order to use this system to manage client portfolios?

g. On a weekly basis Pfeiffer revises the yield estimates for the three funds. Suppose Pfeiffer has 50 clients. Describe how you would envision Pfeiffer making weekly modifications in each client's portfolio and allocating the total funds managed among the three investment funds.

29. La Jolla Beverage Products is considering producing a wine cooler that would be a blend of a white wine, a rosé wine, and fruit juice. To meet taste specifications, the wine cooler must consist of at least 50% white wine, at least 20% and no more than 30% rosé, and exactly 20% fruit juice. La Jolla purchases the wine from local wineries and the fruit juice from a processing plant in San Francisco. For the current production period, 10,000 gallons of white wine and 8000 gallons of rosé wine can be purchased; an unlimited amount of fruit juice can be ordered. The costs for the wine are $1.00 per gallon for the white and $1.50 per gallon for the rosé; the fruit juice can be purchased for $0.50 per gallon. La Jolla Beverage Products can sell all of the wine cooler it can produce for $2.50 per gallon.

a. Is the cost of the wine and fruit juice a sunk cost or a relevant cost in this situation? Explain.

b. Formulate a linear program to determine the blend of the three ingredients that will maximize the total profit contribution. Solve the linear program to determine the number of gallons of each ingredient La Jolla should purchase and the total profit contribution it will realize from this blend.

c. If La Jolla could obtain additional amounts of the white wine, should it do so? If so, how much should it be willing to pay for each additional gallon, and how many additional gallons would it want to purchase?

d. If La Jolla Beverage Products could obtain additional amounts of the rosé wine, should it do so? If so, how much should it be willing to pay for each additional gallon, and how many additional gallons would it want to purchase?

e. Interpret the shadow price for the constraint corresponding to the requirement that the wine cooler must contain at least 50% white wine. What is your advice to management given this shadow price?

f. Interpret the shadow price for the constraint corresponding to the requirement that the wine cooler must contain exactly 20% fruit juice. What is your advice to management given this shadow price?

30. The program manager for Channel 10 would like to determine the best way to allocate the time for the 11:00–11:30 evening news broadcast. Specifically, she would like to determine the number of minutes of broadcast time to devote to local news, national news, weather, and sports. Over the 30-minute broadcast, 10 minutes are set aside for advertising. The station's broadcast policy states that at least 15% of the time available should be devoted to local news coverage; the time devoted to the combination of local news and national news must be at least 50% of the total broadcast time; the time devoted to the weather segment must be less than or equal to the time devoted to the sports segment; the time devoted to the sports segment should be no longer than the total time spent on the local and national news; and at least 20% of the time should be devoted to the weather segment. The production costs per minute are $300 for local news, $200 for national news, $100 for weather, and $100 for sports.

a. Formulate and solve a linear program that can determine how the 20 available minutes should be used to minimize the total cost of producing the program.

b. Interpret the shadow price for the constraint corresponding to the available time. What advice would you give the station manager given this shadow price?

c. Interpret the shadow price for the constraint corresponding to the requirement that at least 15% of the available time should be devoted to local coverage. What advice would you give the station manager given this shadow price?

d. Interpret the shadow price for the constraint corresponding to the requirement that the time devoted to the local and the national news must be at least 50% of the total broadcast time. What advice would you give the station manager given this shadow price?

e. Interpret the shadow price for the constraint corresponding to the requirement that the time devoted to the weather segment must be less than or equal to the time devoted to the sports segment. What advice would you give the station manager given this shadow price?

31. Gulf Coast Electronics is ready to award contracts to suppliers for providing reservoir capacitors for use in its electronic devices. For the past several years, Gulf Coast Electronics has relied on two suppliers for its reservoir capacitors: Able Controls and Lyshenko Industries. A new firm, Boston Components, inquired into the possibility of providing a portion of the reservoir capacitors needed by Gulf Coast. The quality of products provided by Lyshenko Industries has been extremely high; in fact, only 0.5% of the capacitors provided by Lyshenko had to be discarded because of quality problems. Able Controls has also had a high quality level historically, producing an average of only 1% unacceptable capacitors. Because Gulf Coast Electronics has had no experience with Boston Components, it estimated Boston's defective rate to be 10%. Gulf Coast would like to determine how many reservoir capacitors should be ordered from each firm to obtain 75,000 acceptable-quality capacitors to use in its electronic devices. To ensure that Boston Components will receive some of the contract, management specified that the volume of reservoir capacitors awarded to Boston Components must be at least 10% of the volume given to Able Controls. In addition, the total volume assigned to Boston

Components, Able Controls, and Lyshenko Industries should not exceed 30,000, 50,000, and 50,000 capacitors, respectively. Because of the long-term relationship with Lyshenko Industries, management also specified that at least 30,000 capacitors should be ordered from Lyshenko. The cost per capacitor is $2.45 for Boston Components, $2.50 for Able Controls, and $2.75 for Lyshenko Industries.

a.   Formulate and solve a linear program for determining how many reservoir capacitors should be from each supplier to minimize the total cost of obtaining 75,000 acceptable-quality reservoir capacitors.

b.   Suppose that the quality level for Boston Components is much better than estimated. What effect, if any, would this quality level have?

c.   Suppose that management is willing to reconsider its requirement that at least 30,000 capacitors must be ordered from Lyshenko Industries. What effect, if any, would this consideration have?

32.   PartsTech, Inc., a manufacturer of rechargeable batteries for phones, cameras, and other personal electronic devices, signed a contract with an electronics company to produce three different lithium-ion battery packs for a new line of smartphones. The contract calls for the following:

Battery Pack	Production Quantity
PT-100	200,000
PT-200	100,000
PT-300	150,000

PartsTech can manufacture the battery packs at manufacturing plants located in the Philippines and Mexico. The unit cost of the battery packs differs at the two plants because of differences in production equipment and wage rates. The unit costs for each battery pack at each manufacturing plant are as follows:

	Plant	
Product	Philippines	Mexico
PT-100	$0.95	$0.98
PT-200	$0.98	$1.06
PT-300	$1.34	$1.15

The PT-100 and PT-200 battery packs are produced using similar production equipment available at both plants. However, each plant has a limited capacity for the total number of PT-100 and PT-200 battery packs produced. The combined PT-100 and PT-200 production capacities are 175,000 units at the Philippines plant and 160,000 units at the Mexico plant. The PT-300 production capacities are 75,000 units at the Philippines plant and 100,000 units at the Mexico plant. The cost of shipping from the Philippines plant is $0.18 per unit, and the cost of shipping from the Mexico plant is $0.10 per unit.

a.   Develop a linear program that PartsTech can use to determine how many units of each battery pack to produce at each plant in order to minimize the total production and shipping cost associated with the new contract.

b.   Solve the linear program developed in part (a) to determine the optimal production plan.

c.   Use sensitivity analysis to determine how much the production and/or shipping cost per unit would have to change in order to produce additional units of the PT-100 in the Philippines plant.

d.   Use sensitivity analysis to determine how much the production and/or shipping cost per unit would have to change in order to produce additional units of the PT-200 in the Mexico plant.

Case Problem 1   Product Mix

TJ, Inc., makes three nut mixes for sale to grocery chains located in the Southeast. The three mixes, referred to as the Regular Mix, the Deluxe Mix, and the Holiday Mix, are made by mixing different percentages of five types of nuts.

In preparation for the fall season, TJ, Inc., purchased the following shipments of nuts at the prices shown:

Type of Nut	Shipment Amount (pounds)	Cost per Shipment
Almond	6000	$7500
Brazil	7500	$7125
Filbert	7500	$6750
Pecan	6000	$7200
Walnut	7500	$7875

The Regular Mix consists of 15% almonds, 25% Brazil nuts, 25% filberts, 10% pecans, and 25% walnuts. The Deluxe Mix consists of 20% of each type of nut, and the Holiday Mix consists of 25% almonds, 15% Brazil nuts, 15% filberts, 25% pecans, and 20% walnuts.

An accountant at TJ, Inc., analyzed the cost of packaging materials, sales price per pound, and so forth, and determined that the profit contribution per pound is $1.65 for the Regular Mix, $2.00 for the Deluxe Mix, and $2.25 for the Holiday Mix. These figures do not include the cost of specific types of nuts in the different mixes because that cost can vary greatly in the commodity markets.

Customer orders already received are summarized here:

Type of Mix	Orders (pounds)
Regular	10,000
Deluxe	3,000
Holiday	5,000

Because demand is running high, TJ, Inc., expects to receive many more orders than can be satisfied.

TJ, Inc., is committed to using the available nuts to maximize profit over the fall season; nuts not used will be given to the Free Store. Even if it is not profitable to do so, the president of TJ, Inc., indicated that the orders already received must be satisfied.

Managerial Report

Perform an analysis of the TJ, Inc. product mix problem. Prepare a summary report of your findings for TJ, Inc.'s president. Be sure to include information and analysis on the following:

1. The cost per pound of the nuts included in the Regular, Deluxe, and Holiday mixes
2. The optimal product mix and the total profit contribution
3. Recommendations regarding how the total profit contribution can be increased if additional quantities of nuts can be purchased
4. A recommendation as to whether TJ, Inc., should purchase an additional 1000 pounds of almonds for $1000 from a supplier who overbought
5. Recommendations on how profit contribution could be increased (if at all) if TJ, Inc., does not satisfy all existing orders

Case Problem 2   Investment Strategy

J. D. Williams, Inc., is an investment advisory firm that manages more than $120 million in funds for its numerous clients. The company uses an asset allocation model that recommends the portion of each client's portfolio to be invested in a growth stock fund, an income fund, and a money market fund. To maintain diversity in each client's portfolio, the firm places limits on the percentage of each portfolio that may be invested in each of the three funds. General guidelines indicate that the amount invested in the growth fund must be between 20% and 40% of the total portfolio value. Similar percentages for the other two funds stipulate that between 20% and 50% of the total portfolio value must be in the income fund and at least 30% of the total portfolio value must be in the money market fund.

In addition, the company attempts to assess the risk tolerance of each client and adjust the portfolio to meet the needs of the individual investor. For example, Williams just contracted with a new client who has $800,000 to invest. Based on an evaluation of the client's risk tolerance, Williams assigned a maximum risk index of 0.05 for the client. The firm's risk indicators show the risk of the growth fund at 0.10, the income fund at 0.07, and the money market fund at 0.01. An overall portfolio risk index is computed as a weighted average of the risk rating for the three funds, where the weights are the fraction of the client's portfolio invested in each of the funds.

Additionally, Williams is currently forecasting annual yields of 18% for the growth fund, 12.5% for the income fund, and 7.5% for the money market fund. Based on the information provided, how should the new client be advised to allocate the $800,000 among the growth, income, and money market funds? Develop a linear programming model that will provide the maximum yield for the portfolio. Use your model to develop a managerial report.

Managerial Report

1. Recommend how much of the $800,000 should be invested in each of the three funds. What is the annual yield you anticipate for the investment recommendation?
2. Assume that the client's risk index could be increased to 0.055. How much would the yield increase, and how would the investment recommendation change?
3. Refer again to the original situation, where the client's risk index was assessed to be 0.05. How would your investment recommendation change if the annual yield for the growth fund were revised downward to 16% or even to 14%?
4. Assume that the client expressed some concern about having too much money in the growth fund. How would the original recommendation change if the amount invested in the growth fund is not allowed to exceed the amount invested in the income fund?
5. The asset allocation model you developed may be useful in modifying the portfolios for all of the firm's clients whenever the anticipated yields for the three funds are periodically revised. What is your recommendation as to whether use of this model is possible?

Case Problem 3   Truck Leasing Strategy

Reep Construction recently won a contract for the excavation and site preparation of a new rest area on Interstate Highway 5 in California. In preparing his bid for the job, Bob Reep, founder and president of Reep Construction, estimated that it would take four months to perform the work and that 10, 12, 14, and 8 trucks would be needed in months 1 through 4, respectively.

The firm currently has 20 trucks of the type needed to perform the work on the new project. These trucks were obtained last year when Bob signed a long-term lease with CalState Leasing. Although most of these trucks are currently being used on existing jobs, Bob estimates that one truck will be available for use on the new project in month 1, two trucks will be available in month 2, three trucks will be available in month 3, and one truck will be available in month 4. Thus, to complete the project, Bob will have to lease additional trucks.

The long-term leasing contract with CalState charges a monthly cost of $600 per truck. Reep Construction pays its truck drivers $20 an hour, and daily fuel costs are approximately $100 per truck. All maintenance costs are paid by CalState Leasing. For planning purposes, Bob estimates that each truck used on the new project will be operating eight hours a day, five days a week for approximately four weeks each month.

Bob does not believe that current business conditions justify committing the firm to additional long-term leases. In discussing the short-term leasing possibilities with CalState Leasing, Bob learned that he can obtain short-term leases of one to four months. Short-term leases differ from long-term leases in that the short-term leasing plans include the cost of both a truck and a driver. Maintenance costs for short-term leases also are paid by CalState Leasing. The following costs for each of the four months cover the lease of a truck and driver:

Length of Lease	Cost per Month
1	$4000
2	$3700
3	$3225
4	$3040

Bob Reep would like to acquire a lease that minimizes the cost of meeting the monthly trucking requirements for his new project, but he also takes great pride in the fact that his company has never laid off employees. Bob is committed to maintaining his no-layoff policy; that is, he will use his own drivers even if costs are higher.

Managerial Report

Perform an analysis of Reep Construction's leasing problem and prepare a report for Bob Reep that summarizes your findings. Be sure to include information on, and analysis of, the following items:

1. The optimal leasing plan
2. The costs associated with the optimal leasing plan
3. The cost for Reep Construction to maintain its current policy of no layoffs

Appendix 8.1   # Sensitivity Analysis with Excel Solver

In Appendix 7.1 we showed how Excel Solver can be used to solve a linear program by using it to solve the RMC problem. We used reports similar to Excel's Answer Report in Chapter 7, but these reports do not contain the sensitivity analysis information discussed in this chapter. Let us now see how Excel Solver can be used to provide sensitivity analysis information.

When Excel Solver has found the optimal solution to a linear program, the **Solver Results** dialog box (see Figure 8.23) will appear on the screen. If only the solution is desired, simply

FIGURE 8.23   EXCEL SOLVER RESULTS DIALOG BOX TO PRODUCE SENSITIVITY
REPORT

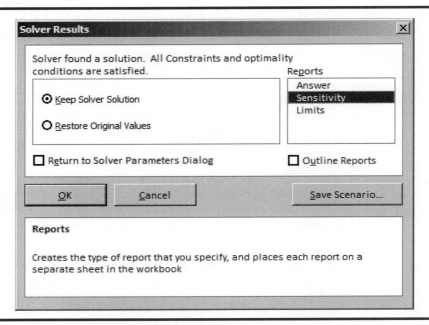

click **OK**. To obtain the optimal solution and the sensitivity analysis output, you must select **Sensitivity** in the **Reports** box before clicking **OK**; the Sensitivity Report is created
on another worksheet in the same Excel workbook. Following this procedure for the RMC
problem, we obtained the optimal solution shown in Figure 8.24. Figure 8.25 shows the
Sensitivity Report as generated by Excel Solver. Note that there are no columns for Model
Variables or Constraint Numbers as shown in the reports in Chapter 8. The Cell columns in
Figure 8.25 correspond to the location of the decision variables and constraints in the Excel
model (Figure 8.24).

Appendix 8.2   Sensitivity Analysis with LINGO

In Appendix 7.2 we showed how LINGO can be used to solve a linear program by using it
to solve the RMC problem. A copy of the Solution Report is shown in Figure 8.26. As we
discussed previously, the value of the objective function is 1600, the optimal solution is
$F = 25$ and $S = 20$, and the values of the slack variables corresponding to the three constraints (rows 2–4) are 0.0, 1.0, and 0.0. Now, let us consider the information in the Reduced
Cost column and the Dual Price column.

For the RMC problem, the reduced costs for both decision variables are zero because
both variables are at a positive value. LINGO reports a *dual price* rather than a shadow price.
For a maximization problem, the dual price and shadow price are identical. For a minimization problem, the dual price is equal to the negative of the shadow price. When interpreting
the LINGO output for a minimization problem, multiply the dual prices by -1, treat the
resulting number as a shadow price, and interpret the number as described in Section 8.3. The
nonzero dual prices of 33.3333 for constraint 1 (material 1 constraint in row 2) and 44.4444

*LINGO always takes
the absolute value of the
reduced cost.*

FIGURE 8.24   EXCEL SOLUTION FOR THE RMC PROBLEM

RMC

	A	B	C	D	E
1	RMC				
2					
3		**Material Requirements**			
4	**Material**	**Fuel Additive**	**Solvent Base**	**Amount Available**	
5	Material 1	0.4	0.5	20	
6	Material 2	0	0.2	5	
7	Material 3	0.6	0.3	21	
8	**Profit Per Ton**	40	30		
9					
10					
11	**Model**				
12					
13		**Decision Variables**			
14		**Fuel Additive**	**Solvent Base**		
15	**Tons Produced**	25	20		
16					
17	**Maximize Total Profit**	1600			
18					
19	**Constraints**	**Amount Used**		**Amount Available**	
20	Material 1	20	<=	20	
21	Material 2	4	<=	5	
22	Material 3	21	<=	21	
23					

FIGURE 8.25   EXCEL SOLVER SENSITIVITY REPORT FOR THE RMC PROBLEM

Adjustable Cells

Cell	Name	Final Value	Reduced Cost	Objective Coefficient	Allowable Increase	Allowable Decrease
$B$15	Tons Produced Fuel Additive	25.000	0.000	40.000	20.000	16.000
$C$15	Tons Produced Solvent Base	20.000	0.000	30.000	20.000	10.000

Constraints

Cell	Name	Final Value	Shadow Price	Constraint R.H. Side	Allowable Increase	Allowable Decrease
$B$20	Material 1 Amount Used	20.000	33.333	20.000	1.500	6.000
$B$21	Material 2 Amount Used	4.000	0.000	5.000	1E+30	1.000
$B$22	Material 3 Amount Used	21.000	44.444	21.000	9.000	2.250

for constraint 3 (material 3 constraint in row 4) tell us that an additional ton of material 1 increases the value of the optimal solution by $33.33 and an additional ton of material 3 increases the value of the optimal solution by $44.44.

FIGURE 8.26   LINGO SOLUTION REPORT FOR THE RMC PROBLEM

```
Global optimal solution found.        1600.000
Objective value:                           2
Total solver iterations:

Model Title: RMC CORPORATION

        Variable              Value              Reduced Cost
      -------------      ----------------       ----------------
            F                25.00000                0.00000
            S                20.00000                0.00000

          Row             Slack/Surplus            Dual Price
      -------------      ----------------       ----------------
            1              1600.00000                1.00000
            2                 0.00000               33.33333
            3                 1.00000                0.00000
            4                 0.00000               44.44444
```

Next, let us consider how LINGO can be used to compute the range of optimality for each objective function coefficient and the range of feasibility for each of the dual prices. By default, range computations are not enabled in LINGO. To enable range computations, perform the following steps:

Step 1. Choose the **LINGO** menu
Step 2. Select **Options**
Step 3. When the **LINGO Options** dialog box appears:
   Select the **General Solver** tab
   Choose **Prices & Ranges** in the **Dual Computations:** box
   Click **Apply**
   Click **OK**

You will now have to re-solve the RMC problem in order for LINGO to perform the range computations. After re-solving the problem, close or minimize the **Solution Report** window. To display the range information, select the **Range** command from the **LINGO** menu. LINGO displays the range information in a new window titled **Range Report**. The output that appears in the Range Report window for the RMC problem is shown in Figure 8.27.

We will use the information in the Objective Coefficient Ranges: section of the range report to compute the range of optimality for the objective function coefficients. For example, the current objective function coefficient for F (fuel additive) is 40. Note that the corresponding allowable increase is 20.0 and the corresponding allowable decrease is 16.0. Thus the range of optimality for the contribution to profit for F, the objective function coefficient for F, is $40.0 - 16.0 = 24.0$ to $40.0 + 20.0 = 60.0$. Using PF to denote the contribution to profit for fuel additive, the range of optimality for PF is $24.0 \leq PF \leq 60.0$. Similarly, with an allowable increase of 20.0 and an allowable decrease of 10.0, the range of optimality for PS, the profit contribution for solvent is $20.0 \leq PS \leq 50.0$.

FIGURE 8.27   LINGO RANGE REPORT FOR THE RMC PROBLEM

```
Ranges in which the basis is unchanged:

OBJECTIVE COEFFICIENT RANGES

                      Current        Allowable        Allowable
       Variable     Coefficient       Increase         Decrease
      ------------  -------------   -------------    -------------
          F          40.00000        20.00000         16.00000
          S          30.00000        20.00000         10.00000

RIGHTHAND SIDE RANGES

                      Current        Allowable        Allowable
       Row              RHS           Increase         Decrease
      ------------  -------------   -------------    -------------
          2          20.00000         1.50000          6.00000
          3           5.00000        INFINITY          1.00000
          4          21.00000         9.00000          2.25000
```

To compute the range of feasibility for each dual price, we will use the information in the Righthand Side Ranges section of the Range Report. For example, the current right-hand-side value for material 1 constraint (row 2) is 20, the allowable increase is 1.5, and the allowable decrease is 6.0. Because the dual price for this constraint is 33.33 (shown in the LINGO Solution Report), we can conclude that an additional ton will increase the objective function by $33.33 per ton. From the range information given, we see that after rounding, the dual price of $33.33 is valid for increases up to $20.0 + 1.5 = 21.5$ and decreases to $20.0 − 6.0 = 14.0$. Thus, the range of feasibility for material 1 is 14.0 to 21.5. The ranges of feasibility for the other constraints can be determined in a similar manner.

CHAPTER 9

Linear Programming Applications in Marketing, Finance, and Operations Management

Linear programming has proven to be one of the most successful quantitative approaches to decision making. Applications have been reported in almost every industry. These applications include production scheduling, media selection, financial planning, capital budgeting, supply chain design, product mix, staffing, and blending.

The Q.M. in Action, A Marketing Planning Model at Marathon Oil Company, provides an example of the use of linear programming by showing how Marathon uses a large-scale linear programming model to solve a wide variety of planning problems. Later in the chapter, other Q.M. in Action features illustrate how General Electric uses linear programming for deciding on investments in solar energy; how Jeppesen Sanderson uses linear programming to optimize production of flight manuals; and how the Kellogg Company uses a large-scale linear programming model to integrate production, distribution, and inventory planning.

In this chapter we present a variety of applications from the traditional business areas of marketing, finance, and operations management. Modeling, computer solution, and interpretation of output are emphasized. A mathematical model is developed for each problem studied, and solutions obtained using Excel Solver are presented for most of the applications. In the chapter appendix we illustrate the use of Excel Solver by solving a financial planning problem.

Q.M. *in* ACTION

A MARKETING PLANNING MODEL AT MARATHON OIL COMPANY*

Marathon Oil Company has four refineries within the United States, operates 50 light product terminals, and has product demand at more than 95 locations. The Supply and Transportation Division faces the problem of determining which refinery should supply which terminal and, at the same time, determining which products should be transported via pipeline, barge, or tanker to minimize cost. Product demand must be satisfied, and the supply capability of each refinery must not be exceeded. To help solve this difficult problem, Marathon Oil developed a marketing planning model.

The marketing planning model is a large-scale linear programming model that takes into account sales not only at Marathon product terminals but also at all exchange locations. An exchange contract is an agreement with other oil product marketers that involves exchanging or trading

Marathon's products for theirs at different locations. All pipelines, barges, and tankers within Marathon's marketing area are also represented in the linear programming model. The objective of the model is to minimize the cost of meeting a given demand structure, taking into account sales price, pipeline tariffs, exchange contract costs, product demand, terminal operating costs, refining costs, and product purchases.

The marketing planning model is used to solve a wide variety of planning problems that vary from evaluating gasoline blending economics to analyzing the economics of a new terminal or pipeline. With daily sales of about 10 million gallons of refined light product, a savings of even one-thousandth of a cent per gallon can result in significant long-term savings. At the same time, what may appear to be a savings in one area, such as refining or transportation, may actually add to overall costs when the effects are fully realized throughout the system. The marketing planning model allows a simultaneous examination of this total effect.

*Based on information provided by Robert W. Wernert at Marathon Oil Company, Findlay, Ohio.

9.1 Marketing Applications

Applications of linear programming in marketing are numerous. In this section we discuss applications in media selection and marketing research.

Media Selection

Online advertising includes search engine marketing, website banner advertisements, mobile-device ads and email marketing.

Media selection applications of linear programming are designed to help marketing managers allocate a fixed advertising budget to various advertising media. Potential media include newspapers, magazines, radio, television, direct mail, and online. In these applications, the objective is to maximize reach, frequency, and quality of exposure. Restrictions on the allowable allocation usually arise during consideration of company policy, contract requirements, and media availability. In the application that follows, we illustrate how a media selection problem might be formulated and solved using a linear programming model.

Relax-and-Enjoy Lake Development Corporation is developing a lakeside community at a privately owned lake. The primary market for the lakeside lots and homes includes all middle- and upper-income families within approximately 100 miles of the development. Relax-and-Enjoy employed the advertising firm of Boone, Phillips, and Jackson (BP&J) to design the promotional campaign.

After considering possible advertising media and the market to be covered, BP&J recommended that the first month's advertising be restricted to five media. At the end of the month, BP&J will then reevaluate its strategy based on the month's results. BP&J collected data on the number of potential customers reached, the cost per advertisement, the maximum number of times each medium is available, and the exposure quality rating for each of the five media. The quality rating is measured in terms of an exposure quality unit, a measure of the relative value of one advertisement in each of the media. This measure, based on BP&J's experience in the advertising business, takes into account factors such as audience demographics (age, income, and education of the audience reached), image presented, and quality of the advertisement. The information collected is presented in Table 9.1.

TABLE 9.1 ADVERTISING MEDIA ALTERNATIVES FOR THE RELAX-AND-ENJOY LAKE DEVELOPMENT CORPORATION

Advertising Media	Number of Potential Customers Reached	Cost ($) per Advertisement	Maximum Times Available per Month*	Exposure Quality Units
1. Daytime TV (1 min), station WKLA	1000	1500	15	65
2. Evening TV (30 sec), station WKLA	2000	3000	10	90
3. Website advertisement (banner ad)	1500	400	25	40
4. Sunday newspaper magazine (½ page color), *The Sunday Press*	2500	1000	4	60
5. Radio, 8:00 A.M. or 5:00 P.M. news (30 sec), station KNOP	300	100	30	20

*The maximum number of times the medium is available is either the maximum number of times the advertising medium occurs (e.g., four Sundays per month) or the maximum number of times BP&J recommends that the medium be used.

In Section 7.1 we provided some general guidelines for modeling linear programming problems. You may want to review Section 7.1 before proceeding with the linear programming applications in this chapter.

Relax-and-Enjoy provided BP&J with an advertising budget of $30,000 for the first month's campaign. In addition, Relax-and-Enjoy imposed the following restrictions on how BP&J may allocate these funds: At least 10 television commercials must be used, at least 50,000 potential customers must be reached, and no more than $18,000 may be spent on television advertisements. What advertising media selection plan should be recommended?

The decision to be made is how many times to use each medium. We begin by defining the decision variables:

$$DTV = \text{number of times daytime TV is used}$$
$$ETV = \text{number of times evening TV is used}$$
$$W = \text{number of times website banner ads are used}$$
$$SN = \text{number of times Sunday newspaper is used}$$
$$R = \text{number of times radio is used}$$

The data on quality of exposure in Table 9.1 show that each daytime TV (DTV) advertisement is rated at 65 exposure quality units. Thus, an advertising plan with DTV advertisements will provide a total of $65DTV$ exposure quality units. Continuing with the data in Table 9.1, we find evening TV (ETV) rated at 90 exposure quality units, website banner ads (W) rated at 40 exposure quality units, Sunday newspaper (SN) rated at 60 exposure quality units, and radio (R) rated at 20 exposure quality units. With the objective of maximizing the total exposure quality units for the overall media selection plan, the objective function becomes

$$\text{Max}\quad 65DTV + 90ETV + 40W + 60SN + 20R \qquad \text{Exposure quality}$$

We now formulate the constraints for the model from the information given:

$$
\begin{aligned}
DTV &\leq 15 \\
ETV &\leq 10 \\
W &\leq 25 \quad \left.\right\} \text{Availability of media} \\
SN &\leq 4 \\
R &\leq 30
\end{aligned}
$$

$$1500DTV + 3000ETV + 400W + 1000SN + 100R \leq 30{,}000 \quad \text{Budget}$$
$$
\begin{aligned}
DTV + ETV &\geq 10 \quad \left.\right\} \text{Television} \\
1500DTV + 3000ETV &\leq 18{,}000 \quad \text{restrictions}
\end{aligned}
$$
$$1000DTV + 2000ETV + 1500W + 2500SN + 300R \geq 50{,}000 \quad \text{Customers reached}$$
$$DTV, ETV, W, SN, R \geq 0$$

Care must be taken to ensure the linear programming model accurately reflects the real problem. Always review your formulation thoroughly before attempting to solve the model.

Problem 1 provides practice at formulating a similar media selection model.

The optimal solution to this five-variable, nine-constraint linear programming model is shown in Figure 9.1; a summary is presented in Table 9.2.

The optimal solution calls for advertisements to be distributed among daytime TV, websites, Sunday newspaper, and radio. The maximum number of exposure quality units is $65(10) + 90(0) + 40(25) + 60(2) + 20(30) = 2370$, and the total number of customers reached is 61,500. Note that in the constraint section the simple bound constraints on the availability of media are not listed. However, for each variable at its bound, the Reduced Cost gives the shadow price for that constraint. So, for example, the reduced cost of 65 for evening TV indicates that forcing the use of this type of ad would actually drop exposure quality by 65 points. On the other hand, allowing another website banner ad (26 instead of a limit of 25) would increase exposure quality by 16 units. Note that the budget constraint has a shadow price of 0.060. Therefore, a $1.00 increase in the advertising budget will lead

FIGURE 9.1 SENSITIVITY REPORT FOR THE RELAX-AND-ENJOY LAKE
DEVELOPMENT CORPORATION PROBLEM

Variable Cells

Model Variable	Name	Final Value	Reduced Cost	Objective Coefficient	Allowable Increase	Allowable Decrease
DTV	Ads Placed DTV	10.000	0.000	65.000	25.000	65.000
EVT	Ads Placed ETV	0.000	−65.000	90.000	65.000	1E+30
W	Ads Placed W	25.000	16.000	40.000	1E+30	16.000
SN	Ads Placed SN	2.000	0.000	60.000	40.000	16.667
R	Ads Placed R	30.000	14.000	20.000	1E+30	14.000

Constraints

Constraint Number	Name	Final Value	Shadow Price	Constraint R.H. Side	Allowable Increase	Allowable Decrease
1	Budget	30000.000	0.060	30000.000	2000.000	2000.000
2	Num TV Ads	10.000	−25.000	10.000	1.333	1.333
3	TV Budget	15000.000	0.000	18000.000	1E+30	3000.000
4	Customers Reached	61500.000	0.000	50000.000	11500.000	1E+30

More complex media selection models may include considerations such as the reduced exposure quality value for repeat media usage, cost discounts for repeat media usage, audience overlap by different media, and/or timing recommendations for the advertisements.

to an increase of 0.06 exposure quality units. The shadow price of −25.000 for the number of TV ads indicates that reducing the number of required television commercials by 1 will increase the exposure quality of the advertising plan by 25 units. Thus, Relax-and-Enjoy should consider reducing the requirement of having at least 10 television commercials.

A possible shortcoming of this model is that, even if the exposure quality measure were not subject to error, it offers no guarantee that maximization of total exposure quality will lead to a maximization of profit or of sales (a common surrogate for profit). However, this issue is not a shortcoming of linear programming; rather, it is a shortcoming of the use of exposure quality as a criterion. If we could directly measure the effect of an advertisement on profit, we could use total profit as the objective to be maximized.

TABLE 9.2 ADVERTISING PLAN FOR THE RELAX-AND-ENJOY
LAKE DEVELOPMENT CORPORATION

Media	Frequency	Budget
Daytime TV	10	$15,000
Websites	25	10,000
Sunday newspaper	2	2,000
Radio	30	3,000
		$30,000

Exposure quality units = 2370
Total customers reached = 61,500

NOTES AND COMMENTS

1. The media selection model required subjective evaluations of the exposure quality for the media alternatives. Marketing managers may have substantial data concerning exposure quality, but the final coefficients used in the objective

function may also include considerations based primarily on managerial judgment.

2. The media selection model presented in this section uses exposure quality as the objective function and places a constraint on the number of customers reached. An alternative formulation of this problem would be to use the number of customers reached as the objective function and add a constraint indicating the minimum total exposure quality required for the media plan.

Marketing Research

An organization conducts marketing research to learn about consumer characteristics, attitudes, and preferences. Marketing research firms that specialize in providing such information often do the actual research for client organizations. Typical services offered by a marketing research firm include designing the study, conducting market surveys, analyzing the data collected, and providing summary reports and recommendations for the client. In the research design phase, targets or quotas may be established for the number and types of respondents to be surveyed. The marketing research firm's objective is to conduct the survey so as to meet the client's needs at a minimum cost.

Market Survey, Inc. (MSI) specializes in evaluating consumer reaction to new products, services, and advertising campaigns. A client firm requested MSI's assistance in ascertaining consumer reaction to a recently marketed household product. During meetings with the client, MSI agreed to conduct door-to-door personal interviews to obtain responses from households with children and households without children. In addition, MSI agreed to conduct both day and evening interviews. Specifically, the client's contract called for MSI to conduct 1000 interviews under the following quota guidelines:

1. Interview at least 400 households with children.
2. Interview at least 400 households without children.
3. The total number of households interviewed during the evening must be at least as great as the number of households interviewed during the day.
4. At least 40% of the interviews for households with children must be conducted during the evening.
5. At least 60% of the interviews for households without children must be conducted during the evening.

Because the interviews for households with children take additional interviewer time and because evening interviewers are paid more than daytime interviewers, the cost varies with the type of interview. Based on previous research studies, estimates of the interview costs are as follows:

	Interview Cost	
Household	**Day**	**Evening**
Children	$20	$25
No children	$18	$20

What is the household, time-of-day interview plan that will satisfy the contract requirements at a minimum total interviewing cost?

In formulating the linear programming model for the MSI problem, we utilize the following decision-variable notation:

$$DC = \text{the number of daytime interviews of households with children}$$
$$EC = \text{the number of evening interviews of households with children}$$

> DNC = the number of daytime interviews of households without children
>
> ENC = the number of evening interviews of households without children

We begin the linear programming model formulation by using the cost-per-interview data to develop the objective function:

$$\text{Min} \quad 20DC + 25EC + 18DNC + 20ENC$$

The constraint requiring a total of 1000 interviews is

$$DC + EC + DNC + ENC = 1000$$

The five specifications concerning the types of interviews are as follows:

- Households with children:

$$DC + EC \geq 400$$

- Households without children:

$$DNC + ENC \geq 400$$

- At least as many evening interviews as day interviews:

$$EC + ENC \geq DC + DNC$$

The usual format for linear programming model formulation places all decision variables on the left side of the inequality and a constant (possibly zero) on the right side. Thus, we rewrite this constraint as

$$-DC + EC - DNC + ENC \geq 0$$

- At least 40% of interviews of households with children during the evening:

$$EC \geq 0.4(DC + EC) \quad \text{or} \quad -0.4DC + 0.6EC \geq 0$$

- At least 60% of interviews of households without children during the evening:

$$ENC \geq 0.6(DNC + ENC) \quad \text{or} \quad -0.6DNC + 0.4ENC \geq 0$$

When we add the nonnegativity requirements, the four-variable and six-constraint linear programming model becomes

Min $20DC + 25EC + 18DNC + 20ENC$
s.t.

$DC +$	$EC +$	$DNC +$	$ENC =$	1000	Total interviews
$DC +$	EC			$\geq$ 400	Households with children
		$DNC +$	$ENC \geq$	400	Households without children
$-DC +$	$EC -$	$DNC +$	$ENC \geq$	0	Evening interviews
$-0.4DC +$	$0.6EC$			$\geq$ 0	Evening interviews in households with children
		$-0.6DNC +$	$0.4ENC \geq$	0	Evening interviews in households without children

$$DC, EC, DNC, ENC \geq 0$$

The sensitivity report based on Excel Solver is shown in Figure 9.2. The solution reveals that the minimum cost of $20(240) + 25(160) + 18(240) + 20(360) = \$20,320$ occurs with the following interview schedule:

Household	Number of Interviews		
	Day	**Evening**	**Totals**
Children	240	160	400
No children	240	360	600
Totals	480	520	1000

Hence, 480 interviews will be scheduled during the day and 520 during the evening. Households with children will be covered by 400 interviews, and households without children will be covered by 600 interviews.

Selected sensitivity analysis information from Figure 9.2 shows a shadow price of 19.200 for the Total Interviews constraint. This indicates that the total interviewing cost will increase by $19.20 if the number of interviews is increased from 1000 to 1001. Thus, $19.20 is the incremental cost of obtaining additional interviews. It also is the savings that could be realized by reducing the number of interviews from 1000 to 999.

In this solution, exactly 400 households with children are interviewed and we exceed the minimum requirement on households without children by 200 (600 versus the minimum requirement of 400). The shadow price of 5.000 for the fifth constraint indicates that if one more household (with children) than the minimum requirement must be interviewed during the evening, the total interviewing cost will go up by $5.00. Similarly, the sixth constraint shows that requiring one more household (without children) to be interviewed during the evening will increase costs by $2.00.

FIGURE 9.2   SENSITIVITY REPORT FOR THE MARKET SURVEY PROBLEM

Variable Cells

Model Variable	Name	Final Value	Reduced Cost	Objective Coefficient	Allowable Increase	Allowable Decrease
DC	Children Day	240.000	0.000	20.000	5.000	4.667
EC	Children Evening	160.000	0.000	25.000	1E+30	5.000
DNC	No Children Day	240.000	0.000	18.000	2.000	1E+30
ENC	No Children Evening	360.000	0.000	20.000	4.667	2.000

Constraints

Constraint Number	Name	Final Value	Shadow Price	Constraint R.H. Side	Allowable Increase	Allowable Decrease
1	Total Interviews	1000.000	19.200	1000.000	1E+30	200.000
2	Children	400.000	2.800	400.000	100.000	400.000
3	No Children	600.000	0.000	400.000	200.000	1E+30
4	Eve. Interviews	520.000	0.000	0.000	40.000	1E+30
5	Eve. Children	160.000	5.000	0.000	240.000	20.000
6	Eve. No Children	360.000	2.000	0.000	240.000	20.000

9.2 # Financial Applications

In finance, linear programming can be applied in problem situations involving capital budgeting, make-or-buy decisions, asset allocation, portfolio selection, financial planning, and many more. In this section we describe a portfolio selection problem and a problem involving funding of an early retirement program.

Portfolio Selection

Portfolio selection problems involve situations in which a financial manager must select specific investments—for example, stocks and bonds—from a variety of investment alternatives. Managers of mutual funds, credit unions, insurance companies, and banks frequently encounter this type of problem. The objective function for portfolio selection problems usually is maximization of expected return or minimization of risk. The constraints usually reflect restrictions on the type of permissible investments, state laws, company policy, maximum permissible risk, and so on. Problems of this type have been formulated and solved using a variety of mathematical programming techniques. In this section we formulate and solve a portfolio selection problem as a linear program.

Consider the case of Welte Mutual Funds, Inc., located in New York City. Welte just obtained $100,000 by converting industrial bonds to cash and is now looking for other investment opportunities for these funds. Based on Welte's current investments, the firm's top financial analyst recommends that all new investments be made in the oil industry, in the steel industry, or in government bonds. Specifically, the analyst identified five investment opportunities and projected their annual rates of return. The investments and rates of return are shown in Table 9.3.

Management of Welte imposed the following investment guidelines:

1. Neither industry (oil or steel) should receive more than $50,000.
2. Government bonds should be at least 25% of the steel industry investments.
3. The investment in Pacific Oil, the high-return but high-risk investment, cannot be more than 60% of the total oil industry investment.

What portfolio recommendations—investments and amounts—should be made for the available $100,000? Given the objective of maximizing projected return subject to the budgetary and managerially imposed constraints, we can answer this question by formulating and solving a linear programming model of the problem. The solution will provide investment recommendations for the management of Welte Mutual Funds.

TABLE 9.3   INVESTMENT OPPORTUNITIES FOR WELTE MUTUAL FUNDS

Investment	Projected Rate of Return (%)
Atlantic Oil	7.3
Pacific Oil	10.3
Midwest Steel	6.4
Huber Steel	7.5
Government bonds	4.5

Let

$$A = \text{dollars invested in Atlantic Oil}$$
$$P = \text{dollars invested in Pacific Oil}$$
$$M = \text{dollars invested in Midwest Steel}$$
$$H = \text{dollars invested in Huber Steel}$$
$$G = \text{dollars invested in government bonds}$$

Using the projected rates of return shown in Table 9.3, we write the objective function for maximizing the total return for the portfolio as

$$\text{Max} \quad 0.073A + 0.103P + 0.064M + 0.075H + 0.045G$$

The constraint specifying investment of the available $100,000 is

$$A + P + M + H + G = 100{,}000$$

The requirements that neither the oil nor the steel industry should receive more than $50,000 are

$$A + P \leq 50{,}000$$
$$M + H \leq 50{,}000$$

The requirement that government bonds be at least 25% of the steel industry investment is expressed as

$$G \geq 0.25(M + H) \quad \text{or} \quad -0.25M - 0.25H + G \geq 0$$

Finally, the constraint that Pacific Oil cannot be more than 60% of the total oil industry investment is

$$P \leq 0.60(A + P) \quad \text{or} \quad -0.60A + 0.40P \leq 0$$

By adding the nonnegativity restrictions, we obtain the complete linear programming model for the Welte Mutual Funds investment problem:

Max $0.073A + 0.103P + 0.064M + 0.075H + 0.045G$

s.t.

$A +$	$P +$	$M +$	$H +$	$G =$	100,000	Available funds
$A +$	P			$\leq$	50,000	Oil industry maximum
		$M +$	H	$\leq$	50,000	Steel industry maximum
	$- 0.25M -$	$0.25H +$	$G \geq$	0	Government bonds minimum
$-0.6A +$	$0.4P$			$\leq$	0	Pacific Oil restriction

$$A, P, M, H, G \geq 0$$

The sensitivity report based on Excel Solver for this linear program is shown in Figure 9.3. Table 9.4 shows how the funds are allocated among the securities. Note that the optimal solution indicates that the portfolio should be diversified among all the investment opportunities except

FIGURE 9.3 SENSITIVITY REPORT FOR THE WELTE MUTUAL FUNDS PROBLEM

Variable Cells

Model Variable	Name	Final Value	Reduced Cost	Objective Coefficient	Allowable Increase	Allowable Decrease
A	Atlantic Oil Amount Invested	20000.000	0.000	0.073	0.030	0.055
P	Pacific Oil Amount Invested	30000.000	0.000	0.103	1E+30	0.030
M	Midwest Steel Amount Invested	0.000	−0.011	0.064	0.011	1E+30
H	Huber Steel Amount Invested	40000.000	0.000	0.075	0.0275	0.011
G	Gov't Bonds Amount Invested	10000.000	0.000	0.045	0.030	1E+30

Constraints

Constraint Number	Name	Final Value	Shadow Price	Constraint R.H. Side	Allowable Increase	Allowable Decrease
1	Avl. Funds	100000.000	0.069	100000.000	12500.000	50000.000
2	Oil Max	50000.000	0.022	50000.000	50000.000	12500.000
3	Steel Max	40000.000	0.000	50000.000	1E+30	10000.000
4	Gov't Bonds	10000.000	−0.024	0.000	50000.000	12500.000
5	Pacific Oil	30000.000	0.030	0.000	20000.000	30000.000

Midwest Steel. The projected annual return for this portfolio is 0.073(20000) + 0.103(30000) + 0.064(0) + 0.075(40000) + 0.045(10000) = $8000, which is an overall return of 8%.

The optimal solution shows the shadow price for the third constraint is zero. The reason is that the steel industry maximum constraint is not binding; increases in the steel industry limit of $50,000 will not improve the value of the optimal solution. Indeed, the final value for the left hand side of the third constraint shows that the current steel industry investment is $10,000 below its limit of $50,000. The shadow prices for the other constraints are non-zero, indicating that these constraints are binding.

The shadow price of 0.069 for the first constraint shows that the optimal value of objective function can be increased by 0.069 if one more dollar can be made available for the portfolio investment. If more funds can be obtained at a cost of less than 6.9%, management should consider obtaining them. However, if a return in excess of 6.9% can be obtained by investing funds elsewhere (other than in these five securities), management should question the wisdom of investing the entire $100,000 in this portfolio.

TABLE 9.4 OPTIMAL PORTFOLIO SELECTION FOR WELTE MUTUAL FUNDS

Investment	Amount	Expected Annual Return
Atlantic Oil	$ 20,000	$1460
Pacific Oil	30,000	3090
Huber Steel	40,000	3000
Government bonds	10,000	450
Totals	$100,000	$8000

Expected annual return of $8000
Overall rate of return = 8%

The shadow price for the available funds constraint provides information on the rate of return from additional investment funds.

Similar interpretations can be given to the other shadow prices. Note that the shadow price for the government bonds constraint is -0.024. This result indicates that increasing the value on the right-hand side of the constraint by one unit can be expected to decrease the value of the optimal solution by 0.024. In terms of the optimal portfolio, then, if Welte invests one more dollar in government bonds (beyond the minimum requirement), the total return will decrease by $0.024. To see why this decrease occurs, note again from the shadow price for the first constraint that the marginal return on the funds invested in the portfolio is 6.9% (the average return is 8%). The rate of return on government bonds is 4.5%. Thus, the cost of investing one more dollar in government bonds is the difference between the marginal return on the portfolio and the marginal return on government bonds: $6.9\% - 4.5\% = 2.4\%$.

Note that the optimal solution shows that Midwest Steel should not be included in the portfolio ($M = 0$). The associated reduced cost for M of -0.011 tells us that the objective function value will decrease by 0.011 for every dollar we invest in Midwest Steel. Stated differently, the coefficient for Midwest Steel would have to increase by 0.011 before considering the Midwest Steel investment alternative would be advisable. With such an increase the Midwest Steel return would be $0.064 + 0.011 = 0.075$, making this investment just as desirable as the currently used Huber Steel investment alternative.

Finally, a simple modification of the Welte linear programming model permits us to determine the fraction of available funds invested in each security. That is, we divide each of the right-hand-side values by 100,000. Then the optimal values for the variables will give the fraction of funds that should be invested in each security for a portfolio of any size.

NOTES AND COMMENTS

1. The optimal solution to the Welte Mutual Funds problem indicates that $20,000 is to be spent on the Atlantic Oil stock. If Atlantic Oil sells for $75 per share, we would have to purchase exactly 266⅔ shares in order to spend exactly $20,000. The difficulty of purchasing fractional shares can be handled by purchasing the largest possible integer number of shares with the allotted funds (e.g., 266 shares of Atlantic Oil). This approach guarantees that the budget constraint will not be violated. This approach, of course, introduces the possibility that the solution will no longer be optimal, but the danger is slight if a large number of securities are involved. In cases where the analyst believes that the decision variables *must* have integer values, the problem must be formulated as an integer linear programming model. Integer linear programming is the topic of Chapter 11.

2. Financial portfolio theory stresses obtaining a proper balance between risk and return. In the Welte problem, we explicitly considered return in the objective function. Risk is controlled by choosing constraints that ensure diversity among oil and steel stocks and a balance between government bonds and the steel industry investment.

Financial Planning

Linear programming has been used for a variety of investment planning applications. The Q.M. in Action, General Electric Uses Linear Programming for Solar Energy Investment Decisions, describes how linear programming is used to guide GE's investment in solar energy.

Q.M. *in* ACTION

GENERAL ELECTRIC USES LINEAR PROGRAMMING FOR SOLAR ENERGY INVESTMENT DECISIONS*

With growing concerns about the environment and our ability to continue to utilize limited nonrenewable sources for energy, companies have begun to place much more emphasis on renewable forms of energy. Water, wind, and solar energy are renewable forms of energy that have become the focus of considerable investment by companies.

General Electric (GE) has products in a variety of areas within the energy sector. One such area of interest to GE is solar energy. Solar energy is a relatively new concept with rapidly changing technologies; for example, solar cells and solar power systems. Solar cells can convert sunlight directly into electricity. Concentrating solar power systems focus a larger area of sunlight into a small beam that can be used as a heat source for conventional power generation. Solar cells can be placed on rooftops and hence can be used by both commercial and residential customers, whereas solar power systems are

mostly used in commercial settings. In recent years, GE has invested in several solar cell technologies.

Uncertainties in technology development, costs, and demand for solar energy make determining the appropriate amount of production capacity in which to invest a difficult problem. GE uses a set of decision support tools to solve this problem. A detailed descriptive analytical model is used to estimate the cost of newly developed or proposed solar cells. Statistical models developed for new product introductions are used to estimate annual solar demand 10 to 15 years into the future. Finally, the cost and demand estimates are used in a multiperiod linear program to determine the best production capacity investment plan.

The linear program finds an optimal expansion plan by taking into account inventory, capacity, production, and budget constraints. Because of the high level of uncertainty, the linear program is solved over multiple future scenarios. A solution to each individual scenario is found and evaluated in the other scenarios to assess the risk associated with that plan. GE planning analysts have used these tools to support management's strategic investment decisions in the solar energy sector.

*Based on B. G. Thomas and S. Bollapragada, "General Electric Uses an Integrated Framework for Product Costing, Demand Forecasting and Capacity Planning for New Photovoltaic Technology Products," *Interfaces* 40, no. 5 (September/October 2010): 353–367.

Hewlitt Corporation established an early retirement program as part of its corporate restructuring. At the close of the voluntary sign-up period, 68 employees had elected early retirement. As a result of these early retirements, the company incurs the following obligations over the next eight years:

Year	1	2	3	4	5	6	7	8
Cash Requirement	430	210	222	231	240	195	225	255

The cash requirements (in thousands of dollars) are due at the beginning of each year.

The corporate treasurer must determine how much money must be set aside today to meet the eight yearly financial obligations as they come due. The financing plan for the retirement program includes investments in government bonds as well as savings. The investments in government bonds are limited to three choices:

Bond	Price	Rate (%)	Years to Maturity
1	$1150	8.875	5
2	1000	5.500	6
3	1350	11.750	7

The government bonds have a par value of $1000, which means that even with different prices each bond pays $1000 at maturity. The rates shown are based on the par value. For purposes of planning, the treasurer assumed that any funds not invested in bonds will be placed in savings and earn interest at an annual rate of 4%.

We define the decision variables as follows:

F = total dollars required to meet the retirement plan's eight-year obligation
B_1 = units of bond 1 purchased at the beginning of year 1
B_2 = units of bond 2 purchased at the beginning of year 1
B_3 = units of bond 3 purchased at the beginning of year 1
S_i = amount placed in savings at the beginning of year i for $i = 1, \ldots, 8$

The objective function is to minimize the total dollars needed to meet the retirement plan's eight-year obligation, or

$$\text{Min} \quad F$$

A key feature of this type of financial planning problem is that a constraint must be formulated for each year of the planning horizon. In general, each constraint takes the form

$$\begin{pmatrix} \text{Funds available at} \\ \text{the beginning of the year} \end{pmatrix} - \begin{pmatrix} \text{Funds invested in bonds} \\ \text{and placed in savings} \end{pmatrix} = \begin{pmatrix} \text{Cash obligation for} \\ \text{the current year} \end{pmatrix}$$

The funds available at the beginning of year 1 are given by F. With a current price of $1150 for bond 1 and investments expressed in thousands of dollars, the total investment for B_1 units of bond 1 would be $1.15B_1$. Similarly, the total investment in bonds 2 and 3 would be $1B_2$ and $1.35B_3$, respectively. The investment in savings for year 1 is S_1. Using these results and the first-year obligation of 430, we obtain the constraint for year 1:

$$F - 1.15B_1 - 1B_2 - 1.35B_3 - S_1 = 430 \quad \text{Year 1}$$

Investments in bonds can take place only in this first year, and the bonds will be held until maturity.

The funds available at the beginning of year 2 include the investment returns of 8.875% on the par value of bond 1, 5.5% on the par value of bond 2, 11.75% on the par value of bond 3, and 4% on savings. The new amount to be invested in savings for year 2 is S_2. With an obligation of 210, the constraint for year 2 is

$$0.08875B_1 + 0.055B_2 + 0.1175B_3 + 1.04S_1 - S_2 = 210 \quad \text{Year 2}$$

Similarly, the constraints for years 3 to 8 are

$$0.08875B_1 + 0.055B_2 + 0.1175B_3 + 1.04S_2 - S_3 = 222 \quad \text{Year 3}$$
$$0.08875B_1 + 0.055B_2 + 0.1175B_3 + 1.04S_3 - S_4 = 231 \quad \text{Year 4}$$
$$0.08875B_1 + 0.055B_2 + 0.1175B_3 + 1.04S_4 - S_5 = 240 \quad \text{Year 5}$$
$$1.08875B_1 + 0.055B_2 + 0.1175B_3 + 1.04S_5 - S_6 = 195 \quad \text{Year 6}$$
$$1.055B_2 + 0.1175B_3 + 1.04S_6 - S_7 = 225 \quad \text{Year 7}$$
$$1.1175B_3 + 1.04S_7 - S_8 = 255 \quad \text{Year 8}$$

We do not consider future investments in bonds because the future price of bonds depends on interest rates and cannot be known in advance.

Note that the constraint for year 6 shows that funds available from bond 1 are $1.08875B_1$. The coefficient of 1.08875 reflects the fact that bond 1 matures at the end of year 5. As a result, the par value plus the interest from bond 1 during year 5 is available at the beginning of year 6. Also, because bond 1 matures in year 5 and becomes available for use at the beginning of year 6, the variable B_1 does not appear in the constraints for years 7 and 8. Note the similar interpretation for bond 2, which matures at the end of year 6 and has the

FIGURE 9.4 SENSITIVITY REPORT FOR THE HEWLITT CORPORATION CASH
REQUIREMENTS PROBLEM

Variable Cells

Model Variable	Name	Final Value	Reduced Cost	Objective Coefficient	Allowable Increase	Allowable Decrease
F	Dollars Needed	1728.794	0.000	1.000	1E+30	1.000
B1	Bond 1 - Year 1	144.988	0.000	0.000	0.067	0.013
B2	Bond 2 - Year 2	187.856	0.000	0.000	0.013	0.020
B3	Bond 3 - Year 3	228.188	0.000	0.000	0.023	0.750
S1	Savings Year 1	636.148	0.000	0.000	0.110	0.055
S2	Savings Year 2	501.606	0.000	0.000	0.143	0.057
S3	Savings Year 3	349.682	0.000	0.000	0.211	0.059
S4	Savings Year 4	182.681	0.000	0.000	0.414	0.061
S5	Savings Year 5	0.000	0.064	0.000	1E+30	0.064
S6	Savings Year 6	0.000	0.013	0.000	1E+30	0.013
S7	Savings Year 7	0.000	0.021	0.000	1E+30	0.021
S8	Savings Year 8	0.000	0.671	0.000	1E+30	0.671

WEB file

Hewlitt

Constraints

Constraint Number	Name	Final Value	Shadow Price	Constraint R.H. Side	Allowable Increase	Allowable Decrease
1	Year 1 Flow	430.000	1.000	430.000	1E+30	1728.794
2	Year 2 Flow	210.000	0.962	210.000	1E+30	661.594
3	Year 3 Flow	222.000	0.925	222.000	1E+30	521.670
4	Year 4 Flow	231.000	0.889	231.000	1E+30	363.669
5	Year 5 Flow	240.000	0.855	240.000	1E+30	189.988
6	Year 6 Flow	195.000	0.760	195.000	2149.928	157.856
7	Year 7 Flow	225.000	0.719	225.000	3027.962	198.188
8	Year 8 Flow	255.000	0.671	255.000	1583.882	255.000

par value plus interest available at the beginning of year 7. In addition, bond 3 matures at the end of year 7 and has the par value plus interest available at the beginning of year 8.

Finally, note that a variable S_8 appears in the constraint for year 8. The retirement fund obligation will be completed at the beginning of year 8, so we anticipate that S_8 will be zero and no funds will be put into savings. However, the formulation includes S_8 in the event that the bond income plus interest from the savings in year 7 exceed the 255 cash requirement for year 8. Thus, S_8 is a surplus variable that shows any funds remaining after the eight-year cash requirements have been satisfied.

The optimal solution and sensitivity report based on Excel Solver is shown in Figure 9.4. With an objective function value of $F = 1728.794$, the total investment required to meet the retirement plan's eight-year obligation is $1,728,794. Using the current prices of $1150, $1000, and $1350 for each of the bonds, respectively, we can summarize the initial investments in the three bonds as follows:

Bond	Units Purchased	Investment Amount
1	$B_1 = 144.988$	$1150(144.988) = $166,736
2	$B_2 = 187.856$	$1000(187.856) = $187,856
3	$B_3 = 228.188$	$1350(228.188) = $308,054

The solution also shows that $636,148 (see S_1) will be placed in savings at the beginning of the first year. By starting with $1,728,794, the company can make the specified bond and savings investments and have enough left over to meet the retirement program's first-year cash requirement of $430,000.

The optimal solution in Figure 9.4 shows that the decision variables S_1, S_2, S_3, and S_4 all are greater than zero, indicating that investments in savings are required in each of the first four years. However, interest from the bonds plus the bond maturity incomes will be sufficient to cover the retirement program's cash requirements in years 5 through 8.

In this application, the shadow price can be thought of as the present value of each dollar in the cash requirement. For example, each dollar that must be paid in year 8 has a present value of $0.671.

The shadow prices have an interesting interpretation in this application. Each right-hand-side value corresponds to the payment that must be made in that year. Note that the shadow prices are positive, indicating that increasing the requirements in any year causes the needed cash to increase. However, *reducing* the payment in any year would be beneficial because the total funds required for the retirement program's obligation would be less. Note that the shadow prices show that reductions in required funds are more beneficial in the early years, with decreasing benefits in subsequent years. As a result, Hewlitt would benefit by reducing cash requirements in the early years even if it had to make equivalently larger cash payments in later years.

NOTES AND COMMENTS

1. The optimal solution for the Hewlitt Corporation problem shows fractional numbers of government bonds at 144.988, 187.856, and 228.188 units, respectively. However, fractional bond units usually are not available. If we were conservative and rounded up to 145, 188, and 229 units, respectively, the total funds required for the eight-year retirement program obligation would be approximately $1254 more than the total funds indicated by the objective function. Because of the magnitude of the funds involved, rounding up probably would provide a workable solution. If an optimal integer solution were required, the methods of integer linear programming covered in Chapter 11 would have to be used.

2. We implicitly assumed that interest from the government bonds is paid annually. Investments such as treasury notes actually provide interest payments every six months. In such cases, the model can be reformulated using six-month periods, with interest and/or cash payments occurring every six months.

9.3 Operations Management Applications

Linear programming applications developed for production and operations management include scheduling, staffing, inventory control, and capacity planning. In this section we describe examples of make-or-buy decisions, production scheduling, and workforce assignments.

A Make-or-Buy Decision

We illustrate the use of a linear programming model to determine how much of each of several component parts a company should manufacture and how much it should purchase from an outside supplier. Such a decision is referred to as a make-or-buy decision.

The Janders Company markets various business and engineering products. Currently, Janders is preparing to introduce two new calculators: one for the business market, called the Financial Manager, and one for the engineering market, called the Technician. Each calculator has three components: a base, an electronic cartridge, and a faceplate or top. The same base is used for both calculators, but the cartridges and tops are different. All

TABLE 9.5   MANUFACTURING COSTS AND PURCHASE PRICES FOR JANDERS
CALCULATOR COMPONENTS

	Cost per Unit	
Component	**Manufacture (regular time)**	**Purchase**
Base	$0.50	$0.60
Financial cartridge	$3.75	$4.00
Technician cartridge	$3.30	$3.90
Financial top	$0.60	$0.65
Technician top	$0.75	$0.78

components can be manufactured by the company or purchased from outside suppliers. The manufacturing costs and purchase prices for the components are summarized in Table 9.5.

Company forecasters indicate that 3000 Financial Manager calculators and 2000 Technician calculators will be needed. However, manufacturing capacity is limited. The company has 200 hours of regular manufacturing time and 50 hours of overtime that can be scheduled for the calculators. Overtime involves a premium at the additional cost of $9 per hour. Table 9.6 shows manufacturing times (in minutes) for the components.

The problem for Janders is to determine how many units of each component to manufacture and how many units of each component to purchase. We define the decision variables as follows:

$$BM = \text{number of bases manufactured}$$
$$BP = \text{number of bases purchased}$$
$$FCM = \text{number of Financial cartridges manufactured}$$
$$FCP = \text{number of Financial cartridges purchased}$$
$$TCM = \text{number of Technician cartridges manufactured}$$
$$TCP = \text{number of Technician cartridges purchased}$$
$$FTM = \text{number of Financial tops manufactured}$$
$$FTP = \text{number of Financial tops purchased}$$
$$TTM = \text{number of Technician tops manufactured}$$
$$TTP = \text{number of Technician tops purchased}$$

One additional decision variable is needed to determine the hours of overtime that must be scheduled:

$$OT = \text{number of hours of overtime to be scheduled}$$

TABLE 9.6   MANUFACTURING TIMES IN MINUTES PER UNIT FOR JANDERS
CALCULATOR COMPONENTS

Component	**Manufacturing Time**
Base	1.0
Financial cartridge	3.0
Technician cartridge	2.5
Financial top	1.0
Technician top	1.5

The objective function is to minimize the total cost, including manufacturing costs, purchase costs, and overtime costs. Using the cost-per-unit data in Table 9.5 and the overtime premium cost rate of $9 per hour, we write the objective function as

$$\text{Min} \quad 0.5BM + 0.6BP + 3.75FCM + 4FCP + 3.3TCM + 3.9TCP + 0.6FTM$$
$$+ 0.65FTP + 0.75TTM + 0.78TTP + 9OT$$

The first five constraints specify the number of each component needed to satisfy the demand for 3000 Financial Manager calculators and 2000 Technician calculators. A total of 5000 base components are needed, with the number of other components depending on the demand for the particular calculator. The five demand constraints are

$$BM + BP = 5000 \quad \text{Bases}$$
$$FCM + FCP = 3000 \quad \text{Financial cartridges}$$
$$TCM + TCP = 2000 \quad \text{Technician cartridges}$$
$$FTM + FTP = 3000 \quad \text{Financial tops}$$
$$TTM + TTP = 2000 \quad \text{Technician tops}$$

Two constraints are needed to guarantee that manufacturing capacities for regular time and overtime cannot be exceeded. The first constraint limits overtime capacity to 50 hours, or

$$OT \leq 50$$

The second constraint states that the total manufacturing time required for all components must be less than or equal to the total manufacturing capacity, including regular time plus overtime. The manufacturing times for the components are expressed in minutes, so we state the total manufacturing capacity constraint in minutes, with the 200 hours of regular time capacity becoming $60(200) = 12{,}000$ minutes. The actual overtime required is unknown at this point, so we write the overtime as $60OT$ minutes. Using the manufacturing times from Table 9.6, we have

$$BM + 3FCM + 2.5TCM + FTM + 1.5TTM \leq 12{,}000 + 60OT$$

Moving the decision variable for overtime to the left-hand side of the constraint provides the manufacturing capacity constraint:

$$BM + 3FCM + 2.5TCM + FTM + 1.5TTM - 60OT \leq 12{,}000$$

The complete formulation of the Janders make-or-buy problem with all decision variables greater than or equal to zero is

$$\text{Min} \quad 0.5BM + 0.6BP + 3.75FCM + 4FCP + 3.3TCM + 3.9TCP$$
$$+ 0.6FTM + 0.65FTP + 0.75TTM + 0.78TTP + 9OT$$

s.t.

BM				$+$	$BP =$	5000	Bases
	FCM			$+$	$FCP =$	3000	Financial cartridges
		TCM		$+$	$TCP =$	2000	Technician cartridges
			FTM	$+$	$FTP =$	3000	Financial tops
			$TTM +$		$TTP =$	2000	Technician tops
					$OT \leq$	50	Overtime hours

$$BM + 3FCM + 2.5TCM + FTM + 1.5TTM - 60OT \leq 12{,}000 \quad \text{Manufacturing capacity}$$

FIGURE 9.5   SENSITIVITY REPORT FOR THE JANDERS MAKE-OR-BUY PROBLEM

Variable Cells

Model Variable	Name	Final Value	Reduced Cost	Objective Coefficient	Allowable Increase	Allowable Decrease
BM	Base Make	5000.000	0.000	0.500	0.017	1E+30
BP	Base Purchase	0.000	0.017	0.600	1E+30	0.017
FCM	Fin. Cart. Make	666.667	0.000	3.750	0.100	0.050
FCP	Fin. Cart. Purchase	2333.333	0.000	4.000	0.050	0.100
TCM	Tech. Cart. Make	2000.000	0.000	3.300	0.392	1E+30
TCP	Tech. Cart. Purchase	0.000	0.392	3.900	1E+30	0.392
FTM	Fin. Top Make	0.000	0.033	0.600	1E+30	0.033
FTP	Fin. Top Purchase	3000.000	0.000	0.650	0.033	1E+30
TTM	Tech. Top Make	0.000	0.095	0.750	1E+30	0.095
TTP	Tech. Top Purchase	2000.000	0.000	0.780	0.095	1E+30
OT	Overtime Used	0.000	4.000	9.000	1E+30	4.000

WEB file

Janders

Constraints

Constraint Number	Name	Final Value	Shadow Price	Constraint R.H. Side	Allowable Increase	Allowable Decrease
1	Base Available	5000.0000	0.583	5000.000	2000.000	5000.000
2	Fin. Cart. Available	3000.0000	4.000	3000.000	1E+30	2333.333
3	Tech. Cart. Available	2000.0000	3.508	2000.000	800.000	2000.000
4	Fin. Top Available	3000.0000	0.650	3000.000	1E+30	3000.000
5	Tech. Top Available	2000.0000	0.780	2000.000	1E+30	2000.000
6	Overtime Time Used	0.0000	0.000	0.000	1E+30	50.000
7	Mfg. Time Time Used	12000.0000	−0.083	0.000	7000.000	2000.000

Since we cannot produce or purchase fractional amounts, in reality we would likely purchase 2334 units and produce 666 units of the Financial Manager catridges.

The sensitivity report based on Excel Solver for this 11-variable, 7-constraint linear program is shown in Figure 9.5. The optimal solution indicates that all 5000 bases (*BM*), 666.67 Financial Manager cartridges (*FCM*), and 2000 Technician cartridges (*TCM*) should be manufactured. The remaining 2333.333 Financial Manager cartridges (*FCP*), all the Financial Manager tops (*FTP*), and all Technician tops (*TTP*) should be purchased. No overtime manufacturing is necessary. This plan results in a total cost of 0.5(5000) + 0.6(0) + 3.75(666.67) + 4(2333.333) + 3.3(2000) + 3.9(0) + 0.6(0) + 0.65(3000) + 0.75(0) + 0.78(2000) + 9(0) = $24,443.33.

The same units of measure must be used for both the left-hand side and right-hand side of the constraint. In this case, minutes are used.

Sensitivity analysis provides some additional information about the unused overtime capacity. The Reduced Costs column shows that the overtime (*OT*) premium would have to decrease by $4 per hour before overtime production should be considered. That is, if the overtime premium is $9 − $4 = $5 or less, Janders may want to replace some of the purchased components with components manufactured on overtime.

The shadow price for the manufacturing capacity constraint time (constraint 7) is −0.083. This price indicates that an additional hour of manufacturing capacity is worth $0.083 per minute or ($0.083)(60) = $5 per hour. The right-hand-side range for constraint 7 shows that this conclusion is valid until the amount of regular time increases to 19,000 minutes, or 316.7 hours.

Sensitivity analysis also indicates that a change in prices charged by the outside suppliers can affect the optimal solution. For instance, the objective coefficient range for *BP* is 0.600 − 0.017 = 0.583 to no upper limit. If the purchase price for bases remains at $0.583

or more, the number of bases purchased (*BP*) will remain at zero. However, if the purchase price drops below $0.583, Janders should begin to purchase rather than manufacture the base component. Similar sensitivity analysis conclusions about the purchase price ranges can be drawn for the other components.

NOTES AND COMMENTS

1. The proper interpretation of the shadow price for manufacturing capacity (constraint 7) in the Janders problem is that an additional hour of manufacturing capacity is worth ($0.083)(60) = $5 per hour. Thus, the company should be willing to pay a premium of $5 per hour over and above the current regular time cost per hour, which is already included in the manufacturing cost of the product. Thus, if the regular time cost is $18 per hour, Janders should be willing to pay up to $18 + $5 = $23 per hour to obtain additional labor capacity.

Production Scheduling

One of the most important applications of linear programming deals with multiperiod planning such as production scheduling. The solution to a production scheduling problem enables the manager to establish an efficient low-cost production schedule for one or more products over several time periods (weeks or months). Essentially, a production scheduling problem can be viewed as a product-mix problem for each of several periods in the future. The manager must determine the production levels that will allow the company to meet product demand requirements, given limitations on production capacity, labor capacity, and storage space, while minimizing total production costs.

One advantage of using linear programming for production scheduling problems is that they recur. A production schedule must be established for the current month, then again for the next month, for the month after that, and so on. When looking at the problem each month, the production manager will find that, although demand for the products has changed, production times, production capacities, storage space limitations, and so on are roughly the same. Thus, the production manager is basically re-solving the same problem handled in previous months, and a general linear programming model of the production scheduling procedure may be frequently applied. Once the model has been formulated, the manager can simply supply the data—demand, capacities, and so on—for the given production period and use the linear programming model repeatedly to develop the production schedule. The Q.M. in Action, Optimizing Production of Flight Manuals at Jeppesen Sanderson, Inc., describes how linear programming is used to minimize the cost of producing weekly revisions to flight manuals.

Q.M. *in* ACTION

OPTIMIZING PRODUCTION OF FLIGHT MANUALS AT JEPPESEN SANDERSON, INC.*

Jeppesen Sanderson, Inc., manufactures and distributes flight manuals that contain safety information to more than 300,000 pilots and 4000 airlines. Every week Jeppe-

*Based on E. Katok, W. Tarantino, and R. Tiedman, "Improving Performance and Flexibility at Jeppesen: The World's Leading Aviation-Information Company," *Interfaces* (January/February 2001): 7–29.

sen mails between 5 and 30 million pages of chart revisions to 200,000 customers worldwide and receives about 1500 new orders each week. In the late 1990s, its customer service deteriorated as its existing production and supporting systems failed to keep up with this level of activity. To meet customer service goals, Jeppesen turned to optimization-based decision support tools for production planning.

(continued)

Jeppesen developed a large-scale linear program called Scheduler to minimize the cost of producing the weekly revisions. Model constraints included capacity constraints and numerous internal business rules. The model includes 250,000 variables and 40,000–50,000 constraints. Immediately after introducing the model, Jeppesen established a new record for the number of consecutive weeks with 100% on-time revisions. Scheduler decreased tardiness of revisions from approximately 9% to 3% and dramatically improved customer satisfaction. Even more importantly, Scheduler provided a model of the production system for Jeppesen to use in strategic economic analysis. Overall, the use of optimization techniques at Jeppesen resulted in cost reductions of nearly 10% and a 24% increase in profit.

Let us consider the case of the Bollinger Electronics Company, which produces two different electronic components for a major airplane engine manufacturer. The airplane engine manufacturer notifies the Bollinger sales office each quarter of its monthly requirements for components for each of the next three months. The monthly requirements for the components may vary considerably depending on the type of engine the airplane engine manufacturer is producing. The order shown in Table 9.7 has just been received for the next three-month period.

After the order is processed, a demand statement is sent to the production control department. The production control department must then develop a three-month production plan for the components. In arriving at the desired schedule, the production manager will want to identify the following:

1. Total production cost
2. Inventory holding cost
3. Change-in-production-level costs

In the remainder of this section, we show how to formulate a linear programming model of the production and inventory process for Bollinger Electronics to minimize the total cost.

To develop the model, we let x_{im} denote the production volume in units for product i in month m. Here $i = 1, 2$, and $m = 1, 2, 3$; $i = 1$ refers to component 322A, $i = 2$ refers to component 802B, $m = 1$ refers to April, $m = 2$ refers to May, and $m = 3$ refers to June. The purpose of the double subscript is to provide a more descriptive notation. We could simply use x_6 to represent the number of units of product 2 produced in month 3, but x_{23} is more descriptive, identifying directly the product and month represented by the variable.

If component 322A costs \$20 per unit produced and component 802B costs \$10 per unit produced, the total production cost part of the objective function is

$$\text{Total production cost} = 20x_{11} + 20x_{12} + 20x_{13} + 10x_{21} + 10x_{22} + 10x_{23}$$

Because the production cost per unit is the same each month, we don't need to include the production costs in the objective function; that is, regardless of the production schedule selected, the total production cost will remain the same. In other words, production costs are not relevant costs for the production scheduling decision under consideration. In cases in which the production cost per unit is expected to change each month, the variable

TABLE 9.7   THREE-MONTH DEMAND SCHEDULE FOR BOLLINGER ELECTRONICS COMPANY

Component	April	May	June
322A	1000	3000	5000
802B	1000	500	3000

production costs per unit per month must be included in the objective function. The solution for the Bollinger Electronics problem will be the same regardless of whether these costs are included; therefore, we included them so that the value of the linear programming objective function will include all the costs associated with the problem.

To incorporate the relevant inventory holding costs into the model, we let s_{im} denote the inventory level for product i at the end of month m. Bollinger determined that on a monthly basis, inventory holding costs are 1.5% of the cost of the product; that is, $(0.015)(\$20) = \$0.30$ per unit for component 322A and $(0.015)(\$10) = \$0.15$ per unit for component 802B. A common assumption made in using the linear programming approach to production scheduling is that monthly ending inventories are an acceptable approximation to the average inventory levels throughout the month. Making this assumption, we write the inventory holding cost portion of the objective function as

$$\text{Inventory holding cost} = 0.30s_{11} + 0.30s_{12} + 0.30s_{13} + 0.15s_{21} + 0.15s_{22} + 0.15s_{23}$$

To incorporate the costs of fluctuations in production levels from month to month, we need to define two additional variables:

$$I_m = \text{increase in the total production level necessary during month } m$$
$$D_m = \text{decrease in the total production level necessary during month } m$$

After estimating the effects of employee layoffs, turnovers, reassignment training costs, and other costs associated with fluctuating production levels, Bollinger estimates that the cost associated with increasing the production level for any month is $0.50 per unit increase. A similar cost associated with decreasing the production level for any month is $0.20 per unit. Thus, we write the third portion of the objective function as

$$\text{Change-in production-level costs} = 0.50I_1 + 0.50I_2 + 0.50I_3$$
$$+ 0.20D_1 + 0.20D_2 + 0.20D_3$$

Note that the cost associated with changes in production level is a function of the change in the total number of units produced in month m compared to the total number of units produced in month $m - 1$. In other production scheduling applications, fluctuations in production level might be measured in terms of machine-hours or labor-hours required rather than in terms of the total number of units produced.

Combining all three costs, the complete objective function becomes

$$\text{Min} \quad 20x_{11} + 20x_{12} + 20x_{13} + 10x_{21} + 10x_{22} + 10x_{23} + 0.30s_{11}$$
$$+ 0.30s_{12} + 0.30s_{13} + 0.15s_{21} + 0.15s_{22} + 0.15s_{23} + 0.50I_1$$
$$+ 0.50I_2 + 0.50I_3 + 0.20D_1 + 0.20D_2 + 0.20D_3$$

We now consider the constraints. First, we must guarantee that the schedule meets customer demand. Because the units shipped can come from the current month's production or from inventory carried over from previous months, the demand requirement takes the form

$$\begin{pmatrix} \text{Ending} \\ \text{inventory} \\ \text{from previous} \\ \text{month} \end{pmatrix} + \begin{pmatrix} \text{Current} \\ \text{production} \end{pmatrix} - \begin{pmatrix} \text{Ending} \\ \text{inventory} \\ \text{for this} \\ \text{month} \end{pmatrix} = \begin{pmatrix} \text{This month's} \\ \text{demand} \end{pmatrix}$$

Suppose that the inventories at the beginning of the three-month scheduling period were 500 units for component 322A and 200 units for component 802B. The demand for both products in the first month (April) was 1000 units, so the constraints for meeting demand in the first month become

$$500 + x_{11} - s_{11} = 1000$$
$$200 + x_{21} - s_{21} = 1000$$

Moving the constants to the right-hand side, we have

$$x_{11} - s_{11} = 500$$
$$x_{21} - s_{21} = 800$$

Similarly, we need demand constraints for both products in the second and third months. We write them as follows:

Month 2

$$s_{11} + x_{12} - s_{12} = 3000$$
$$s_{21} + x_{22} - s_{22} = 500$$

Month 3

$$s_{12} + x_{13} - s_{13} = 5000$$
$$s_{22} + x_{23} - s_{23} = 3000$$

If the company specifies a minimum inventory level at the end of the three-month period of at least 400 units of component 322A and at least 200 units of component 802B, we can add the constraints

$$s_{13} \geq 400$$
$$s_{23} \geq 200$$

Suppose that we have the additional information on machine, labor, and storage capacity shown in Table 9.8. Machine, labor, and storage space requirements are given in Table 9.9. To reflect these limitations, the following constraints are necessary:

TABLE 9.8   MACHINE, LABOR, AND STORAGE CAPACITIES FOR BOLLINGER ELECTRONICS

Month	Machine Capacity (hours)	Labor Capacity (hours)	Storage Capacity (square feet)
April	400	300	10,000
May	500	300	10,000
June	600	300	10,000

TABLE 9.9   MACHINE, LABOR, AND STORAGE REQUIREMENTS FOR COMPONENTS 322A AND 802B

Component	Machine (hours/unit)	Labor (hours/unit)	Storage (square feet/unit)
322A	0.10	0.05	2
802B	0.08	0.07	3

Machine Capacity

$$0.10x_{11} + 0.08x_{21} \leq 400 \quad \text{Month 1}$$
$$0.10x_{12} + 0.08x_{22} \leq 500 \quad \text{Month 2}$$
$$0.10x_{13} + 0.08x_{23} \leq 600 \quad \text{Month 3}$$

Labor Capacity

$$0.05x_{11} + 0.07x_{21} \leq 300 \quad \text{Month 1}$$
$$0.05x_{12} + 0.07x_{22} \leq 300 \quad \text{Month 2}$$
$$0.05x_{13} + 0.07x_{23} \leq 300 \quad \text{Month 3}$$

Storage Capacity

$$2s_{11} + 3s_{21} \leq 10,000 \quad \text{Month 1}$$
$$2s_{12} + 3s_{22} \leq 10,000 \quad \text{Month 2}$$
$$2s_{13} + 3s_{23} \leq 10,000 \quad \text{Month 3}$$

One final set of constraints must be added to guarantee that I_m and D_m will reflect the increase or decrease in the total production level for month m. Suppose that the production levels for March, the month before the start of the current production scheduling period, had been 1500 units of component 322A and 1000 units of component 802B for a total production level of $1500 + 1000 = 2500$ units. We can find the amount of the change in production for April from the relationship

$$\text{April production} - \text{March production} = \text{Change}$$

Using the April production variables, x_{11} and x_{21}, and the March production of 2500 units, we have

$$(x_{11} + x_{21}) - 2500 = \text{Change}$$

Note that the change can be positive or negative. A positive change reflects an increase in the total production level, and a negative change reflects a decrease in the total production level. We can use the increase in production for April, I_1, and the decrease in production for April, D_1, to specify the constraint for the change in total production for the month of April:

$$(x_{11} + x_{21}) - 2500 = I_1 - D_1$$

Of course, we cannot have an increase in production and a decrease in production during the same one-month period; thus, either I_1 or D_1 will be zero. If April requires 3000 units of production, $I_1 = 500$ and $D_1 = 0$. If April requires 2200 units of production, $I_1 = 0$ and $D_1 = 300$. This approach of denoting the change in production level as the difference between two nonnegative variables, I_1 and D_1, permits both positive and negative changes in the total production level. If a single variable (say, c_m) had been used to represent the change in production level, only positive changes would be possible because of the nonnegativity requirement.

Using the same approach in May and June (always subtracting the previous month's total production from the current month's total production), we obtain the constraints for the second and third months of the production scheduling period:

$$(x_{12} + x_{22}) - (x_{11} + x_{21}) = I_2 - D_2$$
$$(x_{13} + x_{23}) - (x_{12} + x_{22}) = I_3 - D_3$$

Placing the variables on the left-hand side and the constants on the right-hand side yields the complete set of what are commonly referred to as production-smoothing constraints:

$$x_{11} + x_{21} \qquad\qquad -I_1 + D_1 = 2500$$
$$-x_{11} - x_{21} + x_{12} + x_{22} \qquad\qquad -I_2 + D_2 = 0$$
$$-x_{12} - x_{22} + x_{13} + x_{23} - I_3 + D_3 = 0$$

The initially small, two-product, three-month scheduling problem has now developed into an 18-variable, 20-constraint linear programming problem. Note that in this problem we were concerned only with one type of machine process, one type of labor, and one type of storage area. Actual production scheduling problems usually involve several machine types, several labor grades, and/or several storage areas, requiring large-scale linear programs. For instance, a problem involving 100 products over a 12-month period could have more than 1000 variables and constraints.

Problem 19 involves a production scheduling application with labor-smoothing constraints.

Figure 9.6 shows the optimal solution to the Bollinger Electronics production scheduling problem. Table 9.10 contains a portion of the managerial report based on the optimal solution.

Consider the monthly variation in the production and inventory schedule shown in Table 9.10. Recall that the inventory cost for component 802B is one-half the inventory

TABLE 9.10   MINIMUM COST PRODUCTION SCHEDULE INFORMATION
FOR THE BOLLINGER ELECTRONICS PROBLEM

Activity	April	May	June
Production			
Component 322A	500	3200	5200
Component 802B	2500	2000	0
Totals	3000	5200	5200
Ending inventory			
Component 322A	0	200	400
Component 802B	1700	3200	200
Machine usage			
Scheduled hours	250	480	520
Slack capacity hours	150	20	80
Labor usage			
Scheduled hours	200	300	260
Slack capacity hours	100	0	40
Storage usage			
Scheduled storage	5100	10,000	1400
Slack capacity	4900	0	8600
Total production, inventory, and production-smoothing cost = $225,295			

FIGURE 9.6 SENSITIVITY REPORT FOR THE BOLLINGER ELECTRONICS PROBLEM

Variable Cells

Model Variable	Name	Final Value	Reduced Cost	Objective Coefficient	Allowable Increase	Allowable Decrease
X11	322A April Production	500.000	0.000	20.000	1E+30	0.172
X12	322A May Production	3200.000	0.000	20.000	0.093	0.100
X13	322A June Production	5200.000	0.000	20.000	0.100	0.093
S11	322A April Ending Inv	0.000	0.172	0.300	1E+30	0.172
S12	322A May Ending Inv	200.000	0.000	0.300	0.093	0.100
S13	322A June Ending Inv	400.000	0.000	0.300	1E+30	20.728
X21	802B April Production	2500.000	0.000	10.000	0.130	0.050
X22	802B May Production	2000.000	0.000	10.000	0.050	0.130
X23	802B June Production	0.000	0.128	10.000	1E+30	0.128
S21	802B April Ending Inv	1700.000	0.000	0.150	0.130	0.050
S22	802B May Ending Inv	3200.000	0.000	0.150	0.128	10.450
S23	802B June Ending Inv	200.000	0.000	0.150	1E+30	10.450
I1	Increase April	500.000	0.000	0.500	0.130	0.050
I2	Increase May	2200.000	0.000	0.500	0.033	0.192
I3	Increase June	0.000	0.072	0.500	1E+30	0.072
D1	Decrease April	0.000	0.700	0.200	1E+30	0.700
D2	Decrease May	0.000	0.700	0.200	1E+30	0.700
D3	Decrease June	0.000	0.628	0.200	1E+30	0.628

WEB file

Bollinger

Constraints

Constraint Number	Name	Final Value	Shadow Price	Constraint R.H. Side	Allowable Increase	Allowable Decrease
1	322A/April Balance Equation	1000.000	20.000	1000.000	1500.000	500.000
2	802B/April Balance Equation	1000.000	10.000	1000.000	1428.571	500.000
3	322A/May Balance Equation	3000.000	20.128	3000.000	600.000	0.000
4	802B/May Balance Equation	500.000	10.150	500.000	1428.571	500.000
5	322A/June Balance Equation	5000.000	20.428	5000.000	0.000	257.143
6	802B/June Balance Equation	3000.000	10.300	3000.000	0.000	500.000
7	322A Ending Inventory	400.000	20.728	400.000	0.000	257.143
8	802B Ending Inventory	200.000	10.450	200.000	0.000	200.000
9	Mach/Apr Used	250.000	0.000	400.000	1E+30	150.000
10	Mach/May Used	480.000	0.000	500.000	1E+30	20.000
11	Mach/June Used	520.000	0.000	600.000	1E+30	80.000
12	Labor/Apr Used	200.000	0.000	300.000	1E+30	100.000
13	Labor/May Used	300.000	−1.111	300.000	18.000	1.00044E-13
14	Labor/June Used	260.000	0.000	300.000	1E+30	40.000
15	Storage/Apr Used	5100.000	0.000	10000.000	1E+30	4900.000
16	Storage/May Used	10000.000	0.000	10000.000	1E+30	0.000
17	Storage/June Used	1400.000	0.000	10000.000	1E+30	8600.000
18	April Difference	500.000	−0.500	0.000	500.000	1E+30
19	May Difference	2200.000	−0.500	0.000	2200.000	1E+30
20	June Difference	0.000	−0.428	0.000	257.143	0.000

Linear programming models for production scheduling are often very large. Thousands of decision variables and constraints are necessary when the problem involves numerous products, machines, and time periods. Data collection for large-scale models can be more time-consuming than either the formulation of the model or the development of the computer solution.

cost for component 322A. Therefore, as might be expected, component 802B is produced heavily in the first month (April) and then held in inventory for the demand that will occur in future months. Component 322A tends to be produced when needed, and only small amounts are carried in inventory.

The costs of increasing and decreasing the total production volume tend to smooth the monthly variations. In fact, the minimum-cost schedule calls for a 500-unit increase in total production in April and a 2200-unit increase in total production in May. The May production level of 5200 units is then maintained during June.

The machine usage section of the report shows ample machine capacity in all three months. However, labor capacity is at full utilization in the month of May (see constraint 13 in Figure 9.6). The shadow price shows that an additional hour of labor capacity in May will decrease the optimal cost by approximately $1.11.

A linear programming model of a two-product, three-month production system can provide valuable information in terms of identifying a minimum-cost production schedule. In larger production systems, where the number of variables and constraints is too large to track manually, linear programming models can provide a significant advantage in developing cost-saving production schedules. The Q.M. in Action, Optimizing Production, Inventory, and Distribution at the Kellogg Company, illustrates the use of a large-scale multiperiod linear program for production planning and distribution.

Q.M. *in* ACTION

OPTIMIZING PRODUCTION, INVENTORY, AND DISTRIBUTION AT THE KELLOGG COMPANY*

The Kellogg Company is the largest cereal producer in the world and a leading producer of convenience foods, such as Kellogg's Pop-Tarts and Nutri-Grain cereal bars. Kellogg produces more than 40 different cereals at plants in 19 countries, on six continents. The company markets its products in more than 160 countries and employs more than 15,600 people in its worldwide organization. In the cereal business alone, Kellogg coordinates the production of about 80 products using a total of approximately 90 production lines and 180 packaging lines.

Kellogg has a long history of using linear programming for production planning and distribution. The

*Based on G. Brown, J. Keegan, B. Vigus, and K. Wood, "The Kellogg Company Optimizes Production, Inventory, and Distribution," *Interfaces* (November/December 2001): 1–15.

Kellogg Planning System (KPS) is a large-scale, multiperiod linear program. The operational version of KPS makes production, packaging, inventory, and distribution decisions on a weekly basis. The primary objective of the system is to minimize the total cost of meeting estimated demand; to deal with constraints involving processing line capacities and packaging line capacities; and to satisfy safety stock requirements.

A tactical version of KPS helps to establish plant budgets and make capacity-expansion and consolidation decisions on a monthly basis. The tactical version was recently used to guide a consolidation of production capacity that resulted in projected savings of $35 to $40 million per year. Because of the success Kellogg has had using KPS in its North American operations, the company is now introducing KPS into Latin America and is studying the development of a global KPS model.

Workforce Assignment

Workforce assignment problems frequently occur when production managers must make decisions involving staffing requirements for a given planning period. Workforce assignments often have some flexibility, and at least some personnel can be assigned to more than one department or work center. Such is the case when employees have been cross-trained on two or more jobs or, for instance, when sales personnel can be transferred between stores.

In the following application, we show how linear programming can be used to determine not only an optimal product mix, but also an optimal workforce assignment.

McCormick Manufacturing Company produces two products with contributions to profit per unit of \$10 and \$9, respectively. The labor requirements per unit produced and the total hours of labor available from personnel assigned to each of four departments are shown in Table 9.11. Assuming that the number of hours available in each department is fixed, we can formulate McCormick's problem as a standard product-mix linear program with the following decision variables:

$$P_1 = \text{units of product 1}$$
$$P_2 = \text{units of product 2}$$

The linear program is

$$\text{Max} \quad 10P_1 + 9P_2$$
$$\text{s.t.}$$
$$0.65P_1 + 0.95P_2 \leq 6500$$
$$0.45P_1 + 0.85P_2 \leq 6000$$
$$1.00P_1 + 0.70P_2 \leq 7000$$
$$0.15P_1 + 0.30P_2 \leq 1400$$
$$P_1 P_2 \geq 0$$

The answer report to the linear programming model is shown in Figure 9.7. The product mix calls for approximately 5744 units of product 1, 1795 units of product 2, and a total profit of \$73,590. With this optimal solution, departments 3 and 4 are operating at capacity, and departments 1 and 2 have a slack of approximately 1062 and 1890 hours, respectively. We would anticipate that the product mix would change and that the total profit would increase if the workforce assignment could be revised so that the slack, or unused hours, in departments 1 and 2 could be transferred to the departments currently working at capacity. However, the production manager may be uncertain as to how the workforce should be reallocated among the four departments. Let us expand the linear programming model to include decision variables that will help determine the optimal workforce assignment in addition to the profit-maximizing product mix.

TABLE 9.11   DEPARTMENTAL LABOR-HOURS PER UNIT AND TOTAL HOURS AVAILABLE FOR THE MCCORMICK MANUFACTURING COMPANY

	Labor-Hours per Unit		
Department	Product 1	Product 2	Total Hours Available
1	0.65	0.95	6500
2	0.45	0.85	6000
3	1.00	0.70	7000
4	0.15	0.30	1400

FIGURE 9.7 ANSWER REPORT FOR THE McCORMICK MANUFACTURING COMPANY PROBLEM WITH NO WORKFORCE TRANSFERS PERMITTED

WEB file

McCormick

Objective Cell (Max)

Name	Original Value	Final Value
Max Profit	0.000	73589.744

Variable Cells

Model Variable	Name	Original Value	Final Value	Integer
P1	Product 1	0.000	5743.590	Contin
P2	Product 2	0.000	1794.872	Contin

Constraints

Constraint Number	Name	Cell Value	Status	Slack
1	Dept 1 Hours	5438.462	Not Binding	1061.538
2	Dept 2 Hours	4110.256	Not Binding	1889.744
3	Dept 3 Hours	7000.000	Binding	0.000
4	Dept 4 Hours	1400.000	Binding	0.000

Suppose that McCormick has a cross-training program that enables some employees to be transferred between departments. By taking advantage of the cross-training skills, a limited number of employees and labor-hours may be transferred from one department to another. For example, suppose that the cross-training permits transfers as shown in Table 9.12. Row 1 of this table shows that some employees assigned to department 1 have cross-training skills that permit them to be transferred to department 2 or 3. The right-hand column shows that, for the current production planning period, a maximum of 400 hours can be transferred from department 1. Similar cross-training transfer capabilities and capacities are shown for departments 2, 3, and 4.

When workforce assignments are flexible, we do not automatically know how many hours of labor should be assigned to or be transferred from each department. We need to add decision variables to the linear programming model to account for such changes.

The right-hand sides are now treated as decision variables.

b_i = the labor-hours allocated to department i for $i = 1, 2, 3,$ and 4

t_{ij} = the labor-hours transferred from department i to department j

TABLE 9.12 CROSS-TRAINING ABILITY AND CAPACITY INFORMATION

From Department	Cross-Training Transfers Permitted to Department				Maximum Hours Transferable
	1	2	3	4	
1	—	yes	yes	—	400
2	—	—	yes	yes	800
3	—	—	—	yes	100
4	yes	yes	—	—	200

With the addition of decision variables b_1, b_2, b_3, and b_4, we write the capacity restrictions for the four departments as follows:

$$0.65P_1 + 0.95P_2 \leq b_1$$
$$0.45P_1 + 0.85P_2 \leq b_2$$
$$1.00P_1 + 0.70P_2 \leq b_3$$
$$0.15P_1 + 0.30P_2 \leq b_4$$

Because b_1, b_2, b_3, and b_4 are now decision variables, we follow the standard practice of placing these variables on the left side of the inequalities, and the first four constraints of the linear programming model become

$$0.65P_1 + 0.95P_2 - b_1 \qquad\qquad\qquad \leq 0$$
$$0.45P_1 + 0.85P_2 \qquad - b_2 \qquad\qquad \leq 0$$
$$1.00P_1 + 0.70P_2 \qquad\qquad - b_3 \qquad \leq 0$$
$$0.15P_1 + 0.30P_2 \qquad\qquad\qquad - b_4 \leq 0$$

The labor-hours ultimately allocated to each department must be determined by a series of labor balance equations, or constraints, that include the number of hours initially assigned to each department plus the number of hours transferred into the department minus the number of hours transferred out of the department. Using department 1 as an example, we determine the workforce allocation as follows:

$$b_1 = \begin{pmatrix} \text{Hours} \\ \text{initially in} \\ \text{department 1} \end{pmatrix} + \begin{pmatrix} \text{Hours} \\ \text{transferred into} \\ \text{department 1} \end{pmatrix} - \begin{pmatrix} \text{Hours} \\ \text{transferred out of} \\ \text{department 1} \end{pmatrix}$$

Table 9.11 shows 6500 hours initially assigned to department 1. We use the transfer decision variables t_{i1} to denote transfers into department 1 and t_{1j} to denote transfers from department 1. Table 9.12 shows that the cross-training capabilities involving department 1 are restricted to transfers from department 4 (variable t_{41}) and transfers to either department 2 or department 3 (variables t_{12} and t_{13}). Thus, we can express the total workforce allocation for department 1 as

$$b_1 = 6500 + t_{41} - t_{12} - t_{13}$$

Moving the decision variables for the workforce transfers to the left-hand side, we have the labor balance equation or constraint

$$b_1 - t_{41} + t_{12} + t_{13} = 6500$$

This form of constraint will be needed for each of the four departments. Thus, the following labor balance constraints for departments 2, 3, and 4 would be added to the model:

$$b_2 - t_{12} - t_{42} + t_{23} + t_{24} = 6000$$
$$b_3 - t_{13} - t_{23} + t_{34} \qquad = 7000$$
$$b_4 - t_{24} - t_{34} + t_{41} + t_{42} = 1400$$

Finally, Table 9.12 shows the number of hours that may be transferred from each department is limited, indicating that a transfer capacity constraint must be added for each of the four departments. The additional constraints are

$$t_{12} + t_{13} \leq 400$$
$$t_{13} + t_{24} \leq 800$$
$$t_{34} \leq 100$$
$$t_{41} + t_{42} \leq 200$$

The complete linear programming model has two product decision variables (P_1 and P_2), four department workforce assignment variables (b_1, b_2, b_3, and b_4), seven transfer variables (t_{12}, t_{13}, t_{23}, t_{24}, t_{34}, t_{41}, and t_{42}), and 12 constraints. Figure 9.8 shows the optimal solution to this linear program based on Excel Solver.

FIGURE 9.8 ANSWER REPORT FOR THE MODIFIED McCORMICK MANUFACTURING COMPANY PROBLEM

Objective Cell (Max)

Name	Original Value	Final Value
Max Profit	0.000	84011.299

Variable Cells

Model Name	Name	Original Value	Final Value	Integer
P1	Product 1	0.000	6824.859	Contin
P2	Product 2	0.000	1751.412	Contin
B1	Dept 1 Hours Allocated	0.000	6100.000	Contin
B2	Dept 2 Hours Allocated	0.000	5200.000	Contin
B3	Dept 3 Hours Allocated	0.000	8050.847	Contin
B4	Dept 4 Hours Allocated	0.000	1549.153	Contin
T12	From 1 To 2	0.000	0.000	Contin
T13	From 1 To 3	0.000	400.000	Contin
T23	From 2 To 3	0.000	650.847	Contin
T24	From 2 To 4	0.000	149.153	Contin
T34	From 3 To 4	0.000	0.000	Contin
T41	From 4 To 1	0.000	0.000	Contin
T42	From 4 To 2	0.000	0.000	Contin

Constraints

Constraint Number	Name	Cell Value	Status	Slack
1	Dept 1 Hours	6100.000	Binding	0.000
2	Dept 2 Hours	4559.887	Not Binding	640.113
3	Dept 3 Hours	8050.847	Binding	0.000
4	Dept 4 Hours	1549.153	Binding	0.000
5	Dept 1 Hours Allocated	6100.000	Binding	0.000
6	Dept 2 Hours Allocated	5200.000	Binding	0.000
7	Dept 3 Hours Allocated	8050.847	Binding	0.000
8	Dept 4 Hours Allocated	1549.153	Binding	0.000
9	From 1 Total	400.000	Binding	0.000
10	From 2 Total	800.000	Binding	0.000
11	From 3 Total	0.000	Not Binding	100.000
12	From 4 Total	0.000	Not Binding	200.000

*Variations in the workforce
assignment model could
be used in situations such
as allocating raw material
resources to products,
allocating machine time
to products, and allocating
salesforce time to stores
or sales territories.*

McCormick's profit can be increased by $84,011 − $73,590 = $10,421 by taking advantage of cross-training and workforce transfers. The optimal product mix of 6825 units of product 1 and 1751 units of product 2 can be achieved if $t_{13} = 400$ hours are transferred from department 1 to department 3; $t_{23} = 651$ hours are transferred from department 2 to department 3; and $t_{24} = 149$ hours are transferred from department 2 to department 4. The resulting workforce assignments for departments 1–4 would provide 6100, 5200, 8051, and 1549 hours, respectively, after rounding.

If a manager has the flexibility to assign personnel to different departments, reduced workforce idle time, improved workforce utilization, and improved profit should result. The linear programming model in this section automatically assigns employees and labor-hours to the departments in the most profitable manner.

Blending Problems

Blending problems arise whenever a manager must decide how to blend two or more resources to produce one or more products. In these situations, the resources contain one or more essential ingredients that must be blended into final products that will contain specific percentages of each. In most of these applications, then, management must decide how much of each resource to purchase to satisfy product specifications and product demands at minimum cost.

Blending problems occur frequently in the petroleum industry (e.g., blending crude oil to produce different octane gasolines), the chemical industry (e.g., blending chemicals to produce fertilizers and weed killers), and the food industry (e.g., blending ingredients to produce soft drinks and soups). In this section we illustrate how to apply linear programming to a blending problem in the petroleum industry.

The Grand Strand Oil Company produces regular and premium gasoline for independent service stations in the southeastern United States. The Grand Strand refinery manufactures the gasoline products by blending three petroleum components. The gasolines are sold at different prices, and the petroleum components have different costs. The firm wants to determine how to mix or blend the three components into the two gasoline products and maximize profits.

Data available show that regular gasoline can be sold for $2.90 per gallon and premium gasoline for $3.00 per gallon. For the current production planning period, Grand Strand can obtain the three petroleum components at the cost per gallon and in the quantities shown in Table 9.13.

Product specifications for the regular and premium gasolines restrict the amounts of each component that can be used in each gasoline product. Table 9.14 lists the product specifications. Current commitments to distributors require Grand Strand to produce at least 10,000 gallons of regular gasoline.

TABLE 9.13   PETROLEUM COST AND SUPPLY FOR THE GRAND STRAND
BLENDING PROBLEM

Petroleum Component	Cost/Gallon	Maximum Available
1	$2.50	5,000 gallons
2	$2.60	10,000 gallons
3	$2.84	10,000 gallons

TABLE 9.14   PRODUCT SPECIFICATIONS FOR THE GRAND STRAND
BLENDING PROBLEM

Product	Specifications
Regular gasoline	At most 30% component 1
	At least 40% component 2
	At most 20% component 3
Premium gasoline	At least 25% component 1
	At most 45% component 2
	At least 30% component 3

The Grand Strand blending problem is to determine how many gallons of each component should be used in the regular gasoline blend and how many should be used in the premium gasoline blend. The optimal blending solution should maximize the firm's profit, subject to the constraints on the available petroleum supplies shown in Table 9.13, the product specifications shown in Table 9.14, and the required 10,000 gallons of regular gasoline. We define the decision variables as

$$x_{ij} = \text{gallons of component } i \text{ used in gasoline } j,$$
$$\text{where } i = 1, 2, \text{ or } 3 \text{ for components 1, 2, or 3,}$$
$$\text{and } j = r \text{ if regular or } j = p \text{ if premium}$$

The six decision variables are

$$x_{1r} = \text{gallons of component 1 in regular gasoline}$$
$$x_{2r} = \text{gallons of component 2 in regular gasoline}$$
$$x_{3r} = \text{gallons of component 3 in regular gasoline}$$
$$x_{1p} = \text{gallons of component 1 in premium gasoline}$$
$$x_{2p} = \text{gallons of component 2 in premium gasoline}$$
$$x_{3p} = \text{gallons of component 3 in premium gasoline}$$

The total number of gallons of each type of gasoline produced is the sum of the number of gallons produced using each of the three petroleum components.

Total Gallons Produced

$$\text{Regular gasoline} = x_{1r} + x_{2r} + x_{3r}$$
$$\text{Premium gasoline} = x_{1p} + x_{2p} + x_{3p}$$

The total gallons of each petroleum component are computed in a similar fashion.

Total Petroleum Component Use

$$\text{Component 1} = x_{1r} + x_{1p}$$
$$\text{Component 2} = x_{2r} + x_{2p}$$
$$\text{Component 3} = x_{3r} + x_{3p}$$

We develop the objective function of maximizing the profit contribution by identifying the difference between the total revenue from both gasolines and the total cost of the three petroleum components. By multiplying the $2.90 per gallon price by the total gallons of regular gasoline, the $3.00 per gallon price by the total gallons of premium gasoline, and the component cost per gallon figures in Table 9.13 by the total gallons of each component used, we obtain the objective function:

$$\text{Max} \quad 2.90(x_{1r} + x_{2r} + x_{3r}) + 3.00(x_{1p} + x_{2p} + x_{3p}) \\ - 2.50(x_{1r} + x_{1p}) - 2.60(x_{2r} + x_{2p}) - 2.84(x_{3r} + x_{3p})$$

When we combine terms, the objective function becomes

$$\text{Max} \quad 0.40x_{1r} + 0.30x_{2r} + 0.06x_{3r} + 0.50x_{1p} + 0.40x_{2p} + 0.16x_{3p}$$

The limitations on the availability of the three petroleum components are

$$\begin{aligned} x_{1r} + x_{1p} &\leq 5{,}000 \quad \text{Component 1} \\ x_{2r} + x_{2p} &\leq 10{,}000 \quad \text{Component 2} \\ x_{3r} + x_{3p} &\leq 10{,}000 \quad \text{Component 3} \end{aligned}$$

Six constraints are now required to meet the product specifications stated in Table 9.14. The first specification states that component 1 can account for no more than 30% of the total gallons of regular gasoline produced. That is,

$$x_{1r} \leq 0.30(x_{1r} + x_{2r} + x_{3r})$$

Rewriting this constraint with the variables on the left-hand side and a constant on the right-hand side yields

$$0.70x_{1r} - 0.30x_{2r} - 0.30x_{3r} \leq 0$$

The second product specification listed in Table 9.14 becomes

$$x_{2r} \geq 0.40(x_{1r} + x_{2r} + x_{3r})$$

and thus

$$-0.40x_{1r} + 0.60x_{2r} - 0.40x_{3r} \geq 0$$

Similarly, we write the four remaining blending specifications listed in Table 9.14 as

$$\begin{aligned} -0.20x_{1r} - 0.20x_{2r} + 0.80x_{3r} &\leq 0 \\ +0.75x_{1p} - 0.25x_{2p} - 0.25x_{3p} &\geq 0 \\ -0.45x_{1p} + 0.55x_{2p} - 0.45x_{3p} &\leq 0 \\ -0.30x_{1p} - 0.30x_{2p} + 0.70x_{3p} &\geq 0 \end{aligned}$$

The constraint for at least 10,000 gallons of regular gasoline is

$$x_{1r} + x_{2r} + x_{3r} \geq 10{,}000$$

The complete linear programming model with 6 decision variables and 10 constraints is

$$\text{Max} \quad 0.40x_{1r} + 0.30x_{2r} + 0.06x_{3r} + 0.50x_{1p} + 0.40x_{2p} + 0.16x_{3p}$$

s.t.

$$
\begin{array}{rcl}
x_{1r} + x_{1p} & \leq & 5{,}000 \\
x_{2r} + x_{2p} & \leq & 10{,}000 \\
x_{3r} + x_{3p} & \leq & 10{,}000 \\
0.70x_{1r} - 0.30x_{2r} - 0.30x_{3r} & \leq & 0 \\
-0.40x_{1r} + 0.60x_{2r} - 0.40x_{3r} & \geq & 0 \\
-0.20x_{1r} - 0.20x_{2r} + 0.80x_{3r} & \leq & 0 \\
0.75x_{1p} - 0.25x_{2p} - 0.25x_{3p} & \geq & 0 \\
-0.45x_{1p} + 0.55x_{2p} - 0.45x_{3p} & \leq & 0 \\
-0.30x_{1p} - 0.30x_{2p} + 0.70x_{3p} & \geq & 0 \\
x_{1r} + x_{2r} + x_{3r} & \geq & 10{,}000 \\
\end{array}
$$

$$x_{1r}, x_{2r}, x_{3r}, x_{1p}, x_{2p}, x_{3p} \geq 0$$

The optimal solution to the Grand Strand blending problem is shown in Figure 9.9. The optimal solution, which provides a profit of $7100, is summarized in Table 9.15. The optimal blending strategy shows that 10,000 gallons of regular gasoline should be produced. The regular gasoline will be manufactured as a blend of 8000 gallons of component 2 and 2000 gallons of component 3. The 15,000 gallons of premium gasoline will be manufactured as a blend of 5000 gallons of component 1, 2000 gallons of component 2, and 8000 gallons of component 3.

Try Problem 15 as another example of a blending model.

The interpretation of the slack and surplus variables associated with the product specification constraints (constraints 4–9) in Figure 9.9 needs some clarification. If the constraint is a $\leq$ constraint, the value of the slack variable can be interpreted as the gallons of component use below the maximum amount of the component use specified by the constraint. For example, the slack of 3000.000 for constraint 4 shows that component 1 use is 3000 gallons below the maximum amount of component 1 that could have been used in the production of 10,000 gallons of regular gasoline. If the product specification constraint is a $\geq$ constraint, a surplus variable shows the gallons of component use above the minimum amount of component use specified by the blending constraint. For example, the surplus of 4000.000 for constraint 5 shows that component 2 use is 4000 gallons above the minimum amount of component 2 that must be used in the production of 10,000 gallons of regular gasoline.

TABLE 9.15 GRAND STRAND GASOLINE BLENDING SOLUTION

	Gallons of Component (percentage)			
Gasoline	**Component 1**	**Component 2**	**Component 3**	**Total**
Regular	0 (0.0%)	8000 (80%)	2000 (20%)	10,000
Premium	5000 (33⅓%)	2000 (13⅓%)	8000 (53⅓%)	15,000

FIGURE 9.9 ANSWER REPORT FOR THE GRAND STRAND BLENDING PROBLEM

Objective Cell (Max)

Name	Original Value	Final Value
Max Profit	0.000	7100.000

Variable Cells

Model Variable	Name	Original Value	Final Value	Integer
X1R	Regular Component 1	0.000	0.000	Contin
X2R	Regular Component 2	0.000	8000.000	Contin
X3R	Regular Component 3	0.000	2000.000	Contin
X1P	Premium Component 1	0.000	5000.000	Contin
X2P	Premium Component 2	0.000	2000.000	Contin
X3P	Premium Component 3	0.000	8000.000	Contin

Constraints

Constraint Number	Name	Cell Value	Status	Slack
1	Total Component 1	5000.000	Binding	0.000
2	Total Component 2	10000.000	Binding	0.000
3	Total Component 3	10000.000	Binding	0.000
4	Max Comp 1 Regular	0.000	Not Binding	3000.000
5	Min Comp 2 Regular	8000.000	Not Binding	4000.000
6	Max Comp 3 Regular	2000.000	Binding	0.000
7	Min Comp 1 Premium	5000.000	Not Binding	1250.000
8	Max Comp 2 Premium	2000.000	Not Binding	4000.000
9	Min Comp 3 Premium	8000.000	Not Binding	3500.000
10	Regular Total	10000.000	Binding	0.000

NOTES AND COMMENTS

1. A convenient way to define the decision variables in a blending problem is to use a matrix in which the rows correspond to the raw materials and the columns correspond to the final products. For example, in the Grand Strand blending problem, we define the decision variables as follows:

This approach has two advantages: (1) It provides a systematic way to define the decision variables for any blending problem; and (2) it provides a visual image of the decision variables in terms of how they are related to the raw materials, products, and each other.

		Final Products	
		Regular Gasoline	**Premium Gasoline**
Raw Materials	**Component 1**	x_{1r}	x_{1p}
	Component 2	x_{2r}	x_{2p}
	Component 3	x_{3r}	x_{3p}

Summary

In this chapter we presented a broad range of applications that demonstrate how to use linear programming to assist in the decision-making process. We formulated and solved problems from marketing, finance, and operations management, and interpreted the computer output.

Many of the illustrations presented in this chapter are scaled-down versions of actual situations in which linear programming has been applied. In real-world applications, the problem may not be so concisely stated, the data for the problem may not be as readily available, and the problem most likely will involve numerous decision variables and/or constraints. However, a thorough study of the applications in this chapter is a good place to begin in applying linear programming to real problems.

Problems

Note: The following problems have been designed to give you an understanding and appreciation of the broad range of problems that can be formulated as linear programs. You should be able to formulate a linear programming model for each of the problems. However, you will need access to a linear programming computer package to develop the solutions and make the requested interpretations.

1. The Westchester Chamber of Commerce periodically sponsors public service seminars and programs. Currently, promotional plans are under way for this year's program. Advertising alternatives include television, radio, and online. Audience estimates, costs, and maximum media usage limitations are as shown:

Constraint	Television	Radio	Online
Audience per advertisement	100,000	18,000	40,000
Cost per advertisement	$2000	$300	$600
Maximum media usage	10	20	10

To ensure a balanced use of advertising media, radio advertisements must not exceed 50% of the total number of advertisements authorized. In addition, television should account for at least 10% of the total number of advertisements authorized.
   a. If the promotional budget is limited to $18,200, how many commercial messages should be run on each medium to maximize total audience contact? What is the allocation of the budget among the three media, and what is the total audience reached?
   b. By how much would audience contact increase if an extra $100 were allocated to the promotional budget?

2. The management of Hartman Company is trying to determine the amount of each of two products to produce over the coming planning period. The following information concerns labor availability, labor utilization, and product profitability:

Department	Product (hours/unit) 1	Product (hours/unit) 2	Labor-Hours Available
A	1.00	0.35	100
B	0.30	0.20	36
C	0.20	0.50	50
Profit contribution/unit	$30.00	$15.00	

   a. Develop a linear programming model of the Hartman Company problem. Solve the model to determine the optimal production quantities of products 1 and 2.

b. In computing the profit contribution per unit, management doesn't deduct labor costs because they are considered fixed for the upcoming planning period. However, suppose that overtime can be scheduled in some of the departments. Which departments would you recommend scheduling for overtime? How much would you be willing to pay per hour of overtime in each department?

c. Suppose that 10, 6, and 8 hours of overtime may be scheduled in departments A, B, and C, respectively. The cost per hour of overtime is $18 in department A, $22.50 in department B, and $12 in department C. Formulate a linear programming model that can be used to determine the optimal production quantities if overtime is made available. What are the optimal production quantities, and what is the revised total contribution to profit? How much overtime do you recommend using in each department? What is the increase in the total contribution to profit if overtime is used?

3. The employee credit union at State University is planning the allocation of funds for the coming year. The credit union makes four types of loans to its members. In addition, the credit union invests in risk-free securities to stabilize income. The various revenue-producing investments together with annual rates of return are as follows:

Type of Loan/Investment	Annual Rate of Return (%)
Automobile loans	8
Furniture loans	10
Other secured loans	11
Signature loans	12
Risk-free securities	9

The credit union will have $2 million available for investment during the coming year. State laws and credit union policies impose the following restrictions on the composition of the loans and investments:

- Risk-free securities may not exceed 30% of the total funds available for investment.
- Signature loans may not exceed 10% of the funds invested in all loans (automobile, furniture, other secured, and signature loans).
- Furniture loans plus other secured loans may not exceed the automobile loans.
- Other secured loans plus signature loans may not exceed the funds invested in risk-free securities.

How should the $2 million be allocated to each of the loan/investment alternatives to maximize total annual return? What is the projected total annual return?

4. The Bahama Nut Company sells three different half-pound bags of peanut mixes: Party Nuts, Mixed, and Premium Mix. These generate per-bag revenue of $1.00, $2.10, and $3.63, respectively. The tables below show the makeup of each mix, the available ingredients for the next week, and the cost of each ingredient.

		Ingredients		
	Peanuts	**Cashews**	**Brazil Nuts**	**Hazelnuts**
Party Nuts	100%			
Mixed	55%	25%	10%	10%
Premium Mix		40%	20%	40%

	Pounds Available	**Cost per Pound**
Peanuts	500	$1.50
Cashews	180	$5.35
Brazil nuts	100	$6.25
Hazelnuts	80	$7.50

Develop a linear programming model to help Bahama determine how many bags of each type to produce to maximize contribution to profit. How many bags of each type should be produced and what is the maximal profit? Which constraints are binding?

5. Kilgore's Deli is a small delicatessen located near a major university. Kilgore's does a large walk-in carry-out lunch business. The deli offers two luncheon chili specials, Wimpy and Dial 911. At the beginning of the day, Kilgore needs to decide how much of each special to make (he always sells out of whatever he makes). The profit on one serving of Wimpy is $.45, on one serving of Dial 911, $.58. Each serving of Wimpy requires .25 pound of beef, .25 cup of onions, and 5 ounces of Kilgore's special sauce. Each serving of Dial 911 requires .25 pound of beef, .4 cup of onions, 2 ounces of Kilgore's special sauce, and 5 ounces of hot sauce. Today, Kilgore has 20 pounds of beef, 15 cups of onions, 88 ounces of Kilgore's special sauce, and 60 ounces of hot sauce on hand.

   a. Develop a linear programming model that will tell Kilgore how many servings of Wimpy and Dial 911 to make in order to maximize his profit today.
   b. Find an optimal solution.
   c. What is the shadow price for special sauce? Interpret the shadow price.
   d. Increase the amount of special sauce available by 1 ounce and re-solve. Does the solution confirm the answer to part (c)? Give the new solution.

6. G. Kunz and Sons, Inc., manufactures two products used in the heavy equipment industry. Both products require manufacturing operations in two departments. The following are the production time (in hours) and profit contribution figures for the two products:

		Labor-Hours	
Product	**Profit per Unit**	**Dept. A**	**Dept. B**
1	$25	6	12
2	$20	8	10

   For the coming production period, Kunz has available a total of 900 hours of labor that can be allocated to either of the two departments. Find the production plan and labor allocation (hours assigned in each department) that will maximize the total contribution to profit.

7. As part of the settlement for a class action lawsuit, Hoxworth Corporation must provide sufficient cash to make the following annual payments (in thousands of dollars):

Year	1	2	3	4	5	6
Payment	190	215	240	285	315	460

   The annual payments must be made at the beginning of each year. The judge will approve an amount that, along with earnings on its investment, will cover the annual payments. Investment of the funds will be limited to savings (at 4% annually) and government securities, at prices and rates currently quoted in *The Wall Street Journal*.

   Hoxworth wants to develop a plan for making the annual payments by investing in the following securities (par value = $1000). Funds not invested in these securities will be placed in savings.

Security	**Current Price**	**Rate (%)**	**Years to Maturity**
1	$1055	6.750	3
2	$1000	5.125	4

Assume that interest is paid annually. The plan will be submitted to the judge and, if approved, Hoxworth will be required to pay a trustee the amount that will be required to fund the plan.

    a.   Use linear programming to find the minimum cash settlement necessary to fund the annual payments.

    b.   Use the shadow price to determine how much more Hoxworth should be willing to pay now to reduce the payment at the beginning of year 6 to $400,000.

    c.   Use the shadow price to determine how much more Hoxworth should be willing to pay to reduce the year 1 payment to $150,000.

    d.   Suppose that the annual payments are to be made at the end of each year. Reformulate the model to accommodate this change. How much would Hoxworth save if this change could be negotiated?

8.   The Clark County Sheriff's Department schedules police officers for 8-hour shifts. The beginning times for the shifts are 8:00 A.M., noon, 4:00 P.M., 8:00 P.M., midnight, and 4:00 A.M. An officer beginning a shift at one of these times works for the next 8 hours. During normal weekday operations, the number of officers needed varies depending on the time of day. The department staffing guidelines require the following minimum number of officers on duty:

Time of Day	Minimum Officers on Duty
8:00 A.M.–Noon	5
Noon–4:00 P.M.	6
4:00 P.M.–8:00 P.M.	10
8:00 P.M.–Midnight	7
Midnight–4:00 A.M.	4
4:00 A.M.–8:00 A.M.	6

Determine the number of police officers that should be scheduled to begin the 8-hour shifts at each of the six times (8:00 A.M., noon, 4:00 P.M., 8:00 P.M., midnight, and 4:00 A.M.) to minimize the total number of officers required. (*Hint:* Let $x_1 =$ the number of officers beginning work at 8:00 A.M., $x_2 =$ the number of officers beginning work at noon, and so on.)

9.   Epsilon Airlines services predominantly the eastern and southeastern United States. The vast majority of Epsilon's customers make reservations through Epsilon's website, but a small percentage of customers make reservations via phones. Epsilon employs call center personnel to handle these reservations and to deal with website reservation system problems and for the rebooking of flights for customers whose plans have changed or whose travel is disrupted. Staffing the call center appropriately is a challenge for Epsilon's management team. Having too many employees on hand is a waste of money, but having too few results in very poor customer service and the potential loss of customers.

    Epsilon analysts have estimated the minimum number of call center employees needed by day of the week for the upcoming vacation season (June, July, and the first two weeks of August). These estimates are as follows:

Day	Minimum Number of Employees Needed
Monday	75
Tuesday	50
Wednesday	45
Thursday	60
Friday	90
Saturday	75
Sunday	45

The call center employees work for five consecutive days and then have two consecutive days off. An employee may start work on any day of the week. Each call center employee receives the same salary. Assume that the schedule cycles and ignore start up and stopping of the schedule. Develop a model that will minimize the total number of call center employees needed to meet the minimum requirements. Find the optimal solution. Give the number of call center employees that exceed the minimum required.

10. An investment advisor at Shore Financial Services wants to develop a model that can be used to allocate investment funds among four alternatives: stocks, bonds, mutual funds, and cash. For the coming investment period, the company developed estimates of the annual rate of return and the associated risk for each alternative. Risk is measured using an index between 0 and 1, with higher risk values denoting more volatility and thus more uncertainty.

Investment	Annual Rate of Return (%)	Risk
Stocks	10	0.8
Bonds	3	0.2
Mutual funds	4	0.3
Cash	1	0.0

Because cash is held in a money market fund, the annual return is lower, but it carries essentially no risk. The objective is to determine the portion of funds allocated to each investment alternative in order to maximize the total annual return for the portfolio subject to the risk level the client is willing to tolerate.

Total risk is the sum of the risk for all investment alternatives. For instance, if 40% of a client's funds are invested in stocks, 30% in bonds, 20% in mutual funds, and 10% in cash, the total risk for the portfolio would be $0.40(0.8) + 0.30(0.2) + 0.20(0.3) + 0.10(0.0) = 0.44$. An investment advisor will meet with each client to discuss the client's investment objectives and to determine a maximum total risk value for the client. A maximum total risk value of less than 0.3 would be assigned to a conservative investor; a maximum total risk value of between 0.3 and 0.5 would be assigned to a moderate tolerance to risk; and a maximum total risk value greater than 0.5 would be assigned to a more aggressive investor.

Shore Financial Services specified additional guidelines that must be applied to all clients. The guidelines are as follows:

- No more than 75% of the total investment may be in stocks.
- The amount invested in mutual funds must be at least as much as invested in bonds.
- The amount of cash must be at least 10%, but no more than 30% of the total investment funds.

a. Suppose the maximum risk value for a particular client is 0.4. What is the optimal allocation of investment funds among stocks, bonds, mutual funds, and cash? What is the annual rate of return and the total risk for the optimal portfolio?

b. Suppose the maximum risk value for a more conservative client is 0.18. What is the optimal allocation of investment funds for this client? What is the annual rate of return and the total risk for the optimal portfolio?

c. Another more aggressive client has a maximum risk value of 0.7. What is the optimal allocation of investment funds for this client? What is the annual rate of return and the total risk for the optimal portfolio?

d. Refer to the solution for the more aggressive client in part (c). Would this client be interested in having the investment advisor increase the maximum percentage allowed in stocks or decrease the requirement that the amount of cash must be at least 10% of the funds invested? Explain.

e. What is the advantage of defining the decision variables as is done in this model rather than stating the amount to be invested and expressing the decision variables directly in dollar amounts?

11. Edwards Manufacturing Company purchases two component parts from three different suppliers. The suppliers have limited capacity, and no one supplier can meet all the company's needs. In addition, the suppliers charge different prices for the components. Component price data (in price per unit) are as follows:

Component	Supplier		
	1	2	3
1	$12	$13	$14
2	$10	$11	$10

Each supplier has a limited capacity in terms of the total number of components it can supply. However, as long as Edwards provides sufficient advance orders, each supplier can devote its capacity to component 1, component 2, or any combination of the two components, if the total number of units ordered is within its capacity. Supplier capacities are as follows:

Supplier	1	2	3
Capacity	600	1000	800

If the Edwards production plan for the next period includes 1000 units of component 1 and 800 units of component 2, what purchases do you recommend? That is, how many units of each component should be ordered from each supplier? What is the total purchase cost for the components?

12. The Atlantic Seafood Company (ASC) is a buyer and distributor of seafood products that are sold to restaurants and specialty seafood outlets throughout the Northeast. ASC has a frozen storage facility in New York City that serves as the primary distribution point for all products. One of the ASC products is frozen large black tiger shrimp, which are sized at 16–20 pieces per pound. Each Saturday ASC can purchase more tiger shrimp or sell the tiger shrimp at the existing New York City warehouse market price. The ASC goal is to buy tiger shrimp at a low weekly price and sell it later at a higher price. ASC currently has 20,000 pounds of tiger shrimp in storage. Space is available to store a maximum of 100,000 pounds of tiger shrimp each week. In addition, ASC developed the following estimates of tiger shrimp prices for the next four weeks:

Week	Price/lb.
1	$6.00
2	$6.20
3	$6.65
4	$5.55

ASC would like to determine the optimal buying/storing/selling strategy for the next four weeks. The cost to store a pound of shrimp for one week is $0.15, and to account for unforeseen changes in supply or demand, management also indicated that 25,000 pounds of tiger shrimp must be in storage at the end of week 4. Determine the optimal buying/storing/selling strategy for ASC. What is the projected four-week profit?

13. Romans Food Market, located in Saratoga, New York, carries a variety of specialty foods from around the world. Two of the store's leading products use the Romans Food Market name: Romans Regular Coffee and Romans DeCaf Coffee. These coffees are blends of Brazilian Natural and Colombian Mild coffee beans, which are purchased from a distributor located in New York City. Because Romans purchases large quantities, the coffee beans may be purchased on an as-needed basis for a price 10% higher than the market price the distributor pays for the beans. The current market price is $0.47 per pound for Brazilian Natural and $0.62 per pound for Colombian Mild. The compositions of each coffee blend are as follows:

	Blend	
Bean	**Regular**	**DeCaf**
Brazilian Natural	75%	40%
Colombian Mild	25%	60%

Romans sells the Regular blend for $3.60 per pound and the DeCaf blend for $4.40 per pound. Romans would like to place an order for the Brazilian and Colombian coffee beans that will enable the production of 1000 pounds of Romans Regular coffee and 500 pounds of Romans DeCaf coffee. The production cost is $0.80 per pound for the Regular blend. Because of the extra steps required to produce DeCaf, the production cost for the DeCaf blend is $1.05 per pound. Packaging costs for both products are $0.25 per pound. Formulate a linear programming model that can be used to determine the pounds of Brazilian Natural and Colombian Mild that will maximize the total contribution to profit. What is the optimal solution, and what is the contribution to profit?

14. The production manager for the Classic Boat Corporation must determine how many units of the Classic 21 model to produce over the next four quarters. The company has a beginning inventory of 100 Classic 21 boats, and demand for the four quarters is 2000 units in quarter 1, 4000 units in quarter 2, 3000 units in quarter 3, and 1500 units in quarter 4. The firm has limited production capacity in each quarter. That is, up to 4000 units can be produced in quarter 1, 3000 units in quarter 2, 2000 units in quarter 3, and 4000 units in quarter 4. Each boat held in inventory in quarters 1 and 2 incurs an inventory holding cost of $250 per unit; the holding cost for quarters 3 and 4 is $300 per unit. The production costs for the first quarter are $10,000 per unit; these costs are expected to increase by 10% each quarter because of increases in labor and material costs. Management specified that the ending inventory for quarter 4 must be at least 500 boats.

a.   Formulate a linear programming model that can be used to determine the production schedule that will minimize the total cost of meeting demand in each quarter subject to the production capacities in each quarter and also to the required ending inventory in quarter 4.

b.   Solve the linear program formulated in part (a). Then develop a table that will show for each quarter the number of units to manufacture, the ending inventory, and the costs incurred.

c.   Interpret each of the shadow prices corresponding to the constraints developed to meet demand in each quarter. Based on these shadow prices, what advice would you give the production manager?

d.   Interpret each of the shadow prices corresponding to the production capacity in each quarter. Based on each of these shadow prices, what advice would you give the production manager?

15. Bay Oil produces two types of fuels (regular and super) by mixing three ingredients. The major distinguishing feature of the two products is the octane level required.

Regular fuel must have a minimum octane level of 90 while super must have a level of at least 100. The cost per barrel, octane levels, and available amounts (in barrels) for the upcoming two-week period are shown in the following table. Likewise, the maximum demand for each end product and the revenue generated per barrel are shown.

Input	Cost/Barrel	Octane	Available (barrels)
1	$16.50	100	110,000
2	$14.00	87	350,000
3	$17.50	110	300,000

	Revenue/Barrel	Max Demand (barrels)
Regular	$18.50	350,000
Super	$20.00	500,000

Develop and solve a linear programming model to maximize contribution to profit. What is the optimal contribution to profit?

16. The Ferguson Paper Company produces rolls of paper for use in cash registers. The rolls, which are 200 feet long, are produced in widths of $1\frac{1}{2}$, $2\frac{1}{2}$, and $3\frac{1}{2}$ inches. The production process provides 200-foot rolls in 10-inch widths only. The firm must therefore cut the rolls to the desired final product sizes. The seven cutting alternatives and the amount of waste generated by each are as follows:

Cutting Alternative	Number of Rolls			Waste (inches)
	$1\frac{1}{2}$ in.	$2\frac{1}{2}$ in.	$3\frac{1}{2}$ in.	
1	6	0	0	1
2	0	4	0	0
3	2	0	2	0
4	0	1	2	$\frac{1}{2}$
5	1	3	0	1
6	1	2	1	0
7	4	0	1	$\frac{1}{2}$

The minimum requirements for the three products are

Roll Width (inches)	$1\frac{1}{2}$	$2\frac{1}{2}$	$3\frac{1}{2}$
Units	1000	2000	4000

a. If the company wants to minimize the number of 10-inch rolls that must be manufactured, how many 10-inch rolls will be processed on each cutting alternative? How many rolls are required, and what is the total waste (inches)?

b. If the company wants to minimize the waste generated, how many 10-inch rolls will be processed on each cutting alternative? How many rolls are required, and what is the total waste (inches)?

c. What are the differences between parts (a) and (b) of this problem? In this case, which objective do you prefer? Explain. What types of situations would make the other objective more desirable?

17. Frandec Company manufactures, assembles, and rebuilds material handling equipment used in warehouses and distribution centers. One product, called a Liftmaster, is assembled from four components: a frame, a motor, two supports, and a metal strap. Frandec's production

schedule calls for 5000 Liftmasters to be made next month. Frandec purchases the motors from an outside supplier, but the frames, supports, and straps may be either manufactured by the company or purchased from an outside supplier. Manufacturing and purchase costs per unit are shown.

Component	Manufacturing Cost	Purchase Cost
Frame	$38.00	$51.00
Support	$11.50	$15.00
Strap	$ 6.50	$ 7.50

Three departments are involved in the production of these components. The time (in minutes per unit) required to process each component in each department and the available capacity (in hours) for the three departments are as follows:

	Department		
Component	Cutting	Milling	Shaping
Frame	3.5	2.2	3.1
Support	1.3	1.7	2.6
Strap	0.8	—	1.7
Capacity (hours)	350	420	680

a. Formulate and solve a linear programming model for this make-or-buy application. How many of each component should be manufactured and how many should be purchased?
b. What is the total cost of the manufacturing and purchasing plan?
c. How many hours of production time are used in each department?
d. How much should Frandec be willing to pay for an additional hour of time in the shaping department?
e. Another manufacturer has offered to sell frames to Frandec for $45 each. Could Frandec improve its position by pursuing this opportunity? Why or why not?

18. The Two-Rivers Oil Company near Pittsburgh transports gasoline to its distributors by truck. The company recently contracted to supply gasoline distributors in southern Ohio, and it has $600,000 available to spend on the necessary expansion of its fleet of gasoline tank trucks. Three models of gasoline tank trucks are available.

Truck Model	Capacity (gallons)	Purchase Cost	Monthly Operating Cost, Including Depreciation
Super Tanker	5000	$67,000	$550
Regular Line	2500	$55,000	$425
Econo-Tanker	1000	$46,000	$350

The company estimates that the monthly demand for the region will be 550,000 gallons of gasoline. Because of the size and speed differences of the trucks, the number of deliveries or round trips possible per month for each truck model will vary. Trip capacities are estimated at 15 trips per month for the Super Tanker, 20 trips per month for the Regular Line, and 25 trips per month for the Econo-Tanker. Based on maintenance and driver availability, the firm does not want to add more than 15 new vehicles to its fleet. In addition, the company has decided to purchase at least three of the new Econo-Tankers for use on short-run, low-demand routes. As a final constraint, the company does not want more than half the new models to be Super Tankers.

a. If the company wishes to satisfy the gasoline demand with a minimum monthly operating expense, how many models of each truck should be purchased?

b. If the company did not require at least three Econo-Tankers and did not limit the number of Super Tankers to at most half the new models, how many models of each truck should be purchased?

19. The Silver Star Bicycle Company will be manufacturing both men's and women's models of its Easy-Pedal bicycles during the next two months. Management wants to develop a production schedule indicating how many bicycles of each model should be produced in each month. Current demand forecasts call for 150 men's and 125 women's models to be shipped during the first month and 200 men's and 150 women's models to be shipped during the second month. Additional data are shown:

Model	Production Costs	Labor Requirements (hours)		Current Inventory
		Manufacturing	Assembly	
Men's	$120	2.0	1.5	20
Women's	$ 90	1.6	1.0	30

Last month the company used a total of 1000 hours of labor. The company's labor relations policy will not allow the combined total hours of labor (manufacturing plus assembly) to increase or decrease by more than 100 hours from month to month. In addition, the company charges monthly inventory at the rate of 2% of the production cost based on the inventory levels at the end of the month. The company would like to have at least 25 units of each model in inventory at the end of the two months.

a. Establish a production schedule that minimizes production and inventory costs and satisfies the labor-smoothing, demand, and inventory requirements. What inventories will be maintained, and what are the monthly labor requirements?

b. If the company changed the constraints so that monthly labor increases and decreases could not exceed 50 hours, what would happen to the production schedule? How much will the cost increase? What would you recommend?

20. Filtron Corporation produces filtration containers used in water treatment systems. Although business has been growing, the demand each month varies considerably. As a result, the company utilizes a mix of part-time and full-time employees to meet production demands. Although this approach provides Filtron with great flexibility, it resulted in increased costs and morale problems among employees. For instance, if Filtron needs to increase production from one month to the next, additional part-time employees have to be hired and trained, and costs go up. If Filtron has to decrease production, the workforce has to be reduced and Filtron incurs additional costs in terms of unemployment benefits and decreased morale. Best estimates are that increasing the number of units produced from one month to the next will increase production costs by $1.25 per unit, and that decreasing the number of units produced will increase production costs by $1.00 per unit. In February Filtron produced 10,000 filtration containers but only sold 7500 units; 2500 units are currently in inventory. The sales forecasts for March, April, and May are for 12,000 units, 8000 units, and 15,000 units, respectively. In addition, Filtron has the capacity to store up to 3000 filtration containers at the end of any month. Management would like to determine the number of units to be produced in March, April, and May that will minimize the total cost of the monthly production increases and decreases.

21. Star Power Company is a power company in the Midwest region of the United States. Star buys and sells energy on the spot market. Star can store power in a high-capacity battery that can store up to 60 kWh (kilowatt hours). During a particular period, Star can buy or sell electricity at the market price known as LMP (Locational Marginal Price). The maximum rate that power can be injected or withdrawn from the battery is 20 kWh per period. Star has forecasted the following LMPs for the next 10 periods:

Period	LMP ($/kWh)
1	$ 5
2	$27
3	$ 2
4	$25
5	$22
6	$29
7	$24
8	$20
9	$61
10	$66

The battery is full at the beginning of period 1; that is, at the start of the planning horizon, the battery contains 60 kWh of electricity.

a. Develop a linear programming model Star Power can use to determine when to buy and sell electricity in order to maximize profit over these 10 weeks. What is the maximum achievable profit?

b. Your solution to part (a) should result in a battery level of 0 at the end of period 10. Why does this make sense? Modify your model with the requirement that the battery should be full (60 kWh) at the end of period 10. How does this impact the optimal profit?

c. To further investigate the impact of requirements on the battery level at the end of period 10, solve your model from part (b) with the constraint on the ending battery level varying from 0 kWh to 60 kWh in increments of 10 kWh. Develop a graph with profit on the vertical axis and required ending battery level on the horizontal axis. Given that Star has not forecasted LMPs for periods 11, 12, and so on, what ending battery level do you recommend that Star use in its optimization model?

22. TriCity Manufacturing (TCM) makes Styrofoam cups, plates, and sandwich and meal containers. Next week's schedule calls for the production of 80,000 small sandwich containers, 80,000 large sandwich containers, and 65,000 meal containers. To make these containers, Styrofoam sheets are melted and formed into final products using three machines: M1, M2, and M3. Machine M1 can process Styrofoam sheets with a maximum width of 12 inches. The width capacity of machine M2 is 16 inches, and the width capacity of machine M3 is 20 inches. The small sandwich containers require 10-inch-wide Styrofoam sheets; thus, these containers can be produced on each of the three machines. The large sandwich containers require 12-inch-wide sheets; thus, these containers can also be produced on each of the three machines. However, the meal containers require 16-inch-wide Styrofoam sheets, so the meal containers cannot be produced on machine M1. Waste is incurred in the production of all three containers because Styrofoam is lost in the heating and forming process as well as in the final trimming of the product. The amount of waste generated varies depending upon the container produced and the machine used. The following table shows the waste in square inches for each machine and product combination. The waste material is recycled for future use.

Machine	Small Sandwich	Large Sandwich	Meal
M1	20	15	—
M2	24	28	18
M3	32	35	36

Production rates also depend upon the container produced and the machine used. The following table shows the production rates in units per minute for each machine and product combination. Machine capacities are limited for the next week. Time available is 35 hours for machine M1, 35 hours for machine M2, and 40 hours for machine M3.

Machine	Small Sandwich	Large Sandwich	Meal
M1	30	25	—
M2	45	40	30
M3	60	52	44

a. Costs associated with reprocessing the waste material have been increasing. Thus, TCM would like to minimize the amount of waste generated in meeting next week's production schedule. Formulate a linear programming model that can be used to determine the best production schedule.
b. Solve the linear program formulated in part (a) to determine the production schedule. How much waste is generated? Which machines, if any, have idle capacity?

23. EZ-Windows, Inc., manufactures replacement windows for the home remodeling business. In January, the company produced 15,000 windows and ended the month with 9000 windows in inventory. EZ-Windows' management team would like to develop a production schedule for the next three months. A smooth production schedule is obviously desirable because it maintains the current workforce and provides a similar month-to-month operation. However, given the sales forecasts, the production capacities, and the storage capabilities as shown, the management team does not think a smooth production schedule with the same production quantity each month is possible.

	February	March	April
Sales forecast	15,000	16,500	20,000
Production capacity	14,000	14,000	18,000
Storage capacity	6,000	6,000	6,000

The company's cost accounting department estimates that increasing production by one window from one month to the next will increase total costs by $1.00 for each unit increase in the production level. In addition, decreasing production by one unit from one month to the next will increase total costs by $0.65 for each unit decrease in the production level. Ignoring production and inventory carrying costs, formulate and solve a linear programming model that will minimize the cost of changing production levels while still satisfying the monthly sales forecasts.

24. Morton Financial must decide on the percentage of available funds to commit to each of two investments, referred to as A and B, over the next four periods. The following table shows the amount of new funds available for each of the four periods, as well as the cash expenditure required for each investment (negative values) or the cash income from the investment (positive values). The data shown (in thousands of dollars) reflect the amount of expenditure or income if 100% of the funds available in any period are invested in either A or B. For example, if Morton decides to invest 100% of the funds available in any period in investment A, it will incur cash expenditures of $1000 in period 1, $800 in period 2, $200 in period 3, and income of $200 in period 4. Note, however, that if Morton made the decision to invest 80% in investment A, the cash expenditures or income would be 80% of the values shown.

Period	New Investment Funds Available	Investment	
		A	**B**
1	$1500	−$1000	−$800
2	$ 400	−$ 800	−$500
3	$ 500	−$ 200	−$300
4	$ 100	−$ 200	−$300

The amount of funds available in any period is the sum of the new investment funds for the period, the new loan funds, the savings from the previous period, the cash income from investment A, and the cash income from investment B. The funds available in any period can be used to pay the loan and interest from the previous period, can be placed in savings, can be used to pay the cash expenditures for investment A, or can be used to pay the cash expenditures for investment B.

Assume an interest rate of 10% per period for savings and an interest rate of 18% per period on borrowed funds. Let

$$S_t = \text{the savings for period } t$$
$$L_t = \text{the new loan funds for period } t$$

Then, in any period t, the savings income from the previous period is $1.1S_{t-1}$ and the loan and interest expenditure from the previous period is $1.18L_{t-1}$.

At the end of period 4, investment A is expected to have a cash value of $3200 (assuming a 100% investment in A), and investment B is expected to have a cash value of $2500 (assuming a 100% investment in B). Additional income and expenses at the end of period 4 will be income from savings in period 4 less the repayment of the period 4 loan plus interest.

Suppose that the decision variables are defined as

$$x_1 = \text{the proportion of investment A undertaken}$$
$$x_2 = \text{the proportion of investment B undertaken}$$

For example, if $x_1 = 0.5$, $500 would be invested in investment A during the first period, and all remaining cash flows and ending investment A values would be multiplied by 0.5. The same holds for investment B. The model must include constraints $x_1 \leq 1$ and $x_2 \leq 1$ to make sure that no more than 100% of the investments can be undertaken.

If no more than $200 can be borrowed in any period, determine the proportions of investments A and B and the amount of savings and borrowing in each period that will maximize the cash value for the firm at the end of the four periods.

25.   Western Family Steakhouse offers a variety of low-cost meals and quick service. Other than management, the steakhouse operates with two full-time employees who work 8 hours per day. The rest of the employees are part-time employees who are scheduled for 4-hour shifts during peak meal times. On Saturdays the steakhouse is open from 11:00 A.M. to 10:00 P.M. Management wants to develop a schedule for part-time employees that will minimize labor costs and still provide excellent customer service. The average wage rate for the part-time employees is $7.60 per hour. The total number of full-time and part-time employees needed varies with the time of day as shown.

Time	Total Number of Employees Needed
11:00 A.M.–Noon	9
Noon–1:00 P.M.	9
1:00 P.M.–2:00 P.M.	9
2:00 P.M.–3:00 P.M.	3
3:00 P.M.–4:00 P.M.	3
4:00 P.M.–5:00 P.M.	3
5:00 P.M.–6:00 P.M.	6
6:00 P.M.–7:00 P.M.	12
7:00 P.M.–8:00 P.M.	12
8:00 P.M.–9:00 P.M.	7
9:00 P.M.–10:00 P.M.	7

One full-time employee comes on duty at 11:00 A.M., works 4 hours, takes an hour off, and returns for another 4 hours. The other full-time employee comes to work at 1:00 P.M. and works the same 4-hours-on, 1-hour-off, 4-hours-on pattern.

a.   Develop a minimum-cost schedule for part-time employees.

b.   What is the total payroll for the part-time employees? How many part-time shifts are needed? Use the surplus variables to comment on the desirability of scheduling at least some of the part-time employees for 3-hour shifts.

c.   Assume that part-time employees can be assigned either a 3-hour or a 4-hour shift. Develop a minimum-cost schedule for the part-time employees. How many part-time shifts are needed, and what is the cost savings compared to the previous schedule?

Case Problem 1   Planning an Advertising Campaign

The Flamingo Grill is an upscale restaurant located in St. Petersburg, Florida. To help plan an advertising campaign for the coming season, Flamingo's management team hired the advertising firm of Haskell & Johnson (HJ). The management team requested HJ's recommendation concerning how the advertising budget should be distributed across television, radio, and online. The budget has been set at $279,000.

In a meeting with Flamingo's management team, HJ consultants provided the following information about the industry exposure effectiveness rating per ad, their estimate of the number of potential new customers reached per ad, and the cost for each ad:

Advertising Media	Exposure Rating per Ad	New Customers per Ad	Cost per Ad
Television	90	4000	$10,000
Radio	25	2000	$ 3000
Online	10	1000	$ 1000

The exposure rating is viewed as a measure of the value of the ad to both existing customers and potential new customers. It is a function of such things as image, message recall, visual and audio appeal, and so on. As expected, the more expensive television advertisement has the highest exposure effectiveness rating along with the greatest potential for reaching new customers.

At this point, the HJ consultants pointed out that the data concerning exposure and reach were only applicable to the first few ads in each medium. For television, HJ stated that the exposure rating of 90 and the 4000 new customers reached per ad were reliable for the first 10 television ads. After 10 ads, the benefit is expected to decline. For planning purposes, HJ recommended reducing the exposure rating to 55 and the estimate of the potential new customers reached to 1500 for any television ads beyond 10. For radio ads, the preceding data are reliable up to a maximum of 15 ads. Beyond 15 ads, the exposure rating declines to 20 and the number of new customers reached declines to 1200 per ad. Similarly, for online ads, the preceding data are reliable up to a maximum of 20; the exposure rating declines to 5 and the potential number of new customers reached declines to 800 for additional ads.

Flamingo's management team accepted maximizing the total exposure rating across all media as the objective of the advertising campaign. Because of management's concern with attracting new customers, management stated that the advertising campaign must reach at least 100,000 new customers. To balance the advertising campaign and make use of all advertising media, Flamingo's management team also adopted the following guidelines:

- Use at least twice as many radio advertisements as television advertisements.
- Use no more than 20 television advertisements.
- The television budget should be at least $140,000.
- The radio advertising budget is restricted to a maximum of $99,000.
- The online advertising budget is to be at least $30,000.

HJ agreed to work with these guidelines and provide a recommendation as to how the $279,000 advertising budget should be allocated among television, radio, and online advertising.

Managerial Report

Develop a model that can be used to determine the advertising budget allocation for the Flamingo Grill. Include a discussion of the following items in your report:

1. A schedule showing the recommended number of television, radio, and online advertisements and the budget allocation for each medium. Show the total exposure and indicate the total number of potential new customers reached.
2. A discussion of how the total exposure would change if an additional $10,000 were added to the advertising budget.
3. A discussion of the ranges for the objective function coefficients. What do the ranges indicate about how sensitive the recommended solution is to HJ's exposure rating coefficients?
4. The resulting media schedule if the objective of the advertising campaign was to maximize the number of potential new customers reached instead of maximizing the total exposure rating.
5. A comparison of the two media schedules resulting from items 1 and 4, respectively. What is your recommendation for the Flamingo Grill's advertising campaign?

Case Problem 2   Schneider's Sweet Shop

Schneider's Sweet Shop specializes in homemade candies and ice cream. Schneider's produces its ice cream in-house, in batches of 50 pounds. The first stage in ice cream making is the blending of ingredients to obtain a mix, which meets prespecified requirements on the percentages of certain constituents of the mix. The desired composition is as follows:

1. Fat	16.00%
2. Serum Solids	8.00%
3. Sugar Solids	16.00%
4. Egg Solids	.35%
5. Stabilizer	.25%
6. Emulsifier	.15%
7. Water	59.25%

The mix can be composed of ingredients from the following list:

Ingredient	Cost ($/lb.)
1. 40% Cream	$1.19
2. 23% Cream	.70
3. Butter	2.32
4. Plastic Cream	2.30
5. Butter Oil	2.87
6. 4% Milk	.25
7. Skim Condensed Milk	.35
8. Skim Milk Powder	.65
9. Liquid Sugar	.25
10. Sugared Frozen Fresh Egg Yolk	1.75
11. Powdered Egg Yolk	4.45
12. Stabilizer	2.45
13. Emulsifier	1.68
14. Water	.00

The number of pounds of a constituent found in a pound of an ingredient is shown below. Note that a pound of stabilizer contributes only to the stabilizer requirement (1 pound), 1 pound of emulsifier contributes only to the emulsifier requirement (1 pound), and that water contributes only to the water requirement (1 pound).

Constituent							Ingredient							
	1	2	3	4	5	6	7	8	9	10	11	12	13	14
1	.4	.2	.8	.8	.9	.1				.5	.6			
2	.1			.1		.1	.3	1						
3									.7	.1				
4										.4	.4			
5												1		
6													1	
7	.5	.8	.2	.1	.1	.8	.7		.3					1

Young Jack Schneider has recently acquired the shop from his father. Jack's father has in the past used the following mixture: 9.73 pounds of Plastic Cream, 3.03 pounds of Skim Milk Powder, 11.37 pounds of Liquid Sugar, .44 pounds of Sugared Frozen Fresh Egg Yolk, .12 pounds of Stabilizer, .07 pounds of Emulsifier, and 25.24 pounds of water. (The scale at Schneider's is only accurate to 100ths of a pound.) Jack feels that perhaps it is possible to produce the ice cream in a more cost-effective manner. He would like to find the cheapest mix for producing a batch of ice cream which meets the requirements specified above.

Jack is also curious about the cost effect of being a little more flexible in the requirements listed above. He wants to know the cheapest mix if the composition meets the following tolerances:

1. Fat	15.00–17.00%
2. Serum Solids	7.00–9.00%
3. Sugar Solids	15.50–16.50%
4. Egg Solids	.30–.40%
5. Stabilizer	.20–.30%
6. Emulsifier	.10–20%
7. Water	58.00–59.50%

Managerial Report

Write a managerial report that compares the cost of Papa Jack's approach to (a) the cost-minimized approach using the desired composition and (b) the cost-minimized approach with the more flexible requirements. Include the following in your report:

1. The cost of 50 pounds of ice cream under each of the three approaches.
2. The amount of each ingredient used in the mix for each of the three approaches.
3. A recommendation as to which approach should be used.

Case Problem 3 # Textile Mill Scheduling

The Scottsville Textile Mill[1] produces five different fabrics. Each fabric can be woven on one or more of the mill's 38 looms. The sales department's forecast of demand for the next month is shown in Table 9.16, along with data on the selling price per yard, variable cost per yard, and purchase price per yard. The mill operates 24 hours a day and is scheduled for 30 days during the coming month.

The mill has two types of looms: dobbie and regular. The dobbie looms are more versatile and can be used for all five fabrics. The regular looms can produce only three of the fabrics. The mill has a total of 38 looms: 8 are dobbie and 30 are regular. The rate of production for each fabric on each type of loom is given in Table 9.17. The time required to change over from producing one fabric to another is negligible and does not have to be considered.

The Scottsville Textile Mill satisfies all demand with either its own fabric or fabric purchased from another mill. Fabrics that cannot be woven at the Scottsville Mill because of limited loom capacity will be purchased from another mill. The purchase price of each fabric is also shown in Table 9.16.

---

[1] This case is based on the Calhoun Textile Mill Case by Jeffrey D. Camm, P. M. Dearing, and Suresh K. Tadisnia, 1987.

TABLE 9.16   MONTHLY DEMAND, SELLING PRICE, VARIABLE COST, AND
PURCHASE PRICE DATA FOR SCOTTSVILLE TEXTILE MILL FABRICS

Fabric	Demand (yards)	Selling Price ($/yard)	Variable Cost ($/yard)	Purchase Price ($/yard)
1	16,500	0.99	0.66	0.80
2	22,000	0.86	0.55	0.70
3	62,000	1.10	0.49	0.60
4	7,500	1.24	0.51	0.70
5	62,000	0.70	0.50	0.70

TABLE 9.17   LOOM PRODUCTION RATES FOR THE SCOTTSVILLE TEXTILE MILL

	Loom Rate (yards/hour)	
Fabric	Dobbie	Regular
1	4.63	—
2	4.63	—
3	5.23	5.23
4	5.23	5.23
5	4.17	4.17

Note: Fabrics 1 and 2 can be manufactured only on
the dobbie loom.

Managerial Report

Develop a model that can be used to schedule production for the Scottsville Textile Mill,
and, at the same time, determine how many yards of each fabric must be purchased from
another mill. Include a discussion and analysis of the following items in your report:

1. The final production schedule and loom assignments for each fabric.
2. The projected total contribution to profit.
3. A discussion of the value of additional loom time. (The mill is considering purchasing a ninth dobbie loom. What is your estimate of the monthly profit contribution of this additional loom?)
4. A discussion of the objective coefficients' ranges.
5. A discussion of how the objective of minimizing total costs would provide a different model than the objective of maximizing total profit contribution. (How would the interpretation of the objective coefficients' ranges differ for these two models?)

Case Problem 4   Workforce Scheduling

Davis Instruments has two manufacturing plants located in Atlanta, Georgia. Product
demand varies considerably from month to month, causing Davis extreme difficulty in
workforce scheduling. Recently Davis started hiring temporary workers supplied by Work-
Force Unlimited, a company that specializes in providing temporary employees for firms
in the greater Atlanta area. WorkForce Unlimited offered to provide temporary employees

under three contract options that differ in terms of the length of employment and the cost. The three options are summarized:

Option	Length of Employment	Cost
1	One month	$2000
2	Two months	$4800
3	Three months	$7500

The longer contract periods are more expensive because WorkForce Unlimited experiences greater difficulty finding temporary workers who are willing to commit to longer work assignments.

Over the next six months, Davis projects the following needs for additional employees:

Month	January	February	March	April	May	June
Employees Needed	10	23	19	26	20	14

Each month, Davis can hire as many temporary employees as needed under each of the three options. For instance, if Davis hires five employees in January under Option 2, WorkForce Unlimited will supply Davis with five temporary workers who will work two months: January and February. For these workers, Davis will have to pay 5($4800) = $24,000. Because of some merger negotiations under way, Davis does not want to commit to any contractual obligations for temporary employees that extend beyond June.

Davis's quality control program requires each temporary employee to receive training at the time of hire. The training program is required even if the person worked for Davis Instruments in the past. Davis estimates that the cost of training is $875 each time a temporary employee is hired. Thus, if a temporary employee is hired Davis will incur a training cost of $875 in the first month of hire, but will incur no additional training cost if the employee is on a two- or three-month contract.

Managerial Report

Develop a model that can be used to determine the number of temporary employees Davis should hire each month under each contract plan in order to meet the projected needs at a minimum total cost. Include the following items in your report:

1. A schedule that shows the number of temporary employees that Davis should hire each month for each contract option.
2. A summary table that shows the number of temporary employees that Davis should hire under each contract option, the associated contract cost for each option, and the associated training cost for each option. Provide summary totals showing the total number of temporary employees hired, total contract costs, and total training costs.
3. An explanation of how reducing the cost to train each temporary employee to $700 per month affects the hiring plan. Discuss the implications that this effect on the hiring plan has for identifying methods for reducing training costs. How much of a reduction in training costs would be required to change the hiring plan based on a training cost of $875 per temporary employee?
4. A recommendation regarding the decision to hire additional full-time employees if Davis can hire 10 full-time employees at the beginning of January in order to satisfy part of the labor requirements over the next six months. Assume that Davis

can hire full-time employees at \$16.50 per hour, including fringe benefits, and that full-time and temporary employees both work approximately 160 hours per month. What effect would does the hiring of additional full-time employees have on total labor and training costs over the six-month period as compared to hiring only temporary employees?

Case Problem 5   Duke Energy Coal Allocation[2]

Duke Energy manufactures and distributes electricity to customers in the United States and Latin America. Duke Energy acquired Cinergy Corporation in 2005, which had generating facilities and energy customers in Indiana, Kentucky, and Ohio. For these customers Cinergy has been spending \$725 to \$750 million each year for the fuel needed to operate its coal-fired and gas-fired power plants; 92% to 95% of the fuel used is coal. In this region, Duke Energy uses 10 coal-burning generating plants: 5 located inland and 5 located on the Ohio River. Some plants have more than one generating unit. Duke Energy uses 28–29 million tons of coal per year at a cost of approximately \$2 million every day in this region.

Duke Energy purchases coal using fixed-tonnage or variable-tonnage contracts from mines in Indiana (49%), West Virginia (20%), Ohio (12%), Kentucky (11%), Illinois (5%), and Pennsylvania (3%). Duke Energy must purchase all of the coal contracted for on fixed-tonnage contracts, but on variable-tonnage contracts it can purchase varying amounts up to the limit specified in the contract. The coal is shipped from the mines to Duke Energy's generating facilities in Ohio, Kentucky, and Indiana. The cost of coal varies from \$19 to \$35 per ton, and transportation/delivery charges range from \$1.50 to \$5.00 per ton.

A model is used to determine the megawatt-hours (MWh) of electricity that each generating unit is expected to produce and to provide a measure of each generating unit's efficiency, referred to as the heat rate. The heat rate is the total British thermal units (BTUs) required to produce 1 kilowatt-hour (kWh) of electrical power.

Coal Allocation Model

Duke Energy uses a linear programming model, called the coal allocation model, to allocate coal to its generating facilities. The objective of the coal allocation model is to determine the lowest-cost method for purchasing and distributing coal to the generating units. The supply/availability of the coal is determined by the contracts with the various mines, and the demand for coal at the generating units is determined indirectly by the megawatt-hours of electricity each unit must produce.

The cost to process coal, called the add-on cost, depends upon the characteristics of the coal (moisture content, ash content, BTU content, sulfur content, and grindability) and the efficiency of the generating unit. The add-on cost plus the transportation cost are added to the purchase cost of the coal to determine the total cost to purchase and use the coal.

Current Problem

Duke Energy signed three fixed-tonnage contracts and four variable-tonnage contracts. The company would like to determine the least-cost way to allocate the coal available through

---

[2] The authors are indebted to Thomas Mason and David Bossee of Duke Energy Corporation, formerly Cinergy Corp., for their contribution to this case problem.

these contracts to five generating units. The relevant data for the three fixed-tonnage contracts are as follows:

Supplier	Number of Tons Contracted For	Cost ($/ton)	BTU/lb
RAG	350,000	22	13,000
Peabody Coal Sales	300,000	26	13,300
American Coal Sales	275,000	22	12,600

For example, the contract signed with RAG requires Duke Energy to purchase 350,000 tons of coal at a price of $22 per ton; each pound of this particular coal provides 13,000 BTUs.

The data for the four variable-tonnage contracts follow:

Supplier	Number of Tons Available	Cost ($/ton)	BTU/lb
Consol, Inc.	200,000	32	12,250
Cyprus Amax	175,000	35	12,000
Addington Mining	200,000	31	12,000
Waterloo	180,000	33	11,300

For example, the contract with Consol, Inc., enables Duke Energy to purchase up to 200,000 tons of coal at a cost of $32 per ton; each pound of this coal provides 12,250 BTUs.

The number of megawatt-hours of electricity that each generating unit must produce and the heat rate provided are as follows:

Generating Unit	Electricity Produced (MWh)	Heat Rate (BTU per kWh)
Miami Fort Unit 5	550,000	10,500
Miami Fort Unit 7	500,000	10,200
Beckjord Unit 1	650,000	10,100
East Bend Unit 2	750,000	10,000
Zimmer Unit 1	1,100,000	10,000

For example, Miami Fort Unit 5 must produce 550,000 megawatt-hours of electricity, and 10,500 BTUs are needed to produce each kilowatt-hour.

The transportation cost and the add-on cost in dollars per ton are shown here:

	Transportation Cost ($/ton)				
Supplier	Miami Fort Unit 5	Miami Fort Unit 7	Beckjord Unit 1	East Bend Unit 2	Zimmer Unit 1
RAG	5.00	5.00	4.75	5.00	4.75
Peabody	3.75	3.75	3.50	3.75	3.50
American	3.00	3.00	2.75	3.00	2.75
Consol	3.25	3.25	2.85	3.25	2.85
Cyprus	5.00	5.00	4.75	5.00	4.75
Addington	2.25	2.25	2.00	2.25	2.00
Waterloo	2.00	2.00	1.60	2.00	1.60

	Add-On Cost (\$/ton)				
Supplier	Miami Fort Unit 5	Miami Fort Unit 7	Beckjord Unit 1	East Bend Unit 2	Zimmer Unit 1
RAG	10.00	10.00	10.00	5.00	6.00
Peabody	10.00	10.00	11.00	6.00	7.00
American	13.00	13.00	15.00	9.00	9.00
Consol	10.00	10.00	11.00	7.00	7.00
Cyprus	10.00	10.00	10.00	5.00	6.00
Addington	5.00	5.00	6.00	4.00	4.00
Waterloo	11.00	11.00	11.00	7.00	9.00

Managerial Report

Prepare a report that summarizes your recommendations regarding Duke Energy's coal allocation problem. Be sure to include information and analysis for the following issues:

1. Determine how much coal to purchase from each of the mining companies and how it should be allocated to the generating units. What is the cost to purchase, deliver, and process the coal?
2. Compute the average cost of coal in cents per million BTUs for each generating unit (a measure of the cost of fuel for the generating units).
3. Compute the average number of BTUs per pound of coal received at each generating unit (a measure of the energy efficiency of the coal received at each unit).
4. Suppose that Duke Energy can purchase an additional 80,000 tons of coal from American Coal Sales as an "all or nothing deal" for \$30 per ton. Should Duke Energy purchase the additional 80,000 tons of coal?
5. Suppose that Duke Energy learns that the energy content of the coal from Cyprus Amax is actually 13,000 BTUs per pound. Should Duke Energy revise its procurement plan?
6. Duke Energy has learned from its trading group that Duke Energy can sell 50,000 megawatt-hours of electricity over the grid (to other electricity suppliers) at a price of \$30 per megawatt-hour. Should Duke Energy sell the electricity? If so, which generating units should produce the additional electricity?

Appendix 9.1 Excel Solution of Hewlitt Corporation Financial Planning Problem

In Appendix 7.1 we showed how Excel could be used to solve the RMC linear programming problem. To illustrate the use of Excel in solving a more complex linear programming problem, we show the solution to the Hewlitt Corporation financial planning problem presented in Section 9.2.

The spreadsheet formulation and solution of the Hewlitt Corporation problem are shown in Figure 9.10. As described in Appendix 7.1, our practice is to put the data required for the problem in the top part of the worksheet and build the model in the bottom part of the worksheet. The model consists of a set of cells for the decision variables, a cell for the objective function, a set of cells for the left-hand-side functions, and a set of cells for the right-hand sides of the constraints. The cells for the decision variables are also enclosed by a boldface line. Descriptive labels are used to make the spreadsheet easy to read.

FIGURE 9.10 EXCEL SOLUTION FOR THE HEWLITT CORPORATION PROBLEM

	A	B	C	D	E	F	G	H	I	J	K	L
1	**Hewlitt Corporation Cash Requirements**											
2												
3		**Cash**										
4	**Year**	**Rqmt.**				**Bond**						
5	1	430.000			1	2	3					
6	2	210.000	**Price ($1000)**		1.1500	1.0000	1.3500					
7	3	222.000	**Rate**		0.0888	0.0550	0.1175					
8	4	231.000	**Years to Maturity**		5.0000	6.0000	7.0000					
9	5	240.000										
10	6	195.000	**Annual Savings Multiple**		1.040							
11	7	225.000										
12	8	255.000										
13												
14	**Model**											
15												
16	F	B1	B2	B3	S1	S2	S3	S4	S5	S6	S7	S8
17	1728.794	144.988	187.856	228.188	636.148	501.606	349.682	182.681	0.000	0.000	0.000	0.000
18												
19					**Cash Flow**		**Net Cash**		**Cash**			
20	**Min Funds**	1728.794		**Constraint**	**In**	**Out**	**Flow**		**Rqmt.**			
21				Year 1	1728.794	1298.794	430.000	=	430.000			
22				Year 2	711.606	501.606	210.000	=	210.000			
23				Year 3	571.682	349.682	222.000	=	222.000			
24				Year 4	413.681	182.681	231.000	=	231.000			
25				Year 5	240.000	0.000	240.000	=	240.000			
26				Year 6	195.000	0.000	195.000	=	195.000			
27				Year 7	225.000	0.000	225.000	=	225.000			
28				Year 8	255.000	0.000	255.000	=	255.000			
29												

WEB file

Hewlitt

Formulation

The data and descriptive labels are contained in cells A1:G12. The cells in the bottom portion of the spreadsheet contain the key elements of the model required by the Excel Solver.

Decision Variables Cells A17:L17 are reserved for the decision variables. The optimal values (rounded to three places), are shown to be $F = 1728.794$, $B_1 = 144.988$, $B_2 = 187.856$, $B_3 = 228.188$, $S_1 = 636.148$, $S_2 = 501.606$, $S_3 = 349.682$, $S_4 = 182.681$, and $S_5 = S_6 = S_7 = S_8 = 0$.

Objective Function The formula $=A17$ has been placed into cell B20 to reflect the total funds required. It is simply the value of the decision variable, F. The total funds required by the optimal solution are shown to be $1,728,794.

Left-Hand Sides The left-hand sides for the eight constraints represent the annual net cash flow. They are placed into cells G21:G28.

Cell G21 $= E21 - F21$ (Copy to G22:G28)

For this problem, some of the left-hand-side cells reference other cells that contain formulas. These referenced cells provide Hewlitt's cash flow in and cash flow out for each of the eight years.[3] The cells and their formulas are as follows:

$$\text{Cell E21} = \text{A17}$$
$$\text{Cell E22} = \text{SUMPRODUCT(\$E\$7:\$G\$7,\$B\$17:\$D\$17)} + \text{\$F\$10*E17}$$
$$\text{Cell E23} = \text{SUMPRODUCT(\$E\$7:\$G\$7,\$B\$17:\$D\$17)} + \text{\$F\$10*F17}$$
$$\text{Cell E24} = \text{SUMPRODUCT(\$E\$7:\$G\$7,\$B\$17:\$D\$17)} + \text{\$F\$10*G17}$$
$$\text{Cell E25} = \text{SUMPRODUCT(\$E\$7:\$G\$7,\$B\$17:\$D\$17)} + \text{\$F\$10*H17}$$
$$\text{Cell E26} = (1+\text{E7})*\text{B17} + \text{F7}*\text{C17} + \text{G7}*\text{D17} + \text{F10}*\text{I17}$$
$$\text{Cell E27} = (1+\text{F7})*\text{C17} + \text{G7}*\text{D17} + \text{F10}*\text{J17}$$
$$\text{Cell E28} = (1+\text{G7})*\text{D17} + \text{F10}*\text{K17}$$
$$\text{Cell F21} = \text{SUMPRODUCT(E6:G6,B17:D17)} + \text{E17}$$
$$\text{Cell F22} = \text{F17}$$
$$\text{Cell F23} = \text{G17}$$
$$\text{Cell F24} = \text{H17}$$
$$\text{Cell F25} = \text{I17}$$
$$\text{Cell F26} = \text{J17}$$
$$\text{Cell F27} = \text{K17}$$
$$\text{Cell F28} = \text{L17}$$

Right-Hand Sides   The right-hand sides for the eight constraints represent the annual cash requirements. They are placed into cells I21:I28.

$$\text{Cell I21} = \text{B5 (Copy to I22:I28)}$$

Excel Solution

We are now ready to use the information in the worksheet to determine the optimal solution to the Hewlitt Corporation problem. The following steps describe how to use Excel to obtain the optimal solution:

Step 1. Select the **Data** tab from the **Ribbon**
Step 2. Select **Solver** from the **Analysis** group
Step 3. When the **Solver Parameters** dialog box appears (see Figure 9.11):
　　　　　Enter *B20* in the Set **Objective Cell** box
　　　　　Select the To**: Min** option
　　　　　Enter *A17:L17* in the **By Changing Variable Cells** box
Step 4. Select **Add**
　　　　When the **Add Constraint** dialog box appears:
　　　　　Enter *G21:G28* in the left-hand box of the **Cell Reference** box
　　　　　From the middle drop-down button, select **=**
　　　　　Enter *I21:I28* in **Constraint** box
　　　　　Click **OK**

---

[3] The cash flow in is the sum of the positive terms in each constraint equation in the mathematical model, and the cash flow out is the sum of the negative terms in each constraint equation.

FIGURE 9.11   EXCEL SOLVER PARAMETERS DIALOG BOX FOR THE HEWLITT
CORPORATION PROBLEM

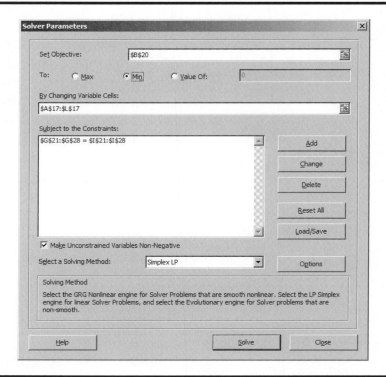

Step 5. When the **Solver Parameters** dialog box reappears (see Figure 9.11):
   Click the checkbox for **Make Unconstrained Variables Non-negative**
Step 6. Select the **Select a Solving Method** drop-down button Select
   Simplex LP
Step 7. Choose **Solve**
Step 8. When the **Solver Results** dialog box appears:
   Select **Keep Solver Solution**
   Select **Sensitivity** in the **Reports** box
   Click **OK**

The Solver Parameters dialog box is shown in Figure 9.11. The optimal solution is
shown in Figure 9.10; the accompanying sensitivity report is shown in Figure 9.12.

Discussion

Recall that the Excel sensitivity report uses the term *shadow price* to describe the *change*
in value of the solution per unit increase in the right-hand side of a constraint. LINGO uses
the term *dual price* to describe the *improvement* in value of the solution per unit increase
in the right-hand side of a constraint. For maximization problems, the shadow price and
dual price are the same; for minimization problems, the shadow price and dual price have
opposite signs.

FIGURE 9.12   EXCEL SOLVER SENSITIVITY REPORT FOR THE HEWLITT CORPORATION PROBLEM

Variable Cells

Cell	Name	Final Value	Reduced Cost	Objective Coefficient	Allowable Increase	Allowable Decrease
$A$17	Dollars Needed	1728.794	0.000	1.000	1E+30	1.000
$B$17	Bond 1 - Year 1	144.988	0.000	0.000	0.0670	0.013
$C$17	Bond 2 - Year 2	187.856	0.000	0.000	0.0128	0.020
$D$17	Bond 3 - Year 3	228.188	0.000	0.000	0.0229	0.750
$E$17	Savings Year 1	636.148	0.000	0.000	0.1096	0.055
$F$17	Savings Year 2	501.606	0.000	0.000	0.1433	0.057
$G$17	Savings Year 3	349.682	0.000	0.000	0.2109	0.059
$H$17	Savings Year 4	182.681	0.000	0.000	0.4136	0.061
$I$17	Savings Year 5	0.000	0.064	0.000	1E+30	0.064
$J$17	Savings Year 6	0.000	0.013	0.000	1E+30	0.013
$K$17	Savings Year 7	0.000	0.021	0.000	1E+30	0.021
$L$17	Savings Year 8	0.000	0.671	0.000	1E+30	0.671

Constraints

Cell	Name	Final Value	Shadow Price	Constraint R.H. Side	Allowable Increase	Allowable Decrease
$G$21	Year 1 Flow	430.000	1.000	430.000	1E+30	1728.794
$G$22	Year 2 Flow	210.000	0.962	210.000	1E+30	661.594
$G$23	Year 3 Flow	222.000	0.925	222.000	1E+30	521.670
$G$24	Year 4 Flow	231.000	0.889	231.000	1E+30	363.669
$G$25	Year 5 Flow	240.000	0.855	240.000	1E+30	189.988
$G$26	Year 6 Flow	195.000	0.760	195.000	2149.928	157.856
$G$27	Year 7 Flow	225.000	0.719	225.000	3027.962	198.188
$G$28	Year 8 Flow	225.000	0.671	225.000	1583.882	255.000

CHAPTER 10

Distribution and Network Models

CONTENTS

The models discussed in this chapter belong to a special class of linear programming problems called *network flow* problems. We begin by discussing models commonly encountered when dealing with problems related to supply chains, specifically transportation and transshipment problems. We then consider three other types of network problems: assignment problems, shortest-route problems, and maximal flow problems.

In each case, we present a graphical representation of the problem in the form of a *network*. We then show how the problem can be formulated and solved as a linear program. In the last section of the chapter we present a production and inventory problem that is an interesting application of the transshipment problem.

10.1 Supply Chain Models

A **supply chain** describes the set of all interconnected resources involved in producing and distributing a product. For instance, a supply chain for automobiles could include raw material producers, automotive-parts suppliers, distribution centers for storing automotive parts, assembly plants, and car dealerships. All the materials needed to produce a finished automobile must flow through the supply chain. In general, supply chains are designed to satisfy customer demand for a product at minimum cost. Those that control the supply chain must make decisions such as where to produce the product, how much should be produced, and where it should be sent. We will look at two specific types of problems common in supply chain models that can be solved using linear programing: transportation problems and transshipment problems.

Transportation Problem

The **transportation problem** arises frequently in planning for the distribution of goods and services from several supply locations to several demand locations. Typically, the quantity of goods available at each supply location (origin) is limited, and the quantity of goods needed at each of several demand locations (destinations) is known. The usual objective in a transportation problem is to minimize the cost of shipping goods from the origins to the destinations.

Let us illustrate by considering a transportation problem faced by Foster Generators. This problem involves the transportation of a product from three plants to four distribution centers. Foster Generators operates plants in Cleveland, Ohio; Bedford, Indiana; and York, Pennsylvania. Production capacities over the next three-month planning period for one particular type of generator are as follows:

Origin	Plant	Three-Month Production Capacity (units)
1	Cleveland	5,000
2	Bedford	6,000
3	York	2,500
	Total	13,500

The firm distributes its generators through four regional distribution centers located in Boston, Chicago, St. Louis, and Lexington; the three-month forecast of demand for the distribution centers is as follows:

Destination	Distribution Center	Three-Month Demand Forecast (units)
1	Boston	6,000
2	Chicago	4,000
3	St. Louis	2,000
4	Lexington	1,500
	Total	13,500

Management would like to determine how much of its production should be shipped from each plant to each distribution center. Figure 10.1 shows graphically the 12 distribution routes Foster can use. Such a graph is called a **network**; the circles are referred to as

FIGURE 10.1   THE NETWORK REPRESENTATION OF THE FOSTER GENERATORS TRANSPORTATION PROBLEM

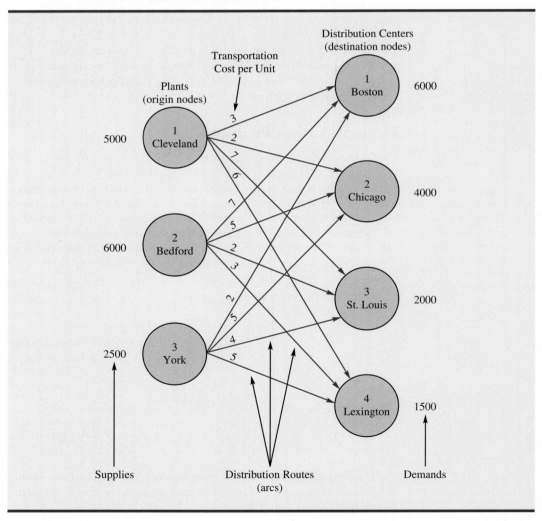

TABLE 10.1 TRANSPORTATION COST PER UNIT FOR THE FOSTER GENERATORS TRANSPORTATION PROBLEM

	Destination			
Origin	**Boston**	**Chicago**	**St. Louis**	**Lexington**
Cleveland	3	2	7	6
Bedford	7	5	2	3
York	2	5	4	5

nodes and the lines connecting the nodes as **arcs**. Each origin and destination is represented by a node, and each possible shipping route is represented by an arc. The amount of the supply is written next to each origin node, and the amount of the demand is written next to each destination node. The goods shipped from the origins to the destinations represent the flow in the network. Note that the direction of flow (from origin to destination) is indicated by the arrows.

Try Problem 1 for practice in developing a network model of a transportation problem.

For Foster's transportation problem, the objective is to determine the routes to be used and the quantity to be shipped via each route that will provide the minimum total transportation cost. The cost for each unit shipped on each route is given in Table 10.1 and is shown on each arc in Figure 10.1.

A linear programming model can be used to solve this transportation problem. We use double-subscripted decision variables, with x_{11} denoting the number of units shipped from origin 1 (Cleveland) to destination 1 (Boston), x_{12} denoting the number of units shipped from origin 1 (Cleveland) to destination 2 (Chicago), and so on. In general, the decision variables for a transportation problem having m origins and n destinations are written as follows:

The first subscript identifies the "from" node of the corresponding arc and the second subscript identifies the "to" node of the arc.

$$x_{ij} = \text{number of units shipped from origin } i \text{ to destination } j$$
$$\text{where } i = 1, 2, \ldots, m \text{ and } j = 1, 2, \ldots, n$$

Because the objective of the transportation problem is to minimize the total transportation cost, we can use the cost data in Table 10.1 or on the arcs in Figure 10.1 to develop the following cost expressions:

Transportation costs for
units shipped from Cleveland $= 3x_{11} + 2x_{12} + 7x_{13} + 6x_{14}$

Transportation costs for
units shipped from Bedford $\quad = 7x_{21} + 5x_{22} + 2x_{23} + 3x_{24}$

Transportation costs for
units shipped from York $\quad = 2x_{31} + 5x_{32} + 4x_{33} + 5x_{34}$

The sum of these expressions provides the objective function showing the total transportation cost for Foster Generators.

Transportation problems need constraints because each origin has a limited supply and each destination has a demand requirement. We consider the supply constraints first. The capacity at the Cleveland plant is 5000 units. With the total number of units shipped from the Cleveland plant expressed as $x_{11} + x_{12} + x_{13} + x_{14}$, the supply constraint for the Cleveland plant is

$$x_{11} + x_{12} + x_{13} + x_{14} \leq 5000 \quad \text{Cleveland supply}$$

With three origins (plants), the Foster transportation problem has three supply constraints. Given the capacity of 6000 units at the Bedford plant and 2500 units at the York plant, the two additional supply constraints are

$$x_{21} + x_{22} + x_{23} + x_{24} \leq 6000 \quad \text{Bedford supply}$$
$$x_{31} + x_{32} + x_{33} + x_{34} \leq 2500 \quad \text{York supply}$$

With the four distribution centers as the destinations, four demand constraints are needed to ensure that destination demands will be satisfied:

To obtain a feasible solution, the total supply must be greater than or equal to the total demand.

$$x_{11} + x_{21} + x_{31} = 6000 \quad \text{Boston demand}$$
$$x_{12} + x_{22} + x_{32} = 4000 \quad \text{Chicago demand}$$
$$x_{13} + x_{23} + x_{33} = 2000 \quad \text{St. Louis demand}$$
$$x_{14} + x_{24} + x_{34} = 1500 \quad \text{Lexington demand}$$

Combining the objective function and constraints into one model provides a 12-variable, 7-constraint linear programming formulation of the Foster Generators transportation problem:

$$\text{Min} \quad 3x_{11} + 2x_{12} + 7x_{13} + 6x_{14} + 7x_{21} + 5x_{22} + 2x_{23} + 3x_{24} + 2x_{31} + 5x_{32} + 4x_{33} + 5x_{34}$$

s.t.

$$
\begin{aligned}
x_{11} + x_{12} + x_{13} + x_{14} &\leq 5000 \\
x_{21} + x_{22} + x_{23} + x_{24} &\leq 6000 \\
x_{31} + x_{32} + x_{33} + x_{34} &\leq 2500 \\
x_{11} \qquad\qquad + x_{21} \qquad\qquad + x_{31} &= 6000 \\
x_{12} \qquad\qquad + x_{22} \qquad\qquad + x_{32} &= 4000 \\
x_{13} \qquad\qquad + x_{23} \qquad\qquad + x_{33} &= 2000 \\
x_{14} \qquad\qquad + x_{24} \qquad\qquad + x_{34} &= 1500
\end{aligned}
$$

$$x_j \geq 0 \quad \text{for } i = 1, 2, 3 \text{ and } j = 1, 2, 3, 4$$

Comparing the linear programming formulation to the network in Figure 10.1 leads to several observations: All the information needed for the linear programming formulation is on the network. Each node has one constraint and each arc has one variable. The sum of the variables corresponding to arcs from an origin node must be less than or equal to the origin's supply, and the sum of the variables corresponding to the arcs into a destination node must be equal to the destination's demand.

Can you now use Excel to solve a linear programming model of a transportation problem? Try Problem 2.

We solved the Foster Generators problem using Excel Solver. The optimal objective function values and optimal decision variable values are shown in Figure 10.2, which indicates that the minimum total transportation cost is $39,500. The values for the decision variables show the optimal amounts to ship over each route. For example, 3500 units should be shipped from Cleveland to Boston, and 1500 units should be shipped from Cleveland to Chicago. Other values of the decision variables indicate the remaining shipping quantities and routes. Table 10.2 shows the minimum cost transportation schedule, and Figure 10.3 summarizes the optimal solution on the network.

Problem Variations

The Foster Generators problem illustrates use of the basic transportation model. Variations of the basic transportation model may involve one or more of the following situations:

1. Total supply not equal to total demand
2. Maximization objective function
3. Route capacities or route minimums
4. Unacceptable routes

FIGURE 10.2 OPTIMAL SOLUTION FOR THE FOSTER GENERATORS TRANSPORTATION PROBLEM

Objective Cell (Min)

Name	Original Value	Final Value
Minimize Total Cost	0.000	39500.000

Variable Cells

Foster

Model Variable	Name	Original Value	Final Value	Integer
X11	Cleveland to Boston	0.000	3500.000	Contin
X12	Cleveland to Chicago	0.000	1500.000	Contin
X13	Cleveland to St. Louis	0.000	0.000	Contin
X14	Cleveland to Lexington	0.000	0.000	Contin
X21	Bedford to Boston	0.000	0.000	Contin
X22	Bedford to Chicago	0.000	2500.000	Contin
X23	Bedford to St. Louis	0.000	2000.000	Contin
X24	Bedford to Lexington	0.000	1500.000	Contin
X31	York to Boston	0.000	2500.000	Contin
X32	York to Chicago	0.000	0.000	Contin
X33	York to St. Louis	0.000	0.000	Contin
X34	York to Lexington	0.000	0.000	Contin

TABLE 10.2 OPTIMAL SOLUTION TO THE FOSTER GENERATORS TRANSPORTATION PROBLEM

Route From	To	Units Shipped	Cost per Unit	Total Cost
Cleveland	Boston	3500	$3	$10,500
Cleveland	Chicago	1500	$2	$ 3,000
Bedford	Chicago	2500	$5	$12,500
Bedford	St. Louis	2000	$2	$ 4,000
Bedford	Lexington	1500	$3	$ 4,500
York	Boston	2500	$2	$ 5,000
				$39,500

With slight modifications in the linear programming model, we can easily accommodate these situations.

Total Supply Not Equal to Total Demand Often *the total supply is not equal to the total demand*. If total supply exceeds total demand, no modification in the linear programming formulation is necessary. Excess supply will appear as slack in the linear programming solution. Slack for any particular origin can be interpreted as the unused supply or amount not shipped from the origin.

Whenever total supply is less than total demand, the model does not determine how the unsatisfied demand is handled (e.g., backorders). The manager must handle this aspect of the problem.

If total supply is less than total demand, the linear programming model of a transportation problem will not have a feasible solution. In this case, we modify the network representation by adding a **dummy origin** with a supply equal to the difference between the total demand and the total supply. With the addition of the dummy origin and an arc from the

FIGURE 10.3   NETWORK DIAGRAM FOR THE OPTIMAL SOLUTION TO THE FOSTER
GENERATORS TRANSPORTATION PROBLEM

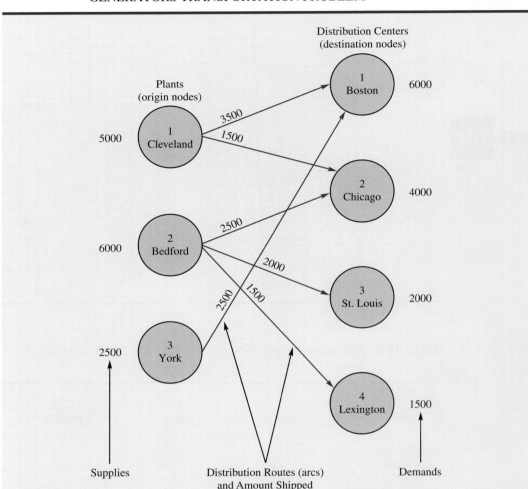

dummy origin to each destination, the linear programming model will have a feasible solution. A zero cost per unit is assigned to each arc leaving the dummy origin so that the value of the optimal solution for the revised problem will represent the shipping cost for the units actually shipped (no shipments actually will be made from the dummy origin). When the optimal solution is implemented, the destinations showing shipments being received from the dummy origin will be the destinations experiencing a shortfall or unsatisfied demand.

Try Problem 6 for practice with a case in which demand is greater than supply with a maximization objective.

Maximization Objective Function   In some transportation problems, the objective is to find a solution that maximizes profit or revenue. Using the values for profit or revenue per unit as coefficients in the objective function, we simply solve a maximization rather than a minimization linear program. This change does not affect the constraints.

Route Capacities or Route Minimums   The linear programming formulation of the transportation problem also can accommodate capacities or minimum quantities for one or more of the routes. For example, suppose that in the Foster Generators problem the York–Boston route (origin 3 to destination 1) had a capacity of 1000 units because of limited space availability on its normal mode of transportation. With x_{31} denoting the amount shipped from York to Boston, the route capacity constraint for the York–Boston route would be

$$x_{31} \leq 1000$$

Similarly, route minimums can be specified. For example,

$$x_{22} \geq 2000$$

would guarantee that a previously committed order for a Bedford–Chicago delivery of at least 2000 units would be maintained in the optimal solution.

Unacceptable Routes Finally, establishing a route from every origin to every destination may not be possible. To handle this situation, we simply drop the corresponding arc from the network and remove the corresponding variable from the linear programming formulation. For example, if the Cleveland–St. Louis route were unacceptable or unusable, the arc from Cleveland to St. Louis could be dropped in Figure 10.1, and x_{13} could be removed from the linear programming formulation. Solving the resulting 11-variable, 7-constraint model would provide the optimal solution while guaranteeing that the Cleveland–St. Louis route is not used.

A General Linear Programming Model

To show the general linear programming model for a transportation problem with m origins and n destinations, we use the following notation:

x_{ij} = number of units shipped from origin i to destination j

c_{ij} = cost per unit of shipping from origin i to destination j

s_i = supply or capacity in units at origin i

d_j = demand in units at destination j

The general linear programming model is as follows:

$$\text{Min} \quad \sum_{i=1}^{m} \sum_{j=1}^{n} c_{ij} x_{ij}$$

$$\text{s.t.}$$

$$\sum_{j=1}^{n} x_{ij} \leq s_i \qquad i = 1, 2, \ldots, m \quad \text{Supply}$$

$$\sum_{i=1}^{m} x_{ij} = d_j \qquad j = 1, 2, \ldots, n \quad \text{Demand}$$

$$x_{ij} \geq 0 \qquad \text{for all } i \text{ and } j$$

As mentioned previously, we can add constraints of the form $x_{ij} \leq L_{ij}$ if the route from origin i to destination j has capacity L_{ij}. A transportation problem that includes constraints of this type is called a **capacitated transportation problem**. Similarly, we can add route minimum constraints of the form $x_{ij} \geq M_{ij}$ if the route from origin i to destination j must handle at least M_{ij} units.

The Q.M. in Action, Optimizing Freight Car Assignments at Union Pacific, describes how Union Pacific railroad used an optimization model to solve a transportation problem of assigning empty freight cars to customer requests.

OPTIMIZING FREIGHT CAR ASSIGNMENTS AT UNION PACIFIC*

Union Pacific (UP) is one of the largest railroads in North America. It owns over 100,000 freight cars, which it uses to service its customers via a network of over 30,000 miles of railroad track. In response to customer demand, UP moves empty freight cars to its customer locations, where the cars are loaded. UP then transports the loaded cars to destinations designated by the customers.

At any point in time, Union Pacific may have hundreds of customer requests for empty freight cars to transport their products. Empty freight cars are typically scattered throughout UP's rail network at previous delivery destinations. A day-to-day decision faced by UP operations managers is how to assign these empty freight cars to current freight car requests from its customers. The assignments need to be cost effective but also must meet the customers' needs in terms of service time.

*Based on A. Narisetty et al., "An Optimization Model for Empty Freight Car Assignment at Union Pacific Railroad," Interfaces 38, no. 2 (March/April 2008): 89–102.

UP partnered with researchers from Purdue University to develop an optimization model to assist with the empty freight car assignment problem. In order to be useful, the model had to be simple enough to be solved quickly and had to run within UP's existing information systems. A transportation model was developed, with supply being the empty freight cars at their current locations and demand being the current and forecasted requests at the customer locations. The objective function includes not just the cost of transporting the cars, but other factors such as early and late delivery penalties and customer priority. This allows the managers to trade off a variety of factors with the cost of assignments to ensure that the proper level of service is achieved. The model outputs the number of empty cars to move from each current location to the locations of customers requesting cars. The model is used on a daily basis for operations planning and is also used to study the potential impact of changes in operational policies.

Transshipment Problem

The **transshipment problem** is an extension of the transportation problem in which intermediate nodes, referred to as *transshipment nodes*, are added to account for locations such as warehouses. In this more general type of distribution problem, shipments may be made between any pair of the three general types of nodes: origin nodes, transshipment nodes, and destination nodes. For example, the transshipment problem permits shipments of goods from origins to intermediate nodes and on to destinations, from one origin to another origin, from one intermediate location to another, from one destination location to another, and directly from origins to destinations.

As was true for the transportation problem, the supply available at each origin is limited, and the demand at each destination is specified. The objective in the transshipment problem is to determine how many units should be shipped over each arc in the network so that all destination demands are satisfied with the minimum possible transportation cost.

Try Problem 11, part (a), for practice in developing a network representation of a transshipment problem.

Let us consider the transshipment problem faced by Ryan Electronics. Ryan is an electronics company with production facilities in Denver and Atlanta. Components produced at either facility may be shipped to either of the firm's regional warehouses, which are located in Kansas City and Louisville. From the regional warehouses, the firm supplies retail outlets in Detroit, Miami, Dallas, and New Orleans. The key features of the problem are shown in the network model depicted in Figure 10.4. Note that the supply at each origin and demand at each destination are shown in the left and right margins, respectively. Nodes 1 and 2 are the origin nodes; nodes 3 and 4 are the transshipment nodes; and nodes 5, 6, 7, and 8 are the destination nodes. The transportation cost per unit for each distribution route is shown in Table 10.3 and on the arcs of the network model in Figure 10.4.

FIGURE 10.4 NETWORK REPRESENTATION OF THE RYAN ELECTRONICS
TRANSSHIPMENT PROBLEM

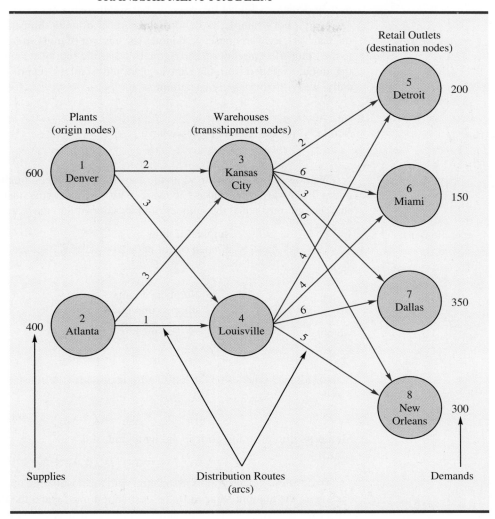

TABLE 10.3 TRANSPORTATION COST PER UNIT FOR THE RYAN ELECTRONICS
TRANSSHIPMENT PROBLEM

	Warehouse	
Plant	**Kansas City**	**Louisville**
Denver	2	3
Atlanta	3	1

	Retail Outlet			
Warehouse	**Detroit**	**Miami**	**Dallas**	**New Orleans**
Kansas City	2	6	3	6
Louisville	4	4	6	5

As with the transportation problem, we can formulate a linear programming model of the transshipment problem from a network representation. Again, we need a constraint for each node and a variable for each arc. Let x_{ij} denote the number of units shipped from node i to node j. For example, x_{13} denotes the number of units shipped from the Denver plant to the Kansas City warehouse, x_{14} denotes the number of units shipped from the Denver plant to the Louisville warehouse, and so on. Because the supply at the Denver plant is 600 units, the amount shipped from the Denver plant must be less than or equal to 600. Mathematically, we write this supply constraint as

$$x_{13} + x_{14} \leq 600$$

Similarly, for the Atlanta plant we have

$$x_{23} + x_{24} \leq 400$$

We now consider how to write the constraints corresponding to the two transshipment nodes. For node 3 (the Kansas City warehouse), we must guarantee that the number of units shipped out must equal the number of units shipped into the warehouse. If

$$\text{Number of units shipped out of node 3} = x_{35} + x_{36} + x_{37} + x_{38}$$

and

$$\text{Number of units shipped into node 3} = x_{13} + x_{23}$$

we obtain

$$x_{35} + x_{36} + x_{37} + x_{38} = x_{13} + x_{23}$$

Placing all the variables on the left-hand side provides the constraint corresponding to node 3 as

$$- x_{13} - x_{23} + x_{35} + x_{36} + x_{37} + x_{38} = 0$$

Similarly, the constraint corresponding to node 4 is

$$- x_{14} - x_{24} + x_{45} + x_{46} + x_{47} + x_{48} = 0$$

To develop the constraints associated with the destination nodes, we recognize that for each node the amount shipped to the destination must equal the demand. For example, to satisfy the demand for 200 units at node 5 (the Detroit retail outlet), we write

$$x_{35} + x_{45} = 200$$

Similarly, for nodes 6, 7, and 8, we have

$$x_{36} + x_{46} = 150$$
$$x_{37} + x_{47} = 350$$
$$x_{38} + x_{48} = 300$$

Try Problem 11, parts (b) and (c), for practice in developing the linear programming model and in solving a transshipment problem on the computer.

As usual, the objective function reflects the total shipping cost over the 12 shipping routes. Combining the objective function and constraints leads to a 12-variable, 8-constraint linear programming model of the Ryan Electronics transshipment problem (see Figure 10.5). Figure 10.6 shows the optimal solution from the answer report, and Table 10.4 summarizes the optimal solution.

As mentioned at the beginning of this section, in the transshipment problem, arcs may connect any pair of nodes. All such shipping patterns are possible in a transshipment

FIGURE 10.5 LINEAR PROGRAMMING FORMULATION OF THE RYAN ELECTRONICS TRANSSHIPMENT PROBLEM

$$\text{Min } 2x_{13} + 3x_{14} + 3x_{23} + 1x_{24} + 2x_{35} + 6x_{36} + 3x_{37} + 6x_{38} + 4x_{45} + 4x_{46} + 6x_{47} + 5x_{48}$$

s.t.

$$
\begin{aligned}
x_{13} + x_{14} && \le 600 \left.\right\} \text{ Origin node} \\
x_{23} + x_{24} && \le 400 \left.\right\} \text{ constraints} \\
-x_{13} \quad - x_{23} \quad + x_{35} + x_{36} + x_{37} + x_{38} && = 0 \left.\right\} \text{ Transshipment node} \\
- x_{14} \quad - x_{24} \quad\quad\quad + x_{45} + x_{46} + x_{47} + x_{48} && = 0 \left.\right\} \text{ constraints} \\
x_{35} \quad\quad\quad + x_{45} && = 200 \left.\right\} \\
x_{36} \quad\quad\quad + x_{46} && = 150 \left.\right\} \text{ Destination node} \\
x_{37} \quad\quad\quad + x_{47} && = 350 \left.\right\} \text{ constraints} \\
x_{38} \quad\quad\quad + x_{48} && = 300 \left.\right\}
\end{aligned}
$$

$x_{ij} \ge 0$ for all i and j

FIGURE 10.6 OPTIMAL SOLUTION FOR THE RYAN ELECTRONICS TRANSSHIPMENT PROBLEM

Objective Cell (Min)

Name	Original Value	Final Value
Minimize Total Cost	0.000	5200.000

Variable Cells

Model Variable	Name	Original Value	Final Value	Integer
X13	Denver–Kansas City	0.000	550.000	Contin
X14	Denver–Louisville	0.000	50.000	Contin
X23	Atlanta–Kansas City	0.000	0.000	Contin
X24	Atlanta–Louisville	0.000	400.000	Contin
X35	Kansas City–Detroit	0.000	200.000	Contin
X36	Kansas City–Miami	0.000	0.000	Contin
X37	Kansas City–Dallas	0.000	350.000	Contin
X38	Kansas City–New Orleans	0.000	0.000	Contin
X45	Louisville–Detroit	0.000	0.000	Contin
X46	Louisville–Miami	0.000	150.000	Contin
X47	Louisville–Dallas	0.000	0.000	Contin
X48	Louisville–New Orleans	0.000	300.000	Contin

WEB file

Ryan

problem. We still require only one constraint per node, but the constraint must include a variable for every arc entering or leaving the node. For origin nodes, the sum of the shipments out minus the sum of the shipments in must be less than or equal to the origin supply. For destination nodes, the sum of the shipments in minus the sum of the shipments out must equal demand. For transshipment nodes, the sum of the shipments out must equal the sum of the shipments in, as before.

For an illustration of this more general type of transshipment problem, let us modify the Ryan Electronics problem. Suppose that it is possible to ship directly from Atlanta to New Orleans at $4 per unit and from Dallas to New Orleans at $1 per unit. The network model corresponding to this modified Ryan Electronics problem is shown in Figure 10.7,

TABLE 10.4   OPTIMAL SOLUTION TO THE RYAN ELECTRONICS TRANSSHIPMENT
PROBLEM

Route				
From	**To**	**Units Shipped**	**Cost per Unit**	**Total Cost**
Denver	Kansas City	550	$2	$1100
Denver	Louisville	50	$3	$ 150
Atlanta	Louisville	400	$1	$ 400
Kansas City	Detroit	200	$2	$ 400
Kansas City	Dallas	350	$3	$1050
Louisville	Miami	150	$4	$ 600
Louisville	New Orleans	300	$5	$1500
				$5200

FIGURE 10.7   NETWORK REPRESENTATION OF THE MODIFIED RYAN ELECTRONICS
TRANSSHIPMENT PROBLEM

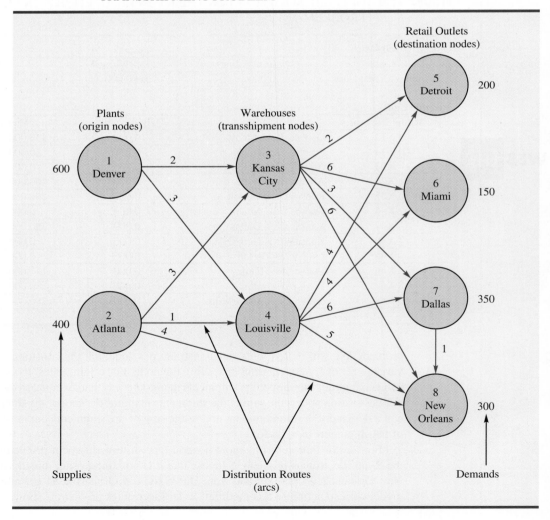

FIGURE 10.8   LINEAR PROGRAMMING FORMULATION OF THE MODIFIED RYAN ELECTRONICS
TRANSSHIPMENT PROBLEM

$$\text{Min} \quad 2x_{13} + 3x_{14} + 3x_{23} + 1x_{24} + 2x_{35} + 6x_{36} + 3x_{37} + 6x_{38} + 4x_{45} + 4x_{46} + 6x_{47} + 5x_{48} + 4x_{28} + 1x_{78}$$

s.t.

$$
\begin{aligned}
x_{13} + x_{14} & \le 600 \\
x_{23} + x_{24} & \qquad\qquad + x_{28} \le 400 \\
-x_{13} \quad - x_{23} \quad + x_{35} + x_{36} + x_{37} + x_{38} & = 0 \\
- x_{14} \quad - x_{24} \qquad\qquad + x_{45} + x_{46} + x_{47} + x_{48} & = 0 \\
x_{35} \qquad\qquad + x_{45} & = 200 \\
x_{36} \qquad\qquad + x_{46} & = 150 \\
x_{37} \qquad\qquad + x_{47} \quad - x_{78} & = 350 \\
x_{38} \qquad\qquad + x_{48} + x_{28} + x_{78} & = 300
\end{aligned}
$$

Origin node constraints

Transshipment node constraints

Destination node constraints

$x_{ij} \ge 0$ for all i and j

FIGURE 10.9   OPTIMAL SOLUTION FOR THE MODIFIED RYAN ELECTRONICS
TRANSSHIPMENT PROBLEM

Objective Cell (Min)

Name	Original Value	Final Value
Total Cost	0.000	4600.000

ModifiedRyan

Variable Cells

Model Variable	Name	Original Value	Final Value	Integer
X13	Denver–Kansas City	0.000	550.000	Contin
X14	Denver–Louisville	0.000	50.000	Contin
X23	Atlanta–Kansas City	0.000	0.000	Contin
X24	Atlanta–Louisville	0.000	100.000	Contin
X35	Kansas City–Detroit	0.000	200.000	Contin
X36	Kansas City–Miami	0.000	0.000	Contin
X37	Kansas City–Dallas	0.000	350.000	Contin
X38	Kansas City–New Orleans	0.000	0.000	Contin
X45	Louisville–Detroit	0.000	0.000	Contin
X46	Louisville–Miami	0.000	150.000	Contin
X47	Louisville–Dallas	0.000	0.000	Contin
X48	Louisville–New Orleans	0.000	0.000	Contin
X28	Atlanta–New Orleans	0.000	300.000	Contin
X78	Dallas–New Orleans	0.000	0.000	Contin

the linear programming formulation is shown in Figure 10.8, and the optimal solution from the answer report is shown in Figure 10.9.

Try Problem 12 for practice working with transshipment problems with this more general structure.

In Figure 10.7 we added two new arcs to the network model. Thus, two new variables are necessary in the linear programming formulation. Figure 10.8 shows that the new variables x_{28} and x_{78} appear in the objective function and in the constraints corresponding to the nodes to which the new arcs are connected. Figure 10.9 shows that the value of the optimal solution has been reduced $600 by allowing these additional shipping routes. The value of $x_{28} = 300$ indicates that 300 units are being shipped directly from Atlanta to New Orleans.

The value of $x_{78} = 0$ indicates that no units are shipped from Dallas to New Orleans in this solution.[1]

Problem Variations

As with transportation problems, transshipment problems may be formulated with several variations, including

1. Total supply not equal to total demand
2. Maximization objective function
3. Route capacities or route minimums
4. Unacceptable routes

The linear programming model modifications required to accommodate these variations are identical to the modifications required for the transportation problem. When we add one or more constraints of the form $x_{ij} \leq L_{ij}$ to show that the route from node i to node j has capacity L_{ij}, we refer to the transshipment problem as a **capacitated transshipment problem**.

A General Linear Programming Model

To show the general linear programming model for the transshipment problem, we use the following notation:

$$x_{ij} = \text{number of units shipped from node } i \text{ to node } j$$
$$c_{ij} = \text{cost per unit of shipping from node } i \text{ to node } j$$
$$s_i = \text{supply at origin node } i$$
$$d_j = \text{demand at destination node } j$$

The general linear programming model for the transshipment problem is as follows:

$$\text{Min} \quad \sum_{\text{all arcs}} c_{ij} x_{ij}$$

$$\text{s.t.}$$

$$\sum_{\text{arcs out}} x_{ij} - \sum_{\text{arcs in}} x_{ij} \leq s_i \qquad \text{Origin nodes } i$$

$$\sum_{\text{arcs out}} x_{ij} - \sum_{\text{arcs in}} x_{ij} = 0 \qquad \text{Transshipment nodes}$$

$$\sum_{\text{arcs in}} x_{ij} - \sum_{\text{arcs out}} x_{ij} = d_j \qquad \text{Destination nodes } j$$

$$x_{ij} \geq 0 \text{ for all } i \text{ and } j$$

The Q.M. in Action, Product Sourcing Heuristic at Procter & Gamble, describes a transshipment model used by Procter & Gamble to help make strategic decisions related to sourcing and distribution.

---

[1]This is an example of a linear programming with alternate optimal solutions. The solution $x_{13} = 600$, $x_{14} = 0$, $x_{23} = 0$, $x_{24} = 150$, $x_{28} = 250$, $x_{35} = 200$, $x_{36} = 0$, $x_{37} = 400$, $x_{38} = 0$, $x_{45} = 0$, $x_{46} = 150$, $x_{47} = 0$, $x_{48} = 0$, $x_{78} = 50$ is also optimal. Thus, in this solution both new routes are used: $x_{28} = 250$ units are shipped from Atlanta to New Orleans and $x_{78} = 50$ units are shipped from Dallas to New Orleans.

NOTES AND COMMENTS

1. Supply chain models used in practice usually lead to large linear programs. Problems with 100 origins and 100 destinations are not unusual. Such a problem would involve $(100 \times 100) = 10,000$ variables.

2. To handle a situation in which some routes may be unacceptable, we stated that you could drop the corresponding arc from the network and remove the corresponding variable from the linear programming formulation. Another approach often used is to assign an extremely large objective function cost coefficient to any unacceptable arc. If the problem has already been formulated, another option is to add a constraint to the formulation that sets the variable you want to remove equal to zero.

3. The optimal solution to a transportation model will consist of integer values for the decision variables as long as all supply and demand values are integers. The reason is the special mathematical structure of the linear programming model. Each variable appears in exactly one supply and one demand constraint, and all coefficients in the constraint equations are 1 or 0.

4. In the general linear programming formulation of the transshipment problem, the constraints for the destination nodes are often written as

$$\sum_{\text{arcs out}} x_{ij} - \sum_{\text{arcs in}} x_{ij} = -d_j$$

The advantage of writing the constraints this way is that the left-hand side of each constraint then represents the flow out of the node minus the flow in.

Q.M. *in* ACTION

PRODUCT SOURCING HEURISTIC AT PROCTER & GAMBLE*

During a period of planning for possible changes to its supply chain, Procter & Gamble (P&G) embarked on a major strategic initiative called the North American Product Sourcing Study. P&G wanted to consolidate its product sources and optimize its distribution system design throughout North America. A decision support system used to aid in this project was called the Product Sourcing Heuristic (PSH) and was based on a transshipment model much like the ones described in this chapter.

In a preprocessing phase, the many P&G products were aggregated into groups that shared the same technology and could be made at the same plant. The PSH employing the transshipment model was then used by product strategy teams responsible for developing product sourcing options for these product groups. The various plants that could produce the product group were the source nodes, the company's regional distribution centers were the transshipment nodes, and P&G's customer zones were the destinations. Direct shipments to customer zones as well as shipments through distribution centers were employed.

The product strategy teams used the heuristic interactively to explore a variety of questions concerning product sourcing and distribution. For instance, the team might be interested in the impact of closing two of five plants and consolidating production in the three remaining plants. The product sourcing heuristic would then delete the source nodes corresponding to the two closed plants, make any capacity modifications necessary to the sources corresponding to the remaining three plants, and re-solve the transshipment problem. The product strategy team could then examine the new solution, make some more modifications, solve again, and so on.

The Product Sourcing Heuristic was viewed as a valuable decision support system by all who used it. When P&G implemented the results of the study, it realized annual savings in the $200 million range. The PSH proved so successful in North America that P&G used it in other markets around the world.

*Based on information provided by Franz Dill and Tom Chorman of Procter & Gamble.

Assignment Problem

10.2

The **assignment problem** arises in a variety of decision-making situations; typical assignment problems involve assigning jobs to machines, agents to tasks, sales personnel to sales territories, contracts to bidders, and so on. A distinguishing feature of the assignment problem is that *one* agent is assigned to *one and only one* task. Specifically, we look for the set of assignments that will optimize a stated objective, such as minimize cost, minimize time, or maximize profits.

To illustrate the assignment problem, let us consider the case of Fowle Marketing Research, which has just received requests for market research studies from three new clients. The company faces the task of assigning a project leader (agent) to each client (task). Currently, three individuals have no other commitments and are available for the project leader assignments. Fowle's management realizes, however, that the time required to complete each study will depend on the experience and ability of the project leader assigned. The three projects have approximately the same priority, and management wants to assign project leaders to minimize the total number of days required to complete all three projects. If a project leader is to be assigned to one client only, which assignments should be made?

To answer the assignment question, Fowle's management must first consider all possible project leader–client assignments and then estimate the corresponding project completion times. With three project leaders and three clients, nine assignment alternatives are possible. The alternatives and the estimated project completion times in days are summarized in Table 10.5.

Try Problem 17, part (a), for practice in developing a network model for an assignment problem.

Figure 10.10 shows the network representation of Fowle's assignment problem. The nodes correspond to the project leaders and clients, and the arcs represent the possible assignments of project leaders to clients. The supply at each origin node and the demand at each destination node are 1; the cost of assigning a project leader to a client is the time it takes that project leader to complete the client's task. Note the similarity between the network models of the assignment problem (Figure 10.10) and the transportation problem (Figure 10.1). The assignment problem is a special case of the transportation problem in which all supply and demand values equal 1, and the amount shipped over each arc is either 0 or 1.

Because the assignment problem is a special case of the transportation problem, a linear programming formulation can be developed. Again, we need a constraint for each node and a variable for each arc. As in the transportation problem, we use double-subscripted decision variables, with x_{11} denoting the assignment of project leader 1 (Terry) to client 1,

TABLE 10.5   ESTIMATED PROJECT COMPLETION TIMES (DAYS) FOR THE FOWLE MARKETING RESEARCH ASSIGNMENT PROBLEM

		Client	
Project Leader	**1**	**2**	**3**
1. Terry	10	15	9
2. Carle	9	18	5
3. McClymonds	6	14	3

**FIGURE 10.10   A NETWORK MODEL OF THE FOWLE MARKETING RESEARCH
ASSIGNMENT PROBLEM**

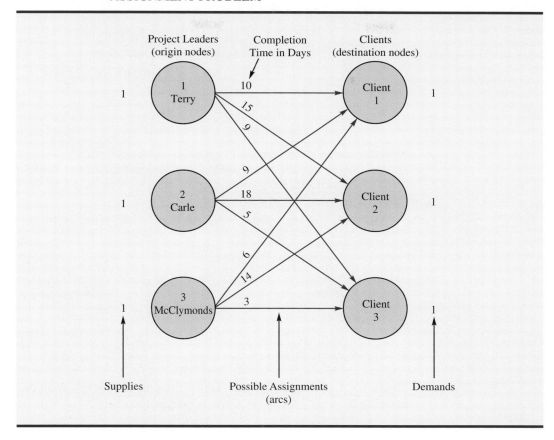

x_{12} denoting the assignment of project leader 1 (Terry) to client 2, and so on. In general, we interpret the decision variables for Fowle's assignment problem as

Due to the special structure of the assignment problem, the x_{ij} variables will either be 0 or 1 and not any value in between, e.g., 0.6. In Chapter 11, we discuss optimization problems which represent discrete choices with 0-1 (or binary) variables that must be explicitly constrained to avoid fractional values.

$$x_{ij} = \begin{cases} 1 & \text{if project leader } i \text{ is assigned to client } j \\ 0 & \text{otherwise} \end{cases}$$

where $i = 1, 2, 3$, and $j = 1, 2, 3$

Using this notation and the completion time data in Table 10.5, we develop completion time expressions:

Days required for Terry's assignment $= 10x_{11} + 15x_{12} + 9x_{13}$

Days required for Carle's assignment $= 9x_{21} + 18x_{22} + 5x_{23}$

Days required for McClymonds's assignment $= 6x_{31} + 14x_{32} + 3x_{33}$

The sum of the completion times for the three project leaders will provide the total days required to complete the three assignments. Thus, the objective function is

$$\text{Min } 10x_{11} + 15x_{12} + 9x_{13} + 9x_{21} + 18x_{22} + 5x_{23} + 6x_{31} + 14x_{32} + 3x_{33}$$

Because the number of project leaders equals the number of clients, all the constraints could be written as equalities. But when the number of project leaders exceeds the number of clients, less-than-or-equal-to constraints must be used for the project leader constraints.

The constraints for the assignment problem reflect the conditions that each project leader can be assigned to at most one client and that each client must have one assigned project leader. These constraints are written as follows:

$$x_{11} + x_{12} + x_{13} \leq 1 \quad \text{Terry's assignment}$$
$$x_{21} + x_{22} + x_{23} \leq 1 \quad \text{Carle's assignment}$$
$$x_{31} + x_{32} + x_{33} \leq 1 \quad \text{McClymonds's assignment}$$
$$x_{11} + x_{21} + x_{31} = 1 \quad \text{Client 1}$$
$$x_{12} + x_{22} + x_{32} = 1 \quad \text{Client 2}$$
$$x_{13} + x_{23} + x_{33} = 1 \quad \text{Client 3}$$

Note that each node in Figure 10.10 has one constraint.

Combining the objective function and constraints into one model provides the following nine-variable, six-constraint linear programming model of the Fowle Marketing Research assignment problem:

Try Problem 17, part (b), for practice in formulating and solving a linear programming model for an assignment problem on the computer.

$$\text{Min} \quad 10x_{11} + 15x_{12} + 9x_{13} + 9x_{21} + 18x_{22} + 5x_{23} + 6x_{31} + 14x_{32} + 3x_{33}$$

s.t.

$$
\begin{aligned}
x_{11} + x_{12} + x_{13} & & & \leq 1 \\
& x_{21} + x_{22} + x_{23} & & \leq 1 \\
& & x_{31} + x_{32} + x_{33} & \leq 1 \\
x_{11} & + x_{21} & + x_{31} & = 1 \\
x_{12} & + x_{22} & + x_{32} & = 1 \\
x_{13} & + x_{23} & + x_{33} & = 1
\end{aligned}
$$

$$x_{ij} \geq 0 \quad \text{for } i = 1, 2, 3; j = 1, 2, 3$$

Figure 10.11 shows the optimal solution from the answer report for this model. Terry is assigned to client 2 ($x_{12} = 1$), Carle is assigned to client 3 ($x_{23} = 1$), and McClymonds

FIGURE 10.11 OPTIMAL SOLUTION FOR THE FOWLE MARKETING RESEARCH ASSIGNMENT PROBLEM

Objective Cell (Min)

Name	Original Value	Final Value
Minimize Completion Time	0.000	26.000

WEB file

Fowle

Variable Cells

Model Variable	Name	Original Value	Final Value	Integer
X11	Terry to Client 1	0.000	0.000	Contin
X12	Terry to Client 2	0.000	1.000	Contin
X13	Terry to Client 3	0.000	0.000	Contin
X21	Carle to Client 1	0.000	0.000	Contin
X22	Carle to Client 2	0.000	0.000	Contin
X23	Carle to Client 3	0.000	1.000	Contin
X31	McClymonds to Client 1	0.000	1.000	Contin
X32	McClymonds to Client 2	0.000	0.000	Contin
X33	McClymonds to Client 3	0.000	0.000	Contin

TABLE 10.6   OPTIMAL PROJECT LEADER ASSIGNMENTS FOR THE FOWLE
MARKETING RESEARCH ASSIGNMENT PROBLEM

Project Leader	Assigned Client	Days
Terry	2	15
Carle	3	5
McClymonds	1	6
	Total	26

is assigned to client 1 ($x_{31} = 1$). The total completion time required is 26 days. This
solution is summarized in Table 10.6.

Problem Variations

Because the assignment problem can be viewed as a special case of the transportation problem, the problem variations that may arise in an assignment problem parallel those for the
transportation problem. Specifically, we can handle

1. Total number of agents (supply) not equal to the total number of tasks (demand)
2. A maximization objective function
3. Unacceptable assignments

The situation in which the number of agents does not equal the number of tasks is analogous
to total supply not equaling total demand in a transportation problem. If the number of agents
exceeds the number of tasks, the extra agents simply remain unassigned in the linear programming solution. If the number of tasks exceeds the number of agents, the linear programming
model will not have a feasible solution. In this situation, a simple modification is to add enough
dummy agents to equalize the number of agents and the number of tasks. For instance, in the
Fowle problem we might have had five clients (tasks) and only three project leaders (agents). By
adding two dummy project leaders, we can create a new assignment problem with the number of
project leaders equal to the number of clients. The objective function coefficients for the assignment of dummy project leaders would be zero so that the value of the optimal solution would
represent the total number of days required by the assignments actually made (no assignments
will actually be made to the clients receiving dummy project leaders).

If the assignment alternatives are evaluated in terms of revenue or profit rather than
time or cost, the linear programming formulation can be solved as a maximization rather
than a minimization problem. In addition, if one or more assignments are unacceptable, the
corresponding decision variable can be removed from the linear programming formulation.
This situation could happen, for example, if an agent did not have the experience necessary
for one or more of the tasks.

A General Linear Programming Model

To show the general linear programming model for an assignment problem with m agents
and n tasks, we use the following notation:

$$x_{ij} = \begin{cases} 1 & \text{if agent } i \text{ is assigned to task } j \\ 0 & \text{otherwise} \end{cases}$$

$$c_{ij} = \text{the cost of assigning agent } i \text{ to task } j$$

The general linear programming model is as follows:

$$\text{Min} \quad \sum_{i=1}^{m} \sum_{j=1}^{n} c_{ij} x_{ij}$$

s.t.

$$\sum_{j=1}^{n} x_{ij} \leq 1 \qquad i = 1, 2, \ldots, m \quad \text{Agents}$$

$$\sum_{i=1}^{m} x_{ij} = 1 \qquad j = 1, 2, \ldots, n \quad \text{Tasks}$$

$$x_{ij} \geq 0 \qquad \text{for all } i \text{ and } j$$

At the beginning of this section, we indicated that a distinguishing feature of the assignment problem is that *one* agent is assigned to *one and only one* task. In generalizations of the assignment problem where one agent can be assigned to two or more tasks, the linear programming formulation of the problem can be easily modified. For example, let us assume that in the Fowle Marketing Research problem Terry could be assigned up to two clients; in this case, the constraint representing Terry's assignment would be $x_{11} + x_{12} + x_{13} \leq 2$. In general, if a_i denotes the upper limit for the number of tasks to which agent i can be assigned, we write the agent constraints as

$$\sum_{j=1}^{n} x_{ij} \leq a_i \qquad i = 1, 2, \ldots, m$$

If some tasks require more than one agent, the linear programming formulation can also accommodate the situation. Use the number of agents required as the right-hand side of the appropriate task constraint.

NOTES AND COMMENTS

1. As noted, the assignment model is a special case of the transportation model. We stated in the Notes and Comments at the end of the preceding section that the optimal solution to the transportation problem will consist of integer values for the decision variables as long as the supplies and demands are integers. For the assignment problem, all supplies and demands equal 1; thus, the optimal solution must be integer valued and the integer values must be 0 or 1.
2. Combining the method for handling multiple assignments with the notion of a dummy agent

provides another means of dealing with situations when the number of tasks exceeds the number of agents. That is, we add one dummy agent but provide the dummy agent with the capability to handle multiple tasks. The number of tasks the dummy agent can handle is equal to the difference between the number of tasks and the number of agents.
3. The Q.M. in Action, Assigning Consultants to Clients at Energy Education, Inc., describes how a consulting company uses an assignment problem as part of an innovative model to minimize the travel costs for their clients.

Q.M. *in* ACTION

ASSIGNING CONSULTANTS TO CLIENTS AT ENERGY EDUCATION, INC.*

Energy Education, Inc. (EEI) is a consulting firm that provides experts to schools, universities, and other orga-

nizations to implement energy conservation programs. It is estimated that EEI has helped more than 1100 clients save in excess of $2.3 billion in energy costs over

*Based on Junfang Yu and Randy Hoff, "Optimal Routing and Assignment of Consultants for Energy Education, Inc.," *Interfaces* (March–April 2013), 142–151.

(*continued*)

the course of the 25 years in which EEI has provided consulting services. EEI consultants spend almost all of their time working at the client location, which results in frequent travel and high travel costs for the company. On average, a consultant for EEI spends about $1000 per week for air travel costs alone.

Because of the large expense associated with consultant travel, EEI seeks to minimize travel costs whenever possible. To help minimize consultant travel cost, EEI created models that assign consultants to clients. The objective of these models is to minimize the total number of flights required each week while meeting all client needs. These models include an assignment-type problem similar to those described in this chapter as part of a more complicated framework that also considers the optimal routing of consultants among client locations.

The models developed by EEI are solved using dedicated optimization software, and the output of the models provides a weekly assignment and travel route for each consultant. The new models resulted in a 44% reduction in flight costs for EEI over a 12-week period in comparison to the consultant assignments and travel plans used previously. The number of consultants required to meet all client demand was also reduced using the new models, leading to a direct labor cost reduction of 15%. In total, EEI realized an annual cost savings of nearly $500,000 from implementing their models for assigning consultants to clients and optimizing consultant travel.

Shortest-Route Problem

In this section we consider a problem in which the objective is to determine the **shortest route**, or *path*, between two nodes in a network. We will demonstrate the shortest-route problem by considering the situation facing the Gorman Construction Company. Gorman has several construction sites located throughout a three-county area. With multiple daily trips carrying personnel, equipment, and supplies from Gorman's office to the construction sites, the costs associated with transportation activities are substantial. The travel alternatives between Gorman's office and each construction site can be described by the road network shown in Figure 10.12. The road distances in miles between the nodes are shown above the corresponding arcs. In this application, Gorman would like to determine the route that will minimize the total travel distance between Gorman's office (located at node 1) and the construction site located at node 6.

A key to developing a model for the shortest-route problem is to understand that the problem is a special case of the transshipment problem. Specifically, the Gorman shortest-route problem can be viewed as a transshipment problem with one origin node (node 1), one destination node (node 6), and four transshipment nodes (nodes 2, 3, 4 and 5). The transshipment network for the Gorman shortest-route problem is shown in Figure 10.13. Arrows added to the arcs show the direction of flow, which is always *out* of the origin node and *into* the destination node. Note also that two directed arcs are shown between the pairs of transshipment nodes. For example, one arc going from node 2 to node 3 indicates that the shortest route may go from node 2 to node 3, and one arc going from node 3 to node 2 indicates that the shortest route may go from node 3 to node 2. The distance between two transshipment nodes is the same in either direction.

To find the shortest route between node 1 and node 6, think of node 1 as having a supply of 1 unit and node 6 as having a demand of 1 unit. Let x_{ij} denote the number of units that flow or are shipped from node i to node j. Because only 1 unit will be shipped from node 1 to node 6, the value of x_{ij} will be either 1 or 0. Thus, if $x_{ij} = 1$, the arc from node i to node j is

FIGURE 10.12   ROAD NETWORK FOR THE GORMAN COMPANY SHORTEST-ROUTE PROBLEM

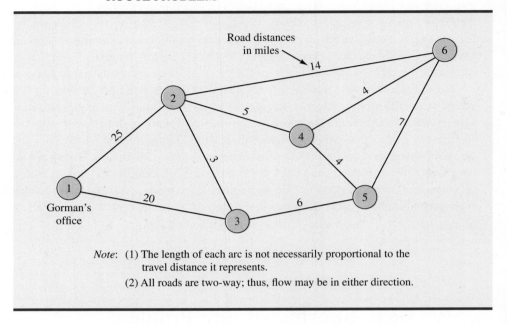

Note: (1) The length of each arc is not necessarily proportional to the travel distance it represents.
(2) All roads are two-way; thus, flow may be in either direction.

FIGURE 10.13   TRANSSHIPMENT NETWORK FOR THE GORMAN SHORTEST-ROUTE PROBLEM

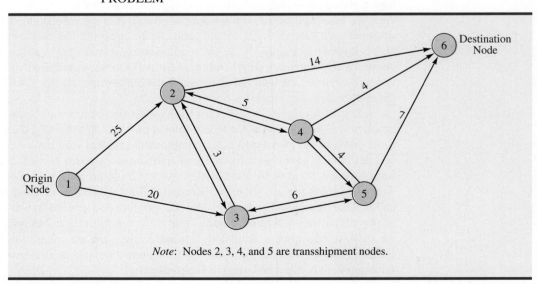

Note: Nodes 2, 3, 4, and 5 are transshipment nodes.

on the shortest route from node 1 to node 6; if $x_{ij} = 0$, the arc from node i to node j is not on the shortest route. Because we are looking for the shortest route between node 1 and node 6, the objective function for the Gorman problem is

$$\text{Min} \quad 25x_{12} + 20x_{13} + 3x_{23} + 3x_{32} + 5x_{24} + 5x_{42} + 14x_{26} + 6x_{35} + 6x_{53}$$
$$+ 4x_{45} + 4x_{54} + 4x_{46} + 7x_{56}$$

To develop the constraints for the model, we begin with node 1. Because the supply at node 1 is 1 unit, the flow out of node 1 must equal 1. Thus, the constraint for node 1 is written

$$x_{12} + x_{13} = 1$$

For transshipment nodes 2, 3, 4, and 5, the flow out of each node must equal the flow into each node; thus, the flow out minus the flow in must be 0. The constraints for the four transshipment nodes are as follows:

	Flow Out	Flow In
Node 2	$x_{23} + x_{24} + x_{26}$	$-x_{12} - x_{32} - x_{42} = 0$
Node 3	$x_{32} + x_{35}$	$-x_{13} - x_{23} - x_{53} = 0$
Node 4	$x_{42} + x_{45} + x_{46}$	$-x_{24} - x_{54} \quad\quad = 0$
Node 5	$x_{53} + x_{54} + x_{56}$	$-x_{35} - x_{45} \quad\quad = 0$

Because node 6 is the destination node with a demand of 1 unit, the flow into node 6 must equal 1. Thus, the constraint for node 6 is written as

$$x_{26} + x_{46} + x_{56} = 1$$

Including the negative constraints $x_{ij} \geq 0$ for all i and j, the linear programming model for the Gorman shortest-route problem is shown in Figure 10.14.

The optimal solution from the answer report for the Gorman shortest-route problem is shown in Figure 10.15. The objective function value of 32 indicates that the shortest route between Gorman's office located at node 1 to the construction site located at node 6 is 32 miles. With $x_{13} = 1$, $x_{32} = 1$, $x_{24} = 1$, and $x_{46} = 1$, the shortest route from node 1 to node 6

FIGURE 10.14 LINEAR PROGRAMMING FORMULATION OF THE GORMAN SHORTEST-ROUTE PROBLEM

Min $25x_{12} + 20x_{13} + 3x_{23} + 3x_{32} + 5x_{24} + 5x_{42} + 14x_{26} + 6x_{35} + 6x_{53} + 4x_{45} + 4x_{54} + 4x_{46} + 7x_{56}$
s.t.

$$
\begin{array}{llll}
x_{12} + x_{13} & = 1 & \text{Origin node} \\
-x_{12} + x_{23} - x_{32} + x_{24} - x_{42} + x_{26} & = 0 \\
- x_{13} - x_{23} + x_{32} + x_{35} - x_{53} & = 0 \\
- x_{24} + x_{42} + x_{45} - x_{54} + x_{46} & = 0 \\
- x_{35} + x_{53} - x_{45} + x_{54} + x_{56} = 0 \\
x_{26} + x_{46} + x_{56} = 1 & \text{Destination node}
\end{array}
$$

$x_{ij} \geq 0$ for all i and j

FIGURE 10.15   OPTIMAL SOLUTION FOR THE GORMAN SHORTEST-ROUTE PROBLEM

Objective Cell (Min)

Name	Original Value	Final Value
Total Distance	0.000	32.000

Variable Cells

Cell	Name	Original Value	Final Value	Integer
X12	Flow from Node 1 to 2	0.000	0.000	Contin
X13	Flow from Node 1 to 3	0.000	1.000	Contin
X23	Flow from Node 2 to 3	0.000	0.000	Contin
X32	Flow from Node 3 to 2	0.000	1.000	Contin
X24	Flow from Node 2 to 4	0.000	1.000	Contin
X42	Flow from Node 4 to 2	0.000	0.000	Contin
X26	Flow from Node 2 to 6	0.000	0.000	Contin
X35	Flow from Node 3 to 5	0.000	0.000	Contin
X53	Flow from Node 5 to 3	0.000	0.000	Contin
X45	Flow from Node 4 to 5	0.000	0.000	Contin
X54	Flow from Node 5 to 4	0.000	0.000	Contin
X46	Flow from Node 4 to 6	0.000	1.000	Contin
X56	Flow from Node 5 to 6	0.000	0.000	Contin

Gorman

Try Problem 23 to practice solving a shortest-route problem.

is 1–3–2–4–6; in other words, the shortest route takes us from node 1 to node 3; then from node 3 to node 2; then from node 2 to node 4; and finally from node 4 to node 6.

A General Linear Programming Model

To show the general linear programming model for the shortest-route problem, we use the following notation:

$$x_{ij} = \begin{cases} 1 & \text{if the arc from node } i \text{ to node } j \text{ is on the shortest route} \\ 0 & \text{otherwise} \end{cases}$$

c_{ij} = the distance, time, or cost associated with the arc from node i to node j

The general linear programming model for the shortest-route problem is as follows:

$$\text{Min} \sum_{\text{all arcs}} c_{ij} x_{ij}$$

s.t.

$$\sum_{\text{arcs out}} x_{ij} = 1 \qquad \text{Origin node } i$$

$$\sum_{\text{arcs out}} x_{ij} - \sum_{\text{arcs in}} x_{ij} = 0 \qquad \text{Transshipment nodes}$$

$$\sum_{\text{arcs in}} x_{ij} = 1 \qquad \text{Destination node } j$$

NOTES AND COMMENTS

1. In the Gorman problem we assumed that all roads in the network are two-way. As a result, the road connecting nodes 2 and 3 in the road network resulted in the creation of two corresponding arcs in the transshipment network. Two decision variables, x_{23} and x_{32}, were required to show that the shortest route might go from node 2 to node 3 or from node 3 to node 2. If the road connecting nodes 2 and 3 had been a one-way road allowing flow only from node 2 to node 3, decision variable x_{32} would not have been included in the model.

10.4 Maximal Flow Problem

The objective in a **maximal flow** problem is to determine the maximum amount of flow (vehicles, messages, fluid, etc.) that can enter and exit a network system in a given period of time. In this problem, we attempt to transmit flow through all arcs of the network as efficiently as possible. The amount of flow is limited due to capacity restrictions on the various arcs of the network. For example, highway types limit vehicle flow in a transportation system, while pipe sizes limit oil flow in an oil distribution system. The maximum or upper limit on the flow in an arc is referred to as the **flow capacity** of the arc. Even though we do not specify capacities for the nodes, we do assume that the flow out of a node is equal to the flow into the node.

As an example of the maximal flow problem, consider the north–south interstate highway system passing through Cincinnati, Ohio. The north–south vehicle flow reaches a level of 15,000 vehicles per hour at peak times. Due to a summer highway maintenance program, which calls for the temporary closing of lanes and lower speed limits, a network of alternate routes through Cincinnati has been proposed by a transportation planning committee. The alternate routes include other highways as well as city streets. Because of differences in speed limits and traffic patterns, flow capacities vary depending on the particular streets and roads used. The proposed network with arc flow capacities is shown in Figure 10.16.

FIGURE 10.16   NETWORK OF HIGHWAY SYSTEM AND FLOW CAPACITIES (1000S/HOUR) FOR CINCINNATI

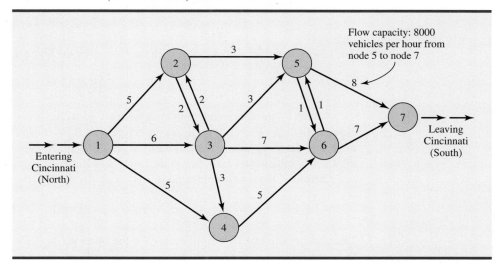

FIGURE 10.17 FLOW OVER ARC FROM NODE 7 TO NODE 1 TO REPRESENT TOTAL FLOW THROUGH THE CINCINNATI HIGHWAY SYSTEM

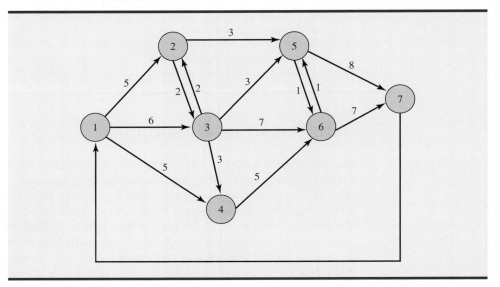

The direction of flow for each arc is indicated, and the arc capacity is shown next to each arc. Note that most of the streets are one-way. However, a two-way street can be found between nodes 2 and 3 and between nodes 5 and 6. In both cases, the capacity is the same in each direction.

We will show how to develop a capacitated transshipment model for the maximal flow problem. First, we will add an arc from node 7 back to node 1 to represent the total flow through the highway system. Figure 10.17 shows the modified network. The newly added arc shows no capacity; indeed, we will want to maximize the flow over that arc. Maximizing the flow over the arc from node 7 to node 1 is equivalent to maximizing the number of cars that can get through the north–south highway system passing through Cincinnati.

The decision variables are as follows:

$$x_{ij} = \text{amount of traffic flow from node } i \text{ to node } j$$

The objective function that maximizes the flow over the highway system is

$$\text{Max } x_{71}$$

As with all transshipment problems, each arc generates a variable and each node generates a constraint. For each node, a conservation of flow constraint represents the requirement that the flow out must equal the flow in. Or, stated another way, the flow out minus the flow in must equal zero. For node 1, the flow out is $x_{12} + x_{13} + x_{14}$, and the flow in is x_{71}. Therefore, the constraint for node 1 is

$$x_{12} + x_{13} + x_{14} - x_{71} = 0$$

The conservation of flow constraints for the other six nodes are developed in a similar fashion.

	Flow Out	**Flow In**	
Node 2	$x_{23} + x_{25}$	$-x_{12} - x_{32}$	$= 0$
Node 3	$x_{32} + x_{34} + x_{35} + x_{36}$	$-x_{13} - x_{23}$	$= 0$
Node 4	x_{46}	$-x_{14} - x_{34}$	$= 0$
Node 5	$x_{56} + x_{57}$	$-x_{25} - x_{35} - x_{65}$	$= 0$
Node 6	$x_{65} + x_{67}$	$-x_{36} - x_{46} - x_{56}$	$= 0$
Node 7	x_{71}	$-x_{57} - x_{67}$	$= 0$

Additional constraints are needed to enforce the capacities on the arcs. These 14 simple upper-bound constraints are given.

$$x_{12} \leq 5 \quad x_{13} \leq 6 \quad x_{14} \leq 5$$
$$x_{23} \leq 2 \quad x_{25} \leq 3$$
$$x_{32} \leq 2 \quad x_{34} \leq 3 \quad x_{35} \leq 5 \quad x_{36} \leq 7$$
$$x_{46} \leq 5$$
$$x_{56} \leq 1 \quad x_{57} \leq 8$$
$$x_{65} \leq 1 \quad x_{67} \leq 7$$

Note that the only arc without a capacity is the one we added from node 7 to node 1.

The optimal solution from the answer report for this 15-variable, 21-constraint linear programming problem is shown in Figure 10.18. We note that the value of the optimal

FIGURE 10.18   OPTIMAL SOLUTION FOR THE CINCINNATI HIGHWAY SYSTEM MAXIMAL FLOW PROBLEM

Objective Cell (Max)

Name	Original Value	Final Value
Max Flow	0.000	14.000

Variable Cells

Cell	Name	Original Value	Final Value	Integer
X12	Flow from 1 to 2	0.000	3.000	Contin
X13	Flow from 1 to 3	0.000	6.000	Contin
X14	Flow from 1 to 4	0.000	5.000	Contin
X23	Flow from 2 to 3	0.000	0.000	Contin
X25	Flow from 2 to 5	0.000	3.000	Contin
X34	Flow from 3 to 4	0.000	0.000	Contin
X35	Flow from 3 to 5	0.000	3.000	Contin
X36	Flow from 3 to 6	0.000	3.000	Contin
X32	Flow from 3 to 2	0.000	0.000	Contin
X46	Flow from 4 to 6	0.000	5.000	Contin
X56	Flow from 5 to 6	0.000	0.000	Contin
X57	Flow from 5 to 7	0.000	7.000	Contin
X65	Flow from 6 to 5	0.000	1.000	Contin
X67	Flow from 6 to 7	0.000	7.000	Contin
X71	Flow from 7 to 1	0.000	14.000	Contin

WEB file

Cincinnati

FIGURE 10.19   MAXIMAL FLOW PATTERN FOR THE CINCINNATI HIGHWAY
SYSTEM NETWORK

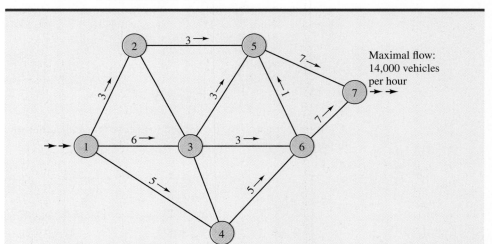

*Try Problem 29 for practice
in solving a maximal flow
problem.*

solution is 14. This result implies that the maximal flow over the highway system is 14,000
vehicles. Figure 10.19 shows how the vehicle flow is routed through the original highway
network. We note, for instance, that 3000 vehicles per hour are routed between nodes 1 and
2, 6000 vehicles per hour are routed between nodes 1 and 3, 0 vehicles are routed between
nodes 2 and 3, and so on.

The results of the maximal flow analysis indicate that the planned highway network
system will not handle the peak flow of 15,000 vehicles per hour. The transportation
planners will have to expand the highway network, increase current arc flow capacities,
or be prepared for serious traffic problems. If the network is extended or modified, another maximal flow analysis will determine the extent of any improved flow. The Q.M.
in Action, Finding the Shortest Paths for Containerships, describes how Danaos Corporation computes shortest path routes for their containerships to save millions of dollars in
reduced fuel costs.

NOTES AND COMMENTS

1. The maximal flow problem of this section can
also be solved with a slightly different formulation if the extra arc between nodes 7 and 1 is not
used. The alternate approach is to maximize the
flow into node 7 ($x_{57} + x_{67}$) and drop the conservation of flow constraints for nodes 1 and 7.
However, the formulation used in this section is
most common in practice.

2. Network models can be used to describe a variety of important problems. Unfortunately, no
one network solution algorithm can be used to
solve every network problem. It is important to
recognize the specific type of problem being
modeled in order to select the correct specialized solution algorithm.

FINDING THE SHORTEST PATHS FOR CONTAINERSHIPS*

Danaos Corporation is an international shipping company based in Greece that owns more than 60 containerships. Danaos' containerships travel millions of miles each year to transport millions of containers all around the world. Danaos has developed a powerful tool to improve shipping operations, known as the Operations Research in Ship Management (ORISMA) tool. Part of this tool involves the solving of shortest-path problems to determine a containership's optimal route.

Optimizing the travel route for a containership generates substantial savings through the use of less fuel and because it allows the ship to generate more revenue

---

*Based on Takis Varelas, Sofia Archontaki, John Dimotikalis, Osman Turan, Iraklis Lazakis, and Orestis Varelas, "Optimizing Ship Routing to Maximize Fleet Revenue at Danaos," *Interfaces* (January–February 2013), 37–47.

in less time by visiting additional ports to pick up and deliver containers. A subcomponent of ORISMA determines the shortest-path route between two given waypoints (intermediate points of a ship's complete voyage) by defining nodes in the feasible sailing space for the containership.

Danaos determined that it generated $1.3 million in additional revenue in a single year by using ORISMA to reduce the amount of time containerships spent traveling between ports. Furthermore, it saved $3.2 million in reduced fuel costs during the same year. Danaos estimates that further use of ORISMA will increase profitability by 7–10% annually in the future. As a nice byproduct of Danaos' reduced travel times and decreased fuel usage, carbon emissions have been cut substantially, and customers are happier to get their products with less lead time.

A Production and Inventory Application

The introduction to supply chain models in Section 10.1 involved applications for the shipment of goods from several supply locations or origins to several demand sites or destinations. Although the shipment of goods is the subject of many supply chain problems, supply chain models can be developed for applications that have nothing to do with the physical shipment of goods from origins to destinations. In this section we show how to use a transshipment model to solve a production and inventory problem.

Contois Carpets is a small manufacturer of carpeting for home and office installations. Production capacity, demand, production cost per square yard, and inventory holding cost per square yard for the next four quarters are shown in Table 10.7. Note that production capacity, demand, and production costs vary by quarter, whereas the cost of carrying inventory from one quarter to the next is constant at $0.25 per yard. Contois wants to

TABLE 10.7   PRODUCTION, DEMAND, AND COST ESTIMATES FOR CONTOIS CARPETS

Quarter	Production Capacity (square yards)	Demand (square yards)	Production Cost ($/square yard)	Inventory Cost ($/square yard)
1	600	400	2	0.25
2	300	500	5	0.25
3	500	400	3	0.25
4	400	400	3	0.25

determine how many yards of carpeting to manufacture each quarter to minimize the total production and inventory cost for the four-quarter period.

The network flows into and out of demand nodes are what make the model a transshipment model.

We begin by developing a network representation of the problem. First, we create four nodes corresponding to the production in each quarter and four nodes corresponding to the demand in each quarter. Each production node is connected by an outgoing arc to the demand node for the same period. The flow on the arc represents the number of square yards of carpet manufactured for the period. For each demand node, an outgoing arc represents the amount of inventory (square yards of carpet) carried over to the demand node for the next period. Figure 10.20 shows the network model. Note that nodes 1–4 represent the production for each quarter and that nodes 5–8 represent the demand for each quarter. The quarterly production capacities are shown in the left margin, and the quarterly demands are shown in the right margin.

FIGURE 10.20   NETWORK REPRESENTATION OF THE CONTOIS CARPETS PROBLEM

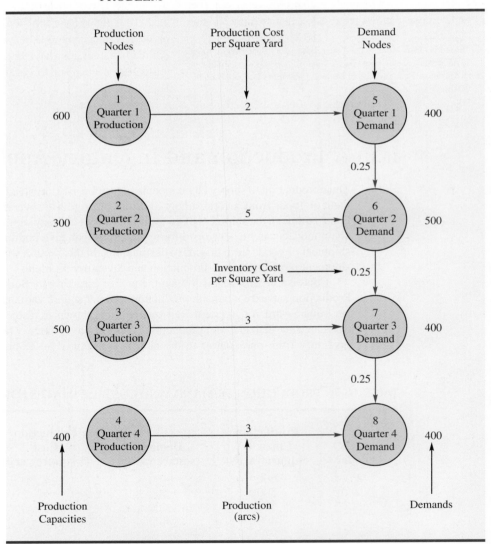

The objective is to determine a production scheduling and inventory policy that will minimize the total production and inventory cost for the four quarters. Constraints involve production capacity and demand in each quarter. As usual, a linear programming model can be developed from the network by establishing a constraint for each node and a variable for each arc.

Let x_{15} denote the number of square yards of carpet manufactured in quarter 1. The capacity of the facility is 600 square yards in quarter 1, so the production capacity constraint is

$$x_{15} \leq 300$$

Using similar decision variables, we obtain the production capacities for quarters 2–4:

$$x_{26} \leq 300$$
$$x_{37} \leq 500$$
$$x_{48} \leq 400$$

We now consider the development of the constraints for each of the demand nodes. For node 5, one arc enters the node, which represents the number of square yards of carpet produced in quarter 1, and one arc leaves the node, which represents the number of square yards of carpet that will not be sold in quarter 1 and will be carried over for possible sale in quarter 2. In general, for each quarter the beginning inventory plus the production minus the ending inventory must equal demand. However, because quarter 1 has no beginning inventory, the constraint for node 5 is

$$x_{15} - x_{56} = 400$$

The constraints associated with the demand nodes in quarters 2, 3, and 4 are

$$x_{56} + x_{26} - x_{67} = 500$$
$$x_{67} + x_{37} - x_{78} = 400$$
$$x_{78} + x_{48} = 400$$

Note that the constraint for node 8 (fourth-quarter demand) involves only two variables because no provision is made for holding inventory for a fifth quarter.

The objective is to minimize total production and inventory cost, so we write the objective function as

$$\text{Min} \quad 2x_{15} + 5x_{26} + 3x_{37} + 3x_{48} + 0.25x_{56} + 0.25x_{67} + 0.25x_{78}$$

The complete linear programming formulation of the Contois Carpets problem is

$$\text{Min} \quad 2x_{15} + 5x_{26} + 3x_{37} + 3x_{48} + 0.25x_{56} + 0.25x_{67} + 0.25x_{78}$$

s.t.

$$
\begin{array}{llllllll}
x_{15} & & & & & & & \leq 600 \\
& x_{26} & & & & & & \leq 300 \\
& & x_{37} & & & & & \leq 500 \\
& & & x_{48} & & & & \leq 400 \\
x_{15} & & & & - x_{56} & & & = 400 \\
& x_{26} & & & + x_{56} & - x_{67} & & = 500 \\
& & x_{37} & & & + x_{67} & - x_{78} & = 400 \\
& & & x_{48} & & & + x_{78} & = 400 \\
\end{array}
$$

$$x_{ij} \geq 0 \quad \text{for all } i \text{ and } j$$

FIGURE 10.21   OPTIMAL SOLUTION FOR THE CONTOIS CARPETS PROBLEM

Objective Cell (Min)

Name	Original Value	Final Value
Total Cost	0.000	5150.000

Contois

Variable Cells

Model Variable	Name	Original Value	Final Value	Integer
X15	Flow from Node 1 to 5	0.000	600.000	Contin
X26	Flow from Node 2 to 6	0.000	300.000	Contin
X37	Flow from Node 3 to 7	0.000	400.000	Contin
X48	Flow from Node 4 to 8	0.000	400.000	Contin
X56	Flow from Node 5 to 6	0.000	200.000	Contin
X67	Flow from Node 6 to 7	0.000	0.000	Contin
X78	Flow from Node 7 to 8	0.000	0.000	Contin

Figure 10.21 shows the optimal solution from the answer report for this problem. Contois Carpets should manufacture 600 square yards of carpet in quarter 1, 300 square yards in quarter 2, 400 square yards in quarter 3, and 400 square yards in quarter 4. Note also that 200 square yards will be carried over from quarter 1 to quarter 2. The total production and inventory cost is $5150.

NOTES AND COMMENTS

1. For the network models presented in this chapter, the amount leaving the starting node for an arc is always equal to the amount entering the ending node for that arc. An extension of such a network model is the case where a gain or a loss occurs as an arc is traversed. The amount entering the destination node may be greater or smaller than the amount leaving the origin node. For instance, if cash is the commodity flowing across an arc, the cash earns interest from one period to the next. Thus, the amount of cash entering the next period is greater than the amount leaving the previous period by the amount of interest earned. Networks with gains or losses are treated in more advanced texts on network flow programming.

Summary

In this chapter we introduced models related to supply chain problems—specifically, transportation and transshipment problems—as well as assignment, shortest-route, and maximal flow problems. All of these types of problems belong to the special category of linear programs called *network flow problems*. In general, the network model for these problems consists of nodes representing origins, destinations, and, if necessary, transshipment points in the network system. Arcs are used to represent the routes for shipment, travel, or flow between the various nodes.

Transportation problems and transshipment problems are commonly encountered when dealing with supply chains. The general transportation problem has *m* origins and *n* destinations. Given the supply at each origin, the demand at each destination, and unit shipping cost between each origin and each destination, the transportation model determines the optimal amounts to ship from each origin to each destination. The transshipment problem is an extension of the transportation problem involving transfer points referred to as transshipment nodes. In this more general model, we allow arcs between any pair of nodes in the network.

The assignment problem is a special case of the transportation problem in which all supply and all demand values are 1. We represent each agent as an origin node and each task as a destination node. The assignment model determines the minimum cost or maximum profit assignment of agents to tasks.

The shortest-route problem finds the shortest route or path between two nodes of a network. Distance, time, and cost are often the criteria used for this model. The shortest-route problem can be expressed as a transshipment problem with one origin and one destination. By shipping one unit from the origin to the destination, the solution will determine the shortest route through the network.

The maximal flow problem can be used to allocate flow to the arcs of the network so that flow through the network system is maximized. Arc capacities determine the maximum amount of flow for each arc. With these flow capacity constraints, the maximal flow problem is expressed as a capacitated transshipment problem.

In the last section of the chapter, we showed how a variation of the transshipment problem could be used to solve a production and inventory problem. In the chapter appendix we show how to use Excel to solve three of the distribution and network problems presented in the chapter.

Glossary

Arcs The lines connecting the nodes in a network.

Assignment problem A network flow problem that often involves the assignment of agents to tasks; it can be formulated as a linear program and is a special case of the transportation problem.

Capacitated transportation problem A variation of the basic transportation problem in which some or all of the arcs are subject to capacity restrictions.

Capacitated transshipment problem A variation of the transshipment problem in which some or all of the arcs are subject to capacity restrictions.

Dummy origin An origin added to a transportation problem to make the total supply equal to the total demand. The supply assigned to the dummy origin is the difference between the total demand and the total supply.

Flow capacity The maximum flow for an arc of the network. The flow capacity in one direction may not equal the flow capacity in the reverse direction.

Maximal flow The maximum amount of flow that can enter and exit a network system during a given period of time.

Network A graphical representation of a problem consisting of numbered circles (nodes) interconnected by a series of lines (arcs); arrowheads on the arcs show the direction of flow. Transportation, assignment, and transshipment problems are network flow problems.

Nodes The intersection or junction points of a network.

Shortest route Shortest path between two nodes in a network.

Supply chain The set of all interconnected resources involved in producing and distributing a product.

Transportation problem A network flow problem that often involves minimizing the cost of shipping goods from a set of origins to a set of destinations; it can be formulated and solved as a linear program by including a variable for each arc and a constraint for each node.

Transshipment problem An extension of the transportation problem to distribution problems involving transfer points and possible shipments between any pair of nodes.

Problems

1. A company imports goods at two ports: Philadelphia and New Orleans. Shipments of one product are made to customers in Atlanta, Dallas, Columbus, and Boston. For the next planning period, the supplies at each port, customer demands, and shipping costs per case from each port to each customer are as follows:

Port	Customers Atlanta	Dallas	Columbus	Boston	Port Supply
Philadelphia	2	6	6	2	5000
New Orleans	1	2	5	7	3000
Demand	1400	3200	2000	1400	

Develop a network representation of the distribution system (transportation problem).

2. Consider the following network representation of a transportation problem:

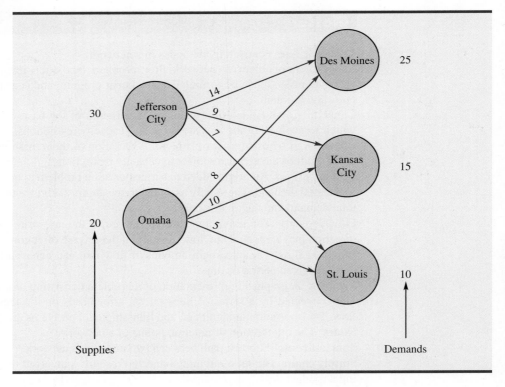

The supplies, demands, and transportation costs per unit are shown on the network.
a. Develop a linear programming model for this problem; be sure to define the variables in your model.
b. Solve the linear program to determine the optimal solution.

3. Tri-County Utilities, Inc., supplies natural gas to customers in a three-county area. The company purchases natural gas from two companies: Southern Gas and Northwest Gas. Demand forecasts for the coming winter season are as follows: Hamilton County, 400 units; Butler County, 200 units; and Clermont County, 300 units. Contracts to provide the following quantities have been written: Southern Gas, 500 units; and Northwest Gas, 400 units. Distribution costs for the counties vary, depending upon the location of the suppliers. The distribution costs per unit (in thousands of dollars) are as follows:

| | | To | |
From	Hamilton	Butler	Clermont
Southern Gas	10	20	15
Northwest Gas	12	15	18

a. Develop a network representation of this problem.
b. Develop a linear programming model that can be used to determine the plan that will minimize total distribution costs.
c. Describe the distribution plan and show the total distribution cost.
d. Recent residential and industrial growth in Butler County has the potential for increasing demand by as much as 100 units. Which supplier should Tri-County contract with to supply the additional capacity?

4. GloFish, Inc. has genetically engineered a species of fish that glows in normal lighting conditions. The company believes the new fish will be a huge success as a new pet option for children and adults alike. GloFish, Inc. has developed two varieties of its glowing fish: one that glows red and one that glows blue. GloFish currently "grows" its fish at two different fish farms in the United States: one in Michigan and one in Texas. The Michigan farm can produce up to 1 million red and 1 million blue GloFish per year; the Texas farm can produce up to 600,000 GloFish, but only in the blue variety. GloFish ships its fish between the fish farms and its three retail stores using a third-party shipper. The shipment rates between origins and destinations are shown in the following table. These costs are per fish and do not depend on the color of the fish being shipped.

| | Cost of Shipping GloFish | | |
	Retailer 1	Retailer 2	Retailer 3
Michigan	$1.00	$2.50	$0.50
Texas	$2.00	$1.50	$2.80

Estimated demands by each retailer for each color of fish are shown in the following table.

| | Demand for GloFish | | |
	Retailer 1	Retailer 2	Retailer 3
Red	320,000	300,000	160,000
Blue	380,000	450,000	290,000

a. What is the optimal policy for the fish farms? How many red and blue fish should be produced in Michigan and shipped to each retailer? How many blue fish should be produced in Texas and shipped to each retailer?

b. What is the minimum shipping cost that can be incurred and still meet demand requirements at retailers 1, 2, and 3?

c. How much should GloFish be willing to invest to enable the Texas farm to produce both red and blue GloFish while maintaining the maximum of 600,000 total fish produced at the Texas farm?

5. Premier Consulting's two consultants, Avery and Baker, can be scheduled to work for clients up to a maximum of 160 hours each over the next four weeks. A third consultant, Campbell, has some administrative assignments already planned and is available for clients up to a maximum of 140 hours over the next four weeks. The company has four clients with projects in process. The estimated hourly requirements for each of the clients over the four-week period are as follows:

Client	Hours
A	180
B	75
C	100
D	85

Hourly rates vary for the consultant–client combination and are based on several factors, including project type and the consultant's experience. The rates (dollars per hour) for each consultant–client combination are as follows:

			Client	
Consultant	A	B	C	D
Avery	100	125	115	100
Baker	120	135	115	120
Campbell	155	150	140	130

a. Develop a network representation of the problem.

b. Formulate the problem as a linear program, with the optimal solution providing the hours each consultant should be scheduled for each client to maximize the consulting firm's billings. What is the schedule and what is the total billing?

c. New information shows that Avery doesn't have the experience to be scheduled for client B. If this consulting assignment is not permitted, what impact does it have on total billings? What is the revised schedule?

6. Klein Chemicals, Inc., produces a special oil-based material that is currently in short supply. Four of Klein's customers have already placed orders that together exceed the combined capacity of Klein's two plants. Klein's management faces the problem of deciding how many units it should supply to each customer. Because the four customers are in different industries, different prices can be charged because of the various industry pricing structures. However, slightly different production costs at the two plants and varying transportation costs between the plants and customers make a "sell to the highest bidder"

strategy unacceptable. After considering price, production costs, and transportation costs, Klein established the following profit per unit for each plant–customer alternative:

	Customer			
Plant	D_1	D_2	D_3	D_4
Clifton Springs	$32	$34	$32	$40
Danville	$34	$30	$28	$38

The plant capacities and customer orders are as follows:

Plant	**Capacity (units)**	**Distributor Orders (units)**
Clifton Springs	5000	D_1 2000
		D_2 5000
Danville	3000	D_3 3000
		D_4 2000

How many units should each plant produce for each customer to maximize profits? Which customer demands will not be met? Show your network model and linear programming formulation.

7. Aggie Power Generation supplies electrical power to residential customers for many U.S. cities. Its main power generation plants are located in Los Angeles, Tulsa, and Seattle. The following table shows Aggie Power Generation's major residential markets, the annual demand in each market (in megawatts or MW), and the cost to supply electricity to each market from each power generation plant (prices are in $/MW).

	Distribution Costs			
City	**Los Angeles**	**Tulsa**	**Seattle**	**Demand (MW)**
Seattle	$356.25	$593.75	$59.38	950.00
Portland	$356.25	$593.75	$178.13	831.25
San Francisco	$178.13	$475.00	$296.88	2375.00
Boise	$356.25	$475.00	$296.88	593.75
Reno	$237.50	$475.00	$356.25	950.00
Bozeman	$415.63	$415.63	$296.88	593.75
Laramie	$356.25	$415.63	$356.25	1187.50
Park City	$356.25	$356.25	$475.00	712.50
Flagstaff	$178.13	$475.00	$593.75	1187.50
Durango	$356.25	$296.88	$593.75	1543.75

a. If there are no restrictions on the amount of power that can be supplied by any of the power plants, what is the optimal solution to this problem? Which cities should be supplied by which power plants? What is the total annual power distribution cost for this solution?

b. If at most 4000 MW of power can be supplied by any one of the power plants, what is the optimal solution? What is the annual increase in power distribution cost that results from adding these constraints to the original formulation?

8. Forbelt Corporation has a one-year contract to supply motors for all refrigerators produced by the Ice Age Corporation. Ice Age manufactures the refrigerators at four locations around the country: Boston, Dallas, Los Angeles, and St. Paul. Plans call for the following number (in thousands) of refrigerators to be produced at each location:

Boston	50
Dallas	70
Los Angeles	60
St. Paul	80

Forbelt's three plants are capable of producing the motors. The plants and production capacities (in thousands) are as follows:

Denver	100
Atlanta	100
Chicago	150

Because of varying production and transportation costs, the profit that Forbelt earns on each lot of 1000 units depends on which plant produced the lot and which destination it was shipped to. The following table gives the accounting department estimates of the profit per unit (shipments will be made in lots of 1000 units):

	Shipped To			
Produced At	**Boston**	**Dallas**	**Los Angeles**	**St. Paul**
Denver	7	11	8	13
Atlanta	20	17	12	10
Chicago	8	18	13	16

With profit maximization as a criterion, Forbelt's management wants to determine how many motors should be produced at each plant and how many motors should be shipped from each plant to each destination.
a. Develop a network representation of this problem.
b. Find the optimal solution.

9. The Ace Manufacturing Company has orders for three similar products:

Product	Orders (units)
A	2000
B	500
C	1200

Three machines are available for the manufacturing operations. All three machines can produce all the products at the same production rate. However, due to varying defect percentages of each product on each machine, the unit costs of the products vary depending on the machine used. Machine capacities for the next week and the unit costs are as follows:

Machine	Capacity (units)
1	1500
2	1500
3	1000

Machine	Product A	B	C
1	$1.00	$1.20	$0.90
2	$1.30	$1.40	$1.20
3	$1.10	$1.00	$1.20

Use the transportation model to develop the minimum cost production schedule for the products and machines. Show the linear programming formulation.

10. Hatcher Enterprises uses a chemical called Rbase in production operations at five divisions. Only six suppliers of Rbase meet Hatcher's quality control standards. All six suppliers can produce Rbase in sufficient quantities to accommodate the needs of each division. The quantity of Rbase needed by each Hatcher division and the price per gallon charged by each supplier are as follows:

Division	Demand (1000s of gallons)
1	40
2	45
3	50
4	35
5	45

Supplier	Price per gallon ($)
1	12.60
2	14.00
3	10.20
4	14.20
5	12.00
6	13.00

The cost per gallon ($) for shipping from each supplier to each division is provided in the following table:

Division	Supplier 1	2	3	4	5	6
1	2.75	2.50	3.15	2.80	2.75	2.75
2	0.80	0.20	5.40	1.20	3.40	1.00
3	4.70	2.60	5.30	2.80	6.00	5.60
4	2.60	1.80	4.40	2.40	5.00	2.80
5	3.40	0.40	5.00	1.20	2.60	3.60

Hatcher believes in spreading its business among suppliers so that the company will be less affected by supplier problems (e.g., labor strikes or resource availability). Company policy requires that each division have a separate supplier.

a. For each supplier–division combination, compute the total cost of supplying the division's demand.

b. Determine the optimal assignment of suppliers to divisions.

11. The distribution system for the Herman Company consists of three plants, two warehouses, and four customers. Plant capacities and shipping costs per unit (in $) from each plant to each warehouse are as follows:

| | Warehouse | | |
Plant	1	2	Capacity
1	4	7	450
2	8	5	600
3	5	6	380

Customer demand and shipping costs per unit (in $) from each warehouse to each customer are as follows:

| | Customer | | | |
Warehouse	1	2	3	4
1	6	4	8	4
2	3	6	7	7
Demand	300	300	300	400

a. Develop a network representation of this problem.
b. Formulate a linear programming model of the problem.
c. Solve the linear program to determine the optimal shipping plan.

12. Refer to Problem 11. Suppose that shipments between the two warehouses are permitted at $2 per unit and that direct shipments can be made from plant 3 to customer 4 at a cost of $7 per unit.
a. Develop a network representation of this problem.
b. Formulate a linear programming model of this problem.
c. Solve the linear program to determine the optimal shipping plan.

13. Sports of All Sorts produces, distributes, and sells high-quality skateboards. Its supply chain consists of three factories (located in Detroit, Los Angeles, and Austin) that produce skateboards. The Detroit and Los Angeles facilities can produce 350 skateboards per week, but the Austin plant is larger and can produce up to 700 skateboards per week. Skateboards must be shipped from the factories to one of four distribution centers, or DCs (located in Iowa, Maryland, Idaho, and Arkansas). Each distribution center can process (repackage, mark for sale, and ship) at most 500 skateboards per week.

Skateboards are then shipped from the distribution centers to retailers. Sports of All Sorts supplies three major U.S. retailers: Just Sports, Sports 'N Stuff, and The Sports Dude. The weekly demands are 200 skateboards at Just Sports, 500 skateboards at Sports 'N Stuff, and 650 skateboards at The Sports Dude. The following tables display the per-unit costs for shipping skateboards between the factories and DCs and for shipping between the DCs and the retailers.

	Shipping Costs (\$ per skateboard)			
Factory/DCs	**Iowa**	**Maryland**	**Idaho**	**Arkansas**
Detroit	25.00	25.00	35.00	40.00
Los Angeles	35.00	45.00	35.00	42.50
Austin	40.00	40.00	42.50	32.50

Retailers/DCs	**Iowa**	**Maryland**	**Idaho**	**Arkansas**
Just Sports	30.00	20.00	35.00	27.50
Sports 'N Stuff	27.50	32.50	40.00	25.00
The Sports Dude	30.00	40.00	32.50	42.50

    a. Draw the network representation for this problem.
    b. Build a model to minimize the transportation cost of a logistics system that will deliver skateboards from the factories to the distribution centers and from the distribution centers to the retailers. What is the optimal production strategy and shipping pattern for Sports of All Sorts? What is the minimum attainable transportation cost?
    c. Sports of All Sorts is considering expansion of the Iowa DC capacity to 800 units per week. The annual amortized cost of expansion is \$40,000. Should the company expand the Iowa DC capacity so that it can process 800 skateboards per week? (Assume 50 operating weeks per year.)

14. The Moore & Harman Company is in the business of buying and selling grain. An important aspect of the company's business is arranging for the purchased grain to be shipped to customers. If the company can keep freight costs low, profitability will improve.

    The company recently purchased three rail cars of grain at Muncie, Indiana; six rail cars at Brazil, Indiana; and five rail cars at Xenia, Ohio. Twelve carloads of grain have been sold. The locations and the amount sold at each location are as follows:

Location	**Number of Rail Car Loads**
Macon, GA	2
Greenwood, SC	4
Concord, SC	3
Chatham, NC	3

All shipments must be routed through either Louisville or Cincinnati. Shown are the shipping costs per bushel (in cents) from the origins to Louisville and Cincinnati and the costs per bushel to ship from Louisville and Cincinnati to the destinations.

	To	
From	**Louisville**	**Cincinnati**
Muncie	8	6 ← Cost per bushel
Brazil	3	8 from Muncie to
Xenia	9	3 Cincinnati is 6¢

From	To			
	Macon	**Greenwood**	**Concord**	**Chatham**
Louisville	44	34	34	32
Cincinnati	57	35	28	24

Cost per bushel from
Cincinnati to Greenwood is 35¢

Determine a shipping schedule that will minimize the freight costs necessary to satisfy demand. Which (if any) rail cars of grain must be held at the origin until buyers can be found?

15. The following linear programming formulation is for a transshipment problem:

$$\text{Min} \quad 11x_{13} + 12x_{14} + 10x_{21} + 8x_{34} + 10x_{35} + 11x_{42} + 9x_{45} + 12x_{52}$$

s.t.

$$
\begin{aligned}
x_{13} + x_{14} - x_{21} &\le 5 \\
x_{21} \quad\quad - x_{42} \quad\quad - x_{52} &\le 3 \\
x_{13} \quad - x_{34} - x_{35} &= 6 \\
- x_{14} \quad - x_{34} \quad + x_{42} + x_{45} &\le 2 \\
x_{35} \quad\quad + x_{45} - x_{52} &= 4
\end{aligned}
$$

$$x_{ij} \ge 0 \quad \text{for all } i, j$$

Show the network representation of this problem.

16. A rental car company has an imbalance of cars at seven of its locations. The following network shows the locations of concern (the nodes) and the cost to move a car between locations. A positive number by a node indicates an excess supply at the node, and a negative number indicates an excess demand.

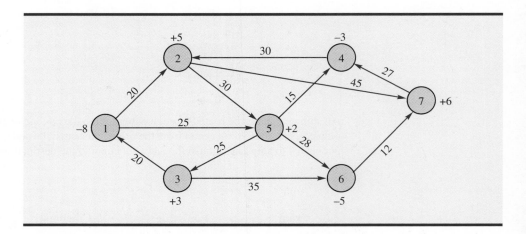

a.   Develop a linear programming model of this problem.
b.   Solve the model formulated in part (a) to determine how the cars should be redistributed among the locations.

17. Scott and Associates, Inc., is an accounting firm that has three new clients. Project leaders will be assigned to the three clients. Based on the different backgrounds and experiences of the leaders, the various leader–client assignments differ in terms of projected completion times. The possible assignments and the estimated completion times in days are as follows:

| | | Client | |
Project Leader	1	2	3
Jackson	10	16	32
Ellis	14	22	40
Smith	22	24	34

a. Develop a network representation of this problem.
b. Formulate the problem as a linear program, and solve. What is the total time required?

18. CarpetPlus sells and installs floor covering for commercial buildings. Brad Sweeney, a CarpetPlus account executive, was just awarded the contract for five jobs. Brad must now assign a CarpetPlus installation crew to each of the five jobs. Because the commission Brad will earn depends on the profit CarpetPlus makes, Brad would like to determine an assignment that will minimize total installation costs. Currently, five installation crews are available for assignment. Each crew is identified by a color code, which aids in tracking of job progress on a large white board. The following table shows the costs (in hundreds of dollars) for each crew to complete each of the five jobs:

| | | | Job | | |
Crew	1	2	3	4	5
Red	30	44	38	47	31
White	25	32	45	44	25
Blue	23	40	37	39	29
Green	26	38	37	45	28
Brown	26	34	44	43	28

a. Develop a network representation of the problem.
b. Formulate and solve a linear programming model to determine the minimum cost assignment.

19. A local television station plans to drop four Friday evening programs at the end of the season. Steve Botuchis, the station manager, developed a list of six potential replacement programs. Estimates of the advertising revenue ($) that can be expected for each of the new programs in the four vacated time slots are as follows. Mr. Botuchis asked you to find the assignment of programs to time slots that will maximize total advertising revenue.

	5:00– 5:30 P.M.	5:30– 6:00 P.M.	7:00– 7:30 P.M.	8:00– 8:30 P.M.
Home Improvement	5000	3000	6000	4000
World News	7500	8000	7000	5500
NASCAR Live	8500	5000	6500	8000
Wall Street Today	7000	6000	6500	5000
Hollywood Briefings	7000	8000	3000	6000
Ramundo & Son	6000	4000	4500	7000

20. The U.S. Cable Company uses a distribution system with five distribution centers and eight customer zones. Each customer zone is assigned a sole source supplier; each customer zone receives all of its cable products from the same distribution center. In an effort to balance demand and workload at the distribution centers, the company's vice president of logistics specified that distribution centers may not be assigned more than three customer zones. The following table shows the five distribution centers and cost of supplying each customer zone (in thousands of dollars):

	Customer Zones							
Distribution Centers	**Los Angeles**	**Chicago**	**Columbus**	**Atlanta**	**Newark**	**Kansas City**	**Denver**	**Dallas**
Plano	70	47	22	53	98	21	27	13
Nashville	75	38	19	58	90	34	40	26
Flagstaff	15	78	37	82	111	40	29	32
Springfield	60	23	8	39	82	36	32	45
Boulder	45	40	29	75	86	25	11	37

a. Determine the assignment of customer zones to distribution centers that will minimize cost.
b. Which distribution centers, if any, are not used?
c. Suppose that each distribution center is limited to a maximum of two customer zones. How does this constraint change the assignment and the cost of supplying customer zones?

21. United Express Service (UES) uses large quantities of packaging materials at its four distribution hubs. After screening potential suppliers, UES identified six vendors that can provide packaging materials that will satisfy its quality standards. UES asked each of the six vendors to submit bids to satisfy annual demand at each of its four distribution hubs over the next year. The following table lists the bids received (in thousands of dollars). UES wants to ensure that each of the distribution hubs is serviced by a different vendor. Which bids should UES accept, and which vendors should UES select to supply each distribution hub?

	Distribution Hub			
Bidder	**1**	**2**	**3**	**4**
Martin Products	190	175	125	230
Schmidt Materials	150	235	155	220
Miller Containers	210	225	135	260
D&J Burns	170	185	190	280
Larbes Furnishings	220	190	140	240
Lawler Depot	270	200	130	260

22. The analytics department head at a major midwestern university will be scheduling faculty to teach courses during the coming autumn term. Four core courses need to be covered. The four courses are at the undergraduate (UG), master of business administration (MBA), master of science (MS), and doctor of philosophy (Ph.D.) levels. Four professors will be assigned to the courses, with each professor receiving one of the courses. Student evaluations of professors are available from previous terms. Based on a rating scale of 4 (excellent), 3 (very good), 2 (average), 1 (fair), and 0 (poor), the average student evaluations for each professor are shown. Professor D does not have a Ph.D. and cannot

be assigned to teach the Ph.D. level course. If the department head makes teaching assignments based on maximizing the student evaluation ratings over all four courses, what staffing assignments should be made?

Professor	UG	MBA	MS	Ph.D.
		Course		
A	2.8	2.2	3.3	3.0
B	3.2	3.0	3.6	3.6
C	3.3	3.2	3.5	3.5
D	3.2	2.8	2.5	—

SELF test

23. Find the shortest route from node 1 to node 7 in the network shown.

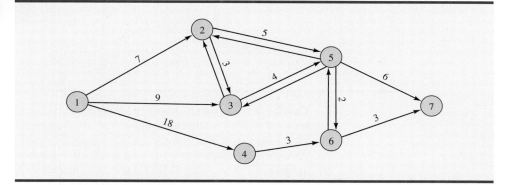

24. In the original Gorman Construction Company problem, we found the shortest distance from the office (node 1) to the construction site located at node 6. Because some of the roads are highways and others are city streets, the shortest-distance routes between the office and the construction site may not necessarily provide the quickest or shortest-time route. Shown here is the Gorman road network with travel time rather than distance. Find the shortest route from Gorman's office to the construction site at node 6 if the objective is to minimize travel time rather than distance.

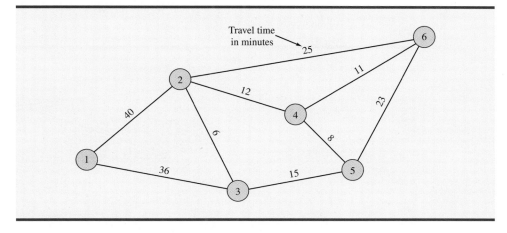

25. Cleveland Area Rapid Delivery (CARD) operates a delivery service in the Cleveland metropolitan area. Most of CARD's business involves rapid delivery of documents and

parcels between offices during the business day. CARD promotes its ability to make fast and on-time deliveries anywhere in the metropolitan area. When a customer calls with a delivery request, CARD quotes a guaranteed delivery time. The following network shows the street routes available. The numbers above each arc indicate the travel time in minutes between the two locations.

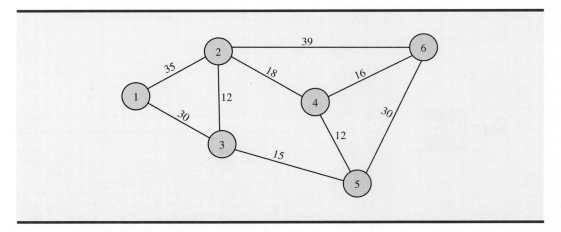

a. Develop a linear programming model that can be used to find the minimum time required to make a delivery from location 1 to location 6.
b. How long does it take to make a delivery from location 1 to location 6?
c. Assume that it is now 1:00 P.M. and that CARD just received a request for a pickup at location 1. The closest CARD courier is 8 minutes away from location 1. If CARD provides a 20% safety margin in guaranteeing a delivery time, what is the guaranteed delivery time if the package picked up at location 1 is to be delivered to location 6?

26. Morgan Trucking Company operates a special pickup and delivery service between Chicago and six other cities located in a four-state area. When Morgan receives a request for service, it dispatches a truck from Chicago to the city requesting service as soon as possible. With both fast service and minimum travel costs as objectives for Morgan, it is important that the dispatched truck take the shortest route from Chicago to the specified city. Assume that the following network (not drawn to scale) with distances given in miles represents the highway network for this problem. Find the shortest-route distances from Chicago to node 6.

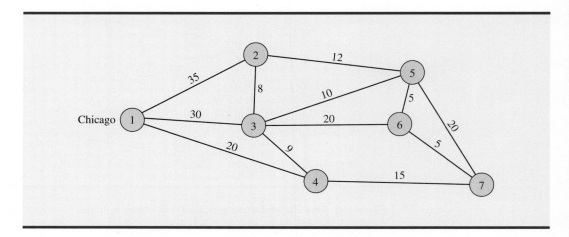

27. City Cab Company identified 10 primary pickup and drop locations for cab riders in New York City. In an effort to minimize travel time and improve customer service and the utilization of the company's fleet of cabs, management would like the cab drivers to take the shortest route between locations whenever possible. Using the following network of roads and streets, what is the route a driver beginning at location 1 should take to reach location 10? The travel times in minutes are shown on the arcs of the network. Note that there are two one-way streets and that the direction is shown by the arrows.

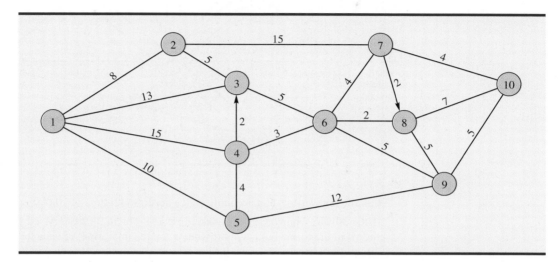

28. The five nodes in the following network represent points one year apart over a four-year period. Each node indicates a time when a decision is made to keep or replace a firm's computer equipment. If a decision is made to replace the equipment, a decision must also be made as to how long the new equipment will be used. The arc from node 0 to node 1 represents the decision to keep the current equipment one year and replace it at the end of the year. The arc from node 0 to node 2 represents the decision to keep the current equipment two years and replace it at the end of year 2. The numbers above the arcs indicate the total cost associated with the equipment replacement decisions. These costs include discounted purchase price, trade-in value, operating costs, and maintenance costs. Use a shortest-route model to determine the minimum cost equipment replacement policy for the four-year period.

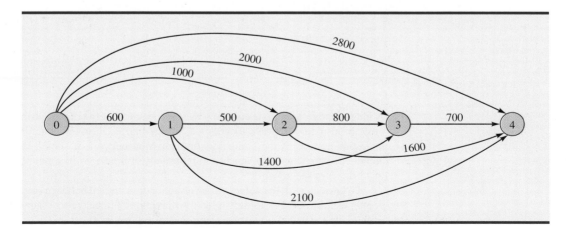

29.   The north–south highway system passing through Albany, New York, can accommodate the capacities shown.

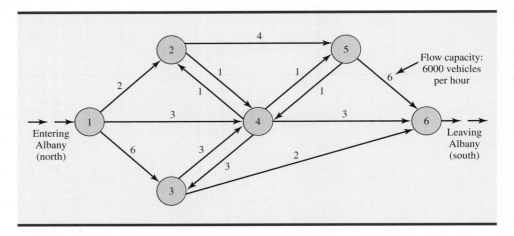

Can the highway system accommodate a north–south flow of 10,000 vehicles per hour?

30.   If the Albany highway system described in Problem 29 has revised flow capacities as shown in the following network, what is the maximal flow in vehicles per hour through the system? How many vehicles per hour must travel over each road (arc) to obtain this maximal flow?

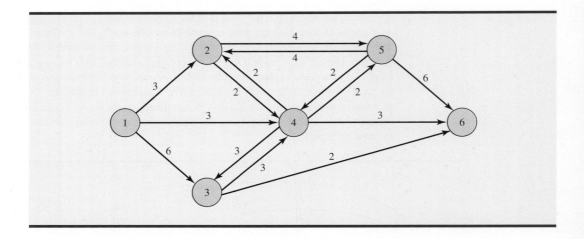

31.   A long-distance telephone company uses a fiber-optic network to transmit phone calls and other information between locations. Calls are carried through cable lines and switching nodes. A portion of the company's transmission network is shown here. The numbers above each arc show the capacity in thousands of messages that can be transmitted over that branch of the network.

   To keep up with the volume of information transmitted between origin and destination points, use the network to determine the maximum number of messages that may be sent from a city located at node 1 to a city located at node 7.

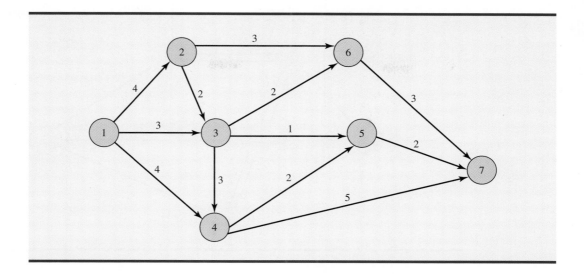

32. The High-Price Oil Company owns a pipeline network that is used to convey oil from its source to several storage locations. A portion of the network is as follows:

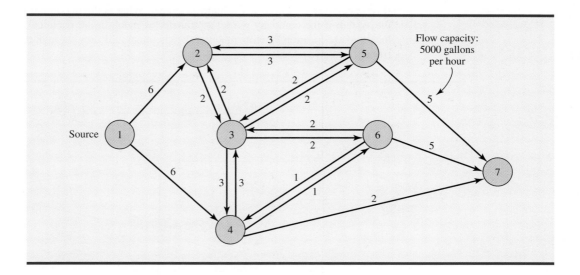

Due to the varying pipe sizes, the flow capacities vary. By selectively opening and closing sections of the pipeline network, the firm can supply any of the storage locations.

a. If the firm wants to fully utilize the system capacity to supply storage location 7, how long will it take to satisfy a location 7 demand of 100,000 gallons? What is the maximal flow for this pipeline system?

b. If a break occurs on line 2–3 and that line is closed down, what is the maximal flow for the system? How long will it take to transmit 100,000 gallons to location 7?

33. For the following highway network system, determine the maximal flow in vehicles per hour:

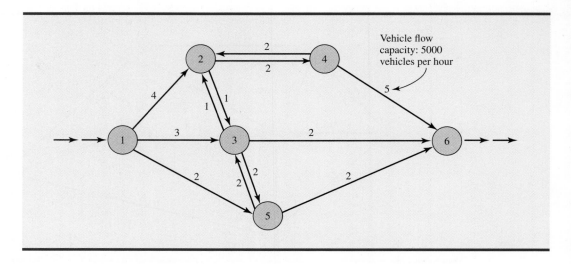

The highway commission is considering adding highway section 3–4 to permit a flow of 2000 vehicles per hour or, at an additional cost, a flow of 3000 vehicles per hour. What is your recommendation for the 3–4 arc of the network?

34. A chemical processing plant has a network of pipes that are used to transfer liquid chemical products from one part of the plant to another. The following pipe network has pipe flow capacities in gallons per minute as shown. What is the maximum flow capacity for the system if the company wishes to transfer as much liquid chemical as possible from location 1 to location 9? How much of the chemical will flow through the section of pipe from node 3 to node 5?

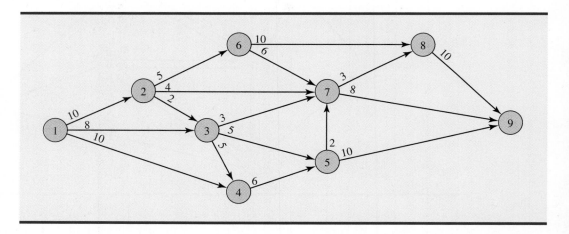

35. Refer to the Contois Carpets problem, for which the network representation is shown in Figure 10.20. Suppose that Contois has a beginning inventory of 50 yards of carpet and requires an inventory of 100 yards at the end of quarter 4.
   a. Develop a network representation of this modified problem.
   b. Develop a linear programming model and solve for the optimal solution.

36. Sanders Fishing Supply of Naples, Florida, manufactures a variety of fishing equipment that it sells throughout the United States. For the next three months, Sanders estimates demand for a particular product at 150, 250, and 300 units, respectively. Sanders can

supply this demand by producing on regular time or overtime. Because of other commitments and anticipated cost increases in month 3, the production capacities in units and the production costs per unit are as follows:

Production	Capacity (units)	Cost per Unit ($)
Month 1—Regular	275	50
Month 1—Overtime	100	80
Month 2—Regular	200	50
Month 2—Overtime	50	80
Month 3—Regular	100	60
Month 3—Overtime	50	100

Inventory may be carried from one month to the next, but the cost is $20 per unit per month. For example, regular production from month 1 used to meet demand in month 2 would cost Sanders $50 + $20 = $70 per unit. This same month 1 production used to meet demand in month 3 would cost Sanders $50 + 2($20) = $90 per unit.

a. Develop a network representation of this production scheduling problem as a transportation problem. (*Hint*: Use six origin nodes; the supply for origin node 1 is the maximum that can be produced in month 1 on regular time, and so on.)

b. Develop a linear programming model that can be used to schedule regular and overtime production for each of the three months.

c. What is the production schedule, how many units are carried in inventory each month, and what is the total cost?

d. Is there any unused production capacity? If so, where?

Case Problem 1   Solutions Plus

Solutions Plus is an industrial chemicals company that produces specialized cleaning fluids and solvents for a wide variety of applications. Solutions Plus just received an invitation to submit a bid to supply Great North American railroad with a cleaning fluid for locomotives. Great North American needs the cleaning fluid at 11 locations (railway stations); it provided the following information to Solutions Plus regarding the number of gallons of cleaning fluid required at each location (see Table 10.8).

Solutions Plus can produce the cleaning fluid at its Cincinnati plant for $1.20 per gallon. Even though the Cincinnati location is its only plant, Solutions Plus has negotiated

TABLE 10.8   GALLONS OF CLEANING FLUID REQUIRED AT EACH LOCATION

Location	Gallons Required	Location	Gallons Required
Santa Ana	22,418	Glendale	33,689
El Paso	6,800	Jacksonville	68,486
Pendleton	80,290	Little Rock	148,586
Houston	100,447	Bridgeport	111,475
Kansas City	24,570	Sacramento	112,000
Los Angeles	64,761		

TABLE 10.9   FREIGHT COST ($ PER GALLON)

	Cincinnati	Oakland
Santa Ana	—	0.22
El Paso	0.84	0.74
Pendleton	0.83	0.49
Houston	0.45	—
Kansas City	0.36	—
Los Angeles	—	0.22
Glendale	—	0.22
Jacksonville	0.34	—
Little Rock	0.34	—
Bridgeport	0.34	—
Sacramento	—	0.15

with an industrial chemicals company located in Oakland, California, to produce and ship up to 500,000 gallons of the locomotive cleaning fluid to selected Solutions Plus customer locations. The Oakland company will charge Solutions Plus $1.65 per gallon to produce the cleaning fluid, but Solutions Plus thinks that the lower shipping costs from Oakland to some customer locations may offset the added cost to produce the product.

The president of Solutions Plus, Charlie Weaver, contacted several trucking companies to negotiate shipping rates between the two production facilities (Cincinnati and Oakland) and the locations where the railroad locomotives are cleaned. Table 10.9 shows the quotes received in terms of dollars per gallon. The "—" entries in Table 10.9 identify shipping routes that will not be considered because of the large distances involved. These quotes for shipping rates are guaranteed for one year.

To submit a bid to the railroad company, Solutions Plus must determine the price per gallon it will charge. Solutions Plus usually sells its cleaning fluids for 15% more than its cost to produce and deliver the product. For this big contract, however, Fred Roedel, the director of marketing, suggested that maybe the company should consider a smaller profit margin. In addition, to ensure that if Solutions Plus wins the bid, it will have adequate capacity to satisfy existing orders as well as accept orders for other new business, the management team decided to limit the number of gallons of the locomotive cleaning fluid produced in the Cincinnati plant to 500,000 gallons at most.

Managerial Report

You are asked to make recommendations that will help Solutions Plus prepare a bid. Your report should address, but not be limited to, the following issues:

1. If Solutions Plus wins the bid, which production facility (Cincinnati or Oakland) should supply the cleaning fluid to the locations where the railroad locomotives are cleaned? How much should be shipped from each facility to each location?
2. What is the breakeven point for Solutions Plus? That is, how low can the company go on its bid without losing money?
3. If Solutions Plus wants to use its standard 15% markup, how much should it bid?
4. Freight costs are significantly affected by the price of oil. The contract on which Solutions Plus is bidding is for two years. Discuss how fluctuation in freight costs might affect the bid Solutions Plus submits.

Case Problem 2   Supply Chain Design for the Darby Company

The Darby Company manufactures and distributes meters used to measure electric power consumption. The company started with a small production plant in El Paso and gradually built a customer base throughout Texas. A distribution center was established in Fort Worth, Texas, and later, as business expanded, a second distribution center was established in Santa Fe, New Mexico.

The El Paso plant was expanded when the company began marketing its meters in Arizona, California, Nevada, and Utah. With the growth of the West Coast business, the Darby Company opened a third distribution center in Las Vegas and just two years ago opened a second production plant in San Bernardino, California.

Manufacturing costs differ between the company's production plants. The cost of each meter produced at the El Paso plant is $10.50. The San Bernardino plant utilizes newer and more efficient equipment; as a result, manufacturing costs are $0.50 per meter less than at the El Paso plant.

Due to the company's rapid growth, not much attention had been paid to the efficiency of its supply chain, but Darby's management decided that it is time to address this issue. The cost of shipping a meter from each of the two plants to each of the three distribution centers is shown in Table 10.10.

The quarterly production capacity is 30,000 meters at the older El Paso plant and 20,000 meters at the San Bernardino plant. Note that no shipments are allowed from the San Bernardino plant to the Fort Worth distribution center.

The company serves nine customer zones from the three distribution centers. The forecast of the number of meters needed in each customer zone for the next quarter is shown in Table 10.11.

TABLE 10.10   SHIPPING COST PER UNIT FROM PRODUCTION PLANTS TO DISTRIBUTION CENTERS ($)

	Distribution Center		
Plant	**Fort Worth**	**Santa Fe**	**Las Vegas**
El Paso	3.20	2.20	4.20
San Bernardino	—	3.90	1.20

TABLE 10.11   QUARTERLY DEMAND FORECAST

Customer Zone	Demand (meters)
Dallas	6300
San Antonio	4880
Wichita	2130
Kansas City	1210
Denver	6120
Salt Lake City	4830
Phoenix	2750
Los Angeles	8580
San Diego	4460

TABLE 10.12   SHIPPING COST FROM THE DISTRIBUTION CENTERS TO THE CUSTOMER ZONES

Distribution Center	Customer Zone								
	Dallas	San Antonio	Wichita	Kansas City	Denver	Salt Lake City	Phoenix	Los Angeles	San Diego
Fort Worth	0.3	2.1	3.1	4.4	6.0	—	—	—	—
Santa Fe	5.2	5.4	4.5	6.0	2.7	4.7	3.4	3.3	2.7
Las Vegas	—	—	—	—	5.4	3.3	2.4	2.1	2.5

The cost per unit of shipping from each distribution center to each customer zone is given in Table 10.12; note that some distribution centers cannot serve certain customer zones. These are indicated by a dash, "—".

In its current supply chain, demand at the Dallas, San Antonio, Wichita, and Kansas City customer zones is satisfied by shipments from the Fort Worth distribution center. In a similar manner, the Denver, Salt Lake City, and Phoenix customer zones are served by the Santa Fe distribution center, and the Los Angeles and San Diego customer zones are served by the Las Vegas distribution center. To determine how many units to ship from each plant, the quarterly customer demand forecasts are aggregated at the distribution centers, and a transportation model is used to minimize the cost of shipping from the production plants to the distribution centers.

Managerial Report

You are asked to make recommendations for improving Darby Company's supply chain. Your report should address, but not be limited to, the following issues:

1. If the company does not change its current supply chain, what will its distribution costs be for the following quarter?
2. Suppose that the company is willing to consider dropping the distribution center limitations; that is, customers could be served by any of the distribution centers for which costs are available. Can costs be reduced? If so, by how much?
3. The company wants to explore the possibility of satisfying some of the customer demand directly from the production plants. In particular, the shipping cost is $0.30 per unit from San Bernardino to Los Angeles and $0.70 from San Bernardino to San Diego. The cost for direct shipments from El Paso to San Antonio is $3.50 per unit. Can distribution costs be further reduced by considering these direct plant-to-customer shipments?
4. Over the next five years, Darby is anticipating moderate growth (5000 meters) to the north and west. Would you recommend that Darby consider plant expansion at this time?

Case Problem 3   DK Dental Care

DK Dental Care produces electric toothbrushes at facilities in Omaha, Tampa, Albuquerque, and Eugene. The finished products are shipped every four weeks to warehouses in Boise, Fort Worth, Mobile, Richmond, and Hanover. Each week Omaha produces 2000 cases of electric toothbrushes, Tampa produces 1500 cases of electric toothbrushes, Albuquerque produces 1200 cases of electric toothbrushes, and Eugene produces 2350 cases of electric toothbrushes.

The managers of DK are preparing for the next set of shipments. They have contacted the managers of their five warehouses and found that the Boise warehouse manager anticipates that she will have the capacity to store 8000 cases of electric toothbrushes, the Fort Worth warehouse manager anticipates that she will have the capacity to store 6400 cases of electric toothbrushes, the Mobile warehouse manager anticipates that he will have the capacity to store 5600 cases of electric toothbrushes, the Richmond warehouse manager anticipates that he will have the capacity to store 9200 cases of electric toothbrushes, and the Hanover warehouse manager anticipates that she will have the capacity to store 4800 cases of electric toothbrushes.

Typically, all existing inventory at the warehouses are shipped to retailers before the next shipment of toothbrushes arrives from the manufacturing facilities; however, the Hanover warehouse manager has also asked DK management to consider the large winter storm that is currently offshore in the northern Atlantic Ocean. There is a chance that this storm could develop into a major blizzard and move through Hanover at the time the shipments are due to arrive from the manufacturing facilities. If this happens, the Hanover warehouse will not be able to ship any of its current inventory to retailers and so would have no capacity for additional inventory of electric toothbrushes. Under these circumstances, the shipments to Hanover would be returned to the production facilities where they were produced and then reshipped to other warehouses, and DK would incur both the cost of shipping these electric toothbrushes to the Hanover warehouse and the cost of subsequently shipping them to alternative warehouses.

The transportation costs associated with shipping a case of electric toothbrushes from each production facility to each warehouse are provided in the following table.

Production Facility	Warehouse				
	Boise	Fort Worth	Mobile	Richmond	Hanover
Omaha	$2.15	$1.60	$2.10	$2.15	$2.20
Tampa	$2.30	$2.10	$1.25	$2.10	$2.35
Albuquerque	$1.95	$1.95	$2.25	$2.35	$2.90
Eugene	$1.85	$2.45	$2.75	$2.95	$2.75

Managerial Report

Find DK's optimal shipping plan for this month and prepare a report for the managers of DK that summarizes your findings and recommendations. Include the following:

1. Develop a "no blizzard" plan that tells DK how many cases of electric toothbrushes to ship from each production facility to each warehouse and the total cost associated with these shipments if DK were certain the potential blizzard would not prevent delivery of shipments to Hanover this month.
2. Develop an alternative "blizzard" plan that tells DK how many cases of electric toothbrushes to ship from each production facility to each warehouse and the total cost associated with these shipments if DK were certain the potential blizzard would prevent delivery of shipments to Hanover this month.
3. Suppose the National Weather Service has estimated that the probability this storm will develop into a major blizzard is 0.10, and so DK believes the probability is 0.10 that any shipment to Hanover will have to be returned to the original production facility and then shipped again to a different warehouse. Make a recommendation on whether DK should utilize the "no blizzard" plan or the "blizzard" plan and explain your recommendation.

4. For what probability of the blizzard preventing shipments to the Hanover warehouse are the expected shipping costs equal under the "no blizzard" and "blizzard" plans?

Excel Solver Solution of Transportation, Transshipment, and Assignment Problems

In this appendix we will use an Excel worksheet and Excel Solver to solve transportation, transshipment, and assignment problems. We start with the Foster Generators transportation problem (see Section 10.1).

Transportation Problem

The first step is to enter the data for the transportation costs, the origin supplies, and the destination demands in the top portion of the worksheet. Then the linear programming model is developed in the bottom portion of the worksheet. As with all linear programs, the worksheet model has four key elements: the decision variables, the objective function, the constraint left-hand sides, and the constraint right-hand sides. For a transportation problem, the decision variables are the amounts shipped from each origin to each destination; the objective function is the total transportation cost; the left-hand sides are the number of units shipped from each origin and the number of units shipped into each destination; and the right-hand sides are the origin supplies and the destination demands.

The formulation and solution of the Foster Generators problem are shown in Figure 10.22. The data are in the top portion of the worksheet. The model appears in the bottom portion of the worksheet.

Formulation

The data and descriptive labels are contained in cells A1:F8. The transportation costs are in cells B5:E7. The origin supplies are in cells F5:F7, and the destination demands are in cells B8:E8. The key elements of the model required by the Excel Solver are the decision variables, the objective function, the constraint left-hand sides, and the constraint right-hand sides.

Decision Variables   Cells B17:E19 are reserved for the decision variables. The optimal values are shown to be $x_{11} = 3500$, $x_{12} = 1500$, $x_{22} = 2500$, $x_{23} = 2000$, $x_{24} = 1500$, and $x_{41} = 2500$. All other decision variables equal zero, indicating that nothing will be shipped over the corresponding routes.

Objective Function   The formula SUMPRODUCT(B5:E7,B17:E19) has been placed into cell A13 to compute the cost of the solution. The minimum cost solution is shown to have a value of $39,500.

Left-Hand Sides   Cells F17:F19 contain the left-hand sides for the supply constraints, and cells B20:E20 contain the left-hand sides for the demand constraints.

     Cell F17 = SUM(B17:E17) (Copy to F18:F19)
     Cell B20 = SUM(B17:B19) (Copy to C20:E20)

FIGURE 10.22   EXCEL SOLVER SOLUTION OF THE FOSTER GENERATORS PROBLEM

WEB file

Foster

	A	B	C	D	E	F	G	H
1	**Foster Generators**							
2								
3				**Destination**				
4	**Origin**	to Boston	to Chicago	to St. Louis	to Lexington	**Supply**		
5	Cleveland	3	2	7	6	5000		
6	Bedford	7	5	2	3	6000		
7	York	2	5	4	5	2500		
8	**Demand**	6000	4000	2000	1500			
9								
10								
11	**Model**							
12	**Minimize Total Cost**							
13	39500							
14								
15				**Destination**				
16	**Origin**	to Boston	to Chicago	to St. Louis	to Lexington	**Total**		
17	Cleveland	3500	1500	0	0	5000	<=	5000
18	Bedford	0	2500	2000	1500	6000	<=	6000
19	York	2500	0	0	0	2500	<=	2500
20	**Total**	6000	4000	2000	1500			
21		=	=	=	=			
22		6000	4000	2000	1500			
23								

Right-Hand Sides   Cells H17:H19 contain the right-hand sides for the supply constraints, and cells B22:E22 contain the right-hand sides for the demand constraints.

Cell H17 = F5 (Copy to H18:H19)
Cell B22 = B8 (Copy to C22:E22)

Excel Solver Solution

The solution shown in Figure 10.22 can be obtained by selecting **Solver** from the **Analysis Group** in the **Data Ribbon**. When the **Solver Parameters** dialog box appears, enter the proper values for the constraints and the objective function, select **Simplex LP,** and click the checkbox for **Make Unconstrained Variables Non-negative.** Then click **Solve.** The information entered into the **Solver Parameters** dialog box is shown in Figure 10.23.

Transshipment Problem

The worksheet model we present for the transshipment problem can be used for all the network flow problems (transportation, transshipment, and assignment) in this chapter. We organize the worksheet into two sections: an arc section and a node section. Let us illustrate by showing the worksheet formulation and solution of the Ryan Electronics transshipment problem. Refer to Figure 10.24 as we describe the steps involved.

FIGURE 10.23   EXCEL SOLVER PARAMETERS DIALOG BOX FOR THE FOSTER
GENERATORS PROBLEM

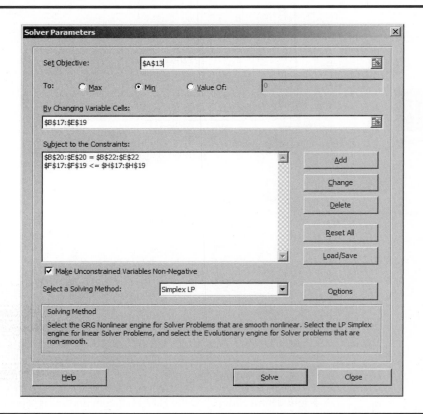

FIGURE 10.24   EXCEL SOLVER SOLUTION FOR THE RYAN ELECTRONICS PROBLEM

Ryan

	A	B	C	D	E	F	G	H	I	J	K
1	**Ryan Electronics Transshipment**										
2											
3											
4	**Arc**	**Cost**									
5	Denver - Kansas City	2	550				**Units Shipped**		**Net**		
6	Denver - Louisville	3	50			**Node**	**In**	**Out**	**Shipments**		**Supply**
7	Atlanta - Kansas City	3	0			Denver		600	600	<=	600
8	Atlanta - Louisville	1	400			Atlanta		400	400	<=	400
9	Kansas City - Detroit	2	200			Kansas City	550	550	0	=	0
10	Kansas City - Miami	6	0			Louisville	450	450	0	=	0
11	Kansas City - Dallas	3	350			Detroit	200		-200	=	-200
12	Kansas City - New Orleans	6	0			Miami	150		-150	=	-150
13	Louisville - Detroit	4	0			Dallas	350		-350	=	-350
14	Louisville - Miami	4	150			New Orleans	300		-300	=	-300
15	Louisville - Dallas	6	0								
16	Louisville - New Orleans	5	300								
17											
18					**Minimize Total Cost**		5200				
19											

Formulation

The arc section uses cells A4:C16. Each arc is identified in cells A5:A16. The arc costs are identified in cells B5:B16, and cells C5:C16 are reserved for the values of the decision variables (the amount shipped over the arcs).

The node section uses cells F5:K14. Each of the nodes is identified in cells F7:F14. The following formulas are entered into cells G7:H14 to represent the flow out and the flow in for each node:

Units shipped in: Cell G9 = C5+C7
                    Cell G10 = C6+C8
                    Cell G11 = C9+C13
                    Cell G12 = C10+C14
                    Cell G13 = C11+C15
                    Cell G14 = C12+C16

Units shipped out: Cell H7 = SUM(C5:C6)
                    Cell H8 = SUM(C7:C8)
                    Cell H9 = SUM(C9:C12)
                    Cell H10 = SUM(C13:C16)

The net shipments in cells I7:I14 are the flows out minus the flows in for each node. For supply nodes, the flow out will exceed the flow in, resulting in positive net shipments. For demand nodes, the flow out will be less than the flow in, resulting in negative net shipments. The "net" supply appears in cells K7:K14. Note that the net supply is negative for demand nodes.

Decision Variables	Cells C5:C16 are reserved for the decision variables. The optimal number of units to ship over each arc is shown.
Objective Function	The formula =SUMPRODUCT(B5:B16,C5:C16) is placed into cell G18 to show the total cost associated with the solution. As shown, the minimum total cost is $5200.
Left-Hand Sides	The left-hand sides of the constraints represent the net shipments for each node. Cells I7:I14 are reserved for these constraints. Cell I7 = H7-G7 (Copy to I8:I14)
Right-Hand Sides	The right-hand sides of the constraints represent the supply at each node. Cells K7:K14 are reserved for these values. (Note the negative supply at the four demand nodes.)

Excel Solver Solution

The solution can be obtained by selecting **Solver** from the **Analysis Group** in the **Data Ribbon**. When the **Solver Parameters** dialog box appears, enter the proper values for the constraints and the objective function, select **Simplex LP**, and click the checkbox for **Make Unconstrained Variables Non-negative.** Then click **Solve.** The information entered into the **Solver Parameters** dialog box is shown in Figure 10.25.

FIGURE 10.25   EXCEL SOLVER PARAMETERS DIALOG BOX FOR THE RYAN
ELECTRONICS PROBLEM

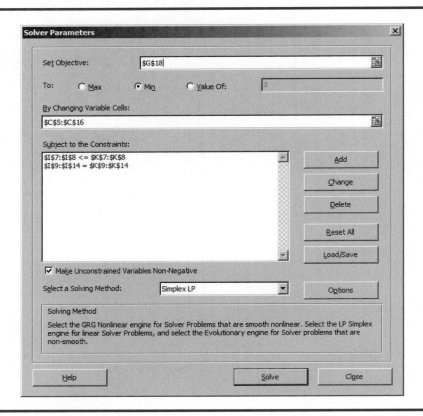

Assignment Problem

The first step is to enter the data for the assignment costs in the top portion of the work-sheet. Even though the assignment model is a special case of the transportation model, it is not necessary to enter values for origin supplies and destination demands because they are always equal to 1.

The linear programming model is developed in the bottom portion of the worksheet. As with all linear programs, the model has four key elements: the decision variables, the objective function, the constraint left-hand sides, and the constraint right-hand sides. For an assignment problem the decision variables indicate whether an agent is assigned to a task (with a 1 for yes or 0 for no); the objective function is the total cost of all assign-ments; the constraint left-hand sides are the number of tasks that are assigned to each agent and the number of agents that are assigned to each task; and the right-hand sides are the number of tasks each agent can handle (1) and the number of agents each task requires (1). The worksheet formulation and solution for the Fowle marketing research problem are shown in Figure 10.26.

FIGURE 10.26   EXCEL SOLVER SOLUTION OF THE FOWLE MARKETING RESEARCH
PROBLEM

WEB file

Fowle

	A	B	C	D	E	F	G
1	**Fowle Marketing Research**						
2							
3			**Client**				
4	**Project Leader**	1	2	3			
5	Terry	10	15	9			
6	Carle	9	18	5			
7	McClymonds	6	14	3			
8							
9							
10	**Model**						
11							
12	**Minimize Completion Time**		26				
13							
14							
15	**Project Leader**	to Client 1	to Client 2	to Client 3	**Total**		
16	Terry	0	1	0	1	<=	1
17	Carle	0	0	1	1	<=	1
18	McClymonds	1	0	0	1	<=	1
19	**Total**	1	1	1			
20		=	=	=			
21		1	1	1			
22							

Formulation

The data and descriptive labels are contained in cells A3:D7. Note that we have not inserted
supply and demand values because they are always equal to 1 in an assignment problem.
The model appears in the bottom portion of the worksheet.

Decision Variables	Cells B16:D18 are reserved for the decision variables. The optimal values are shown to be $x_{12} = 1$, $x_{23} = 1$, and $x_{31} = 1$, with all other variables = 0.
Objective Function	The formula =SUMPRODUCT(B5:D7,B16:D18) has been placed into cell C12 to compute the number of days required to complete all the jobs. The minimum time solution has a value of 26 days.

Left-Hand Sides	Cells E16:E18 contain the left-hand sides of the constraints for the number of clients each project leader can handle. Cells B19:D19 contain the left-hand sides of the constraints requiring that each client must be assigned a project leader.
	    Cell E16 = SUM(B16:D16) (Copy to E17:E18)
	    Cell B19 = SUM(B16:B18) (Copy to C19:D19)

Right-Hand Sides	Cells G16:G18 contain the right-hand sides for the project leader constraints, and cells B21:D21 contain the right-hand sides for the client constraints. All right-hand-side cell values are 1.

Excel Solver Solution

The solution shown in Figure 10.26 can be obtained by selecting **Solver** from the **Analysis Group** in the **Data Ribbon**. When the **Solver Parameters** dialog box appears, enter the proper values for the constraints and the objective function, select **Simplex LP,** and click the checkbox for **Make Unconstrained Variables Non-negative.** Then click **Solve.** The information entered into the **Solver Parameters** dialog box is shown in Figure 10.27.

FIGURE 10.27   EXCEL SOLVER PARAMETERS DIALOG BOX FOR THE FOWLE
                    MARKETING RESEARCH PROBLEM

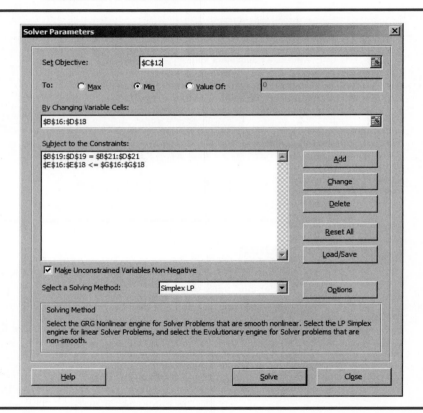

CHAPTER 11

Integer Linear Programming

CONTENTS

In this chapter we discuss a class of problems that are modeled as linear programs with the additional requirement that one or more variables must be integer. Such problems are called **integer linear programs**. If all variables must be integer, we have an all-integer linear program. If some, but not all, variables must be integer, we have a mixed-integer linear program. In many applications of integer linear programming, one or more integer variables are required to equal either 0 or 1. Such variables are called 0-1 or *binary variables*. If all variables are 0-1 variables, we have a 0-1 integer linear program.

Integer variables—especially 0-1 variables—provide substantial modeling flexibility. As a result, the number of applications that can be addressed with linear programming methodology is expanded. For instance, the Q.M. in Action, Optimizing the Transport of Oil Rig Crews, describes how Petrobras uses a model with 0-1 variables for assigning helicopters to flights for transporting crews to and from its oil rigs. Later Q.M. in Action articles describe how the Virginia Court of Appeals uses a 0-1 integer program for scheduling panels of judges to preside over appeal hearings, and how a series of three integer programming models was used to schedule volunteers for the 2003 Edmonton Folk Festival. Many other applications of integer programming are described throughout the chapter.

The objective of this chapter is to provide an applications-oriented introduction to integer linear programming. First, we discuss the different types of integer linear programming models. Then we show the formulation, graphical solution, and computer solution of an all-integer linear program. In Section 11.3 we discuss five applications of integer linear programming that make use of 0-1 variables: capital budgeting, fixed cost, supply chain design, bank location, and market share optimization problems. In Section 11.4 we provide additional illustrations of the modeling flexibility provided by 0-1 variables. Appendix 11.1 and Appendix 11.2 illustrate the use of Excel and LINGO for solving integer programs.

The cost of the added modeling flexibility provided by integer programming is that problems involving integer variables are often much more difficult to solve than linear programs. A linear programming problem with several thousand continuous variables can be solved with any of several commercial linear programming solvers. However, an all-integer linear programming problem with less than 100 variables can be extremely difficult to solve. Experienced management scientists can help identify the types of integer linear programs that are easy, or at least reasonable, to solve. Excel Solver has the capability to solve integer linear programs. Additionally, commercial computer software packages, such as LINGO, CPLEX, Xpress-MP, have extensive integer programming capability, and very robust open-source software packages for integer programming are also available.

Q.M. (in) ACTION

OPTIMIZING THE TRANSPORT OF OIL RIG CREWS*

Petrobras, the largest corporation in Brazil, operates approximately 80 offshore oil production and exploration platforms in the oil-rich Campos Basin. One of Petrobras' biggest challenges is the planning of its logistics,

*Based on F. Menezes et al., "Optimizing Helicopter Transport of Oil Rig Crews at Petrobras," *Interfaces* 40, no. 5 (September–October 2010): 408–416.

including how to efficiently and safely transport nearly 1900 employees per day from its four mainland bases to the offshore platforms. Every day, planners must route and schedule the helicopters used to transport Petrobras employees from the mainland to the offshore locations and back to the mainland. This routing and scheduling

(*continued*)

problem is challenging because there are over a billion possible combinations of schedules and routes.

Petrobras uses mixed integer linear optimization to solve its helicopter transport scheduling and routing problem. The objective function of the optimization model is a weighted function designed to ensure safety, minimize unmet demand, and minimize the cost of the transport of its crews. Because offshore landings are the riskiest part of the transport, the safety objective is met by minimizing the number of offshore landings required in the schedule. Numerous constraints must be met in planning these routes and schedule. These include limiting the number of departures from a platform at certain times; ensuring no time conflicts for a given helicopter and pilot; ensuring proper breaks for pilots; limiting the number of flights per day for a given helicopter and routing restrictions. The decision variables include binary variables for assigning helicopters to flights and pilots to break times, as well as variables on the number of passengers per flight.

Compared to the previously-used manual approach to this problem, the new approach using the integer optimization model transports the same number of passengers but with 18% fewer offshore landings, 8% less flight time, and a reduction in cost of 14%. The annual cost savings is estimated to be approximately $24 million.

NOTES AND COMMENTS

1. Because integer linear programs are harder to solve than linear programs, one should not try to solve a problem as an integer program if simply rounding the linear programming solution is adequate. In many linear programming problems, such as those in previous chapters, rounding has little economic consequence on the objective function, and feasibility is not an issue. But, in problems such as determining how many jet engines to manufacture, the consequences of rounding can be substantial, and integer programming methodology should be employed.

2. Some linear programming problems have a special structure, which guarantees that the variables will have integer values. The assignment, transportation, and transshipment problems of Chapter 10 have such structures. If the supply and the demand for transportation and transshipment problems are integer, the optimal linear programming solution will provide integer amounts shipped. For the assignment problem, the optimal linear programming solution will consist of 0s and 1s. So, for these specially structured problems, linear programming methodology can be used to find optimal integer solutions. Integer linear programming algorithms are not necessary.

 # Types of Integer Linear Programming Models

The only difference between the problems studied in this chapter and the ones studied in earlier chapters on linear programming is that one or more variables are required to be integer. If all variables are required to be integer, we have an **all-integer linear program**. The following is a two-variable, all-integer linear programming model:

$$\text{Max}\quad 2x_1 + 3x_2$$
$$\text{s.t.}$$
$$3x_1 + 3x_2 \le 12$$
$$\tfrac{2}{3}x_1 + 1x_2 \le 4$$
$$1x_1 + 2x_2 \le 6$$
$$x_1, x_2 \ge 0 \text{ and integer}$$

If we drop the phrase "and integer" from the last line of this model, we have the familiar two-variable linear program. The linear program that results from dropping the integer requirements is called the **LP Relaxation** of the integer linear program.

If some, but not necessarily all, variables are required to be integer, we have a **mixed-integer linear program**. The following is a two-variable, mixed-integer linear program:

$$\text{Max} \quad 3x_1 + 4x_2$$
$$\text{s.t.}$$
$$-1x_1 + 2x_2 \leq 8$$
$$1x_1 + 2x_2 \leq 12$$
$$2x_1 + 1x_2 \leq 16$$
$$x_1, x_2 \geq 0 \text{ and } x_2 \text{ integer}$$

We obtain the LP Relaxation of this mixed-integer linear program by dropping the requirement that x_2 be integer.

In some applications, the integer variables may only take on the values 0 or 1. Then we have a **0-1 linear integer program**. As we see later in the chapter, 0-1 variables provide additional modeling capability. The Q.M. in Action, Scheduling the Virginia Court of Appeals, describes how the Virginia Court of Appeals uses a 0-1 integer program to schedule hearings for its appeals and how it constructs the panels of judges to ensure that laws governing the process are followed.

Q.M. *in* ACTION

SCHEDULING THE VIRGINIA COURT OF APPEALS*

Every city and county in the state of Virginia has a circuit court that hears felony cases as well as claims of more than $25,000. In order to ensure fair outcomes, the Court of Appeals of the state of Virginia hears appeals of decisions handed down by the circuit courts. The Court of Appeals consists of 11 judges, who sit in panels of three judges for hearing sessions. A number of full-court sessions are also held, which by law must consist of at least 8 of the 11 judges. In order to ensure a fair and equitable judicial system for its citizens, Virginia law specifies a variety of constraints for how often, when, and where these sessions are scheduled and the makeup of each panel of judges.

The scheduling of the appeal hearings is based on forecasted case load. The construction of each panel of judges, when done by hand, is a complex and arduous

*Based on J. Paul Brooks, "The Court of Appeals of Virginia Uses Integer Programming and Cloud Computing to Schedule Sessions," *Interfaces* (November/December, 2012): 544–553.

task. The manual process was to use a wall-sized calendar with color-coded magnets to construct a full schedule based on extensive trial and error, often requiring 150 hours to complete. Court of Appeals staff members approached Virginia Commonwealth University about the possibility of automating the scheduling process. Working with the information technology department of the Court of Appeals, the Department of Statistics and Operations Research at Virginia Commonwealth developed a binary integer program to solve this complex problem.

Virginia law dictates that numerous restrictions must be satisfied with the schedule for the hearings. For example, no panel sessions may be scheduled during a week of a full-court session. Panels must be held in each of the state's four districts; in a given district, hearings must be at least three weeks apart. Each of the four districts must have a session in the month of September, and dates on which there are judge's conferences or retreats as well as certain holidays, must be avoided.

(*continued*)

Likewise, restrictions exist on the makeup of the judges' panel for each session. Each judge must serve on a panel with every other judge at least once, and any two judges can be on at most three of the same three-judge panels. Each judge must have a panel in each district but can have at most two panels in any district that is not his/her home district. Other constraints similar to these must also be enforced.

In addition to the restrictions mentioned, each judge specifies times to be avoided if possible. The objective of the integer programing model is to minimize the number of assignments where a judge is assigned to a session that he/she requested to be avoided. The decision variables for the model are binary variables that indicate (1) if a judge is assigned to a session or not, (2) if a session is held or not, (3) if a judge serves in a given month or not, and (4) if a pair of judges works in a given session or not.

The resulting integer programming model is quite large, but with some preprocessing to eliminate obvious infeasible options, the model size was reduced from more than 80,000 variables and millions of constraints to 10,000 variables and approximately 100,000 constraints. Rather than buying software to solve the problem, the team used an optimization service available over the web to solve the problem. The solution time was about 10 hours. The team also constructed a backend solution processor in Microsoft Access to allow easy visualization of the schedule, which is important for presenting the proposed solution for approval. Through the use of the optimization model, the deputy clerk is now free to use the 150 hours that were previously spent on scheduling for more productive activities.

Graphical and Computer Solutions for an All-Integer Linear Program

Eastborne Realty has $2 million available for the purchase of new rental property. After an initial screening, Eastborne reduced the investment alternatives to townhouses and apartment buildings. Each townhouse can be purchased for $282,000, and five are available. Each apartment building can be purchased for $400,000, and the developer will construct as many buildings as Eastborne wants to purchase.

Eastborne's property manager can devote up to 140 hours per month to these new properties; each townhouse is expected to require 4 hours per month, and each apartment building is expected to require 40 hours per month. The annual cash flow, after deducting mortgage payments and operating expenses, is estimated to be $10,000 per townhouse and $15,000 per apartment building. Eastborne's owner would like to determine the number of townhouses and the number of apartment buildings to purchase to maximize annual cash flow.

We begin by defining the decision variables as follows:

$$T = \text{number of townhouse}$$
$$A = \text{number of apartment buildings}$$

The objective function for cash flow (in thousands of dollars) is

$$\text{Max } 10T + 15A$$

Three constraints must be satisfied:

$$
\begin{array}{lll}
282T + 400A \leq 2000 & \quad \text{Funds available (\$1000s)} \\
4T + 40A \leq 140 & \quad \text{Manager's time (hours)} \\
T \leq 5 & \quad \text{Townhouses available}
\end{array}
$$

The variables T and A must be nonnegative. In addition, the purchase of a fractional number of townhouses and/or a fractional number of apartment buildings is unacceptable. Thus, T and A must be integer. The model for the Eastborne Realty problem is the following all-integer linear program:

$$\text{Max} \quad 10T + 15A$$
$$\text{s.t.}$$
$$282T + 400A \leq 2000$$
$$4T + 40A \leq 140$$
$$T \leq 5$$
$$T, A \geq 0 \text{ and integer}$$

Graphical Solution of the LP Relaxation

Suppose that we drop the integer requirements for T and A and solve the LP Relaxation of the Eastborne Realty problem. Using the graphical solution procedure, as presented in Chapter 7, the optimal linear programming solution is shown in Figure 11.1. It is $T = 2.479$ townhouses and $A = 3.252$ apartment buildings. The optimal value of the objective function is 73.574, which indicates an annual cash flow of \$73,574. Unfortunately,

FIGURE 11.1   GRAPHICAL SOLUTION TO THE LP RELAXATION OF THE EASTBORNE REALTY PROBLEM

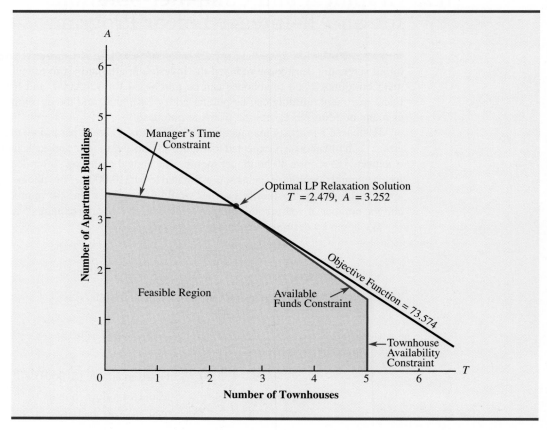

Eastborne cannot purchase fractional numbers of townhouses and apartment buildings; further analysis is necessary.

Rounding to Obtain an Integer Solution

In many cases, a noninteger solution can be rounded to obtain an acceptable integer solution. For instance, a linear programming solution to a production scheduling problem might call for the production of 15,132.4 cases of breakfast cereal. The rounded integer solution of 15,132 cases would probably have minimal impact on the value of the objective function and the feasibility of the solution. Rounding would be a sensible approach. Indeed, whenever rounding has a minimal impact on the objective function and constraints, most managers find it acceptable. A near-optimal solution is fine.

However, rounding may not always be a good strategy. When the decision variables take on small values that have a major impact on the value of the objective function or feasibility, an optimal integer solution is needed. Let us return to the Eastborne Realty problem and examine the impact of rounding. The optimal solution to the LP Relaxation for Eastborne Realty resulted in $T = 2.479$ townhouses and $A = 3.252$ apartment buildings. Because each townhouse costs \$282,000 and each apartment building costs \$400,000, rounding to an integer solution can be expected to have a significant economic impact on the problem.

If a problem has only less-than-or-equal-to constraints with positive coefficients for the variables, rounding down will always provide a feasible integer solution.

Suppose that we round the solution to the LP Relaxation to obtain the integer solution $T = 2$ and $A = 3$, with an objective function value of $10(2) + 15(3) = 65$. The annual cash flow of \$65,000 is substantially less than the annual cash flow of \$73,574 provided by the solution to the LP Relaxation. Do other rounding possibilities exist? Exploring other rounding alternatives shows that the integer solution $T = 3$ and $A = 3$ is infeasible because it requires more funds than the \$2,000,000 Eastborne has available. The rounded solution of $T = 2$ and $A = 4$ is also infeasible for the same reason. At this point, rounding has led to two townhouses and three apartment buildings with an annual cash flow of \$65,000 as the best feasible integer solution to the problem. Unfortunately, we don't know whether this solution is the best integer solution to the problem.

Rounding to an integer solution is a trial-and-error approach. Each rounded solution must be evaluated for feasibility as well as for its impact on the value of the objective function. Even in cases where a rounded solution is feasible, we do not have a guarantee that we have found the optimal integer solution. We will see shortly that the rounded solution ($T = 2$ and $A = 3$) is not optimal for Eastborne Realty.

Graphical Solution of the All-Integer Problem

Figure 11.2 shows the changes in the linear programming graphical solution procedure required to solve the Eastborne Realty integer linear programming problem. First, the graph of the feasible region is drawn exactly as in the LP Relaxation of the problem. Then, because the optimal solution must have integer values, we identify the feasible integer solutions with the dots shown in Figure 11.2. Finally, instead of moving the objective function line to the best extreme point in the feasible region, we move it in an improving direction as far as possible until reaching the dot (feasible integer point) providing the best value for the objective function. Viewing Figure 11.2, we see that the optimal integer solution occurs at $T = 4$ townhouses and $A = 2$ apartment buildings. The objective function value is $10(4) + 15(2) = 70$, providing an annual cash flow of \$70,000. This solution is significantly better than the best solution found by rounding: $T = 2$, $A = 3$ with an annual cash flow of \$65,000. Thus, we see that rounding would not have been the best strategy for Eastborne Realty.

Try Problem 2 for practice with the graphical solution of an integer program.

FIGURE 11.2   GRAPHICAL SOLUTION OF THE EASTBORNE REALTY INTEGER PROBLEM

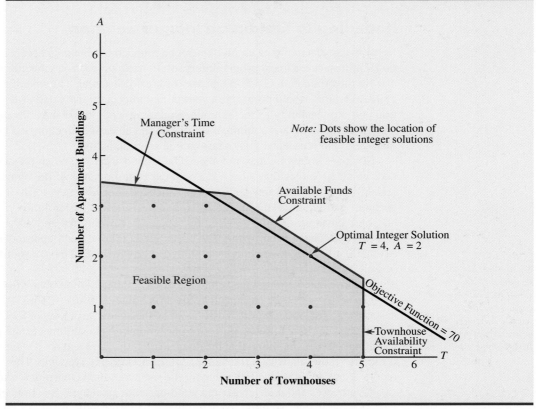

Using the LP Relaxation to Establish Bounds

An important observation can be made from the analysis of the Eastborne Realty problem. It has to do with the relationship between the value of the optimal integer solution and the value of the optimal solution to the LP Relaxation.

> For integer linear programs involving maximization, the value of the optimal solution to the LP Relaxation provides an upper bound on the value of the optimal integer solution. For integer linear programs involving minimization, the value of the optimal solution to the LP Relaxation provides a lower bound on the value of the optimal integer solution.

This observation is valid for the Eastborne Realty problem. The value of the optimal integer solution is $70,000, and the value of the optimal solution to the LP Relaxation is $73,574. Thus, we know from the LP Relaxation solution that the upper bound for the value of the objective function is $73,574.

The bounding property of the LP Relaxation allows us to conclude that if, by chance, the solution to an LP Relaxation turns out to be an integer solution, it is also optimal for

Try Problem 5 for the graphical solution of a mixed-integer program.

the integer linear program. This bounding property can also be helpful in determining whether a rounded solution is "good enough." If a rounded LP Relaxation solution is feasible and provides a value of the objective function that is "almost as good as" the value of the objective function for the LP Relaxation, we know the rounded solution is a near-optimal integer solution. In this case, we can avoid having to solve the problem as an integer linear program.

Computer Solution

As mentioned earlier, commercial software packages that can solve integer linear programs are widely available. Excel Solver can be used to solve all of the integer linear programs in this chapter. To use Excel Solver to solve the Eastborne Realty problem, the model worksheet is completed in the same way as for any linear program. Then variables can be defined as integer thorugh the the constraint dialog box. The step-by-step details for how to do this are given in Appnedix 11.1. Specifying both T and A as integers provides the optimal integer solution as shown in Figure 11.3. Note that in the far right column of the variables section, Excel Solver indicates that both variables have been declared integer. The solution of $T = 4$ townhouses and $A = 2$ apartment buildings has a maximum annual cash flow of $70,000. The values of the slack variables tell us that the optimal solution has $72,000 of available funds unused, 44 hours of the manager's time still available, and 1 of the available townhouses not purchased.

NOTES AND COMMENTS

1. In Appendix 11.1, we show the details of how Excel Solver can be used to solve integer linear programs such as the Eastborne Realty problem. Appendix 11.2 shows how to use LINGO to solve integer programs.

FIGURE 11.3   ANSWER REPORT FOR THE EASTBORNE REALTY PROBLEM

Objective Cell (Max)

Name	Original Value	Final Value
Max Cash Flow	0.000	70.000

Variable Cells

Eastborne

Model Variable	Name	Original Value	Final Value	Integer
T	Townhouses	0.000	4.000	Integer
A	Apt. Bldgs.	0.000	2.000	Integer

Constraints

Constraint Number	Name	Cell Value	Status	Slack
1	Funds	1928.000	Not Binding	72.000
2	Manager's Time	96.000	Not Binding	44.000
3	Townhouses	4.000	Not Binding	1.000

11.3 Applications Involving 0-1 Variables

Much of the modeling flexibility provided by integer linear programming is due to the use of 0-1 variables. In many applications, 0-1 variables provide selections or choices with the value of the variable equal to 1 if a corresponding activity is undertaken and equal to 0 if the corresponding activity is not undertaken. The capital budgeting, fixed cost, supply chain design, bank location, and product design/market share applications presented in this section make use of 0-1 variables.

Capital Budgeting

The Ice-Cold Refrigerator Company is considering investing in several projects that have varying capital requirements over the next four years. Faced with limited capital each year, management would like to select the most profitable projects. The estimated net present value for each project,[1] the capital requirements, and the available capital over the four-year period are shown in Table 11.1.

The four 0-1 decision variables are as follows:

$P = 1$ if the plant expansion project is accepted; 0 if rejected

$W = 1$ if the warehouse expansion project is accepted; 0 if rejected

$M = 1$ if the new machinery project is accepted; 0 if rejected

$R = 1$ if the new product research project is accepted; 0 if rejected

In a **capital budgeting problem,** the company's objective function is to maximize the net present value of the capital budgeting projects. This problem has four constraints: one for the funds available in each of the next four years.

A 0-1 integer linear programming model with dollars in thousands is as follows:

$$\text{Max} \quad 90P + 40W + 10M + 37R$$

s.t.

$$
\begin{array}{ll}
15P + 10W + 10M + 15R \le 40 & \text{(Year 1 capital available)} \\
20P + 15W + 10R \le 50 & \text{(Year 2 capital available)} \\
20P + 20W + 10R \le 40 & \text{(Year 3 capital available)} \\
15P + 5W + 4M + 10R \le 35 & \text{(Year 4 capital available)} \\
\multicolumn{2}{l}{P, W, M, R = 0, 1}
\end{array}
$$

---

[1]The estimated net present value is the net cash flow discounted back to the beginning of year 1.

TABLE 11.1   PROJECT NET PRESENT VALUE, CAPITAL REQUIREMENTS, AND AVAILABLE CAPITAL FOR THE ICE-COLD REFRIGERATOR COMPANY

	Project				
	Plant Expansion	**Warehouse Expansion**	**New Machinery**	**New Product Research**	**Total Capital Available**
Present Value	$90,000	$40,000	$10,000	$37,000	
Year 1 Cap Rqmt	$15,000	$10,000	$10,000	$15,000	$40,000
Year 2 Cap Rqmt	$20,000	$15,000		$10,000	$50,000
Year 3 Cap Rqmt	$20,000	$20,000		$10,000	$40,000
Year 4 Cap Rqmt	$15,000	$ 5,000	$ 4,000	$10,000	$35,000

FIGURE 11.4   ANSWER REPORT FOR THE ICE-COLD REFRIGERATOR COMPANY PROBLEM

Objective Cell (Max)

Name	Original Value	Final Value
Max Net Present Value	0.000	140.000

Variable Cells

Model Variable	Name	Original Value	Final Value	Integer
P	Plant Expansion	0.000	1.000	Binary
W	Warehouse Expansion	0.000	1.000	Binary
M	New Machinery	0.000	1.000	Binary
R	New Prod. Research	0.000	0.000	Binary

WEB file

Ice-Cold

Constraints

Constraint Number	Name	Cell Value	Status	Slack
1	Year 1 Capital	35.000	Not Binding	5.000
2	Year 2 Capital	35.000	Not Binding	15.000
3	Year 3 Capital	40.000	Binding	0.000
4	Year 4 Capital	24.000	Not Binding	11.000

The integer programming solution is shown in Figure 11.4. The optimal solution is $P = 1$, $W = 1$, $M = 1$, $R = 0$, with a total estimated net present value of $140,000. Thus, the company should fund the plant expansion, the warehouse expansion, and the new machinery projects. The new product research project should be put on hold unless additional capital funds become available. The values of the slack variables (see Figure 11.4) show that the company will have $5,000 remaining in year 1, $15,000 remaining in year 2, and $11,000 remaining in year 4. Checking the capital requirements for the new product research project, we see that enough funds are available for this project in year 2 and year 4. However, the company would have to find additional capital funds of $10,000 in year 1 and $10,000 in year 3 to fund the new product research project.

Fixed Cost

In many applications, the cost of production has two components: a setup cost, which is a fixed cost, and a variable cost, which is directly related to the production quantity. The use of 0-1 variables makes including the setup cost possible in a model for a production application.

As an example of a **fixed cost problem**, consider the RMC problem discussed in Chapters 7 and 8. Three raw materials are used to produce three products: a fuel additive, a solvent base, and a carpet cleaning fluid. The following decision variables are used:

$$F = \text{tons of fuel additive produced}$$
$$S = \text{tons of solvent base produced}$$
$$C = \text{tons of carpet cleaning fluid produced}$$

The profit contributions are $40 per ton for the fuel additive, $30 per ton for the solvent base, and $50 per ton for the carpet cleaning fluid. Each ton of fuel additive is a blend of 0.4 tons of material 1 and 0.6 tons of material 3. Each ton of solvent base requires 0.5 tons of material 1, 0.2 tons of material 2, and 0.3 tons of material 3. Each ton of carpet cleaning fluid is a blend of 0.6 tons of material 1, 0.1 tons of material 2, and 0.3 tons of material 3. RMC has 20 tons of material 1, 5 tons of material 2, and 21 tons of material 3 and is interested in determining the optimal production quantities for the upcoming planning period.

A linear programming model of the RMC problem is shown:

$$\text{Max} \quad 40F + 30S + 50C$$

$$\text{s.t.}$$

$$
\begin{array}{ll}
0.4F + 0.5S + 0.6C \leq 20 & \text{Material 1} \\
0.2S + 0.1C \leq 5 & \text{Material 2} \\
0.6F + 0.3S + 0.3C \leq 21 & \text{Material 3} \\
F, S, C \geq 0 &
\end{array}
$$

Using Excel Solver, we obtained an optimal solution consisting of 27.5 tons of fuel additive, 0 tons of solvent base, and 15 tons of carpet cleaning fluid, with a value of $1850, as shown in Figure 11.5.

This linear programming formulation of the RMC problem does not include a fixed cost for production setup of the products. Suppose that the following data are available concerning the setup cost and the maximum production quantity for each of the three products:

Product	Setup Cost	Maximum Production
Fuel additive	$200	50 tons
Solvent base	$ 50	25 tons
Carpet cleaning fluid	$400	40 tons

The modeling flexibility provided by 0-1 variables can now be used to incorporate the fixed setup costs into the production model. The 0-1 variables are defined as follows:

$$SF = 1 \text{ if the fuel additive is produced; 0 if not}$$

$$SS = 1 \text{ if the solvent base is produced; 0 if not}$$

$$SC = 1 \text{ if the carpet cleaning fluid is produced; 0 if not}$$

Using these setup variables, the total setup cost is

$$200SF + 50SS + 400SC$$

FIGURE 11.5   ANSWER REPORT FOR THE RMC PROBLEM

Objective Cell (Max)

Name	Original Value	Final Value
Max Net Profit	0.000	1850.000

Variable Cells

Model Variable	Name	Original Value	Final Value	Integer
F	Fuel Additive	0.000	27.500	Contin
S	Solvent Base	0.000	0.000	Contin
C	Cleaning Fluid	0.000	15.000	Contin

Constraints

Constraint Number	Name	Cell Value	Status	Slack
1	Material 1	20.000	Binding	0.000
2	Material 2	1.500	Not Binding	3.500
3	Material 3	21.000	Binding	0.000

We can now rewrite the objective function to include the setup cost. Thus, the net profit objective function becomes

$$\text{Max } 40F + 30S + 50C - 200SF - 50SS - 400SC$$

Next, we must write production capacity constraints so that if a setup variable equals 0, production of the corresponding product is not permitted and, if a setup variable equals 1, production is permitted up to the maximum quantity. For the fuel additive, we do so by adding the following constraint:

$$F \leq 50SF$$

Note that, with this constraint present, production of the fuel additive is not permitted when $SF = 0$. When $SF = 1$, production of up to 50 tons of fuel additive is permitted. We can think of the setup variable as a switch. When it is off ($SF = 0$), production is not permitted; when it is on ($SF = 1$), production is permitted.

Similar production capacity constraints, using 0-1 variables, are added for the solvent base and carpet cleaning products:

$$S \leq 25SS$$

$$C \leq 40SC$$

Moving all the variables to the left-hand side of the constraints provides the following fixed cost model for the RMC problem:

$$
\begin{array}{llll}
\text{Max} & 40F + 30S + 50C - 200SF - 50SS - 400SC & & \\
\text{s.t.} & & & \\
& 0.4F + 0.5S + 0.6C & \leq 20 & \text{Material 1} \\
& 0.2S + 0.1C & \leq 5 & \text{Material 2} \\
& 0.6F + 0.3S + 0.3C & \leq 21 & \text{Material 3} \\
& F - 50SF & \leq 0 & \text{Maximum } F \\
& S - 25SS & \leq 0 & \text{Maximum } S \\
& C - 40SC & \leq 0 & \text{Maximum } C \\
& F, S, C \geq 0; SF, SS, SC = 0, 1 & &
\end{array}
$$

We solved the RMC problem with setup costs using Excel Solver. As shown in Figure 11.6, the optimal solution requires 25 tons of fuel additive and 20 tons of solvent base. The value of the objective function after deducting the setup cost is $1350. The setup cost for the fuel additive and the solvent base is $200 + $50 = $250. The optimal solution includes $SC = 0$, which indicates that the more expensive $400 setup cost for the carpet cleaning fluid should be avoided. Thus, the carpet cleaning fluid is not produced.

The key to developing a fixed-cost model is the introduction of a 0-1 variable for each fixed cost and the specification of an upper bound for the corresponding production variable. For a production quantity x, a constraint of the form $x \leq My$ can then be used to allow production when the setup variable $y = 1$ and not to allow production when the setup variable $y = 0$. The value of the maximum production quantity M should be large enough to allow for all reasonable levels of production. However, research has shown that choosing values of M excessively large will slow the solution procedure.

Supply Chain Design

The Martin-Beck Company operates a plant in St. Louis with an annual capacity of 30,000 units. Product is shipped to regional distribution centers located in Boston, Atlanta, and Houston. Because of an anticipated increase in demand, Martin-Beck plans to increase capacity by

FIGURE 11.6   ANSWER REPORT FOR THE RMC PROBLEM WITH SETUP COSTS

Objective Cell (Max)

Name	Original Value	Final Value
Max Net Profit	0.000	1350.000

Variable Cells

Model Variable	Name	Original Value	Final Value	Integer
F	Fuel Additive	0.000	25.000	Contin
S	Solvent Base	0.000	20.000	Contin
C	Cleaning Fluid	0.000	0.000	Contin
SF	Setup Fuel Additive	0.000	1.000	Binary
SS	Setup Solvent Base	0.000	1.000	Binary
SC	Setup Cleaning Fluid	0.000	0.000	Binary

WEB file

RMC-Setup

Constraints

Constraint Number	Name	Cell Value	Status	Slack
1	Material 1	20.000	Binding	0.000
2	Material 2	4.000	Not Binding	1.000
3	Material 3	21.000	Binding	0.000
4	Max Fuel Additive	25.000	Not Binding	25.000
5	Max Solvent Base	20.000	Not Binding	5.000
6	Max Cleaning Fluid	0.000	Binding	0.000

constructing a new plant in one or more of the following cities: Detroit, Toledo, Denver, or Kansas City. The estimated annual fixed cost and the annual capacity for the four proposed plants are as follows:

Proposed Plant	Annual Fixed Cost	Annual Capacity
Detroit	$175,000	10,000
Toledo	$300,000	20,000
Denver	$375,000	30,000
Kansas City	$500,000	40,000

The company's long-range planning group developed forecasts of the anticipated annual demand at the distribution centers as follows:

Distribution Center	Annual Demand
Boston	30,000
Atlanta	20,000
Houston	20,000

The shipping cost per unit from each plant to each distribution center is shown in Table 11.2. A network representation of the potential Martin-Beck supply chain is shown in Figure 11.7. Each potential plant location is shown; capacities and demands are shown in thousands of units. This network representation is for a transportation problem with a plant

TABLE 11.2   SHIPPING COST PER UNIT FOR THE MARTIN-BECK SUPPLY CHAIN

| | Distribution Centers | | |
Plant Site	Boston	Atlanta	Houston
Detroit	5	2	3
Toledo	4	3	4
Denver	9	7	5
Kansas City	10	4	2
St. Louis	8	4	3

FIGURE 11.7   THE NETWORK REPRESENTATION OF THE MARTIN-BECK COMPANY
SUPPLY CHAIN DESIGN PROBLEM

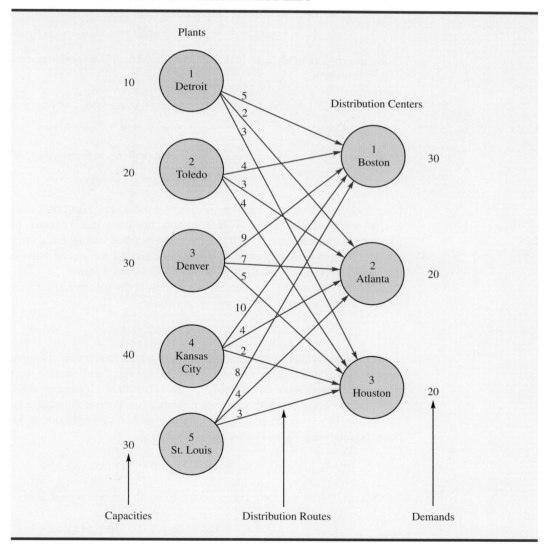

at St. Louis and at all four proposed sites. However, the decision has not yet been made as to which new plant or plants will be constructed.

Let us now show how 0-1 variables can be used in this **supply chain design problem** to develop a model for choosing the best plant locations and for determining how much to ship from each plant to each distribution center. We can use the following 0-1 variables to represent the plant construction decision:

$$y_1 = 1 \text{ if a plant is constructed in Detroit; } 0 \text{ if not}$$
$$y_2 = 1 \text{ if a plant is constructed in Toledo; } 0 \text{ if not}$$
$$y_3 = 1 \text{ if a plant is constructed in Denver; } 0 \text{ if not}$$
$$y_4 = 1 \text{ if a plant is constructed in Kansas City; } 0 \text{ if not}$$

The variables representing the amount shipped from each plant site to each distribution center are defined just as for a transportation problem.

$$x_{ij} = \text{ the units shipped in thousands from plant } i \text{ to distribution center } j$$
$$i = 1, 2, 3, 4, 5 \text{ and } j = 1, 2, 3$$

Using the shipping cost data in Table 11.2, the annual transportation cost in thousands of dollars is written

$$5x_{11} + 2x_{12} + 3x_{13} + 4x_{21} + 3x_{22} + 4x_{23} + 9x_{31} + 7x_{32} + 5x_{33}$$
$$+ 10x_{41} + 4x_{42} + 2x_{43} + 8x_{51} + 4x_{52} + 3x_{53}$$

The annual fixed cost of operating the new plant or plants in thousands of dollars is written as

$$175y_1 + 300y_2 + 375y_3 + 500y_4$$

Note that the 0-1 variables are defined so that the annual fixed cost of operating the new plants is only calculated for the plant or plants that are actually constructed (i.e., $y_i = 1$). If a plant is not constructed, $y_i = 0$ and the corresponding annual fixed cost is $0.

The Martin-Beck objective function is the sum of the annual transportation cost plus the annual fixed cost of operating the newly constructed plants.

Now let us consider the capacity constraints at the four proposed plants. Using Detroit as an example, we write the following constraint:

$$x_{11} + x_{12} + x_{13} \leq 10y_1$$

If the Detroit plant is constructed, $y_1 = 1$ and the total amount shipped from Detroit to the three distribution centers must be less than or equal to Detroit's 10,000-unit capacity. If the Detroit plant is not constructed, $y_1 = 0$ will result in a 0 capacity at Detroit. In this case, the variables corresponding to the shipments from Detroit must all equal zero: $x_{11} = 0$, $x_{12} = 0$, and $x_{13} = 0$. By placing all variables on the left-hand side of the constraints, we have the following Detroit capacity constraint:

$$x_{11} + x_{12} + x_{13} - 10y_1 \leq 0 \quad \text{Detroit capacity}$$

In a similar fashion, the capacity constraint for the proposed plant in Toledo can be written

$$x_{21} + x_{22} + x_{23} - 20y_2 \leq 0 \quad \text{Toledo capacity}$$

Similar constraints can be written for the proposed plants in Denver and Kansas City. Note that since the plant already exists in St. Louis, we do not define a 0-1 variable for this plant. Its capacity constraint can be written as follows:

$$x_{51} + x_{52} + x_{53} \leq 30 \quad \text{St. Louis capacity}$$

Three demand constraints will be needed, one for each of the three distribution centers. The demand constraint for the Boston distribution center with units in thousands is written as

$$x_{11} + x_{21} + x_{31} + x_{41} + x_{51} = 30 \quad \text{Boston demand}$$

Similar constraints appear for the Atlanta and Houston distribution centers.

The complete model for the Martin-Beck supply chain design problem is as follows:

$$
\begin{aligned}
\text{Min} \quad & 5x_{11} + 2x_{12} + 3x_{13} + 4x_{21} + 3x_{22} + 4x_{23} + 9x_{31} + 7x_{32} + 5x_{33} + 10x_{41} + 4x_{42} \\
& + 2x_{43} + 8x_{51} + 4x_{52} + 3x_{53} + 175y_1 + 300y_2 + 375y_3 + 500y_4
\end{aligned}
$$

s.t.

$$
\begin{aligned}
x_{11} + x_{12} + x_{13} \quad\quad\quad\quad\quad - 10y_1 \quad\quad\quad\quad\quad\quad\quad\quad & \leq 0 \quad \text{Detroit capacity} \\
x_{21} + x_{22} + x_{23} \quad\quad\quad\quad\quad\quad - 20y_2 \quad\quad\quad\quad\quad\quad\quad & \leq 0 \quad \text{Toledo capacity} \\
x_{31} + x_{32} + x_{33} \quad\quad\quad\quad\quad\quad\quad\quad - 30y_3 \quad\quad\quad\quad & \leq 0 \quad \text{Denver capacity} \\
x_{41} + x_{42} + x_{43} \quad\quad\quad\quad\quad\quad\quad\quad\quad - 40y_4 & \leq 0 \quad \text{Kansas City capacity} \\
x_{51} + x_{52} + x_{53} \quad\quad\quad\quad\quad\quad\quad\quad\quad\quad\quad\quad & \leq 30 \quad \text{St. Louis capacity} \\
x_{11} + x_{21} + x_{31} + x_{41} + x_{51} \quad\quad\quad\quad\quad & = 30 \quad \text{Boston demand} \\
x_{12} + x_{22} + x_{32} + x_{42} + x_{52} \quad\quad\quad\quad\quad & = 20 \quad \text{Atlanta demand} \\
x_{13} + x_{23} + x_{33} + x_{43} + x_{53} \quad\quad\quad\quad\quad & = 20 \quad \text{Houston demand}
\end{aligned}
$$

$$x_{ij} \geq \text{ for all } i \text{ and } j; \; y_1, y_2, y_3, y_4 = 0, 1$$

Using Excel Solver, we obtained the solution shown in Figure 11.8. The optimal solution calls for the construction of a plant in Kansas City ($y_4 = 1$); 20,000 units will be shipped from Kansas City to Atlanta ($x_{42} = 20$), 20,000 units will be shipped from Kansas City to Houston ($x_{43} = 20$), and 30,000 units will be shipped from St. Louis to Boston ($x_{51} = 30$). Note that the total cost of this solution including the fixed cost of $500,000 for the plant in Kansas City is $860,000.

This basic model can be expanded to accommodate supply chains involving direct shipments from plants to warehouses, from plants to retail outlets, and multiple products.[2] Using the special properties of 0-1 variables, the model can also be expanded to accommodate a variety of configuration constraints on the plant locations. For example, suppose in another problem site 1 was in Dallas and site 2 was in Fort Worth. A company might not want to locate plants in both Dallas and Fort Worth because the cities are so close together. To prevent this from happening, the following constraint can be added to the model:

Problem 13, which is based on the Martin-Beck supply chain design problem, provides additional practice involving 0-1 variables.

$$y_1 + y_2 \leq 1$$

This constraint allows either y_1 or y_2 to equal 1, but not both. If we had written the constraints as an equality, it would require that a plant be located in either Dallas or Fort Worth.

---

[2]For computational reasons, it is usually preferable to replace the m plant capacity constraints with mn shipping route capacity constraints of the form $x_{ij} \leq \text{Min}\{s_i, d_j\} y_i$ for $i = 1, \ldots, m$, and $j = 1, \ldots, n$. The coefficient for y_i in each of these constraints is the smaller of the origin capacity (s_i) or the destination demand (d_j). These additional constraints often cause the solution of the LP Relaxation to be integer.

FIGURE 11.8   OPTIMAL SOLUTION FOR THE MARTIN-BECK COMPANY
DISTRIBUTION SYSTEM PROBLEM

Objective Cell (Max)

Name	Original Value	Final Value
Min Cost	0.000	860.000

Variable Cells

Model Variable	Name	Original Value	Final Value	Integer
X11	Detroit to Boston	0.000	0.000	Contin
X12	Detroit to Atlanta	0.000	0.000	Contin
X13	Detroit to Houston	0.000	0.000	Contin
X21	Toledo to Boston	0.000	0.000	Contin
X22	Toledo to Atlanta	0.000	0.000	Contin
X23	Toledo to Houston	0.000	0.000	Contin
X31	Denver to Boston	0.000	0.000	Contin
X32	Denver to Atlanta	0.000	0.000	Contin
X33	Denver to Houston	0.000	0.000	Contin
X41	Kansas City to Boston	0.000	0.000	Contin
X42	Kansas City to Atlanta	0.000	20.000	Contin
X43	Kansas City to Houston	0.000	20.000	Contin
X51	St. Louis to Boston	0.000	30.000	Contin
X52	St. Louis to Atlanta	0.000	0.000	Contin
X53	St. Louis to Houston	0.000	0.000	Contin
Y1	Detroit Open or Closed	0.000	0.000	Binary
Y2	Toledo Open or Closed	0.000	0.000	Binary
Y3	Denver Open or Closed	0.000	0.000	Binary
Y4	Kansas City Open or Closed	0.000	1.000	Binary

Martin-Beck

Bank Location

The long-range planning department for the Ohio Trust Company is considering expanding its operation into a 20-county region in northeastern Ohio (see Figure 11.9). Currently, Ohio Trust does not have a principal place of business in any of the 20 counties. According to the banking laws in Ohio, if a bank establishes a principal place of business (PPB) in any county, branch banks can be established in that county and in any adjacent county. However, to establish a new principal place of business, Ohio Trust must either obtain approval for a new bank from the state's superintendent of banks or purchase an existing bank.

Table 11.3 lists the 20 counties in the region and adjacent counties. For example, Ashtabula County is adjacent to Lake, Geauga, and Trumbull counties; Lake County is adjacent to Ashtabula, Cuyahoga, and Geauga counties; and so on.

As an initial step in its planning, Ohio Trust would like to determine the minimum number of PPBs necessary to do business throughout the 20-county region. A 0-1 integer programming model can be used to solve this **location problem** for Ohio Trust. We define the variables as

$$x_i = 1 \text{ if a PPB is established in county } i; 0 \text{ otherwise}$$

To minimize the number of PPBs needed, we write the objective function as

$$\text{Min } x_1 + x_2 + \cdots + x_{20}$$

FIGURE 11.9   THE 20-COUNTY REGION IN NORTHEASTERN OHIO

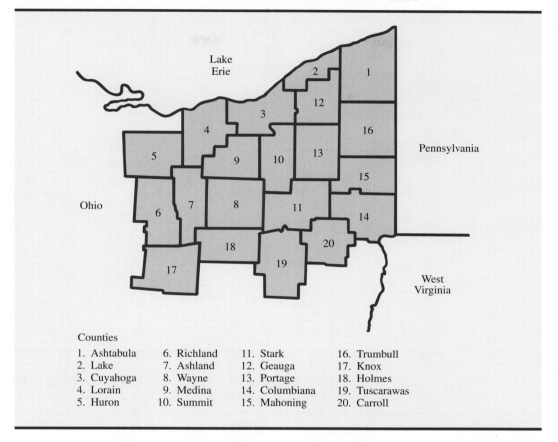

Counties

1. Ashtabula	6. Richland	11. Stark	16. Trumbull
2. Lake	7. Ashland	12. Geauga	17. Knox
3. Cuyahoga	8. Wayne	13. Portage	18. Holmes
4. Lorain	9. Medina	14. Columbiana	19. Tuscarawas
5. Huron	10. Summit	15. Mahoning	20. Carroll

The bank may locate branches in a county if the county contains a PPB or is adjacent to another county with a PPB. Thus, the linear program will need one constraint for each county. For example, the constraint for Ashtabula County is

$$x_1 + x_2 + x_{12} + x_{16} \geq 1 \quad \text{Ashtabula}$$

Note that satisfaction of this constraint ensures that a PPB will be placed in Ashtabula County *or* in one or more of the adjacent counties. This constraint thus guarantees that Ohio Trust will be able to place branch banks in Ashtabula County.

The complete statement of the bank location problem is

$$
\begin{array}{llll}
\text{Min} & x_1 + x_2 + & \cdots & + x_{20} \\
\text{s.t.} & & & \\
& x_1 + x_2 + x_{12} + x_{16} & \geq 1 & \text{Ashtabula} \\
& x_1 + x_2 + x_3 + x_{12} & \geq 1 & \text{Lake} \\
& \quad\quad\vdots & \quad\vdots & \\
& x_{11} + x_{14} + x_{19} + x_{20} \geq 1 & & \text{Carroll} \\
& x_i = 0, 1 \quad i = 1, 2, \ldots, 20 & &
\end{array}
$$

TABLE 11.3   COUNTIES IN THE OHIO TRUST EXPANSION REGION

Counties Under Consideration	Adjacent Counties (by Number)
1. Ashtabula	2, 12, 16
2. Lake	1, 3, 12
3. Cuyahoga	2, 4, 9, 10, 12, 13
4. Lorain	3, 5, 7, 9
5. Huron	4, 6, 7
6. Richland	5, 7, 17
7. Ashland	4, 5, 6, 8, 9, 17, 18
8. Wayne	7, 9, 10, 11, 18
9. Medina	3, 4, 7, 8, 10
10. Summit	3, 8, 9, 11, 12, 13
11. Stark	8, 10, 13, 14, 15, 18, 19, 20
12. Geauga	1, 2, 3, 10, 13, 16
13. Portage	3, 10, 11, 12, 15, 16
14. Columbiana	11, 15, 20
15. Mahoning	11, 13, 14, 16
16. Trumbull	1, 12, 13, 15
17. Knox	6, 7, 18
18. Holmes	7, 8, 11, 17, 19
19. Tuscarawas	11, 18, 20
20. Carroll	11, 14, 19

We used Excel Solver to solve this 20-variable, 20-constraint problem formulation. In Figure 11.10 we show the optimal solution. Using the output, we see that the optimal solution calls for principal places of business in Ashland, Stark, and Geauga counties. With PPBs in these three counties, Ohio Trust can place branch banks in all 20 counties (see Figure 11.11). All other decision variables have an optimal value of zero, indicating that a PPB should not be placed in these counties. Clearly the integer programming model could be enlarged to allow for expansion into a larger area or throughout the entire state.

Product Design and Market Share Optimization

Conjoint analysis is a market research technique that can be used to learn how prospective buyers of a product value the product's attributes. In this section we will show how the results of conjoint analysis can be used in an integer programming model of a **product design and market share optimization problem**. We illustrate the approach by considering a problem facing Salem Foods, a major producer of frozen foods.

Salem Foods is planning to enter the frozen pizza market. Currently, two existing brands, Antonio's and King's, have the major share of the market. In trying to develop a sausage pizza that will capture a significant share of the market, Salem determined that the four most important attributes when consumers purchase a frozen sausage pizza are crust, cheese, sauce, and sausage flavor. The crust attribute has two levels (thin and thick); the cheese attribute has two levels (mozzarella and blend); the sauce attribute has two levels (smooth and chunky); and the sausage flavor attribute has three levels (mild, medium, and hot).

In a typical conjoint analysis, a sample of consumers is asked to express their preference for specially prepared pizzas with chosen levels for the attributes. Then regression analysis is used to determine the part-worth for each of the attribute levels. In essence, the part-worth

FIGURE 11.10 OPTIMAL SOLUTION FOR THE OHIO TRUST PPB LOCATION PROBLEM

Objective Cell (Max)

Name	Original Value	Final Value
Min PPBs	0.000	3.000

Variable Cells

Model Variable	Name	Original Value	Final Value	Integer
X1	Ashtabula	0.000	0.000	Binary
X2	Lake	0.000	0.000	Binary
X3	Cuyahoga	0.000	0.000	Binary
X4	Lorain	0.000	0.000	Binary
X5	Huron	0.000	0.000	Binary
X6	Richland	0.000	0.000	Binary
X7	Ashland	0.000	1.000	Binary
X8	Wayne	0.000	0.000	Binary
X9	Medina	0.000	0.000	Binary
X10	Summit	0.000	0.000	Binary
X11	Stark	0.000	1.000	Binary
X12	Geauga	0.000	1.000	Binary
X13	Portage	0.000	0.000	Binary
X14	Columbiana	0.000	0.000	Binary
X15	Mahoning	0.000	0.000	Binary
Y16	Trumbull	0.000	0.000	Binary
Y17	Knox	0.000	0.000	Binary
Y18	Holmes	0.000	0.000	Binary
Y19	Tuscarawas	0.000	0.000	Binary
Y20	Carroll	0.000	0.000	Binary

WEB file

Ohio-Trust

is the utility value that a consumer attaches to each level of each attribute. A discussion of how to use regression analysis to compute the part-worths is beyond the scope of this text, but we will show how the part-worths can be used to determine the overall value a consumer attaches to a particular pizza.

Table 11.4 shows the part-worths for each level of each attribute provided by a sample of eight potential Salem customers who are currently buying either King's or Antonio's pizza. For consumer 1, the part-worths for the crust attribute are 11 for thin crust and 2 for thick crust, indicating a preference for thin crust. For the cheese attribute, the part-worths are 6 for the mozzarella cheese and 7 for the cheese blend; thus, consumer 1 has a slight preference for the cheese blend. From the other part-worths, we see that consumer 1 shows a strong preference for the chunky sauce over the smooth sauce (17 to 3) and has a slight preference for the medium-flavored sausage. Note that consumer 2 shows a preference for the thin crust, the cheese blend, the chunky sauce, and mild-flavored sausage. The part-worths for the others consumers are interpreted in a similar manner.

The part-worths can be used to determine the overall value (utility) each consumer attaches to a particular type of pizza. For instance, consumer 1's current favorite pizza is the Antonio's brand, which has a thick crust, mozzarella cheese, chunky sauce, and medium-flavored sausage. We can determine consumer 1's utility for this particular type of pizza using the part-worths in Table 11.4. For consumer 1 the part-worths are 2 for thick crust, 6 for mozzarella cheese, 17 for chunky sauce, and 27 for medium-flavored sausage.

FIGURE 11.11 PRINCIPAL PLACE OF BUSINESS COUNTIES FOR OHIO TRUST

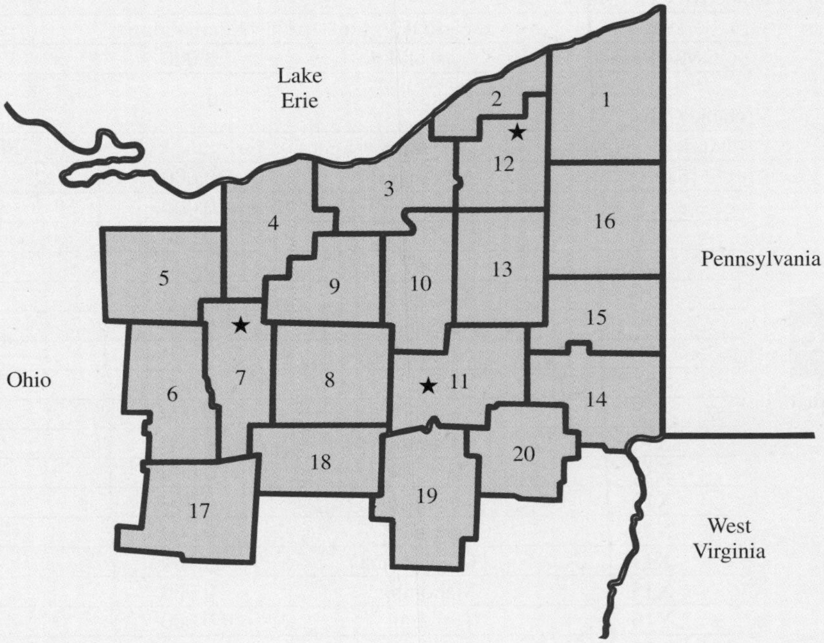
Lake
Erie
Pennsylvania
Ohio
West
Virginia
1
2
3
4
5
6
7
8
9
10
11
12
13
14
15
16
17
18
19
20
Counties
1. Ashtabula
2. Lake
3. Cuyahoga
4. Lorain
5. Huron
6. Richland
7. Ashland
8. Wayne
9. Medina
10. Summit
11. Stark
12. Geauga
13. Portage
14. Columbiana
15. Mahoning
16. Trumbull
17. Knox
18. Holmes
19. Tuscarawas
20. Carroll
★ A principal place of business should be located in these counties.

TABLE 11.4 PART-WORTHS FOR THE SALEM FOODS PROBLEM

	Crust		Cheese		Sauce		Sausage Flavor		
Consumer	Thin	Thick	Mozzarella	Blend	Smooth	Chunky	Mild	Medium	Hot
1	11	2	6	7	3	17	26	27	8
2	11	7	15	17	16	26	14	1	10
3	7	5	8	14	16	7	29	16	19
4	13	20	20	17	17	14	25	29	10
5	2	8	6	11	30	20	15	5	12
6	12	17	11	9	2	30	22	12	20
7	9	19	12	16	16	25	30	23	19
8	5	9	4	14	23	16	16	30	3

Thus, consumer 1's utility for the Antonio's brand pizza is $2 + 6 + 17 + 27 = 52$. We can compute consumer 1's utility for a King's brand pizza in a similar manner. The King's brand pizza has a thin crust, a cheese blend, smooth sauce, and mild-flavored sausage. Because the part-worths for consumer 1 are 11 for thin crust, 7 for cheese blend, 3 for smooth sauce, and 26 for mild-flavored sausage, consumer 1's utility for the King's brand pizza is $11 + 7 + 3 + 26 = 47$. In general, each consumer's utility for a particular type of pizza is just the sum of the appropriate part-worths.

In order to be successful with its brand, Salem Foods realizes that it must entice consumers in the marketplace to switch from their current favorite brand of pizza to the Salem product. That is, Salem must design a pizza (choose the type of crust, cheese, sauce, and sausage flavor) that will have the highest utility for enough people to ensure sufficient sales to justify making the product. Assuming the sample of eight consumers in the current study is representative of the marketplace for frozen sausage pizza, we can formulate and solve an integer programming model that can help Salem come up with such a design. In marketing literature, the problem being solved is called the *share of choice* problem.

The decision variables are defined as follows:

$$l_{ij} = 1 \text{ if Salem chooses level } i \text{ for attribute } j; 0 \text{ otherwise}$$

$$y_k = 1 \text{ if consumer } k \text{ chooses the Salem brand; } 0 \text{ otherwise}$$

The objective is to choose the levels of each attribute that will maximize the number of consumers preferring the Salem brand pizza. Because the number of customers preferring the Salem brand pizza is just the sum of the y_k variables, the objective function is

$$\text{Max } y_1 + y_2 + \cdots + y_8$$

One constraint is needed for each consumer in the sample. To illustrate how the constraints are formulated, let us consider the constraint corresponding to consumer 1. For consumer 1, the utility of a particular type of pizza can be expressed as the sum of the part-worths:

$$\text{Utility for Customer 1} = 11l_{11} + 2l_{21} + 6l_{12} + 7l_{22} + 3l_{13} + 17l_{23} + 26l_{14} + 27l_{24} + 8l_{34}$$

In order for consumer 1 to prefer the Salem pizza, the utility for the Salem pizza must be greater than the utility for consumer 1's current favorite. Recall that consumer 1's current favorite brand of pizza is Antonio's, with a utility of 52. Thus, consumer 1 will only purchase the Salem brand if the levels of the attributes for the Salem brand are chosen such that

$$11l_{11} + 2l_{21} + 6l_{12} + 7l_{22} + 3l_{13} + 17l_{23} + 26l_{14} + 27l_{24} + 8l_{34} > 52$$

Given the definitions of the y_k decision variables, we want $y_1 = 1$ when the consumer prefers the Salem brand and $y_1 = 0$ when the consumer does not prefer the Salem brand. Thus, we write the constraint for consumer 1 as follows:

$$11l_{11} + 2l_{21} + 6l_{12} + 7l_{22} + 3l_{13} + 17l_{23} + 26l_{14} + 27l_{24} + 8l_{34} \geq 1 + 52y_1$$

With this constraint, y_1 cannot equal 1 unless the utility for the Salem design (the left-hand side of the constraint) exceeds the utility for consumer 1's current favorite by at least 1. Because the objective function is to maximize the sum of the y_k variables, the optimization will seek a product design that will allow as many y_k as possible to equal 1.

Placing all the decision variables on the left-hand side of the constraint enables us to rewrite constraint 1 as follows:

$$11l_{11} + 2l_{21} + 6l_{12} + 7l_{22} + 3l_{13} + 17l_{23} + 26l_{14} + 27l_{24} + 8l_{34} - 52y_1 \geq 1$$

A similar constraint is written for each consumer in the sample. The coefficients for the l_{ij} variables in the utility functions are taken from Table 11.4, and the coefficients for the y_k

Antonio's brand is the current favorite pizza for consumers 1, 4, 6, 7, and 8. King's brand is the current favorite pizza for consumers 2, 3, and 5.

variables are obtained by computing the overall utility of the consumer's current favorite brand of pizza. The following constraints correspond to the eight consumers in the study:

$$11l_{11} + 2l_{21} + 6l_{12} + 7l_{22} + 3l_{13} + 17l_{23} + 26l_{14} + 27l_{24} + 8l_{34} - 52y_1 \geq 1$$
$$11l_{11} + 7l_{21} + 15l_{12} + 17l_{22} + 16l_{13} + 26l_{23} + 14l_{14} + 1l_{24} + 10l_{34} - 58y_2 \geq 1$$
$$7l_{11} + 5l_{21} + 8l_{12} + 14l_{22} + 16l_{13} + 7l_{23} + 29l_{14} + 16l_{24} + 19l_{34} - 66y_3 \geq 1$$
$$13l_{11} + 20l_{21} + 20l_{12} + 17l_{22} + 17l_{13} + 14l_{23} + 25l_{14} + 29l_{24} + 10l_{34} - 83y_4 \geq 1$$
$$2l_{11} + 8l_{21} + 6l_{12} + 11l_{22} + 30l_{13} + 20l_{23} + 15l_{14} + 5l_{24} + 12l_{34} - 58y_5 \geq 1$$
$$12l_{11} + 17l_{21} + 11l_{12} + 9l_{22} + 2l_{13} + 30l_{23} + 22l_{14} + 12l_{24} + 20l_{34} - 70y_6 \geq 1$$
$$9l_{11} + 19l_{21} + 12l_{12} + 16l_{22} + 16l_{13} + 25l_{23} + 30l_{14} + 23l_{24} + 19l_{34} - 79y_7 \geq 1$$
$$5l_{11} + 9l_{21} + 4l_{12} + 14l_{22} + 23l_{13} + 16l_{23} + 16l_{14} + 30l_{24} + 3l_{34} - 59y_8 \geq 1$$

Four more constraints must be added, one for each attribute. These constraints are necessary to ensure that one and only one level is selected for each attribute. For attribute 1 (crust), we must add the constraint

$$l_{11} + l_{21} = 1$$

Because l_{11} and l_{21} are both 0-1 variables, this constraint requires that one of the two variables equals 1 and the other equals zero. The following three constraints ensure that one and only one level is selected for each of the other three attributes:

$$l_{12} + l_{22} = 1$$
$$l_{13} + l_{23} = 1$$
$$l_{14} + l_{24} + l_{34} = 1$$

WEB file

Salem

The optimal solution to this 17-variable, 12-constraint integer linear program is $l_{11} = l_{22} = l_{23} = l_{14} = 1$ and $y_2 = y_5 = y_6 = y_7 = 1$. The value of the optimal solution is 4, indicating that if Salem makes this type of pizza, it will be preferable to the current favorite for four of the eight consumers. With $l_{11} = l_{22} = l_{23} = l_{14} = 1$, the pizza design that obtains the largest market share for Salem has a thin crust, a cheese blend, a chunky sauce, and mild-flavored sausage. Note also that with $y_2 = y_5 = y_6 = y_7 = 1$, consumers 2, 5, 6, and 7 will prefer the Salem pizza. With this information Salem may choose to market this type of pizza.

NOTES AND COMMENTS

1. Most practical applications of integer linear programming involve only 0-1 integer variables. Indeed, some mixed-integer computer codes are designed to handle only integer variables with binary values. However, if a clever mathematical trick is employed, these codes can still be used for problems involving general integer variables. The trick is called *binary expansion* and requires that an upper bound be established for each integer variable. More advanced texts on integer programming show how it can be done.

2. The Q.M. in Action, Volunteer Scheduling for the Edmonton Folk Festival, describes how a series of three integer programming models was used to schedule volunteers. Two of the models employ 0-1 variables.

3. General-purpose mixed-integer linear programming codes and some spreadsheet packages can be used for linear programming problems, all-integer problems, and problems involving some continuous and some integer variables. General-purpose codes are seldom the fastest for solving problems with special structure (such as the transportation, assignment, and transshipment problems); however, unless the problems are very large, speed is usually not a critical issue. Thus, most practitioners prefer to use one general-purpose computer package that can be used on a variety of problems rather than to maintain a variety of computer programs designed for special problems.

VOLUNTEER SCHEDULING FOR THE EDMONTON FOLK FESTIVAL*

The Edmonton Folk Festival is a four-day outdoor event that is run almost entirely by volunteers. In 2002, 1800 volunteers worked on 35 different crews and contributed more than 50,000 volunteer hours. With this many volunteers, coordination requires a major effort. For instance, in 2002, two volunteer coordinators used a trial-and-error procedure to develop schedules for the volunteers in the two gate crews. However, developing these schedules proved to be time consuming and frustrating; the coordinators spent as much time scheduling as they did supervising volunteers during the festival. To reduce the time spent on gate-crew scheduling, one of the coordinators asked the Centre for Excellence in Operations at the University of Alberta School of Business for help in automating the scheduling process. The Centre agreed to help.

The scheduling system developed consists of three integer programming models. Model 1 is used to determine daily shift schedules. This model determines the length of each shift (number of hours) and how many volunteers are needed for each shift to meet the peaks and valleys in demand. Model 2 is a binary integer program used to assign volunteers to shifts. The objective is to maximize volunteer preferences subject to several constraints, such as number of hours worked, balance between morning and afternoon shifts, a mix of experienced and inexperienced volunteers on each shift, no conflicting shifts, and so on. Model 3 is used to allocate volunteers between the two gates.

The coordinators of the gate crews were pleased with the results provided by the models and learned to use them effectively. Vicki Fannon, the manager of volunteers for the festival, now has plans to expand the use of the integer programming models to the scheduling of other crews in the future.

*Based on L. Gordon and E. Erkut, "Improving Volunteer Scheduling for the Edmonton Folk Festival," *Interfaces* (September/October 2004): 367–376.

11.4 Modeling Flexibility Provided by 0-1 Integer Variables

In Section 11.3 we presented four applications involving 0-1 integer variables. In this section we continue the discussion of the use of 0-1 integer variables in modeling. First, we show how 0-1 integer variables can be used to model multiple-choice and mutually exclusive constraints. Then, we show how 0-1 integer variables can be used to model situations in which k projects out of a set of n projects must be selected, as well as situations in which the acceptance of one project is conditional on the acceptance of another. We close the section with a cautionary note on the role of sensitivity analysis in integer linear programming.

Multiple-Choice and Mutually Exclusive Constraints

Recall the Ice-Cold Refrigerator capital budgeting problem introduced in Section 11.3. The decision variables were defined as

$$P = 1 \text{ if the plant expansion project is accepted; 0 if rejected}$$
$$W = 1 \text{ if the warehouse expansion project is accepted; 0 if reject}$$
$$M = 1 \text{ if the new machinery project is accepted; 0 if rejected}$$
$$R = 1 \text{ if the new product research project is accepted; 0 if rejected}$$

Suppose that, instead of one warehouse expansion project, the Ice-Cold Refrigerator Company actually has three warehouse expansion projects under consideration. One of the warehouses *must* be expanded because of increasing product demand, but new demand isn't sufficient to make expansion of more than one warehouse necessary. The following variable definitions and **multiple-choice constraint** could be incorporated into the previous 0-1 integer linear programming model to reflect this situation. Let

$W_1 = 1$ if the original warehouse expansion project is accepted; 0 if rejected

$W_2 = 1$ if the second warehouse expansion project is accepted; 0 if rejected

$W_3 = 1$ if the third warehouse expansion project is accepted; 0 if rejected

The multiple-choice constraint reflecting the requirement that exactly one of these projects must be selected is

$$W_1 + W_2 + W_3 = 1$$

If W_1, W_2, and W_3 are allowed to assume only the values 0 or 1, then one and only one of these projects will be selected from among the three choices.

If the requirement that one warehouse must be expanded did not exist, the multiple-choice constraint could be modified as follows:

$$W_1 + W_2 + W_3 \leq 1$$

This modification allows for the case of no warehouse expansion ($W_1 = W_2 = W_3 = 0$) but does not permit more than one warehouse to be expanded. This type of constraint is often called a **mutually exclusive constraint**.

k out of *n* Alternatives Constraint

An extension of the notion of a multiple-choice constraint can be used to model situations in which *k out of a set of n* projects must be selected—a *k* **out of** *n* **alternatives constraint**. Suppose that W_1, W_2, W_3, W_4, and W_5 represent five potential warehouse expansion projects and that two of the five projects must be accepted. The constraint that satisfies this new requirement is

$$W_1 + W_2 + W_3 + W_4 + W_5 = 2$$

If no more than two of the projects are to be selected, we would use the following less-than-or-equal-to constraint:

$$W_1 + W_2 + W_3 + W_4 + W_5 \leq 2$$

Again, each of these variables must be restricted to 0-1 values.

Conditional and Corequisite Constraints

Sometimes the acceptance of one project is conditional on the acceptance of another. For example, suppose for the Ice-Cold Refrigerator Company that the warehouse expansion project was conditional on the plant expansion project. That is, management will not consider expanding the warehouse unless the plant is expanded. With P representing plant expansion and W representing warehouse expansion, a **conditional constraint** could be introduced to enforce this requirement:

$$W \leq P$$

Both P and W must be 0 or 1; whenever P is 0, W will be forced to 0. When P is 1, W is also allowed to be 1; thus, both the plant and the warehouse can be expanded. However, we note that the preceding constraint does not force the warehouse expansion project (W) to be accepted if the plant expansion project (P) is accepted.

If the warehouse expansion project had to be accepted whenever the plant expansion project was, and vice versa, we would say that P and W represented **corequisite constraint** projects. To model such a situation, we simply write the preceding constraint as an equality:

$$W = P$$

Try Problem 7 for practice with the modeling flexibility provided by 0-1 variables.

The constraint forces P and W to take on the same value.

The Q.M. in Action, Customer Order Allocation Model at Ketron, describes how the modeling flexibility provided by 0-1 variables helped Ketron build a customer order allocation model for a sporting goods company.

Q.M. *in* ACTION

CUSTOMER ORDER ALLOCATION MODEL AT KETRON*

Ketron Optimization provides consulting services for the design and implementation of mathematical programming applications. One such application involved the development of a mixed-integer programming model of the customer order allocation problem for a major sporting goods company. The sporting goods company markets approximately 300 products and has about 30 sources of supply (factory and warehouse locations). The problem is to determine how best to allocate customer orders to the various sources of supply such that the total manufacturing cost for the products ordered is minimized. Figure 11.12 provides a graphical representation of this problem. Note in the figure that each customer can receive shipments from only a few of the various sources of supply. For example, we see that customer 1 may be supplied by source A or B, customer 2 may be supplied only by source A, and so on.

The sporting equipment company classifies each customer order as either a "guaranteed" or "secondary" order. Guaranteed orders are single-source orders in that they must be filled by a single supplier to ensure that the

complete order will be delivered to the customer at one time. This single-source requirement necessitates the use of 0-1 integer variables in the model. Approximately 80% of the company's orders are guaranteed orders. Secondary orders can be split among the various sources of supply. These orders are made by customers restocking inventory, and receiving partial shipments from different sources at different times is not a problem. The 0-1 variables are used to represent the assignment of a guaranteed order to a supplier, and continuous variables are used to represent the secondary orders.

Constraints for the problem involve raw material capacities, manufacturing capacities, and individual product capacities. A fairly typical problem has about 800 constraints, 2000 0-1 assignment variables, and 500 continuous variables associated with the secondary orders. The customer order allocation problem is solved periodically as orders are received. In a typical period, between 20 and 40 customers are to be supplied. Because most customers require several products, usually between 600 and 800 orders must be assigned to the sources of supply.

---

*Based on information provided by J. A. Tomlin of Ketron Optimization.

(*continued*)

FIGURE 11.12   GRAPHICAL REPRESENTATION OF THE CUSTOMER ORDER
ALLOCATION PROBLEM

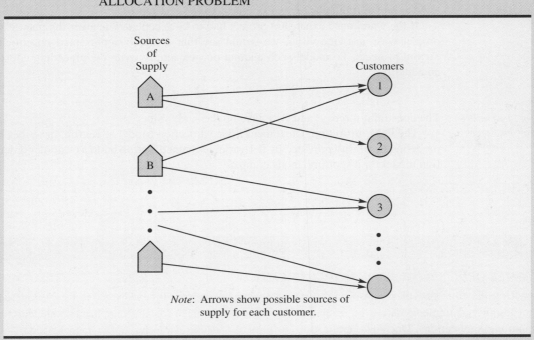

Note: Arrows show possible sources of
supply for each customer.

A Cautionary Note About Sensitivity Analysis

Sensitivity analysis often is more crucial for integer linear programming problems than for
linear programming problems. A small change in one of the coefficients in the constraints
can cause a relatively large change in the value of the optimal solution. To understand why,
consider the following integer programming model of a simple capital budgeting problem
involving four projects and a budgetary constraint for a single time period:

$$\text{Max} \quad 40x_1 + 60x_2 + 70x_3 + 160x_4$$

$$\text{s.t.}$$

$$16x_1 + 35x_2 + 45x_3 + 85x_4 \leq 100$$

$$x_1, x_2, x_3, x_4 = 0, 1$$

*Shadow prices cannot be
used for integer
programming sensitivity
analysis because they are
designed for linear
programs. Multiple
computer runs usually are
necessary for sensitivity
analysis of integer linear
programs.*

We can obtain the optimal solution to this problem by enumerating the alternatives. It is
$x_1 = 1$, $x_2 = 1$, $x_3 = 1$, and $x_4 = 0$, with an objective function value of $170. However, note
that if the budget available is increased by $1 (from $100 to $101), the optimal solution changes
to $x_1 = 1$, $x_2 = 0$, $x_3 = 0$, and $x_4 = 1$, with an objective function value of $200. That is, one
additional dollar in the budget would lead to a $30 increase in the return. Surely management,
when faced with such a situation, would increase the budget by $1. Because of the extreme
sensitivity of the value of the optimal solution to the constraint coefficients, practitioners usually recommend re-solving the integer linear program several times with slight variations in the
coefficients before attempting to choose the best solution for implementation.

Summary

In this chapter we introduced the important extension of linear programming referred to as *integer linear programming.* The only difference between the integer linear programming problems discussed in this chapter and the linear programming problems studied in previous chapters is that one or more of the variables must be integer. If all variables must be integer, we have an all-integer linear program. If some, but not necessarily all, variables must be integer, we have a mixed-integer linear program. Most integer programming applications involve 0-1 or binary variables.

Studying integer linear programming is important for two major reasons. First, integer linear programming may be helpful when fractional values for the variables are not permitted. Rounding a linear programming solution may not provide an optimal integer solution; methods for finding optimal integer solutions are needed when the economic consequences of rounding are significant. A second reason for studying integer linear programming is the increased modeling flexibility provided through the use of 0-1 variables. We showed how 0-1 variables could be used to model important managerial considerations in capital budgeting, fixed cost, supply chain design, bank location, and product design/market share applications.

The number of applications of integer linear programming continues to grow rapidly. This growth is due in part to the availability of good integer linear programming software packages. As researchers develop solution procedures capable of solving larger integer linear programs and as computer speed increases, a continuation of the growth of integer programming applications is expected.

Glossary

0-1 integer linear program An all-integer or mixed-integer linear program in which the integer variables are only permitted to assume the values 0 or 1. Also called *binary integer program.*

All-integer linear program An integer linear program in which all variables are required to be integer.

Capital budgeting problem A 0-1 integer programming problem that involves choosing which possible projects or activities provide the best investment return.

Conditional constraint A constraint involving 0-1 variables that does not allow certain variables to equal 1 unless certain other variables are equal to 1.

Corequisite constraint A constraint requiring that two 0-1 variables be equal. Thus, they are both either in or out of solution together.

Fixed cost problem A 0-1 mixed-integer programming problem in which the binary variables represent whether an activity, such as a production run, is undertaken (variable = 1) or not (variable = 0).

Integer linear program A linear program with the additional requirement that one or

k out of n alternatives constraint An extension of the multiple-choice constraint. This constraint requires that the sum of n 0-1 variables equals k. more of the variables must be integer.

Location problem A 0-1 integer programming problem in which the objective is to select the best locations to meet a stated objective. Variations of this problem (see the bank location problem in Section 11.3) are known as covering problems.

LP Relaxation   The linear program that results from dropping the integer requirements for the variables in an integer linear program.

Mixed-integer linear program   An integer linear program in which some, but not necessarily all, variables are required to be integer.

Multiple-choice constraint   A constraint requiring that the sum of two or more 0-1 variables equals 1. Thus, any feasible solution makes a choice of which variable to set equal to 1.

Mutually exclusive constraint   A constraint requiring that the sum of two or more 0-1 variables be less than or equal to 1. Thus, if one of the variables equals 1, the others must equal 0. However, all variables could equal 0.

Product design and market share optimization problem   Sometimes called the share of choice problem, it involves choosing a product design that maximizes the number of consumers preferring it.

Supply chain design problem   A mixed-integer linear program in which the binary integer variables usually represent sites selected for warehouses or plants and continuous variables represent the amount shipped over arcs in the supply chain.

Problems

1. Indicate which of the following is an all-integer linear program and which is a mixed-integer linear program. Write the LP Relaxation for the problem but do not attempt to solve.

   a. Max $30x_1 + 25x_2$

       s.t.

   $$3x_1 + 1.5x_2 \le 400$$
   $$1.5x_1 + 2x_2 \le 250$$
   $$1x_1 + 1x_2 \le 150$$
   $$x_1, x_2 \ge 0 \text{ and } x_2 \text{ integer}$$

   b. Min $3x_1 + 4x_2$

       s.t.

   $$2x_1 + 4x_2 \ge 8$$
   $$2x_1 + 6x_2 \ge 12$$
   $$x_1, x_2 \ge 0 \text{ and integer}$$

2. Consider the following all-integer linear program:

   $$\text{Max} \quad 5x_1 + 8x_2$$

       s.t.

   $$6x_1 + 5x_2 \le 30$$
   $$9x_1 + 4x_2 \le 36$$
   $$1x_1 + 2x_2 \le 10$$
   $$x_1, x_2 \ge 0 \text{ and integer}$$

   a. Graph the constraints for this problem. Use dots to indicate all feasible integer solutions.

   b. Find the optimal solution to the LP Relaxation. Round down to find a feasible integer solution.

   c. Find the optimal integer solution. Is it the same as the solution obtained in part (b) by rounding down?

3.   Consider the following all-integer linear program:

$$\text{Max} \quad 1x_1 + 1x_2$$

s.t.

$$4x_1 + 6x_2 \le 22$$
$$1x_1 + 5x_2 \le 15$$
$$2x_1 + 1x_2 \le 9$$
$$x_1, x_2 \ge 0 \text{ and integer}$$

a.   Graph the constraints for this problem. Use dots to indicate all feasible integer solutions.
b.   Solve the LP Relaxation of this problem.
c.   Find the optimal integer solution.

4.   Consider the following all-integer linear program:

$$\text{Max} \quad 10x_1 + 3x_2$$

s.t.

$$6x_1 + 7x_2 \le 40$$
$$3x_1 + 1x_2 \le 11$$
$$x_1, x_2 \ge 0 \text{ and integer}$$

a.   Formulate and solve the LP Relaxation of the problem. Solve it graphically, and round down to find a feasible solution. Specify an upper bound on the value of the optimal solution.
b.   Solve the integer linear program graphically. Compare the value of this solution with the solution obtained in part (a).
c.   Suppose the objective function changes to Max $3x_1 + 6x_2$. Repeat parts (a) and (b).

5.   Consider the following mixed-integer linear program:

$$\text{Max} \quad 2x_1 + 3x_2$$

s.t.

$$4x_1 + 9x_2 \le 36$$
$$7x_1 + 5x_2 \le 35$$
$$x_1, x_2 \ge 0 \text{ and } x_1 \text{ integer}$$

a.   Graph the constraints for this problem. Indicate on your graph all feasible mixed-integer solutions.
b.   Find the optimal solution to the LP Relaxation. Round the value of x_1 down to find a feasible mixed-integer solution. Is this solution optimal? Why or why not?
c.   Find the optimal solution for the mixed-integer linear program.

6.   Consider the following mixed-integer linear program:

$$\text{Max} \quad 1x_1 + 1x_2$$

s.t.

$$7x_1 + 9x_2 \le 63$$
$$9x_1 + 5x_2 \le 45$$
$$3x_1 + 1x_2 \le 12$$
$$x_1, x_2 \ge 0 \text{ and } x_2 \text{ integer}$$

a.   Graph the constraints for this problem. Indicate on your graph all feasible mixed-integer solutions.

b.   Find the optimal solution to the LP Relaxation. Round the value of x_2 down to find a feasible mixed-integer solution. Specify upper and lower bounds on the value of the optimal solution to the mixed-integer linear program.

c.   Find the optimal solution to the mixed-integer linear program.

7.   The following questions refer to a capital budgeting problem with six projects represented by 0-1 variables x_1, x_2, x_3, x_4, x_5, and x_6:

a.   Write a constraint modeling a situation in which two of the projects 1, 3, 5, and 6 must be undertaken.

b.   Write a constraint modeling a situation in which, if projects 3 and 5 must be undertaken, they must be undertaken simultaneously.

c.   Write a constraint modeling a situation in which project 1 or 4 must be undertaken, but not both.

d.   Write constraints modeling a situation where project 4 cannot be undertaken unless projects 1 and 3 also are undertaken.

e.   Revise the requirement in part (d) to accommodate the case in which, when projects 1 and 3 are undertaken, project 4 also must be undertaken.

 8.   Spencer Enterprises is attempting to choose among a series of new investment alternatives. The potential investment alternatives, the net present value of the future stream of returns, the capital requirements, and the available capital funds over the next three years are summarized as follows:

| | Net Present | Capital Requirements ($) | | |
Alternative	Value ($)	Year 1	Year 2	Year 3
Limited warehouse expansion	4,000	3,000	1,000	4,000
Extensive warehouse expansion	6,000	2,500	3,500	3,500
Test market new product	10,500	6,000	4,000	5,000
Advertising campaign	4,000	2,000	1,500	1,800
Basic research	8,000	5,000	1,000	4,000
Purchase new equipment	3,000	1,000	500	900
Capital funds available		10,500	7,000	8,750

a.   Develop and solve an integer programming model for maximizing the net present value.

b.   Assume that only one of the warehouse expansion projects can be implemented. Modify your model of part (a).

c.   Suppose that, if test marketing of the new product is carried out, the advertising campaign also must be conducted. Modify your formulation of part (b) to reflect this new situation.

9.   Hawkins Manufacturing Company produces connecting rods for 4- and 6-cylinder automobile engines using the same production line. The cost required to set up the production line to produce the 4-cylinder connecting rods is $2000, and the cost required to set up the production line for the 6-cylinder connecting rods is $3500. Manufacturing costs are $15 for each 4-cylinder connecting rod and $18 for each 6-cylinder connecting rod. Hawkins makes a decision at the end of each week as to which product will be manufactured the following week. If there is a production changeover from one week to the next, the weekend is used to reconfigure the production line. Once the line has been set up, the weekly production capacities are 6000 6-cylinder connecting rods and 8000 4-cylinder connecting rods. Let

x_4 = the number of 4-cylinder connecting rods produced next week

x_6 = the number of 6-cylinder connecting rods produced next week

$s_4 = 1$ if the production line is set up to produce the 4-cylinder connecting rods; 0 if otherwise

$s_6 = 1$ if the production line is set up to produce the 6-cylinder connecting rods; 0 if otherwise

a. Using the decision variables x_4 and s_4, write a constraint that limits next week's production of the 4-cylinder connecting rods to either 0 or 8000 units.
b. Using the decision variables x_6 and s_6, write a constraint that limits next week's production of the 6-cylinder connecting rods to either 0 or 6000 units.
c. Write three constraints that, taken together, limit the production of connecting rods for next week.
d. Write an objective function for minimizing the cost of production for next week.

10. Grave City is considering the relocation of several police substations to obtain better enforcement in high-crime areas. The locations under consideration together with the areas that can be covered from these locations are given in the following table:

Potential Locations for Substations	Areas Covered
A	1, 5, 7
B	1, 2, 5, 7
C	1, 3, 5
D	2, 4, 5
E	3, 4, 6
F	4, 5, 6
G	1, 5, 6, 7

a. Formulate an integer programming model that could be used to find the minimum number of locations necessary to provide coverage to all areas.
b. Solve the problem in part (a).

11. Hart Manufacturing makes three products. Each product requires manufacturing operations in three departments: A, B, and C. The labor-hour requirements, by department, are as follows:

Department	Product 1	Product 2	Product 3
A	1.50	3.00	2.00
B	2.00	1.00	2.50
C	0.25	0.25	0.25

During the next production period, the labor-hours available are 450 in department A, 350 in department B, and 50 in department C. The profit contributions per unit are $25 for product 1, $28 for product 2, and $30 for product 3.

a. Formulate a linear programming model for maximizing total profit contribution.
b. Solve the linear program formulated in part (a). How much of each product should be produced, and what is the projected total profit contribution?
c. After evaluating the solution obtained in part (b), one of the production supervisors noted that production setup costs had not been taken into account. She noted that setup costs are $400 for product 1, $550 for product 2, and $600 for product 3. If the solution developed in part (b) is to be used, what is the total profit contribution after taking into account the setup costs?

    d. Management realized that the optimal product mix, taking setup costs into account, might be different from the one recommended in part (b). Formulate a mixed-integer linear program that takes setup costs into account. Management also stated that we should not consider making more than 175 units of product 1, 150 units of product 2, or 140 units of product 3.

    e. Solve the mixed-integer linear program formulated in part (d). How much of each product should be produced, and what is the projected total profit contribution? Compare this profit contribution to that obtained in part (c).

12. Offhaus Manufacturing produces office supplies, but outsources the delivery of its products to third party carriers. Offhaus ships to 20 cities from its Dayton, Ohio, manufacturing facility and has asked a variety of carriers to bid on its business. Seven carriers have responded with bids. The resulting bids (in dollars per truckload) are shown in the following table. For example, the table shows that Carrier 1 bid on the business to cities 11–20. The right side of the table provides the number of truckloads scheduled for each destination in the next quarter.

Bid $/Truckload	Carrier 1	Carrier 2	Carrier 3	Carrier 4	Carrier 5	Carrier 6	Carrier 7	Destination	Demand (Truckloads)
City 1					$2188	$1666	$1790	City 1	30
City 2		$1453			$2602	$1767		City 2	10
City 3		$1534			$2283	$1857	$1870	City 3	20
City 4		$1687			$2617	$1738		City 4	40
City 5		$1523			$2239	$1771	$1855	City 5	10
City 6		$1521			$1571		$1545	City 6	10
City 7		$2100		$1922	$1938		$2050	City 7	12
City 8		$1800		$1432	$1416		$1739	City 8	25
City 9		$1134		$1233	$1181		$1150	City 9	25
City 10		$ 672		$ 610	$ 669		$ 678	City 10	33
City 11	$724		$723	$ 627	$ 657		$ 706	City 11	11
City 12	$766		$766	$ 721	$ 682		$ 733	City 12	29
City 13	$741		$745		$ 682		$ 733	City 13	12
City 14	$815	$ 800	$828		$ 745		$ 832	City 14	24
City 15	$904		$880		$ 891		$ 914	City 15	10
City 16	$958		$933		$ 891		$ 914	City 16	10
City 17	$925		$929		$ 937		$ 984	City 17	23
City 18	$892		$869	$ 822	$ 829		$ 864	City 18	25
City 19	$927		$969		$ 967		$1008	City 19	12
City 20	$963		$938		$ 955		$ 995	City 20	10
Number of Bids	10	10	10	7	20	5	18		

Because dealing with too many carriers can be a hassle, Offhaus would like to limit the number of carriers it uses to three. Also, for customer relationship reasons, Offhaus wants each city to be assigned to only one carrier (that is, there is no splitting of the demand to a given city across carriers).

    a. Develop a model that will yield the three selected carriers and the city-carrier assignments so as to minimize the cost of shipping. Solve the model and report the solution.

    b. Offhaus is not sure if three is the correct number of carriers to select. Run the model you developed in part (a) for allowable carriers varying from 1 up to 7. Based on results, how many carriers would you recommend and why?

13. Recall the Martin-Beck Company supply chain design problem in Section 11.3.

    a. Modify the formulation shown in Section 11.3 to account for the policy restriction that a plant must be located either in Detroit or in Toledo, but not both.

    b. Modify the formulation shown in Section 11.3 to account for the policy restriction that no more than two plants can be located in Denver, Kansas City, and St. Louis.

14. An automobile manufacturer has five outdated plants: one each in Michigan, Ohio, and California and two in New York. Management is considering modernizing these plants to manufacture engine blocks and transmissions for a new model car. The cost to modernize each plant and the manufacturing capacity after modernization is as follows:

Plant	Cost ($ millions)	Engine Blocks (1000s)	Transmissions (1000s)
Michigan	25	500	300
New York	35	800	400
New York	35	400	800
Ohio	40	900	600
California	20	200	300

The projected needs are for total capacities of 900,000 engine blocks and 900,000 transmissions. Management wants to determine which plants to modernize to meet projected manufacturing needs and, at the same time, minimize the total cost of modernization.

a. Develop a table that lists every possible option available to management. As part of your table, indicate the total engine block capacity and transmission capacity for each possible option, whether the option is feasible based on the projected needs, and the total modernization cost for each option.

b. Based on your analysis in part (a), what recommendation would you provide management?

c. Formulate a 0-1 integer programming model that could be used to determine the optimal solution to the modernization question facing management.

d. Solve the model formulated in part (c) to provide a recommendation for management.

OhioTrustFull

15. Consider again the Ohio Trust bank location problem discussed in Section 11.3. The file OhioTrustFull contains data for all of Ohio's 88 counties. The file contains an 88 × 88 matrix with the rows and columns each being the 88 counties. The entries in the matrix are zeros and ones and indicate if the county of the row shares a border with the county of the column (1 = yes and 0 = no).

a. Create a model to find the location of required principal places of business (PPBs) to minimize the number of PPBs needed to open all counties to branches.

b. Solve the model constructed in part (a). What is the minimum number of PPBs needed to open up the entire state to Ohio Trust branches?

16. The Northshore Bank is working to develop an efficient work schedule for full-time and part-time tellers. The schedule must provide for efficient operation of the bank, including adequate customer service, employee breaks, and so on. On Fridays the bank is open from 9:00 A.M. to 7:00 P.M. The number of tellers necessary to provide adequate customer service during each hour of operation is summarized in the following table.

Time	Number of Tellers	Time	Number of Tellers
9:00 A.M.–10:00 A.M.	6	2:00 P.M.–3:00 P.M.	6
10:00 A.M.–11:00 A.M.	4	3:00 P.M.–4:00 P.M.	4
11:00 A.M.–Noon	8	4:00 P.M.–5:00 P.M.	7
Noon–1:00 P.M.	10	5:00 P.M.–6:00 P.M.	6
1:00 P.M.–2:00 P.M.	9	6:00 P.M.–7:00 P.M.	6

Each full-time employee starts on the hour and works a 4-hour shift, followed by 1 hour for lunch and then a 3-hour shift. Part-time employees work one 4-hour shift beginning on the hour. Considering salary and fringe benefits, full-time employees cost the bank $15 per hour ($105 a day), and part-time employees cost the bank $8 per hour ($32 per day).

a. Formulate an integer programming model that can be used to develop a schedule that will satisfy customer service needs at a minimum employee cost. (*Hint:* Let x_i = number of full-time employees coming on duty at the beginning of hour i and y_i = number of part-time employees coming on duty at the beginning of hour i.)

b. Solve the LP Relaxation of your model in part (a).

c. Solve for the optimal schedule of tellers. Comment on the solution.

d. After reviewing the solution to part (c), the bank manager realized that some additional requirements must be specified. Specifically, she wants to ensure that one full-time employee is on duty at all times and that there is a staff of at least five full-time employees. Revise your model to incorporate these additional requirements and solve for the optimal solution.

OhioTrustPop

17. Consider again the Ohio Trust Inc. problem described in Problem 15. Suppose only a limited number of PPBs can be placed. Ohio Trust would like to place this limited number of PPBs in counties so that the allowable branches can reach the maximum possible population. The file OhioTrustPop contains the county adjacency matrix described in Problem 15 as well as the population of each county.

a. Assume that only a fixed number of PPBs, denoted k. can be established. Formulate a linear binary integer program that will tell Ohio Trust Inc. where to locate the fixed number of PPBs in order to maximize the population reached. (*Hint:* Introduce variable y_i = 1 if it is possible to establish a branch in county i, and y_i = 0 otherwise; that is, if county i is covered by a PPB, then the population can be counted as covered.)

b. Suppose that two PPBs can be established. Where should they be located to maximize the population served?

c. Solve your model from part a for allowable number of PPBs ranging from 1 to 10. In other words, solve the model 10 times, k set to 1,2, ... , 10. Record the population reached for each value of k. Graph the results of this analysis by plotting the population reached versus number of PPBs allowed. Based on their cost calculations, Ohio Trust considers an additional PPB to be fiscally prudent only if it increases the population reached by at least 500,000 people. Based on this graph, what is the number of PPBs you recommend to be implemented?

18. Refer to the Salem Foods share of choices problem in Section 11.3 and address the following issues. It is rumored that King's is getting out of the frozen pizza business. If so, the major competitor for Salem Foods will be the Antonio's brand pizza.

a. Compute the overall utility for the Antonio's brand pizza for each of the consumers in Table 11.4.

b. Assume that Salem's only competitor is the Antonio's brand pizza. Formulate and solve the share of choices problem that will maximize market share. What is the best product design, and what share of the market can be expected?

19. Burnside Marketing Research conducted a study for Barker Foods on some designs for a new dry cereal. Three attributes were found to be most influential in determining which cereal had the best taste: ratio of wheat to corn in the cereal flake, type of sweetener (sugar, honey, or artificial), and the presence or absence of flavor bits. Seven children participated in taste tests and provided the following part-worths for the attributes:

Child	Wheat/Corn		Sweetener			Flavor Bits	
	Low	High	Sugar	Honey	Artificial	Present	Absent
1	15	35	30	40	25	15	9
2	30	20	40	35	35	8	11
3	40	25	20	40	10	7	14
4	35	30	25	20	30	15	18
5	25	40	40	20	35	18	14
6	20	25	20	35	30	9	16
7	30	15	25	40	40	20	11

a. Suppose the overall utility (sum of part-worths) of the current favorite cereal is 75 for each child. What is the product design that will maximize the share of choices for the seven children in the sample?

b. Assume the overall utility of the current favorite cereal for children 1–4 is 70, and the overall utility of the current favorite cereal for children 5–7 is 80. What is the product design that will maximize the share of choice for the seven children in the sample?

20. Refer to Problem 14. Suppose that management determined that its cost estimates to modernize the New York plants were too low. Specifically, suppose that the actual cost is $40 million to modernize each plant.

a. What changes in your previous 0-1 integer linear programming model are needed to incorporate these changes in costs?

b. For these cost changes, what recommendations would you now provide management regarding the modernization plan?

c. Reconsider the solution obtained using the revised cost figures. Suppose that management decides that closing two plants in the same state is not acceptable. How could this policy restriction be added to your 0-1 integer programming model?

d. Based on the cost revision and the policy restriction presented in part (c), what recommendations would you now provide management regarding the modernization plan?

21. The Bayside Art Gallery is considering installing a video camera security system to reduce its insurance premiums. A diagram of the eight display rooms that Bayside uses for exhibitions is shown in Figure 11.13; the openings between the rooms are numbered 1–13. A security firm proposed that two-way cameras be installed at some room openings. Each camera has the ability to monitor the two rooms between which the camera is located. For example, if a camera were located at opening number 4, rooms 1 and 4 would be covered; if a camera were located at opening 11, rooms 7 and 8 would be covered; and so on. Management decided not to locate a camera system at the entrance to the display rooms. The objective is to provide security coverage for all eight rooms using the minimum number of two-way cameras.

a. Formulate a 0-1 integer linear programming model that will enable Bayside's management to determine the locations for the camera systems.

b. Solve the model formulated in part (a) to determine how many two-way cameras to purchase and where they should be located.

c. Suppose that management wants to provide additional security coverage for room 7. Specifically, management wants room 7 to be covered by two cameras. How would your model formulated in part (a) have to change to accommodate this policy restriction?

d. With the policy restriction specified in part (c), determine how many two-way camera systems will need to be purchased and where they will be located.

FIGURE 11.13 DIAGRAM OF DISPLAY ROOMS FOR BAYSIDE ART GALLERY

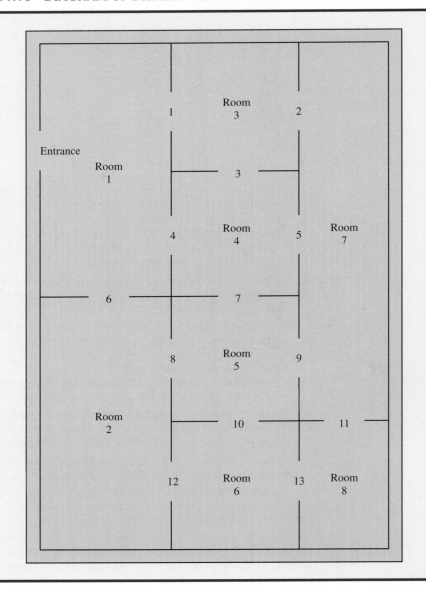

22. The Delta Group is a management consulting firm specializing in the health care industry. A team is being formed to study possible new markets, and a linear programming model has been developed for selecting team members. However, one constraint the president imposed is a team size of three, five, or seven members. The staff cannot figure out how to incorporate this requirement in the model. The current model requires that team members be selected from three departments and uses the following variable definitions:

$$x_1 = \text{the number of employees selected from department 1}$$
$$x_2 = \text{the number of employees selected from department 2}$$
$$x_3 = \text{the number of employees selected from department 3}$$

Show the staff how to write constraints that will ensure that the team will consist of three, five, or seven employees. The following integer variables should be helpful:

$$y_1 = \begin{cases} 1 & \text{if team size is 3} \\ 0 & \text{otherwise} \end{cases}$$

$$y_2 = \begin{cases} 1 & \text{if team size is 5} \\ 0 & \text{otherwise} \end{cases}$$

$$y_3 = \begin{cases} 1 & \text{if team size is 7} \\ 0 & \text{otherwise} \end{cases}$$

23. Roedel Electronics produces a variety of electrical components, including a remote control for televisions and a remote control for DVD players. Each remote control consists of three subassemblies that are manufactured by Roedel: a base, a cartridge, and a keypad. Both remote controls use the same base subassembly, but different cartridge and keypad subassemblies.

   Roedel's sales forecast indicates that 7000 TV remote controls and 5000 DVD remote controls will be needed to satisfy demand during the upcoming Christmas season. Because only 500 hours of in-house manufacturing time are available, Roedel is considering purchasing some, or all, of the subassemblies from outside suppliers. If Roedel manufactures a subassembly in-house, it incurs a fixed setup cost as well as a variable manufacturing cost. The following table shows the setup cost, the manufacturing time per subassembly, the manufacturing cost per subassembly, and the cost to purchase each of the subassemblies from an outside supplier:

Subassembly	Setup Cost ($)	Manufacturing Time per Unit (min.)	Manufacturing Cost per Unit ($)	Purchase Cost per Unit ($)
Base	1000	0.9	0.40	0.65
TV cartridge	1200	2.2	2.90	3.45
DVD cartridge	1900	3.0	3.15	3.70
TV keypad	1500	0.8	0.30	0.50
DVD keypad	1500	1.0	0.55	0.70

   a. Determine how many units of each subassembly Roedel should manufacture and how many units Roedel should purchase. What is the total manufacturing and purchase cost associated with your recommendation?

   b. Suppose Roedel is considering purchasing new machinery to produce DVD cartridges. For the new machinery, the setup cost is $3000; the manufacturing time is 2.5 minutes per cartridge, and the manufacturing cost is $2.60 per cartridge. Assuming that the new machinery is purchased, determine how many units of each subassembly Roedel should manufacture and how many units of each subassembly Roedel should purchase. What is the total manufacturing and purchase cost associated with your recommendation? Do you think the new machinery should be purchased? Explain.

24. A mathematical programming system named SilverScreener uses a 0-1 integer programming model to help theater managers decide which movies to show on a weekly basis in a multiple-screen theater. Suppose that management of Valley Cinemas would like to investigate the potential of using a similar scheduling system for their chain of multiple-screen theaters. Valley selected a small two-screen movie theater for the pilot testing and would like to develop an integer programming model to help schedule movies for the next four weeks. Six movies are available. The first week each movie is available, the last week

each movie can be shown, and the maximum number of weeks that each movie can run are shown here:

Movie	First Week Available	Last Week Available	Max. Run (weeks)
1	1	2	2
2	1	3	2
3	1	1	2
4	2	4	2
5	3	6	3
6	3	5	3

The overall viewing schedule for the theater is composed of the individual schedules for each of the six movies. For each movie a schedule must be developed that specifies the week the movie starts and the number of consecutive weeks it will run. For instance, one possible schedule for movie 2 is for it to start in week 1 and run for two weeks. Theater policy requires that once a movie is started, it must be shown in consecutive weeks. It cannot be stopped and restarted again. To represent the schedule possibilities for each movie, the following decision variables were developed:

$$x_{ijw} = \begin{cases} 1 & \text{if movie } i \text{ is scheduled to start in week } j \text{ and run for } w \text{ weeks} \\ 0 & \text{otherwise} \end{cases}$$

For example, $x_{532} = 1$ means that the schedule selected for movie 5 is to begin in week 3 and run for two weeks. For each movie, a separate variable is given for each possible schedule.

a. Three schedules are associated with movie 1. List the variables that represent these schedules.
b. Write a constraint requiring that only one schedule be selected for movie 1.
c. Write a constraint requiring that only one schedule be selected for movie 5.
d. What restricts the number of movies that can be shown in week 1? Write a constraint that restricts the number of movies selected for viewing in week 1.
e. Write a constraint that restricts the number of movies selected for viewing in week 3.

25. East Coast Trucking provides service from Boston to Miami using regional offices located in Boston, New York, Philadelphia, Baltimore, Washington, Richmond, Raleigh, Florence, Savannah, Jacksonville, and Tampa. The number of miles between each of the regional offices is provided in the following table:

	New York	Philadelphia	Baltimore	Washington	Richmond	Raleigh	Florence	Savannah	Jacksonville	Tampa	Miami
Boston	211	320	424	459	565	713	884	1056	1196	1399	1669
New York		109	213	248	354	502	673	845	985	1188	1458
Philadelphia			104	139	245	393	564	736	876	1079	1349
Baltimore				35	141	289	460	632	772	975	1245
Washington					106	254	425	597	737	940	1210
Richmond						148	319	491	631	834	1104
Raleigh							171	343	483	686	956
Florence								172	312	515	785
Savannah									140	343	613
Jacksonville										203	473
Tampa											270

The company's expansion plans involve constructing service facilities in some of the cities where a regional office is located. Each regional office must be within 400 miles of a service facility. For instance, if a service facility is constructed in Richmond, it can provide service to regional offices located in New York, Philadelphia, Baltimore, Washington, Richmond, Raleigh, and Florence. Management would like to determine the minimum number of service facilities needed and where they should be located.

a. Formulate an integer linear program that can be used to determine the minimum number of service facilities needed and their locations.

b. Solve the integer linear program formulated in part (a). How many service facilities are required and where should they be located?

c. Suppose that each service facility can only provide service to regional offices within 300 miles. How many service facilities are required and where should they be located?

26. Dave has $100,000 to invest in 10 mutual fund alternatives with the following restrictions. For diversification, no more than $25,000 can be invested in any one fund. If a fund is chosen for investment, then at least $10,000 will be invested in it. No more than two of the funds can be pure growth funds, and at least one pure bond fund must be selected. The total amount invested in pure bond funds must be at least as much as the amount invested in pure growth funds. Using the following expected returns, formulate and solve a model that will determine the investment strategy that will maximize expected annual return. What assumptions have you made in your model? How often would you expect to run your model?

Fund	Type	Expected Return
1	Growth	6.70%
2	Growth	7.65%
3	Growth	7.55%
4	Growth	7.45%
5	Growth & Income	7.50%
6	Growth & Income	6.45%
7	Growth & Income	7.05%
8	Stock & Bond	6.90%
9	Bond	5.20%
10	Bond	5.90%

Case Problem 1   Textbook Publishing

ASW Publishing, Inc., a small publisher of college textbooks, must make a decision regarding which books to publish next year. The books under consideration are listed in the following table, along with the projected three-year sales expected from each book:

Book Subject	Type of Book	Projected Sales (1000s)
Business calculus	New	20
Finite mathematics	Revision	30
General statistics	New	15
Mathematical statistics	New	10
Business statistics	Revision	25
Finance	New	18
Financial accounting	New	25
Managerial accounting	Revision	50
English literature	New	20
German	New	30

The books listed as revisions are texts that ASW already has under contract; these texts are being considered for publication as new editions. The books that are listed as new have been reviewed by the company, but contracts have not yet been signed.

Three individuals in the company can be assigned to these projects, all of whom have varying amounts of time available; John has 60 days available, and Susan and Monica both have 40 days available. The days required by each person to complete each project are shown in the following table. For instance, if the business calculus book is published, it will require 30 days of John's time and 40 days of Susan's time. An "X" indicates that the person will not be used on the project. Note that at least two staff members will be assigned to each project except the finance book.

Book Subject	John	Susan	Monica
Business calculus	30	40	X
Finite mathematics	16	24	X
General statistics	24	X	30
Mathematical statistics	20	X	24
Business statistics	10	X	16
Finance	X	X	14
Financial accounting	X	24	26
Managerial accounting	X	28	30
English literature	40	34	30
German	X	50	36

ASW will not publish more than two statistics books or more than one accounting text in a single year. In addition, management decided that one of the mathematics books (business calculus or finite math) must be published, but not both.

Managerial Report

Prepare a report for the managing editor of ASW that describes your findings and recommendations regarding the best publication strategy for next year. In carrying out your analysis, assume that the fixed costs and the sales revenues per unit are approximately equal for all books; management is interested primarily in maximizing the total unit sales volume.

The managing editor also asked that you include recommendations regarding the following possible changes:

1. If it would be advantageous to do so, Susan can be moved off another project to allow her to work 12 more days.
2. If it would be advantageous to do so, Monica can also be made available for another 10 days.
3. If one or more of the revisions could be postponed for another year, should they be? Clearly the company will risk losing market share by postponing a revision.

Include details of your analysis in an appendix to your report.

Case Problem 2 Yeager National Bank

Using aggressive mail promotion with low introductory interest rates, Yeager National Bank (YNB) built a large base of credit card customers throughout the continental United States. Currently, all customers send their regular payments to the bank's corporate office located in Charlotte, North Carolina. Daily collections from customers making their regular payments are substantial, with an average of approximately $600,000. YNB estimates that it makes about 15% on its funds and would like to ensure that customer payments are credited to the bank's account as soon as possible. For instance, if it takes five days for a customer's payment to be sent through the mail, processed, and credited to the bank's account, YNB has potentially lost five days' worth of interest income. Although the time needed for this collection process cannot be completely eliminated, reducing it can be beneficial given the large amounts of money involved.

Instead of having all its credit card customers send their payments to Charlotte, YNB is considering having customers send their payments to one or more regional collection centers, referred to in the banking industry as lockboxes. Four lockbox locations have been proposed: Phoenix, Salt Lake City, Atlanta, and Boston. To determine which lockboxes to open and where lockbox customers should send their payments, YNB divided its customer base into five geographical regions: Northwest, Southwest, Central, Northeast, and Southeast. Every customer in the same region will be instructed to send his or her payment to the same lockbox. The following table shows the average number of days it takes before a customer's payment is credited to the bank's account when the payment is sent from each of the regions to each of the potential lockboxes:

Customer	Location of Lockbox				Daily Collection
Zone	Phoenix	Salt Lake City	Atlanta	Boston	($1000s)
Northwest	4	2	4	4	80
Southwest	2	3	4	6	90
Central	5	3	3	4	150
Northeast	5	4	3	2	180
Southeast	4	6	2	3	100

Managerial Report

Dave Wolff, the vice president for cash management, asked you to prepare a report containing your recommendations for the number of lockboxes and the best lockbox locations. Mr. Wolff is primarily concerned with minimizing lost interest income, but he wants you to also consider the effect of an annual fee charged for maintaining a lockbox at any location. Although the amount of the fee is unknown at this time, we can assume that the fees will be in the range of $20,000 to $30,000 per location. Once good potential locations have been selected, Mr. Wolff will inquire as to the annual fees.

Case Problem 3

Production Scheduling with Changeover Costs

Buckeye Manufacturing produces heads for engines used in the manufacture of trucks. The production line is highly complex, and it measures 900 feet in length. Two types of engine heads are produced on this line: the P-Head and the H-Head. The P-Head is used in heavy-duty trucks and the H-Head is used in smaller trucks. Because only one type of head can be produced at a time, the line is set up to manufacture either the P-Head or the H-Head, but not both. Changeovers are made over a weekend; costs are $500 in going from a setup for the P-Head to a setup for the H-Head, and vice versa. When set up for the P-Head, the maximum production rate is 100 units per week and when set up for the H-Head, the maximum production rate is 80 units per week.

Buckeye just shut down for the week after using the line to produce the P-Head. The manager wants to plan production and changeovers for the next eight weeks. Currently, Buckeye's inventory consists of 125 P-Heads and 143 H-Heads. Inventory carrying costs are charged at an annual rate of 19.5% of the value of inventory. The production cost for the P-Head is $225, and the production cost for the H-Head is $310. The objective in developing a production schedule is to minimize the sum of production cost, plus inventory carrying cost, plus changeover cost.

Buckeye received the following requirements schedule from its customer (an engine assembly plant) for the next nine weeks:

| | **Product Demand** | |
Week	P-Head	H-Head
1	55	38
2	55	38
3	44	30
4	0	0
5	45	48
6	45	48
7	36	58
8	35	57
9	35	58

Safety stock requirements are such that week-ending inventory must provide for at least 80% of the next week's demand.

Managerial Report

Prepare a report for Buckeye's management with a production and changeover schedule for the next eight weeks. Be sure to note how much of the total cost is due to production, how much is due to inventory, and how much is due to changeover.

Case Problem 4   # Applecore Children's Clothing

Applecore Children's Clothing is a retailer that sells high-end clothes for toddlers (ages 1–3) primarily in shopping malls. Applecore also has a successful Internet-based sales division. Recently Dave Walker, vice president of the e-commerce division, has been given the directive to expand the company's Internet sales. He commissioned a major study on the effectiveness of Internet ads placed on news websites. The results were favorable: Current patrons who purchased via the Internet and saw the ads on news websites spent more, on average, than did comparable Internet customers who did not see the ads.

With this new information on Internet ads, Walker continued to investigate how new Internet customers could most effectively be reached. One of these ideas involved strategically purchasing ads on news websites prior to and during the holiday season. To determine which news sites might be the most effective for ads, Walker conducted a follow-up study. An e-mail questionnaire was administered to a sample of 1200 current Internet customers to ascertain which of 30 news sites they regularly visit. The idea is that websites with high proportions of current customer visits would be viable sources of future customers of Applecore products.

Walker would like to ascertain which news sites should be selected for ads. The problem is complicated because Walker does not want to count multiple exposures. So, if a respondent visits multiple sites with Applecore ads or visits a given site multiple times, that respondent should be counted as reached but not more than once. In other words, a customer is considered reached if he or she has visited at least one website with an Applecore ad.

Data from the customer e-mail survey have begun to trickle in. Walker wants to develop a prototype model based on the current survey results. So far, 53 surveys have been returned. To keep the prototype model manageable, Walker wants to proceed with model development using the data from the 53 returned surveys and using only the first ten news sites in the questionnaire. The costs of ads per week for the 10 websites are given in the following table, and the budget is $10,000 per week. For each of the 53 responses received, which of the 10 websites are regularly visited is given as shown below. For a given customer–website pair, a one indicates that the customer regularly visits that website, and a zero indicates that the customer does not regularly visit that site.

Data for Applecore Customer Visits to News Websites (respondents 5–33 hidden).

	Website									
	1	2	3	4	5	6	7	8	9	10
Cost/Wk ($000)	$5.0	$8.0	$3.5	$5.5	$7.0	$4.5	$6.0	$5.0	$3.0	$2.2
	Website									
Customer	1	2	3	4	5	6	7	8	9	10
1	0	0	0	0	0	0	0	0	0	1
2	1	0	0	1	0	0	0	0	0	0
3	1	0	0	0	0	0	0	0	0	0
4	0	0	0	0	1	1	0	0	0	0
34	0	0	0	1	1	0	0	0	0	0
35	1	0	0	0	1	1	0	0	0	0
36	1	0	1	0	0	0	0	0	0	0
37	0	0	1	0	1	0	0	1	0	0
38	0	0	1	0	0	0	0	0	0	0
39	0	1	0	0	0	0	1	0	0	0
40	0	1	0	0	0	0	1	0	0	0
41	0	0	0	0	0	0	1	0	0	0
42	0	0	0	1	1	1	0	0	0	0
43	0	0	0	0	0	0	0	0	0	0
44	0	0	0	0	1	0	0	0	0	1
45	1	1	0	0	0	0	0	0	0	0
46	0	0	0	0	0	0	1	0	0	0
47	1	0	0	0	1	0	0	0	0	1
48	0	0	1	0	0	0	0	0	0	0
49	1	0	1	1	0	0	0	0	0	0
50	0	0	0	0	0	0	0	0	0	0
51	0	1	0	0	0	1	0	0	0	0
52	0	0	0	0	0	0	0	0	0	0
53	0	1	0	0	1	0	0	1	1	1

WEB file

Applecore

Managerial Report

1. Develop a model that will allow Applecore to maximize the number of customers reached for a budget of $10,000 for one week of promotion.
2. Solve the model. What is the maximum number of customers reached for the $10,000 budget?

3. Perform a sensitivity analysis on the budget for values from $5,000 to $35,000 in increments of $5,000. Construct a graph of percentage reach versus budget. Is the additional increase in percentage reach monotonically decreasing as the budget allocation increases? Why or why not? What is your recommended budget? Explain.

Appendix 11.1   Excel Solver Solution of Integer Linear Programs

Worksheet formulation and solution for integer linear programs is similar to that for linear programming problems. Actually the worksheet formulation is exactly the same, but some additional information must be provided when setting up the Solver Parameters and Integer Options dialog boxes. First, constraints must be added in the Solver Parameters dialog box to identify the integer variables. In addition, the value for Tolerance in the Integer Options dialog box may need to be adjusted to obtain a solution.

Let us demonstrate the Excel solution of an integer linear program by showing how Excel Solver can be used to solve the Eastborne Realty problem. The worksheet with the optimal solution is shown in Figure 11.14. We will describe the key elements of the worksheet and how to obtain the solution, and then interpret the solution.

Formulation

The data and descriptive labels appear in cells A1:G7 of the worksheet in Figure 11.14. The cells in the lower portion of the worksheet contain the information required by Excel Solver (decision variables, objective function, constraint left-hand sides, and constraint right-hand sides).

Decision Variables   Cells B17:C17 are reserved for the decision variables. The optimal solution is to purchase four townhouses and two apartment buildings.

FIGURE 11.14   EXCEL SOLVER SOLUTION FOR THE EASTBORNE REALTY PROBLEM

WEB file

Eastborne

	A	B	C	D	E	F	G	H	I
1	Eastborne Realty Problem								
2									
3		Townhouse	Apt. Bldg.						
4	Price($1000s)	282	400		Funds Avl.($1000s)		2000		
5	Mgr. Time	4	40		Mgr. Time Avl.		140		
6					Townhouses Avl.		5		
7	Ann. Cash Flow ($1000s)	10	15						
8									
9									
10	Model								
11									
12									
13	Max Cash Flow	70							
14					Constraints	LHS		RHS	
15		Number of			Funds	1928	<=	2000	
16		Townhouses	Apt. Bldgs.		Time	96	<=	140	
17	Purchase Plan	4	2		Townhouses	4	<=	5	
18									
19									
20									
21									

Objective Function	The formula =*SUMPRODUCT(B7:C7,B17:C17)* has been placed into cell B13 to reflect the annual cash flow associated with the solution. The optimal solution provides an annual cash flow of $70,000.
Left-Hand Sides	The left-hand sides for the three constraints are placed into cells F15:F17. Cell F15 =*SUMPRODUCT(B4:C4, $B$17:$C$17)* (Copy to cell F16) Cell F17 =*B17*
Right-Hand Sides	The right-hand sides for the three constraints are placed into cells H15:H17. Cell H15 =*G4* (Copy to cells H16:H17)

Excel Solver Solution

0-1 variables are identified with the "bin" designation in the Solver Parameters dialog box.

Begin the solution procedure by selecting the **Data** tab from the Ribbon and then select **Solver** in the **Analysis** group. Enter the proper values into the **Solver Parameters** dialog box as shown in Figure 11.15. The first constraint shown is $B$17:$C$17 = integer. This

FIGURE 11.15 EXCEL SOLVER PARAMETERS DIALOG BOX FOR THE EASTBORNE REALTY PROBLEM

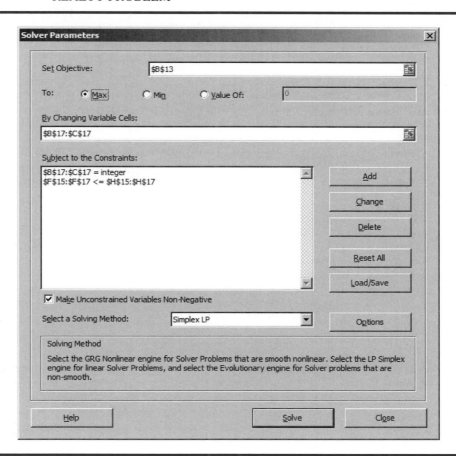

constraint tells Solver that the decision variables in cell B17 and cell C17 must be integer. The integer requirement is created by using the **Add-Constraint** procedure. $B$17:$C$17 is entered as the **Cell Reference** and **int** rather than ≤, =, or ≥ is selected as the form of the constraint. When **int** is selected, the term "integer" automatically appears as the right-hand side of the constraint. Figure 11.15 shows the additional information required to complete the **Solver Parameters** dialog box.

Check the **Make Unconstrained Variables Non-Negative** option and select **Simplex LP** as the **Solving Method**. Next the **Options** button must be selected. Figure 11.16 shows the completed **Solver Options** dialog box for the Eastborne Realty problem. To ensure we find the optimal integer solution, under the **All Methods** tab, we must set the **Integer Optimality (%):** to zero as shown in Figure 11.16.

Clicking **OK** in the **Solver Options** dialog box and selecting **Solve** in the **Solver Parameters** dialog box will instruct Excel Solver to compute the optimal integer solution. The worksheet in Figure 11.14 shows that the optimal solution is to purchase four town-houses and two apartment buildings. The annual cash flow is $70,000.

FIGURE 11.16 EXCEL SOLVER OPTIONS DIALOG BOX FOR THE EASTBORNE REALTY PROBLEM

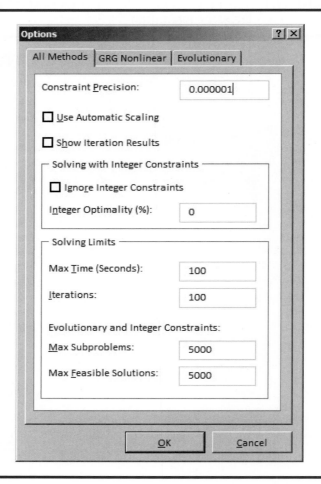

If binary variables are present in an integer linear programming problem, you must select the designation **bin** instead of int when setting up the constraints in the **Solver Parameters** dialog box.

The time required to obtain an optimal solution can be highly variable for integer linear programs. If an optimal solution cannot be found within a reasonable amount of time, the **Integer Optimality (%)**: can be reset to 5%, or some higher value, so that the search procedure may stop when a near-optimal solution (within the tolerance of being optimal) has been found. This can shorten the solution time, since if the **Integer Optimality (%)**: is set to 5%, Solver can stop when it knows it is within 5% of optimal rather then having to complete the search. In general, unless you are experiencing excessive run times, we recommend you set the **Integer Optimaility (%)**: to zero.

Appendix 11.2   LINGO Solution of Integer Linear Programs

LINGO may be used to solve linear integer programs. An integer linear model is entered into LINGO exactly as described in Appendix 7.2, but with additional statements for declaring variables as either general integer or binary. For example, to declare a variable x integer, you need to include the following statement:

```
@GIN(x) ;
```

Note the use of the semicolon to end the statement. GIN stands for general integer. Likewise to declare a variable y a binary variable, the following statement is required:

```
@BIN(y) ;
```

BIN stands for binary.

To illustrate the use of integer variables, we will use LINGO statements to model the Eastborne Realty problem discussed in this chapter. First we enter the following:

```
MODEL:
TITLE    EASTBORNE REALTY;
```

This statement gives the LINGO model the title Eastborne Realty. Next we enter the following two lines to document the definition of our decision variables (recall that ! denotes a comment, and each comment ends with a semicolon).

```
! T = NUMBER OF TOWNHOUSES PURCHASED;
! A = NUMBER OF APARTMENT BUILDINGS PURCHASED;
```

Next we enter the objective function and constraints, each with a descriptive comment.

```
! MAXIMIZE THE CASH FLOW;
MAX = 10*T + 15*A;

! FUNDS AVAILABLE ($1000);
282*T + 400*A <= 2000;
```

```
! TIME AVAILABLILITY;
4*T + 40*A <= 140;

! TOWNHOUSES AVAILABLE;
T <= 5;
```

Finally, we must declare the variables T and A as general integer variables. Again, to document the model we begin with a descriptive comment and then declare each variable as a general integer variable:

```
! DECLARE THE VARIABLES TO BE GENERAL INTEGER VARIABLES;
@GIN(T);
@GIN(A);
```

The complete LINGO model is available on the website that accompanies this book.

CHAPTER 12

Advanced Optimization Applications

CONTENTS

This chapter begins with the study of linear programming applications. Three new applications of linear programming are introduced. The first is data envelopment analysis (DEA), which is an application of linear programming used to measure the relative efficiency of operating units with the same goals and objectives. We illustrate how this technique is used to evaluate the performance of hospitals. In Section 12.2 we introduce the topic of revenue management. Revenue management involves managing the short-term demand for a fixed perishable inventory in order to maximize the revenue potential for an organization. For example, revenue management is critically important in the airline industry. After a flight departs, empty seats are worthless (a perishable good), so airlines try to price their seats in such a way as to maximize revenue. We illustrate the concept by determining the optimal full-fare and discount-fare seat allocations for flights among five cities. Management science has also made a major impact in finance. In Section 12.3 we show how linear programming is used to design portfolios that are consistent with a client's risk preferences.

Although linear programming is used to solve a wide variety of important business problems, many business processes are nonlinear. For example, the price of a bond is a nonlinear function of interest rates, and the price of a stock option is a nonlinear function of the price of the underlying stock. The marginal cost of production often decreases with the quantity produced, and the profit function for most products is usually a nonlinear function of the price. These and many other nonlinear relationships are present in many business applications.

In Section 12.4 we allow the optimization model to be nonlinear. A **nonlinear optimization problem** is any optimization problem in which at least one term in the objective function or a constraint is nonlinear. We begin our study of nonlinear applications by considering a production problem in which the objective function is a nonlinear function of the decision variables. In Section 12.5 we develop a nonlinear application that involves designing a portfolio of securities to track a stock market index. As a further illustration of the use of nonlinear optimization in practice, there are two Q.M. in Action inserts that describe applications of nonlinear programming. The first, Pricing for Environmental Compliance in the Auto Industry, describes a nonlinear pricing application in the auto industry in order to meet overall federal government requirements on average miles per gallon across all cars in an auto company's fleet; there is also a case based on this Q.M. in Action. The second, Scheduling Flights and Crews for Bombardier Flexjet, discusses how Flexjet used nonlinear optimization to assign aircraft and crews to flights.

The computer solutions presented in the chapter were developed using Excel Solver. However, LINGO can also be used to solve these problems. Chapter appendixes describe how to solve nonlinear programs using LINGO and Excel Solver.

(12.1) Data Envelopment Analysis

Data envelopment analysis (DEA) is an application of linear programming used to measure the relative efficiency of operating units with the same goals and objectives. For example, DEA has been used within individual fast-food outlets in the same chain. In this case, the goal of DEA was to identify the inefficient outlets that should be targeted for further study and, if necessary, corrective action. Other applications of DEA have measured the relative efficiencies of hospitals, banks, courts, schools, and so on. In these applications, the performance of each institution or organization was measured relative to the performance of all operating units in the same system. The Q.M. in Action, American Red Cross Evaluates the Efficiency of Service, describes how the American Red Cross used DEA to identify underperforming chapters.

Q.M. *in* ACTION

AMERICAN RED CROSS EVALUATES THE EFFICIENCY OF SERVICE*

The American Red Cross (ARC) is one of the largest nonprofit service organizations in the world. ARC has approximately 1000 chapters in the United States. Each chapter covers a geographic territory, providing disaster relief, armed forces emergency communications, and health and safety training to the general public.

Historically, ARC chapters reported their performance data to the national headquarters in Washington, D.C., but little feedback was provided and no analysis was given for chapters to compare their performance to the performances of other similar chapters. Like many other nonprofit service agencies, ARC is under increased pressure to be more efficient and accountable for its budget. As a result, ARC sought a system that would provide relevant performance feedback to the chapters, with the ultimate goal of improving performance.

ARC developed a system based on data envelopment analysis (DEA) to identify underperforming chapters. DEA is a data-driven approach for measuring the relative performance of an operating unit based on how it converts inputs into outputs. In the case of ARC, chapter inputs include revenues from contracts and donations, the number of volunteers, the number of paid staff, and others. Measures of chapter outputs include metrics such as the number of clients receiving disaster relief, the number of emergency communications provided, and the number of people trained in safety and health courses. Using linear programming models, DEA assesses if a chapter is efficient or inefficient relative to other similar chapters.

The ARC chapter evaluation system was created using Visual Basic for Applications (VBA). VBA is used to clean and format the data, automate the solution of thousands of linear optimization models needed to use DEA to evaluate the chapters, and to generate reports that will be useful to chapter management. By identifying inefficient chapters and peer groups from which they can learn, DEA provides a way for inefficient chapters to improve their performance.

In the previous approach, chapters had to collect and analyze their own data, generate a report, and send it to headquarters, and then they would receive little feedback. Based on past experience, this process consumed at least 160,000 person hours each year. The new automated system saves at least $700,000 in analysis and report generating costs per year. More importantly, it has fostered a culture of continuous improvement at ARC, so that chapter managers can learn from one another, and this has led to improved effectiveness in service.

---

*K. S. Pasupathy and A. Medina-Borja, "Integrating Excel, Access and Visual Basic to Deploy Performance Measurement and Evaluation at American Red Cross," *Interfaces* 38, no. 4 (July–August 2008): pp. 324–337.

The operating units of most organizations have multiple inputs such as staff size, salaries, hours of operation, and advertising budget, as well as multiple outputs such as profit, market share, and growth rate. In these situations, it is often difficult for a manager to determine which operating units are inefficient in converting their multiple inputs into multiple outputs. This particular area is where data envelopment analysis has proven to be a helpful managerial tool. We illustrate the application of data envelopment analysis by evaluating the performance of a group of four hospitals.

Evaluating the Performance of Hospitals

Problem 1 asks you to formulate and solve a linear program to assess the relative efficiency of General Hospital.

The hospital administrators at General Hospital, University Hospital, County Hospital, and State Hospital have been meeting to discuss ways in which they can help one another improve the performance at each of their hospitals. A consultant suggested that they consider using DEA to measure the performance of each hospital relative to the performance of all

TABLE 12.1   ANNUAL RESOURCES CONSUMED (INPUTS) BY THE FOUR HOSPITALS

	Hospital			
Input Measure	General	University	County	State
Full-time equivalent nonphysicians	285.20	162.30	275.70	210.40
Supply expense ($1000s)	123.80	128.70	348.50	154.10
Bed-days available (1000s)	106.72	64.21	104.10	104.04

four hospitals. In discussing how this evaluation could be done, the following three input measures and four output measures were identified:

Input Measures

1. The number of full-time equivalent (FTE) nonphysician personnel
2. The amount spent on supplies
3. The number of bed-days available

Output Measures

1. Patient-days of service under Medicare
2. Patient-days of service not under Medicare
3. Number of nurses trained
4. Number of interns trained

Summaries of the input and output measures for a one-year period at each of the four hospitals are shown in Tables 12.1 and 12.2. Let us show how DEA can use these data to identify relatively inefficient hospitals.

Overview of the DEA Approach

In this application of DEA, a linear programming model is developed for each hospital whose efficiency is to be evaluated. To illustrate the modeling process, we formulate a linear program that can be used to determine the relative efficiency of County Hospital.

First, using a linear programming model, we construct a **hypothetical composite**, in this case a composite hospital, based on the outputs and inputs for all operating units with the same goals. For each of the four hospitals' output measures, the output for the composite hospital is determined by computing a weighted average of the corresponding outputs for all four hospitals. For each of the three input measures, the input for the composite hospital is determined by using the same weights to compute a weighted average of the corresponding

TABLE 12.2   ANNUAL SERVICES PROVIDED (OUTPUTS) BY THE FOUR HOSPITALS

	Hospital			
Output Measure	General	University	County	State
Medicare patient-days (1000s)	48.14	34.62	36.72	33.16
Non-Medicare patient-days (1000s)	43.10	27.11	45.98	56.46
Nurses trained	253	148	175	160
Interns trained	41	27	23	84

inputs for all four hospitals. Constraints in the linear programming model require all outputs for the composite hospital to be *greater than or equal to* the outputs of County Hospital, the hospital being evaluated. If the inputs for the composite unit can be shown to be *less than* the inputs for County Hospital, the composite hospital is shown to have the same, or more, output for *less input*. In this case, the model shows that the composite hospital is more efficient than County Hospital. In other words, the hospital being evaluated is *less efficient* than the composite hospital. Because the composite hospital is based on all four hospitals, the hospital being evaluated can be judged *relatively inefficient* when compared to the other hospitals in the group.

DEA Linear Programming Model

To determine the weight that each hospital will have in computing the outputs and inputs for the composite hospital, we use the following decision variables:

wg = weight applied to inputs and outputs for General Hospital

wu = weight applied to inputs and outputs for University Hospital

wc = weight applied to inputs and outputs for County Hospital

ws = weight applied to inputs and outputs for State Hospital

The DEA approach requires that the sum of these weights equal 1. Thus, the first constraint is

$$wg + wu + wc + ws = 1$$

In general, every DEA linear programming model will include a constraint that requires the weights for the operating units to sum to 1.

As we stated previously, for each output measure, the output for the composite hospital is determined by computing a weighted average of the corresponding outputs for all four hospitals. For instance, for output measure 1, the number of patient days of service under Medicare, the output for the composite hospital is

$$\begin{pmatrix} \text{Medicare patient-days} \\ \text{for Composite Hospital} \end{pmatrix} = \begin{pmatrix} \text{Medicare patient-days} \\ \text{for General Hospital} \end{pmatrix}wg + \begin{pmatrix} \text{Medicare patient-days} \\ \text{for University Hospital} \end{pmatrix}wu$$
$$+ \begin{pmatrix} \text{Medicare patient-days} \\ \text{for County Hospital} \end{pmatrix}wc + \begin{pmatrix} \text{Medicare patient-days} \\ \text{for State Hospital} \end{pmatrix}ws$$

Substituting the number of Medicare patient-days for each hospital as shown in Table 12.2, we obtain the following expression:

$$\begin{pmatrix} \text{Medicare patient-days} \\ \text{for Composite Hospital} \end{pmatrix} = 48.14wg + 34.62wu + 36.72wc + 33.16ws$$

The other output measures for the composite hospital are computed in a similar fashion. Figure 12.1 provides a summary of the results.

For each of the four output measures, we need to write a constraint that requires the output for the composite hospital to be greater than or equal to the output for County Hospital. Thus, the general form of the output constraints is

$$\begin{pmatrix} \text{Output for the} \\ \text{Composite Hospital} \end{pmatrix} \geq \begin{pmatrix} \text{Output for} \\ \text{County Hospital} \end{pmatrix}$$

Because the number of Medicare patient-days for County Hospital is 36.72, the output constraint corresponding to the number of Medicare patient-days is

$$48.14wg + 34.62wu + 36.72wc + 33.16ws \geq 36.72$$

FIGURE 12.1   RELATIONSHIP BETWEEN THE OUTPUT MEASURES FOR THE FOUR HOSPITALS AND THE OUTPUT MEASURES FOR THE COMPOSITE HOSPITAL

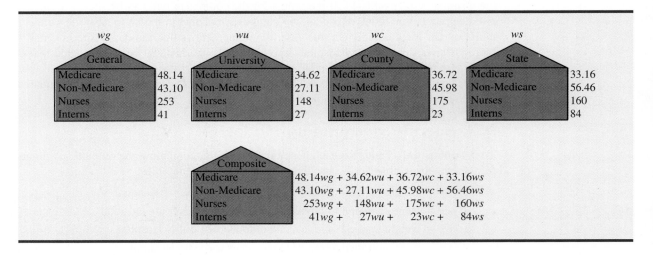

In a similar fashion, we formulated a constraint for each of the other three output measures, with the results as shown:

$$43.10wg + 27.11wu + 45.98wc + 56.46ws \geq 45.98 \quad \text{Non-Medicare}$$
$$253wg + 148wu + 175wc + 160ws \geq 175 \quad \text{Nurses}$$
$$41wg + 27wu + 23wc + 84ws \geq 23 \quad \text{Interns}$$

The four output constraints require the linear programming solution to provide weights that will make each output measure for the composite hospital greater than or equal to the corresponding output measure for County Hospital. Thus, if a solution satisfying the output constraints can be found, the composite hospital will have produced at least as much of each output as County Hospital.

Next, we need to consider the constraints needed to model the relationship between the inputs for the composite hospital and the resources available to the composite hospital. A constraint is required for each of the three input measures. The general form for the input constraints is as follows:

$$\frac{\text{Input for the}}{\text{Composite Hospital}} \leq \frac{\text{Resources available to}}{\text{the Composite Hospital}}$$

The logic of a DEA model is to determine whether a hypothetical composite facility can achieve the same or more output while requiring less input. If more output with less input can be achieved, the facility being evaluated is judged to be relatively inefficient.

For each input measure, the input for the composite hospital is a weighted average of the corresponding input for each of the four hospitals. Thus, for input measure 1, the number of full-time equivalent nonphysicians, the input for the composite hospital is

$$\binom{\text{FTE nonphysicians}}{\text{for Composite Hospital}} = \binom{\text{FTE nonphysicians}}{\text{for General Hospital}}wg + \binom{\text{FTE nonphysicians}}{\text{for University Hospital}}wu$$

$$+ \binom{\text{FTE nonphysicians}}{\text{for County Hospital}}wc + \binom{\text{FTE nonphysicians}}{\text{for State Hospital}}ws$$

FIGURE 12.2   RELATIONSHIP BETWEEN THE INPUT MEASURES FOR THE FOUR HOSPITALS
AND THE INPUT MEASURES FOR THE COMPOSITE HOSPITAL

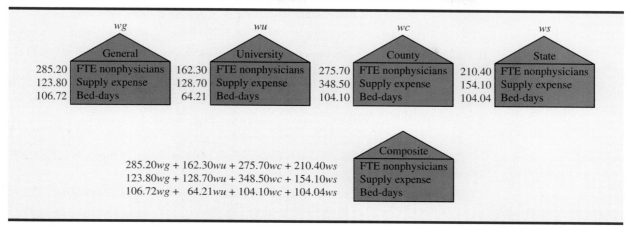

Substituting the values for the number of full-time equivalent nonphysicians for each hospital as shown in Table 12.1, we obtain the following expression for the number of full-time equivalent nonphysicians for the composite hospital:

$$285.20wg + 162.30wu + 275.70wc + 210.40ws$$

In a similar manner, we can write expressions for each of the other two input measures as shown in Figure 12.2.

To complete the formulation of the input constraints, we must write expressions for the right-hand-side values for each constraint. First, note that the right-hand-side values are the resources available to the composite hospital. In the DEA approach, these right-hand-side values are a percentage of the input values for County Hospital. Thus, we must introduce the following decision variable:

E = the fraction of County Hospital's input available to the composite hospital

To illustrate the important role that E plays in the DEA approach, we show how to write the expression for the number of FTE nonphysicians available to the composite hospital. Table 12.1 shows that the number of FTE nonphysicians used by County Hospital was 275.70; thus, 275.70E is the number of FTE nonphysicians available to the composite hospital. If $E = 1$, the number of FTE nonphysicians available to the composite hospital is 275.70, the same as the number of FTE nonphysicians used by County Hospital. However, if E is greater than 1, the composite hospital would have available proportionally more nonphysicians, while if E is less than 1, the composite hospital would have available proportionally fewer FTE nonphysicians. Because of the effect that E has in determining the resources available to the composite hospital, E is referred to as the **efficiency index**.

We can now write the input constraint corresponding to the number of FTE nonphysicians available to the composite hospital:

$$285.50wg + 162.30wu + 275.70wc + 210.40ws \leq 275.70E$$

In a similar manner, we can write the input constraints for the supplies and bed-days available to the composite hospital. First, using the data in Table 12.1, we note that for each of these resources, the amount that is available to the composite hospital is 348.50E and

104.10E, respectively. Thus, the input constraints for the supplies and bed-days are written as follows:

$$123.80wg + 128.70wu + 348.50wc + 154.10ws \leq 348.50E \quad \text{Supplies}$$
$$106.72wg + 64.21wu + 104.10wc + 104.04ws \leq 104.10E \quad \text{Bed-days}$$

If a solution with $E < 1$ can be found, the composite hospital does not need as many resources as County Hospital needs to produce the same level of output.

The objective function for the DEA model is to minimize the value of E, which is equivalent to minimizing the input resources available to the composite hospital. Thus, the objective function is written as

Min E

The objective function in a DEA model is always Min E. The facility being evaluated (County Hospital in this example) can be judged relatively inefficient if the optimal solution provides E less than 1, indicating that the composite facility requires less in input resources.

The DEA efficiency conclusion is based on the optimal objective function value for E. The decision rule is as follows:

If $E = 1$, the composite hospital requires *as much input* as County Hospital does. There is no evidence that County Hospital is inefficient.

If $E < 1$, the composite hospital requires *less input* to obtain the output achieved by County Hospital. The composite hospital is more efficient; thus, County Hospital can be judged relatively inefficient.

The DEA linear programming model for the efficiency evaluation of County Hospital has five decision variables and eight constraints. The complete model is rewritten as follows:

Min E

s.t.

$$
\begin{aligned}
wg + wu + wc + ws &= 1 \\
48.14wg + 34.62wu + 36.72wc + 33.16ws &\geq 36.72 \\
43.10wg + 27.11wu + 45.98wc + 56.46ws &\geq 45.98 \\
253wg + 148wu + 175wc + 160ws &\geq 175 \\
41wg + 27wu + 23wc + 84ws &\geq 23 \\
-275.70E + 285.20wg + 162.30wu + 275.70wc + 210.40ws &\leq 0 \\
-348.50E + 123.80wg + 128.70wu + 348.50wc + 154.10ws &\leq 0 \\
-104.10E + 106.72wg + 64.21wu + 104.10wc + 104.04ws &\leq 0 \\
E, wg, wu, wc, ws &\geq 0
\end{aligned}
$$

The optimal solution is shown in Figure 12.3. We first note that the value of the objective function shows that the efficiency score for County Hospital is 0.905. This score tells us that the composite hospital can obtain at least the level of each output that County Hospital obtains by having available no more than 90.5% of the input resources required by County Hospital. Thus, the composite hospital is more efficient, and the DEA analysis identified County Hospital as being relatively inefficient.

From the solution in Figure 12.3, we see that the composite hospital is formed from the weighted average of General Hospital ($wg = 0.212$), University Hospital ($wu = 0.260$), and State Hospital ($ws = 0.527$). Each input and output of the composite hospital is determined by the same weighted average of the inputs and outputs of these three hospitals.

The Slack column provides some additional information about the efficiency of County Hospital compared to the composite hospital. Specifically, the composite hospital has at least as much of each output as County Hospital has (constraints 2–5) and provides 1.6 more nurses trained (surplus for constraint 4) and 37 more interns trained (surplus for constraint 5). The slack of zero from constraint 8 shows that the composite hospital uses

WEB file

County

FIGURE 12.3   ANSWER REPORT FOR THE COUNTY HOSPITAL DATA ENVELOPMENT ANALYSIS
PROBLEM

Objective Cell (Min)

Name	Original Value	Final Value
Min E	0.000	0.905

Variable Cells

Model Variable	Name	Original Value	Final Value	Integer
WG	Weight WG	0.000	0.212	Contin
WU	Weight WU	0.000	0.260	Contin
WC	Weight WC	0.000	0.000	Contin
WS	Weight WS	0.000	0.527	Contin
E	Weight E	0.000	0.905	Contin

Constraints

Constraint Number	Name	Cell Value	Status	Slack
1	Sum of Weights	1.000	Binding	0.000
2	Med. Pat. Days (1000s) (Output)	36.720	Binding	0.000
3	Non-Med. Pat. Days (1000s) (Output)	45.980	Binding	0.000
4	Nurses Trained (Output)	176.615	Not Binding	1.615
5	Interns Trained (Output)	60.027	Not Binding	37.027
6	FTE nonphys. (Input)	213.750	Not Binding	35.824
7	Supply Expense ($1000s) (Input)	141.053	Not Binding	174.422
8	Bed Days Available (1000s) (Input)	94.235	Binding	0.000

approximately 90.5% of the bed-days used by County Hospital. The slack values for constraints 6 and 7 show that less than 90.5% of the FTE nonphysician and the supply expense resources used at County Hospital are used by the composite hospital.

Clearly, the composite hospital is more efficient than County Hospital, and we are justified in concluding that County Hospital is relatively inefficient compared to the other hospitals in the group. Given the results of the DEA, hospital administrators should examine operations to determine how County Hospital resources can be more effectively utilized.

Summary of the DEA Approach

To use data envelopment analysis to measure the relative efficiency of County Hospital, we used a linear programming model to construct a hypothetical composite hospital based on the outputs and inputs for the four hospitals in the problem. The approach to solving other types of problems using DEA is similar. For each operating unit whose efficiency we want to measure, we must formulate and solve a linear programming model similar to the linear program we solved to measure the relative efficiency of County Hospital. The following step-by-step procedure should help you in formulating a linear programming model for other types of DEA applications. Note that the operating unit for which we want to measure the relative efficiency is referred to as the jth operating unit.

Step 1. Define decision variables or weights (one for each operating unit) that can be used to determine the inputs and outputs for the composite operating unit.

Step 2. Write a constraint that requires the weights to sum to 1.

Step 3. For each output measure, write a constraint that requires the output for the composite operating unit to be greater than or equal to the corresponding output for the jth operating unit.

Step 4. Define a decision variable, E, which determines the fraction of the jth operating unit's input available to the composite operating unit.

Step 5. For each input measure, write a constraint that requires the input for the composite operating unit to be less than or equal to the resources available to the composite operating unit.

Step 6. Write the objective function as Min E.

NOTES AND COMMENTS

1. Remember that the goal of data envelopment analysis is to identify operating units that are relatively inefficient. The method *does not* necessarily identify the operating units that are *relatively efficient*. Just because the efficiency index is $E = 1$, we cannot conclude that the unit being analyzed is relatively efficient. Indeed, any unit that has the largest output on any one of the output measures cannot be judged relatively inefficient.

2. It is possible for DEA to show all but one unit to be relatively inefficient. Such would be the case

if a unit producing the most of every output also consumes the least of every input. Such cases are extremely rare in practice.

3. In applying data envelopment analysis to problems involving a large group of operating units, practitioners have found that roughly 50% of the operating units can be identified as inefficient. Comparing each relatively inefficient unit to the units contributing to the composite unit may be helpful in understanding how the operation of each relatively inefficient unit can be improved.

12.2 Revenue Management

Revenue management involves managing the short-term demand for a fixed perishable inventory in order to maximize the revenue potential for an organization. The methodology, originally developed for American Airlines, was first used to determine how many airline flight seats to sell at an early reservation discount fare and how many airline flight seats to sell at a full fare. By making the optimal decision for the number of discount-fare seats and the number of full-fare seats on each flight, the airline is able to increase its average number of passengers per flight and maximize the total revenue generated by the combined sale of discount-fare and full-fare seats. Today, all major airlines use some form of revenue management.

Given the success of revenue management in the airline industry, it was not long before other industries began using this approach. Revenue management systems often include pricing strategies and overbooking policies. Overbooking policies attempt to determine the number of items to sell over and above capacity so as to compensate for no-shows. Application areas now include hotels, apartment rentals, car rentals, cruise lines, and sports events. The Q.M. in Action, Revenue Management at Harrah's Cherokee Casino & Hotel, discusses how Harrah's successfully implemented revenue management in its operations.

The development of a revenue management system can be expensive and time-consuming, but the potential payoffs may be substantial. For instance, the revenue management system used at American Airlines generates nearly $1 billion in annual incremental revenue. To illustrate the fundamentals of revenue management, we will use a linear programming model to develop a revenue management plan for Leisure Air, a regional airline that provides service for Pittsburgh, Newark, Charlotte, Myrtle Beach, and Orlando.

Leisure Air has two Boeing 737-400 airplanes, one based in Pittsburgh and the other in Newark. Both airplanes have a coach section with a 132-seat capacity. Each morning the Pittsburgh-based plane flies to Orlando with a stopover in Charlotte, and the Newark-based plane flies to Myrtle Beach, also with a stopover in Charlotte. At the end of the day, both planes return to their home bases. To keep the size of the problem reasonable, we restrict our attention to the Pittsburgh–Charlotte, Charlotte–Orlando, Newark–Charlotte, and Charlotte–Myrtle Beach flight legs for the morning flights. Figure 12.4 illustrates the logistics of the Leisure Air problem situation.

Leisure Air uses two fare classes: a discount-fare Q class and a full-fare Y class. Reservations using the discount-fare Q class must be made 14 days in advance and must include a Saturday night stay in the destination city. Reservations using the full-fare Y class may be made any time, with no penalty for changing the reservation at a later date. To determine the itinerary and fare alternatives that Leisure Air can offer its customers, we must consider not only the origin and the destination of each flight, but also the fare class. For instance, possible products include Pittsburgh to Charlotte using Q class, Newark to Orlando using Q class, Charlotte to Myrtle Beach using Y class, and so on. Each product is referred to as an origin-destination-itinerary fare (ODIF). For May 5, Leisure Air established fares and developed forecasts of customer demand for each of 16 ODIFs. These data are shown in Table 12.3.

Suppose that on April 4 a customer calls the Leisure Air reservation office and requests a Q class seat on the May 5 flight from Pittsburgh to Myrtle Beach. Should Leisure Air accept the reservation? The difficulty in making this decision is that even though Leisure Air may have seats available, the company may not want to accept this reservation at the Q class fare of $268, especially if it is possible to sell the same reservation later at the Y class fare of $456. Thus, determining how many Q and Y class seats to make available are important decisions that Leisure Air must make in order to operate its reservation system.

Q.M. *in* ACTION

REVENUE MANAGEMENT AT HARRAH'S CHEROKEE CASINO & HOTEL*

Harrah's Cherokee Casino & Hotel has benefited greatly from the use of revenue management. Harrah's tracks customer spending habits using its customers' Total Rewards cards. This allows Harrah's to distinguish between high-spending and lower-spending customers. The premise of revenue management for Harrah's is to maximize its revenue by reserving rooms for its highest-spending customers. This means that Harrah's may tell a low-spending customer that no rooms are available at its hotel in order to reserve the room for a potential future high-spending customer. To preserve goodwill, Harrah's typically offers these low-spending customers complimentary rooms at nearby hotels. Harrah's is betting that the payoff from a potential future high-spending customer reservation will more than compensate for the cost of the complimentary room.

Quantitative methods play a key role in Harrah's revenue management system, and Harrah's has a long history of using management science in its operations. The company uses a linear optimization model to determine how many hotel rooms to reserve for high-spending customers. The optimization model is updated frequently over time to account for current customer reservations and expected future reservations. The key to this model is in calculating the "opportunity cost" of selling a room to a low-spending customer. This can be determined by using Harrah's Total Rewards program to track customer spending habits in combination with a forecast for future reservations of low-spending and high-spending customers.

Harrah's Cherokee Casino & Hotel has enjoyed great success in its use of revenue management. While typical revenue management implementations result in revenue increases of 3 to 7%, Harrah's has experienced 15% improvements. Harrah's believes that revenue management systems, and management science in general, are central to its continued success.

*From: R. Metters et al., "The 'Killer Application' of Revenue Management: Harrah's Cherokee Casino & Hotel," *Interfaces* 38, no. 3 (May/June 2008): 161–175.

FIGURE 12.4   LOGISTICS OF THE LEISURE AIR PROBLEM

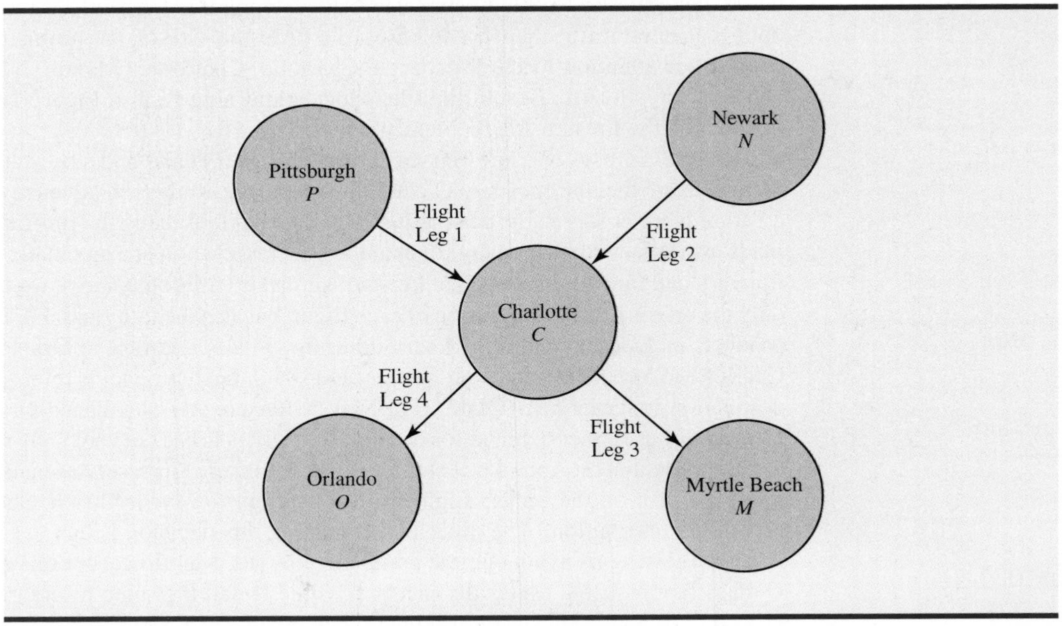

TABLE 12.3   FARE AND DEMAND DATA FOR 16 LEISURE AIR
ORIGIN-DESTINATION-ITINERARY FARES (ODIFS)

	Origin	Destination	Fare Class	ODIF Code	Fare	Forecasted ODIF Demand
1	Pittsburgh	Charlotte	Q	PCQ	$178	33
2	Pittsburgh	Myrtle Beach	Q	PMQ	268	44
3	Pittsburgh	Orlando	Q	POQ	228	45
4	Pittsburgh	Charlotte	Y	PCY	380	16
5	Pittsburgh	Myrtle Beach	Y	PMY	456	6
6	Pittsburgh	Orlando	Y	POY	560	11
7	Newark	Charlotte	Q	NCQ	199	26
8	Newark	Myrtle Beach	Q	NMQ	249	56
9	Newark	Orlando	Q	NOQ	349	39
10	Newark	Charlotte	Y	NCY	385	15
11	Newark	Myrtle Beach	Y	NMY	444	7
12	Newark	Orlando	Y	NOY	580	9
13	Charlotte	Myrtle Beach	Q	CMQ	179	64
14	Charlotte	Myrtle Beach	Y	CMY	380	8
15	Charlotte	Orlando	Q	COQ	224	46
16	Charlotte	Orlando	Y	COY	582	10

To develop a linear programming model that can be used to determine how many seats Leisure Air should allocate to each fare class, we need to define 16 decision variables, one for each ODIF alternative. Using P for Pittsburgh, N for Newark, C for Charlotte, M for Myrtle Beach, and O for Orlando, the decision variables take the following form:

PCQ = number of seats allocated to Pittsburgh–Charlotte Q class

PMQ = number of seats allocated to Pittsburgh–Myrtle Beach Q class

POQ = number of seats allocated to Pittsburgh–Orlando Q class

PCY = number of seats allocated to Pittsburgh–Charlotte Y class

$\vdots$

NCQ = number of seats allocated to Newark–Charlotte Q class

$\vdots$

COY = number of seats allocated to Charlotte–Orlando Y class

The objective is to maximize total revenue. Using the fares shown in Table 12.3, we can write the objective function for the linear programming model as follows:

$$\text{Max} \quad 178PCQ + 268PMQ + 228POQ + 380PCY + 456PMY + 560POY$$
$$+ 199NCQ + 249NMQ + 349NOQ + 385NCY + 444NMY$$
$$+ 580NOY + 179CMQ + 380CMY + 224COQ + 582COY$$

Next, we must write the constraints. We need two types of constraints: capacity and demand. We begin with the capacity constraints.

Consider the Pittsburgh–Charlotte flight leg shown in Figure 12.4. The Boeing 737-400 airplane has a 132-seat capacity. Three possible final destinations for passengers on this flight (Charlotte, Myrtle Beach, or Orlando) and two fare classes (Q and Y) provide six ODIF alternatives: (1) Pittsburgh–Charlotte Q class; (2) Pittsburgh–Myrtle Beach Q class; (3) Pittsburgh–Orlando Q class; (4) Pittsburgh–Charlotte Y class; (5) Pittsburgh–Myrtle Beach Y class; and (6) Pittsburgh–Orlando Y class. Thus, the number of seats allocated to the Pittsburgh–Charlotte flight leg is $PCQ + PMQ + POQ + PCY + PMY + POY$. With the capacity of 132 seats, the capacity constraint is as follows:

$$PCQ + PMQ + POQ + PCY + PMY + POY \leq 132 \quad \text{Pittsburgh–Charlotte}$$

The capacity constraints for the Newark–Charlotte, Charlotte–Myrtle Beach, and Charlotte–Orlando flight legs are developed in a similar manner. These three constraints are as follows:

$$NCQ + NMQ + NOQ + NCY + NMY + NOY \leq 132 \quad \text{Newark–Charlotte}$$
$$PMQ + PMY + NMQ + NMY + CMQ + CMY \leq 132 \quad \text{Charlotte–Myrtle Beach}$$
$$POQ + POY + NOQ + NOY + COQ + COY \leq 132 \quad \text{Charlotte–Orlando}$$

The demand constraints limit the number of seats for each ODIF based on the forecasted demand. Using the demand forecasts in Table 12.3, 16 demand constraints must be added to the model. The first four demand constraints are as follows:

$$PCQ \leq 33 \quad \text{Pittsburgh–Charlotte Q class}$$
$$PMQ \leq 44 \quad \text{Pittsburgh–Myrtle Beach Q class}$$
$$POQ \leq 45 \quad \text{Pittsburgh–Orlando Q class}$$
$$PCY \leq 16 \quad \text{Pittsburgh–Charlotte Y class}$$

The complete linear programming model with 16 decision variables, 4 capacity constraints, and 16 demand constraints is as follows:

Max $178PCQ + 268PMQ + 228POQ + 380PCY + 456PMY + 560POY$
       $+ 199NCQ + 249NMQ + 349NOQ + 385NCY + 444NMY$
       $+ 580NOY + 179CMQ + 380CMY + 224COQ + 582COY$

s.t.

$$PCQ + PMQ + POQ + PCY + PMY + POY \leq 132 \quad \text{Pittsburgh–Charlotte}$$
$$NCQ + NMQ + NOQ + NCY + NMY + NOY \leq 132 \quad \text{Newark–Charlotte}$$
$$PMQ + PMY + NMQ + NMY + CMQ + CMY \leq 132 \quad \text{Charlotte–Myrtle Beach}$$
$$POQ + POY + NOQ + NOY + COQ + COY \leq 132 \quad \text{Charlotte–Orlando}$$

$$
\left.
\begin{array}{r}
PCQ \leq 33 \\
PMQ \leq 44 \\
POQ \leq 45 \\
PCY \leq 16 \\
PMY \leq 6 \\
POY \leq 11 \\
NCQ \leq 26 \\
NMQ \leq 56 \\
NOQ \leq 39 \\
NCY \leq 15 \\
NMY \leq 7 \\
NOY \leq 9 \\
CMQ \leq 64 \\
CMY \leq 8 \\
COQ \leq 46 \\
COY \leq 10
\end{array}
\right\} \quad \text{Demand Constraints}
$$

$$PCQ, PMQ, POQ, PCY, \ldots, COY \geq 0$$

Leisure

The sensitivity report for the Leisure Air revenue management problem is shown in Figure 12.5. The value of the optimal solution is $178(33) + 268(44) + 228(22) + 380(16) + 456(6) + 560(11) + 199(26) + 249(36) + 349(39) + 385(15) + 444(7) + 580(9) + 179(31) + 380(8) + 224(41) + 582(10) = \$103,103$. The optimal solution shows that $PCQ = 33$, $PMQ = 44$, $POQ = 22$, $PCY = 16$, and so on. Thus, to maximize revenue, Leisure Air should allocate 33 Q class seats to Pittsburgh–Charlotte, 44 Q class seats to Pittsburgh–Myrtle Beach, 22 Q class seats to Pittsburgh–Orlando, 16 Y class seats to Pittsburgh–Charlotte, and so on.

Over time, reservations will come into the system and the number of remaining seats available for each ODIF will decrease. For example, the optimal solution allocated 44 Q class seats to Pittsburgh–Myrtle Beach. Suppose that two weeks prior to the departure date of May 5, all 44 seats have been sold. Now, suppose that a new customer calls the Leisure Air reservation office and requests a Q class seat for the Pittsburgh–Myrtle Beach flight. Should Leisure Air accept the new reservation even though it exceeds the original 44-seat allocation? The shadow price for the Pittsburgh–Myrtle Beach Q class demand constraint will provide information that will help a Leisure Air reservation agent make this decision.

Constraint 6, $PMQ \leq 44$, restricts the number of Q class seats that can be allocated to Pittsburgh–Myrtle Beach to 44 seats. In Figure 12.5 we see that the shadow price for

FIGURE 12.5 SENSITIVITY REPORT FOR THE LEISURE AIR REVENUE MANAGEMENT PROBLEM

Variable Cells

Model Variable	Name	Final Value	Reduced Cost	Objective Coefficient	Allowable Increase	Allowable Decrease
PCQ	ODIF 1 Allocation	33.000	0.000	178.000	1E+30	174.000
PMQ	ODIF 2 Allocation	44.000	0.000	268.000	1E+30	85.000
POQ	ODIF 3 Allocation	22.000	0.000	228.000	85.000	4.000
PCY	ODIF 4 Allocation	16.000	0.000	380.000	1E+30	376.000
PMY	ODIF 5 Allocation	6.000	0.000	456.000	1E+30	273.000
POY	ODIF 6 Allocation	11.000	0.000	560.000	1E+30	332.000
NCQ	ODIF 7 Allocation	26.000	0.000	199.000	1E+30	129.000
NMQ	ODIF 8 Allocation	36.000	0.000	249.000	55.000	70.000
NOQ	ODIF 9 Allocation	39.000	0.000	349.000	1E+30	55.000
NCY	ODIF 10 Allocation	15.000	0.000	385.000	1E+30	315.000
NMY	ODIF 11 Allocation	7.000	0.000	444.000	1E+30	195.000
NOY	ODIF 12 Allocation	9.000	0.000	580.000	1E+30	286.000
CMQ	ODIF 13 Allocation	31.000	0.000	179.000	70.000	55.000
CMY	ODIF 14 Allocation	8.000	0.000	380.000	1E+30	201.000
COQ	ODIF 15 Allocation	41.000	0.000	224.000	4.000	85.000
COY	ODIF 16 Allocation	10.000	0.000	582.000	1E+30	358.000

Constraints

Constraint Number	Name	Final Value	Shadow Price	Constraint R.H. Side	Allowable Increase	Allowable Decrease
1	Leg 1 Capacity	132.000	4.000	132.000	23.000	5.000
2	Leg 2 Capacity	132.000	70.000	132.000	20.000	33.000
3	Leg 3 Capacity	132.000	179.000	132.000	33.000	31.000
4	Leg 4 Capacity	132.000	224.000	132.000	5.000	41.000
5	ODIF 1 Demand	33.000	174.000	33.000	5.000	23.000
6	ODIF 2 Demand	44.000	85.000	44.000	5.000	23.000
7	ODIF 3 Demand	22.000	0.000	45.000	1E+30	23.000
8	ODIF 4 Demand	16.000	376.000	16.000	5.000	16.000
9	ODIF 5 Demand	6.000	273.000	6.000	5.000	6.000
10	ODIF 6 Demand	11.000	332.000	11.000	22.000	11.000
11	ODIF 7 Demand	26.000	129.000	26.000	33.000	20.000
12	ODIF 8 Demand	36.000	0.000	56.000	1E+30	20.000
13	ODIF 9 Demand	39.000	55.000	39.000	33.000	5.000
14	ODIF 10 Demand	15.000	315.000	15.000	33.000	15.000
15	ODIF 11 Demand	7.000	195.000	7.000	36.000	7.000
16	ODIF 12 Demand	9.000	286.000	9.000	33.000	5.000
17	ODIF 13 Demand	31.000	0.000	64.000	1E+30	33.000
18	ODIF 14 Demand	8.000	201.000	8.000	31.000	8.000
19	ODIF 15 Demand	41.000	0.000	46.000	1E+30	5.000
20	ODIF 16 Demand	10.000	358.000	10.000	41.000	5.000

Shadow prices tell reservation agents the additional revenue associated with overbooking each ODIF.

constraint 6 is \$85. The shadow price tells us that if one more Q class seat were available from Pittsburgh to Myrtle Beach, revenue would improve by \$85. This increase in revenue is referred to as the bid price for this ODIF. In general, the bid price for an ODIF tells a Leisure Air reservation agent the value of one additional reservation once a particular ODIF has been sold out.

By looking at the shadow prices for the demand constraints in Figure 12.5, we see that the highest shadow price (bid price) is \$376 for constraint 8, $PCY \leq 16$. This constraint corresponds to the Pittsburgh–Charlotte Y class itinerary. Thus, if all 16 seats allocated to this itinerary have been sold, accepting another reservation will provide additional revenue of \$376. Given this revenue contribution, a reservation agent would most likely accept the additional reservation even if it resulted in an overbooking of the flight. Other shadow prices for the demand constraints show a bid price of \$358 for constraint 20 (COY) and a bid price of \$332 for constraint 10 (POY). Thus, accepting additional reservations for the Charlotte–Orlando Y class and the Pittsburgh–Orlando Y class itineraries is a good choice for increasing revenue.

A revenue management system like the one at Leisure Air must be flexible and adjust to the ever-changing reservation status. Conceptually, each time a reservation is accepted for an ODIF that is at its capacity, the linear programming model should be updated and re-solved to obtain new seat allocations along with the revised bid price information. In practice, updating the allocations on a real-time basis is not practical because of the large number of itineraries involved. However, the bid prices from a current solution and some simple decision rules enable reservation agents to make decisions that improve the revenue for the firm. Then, on a periodic basis such as once a day or once a week, the entire linear programming model can be updated and re-solved to generate new seat allocations and revised bid price information.

12.3 Portfolio Models and Asset Allocation

Asset allocation refers to the process of determining how to allocate investment funds across a variety of asset classes such as stocks, bonds, mutual funds, real estate, and cash. Portfolio models are used to determine the percentage of the investment funds that should be made in each asset class. The goal is to create a portfolio that provides the best balance between risk and return. In this section we show how linear programming models can be developed to determine an optimal portfolio involving a mix of mutual funds. The first model is designed for conservative investors who are strongly averse to risk. The second model is designed for investors with a variety of risk tolerances.

In 1952 Harry Markowitz showed how to develop a portfolio that optimized the trade-off between risk and return. His work earned him a share of the 1990 Nobel Prize in Economics.

A Portfolio of Mutual Funds

Hauck Investment Services designs annuities, IRAs, 401(k) plans, and other investment vehicles for investors with a variety of risk tolerances. Hauck would like to develop a portfolio model that can be used to determine an optimal portfolio involving a mix of six mutual funds. A variety of measures can be used to indicate risk, but for portfolios of financial assets all of these measures are related to variability in return. Table 12.4 shows the annual return (%) for five 1-year periods for the six mutual funds. Scenario 1 represents a year in which the annual returns are good for all the mutual funds. Scenario 2 is also a good year for most of the mutual funds. But scenario 3 is a bad year for the small-cap value fund; scenario 4 is a bad year for the intermediate-term bond fund; and scenario 5 is a bad year for four of the six mutual funds.

It is not possible to predict exactly the returns for any of the funds over the next 12 months, but the portfolio managers at Hauck Financial Services think that the returns

TABLE 12.4   MUTUAL FUND PERFORMANCE IN FIVE SELECTED YEARLY SCENARIOS

Mutual Fund	Annual Return (%)				
	Scenario 1	Scenario 2	Scenario 3	Scenario 4	Scenario 5
Foreign Stock	10.06	13.12	13.47	45.42	−21.93
Intermediate-Term Bond	17.64	3.25	7.51	−1.33	7.36
Large-Cap Growth	32.41	18.71	33.28	41.46	−23.26
Large-Cap Value	32.36	20.61	12.93	7.06	−5.37
Small-Cap Growth	33.44	19.40	3.85	58.68	−9.02
Small-Cap Value	24.56	25.32	−6.70	5.43	17.31

for the five years shown in Table 12.4 are scenarios that can be used to represent the possibilities for the next year. For the purpose of building portfolios for their clients, Hauck's portfolio managers will choose a mix of these six mutual funds and assume that one of the five possible scenarios will describe the return over the next 12 months.

Conservative Portfolio

One of Hauck's portfolio managers has been asked to develop a portfolio for the firm's conservative clients who express a strong aversion to risk. The manager's task is to determine the proportion of the portfolio to invest in each of the six mutual funds so that the portfolio provides the best return possible with a minimum risk. Let us see how linear programming can be used to develop a portfolio for these clients.

In portfolio models, risk is minimized by diversification. To see the value of diversification, suppose we first consider investing the entire portfolio in just one of the six mutual funds. Assuming the data in Table 12.4 represent the possible outcomes over the next 12 months, the clients run the risk of losing 21.93% over the next 12 months if the entire portfolio is invested in the foreign stock mutual fund. Similarly, if the entire portfolio is invested in any one of the other five mutual funds, the clients will also run the risk of losing money; that is, the possible losses are 1.33% for the intermediate-term bond fund, 23.26% for the large-cap growth fund, 5.37% for the large-cap value fund, 9.02% for the small-cap growth fund, and 6.70% for the small-cap value fund. Let us now see how we can construct a diversified portfolio of these mutual funds that minimizes the risk of a loss.

To determine the proportion of the portfolio that will be invested in each of the mutual funds, we use the following decision variables:

FS = proportion of portfolio invested in the foreign stock mutual fund

IB = proportion of portfolio invested in the intermediate-term bond fund

LG = proportion of portfolio invested in the large-cap growth fund

LV = proportion of portfolio invested in the large-cap value fund

SG = proportion of portfolio invested in the small-cap growth fund

SV = proportion of portfolio invested in the small-cap value fund

Because the sum of these proportions must equal 1, we need the following constraint:

$$FS + IB + LG + LV + SG + SV = 1$$

The other constraints are concerned with the return that the portfolio will earn under each of the planning scenarios in Table 12.4.

The portfolio return over the next 12 months depends on which of the possible scenarios in Table 12.4 occurs. Let $R1$ denote the portfolio return if scenario 1 occurs, $R2$ denote the portfolio return if scenario 2 occurs, and so on. The portfolio returns for the five planning scenarios are as follows:

Scenario 1 return

$$R1 = 10.06FS + 17.64IB + 32.41LG + 32.36LV + 33.44SG + 24.56SV$$

Scenario 2 return

$$R2 = 13.12FS + 3.25IB + 18.71LG + 20.61LV + 19.40SG + 25.32SV$$

Scenario 3 return

$$R3 = 13.47FS + 7.51IB + 33.28LG + 12.93LV + 3.85SG - 6.70SV$$

Scenario 4 return

$$R4 = 45.42FS - 1.33IB + 41.46LG + 7.06LV + 58.68SG + 5.43SV$$

Scenario 5 return

$$R5 = -21.93FS + 7.36IB - 23.26LG - 5.37LV - 9.02SG + 17.31SV$$

Let us now introduce a variable M to represent the minimum return for the portfolio. As we have already shown, one of the five possible scenarios in Table 12.4 will determine the portfolio return. Thus, the minimum possible return for the portfolio will be determined by the scenario that provides the worst-case return. But we don't know which of the scenarios will turn out to represent what happens over the next 12 months. To ensure that the return under each scenario is at least as large as the minimum return M, we must add the following minimum-return constraints:

$R1 \geq M$	Scenario 1 minimum return
$R2 \geq M$	Scenario 2 minimum return
$R3 \geq M$	Scenario 3 minimum return
$R4 \geq M$	Scenario 4 minimum return
$R5 \geq M$	Scenario 5 minimum return

Substituting the values shown previously for $R1$, $R2$, and so on provides the following five minimum-return constraints:

Scenario 1

$$10.06FS + 17.64IB + 32.41LG + 32.36LV + 33.44SG + 24.56SV \geq M$$

Scenario 2

$$13.12FS + 3.25IB + 18.71LG + 20.61LV + 19.40SG + 25.32SV \geq M$$

Scenario 3

$$13.47FS + 7.51IB + 33.28LG + 12.93LV + 3.85SG - 6.70SV \geq M$$

Scenario 4

$$45.42FS - 1.33IB + 41.46LG + 7.06LV + 58.68SG + 5.43SV \geq M$$

Scenario 5

$$-21.93FS + 7.36IB - 23.26LG - 5.37LV - 9.02SG + 17.31SV \geq M$$

To develop a portfolio that provides the best return possible with a minimum risk, we need to maximize the minimum return for the portfolio. Thus, the objective function is simple:

$$\text{Max } M$$

With the five minimum-return constraints present, the optimal value of M will equal the value of the minimum return scenario. The objective is to maximize the value of the minimum return scenario.

Because the linear programming model was designed to maximize the minimum return over all the scenarios considered, we refer to it as the maximin model. The complete maximin model for the problem of choosing a portfolio of mutual funds for a conservative, risk-averse investor involves seven variables and six constraints. After moving all the variables in the five minimum return constraints to the left-hand side, the complete maximin model is rewritten as follows:

$$\text{Max} \qquad M$$

s.t.

$$-M + 10.06FS + 17.64IB + 32.41LG + 32.36LV + 33.44SG + 24.56SV \geq 0$$
$$-M + 13.12FS + 3.25IB + 18.71LG + 20.61LV + 19.40SG + 25.32SV \geq 0$$
$$-M + 13.47FS + 7.51IB + 33.28LG + 12.93LV + 3.85SG - 6.70SV \geq 0$$
$$-M + 45.42FS - 1.33IB + 41.46LG + 7.06LV + 58.68SG + 5.43SV \geq 0$$
$$-M - 21.93FS + 7.36IB - 23.26LG - 5.37LV - 9.02SG + 17.31SV \geq 0$$
$$FS + IB + LG + LV + SG + SV = 1$$
$$M, FS, IB, LG, LV, SG, SV \geq 0$$

Note that we have written the constraint that requires the sum of the proportion of the portfolio invested in each mutual fund as the last constraint in the model. In this way, when we interpret the computer solution of the model, constraint 1 will correspond to planning scenario 1, constraint 2 will correspond to planning scenario 2, and so on.

WEB file

Maximin

The optimal solution to the Hauck maximin model is shown in Figure 12.6. The optimal value of the objective function is 6.445; thus, the optimal portfolio will earn 6.445% in the worst-case scenario. The optimal solution calls for 55.4% of the portfolio to be invested in the intermediate-term bond fund, 13.2% of the portfolio to be invested in the large-cap growth fund, and 31.4% of the portfolio to be invested in the small-cap value fund.

Because we do not know at the time of solving the model which of the five possible scenarios will occur, we cannot say for sure that the portfolio return will be 6.445%. However, using the slack variables, we can learn what the portfolio return will be under each of the scenarios. Constraints 3, 4, and 5 correspond to scenarios 3, 4, and 5 in Table 12.4. The slack variables for these constraints are zero to indicate that the portfolio return will be $M = 6.445\%$ if any of these three scenarios occur. The slack variable for constraint 1 is 15.321, indicating that the portfolio return will exceed $M = 6.445$ by 15.321 if scenario 1 occurs. So, if scenario 1 occurs, the portfolio return will be 6.445% + 15.321% = 21.766%. Referring to the slack variable for constraint 2, we see that the portfolio return will be 6.445% + 5.785% = 12.230% if scenario 2 occurs.

We must also keep in mind that in order to develop the portfolio model, Hauck made the assumption that over the next 12 months one of the five possible scenarios in Table 12.4 will occur. But we also recognize that the actual scenario that occurs over the next 12 months may be different from the scenarios Hauck considered. Thus, Hauck's experience and judgment in selecting representative scenarios plays a key part in determining how valuable the model recommendations will be for the client.

FIGURE 12.6   ANSWER REPORT FOR THE HAUCK MAXIMIN PORTFOLIO PROBLEM

Objective Cell (Max)

Name	Original Value	Final Value
Maximin Return	0.000	6.445

Variable Cells

Model Variable	Name	Original Value	Final Value	Integer
FS	Foreign Stock	0.000	0.000	Contin
IB	Intermediate-Term Bond	0.000	0.554	Contin
LG	Large-Cap Growth	0.000	0.132	Contin
LV	Large-Cap Value	0.000	0.000	Contin
SG	Small-Cap Growth	0.000	0.000	Contin
SV	Small-Cap Value	0.000	0.314	Contin
M	Maximin Return	0.000	6.445	Contin

Constraints

Constraint Number	Name	Cell Value	Status	Slack
1	Return Year 1	21.766	Not Binding	15.321
2	Return Year 2	12.230	Not Binding	5.785
3	Return Year 3	6.445	Binding	0.000
4	Return Year 4	6.445	Binding	0.000
5	Return Year 5	6.445	Binding	0.000
6	Prop. Sum	1.000	Binding	0.000

Moderate Risk Portfolio

Hauck's portfolio manager would like to also construct a portfolio for clients who are willing to accept a moderate amount of risk in order to attempt to achieve better returns. Suppose that clients in this risk category are willing to accept some risk, but do not want the annual return for the portfolio to drop below 2%. By setting $M = 2$ in the minimum return constraints in the maximin model, we can constrain the model to provide a solution with an annual return of at least 2%. The minimum return constraints needed to provide an annual return of at least 2% are as follows:

$$R1 \geq 2 \quad \text{Scenario 1 minimum return}$$
$$R2 \geq 2 \quad \text{Scenario 2 minimum return}$$
$$R3 \geq 2 \quad \text{Scenario 3 minimum return}$$
$$R4 \geq 2 \quad \text{Scenario 4 minimum return}$$
$$R5 \geq 2 \quad \text{Scenario 5 minimum return}$$

Substituting the expressions previously developed for $R1$, $R2$, and so on provides the following five minimum return constraints:

Scenario 1

$$10.06FS + 17.64IB + 32.41LG + 32.36LV + 33.44SG + 24.56SV \geq 2$$

Scenario 2

$$13.12FS + 3.25IB + 18.71LG + 20.61LV + 19.40SG + 25.32SV \geq 2$$

Scenario 3

$$13.47FS + 7.51IB + 33.28LG + 12.93LV + 3.85SG - 6.70SV \geq 2$$

Scenario 4

$$45.42FS - 1.33IB + 41.46LG + 7.06LV + 58.68SG + 5.43SV \geq 2$$

Scenario 5

$$-21.93FS + 7.36IB - 23.26LG - 5.37LV - 9.02SG + 17.31SV \geq 2$$

In addition to these five minimum return constraints, we still need the constraint that requires that the sum of the proportions invested in the separate mutual funds add to 1.

$$FS + IB + LG + LV + SG + SV = 1$$

A different objective is needed for this portfolio optimization problem. A common approach is to maximize the expected value of the return for the portfolio. For instance, if we assume that the planning scenarios are equally likely, we would assign a probability of 0.20 to each scenario. In this case the objective function is

$$\text{Expected value of the return} = 0.2R1 + 0.2R2 + 0.2R3 + 0.2R4 + 0.2R5$$

The coefficient of FS in the objective function is given by $0.2(10.06) + 0.2(13.12) + 0.2(13.47) + 0.2(45.42) + 0.2(-21.93) = 12.03$; the coefficient of IB is $0.2(17.64) + 0.2(3.25) + 0.2(7.51) + 0.2(-1.33) + 0.2(7.36) = 6.89$; and so on. Thus, the objective function is

$$12.03FS + 6.89IB + 20.52LG + 13.52LV + 21.27SG + 13.18SV$$

Because the objective is to maximize the expected value of the return, we write Hauck's objective function as follows:

$$\text{Max } 12.03FS + 6.89IB + 20.52LG + 13.52LV + 21.27SG + 13.18SV$$

The complete linear programming formulation for this version of the portfolio optimization problem involves six variables and six constraints.

$$\text{Max } 12.03FS + 6.89IB + 20.52LG + 13.52LV + 21.27SG + 13.18SV$$

s.t.

$$10.06FS + 17.64IB + 32.41LG + 32.36LV + 33.44SG + 24.56SV \geq 2$$
$$13.12FS + 3.25IB + 18.71LG + 20.61LV + 19.40SG + 25.32SV \geq 2$$
$$13.47FS + 7.51IB + 33.28LG + 12.93LV + 3.85SG - 6.70SV \geq 2$$
$$45.42FS - 1.33IB + 41.46LG + 7.06LV + 58.68SG + 5.43SV \geq 2$$
$$-21.93FS + 7.36IB - 23.26LG - 5.37LV - 9.02SG + 17.31SV \geq 2$$
$$FS + IB + LG + LV + SG + SV = 1$$
$$FS, IB, LG, LV, SG, SV \geq 0$$

WEB file

ModerateRisk

The optimal solution is shown in Figure 12.7. The optimal allocation is to invest 10.8% of the portfolio in a large-cap growth mutual fund, 41.5% in a small-cap growth mutual fund, and 47.7% in a small-cap value mutual fund. The objective function value shows that this allocation provides a maximum expected return of 17.33%. From the slack variables, we see that the portfolio return will only be 2% if scenarios 3 or 5 occur (constraints 3 and 5 are binding). The returns will be excellent if scenarios 1, 2, or 4 occur: The portfolio return will be 29.093% if scenario 1 occurs, 22.149% if scenario 2 occurs, and 31.417% if scenario 4 occurs.

FIGURE 12.7 ANSWER REPORT FOR THE MODERATE RISK PORTFOLIO PROBLEM

Objective Cell (Max)

Name	Original Value	Final Value
Expected Return	0.000	17.332

Variable Cells

Model Variable	Name	Original Value	Final Value	Integer
FS	Foreign Stock	0.000	0.000	Contin
IB	Intermediate-Term Bond	0.000	0.000	Contin
LG	Large-Cap Growth	0.000	0.108	Contin
LV	Large-Cap Value	0.000	0.000	Contin
SG	Small-Cap Growth	0.000	0.415	Contin
SV	Small-Cap Value	0.000	0.477	Contin

Constraints

Constraint Number	Name	Cell Value	Status	Slack
1	Return Scenario 1	29.093	Not Binding	27.093
2	Return Scenario 2	22.149	Not Binding	20.149
3	Return Scenario 3	2.000	Binding	0.000
4	Return Scenario 4	31.417	Not Binding	29.417
5	Return Scenario 5	2.000	Binding	0.000
6	Prop. Sum	1.000	Binding	0.000

The moderate risk portfolio exposes Hauck's clients to more risk than the maximin portfolio developed for a conservative investor. With the maximin portfolio, the worst-case scenario provided a return of 6.44%. With the moderate risk portfolio, the worst-case scenarios (scenarios 3 and 5) only provide a return of 2%, but there is also the possibility of higher returns in the other scenarios.

The formulation we have developed for a moderate risk portfolio can be modified to account for other risk tolerances. If an investor can tolerate the risk of no return, the right-hand sides of the minimum return constraints would be set to 0. If an investor can tolerate a loss of 3%, the right-hand side of the minimum return constraints would be set equal to −3.

NOTES AND COMMENTS

1. The Q.M. in Action, Asset Allocation and Variable Annuities, describes how insurance companies use asset allocation models to choose a portfolio of mutual funds for their clients' variable annuity investments.

2. Other constraints may be added to portfolio models to make them more flexible. For instance, if a client wanted to have at least 10% of the portfolio invested in foreign stocks, we would add the constraint $FS \geq 0.10$ to either the maximin or moderate risk portfolio models.

3. The portfolio models developed in this section are based on "Risk Management Strategies via Minimax Portfolio Optimization," *European Journal of Operational Research* (2010) by George G. Polak, David F. Rogers, and Dennis J. Sweeney. Related models can be found in "A Minimax Portfolio Selection Rule with Linear Programming," by Martin R. Young, *Management Science* (1998).

4. Harry Markowitz pioneered the use of mathematical models for portfolio selection. The primary model he developed is nonlinear and uses the statistical variance of returns for the portfolio as a measure of risk.

ASSET ALLOCATION AND VARIABLE ANNUITIES*

Insurance companies use portfolio models for asset allocation to structure a portfolio for their clients who purchase variable annuities. A variable annuity is an insurance contract that involves an accumulation phase and a distribution phase. In the accumulation phase the individual either makes a lump sum contribution or contributes to the annuity over a period of time. In the distribution phase the investor receives payments either in a lump sum or over a period of time. The distribution phase usually occurs at retirement, but because a variable annuity is an insurance product, a benefit is paid to a beneficiary should the annuitant die before or during the distribution period.

   Most insurance companies selling variable annuities offer their clients the benefit of an asset allocation model to

help them decide how to allocate their investment among a family of mutual funds. Usually the client fills out a questionnaire to assess his or her level of risk tolerance. Then, given that risk tolerance, the insurance company's asset allocation model recommends how the client's investment should be allocated over a family of mutual funds. American Skandia, a Prudential Financial Company, markets variable annuities that provide the types of services mentioned. A questionnaire is used to assess the client's risk tolerance, and the Morningstar Asset Allocator is used to develop portfolios for five levels of risk tolerance. Clients with low levels of risk tolerance are guided to portfolios consisting of bond funds and T-bills, and the most risk-tolerant investors are guided to portfolios consisting of a large proportion of growth stock mutual funds. Investors with intermediate, or moderate, risk tolerances are guided to portfolios that may consist of suitable mixtures of value and growth stock funds as well as some bond funds.

*Based on information provided by James R. Martin of the Martin Company, a financial services company.

12.4   Nonlinear Optimization—The RMC Problem Revisited

We introduce constrained and unconstrained nonlinear optimization problems by considering an extension of the RMC linear program introduced in Chapter 7. We first consider the case in which the relationship between price and quantity sold causes the objective function to become nonlinear. The resulting unconstrained nonlinear program is then solved, and we observe that the unconstrained optimal solution does not satisfy the production constraints. Adding the production constraints back into the problem allows us to show the formulation and solution of a constrained nonlinear program. The section closes with a discussion of local and global optima.

PRICING FOR ENVIRONMENTAL COMPLIANCE IN THE AUTO INDUSTRY*

As a result of the 1973 oil embargo, Congress put into law the Corporate Average Fuel Economy (CAFE) regulations in 1975. The CAFE standards are designed to promote the sale of fuel-efficient automobiles and light

*Based on Stephan Biller and Julie Swann, "Pricing for Environmental Compliance in the Auto Industry," *Interfaces* 36, no. 2 (March/April 2006): 118–125.

trucks, thus reducing dependence on oil. The CAFE standards were modified when President Bush signed into law the Clean Energy Act of 2007. This law requires that automakers boost fleet gas mileage average to 35 mpg by the year 2020. Although polls reveal strong support for such regulatory action, actual consumer behavior runs counter to supporting the purchase of

(*continued*)

fuel-efficient cars. Indeed, car manufacturers are faced with the problem of influencing consumers to purchase more fuel-efficient cars in order for the manufacturer to meet the CAFE-mandated standard. One way to influence consumer purchase behavior is through price. Lowering the price of fuel-efficient cars is one way to shift demand to this market. Of course, this should be done in a way to keep profits as large as possible subject to the CAFE constraints.

In order to meet the CAFE constraints while maximizing profits, General Motors (GM) used a mathematical model for coordinated pricing and production called Visual CAFÉ. This was built into an Excel spreadsheet with data input from Microsoft Access. The objective function for this model is much like the objective function for the nonlinear version of RMC that we develop in this section. In both cases the objective is to maximize profit, and the profit function is the product of quantity sold times the contribution margin of each product. The quantity sold is based on a linear demand function. A key constraint is the CAFE constraint, which is a constraint on the average miles per gallon for the GM fleet of cars. In addition, there are constraints on assembly, engine, and transmission capacity.

An Unconstrained Problem

Let us consider a revision of the RMC problem from Chapter 7. Recall that RMC produced a variety of chemical-based products, including a fuel additive and a solvent base. In formulating the linear programming model for the RMC problem, we assumed that it could sell all of the fuel additive and solvent base produced. However, depending on the price of the fuel additive and solvent base, this assumption may not hold. An inverse relationship usually exists between price and demand. As price goes up, the quantity demanded goes down. Let P_F denote the price RMC charges for each ton of fuel additive and P_S denote the price for each ton of solvent base. Assume that the demand for tons of fuel additive F and the demand for tons of solvent base S are

$$F = 580 - 2P_F \qquad (12.1)$$

$$S = 840 - 2.5P_S \qquad (12.2)$$

The revenue generated from selling fuel additive is the price per ton P_F times the number of tons of fuel additive sold, F. If the cost to produce a ton of fuel additive is \$250, the cost to produce F tons of fuel additive is $250F$. Thus, the profit contribution for producing and selling F tons of fuel additive (revenue − cost) is

$$P_F F - 250F \qquad (12.3)$$

We can solve equation (12.1) for P_F to show how the price of a ton of fuel additive is related to the number of tons of fuel additive sold. It is $P_F = 290 - \frac{1}{2}F$. Substituting $290 - \frac{1}{2}F$ for P_F in equation (12.3), the profit contribution for fuel additive is

$$P_F F - 250F = (290 - F/2)F - 250F = 40F - 0.5F^2 \qquad (12.4)$$

Suppose that the cost to produce each ton of solvent base is \$300. Using the same logic we used to develop equation (12.4), the profit contribution for solvent base is

$$P_S S - 300S = (336 - S/2.5)S - 300S = 36S - 0.4S^2$$

(Note we have written $1/2.5 = 0.4$.) Total profit contribution is the sum of the profit contribution from the fuel additive and the profit contribution for the solvent base. Thus, total profit contribution is written as

$$\text{Total profit contribution} = 40F - 0.5F^2 + 36S - 0.4S^2 \qquad \textbf{(12.5)}$$

Note that the two linear demand functions, equations (12.1) and (12.2), give a nonlinear total profit contribution function, equation (12.5). This function is an example of a quadratic function because the nonlinear terms have a power of 2.

RMCNonlinearUncon

Using Excel Solver (see Appendix 12.2), we find that the values of F and S that maximize the profit contribution function are $F = 40$ and $S = 45$. The corresponding prices are \$270 for a ton of fuel additive and \$318 for solvent base, and the profit contribution is \$1610. These values provide the optimal solution for RMC if all material limit constraints are also satisfied.

A Constrained Problem

Unfortunately, RMC cannot make the profit contribution associated with the optimal solution to the unconstrained problem because the constraints defining the feasible region are violated. For instance, the Material 1 constraint is $0.4F + 0.5S \leq 20$.

A production quantity of 40 tons of fuel additive and solvent base will require $0.4(40) + 0.5(45) = 38.5$ tons, which exceeds the limit of 20 tons by 18.5. The feasible region for the original RMC problem, along with the unconstrained optimal solution point (40, 45), is shown in Figure 12.8. The unconstrained optimum of (40, 45) is obviously outside the feasible region.

FIGURE 12.8   THE RMC FEASIBLE REGION AND THE OPTIMAL SOLUTION FOR THE UNCONSTRAINED OPTIMIZATION PROBLEM

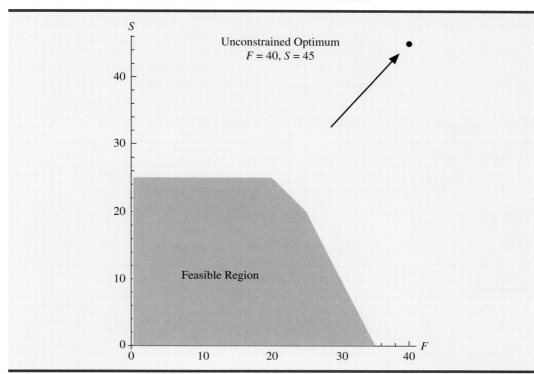

Clearly the problem that RMC must solve is to maximize the total profit contribution

$$40F - 0.5F^2 + 36S - 0.4S^2$$

subject to all of the material tonnage constraints that were given in Chapter 7. The complete mathematical model for the RMC constrained nonlinear maximization problem follows:

$$\text{Max} \quad 40F - 0.5F^2 + 36S - 0.4S^2$$

s.t.

$$
\begin{aligned}
0.4F + 0.5S &\leq 20 \quad \text{Material 1} \\
0.2S &\leq 5 \quad \text{Material 2} \\
0.6F + 0.3S &\leq 21 \quad \text{Material 3} \\
F, S &\geq 0
\end{aligned}
$$

RMCNonlinear

This maximization problem is exactly the same as the RMC problem in Chapter 7 except for the nonlinear objective function. The solution to this constrained nonlinear maximization problem is shown in Figure 12.9.

The optimal value of the objective function is $1247.83. The Variable Cells section shows that the optimal solution is to produce 24.339 tons of fuel additive and 20.529 tons of solvent base. In the Constraints section, constraints 1–3 correspond to the three material tonnage constraints. In the Slack column, the value of 0 in constraint 1 indicates that the optimal solution uses all of Material 1 that is available; but the nonzero values for constraints 2 and 3 indicate that there is excess tonnage of Materials 2 and 3.

A graphical view of the optimal solution of 24.339 tons of fuel additive and 20.529 tons of solvent base is shown in Figure 12.10.

Note that the optimal solution is no longer at an extreme point of the feasible region. The optimal solution lies on the Material 1 constraint line

$$0.4F + 0.5S = 20$$

but not at the extreme point formed by the intersection of the Material 1 constraint and Material 2 constraint, nor the extreme point formed by the intersection of the Material 1 constraint and the Material 3 constraint. To understand why, we look at Figure 12.10.

In Figure 12.10 we see three profit contribution contour lines. Each point on the same contour line is a point of equal profit. Here, the contour lines show profit contributions of

FIGURE 12.9   ANSWER REPORT FOR THE NONLINEAR RMC PROBLEM

Objective Cell (Max)

Name	Original Value	Final Value
Maximize Total Profit	0.000	1247.831

Variable Cells

Model Variable	Name	Original Value	Final Value	Integer
F	Tons Fuel Additive	0.000	24.339	Contin
S	Tons Solvent Base	0.000	20.529	Contin

Constraints

Constraint Number	Name	Cell Value	Status	Slack
1	Material 1	20.000	Binding	0.000
2	Material 2	4.106	Not Binding	0.894
3	Material 3	20.762	Not Binding	0.238

FIGURE 12.10 THE RMC FEASIBLE REGION WITH OBJECTIVE FUNCTION
CONTOUR LINES

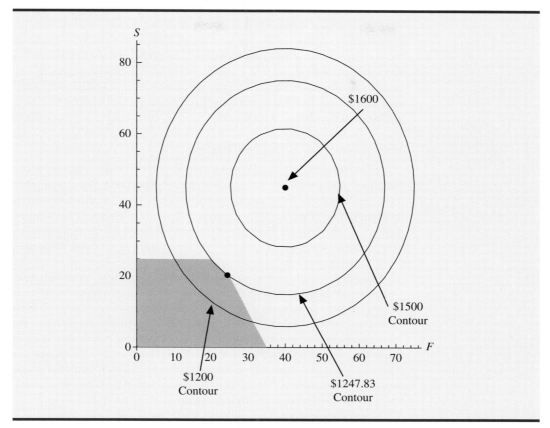

$1200, $1247.83, and $1500. In the original RMC problem described in Chapter 7, the objective function is linear and thus the profit contours are straight lines. However, for the RMC problem with a quadratic objective function, the profit contours are ellipses.

Because part of the $1200 profit contour line cuts through the feasible region, we know an infinite number of combinations of fuel additive and solvent base tonnages will yield a profit of $1200. An infinite number of combinations of fuel additive and solvent base tonnages provide a profit of $1500. However, none of the points on the $1500 contour profit line are in the feasible region. As the contour lines move farther out from the unconstrained optimum of (40, 45) the profit contribution associated with each contour line decreases. The contour line representing a profit of $1247.83 intersects the feasible region at a single point. This solution provides the maximum possible profit. No contour line that has a profit contribution greater than 1247.83 will intersect the feasible region. Because the contour lines are nonlinear, the contour line with the highest profit can touch the boundary of the feasible region at any point, not just an extreme point. In the RMC case, the optimal solution is on the Material 1 constraint line partway between two extreme points.

It is also possible for the optimal solution to a nonlinear optimization problem to lie in the interior of the feasible region. For instance, if the right-hand sides of the constraints in the RMC problem were all increased by a sufficient amount, the feasible region would expand so that the optimal unconstrained solution point of (40, 45) in Figure 12.10 would be in the interior of the feasible region. Many linear programming algorithms (e.g., the simplex method) optimize by examining only the extreme points and selecting the extreme point that gives the best solution value. As the solution to the constrained RMC nonlinear problem illustrates, such a method will not work in the nonlinear case because the optimal solution is generally not an extreme point solution. Hence, nonlinear programming algorithms are more complex than linear programming algorithms, and the details are beyond the scope of this text. Fortunately, we don't need to know how nonlinear algorithms work, we just need to know how to use them. Computer software such as LINGO and Excel Solver are available to solve nonlinear programming problems, and we describe how to use these software packages in the chapter appendices.

Local and Global Optima

A feasible solution is a **local optimum** if no other feasible solutions with a better objective function value are found in the immediate neighborhood. For example, for the constrained RMC problem, the local optimum corresponds to a **local maximum**; a point is a local maximum if no other feasible solutions with a larger objective function value are in the immediate neighborhood. Similarly, for a minimization problem, a point is a **local minimum** if no other feasible solutions with a smaller objective function value are in the immediate neighborhood.

Nonlinear optimization problems can have multiple local optimal solutions, which means we are concerned with finding the best of the local optimal solutions. A feasible solution is a **global optimum** if no other feasible points with a better objective function value are found in the feasible region. In the case of a maximization problem, the global optimum corresponds to a global maximum. A point is a **global maximum** if no other points in the feasible region give a strictly larger objective function value. For a minimization problem, a point is a **global minimum** if no other feasible points with a strictly smaller objective function value are in the feasible region. Obviously a global maximum is also a local maximum, and a global minimum is also a local minimum.

Nonlinear problems with multiple local optima are difficult to solve. But in many nonlinear applications, a single local optimal solution is also the global optimal solution. For such problems, we only need to find a local optimal solution. We will now present some of the more common classes of nonlinear problems of this type.

Consider the function $f(X, Y) = -X^2 - Y^2$. The shape of this function is illustrated in Figure 12.11. A function that is bowl shaped down is called a **concave function**. The maximum value for this particular function is 0, and the point $(0, 0)$ gives the optimal value of 0. The point $(0, 0)$ is a local maximum; but it is also a global maximum because no point

FIGURE 12.11   CONCAVE FUNCTION $f(X, Y) = -X^2 - Y^2$

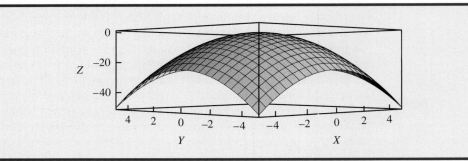

FIGURE 12.12 CONVEX FUNCTION $f(X, Y) = X^2 + Y^2$

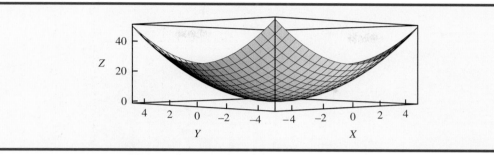

gives a larger function value. In other words, no values of X or Y result in an objective function value greater than 0. Functions that are concave, such as $f(X, Y) = -X^2 - Y^2$, have a single local maximum that is also a global maximum. This type of nonlinear problem is relatively easy to maximize.

The objective function for the nonlinear RMC problem is another example of a concave function:

$$40F - 0.5F^2 + 36S - 0.4S^2$$

In general, if all of the squared terms in a quadratic function have a negative coefficient and there are no cross-product terms, such as xy, then the function is a concave quadratic function. Thus, for the RMC problem, we are assured that the solution identified by Excel Solver in Figure 12.9 is the global maximum.

Let us now consider another type of function with a single local optimum that is also a global optimum. Consider the function $f(X, Y) = X^2 + Y^2$. The shape of this function is illustrated in Figure 12.12. It is bowl shaped up and called a **convex function**. The minimum value for this particular function is 0, and the point (0, 0) gives the minimum value of 0. The point (0, 0) is a local minimum and a global minimum because no values of X or Y give an objective function value less than 0. Functions that are convex, such as $f(X, Y) = X^2 + Y^2$, have a single local minimum and are relatively easy to minimize.

For a concave function, we can be assured that if our computer software finds a local maximum, it is a global maximum. Similarly, for a convex function, we know that if our computer software finds a local minimum, it is a global minimum. Concave and convex functions are well behaved. However, some nonlinear functions have multiple local optima. For example, Figure 12.13 shows the graph of the following function:[1]

$$f(X, Y) = 3(1 - X)^2 e^{-X^2 - (Y+1)^2} - 10(X/5 - X^3 - Y^5)e^{-X^2 - Y^2} - e^{-(X+1)^2 - Y^2}/3$$

The hills and valleys in this graph show that this function has several local maximums and local minimums. These concepts are further illustrated in Figure 12.14, which is the same function as in Figure 12.13 but from a different viewpoint. It indicates two local minimums and three local maximums. One of the local minimums is also the global minimum, and one of the local maximums is also the global maximum.

From a technical standpoint, functions with multiple local optima pose a serious challenge for optimization software; most nonlinear optimization software methods can get "stuck" and terminate at a local optimum. Unfortunately, many applications can be nonlinear, and there is a severe penalty for finding a local optimum that is not a global optimum. Developing algorithms capable of finding the global optimum is currently an active

---

[1]This example is taken from the LINDO API manual available at *http://www.LINDO.com*.

FIGURE 12.13   A FUNCTION WITH LOCAL MAXIMA AND MINIMA

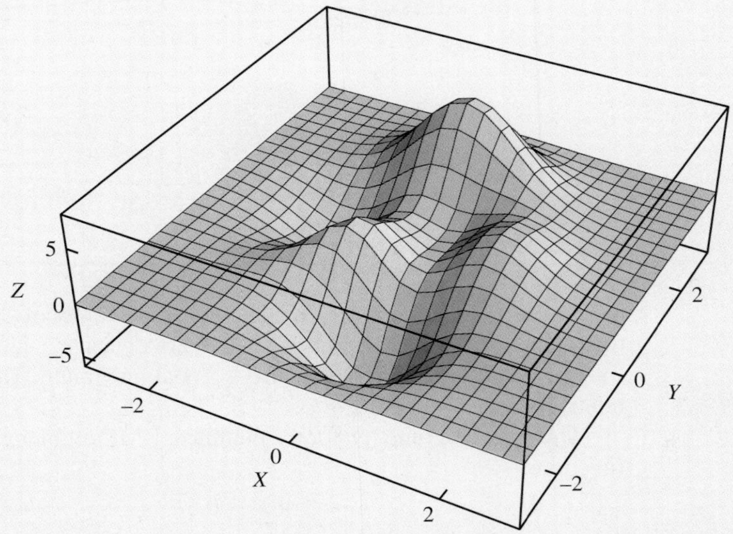

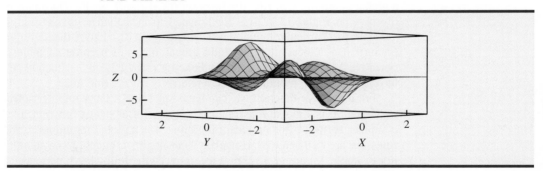

FIGURE 12.14   ANOTHER VIEWPOINT OF A FUNCTION WITH LOCAL MAXIMA
AND MINIMA

research area. But the problem of minimizing a convex quadratic function over a linear
constraint set is relatively easy, and for problems of this type there is no danger in getting
stuck at a local minimum that is not a global minimum. Similarly, the problem of maximizing a concave quadratic function over a linear constraint set is also relatively easy to solve
without getting stuck at a local maximum that is not the global maximum.

Shadow Prices

We conclude this section with a brief discussion of shadow prices. The concept of a shadow
price was introduced in Chapter 8. Recall that the shadow price is the change in the objective value of the optimal solution per unit increase in the right-hand side of the constraint.
Most nonlinear optimization software programs provide shadow price information.

FIGURE 12.15   SENSITIVITY REPORT FOR THE CONSTRAINED NONLINEAR RMC PROBLEM

Variable Cells

Model Variable	Name	Final Value	Reduced Gradient
F	Tons Fuel Additive	24.339	0.000
S	Tons Solvent Base	20.529	0.000

Constraints

Constraint Number	Name	Final Value	Lagrange Multiplier
1	Material 1	20.000	39.153
2	Material 2	4.106	0.000
3	Material 3	20.762	0.000

RMCNonlinear

Figure 12.15 shows output from the sensitivity report for the nonlinear RMC problem. In Figure 12.15, the Lagrange Multiplier column shows the value of the shadow price for each constraint. The interpretation of the shadow price for nonlinear models is exactly the same as it is for linear programs. However, for nonlinear problems the allowable increase and decrease are not usually reported. This is because for typical nonlinear problems the allowable increase and decrease are zero. That is, if you change the right-hand side by even a small amount, the shadow price changes.

Q.M. in ACTION

SCHEDULING FLIGHTS AND CREWS FOR BOMBARDIER FLEXJET*

Bombardier Flexjet is a leading company in the fast-growing fractional aircraft industry. Flexjet sells shares of business jets in share sizes equal to 50 hours of flying per year. A firm with fractional ownership is guaranteed 24-hour access to an aircraft with as little as a 4-hour lead time. Companies with a fractional share pay monthly management and usage fees. In exchange for the management fee, Flexjet provides hangar facilities, maintenance, and flight crews.

Because of the flexibility provided in the fractional aircraft business, the problem of scheduling crews and flights is even more complicated than in the commercial airline industry. Initially, Flexjet attempted to schedule flights by hand. However, this task quickly proved to be infeasible. Indeed, the inadequate manual scheduling resulted in Flexjet maintaining extra business jets and crews. The cost of the extra jets and crews was estimated

at several hundred dollars per flight hour. A scheduling system using optimization was clearly required.

The scheduling system developed for Flexjet includes a large nonlinear optimization model that is integrated with a graphical user interface (GUI) used by Flexjet personnel. The model includes "hard" constraints based on Federal Aviation Administration (FAA) regulations, company rules, and aircraft performance characteristics. It also includes "soft constraints" that involve cost trade-offs. The model is used to assign aircraft and crews to flights.

The resulting model is too large to solve directly with commercial optimization software. Models with too many variables to solve directly are often solved using decomposition methods. Decomposition methods work with a master problem that includes only a small fraction of the total number of variables. Variables that are good candidates to be part of the optimal solution are identified through the solution of a subproblem. In the Flexjet model, the subproblem is a nonlinear integer program.

(continued)

*Based on Richard Hicks et al., "Bombardier Flexjet Significantly Improves Its Fractional Aircraft Ownership Operations," *Interfaces* 35, no. 1 (January/February 2005): 49–60.

The heart of the nonlinearity is the product of a binary variable that is 1 if a particular pair of flight legs is used and a continuous variable that is used to impose a time window on flight times. The subproblem is optimized using a technique called dynamic programming.

The optimization model was a big success. The model initially saved Flexjet $54 million, with a projected annual savings of $27 million. Much of this cost saving is the result of reducing crew levels by 20% and aircraft inventory by 40%. Aircraft utilization also increased by 10%.

 ## Constructing an Index Fund

In Section 12.3 we studied portfolio and asset allocation models for Hauck Financial Services. Several linear programs were built to model different client attitudes toward risk. In this section we study an important related application.

Index funds are an extremely popular investment vehicle in the mutual fund industry. Indeed, the Vanguard 500 Index Fund is one of the largest mutual funds in the United States. An **index fund** is an example of passive asset management. The key idea behind an index fund is to construct a portfolio of stocks, mutual funds, or other securities that matches as closely as possible the performance of a broad market index such as the S&P 500.

Table 12.5 shows the one-year returns for four Vanguard Index Funds and the returns for the corresponding market indexes. Several interesting issues are illustrated in this table. First, Vanguard has index funds for numerous types of investments. For example, the market indexes for the first two Vanguard funds are stock funds: the S&P 500 Index Fund and the MSCI Broad Market fund. The MSCI REIT fund is an investment in the real estate market, and the Short-Term Bond (Barclays 1-5) fund is an investment in the corporate bond market. Second, notice that even though the returns show considerable variation among the funds, the index funds do a good job of matching the return of the corresponding market index.

Why are index funds so popular? Behind the popularity of index funds is a substantial amount of research in finance that basically says, "You can't beat the market." In fact, the vast majority of mutual fund managers actually underperform leading market indexes such as the S&P 500. Therefore, many investors are satisfied with investments that provide a return that more closely matches the market return.

Now, let us revisit the Hauck Financial Services example. Assume that Hauck has a substantial number of clients who wish to own a mutual fund portfolio with the characteristic that the portfolio, as a whole, closely matches the performance of the S&P 500 stock index. What percentage of the portfolio should be invested in each mutual fund in order to most closely mimic the performance of the entire S&P 500 index?

TABLE 12.5   ONE-YEAR RETURNS FOR FOUR VANGUARD INDEX FUNDS

Vanguard Fund	Vanguard Fund Return	Market Index	Market Index Return
500 Index Fund	4.77%	S&P 500	4.91%
Total Stock Index	5.98%	MSCI Broad Market	6.08%
REIT Index	11.90%	MSCI REIT	12.13%
Short-Term Bond	1.31%	Barclays 1-5 Index	1.44%

TABLE 12.6 MUTUAL FUND PERFORMANCE IN FIVE SELECTED YEARLY SCENARIOS

Mutual Fund	Planning Scenarios				
	Scenario 1	**Scenario 2**	**Scenario 3**	**Scenario 4**	**Scenario 5**
Foreign Stock	10.06	13.12	13.47	45.42	−21.93
Intermediate-Term Bond	17.64	3.25	7.51	−1.33	7.36
Large-Cap Growth	32.41	18.71	33.28	41.46	−23.26
Large-Cap Value	32.36	20.61	12.93	7.06	−5.37
Small-Cap Growth	33.44	19.40	3.85	58.68	−9.02
Small-Cap Value	24.56	25.32	−6.70	5.43	17.31
S&P 500 Return	**25.00**	**20.00**	**8.00**	**30.00**	**−10.00**

In Table 12.6 we reproduce Table 12.4 with an additional row that gives the S&P 500 return for each planning scenario. Recall that the columns show the actual percentage return that was earned by each mutual fund in that year. These five columns represent the most likely scenarios for the coming year.

The variables used in the model presented in Section 12.3 represented the proportion of the portfolio invested in each mutual fund.

FS = proportion of portfolio invested in a foreign stock mutual fund

IB = proportion of portfolio invested in an intermediate-term bond fund

LG = proportion of portfolio invested in a large-cap growth fund

LV = proportion of portfolio invested in a large-cap value fund

SG = proportion of portfolio invested in a small-cap growth fund

SV = proportion of portfolio invested in a small-cap value fund

The portfolio models presented in Section 12.3 chose the proportion of the portfolio to invest in each mutual fund in order to maximize return subject to constraints on the portfolio risk. Here we wish to choose the proportion of the portfolio to invest in each mutual fund in order to track as closely as possible the S&P 500 return.

For clarity of model exposition, we introduce variables $R1$, $R2$, $R3$, $R4$, and $R5$ that measure the portfolio return for each scenario. Consider, for example, variable $R1$. If the scenario represented by year 1 reflects what happens over the next 12 months, the portfolio return under scenario 1 is

$$10.06FS + 17.64IB + 32.41LG + 32.36LV + 33.44SG + 24.56SV = R1$$

Similarly, if scenarios 2–5 reflect the returns obtained over the next 12 months, the portfolio returns under scenarios 2–5 are as follows:

Scenario 2 return

$$13.12FS + 3.25IB + 18.71LG + 20.61LV + 19.40SG + 25.32SV = R2$$

Scenario 3 return

$$13.47FS + 7.51IB + 33.28LG + 12.93LV + 3.85SG - 6.70SV = R3$$

Scenario 4 return

$$45.42FS - 1.33IB + 41.46LG + 7.06LV + 58.68SG + 5.43SV = R4$$

Scenario 5 return

$$-21.93FS + 7.36IB - 23.26LG - 5.37LV - 9.02SG + 17.31SV = R5$$

Next, for each scenario we compute the deviation between the return for the scenario and the S&P 500 return. Based on the last row of Table 12.6, the deviations are

$$R1 - 25, \quad R2 - 20, \quad R3 - 8, \quad R4 - 30, \quad R5 - (-10) \qquad \textbf{(12.6)}$$

The objective is for the portfolio returns to match as closely as possible the S&P 500 returns. To do so, we might try minimizing the sum of the deviations given in equation (12.6) as follows:

$$\text{Min} \quad (R1 - 25) + (R2 - 20) + (R3 - 8) + (R4 - 30) + (R5 - (-10)) \qquad \textbf{(12.7)}$$

Unfortunately, if we use equation (12.7), positive and negative deviations will cancel each other out, so a portfolio that has a small value for equation (12.7) might actually behave quite differently than the target index. Also, because we want to get as close to the target returns as possible, it makes sense to assign a higher marginal penalty cost for large deviations than for small deviations. A function that achieves this goal is

$$\text{Min} \ (R1 - 25)^2 + (R2 - 20)^2 + (R3 - 8)^2 + (R4 - 30)^2 + (R5 - (-10))^2$$

When we square each term, positive and negative deviations do not cancel each other out, and the marginal penalty cost for deviations increases as the deviation gets larger. The complete mathematical model we have developed involves 11 variables and 6 constraints (excluding the nonnegativity constraints).

$$\text{Min} \quad (R1 - 25)^2 + (R2 - 20)^2 + (R3 - 8)^2 + (R4 - 30)^2 + (R5 - (-10))^2$$
s.t.
$$10.06FS + 17.64IB + 32.41LG + 32.36LV + 33.44SG + 24.56SV = R1$$
$$13.12FS + 3.25IB + 18.71LG + 20.61LV + 19.40SG + 25.32SV = R2$$
$$13.47FS + 7.51IB + 33.28LG + 12.93LV + 3.85SG - 6.70SV = R3$$
$$45.42FS - 1.33IB + 41.46LG + 7.06LV + 58.68SG + 5.43SV = R4$$
$$-21.93FS + 7.36IB - 23.26LG - 5.37LV - 9.02SG + 17.31SV = R5$$
$$FS + IB + LG + LV + 33.44SG + SV = 1$$
$$FS, IB, LG, LV, SG, SV \geq 0$$

This minimization problem is nonlinear because of the quadratic terms that appear in the objective function. For example, in the term $(R1 - 25)^2$ the variable $R1$ is raised to a power of 2 and is therefore nonlinear. However, because the coefficient of each squared term is positive, and there are no cross-product terms, the objective function is a convex function. Therefore, we are guaranteed that any local minimum is also a global minimum.

The optimal solution is given in Figure 12.16. The optimal value of the objective function is 4.427, the sum of the squares of the return deviations. The portfolio calls for

WEB file

HauckIndex

FIGURE 12.16   ANSWER REPORT FOR THE HAUCK FINANCIAL SERVICES PROBLEM

Objective Cell (Min)

Name	Original Value	Final Value
Deviations Squared	2089.000	4.427

Variable Cells

Variable Name	Name	Original Value	Final Value	Integer
R1	Return Scenario 1	0.000	25.013	Contin
R2	Return Scenario 2	0.000	18.557	Contin
R3	Return Scenario 3	0.000	8.975	Contin
R4	Return Scenario 4	0.000	30.218	Contin
R5	Return Scenario 5	0.000	−8.840	Contin
FS	Foreign Stock	0.000	0.304	Contin
IB	Intermediate-Term Bond	0.000	0.000	Contin
LG	Large-Cap Growth	0.000	0.000	Contin
LV	Large-Cap Value	0.000	0.365	Contin
SG	Small-Cap Growth	0.000	0.226	Contin
SV	Small-Cap Value	0.000	0.105	Contin

Constraints

Constraint Number	Name	Cell Value	Status	Slack
1	Return Scenario 1	25.013	Binding	0.000
2	Return Scenario 2	18.557	Binding	0.000
3	Return Scenario 3	8.975	Binding	0.000
4	Return Scenario 4	30.218	Binding	0.000
5	Return Scenario 5	−8.840	Binding	0.000
6	Prop. Sum	1.000	Binding	0.000
7	Foreign Stock	0.304	Not Binding	0.304
8	Intermediate-Term Bond	0.000	Binding	0.000
9	Large-Cap Growth	0.000	Binding	0.000
10	Large-Cap Value	0.365	Not Binding	0.365
11	Small-Cap Growth	0.226	Not Binding	0.226
12	Small-Cap Value	0.105	Not Binding	0.105

approximately 30% of the funds to be invested in the foreign stock fund ($FS = 0.304$), 37% of the funds to be invested in the large-cap value fund ($LV = 0.365$), 23% of the funds to be invested in the small-cap growth fund ($SG = 0.226$), and 11% of the funds to be invested in the small-cap value fund ($SV = 0.105$). Note that in the Constraint section, constraints 7 through 12 correspond to the nonnegativity constraints (note that the return variables R1 through R5 are not restricted to be nonnegative).

Table 12.7 shows a comparison of the portfolio return (see R1, R2, R3, R4, and R5 in Figure 12.16) to the S&P 500 return for each scenario. Notice how closely the portfolio returns match the S&P 500 returns. Based on historical data, a portfolio with this mix of Hauck mutual funds will indeed closely match the returns for the S&P 500 stock index.

TABLE 12.7   PORTFOLIO RETURN VERSUS S&P 500 RETURN

Scenario	Portfolio Return	S&P 500 Return
1	25.013	25
2	18.557	20
3	8.975	8
4	30.218	30
5	−8.840	−10

NOTES AND COMMENTS

1. The returns for the planning scenarios in Table 12.6 are the actual returns for five years in the past. They were chosen as the past data most likely to represent what could happen over the next year. By using actual past data, the correlation among the mutual funds is automatically incorporated into the model.
2. It would not be practical for an individual investor who desires to receive the same return as the S&P 500 to purchase all the S&P 500 stocks. The index fund we have constructed permits such an investor to approximate the S&P 500 return.
3. In this section we constructed an index fund from among mutual funds. The investment alternatives used to develop the index fund could also be individual stocks that are part of the S&P 500.

Summary

In this chapter we presented three advanced linear programming applications. In particular, we applied linear programming to data envelopment analysis, maximizing revenue for airlines, and constructing mutual fund portfolios. In practice, most of the modeling effort in these types of linear programming applications involves clearly understanding the problem, stating the problem mathematically, and then finding reliable data in the format required by the model.

In this chapter we introduced nonlinear optimization models. A nonlinear optimization model is a model with at least one nonlinear term in either a constraint or the objective function. Because so many processes in business and nature behave in a nonlinear fashion, allowing nonlinear terms greatly increases the number of important applications that can be modeled as an optimization problem. Numerous problems in portfolio optimization, pricing options, blending, economics, facility location, forecasting, and scheduling lend themselves to nonlinear models.

Unfortunately, nonlinear optimization models are not as easy to solve as linear optimization models, or even linear integer optimization models. As a rule of thumb, if a problem can be modeled realistically as a linear or linear integer problem, then it is probably best to do so. Many nonlinear formulations have local optima that are not globally optimal. Because most nonlinear optimization codes will terminate with a local optimum, the solution returned by the code may not be the best solution available. However, as pointed out in this chapter, numerous important classes of optimization problems, such as the index portfolio model, are convex optimization problems. For a convex optimization problem, a local optimum is also the global optimum. Additionally, the development of nonlinear optimization codes that do find globally optimal solutions is proceeding at a rapid rate.

Glossary

Concave function A function that is bowl shaped down: for example, the functions and $f(x) = -5x^2 - 5x$ and $f(x,y) = -x^2 - 11y^2$ are concave functions.

Convex function A function that is bowl shaped up: for example, the functions and $f(x) = x^2 - 5x$ and $f(x,y) = x^2 + 5y^2$ are convex functions.

Data envelopment analysis (DEA) A linear programming application used to measure the relative efficiency of operating units with the same goals and objectives.

Efficiency index Percentage of an individual operating unit's resources that are available to the composite operating unit.

Global maximum A feasible solution is a global maximum if there are no other feasible points with a larger objective function value in the entire feasible region. A global maximum is also a local maximum.

Global minimum A feasible solution is a global minimum if there are no other feasible points with a smaller objective function value in the entire feasible region. A global minimum is also a local minimum.

Global optimum A feasible solution is a global optimum if there are no other feasible points with a better objective function value in the entire feasible region. A global optimum may be either a global maximum or a global minimum.

Hypothetical composite A weighted average of outputs and inputs of all operating units with similar goals.

Index fund A portfolio of stocks, mutual funds, or other securities that matches as closely as possible the performance of a broad market index such as the S&P 500.

Local maximum A feasible solution is a local maximum if there are no other feasible solutions with a larger objective function value in the immediate neighborhood.

Local minimum A feasible solution is a local minimum if there are no other feasible solutions with a smaller objective function value in the immediate neighborhood.

Local optimum A feasible solution is a local optimum if there are no other feasible solutions with a better objective function value in the immediate neighborhood. A local optimum may be either a local maximum or a local minimum.

Nonlinear optimization problem An optimization problem that contains at least one nonlinear term in the objective function or a constraint.

Problems

1. In Section 12.1 data envelopment analysis was used to evaluate the relative efficiencies of four hospitals. Data for three input measures and four output measures were provided in Tables 12.1 and 12.2.
   a. Use these data to develop a linear programming model that could be used to evaluate the performance of General Hospital.
   b. The following solution is optimal. Does the solution indicate that General Hospital is relatively inefficient?

Objective Function Value = 1.000		
Variable	**Value**	**Reduced Costs**
E	1.000	0.000
WG	1.000	0.000
WU	0.000	0.000
WC	0.000	0.331
WS	0.000	0.215

    c.   Explain which hospital or hospitals make up the composite unit used to evaluate General Hospital and why.

2. Data envelopment analysis can measure the relative efficiency of a group of hospitals. The following data from a particular study involving seven teaching hospitals include three input measures and four output measures.

    a.   Formulate a linear programming model so that data envelopment analysis can be used to evaluate the performance of hospital D.

    b.   Solve the model.

    c.   Is hospital D relatively inefficient? What is the interpretation of the value of the objective function?

	Input Measures		
Hospital	**Full-Time Equivalent Nonphysicians**	**Supply Expense (1000s)**	**Bed-Days Available (1000s)**
A	310.0	134.60	116.00
B	278.5	114.30	106.80
C	165.6	131.30	65.52
D	250.0	316.00	94.40
E	206.4	151.20	102.10
F	384.0	217.00	153.70
G	530.1	770.80	215.00

	Output Measures			
Hospital	**Patient-Days (65 or older) (1000s)**	**Patient-Days (under 65) (1000s)**	**Nurses Trained**	**Interns Trained**
A	55.31	49.52	291	47
B	37.64	55.63	156	3
C	32.91	25.77	141	26
D	33.53	41.99	160	21
E	32.48	55.30	157	82
F	48.78	81.92	285	92
G	58.41	119.70	111	89

    d.   How many patient-days of each type are produced by the composite hospital?

    e.   Which hospitals would you recommend hospital D consider emulating to improve the efficiency of its operation?

3. Jim's Camera shop sells two high-end cameras, the Sky Eagle and the Horizon. The demand for these two cameras are as follows: D_S = demand for the Sky Eagle, P_S is the selling price of the Sky Eagle, D_H is the demand for the Horizon, and P_H is the selling price of the Horizon.

$$D_S = 222 - 0.60P_S + 0.35P_H$$
$$D_H = 270 + 0.10P_S - 0.64P_H$$

The store wishes to determine the selling price that maximizes revenue for these two products. Develop the revenue function for these two models, and find the revenue maximizing prices.

4. The Ranch House, Inc., operates five fast-food restaurants. Input measures for the restaurants include weekly hours of operation, full-time equivalent staff, and weekly supply expenses. Output measures of performance include average weekly contribution to profit, market share, and annual growth rate. Data for the input and output measures are shown in the following tables.

	Input Measures		
Restaurant	**Hours of Operation**	**FTE Staff**	**Supplies ($)**
Bardstown	96	16	850
Clarksville	110	22	1400
Jeffersonville	100	18	1200
New Albany	125	25	1500
St. Matthews	120	24	1600
	Output Measures		
Restaurant	**Weekly Profit**	**Market Share (%)**	**Growth Rate (%)**
Bardstown	$3800	25	8.0
Clarksville	$4600	32	8.5
Jeffersonville	$4400	35	8.0
New Albany	$6500	30	10.0
St. Matthews	$6000	28	9.0

a. Develop a linear programming model that can be used to evaluate the performance of the Clarksville Ranch House restaurant.
b. Solve the model.
c. Is the Clarksville Ranch House restaurant relatively inefficient? Discuss.
d. Where does the composite restaurant have more output than the Clarksville restaurant? How much less of each input resource does the composite restaurant require when compared to the Clarksville restaurant?
e. What other restaurants should be studied to find suggested ways for the Clarksville restaurant to improve its efficiency?

5. Reconsider the Leisure Airlines problem from Section 12.2. The demand forecasts shown in Table 12.3 represent Leisure Air's best estimates of demand. But because demand cannot be forecasted perfectly, the number of seats actually sold for each origin-destination-itinerary fare (ODIF) may turn out to be smaller or larger than forecasted. Suppose that Leisure Air believes that economic conditions have improved and that its original forecast may be too low. To account for this possibility, Leisure Air is considering switching the Boeing 737-400 airplanes that are based in Pittsburgh and Newark with Boeing 757-200 airplanes that Leisure Air has available in other markets. The Boeing 757-200 airplane has a seating capacity of 158 in the coach section.
a. Because of scheduling conflicts in other markets, suppose that Leisure Air is only able to obtain one Boeing 757-200. Should the larger plane be based in Pittsburgh or in Newark? Explain.
b. Based upon your answer in part (a), determine a new allocation for the ODIFs. Briefly summarize the major differences between the new allocation using one Boeing 757-200 and the original allocation summarized in Figure 12.5.

c. Suppose that two Boeing 757-200 airplanes are available. Determine a new allocation for the ODIF's using the two larger airplanes. Briefly summarize the major differences between the new allocation using two Boeing 757-200 airplanes and the original allocation shown in Figure 12.5.

d. Consider the new solution obtained in part (b). Which ODIF has the highest bid price? What is the interpretation for this bid price?

6. Reconsider the Leisure Airlines problem from Section 12.2. Suppose that as of May 1 the following number of seats have been sold:

ODIF	1	2	3	4	5	6	7	8	9	10	11	12	13	14	15	16
Seats Sold	25	44	18	12	5	9	20	33	37	11	5	8	27	6	35	7

a. Determine how many seats are still available for sale on each flight leg.

b. Using the original demand forecasted for each ODIF, determine the remaining demand for each ODIF.

c. Revise the linear programming model presented in Section 12.2 to account for the number of seats currently sold and a demand of one additional seat for the Pittsburgh–Myrtle Beach Q class ODIF. Resolve the linear programming model to determine a new allocation schedule for the ODIFs.

7. Hanson Inn is a 96-room hotel located near the airport and convention center in Louisville, Kentucky. When a convention or a special event is in town, Hanson increases its normal room rates and takes reservations based on a revenue management system. The Classic Corvette Owners Association scheduled its annual convention in Louisville for the first weekend in June. Hanson Inn agreed to make at least 50% of its rooms available for convention attendees at a special convention rate in order to be listed as a recommended hotel for the convention. Although the majority of attendees at the annual meeting typically request a Friday and Saturday two-night package, some attendees may select a Friday night only or a Saturday night only reservation. Customers not attending the convention may also request a Friday and Saturday two-night package, or make a Friday night only or Saturday night only reservation. Thus, six types of reservations are possible: convention customers/two-night package; convention customers/Friday night only; convention customers/Saturday night only; regular customers/two-night package; regular customers/Friday night only; and regular customers/Saturday night only.

The cost for each type of reservation is shown here.

	Two-Night Package	Friday Night Only	Saturday Night Only
Convention	$225	$123	$130
Regular	$295	$146	$152

The anticipated demand for each type of reservation is as follows:

	Two-Night Package	Friday Night Only	Saturday Night Only
Convention	40	20	15
Regular	20	30	25

Hanson Inn would like to determine how many rooms to make available for each type of reservation in order to maximize total revenue.

a. Define the decision variables and state the objective function.

b. Formulate a linear programming model for this revenue management application.

c. What is the optimal allocation and the anticipated total revenue?

d. Suppose that one week before the convention, the number of regular customers/ Saturday night only rooms that were made available sell out. If another nonconvention customer calls and requests a Saturday only room, what is the value of accepting this additional reservation?

8. In the latter part of Section 12.3 we developed a moderate risk portfolio model for Hauck Investment Services. Modify the model given so that it can be used to construct a portfolio for more aggressive investors. In particular, do the following:

a. Develop a portfolio model for investors who are willing to risk a portfolio with a return as low as 0%.

b. What is the recommended allocation for this type of investor?

c. How would you modify your recommendation in part (b) for an investor who also wants to have at least 10% of his or her portfolio invested in the foreign stock mutual fund? How does requiring at least 10% of the portfolio be invested in the foreign stock fund affect the expected return?

9. Table 12.8 shows data on the returns over five 1-year periods for six mutual funds. A firm's portfolio managers assume that one of these scenarios will accurately reflect the investing climate over the next 12 months. The probabilities of each of the scenarios occurring are 0.1, 0.3, 0.1, 0.1, and 0.4 for scenarios 1 to 5, respectively.

a. Develop a portfolio model for investors who are willing to risk a portfolio with a return no lower than 2%.

b. Solve the model in part (a) and recommend a portfolio allocation for the investor with this risk tolerance.

c. Modify the portfolio model in part (a) and solve it to develop a portfolio for an investor with a risk tolerance of 0%.

d. Is the expected return greater for investors following the portfolio recommendations in part (c) as compared to the returns for the portfolio in part (b)? If so, do you believe the returns are sufficiently greater to justify investing in that portfolio?

10. The purpose of this exercise is to provide practice using LINGO or Excel Solver. Find the values of X and Y that minimize the function

$$\text{Min } X^2 - 4X + Y^2 + 8Y + 20$$

Do not assume nonnegativity of the X and Y variables. Recall that by default LINGO assumes nonnegative variables. In order to allow the variables to take on negative values, you can add

@FREE(X); @FREE(Y);

TABLE 12.8 RETURNS OVER FIVE 1-YEAR PERIODS FOR SIX MUTUAL FUNDS

Mutual Funds	Planning Scenarios for Next 12 Months				
	Scenario 1	Scenario 2	Scenario 3	Scenario 4	Scenario 5
Large-Cap Stock	35.3	20.0	28.3	10.4	−9.3
Mid-Cap Stock	32.3	23.2	−0.9	49.3	−22.8
Small-Cap Stock	20.8	22.5	6.0	33.3	6.1
Energy/Resources Sector	25.3	33.9	−20.5	20.9	−2.5
Health Sector	49.1	5.5	29.7	77.7	−24.9
Technology Sector	46.2	21.7	45.7	93.1	−20.1
Real Estate Sector	20.5	44.0	−21.1	2.6	5.1

Alternatively, if you want LINGO to allow for negative values by default, in the LINGO menu select **Options** and then click **General Solver,** and then uncheck the **Variables assumed nonnegative** tab.

11. Consider the problem

$$\text{Min} \quad 2X^2 - 20X + 2XY + Y^2 - 14Y + 58$$
$$\text{s.t.} \quad X + 4Y \le 8$$

   a. Find the minimum solution to this problem.
   b. If the right-hand side of the constraint is increased from 8 to 9, how much do you expect the objective function to change?
   c. Re-solve the problem with a new right-hand side of 9. How does the actual change compare with your estimate?

12. GreenLawns provides a lawn fertilizer and weed control service. The company is adding a special aeration treatment as a low-cost extra service option, which it hopes will help attract new customers. Management is planning to promote this new service in two media: radio and direct-mail advertising. A media budget of $3000 is available for this promotional campaign. Based on past experience in promoting its other services, GreenLawns obtained the following estimate of the relationship between sales and the amount spent on promotion in these two media:

$$S = -2R^2 - 10M^2 - 8RM + 18R + 34M$$

where

$$S = \text{total sales in thousands of dollars}$$
$$R = \text{thousands of dollars spent on radio advertising}$$
$$M = \text{thousands of dollars spent on direct-mail advertising}$$

   GreenLawns would like to develop a promotional strategy that will lead to maximum sales subject to the restriction provided by the media budget.
   a. What is the value of sales if $2000 is spent on radio advertising and $1000 is spent on direct-mail advertising?
   b. Formulate an optimization problem that can be solved to maximize sales subject to the media budget.
   c. Determine the optimal amount to spend on radio and direct-mail advertising. How much in sales will be generated?

13. The function

$$f(X, Y) = 3(1 - X)^2 e^{(-X^2 - (Y+1)^2)} - 10(X/5 - X^3 - Y^5) e^{(-X^2 - Y^2)} - e^{(-(X+1)^2 - Y^2)/3}$$

was used to generate Figures 12.13 and 12.14 in order to illustrate the concept of local optima versus global optima.
   a. Minimize this function using LINGO. [*Warning*: Make sure you use the unary minus sign correctly. In other words, rewrite a term such as $-X^2$ as $-(X)^2$.] (See Appendix 12.1.)
   b. Now minimize this function using LINGO with the Global Solver option turned on.

14. The Cobb-Douglas production function is a classic model from economics used to model output as a function of capital and labor. It has the form

$$f(L, C) = c_0 L^{c_1} C^{c_2}$$

where c_0, c_1, and c_2 are constants. The variable L represents the units of input of labor and the variable C represents the units of input of capital.
   a. In this example, assume $c_0 = 5$, $c_1 = 0.25$, and $c_2 = 0.75$. Assume each unit of labor costs $25 and each unit of capital costs $75. With $75,000 available in the budget, develop an optimization model for determining how the budgeted amount should be allocated between capital and labor in order to maximize output.

b. Find the optimal solution to the model you formulated in part (a). *Hint*: When using Excel Solver, start with an initial $L > 0$ and $C > 0$.

15. Let S represent the amount of steel produced (in tons). Steel production is related to the amount of labor used (L) and the amount of capital used (C) by the following function:

$$S = 20L^{0.30}C^{0.70}$$

In this formula L represents the units of labor input and C the units of capital input. Each unit of labor costs \$50, and each unit of capital costs \$100.

a. Formulate an optimization problem that will determine how much labor and capital are needed in order to produce 50,000 tons of steel at minimum cost.

b. Solve the optimization problem you formulated in part (a). *Hint*: When using Excel Solver, start with an initial $L > 0$ and $C > 0$.

16. The profit function for two products is

$$\text{Profit} = -3x_1^2 + 42x_1 - 3x_2^2 + 48x_2 + 700$$

where x_1 represents units of production of product 1 and x_2 represents units of production of product 2. Producing one unit of product 1 requires 4 labor-hours and producing one unit of product 2 requires 6 labor-hours. Currently, 24 labor-hours are available. The cost of labor-hours is already factored into the profit function. However, it is possible to schedule overtime at a premium of \$5 per hour.

a. Formulate an optimization problem that can be used to find the optimal production quantity of product 1 and the optimal number of overtime hours to schedule.

b. Solve the optimization model you formulated in part (a). How much should be produced and how many overtime hours should be scheduled?

17. Heller Manufacturing has two production facilities that manufacture baseball gloves. Production costs at the two facilities differ because of varying labor rates, local property taxes, type of equipment, capacity, and so on. The Dayton plant has weekly costs that can be expressed as a function of the number of gloves produced:

$$TCD(X) = X^2 - X + 5$$

where X is the weekly production volume in thousands of units and $TCD(X)$ is the cost in thousands of dollars. The Hamilton plant's weekly production costs are given by

$$TCH(Y) = Y^2 + 2Y + 3$$

where Y is the weekly production volume in thousands of units and $TCH(Y)$ is the cost in thousands of dollars. Heller Manufacturing would like to produce 8000 gloves per week at the lowest possible cost.

a. Formulate a mathematical model that can be used to determine the optimal number of gloves to produce each week at each facility.

b. Use LINGO or Excel Solver to find the solution to your mathematical model to determine the optimal number of gloves to produce at each facility.

18. Harry Markowitz received the 1990 Nobel Prize for his path-breaking work in portfolio optimization. One version of the Markowitz model is based on minimizing the variance of the portfolio subject to a constraint on return. We use the data and notation developed for the Hauck Index Fund in Section 12.5 to develop an example of the Markowitz mean-variance model. If each of the scenarios is equally likely and occurs with probability 1/5, then the mean return or expected return of the portfolio is

$$\bar{R} = \tfrac{1}{5}\sum_{S=1}^{5} R_s$$

The variance of the portfolio return is

$$\text{Var} = \tfrac{1}{5}\sum_{S=1}^{5}(R_s - \overline{R})^2$$

See Section 3.2 in Chapter 3 for a review of the mean and variance concept. Using the scenario return data given in Table 12.6, formulate the Markowitz mean-variance model. The objective function is the variance of the portfolio and should be minimized. Assume that the required return on the portfolio is 10%. There is also a unity constraint that all of the money must be invested in mutual funds. Solve this mean-variance model using either LINGO or Excel Solver.

19. Many forecasting models use parameters that are estimated using nonlinear optimization. This is true of many of the models developed in Chapter 6. Consider the exponential smoothing forecasting model from Section 6.3. For instance, the basic exponential smoothing model for forecasting sales is

$$\hat{Y}_{t+1} = \alpha Y_t + (1 - \alpha)F_t$$

where

$$\hat{Y}_{t+1} = \text{forecast of sales for period } t+1$$
$$Y_t = \text{actual value of sales for period } t$$
$$F_t = \text{forecast of sales for period } t$$
$$\alpha = \text{smoothing constant } 0 \leq \alpha \leq 1$$

This model is used recursively; the forecast for time period $t + 1$ is based on the forecast for period t, $\hat{Y}_t$; the observed value of sales in period t, Y_t; and the smoothing parameter α. The use of this model to forecast sales for 12 months is illustrated in Table 12.9 with the smoothing constant $\alpha = 0.3$. The forecast errors, $Y_t - \hat{Y}_t$, are calculated in the fourth column. The value of α is often chosen by minimizing the sum of squared forecast errors, commonly referred to as the mean squared error (MSE). The last column of Table 12.9 shows the square of the forecast error and the sum of squared forecast errors.

TABLE 12.9   EXPONENTIAL SMOOTHING MODEL FOR $\alpha = 0.3$

Week (t)	Observed Value (Y_t)	Forecast $(\hat{Y}_t)$	Forecast Error $(Y_t - \hat{Y}_t)$	Squared Forecast Error $(Y_t - \hat{Y}_t)^2$
1	17	17.00	0.00	0.00
2	21	17.00	4.00	16.00
3	19	18.20	0.80	0.64
4	23	18.44	4.56	20.79
5	18	19.81	−1.81	3.27
6	16	19.27	−3.27	10.66
7	20	18.29	1.71	2.94
8	18	18.80	−0.80	0.64
9	22	18.56	3.44	11.83
10	20	19.59	0.41	0.17
11	15	19.71	−4.71	22.23
12	22	18.30	3.70	13.69
				SUM = 102.86

In using exponential smoothing models, we try to choose the value of α that provides the best forecasts. Build an optimization model that will find the smoothing parameter, α, that minimizes the sum of squared forecast errors. You may find it easiest to put Table 12.9 into an Excel spreadsheet and then use Solver to find the optimal value of α.

20. The economic order quantity (EOQ) model is a classical model used for controlling inventory and satisfying demand. Costs included in the model are holding cost per unit, ordering cost, and the cost of goods ordered. The assumptions for that model are that only a single item is considered, that the entire quantity ordered arrives at one time, that the demand for the item is constant over time, and that no shortages are allowed.

Suppose we relax the first assumption and allow for multiple items that are independent except for a budget restriction. The following model describes this situation:

Let D_j = annual demand for item j
   C_j = unit cost of item j
   S_j = cost per order placed for item j
   i = inventory carrying charge as a percentage of the cost per unit
   B = the maximum amount of investment in goods
   N = number of items

The decision variables are Q_j, the amount of item j to order. The model is:

$$\text{Minimize} \sum_{j=1}^{N} \left[C_j D_j + \frac{S_j D_j}{Q_j} + iC_j \frac{Q_j}{2} \right]$$

s.t.

$$\sum_{j=1}^{N} C_j Q_j \leq B$$

$$Q_j \leq 0 \, j = 1, 2, \ldots, N$$

In the objective function, the first term is the annual cost of goods, the second is the annual ordering cost (D_j/Q_j is the number of orders), and the last term is the annual inventory holding cost ($Q_j/2$ is the average amount of inventory).

Set up and solve a nonlinear optimization model for the following data:

	Item 1	Item 2	Item 3
Annual Demand	2000	2000	1000
Item Cost	$100	$50	$80
Order Cost	$150	$135	$125
B = $20,000			
i = 0.20			

21. Formulate and solve the Markowitz portfolio optimization model that was introduced in Problem 18 using the return data in columns five, six, and seven of Table 12.10. In this case, nine scenarios correspond to the yearly returns for years 1 through 9. Treat each scenario as being equally likely.

22. Using the return data in Table 12.10, construct a portfolio from Apple, AMD, and Oracle that matches the Information Technology S&P index as closely as possible. Use the return data for the Information Technology S&P index given in the following table. The model for constructing the portfolio should be similar to the one developed for Hauck Financial Services in Section 12.5.

TABLE 12.10   YEARLY RETURNS FOR AAPL, AMD, AND ORCL

Beginning of Year	AAPL Adj. Close	AMD Adj. Close	ORCL Adj. Close	AAPL Return	AMD Return	ORCL Return
Year 1	4.16	17.57	4.32	0.0962	−0.5537	−0.1074
Year 2	4.58	10.1	3.88	0.8104	0.1272	0.8666
Year 3	10.30	11.47	9.23	0.9236	0.4506	0.9956
Year 4	25.94	18	24.98	−0.8753	0.3124	0.1533
Year 5	10.81	24.6	29.12	0.1340	−0.4270	−0.5230
Year 6	12.36	16.05	17.26	−0.5432	−1.1194	−0.3610
Year 7	7.18	5.24	12.03	0.4517	1.0424	0.1416
Year 8	11.28	14.86	13.86	1.2263	0.0613	−0.0065
Year 9	38.35	15.8	13.77	0.6749	0.9729	−0.0912
Year 10	75.51	41.8	12.57			

WEB file

StockReturns

Year	Information Technology S&P Return
1	28.54%
2	78.14
3	78.74
4	−40.90
5	−25.87
6	−37.41
7	48.40
8	2.56
9	0.99

23. Most investors are happy when their returns are "above average," but not so happy when they are "below average." In the Markowitz portfolio optimization model in Problem 18, the objective function is to minimize variance, which is given by

$$\text{Min } \frac{1}{5}\sum_{s=1}^{5}(R_s - \overline{R})^2$$

where R_s is the portfolio return under scenario s and $\overline{R}$ is the expected or average return of the portfolio.

With this objective function, we are choosing a portfolio that minimizes deviations both above and below the average, $\overline{R}$. However, most investors are happy when $R_s > \overline{R}$, but unhappy when $R_s < \overline{R}$. With this preference in mind, an alternative to the variance measure in the objective function for the Markowitz model is the semivariance. The semivariance is calculated by only considering deviations below $\overline{R}$.

Let $D_{sp} - D_{sn} = R_s - \overline{R}$ and restrict D_{sp} and D_{sn} to be nonnegative. Then D_{sp} measures the positive deviation from the mean return in scenario s (i.e., $D_{sp} = R_s - \overline{R}$ when $R_s > \overline{R}$). In the case where the scenario return is below the average return, $R_s < \overline{R}$, we have $-D_{sn} = R_s - \overline{R}$. Using these new variables, we can reformulate the Markowitz model to only minimize the square of negative deviations below the average return. By doing so, we will use the semivariance rather than the variance in the objective function.

Reformulate the Markowitz portfolio optimization model given in Problem 18 to use semivariance in the objective function. Solve the model using either Excel Solver or LINGO. (*Hint*: When using Excel Solver, assume $\frac{1}{6}$ of the portfolio is allocated to each mutual fund for a starting solution.)

24. A second version of the Markowitz portfolio model maximizes expected return subject to a constraint that the variance of the portfolio must be less than or equal to some specified amount. Consider again the Hauck Financial Service data given in Table 12.4.

Mutual Fund	Annual Return (%)				
	Year 1	Year 2	Year 3	Year 4	Year 5
Foreign Stock	10.06	13.12	13.47	45.42	−21.93
Intermediate-Term Bond	17.64	3.25	7.51	−1.33	7.36
Large-Cap Growth	32.41	18.71	33.28	41.46	−23.26
Large-Cap Value	32.36	20.61	12.93	7.06	−5.37
Small-Cap Growth	33.44	19.40	3.85	58.68	−9.02
Small-Cap Value	24.56	25.32	−6.70	5.43	17.31

a. Construct this version of the Markowitz model for a maximum variance of 30.
b. Solve the model developed in part (a).

25 Refer to Problem 24. Use the model developed for Problem 24 to solve a series of models by varying the maximum allowable variance from 20 to 60 in increments of 5 and solving for the maximum return for each (solve a total of nine models). A graph of maximum return versus allowable maximum variance is called the *efficient frontier*. Based on the nine models you solved, plot the efficient frontier. Comment on the shape of the efficient frontier.

26. The port of Lajitas has three loading docks. The distance (in meters) among the loading docks is given in the following table:

	1	2	3
1	0	100	150
2	100	0	50
3	150	50	0

Three tankers currently at sea are coming into Lajitas. It is necessary to assign a dock for each tanker. Also, only one tanker can anchor in a given dock. Currently, ships 2 and 3 are empty and have no cargo. However, ship 1 has cargo that must be loaded onto the other two ships. The number of tons that must be transferred is as follows:

To		1	2	3
From	1	0	60	80

Formulate and solve with Excel Solver or LINGO an optimization problem that will assign ships to docks so that the product of tonnage moved times distance is minimized. (*Hints*: This problem is an extension of the assignment problem introduced in Chapter 10. Also, be careful with the objective function. Only include the nonzero terms. Each of the 12 nonzero terms in the objective function is a quadratic term, or the product of two variables.) There are 12 nonzero terms in the objective function.

27. Andalus Furniture Company has two manufacturing plants, one at Aynor and another at Spartanburg. The cost in dollars of producing a kitchen chair at each of the two plants is given here.

$$\text{Aynor: Cost} = 75Q_1 + 5Q_1^2 + 100$$
$$\text{Spartanburg: Cost} = 25Q_2 + 2.5Q_2^2 + 150$$

where

Q_1 = number of chairs produced at Aynor
Q_2 = number of chairs produced at Spartanburg

Andalus needs to manufacture a total of 40 kitchen chairs to meet an order just received. How many chairs should be made at Aynor and how many should be made at Spartanburg in order to minimize total production cost?

28. Larosa Job Shop is studying where to locate its tool bin facility on the shop floor. There are five production cells (fabrication, paint, subassembly 1, subassembly 2, and assembly) at fixed locations. The following table contains the cell locations, expressed as x and y coordinates on a shop floor grid, as well as the daily demand for tools (measured in number of trips to the tool bin) at each production cell.

| | Location | | |
Cell	x Coordinate	y Coordinate	Demand
Fabrication	1	4	12
Paint	1	2	24
Subassembly 1	2.5	2	13
Subassembly 2	3	5	7
Assembly	4	4	17

One way to solve this problem is to find the tool bin location that minimizes the sum of the distances from each production cell to the tool bin location. There are a number of ways to measure distance, but Larosa has decided to use Euclidean (straight-line) distance. The Euclidean distance between two points (x, y) and (a, b) is

$$\sqrt{(x - a)^2 + (y - b)^2}$$

However, considering only distance ignores that fact that some production cells make more trips for tools than others. An approach that takes into account that some cell locations use more tools than others is to minimize the sum of the *weighted distances* from each station to the tool bin, where the weights are the demand from each production cell.

a. Develop a model that will find the optimal tool bin location for Larosa, where the objective is to minimize the sum of the distances from the tool bin to the production cell locations (ignoring the demand). Solve your model for the optimal location.

b. Update your model to find the tool bin location that minimizes the sum of the demand-weighted distances form the tool bin to the production cell locations. Solve your model for the optimal location.

c. Compare the results from parts (a) and (b). Explain the differences in the solutions.

29. TN Communications provides cellular telephone services. The company is planning to expand into the Cincinnati area and is trying to determine the best location for its transmission tower. The tower transmits over a radius of 10 miles. The locations that must be reached by this tower are shown in the following figure.

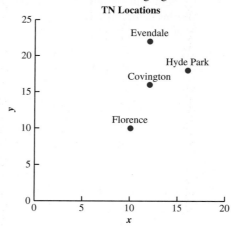
TN Locations

	x	y
Florence	10	10
Covingtokn	12	16
Hyde Park	16	18
Evendale	12	22

    a.   Formulate and solve a model that provides the new tower's location that reaches each of these cities and minimizes the sum of the distances to all locations from the new tower.

    b.   Formulate and solve a model that finds the location of the new tower that reaches every city and minimizes the maximum distance from the transmission tower location to the city locations.

WEB file

Wedding

30.   The distance between two cities in the United States can be approximated by the following formula, where lat_1 and $long_1$ are the latitude and longitude of city 1 and lat_2 and $long_2$ are the latitude and longitude of city 2:

$$69\sqrt{(lat_1 - lat_2)^2 + (long_1 - long_2)^2}$$

Ted's daughter is getting married, and he is inviting relatives from 15 different locations in the United States. The file Wedding gives the longitude, latitude, and number of relatives in each of the 15 locations. Ted would like to find the location to hold the wedding that minimizes the demand-weighted distance, where demand is the number of relatives at each location. Formulate and solve a model for Ted's location problem.

Case Problem   CAFE Compliance in the Auto Industry

This case is based on the Q.M. in Action, Pricing for Environmental Compliance in the Auto Industry. In this case we build a model similar to the one built for General Motors. The CAFE requirement on fleet miles per gallon is based on an average. The harmonic average is used to calculate the CAFE requirement on average miles per gallon.

In order to understand the harmonic average, assume that there is a passenger car and a light truck. The passenger car gets 30 miles per gallon (MPG) and the light truck gets 20 miles per gallon (MPG). Assume each vehicle is driven exactly one mile. Then the passenger car consumes $1/30$ gallon of gasoline in driving one mile and the light truck consumes $1/20$ gallon of gasoline in driving one mile. The amount of gasoline consumed in total is

$$\text{Gas consumption} = (1/30) + (1/20) = (5/60) = (1/12) \text{ gallon}$$

The average MPG of the two vehicles calculated the "normal way" is $(30 + 20)/2 = 25$ MPG. If both vehicles are "average," and each vehicle is driven exactly one mile, then the total gasoline consumption is

$$\text{Gas consumption} = (1/25) + (1/25) = (2/25) \text{ gallon}$$

Because $(2/25)$ is not equal to $(5/60)$, the total gas consumption of two "average vehicles" driving exactly one mile is not equal to the total gas consumption of each of the original vehicles driving exactly one mile. This is unfortunate. In order to make it easy for the government to impose and enforce MPG constraints on the auto companies, it would be nice to have a single target value MPG that every company in the auto industry must meet. As just illustrated, there is a problem with requiring an average MPG on the industry because it will incorrectly estimate the gas mileage consumption of the fleet. Fortunately, there is a statistic called the harmonic average so that total gas consumption by harmonic average vehicles is equal to gas consumption of the actual vehicles.

For simplicity, first assume that there are two types of vehicles in the fleet, passenger cars and light trucks. If there is one passenger car getting 30 miles per gallon and there is one light truck getting 20 miles per gallon, the harmonic average of these two vehicles is

$$\frac{2}{\dfrac{1}{30} + \dfrac{1}{20}} = \frac{2}{\dfrac{5}{60}} = \frac{120}{5} = 24$$

If each vehicle were to drive exactly one mile, each vehicle would consume $1/24$ gallon of gasoline for a total of $2/24 = 1/12$ gallon of gasoline. In this case each "average" vehicle driving exactly one mile results in total gas consumption equal to the total gas consumption of each vehicle with a different MPG rating driving exactly one mile.

If there are three passenger vehicles and two light trucks, the harmonic average is given by

$$\frac{5}{\dfrac{3}{30} + \dfrac{2}{20}} = \frac{5}{0.1 + 0.1} = \frac{5}{0.2} = 25$$

In general, when calculating the harmonic average, the numerator is the total number of vehicles. The denominator is the sum of two terms. Each term is the ratio of the number of vehicles in that class to the MPG of cars in that class. For example, the first ratio in the denominator is $3/30$ because there are 3 cars (the numerator) each getting 30 MPG (the denominator). These calculations are illustrated in Figure 12.17.

Based on Figure 12.17, if each of the five cars is average and drives exactly one mile, $(5/25) = (1/5)$ gallon of gas is consumed. If three cars getting 30 MPG drive exactly one mile each and two cars getting 20 MPG drive exactly one mile, then $(3/30) + (2/20) = (2/10) = (1/5)$ gallon is consumed. Thus the average cars exactly duplicate the gas consumption of the fleet with varying MPG.

Now assume that the demand function for passenger cars is

$$\text{Demand} = 750 - P_C \tag{12.8}$$

FIGURE 12.17   EXCEL SPREADSHEET WITH A CAFE CALCULATION

	A	B	C	D	E
1			**Number**		
2		**MPG**	**Of Vehicles**	**Café Weight**	
3	**Passenger Cars**	30	3	0.1000	
4	**Light Trucks**	20	2	0.1000	
5			5	0.2000	
6					
7	**Café Average**	25			
8					
9					

where P_C is the price of a passenger car. Similarly, the demand function for light trucks is

$$\text{Demand} = 830 - P_T \qquad \textbf{(12.9)}$$

where P_T is the price of a light truck.

Managerial Report

1. Using the formulas given in equations (12.8) and (12.9), develop an expression for the total profit contribution as a function of the price of cars and the price of light trucks. Assume the marginal cost for passenger cars is 15 and the marginal cost for light trucks is 17.
2. Using Excel Solver or LINGO, find the price for each car so that the total profit contribution is maximized.
3. Given the prices determined in Question 2, calculate the number of passenger cars sold and the number of light trucks sold.
4. Duplicate the spreadsheet in Figure 12.17. Your spreadsheet should have formulas in cells D3:D5 and B7 and be able to calculate the harmonic (CAFE) average for any MPG rating and any number of vehicles in each category.
5. Again, assuming that passenger cars get 30 MPG and light trucks get 20 MPG, calculate the CAFE average for the fleet size from Question 3.
6. If you do the calculation in Question 5 correctly, the CAFE average of the fleet is 23.57. Add a constraint that the fleet average must be 25 MPG and re-solve the model to get the maximum total profit contribution subject to meeting the CAFE constraint.

Appendix 12.1 Solving Nonlinear Problems with LINGO

Solving a nonlinear optimization problem in LINGO is no different from solving a linear optimization problem in LINGO. Simply type in the formulation, select the **LINGO** menu, and choose the **Solve** option. Just remember that LINGO uses the ^ sign for exponentiation and the / sign for division. Also note that an asterisk (*) must be used to indicate multiplication.

We show how the unconstrained RMC problem from Section 12.4 is solved using LINGO. After starting LINGO, we type in the problem formulation in the model window as follows:

```
MAX = F*(290 − F/2) − 250*F + S*(336 − S/2.5) − 300*S;
```

Appendix 7.2 shows how to use LINGO to solve linear programs.

To solve the problem, select the **Solve** command from the **LINGO** menu, or press the **Solve** button on the toolbar. Note that the value of the objective function is 1610.00, $F = 40$, and $S = 45$.

Now solve the constrained RMC problem from Section 12.4 using LINGO. The only difference from the unconstrained problem is that three lines must be added to the formulation to account for the constraints. After starting LINGO, we type in the problem formulation in the model window as follows:

```
! MAXIMIZE PROFIT;
MAX = F*(290 − F/2) − 250*F + S*(336 − S/2.5) − 300*S;
!MATERIAL 1 CONSTRAINT;
```

```
0.4*F  +  .5*S  <  20;
!MATERIAL 2 CONSTRAINT;
 .2*S  <  5;
!MATERIAL 3 CONSTRAINT;
0.6*F  +  .3*S  <  21;
```

Note that at the end of the objective function and each constraint, a semicolon is used.

After selecting the **Solve** command from the **LINGO** menu, the solution shown in Figure 12.18 is obtained. The first line shows that a local optimal solution has been found. This local optimum is also a global optimum (see the next paragraph). The optimal value of the objective function is $1247.83. The Variable section shows that the optimal solution is to produce 24.33862 tons of fuel additive and 20.5291 tons of solvent base. In the Row section, row 1 corresponds to the objective function and rows 2 through 4 correspond to the three material tonnage constraints. In the Slack/Surplus column, the value of 0 in row 2 indicates that the optimal solution uses all of Material 1 that is available; but the nonzero value in rows 3 and 4 indicate that there is excess tonnage of Material 2 and Material 3. Note that rather than the shadow price discussed in Chapter 8, LINGO reports a dual price for each constraint. For a maximization problem, the dual price is the shadow price for that constraint. For a minimization problem, the dual price is the negative of the shadow price.

We have discussed the concept of global versus local optimum. By default, LINGO finds a local optimum and the global solver is turned off. In order to turn on the global solver, select **Options** from the **LINGO** menu. When the Options dialog box appears, select the **Global Solver** tab and check the **Use Global Solver** box. By executing LINGO's Global Solver on the RMC problem, we can confirm that the local optimum in Figure 12.18 is indeed a global optimum.

The demo at the LINGO link on the website accompanying this text allows only five variables for problems that use the global solver.

In the RMC problem, all the variables are constrained to be nonnegative. If some of the variables may assume negative values, extra lines must be added to the LINGO formulation and the @FREE command must be used. For instance, the Hauck index fund model shown in Section 12.4 does not have nonnegativity constraints for variables $R1$, $R2$, $R3$, $R4$, and $R5$ because these variables are allowed to assume negative values. Thus, after entering the objective function and constraints, the following five lines must be added to the LINGO model to solve the problem:

$$@FREE(R1);$$
$$@FREE(R2);$$
$$@FREE(R3);$$
$$@FREE(R4);$$
$$@FREE(R5);$$

LINGO also provides the user with a wide variety of nonlinear functions that are useful in finance, inventory management, statistics, and other applications. To get a list of these functions, use the online LINGO User's Manual, which is available under the Help menu. In the User's Manual you will find a chapter entitled LINGO's Operators and Functions. This chapter contains a list of the available functions. When using a LINGO function you must precede the function name with the @ sign. For example, if you wanted to take the natural logarithm of X you would write @LOG(X).

FIGURE 12.18   LINGO SOLUTION FOR THE NONLINEAR RMC PROBLEM

```
Global optimal solution found.
Objective value:                    1247.831
Infeasibilities:                    0.000000
Total solver interations:                  7
Elapsed runtime seconds:                0.06
Model is convex quadratic

Model Class:                             QP

Total variables:            2
Nonlinear variables:        2
Integer variables:          0

Total constraints:          4
Nonlinear constraints:      1

Total nonzeros:             7
Nonlinear Nonlinear:        2


        Variable              Value            Reduced Cost
           F               24.33862           0.3576298E-08
           S               20.52910           0.4246891E-08


          Row          Slack or Surplus        Dual Price
           1             1247.831              1.000000
           2             0.2222080E-08         39.15344
           3             0.8941799             0.9715576E-07
           4             0.2380953             0.5061981E-06
```

When using LINGO one must exercise care in how the minus sign is used. When used in an expression such as $y - x^2$, the minus sign is a binary operator because it connects two terms, y and x^2. By convention, exponentiation has higher "precedence" than the minus; so if $y = 2$ and $x = -1$, the expression $y - x^2$ evaluates to

$$y - x^2 = 2 - (-1)^2 = 2 - 1 = 1$$

However, in the expression $-x^2 + y$, the minus sign is a unary operator because it does not combine terms. LINGO, by default, assigns the unary minus sign higher precedence than exponentiation. Thus, if $y = 2$ and $x = -1$, the expression $-x^2 + y$ evaluates to

$$-x^2 + y = (-x)^2 + y = 1^2 + 2 = 3$$

This is a potential source of confusion. Excel also treats the unary minus sign in this fashion. In this text we, like many authors, expect $-x^2$ to be interpreted as $-(x^2)$, not $(-x)^2$.

Appendix 12.2   Solving Nonlinear Problems with Excel Solver

Excel Solver can be used for nonlinear optimization. The Excel formulation of the non-linear version of the RMC problem developed in Section 12.4 is shown in Figure 12.19. A worksheet model is constructed just as in the linear case. The formula in cell B17 is the objective function. The formulas in cells B20:B22 are the left-hand sides of constraint inequalities. And the formulas in cells D20:D22 provide the right-hand sides for the con-straint inequalities.

Note how the nonlinearity comes into the model. The formula in cell B17, the objective function cell, is

$$=40*B15 - 0.5*B15*B15 + 36*C15 - 0.4*C15*C15$$

In the preceding formula, cell B15 holds the value for the number of tons of fuel additive and C15 holds the value for the number of tons of solvent base. Thus, the objective func-tion cell is a nonlinear function of the decision variables, and Excel Solver cannot solve the model using the standard LP Simplex Solver engine.

However, this is not a problem. Three possible **Solver Methods** are available. One method is Standard LP Simplex and is the option we have used so far in the book for solving linear and linear integer programming problems. If you use this method on the nonlinear version of the RMC problem, you will get the error message: "The linearity conditions required by this LP Solver are not satisfied." This message is not surprising because the objective function is a nonlinear function of the variable cells.

Another solver engine is GRG Nonlinear. For this version of the RMC problem, you should select the **GRG Nonlinear** solver in the Solver Parameters Box. The GRG Nonlinear solver method is based on the (Generalized Reduced Gradient) GRG Nonlinear algorithm,

FIGURE 12.19   EXCEL SPREADSHEET MODEL FOR THE MODIFIED RMC PROBLEM

	A	B	C	D
4	**Material**	**Fuel Additive**	**Solvent Base**	**Amount Available**
5	Material 1	0.4	0.5	20
6	Material 2		0.2	5
7	Material 3	0.6	0.3	21
8	**Profit Per Ton**	40	30	
9				
10				
11	**Model**			
12				
13		**Decision Variables**		
14		**Fuel Additive**	**Solvent Base**	
15	**Tons Produced**	24.3386243386243	20.5291005291005	
16				
17	**Maximize Total Profit**	=40*B15 - 0.5*B15*B15 +36*C15 - 0.4*C15*C15		
18				
19	**Constraints**	**Amount Used (LHS)**		**Amount Available (RHS)**
20	Material 1	=B5*B15+C5*C15	<=	=D5
21	Material 2	=B6*B15+C6*C15	<=	=D6
22	Material 3	=B7*B15+C7*C15	<=	=D7
23				
24				
25				

which uses a calculus tool called the gradient. The gradient essentially calculates a direction of improvement for the objective function based on the contour lines.

The last solver engine is the Evolutionary engine, and it is based on a class of solution techniques called genetic algorithms. These algorithms are designed for nonlinear problems that are nonsmooth. In Section 12.4 we pointed out that some classes of nonlinear problems are more difficult to solve than others. In general, smooth problems are easier to solve than nonsmooth problems. By nonsmooth, we mean the graph of the function may have discontinuities (holes) or may have sharp edges or angles (such as the absolute value function). Standard Excel functions such as ABS, IF, MAX, and MIN are examples of nonsmooth but useful functions.

If you solve a nonsmooth problem using the Evolutionary Solver, you may not find the optimal solution. This outcome often happens with genetic solution algorithms. It is often convenient and easy to develop models using functions such as IF, but you may pay a price and not find the optimal solution.

When using Excel, one must exercise care in how the minus sign is used. When used in a cell formula such as =A1-B1^2, the minus sign is a binary operator because it connects two terms, A1 and B1^2. By convention, exponentiation has higher "precedence" than the minus, so if cell A1 contains 2 and cell B1 contains -1, the expression =A1-B1^2 evaluates to

$$=A1\text{-}B1\verb|^|2=2\text{-}(\text{-}1)^2=2\text{-}1=1$$

However, in the expression -B1^2+A1, the minus sign is a unary operator because it does not combine terms. Excel, by default, assigns the unary minus sign higher precedence than exponentiation. Thus, if cell A1 contains 2 and cell B1 contains -1, the expression -B1^2-A1 evaluates to

$$\text{-}B1\verb|^|2+A1=(\text{-}B1)^2+A1=1^2+2=3$$

LINGO also treats the unary minus sign in this fashion. This is a potential source of confusion. In this text we, like many authors, expect $-x^2$ to be interpreted as $-(x^2)$, not $(-x)^2$.

CHAPTER 13

Project Scheduling: PERT/CPM

CONTENTS

In many situations managers are responsible for planning, scheduling, and controlling projects that consist of numerous separate jobs or tasks performed by a variety of departments and individuals. Often these projects are so large or complex that the manager cannot possibly remember all the information pertaining to the plan, schedule, and progress of the project. In these situations the **program evaluation and review technique (PERT)** and the **critical path method (CPM)** have proven to be extremely valuable.

PERT and CPM can be used to plan, schedule, and control a wide variety of projects. Common applications include:

1. Research and development of new products and processes
2. Construction of plants, buildings, and highways
3. Maintenance of large and complex equipment
4. Design and installation of new systems

Henry L. Gantt developed the Gantt Chart as a graphical aid to scheduling jobs on machines. This application was the first of what has become known as project scheduling techniques.

In these types of projects, project managers must schedule and coordinate the various jobs or **activities** so that the entire project is completed on time. A complicating factor in carrying out this task is the interdependence of the activities; for example, some activities depend on the completion of other activities before they can be started. Because projects may comprise as many as several thousand activities, project managers look for procedures that will help them answer questions such as the following:

1. What is the total time to complete the project?
2. What are the scheduled start and finish dates for each specific activity?
3. Which activities are "critical" and must be completed *exactly* as scheduled to keep the project on schedule?
4. How long can "noncritical" activities be delayed before they cause an increase in the total project completion time?

PERT and CPM can help answer these questions.

Although PERT and CPM have the same general purpose and utilize much of the same terminology, the techniques were developed independently. PERT was developed in the late 1950s by the Navy specifically for the Polaris missile project. Many activities associated with this project had never been attempted previously, so PERT was developed to handle uncertain activity times. CPM was developed originally by DuPont and Remington Rand primarily for industrial projects for which activity times were certain and variability was not a concern. CPM offered the option of reducing activity times by adding more workers and/or resources, usually at an increased cost. Thus, a distinguishing feature of CPM was that it identified trade-offs between time and cost for various project activities.

Today's computerized versions of PERT and CPM combine the best features of both approaches. Thus, the distinction between the two techniques is no longer necessary. As a result, we refer to the project scheduling procedures covered in this chapter as PERT/CPM. We begin the discussion of PERT/CPM by considering a project for the expansion of the Western Hills Shopping Center. At the end of the section, we describe how the investment securities firm of Seasongood & Mayer used PERT/CPM to schedule a $31 million hospital revenue bond project.

(13.1) Project Scheduling Based on Expected Activity Times

The owner of the Western Hills Shopping Center plans to modernize and expand the current 32-business shopping center complex. The project is expected to provide room for 8 to 10 new businesses. Financing has been arranged through a private investor. All that remains is

TABLE 13.1   LIST OF ACTIVITIES FOR THE WESTERN HILLS SHOPPING CENTER PROJECT

Activity	Activity Description	Immediate Predecessor	Expected Activity Time
A	Prepare architectural drawings	—	5
B	Identify potential new tenants	—	6
C	Develop prospectus for tenants	A	4
D	Select contractor	A	3
E	Prepare building permits	A	1
F	Obtain approval for building permits	E	4
G	Perform construction	D, F	14
H	Finalize contracts with tenants	B, C	12
I	Tenants move in	G, H	2
		Total	51

The effort that goes into identifying activities, determining interrelationships among activities, and estimating activity times is crucial to the success of PERT/CPM. A substantial amount of time may be needed to complete this initial phase of the project scheduling process.

Immediate predecessor information determines whether activities can be completed in parallel (worked on simultaneously) or in series (one completed before another begins). Generally, a project with more series relationships will take longer to complete.

A project network is extremely helpful in visualizing the interrelationships among the activities. No rules guide the conversion of a list of activities and immediate predecessor information into a project network. The process of constructing a project network generally improves with practice and experience.

for the owner of the shopping center to plan, schedule, and complete the expansion project. Let us show how PERT/CPM can help.

The first step in the PERT/CPM scheduling process is to develop a list of the activities that make up the project. Table 13.1 shows the list of activities for the Western Hills Shopping Center expansion project. Nine activities are described and denoted A through I for later reference. Table 13.1 also shows the immediate predecessor(s) and the activity time (in weeks) for each activity. For a given activity, the **immediate predecessor** column identifies the activities that must be completed *immediately prior* to the start of that activity. Activities A and B do not have immediate predecessors and can be started as soon as the project begins; thus, a dash is written in the immediate predecessor column for these activities. The other entries in the immediate predecessor column show that activities C, D, and E cannot be started until activity A has been completed; activity F cannot be started until activity E has been completed; activity G cannot be started until both activities D and F have been completed; activity H cannot be started until both activities B and C have been completed; and, finally, activity I cannot be started until both activities G and H have been completed. The project is finished when activity I is completed.

The last column in Table 13.1 shows the expected number of weeks required to complete each activity. For example, activity A is expected to take 5 weeks, activity B is expected to take 6 weeks, and so on. The sum of expected activity times is 51. As a result, you may think that the total time required to complete the project is 51 weeks. However, as we show, two or more activities often may be scheduled concurrently (assuming sufficient availability of other required resources, such as labor and equipment), thus shortening the completion time for the project. Ultimately, PERT/CPM will provide a detailed activity schedule for completing the project in the shortest time possible.

Using the immediate predecessor information in Table 13.1, we can construct a graphical representation of the project, or the **project network**. Figure 13.1 depicts the project network for Western Hills Shopping Center. The activities correspond to the *nodes* of the network (drawn as rectangles), and the *arcs* (the lines with arrows) show the precedence relationships among the activities. In addition, nodes have been added to the network to denote the start and the finish of the project. A project network will help a manager visualize the activity relationships and provide a basis for carrying out the PERT/CPM computations.

FIGURE 13.1   PROJECT NETWORK FOR THE WESTERN HILLS SHOPPING CENTER

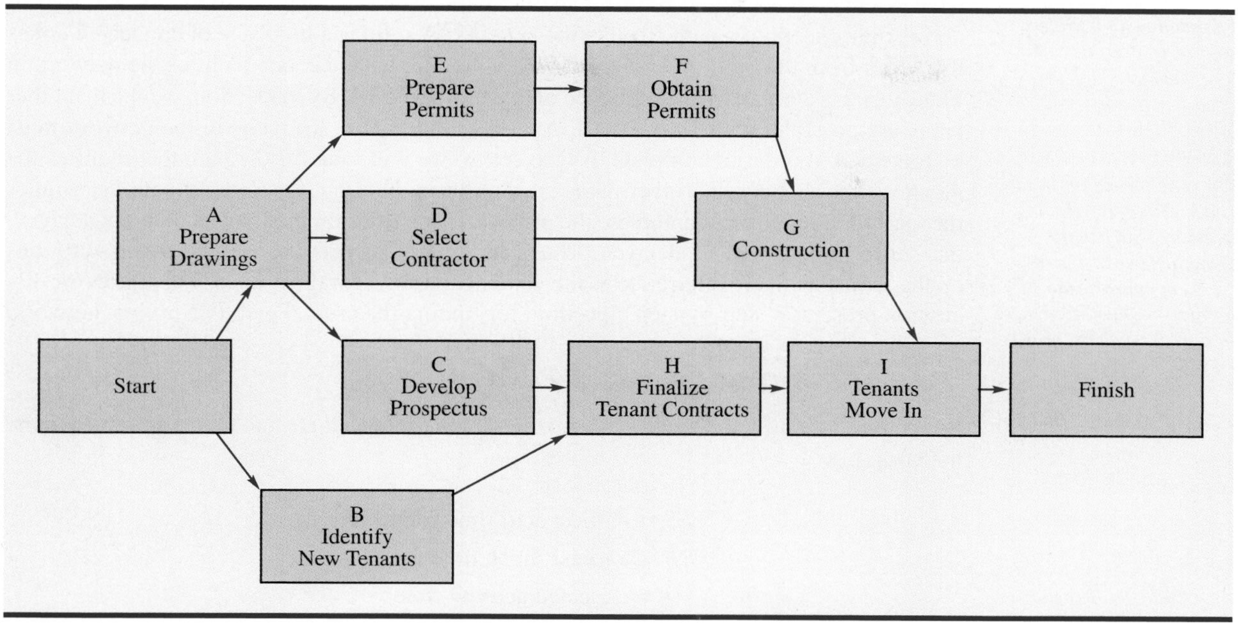

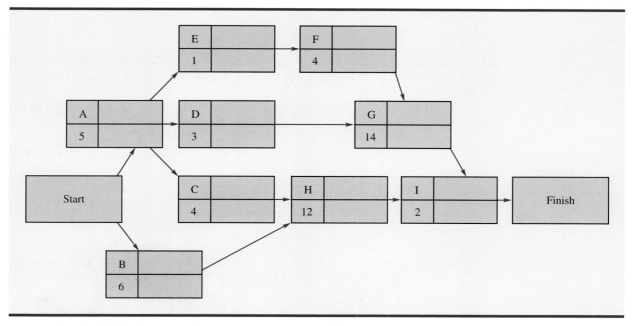

FIGURE 13.2   WESTERN HILLS SHOPPING CENTER PROJECT NETWORK WITH ACTIVITY TIMES

The Concept of a Critical Path

To facilitate the PERT/CPM computations, we modified the project network as shown in Figure 13.2. Note that the upper left-hand corner of each node contains the corresponding activity letter. The activity time appears immediately below the letter.

Problem 3 provides the immediate predecessor information for a project with seven activities and asks you to develop the project network.

For convenience, we use the convention of referencing activities with letters. Generally, we assign the letters in approximate order as we move from left to right through the project network.

To determine the project completion time, we have to analyze the network and identify what is called the **critical path** for the network. However, before doing so, we need to define the concept of a path through the network. A **path** is a sequence of connected nodes that leads from the Start node to the Finish node. For instance, one path for the network in Figure 13.2 is defined by the sequence of nodes A-E-F-G-I. By inspection, we see that other paths are possible, such as A-D-G-I, A-C-H-I, and B-H-I. All paths in the network must be traversed in order to complete the project, so we will look for the path that requires the greatest time. Because all other paths are shorter in duration, this *longest* path determines the total time required to complete the project. If activities on the longest path are delayed, the entire project will be delayed. Thus, the longest path is the *critical path*. Activities on the critical path are referred to as the **critical activities** for the project. The following discussion presents a step-by-step algorithm for finding the critical path in a project network.

Determining the Critical Path

We begin by finding the **earliest start time** and the **latest start time** for all activities in the network. Let

$$ES = \text{earliest start time for an activity}$$
$$EF = \text{earliest finish time for an activity}$$
$$t = \text{expected activity time}$$

The **earliest finish time** for any activity is

$$EF = ES + t \qquad\qquad \textbf{(13.1)}$$

Activity A can start as soon as the project starts, so we set the earliest start time for activity A equal to 0. With an expected activity time of 5 weeks, the earliest finish time for activity A is $EF = ES + t = 0 + 5 = 5$.

We will write the earliest start and earliest finish times in the node to the right of the activity letter. Using activity A as an example, we have

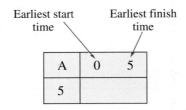

Because an activity cannot be started until *all* immediately preceding activities have been finished, the following rule can be used to determine the earliest start time for each activity:

The earliest start time for an activity is equal to the *largest* (i.e., *latest*) of the earliest finish times for all its immediate predecessors.

Let us apply the earliest start time rule to the portion of the network involving nodes A, B, C, and H, as shown in Figure 13.3. With an earliest start time of 0 and an activity time of 6 for activity B, we show $ES = 0$ and $EF = ES + t = 0 + 6 = 6$ in the node for activity B.

FIGURE 13.3   A PORTION OF THE WESTERN HILLS SHOPPING CENTER PROJECT NETWORK, SHOWING ACTIVITIES A, B, C, AND H

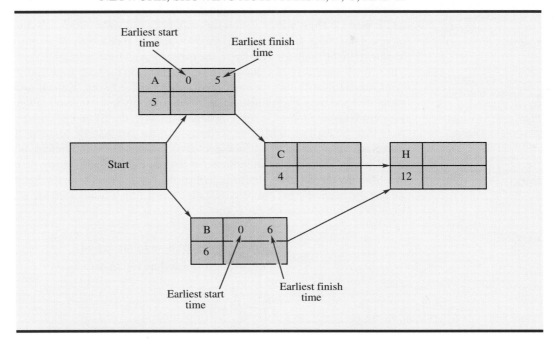

FIGURE 13.4   DETERMINING THE EARLIEST START TIME FOR ACTIVITY H

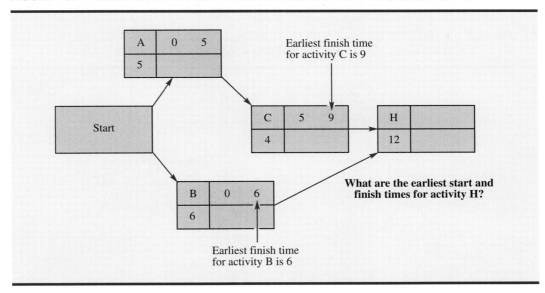

Looking at node C, we note that activity A is the only immediate predecessor for activity C. The earliest finish time for activity A is 5, so the earliest start time for activity C must be $ES = 5$. Thus, with an activity time of 4, the earliest finish time for activity C is $EF = ES + t = 5 + 4 = 9$. Both the earliest start time and the earliest finish time can be shown in the node for activity C (see Figure 13.4).

Determining the expected completion time of a project via critical path calculations implicitly assumes that sufficient resources (labor, equipment, supplies, etc.) are available to execute activities in parallel. If the resources available are insufficient to support the schedule generated by PERT/CPM, then more advanced techniques such as an integer linear programming model (Chapter 11) can be applied.

Continuing with Figure 13.4, we move on to activity H and apply the earliest start time rule for this activity. With both activities B and C as immediate predecessors, the earliest start time for activity H must be equal to the largest of the earliest finish times for activities B and C. Thus, with $EF = 6$ for activity B and $EF = 9$ for activity C, we select the largest value, 9, as the earliest start time for activity H ($ES = 9$). With an activity time of 12 as shown in the node for activity H, the earliest finish time is $EF = ES + t = 9 + 12 = 21$. The $ES = 9$ and $EF = 21$ values can now be entered in the node for activity H in Figure 13.4.

Continuing with this **forward pass** through the network, we can establish the earliest start times and the earliest finish times for each activity in the network. Figure 13.5 shows the Western Hills Shopping Center project network with the *ES* and *EF* values for each activity. Note that the earliest finish time for activity I, the last activity in the project, is 26 weeks. Therefore, we now know that the expected completion time for the entire project is 26 weeks.

We now continue the algorithm for finding the critical path by making a **backward pass** through the network. Because the expected completion time for the entire project is 26 weeks, we begin the backward pass with a **latest finish time** of 26 for activity I. Once the latest finish time for an activity is known, the *latest start time* for an activity can be computed as follows. Let

$$LS = \text{latest start time for an activity}$$

$$LF = \text{latest finish time for an activity}$$

Then

$$LS = LF - t \tag{13.2}$$

Beginning the backward pass with activity I, we know that the latest finish time is $LF = 26$ and that the activity time is $t = 2$. Thus, the latest start time for activity I is

FIGURE 13.5   WESTERN HILLS SHOPPING CENTER PROJECT NETWORK WITH EARLIEST START AND EARLIEST FINISH TIMES SHOWN FOR ALL ACTIVITIES

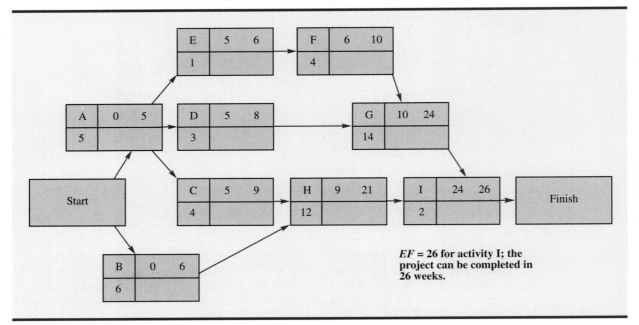

$LS = LF - t = 26 - 2 = 24$. We will write the LS and LF values in the node directly below the earliest start (ES) and earliest finish (EF) times. Thus, for node I, we have

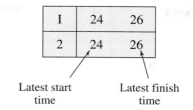

Latest start   Latest finish
time   time

The following rule can be used to determine the latest finish time for each activity in the network:

> The latest finish time for an activity is the smallest (i.e., earliest) of the latest start times for all activities that immediately follow the activity.

Logically, this rule states that the latest time an activity can be finished equals the earliest (smallest) value for the latest start time of following activities. Figure 13.6 shows the complete project network with the LS and LF backward pass results. We can use the latest finish time rule to verify the LS and LF values shown for activity H. The latest finish time for activity H must be the latest start time for activity I. Thus, we set $LF = 24$ for activity H. Using equation (13.2), we find that $LS = LF - t = 24 - 12 = 12$ as the latest start time for activity H. These values are shown in the node for activity H in Figure 13.6.

FIGURE 13.6 WESTERN HILLS SHOPPING CENTER PROJECT NETWORK WITH LATEST START AND LATEST FINISH TIMES SHOWN IN EACH NODE

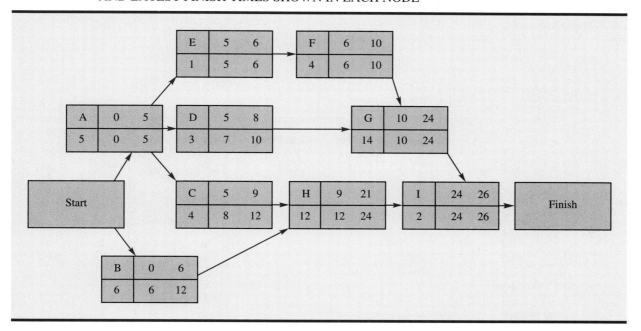

Activity A requires a more involved application of the latest start time rule. First, note that three activities (C, D, and E) immediately follow activity A. Figure 13.6 shows that the latest start times for activities C, D, and E are $LS = 8$, $LS = 7$, and $LS = 5$, respectively. The latest finish time rule for activity A states that the LF for activity A is the smallest of the latest start times for activities C, D, and E. With the smallest value being 5 for activity E, we set the latest finish time for activity A to $LF = 5$. Verify this result and the other latest start times and latest finish times shown in the nodes in Figure 13.6.

After we complete the forward and backward passes, we can determine the amount of slack associated with each activity. **Slack** is the length of time an activity can be delayed without increasing the project completion time. The amount of slack for an activity is computed as follows:

$$\text{Slack} = LS - ES = LF - EF \qquad \textbf{(13.3)}$$

One of the primary contributions of PERT/CPM is the identification of the critical activities. The project manager will want to monitor critical activities closely because a delay in any one of these activities will lengthen the project completion time.

For example, the slack associated with activity C is $LS - ES = 8 - 5 = 3$ weeks. Hence, activity C can be delayed up to 3 weeks, and the entire project can still be completed in 26 weeks. In this sense, activity C is not critical to the completion of the entire project in 26 weeks. Next, we consider activity E. Using the information in Figure 13.6, we find that the slack is $LS - ES = 5 - 5 = 0$. Thus, activity E has zero, or no, slack. Consequently, this activity cannot be delayed without increasing the completion time for the entire project. In other words, completing activity E exactly as scheduled is critical in terms of keeping the project on schedule, and so activity E is a critical activity. In general, the *critical activities* are the activities with zero slack.

The critical path algorithm is essentially a longest path algorithm. From the start node to the finish node, the critical path identifies the path that requires the most time.

The start and finish times shown in Figure 13.6 can be used to develop a detailed start time and finish time schedule for all activities. Putting this information in tabular form provides the activity schedule shown in Table 13.2. Note that the slack column shows that activities A, E, F, G, and I have zero slack. Hence, these activities are the critical activities for the project; the path formed by nodes A-E-F-G-I is the *critical path* in the Western Hills Shopping Center project network. The detailed schedule shown in Table 13.2 indicates the slack or delay that can be tolerated for the noncritical activities before these activities will increase project completion time.

TABLE 13.2 ACTIVITY SCHEDULE FOR THE WESTERN HILLS SHOPPING CENTER PROJECT

Activity	Earliest Start (ES)	Latest Start (LS)	Earliest Finish (EF)	Latest Finish (LF)	Slack (LS − ES)	Critical Path?
A	0	0	5	5	0	Yes
B	0	6	6	12	6	
C	5	8	9	12	3	
D	5	7	8	10	2	
E	5	5	6	6	0	Yes
F	6	6	10	10	0	Yes
G	10	10	24	24	0	Yes
H	9	12	21	24	3	
I	24	24	26	26	0	Yes

Contributions of PERT/CPM

We previously stated that project managers look for procedures that will help answer important questions regarding the planning, scheduling, and controlling of projects. Let us reconsider these questions in light of the information that the critical path calculations have given us.

1. How long will the project take to complete?
   Answer: The project can be completed in 26 weeks if each activity is completed on schedule.
2. What are the scheduled start and completion times for each activity?
   Answer: The activity schedule (see Table 13.2) shows the earliest start, latest start, earliest finish, and latest finish times for each activity.
3. Which activities are critical and must be completed *exactly* as scheduled to keep the project on schedule?
   Answer: A, E, F, G, and I are the critical activities.
4. How long can noncritical activities be delayed before they cause an increase in the completion time for the project?
   Answer: The activity schedule (see Table 13.2) shows the slack associated with each activity.

Such information is valuable in managing any project. Although the effort required to develop the immediate predecessor relationships and the activity time estimates generally increases with the size of the project, the procedure and contribution of PERT/CPM to larger projects are identical to those shown for the shopping center expansion project. The Q.M. in Action, Hospital Revenue Bond at Seasongood & Mayer, describes a 23-activity project that introduced a $31 million hospital revenue bond. PERT/CPM was used to identify the critical activities, the expected project completion time of 29 weeks, and the activity start times and finish times necessary to keep the entire project on schedule.

Summary of the PERT/CPM Critical Path Procedure

Before leaving this section, let us summarize the PERT/CPM critical path procedure.

Step 1. Develop a list of the activities that make up the project.
Step 2. Determine the immediate predecessor(s) for each activity in the project.
Step 3. Estimate the expected completion time for each activity.
Step 4. Draw a project network depicting the activities and immediate predecessors listed in steps 1 and 2.
Step 5. Use the project network and the activity time estimates to determine the earliest start and the earliest finish time for each activity by making a forward pass through the network. The earliest finish time for the last activity in the project identifies the expected time required to complete the entire project.
Step 6. Use the expected project completion time identified in step 5 as the latest finish time for the last activity and make a backward pass through the network to identify the latest start and latest finish time for each activity.
Step 7. Use the difference between the latest start time and the earliest start time for each activity to determine the slack for each activity.
Step 8. Find the activities with zero slack; these are the critical activities.
Step 9. Use the information from steps 5 and 6 to develop the activity schedule for the project.

Q.M. *in* ACTION

HOSPITAL REVENUE BOND AT SEASONGOOD & MAYER

Seasongood & Mayer is an investment securities firm located in Cincinnati, Ohio. The firm engages in municipal financing, including the underwriting of new issues of municipal bonds, acting as a market maker for previously issued bonds, and performing other investment banking services.

Seasongood & Mayer provided the underwriting for a $31 million issue of hospital facilities revenue bonds for Providence Hospital in Hamilton County, Ohio. The project of underwriting this municipal bond issue began with activities such as drafting the legal documents, drafting a description of the existing hospital facilities, and completing a feasibility study. A total of 23 activities defined the project that would be completed when the hospital signed the construction contract and then made the bond proceeds available. The immediate predecessor relationships for the activities and the activity times were developed by a project management team.

PERT/CPM analysis of the project network identified the 10 critical path activities. The analysis also provided the expected completion time of 29 weeks, or approximately seven months. The activity schedule showed the start time and finish time for each activity and provided the information necessary to monitor the project and keep it on schedule. PERT/CPM was instrumental in helping Seasongood & Mayer obtain the financing for the project within the time specified in the construction bid.

NOTES AND COMMENTS

1. Software packages such as Microsoft Project perform the critical path calculations quickly and efficiently. Program inputs include the activities, their immediate predecessors, and expected activity times. The project manager can modify any aspect of the project and quickly determine how the modification affects the activity schedule and the expected time required to complete the project.

2. After analyzing a PERT/CPM network, if the project manager finds that the project completion time is unacceptable (i.e., the project is going to take too long), judgment about where and how to shorten the time of critical activities must be exercised. The manager can: (a) review the original PERT/CPM network to see whether any immediate predecessor relationships can be modified so that at least some of the critical path activities can be done simultaneously, and/or (b) consider adding resources to critical path activities in an attempt to shorten the critical path. In Section 13.3, we discuss the second course of action, referred to as *crashing*, and show how to use linear programming to identify the least-cost way to shorten the project completion time.

13.2 Project Scheduling Considering Uncertain Activity Times

In this section we consider the details of project scheduling for a problem involving new-product research and development. Because many of the activities in such a project have never been attempted by this organization, the project manager wants to account for uncertainties in the activity times. Let us show how project scheduling can be conducted with uncertain activity times.

The Daugherty Porta-Vac Project

The H. S. Daugherty Company has manufactured industrial vacuum cleaning systems for many years. Recently, a member of the company's new-product research team submitted a report suggesting that the company consider manufacturing a cordless vacuum cleaner. The

Accurate activity time estimates are important in the development of an activity schedule. When activity times are uncertain, the three time estimates— optimistic, most probable, and pessimistic—allow the project manager to take uncertainty into consideration in determining the critical path and the activity schedule. This approach was developed by the designers of PERT.

new product, referred to as Porta-Vac, could contribute to Daugherty's expansion into the household market. Management hopes that the Porta-Vac can be manufactured at a reasonable cost and that its portability and no-cord convenience will make it extremely attractive to potential consumers.

Daugherty's management wants to study the feasibility of manufacturing the Porta-Vac product. The feasibility study will provide a recommendation on the action to be taken. To complete this study, information must be obtained from the firm's research and development (R&D), product testing, manufacturing, cost estimating, and market research groups. How long will it take to complete this feasibility study? In the following discussion, we show how to answer this question and provide an activity schedule for the project.

Again, the first step in the project scheduling process is to identify all activities that make up the project and determine the immediate predecessor(s) for each activity. Table 13.3 shows this information for the Porta-Vac project.

The Porta-Vac project network is shown in Figure 13.7. Verify that the network does in fact maintain the immediate predecessor relationships shown in Table 13.3.

Uncertain Activity Times

Once we develop the project network, we will need information on the time required to complete each activity. This information is used in the calculating the total time required to complete the project and in the scheduling of specific activities. For repeat projects, such as construction and maintenance projects, managers may have the experience and historical data necessary to provide accurate activity time estimates. However, for new or unique projects, estimating the time for each activity may be quite difficult. In fact, in many cases activity times are uncertain and are best described by a range of possible values rather than by one specific time estimate. In these instances, the uncertain activity times are treated as random variables with associated probability distributions. As a result, probability statements will be provided about the ability to meet a specific project completion date.

To incorporate uncertain activity times into the analysis, we need to obtain three time estimates for each activity:

Optimistic time a = the minimum activity time if everything progresses ideally

Most probable time m = the most probable activity time under normal conditions

Pessimistic time b = the maximum activity time if substantial delays are encountered

TABLE 13.3   ACTIVITY LIST FOR THE PORTA-VAC PROJECT

Activity	Description	Immediate Predecessor
A	Develop product design	—
B	Plan market research	—
C	Prepare routing (manufacturing engineering)	A
D	Build prototype model	A
E	Prepare marketing brochure	A
F	Prepare cost estimates (industrial engineering)	C
G	Do preliminary product testing	D
H	Complete market survey	B, E
I	Prepare pricing and forecast report	H
J	Prepare final report	F, G, I

FIGURE 13.7   PORTA-VAC CORDLESS VACUUM CLEANER PROJECT NETWORK

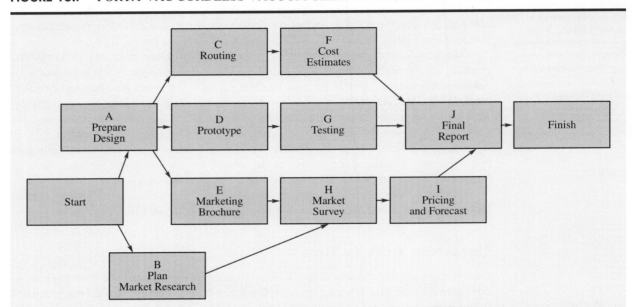

To illustrate the PERT/CPM procedure with uncertain activity times, let us consider the optimistic, most probable, and pessimistic time estimates for the Porta-Vac activities as presented in Table 13.4. Using activity A as an example, we see that the most probable time is 5 weeks, with a range from 4 weeks (optimistic) to 12 weeks (pessimistic). If the activity could be repeated a large number of times, what is the average time for the activity? This average or **expected time** (t) is as follows:

$$t = \frac{a + 4m + b}{6} \qquad \textbf{(13.4)}$$

TABLE 13.4   OPTIMISTIC, MOST PROBABLE, AND PESSIMISTIC ACTIVITY TIME ESTIMATES (IN WEEKS) FOR THE PORTA-VAC PROJECT

Activity	Optimistic (a)	Most Probable (m)	Pessimistic (b)
A	4	5	12
B	1	1.5	5
C	2	3	4
D	3	4	11
E	2	3	4
F	1.5	2	2.5
G	1.5	3	4.5
H	2.5	3.5	7.5
I	1.5	2	2.5
J	1	2	3

For activity A we have an average or expected time of

$$t_A = \frac{4 + 4(5) + 12}{6} = \frac{36}{6} = 6 \text{ weeks}$$

With uncertain activity times, we can use the *variance* to describe the dispersion or variation in the activity time values. The variance of the activity time is given by the formula[1]

$$\sigma^2 = \left(\frac{b - a}{6}\right)^2 \qquad \qquad \textbf{(13.5)}$$

The difference between the pessimistic (*b*) and optimistic (*a*) time estimates greatly affects the value of the variance. Large differences in these two values reflect a high degree of uncertainty in the activity time. Using equation (13.5), we obtain the measure of uncertainty—that is, the variance—of activity A, denoted σ_A^2:

$$\sigma_A^2 = \left(\frac{12 - 4}{6}\right)^2 = \left(\frac{8}{6}\right)^2 - 1.78$$

Equations (13.4) and (13.5) are based on the assumption that the activity time distribution can be described by a **beta probability distribution**.[2] With this assumption, the probability distribution for the time to complete activity A is as shown in Figure 13.8. Using equations (13.4) and (13.5) and the data in Table 13.4, we calculated the expected time and variance for each Porta-Vac activity; the results are summarized in Table 13.5. The Porta-Vac project network with expected activity times is shown in Figure 13.9.

FIGURE 13.8   ACTIVITY TIME DISTRIBUTION FOR PRODUCT DESIGN (ACTIVITY A)
FOR THE PORTA-VAC PROJECT

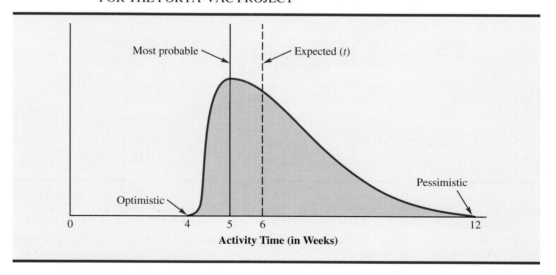

---

[1] The variance equation is based on the notion that a standard deviation is approximately $\frac{1}{6}$ of the difference between the extreme values of the distribution: $(b - a)/6$. The variance is the square of the standard deviation.

[2] The equations for *t* and σ^2 require additional assumptions about the parameters of the beta probability distribution. However, even when these additional assumptions are not made, the equations still provide good approximations of *t* and σ^2.

TABLE 13.5   EXPECTED TIMES AND VARIANCES FOR THE PORTA-VAC PROJECT ACTIVITIES

Activity	Expected Time (weeks)	Variance
A	6	1.78
B	2	0.44
C	3	0.11
D	5	1.78
E	3	0.11
F	2	0.03
G	3	0.25
H	4	0.69
I	2	0.03
J	2	0.11
	Total 32	

FIGURE 13.9   PORTA-VAC PROJECT NETWORK WITH EXPECTED ACTIVITY TIMES

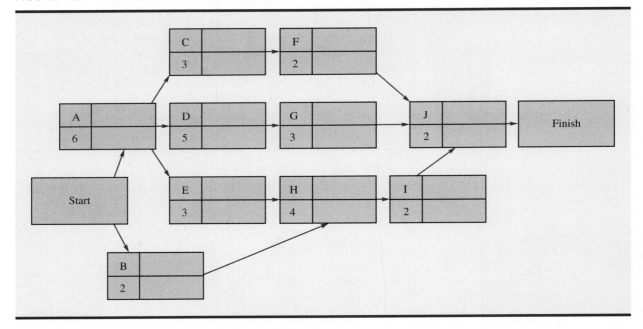

When uncertain activity times are considered, the actual time required to complete the project may differ from the expected time to complete the project provided by the critical path calculations. However, for planning purposes, the expected time provides valuable information to the project manager.

The Critical Path

When we have the project network and the expected activity times, we are ready to proceed with the critical path calculations necessary to determine the expected time required to complete the project and determine the activity schedule. In these calculations, we find the critical path for the Porta-Vac project by applying the critical path procedure introduced in Section 13.1 to the expected activity times (Table 13.5). After the critical activities and the expected time to complete the project have been determined, we analyze the effect of the activity time variability.

Proceeding with a forward pass through the network shown in Figure 13.9, we can establish the earliest start (*ES*) and earliest finish (*EF*) times for each activity. Figure 13.10 shows the project network with the *ES* and *EF* values. Note that the earliest finish time for activity J, the last activity, is 17 weeks. Thus, the expected completion time for the project is 17 weeks. Next, we make a backward pass through the network. The backward pass provides the latest start (*LS*) and latest finish (*LF*) times shown in Figure 13.11.

FIGURE 13.10   PORTA-VAC PROJECT NETWORK WITH EARLIEST START AND EARLIEST FINISH TIMES

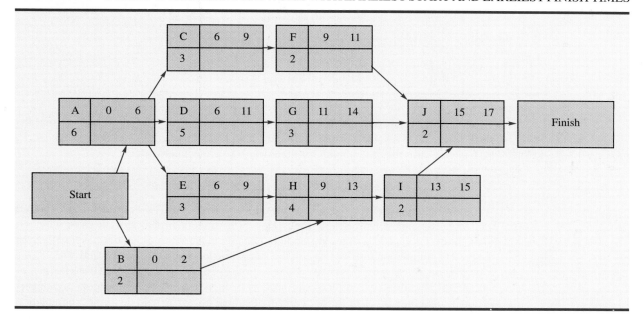

FIGURE 13.11   PORTA-VAC PROJECT NETWORK WITH LATEST START AND LATEST FINISH TIMES

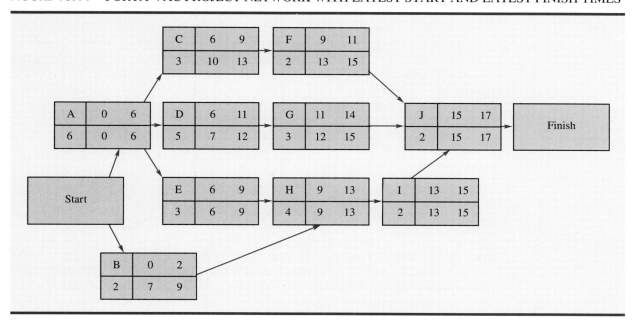

TABLE 13.6 ACTIVITY SCHEDULE FOR THE PORTA-VAC PROJECT

Activity	Earliest Start (ES)	Latest Start (LS)	Earliest Finish (EF)	Latest Finish (LF)	Slack (LS − ES)	Critical Path?
A	0	0	6	6	0	Yes
B	0	7	2	9	7	
C	6	10	9	13	4	
D	6	7	11	12	1	
E	6	6	9	9	0	Yes
F	9	13	11	15	4	
G	11	12	14	15	1	
H	9	9	13	13	0	Yes
I	13	13	15	15	0	Yes
J	15	15	17	17	0	Yes

The activity schedule for the Porta-Vac project is shown in Table 13.6. Note that the slack time (LS − ES) is also shown for each activity. The activities with zero slack (A, E, H, I, and J) form the critical path for the Porta-Vac project network.

Variability in Project Completion Time

We know that for the Porta-Vac project the critical path of A-E-H-I-J resulted in an expected total project completion time of 17 weeks. However, variation in activities can cause variation in the project completion time. Variation in noncritical activities ordinarily has no effect on the project completion time because of the slack time associated with these activities. However, if a noncritical activity is delayed long enough to expend its slack time, it becomes part of a new critical path and may affect the project completion time. Variability leading to a longer-than-expected total time for the critical activities will always extend the project completion time. Conversely, variability that results in a shorter-than-expected total time for the critical activities will reduce the project completion time, unless other activities become critical.

For a project involving uncertain activity times, the probability that the project can be completed within a specified amount of time is helpful managerial information. To understand the effect of variability on project management, we consider the variation along every path through the Porta-Vac project network. Examining Figure 13.11, we observe four paths through the project network: path 1 = A–E–H–I–J, path 2 = A–C–F–J, path 3 = A–D–G–J, and path 4 = B–H–I–J. Let the random variable T_i denote the total time to complete path i. The expected value of T_i is equal to the sum of the expected times of the activities along path i. For path 1 (the critical path), the expected time is

$$E(T_1) = t_A + t_E + t_H + t_I + t_J = 6 + 3 + 4 + 2 + 2 = 17 \text{ weeks}$$

The variance of T_i is the sum of the variances of the activities along path i. For path 1 (the critical path), the variance in completion time is

$$\sigma_1^2 = \sigma_A^2 + \sigma_E^2 + \sigma_H^2 + \sigma_I^2 + \sigma_J^2 = 1.78 + 0.11 + 0.69 + 0.03 + 0.11 = 2.72 \text{ weeks}$$

where σ_A^2, σ_E^2, σ_H^2, σ_I^2, and σ_J^2 are the variances of the activities A, E, H, I, and J. The formula for σ_1^2 is based on the assumption that the activity times are independent.

If two or more activities are dependent, the formula provides only an approximation of the variance of the path completion time. The closer the activities are to being independent, the better the approximation.

Knowing that the standard deviation is the square root of the variance, we compute the standard deviation σ_1 for the path 1 completion time as

$$\sigma_1 - \sqrt{\sigma_1^2} = \sqrt{2.72} = 1.65$$

The normal distribution tends to be a better approximation of the distribution of completion time for larger projects.

Appendix 13.1 describes how to compute cumulative probabilities for normal random variables in Excel.

Assuming that the distribution of the path completion time T_1 follows a normal or bell-shaped distribution[3] allows us to draw the distribution shown in Figure 13.12. With this distribution, we can compute the probability that a path of activities will meet be completed within a specified time. For example, suppose that management allotted 20 weeks for the Porta-Vac project. What is the probability that path 1 will be completed within 20 weeks? We are asking for the probability that $T_1 \leq 20$, which corresponds graphically to the shaded area in Figure 13.13. The z-score for the normal probability distribution at $T_1 = 20$ is

$$z_1 = \frac{20 - 17}{1.65} = 1.82$$

FIGURE 13.12   NORMAL DISTRIBUTION OF THE CRITICAL PATH COMPLETION TIME FOR THE PORTA-VAC PROJECT

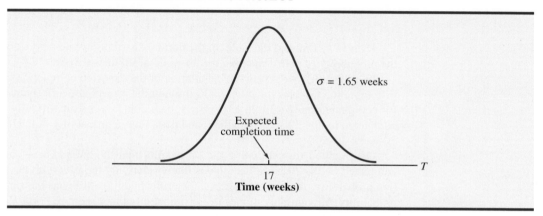

FIGURE 13.13   PROBABILITY THE CRITICAL PATH WILL MEET THE 20-WEEK DEADLINE

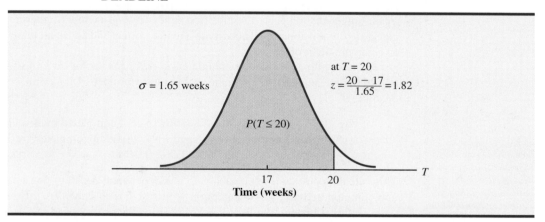

[3]Use of the normal distribution as an approximation is based on the central limit theorem, which indicates that the sum of independent activity times follows a normal distribution as the number of activity times becomes large.

TABLE 13.7   COMPUTING THE PROBABILITY OF EACH PROJECT PATH MEETING THE 20-WEEK DEADLINE

Expected Path Completion Time	Standard Deviation of Path Completion Time	z-Score	Probability of Meeting Deadline
$E(T_1) = 6 + 3 + 4 + 2 + 2 = 17$	$\sigma_1^2 = 1.78 + 0.11 + 0.69 + 0.03 + 0.11 = 2.72$	$z_1 = \dfrac{20 - 17}{\sqrt{2.72}} = 1.82$	0.9656
$E(T_2) = 6 + 3 + 2 + 2 = 13$	$\sigma_2^2 = 1.78 + 0.11 + 0.03 + 0.11 = 2.03$	$z_2 = \dfrac{20 - 13}{\sqrt{2.03}} = 4.91$	>0.9999
$E(T_3) = 6 + 5 + 3 + 2 = 16$	$\sigma_3^2 = 1.78 + 1.78 + 0.25 + 0.11 = 3.92$	$z_3 = \dfrac{20 - 16}{\sqrt{3.92}} = 2.02$	0.9783
$E(T_4) = 2 + 4 + 2 + 2 = 10$	$\sigma_4^2 = 0.44 + 0.69 + 0.03 + 0.11 = 1.27$	$z_4 = \dfrac{20 - 10}{\sqrt{1.27}} = 7.02$	>0.9999

Using $z = 1.82$ and the table for the normal distribution (see Appendix D), we find that the probability of path 1 meeting the 20-week deadline is 0.9656.

In Table 13.7, we repeat the calculation of the expected completion time and variance in completion time for the other paths through the project network (including path 1 again for completeness). As Table 13.7 shows, path 2 and path 4 are virtually guaranteed to be completed by the 20-week deadline, and path 3 has a probability of 0.9783 of meeting the 20-week deadline.

One method for estimating the probability that the entire Porta-Vac project will be completed by the 20-week deadline is to consider only the path with the smallest completion probability. As is often the case, the critical path (path 1) has the smallest completion probability. So a simple estimate of the probability that the entire Porta-Vac project will be complete within 20 weeks is 0.9656.

A common computational shortcut is to base the probability estimate of the entire project being complete by a deadline solely on the critical path. However, a probability estimate based only on the critical activities may be overly optimistic. When uncertain activity times exist, longer-than-expected completion times for one or more noncritical activities may cause an original noncritical activity to become critical and hence increase the time required to complete the project.

Because all paths must be completed in order for the entire project to be completed, an alternative method for computing the entire project's chance of completion by the deadline is:

$$P(\text{path 1 completed by deadline}) \times P(\text{path 2 completed by deadline})$$
$$\times \, P(\text{path 3 completed by deadline}) \times P(\text{path 4 completed by deadline})$$
$$= 0.9656 \times 1.0 \times 0.9783 \times 1.0 = 0.9446$$

Simulation is another technique used in project management and is particularly useful for estimating the probability of an extremely complex project being completed by a specified deadline.

This calculation assumes that each path is independent. As all of these paths share at least one common activity, this assumption is violated. Consequently, this estimate will be a pessimistic estimate of the likelihood of meeting the project deadline.

Regardless of the method used to estimate the completion probability, a project manager should frequently monitor the progress of the project. In particular, the project manager should monitor activities with large variances in their activity times. The Q.M. in Action, Project Management Helps the U.S. Air Force Reduce Maintenance Time, describes how closely managing the progress of individual activities and the assignment of resources led to dramatic improvements in the maintenance of military aircraft.

Q.M. *in* ACTION

PROJECT MANAGEMENT HELPS THE U.S. AIR FORCE REDUCE MAINTENANCE TIME*

Warner Robins Air Logistics Center (WR-ALC) provides maintenance and repair services for U.S. Air Force aircraft and ground equipment. To support combat zone efforts, the U.S. Air Force requested that WR-ALC reduce the amount of time it took to complete maintenance service on its C-5 transporter aircraft.

To identify ways to improve the management of its repair and overhaul process, WR-ALC adopted the method of critical chain project management (CCPM) by viewing each aircraft at its facility as a project with a series of tasks, precedence dependencies between these

*M. M. Srinivasan, W. D. Best, and S. Chandrasekaran, "Warner Robins Air Logistics Center Streamlines Aircraft Repair and Overhaul," Interfaces 37, no. 1 (2007): pp. 7–21.

tasks, and resource requirements. Identifying tasks at a level of detail that allowed supervisors to clearly assign mechanics, maintenance tools, and facilities resulted in a project network of approximately 450 activities.

By explicitly accounting for each task's resource requirements (mechanics, aircraft parts, maintenance tools, etc.), CCPM identifies a "critical chain" of activities. Efforts to reduce the critical chain led to the insight that a task should not be started until all resources needed to complete the task are available. While this approach, called "pipelining," often results in an initial delay to the start of a task, it allows for the quicker completion of the task by eliminating delays after the task's launch and by reducing efficiency-robbing multitasking (across tasks) by the mechanics.

 13.3 # Considering Time–Cost Trade-Offs

Using additional resources to reduce activity times was proposed by the developers of CPM. The shortening of activity times is referred to as crashing.

When determining the time estimates for activities in a project, the project manager bases these estimates on the amount of resources (workers, equipment, etc.) that will be assigned to an activity. The original developers of CPM provided the project manager with the option of adding resources to selected activities to reduce project completion time. Added resources (such as more workers, overtime, and so on) generally increase project costs, so the decision to reduce activity times must take into consideration the additional cost involved. In effect, the project manager must make a decision that involves trading additional project costs for reduced activity time.

Table 13.8 defines a two-machine maintenance project consisting of five activities. Management has substantial experience with similar projects and the times for maintenance activities have very little variability; hence, a single time estimate is given for each activity. The project network is shown in Figure 13.14.

The procedure for making critical path calculations for the maintenance project network is the same one that was used to find the critical path in the networks for both the Western Hills Shopping Center expansion project and the Porta-Vac project. Making the forward pass and backward pass calculations for the network in Figure 13.14, we obtained the activity schedule shown in Table 13.9. The zero slack times, and thus the critical path, are associated with activities A-B-E. The length of the critical path, and thus the total time required to complete the project, is 12 days.

TABLE 13.8   ACTIVITY LIST FOR THE TWO-MACHINE MAINTENANCE PROJECT

Activity	Description	Immediate Predecessor	Expected Time (days)
A	Overhaul machine I	—	7
B	Adjust machine I	A	3
C	Overhaul machine II	—	6
D	Adjust machine II	C	3
E	Test system	B, D	2

FIGURE 13.14   TWO-MACHINE MAINTENANCE PROJECT NETWORK

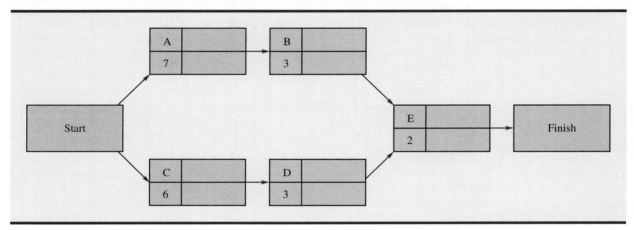

TABLE 13.9   ACTIVITY SCHEDULE FOR THE TWO-MACHINE MAINTENANCE PROJECT

Activity	Earliest Start (ES)	Latest Start (LS)	Earliest Finish (EF)	Latest Finish (LF)	Slack ($LS - ES$)	Critical Path?
A	0	0	7	7	0	Yes
B	7	7	10	10	0	Yes
C	0	1	6	7	1	
D	6	7	9	10	1	
E	10	10	12	12	0	Yes

Crashing Activity Times

Now suppose that current production levels make completing the maintenance project within 10 days imperative. By looking at the length of the critical path of the network (12 days), we realize that meeting the desired project completion time is impossible unless we can shorten selected activity times. This shortening of activity times, which usually can be achieved by adding resources, is referred to as **crashing**. Because the added resources associated with crashing activity times usually result in added project costs, we will want to identify the activities that cost the least to crash and then crash those activities by only the amount necessary to meet the desired project completion time.

To determine where and how much to crash activity times, we need information on how much each activity can be crashed and how much the crashing process costs. Hence, we must ask for the following information:

1. Activity cost under the normal or expected activity time
2. Time to complete the activity under maximum crashing (i.e., the shortest possible activity time)
3. Activity cost under maximum crashing

Let

$$\tau_i = \text{expected time for activity } i$$
$$\tau_i' = \text{time for activity } i \text{ under maximum crashing}$$
$$M_i = \text{maximum possible reduction in time for activity } i \text{ due to crashing}$$

Given τ_i and τ_i', we can compute M_i:

$$M_i = \tau_i - \tau_i' \tag{13.6}$$

This assumes that each unit of time gained by crashing an activity has the same associated cost. It is possible that the first few units of time gained by crashing an activity cost less than ensuing units of time gained by crashing the activity.

Next, let C_i denote the cost for activity i under the normal or expected activity time and let C_i' denote the cost for activity i under maximum crashing. Thus, per unit of time (e.g., per day), the crashing cost K_i for each activity is given by

$$K_i = \frac{C_i' - C_i}{M_i} \tag{13.7}$$

For example, if the normal or expected time for activity A is 7 days at a cost of $C_A = \$500$ and the time under maximum crashing is 4 days at a cost of $C_A = \$800$, equations (13.6) and (13.7) show that the maximum possible reduction in time for activity A is

$$M_A = 7 - 4 = 3 \text{ days}$$

with a crashing cost of

$$K_A = \frac{C_A' - C_A}{M_A} = \frac{800 - 500}{3} = \frac{300}{3} = \$100 \text{ per day}$$

We make the assumption that any portion or fraction of the activity crash time can be achieved for a corresponding portion of the activity crashing cost. For example, if we decided to crash activity A by only 1.5 days, the added cost would be 1.5($100) = $150, which results in a total activity cost of $500 + $150 = $650. Figure 13.15 shows the graph of the time–cost relationship for activity A. The complete normal and crash activity data for the two-machine maintenance project are given in Table 13.10.

Which activities should be crashed—and by how much—to meet the 10-day project completion deadline at minimum cost? Your first reaction to this question may be to consider crashing the critical activities—A, B, or E. Activity A has the lowest crashing cost per day of the three, and crashing this activity by 2 days will reduce the A-B-E path to the desired 10 days. Keep in mind, however, that as you crash the current critical activities, other paths may become critical. Thus, you will need to check the critical path in the revised network and perhaps either

FIGURE 13.15   TIME–COST RELATIONSHIP FOR ACTIVITY A

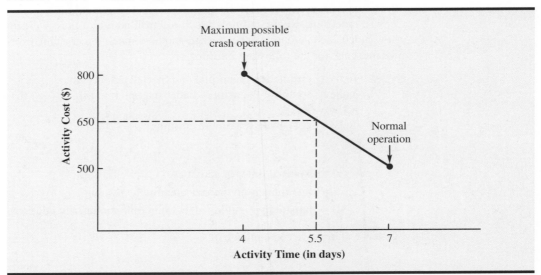

TABLE 13.10   NORMAL AND CRASH ACTIVITY DATA FOR THE TWO-MACHINE MAINTENANCE PROJECT

Activity	Time (days) Normal	Time (days) Crash	Total Cost Normal (C_i)	Total Cost Crash (C_i')	Maximum Reduction in Time (M_i)	Crash Cost per Day $\left(K_i = \dfrac{C_i' - C_i}{M_i}\right)$
A	7	4	$ 500	$ 800	3	$100
B	3	2	200	350	1	150
C	6	4	500	900	2	200
D	3	1	200	500	2	150
E	2	1	300	550	1	250
			$1700	$3100		

identify additional activities to crash or modify your initial crashing decision. For a small net-work, this trial-and-error approach can be used to make crashing decisions; in larger networks, however, a mathematical procedure is required to determine the optimal crashing decisions.

Linear Programming Model for Crashing

Let us describe how linear programming can be used to solve the network crashing problem. With PERT/CPM, we know that when an activity starts at its earliest start time, then

$$\text{Finish time} = \text{Earliest start time} + \text{Activity time}$$

However, if slack time is associated with an activity, then the activity need not start at its earliest start time. In this case, we may have

$$\text{Finish time} > \text{Earliest start time} + \text{Activity time}$$

Because we do not know ahead of time whether an activity will start at its earliest start time, we use the following inequality to show the general relationship among finish time, earliest start time, and activity time for each activity:

$$\text{Finish time} \geq \text{Earliest start time} + \text{Activity time}$$

Consider activity A, which has an expected time of 7 days. Let x_A = finish time for activity A, and y_A = amount of time activity A is crashed. If we assume that the project begins at time 0, the earliest start time for activity A is 0. Because the time for activity A is reduced by the amount of time that activity A is crashed, the finish time for activity A must satisfy the relationship

$$x_A \geq 0 + (7 - y_A)$$

Moving y_A to the left side,

$$x_A + y_A \geq 7$$

In general, let

$$x_i = \text{the finish time for activity } i \qquad i = A, B, C, D, E$$
$$y_i = \text{the amount of time activity } i \text{ is crashed} \quad i = A, B, C, D, E$$

If we follow the same approach that we used for activity A, the constraint corresponding to the finish time for activity C (expected time = 6 days) is

$$x_C \geq 0 + (6 - y_C) \quad \text{or} \quad x_C + y_C \geq 6$$

Continuing with the forward pass of the PERT/CPM procedure, we see that the earliest start time for activity B is x_A, the finish time for activity A. Thus, the constraint corresponding to the finish time for activity B is

$$x_B \geq x_A + (3 - y_B) \quad \text{or} \quad x_B + y_B - x_A \geq 3$$

Similarly, we obtain the constraint for the finish time for activity D:

$$x_D \geq x_C + (3 - y_D) \quad \text{or} \quad x_D + y_D - x_C \geq 3$$

Finally, we consider activity E. The earliest start time for activity E equals the *largest* of the finish times for activities B and D. Because the finish times for both activities B and D will be determined by the crashing procedure, we must write two constraints for activity E, one based on the finish time for activity B and one based on the finish time for activity D:

$$x_E + y_E - x_B \geq 2 \quad \text{and} \quad x_E + y_E - x_D \geq 2$$

Recall that current production levels made completing the maintenance project within 10 days imperative. Thus, the constraint for the finish time for activity E is

$$x_E \leq 10$$

In addition, we must add the following five constraints corresponding to the maximum allowable crashing time for each activity:

$$y_A \leq 3, \quad y_B \leq 1, \quad y_C \leq 2, \quad y_D \leq 2, \quad \text{and} \quad y_E \leq 1$$

As with all linear programs, we add the usual nonnegativity requirements for the decision variables.

All that remains is to develop an objective function for the model. Because the total project cost for a normal completion time is fixed at $1700 (see Table 13.10), we can minimize the total project cost (normal cost plus crashing cost) by minimizing the total crashing costs. Thus, the linear programming objective function becomes

$$\text{Min } 100y_A + 150y_B + 200y_C + 150y_D + 250y_E$$

Thus, to determine the optimal crashing for each of the activities, we must solve a 10-variable, 12-constraint linear programming model. Optimization software, such as Excel Solver, provides the optimal solution of crashing activity A by 1 day and activity E by 1 day, with a total crashing cost of $100 + $250 = $350. With the minimum cost crashing solution, the activity times are as follows:

Activity	Time in Days
A	6 (Crash 1 day)
B	3
C	6
D	3
E	1 (Crash 1 day)

The linear programming solution provided the revised activity times, but not the revised earliest start time, latest start time, and slack information. The revised activity times and the usual PERT/CPM procedure must be used to develop the activity schedule for the project.

NOTES AND COMMENTS

1. Note that the two-machine maintenance project network for the crashing illustration (see Figure 13.14) has only one activity, activity E, leading directly to the Finish node. As a result, the project completion time is equal to the completion time for activity E. Thus, the linear programming constraint requiring the project completion in 10 days or less could be written $x_E \leq 10$.

If two or more activities lead directly to the Finish node of a project network, a slight modification is required in the linear programming model for crashing. Consider the portion of the project network shown here. In this case, we

suggest creating an additional variable, x_{FIN}, which indicates the finish or completion time for the entire project. The fact that the project cannot be finished until both activities E and G are completed can be modeled by the two constraints

$$x_{FIN} \geq x_E \quad \text{or} \quad x_{FIN} - x_E \geq 0$$
$$x_{FIN} \geq x_G \quad \text{or} \quad x_{FIN} - x_G \geq 0$$

The constraint that the project must be finished by time T can be added as $x_{FIN} \leq T$. Problem 22 gives you practice with this type of project network.

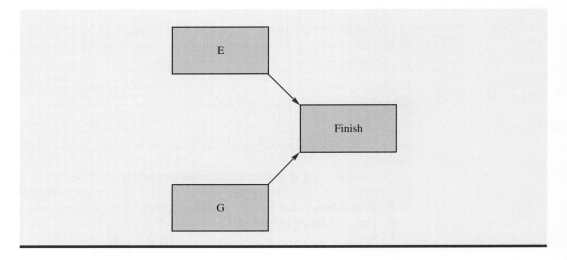

Summary

In this chapter we showed how PERT/CPM can be used to plan, schedule, and control a wide variety of projects. The key to this approach to project scheduling is the development of a PERT/CPM project network that depicts the activities and their precedence relationships. From this project network and activity time estimates, the critical path for the network and the associated critical activities can be identified. In the process, an activity schedule showing the earliest start and earliest finish times, the latest start and latest finish times, and the slack for each activity can be identified.

We showed how we can include capabilities for handling variable or uncertain activity times and how to use this information to provide a probability statement about the chances the project can be completed in a specified period of time. We introduced crashing as a procedure for reducing activity times to meet project completion deadlines, and we showed how a linear programming model can be used to determine the crashing decisions that will minimize the cost of reducing the project completion time.

Glossary

Activities Specific jobs or tasks that are components of a project. Activities are represented by nodes in a project network.

Backward pass Part of the PERT/CPM procedure that involves moving backward through the network to determine the latest start and latest finish times for each activity.

Beta probability distribution A probability distribution used to describe activity times.

Crashing The shortening of activity times by adding resources and hence usually increasing cost.

Critical activities The activities on the critical path.

Critical path The longest path in a project network.

Critical path method (CPM) A network-based project scheduling procedure.

Earliest finish time The earliest time an activity may be completed.

Earliest start time The earliest time an activity may begin.

Expected time The average activity time.

Forward pass Part of the PERT/CPM procedure that involves moving forward through the project network to determine the earliest start and earliest finish times for each activity.

Immediate predecessors The activities that must be completed immediately prior to the start of a given activity.

Latest finish time The latest time an activity may be completed without increasing the project completion time.

Latest start time The latest time an activity may begin without increasing the project completion time.

Most probable time The most probable activity time under normal conditions.

Optimistic time The minimum activity time if everything progresses ideally.

Path A sequence of connected nodes that leads from the Start node to the Finish node.

Pessimistic time The maximum activity time if substantial delays are encountered.

Program evaluation and review technique (PERT) A network-based project scheduling procedure.

Project network A graphical representation of a project that depicts the activities and shows the predecessor relationships among the activities.

Slack The length of time an activity can be delayed without affecting the project completion time.

Problems

1. The Mohawk Discount Store is designing a management training program for individuals at its corporate headquarters. The company wants to design the program so that trainees can complete it as quickly as possible. Important precedence relationships must be maintained between assignments or activities in the program. For example, a trainee cannot serve as an assistant to the store manager until the trainee has obtained experience in the credit department and at least one sales department. The following activities are the assignments that must be completed by each trainee in the program. Construct a project network for this problem. Do not perform any further analysis.

Activity	A	B	C	D	E	F	G	H
Immediate Predecessor	—	—	A	A, B	A, B	C	D, F	E, G

2. Bridge City Developers is coordinating the construction of an office complex. As part of the planning process, the company generated the following activity list. Draw a project network that can be used to assist in the scheduling of the project activities.

Activity	A	B	C	D	E	F	G	H	I	J
Immediate Predecessor	—	—	—	A, B	A, B	D	E	C	C	F, G, H, I

3. Construct a project network for the following project. The project is completed when activities F and G are both complete.

Activity	A	B	C	D	E	F	G
Immediate Predecessor	—	—	A	A	C, B	C, B	D, E

4. Assume that the project in Problem 3 has the following activity times (in months):

Activity	A	B	C	D	E	F	G
Time	4	6	2	6	3	3	5

   a. Find the critical path.
   b. The project must be completed in 1.5 years. Do you anticipate difficulty in meeting the deadline? Explain.

5. Consider the Western Hills Shopping Center Project summarized by Figure 13.6 and Table 13.2. Suppose the project has been under way for seven weeks. Activities A and E have been completed. Activity F has commenced but has three weeks remaining. Activities C and D have not started yet. Activity B has one week remaining (it was not started until week 2). Update the activity schedule for the project. In particular, how has the slack for each activity changed?

6. Consider the following project network and activity times (in weeks):

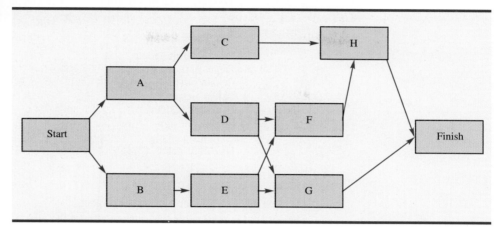

Activity	A	B	C	D	E	F	G	H
Time	5	3	7	6	7	3	10	8

a. Identify the critical path.
b. How much time will be needed to complete this project?
c. Can activity D be delayed without delaying the entire project? If so, by how many weeks?
d. Can activity C be delayed without delaying the entire project? If so, by how many weeks?
e. What is the schedule for activity E?

7. Embassy Club Condominium, located on the west coast of Florida, is undertaking a summer renovation of its main building. The project is scheduled to begin May 1, and a September 1 (17-week) completion date is desired. The condominium manager identified the following renovation activities and their estimated times:

Activity	Immediate Predecessor	Time
A	—	3
B	—	1
C	—	2
D	A, B, C	4
E	C, D	5
F	A	3
G	D, F	6
H	E	4

a. Draw a project network.
b. What are the critical activities?
c. What activity has the most slack time?
d. Will the project be completed by September 1?

8. Colonial State College is considering building a new multipurpose athletic complex on campus. The complex would provide a new gymnasium for intercollegiate basketball

games, expanded office space, classrooms, and intramural facilities. The following activities would have to be undertaken before construction can begin:

Activity	Description	Immediate Predecessor	Time (weeks)
A	Survey building site	—	6
B	Develop initial design	—	8
C	Obtain board approval	A, B	12
D	Select architect	C	4
E	Establish budget	C	6
F	Finalize design	D, E	15
G	Obtain financing	E	12
H	Hire contractor	F, G	8

a. Draw a project network.
b. Identify the critical path.
c. Develop the activity schedule for the project.
d. Does it appear reasonable that construction of the athletic complex could begin one year after the decision to begin the project with the site survey and initial design plans? What is the expected completion time for the project?

9. At a local university, the Student Commission on Programming and Entertainment (SCOPE) is preparing to host its first rock concert of the school year. To successfully produce this rock concert, SCOPE has listed the requisite activities and related information in the following table (duration estimates measured in days).

Activity	Immediate Predecessor(s)	Optimistic	Most Probable	Pessimistic
A: Negotiate contract with selected musicians	—	8	10	15
B: Reserve site	—	7	8	9
C: Manage travel logistics for music group	A	5	6	10
D: Screen & hire security personnel	B	3	3	3
E: Arrange advertising & ticketing	B, C	1	5	9
F: Hire parking staff	D	4	7	10
G: Arrange concession sales	E	3	8	10

a. Draw the project network.
b. Compute the expected duration and variance of each activity.
c. Determine the critical path in the project network.
d. What is the expected duration and variance of the critical path?
e. What is the likelihood that the project will be completed within 30 days?
f. If activity B is delayed by six days beyond its early start time, how does this affect the expected project duration?

10. The following estimates of activity times (in days) are available for a small project:

Activity	Optimistic	Most Probable	Pessimistic
A	4	5.0	6
B	8	9.0	10
C	7	7.5	11
D	7	9.0	10
E	6	7.0	9
F	5	6.0	7

a. Compute the expected activity completion times and the variance for each activity.

b. An analyst determined that the critical path consists of activities B-D-F. Compute the expected project completion time and the variance of this path.

11. Building a backyard swimming pool consists of nine major activities. The activities and their immediate predecessors are shown. Develop the project network.

Activity	A	B	C	D	E	F	G	H	I
Immediate Predecessor	—	—	A, B	A, B	B	C	D	D, F	E, G, H

12. Assume that the activity time estimates (in days) for the swimming pool construction project in Problem 11 are as follows:

Activity	Optimistic	Most Probable	Pessimistic
A	3	5	6
B	2	4	6
C	5	6	7
D	7	9	10
E	2	4	6
F	1	2	3
G	5	8	10
H	6	8	10
I	3	4	5

a. What are the critical activities?

b. What is the expected time to complete the project?

c. Based only on the critical path, what is the estimated probability that the project can be completed in 25 or fewer days?

13. Suppose that the following estimates of activity times (in weeks) were provided for the network shown in Problem 6:

Activity	Optimistic	Most Probable	Pessimistic
A	4.0	5.0	6.0
B	2.5	3.0	3.5
C	6.0	7.0	8.0
D	5.0	5.5	9.0
E	5.0	7.0	9.0
F	2.0	3.0	4.0
G	8.0	10.0	12.0
H	6.0	7.0	14.0

Based only on the critical path, what is the estimated probability that the project will be completed

a. Within 21 weeks?

b. Within 22 weeks?

c. Within 25 weeks?

14. Davison Construction Company is building a luxury lakefront home in the Finger Lakes region of New York. Coordination of the architect and subcontractors will require a major

effort to meet the 44-week (approximately 10-month) completion date requested by the owner. The Davison project manager prepared the following project network:

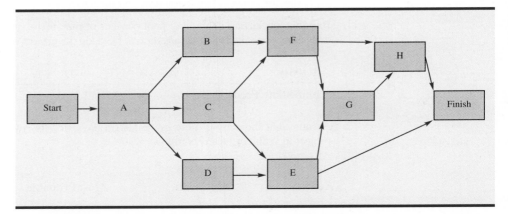

Estimates of the optimistic, most probable, and pessimistic times (in weeks) for the activities are as follows:

Activity	Optimistic	Most Probable	Pessimistic
A	4	8	12
B	6	7	8
C	6	12	18
D	3	5	7
E	6	9	18
F	5	8	17
G	10	15	20
H	5	6	13

a. Find the critical path.
b. What is the expected project completion time?
c. Based only on the critical path, what is the estimated probability the project can be completed in the 44 weeks as requested by the owner?
d. Based only on the critical path, what is the estimated probability the building project could run more than 3 months late? Use 57 weeks for this calculation.
e. What should the construction company tell the owner?

15. Doug Casey is in charge of planning and coordinating next spring's sales management training program for his company. Doug listed the following activity information for this project:

Activity	Description	Immediate Predecessor	Time (weeks) Optimistic	Most Probable	Pessimistic
A	Plan topic	—	1.5	2.0	2.5
B	Obtain speakers	A	2.0	2.5	6.0
C	List meeting locations	—	1.0	2.0	3.0
D	Select location	C	1.5	2.0	2.5
E	Finalize speaker travel plans	B, D	0.5	1.0	1.5
F	Make final check with speakers	E	1.0	2.0	3.0
G	Prepare and mail brochure	B, D	3.0	3.5	7.0
H	Take reservations	G	3.0	4.0	5.0
I	Handle last-minute details	F, H	1.5	2.0	2.5

a. Draw a project network.
b. Prepare an activity schedule.
c. What are the critical activities and what is the expected project completion time?
d. If Doug wants a 0.99 probability of completing the project on time, how far ahead of the scheduled meeting date should he begin working on the project?

16. Management Decision Systems (MDS) is a consulting company that specializes in the development of decision support systems. MDS has a four-person team working on a current project with a small company to set up a system that scrapes data from a collection of websites and then automatically generates a report for management on a daily basis.

Activity	Description	Immediate Predecessor	Optimistic	Most Probable	Pessimistic
				Time (Weeks)	
A	Report generation	—	1	7	11
B	Web scraping	—	3	8	10
C	Testing	A, B	1	1	1

a. Construct the project network.
b. Based solely on the critical path, estimate the probability that the project will be complete within 10 weeks.
c. Using all paths through the project network, estimate the probability that the project will be complete within 10 weeks.
d. Should you use the estimate in part (b) or (c)?

17. The Porsche Shop, founded in 1985 by Dale Jensen, specializes in the restoration of vintage Porsche automobiles. One of Jensen's regular customers asked him to prepare an estimate for the restoration of a 1964 model 356SC Porsche. To estimate the time and cost to perform such a restoration, Jensen broke the restoration process into four separate activities: disassembly and initial preparation work (A), body restoration (B), engine restoration (C), and final assembly (D). Once activity A has been completed, activities B and C can be performed independently of each other; however, activity D can be started only if both activities B and C have been completed. Based on his inspection of the car, Jensen believes that the following time estimates (in days) are applicable:

Activity	Optimistic	Most Probable	Pessimistic
A	3	4	8
B	5	8	11
C	2	4	6
D	4	5	12

Jensen estimates that the parts needed to restore the body will cost $3000 and that the parts needed to restore the engine will cost $5000. His current labor costs are $400 a day.

a. Develop a project network.
b. What is the expected project completion time?
c. Jensen's business philosophy is based on making decisions using a best- and worst-case scenario. Develop cost estimates for completing the restoration based on both a best- and worst-case analysis. Assume that the total restoration cost is the sum of the labor cost plus the material cost.
d. If Jensen obtains the job with a bid that is based on the costs associated with an expected completion time, what is the probability that he will lose money on the job?
e. If Jensen obtains the job based on a bid of $16,800, what is the probability that he will lose money on the job?

18. The manager of the Oak Hills Swimming Club is planning the club's swimming team program. The first team practice is scheduled for May 1. The activities, their immediate predecessors, and the activity time estimates (in weeks) are as follows:

Activity	Description	Immediate Predecessor	Optimistic	Time (weeks) Most Probable	Pessimistic
A	Meet with board	—	1	1	2
B	Hire coaches	A	4	6	8
C	Reserve pool	A	2	4	6
D	Announce program	B, C	1	2	3
E	Meet with coaches	B	2	3	4
F	Order team suits	A	1	2	3
G	Register swimmers	D	1	2	3
H	Collect fees	G	1	2	3
I	Plan first practice	E, H, F	1	1	1

a. Draw a project network.
b. Develop an activity schedule.
c. What are the critical activities, and what is the expected project completion time?
d. If the club manager plans to start the project on February 1, what is the probability the swimming program will be ready by the scheduled May 1 date (13 weeks)? Should the manager begin planning the swimming program before February 1?

19. The product development group at Landon Corporation has been working on a new computer software product that has the potential to capture a large market share. Through outside sources, Landon's management learned that a competitor is working to introduce a similar product. As a result, Landon's top management increased its pressure on the product development group. The group's leader turned to PERT/CPM as an aid to scheduling the activities remaining before the new product can be brought to the market. The project network is as follows:

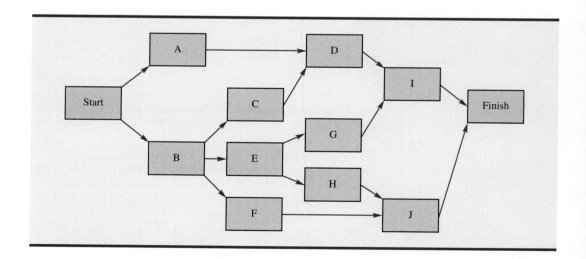

The activity time estimates (in weeks) are as follows:

Activity	Optimistic	Most Probable	Pessimistic
A	3.0	4.0	5.0
B	3.0	3.5	7.0
C	4.0	5.0	6.0
D	2.0	3.0	4.0
E	6.0	10.0	14.0
F	7.5	8.5	12.5
G	4.5	6.0	7.5
H	5.0	6.0	13.0
I	2.0	2.5	6.0
J	4.0	5.0	6.0

a. Develop an activity schedule for this project and identify the critical path activities.
b. What is the probability that the project will be completed so that Landon Corporation may introduce the new product within 25 weeks? Within 30 weeks?

20. Norton Industries is installing a new computer system. The activities, the activity times, and the project network are as follows:

Activity	Time	Activity	Time
A	3	E	4
B	6	F	3
C	2	G	9
D	5	H	3

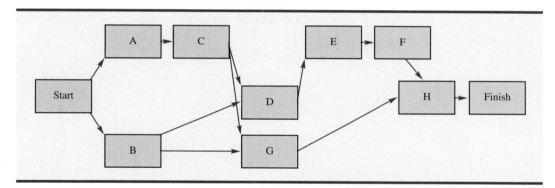

The critical path calculation shows B-D-E-F-H is the critical path, and the expected project completion time is 21 weeks. After viewing this information, management requested overtime be used to complete the project in 16 weeks. Thus, crashing of the project is necessary. The following information is relevant:

Activity	Time (weeks) Normal	Crash	Cost ($) Normal	Crash
A	3	1	900	1700
B	6	3	2000	4000
C	2	1	500	1000
D	5	3	1800	2400
E	4	3	1500	1850
F	3	1	3000	3900
G	9	4	8000	9800
H	3	2	1000	2000

a. Formulate a linear programming model that can be used to make the crashing decisions for this project.
b. Solve the linear programming model and make the minimum cost crashing decisions. What is the added cost of meeting the 16-week completion time?
c. Develop a complete activity schedule based on the crashed activity times.

21. Consider the following project network and activity times (in days):

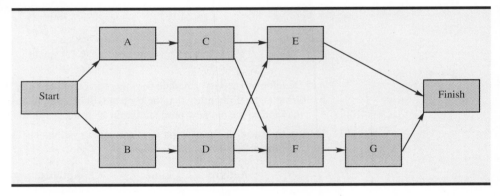

Activity	A	B	C	D	E	F	G
Time	3	2	5	5	6	2	2

The crashing data for this project are as follows:

Activity	Time (days)		Cost ($)	
	Normal	Crash	Normal	Crash
A	3	2	800	1400
B	2	1	1200	1900
C	5	3	2000	2800
D	5	3	1500	2300
E	6	4	1800	2800
F	2	1	600	1000
G	2	1	500	1000

a. Find the critical path and the expected project completion time.
b. What is the total project cost using the normal times?

22. Refer to Problem 21. Assume that management desires a 12-day project completion time.
a. Formulate a linear programming model that can be used to assist with the crashing decisions.
b. What activities should be crashed?
c. What is the total project cost for the 12-day completion time?

23. Consider the following project network. Note that the normal or expected activity times are denoted τ_i, i = A, B, . . . , I. Let x_i = the earliest finish time for activity i. Formulate a linear programming model that can be used to determine the length of the critical path.

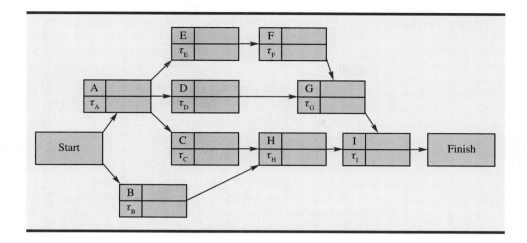

24. Office Automation, Inc., developed a proposal for introducing a new computerized office system that will standardize the electronic archiving of invoices for a particular company. Contained in the proposal is a list of activities that must be accomplished to complete the new office system project. Use the following relevant information about the activities:

Activity	Description	Immediate Predecessor	Time (weeks)		Cost ($1000s)	
			Normal	Crash	Normal	Crash
A	Plan needs	—	10	8	30	70
B	Order equipment	A	8	6	120	150
C	Install equipment	B	10	7	100	160
D	Set up training lab	A	7	6	40	50
E	Conduct training course	D	10	8	50	75
F	Test system	C, E	3	3	60	—

a. Develop a project network.
b. Develop an activity schedule.
c. What are the critical activities, and what is the expected project completion time?
d. Assume that the company wants to complete the project in six months or 26 weeks. What crashing decisions do you recommend to meet the desired completion time at the least possible cost? Work through the network and attempt to make the crashing decisions by inspection.
e. Develop an activity schedule for the crashed project.
f. What added project cost is required to meet the six-month completion time?

25. Because Landon Corporation (see Problem 19) is being pressured to complete the product development project at the earliest possible date, the project leader requested that the possibility of crashing the project be evaluated.
a. Formulate a linear programming model that could be used in making the crashing decisions.
b. What information would have to be provided before the linear programming model could be implemented?

Case Problem # R. C. Coleman

R. C. Coleman distributes a variety of food products that are sold through grocery store and supermarket outlets. The company receives orders directly from the individual outlets, with a typical order requesting the delivery of several cases of anywhere from 20 to 50 different products. Under the company's current warehouse operation, warehouse clerks dispatch order-picking personnel to fill each order and have the goods moved to the warehouse shipping area. Because of the high labor costs and relatively low productivity of hand order-picking, management has decided to automate the warehouse operation by installing a computer-controlled order-picking system, along with a conveyor system for moving goods from storage to the warehouse shipping area.

R. C. Coleman's director of material management has been named the project manager in charge of the automated warehouse system. After consulting with members of the engineering staff and warehouse management personnel, the director compiled a list of activities associated with the project. The optimistic, most probable, and pessimistic times (in weeks) have also been provided for each activity.

Activity	Description	Immediate Predecessor
A	Determine equipment needs	—
B	Obtain vendor proposals	—
C	Select vendor	A, B
D	Order system	C
E	Design new warehouse layout	C
F	Design warehouse	E
G	Design computer interface	C
H	Interface computer	D, F, G
I	Install system	D, F
J	Train system operators	H
K	Test system	I, J

	Time (weeks)		
Activity	Optimistic	Most Probable	Pessimistic
A	4	6	8
B	6	8	16
C	2	4	6
D	8	10	24
E	7	10	13
F	4	6	8
G	4	6	20
H	4	6	8
I	4	6	14
J	3	4	5
K	2	4	6

Managerial Report

Develop a report that presents the activity schedule and expected project completion time for the warehouse expansion project. Include a project network in the report. In addition, take into consideration the following issues:

1. R. C. Coleman's top management established a required 40-week completion time for the project. Can this completion time be achieved? Include probability information in your discussion. What recommendations do you have if the 40-week completion time is required?

2. Suppose that management requests that activity times be shortened to provide an 80% chance of meeting the 40-week completion time. If the variance in the project completion time is the same as you found in part (1), how much should the expected project completion time be shortened to achieve the goal of an 80% chance of completion within 40 weeks?

3. Using the expected activity times as the normal times and the following crashing information, determine the activity crashing decisions and revised activity schedule for the warehouse expansion project:

Activity	Crashed Activity Time (weeks)	Cost ($) Normal	Cost ($) Crashed
A	4	1,000	1,900
B	7	1,000	1,800
C	2	1,500	2,700
D	8	2,000	3,200
E	7	5,000	8,000
F	4	3,000	4,100
G	5	8,000	10,250
H	4	5,000	6,400
I	4	10,000	12,400
J	3	4,000	4,400
K	3	5,000	5,500

Appendix 13.1 Finding Cumulative Probabilities for Normally Distributed Random Variables

Excel can be used to find the probability a project with uncertain activity times will be completed in some given completion time (assuming the project completion time is normally distributed). We demonstrate this on the Porta-Vac Project we considered in Section 13.2. Recall that management allotted 20 days to complete the project. We have found the z value that corresponds to $T = 20$:

$$z = \frac{20 - 17}{1.65} = 1.82$$

The Excel function NORM.S.DIST is only recognized by Excel 2010 and later versions. Earlier versions of Excel use the function name NORMS-DIST to compute the same value.

Now we will make use the Excel function

$$=\text{NORM.S.DIST}(z, \text{TRUE})$$

by substituting the value of z we have found into the function (entering "TRUE" for the second argument signifies that we desire the cumulative probability associated with z). Enter the following function into any empty cell in an Excel worksheet:

$$=\text{NORM.S.DIST}(1.82, \text{TRUE})$$

The resulting value is 0.96562, which is the probability that the completion time for the Porta-Vac project will be no more than 20 days.

CHAPTER 14

Inventory Models

CONTENTS

Inventory refers to idle goods or materials held by an organization for use sometime in the future. Items carried in inventory include raw materials, purchased parts, components, subassemblies, work-in-process, finished goods, and supplies. Two primary reasons organizations stock inventory are: (1) to take advantage of economies-of-scale that exist due to the fixed cost of ordering items, and (2) to buffer against uncertainty in customer demand or disruptions in supply. Even though inventory serves an important and essential role, the expense associated with financing and maintaining inventories is a substantial part of the cost of doing business. In large organizations, the cost associated with inventory can run into the millions of dollars.

In applications involving inventory, managers must answer two important questions.

1. *How much* should be ordered when the inventory is replenished?
2. *When* should the inventory be replenished?

Virtually every business uses some sort of inventory management model or system to address the preceding questions. Hewlett-Packard works with its retailers to help determine the retailer's inventory replenishment strategies for the printers and other HP products. IBM developed inventory management policies for a range of microelectronic parts that are used in IBM plants as well as sold to a number of outside customers. The Q.M. in Action, Inventory Management at CVS Corporation, describes an inventory system used to determine order quantities in the drugstore industry.

The inventory procedure described for the drugstore industry is discussed in detail in Section 14.7.

The purpose of this chapter is to show how quantitative models can assist in making the how-much-to-order and when-to-order inventory decisions. We will first consider *deterministic* inventory models, in which we assume that the rate of demand for the item is constant or nearly constant. Later we will consider *probabilistic* inventory models, in which the demand for the item fluctuates and can be described only in probabilistic terms.

Q.M. *(in)* ACTION

INVENTORY MANAGEMENT AT CVS CORPORATION*

CVS is one of the largest drugstore chains in the United States. The primary inventory management area in the drugstore involves the numerous basic products that are carried in inventory on an everyday basis. For these items, the most important issue is the replenishment quantity or order size each time an order is placed. In most drugstore chains, basic products are ordered under a periodic review inventory system, with the review period being one week.

The weekly review system uses electronic ordering equipment that scans an order label affixed to the shelf directly below each item. Among other information on the label is the item's replenishment level or order-to-quantity. The store employee placing the order determines the weekly order quantity by counting the number of units of the product on the shelf and subtracting this quantity from the replenishment level. A computer program determines the replenishment quantity for each item in each individual store, based on each store's movement rather than on the company movement. To minimize stock-outs the replenishment quantity is set equal to the store's three-week demand or movement for the product.

*Based on information provided by Bob Carver. (The inventory system described was originally implemented in the CVS stores formerly known as SupeRX.)

Economic Order Quantity (EOQ) Model

The **economic order quantity (EOQ)** model is applicable when the demand for an item shows a constant, or nearly constant, rate and when the entire quantity ordered arrives in inventory at one point in time. The **constant demand rate** assumption means that the same number of units is taken from inventory each period of time such as 5 units every day, 25 units every week, 100 units every four-week period, and so on.

To illustrate the EOQ model, let us consider the situation faced by the R&B Beverage Company. R&B Beverage is a distributor of beer, wine, and soft drink products. From a main warehouse located in Columbus, Ohio, R&B supplies nearly 1000 retail stores with beverage products. The beer inventory, which constitutes about 40% of the company's total inventory, averages approximately 50,000 cases. With an average cost per case of approximately $8, R&B estimates the value of its beer inventory to be $400,000.

The warehouse manager decided to conduct a detailed study of the inventory costs associated with Bub Beer, the number-one-selling R&B beer. The purpose of the study is to establish the how-much-to-order and the when-to-order decisions for Bub Beer that will result in the lowest possible total cost. As the first step in the study, the warehouse manager obtained the following demand data for the past 10 weeks:

The cost associated with developing and maintaining inventory is larger than many people think. Models such as the ones presented in this chapter can be used to develop cost-effective inventory management decisions.

Week	Demand (cases)
1	2000
2	2025
3	1950
4	2000
5	2100
6	2050
7	2000
8	1975
9	1900
10	2000
Total cases	20,000
Average cases per week	2000

One of the most criticized assumptions of the EOQ model is the constant demand rate. Obviously, the model would be inappropriate for items with widely fluctuating and variable demand rates. However, as this example shows, the EOQ model can provide a realistic approximation of the optimal order quantity when demand is relatively stable and occurs at a nearly constant rate.

Strictly speaking, these weekly demand figures do not show a constant demand rate. However, given the relatively low variability exhibited by the weekly demand, inventory planning with a constant demand rate of 2000 cases per week appears acceptable. In practice, you will find that the actual inventory situation seldom, if ever, satisfies the assumptions of the model exactly. Thus, in any particular application, the manager must determine whether the model assumptions are close enough to reality for the model to be useful. In this situation, because demand varies from a low of 1900 cases to a high of 2100 cases, the assumption of constant demand of 2000 cases per week appears to be a reasonable approximation.

The how-much-to-order decision involves selecting an order quantity that draws a compromise between (1) keeping small inventories and ordering frequently, and (2) keeping large inventories and ordering infrequently. The first alternative can result in undesirably high ordering costs, while the second alternative can result in undesirably high inventory holding costs. To find an optimal compromise between these conflicting alternatives, let us consider a mathematical model that shows the total cost as the sum of the holding cost and the ordering cost.[1]

Holding costs are the costs associated with maintaining or carrying a given level of inventory; these costs depend on the size of the inventory. The first holding cost to consider is the cost of financing the inventory investment. When a firm borrows money, it incurs an interest charge. If the firm uses its own money, it experiences an opportunity cost associated with not being able to use the money for other investments. In either case, an interest cost exists for the capital tied up in inventory. This **cost of capital** is usually expressed as a percentage of the amount invested. R&B estimates its cost of capital at an annual rate of 18%.

A number of other holding costs, such as insurance, taxes, breakage, pilferage, and warehouse overhead, also depend on the value of the inventory. R&B estimates these other costs at an annual rate of approximately 7% of the value of its inventory. Thus, the total holding cost for the R&B beer inventory is 18% + 7% = 25% of the value of the inventory. The cost of one case of Bub Beer is $8. With an annual holding cost rate of 25%, the cost of holding one case of Bub Beer in inventory for 1 year is 0.25($8) = $2.00.

The next step in the inventory analysis is to determine the **ordering cost**. This cost, which is considered fixed regardless of the order quantity, covers the preparation of the voucher; and the processing of the order, including payment, postage, telephone, transportation, invoice verification, receiving, and so on. For R&B Beverage, the largest portion of the ordering cost involves the salaries of the purchasers. An analysis of the purchasing process showed that a purchaser spends approximately 45 minutes preparing and processing an order for Bub Beer. With a wage rate and fringe benefit cost for purchasers of $20 per hour, the labor portion of the ordering cost is $15. Making allowances for paper, postage, telephone, transportation, and receiving costs at $17 per order, the manager estimates that the ordering cost is $32 per order. That is, R&B is paying $32 per order regardless of the quantity requested in the order.

The holding cost, ordering cost, and demand information are the three data items that must be known prior to the use of the EOQ model. After developing these data for the R&B problem, we can look at how they are used to develop a total cost model. We begin by defining Q as the order quantity. Thus, the how-much-to-order decision involves finding the value of Q that will minimize the sum of holding and ordering costs.

The inventory for Bub Beer will have a maximum value of Q units when an order of size Q is received from the supplier. R&B will then satisfy customer demand from inventory until the inventory is depleted, at which time another shipment of Q units will be received. Thus, assuming a constant demand, the graph of the inventory for Bub Beer is as shown in Figure 14.1. Note that the graph indicates an average inventory of $\frac{1}{2}Q$ for the period in question. This level should appear reasonable because the maximum inventory is Q, the minimum is zero, and the inventory declines at a constant rate over the period.

Figure 14.1 shows the inventory pattern during one order cycle of length T. As time goes on, this pattern will repeat. The complete inventory pattern is shown in Figure 14.2. If the average inventory during each cycle is $\frac{1}{2}Q$, the average inventory over any number of cycles is also $\frac{1}{2}Q$.

The holding cost can be calculated using the average inventory. That is, we can calculate the holding cost by multiplying the average inventory by the cost of carrying one unit in inventory for the stated period. The period selected for the model is up to you; it could be one week, one month, one year, or more. However, because the holding cost for many

---

[1]Even though analysts typically refer to "total cost" models for inventory systems, often these models describe only the total variable or total relevant costs for the decision being considered. Costs that are not affected by the how-much-to-order decision are considered fixed or constant and are not included in the model.

FIGURE 14.1   INVENTORY FOR BUB BEER

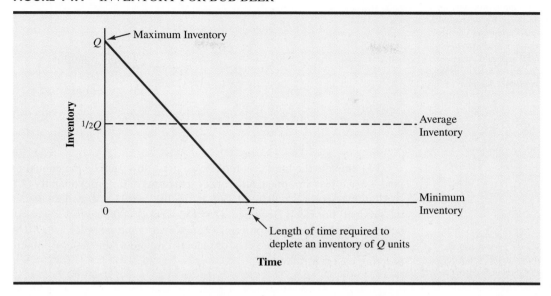

FIGURE 14.2   INVENTORY PATTERN FOR THE EOQ INVENTORY MODEL

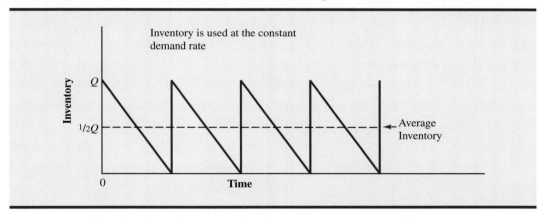

industries and businesses is expressed as an *annual* percentage, most inventory models are developed on an *annual* cost basis.

Let

$$I = \text{annual holding cost rate}$$
$$C = \text{unit cost of the inventory item}$$
$$C_h = \text{annual cost of holding one unit in inventory}$$

The annual cost of holding one unit in inventory is

$$C_h = IC \qquad\qquad (14.1)$$

C_h is the cost of holding one unit in inventory for one year. Because smaller order quantities Q will result in lower inventory, total annual holding cost can be reduced by using smaller order quantities.

The general equation for the annual holding cost for the average inventory of $\frac{1}{2}Q$ units is as follows:

$$
\begin{pmatrix} \text{Annual} \\ \text{holding cost} \end{pmatrix} = \begin{pmatrix} \text{Average} \\ \text{inventory} \end{pmatrix} \begin{pmatrix} \text{Annual holding} \\ \text{cost} \\ \text{per unit} \end{pmatrix}
$$

$$
= \frac{1}{2} Q C_h \tag{14.2}
$$

To complete the total cost model, we must now include the annual ordering cost. The goal is to express the annual ordering cost in terms of the order quantity Q. The first question is, How many orders will be placed during the year? Let D denote the annual demand for the product. For R&B Beverage, $D = (52 \text{ weeks})(2000 \text{ cases per week}) = 104,000$ cases per year. We know that by ordering Q units every time we order, we will have to place D/Q orders per year. If C_o is the cost of placing one order, the general equation for the annual ordering cost is as follows:

C_o, the fixed cost per order, is independent of the amount ordered. For a given annual demand of D units, the total annual ordering cost can be reduced by using larger order quantities.

$$
\begin{pmatrix} \text{Annual} \\ \text{ordering cost} \end{pmatrix} = \begin{pmatrix} \text{Number of} \\ \text{orders} \\ \text{per year} \end{pmatrix} \begin{pmatrix} \text{Cost} \\ \text{per} \\ \text{order} \end{pmatrix}
$$

$$
= \left(\frac{D}{Q} \right) C_o \tag{14.3}
$$

Thus, the total annual cost, denoted TC, can be expressed as follows:

$$
\begin{matrix} \text{Total} & & \text{Annual} & & \text{Annual} \\ \text{annual} & = & \text{holding} & + & \text{ordering} \\ \text{cost} & & \text{cost} & & \text{cost} \end{matrix}
$$

$$
TC = \frac{1}{2} Q C_h + \frac{D}{Q} C_o \tag{14.4}
$$

Using the Bub Beer data $[C_h = IC = (0.25)(\$8) = \$2, C_o = \$32, \text{ and } D = 104,000]$, the total annual cost model is

$$
TC = \frac{1}{2} Q(\$2) + \frac{104,000}{Q} (\$32) = Q + \frac{3,328,000}{Q}
$$

The development of the total cost model goes a long way toward solving the inventory problem. We now are able to express the total annual cost as a function of *how much* should be ordered. The development of a realistic total cost model is perhaps the most important part of the application of quantitative methods to inventory decision making. Equation (14.4) is the general total cost equation for inventory situations in which the assumptions of the economic order quantity model are valid.

The How-Much-to-Order Decision

The next step is to find the order quantity Q that will minimize the total annual cost for Bub Beer. Using a trial-and-error approach, we can compute the total annual cost for several possible order quantities. As a starting point, let us consider $Q = 8000$. The total annual cost for Bub Beer is

$$TC = Q + \frac{3{,}328{,}000}{Q}$$

$$= 8000 + \frac{3{,}328{,}000}{8000} = \$8416$$

A trial order quantity of 5000 gives

$$TC = 5000 + \frac{3{,}328{,}000}{5000} = \$5666$$

The results of several other trial order quantities are shown in Table 14.1. It shows the lowest cost solution to be about 2000 cases. Graphs of the annual holding and ordering costs and total annual costs are shown in Figure 14.3.

The advantage of the trial-and-error approach is that it is rather easy to do and provides the total annual cost for a number of possible order quantity decisions. In this case, the minimum cost order quantity appears to be approximately 2000 cases. The disadvantage of this approach, however, is that it does not provide the exact minimum cost order quantity.

The EOQ formula determines the optimal order quantity by balancing the annual holding cost and the annual ordering cost.

Refer to Figure 14.3. The minimum total cost order quantity is denoted by an order size of Q^*. By using differential calculus, it can be shown (see Appendix 14.1) that the value of Q^* that minimizes the total annual cost is given by the formula

$$Q^* = \sqrt{\frac{2DC_o}{C_h}} \qquad \text{(14.5)}$$

This formula is referred to as the *economic order quantity (EOQ) formula*.

Using equation (14.5), the minimum total annual cost order quantity for Bub Beer is

$$Q^* = \sqrt{\frac{2(104{,}000)32}{2}} = 1824 \text{ cases}$$

TABLE 14.1 ANNUAL HOLDING, ORDERING, AND TOTAL COSTS FOR VARIOUS ORDER QUANTITIES OF BUB BEER

	Annual Cost		
Order Quantity	**Holding**	**Ordering**	**Total**
5000	$5000	$ 666	$5666
4000	$4000	$ 832	$4832
3000	$3000	$1109	$4109
2000	$2000	$1664	$3664
1000	$1000	$3328	$4328

FIGURE 14.3   ANNUAL HOLDING, ORDERING, AND TOTAL COSTS FOR BUB BEER

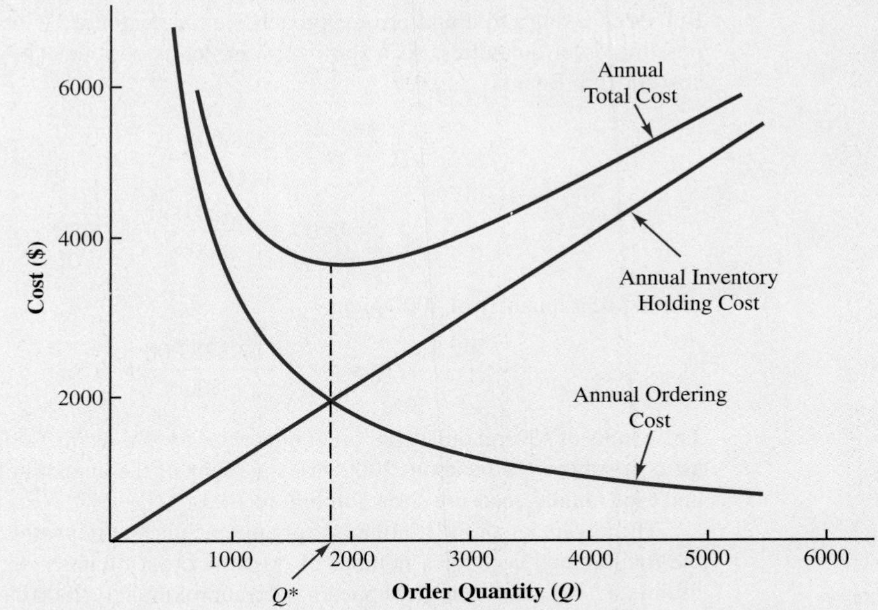

Problem 2 at the end of the chapter asks you to show that equal holding and ordering costs is a property of the EOQ model.

The use of an order quantity of 1824 in equation (14.4) shows that the minimum cost inventory policy for Bub Beer has a total annual cost of $3649. Note that $Q^* = 1824$ balances the holding and ordering costs. Check for yourself to see that these costs are equal.[2]

The When-to-Order Decision

The reorder point is expressed in terms of inventory position, the amount of inventory on hand plus the amount on order. With short lead times, inventory position is usually the same as the inventory on hand. However, with long lead times, inventory position may be larger than inventory on hand.

Now that we know how much to order, we want to address the question of *when* to order. To answer this question, we need to introduce the concept of inventory position. The **inventory position** is defined as the amount of inventory on hand plus the amount of inventory on order. The when-to-order decision is expressed in terms of a **reorder point**—the inventory position at which a new order should be placed.

The manufacturer of Bub Beer guarantees a two-day delivery on any order placed by R&B Beverage. Hence, assuming R&B Beverage operates 250 days per year, the annual demand of 104,000 cases implies a daily demand of $104,000/250 = 416$ cases. Thus, we expect (2 days)(416 cases per day) = 832 cases of Bub to be sold during the two days it takes a new order to reach the R&B warehouse. In inventory terminology, the two-day delivery period is referred to as the **lead time** for a new order, and the 832-case demand anticipated during this period is referred to as the **lead-time demand**. Thus, R&B should order a new shipment of Bub Beer from the manufacturer when the inventory reaches 832 cases. For inventory systems using the constant demand rate assumption and a fixed

---

[2]Actually, Q^* from equation (14.5) is 1824.28, but because we cannot order fractional cases of beer, a Q^* of 1824 is shown. This value of Q^* may cause a few cents deviation between the two costs. If Q^* is used at its exact value, the holding and ordering costs will be exactly the same.

lead time, the reorder point is the same as the lead-time demand. For these systems, the general expression for the reorder point is as follows:

$$r = dm \qquad\qquad \textbf{(14.6)}$$

where

$$r = \text{reorder point}$$
$$d = \text{demand per day}$$
$$m = \text{lead time for a new order in days}$$

The question of how frequently the order will be placed can now be answered. The period between orders is referred to as the **cycle time**. Previously in equation (14.3), we defined D/Q as the number of orders that will be placed in a year. Thus, $D/Q^* = 104,000/1824 = 57$ is the number of orders R&B Beverage will place for Bub Beer each year. If R&B places 57 orders over 250 working days, it will order approximately every $250/57 = 4.39$ working days. Thus, the cycle time is 4.39 working days. The general expression for a cycle time[3] of T days is given by

$$T = \frac{250}{D/Q^*} = \frac{250Q^*}{D} \qquad\qquad \textbf{(14.7)}$$

Sensitivity Analysis for the EOQ Model

Even though substantial time may have been spent in arriving at the cost per order ($32) and the holding cost rate (25%), we should realize that these figures are at best good estimates. Thus, we may want to consider how much the recommended order quantity would change with different estimated ordering and holding costs. To determine the effects of various cost scenarios, we can calculate the recommended order quantity under several different cost conditions. Table 14.2 shows the minimum total cost order quantity for several cost possibilities. As you can see from the table, the value of Q^* appears relatively stable, even with some variations in the cost estimates. Based on these results, the best order quantity for Bub Beer is in the range of 1700–2000 cases. If operated properly, the total cost for the Bub Beer inventory system should be close to $3400–$3800 per year. We also note that little risk is associated with implementing the calculated order quantity of 1824. For example, if R&B implements an order quantity of 1824 cases (using cost estimates based on $32 per order and 25% annual holding rate), but the actual cost per order turns out to be $34 and the actual annual holding rate turns out to be 24%, then R&B experiences only a $5 increase ($3690–$3685) in the total annual cost.

From the preceding analysis, we would say that this EOQ model is insensitive to small variations or errors in the cost estimates. This insensitivity is a property of EOQ models in general, which indicates that if we have at least reasonable estimates of ordering cost and holding cost, we can expect to obtain a good approximation of the true minimum cost order quantity.

---

[3]This general expression for cycle time is based on 250 working days per year. If the firm operated 300 working days per year and wanted to express cycle time in terms of working days, the cycle time would be given by $T = 300Q^*/D$.

TABLE 14.2   OPTIMAL ORDER QUANTITIES FOR SEVERAL COST POSSIBILITIES

Possible Inventory Holding Cost (%)	Possible Cost per Order	Optimal Order Quantity (Q^*)	Projected Total Annual Cost	
			Using Q^*	Using $Q = 1824$
24	$30	1803	$3461	$3462
24	34	1919	3685	3690
26	30	1732	3603	3607
26	34	1844	3835	3836

Excel Solution of the EOQ Model

Inventory models such as the EOQ model are easily implemented with the aid of spreadsheets. The Excel EOQ worksheet for Bub Beer is shown in Figure 14.4. The worksheet view of the formulas is on the left, and the worksheet view of the values is on the right. Data on annual demand, ordering cost, annual inventory holding cost rate, cost per unit, working days per year, and lead time in days are input in cells B3 to B8. The appropriate EOQ model formulas, which determine the optimal inventory policy, are placed in cells B13 to B21. For example, cell B13 computes the optimal economic order quantity 1824.28, and cell B16 computes the total annual cost $3648.56. If sensitivity analysis is desired, one or

FIGURE 14.4   WORKSHEET FOR THE BUB BEER EOQ INVENTORY MODEL

WEB file

EOQ

TABLE 14.3   THE EOQ MODEL ASSUMPTIONS

1. Demand D is deterministic and occurs at a constant rate.
2. The order quantity Q is the same for each order. The inventory level increases by Q units each time an order is received.
3. The cost per order, C_o, is constant and does not depend on the quantity ordered.
4. The purchase cost per unit, C, is constant and does not depend on the quantity ordered.
5. The inventory holding cost per unit per time period, C_h, is constant. The total inventory holding cost depends on both C_h and the size of the inventory.
6. Shortages such as stock-outs or backorders are not permitted.
7. The lead time for an order is constant.
8. The inventory position is reviewed continuously. As a result, an order is placed as soon as the inventory position reaches the reorder point.

more of the input data values can be modified. The impact of any change or changes on the optimal inventory policy will then appear in the worksheet.

The Excel worksheet in Figure 14.4 is a template that can be used for the EOQ model. This worksheet and similar Excel worksheets for the other inventory models presented in this chapter are available at the WEBfiles link on the website that accompanies this text.

Summary of the EOQ Model Assumptions

You should carefully review the assumptions of the inventory model before applying it in an actual situation. Several inventory models discussed later in this chapter alter one or more of the assumptions of the EOQ model.

To use the optimal order quantity and reorder point model described in this section, an analyst must make assumptions about how the inventory system operates. The EOQ model with its economic order quantity formula is based on some specific assumptions about the R&B inventory system. A summary of the assumptions for this model is provided in Table 14.3. Before using the EOQ formula, carefully review these assumptions to ensure that they are applicable to the inventory system being analyzed. If the assumptions are not reasonable, seek a different inventory model.

Various types of inventory systems are used in practice, and the inventory models presented in the following sections alter one or more of the EOQ model assumptions shown in Table 14.3. When the assumptions change, a different inventory model with different optimal operating policies becomes necessary.

NOTES AND COMMENTS

1. With relatively long lead times, the lead-time demand and the resulting reorder point r, determined by equation (14.6), may exceed Q^*. If this condition occurs, at least one order will be outstanding when a new order is placed. For example, assume that Bub Beer has a lead time of $m = 6$ days. With a daily demand of $d = 432$ cases, equation (14.6) shows that the reorder point would be $r = dm = 6 \times 432 = 2592$ cases. Note that this reorder point exceeds $Q^* = 1824$ which also corresponds to the maximum inventory level (see Figure 14.1). At first glance, this seems impossible—how can we order when inventory

drops to 2592 cases when if the maximum inventory level is 1824? The key is to remember that the reorder point is expressed in terms of inventory position which equals cases "on-hand" + cases "on the way." Thus, to interpret the $r = 2952$, realize that 2592 total cases will occur when there are 1824 cases on the way (from a previous order) and 768 on-hand. So, the model states that we should place another order when the on-hand inventory level is 768 cases. That is, because the lead time is so long (6 days), we have to place an order of Q units before the last order of Q units has even arrived!

14.2 Economic Production Lot Size Model

The inventory model in this section alters assumption 2 of the EOQ model (see Table 14.3). The assumption concerning the arrival of Q units each time an order is received is changed to a constant production supply rate.

The inventory model presented in this section is similar to the EOQ model in that we are attempting to determine *how much* we should order and *when* the order should be placed. We again assume a constant demand rate. However, instead of assuming that the order arrives in a shipment of size Q^*, as in the EOQ model, we assume that units are supplied to inventory at a constant rate over several days or several weeks. The **constant supply rate** assumption implies that the same number of units is supplied to inventory each period of time (e.g., 10 units every day or 50 units every week). This model is designed for production situations in which, once an order is placed, production begins and a constant number of units is added to inventory each day until the production run has been completed.

If we have a production system that produces 50 units per day and we decide to schedule 10 days of production, we have a 50(10) = 500-unit production lot size. The **lot size** is the number of units in an order. In general, if we let Q indicate the production lot size, the approach to the inventory decisions is similar to the EOQ model; that is, we build a holding and ordering cost model that expresses the total cost as a function of the production lot size. Then we attempt to find the production lot size that minimizes the total cost.

One other condition that should be mentioned at this time is that the model only applies to situations where the production rate is greater than the demand rate; the production system must be able to satisfy demand. For instance, if the constant demand rate is 400 units per day, the production rate must be at least 400 units per day to satisfy demand.

During the production run, demand reduces the inventory while production adds to inventory. Because we assume that the production rate exceeds the demand rate, each day during a production run we produce more units than are demanded. Thus, the excess production causes a gradual inventory buildup during the production period. When the production run is completed, the continuing demand causes the inventory to gradually decline until a new production run is started. The inventory pattern for this system is shown in Figure 14.5.

This model differs from the EOQ model in that a setup cost replaces the ordering cost, and the saw-tooth inventory pattern shown in Figure 14.5 differs from the inventory pattern shown in Figure 14.2.

As in the EOQ model, we are now dealing with two costs, the holding cost and the ordering cost. Here the holding cost is identical to the definition in the EOQ model, but the interpretation of the ordering cost is slightly different. In fact, in a production situation the ordering cost is more correctly referred to as the production **setup cost**. This cost, which includes labor, material, and lost production costs incurred while preparing the production

FIGURE 14.5 INVENTORY PATTERN FOR THE PRODUCTION LOT SIZE INVENTORY MODEL

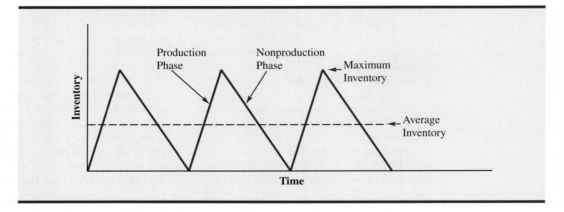

system for operation, is a fixed cost that occurs for every production run regardless of the production lot size.

Total Cost Model

Let us begin building the production lot size model by writing the holding cost in terms of the production lot size Q. Again, the approach is to develop an expression for average inventory and then establish the holding costs associated with the average inventory. We use a one-year time period and an annual cost for the model.

In the EOQ model the average inventory is one-half the maximum inventory, or $\frac{1}{2}Q$. Figure 14.5 shows that for a production lot size model, a constant inventory buildup rate occurs during the production run, and a constant inventory depletion rate occurs during the nonproduction period; thus, the average inventory will be one-half the maximum inventory. However, in this inventory system the production lot size Q does not go into inventory at one point in time, and thus the inventory never reaches a level of Q units.

To show how we can compute the maximum inventory, let

$$d = \text{daily demand rate}$$
$$p = \text{daily production rate}$$
$$t = \text{number of days for a production run}$$

At this point, the logic of the production lot size model is easier to follow using a daily demand rate d and a daily production rate p. However, when the total annual cost model is eventually developed, we recommend that inputs to the model be expressed in terms of the annual demand rate D and the annual production rate P.

Because we are assuming that p will be larger than d, the daily inventory buildup rate during the production phase is $p - d$. If we run production for t days and place $p - d$ units in inventory each day, the inventory at the end of the production run will be $(p - d)t$. From Figure 14.5 we can see that the inventory at the end of the production run is also the maximum inventory. Thus,

$$\text{Maximum inventory} = (p - d)t \tag{14.8}$$

If we know we are producing a production lot size of Q units at a daily production rate of p units, then $Q = pt$, and the length of the production run t must be

$$t = \frac{Q}{p} \text{ days} \tag{14.9}$$

Thus,

$$\text{Maximum inventory} = (p - d)t = (p - d)\left(\frac{Q}{p}\right)$$
$$= \left(1 - \frac{d}{p}\right)Q \tag{14.10}$$

The average inventory, which is one-half the maximum inventory, is given by

$$\text{Average inventory} = \frac{1}{2}\left(1 - \frac{d}{p}\right)Q \tag{14.11}$$

With an annual per-unit holding cost of C_h, the general equation for annual holding cost is as follows:

$$\begin{pmatrix} \text{Annual} \\ \text{holding cost} \end{pmatrix} = \begin{pmatrix} \text{Average} \\ \text{inventory} \end{pmatrix} \begin{pmatrix} \text{Annual} \\ \text{cost} \\ \text{per unit} \end{pmatrix}$$

$$= \frac{1}{2}\left(1 - \frac{d}{p}\right)QC_h \qquad \textbf{(14.12)}$$

If D is the annual demand for the product and C_o is the setup cost for a production run, then the annual setup cost, which takes the place of the annual ordering cost in the EOQ model, is as follows:

$$\text{Annual setup cost} = \begin{pmatrix} \text{Number of production} \\ \text{runs per year} \end{pmatrix}\begin{pmatrix} \text{Setup cost} \\ \text{per run} \end{pmatrix}$$

$$= \frac{D}{Q}C_o \qquad \textbf{(14.13)}$$

Thus, the total annual cost (*TC*) model is

$$TC = \frac{1}{2}\left(1 - \frac{d}{p}\right)QC_h + \frac{D}{Q}C_o \qquad \textbf{(14.14)}$$

Suppose that a production facility operates 250 days per year. Then we can write daily demand d in terms of annual demand D as follows:

$$d = \frac{D}{250}$$

Now let P denote the annual production for the product if the product were produced every day. Then

$$P = 250p \qquad \text{and} \qquad p = \frac{P}{250}$$

Thus,[4]

$$\frac{d}{p} = \frac{D/250}{P/250} = \frac{D}{P}$$

Therefore, we can write the total annual cost model as follows:

$$TC = \frac{1}{2}\left(1 - \frac{D}{P}\right)QC_h + \frac{D}{Q}C_o \qquad \textbf{(14.15)}$$

___

[4]The ratio $d/p = D/P$ holds regardless of the number of days of operation; 250 days is used here merely as an illustration.

Equations (14.14) and (14.15) are equivalent. However, equation (14.15) may be used more frequently because an *annual* cost model tends to make the analyst think in terms of collecting *annual* demand data (*D*) and *annual* production data (*P*) rather than daily data.

Economic Production Lot Size

As the production rate P approaches infinity, D/P approaches zero. In this case, equation (14.16) is equivalent to the EOQ model in equation (14.5).

Given estimates of the holding cost (C_h), setup cost (C_o), annual demand rate (*D*), and annual production rate (*P*), we could use a trial-and-error approach to compute the total annual cost for various production lot sizes (*Q*). However, trial and error is not necessary; we can use the minimum cost formula for Q^* that has been developed using differential calculus (see Appendix 14.2). The equation is as follows:

$$Q^* = \sqrt{\frac{2DC_o}{(1 - D/P)C_h}} \tag{14.16}$$

LotSize

An Example Beauty Bar Soap is produced on a production line that has an annual capacity of 60,000 cases. The annual demand is estimated at 26,000 cases, with the demand rate essentially constant throughout the year. The cleaning, preparation, and setup of the production line cost approximately $135. The manufacturing cost per case is $4.50, and the annual holding cost is figured at a 24% rate. Thus, $C_h = IC = 0.24(\$4.50) = \$1.08$. What is the recommended production lot size?

Using equation (14.16), we have

$$Q^* = \sqrt{\frac{2(26,000)(135)}{(1 - 26,000/60,000)(1.08)}} = 3387$$

Work Problem 13 as an example of an economic production lot size model.

The total annual cost using equation (14.15) and $Q^* = 3387$ is $2073.

Other relevant data include a five-day lead time to schedule and set up a production run and 250 working days per year. Thus, the lead-time demand of $(26,000/250)(5) = 520$ cases is the reorder point. The cycle time is the time between production runs. Using equation (14.7), the cycle time is $T = 250Q^*/D = [(250)(3387)]/26,000$, or 33 working days. Thus, we should plan a production run of 3387 units every 33 working days.

Inventory Model with Planned Shortages

A **shortage** or **stock-out** occurs when demand exceeds the amount of inventory on hand. In many situations, shortages are undesirable and should be avoided if at all possible. However, in other cases it may be desirable—from an economic point of view—to plan for and allow shortages. In practice, these types of situations are most commonly found where the value of the inventory per unit is high and hence the holding cost is high. An example of this type of situation is a new car dealer's inventory. Often a specific car that a customer wants is not in stock. However, if the customer is willing to wait a few weeks, the dealer is usually able to order the car.

The assumptions of the EOQ model in Table 14.3 apply to this inventory model with the exception that shortages, referred to as backorders, are now permitted.

The model developed in this section takes into account a type of shortage known as a **backorder**. In a backorder situation, we assume that when a customer places an order and discovers that the supplier is out of stock, the customer waits until the new shipment arrives, and then the order is filled. Frequently, the waiting period in backorder situations is relatively short. Thus, by promising the customer top priority and immediate delivery when the goods become available, companies may be able to convince the customer to wait until the order arrives. In these cases, the backorder assumption is valid.

The backorder model that we develop is an extension of the EOQ model presented in Section 14.1. We use the EOQ model for which all goods arrive in inventory at one time and are subject to a constant demand rate. If we let S indicate the number of backorders that have accumulated by the time a new shipment of size Q is received, then the inventory system for the backorder case has the following characteristics:

- If S backorders exist when a new shipment of size Q arrives, then S backorders are shipped to the appropriate customers, and the remaining $Q - S$ units are placed in inventory. Therefore, $Q - S$ is the maximum inventory.
- The inventory cycle of T days is divided into two distinct phases: t_1 days when inventory is on hand and orders are filled as they occur, and t_2 days when stock-outs occur and all new orders are placed on backorder.

The inventory pattern for the inventory model with backorders, where negative inventory represents the number of backorders, is shown in Figure 14.6.

With the inventory pattern now defined, we can proceed with the basic step of all inventory models—namely, the development of a total cost model. For the inventory model with backorders, we encounter the usual holding costs and ordering costs. We also incur a backorder cost in terms of the labor and special delivery costs directly associated with the handling of the backorders. Another portion of the backorder cost accounts for the loss of goodwill because some customers will have to wait for their orders. Because the **goodwill cost** depends on how long a customer has to wait, it is customary to adopt the convention of expressing backorder cost in terms of the cost of having a unit on backorder for a stated period of time. This method of costing backorders on a time basis is similar to the method used to compute the inventory holding cost, and we can use it to compute a total annual cost of backorders once the average backorder level and the backorder cost per unit per period are known.

Let us begin the development of a total cost model by calculating the average inventory for a hypothetical problem. If we have an average inventory of two units for three days and no inventory on the fourth day, what is the average inventory over the four-day period? It is

$$\frac{2 \text{ units (3 days)} + 0 \text{ units (1 day)}}{4 \text{ days}} = \frac{6}{4} = 1.5 \text{ units}$$

FIGURE 14.6   INVENTORY PATTERN FOR AN INVENTORY MODEL WITH BACKORDERS

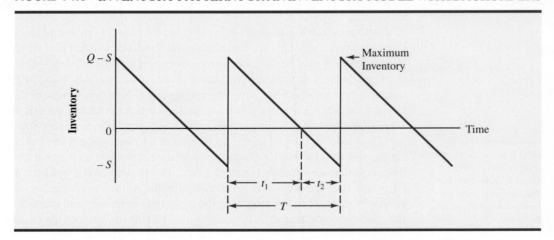

Refer to Figure 14.6. You can see that this situation is what happens in the backorder model. With a maximum inventory of $Q - S$ units, the t_1 days we have inventory on hand will have an average inventory of $(Q - S)/2$. No inventory is carried for the t_2 days in which we experience backorders. Thus, over the total cycle time of $T = t_1 + t_2$ days, we can compute the average inventory as follows:

$$\text{Average inventory} = \frac{\frac{1}{2}(Q - S)t_1 + 0t_2}{t_1 + t_2} = \frac{\frac{1}{2}(Q - S)t_1}{T} \qquad \textbf{(14.17)}$$

Can we find other ways of expressing t_1 and T? Because we know that the maximum inventory is $Q - S$ and that d represents the constant daily demand, we have

$$t_1 = \frac{Q - S}{d} \text{ days} \qquad \textbf{(14.18)}$$

That is, the maximum inventory of $Q - S$ units will be used up in $(Q - S)/d$ days. Because Q units are ordered each cycle, we know the length of a cycle must be

$$T = \frac{Q}{d} \text{ days} \qquad \textbf{(14.19)}$$

Combining equations (14.18) and (14.19) with equation (14.17), we can compute the average inventory as follows:

$$\text{Average inventory} = \frac{\frac{1}{2}(Q - S)[(Q - S)/d]}{Q/d} = \frac{(Q - S)^2}{2Q} \qquad \textbf{(14.20)}$$

Thus, the average inventory is expressed in terms of two inventory decisions: how much we will order (Q) and the maximum number of backorders (S).

The formula for the annual number of orders placed using this model is identical to that for the EOQ model. With D representing the annual demand, we have

$$\text{Annual number of orders} = \frac{D}{Q} \qquad \textbf{(14.21)}$$

The next step is to develop an expression for the average backorder level. Because we know the maximum for backorders is S, we can use the same logic we used to establish average inventory in finding the average number of backorders. We have an average number of backorders during the period t_2 of $\frac{1}{2}$ the maximum number of backorders or $\frac{1}{2}S$. We do not have any backorders during the t_1 days we have inventory; therefore we can calculate the average backorders in a manner similar to equation (14.17). Using this approach, we have

$$\text{Average backorders} = \frac{0t_1 + (S/2)t_2}{T} = \frac{(S/2)t_2}{T} \quad \textbf{(14.22)}$$

When we let the maximum number of backorders reach an amount S at a daily rate of d, the length of the backorder portion of the inventory cycle is

$$t_2 = \frac{S}{d} \quad \textbf{(14.23)}$$

Using equations (14.23) and (14.19) in equation (14.22), we have

$$\text{Average backorders} = \frac{(S/2)(S/d)}{Q/d} = \frac{S^2}{2Q} \quad \textbf{(14.24)}$$

The backorder cost C_b is one of the most difficult costs to estimate in inventory models. The reason is that it attempts to measure the cost associated with the loss of goodwill when a customer must wait for an order. Expressing this cost on an annual basis adds to the difficulty.

Let

C_h = cost to hold one unit in inventory for one year

C_o = cost per order

C_b = cost to maintain one unit on backorder for one year

The total annual cost (TC) for the inventory model with backorders becomes

$$TC = \frac{(Q - S)^2}{2Q} C_h + \frac{D}{Q} C_o + \frac{S^2}{2Q} C_b \quad \textbf{(14.25)}$$

Given C_h, C_o, and C_b and the annual demand D, differential calculus can be used to show that the minimum cost values for the order quantity Q^* and the planned backorders S^* are as follows:

$$Q^* = \sqrt{\frac{2DC_o}{C_h}\left(\frac{C_h + C_b}{C_b}\right)} \quad \textbf{(14.26)}$$

$$S^* = Q^*\left(\frac{C_h}{C_h + C_b}\right) \quad \textbf{(14.27)}$$

Shortage

An Example Suppose that the Higley Radio Components Company has a product for which the assumptions of the inventory model with backorders are valid. Information obtained by the company is as follows:

$D = 2000$ units per year

$I = 20\%$

$C = \$50$ per unit

$C_h = IC = (0.20)(\$50) = \$10$ per unit per year

$C_o = \$25 =$ per order

An inventory situation that incorporates backorder costs is considered in Problem 15.

The company is considering the possibility of allowing some backorders to occur for the product. The annual backorder cost is estimated to be $30 per unit per year. Using equations (14.26) and (14.27), we have

$$Q^* = \sqrt{\frac{2(2000)(25)}{10}\left(\frac{10 + 30}{30}\right)} = 115$$

and

$$S^* = 115\left(\frac{10}{10 + 30}\right) = 29$$

If this solution is implemented, the system will operate with the following properties:

$$\text{Maximum inventory} = Q - S = 115 - 29 = 86$$

$$\text{Cycle time} = T = \frac{Q}{D}(250) = \frac{115}{2000}(250) = 14 \text{ working days}$$

The total annual cost is

If backorders can be tolerated, the total cost including the backorder cost will be less than the total cost of the EOQ model. Some people think the model with backorders will have a greater cost because it includes a backorder cost in addition to the usual inventory holding and ordering costs. You can point out the fallacy in this thinking by noting that the backorder model leads to lower inventory and hence lower inventory holding costs.

$$\text{Holding cost} = \frac{(86)^2}{2(115)}(10) \; = \$322$$

$$\text{Ordering cost} = \frac{2000}{115}(25) \;\;\; = \$435$$

$$\text{Backorder cost} = \frac{(29)^2}{2(115)}(30) \; = \$110$$

$$\text{Total cost} = \$867$$

If the company chooses to prohibit backorders and adopts the regular EOQ model, the recommended inventory decision would be

$$Q^* = \sqrt{\frac{2(2000)(25)}{10}} = \sqrt{10,000} = 100$$

This order quantity would result in a holding cost and an ordering cost of $500 each or a total annual cost of $1000. Thus, in this problem, allowing backorders is projecting a $1000 − $867 = $133, or 13.3%, savings in cost from the no-stock-out EOQ model. The preceding comparison and conclusion are based on the assumption that the backorder model with an annual cost per backordered unit of $30 is a valid model for the actual inventory situation. If the company is concerned that stock-outs might lead to lost sales, then the savings might not be enough to warrant switching to an inventory policy that allows for planned shortages.

NOTES AND COMMENTS

1. Equation (14.27) shows that the optimal number of planned backorders S^* is proportional to the ratio $C_h/(C_h + C_b)$, where C_h is the annual holding cost per unit and C_b is the annual backorder cost per unit. Whenever C_h increases, this ratio becomes larger, and the number of planned backorders increases. This relationship explains why items that have a high per-unit cost and a correspondingly high annual holding cost are more economically handled on a backorder basis. On the other hand, whenever the backorder cost C_b increases, the ratio becomes smaller, and the number of planned backorders decreases. Thus, the model provides the intuitive result that items with high backorder costs will be handled with few backorders. In fact, with high backorder costs, the backorder model and the EOQ model with no backordering allowed provide similar inventory policies.

14.4   Quantity Discounts for the EOQ Model

In the quantity discount model, assumption 4 of the EOQ model in Table 14.3 is altered. The cost per unit varies depending on the quantity ordered.

Quantity discounts occur in numerous situations in which suppliers provide an incentive for large order quantities by offering a lower purchase cost when items are ordered in larger quantities. In this section we show how the EOQ model can be used when quantity discounts are available.

Assume that we have a product in which the basic EOQ model (see Table 14.3) is applicable. Instead of a fixed unit cost, the supplier quotes the following discount schedule:

Discount Category	Order Size	Discount (%)	Unit Cost
1	0 to 999	0	$5.00
2	1000 to 2499	3	4.85
3	2500 and over	5	4.75

The 5% discount for the 2500-unit minimum order quantity looks tempting. However, realizing that higher order quantities result in higher inventory holding costs, we should prepare a thorough cost analysis before making a final ordering and inventory policy recommendation.

Suppose that the data and cost analyses show an annual holding cost rate of 20%, an ordering cost of $49 per order, and an annual demand of 5000 units; what order quantity should we select? The following three-step procedure shows the calculations necessary to make this decision. In the preliminary calculations, we use Q_1 to indicate the order quantity for discount category 1, Q_2 for discount category 2, and Q_3 for discount category 3.

Step 1. For each discount category, compute a Q^* using the EOQ formula based on the unit cost associated with the discount category.

Recall that the EOQ model provides $Q^* = \sqrt{2DC_o/C_h}$, where $C_h = IC = (0.20)C$. With three discount categories providing three different unit costs C, we obtain

$$Q_1^* = \sqrt{\frac{2(5000)49}{(0.20)(5.00)}} = 700$$

$$Q_2^* = \sqrt{\frac{2(5000)49}{(0.20)(4.85)}} = 711$$

$$Q_3^* = \sqrt{\frac{2(5000)49}{(0.20)(4.75)}} = 718$$

Because the only differences in the EOQ formulas come from slight differences in the holding cost, the economic order quantities resulting from this step will be approximately the same. However, these order quantities will usually not all be of the size necessary to qualify for the discount price assumed. In the preceding case, both Q_2^* and Q_3^* are insufficient order quantities to obtain their assumed discounted costs of $4.85 and $4.75, respectively.

For those order quantities for which the assumed price cannot be obtained, the following procedure must be used:

Step 2. For the Q^* that is too small to qualify for the assumed discount price, adjust the order quantity upward to the nearest order quantity that will allow the product to be purchased at the assumed price.

In our example, this adjustment causes us to set

$$Q_2^* = 1000$$

and

$$Q_3^* = 2500$$

If a calculated Q^* for a given discount price is large enough to qualify for a bigger discount, that value of Q^* cannot lead to an optimal solution. Although the reason may not be obvious, it does turn out to be a property of the EOQ quantity discount model.

In the previous inventory models considered, the annual purchase cost of the item was not included because it was constant and never affected by the inventory order policy decision. However, in the quantity discount model, the annual purchase cost depends on the order quantity and the associated unit cost. Thus, annual purchase cost (annual demand $D \times$ unit cost C) is included in the equation for total cost as shown here.

In the EOQ model with quantity discounts, the annual purchase cost must be included because purchase cost depends on the order quantity. Thus, it is a relevant cost.

$$TC = \frac{Q}{2} C_h + \frac{D}{Q} C_o + DC \qquad \textbf{(14.28)}$$

Using this total cost equation, we can determine the optimal order quantity for the EOQ discount model in step 3.

Problem 21 will give you practice in applying the EOQ model to situations with quantity discounts.

Step 3. For each order quantity resulting from steps 1 and 2, compute the total annual cost using the unit price from the appropriate discount category and equation (14.28). The order quantity yielding the minimum total annual cost is the optimal order quantity.

The step 3 calculations for the example problem are summarized in Table 14.4. As you can see, a decision to order 1000 units at the 3% discount rate yields the minimum cost solution. Even though the 2500-unit order quantity would result in a 5% discount, its excessive holding cost makes it the second-best solution. Figure 14.7 shows the total cost curve for each of the three discount categories. Note that $Q^* = 1000$ provides the minimum cost order quantity.

TABLE 14.4 TOTAL ANNUAL COST CALCULATIONS FOR THE EOQ MODEL WITH QUANTITY DISCOUNTS

Discount Category	Unit Cost	Order Quantity	Annual Cost			
			Holding	Ordering	Purchase	Total
1	$5.00	700	$ 350	$350	$25,000	$25,700
2	4.85	1000	$ 485	$245	$24,250	$24,980
3	4.75	2500	$1188	$ 98	$23,750	$25,036

FIGURE 14.7   TOTAL COST CURVES FOR THE THREE DISCOUNT CATEGORIES

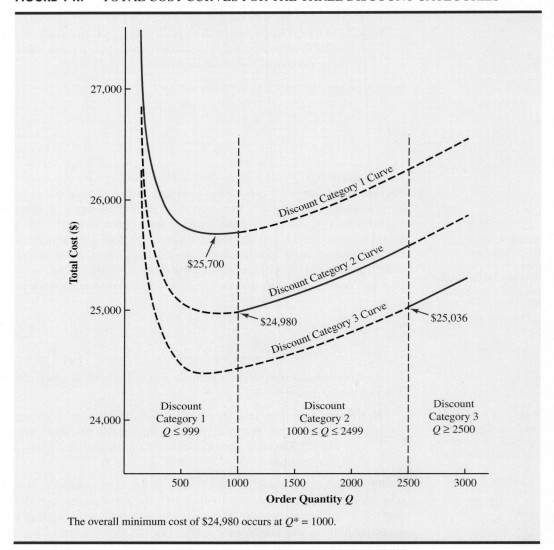

The overall minimum cost of $24,980 occurs at $Q^* = 1000$.

(14.5) Single-Period Inventory Model with Probabilistic Demand

The inventory models discussed thus far were based on the assumption that the demand rate is constant and **deterministic** throughout the year. We developed minimum cost order quantity and reorder point policies based on this assumption. In situations in which the demand rate is not deterministic, other models treat demand as **probabilistic** and best described by a probability distribution. In this section we consider a single-period inventory model with probabilistic demand.

The single-period inventory model refers to inventory situations in which *one* order is placed for the product; at the end of the period, the product has either sold out, or a surplus of

This inventory model is the first in the chapter that explicitly treats probabilistic demand. Unlike the EOQ model, it is for a single period, and unused inventory is not carried over to future periods.

unsold items will be sold for a salvage value. The single-period inventory model is applicable in situations involving seasonal or perishable items that cannot be carried in inventory and sold in future periods. Seasonal clothing (such as bathing suits and winter coats) are typically handled in a single-period manner. In these situations, a buyer places one preseason order for each item and then experiences a stock-out or holds a clearance sale on the surplus stock at the end of the season. No items are carried in inventory and sold the following year. Newspapers are another example of a product that is ordered one time and is either sold or not sold during the single period. Although newspapers are ordered daily, they cannot be carried in inventory and sold in later periods. Thus, newspaper orders may be treated as a sequence of single-period models; that is, each day or period is separate, and a single-period inventory decision must be made each period (day). Because we order only once for the period, the only inventory decision we must make is *how much* of the product to order at the start of the period.

Obviously, if the demand were known for a single-period inventory situation, the solution would be easy; we would simply order the amount we knew would be demanded. However, in most single-period models, the exact demand is not known. In fact, forecasts may show that demand can have a wide variety of values. If we are going to analyze this type of inventory problem in a quantitative manner, we need information about the probabilities associated with the various demand values. Thus, the single-period model presented in this section is based on probabilistic demand.

Neiman Marcus

Let us consider a single-period inventory model that could be used to make a how-much-to-order decision for Neiman Marcus, a high-end fashion store. The buyer for Neiman Marcus decided to order Manolo Blahnik heels shown at a buyers' meeting in New York City. The shoe will be part of the company's spring–summer promotion and will be sold through nine retail stores in the Chicago area. Because the shoe is designed for spring and summer months, it cannot be expected to sell in the fall. Neiman Marcus plans to hold a special August clearance sale in an attempt to sell all shoes not sold by July 31. The shoes cost $700 a pair and retail for $900 a pair. At the sale price of $600 a pair, all surplus shoes can be expected to sell during the August sale. If you were the buyer for Neiman Marcus, how many pairs of the shoes would you order?

To answer the question of how much to order, we need information on the demand for the shoe. Specifically, we would need to construct a probability distribution for the possible values of demand. Let us suppose that the uniform probability distribution shown in Figure 14.8 can be used to describe the demand for the Manolo Blahnik heels. In particular,

FIGURE 14.8   UNIFORM PROBABILITY DISTRIBUTION OF DEMAND FOR NEIMAN MARCUS PROBLEM

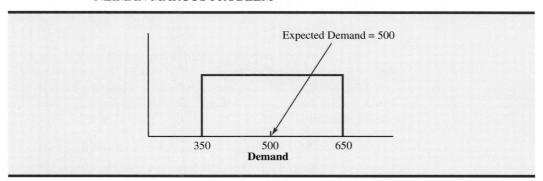

note that the range of demand is from 350 to 650 pairs of shoes, with an average, or expected, demand of 500 pairs of shoes.

Incremental analysis is a method that can be used to determine the optimal order quantity for a single-period inventory model. Incremental analysis addresses the how-much-to-order question by comparing the cost or loss of *ordering one additional unit* with the cost or loss of *not ordering one additional unit*. The costs involved are defined as follows:

c_o = cost per unit of *overestimating* demand. This cost represents the loss of ordering one additional unit and finding that it cannot be sold.

c_u = cost per unit of *underestimating* demand. This cost represents the opportunity loss of not ordering one additional unit and finding that it could have been sold.

In the Neiman Marcus problem, the company will incur the cost of overestimating demand whenever it orders too many pairs and has to sell the extra shoes during the August clearance sale. Thus, the cost per unit of overestimating demand is equal to the purchase cost per unit minus the August sales price per unit; that is, c_o = \$700 − \$600 = \$100. Therefore, Neiman Marcus will lose \$100 for each pair of shoes that it orders over the quantity demanded. The cost of underestimating demand is the lost profit (often referred to as an opportunity cost) because a pair of shoes that could have been sold was not available in inventory. Thus, the per-unit cost of underestimating demand is the difference between the regular selling price per unit and the purchase cost per unit; that is, c_u = \$900 − \$700 = \$200.

The cost of underestimating demand is usually harder to determine than the cost of overestimating demand. The reason is that the cost of underestimating demand includes a lost profit and may include a customer loss of goodwill cost because the customer is unable to purchase the item when desired.

Because the exact level of demand for the Manolo Blahnik heels is unknown, we have to consider the probability of demand and thus the probability of obtaining the associated costs or losses. For example, let us assume that Neiman Marcus management wishes to consider an order quantity equal to the average or expected demand for 500 pairs of shoes. In incremental analysis, we consider the possible losses associated with an order quantity of 501 (ordering one additional unit) and an order quantity of 500 (not ordering one additional unit). The order quantity alternatives and the possible losses are summarized here.

The key to incremental analysis is to focus on the costs that are different when comparing an order quantity Q + 1 to an order quantity Q.

Order Quantity Alternatives	Loss Occurs If	Possible Loss	Probability Loss Occurs
Q = 501	Demand overestimated; the additional unit *cannot* be sold	c_o = \$100	P(demand ≤ 500)
Q = 500	Demand underestimated; an additional unit *could have* been sold	c_u = \$200	P(demand > 500)

Using the demand probability distribution in Figure 14.8, we see that P(demand ≤ 500) = 0.50 and that P(demand > 500) = 0.50. By multiplying the possible losses, c_o = \$100 and c_u = \$200, by the probability of obtaining the loss, we can compute the expected value of the loss, or simply the *expected loss* (EL), associated with the order quantity alternatives. Thus,

$$\text{EL}(Q = 501) = c_o P(\text{demand} \leq 500) = \$100(0.50) = \$50$$
$$\text{EL}(Q = 500) = c_u P(\text{demand} > 500) = \$200(0.50) = \$100$$

Based on these expected losses, do you prefer an order quantity of 501 or 500 pairs of shoes? Because the expected loss is greater for $Q = 500$, and because we want to avoid this higher cost or loss, we should make $Q = 501$ the preferred decision. We could now consider incrementing the order quantity one additional unit to $Q = 502$ and repeating the expected loss calculations.

Although we could continue this unit-by-unit analysis, it would be time-consuming and cumbersome. We would have to evaluate $Q = 502$, $Q = 503$, $Q = 504$, and so on until we found the value of Q where the expected loss of ordering one incremental unit is equal to the expected loss of not ordering one incremental unit; that is, the optimal order quantity $Q*$ occurs when the incremental analysis shows that

$$EL(Q* + 1) = EL(Q*) \tag{14.29}$$

When this relationship holds, increasing the order quantity by one additional unit has no economic advantage. Using the logic with which we computed the expected losses for the order quantities of 501 and 500, the general expressions for $EL(Q* + 1)$ and $EL(Q*)$ can be written

$$EL(Q* + 1) = c_o P(\text{demand} \leq Q*) \tag{14.30}$$

$$EL(Q*) = c_u P(\text{demand} > Q*) \tag{14.31}$$

Because demand $\leq Q*$ and demand $> Q*$ are complimentary events, we know from basic probability that

$$P(\text{demand} \leq Q*) + P(\text{demand} > Q*) = 1 \tag{14.32}$$

and we can write

$$P(\text{demand} > Q*) = 1 - P(\text{demand} \leq Q*) \tag{14.33}$$

Using this expression, equation (14.31) can be rewritten as

$$EL(Q*) = c_u[1 - P(\text{demand} \leq Q*)] \tag{14.34}$$

Equations (14.30) and (14.34) can be used to show that $EL(Q* + 1) = EL(Q*)$ whenever

$$c_o P(\text{demand} \leq Q*) = c_u[1 - P(\text{demand} \leq Q*)] \tag{14.35}$$

Solving for $P(\text{demand} \leq Q*)$, we have

$$P(\text{demand} \leq Q*) = \frac{c_u}{c_u + c_o} \tag{14.36}$$

This expression provides the general condition for the optimal order quantity $Q*$ in the single-period inventory model.

In the Neiman Marcus problem, $c_o = \$100$ and $c_u = \$200$. Thus, equation (14.36) shows that the optimal order size for the Manolo Blahnik heels must satisfy the following condition:

$$P(\text{demand} \leq Q*) = \frac{c_u}{c_u + c_o} = \frac{200}{200 + 100} = \frac{200}{300} = \frac{2}{3}$$

We can find the optimal order quantity Q^* by referring to the probability distribution shown in Figure 14.8 and finding the value of Q that will provide $P(\text{demand} \leq Q^*) = {}^2/_3$. To find this solution, we note that in the uniform distribution the probability is evenly distributed over the entire range of 350–650 pairs of shoes. Thus, we can satisfy the expression for Q^* by moving two-thirds of the way from 350 to 650. Because this range is $650 - 350 = 300$, we move 200 units from 350 toward 650.

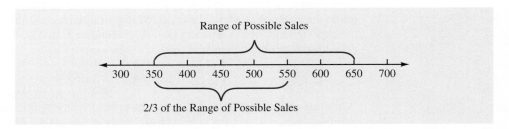

Doing so provides the optimal order quantity of 550 pairs of shoes.

In summary, the key to establishing an optimal order quantity for single-period inventory models is to identify the probability distribution that describes the demand for the item and to calculate the per-unit costs of overestimation and underestimation. Then, using the information for the per-unit costs of overestimation and underestimation, equation (14.36) can be used to find the location of Q^* in the probability distribution.

Nationwide Car Rental

As another example of a single-period inventory model with probabilistic demand, consider the situation faced by Nationwide Car Rental. Nationwide must decide how many automobiles to have available at each car rental location at specific points in time throughout the year. Using the Myrtle Beach, South Carolina, location as an example, management would like to know the number of full-sized automobiles to have available for the Labor Day weekend. Based on previous experience, customer demand for full-sized automobiles for the Labor Day weekend has a normal distribution with a mean of 150 automobiles and a standard deviation of 14 automobiles.

The Nationwide Car Rental situation can benefit from use of a single-period inventory model. The company must establish the number of full-sized automobiles to have available prior to the weekend. Customer demand over the weekend will then result in either a stock-out or a surplus. Let us denote the number of full-sized automobiles available by Q. If Q is greater than customer demand, Nationwide will have a surplus of cars. The cost of a surplus is the cost of overestimating demand. This cost is set at $80 per car, which reflects, in part, the opportunity cost of not having the car available for rent elsewhere.

If Q is less than customer demand, Nationwide will rent all available cars and experience a stock-out or shortage. A shortage results in an underestimation cost of $200 per car. This figure reflects the cost due to lost profit and the lost goodwill of not having a car available for a customer. Given this information, how many full-sized automobiles should Nationwide make available for the Labor Day weekend?

Using the cost of underestimation, $c_u = \$200$, and the cost of overestimation, $c_o = \$80$, equation (14.36) indicates that the optimal order quantity must satisfy the following condition:

$$P(\text{demand} \leq Q^*) = \frac{c_u}{(c_u + c_o)} = \frac{200}{200 + 80} = 0.7143$$

FIGURE 14.9   PROBABILITY DISTRIBUTION OF DEMAND FOR THE NATIONWIDE
CAR RENTAL PROBLEM SHOWING THE LOCATION OF $Q*$

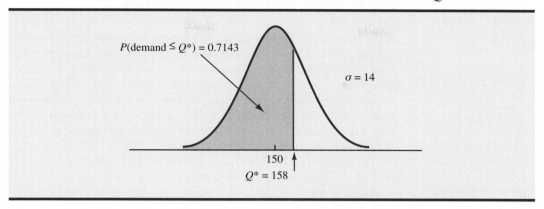

We can use the normal probability distribution for demand as shown in Figure 14.9 to find the order quantity that satisfies the condition that $P(\text{demand} \leq Q*) = 0.7143$. From Appendix D, we see that 0.7143 of the area in the left tail of the normal probability distribution occurs at $z = 0.57$ standard deviations *above* the mean. With a mean demand of $\mu = 150$ automobiles and a standard deviation of $\sigma = 14$ automobiles, we have

$$Q* = \mu + 0.57\sigma$$
$$= 150 + 0.57(14) = 158$$

WEB file

SinglePeriod

An example of a single-period inventory model with probabilistic demand described by a normal probability distribution is considered in Problem 25.

Thus, Nationwide Car Rental should plan to have 158 full-sized automobiles available in Myrtle Beach for the Labor Day weekend. Note that in this case the cost of overestimation is less than the cost of underestimation. Thus, Nationwide is willing to risk a higher probability of overestimating demand and hence a higher probability of a surplus. In fact, Nationwide's optimal order quantity has a 0.7143 probability of a surplus and a $1 - 0.7143 = 0.2857$ probability of a stock-out. As a result, the probability is 0.2857 that all 158 full-sized automobiles will be rented during the Labor Day weekend.

NOTES AND COMMENTS

1. In any probabilistic inventory model, the assumption about the probability distribution for demand is critical and can affect the recommended inventory decision. In the problems presented in this section, we used the uniform and the normal probability distributions to describe demand. In some situations, other probability distributions may be more appropriate. In using probabilistic inventory models, we must exercise care in selecting the probability distribution that most realistically describes demand.

2. In the single-period inventory model, the value of $c_u/(c_u + c_o)$ plays a critical role in selecting the order quantity [see equation (14.36)]. Whenever $c_u = c_o$, $c_u/(c_u + c_o)$ equals 0.50; in this case, we should select an order quantity corresponding to the median demand. With this choice, a stock-out is just as likely as a surplus because the two costs are equal. However, whenever $c_u < c_o$, a smaller order quantity will be recommended. In this case, the smaller order quantity will provide a higher probability of a stock-out; however, the more expensive cost of overestimating demand and having a surplus will tend to be avoided. Finally, whenever $c_u > c_o$, a larger order quantity will be recommended. In this case, the larger order quantity provides a lower probability of a stock-out in an attempt to avoid the more expensive cost of underestimating demand and experiencing a stock-out.

14.6 Order-Quantity, Reorder Point Model with Probabilistic Demand

In the previous section we considered a single-period inventory model with probabilistic demand. In this section we extend our discussion to a multiperiod order-quantity, reorder point inventory model with probabilistic demand. In the multiperiod model, the inventory system operates continuously with many repeating periods or cycles; inventory can be carried from one period to the next. Whenever the inventory position reaches the reorder point, an order for Q units is placed. Because demand is probabilistic, the time the reorder point will be reached, the time between orders, and the time the order of Q units will arrive in inventory cannot be determined in advance.

The inventory model in this section is based on the assumptions of the EOQ model shown in Table 14.3, with the exception that demand is probabilistic rather than deterministic. With probabilistic demand, occasional shortages may occur.

The inventory pattern for the order-quantity, reorder point model with probabilistic demand will have the general appearance shown in Figure 14.10. Note that the increases, or jumps, in the inventory occur whenever an order of Q units arrives. The inventory decreases at a nonconstant rate based on the probabilistic demand. A new order is placed whenever the reorder point is reached. At times, the order quantity of Q units will arrive before inventory reaches zero. However, at other times, higher demand will cause a stock-out before a new order is received. As with other order-quantity, reorder point models, the manager must determine the order quantity Q and the reorder point r for the inventory system.

The exact mathematical formulation of an order-quantity, reorder point inventory model with probabilistic demand is beyond the scope of this text. However, we present a procedure that can be used to obtain good, workable order-quantity and reorder point inventory policies. The solution procedure can be expected to provide only an approximation of the optimal solution, but it can yield good solutions in many practical situations.

Let us consider the inventory problem of Dabco Industrial Lighting Distributors. Dabco purchases a special high-intensity lightbulb for industrial lighting systems from a well-known

FIGURE 14.10   INVENTORY PATTERN FOR AN ORDER-QUANTITY, REORDER POINT MODEL WITH PROBABILISTIC DEMAND

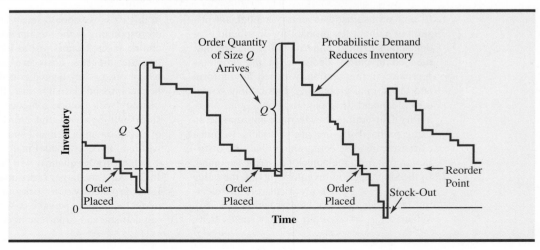

FIGURE 14.11   LEAD-TIME DEMAND PROBABILITY DISTRIBUTION
FOR DABCO LIGHTBULBS

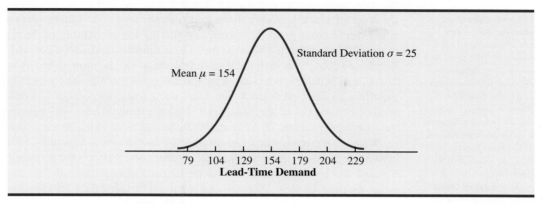

Standard Deviation $\sigma = 25$

Mean $\mu = 154$

79   104   129   154   179   204   229
Lead-Time Demand

lightbulb manufacturer. Dabco would like a recommendation on how much to order and when to order so that a low-cost inventory policy can be maintained. Pertinent facts are that the ordering cost is $12 per order, one bulb costs $6, and Dabco uses a 20% annual holding cost rate for its inventory ($C_h = IC = 0.20 \times \$6 = \$1.20$). Dabco, which has more than 1000 customers, experiences a probabilistic demand; in fact, the number of units demanded varies considerably from day to day and from week to week. The lead time for a new order of lightbulbs is one week. Historical sales data indicate that demand during a one-week lead time can be described by a normal probability distribution with a mean of 154 lightbulbs and a standard deviation of 25 lightbulbs. The normal distribution of demand during the lead time is shown in Figure 14.11. Because the mean demand during one week is 154 units, Dabco can anticipate a mean or expected annual demand of 154 units per week $\times$ 52 weeks per year = 8008 units per year.

The How-Much-to-Order Decision

Although we are in a probabilistic demand situation, we have an estimate of the expected annual demand of 8008 units. We can apply the EOQ model from Section 14.1 as an approximation of the best order quantity, with the expected annual demand used for D. In Dabco's case

ProbDemandQ

$$Q^* = \sqrt{\frac{2DC_o}{C_h}} = \sqrt{\frac{2(8008)(12)}{(1.20)}} = 400 \text{ units}$$

When we studied the sensitivity of the EOQ model, we learned that the total cost of operating an inventory system was relatively insensitive to order quantities that were in the neighborhood of Q^*. Using this knowledge, we expect 400 units per order to be a good approximation of the optimal order quantity. Even if annual demand were as low as 7000 units or as high as 9000 units, an order quantity of 400 units should be a relatively good low-cost order size. Thus, given our best estimate of annual demand at 8008 units, we will use $Q^* = 400$.

We have established the 400-unit order quantity by ignoring the fact that demand is probabilistic. Using $Q^* = 400$, Dabco can anticipate placing approximately $D/Q^* = 8008/400 = 20$ orders per year with an average of approximately $250/20 = 12.5$ working days between orders.

The When-to-Order Decision

We now want to establish a when-to-order decision rule or reorder point that will trigger the ordering process. With a mean lead-time demand of 154 units, you might first suggest a 154-unit reorder point. However, considering the probability of demand now becomes extremely important. If 154 is the mean lead-time demand, and if demand is symmetrically distributed about 154, then the lead-time demand will be more than 154 units roughly 50% of the time. When the demand during the one-week lead time exceeds 154 units, Dabco will experience a shortage or stock-out. Thus, using a reorder point of 154 units, approximately 50% of the time (10 of the 20 orders a year on average) Dabco will be short of bulbs before the new supply arrives. This shortage rate would most likely be viewed as unacceptable.

The probability of a stock-out during any one inventory cycle is easiest to estimate by first determining the number of orders that are expected during the year. The inventory manager can usually state a willingness to allow perhaps one, two, or three stock-outs during the year. The allowable stock-outs per year divided by the number of orders per year will provide the desired probability of a stock-out.

Refer to the **lead-time demand distribution** shown in Figure 14.11. Given this distribution, we can now determine how the reorder point r affects the probability of a stock-out. Because stock-outs occur whenever the demand during the lead time exceeds the reorder point, we can find the probability of a stock-out by using the lead-time demand distribution to compute the probability that demand will exceed r.

We could now approach the when-to-order problem by defining a cost per stock-out and then attempting to include this cost in a total cost equation. Alternatively, we can ask management to specify the average number of stock-outs that can be tolerated per year. If demand for a product is probabilistic, a manager who will never tolerate a stock-out is being somewhat unrealistic because attempting to avoid stock-outs completely will require high reorder points, high inventory, and an associated high holding cost.

Suppose in this case that Dabco management is willing to tolerate an average of one stock-out per year. Because Dabco places 20 orders per year, this decision implies that management is willing to allow demand during lead time to exceed the reorder point one time in 20, or 5% of the time. The reorder point r can be found by using the lead-time demand distribution to find the value of r with a 5% chance of having a lead-time demand that will exceed it. This situation is shown graphically in Figure 14.12.

From the standard normal probability distribution table in Appendix D, we see that $1 - 0.05 = 0.95$ of the area in the left tail of the normal probability distribution occurs at $z = 1.645$ standard deviations above the mean. Therefore, for the assumed normal distribution for lead-time demand with $\mu = 154$ and $\sigma = 25$, the reorder point r is

$$r = 154 + 1.645(25) = 195$$

FIGURE 14.12 REORDER POINT r THAT ALLOWS A 5% CHANCE OF A STOCK-OUT FOR DABCO LIGHTBULBS

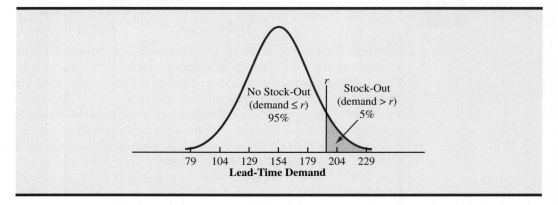

If a normal distribution is used for lead-time demand, the general equation for r is

$$r = \mu + z\sigma \qquad \textbf{(14.37)}$$

where z is the number of standard deviations necessary to obtain the acceptable stock-out probability.

Try Problem 29 as an example of an order-quantity, reorder point model with probabilistic demand.

Thus, the recommended inventory decision is to order 400 units whenever the inventory reaches the reorder point of 195. Because the mean or expected demand during the lead time is 154 units, the $195 - 154 = 41$ units serve as a **safety stock**, which absorbs higher-than-usual demand during the lead time. Roughly 95% of the time, the 195 units will be able to satisfy demand during the lead time. The anticipated annual cost for this system is as follows:

Holding cost, normal inventory $(Q/2)C_h = (400/2)(1.20) = \$240$
Holding cost, safety stock $\qquad (41)C_h = \quad 41(1.20) \quad = \$\ 49$
Ordering cost $\qquad\qquad (D/Q)C_o = (8008/400)12 = \underline{\$240}$
$\qquad\qquad\qquad\qquad\qquad\qquad\qquad\qquad\qquad$ Total $\quad \$529$

If Dabco could assume that a known, constant demand rate of 8008 units per year existed for the lightbulbs, then $Q^* = 400$, $r = 154$, and a total annual cost of $\$240 + \$240 = \$480$ would be optimal. When demand is uncertain and can only be expressed in probabilistic terms, a larger total cost can be expected. The larger cost occurs in the form of larger holding costs because more inventory must be maintained to limit the number of stock-outs. For Dabco, this additional inventory or safety stock was 41 units, with an additional annual holding cost of $49. The Q.M. in Action, Inventory Models at Microsoft, describes how Microsoft has employed inventory models to increase customer service levels as well as reduce inventory costs.

Q.M. *in* ACTION

INVENTORY MODELS AT MICROSOFT*

While known more for its operating system software, Microsoft has steadily increased its presence in consumer electronics. Microsoft produces Xbox video game consoles and a variety of personal-computer accessories such as mice and keyboards. In 2008 the consumer-electronics division of Microsoft generated over $8 billion in revenue compared to $52 billion in revenue from software. While products such as the Xbox are sold year-round, approximately 40% of annual sales occur in October, November, and December. Therefore, it is critical that Microsoft have sufficient inventory available to meet demand during this holiday season.

In conjunction with the supply-chain-services company Optiant, Microsoft began an ambitious effort in 2005

to improve its inventory management systems. Microsoft developed new forecasting techniques to better estimate future demand for its products. It then set service-level requirements for each product based on profit margins and demand forecasts. These service levels were used in safety-stock model calculations to determine target inventory levels that drove production plans. The new safety-stock models were used for more than 10,000 different consumer-electronics products sold by Microsoft.

Microsoft has experienced substantial inventory level reductions since implementing its new models and policies. Corporatewide, Microsoft has reduced its inventories by $1.5 billion (60%). The consumer-electronics division of Microsoft posted its first ever profitable year in 2008. Microsoft largely credits these cost savings and profitability to superior forecasting and inventory models.

*Based on J. J. Neale and S. P. Willems, "Managing Inventory in Supply Chains with Nonstationary Demand," *Interfaces* 39, no. 5 (September 2009): 388–399.

NOTES AND COMMENTS

1. The safety stock required at Microsoft in the Q.M. in Action, Inventory Models at Microsoft, was based on a service level defined by the probability of being able to satisfy all customer demand during an order cycle. If Microsoft wanted to guarantee that it would be able to meet all demand in 95% of all order cycles, then we would say that Microsoft has a 95% service level. This is sometimes referred to as a *Type-I* service level or a *cycle service level*. However, other definitions of *service level* may include the percentage of all customer demand that can be satisfied from inventory. Thus, when an inventory manager expresses a desired service level, it is a good idea to clarify exactly what the manager means by the term *service level*.

14.7 Periodic Review Model with Probabilistic Demand

Up to this point, we have assumed that the inventory position is reviewed continuously so that an order can be placed as soon as the inventory position reaches the reorder point. The inventory model in this section assumes probabilistic demand and a periodic review of the inventory position.

The order-quantity, reorder point inventory models previously discussed require a **continuous review inventory system**. In a continuous review inventory system, the inventory position is monitored continuously so that an order can be placed whenever the reorder point is reached. Computerized inventory systems can easily provide the continuous review required by the order-quantity, reorder point models.

An alternative to the continuous review system is the **periodic review inventory system**. With a periodic review system, the inventory is checked and reordering is done only at specified points in time. For example, inventory may be checked and orders placed on a weekly, biweekly, monthly, or some other periodic basis. When a firm or business handles multiple products, the periodic review system offers the advantage of requiring that orders for several items be placed at the same preset periodic review time. With this type of inventory system, the shipping and receiving of orders for multiple products are easily coordinated. Under the previously discussed order-quantity, reorder point systems, the reorder points for various products can be encountered at substantially different points in time, making the coordination of orders for multiple products more difficult.

To illustrate this system, let us consider Dollar Discounts, a firm with several retail stores that carry a wide variety of products for household use. The company operates its inventory system with a two-week periodic review. Under this system, a retail store manager may order any number of units of any product from the Dollar Discounts central warehouse every two weeks. Orders for all products going to a particular store are combined into one shipment. When making the order quantity decision for each product at a given review period, the store manager knows that a reorder for the product cannot be made until the next review period.

Assuming that the lead time is less than the length of the review period, an order placed at a review period will be received prior to the next review period. In this case, the how-much-to-order decision at any review period is determined using the following:

$$Q = M - H \tag{14.38}$$

where

$$Q = \text{the order quantity}$$
$$M = \text{the replenishment level}$$
$$H = \text{the inventory on hand at the review period}$$

FIGURE 14.13 INVENTORY PATTERN FOR PERIODIC REVIEW MODEL
WITH PROBABILISTIC DEMAND

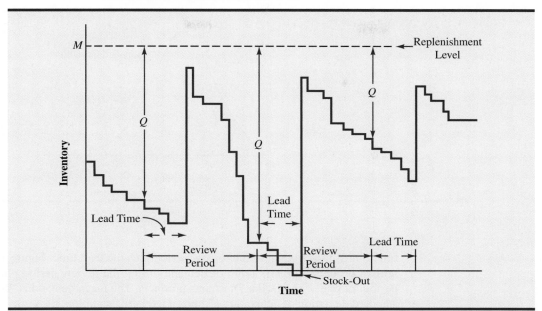

Because the demand is probabilistic, the inventory on hand at the review period, H, will vary. Thus, the order quantity that must be sufficient to bring the inventory position back to its maximum or replenishment level M can be expected to vary each period. For example, if the replenishment level for a particular product is 50 units and the inventory on hand at the review period is $H = 12$ units, an order of $Q = M - H = 50 - 12 = 38$ units should be made. Thus, under the periodic review model, enough units are ordered each review period to bring the inventory position back up to the replenishment level.

A typical inventory pattern for a periodic review system with probabilistic demand is shown in Figure 14.13. Note that the time between periodic reviews is predetermined and fixed. The order quantity Q at each review period can vary and is shown to be the difference between the replenishment level and the inventory on hand. Finally, as with other probabilistic models, an unusually high demand can result in an occasional stock-out.

The decision variable in the periodic review model is the replenishment level M. To determine M, we could begin by developing a total cost model, including holding, ordering, and stock-out costs. Instead, we describe an approach that is often used in practice. In this approach, the objective is to determine a replenishment level that will meet a desired performance level, such as a reasonably low probability of stock-out or a reasonably low number of stock-outs per year.

In the Dollar Discounts problem, we assume that management's objective is to determine the replenishment level with only a 1% chance of a stock-out. In the periodic review model, the order quantity at each review period must be sufficient to cover *demand for the review period plus the demand for the following lead time.* Suppose that an order is to be placed at time t. To determine this order quantity, we must realize that the quantity ordered at time t must last until the next time inventory is replenished, which will be time $(t + \text{review period} + \text{lead time})$. Thus the total length of time that the order quantity at

FIGURE 14.14   PROBABILITY DISTRIBUTION OF DEMAND DURING THE REVIEW
PERIOD AND LEAD TIME FOR THE DOLLAR DISCOUNTS PROBLEM

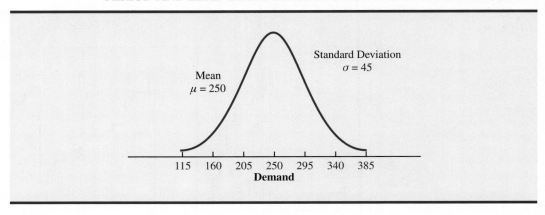

time t must last is equal to the review period plus the lead time. Figure 14.14 shows the
normal probability distribution of demand during the review period plus the lead-time
period for one of the Dollar Discounts products. The mean demand is 250 units, and the
standard deviation of demand is 45 units. Given this situation, the logic used to establish
M is similar to the logic used to establish the reorder point in Section 14.6. Figure 14.15
shows the replenishment level M with a 1% chance that demand will exceed that replenishment level. In other words, Figure 14.15 shows the replenishment level that allows a
1% chance of a stock-out associated with the replenishment decision. Using the normal
probability distribution table in Appendix D, we see that $1 - 0.01 = 0.99$ of the area in
the left tail of the normal probability distribution occurs at $z = 2.33$ standard deviations
above the mean. Therefore, for the assumed normal probability distribution with $\mu = 250$
and $\sigma = 45$, the replenishment level is determined by

$$M = 250 + 2.33(45) = 355$$

WEB file

Periodic

FIGURE 14.15   REPLENISHMENT LEVEL M THAT ALLOWS A 1% CHANCE
OF A STOCK-OUT FOR THE DOLLAR DISCOUNTS PROBLEM

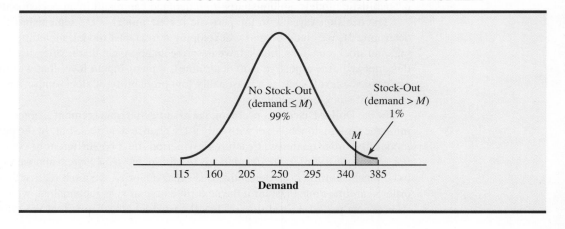

Problem 33 gives you practice in computing the replenishment level for a periodic review model with probabilistic demand.

Although other probability distributions can be used to express the demand during the review period plus the lead-time period, if the normal probability distribution is used, the general expression for *M* is

$$M = \mu + z\sigma \qquad\qquad (14.39)$$

Periodic review systems provide advantages of coordinated orders for multiple items. However, periodic review systems require larger safety-stock levels than corresponding continuous review systems.

where *z* is the number of standard deviations necessary to obtain the acceptable stock-out probability.

If demand had been deterministic rather than probabilistic, the replenishment level would have been the demand during the review period plus the demand during the lead-time period. In this case, the replenishment level would have been 250 units, and no stock-out would have occurred. However, with the probabilistic demand, we have seen that higher inventory is necessary to allow for uncertain demand and to control the probability of a stock-out. In the Dollar Discounts problem, $355 - 250 = 105$ is the safety stock that is necessary to absorb any higher-than-usual demand during the review period plus the demand during the lead-time period. This safety stock limits the probability of a stock-out to 1%.

More Complex Periodic Review Models

The periodic review model just discussed is one approach to determining a replenishment level for the periodic review inventory system with probabilistic demand. More complex versions of the periodic review model incorporate a reorder point as another decision variable; that is, instead of ordering at every periodic review, a reorder point is established. If the inventory on hand at the periodic review is at or below the reorder point, a decision is made to order up to the replenishment level. However, if the inventory on hand at the periodic review is greater than the reorder level, such an order is not placed, and the system continues until the next periodic review. In this case, the cost of ordering is a relevant cost and can be included in a cost model along with holding and stock-out costs. Optimal policies can be reached based on minimizing the expected total cost. Situations with lead times longer than the review period add to the complexity of the model. The mathematical level required to treat these more extensive periodic review models is beyond the scope of this text.

NOTES AND COMMENTS

1. The periodic review model presented in this section is based on the assumption that the lead time for an order is less than the periodic review period. Most periodic review systems operate under this condition. However, the case in which the lead time is longer than the review period can be handled by defining *H* in equation (14.38) as the inventory position, where *H* includes the inventory on hand plus the inventory on order. In this case, the order quantity at any review period is the amount needed for the inventory on hand plus all outstanding orders needed to reach the replenishment level.

2. In the order-quantity, reorder point model discussed in Section 14.6, a continuous review was used to initiate an order whenever the reorder point was reached. The safety stock for this model was based on the probabilistic demand during the lead time. The periodic review model presented in this section also determined a recommended safety stock. However, because the inventory review was only periodic, the safety stock was based on the probabilistic demand during the review period plus the lead-time period. This longer period for the safety stock computation means that periodic review systems tend to require a larger safety stock than do continuous review systems.

Summary

In this chapter we presented some of the approaches used to assist managers in establishing low-cost inventory policies. We first considered cases in which the demand rate for the product is constant. In analyzing these inventory systems, total cost models were developed; these models included ordering costs, holding costs, and, in some cases, backorder costs. Then minimum cost formulas for the order quantity Q were presented. A reorder point r can be established by considering the lead-time demand.

In addition, we discussed inventory models in which a deterministic and constant rate could not be assumed, and thus demand was described by a probability distribution. A critical issue with these probabilistic inventory models is obtaining a probability distribution that most realistically approximates the demand distribution. We first described a single-period model where only one order is placed for the product and, at the end of the period, either the product has sold out or a surplus remains of unsold products that will be sold for a salvage value. Solution procedures were then presented for multiperiod models based on either an order-quantity, reorder point, continuous review system or a replenishment-level, periodic review system.

In closing this chapter, we reemphasize that inventory and inventory systems can be an expensive phase of a firm's operation. It is important for managers to be aware of the cost of inventory systems and to make the best possible operating policy decisions for the inventory system. Inventory models, as presented in this chapter, can help managers to develop good inventory policies.

Glossary

Backorder The receipt of an order for a product when no units are in inventory. These backorders are eventually satisfied when a new supply of the product becomes available.

Constant demand rate An assumption of many inventory models that states that the same number of units are taken from inventory each period of time.

Constant supply rate A situation in which the inventory is built up at a constant rate over a period of time.

Continuous review inventory system A system in which the inventory position is monitored or reviewed on a continuous basis so that a new order can be placed as soon as the reorder point is reached.

Cost of capital The cost a firm incurs to obtain capital for investment. It may be stated as an annual percentage rate, and it is part of the holding cost associated with maintaining inventory.

Cycle time The length of time between the placing of two consecutive orders.

Deterministic inventory model A model where demand is considered known and not subject to uncertainty.

Economic order quantity (EOQ) The order quantity that minimizes the annual holding cost plus the annual ordering cost.

Goodwill cost A cost associated with a backorder, a lost sale, or any form of stock-out or unsatisfied demand. This cost may be used to reflect the loss of future profits because a customer experienced an unsatisfied demand.

Holding cost The cost associated with maintaining an inventory investment, including the cost of the capital investment in the inventory, insurance, taxes, warehouse overhead, and so on. This cost may be stated as a percentage of the inventory investment or as a cost per unit.

Incremental analysis A method used to determine an optimal order quantity by comparing the cost of ordering an additional unit with the cost of not ordering an additional unit.

Inventory position The inventory on hand plus the inventory on order.

Lead time The time between the placing of an order and its receipt in the inventory system.

Lead-time demand The number of units demanded during the lead-time period.

Lead-time demand distribution The distribution of demand that occurs during the lead-time period.

Lot size The order quantity in the production inventory model.

Ordering cost The fixed cost (salaries, paper, transportation, etc.) associated with placing an order for an item.

Periodic review inventory system A system in which the inventory position is checked or reviewed at predetermined periodic points in time. Reorders are placed only at periodic review points.

Probabilistic inventory model A model where demand is not known exactly; probabilities must be associated with the possible values for demand.

Quantity discounts Discounts or lower unit costs offered by the manufacturer when a customer purchases larger quantities of the product.

Reorder point The inventory position at which a new order should be placed.

Safety stock Inventory maintained in order to reduce the number of stock-outs resulting from higher-than-expected demand.

Setup cost The fixed cost (labor, materials, lost production) associated with preparing for a new production run.

Shortage or stock-out Occurrence when demand cannot be supplied from inventory.

Single-period inventory model An inventory model in which only one order is placed for the product, and at the end of the period either the item has sold out, or a surplus of unsold items will be sold for a salvage value.

Problems

1. Suppose that the R&B Beverage Company has a soft drink product that shows a constant annual demand rate of 3600 cases. A case of the soft drink costs R&B $3. Ordering costs are $20 per order and holding costs are 25% of the value of the inventory. R&B has 250 working days per year, and the lead time is 5 days. Identify the following aspects of the inventory policy:
   a. Economic order quantity
   b. Reorder point
   c. Cycle time
   d. Total annual cost

2. A general property of the EOQ inventory model is that total inventory holding and total ordering costs are equal at the optimal solution. Use the data in Problem 1 to show that this result is true. Use equations (14.1), (14.2), and (14.3) to show that, in general, total holding costs and total ordering costs are equal whenever Q^* is used.

3. The reorder point [see equation (14.6)] is defined as the lead-time demand for an item. In cases of long lead times, the lead-time demand and thus the reorder point may exceed the economic order quantity Q^*. In such cases, the inventory position will not equal the

inventory on hand when an order is placed, and the reorder point may be expressed in terms of either the inventory position or the inventory on hand. Consider the economic order quantity model with $D = 5000$, $C_o = \$32$, $C_h = \$2$, and 250 working days per year. Identify the reorder point in terms of the inventory position and in terms of the inventory on hand for each of the following lead times:

a.   5 days
b.   15 days
c.   25 days
d.   45 days

4.   Westside Auto purchases a component used in the manufacture of automobile generators directly from the supplier. Westside's generator production operation, which is operated at a constant rate, will require 1000 components per month throughout the year (12,000 units annually). Assume that the ordering costs are $25 per order, the unit cost is $2.50 per component, and annual holding costs are 20% of the value of the inventory. Westside has 250 working days per year and a lead time of 5 days. Answer the following inventory policy questions:

a.   What is the EOQ for this component?
b.   What is the reorder point?
c.   What is the cycle time?
d.   What are the total annual holding and ordering costs associated with your recommended EOQ?

5.   The Metropolitan Bus Company (MBC) purchases diesel fuel from American Petroleum Supply. In addition to the fuel cost, American Petroleum Supply charges MBC $250 per order to cover the expenses of delivering and transferring the fuel to MBC's storage tanks. The lead time for a new shipment from American Petroleum is 10 days; the cost of holding a gallon of fuel in the storage tanks is $0.04 per month, or $0.48 per year; and annual fuel usage is 150,000 gallons. MBC buses operate 300 days a year.

a.   What is the optimal order quantity for MBC?
b.   How frequently should MBC order to replenish the gasoline supply?
c.   The MBC storage tanks have a capacity of 15,000 gallons. Should MBC consider expanding the capacity of its storage tanks?
d.   What is the reorder point?

6.   The manager at a local university bookstore wishes to apply the EOQ model to determine the respective order quantities for two products: ballpoint pens and mechanical pencils. The annual demand for pens and pencils is 1500 and 400, respectively. The ordering cost for each product is $20 per order and the wholesale price of a pen and pencil is $1.50 and $4, respectively. Assume the bookstore's annual holding rate is 10% and that the bookstore operates 240 days per year.

a.   Determine the optimal order quantity and the order cycle time for each product. What is the total cost (summed over both products)?
b.   The bookstore orders the pens and pencils from the same supplier. If these two products had the same cycle time, the corresponding shipment consolidation would reduce the ordering cost to $15. How much money does the bookstore save by consolidating the orders for these two products? (*Hint:* By setting the cycle times equal, we have $Q_{pens}/(1500/240) = Q_{pencils}/(400/240)$ or $Q_{pens} = 3.75Q_{pencils}$). Make this substitution into the combined cost equation so that it is a function only of $Q_{pencils}$ and apply equation (14.5) with the appropriate values to determine $Q_{pencils}$ (and subsequently Q_{pens}).

7.   A large distributor of oil-well drilling equipment operated over the past two years with EOQ policies based on an annual holding cost rate of 22%. Under the EOQ policy, a particular product has been ordered with a $Q^* = 80$. A recent evaluation of holding costs shows that because of an increase in the interest rate associated with bank loans, the annual

holding cost rate should be 27%. Observe that we cannot directly use the EOQ equation to compute the order quantity considering the new holding cost rate of 27% because we are not given the annual demand, fixed ordering cost, and ordering price. However, we can use the original value of Q and knowledge of how we computed it to determine the revised economic order quantity corresponding to the updated holding cost rate.

a. Develop a general expression showing how the economic order quantity changes when the annual holding cost rate is changed from I to I'.

b. Using the formula you derived in part a, compute the new economic order quantity for the product.

8. Nation-Wide Bus Lines is proud of its six-week bus driver–training program that it conducts for all new Nation-Wide drivers. As long as the class size remains less than or equal to 35, a six-week training program costs Nation-Wide $22,000 for instructors, equipment, and so on. The Nation-Wide training program must provide the company with approximately five new drivers per month. After completing the training program, new drivers are paid $1600 per month but do not work until a full-time driver position is open. Nation-Wide views the $1600 per month paid to each idle new driver as a holding cost necessary to maintain a supply of newly trained drivers available for immediate service. Viewing new drivers as inventory-type units, how large should the training classes be to minimize Nation-Wide's total annual training and new driver idle-time costs? How many training classes should the company hold each year? What is the total annual cost associated with your recommendation?

9. Cress Electronic Products manufactures components used in the automotive industry. Cress purchases parts for use in its manufacturing operation from a variety of different suppliers. One particular supplier provides a part where the assumptions of the EOQ model are realistic. The annual demand is 5000 units, the ordering cost is $80 per order, and the annual holding cost rate is 25%.

a. If the cost of the part is $20 per unit, what is the economic order quantity?

b. Assume 250 days of operation per year. If the lead time for an order is 12 days, what is the reorder point?

c. If the lead time for the part is seven weeks (35 days), what is the reorder point?. Compare this with the economic order quantity from part (a). Explain the relative size of these two quantities. Hint: Remember that the reorder point is expressed in terms of inventory position.

d. What is the reorder point for part (c) if the reorder point is expressed in terms of the inventory on hand rather than the inventory position?

10. All-Star Bat Manufacturing, Inc., supplies baseball bats to major and minor league baseball teams. After an initial order in January, demand over the six-month baseball season is approximately constant at 1000 bats per month. Assuming that the bat production process can handle up to 4000 bats per month, the bat production setup costs are $150 per setup, the production cost is $10 per bat, and the holding costs have a monthly rate of 2%, what production lot size would you recommend to meet the demand during the baseball season? If All-Star operates 20 days per month, how often will the production process operate, and what is the length of a production run?

11. Assume that a production line operates such that the production lot size model of Section 14.2 is applicable. Given $D = 6400$ units per year, $C_o = \$100$, and $C_h = \$2$ per unit per year, compute the minimum cost production lot size for each of the following production rates:

a. 8000 units per year

b. 10,000 units per year

c. 32,000 units per year

d. 100,000 units per year

Compute the EOQ recommended lot size using equation (14.5). What two observations can you make about the relationship between the EOQ model and the production lot size model?

12. EL Computer produces its multimedia notebook computer on a production line that has an annual capacity of 16,000 units. EL Computer estimates the annual demand for this model at 6000 units. The cost to set up the production line is $2345, and the annual holding cost is $20 per unit. Current practice calls for production runs of 500 notebook computers each month.
   a. What is the optimal production lot size?
   b. How many production runs should be made each year? What is the recommended cycle time?
   c. Would you recommend changing the current production lot size policy from the monthly 500-unit production runs? Why or why not? What is the projected savings of your recommendation?

13. Wilson Publishing Company produces books for the retail market. Demand for a current book is expected to occur at a constant annual rate of 7200 copies. The cost of one copy of the book is $14.50. The holding cost is based on an 18% annual rate, and production setup costs are $150 per setup. The equipment with which the book is produced has an annual production volume of 25,000 copies. Wilson has 250 working days per year, and the lead time for a production run is 15 days. Use the production lot size model to compute the following values:
   a. Minimum cost production lot size
   b. Number of production runs per year
   c. Cycle time
   d. Length of a production run
   e. Maximum inventory
   f. Total annual cost
   g. Reorder point

14. A well-known manufacturer of several brands of toothpaste uses the production lot size model to determine production quantities for its various products. The product known as Extra White is currently being produced in production lot sizes of 5000 units. The length of the production run for this quantity is 10 days. Because of a recent shortage of a particular raw material, the supplier of the material announced that a cost increase will be passed along to the manufacturer of Extra White. Current estimates are that the new raw material cost will increase the manufacturing cost of the toothpaste products by 23% per unit. What will be the effect of this price increase on the production lot sizes for Extra White?

15. Suppose that Westside Auto of Problem 4, with $D = 12,000$ units per year, $C_h = (2.50)$ $(0.20) = \$0.50$, and $C_o = \$25$, decided to operate with a backorder inventory policy. Backorder costs are estimated to be $5 per unit per year. Identify the following:
   a. Minimum cost order quantity
   b. Maximum number of backorders
   c. Maximum inventory
   d. Cycle time
   e. Total annual cost

16. Assuming 250 days of operation per year and a lead time of five days, what is the reorder point for Westside Auto in Problem 15? Show the general formula for the reorder point for the EOQ model with backorders. In general, is the reorder point when backorders are allowed greater than or less than the reorder point when backorders are not allowed? Explain.

17. A manager of an inventory system believes that inventory models are important decision-making aids. The manager has experience with the EOQ policy, but has never considered a backorder model because of the assumption that backorders were "bad" and should be avoided. However, with upper management's continued pressure for cost reduction, you have been asked to analyze the economics of a backorder policy for some products that can possibly be backordered. For a specific product with $D = 800$ units per year, $C_o = \$150$, $C_h = \$3$, and $C_b = \$20$, what is the difference in total annual cost between the EOQ model and the planned shortage or backorder model? If the manager adds constraints that no more than 25% of the units can be backordered and that no customer will have to wait more than 15 days for an order, should the backorder inventory policy be adopted? Assume 250 working days per year.

18. If the lead time for new orders is 20 days for the inventory system discussed in Problem 17, find the reorder point for both the EOQ and the backorder models.

19. The A&M Hobby Shop carries a line of radio-controlled model racing cars. Demand for the cars is assumed to be constant at a rate of 40 cars per month. The cars cost $60 each, and ordering costs are approximately $15 per order, regardless of the order size. The annual holding cost rate is 20%.
    a. Determine the economic order quantity and total annual cost under the assumption that no backorders are permitted.
    b. Using a $45 per-unit per-year backorder cost, determine the minimum cost inventory policy and total annual cost for the model racing cars.
    c. What is the maximum number of days a customer would have to wait for a backorder under the policy in part (b)? Assume that the Hobby Shop is open for business 300 days per year.
    d. Would you recommend a no-backorder or a backorder inventory policy for this product? Explain.
    e. If the lead time is six days, what is the reorder point for both the no-backorder and backorder inventory policies?

20. Assume that the following quantity discount schedule is appropriate. If annual demand is 120 units, ordering costs are $20 per order, and the annual holding cost rate is 25%, what order quantity would you recommend?

Order Size	Discount (%)	Unit Cost
0 to 49	0	$30.00
50 to 99	5	$28.50
100 or more	10	$27.00

21. Apply the EOQ model to the following quantity discount situation in which $D = 500$ units per year, $C_o = \$40$, and the annual holding cost rate is 20%. What order quantity do you recommend?

Discount Category	Order Size	Discount (%)	Unit Cost
1	0 to 99	0	$10.00
2	100 or more	3	$ 9.70

22. Keith Shoe Stores carries a basic black dress shoe for men that sells at an approximately constant rate of 500 pairs of shoes every three months. Keith's current buying policy is

to order 500 pairs each time an order is placed. It costs Keith $30 to place an order. The annual holding cost rate is 20%. With the order quantity of 500, Keith obtains the shoes at the lowest possible unit cost of $28 per pair. Other quantity discounts offered by the manufacturer are as follows. What is the minimum cost order quantity for the shoes? What are the annual savings of your inventory policy over the policy currently being used by Keith?

Order Quantity	Price per Pair
0–99	$36
100–199	$32
200–299	$30
300 or more	$28

23.   In the EOQ model with quantity discounts, we stated that if the Q^* for a price category is larger than necessary to qualify for the category price, the category cannot be optimal. Use the two discount categories in Problem 21 to show that this statement is true. That is, plot total cost curves for the two categories and show that if the category 2 minimum cost Q is an acceptable solution, we do not have to consider category 1.

24.   University of Iowa Sports Information (UISI) procures its game-day football magazines from a publishing company at a price of $9.00 per magazine. UISI sells the magazines on the day of the corresponding football game at a retail price of $10.00. To sell these magazines, UISI hires vendors and pays them $0.50 for each program that they sell. For the first game of the season, UISI has determined that demand for the game-day football magazines is normally distributed with a mean of 9000 magazines and a standard deviation of 400 magazines. Any magazines that are not sold on the day of the game are worthless and UISI recycles them.
    a.   What is UISI's optimal order quantity of game-day football magazines for the first game of the season?
    b.   Instead of recycling the unsold programs, suppose the publisher offers to buy back any unsold programs for $8.00. Under this scenario, what is UISI's optimal order quantity?

25.   The Gilbert Air-Conditioning Company is considering the purchase of a special shipment of portable air conditioners manufactured in Japan. Each unit will cost Gilbert $80, and it will be sold for $125. Gilbert does not want to carry surplus air conditioners over until the following year. Thus, all surplus air conditioners will be sold to a wholesaler for $50 per unit. Assume that the air conditioner demand follows a normal probability distribution with $\mu = 20$ and $\sigma = 8$.
    a.   What is the recommended order quantity?
    b.   What is the probability that Gilbert will sell all units it orders?

26.   The Bridgeport city manager and the chief of police agreed on the size of the police force necessary for normal daily operations. However, they need assistance in determining the number of additional police officers needed to cover daily absences due to injuries, sickness, vacations, and personal leave. Records over the past three years show that the daily demand for additional police officers is normally distributed with a mean of 50 officers and a standard deviation of 10 officers. The cost of an additional police officer is based on the average pay rate of $150 per day. If the daily demand for additional police officers exceeds the number of additional officers available, the excess demand will be covered by overtime at the pay rate of $240 per day for each overtime officer.
    a.   If the number of additional police officers available is greater than demand, the city will have to pay for more additional police officers than needed. What is the cost of overestimating demand?

    b.   If the number of additional police officers available is less than demand, the city will have to use overtime to meet the demand. What is the cost of underestimating demand?

    c.   What is the optimal number of additional police officers that should be included in the police force?

    d.   On a typical day, what is the probability that overtime will be necessary?

27. A perishable dairy product is ordered daily at a particular supermarket. The product costs $1.19 per unit and sells for $1.65 per unit. If units are unsold at the end of the day, the supplier takes them back at a rebate of $1 per unit. Assume that daily demand is approximately normally distributed with $\mu = 150$ and $\sigma = 30$.

    a.   What is your recommended daily order quantity for the supermarket?

    b.   What is the probability that the supermarket will sell all the units it orders?

    c.   In problems such as these, why would the supplier offer a rebate as high as $1? For example, why not offer a nominal rebate of, say, 25¢ per unit? What happens to the supermarket order quantity as the rebate is reduced?

28. A retail outlet sells holiday candy for $10 per bag. The cost of the product is $8 per bag. All units not sold during the selling season prior to the holiday are sold for half the retail price in a postholiday clearance sale. Assume that demand for bags of holiday candy during the selling season is uniformly distributed between 200 and 800.

    a.   What is the recommended order quantity?

    b.   What is the probability that at least some customers will ask to purchase the product after the outlet is sold out? That is, what is the probability of a stock-out using your order quantity in part (a)?

    c.   To keep customers happy and returning to the store later, the owner feels that stock-outs should be avoided if at all possible. What is your recommended order quantity if the owner is willing to tolerate a 0.15 probability of a stock-out?

    d.   Using your answer to part (c), what is the goodwill cost you are assigning to a stock-out?

29. Floyd Distributors, Inc., provides a variety of auto parts to small local garages. Floyd purchases parts from manufacturers according to the EOQ model and then ships the parts from a regional warehouse direct to its customers. For a particular type of muffler, Floyd's EOQ analysis recommends orders with $Q^* = 25$ to satisfy an annual demand of 200 mufflers. Floyd's has 250 working days per year, and the lead time averages 15 days.

    a.   What is the reorder point if Floyd assumes a constant demand rate?

    b.   Suppose that an analysis of Floyd's muffler demand shows that the lead-time demand follows a normal probability distribution with $\mu = 12$ and $\sigma = 2.5$. If Floyd's management can tolerate one stock-out per year, what is the revised reorder point?

    c.   What is the safety stock for part (b)? If $C_h = $5/unit/year$, what is the extra cost due to the uncertainty of demand?

30. To serve "to-go" orders, Terrapin Coffeehouse faces normally distributed weekly demand with an average of 300 paper cups and a standard deviation of 75 cups per week. Terrapin orders cups by the box. Each box costs $10 and contains 100 cups. For each order placed, Terrapin pays a fixed $15 shipping fee (regardless of the number of boxes ordered) and the order arrives one week after Terrapin places it with the cup supplier. Terrapin estimates that holding costs are 15% per dollar per year. Due to the importance of cups to business, Terrapin wants no more than a 1% chance of a stock-out during the one-week lead time for cup replenishment. Assume that there are 52 weeks in a year.

    a.   What is the optimal order quantity (in terms of number of boxes)?

    b.   What is the optimal reorder point (in terms of number of cups)?

31. A product with an annual demand of 1000 units has $C_o = \$25.50$ and $C_h = \$8$. The demand exhibits some variability such that the lead-time demand follows a normal probability distribution with $\mu = 25$ and $\sigma = 5$.
    a. What is the recommended order quantity?
    b. What are the reorder point and safety stock if the firm desires at most a 2% probability of stock-out on any given order cycle?
    c. If a manager sets the reorder point at 30, what is the probability of a stock-out on any given order cycle? How many times would you expect a stock-out during the year if this reorder point were used?

32. The B&S Novelty and Craft Shop in Bennington, Vermont, sells a variety of quality hand-made items to tourists. B&S will sell 300 hand-carved miniature replicas of a Colonial soldier each year, but the demand pattern during the year is uncertain. The replicas sell for $20 each, and B&S uses a 15% annual inventory holding cost rate. Ordering costs are $5 per order, and demand during the lead time follows a normal probability distribution with $\mu = 15$ and $\sigma = 6$.
    a. What is the recommended order quantity?
    b. If B&S is willing to accept a stock-out roughly twice a year, what reorder point would you recommend? What is the probability that B&S will have a stock-out in any one order cycle?
    c. What are the safety stock and annual safety stock costs for this product?

33. A firm uses a one-week periodic review inventory system. A two-day lead time is needed for any order, and the firm is willing to tolerate an average of one stock-out per year.
    a. Using the firm's service guideline, what is the probability of a stock-out associated with each replenishment decision?
    b. What is the replenishment level if demand during the review period plus lead-time period is normally distributed with a mean of 60 units and a standard deviation of 12 units?
    c. What is the replenishment level if demand during the review period plus lead-time period is uniformly distributed between 35 and 85 units?

34. Foster Drugs, Inc., handles a variety of health and beauty aid products. A particular hair conditioner product costs Foster Drugs $2.95 per unit. The annual holding cost rate is 20%. An order-quantity, reorder point inventory model recommends an order quantity of 300 units per order.
    a. Lead time is one week, and the lead-time demand is normally distributed with a mean of 150 units and a standard deviation of 40 units. What is the reorder point if the firm is willing to tolerate a 1% chance of stock-out on any one cycle?
    b. What safety stock and annual safety stock costs are associated with your recommendation in part (a)?
    c. The order-quantity, reorder point model requires a continuous review system. Management is considering making a transition to a periodic review system in an attempt to coordinate ordering for many of its products. The demand during the proposed two-week review period and the one-week lead-time period is normally distributed with a mean of 450 units and a standard deviation of 70 units. What is the recommended replenishment level for this periodic review system if the firm is willing to tolerate the same 1% chance of stock-out associated with any replenishment decision?
    d. What safety stock and annual safety stock costs are associated with your recommendation in part (c)?
    e. Compare your answers to parts (b) and (d). The company is seriously considering the periodic review system. Would you support this decision? Explain.
    f. Would you tend to favor the continuous review system for more expensive items? For example, assume that the product in the preceding example sold for $295 per unit. Explain.

35. Statewide Auto Parts uses a four-week periodic review system to reorder parts for its inventory stock. A one-week lead time is required to fill the order. Demand for one

particular part during the five-week replenishment period is normally distributed with a mean of 18 units and a standard deviation of 6 units.

    a.   At a particular periodic review, 8 units are in inventory. The parts manager places an order for 16 units. What is the probability that this part will have a stock-out before an order that is placed at the next four-week review period arrives?

    b.   Assume that the company is willing to tolerate a 2.5% chance of a stock-out associated with a replenishment decision. How many parts should the manager have ordered in part (a)? What is the replenishment level for the four-week periodic review system?

36.   Rose Office Supplies, Inc., which is open six days a week, uses a two-week periodic review for its store inventory. On alternating Monday mornings, the store manager fills out an order sheet requiring a shipment of various items from the company's warehouse. A particular three-ring notebook sells at an average rate of 16 notebooks per week. The standard deviation in sales is 5 notebooks per week. The lead time for a new shipment is three days. The mean lead-time demand is 8 notebooks with a standard deviation of 3.5.

    a.   What is the mean or expected demand during the review period plus the lead-time period?

    b.   Under the assumption of independent demand from week to week, the variances in demands are additive. Thus, the variance of the demand during the review period plus the lead-time period is equal to the variance of demand during the first week plus the variance of demand during the second week plus the variance of demand during the lead-time period. What is the variance of demand during the review period plus the lead-time period? What is the standard deviation of demand during the review period plus the lead-time period?

    c.   Assuming that demand has a normal probability distribution, what is the replenishment level that will provide an expected stock-out rate of one per year?

    d.   On Monday, March 22, 18 notebooks remain in inventory at the store. How many notebooks should the store manager order?

Case Problem 1   Wagner Fabricating Company

Managers at Wagner Fabricating Company are reviewing the economic feasibility of manufacturing a part that the company currently purchases from a supplier. Forecasted annual demand for the part is 3200 units. Wagner operates 250 days per year.

Wagner's financial analysts established a cost of capital of 14% for the use of funds for investments within the company. In addition, over the past year $600,000 was the average investment in the company's inventory. Accounting information shows that a total of $24,000 was spent on taxes and insurance related to the company's inventory. In addition, an estimated $9000 was lost due to inventory shrinkage, which included damaged goods as well as pilferage. A remaining $15,000 was spent on warehouse overhead, including utility expenses for heating and lighting.

An analysis of the purchasing operation shows that approximately two hours are required to process and coordinate an order for the part regardless of the quantity ordered. Purchasing salaries average $28 per hour, including employee benefits. In addition, a detailed analysis of 125 orders showed that $2375 was spent on telephone, paper, and postage directly related to the ordering process.

A one-week lead time is required to obtain the part from the supplier. An analysis of demand during the lead time shows it is approximately normally distributed with a mean of 64 units and a standard deviation of 10 units. Service level guidelines indicate that one stock-out per year is acceptable.

Currently, the company has a contract to purchase the part from a supplier at a cost of $18 per unit. However, over the past few months, the company's production capacity has been expanded. As a result, excess capacity is now available in certain production departments, and the company is considering the alternative of producing the parts itself.

Forecasted utilization of equipment shows that production capacity will be available for the part being considered. The production capacity is available at the rate of 1000 units per month, with up to five months of production time available. Management believes that with a two-week lead time, schedules can be arranged so that the part can be produced whenever needed. The demand during the two-week lead time is approximately normally distributed, with a mean of 128 units and a standard deviation of 20 units. Production costs are expected to be $17 per part.

A concern of management is that setup costs will be substantial. The total cost of labor and lost production time is estimated to be $50 per hour, and a full eight-hour shift will be needed to set up the equipment for producing the part.

Managerial Report

Develop a report for management of Wagner Fabricating that will address the question of whether the company should continue to purchase the part from the supplier or begin to produce the part itself. Include the following factors in your report:

1. An analysis of the holding costs, including the appropriate annual holding cost rate
2. An analysis of ordering costs, including the appropriate cost per order from the supplier
3. An analysis of setup costs for the production operation
4. A development of the inventory policy for the following two alternatives:
   a. Ordering a fixed quantity Q from the supplier
   b. Ordering a fixed quantity Q from in-plant production
5. Include the following in the policies of parts 4(a) and 4(b):
   a. Optimal quantity Q^*
   b. Number of order or production runs per year
   c. Cycle time
   d. Reorder point
   e. Amount of safety stock
   f. Expected maximum inventory
   g. Average inventory
   h. Annual holding cost
   i. Annual ordering cost
   j. Annual cost of the units purchased or manufactured
   k. Total annual cost of the purchase policy and the total annual cost of the production policy
6. Make a recommendation as to whether the company should purchase or manufacture the part. What savings are associated with your recommendation as compared with the other alternative?

Case Problem 2   River City Fire Department

The River City Fire Department (RCFD) fights fires and provides a variety of rescue operations in the River City metropolitan area. The RCFD staffs 13 ladder companies, 26 pumper companies, and several rescue units and ambulances. Normal staffing requires 186 firefighters to be on duty every day.

RCFD is organized with three firefighting units. Each unit works a full 24-hour day and then has two days (48 hours) off. For example, Unit 1 covers Monday, Unit 2 covers Tuesday, and Unit 3 covers Wednesday. Then Unit 1 returns on Thursday, and so on. Over a three-week (21-day) scheduling period, each unit will be scheduled for seven days. On a rotational basis, firefighters within each unit are given one of the seven regularly scheduled days off. This day off is referred to as a Kelley day. Thus, over a three-week scheduling period, each firefighter in a unit works six of the seven scheduled unit days and gets one Kelley day off.

Determining the number of firefighters to be assigned to each unit includes the 186 firefighters who must be on duty plus the number of firefighters in the unit who are off for a Kelley day. Furthermore, each unit needs additional staffing to cover firefighter absences due to injury, sick leave, vacations, or personal time. This additional staffing involves finding the best mix of adding full-time firefighters to each unit and the selective use of overtime. If the number of absences on a particular day brings the number of available firefighters below the required 186, firefighters who are currently off (e.g., on a Kelley day) must be scheduled to work overtime. Overtime is compensated at 1.55 times the regular pay rate.

Analysis of the records maintained over the last several years concerning the number of daily absences shows a normal probability distribution. A mean of 20 and a standard deviation of 5 provides a good approximation of the probability distribution for the number of daily absences.

Managerial Report

Develop a report that will enable Fire Chief O. E. Smith to determine the necessary numbers for the Fire Department. Include, at a minimum, the following items in your report:

1. Assuming no daily absences and taking into account the need to staff Kelley days, determine the base number of firefighters needed by each unit.
2. Using a minimum cost criterion, how many additional firefighters should be added to each unit in order to cover the daily absences? These extra daily needs will be filled by the additional firefighters and, when necessary, the more expensive use of overtime by off-duty firefighters.
3. On a given day, what is the probability that Kelley-day firefighters will be called in to work overtime?
4. Based on the three-unit organization, how many firefighters should be assigned to each unit? What is the total number of full-time firefighters required for the River City Fire Department?

Appendix 14.1   Development of the Optimal Order Quantity (Q*) Formula for the EOQ Model

Given equation (14.4) as the total annual cost for the EOQ model,

$$TC = \frac{1}{2} Q C_h + \frac{D}{Q} C_o \tag{14.4}$$

we can find the order quantity Q that minimizes the total cost by setting the derivative, dTC/dQ, equal to zero and solving for Q^*.

$$\frac{dTC}{dQ} = \frac{1}{2}\,C_\mathrm{h} - \frac{D}{Q^2}\,C_\mathrm{o} = 0$$

$$\frac{1}{2}\,C_\mathrm{h} = \frac{D}{Q^2}\,C_\mathrm{o}$$

$$C_\mathrm{h}Q^2 = 2DC_\mathrm{o}$$

$$Q^2 = \frac{2DC_\mathrm{o}}{C_\mathrm{h}}$$

Hence,

$$Q^* = \sqrt{\frac{2DC_\mathrm{o}}{C_\mathrm{h}}} \tag{14.5}$$

The second derivative is

$$\frac{d^2TC}{dQ^2} = \frac{2D}{Q^3}\,C_\mathrm{o}$$

Because the value of the second derivative is greater than zero, Q^* from equation (14.5) is the minimum-cost solution.

Appendix 14.2 Development of the Optimal Lot Size (Q^*) Formula for the Production Lot Size Model

Given equation (14.15) as the total annual cost for the production lot size model,

$$TC = \frac{1}{2}\left(1 - \frac{D}{P}\right)QC_\mathrm{h} + \frac{D}{Q}\,C_\mathrm{o} \tag{14.15}$$

we can find the order quantity Q that minimizes the total cost by setting the derivative, dTC/dQ, equal to zero and solving for Q^*.

$$\frac{dTC}{dQ} = \frac{1}{2}\left(1 - \frac{D}{P}\right)C_\mathrm{h} - \frac{D}{Q^2}\,C_\mathrm{o} = 0$$

Solving for Q^*, we have

$$\frac{1}{2}\left(1 - \frac{D}{P}\right)C_\mathrm{h} = \frac{D}{Q^2}\,C_\mathrm{o}$$

$$\left(1 - \frac{D}{P}\right)C_\mathrm{h}Q^2 = 2DC_\mathrm{o}$$

$$Q^2 = \frac{2DC_\mathrm{o}}{(1 - D/P)C_\mathrm{h}}$$

Hence,

$$Q^* = \sqrt{\frac{2DC_o}{(1 - D/P)C_h}}$$

(14.16)

The second derivative is

$$\frac{d^2TC}{dQ^2} = \frac{2DC_o}{Q^3}$$

Because the value of the second derivative is greater than zero, Q^* from equation (14.16) is a minimum-cost solution.

CHAPTER 15

Waiting Line Models

CONTENTS

Recall the last time that you had to wait at a supermarket checkout counter, for a teller at your local bank, or to be served at a fast-food restaurant. In these and many other waiting line situations, the time spent waiting is undesirable. Adding more checkout clerks, bank tellers, or servers is not always the most economical strategy for improving service, so businesses need to determine ways to keep waiting times within tolerable limits.

Models have been developed to help managers understand and make better decisions concerning the operation of waiting lines. In management science terminology, a waiting line is also known as a **queue**, and the body of knowledge dealing with waiting lines is known as **queueing theory**. In the early 1900s, A. K. Erlang, a Danish telephone engineer, began a study of the congestion and waiting times occurring in the completion of telephone calls. Since then, queueing theory has grown far more sophisticated, with applications in a wide variety of waiting line situations.

Waiting line models consist of mathematical formulas and relationships that can be used to determine the **operating characteristics** (performance measures) for a waiting line. Operating characteristics of interest include these:

1. The probability that no units are in the system (i.e., the system is idle)
2. The average number of units in the waiting line
3. The average number of units in the system (the number of units in the waiting line plus the number of units being served)
4. The average time a unit spends in the waiting line
5. The average time a unit spends in the system (the waiting time plus the service time)
6. The probability that an arriving unit has to wait for service

Managers who have such information are better able to make decisions that balance desirable service levels against the cost of providing the service.

The Q.M. in Action, ATM Waiting Times at Citibank, describes how a waiting line model was used to help determine the number of automatic teller machines to place at New York City banking centers. A waiting line model prompted the creation of a new kind of line and a chief line director to implement first-come, first-served queue discipline at Whole Foods Market in the Chelsea neighborhood of New York City. In addition, a waiting line model helped the New Haven, Connecticut, fire department develop policies to improve response time for both fire and medical emergencies.

Q.M. *in* ACTION

ATM WAITING TIMES AT CITIBANK*

The waiting line model used at Citibank is discussed in Section 15.3

The New York City franchise of U.S. Citibanking operates more than 250 banking centers. Each center provides one or more automatic teller machines (ATMs) capable of performing a variety of banking transactions. At each center, a waiting line is formed by randomly arriving customers who seek service at one of the ATMs.

In order to make decisions on the number of ATMs to have at selected banking center locations, management needed information about potential waiting times and general customer service. Waiting line operating characteristics such as average number of customers in the waiting line, average time a customer spends waiting, and the probability that an arriving customer has to wait would help management determine the number of ATMs to recommend at each banking center.

For example, one busy Midtown Manhattan center had a peak arrival rate of 172 customers per hour. A multiple-server waiting line model

---

*Based on information provided by Stacey Karter of Citibank.

(*continued*)

with six ATMs showed that 88% of the customers would have to wait, with an average wait time between six and seven minutes. This level of service was judged unacceptable. Expansion to seven ATMs was recommended for this location based on the waiting line model's projection of acceptable waiting times. Use of the waiting line model provided guidelines for making incremental ATM decisions at each banking center location.

Structure of a Waiting Line System

To illustrate the basic features of a waiting line model, we consider the waiting line at the Burger Dome fast-food restaurant. Burger Dome sells hamburgers, cheeseburgers, french fries, soft drinks, and milk shakes, as well as a limited number of specialty items and dessert selections. Although Burger Dome would like to serve each customer immediately, at times more customers arrive than can be handled by the Burger Dome food service staff. Thus, customers wait in line to place and receive their orders.

Burger Dome is concerned that the methods currently used to serve customers are resulting in excessive waiting times and a possible loss of sales. Management wants to conduct a waiting line study to help determine the best approach to reduce waiting times and improve service.

Single-Server Waiting Line

In the current Burger Dome operation, an employee takes a customer's order, determines the total cost of the order, receives payment from the customer, and then fills the order. Once the first customer's order is filled, the employee takes the order of the next customer waiting for service. This operation is an example of a **single-server waiting line**. Each customer entering the Burger Dome restaurant is served by a single order-filling station that handles order placement, bill payment, and food delivery. When more customers arrive than can be served immediately, they form a waiting line and wait for the order-filling station to become available. A diagram of the Burger Dome single-server waiting line is shown in Figure 15.1.

Distribution of Arrivals

Defining the arrival process for a waiting line involves determining the probability distribution for the number of arrivals in a given period of time. For many waiting line situations,

FIGURE 15.1   THE BURGER DOME SINGLE-SERVER WAITING LINE

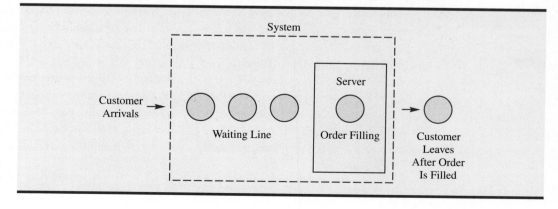

the arrivals occur *randomly and independently* of other arrivals, and we cannot predict when an arrival will occur. In such cases, analysts have found that the **Poisson probability distribution** provides a good description of the arrival pattern.

The Poisson probability function provides the probability of x arrivals in a specific time period. The probability function is as follows:[1]

$$P(x) = \frac{\lambda^x e^{-\lambda}}{x!} \quad \text{for } x = 0, 1, 2, \ldots \tag{15.1}$$

where

$x =$ the number of arrivals in the time period

$\lambda =$ the *mean* number of arrivals per time period

$e = 2.71828$

The mean number of arrivals per time period, λ, is called the **arrival rate**. Values of $e^{-\lambda}$ can be found using a calculator or by using Appendix E.

Suppose that Burger Dome analyzed data on customer arrivals and concluded that the arrival rate is 45 customers per hour. For a one-minute period, the arrival rate would be $\lambda = 45$ customers $\div$ 60 minutes $= 0.75$ customers per minute. Thus, we can use the following Poisson probability function to compute the probability of x customer arrivals during a one-minute period:

$$P(x) = \frac{\lambda^x e^{-\lambda}}{x!} = \frac{0.75^x e^{-0.75}}{x!} \tag{15.2}$$

Thus, the probabilities of 0, 1, and 2 customer arrivals during a one-minute period are

$$P(0) = \frac{(0.75)^0 e^{-0.75}}{0!} = e^{-0.75} = 0.4724$$

$$P(1) = \frac{(0.75)^1 e^{-0.75}}{1!} = 0.75 e^{-0.75} = 0.75(0.4724) = 0.3543$$

$$P(2) = \frac{(0.75)^2 e^{-0.75}}{2!} = \frac{(0.5625)(0.4724)}{2} = 0.1329$$

The probability of no customers in a one-minute period is 0.4724, the probability of one customer in a one-minute period is 0.3543, and the probability of two customers in a one-minute period is 0.1329. Table 15.1 shows the Poisson probabilities for customer arrivals during a one-minute period.

The waiting line models that will be presented in Sections 15.2 and 15.3 use the Poisson probability distribution to describe the customer arrivals at Burger Dome. In practice, you should record the actual number of arrivals per time period for several days or weeks and compare the frequency distribution of the observed number of arrivals to the Poisson probability distribution to determine whether the Poisson probability distribution provides a reasonable approximation of the arrival distribution.

---

[1]The term $x!$, x *factorial*, is defined as $x! = x(x - 1)(x - 2) \ldots (2)(1)$. For example, $4! = (4)(3)(2)(1) = 24$. For the special case of $x = 0$, $0! = 1$ by definition.

TABLE 15.1 POISSON PROBABILITIES FOR THE NUMBER OF CUSTOMER ARRIVALS AT A BURGER DOME RESTAURANT DURING A ONE-MINUTE PERIOD ($\lambda = 0.75$)

Number of Arrivals	Probability
0	0.4724
1	0.3543
2	0.1329
3	0.0332
4	0.0062
5 or more	0.0010

Distribution of Service Times

The service time is the time a customer spends at the service facility once the service has started. At Burger Dome, the service time starts when a customer begins to place the order with the employee and continues until the customer receives the order. Service times are rarely constant. At Burger Dome, the number of items ordered and the mix of items ordered vary considerably from one customer to the next. Small orders can be handled in a matter of seconds, but large orders may require more than two minutes.

If the probability distribution for the service time can be assumed to follow an **exponential probability distribution**, formulas are available for providing useful information about the operation of the waiting line. Using an exponential probability distribution, the probability that the service time will be less than or equal to a time of length t is

$$P(\text{service time} \leq t) = 1 - e^{-\mu t} \tag{15.3}$$

where

μ = the *mean* number of units that can be served per time period

e = 2.71828

The mean number of units that can be served per time period, μ, is called the **service rate**.

Suppose that Burger Dome studied the order-filling process and found that a single employee can process an average of 60 customer orders per hour. On a one-minute basis, the service rate would be $\mu = 60$ customers $\div$ 60 minutes = 1 customer per minute. For example, with $\mu = 1$, we can use equation (15.3) to compute probabilities such as the probability that an order can be processed in $1/2$ minute or less, 1 minute or less, and 2 minutes or less. These computations are

$P(\text{service time} \leq 0.5 \text{ min.}) = 1 - e^{-1(0.5)} = 1 - 0.6065 = 0.3935$

$P(\text{service time} \leq 1.0 \text{ min.}) = 1 - e^{-1(1.0)} = 1 - 0.3679 = 0.6321$

$P(\text{service time} \leq 2.0 \text{ min.}) = 1 - e^{-1(2.0)} = 1 - 0.1353 = 0.8647$

A property of the exponential probability distribution is that there is a 0.6321 probability that the random variable takes on a value less than its mean. In waiting line applications, the exponential probability distribution indicates that approximately 63% of the service times are less than the mean service time and approximately 37% of the service times are greater than the mean service time.

Thus, we would conclude that there is a 0.3935 probability that an order can be processed in $1/2$ minute or less, a 0.6321 probability that it can be processed in 1 minute or less, and a 0.8647 probability that it can be processed in 2 minutes or less.

In several waiting line models presented in this chapter, we assume that the probability distribution for the service time follows an exponential probability distribution. In practice, you should collect data on actual service times to determine whether the exponential probability distribution is a reasonable approximation of the service times for your application.

Queue Discipline

In describing a waiting line system, we must define the manner in which the waiting units are arranged for service. For the Burger Dome waiting line, and in general for most customer-oriented waiting lines, the units waiting for service are arranged on a **first-come, first-served** basis; this approach is referred to as an **FCFS** queue discipline. However, some situations call for different queue disciplines. For example, when people board an airplane, the last passengers to board are typically the first to deplane since many airlines have the passengers with seat assignments in the back of the plane board first. On the other hand, it does not seem prudent for hospital emergency rooms to operate under either of these queue disciplines, and so we have other types of queue disciplines that assign priorities to the waiting units and then serve the unit with the highest priority first. In this chapter we consider only waiting lines based on a first-come, first-served queue discipline.

Steady-State Operation

When the Burger Dome restaurant opens in the morning, no customers are in the restaurant, and the characteristics of the waiting line system fluctuate depending on realized arrival and service times. Gradually, activity builds up to a normal or steady state. The beginning or startup period is referred to as the **transient period**. The transient period ends when the system reaches the normal or **steady-state operation**. Waiting line models describe the steady-state operating characteristics of a waiting line.

15.2   Single-Server Waiting Line Model with Poisson Arrivals and Exponential Service Times

In this section we present formulas that can be used to determine the steady-state operating characteristics for a single-server waiting line. The formulas are applicable if the arrivals follow a Poisson probability distribution and the service times follow an exponential probability distribution. As these assumptions apply to the Burger Dome waiting line problem introduced in Section 15.1, we show how formulas can be used to determine Burger Dome's operating characteristics and thus provide management with helpful decision-making information.

Waiting line models are often based on assumptions such as Poisson arrivals and exponential service times. When applying any waiting line model, data should be collected on the actual system to ensure that the assumptions of the model are reasonable.

The mathematical methodology used to derive the formulas for the operating characteristics of waiting lines is rather complex. However, our purpose in this chapter is not to provide the theoretical development of waiting line models, but rather to show how the formulas that have been developed can provide information about operating characteristics of the waiting line. Readers interested in the mathematical development of the formulas can consult the specialized texts listed in Appendix F at the end of the text.

Operating Characteristics

The following formulas can be used to compute the steady-state operating characteristics for a single-server waiting line with Poisson arrivals and exponential service times, where

λ = the mean number of arrivals per time period (the arrival rate)

μ = the mean number of services per time period (the service rate)

Equations (15.4) through (15.10) do not provide formulas for optimal conditions. Rather, these equations provide information about the steady-state operating characteristics of a waiting line.

1. The probability that no units are in the system:

$$P_0 = 1 - \frac{\lambda}{\mu} \qquad \text{(15.4)}$$

2. The average number of units in the waiting line:

$$L_q = \frac{\lambda^2}{\mu(\mu - \lambda)} \qquad \text{(15.5)}$$

3. The average number of units in the system:

$$L = L_q + \frac{\lambda}{\mu} \qquad \text{(15.6)}$$

4. The average time a unit spends in the waiting line:

$$W_q = \frac{L_q}{\lambda} \qquad \text{(15.7)}$$

5. The average time a unit spends in the system:

$$W = W_q + \frac{1}{\mu} \qquad \text{(15.8)}$$

6. The probability that an arriving unit has to wait for service:

$$P_w = \frac{\lambda}{\mu} \qquad \text{(15.9)}$$

7. The probability of n units in the system:

$$P_n = \left(\frac{\lambda}{\mu}\right)^n P_0 \qquad \text{(15.10)}$$

The values of the arrival rate λ and the service rate μ are clearly important components in determining the operating characteristics. Equation (15.9) shows that the ratio of the arrival rate to the service rate, λ/μ, provides the probability that an arriving unit has to wait because the service facility is in use. Hence, λ/μ is referred to as the *utilization factor* for the service facility.

The operating characteristics presented in equations (15.4) through (15.10) are applicable only when the service rate μ is *greater than* the arrival rate λ—in other words, when $\lambda/\mu < 1$. If this condition does not exist, the waiting line will continue to grow without limit because the service facility does not have sufficient capacity to handle the arriving units. Thus, in using equations (15.4) through (15.10), we must have $\mu > \lambda$.

Operating Characteristics for the Burger Dome Problem

Recall that for the Burger Dome problem we had an arrival rate of $\lambda = 0.75$ customers per minute and a service rate of $\mu = 1$ customer per minute. Thus, with $\mu > \lambda$, equations (15.4) through (15.10) can be used to provide operating characteristics for the Burger Dome single-server waiting line:

$$P_0 = 1 - \frac{\lambda}{\mu} = 1 - \frac{0.75}{1} = 0.25$$

$$L_q = \frac{\lambda^2}{\mu(\mu - \lambda)} = \frac{0.75^2}{1(1 - 0.75)} = 2.25 \text{ customers}$$

$$L = L_q + \frac{\lambda}{\mu} = 2.25 + \frac{0.75}{1} = 3 \text{ customers}$$

$$W_q = \frac{L_q}{\lambda} = \frac{2.25}{0.75} = 3 \text{ minutes}$$

$$W = W_q + \frac{1}{\mu} = 3 + \frac{1}{1} = 4 \text{ minutes}$$

$$P_w = \frac{\lambda}{\mu} = \frac{0.75}{1} = 0.75$$

Problem 5 asks you to compute the operating characteristics for a single-server waiting line application.

Equation (15.10) can be used to determine the probability of any number of customers in the system. Applying this equation provides the probability information in Table 15.2.

Managers' Use of Waiting Line Models

The results of the single-server waiting line for Burger Dome show several important things about the operation of the waiting line. In particular, customers wait an average of three minutes before beginning to place an order, which appears somewhat long for a business based on fast service. In addition, the facts that the average number of customers waiting in line is 2.25 and that 75% of the arriving customers have to wait for service are indicators that something should be done to improve the waiting line operation. Table 15.2 shows a 0.1335 probability that seven or more customers are in the Burger Dome system at one time. This condition indicates a fairly high probability that Burger Dome will experience some long waiting lines if it continues to use the single-server operation.

TABLE 15.2 THE PROBABILITY OF n CUSTOMERS IN THE SYSTEM FOR THE BURGER DOME WAITING LINE PROBLEM

Number of Customers	Probability
0	0.2500
1	0.1875
2	0.1406
3	0.1055
4	0.0791
5	0.0593
6	0.0445
7 or more	0.1335

If the operating characteristics are unsatisfactory in terms of meeting company standards for service, Burger Dome's management should consider alternative designs or plans for improving the waiting line operation.

Improving the Waiting Line Operation

Waiting line models often indicate when improvements in operating characteristics are desirable. However, the decision of how to modify the waiting line configuration to improve the operating characteristics must be based on the insights and creativity of the analyst.

After reviewing the operating characteristics provided by the waiting line model, Burger Dome's management concluded that improvements designed to reduce waiting times were desirable. To make improvements in the waiting line operation, analysts often focus on ways to improve the service rate. Generally, service rate improvements are obtained by making either or both of the following changes:

1. Increase the service rate by making a creative design change or by using new technology.
2. Add one or more servers so that more customers can be served simultaneously.

Assume that in considering Alternative 1, Burger Dome's management decides to employ a design change that allows the customer to fill out and submit a paper order form directly to the kitchen while they are waiting in line. This allows the customer's food to be ready by the time the employee collects payment from the customer. With this design, Burger Dome's management estimates the service rate can be increased from the current 60 customers per hour to 75 customers per hour. Thus, the service rate for the revised system is $\mu = 75$ customers $\div$ 60 minutes $= 1.25$ customers per minute. For $\lambda = 0.75$ customers per minute and $\mu = 1.25$ customers per minute, equations (15.4) through (15.10) can be used to provide the new operating characteristics for the Burger Dome waiting line. These operating characteristics are summarized in Table 15.3.

The information in Table 15.3 indicates that all operating characteristics have improved because of the increased service rate. In particular, the average time a customer spends in the waiting line has been reduced from 3 to 1.2 minutes, and the average time a customer spends in the system has been reduced from 4 to 2 minutes. Are any other alternatives available that Burger Dome can use to increase the service rate? If so, and if the mean service rate μ can be identified for each alternative, equations (15.4) through (15.10) can be used to determine the revised operating characteristics and any improvements in the waiting line system. The added cost of any proposed change can be compared to the corresponding service improvements to help the manager determine whether the proposed service improvements are worthwhile.

TABLE 15.3 OPERATING CHARACTERISTICS FOR THE BURGER DOME SYSTEM WITH THE SERVICE RATE INCREASED TO $\mu = 1.25$ CUSTOMERS PER MINUTE

Probability of no customers in the system	0.400
Average number of customers in the waiting line	0.900
Average number of customers in the system	1.500
Average time in the waiting line	1.200 minutes
Average time in the system	2.000 minutes
Probability that an arriving customer has to wait	0.600
Probability that seven or more customers are in the system	0.028

Problem 11 asks you to determine whether a change in the service rate will meet the company's service guideline for its customers.

As mentioned previously in Alternative 2, another option often available is to add one or more servers so that orders for multiple customers can be filled simultaneously. The extension of the single-server waiting line model to the multiple-server waiting line model is the topic of the next section.

Excel Solution of Waiting Line Model

Waiting line models are easily implemented with the aid of spreadsheets. The Excel worksheet for the Burger Dome single-server waiting line is shown in Figure 15.2. The worksheet view showing the formulas is on the left, and the worksheet view showing the values is on the right. The arrival rate and the service rate are entered in cells B7 and B8. The formulas for the waiting line's operating characteristics are placed in cells C13 to C18. The worksheet computes the same values for the operating characteristics that we obtained earlier. Modifications in the waiting line design can be evaluated by entering different arrival rates and/or service rates into cells B7 and B8. The new operating characteristics of the waiting line will be shown immediately. The Excel worksheet in Figure 15.2 is a template that can be used with any single-server waiting line model with Poisson arrivals and exponential service times.

FIGURE 15.2 WORKSHEET FOR THE BURGER DOME SINGLE-SERVER WAITING LINE

	A	B	C
1	Single-Server Waiting Line Model		
2			
3	Assumptions		
4	Poisson Arrivals		
5	Exponential Service Times		
6			
7	Arrival Rate	0.75	
8	Service Rate	1	
9			
10			
11	Operating Characteristics		
12			
13	Probability that no customers are in the system, P_0		=1-B7/B8
14	Average number of customers in the waiting line, L_q		=B7^2/(B8*(B8-B7))
15	Average number of customers in the system, L		=C14+B7/B8
16	Average time a customer spends in the waiting line, W_q		=C14/B7
17	Average time a customer spends in the system, W		=C16+1/B8
18	Probability an arriving customer has to wait, P_w		=B7/B8

	A	B	C
1	Single-Server Waiting Line Model		
2			
3	Assumptions		
4	Poisson Arrivals		
5	Exponential Service Times		
6			
7	Arrival Rate	0.75	
8	Service Rate	1	
9			
10			
11	Operating Characteristics		
12			
13	Probability that no customers are in the system, P_0		0.2500
14	Average number of customers in the waiting line, L_q		2.2500
15	Average number of customers in the system, L		3.0000
16	Average time a customer spends in the waiting line, W_q		3.0000
17	Average time a customer spends in the system, W		4.0000
18	Probability an arriving customer has to wait, P_w		0.7500

WEB file

Single

NOTES AND COMMENTS

1. The assumption that arrivals follow a Poisson probability distribution is equivalent to the assumption that the time between arrivals has an exponential probability distribution. For example, if the arrivals for a waiting line follow a Poisson probability distribution with a mean of 20 arrivals per hour, the time between arrivals will follow an exponential probability distribution, with a mean time between arrivals of $1/20$ or 0.05 hour.

2. Many individuals believe that whenever the service rate μ is greater than the arrival rate λ, the system should be able to handle or serve all arrivals without any customer waiting for service. This would be true if the time between customer arrivals was constant and the service time was constant. However, as the Burger Dome example shows, the variability of arrival times and service times may result in long waiting times even when the service rate exceeds the arrival rate. A contribution of waiting line models is that they can point out undesirable waiting line operating characteristics even when the $\mu > \lambda$ condition appears satisfactory.

15.3 Multiple–Server Waiting Line Model with Poisson Arrivals and Exponential Service Times

A **multiple-server waiting line** consists of two or more servers that are assumed to be identical in terms of service capability. For multiple-server systems, there are two typical queueing possibilities: (1) arriving customers wait in a single waiting line (called a "pooled" or "shared" queue) and then move to the first available server for processing, or (2) each server has a "dedicated" queue and an arriving customer selects one of these lines to join (and typically is not allowed to switch lines). In this chapter, we focus on the system design with a single shared waiting line for all servers. Operating characteristics for a multiple-server system are typically better when a single shared queue, rather than multiple dedicated waiting lines, is used. The single-server Burger Dome operation can be expanded to a two-server system by opening a second server. Figure 15.3 shows a diagram of the Burger Dome two-server waiting line.

In this section we present formulas that can be used to determine the steady-state operating characteristics for a multiple-server waiting line. These formulas are applicable if the following conditions exist:

1. The arrivals follow a Poisson probability distribution.
2. The service time for each server follows an exponential probability distribution.
3. The service rate μ is the same for each server.
4. The arrivals wait in a single waiting line and then move to the first open server for service.

Operating Characteristics

The following formulas can be used to compute the steady-state operating characteristics for multiple-server waiting lines, where

$$\lambda = \text{the arrival rate for the system}$$
$$\mu = \text{the service rate for } each \text{ server}$$
$$k = \text{the number of servers}$$

FIGURE 15.3   THE BURGER DOME TWO-SERVER WAITING LINE

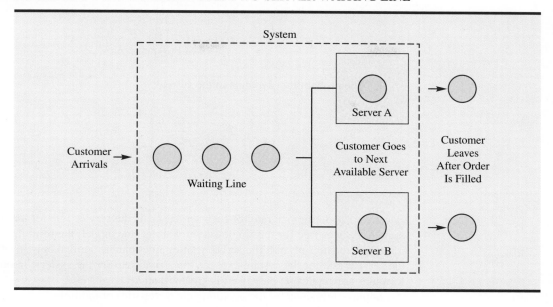

1. The probability that no units are in the system:

$$P_0 = \cfrac{1}{\displaystyle\sum_{n=0}^{k-1} \cfrac{(\lambda/\mu)^n}{n!} + \cfrac{(\lambda/\mu)^k}{k!}\left(\cfrac{k\mu}{k\mu - \lambda}\right)} \qquad \textbf{(15.11)}$$

2. The average number of units in the waiting line:

$$L_q = \cfrac{(\lambda/\mu)^k \lambda\mu}{(k-1)!(k\mu - \lambda)^2} P_0 \qquad \textbf{(15.12)}$$

3. The average number of units in the system:

$$L = L_q + \cfrac{\lambda}{\mu} \qquad \textbf{(15.13)}$$

4. The average time a unit spends in the waiting line:

$$W_q = \cfrac{L_q}{\lambda} \qquad \textbf{(15.14)}$$

5. The average time a unit spends in the system:

$$W = W_q + \cfrac{1}{\mu} \qquad \textbf{(15.15)}$$

6. The probability that an arriving unit has to wait for service:

$$P_w = \frac{1}{k!}\left(\frac{\lambda}{\mu}\right)^k\left(\frac{k\mu}{k\mu - \lambda}\right)P_0 \qquad \textbf{(15.16)}$$

7. The probability of n units in the system:

$$P_n = \frac{(\lambda/\mu)^n}{n!}P_0 \qquad \text{for } n \leq k \qquad \textbf{(15.17)}$$

$$P_n = \frac{(\lambda/\mu)^n}{k!k^{(n-k)}}P_0 \qquad \text{for } n > k \qquad \textbf{(15.18)}$$

Because μ is the service rate for each server, $k\mu$ is the service rate for the multiple-server system. As was true for the single-server waiting line model, the formulas for the operating characteristics of multiple-server waiting lines can be applied only in situations where the service rate for the system exceeds the arrival rate for the system; in other words, the formulas are applicable only if $k\mu$ is greater than λ.

Some expressions for the operating characteristics of multiple-server waiting lines are more complex than their single-server counterparts. However, equations (15.11) through (15.18) provide the same information as provided by the single-server model. To help simplify the use of the multiple-server equations, Table 15.4 contains values of P_0 for selected values of λ/μ and k. The values provided in the table correspond to cases where $k\mu > \lambda$, and hence the service rate is sufficient to process all arrivals.

Operating Characteristics for the Burger Dome Problem

To illustrate the multiple-server waiting line model, we return to the Burger Dome fast-food restaurant waiting line problem. Suppose that management wants to evaluate the desirability of opening a second order-processing station so that two customers can be served simultaneously. Assume a single waiting line with the first customer in line moving to the first available server. Let us evaluate the operating characteristics for this two-server system.

We use equations (15.11) through (15.18) for the $k = 2$-server system. For an arrival rate of $\lambda = 0.75$ customers per minute and a service rate of $\mu = 1$ customer per minute for each server, we obtain the operating characteristics:

WEB file

Multiple

$$P_0 = 0.4545 \quad \text{(from Table 15.4 with } \lambda/\mu = 0.75\text{)}$$

$$L_q = \frac{(0.75/1)^2(0.75)(1)}{(2-1)![2(1) - 0.75]^2}(0.4545) = 0.1227 \text{ customer}$$

$$L = L_q + \frac{\lambda}{\mu} = 0.1227 + \frac{0.75}{1} = 0.8727 \text{ customer}$$

$$W_q = \frac{L_q}{\lambda} = \frac{0.1227}{0.75} = 0.1636 \text{ minute}$$

$$W = W_q + \frac{1}{\mu} = 0.1636 + \frac{1}{1} = 1.1636 \text{ minutes}$$

$$P_w = \frac{1}{2!}\left(\frac{0.75}{1}\right)^2\left[\frac{2(1)}{2(1) - 0.75}\right](0.4545) = 0.2045$$

TABLE 15.4   VALUES OF P_0 FOR MULTIPLE-SERVER WAITING LINES WITH POISSON ARRIVALS AND EXPONENTIAL SERVICE TIMES

Ratio λ/μ	Number of Servers (k)			
	2	3	4	5
0.15	0.8605	0.8607	0.8607	0.8607
0.20	0.8182	0.8187	0.8187	0.8187
0.25	0.7778	0.7788	0.7788	0.7788
0.30	0.7391	0.7407	0.7408	0.7408
0.35	0.7021	0.7046	0.7047	0.7047
0.40	0.6667	0.6701	0.6703	0.6703
0.45	0.6327	0.6373	0.6376	0.6376
0.50	0.6000	0.6061	0.6065	0.6065
0.55	0.5686	0.5763	0.5769	0.5769
0.60	0.5385	0.5479	0.5487	0.5488
0.65	0.5094	0.5209	0.5219	0.5220
0.70	0.4815	0.4952	0.4965	0.4966
0.75	0.4545	0.4706	0.4722	0.4724
0.80	0.4286	0.4472	0.4491	0.4493
0.85	0.4035	0.4248	0.4271	0.4274
0.90	0.3793	0.4035	0.4062	0.4065
0.95	0.3559	0.3831	0.3863	0.3867
1.00	0.3333	0.3636	0.3673	0.3678
1.20	0.2500	0.2941	0.3002	0.3011
1.40	0.1765	0.2360	0.2449	0.2463
1.60	0.1111	0.1872	0.1993	0.2014
1.80	0.0526	0.1460	0.1616	0.1646
2.00		0.1111	0.1304	0.1343
2.20		0.0815	0.1046	0.1094
2.40		0.0562	0.0831	0.0889
2.60		0.0345	0.0651	0.0721
2.80		0.0160	0.0521	0.0581
3.00			0.0377	0.0466
3.20			0.0273	0.0372
3.40			0.0186	0.0293
3.60			0.0113	0.0228
3.80			0.0051	0.0174
4.00				0.0130
4.20				0.0093
4.40				0.0063
4.60				0.0038
4.80				0.0017

Try Problem 18 for practice in determining the operating characteristics for a two-server waiting line.

Using equations (15.17) and (15.18), we can compute the probabilities of n customers in the system. The results from these computations are summarized in Table 15.5.

We can now compare the steady-state operating characteristics of the two-server system to the operating characteristics of the original single-server system discussed in Section 15.2.

1. The average time a customer spends in the system (waiting time plus service time) is reduced from $W = 4$ minutes to $W = 1.1636$ minutes.
2. The average number of customers in the waiting line is reduced from $L_q = 2.25$ customers to $L_q = 0.1227$ customers.

TABLE 15.5   THE PROBABILITY OF n CUSTOMERS IN THE SYSTEM FOR THE BURGER DOME TWO-SERVER WAITING LINE

Number of Customers	Probability
0	0.4545
1	0.3409
2	0.1278
3	0.0479
4	0.0180
5 or more	0.0109

3. The average time a customer spends in the waiting line is reduced from $W_q = 3$ minutes to $W_q = 0.1636$ minutes.
4. The probability that a customer has to wait for service is reduced from $P_w = 0.75$ to $P_w = 0.2045$.

Clearly the two-server system will substantially improve the operating characteristics of the waiting line. The waiting line study provides the operating characteristics that can be anticipated under three configurations: the original single-server system, a single-server system with the design change involving direct submission of paper order form to kitchen, and a two-server system composed of two order-filling employees. After considering these results, what action would you recommend? In this case, Burger Dome adopted the following policy statement: For periods when customer arrivals are expected to average 45 customers per hour, Burger Dome will open two order-processing servers with one employee assigned to each.

By changing the arrival rate λ to reflect arrival rates at different times of the day and then computing the operating characteristics, Burger Dome's management can establish guidelines and policies that tell the store managers when to schedule service operations with a single server, two servers, or perhaps even three or more servers.

NOTES AND COMMENTS

1. The multiple-server waiting line model is based on a single waiting line. You may have also encountered situations where each of the k servers has its own waiting line. Analysts have shown that the operating characteristics of multiple-server systems are better if a single waiting line is used. Also, people tend to like them better; no one who comes in after you can be served ahead of you, and so they appeal to one's sense of fairness. Thus, when possible, banks, airline reservation counters, airport security systems, food-service establishments, and other businesses frequently use a single waiting line for a multiple-server system.

 15.4   # Some General Relationships for Waiting Line Models

In Sections 15.2 and 15.3 we presented formulas for computing the operating characteristics for single-server and multiple-server waiting lines with Poisson arrivals and exponential service times. The operating characteristics of interest included

$$L_q = \text{the average number of units in the waiting line}$$
$$L = \text{the average number of units in the system}$$

W_q = the average time a unit spends in the waiting line

W = the average time a unit spends in the system

John D. C. Little showed that several relationships exist among these four characteristics and that these relationships apply to a variety of different waiting line systems. Two of the relationships, referred to as *Little's flow equations*, are

$$L = \lambda W \qquad \textbf{(15.19)}$$

$$L_q = \lambda W_q \qquad \textbf{(15.20)}$$

Equation (15.19) shows that the average number of units in the system, L, can be found by multiplying the arrival rate, λ, by the average time a unit spends in the system, W. Equation (15.20) shows that the same relationship holds between the average number of units in the waiting line, L_q, and the average time a unit spends in the waiting line, W_q.

Using equation (15.20) and solving for W_q, we obtain

$$W_q = \frac{L_q}{\lambda} \qquad \textbf{(15.21)}$$

Equation (15.21) follows directly from Little's second flow equation. We used it for the single-server waiting line model in Section 15.2 and the multiple-server waiting line model in Section 15.3 [see equations (15.7) and (15.14)]. Once L_q is computed for either of these models, equation (15.21) can then be used to compute W_q.

Another general expression that applies to waiting line models is that the average time in the system, W, is equal to the average time in the waiting line, W_q, plus the average service time. For a system with a service rate μ, the mean service time is $1/\mu$. Thus, we have the general relationship

$$W = W_q + \frac{1}{\mu} \qquad \textbf{(15.22)}$$

Recall that we used equation (15.22) to provide the average time in the system for both the single- and multiple-server waiting line models [see equations (15.8) and (15.15)].

The importance of Little's flow equations is that they apply to *any waiting line model* regardless of whether arrivals follow the Poisson probability distribution and regardless of whether service times follow the exponential probability distribution. For example, in a study of the grocery checkout counters at Murphy's Foodliner, an analyst concluded that arrivals follow the Poisson probability distribution with an arrival rate of 24 customers per hour, or $\lambda = 24/60 = 0.40$ customers per minute. However, the analyst found that service times follow a normal probability distribution rather than an exponential probability distribution. The service rate was found to be 30 customers per hour, or $\mu = 30/60 = 0.50$ customers per minute. A time study of actual customer waiting times showed that, on average, a customer spends 4.5 minutes in the system (waiting time plus checkout time); that is, $W = 4.5$. Using the waiting line relationships discussed in this section, we can now compute other operating characteristics for this waiting line.

First, using equation (15.22) and solving for W_q, we have

$$W_q = W - \frac{1}{\mu} = 4.5 - \frac{1}{0.50} = 2.5 \text{ minutes}$$

The advantage of Little's flow equations is that they show how operating characteristics L, L_q, W, and W_q are related in any waiting line system. Arrivals and service times do not have to follow specific probability distributions for the flow equations to be applicable.

With both W and W_q known, we can use Little's flow equations, (15.19) and (15.20), to compute

$$L = \lambda W = 0.40(4.5) = 1.8 \text{ customers}$$
$$L_q = \lambda W_q = 0.40(2.5) = 1 \text{ customer}$$

The application of Little's flow equations is demonstrated in Problem 24.

The manager of Murphy's Foodliner can now review these operating characteristics to see whether action should be taken to improve the service and to reduce the waiting time and the length of the waiting line.

NOTES AND COMMENTS

1. In waiting line systems where the length of the waiting line is limited (e.g., a small waiting area), some arriving units will be blocked from joining the waiting line and will be lost. In this case, the blocked or lost arrivals will make the mean number of units entering the system some-thing less than the arrival rate. In other instances, arrivals will decide the line is too long and will leave. By defining λ as the mean number of units *joining the system,* rather than the arrival rate, the relationships discussed in this section can be used to determine W, L, W_q, and L_q.

15.5 Economic Analysis of Waiting Lines

Frequently, decisions involving the design of waiting lines will be based on a subjective evaluation of the operating characteristics of the waiting line. For example, a manager may decide that an average waiting time of one minute or less and an average of two customers or fewer in the system are reasonable goals. The waiting line models presented in the preceding sections can be used to determine the number of servers that will meet the manager's waiting line performance goals.

On the other hand, a manager may want to identify the cost of operating the waiting line system and then base the decision regarding system design on a minimum hourly or daily operating cost. Before an economic analysis of a waiting line can be conducted, a total cost model, which includes the cost of waiting and the cost of service, must be developed.

Waiting cost is based on average number of units in the system. It includes the time spent waiting in line plus the time spent being served.

To develop a total cost model for a waiting line, we begin by defining the notation to be used:

$$c_w = \text{the waiting cost per time period for each unit}$$
$$L = \text{the average number of units in the system}$$
$$c_s = \text{the service cost per time period for each server}$$
$$k = \text{the number of servers}$$
$$TC = \text{the total cost per time period}$$

Adding more servers always improves the operating characteristics of the waiting line and reduces the waiting cost. However, additional servers increase the service cost. An economic analysis of waiting lines attempts to find the number of servers that will minimize total cost by balancing the waiting cost and the service cost.

The total cost is the sum of the waiting cost and the service cost; that is,

$$TC = c_w L + c_s k \qquad \text{(15.23)}$$

To conduct an economic analysis of a waiting line, we must obtain reasonable estimates of the waiting cost and the service cost. Of these two costs, the waiting cost is usually the more difficult to evaluate. In the Burger Dome restaurant problem, the waiting cost would be the cost per minute for a customer waiting for service. This cost is not a direct cost to Burger Dome. However, if Burger Dome ignores this cost and allows long waiting lines, customers ultimately will take their business elsewhere. Thus, Burger Dome will experience lost sales and, in effect, incur a cost.

The service cost is generally easier to determine as it relates to any cost associated with establishing each server operation. In the Burger Dome problem, this cost would include the server's wages, benefits, and any other direct costs associated with establishing a server. At Burger Dome, this cost is estimated to be $10 per hour.

To demonstrate the use of equation (15.23), we assume that Burger Dome is willing to assign a cost of $15 per hour for customer waiting time. We use the average number of units in the system, L, as computed in Sections 15.2 and 15.3 to obtain the total hourly cost for the single-server and two-server systems:

Single-server system ($L = 3$ customers):

$$TC = c_w L + c_s k$$
$$= 15(3) + 10(1) = \$55.00 \text{ per hour}$$

Two-server system ($L = 0.8727$ customer):

$$TC = c_w L + c_s k$$
$$= 15(0.8727) + 10(2) = \$33.09 \text{ per hour}$$

Thus, based on the cost data provided by Burger Dome, the two-server system provides the more economical operation. Note that when the cost of serving a customer c_s exceeds the cost of customer waiting time c_w by a sufficient amount, the single-server system will be more economical for Burger Dome.

Problem 21 tests your ability to conduct an economic analysis of proposed single-server and two-server waiting line systems.

Figure 15.4 shows the general shape of the cost curves in the economic analysis of waiting lines. The service cost increases as the number of servers is increased. However, with more servers, the service is better. As a result, waiting time and cost decrease as the number of servers is increased. The number of servers that will provide a good approximation of the minimum total cost design can be found by evaluating the total cost for several design alternatives.

FIGURE 15.4 THE GENERAL SHAPE OF WAITING COST, SERVICE COST, AND TOTAL COST CURVES IN WAITING LINE MODELS

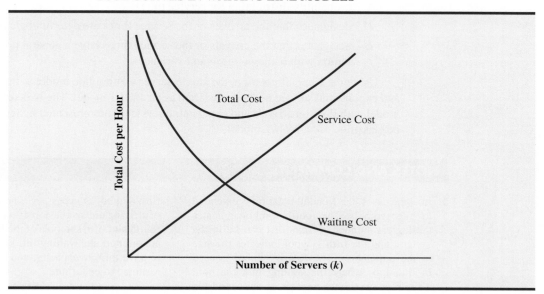

NOTES AND COMMENTS

1. In dealing with government agencies and utility companies, customers may not be able to take their business elsewhere. In these situations, no lost business occurs when long waiting times are encountered. This condition is one reason that service in such organizations may be poor and that customers in such situations may experience long waiting times.

2. In some instances, the organization providing the service also employs the units waiting for the service. For example, consider the case of a company that owns and operates the trucks used to deliver goods to and from its manufacturing plant. In addition to the costs associated with the trucks waiting to be loaded or unloaded, the firm also pays the wages of the truck loaders and unloaders who are effectively operating as servers. In this case, the cost of having the trucks wait and the cost of operating the servers are direct expenses to the firm. An economic analysis of the waiting line system is highly recommended for these types of situations.

15.6   Other Waiting Line Models

D. G. Kendall suggested a notation that is helpful in classifying the wide variety of different waiting line models that have been developed. The three-symbol Kendall notation is as follows:

$$A/B/k$$

where

  A denotes the probability distribution for the arrivals

  B denotes the probability distribution for the service time

  k denotes the number of servers

Depending on the letter appearing in the A or B position, a variety of waiting line systems can be described. The letters that are commonly used are as follows:

  M designates a Poisson probability distribution for the arrivals or an exponential probability distribution for service time

  D designates that the arrivals or the service times are deterministic or constant

  G designates that the arrivals or the service times have a general probability distribution with a known mean and variance

Using the Kendall notation, the single-server waiting line model with Poisson arrivals and exponential service times is classified as an $M/M/1$ model. The two-server waiting line model with Poisson arrivals and exponential service times presented in Section 15.3 would be classified as an $M/M/2$ model.

NOTES AND COMMENTS

1. In some cases, the Kendall notation is extended to five symbols. The fourth symbol indicates the largest number of units that can be in the system, and the fifth symbol indicates the size of the population. The fourth symbol is used in situations where the waiting line can hold a finite or maximum number of units, and the fifth symbol is necessary when the population of arriving units or customers is finite. When the fourth and fifth symbols of the Kendall notation are omitted, the waiting line system is assumed to have infinite capacity, and the population is assumed to be infinite.

15.7

Single-Server Waiting Line Model with Poisson Arrivals and Arbitrary Service Times

Let us return to the single-server waiting line model where arrivals are described by a Poisson probability distribution. However, we now assume that the probability distribution for the service times is not an exponential probability distribution. Thus, using the Kendall notation, the waiting line model that is appropriate is an *M/G*/1 model, where *G* denotes a general or unspecified probability distribution.

Operating Characteristics for the *M/G*/1 Model

When providing input to the M/G/1 model, be consistent in terms of the time period. For example, if λ and μ are expressed in terms of the number of units per hour, the standard deviation of the service time should be expressed in hours. The example that follows uses minutes as the time period for the arrival and service data.

The notation used to describe the operating characteristics for the *M/G*/1 model is

$$\lambda = \text{the arrival rate}$$
$$\mu = \text{the service rate}$$
$$\sigma = \text{the standard deviation of the service time}$$

Some of the steady-state operating characteristics of the *M/G*/1 waiting line model are as follows:

1. The probability that no units are in the system:

$$P_0 = 1 - \frac{\lambda}{\mu} \qquad (15.24)$$

2. The average number of units in the waiting line:

$$L_q = \frac{\lambda^2 \sigma^2 + (\lambda/\mu)^2}{2(1 - \lambda/\mu)} \qquad (15.25)$$

3. The average number of units in the system:

$$L = L_q + \frac{\lambda}{\mu} \qquad (15.26)$$

4. The average time a unit spends in the waiting line:

$$W_q = \frac{L_q}{\lambda} \qquad (15.27)$$

5. The average time a unit spends in the system:

$$W = W_q + \frac{1}{\mu} \qquad (15.28)$$

6. The probability that an arriving unit has to wait for service:

$$P_w = \frac{\lambda}{\mu} \tag{15.29}$$

Note that the relationships for L, W_q, and W are the same as the relationships used for the waiting line models in Sections 15.2 and 15.3. They are given by Little's flow equations.

Problem 27 provides another application of a single-server waiting line with Poisson arrivals and arbitrary service times.

An Example Retail sales at Hartlage's Seafood Supply are handled by one clerk. Customer arrivals follow a Poisson distribution, and the arrival rate is 21 customers per hour or $\lambda = 21/60 = 0.35$ customers per minute. A study of the service process shows that the service time is a random variable with an average of 2 minutes per customer and a standard deviation of $\sigma = 1.2$ minutes. The mean time of 2 minutes per customer shows that the clerk has a service rate of $\mu = 1/2 = 0.50$ customers per minute. The operating characteristics of this $M/G/1$ waiting line system are as follows:

WEB file

SingleArbitrary

$$P_0 = 1 - \frac{\lambda}{\mu} = 1 - \frac{0.35}{0.50} = 0.30$$

$$L_q = \frac{(0.35)^2(1.2)^2 + (0.35/0.50)^2}{2(1 - 0.35/0.50)} = 1.1107 \text{ customers}$$

$$L = L_q + \frac{\lambda}{\mu} = 1.1107 + \frac{0.35}{0.50} = 1.8107 \text{ customers}$$

$$W_q = \frac{L_q}{\lambda} = \frac{1.1107}{0.35} = 3.1733 \text{ minutes}$$

$$W = W_q + \frac{1}{\mu} = 3.1733 + \frac{1}{0.50} = 5.1733 \text{ minutes}$$

$$P_w = \frac{\lambda}{\mu} = \frac{0.35}{0.50} = 0.70$$

Hartlage's manager can review these operating characteristics to determine whether scheduling a second clerk appears to be worthwhile.

Constant Service Times

We want to comment briefly on the single-server waiting line model that assumes random arrivals but constant service times. Such a waiting line can occur in production and manufacturing environments where machine-controlled service times are generally constant. This waiting line is described by the $M/D/1$ model, with the D referring to the deterministic service times. With the $M/D/1$ model, the average number of units in the waiting line, L_q, can be found by using equation (15.25) with the condition that the standard deviation of the constant service time is $\sigma = 0$. Thus, the expression for the average number of units in the waiting line for the $M/D/1$ waiting line becomes

$$L_q = \frac{(\lambda/\mu)^2}{2(1 - \lambda/\mu)} \tag{15.30}$$

The other expressions presented earlier in this section can be used to determine additional operating characteristics of the $M/D/1$ system.

NOTES AND COMMENTS

1. Whenever the operating characteristics of a waiting line are unacceptable, managers often try to improve service by increasing the service rate μ. This approach is good, but equation (15.25) shows that the variation in the service times also affects the operating characteristics of the waiting line. Because the standard deviation of service times, σ, appears in the numerator of equation (15.25), a larger variation in service times results in a larger average number of units in the waiting line. Hence, another alternative for improving the service capabilities of a waiting line is to reduce the variation in the service times. Thus, even when the service rate of the service facility cannot be increased, a reduction in σ will reduce the average number of units in the waiting line and improve the operating characteristics of the system.

Multiple-Server Model with Poisson Arrivals, Arbitrary Service Times, and No Waiting Line

An interesting variation of the waiting line models discussed so far involves a system in which no waiting is allowed. Arriving units or customers seek service from one of several servers. If all servers are busy, arriving units are denied access to the system. In waiting line terminology, arrivals occurring when the system is full are **blocked** and are cleared from the system. Such customers may be lost or may attempt a return to the system later.

The specific model considered in this section is based on the following assumptions:

1. The system has k servers.
2. The arrivals follow a Poisson probability distribution, with arrival rate λ.
3. The service times for each server may have any probability distribution.
4. The service rate μ is the same for each server.
5. An arrival enters the system only if at least one server is available. An arrival occurring when all servers are busy is blocked—that is, denied service and not allowed to enter the system.

With G denoting a general or unspecified probability distribution for service times, the appropriate model for this situation is referred to as an *M/G/k* model with "blocked customers cleared." The question addressed in this type of situation is, How many servers should be used?

A primary application of this model involves the design of telephone and other communication systems where the arrivals are the calls and the servers are the number of telephone or communication lines available. In such a system, the calls are made to one telephone number, with each call automatically switched to an open server if possible. When all servers are busy, additional calls receive a busy signal and are denied access to the system.

Operating Characteristics for the *M/G/k* Model with Blocked Customers Cleared

With no waiting allowed, operating characteristics L_q and W_q considered in previous waiting line models are automatically zero regardless of the number of servers. In this situation, the more important design consideration involves determining how the percentage of blocked customers is affected by the number of servers.

We approach the problem of selecting the best number of servers by computing the steady-state probabilities that j of the k servers will be busy. These probabilities are

$$P_j = \frac{(\lambda/\mu)^j/j!}{\displaystyle\sum_{i=0}^{k} (\lambda/\mu)^i/i!}$$

(15.31)

where

$$\lambda = \text{the arrival rate}$$
$$\mu = \text{the service rate for each server}$$
$$k = \text{the number of servers}$$
$$P_j = \text{the probability that } j \text{ of the } k \text{ servers are busy}$$
$$\text{for } j = 0, 1, 2, \ldots, k$$

The most important probability value is P_k, which is the probability that all k servers are busy. Thus, P_k also indicates the percentage of arrivals that are blocked and denied access to the system.

Another operating characteristic of interest is the average number of units in the system; note that this number is equivalent to the average number of servers in use. Letting L denote the average number of units in the system, we have

$$L = \frac{\lambda}{\mu}(1 - P_k) \tag{15.32}$$

where L will certainly be less than k.

An Example Microdata Software, Inc., uses a telephone ordering system for its computer software products. Callers place orders with Microdata by using the company's 800 telephone number. Assume that calls to this telephone number arrive at a rate of $\lambda = 12$ calls per hour. The time required to process a telephone order varies considerably from order to order. However, each Microdata sales representative can be expected to handle $\mu = 6$ calls per hour. Currently, the Microdata 800 telephone number has three internal lines or servers, each operated by a separate sales representative. Calls received on the 800 number are automatically transferred to an open line or server if available.

Whenever all three lines are busy, callers receive a busy signal. In the past, Microdata's management assumed that callers receiving a busy signal would call back later. However, recent research on telephone ordering showed that a substantial number of callers who are denied access do not call back later. These lost calls represent lost revenues for the firm, so Microdata's management requested an analysis of the telephone ordering system. Specifically, management wanted to know the percentage of callers who get busy signals and are blocked from the system. If management's goal is to provide sufficient capacity to handle 90% of the callers, how many telephone lines and sales representatives should Microdata use?

We can demonstrate the use of equation (15.31) by computing P_3, the probability that all three of the currently available telephone lines will be in use and additional callers will be blocked:

$$P_3 = \frac{(^{12}/_6)^3/3!}{(^{12}/_6)^0/0! + (^{12}/_6)^1/1! + (^{12}/_6)^2/2! + (^{12}/_6)^3/3!} = \frac{1.3333}{6.3333} = 0.2105$$

With $P_3 = 0.2105$, approximately 21% of the calls, or slightly more than one in five calls, are being blocked. Only 79% of the calls are being handled immediately by the three-line system.

Let us assume that Microdata expands to a four-line system. Then, the probability that all four servers will be in use and that callers will be blocked is

TABLE 15.6 PROBABILITIES OF BUSY LINES FOR THE MICRODATA
FOUR-LINE SYSTEM

Number of Busy Lines	Probability
0	0.1429
1	0.2857
2	0.2857
3	0.1905
4	0.0952

$$P_4 = \frac{(^{12}/_6)^4/4!}{(^{12}/_6)^0/0! + (^{12}/_6)^1/1! + (^{12}/_6)^2/2! + (^{12}/_6)^3/3! + (^{12}/_6)^4/4!} = \frac{0.667}{7} = 0.0952$$

Problem 30 provides practice in calculating probabilities for multiple-server systems with no waiting line.

With only 9.52% of the callers blocked, 90.48% of the callers will reach the Microdata sales representatives. Thus, Microdata should expand its order-processing operation to four lines to meet management's goal of providing sufficient capacity to handle at least 90% of the callers. The average number of calls in the four-line system and thus the average number of lines and sales representatives that will be busy is

$$L = \frac{\lambda}{\mu}(1 - P_4) = \frac{12}{6}(1 - 0.0952) = 1.8095$$

Although an average of fewer than two lines will be busy, the four-line system is necessary to provide the capacity to handle at least 90% of the callers. We used equation (15.31) to calculate the probability that 0, 1, 2, 3, or 4 lines will be busy. These probabilities are summarized in Table 15.6.

As discussed in Section 15.5, an economic analysis of waiting lines can be used to guide system design decisions. In the Microdata system, the cost of the additional line and additional sales representative should be relatively easy to establish. This cost can be balanced against the cost of the blocked calls. With 9.52% of the calls blocked and $\lambda = 12$ calls per hour, an eight-hour day will have an average of $8(12)(0.0952) = 9.1$ blocked calls. If Microdata can estimate the cost of possible lost sales, the cost of these blocked calls can be established. The economic analysis based on the service cost and the blocked-call cost can assist in determining the optimal number of lines for the system.

15.9 Waiting Line Models with Finite Calling Populations

For the waiting line models introduced so far, the population of units or customers arriving for service has been considered to be unlimited. In technical terms, when no limit is placed on how many units may seek service, the model is said to have an **infinite calling population**. Under this assumption, the arrival rate λ remains constant regardless of how many units are in the waiting line system. This assumption of an infinite calling population is made in most waiting line models.

In other cases, the maximum number of units or customers that may seek service is assumed to be finite. In this situation the arrival rate for the system changes, depending on

In previous waiting line models, the arrival rate was constant and independent of the number of units in the system. With a finite calling population, the arrival rate decreases as the number of units in the system increases because, with more units in the system, fewer units are available for arrivals.

the number of units in the waiting line, and the waiting line model is said to have a **finite calling population**. The formulas for the operating characteristics of the previous waiting line models must be modified to account for the effect of the finite calling population.

The finite calling population model discussed in this section is based on the following assumptions:

1. The arrivals for *each unit* follow a Poisson probability distribution, with arrival rate λ.
2. The service times follow an exponential probability distribution, with service rate μ.
3. The population of units that may seek service is finite.

With a single server, the waiting line model is referred to as an *M/M/*1 model with a finite calling population.

The arrival rate for the *M/M/*1 model with a finite calling population is defined in terms of how often each unit arrives or seeks service. This situation differs from that for previous waiting line models, in which λ denoted the arrival rate for the system. With a finite calling population, the arrival rate for the system varies depending on the number of units in the system. Instead of adjusting for the changing system arrival rate, in the finite calling population model λ indicates the arrival rate for each unit.

The arrival rate λ is defined differently for the finite calling population model. Specifically, λ is defined in terms of the arrival rate for each unit.

Operating Characteristics for the *M/M/*1 Model with a Finite Calling Population

The following formulas are used to determine the steady-state operating characteristics for an *M/M/*1 model with a finite calling population, where

$$\lambda = \text{the arrival rate for each unit}$$
$$\mu = \text{the service rate}$$
$$N = \text{the size of the population}$$

1. The probability that no units are in the system:

$$P_0 = \frac{1}{\displaystyle\sum_{n=0}^{N} \frac{N!}{(N-n)!}\left(\frac{\lambda}{\mu}\right)^n} \tag{15.33}$$

2. The average number of units in the waiting line:

$$L_q = N - \frac{\lambda + \mu}{\lambda}(1 - P_0) \tag{15.34}$$

3. The average number of units in the system:

$$L = L_q + (1 - P_0) \tag{15.35}$$

4. The average time a unit spends in the waiting line:

$$W_q = \frac{L_q}{(N - L)\lambda} \tag{15.36}$$

5. The average time a unit spends in the system:

$$W = W_q + \frac{1}{\mu} \qquad \textbf{(15.37)}$$

6. The probability an arriving unit has to wait for service:

$$P_w = 1 - P_0 \qquad \textbf{(15.38)}$$

7. The probability of n units in the system:

$$P_n = \frac{N!}{(N-n)!}\left(\frac{\lambda}{\mu}\right)^n P_0 \quad \text{for } n = 0, 1, \ldots, N \qquad \textbf{(15.39)}$$

One of the primary applications of the $M/M/1$ model with a finite calling population is referred to as the *machine repair problem.* In this problem, a group of machines is considered to be the finite population of "customers" that may request repair service. Whenever a machine breaks down, an arrival occurs in the sense that a new repair request is initiated. If another machine breaks down before the repair work has been completed on the first machine, the second machine begins to form a "waiting line" for repair service. Additional breakdowns by other machines will add to the length of the waiting line. The assumption of first-come, first-served indicates that machines are repaired in the order they break down. The $M/M/1$ model shows that one person or one server is available to perform the repair service. To return the machine to operation, each machine with a breakdown must be repaired by the single-server operation. This model is often applied by computer maintenance departments of various organizations.

An Example   The Kolkmeyer Manufacturing Company uses a group of six identical machines, each of which operates an average of 20 hours between breakdowns. Thus, the arrival rate or request for repair service for each machine is $\lambda = \frac{1}{20} = 0.05$ per hour. With randomly occurring breakdowns, the Poisson probability distribution is used to describe the machine breakdown arrival process. One person from the maintenance department provides the single-server repair service for the six machines. The exponentially distributed service times have a mean of two hours per machine, or a service rate of $\mu = \frac{1}{2} = 0.50$ machines per hour.

With $\lambda = 0.05$ and $\mu = 0.50$, we use equations (15.33) through (15.38) to compute the operating characteristics for this system. Note that the use of equation (15.33) makes the computations involved somewhat cumbersome. Confirm for yourself that equation (15.33) provides the value of $P_0 = 0.4845$. The computations for the other operating characteristics are

$$L_q = 6 - \left(\frac{0.05 + 0.50}{0.05}\right)(1 - 0.4845) = 0.3297 \text{ machines}$$

$$L = 0.3295 + (1 - 0.4845) = 0.8451 \text{ machines}$$

$$W_q = \frac{0.3295}{(6 - 0.845)0.50} = 1.279 \text{ hours}$$

$$W = 1.279 + \frac{1}{0.50} = 3.279 \text{ hours}$$

$$P_w = 1 - P_0 = 1 - 0.4845 = 0.5155$$

FIGURE 15.5   WORKSHEET FOR THE KOLKMEYER TWO-SERVER MACHINE REPAIR
PROBLEM

WEB file

Finite

	A	B	C
1	**Waiting Line Model with a Finite Calling Population**		
2			
3	**Assumptions**		
4	**Poisson Arrivals**		
5	**Exponential Service Times**		
6	**Finite Calling Population**		
7			
8	Number of Servers	2	
9	Arrival Rate for Each Unit	0.05	
10	Service Rate for Each Server	0.5	
11	Population Size	6	
12			
13			
14	**Operating Characteristics**		
15			
16	Probability that no customers are in the system, P_0		0.5602
17	Average number of customers in the waiting line, L_q		0.0227
18	Average number of customers in the system, L		0.5661
19	Average time a customer spends in the waiting line, W_q		0.0834
20	Average time a customer spends in the system, W		2.0834
21	Probability an arriving customer has to wait, P_w		0.1036

Operating characteristics of an M/M/1 waiting line with a finite calling population are considered in Problem 34.

Finally, equation (15.39) can be used to compute the probabilities of any number of machines being in the repair system.

As with other waiting line models, the operating characteristics provide the manager with useful information about the operation of the waiting line. In this case, the fact that a machine breakdown waits an average of $W_q = 1.279$ hours before maintenance begins and the fact that more than 50% of the machine breakdowns must wait for service, $P_w = 0.5155$, indicates that a two-server system may be needed to improve the machine repair service.

An Excel worksheet template at the WEBfiles link on the website that accompanies this text may be used to analyze the multiple-server finite calling population model.

Computations of the operating characteristics of a multiple-server finite calling population waiting line are more complex than those for the single-server model. A computer solution is virtually mandatory in this case. The Excel worksheet for the Kolkmeyer two-server machine repair system is shown in Figure 15.5. With two repair personnel, the average machine breakdown waiting time is reduced to $W_q = 0.0834$ hours, or 5 minutes, and only 10%, $P_w = 0.1036$, of the machine breakdowns wait for service. Thus, the two-server system significantly improves the machine repair service operation. Ultimately, by considering the cost of machine downtime and the cost of the repair personnel, management can determine whether the improved service of the two-server system is cost effective.

Summary

In this chapter we presented a variety of waiting line models that have been developed to help managers make better decisions concerning the operation of waiting lines. For each model we presented formulas that could be used to develop operating characteristics or performance measures for the system being studied. The operating characteristics presented include the following:

1. Probability that no units are in the system
2. Average number of units in the waiting line
3. Average number of units in the system
4. Average time a unit spends in the waiting line
5. Average time a unit spends in the system
6. Probability that arriving units will have to wait for service

We also showed how an economic analysis of the waiting line could be conducted by developing a total cost model that includes the cost associated with units waiting for service and the cost required to operate the service facility.

As many of the examples in this chapter show, the most obvious applications of waiting line models are situations in which customers arrive for service such as at a grocery checkout counter, bank, or restaurant. However, with a little creativity, waiting line models can be applied to many different situations, such as telephone calls waiting for connections, mail orders waiting for processing, machines waiting for repairs, manufacturing jobs waiting to be processed, and money waiting to be spent or invested. The Q.M. in Action, Allocating Voting Machines to Polling Locations, describes an application in which a waiting line model helped decrease the waiting times voters experience on Election Day.

The complexity and diversity of waiting line systems found in practice often prevent an analyst from finding an existing waiting line model that fits the specific application being studied. Simulation, the topic discussed in Chapter 16, provides an approach to determining the operating characteristics of such waiting line systems.

Q.M. *in* ACTION

ALLOCATING VOTING MACHINES TO POLLING LOCATIONS*

In the 2004 U.S. presidential election, many voters waited more than ten hours to cast their ballots. Similar problems with long lines at the voting booth were reported in the United States in the 2006 and 2008 elections as well as in the 2010 elections in the United Kingdom. Long lines at a voting booth can result in a voter leaving without casting her/his ballot. Queueing models can be used to diagnose why these long lines are occurring and offer improvements.

Many of the problems occurring in the U.S. elections can be linked to the implementation of direct-recording electronic (DRE) voting machines (better known as touch-screen systems). Because these systems are quite expensive, many election boards had only a relatively few DRE voting machines to allocate to polling locations. Voters' unfamiliarity with the systems also resulted in increased voting times when using DRE machines. Most election boards initially allocated voting machines to polling locations without considering queueing effects.

Starting in 2008, the Board of Elections in Franklin County, Ohio (the location of the state capital, Columbus) has used queueing models to help determine the optimal allocation of voting machines to polling locations. Voting machines can be considered as servers in this context and the voters can be thought of as customers. Queueing models were used to predict voter waiting times based on expected voter turnout, number of registered voters, and ballot lengths. The use of queueing models was credited with greatly reducing the waiting times for Franklin County voters in the 2010 presidential election, even though voter turnout was at a record high.

*Based on work done by Ted Allen (The Ohio State University), Mike Fry and David Kelton (University of Cincinnati), and Muer Yang (University of St. Thomas).

Glossary

Arrival rate The mean number of customers or units arriving in a given period of time.

Blocked When arriving units cannot enter the waiting line because the system is full. Blocked units can occur when waiting lines are not allowed or when waiting lines have a finite capacity.

Exponential probability distribution A probability distribution used to describe the service time for some waiting line models.

Finite calling population The population of customers or units that may seek service has a fixed and finite value.

First-come, first-served (FCFS) The queue discipline that serves waiting units on a first-come, first-served basis.

Infinite calling population The population of customers or units that may seek service has no specified upper limit.

Multiple-server waiting line A waiting line with two or more parallel service facilities.

Operating characteristics The performance measures for a waiting line, including the probability that no units are in the system, the average number of units in the waiting line, the average waiting time, and so on.

Poisson probability distribution A probability distribution used to describe the arrival pattern for some waiting line models.

Queue A waiting line.

Queueing theory The body of knowledge dealing with waiting lines.

Service rate The mean number of customers or units that can be served by one service facility in a given period of time.

Single-server waiting line A waiting line with only one service facility.

Steady-state operation The normal operation of the waiting line after it has gone through a startup or transient period. The operating characteristics of waiting lines are computed for steady-state conditions.

Transient period The startup period for a waiting line, occurring before the waiting line reaches a normal or steady-state operation.

Problems

1. Willow Brook National Bank operates a drive-up teller window that allows customers to complete bank transactions without getting out of their cars. On weekday mornings, arrivals to the drive-up teller window occur at random, with an arrival rate of 24 customers per hour or 0.4 customers per minute.
   a. What is the mean or expected number of customers that will arrive in a five-minute period?
   b. Assume that the Poisson probability distribution can be used to describe the arrival process. Use the arrival rate in part (a) and compute the probabilities that exactly 0, 1, 2, and 3 customers will arrive during a five-minute period.
   c. Delays are expected if more than three customers arrive during any five-minute period. What is the probability that delays will occur?

2. In the Willow Brook National Bank waiting line system (see Problem 1), assume that the service times for the drive-up teller follow an exponential probability distribution with a

service rate of 36 customers per hour, or 0.6 customers per minute. Use the exponential probability distribution to answer the following questions:

a. What is the probability that the service time is one minute or less?
b. What is the probability that the service time is two minutes or less?
c. What is the probability that the service time is more than two minutes?

3. Use the single-server drive-up bank teller operation referred to in Problems 1 and 2 to determine the following operating characteristics for the system:

a. The probability that no customers are in the system
b. The average number of customers waiting
c. The average number of customers in the system
d. The average time a customer spends waiting
e. The average time a customer spends in the system
f. The probability that arriving customers will have to wait for service

4. Use the single-server drive-up bank teller operation referred to in Problems 1–3 to determine the probabilities of 0, 1, 2, and 3 customers in the system. What is the probability that more than three customers will be in the drive-up teller system at the same time?

5. The reference desk of a university library receives requests for assistance. Assume that a Poisson probability distribution with an arrival rate of 10 requests per hour can be used to describe the arrival pattern and that service times follow an exponential probability distribution with a service rate of 12 requests per hour.

a. What is the probability that no requests for assistance are in the system?
b. What is the average number of requests that will be waiting for service?
c. What is the average waiting time in minutes before service begins?
d. What is the average time at the reference desk in minutes (waiting time plus service time)?
e. What is the probability that a new arrival has to wait for service?

6. Movies Tonight is a typical video and DVD movie rental outlet for home-viewing customers. During the weeknight evenings, customers arrive at Movies Tonight with an arrival rate of 1.25 customers per minute. The checkout clerk has a service rate of 2 customers per minute. Assume Poisson arrivals and exponential service times.

a. What is the probability that no customers are in the system?
b. What is the average number of customers waiting for service?
c. What is the average time a customer waits for service to begin?
d. What is the probability that an arriving customer will have to wait for service?
e. Do the operating characteristics indicate that the one-clerk checkout system provides an acceptable level of service?

7. Speedy Oil provides a single-server automobile oil change and lubrication service. Customers provide an arrival rate of 2.5 cars per hour. The service rate is 5 cars per hour. Assume that arrivals follow a Poisson probability distribution and that service times follow an exponential probability distribution.

a. What is the average number of cars in the system?
b. What is the average time that a car waits for the oil and lubrication service to begin?
c. What is the average time a car spends in the system?
d. What is the probability that an arrival has to wait for service?

8. For the Burger Dome single-server waiting line in Section 15.2, assume that the arrival rate is increased to 1 customer per minute and that the service rate is increased to 1.25 customers per minute. Compute the following operating characteristics for the new system: P_0, L_q, L, W_q, W, and P_w. Does this system provide better or poorer service compared to the original system? Discuss any differences and the reason for these differences.

9. Marty's Barber Shop has one barber. Customers have an arrival rate of 2.2 customers per hour, and haircuts are given with a service rate of 5 per hour. Use the Poisson arrivals and exponential service times model to answer the following questions:
    a. What is the probability that no units are in the system?
    b. What is the probability that one customer is receiving a haircut and no one is waiting?
    c. What is the probability that one customer is receiving a haircut and one customer is waiting?
    d. What is the probability that one customer is receiving a haircut and two customers are waiting?
    e. What is the probability that more than two customers are waiting?
    f. What is the average time a customer waits for service?

10. Trosper Tire Company decided to hire a new mechanic to handle all tire changes for customers ordering a new set of tires. Two mechanics applied for the job. One mechanic has limited experience, can be hired for $14 per hour, and can service an average of three customers per hour. The other mechanic has several years of experience, can service an average of four customers per hour, but must be paid $20 per hour. Assume that customers arrive at the Trosper garage at the rate of two customers per hour.
    a. What are the waiting line operating characteristics using each mechanic, assuming Poisson arrivals and exponential service times?
    b. If the company assigns a customer waiting cost of $30 per hour, which mechanic provides the lower operating cost?

11. Agan Interior Design provides home and office decorating assistance to its customers. In normal operation, an average of 2.5 customers arrive each hour. One design consultant is available to answer customer questions and make product recommendations. The consultant averages 10 minutes with each customer.
    a. Compute the operating characteristics of the customer waiting line, assuming Poisson arrivals and exponential service times.
    b. Service goals dictate that an arriving customer should not wait for service more than an average of 5 minutes. Is this goal being met? If not, what action do you recommend?
    c. If the consultant can reduce the average time spent per customer to 8 minutes, what is the mean service rate? Will the service goal be met?

12. Pete's Market is a small local grocery store with only one checkout counter. Assume that shoppers arrive at the checkout lane according to a Poisson probability distribution, with an arrival rate of 15 customers per hour. The checkout service times follow an exponential probability distribution, with a service rate of 20 customers per hour.
    a. Compute the operating characteristics for this waiting line.
    b. If the manager's service goal is to limit the waiting time prior to beginning the checkout process to no more than five minutes, what recommendations would you provide regarding the current checkout system?

13. After reviewing the waiting line analysis of Problem 12, the manager of Pete's Market wants to consider one of the following alternatives for improving service. What alternative would you recommend? Justify your recommendation.
    a. Hire a second person to bag the groceries while the cash register operator is entering the cost data and collecting money from the customer. With this improved single-server operation, the service rate could be increased to 30 customers per hour.
    b. Hire a second person to operate a second checkout counter. The two-server operation would have a service rate of 20 customers per hour for each server.

14. Ocala Software Systems operates a technical support center for its software customers. If customers have installation or use problems with Ocala software products, they may telephone the technical support center and obtain free consultation. Currently, Ocala operates

its support center with one consultant. If the consultant is busy when a new customer call arrives, the customer hears a recorded message stating that all consultants are currently busy with other customers. The customer is then asked to hold and is told that a consultant will provide assistance as soon as possible. The customer calls follow a Poisson probability distribution, with an arrival rate of five calls per hour. On average, it takes 7.5 minutes for a consultant to answer a customer's questions. The service time follows an exponential probability distribution.

a. What is the service rate in terms of customers per hour?
b. What is the probability that no customers are in the system and the consultant is idle?
c. What is the average number of customers waiting for a consultant?
d. What is the average time a customer waits for a consultant?
e. What is the probability that a customer will have to wait for a consultant?
f. Ocala's customer service department recently received several letters from customers complaining about the difficulty in obtaining technical support. If Ocala's customer service guidelines state that no more than 35% of all customers should have to wait for technical support and that the average waiting time should be two minutes or less, does your waiting line analysis indicate that Ocala is or is not meeting its customer service guidelines? What action, if any, would you recommend?

15. To improve customer service, Ocala Software Systems (see Problem 14) wants to investigate the effect of using a second consultant at its technical support center. What effect would the additional consultant have on customer service? Would two technical consultants enable Ocala to meet its service guidelines (no more than 35% of all customers having to wait for technical support and an average customer waiting time of two minutes or less)? Discuss.

16. The new Fore and Aft Marina is to be located on the Ohio River near Madison, Indiana. Assume that Fore and Aft decides to build a docking facility where one boat at a time can stop for gas and servicing. Assume that arrivals follow a Poisson probability distribution, with an arrival rate of 5 boats per hour, and that service times follow an exponential probability distribution, with a service rate of 10 boats per hour. Answer the following questions:

a. What is the probability that no boats are in the system?
b. What is the average number of boats that will be waiting for service?
c. What is the average time a boat will spend waiting for service?
d. What is the average time a boat will spend at the dock?
e. If you were the manager of Fore and Aft Marina, would you be satisfied with the service level your system will be providing? Why or why not?

17. The manager of the Fore and Aft Marina in Problem 16 wants to investigate the possibility of enlarging the docking facility so that two boats can stop for gas and servicing simultaneously. Assume that the arrival rate is 5 boats per hour and that the service rate for each server is 10 boats per hour.

a. What is the probability that the boat dock will be idle?
b. What is the average number of boats that will be waiting for service?
c. What is the average time a boat will spend waiting for service?
d. What is the average time a boat will spend at the dock?
e. If you were the manager of Fore and Aft Marina, would you be satisfied with the service level your system will be providing? Why or why not?

18. All airplane passengers at the Lake City Regional Airport must pass through a security screening area before proceeding to the boarding area. The airport has three screening stations available, and the facility manager must decide how many to have open at any particular time. The service rate for processing passengers at each screening station is 3 passengers per minute. On Monday morning the arrival rate is 5.4 passengers per minute.

Assume that processing times at each screening station follow an exponential distribution and that arrivals follow a Poisson distribution.

a. Suppose two of the three screening stations are open on Monday morning. Compute the operating characteristics for the screening facility.

b. Because of space considerations, the facility manager's goal is to limit the average number of passengers waiting in line to 10 or fewer. Will the two-screening-station system be able to meet the manager's goal?

c. What is the average time required for a passenger to pass through security screening?

19. Refer again to the Lake City Regional Airport described in Problem 18. When the security level is raised to high, the service rate for processing passengers is reduced to 2 passengers per minute at each screening station. Suppose the security level is raised to high on Monday morning. The arrival rate is 5.4 passengers per minute.

a. The facility manager's goal is to limit the average number of passengers waiting in line to 10 or fewer. How many screening stations must be open in order to satisfy the manager's goal?

b. What is the average time required for a passenger to pass through security screening?

20. A Florida coastal community experiences a population increase during the winter months, with seasonal residents arriving from northern states and Canada. Staffing at a local post office is often in a state of change due to the relatively low volume of customers in the summer months and the relatively high volume of customers in the winter months. The service rate of a postal clerk is 0.75 customers per minute. The post office counter has a maximum of three workstations. The target maximum time a customer waits in the system is five minutes.

a. For a particular Monday morning in November, the anticipated arrival rate is 1.2 customers per minute. What is the recommended staffing for this Monday morning? Show the operating characteristics of the waiting line.

b. A new population growth study suggests that over the next two years the arrival rate at the postal office during the busy winter months can be expected to be 2.1 customers per minute. Use a waiting line analysis to make a recommendation to the post office manager.

21. Refer to the Agan Interior Design situation in Problem 11. Agan's management would like to evaluate two alternatives:

- Use one consultant with an average service time of 8 minutes per customer.
- Expand to two consultants, each of whom has an average service time of 10 minutes per customer.

If the consultants are paid $16 per hour and the customer waiting time is valued at $25 per hour for waiting time prior to service, should Agan expand to the two-consultant system? Explain.

22. A fast-food franchise is considering operating a drive-up window food-service operation. Assume that customer arrivals follow a Poisson probability distribution, with an arrival rate of 24 cars per hour, and that service times follow an exponential probability distribution. Arriving customers place orders at an intercom station at the back of the parking lot and then drive to the service window to pay for and receive their orders. The following three service alternatives are being considered:

- A single-server operation in which one employee fills the order and takes the money from the customer. The average service time for this alternative is 2 minutes.
- A single-server operation in which one employee fills the order while a second employee takes the money from the customer. The average service time for this alternative is 1.25 minutes.
- A two-server operation with two service windows and two employees. The employee stationed at each window fills the order and takes the money for customers arriving at the window. The average service time for this alternative is 2 minutes for each server.

Answer the following questions and recommend one of the design options.

a. What is the probability that no cars are in the system?

b. What is the average number of cars waiting for service?

c. What is the average number of cars in the system?

d. What is the average time a car waits for service?

e. What is the average time in the system?

f. What is the probability that an arriving car will have to wait for service?

23. The following cost information is available for the fast-food franchise in Problem 22:

- Customer waiting time is valued at $25 per hour to reflect the fact that waiting time is costly to the fast-food business.
- The cost of each employee is $6.50 per hour.
- To account for equipment and space, an additional cost of $20 per hour is attributable to each server.

What is the lowest-cost design for the fast-food business?

24. A study of the multiple-server food-service operation at the Red Birds baseball park shows that the average time between the arrival of a customer at the food-service counter and his or her departure with a filled order is 10 minutes. During the game, customers arrive at the rate of four per minute. The food-service operation requires an average of 2 minutes per customer order.

a. What is the service rate per server in terms of customers per minute?

b. What is the average waiting time in the line prior to placing an order?

c. On average, how many customers are in the food-service system?

25. To understand how a multiple-server waiting line system with a shared queue compares to a multiple-server waiting line system with a dedicated queue for each server, reconsider the Burger Dome example. Suppose Burger Dome establishes two servers but arranges the restaurant layout so that an arriving customer must decide which server's queue to join. Assume that this system equally splits the customer arrivals so that each server sees half of the customers. How does this system compare with the two-server waiting line system with a shared queue from Section 15.3? Compare the average number of customers waiting, average number of customers in the system, average waiting time, and average time in the system.

26. Manning Autos operates an automotive service. To complete their repair work, Manning mechanics often need to retrieve parts from the company's parts department counter. Mechanics arrive at the parts counter at rate of four per hour. The parts coordinator spends an average of six minutes with each mechanic, discussing the parts the mechanic needs and retrieving the parts from inventory.

a. Currently, Manning has one parts coordinator. On average, each mechanic waits four minutes before the parts coordinator is available to answer questions or retrieve parts from inventory. Find L_q, W, and L for this single-server parts operation.

b. A trial period with a second parts coordinator showed that, on average, each mechanic waited only one minute before a parts coordinator was available. Find L_q, W, and L for this two-server parts operation.

c. If the cost of each mechanic is $20 per hour and the cost of each parts coordinator is $12 per hour, is the one-server or the two-server system more economical?

27. Gubser Welding, Inc., operates a welding service for construction and automotive repair jobs. Assume that the arrival of jobs at the company's office can be described by a Poisson probability distribution with an arrival rate of two jobs per 8-hour day. The time required to complete the jobs follows a normal probability distribution, with a mean time of 3.2 hours and a standard deviation of 2 hours. Answer the following questions, assuming that Gubser uses one welder to complete all jobs:

a. What is the mean arrival rate in jobs per hour?

b. What is the mean service rate in jobs per hour?

c. What is the average number of jobs waiting for service?
d. What is the average time a job waits before the welder can begin working on it?
e. What is the average number of hours between when a job is received and when it is completed?
f. What percentage of the time is Gubser's welder busy?

28. Jobs arrive randomly at a particular assembly plant; assume that the arrival rate is five jobs per hour. Service times (in minutes per job) do not follow the exponential probability distribution. Two proposed designs for the plant's assembly operation are shown.

| | Service Time | |
Design	Mean	Standard Deviation
A	6.0	3.0
B	6.25	0.6

a. What is the service rate in jobs per hour for each design?
b. For the service rates in part (a), what design appears to provide the best or fastest service rate?
c. What are the standard deviations of the service times in hours?
d. Use the *M/G/*1 model to compute the operating characteristics for each design.
e. Which design provides the best operating characteristics? Why?

29. The Robotics Manufacturing Company operates an equipment repair business where emergency jobs arrive randomly at the rate of three jobs per 8-hour day. The company's repair facility is a single-server system operated by a repair technician. The service time varies, with a mean repair time of 2 hours and a standard deviation of 1.5 hours. The company's cost of the repair operation is $28 per hour. In the economic analysis of the waiting line system, Robotics uses $35 per hour cost for customers waiting during the repair process.
a. What are the arrival rate and service rate in jobs per hour?
b. Show the operating characteristics, including the total cost per hour.
c. The company is considering purchasing a computer-based equipment repair system that would enable a constant repair time of 2 hours. For practical purposes, the standard deviation is 0. Because of the computer-based system, the company's cost of the new operation would be $32 per hour. The firm's director of operations rejected the request for the new system because the hourly cost is $4 higher and the mean repair time is the same. Do you agree? What effect will the new system have on the waiting line characteristics of the repair service?
d. Does paying for the computer-based system to reduce the variation in service time make economic sense? How much will the new system save the company during a 40-hour workweek?

30. A large insurance company maintains a central computing system that contains a variety of information about customer accounts. Insurance agents in a six-state area use telephone lines to access the customer information database. Currently, the company's central computer system allows three users to access the central computer simultaneously. Agents who attempt to use the system when it is full are denied access; no waiting is allowed. Management realizes that with its expanding business, more requests will be made to the central information system. Being denied access to the system is inefficient as well as annoying for agents. Access requests follow a Poisson probability distribution, with a mean of 42 calls per hour. The service rate per line is 20 calls per hour.
a. What is the probability that 0, 1, 2, and 3 access lines will be in use?
b. What is the probability that an agent will be denied access to the system?
c. What is the average number of access lines in use?

d. In planning for the future, management wants to be able to handle $\lambda = 50$ calls per hour; in addition, the probability that an agent will be denied access to the system should be no greater than the value computed in part (b). How many access lines should this system have?

31. Mid-West Publishing Company publishes college textbooks. The company operates an 800 telephone number whereby potential adopters can ask questions about forthcoming texts, request examination copies of texts, and place orders. Currently, two extension lines are used, with two representatives handling the telephone inquiries. Calls occurring when both extension lines are being used receive a busy signal; no waiting is allowed. Each representative can accommodate an average of 12 calls per hour. The arrival rate is 20 calls per hour.

a. How many extension lines should be used if the company wants to handle 90% of the calls immediately?

b. What is the average number of extension lines that will be busy if your recommendation in part (a) is used?

c. What percentage of calls receive a busy signal for the current telephone system with two extension lines?

32. City Cab, Inc., uses two dispatchers to handle requests for service and to dispatch the cabs. The telephone calls that are made to City Cab use a common telephone number. When both dispatchers are busy, the caller hears a busy signal; no waiting is allowed. Callers who receive a busy signal can call back later or call another cab service. Assume that the arrival of calls follows a Poisson probability distribution, with a mean of 40 calls per hour, and that each dispatcher can handle a mean of 30 calls per hour.

a. What percentage of time are both dispatchers idle?

b. What percentage of time are both dispatchers busy?

c. What is the probability that callers will receive a busy signal if two, three, or four dispatchers are used?

d. If management wants no more than 12% of the callers to receive a busy signal, how many dispatchers should be used?

33. Kolkmeyer Manufacturing Company (see Section 15.9) is considering adding two machines to its manufacturing operation. This addition will bring the number of machines to eight. The president of Kolkmeyer asked for a study of the need to add a second employee to the repair operation. The arrival rate is 0.05 machines per hour for each machine, and the service rate for each individual assigned to the repair operation is 0.50 machines per hour.

a. Compute the operating characteristics if the company retains the single-employee repair operation.

b. Compute the operating characteristics if a second employee is added to the machine repair operation.

c. Each employee is paid $20 per hour. Machine downtime is valued at $80 per hour. From an economic point of view, should one or two employees handle the machine repair operation? Explain.

34. Five administrative assistants use an office copier. The average time between arrivals for each assistant is 40 minutes, which is equivalent to an arrival rate of $1/40 = 0.025$ arrivals per minute. The mean time each assistant spends at the copier is 5 minutes, which is equivalent to a service rate of $1/5 = 0.20$ per minute. Use the $M/M/1$ model with a finite calling population to determine the following:

a. The probability that the copier is idle

b. The average number of administrative assistants in the waiting line

c. The average number of administrative assistants at the copier

d. The average time an assistant spends waiting for the copier

e. The average time an assistant spends at the copier

     f.   During an 8-hour day, how many minutes does an assistant spend at the copier? How much of this time is waiting time?

     g.   Should management consider purchasing a second copier? Explain.

35.   Schips Department Store operates a fleet of 10 trucks. The trucks arrive at random times throughout the day at the store's truck dock to be loaded with new deliveries or to have incoming shipments from the regional warehouse unloaded. Each truck returns to the truck dock for service two times per 8-hour day. Thus, the arrival rate per truck is 0.25 trucks per hour. The service rate is 4 trucks per hour. Using the Poisson arrivals and exponential service times model with a finite calling population of 10 trucks, determine the following operating characteristics:

     a.   The probability that no trucks are at the truck dock

     b.   The average number of trucks waiting for loading/unloading

     c.   The average number of trucks in the truck dock area

     d.   The average waiting time before loading/unloading begins

     e.   The average waiting time in the system

     f.   What is the hourly cost of operation if the cost is $50 per hour for each truck and $30 per hour for the truck dock?

     g.   Consider a two-server truck dock operation where the second server could be operated for an additional $30 per hour. How much would the average number of trucks waiting for loading/unloading have to be reduced to make the two-server truck dock economically feasible?

     h.   Should the company consider expanding to the two-server truck dock? Explain.

Case Problem 1   Regional Airlines

Regional Airlines is establishing a new telephone system for handling flight reservations. During the 10:00 A.M. to 11:00 A.M. time period, calls to the reservation agent occur randomly at an average of one call every 3.75 minutes. Historical service time data show that a reservation agent spends an average of 3 minutes with each customer. The waiting line model assumptions of Poisson arrivals and exponential service times appear reasonable for the telephone reservation system.

Regional Airlines' management believes that offering an efficient telephone reservation system is an important part of establishing an image as a service-oriented airline. If the system is properly implemented, Regional Airlines will establish good customer relations, which in the long run will increase business. However, if the telephone reservation system is frequently overloaded and customers have difficulty contacting an agent, a negative customer reaction may lead to an eventual loss of business. The cost of a ticket reservation agent is $20 per hour. Thus, management wants to provide good service, but it does not want to incur the cost of overstaffing the telephone reservation operation by using more agents than necessary.

At a planning meeting, Regional's management team agreed that an acceptable customer service goal is to answer at least 85% of the incoming calls immediately. During the planning meeting, Regional's vice president of administration pointed out that the data show that the average service rate for an agent is faster than the average arrival rate of the telephone calls. The vice president's conclusion was that personnel costs could be minimized by using one agent and that the single agent should be able to handle the telephone reservations and still have some idle time. The vice president of marketing restated the importance of customer service and expressed support for at least two reservation agents.

The current telephone reservation system design does not allow callers to wait. Callers who attempt to reach a reservation agent when all agents are occupied receive a busy signal and are blocked from the system. A representative from the telephone company suggested that Regional Airlines consider an expanded system that accommodates waiting. In the expanded system, when a customer calls and all agents are busy, a recorded message tells the customer that the call is being held in the order received and that an agent will be available shortly. The customer can stay on the line and listen to background music while waiting for an agent. Regional's management will need more information before switching to the expanded system.

Managerial Report

Prepare a managerial report for Regional Airlines analyzing the telephone reservation system. Evaluate both the system that does not allow waiting and the expanded system that allows waiting. Include the following information in your report:

1. A detailed analysis of the operating characteristics of the reservation system with one agent as proposed by the vice president of administration. What is your recommendation concerning a single-agent system?
2. A detailed analysis of the operating characteristics of the reservation system based on your recommendation regarding the number of agents Regional should use.
3. A detailed analysis of the advantages or disadvantages of the expanded system. Discuss the number of waiting callers the expanded system would need to accommodate.
4. This report represents a pilot study of the reservation system for the 10:00 A.M. to 11:00 A.M. time period during which an average of one call arrives every 3.75 minutes; however, the arrival rate of incoming calls is expected to change from hour to hour. Describe how your waiting line analysis could be used to develop a ticket agent staffing plan that would enable the company to provide different levels of staffing for the ticket reservation system at different times during the day. Indicate the information that you would need to develop this staffing plan.

Case Problem 2   Office Equipment, Inc.

Office Equipment, Inc. (OEI) leases automatic mailing machines to business customers in Fort Wayne, Indiana. The company built its success on a reputation of providing timely maintenance and repair service. Each OEI service contract states that a service technician will arrive at a customer's business site within an average of three hours from the time that the customer notifies OEI of an equipment problem.

Currently, OEI has 10 customers with service contracts. One service technician is responsible for handling all service calls. A statistical analysis of historical service records indicates that a customer requests a service call at an average rate of one call per 50 hours of operation. If the service technician is available when a customer calls for service, it takes the technician an average of 1 hour of travel time to reach the customer's office and an average of 1.5 hours to complete the repair service. However, if the service technician is busy with another customer when a new customer calls for service, the technician completes the current service call and any other waiting service calls before responding to the new service call. In such cases, once the technician is free from all existing service commitments, the technician takes an average of 1 hour of travel time to reach the new customer's office and an average of 1.5 hours to complete the repair service. The cost of the service technician is $80 per hour. The downtime cost (wait time and service time) for customers is $100 per hour.

OEI is planning to expand its business. Within one year, OEI projects that it will have 20 customers, and within two years, OEI projects that it will have 30 customers. Although OEI is satisfied that one service technician can handle the 10 existing customers, management is concerned about the ability of one technician to meet the average three-hour service call guarantee when the OEI customer base expands. In a recent planning meeting, the marketing manager made a proposal to add a second service technician when OEI reaches 20 customers and to add a third service technician when OEI reaches 30 customers. Before making a final decision, management would like an analysis of OEI service capabilities. OEI is particularly interested in meeting the average three-hour waiting time guarantee at the lowest possible total cost.

Managerial Report

Develop a managerial report summarizing your analysis of the OEI service capabilities. Make recommendations regarding the number of technicians to be used when OEI reaches 20 customers and when OEI reaches 30 customers. Include a discussion of the following issues in your report:

1. What is the arrival rate for each customer per hour?
2. What is the service rate in terms of the number of customers per hour? Note that the average travel time of 1 hour becomes part of the service time because the time that the service technician is busy handling a service call includes the travel time plus the time required to complete the repair.
3. Waiting line models generally assume that the arriving customers are in the same location as the service facility. Discuss the OEI situation in light of the fact that a service technician travels an average of 1 hour to reach each customer. How should the travel time and the waiting time predicted by the waiting line model be combined to determine the total customer waiting time?
4. OEI is satisfied that one service technician can handle the 10 existing customers. Use a waiting line model to determine the following information:
   - Probability that no customers are in the system
   - Average number of customers in the waiting line
   - Average number of customers in the system
   - Average time a customer waits until the service technician arrives
   - Average time a customer waits until the machine is back in operation
   - Probability that a customer will have to wait more than one hour for the service technician to arrive
   - The total cost per hour for the service operation

   Do you agree with OEI management that one technician can meet the average three-hour service call guarantee? Explain.
5. What is your recommendation for the number of service technicians to hire when OEI expands to 20 customers? Use the information that you developed in part (4) to justify your answer.
6. What is your recommendation for the number of service technicians to hire when OEI expands to 30 customers? Use the information that you developed in part (4) to justify your answer.
7. What are the annual savings of your recommendation in part (6) compared to the planning committee's proposal that 30 customers will require three service technicians? Assume 250 days of operation per year.

CHAPTER 16

Simulation

CONTENTS

Q.M. *in* ACTION

REDUCING PATIENT INFECTIONS IN THE ICU*

Approximately 2 million patients acquire an infection after being admitted to the hospital in the United States each year. More than 100,000 of these patients die as a result of their hospital-acquired infections. This problem is expected to worsen as pathogens continue to develop greater resistance to antibiotics.

Two methods of decreasing the rate of hospital-acquired infections are (1) patient isolation and (2) greater adherence to hand-washing hygiene. If infected patients can be identified quickly, they can be quarantined to prevent greater outbreaks. Furthermore, proper hand washing can greatly reduce the number of pathogens present on the skin and thereby also lead to fewer infections. Yet previous studies have found that less than half of all health workers completely and correctly follow hand-hygiene protocols.

*From R. Hagtvedt, P. Griffin, P. Keskinocak, and R. Roberts, "A Simulation Model to Compare Strategies for the Reduction of Health-Care-Associated Infections," *Interfaces* 39, no. 3 (May–June): 2009.

A group of researchers used data from the intensive-care unit (ICU) at Cook County Hospital in Chicago to create a simulation model of the movements of patients, health care workers, hospital visitors, and actual pathogens that lead to infections. The researchers were able to simulate both the creation of a new isolation ward in the ICU and model better hand-hygiene habits. The simulation estimated rates of infection and impacts on hospital costs in each scenario.

The simulation showed that both patient isolation and better hand-hygiene can greatly reduce infection rates. Improving hand-hygiene is considerably cheaper than building and maintaining additional quarantine facilities, but the researchers point out that even the best simulations do not consider psychological responses of health care workers. The simulation cannot detect why hand-hygiene compliance is currently low, so improving adherence in practice could be challenging.

Uncertainty pervades decision making in business, government, and our personal lives. This chapter introduces the use of **simulation** to evaluate the impact of uncertainty on a decision. Simulation models have been successfully used in a variety of disciplines. Financial applications include investment planning, project selection, and option pricing. Marketing applications include new product development and the timing of market entry for a product. Management applications include project management, inventory ordering (especially important for seasonal products), capacity planning, and revenue management (prominent in the airline, hotel, and car rental industries). In each of these applications, there are uncertain quantities that complicate the decision process.

As we will demonstrate, a spreadsheet simulation analysis requires a model foundation of logical formulas that correctly express the relationships between **parameters** and decisions to generate outputs of interest. A simulation model replaces the use of single values for parameters with a range of possible values. For example, a simple spreadsheet model may compute a clothing retailer's profit, given values for the number of ski jackets ordered from the manufacturer and the number of ski jackets demanded by customers. A simulation analysis extends this model by replacing the single value used for ski jacket demand with a **probability distribution** of possible values of ski jacket demand. A probability distribution of ski jacket demand represents not only the range of possible values but also the relative likelihood of various levels of demand.

To evaluate a decision with a simulation model, an analyst identifies parameters that are not known with a high degree of certainty and treats these parameters as random, or uncertain, variables. The values for the **random variables** or **uncertain variables** are randomly generated from the specified probability distributions. The simulation model uses the randomly generated values of the random variables and the relationships between parameters and decisions to compute the corresponding values of an output. Specifically, a simulation experiment produces a *distribution* of output values that correspond to the randomly generated values of the uncertain input variables. This probability distribution of the output values describes the range of possible outcomes as well as the relative likelihood of each outcome. After reviewing the simulation results, the analyst is often able to make decision recommendations for the **controllable inputs** that not only address the *average* output but also the *variability* of the output.

(16.1) What–If Analysis

When making a decision in the presence of uncertainty, decision makers should not only be interested in the average, or expected, outcome, but they should also be interested in information regarding the range of possible outcomes. In particular, decision makers are interested **risk analysis** (i.e., quantifying the likelihood and magnitude of an undesirable outcome). In this section, we show how to perform a basic risk analysis by considering a small set of what-if scenarios.

Sanotronics

Sanotronics is a startup company that manufactures medical devices for use in hospital clinics. Inspired by experiences with family members who have battled cancer, Sanotronics's founders have developed a prototype for a new device that limits health care workers' exposure to chemotherapy treatments while they are preparing, administering, and disposing of these hazardous medications. This new device features an innovative design and has the potential to capture a substantial share of the market.

Santronics would like an analysis of the first-year profit potential of the device. Because of Sanotronics's tight cash flow situation, management is particularly concerned about the potential for a loss. Sanotronics has identified the key parameters in determining first-year profit: selling price per unit (p), first-year administrative and advertising costs (c_a), direct labor cost per unit (c_l), parts cost per unit (c_p), and first-year demand (d). After conducting market research and a financial analysis, Sanotronics estimates with a high level of certainty that the device's selling price will be $249 per unit, and the first-year administrative and advertising costs will total $1,000,000.

Sanotronics is not certain about the values for the cost of direct labor, the cost of parts, and the first-year demand. At this stage of the planning process, Sanotronics's base estimates of these inputs are $45 per unit for the direct labor cost, $90 per unit for the parts cost, and 15,000 units for the first-year demand.

Base-Case Scenario

Sanotronics' first-year profit is computed by

$$\text{Profit} = (p - c_l - c_p) \times d - c_a \tag{16.1}$$

Recall that Sanotronics is certain of a selling price of $249 per unit, and administrative and advertising costs total $1,000,000. Substituting these values into equation (16.1) yields

$$\text{Profit} = (249 - c_l - c_p) \times d - 1,000,000 \tag{16.2}$$

Sanotronics's base-case estimates of the direct labor cost per unit, the parts cost per unit, and first-year demand are $45, $90, and 15,000 units, respectively. These values constitute the **base-case scenario** for Sanotronics. Substituting these values into equation (16.2) yields the following profit projection:

$$\text{Profit} = (249 - 45 - 90)(15,000) - 1,000,000 = 710,000$$

Thus, the base-case scenario leads to an anticipated profit of $710,000.

While the base-case scenario looks appealing, Sanotronics is aware that the values of direct labor cost per unit, parts cost per unit, and first-year demand are uncertain, so the base-case scenario may not occur. To help Sanotronics gauge the impact of the uncertainty, a **what-if analysis** involves considering alternative values for the random variables (direct labor cost, parts cost, and first-year demand) and computing the resulting value for the output (profit).

Sanotronics is interested in what happens if the estimates of the direct labor cost per unit, parts cost per unit, and first-year demand do not turn out to be as expected under the base-case scenario. For instance, suppose that Sanotronics believes that direct labor costs could range from $43 to $47 per unit, the parts cost could range from $80 to $100 per unit, and the first-year demand could range from 0 to 30,000 units. Using these ranges, what-if analysis can be used to evaluate a **worst-case scenario** and a **best-case scenario**.

Worst-Case Scenario

The worst-case value for the direct labor cost is $47 (the highest value), the worst-case value for the parts cost is $100 (the highest value), and the worst-case value for demand is 0 units (the lowest value). Substituting these values into equation (16.2) leads to the following profit projection:

$$\text{Profit} = (249 - 47 - 100)(0) - 1,000,000 = -1,000,000$$

So, the worst-case scenario leads to a projected *loss* of $1,000,000.

Best-Case Scenario

The best-case value for the direct labor cost is $43 (the lowest value), the best-case value for the parts cost is $80 (the lowest value), and the best-case value for demand is 30,000 units (the highest value). Substituting these values into equation (16.2) leads to the following profit projection:

$$\text{Profit} = (249 - 43 - 80)(30,000) - 1,000,000 = 2,780,000$$

So the best-case scenario leads to a projected profit of $2,780,000.

At this point the what-if analysis provides the conclusion that profits may range from a loss of $1,000,000 to a profit of $2,780,000 with a base-case profit of $710,000. Although the base-case profit of $710,000 is possible, the what-if analysis indicates that either a substantial loss or a substantial profit is also possible. Sanotronics can repeat this what-if analysis for other scenarios. However, simple what-if analyses do not indicate the likelihood of the various profit or loss values. In particular, we do not know anything about the probability of a loss. To conduct a more thorough evaluation of risk by obtaining insight on the potential magnitude and probability of undesirable outcomes, we now turn to developing a spreadsheet simulation model.

16.2 Simulation of Sanotronics Problem

In this section, we show how to construct a simulation model and conduct a risk analysis using native Excel functionality. The first step in constructing a spreadsheet simulation model is to express the relationship between the inputs and the outputs with appropriate formula logic. Figure 16.1 provides the formula and value view for the Sanotronics spreadsheet. Data on selling price per unit, administrative and advertising cost, direct labor cost per unit, parts cost per unit, and demand are in cells B4 to B8. The profit calculation, corresponding to equation (16.1), is expressed in cell B11 using appropriate cell references and formula logic. For the values shown in Figure 16.1, the spreadsheet model computes profit for the base-case scenario. By changing one or more values for the input parameters, the spreadsheet model can be used to conduct a manual what-if analysis (e.g., the best-case and worst-case scenarios).

In the chapter appendix we demonstrate how the Excel add-in Analytic Solver Platform facilitates the construction of simulation models.

Use of Probability Distributions to Represent Random Variables

Sanotronics

Using the what-if approach to risk analysis, we manually select values for the random variables (direct labor cost per unit, parts cost per unit, and first-year demand) and then compute the resulting profit. Instead of manually selecting the values for the random variables, a simulation model randomly generates values for the random variables so that the values used reflect what we might observe in practice. A probability distribution describes the possible values of a random variable and the relative likelihood of the random variable realizing these values. The analyst can use historical data and knowledge of the random variable (such as the range, mean, mode, standard deviation) to specify the probability distribution for a random variable. As described below, Sanotronics examined the random variables to identify probability distributions for the direct labor cost per unit, the parts cost per unit, and first-year demand.

FIGURE 16.1 EXCEL WORKSHEET FOR SANOTRONICS

	A	B
1	Sanotronics	
2		
3	Parameters	
4	Selling Price per Unit	249
5	Administrative & Advertising Cost	1000000
6	Direct Labor Cost per Unit	45
7	Parts Cost per Unit	90
8	Demand	15000
9		
10	Model	
11	Profit	=((B4-B6-B7)*B8)-B5
12		

	A	B
1	Sanotronics	
2		
3	Parameters	
4	Selling Price per Unit	$249.00
5	Administrative & Advertising Cost	$1,000,000
6	Direct Labor Cost per Unit	$45.00
7	Parts Cost per Unit	$90.00
8	Demand	15,000
9		
10	Model	
11	Profit	$710,000.00

Direct Labor Cost Based on recent wage rates and estimated processing requirements of the device, Sanotronics believes that the direct labor cost will range from $43 to $47 per unit and is described by the discrete probability distribution shown in Figure 16.2. Thus, we see that there is 0.1 probability that the direct labor cost will be $43 per unit, a 0.2 probability that the direct labor cost will be $44 per unit, and so on. The highest probability of 0.4 is associated with a direct labor cost of $45 per unit. Because we have assumed that the direct labor cost per unit is best described by a **discrete probability distribution**, this means that the direct labor cost per unit can *only* take on a value of $43, $44, $45, $46, or $47.

Parts Cost Sanotronics is relatively unsure of the value of the parts cost because it depends on many factors, including the general economy, the overall demand for parts, and the pricing policy of Sanotronics's parts suppliers. Sanotronics is confident that the parts cost will be between $80 and $100 per unit but is unsure if any particular values between $80 and $100 are more likely than others. Therefore, Sanotronics decides to describe the uncertainty in parts cost with a uniform probability distribution, as shown in Figure 16.3. Costs per unit between $80 and $100 are equally likely. A uniform probability distribution is an example of a **continuous probability distribution**; this means that the parts cost can take on *any* value between $80 and $100 with equal likelihood.

FIGURE 16.2 PROBABILITY DISTRIBUTION FOR DIRECT LABOR COST PER UNIT

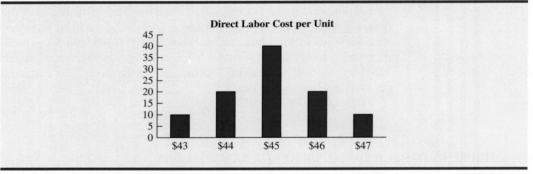

FIGURE 16.3 UNIFORM PROBABILITY DISTRIBUTION FOR PARTS COST PER UNIT

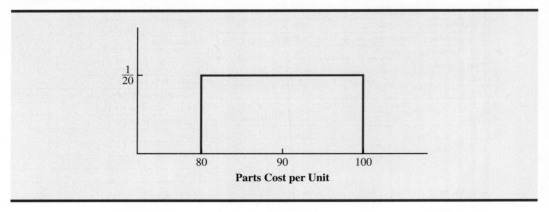

FIGURE 16.4   NORMAL PROBABILITY DISTRIBUTION FOR FIRST-YEAR DEMAND

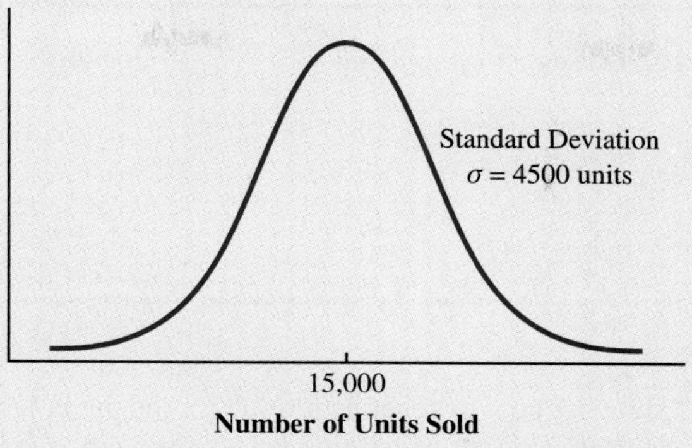

One advantage of simulation is that the analyst can adjust the probability distributions of the random variables to determine the impact of the assumptions about the "shape" of the uncertainty on the results (and ultimately the sensitivity of the decision to the distribution assumptions about the random variables).

First-Year Demand   Based on sales of comparable medical devices, Sanotronics believes that first-year demand is described by the normal probability distribution shown in Figure 16.4. The mean or expected value of first-year demand is 15,000 units. The standard deviation of 4500 units describes the variability in the first-year demand. The normal probability distribution is a continuous probability distribution in which any value is possible, but values far larger or smaller than the mean are increasingly unlikely.

Generating Values for Random Variables with Excel

To simulate the Sanotronics problem, we must generate values for the three random variables and compute the resulting profit. A set of values for the random variables is called a trial. We then generate another trial, compute a second value for profit, and so on. We continue this process until we are satisfied that sufficient trials have been conducted to describe the probability distribution for profit. Put simply, simulation is the process of generating values of random variables and computing the corresponding output measures.

In the Sanotronics model, representative values must be generated for the random variables corresponding to the direct labor cost per unit, the parts cost per unit, and the first-year demand. To illustrate how to generate these values, we need to introduce the concept of computer-generated random numbers.

Computer-generated random numbers[1] are randomly selected numbers from 0 up to, but not including, 1; this interval is denoted [0, 1). All values of the computer-generated random numbers are equally likely and so are uniformly distributed over the interval from 0 to 1. Computer-generated random numbers can be obtained using built-in functions available in computer simulation packages and spreadsheets. For example, placing the formula =RAND() in a cell of an Excel worksheet will result in a random number between 0 and 1 being placed into that cell.

Let us show how random numbers can be used to generate values corresponding to the probability distributions for the random variables in the Sanotronics example. We begin by

---

[1]Computer-generated random numbers are formally called pseudorandom numbers because they are generated through the use of mathematical formulas and are therefore not technically random. The difference between random numbers and pseudorandom numbers is primarily philosophical, and we use the term random numbers regardless of whether they are generated by a computer.

TABLE 16.1   RANDOM NUMBER INTERVALS FOR GENERATING VALUE OF DIRECT LABOR COST PER UNIT

Direct Labor Cost per Unit	Probability	Interval of Random Numbers
$43	0.1	[0.0, 0.1)
$44	0.2	[0.1, 0.3)
$45	0.4	[0.3, 0.7)
$46	0.2	[0.7, 0.9)
$47	0.1	[0.9, 1.0)

showing how to generate a value for the direct labor cost per unit. The approach described is applicable for generating values from any discrete probability distribution.

Table 16.1 illustrates the process of partitioning the interval from 0 to 1 into subintervals so that the probability of generating a random number in a subinterval is equal to the probability of the corresponding direct labor cost. The interval of random numbers from 0 up to but not including 0.1, [0, 0.1), is associated with a direct labor cost of $43, the interval of random numbers from 0.1 up to but not including 0.3, [0.1, 0.3), is associated with a direct labor cost of $44, and so on. With this assignment of random number intervals to the possible values of the direct labor cost, the probability of generating a random number in any interval is equal to the probability of obtaining the corresponding value for the direct labor cost. Thus, to select a value for the direct labor cost, we generate a random number between 0 and 1 using the RAND function in Excel. If the random number is at least 0.0 but less than 0.1, we set the direct labor cost equal to $43. If the random number is at least 0.1 but less than 0.3, we set the direct labor cost equal to $44, and so on.

Each trial of the simulation requires a value for the direct labor cost. Suppose that on the first trial the random number is 0.9109. From Table 16.1, because 0.9109 is in the interval [0.9, 1.0), the corresponding simulated value for the direct labor cost is $47 per unit. Suppose that on the second trial the random number is 0.2841. From Table 16.1, the simulated value for the direct labor cost is $44 per unit.

Each trial in the simulation also requires a value of the parts cost and first-year demand. Let us now turn to the issue of generating values for the parts cost. The probability distribution for the parts cost per unit is the uniform distribution shown in Figure 16.3. Because this random variable has a different probability distribution than direct labor cost, we use random numbers in a slightly different way to generate simulated values for parts cost. To generate a value for a random variable characterized by a continuous uniform distribution, the following Excel formula is used:

$$\text{Value of uniform random variable} = \text{lower bound} + (\text{upper bound} - \text{lower bound}) \times \text{RAND()} \tag{16.3}$$

For Sanotronics, parts cost per unit is a uniformly distributed random variable with a lower bound of $80 and an upper bound of $100. Applying equation (16.3) leads to the following formula for generating the parts cost:

$$\text{Parts cost} = 80 + 20 \times \text{RAND()} \tag{16.4}$$

FIGURE 16.5   GENERATION OF VALUE FOR PARTS COST PER UNIT CORRESPONDING
TO RANDOM NUMBER 0.4576

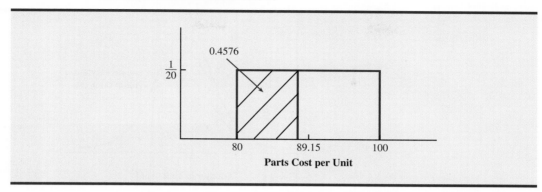

By closely examining equation (16.4), we can understand how it uses random numbers to gen-erate uniformly distributed values for parts cost. The first term of equation (16.4) is 80, since Sanotronics is assuming that the parts cost will never drop below \$80 per unit. Since RAND is between 0 and 1, the second term, $20 \times$ RAND(), corresponds to how much more than the lower bound the simulated value of parts cost is. Since RAND is equally likely to be any value between 0 and 1, the simulated value for the parts cost is equally likely to be between the lower bound $(80 + 0 = 80)$ and the upper bound $(80 + 20 = 100)$. For example, suppose that a ran-dom number of 0.4576 is obtained. As illustrated by Figure 16.5, the value for the parts cost is

$$\text{Parts cost} = 80 + 20 \times 0.4576 = 80 + 9.15 = 89.15 \text{ per unit}$$

Suppose that a random number of 0.5842 is generated on the next trial. The value for the parts cost is

$$\text{Parts cost} = 80 + 20 \times 0.5842 = 80 + 11.68 = 91.68 \text{ per unit}$$

With appropriate choices of the lower bound and the upper bound, equation (16.3) can be used to generate values for any uniform probability distribution.

Lastly, we need a procedure for generating the first-year demand from computer-generated random numbers. Because first-year demand is normally distributed with a mean of 15,000 units and a standard deviation of 4500 units (see Figure 16.4), we need a proce-dure for generating random values from this normal probability distribution.

Once again we will use random numbers between 0 and 1 to simulate values for first-year demand. To generate a value for a random variable characterized by a normal distri-bution with a specified mean and standard deviation, the following Excel formula is used:

$$\text{Value of normal random variable} = \text{NORM.INV(RAND(),}$$
$$\text{mean, standard deviation)} \qquad \textbf{(16.5)}$$

Versions of Excel prior to Excel 2010 do not recognize the function NORM.INV; in these earlier versions of Excel, one can use the function NORMINV. The results will be identical.

For Sanotronics, first-year demand is a normally distributed random variable with a mean of 15,000 and a standard deviation of 4500. Applying equation (16.5) leads to the following formula for generating the first-year demand:

$$\text{Demand} = \text{NORM.INV(RAND(),15000,4500)} \qquad \textbf{(16.6)}$$

FIGURE 16.6   GENERATION OF VALUE FOR FIRST-YEAR DEMAND CORRESPONDING
TO RANDOM NUMBER 0.6026

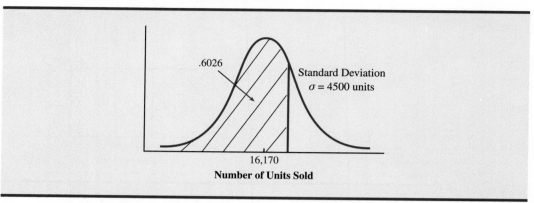

Suppose that the random number of 0.6026 is produced by the RAND function; applying equation (16.6) then results in Demand =NORM.INV(0.6026, 15000, 4500) = 16,170 units. To understand how equation (16.6) uses random numbers to generate normally distributed values for first-year demand, we note that the Excel expression =NORM.INV(0.6026, 15000, 4500) provides the value for a normal distribution with a mean of 15,000 and a standard deviation of 4500, such that 60.26% of the area under the normal curve is to the left of this value (see Figure 16.6). Now suppose that the random number produced by the RAND function is 0.3551; applying equation (16.6) then results in Demand =NORM.INV(0.3551, 15000, 4500) = 13,328 units. Because half of this normal distribution lies below the mean of 15,000 and half lies above, RAND values less than 0.5 result in values of first-year demand below the average of 15,000 units and RAND value above 0.5 correspond to values of first-year demand above the average of 15,000 units.

With appropriate specification of the mean and standard deviation, equation (16.5) can be used to generate values for any normal probability distribution.

Now that we know how to randomly generate values for the random variables (direct labor cost, parts cost, first-year demand) from their respective probability distributions, we modify the spreadsheet by adding this information. The static values in Figure 16.1 for these parameters in cells B6, B7, and B8 are replaced with cell formulas that will randomly generate values whenever the spreadsheet is recalculated (as shown in Figure 16.7). Corresponding to Table 16.1, cell B6 uses a random number generated by the RAND function and looks up the corresponding cost per unit by applying the VLOOKUP function to the table of intervals contained in cells A15:C19 (which corresponds to Table 16.1). Cell B7 executes equation (16.4) using references to the lower bound and upper bound of the uniform distribution of the parts cost in cells F14 and F15, respectively.[2] Cell B8 executes equation (16.6) using references to the mean and standard deviation of the normal distribution of the first-year demand in cells F18 and F19, respectively.[3]

For further description of the VLOOKUP function, refer to Appendix A.

---

[2]Technically, random variables modeled with continuous probability distributions should be appropriately rounded to avoid modeling error (e.g., the simulated values of parts cost per unit should be rounded to the nearest penny). To simplify exposition, we do not worry about the small amount of error that occurs in this case. To model these random variables more accurately, the formula in cell B7 should be =ROUND(F12+(F13-F12)*RAND(),2).

[3]In addition to being a continuous distribution that technically requires rounding when applied to discrete phenomena (like units of medical device demand), the normal distribution also allows negative values. The probability of a negative value is quite small in the case of first-year demand, and we simply ignore the small amount of modeling error for the sake of simplicity. To model first-year demand more accurately, the formula in cell B8 should be =MAX(ROUND(NORM.INV(RAND(),F16,F17),0),0).

FIGURE 16.7   FORMULA WORKSHEET FOR SANOTRONICS

	A	B	C	D	E	F
1	**Sanotronics**					
2						
3	**Parameters**					
4	**Selling Price per Unit**	249				
5	**Administrative & Advertising Cost**	1000000				
6	**Direct Labor Cost per Unit**	=VLOOKUP(RAND(),A15:C19,3,TRUE)				
7	**Parts Cost per Unit**	=F14+(F15-F14)*RAND()				
8	**Demand**	=NORM.INV(RAND(),F18,F19)				
9						
10	**Model**					
11	**Profit**	=((B4-B6-B7)*B8)-B5				
12						
13	**Direct Labor Cost**				**Parts Cost (Uniform Distribution)**	
14	Lower End of Interval	Upper End of Interval	Cost per Unit	Probability	Lower Bound	80
15	0	=D15+A15	43	0.1	Upper Bound	100
16	=B15	=D16+A16	44	0.2		
17	=B16	=D17+A17	45	0.4	**Demand (Normal Distribution)**	
18	=B17	=D18+A18	46	0.2	Mean	15000
19	=B18	1	47	0.1	Standard Deviation	4500
20						

Executing Simulation Trials with Excel

For a detailed description of Excel's Data Table functionality, see Appendix A.

Each trial in the simulation involves randomly generating values for the random variables (direct labor cost, parts cost, and first-year demand) and computing profit. To facilitate the execution of multiple simulation trials, we use Excel's Data Table functionality in an unorthodox, but effective, manner. To set up the spreadsheet for the execution of 1000 simulation trials, we structure a table as shown in cells A21 through E1021 in Figure 16.8. As Figure 16.8 shows, A22:A1021 numbers the 1000 simulation trials (rows 25 through 1019 are hidden). To populate the data table in cells A23 through E1021, we execute the following steps:

Sanotronics

These steps iteratively select the simulation trial number from the range A22 through A1021 and substitute it into the blank cell selected in Step 4 (D1). This substitution has no bearing on the spreadsheet, but it forces Excel to recalculate the spreadsheet each time, thereby generating new random numbers with the RAND functions in cells B6, B7, and B8.

Step 1. Select cell range A22:E1021
Step 2. Click the **DATA** tab in the Ribbon
Step 3. Click **What-If Analysis** in the **Data Tools** group and select **Data Table**
Step 4. When the **Data Table** dialog box appears, enter any blank cell in the spreadsheet (e.g., D1) into the **Column input cell:** box
Step 6. Click **OK**

Figure 16.8 shows the results of our simulation. After executing the simulation with the data table, each row in this table corresponds to a distinct simulation trial consisting of different values of the random variables. In trial 1 (row 22 in the spreadsheet), we see that the direct labor cost is $45 per unit, the parts cost is $86.29 per unit, and first-year demand is 19,976 units, resulting in profit of $1,351,439. In trial 2 (row 23 in the spreadsheet), we observe random variables of $45 for the direct labor cost, $81.02 for the parts cost, and 14,910 for first-year demand. These values provide a simulated profit of $833,700 on the second simulation trial.

FIGURE 16.8   SETTING UP SANOTRONICS SPREADSHEET FOR MULTIPLE SIMULATION
TRIALS

	A	B	C	D	E	F
1	**Sanotronics**					
2						
3	**Parameters**					
4	Selling Price per Unit	249				
5	Administrative & Advertising Cost	1000000				
6	Direct Labor Cost per Unit	-VLOOKUP(RAND(), A15:C19,3,TRUE)				
7	Parts Cost per Unit	-F14+(F15-F14)*RAND()				
8	Demand	-NORM.INV(RAND(),F18,F19)				
9						
10	**Model**					
11	Profit	-((B4-B6-B7)*B8)-B5				
12						
13	Direct Labor Cost				Parts Cost (Uniform Distribution)	
14	Lower End of Interval	Upper End of Interval	Cost per Unit	Probability	Lower Bound	80
15	0	-D15+A15	43	0.1	Upper Bound	100
16	-B15	-D16+A16	44	0.2		
17	-B16	-D17+A17	45	0.4	Demand (Normal Distribution)	
18	-B17	-D18+A18	46	0.2	Mean	15000
19	-B18	1	47	0.1	Standard Deviation	4500
20						
21	Simulation Trial	Direct Labor Cost per Unit	Parts Cost per Unit	Demand	Profit	
22	1	-B6	-B7	-B8	-B11	
23	2					
24	3					
1019	998					
1020	999					
1021	1000					

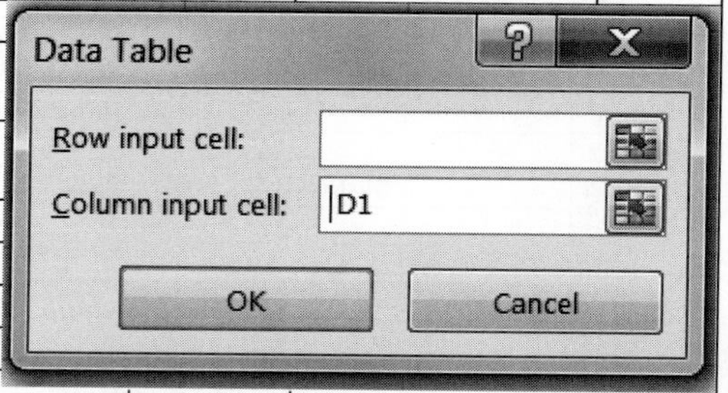

(Data Table dialog box overlaid on cells C4–F11:)

Data Table

Row input cell: [   ]

Column input cell: [D1   ]

OK   Cancel

Measuring and Analyzing Simulation Output

Pressing the F9 key recalculates the spreadsheet, thereby generating a new set of simulation trials.

The analysis of the output observed over the set of simulation trials is a critical part of the simulation process. For the collection of simulation trials, it is helpful to compute descriptive statistics such as sample average, sample standard deviation, minimum, maximum, and sample proportion. To compute these statistics for the Sanotronics example, we use the following Excel functions:

Excel versions prior to Excel 2010 do not recognize the STDEV.S function; in these versions of Excel one can use the function STDEV. The results will be identical.

Cell H22   =AVERAGE(E22:E1021)

Cell H23   =STDEV.S(E22:E1021)

Cell H24   =MIN(E22:E1021)

Cell H25   =MAX(E22:E1021)

Cell H26   =COUNTIF(E22:E1021,"<0") / COUNT(E22:E1021)

Simulation studies enable an objective estimate of the probability of a loss, which is an important aspect of risk analysis.

Cell H26 computes the ratio of the number of trials whose profit is less than zero over the total number of trials. By changing the value of the second argument in the COUNTIF function, the probability that the profit is less than any specified value can be computed in cell H26.

As shown in Figure 16.9, we observe a mean profit of $717,663, standard deviation of $521,536, extremes ranging between −$996,547 and $2,253,674, and a 0.078 estimated probability of a loss.

To visualize the distribution of profit on which these descriptive statistics are based, we create a histogram using the FREQUENCY function and a column chart. We note that the

FIGURE 16.9 OUTPUT FROM SANOTRONICS SIMULATION

	A	B	C	D	E	F	G	H	I	J	K
1	Sanotronics										
2											
3	**Parameters**										
4	Selling Price per Unit	$249									
5	Administrative & Advertising Cost	$1,000,000									
6	Direct Labor Cost per Unit	$45									
7	Parts Cost per Unit	$86.29									
8	Demand	19,976									
9											
10	**Model**										
11	Profit	$1,351,439									
12											
13	Direct Labor Cost				Parts Cost (Uniform Distribution)						
14	Lower End of Interval	Upper End of Interval	Cost per Unit	Probability	Lower Bound	$80					
15	0.0	0.1	$43	0.1	Upper Bound	$100					
16	0.1	0.3	$44	0.2							
17	0.3	0.7	$45	0.4	Demand (Normal Distribution)						
18	0.7	0.9	$46	0.2	Mean	15,000					
19	0.9	1.0	$47	0.1	Standard Deviation	4,500					
20											
21	Simulation Trial	Direct Labor Cost per Unit	Parts Cost per Unit	Demand	Profit		Profit Summary Statistics				
22	1	$45	$86.29	19,976	$1,351,439		Mean	$717,663		Bin	Frequency
23	2	$45	$81.02	14,910	$833,700		Standard Deviation	$521,536		−$1,500,000	0
24	3	$46	$98.15	18,570	$947,064		Minimum Profit	−$996,547		−$1,250,000	0
25	4	$45	$92.29	12,561	$403,085		Maximum Profit	$2,253,674		−$1,000,000	0
26	5	$47	$88.82	6,844	−$225,345		P(Profit < $0)	0.078		−$750,000	3
27	6	$45	$95.98	15,337	$656,778					−$500,000	4
28	7	$44	$88.23	18,723	$1,186,276					−$250,000	22
29	8	$47	$96.20	17,589	$861,005					$0	49
30	9	$44	$85.97	19,967	$1,376,760					$250,000	113
31	10	$45	$89.62	14,056	$607,650					$500,000	151
32	11	$45	$85.96	11,204	$322,448					$750,000	188
33	12	$45	$92.06	11,150	$248,172					$1,000,000	193
34	13	$47	$85.34	11,880	$385,901					$1,250,000	122
35	14	$44	$80.05	24,733	$2,090,469					$1,500,000	79
36	15	$46	$92.47	10,933	$208,447					$1,750,000	47
37	16	$45	$81.61	17,453	$1,136,087					$2,000,000	20
38	17	$45	$84.16	13,205	$582,483					$2,250,000	7
39	18	$45	$93.07	15,809	$753,735					$2,500,000	2
40	19	$47	$85.33	9,422	$99,247					$2,750,000	0
41	20	$43	$83.58	13,599	$664,800					$3,000,000	0
42	21	$47	$92.23	17,168	$884,578					>$3,000,000	0
1021	1,000	$45	$92.87	22,467	$1,496,677						
1022											

For a detailed description of the FREQUENCY function, see Appendix A.

distribution of profit values is fairly symmetric, with a large number of values in the range of $250,000 to $1,250,000. The probability of a large loss or a large gain is small. Only 7 trials out of 1000 resulted in a loss of more than $500,000, and only 9 trials resulted in a profit greater than $2,000,000. The bin with the largest number of values has profit ranging between $750,000 and $1,000,000.

In comparing the simulation approach to the manual what-if approach, we observe that much more information is obtained by using simulation. Recall from the what-if analysis in Section 16.1, we learned that the base-case scenario projected a profit of $710,000, the worst-case scenario projected a loss of $1,000,000, and the best-case scenario projected a profit of $2,591,000. From the 1000 trials of the simulation run, we see that the worst- and best-case scenarios, although possible, are unlikely. Indeed, the advantage of simulation for risk analysis is the information it provides on the likely values of the output. We now know the probability of a loss, how the profit values are distributed over their range, and what profit values are most likely.

The simulation results help Sanotronics's management better understand the profit/loss potential of the new medical device. The 0.078 probability of a loss may be acceptable to management. On the other hand, Sanotronics might want to conduct further market research before deciding whether to introduce the product. In any case, the simulation results should be helpful in reaching an appropriate decision.

NOTES AND COMMENTS

1. In general, the value k of a random variable X corresponding to a computer-generated random number r between 0 and 1 is the smallest value k such that $P(X \leq k) \geq r$.
2. In the preceding section, we showed how to generate values for random variables from a custom discrete distribution, a uniform distribution, and an normal distribution. Generating values for a normally distributed random variable required the use of NORM.INV and the RAND functions. In Appendix 16.1, we describe several additional types of random variables and how to generate them with Excel functions. Using a different probablity distribution for a random variable simply changes the relative likelihood of the random variable realizing certain values. The choice of probability distribution to use for a random variable should be based on historical data and knowledge of the analyst.

16.3 Inventory Simulation

In this section, we describe how simulation can be used to establish an inventory policy for a product that has an uncertain demand. In our example, we consider the Butler Internet Company, which distributes a wireless router. Each router costs Butler $75 and sells for $125. Thus Butler realizes a gross profit of $125 − $75 = $50 for each router sold. Monthly demand for the router is described by a normal probability distribution with a mean of 100 units and a standard deviation of 20 units.

Butler receives monthly deliveries from its supplier and replenishes its inventory to a level of Q at the beginning of each month. This beginning inventory level is referred to as the replenishment level. If monthly demand is less than the replenishment level, an inventory holding cost of $15 is charged for each unit that is not sold. However, if monthly demand is greater than the replenishment level, a stock-out occurs and a shortage cost is incurred. Because Butler assigns a loss-of-goodwill cost of $30 for each customer turned away, a shortage cost of $30 is charged for each unit of demand that cannot be satisfied.

Management would like to use a simulation model to determine the average monthly net profit resulting from using particular replenishment levels. Management would also like information on the percentage of total demand that will be satisfied. This percentage is referred to as the *service level*.

The controllable input to the Butler simulation model is the replenishment level, Q. The monthly demand, D, is a random variable. The two output measures are the average monthly net profit and the service level. Computation of the service level requires that we keep track of the number of routers sold each month and the total demand for routers for each month. The service level will be computed at the end of the simulation run as the ratio of total units sold to total demand.

When demand is less than or equal to the replenishment level ($D \leq Q$), D units are sold, and an inventory holding cost of $15 is incurred for each of the $Q - D$ units that remain in inventory. Net profit for this case is computed as follows:

Case 1: $D \leq Q$

$$\text{Gross profit} = \$50D$$
$$\text{Holding cost} = \$15(Q - D)$$
$$\text{Net profit} = \text{Gross profit} - \text{Holding cost} = \$50D - \$15(Q - D)$$

When demand is greater than the replenishment level ($D > Q$), Q routers are sold, and a shortage cost of $30 is imposed for each of the $D - Q$ units of demand not satisfied. Net profit for this case is computed as follows:

Case 2: $D > Q$

$$\text{Gross profit} = \$50Q$$
$$\text{Holding cost} = \$30(D - Q)$$
$$\text{Net profit} = \text{Gross profit} - \text{Holding cost} = \$50Q - \$30(D - Q)$$

Figure 16.10 shows a flowchart that defines the sequence of logical and mathematical operations required to simulate the Butler inventory system. Each trial in the simulation represents one month of operation. The simulation is run for 1000 months using a given replenishment level, Q. Then, the average profit and service level output measures are computed. Let us describe the steps involved in the simulation by illustrating the results for the first two months of a simulation run using a replenishment level of $Q = 100$.

The first block of the flowchart in Figure 16.10 sets the values of the model parameters: gross profit = $50 per unit, holding cost = $15 per unit, and shortage cost = $30 per unit. The next block shows that a replenishment level of Q is selected; in our illustration, $Q = 100$. A value for monthly demand is then generated from a normal distribution with a mean of 100 units and a standard deviation of 20 units; this can be done in Excel with the command =NORM.INV(RAND(), 100, 20). Suppose that a value of $D = 79$ is generated on the first trial. This value of demand is then compared with the replenishment level, Q. With the replenishment level set at $Q = 100$, demand is less than the replenishment level, and the left branch of the flowchart is followed. Sales are set equal to demand (79), and gross profit, holding cost, and net profit are computed as follows:

$$\text{Gross profit} = 50D = 50(79) = 3950$$
$$\text{Holding cost} = 15(Q - D) = 15(100 - 79) = 315$$
$$\text{Net profit} = \text{Gross profit} - \text{Holding cost} = 3950 - 315 = 3635$$

FIGURE 16.10   FLOWCHART FOR THE BUTLER INVENTORY SIMULATION

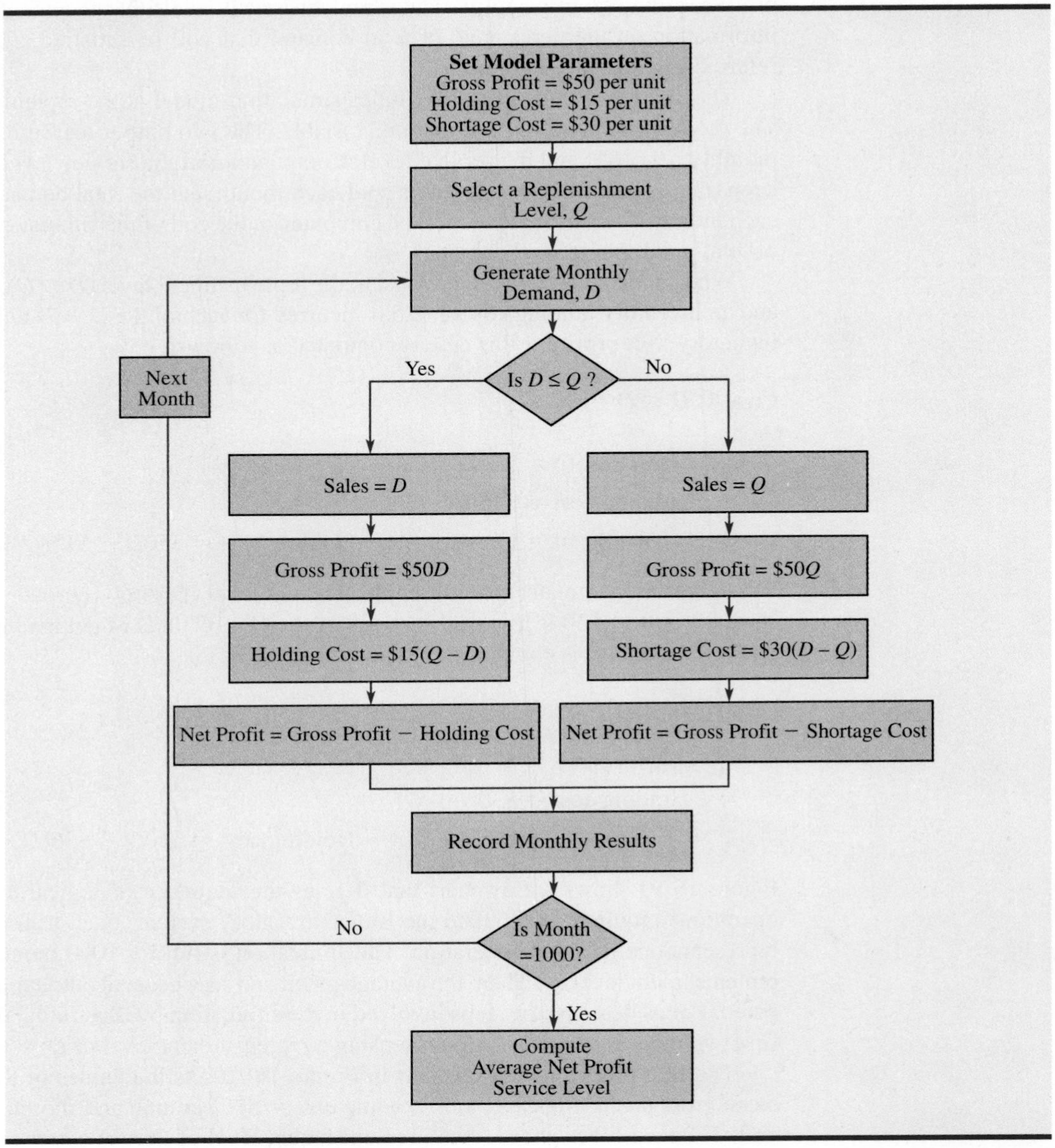

The values of demand, sales, gross profit, holding cost, and net profit are recorded for the first month. The first row of Table 16.2 summarizes the information for this first trial.

For the second month, suppose that a value of 111 is generated for monthly demand. Because demand is greater than the replenishment level, the right branch of the flowchart is followed. Sales are set equal to the replenishment level (100), and gross profit, shortage cost, and net profit are computed as follows:

$$\text{Gross profit} = 50Q = 50(100) = 5000$$
$$\text{Shortage cost} = 30(D - Q) = 30(111 - 100) = 330$$
$$\text{Net profit} = \text{Gross profit} - \text{Shortage cost} = 5000 - 330 = 4670$$

TABLE 16.2   BUTLER INVENTORY SIMULATION RESULTS FOR FIVE TRIALS
WITH $Q = 100$

Month	Demand	Sales	Gross Profit ($)	Holding Cost ($)	Shortage Cost ($)	Net Profit ($)
1	79	79	3,950	315	0	3,635
2	111	100	5,000	0	330	4,670
3	93	93	4,650	105	0	4,545
4	100	100	5,000	0	0	5,000
5	118	100	5,000	0	540	4,460
Totals	501	472	23,600	420	870	22,310
Average	100	94	$4,720	$84	$174	$4,462

The values of demand, sales, gross profit, holding cost, shortage cost, and net profit are recorded for the second month. The second row of Table 16.2 summarizes the information generated in the second trial.

Table 16.2 shows results for five trials (months) of the simulation. The totals show an accumulated total net profit of $22,310, which is an average monthly net profit of $22,310/5 = $4,462. Total unit sales are 472, and total demand is 501. Thus, the service level is 472/501 = 0.942, indicating Butler has been able to satisfy 94.2% of demand during the five-month period.

Simulation of the Butler Inventory Problem

Butler

Using Excel, we simulate the Butler inventory operation for 1000 months. The worksheet used to carry out the simulation is shown in Figure 16.11. Note that the simulation results for months 22 through 999 have been hidden so that the results can be displayed in a reasonably sized figure. If desired, the rows for these months can be shown and the simulation results displayed for all 1000 months. Let us describe the details of the Excel worksheet that provided the Butler inventory simulation.

The gross profit per unit, holding cost per unit, and shortage cost per unit data are entered directly into cells B4, B5, and B6. The mean and standard deviation of the normal probability distribution for demand are entered into cells E6 and E7. The replenishment level (a controllable input) is entered into cell B10. At this point, we are ready to insert Excel formulas that will be executed for each simulation month or trial.

To generate values for demand, the cell formula in cell B7 is =NORM. INV(RAND(),E6,E7). Next, compute the sales, which is equal to demand (cell B7) if demand is less than or equal to the replenishment level, or is equal to the replenishment level (cell B10) if demand is greater than the replenishment level.

Cell B11   Compute sales =MIN(B7,B10)

Cell B12   Calculate gross profit =B11*B4

Cell B13   Calculate the holding cost if demand is less than or equal to the replenishment level

=IF(B10>B7,(B10−B7)*B5,0)

Cell B14   Calculate the shortage cost if demand is greater than the replenishment level

=IF(B7>B10,(B7−B10)*B6,0)

Cell B15   Calculate net profit =B12−B13−B14

FIGURE 16.11   OUTPUT FROM BUTLER INVENTORY SIMULATION

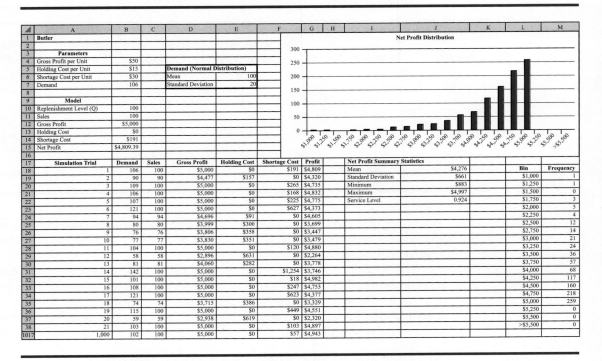

The table of simulation trials in cells A18:G1017 and the summary statistics are generated using the steps described in Section 16.2. The summary statistics in Figure 16.11 show what can be anticipated over 1000 months if Butler operates its inventory system using a replenishment level of 100. The average net profit is $4276 per month and the service level is 92.4%. A closer look at the distribution of net profit shows that the maximum net profit never exceeds $5000 (indeed the maximum monthly net profit of $5000 occurs when monthly demand is 100 routers and matches the replenishment level). The most likely monthly net profit levels are between $4750 and $5000, but net profits below $1000 are also possible.

By varying the values of controllable inputs, simulation models can be used to identify good operating policies and decisions. For Butler, the simulation model can be used to test the impact of different replenishment levels on the monthly net profit. Table 16.3 summarizes the results of varying the replenishment levels of 110, 120, 130, and 140 units by showing the average monthly net profit, standard deviation of monthly net profit, and the service level for the respective replenishment levels. From Table 16.3, we observe that average monthly net profit increases as the replenishment level increases from 100 to 120, but then decreases as the replenishment level is further increased to 130 and beyond. The standard deviation of monthly net profit increases as the replenishment level increases, suggesting that the monthly profit is more variable as Butler stocks more inventory. This occurs because as Butler increases its replenishment level, it can achieve more sales during months with high demand, but also is exposed to increased holding costs during months with low demand. The service level increases as the replenishment level increases because with more inventory on-hand, Butler is more likely to be able to satisfy demand.

TABLE 16.3 BUTLER INVENTORY SIMULATION RESULTS FOR 1000 TRIALS

Replenishment Level	Average Net Profit ($)	Standard Deviation Profit ($)	Service Level (%)
100	4276	661	92.4
110	4498	853	96.2
120	4573	1078	98.1
130	4462	1201	99.4
140	4327	1247	99.9

Simulation allows the user to consider different operating policies and changes to model parameters and then observe the impact of the changes on output measures such as profit or service level.

On the basis of these results, Butler selected a replenishment level of $Q = 120$, which achieves the highest monthly net profit of $4573 with an acceptable service level of 98.1%. Experimental simulation studies, such as this one for Butler's inventory policy, can help identify good operating policies and decisions. Butler's management used simulation to choose a replenishment level of 120 for the wireless router. With the simulation model in place, management can also explore the sensitivity of this decision to some of the model parameters. For instance, we assigned a shortage cost of $30 for any customer demand not met. With this shortage cost, the replenishment level was $Q = 120$ and the service level was 98.6%. If management felt a more appropriate shortage cost was $10 per unit, running the simulation again using $10 as the shortage cost would be a simple matter.

Earlier we mentioned that simulation is not an optimization technique. Even though we used simulation to choose a replenishment level, it does not guarantee that this choice is optimal. All possible replenishment levels were not tested. Perhaps a manager would like to consider additional simulation runs with replenishment levels of $Q = 115$ and $Q = 125$ to search for a superior inventory policy. We also have no guarantee that the replenishment level with the highest profit would be the same for another set of 300 randomly generated demand values. However, with a large number of simulation trials, we should find a near-optimal solution.

16.4 Waiting Line Simulation

The simulation models discussed thus far have been based on independent trials (i.e., trials in which the results for one trial do not affect what happens in subsequent trials). In this sense, the system being modeled does not change or evolve over time. Simulation models such as these are referred to as **static simulation models**. In this section, we develop a simulation model of a waiting line system where the state of the system, including the number of customers in the waiting line and whether the service facility is busy or idle, changes or evolves over time. To incorporate time into the simulation model, we use a simulation clock to record the time that each customer arrives for service as well as the time that each customer completes service. Simulation models that must take into account how the system changes or evolves over time are referred to as **dynamic simulation models**. In a situation in which the simulation experiment is managed as a discrete sequence of events (e.g., arrivals and departures of customers) over time, the simulation models is also referred to as a **discrete-event simulation**.

One common application of discrete-event simulation is the analysis of waiting lines. In a waiting line simulation, the random variables are the interarrival times of the customers and the service times of the servers, which together determine the waiting time and completion time of the customers. In Chapter 15 we presented formulas that could be used to compute the steady-state operating characteristics of a waiting line, including the average waiting time, the average number of units in the waiting line, the probability of waiting, and so on. In most cases, the waiting line formulas were based on specific assumptions about the probability distribution for arrivals, the probability distribution for service times, the queue discipline, and so on. Simulation, as an alternative for studying waiting lines, is more flexible. In applications where the assumptions required by the waiting line formulas are not reasonable, simulation may be the only feasible approach to studying the waiting line system. In this section, we discuss the simulation of the waiting line at the quality inspection department for Black Sheep Scarves.

Black Sheep Scarves

Black Sheep Scarves will open several new production facilities during the coming year. Each new production facility is designed to have one quality inspector who checks the knitting of the wool scarves before they are shipped to retailers. The arrival of hand-knit wool scarves to the quality inspection department is variable over the 24-hour work day. A concern is that during busy periods, the shipment of scarves to retailers may be delayed as they wait to be inspected. This concern prompted Black Sheep Scarves to undertake a study of the flow of scarves into the quality inspection department as a waiting line. Black Sheep Scarves's vice president wants to determine whether one quality inspector per facility will be sufficient. Black Sheep Scarves established service guidelines stating that the average delay waiting for quality inspection should be no more than one minute. Let us show how a simulation model can be used to study the quality inspection for a particular production facility. Note that each scarf can be viewed as a customer in this example, since scarves are the flow unit passing through the system.

Customer (Scarf) Arrival Times

A uniform probability distribution of interarrival times is used here to illustrate the simulation computations. Actually, any interarrival time probability distribution can be assumed, and the fundamental logic of the waiting line simulation model will not change.

One random variable in the Black Sheep Scarves simulation model is the arrival times of scarves to the quality inspection department. In waiting line simulations, arrival times are determined by randomly generating the time between successive arrivals, referred to as the *interarrival time*. For the quality inspection department being studied, the scarf interarrival times are assumed to be uniformly distributed between 0 and 5 minutes, as shown in Figure 16.12. As shown by equation (16.3) in Section 16.2, values from a uniform probability distribution with a lower bound of 0 and upper bound of 5 can be generated using the Excel function =RAND()*5.

Assume that the simulation run begins at time = 0. A random number of 0.2804 generates an interarrival time of 5(0.2804) = 1.4 minutes for scarf 1. Thus, scarf 1 arrives

FIGURE 16.12   UNIFORM PROBABILITY DISTRIBUTION OF INTERARRIVAL TIMES FOR THE BLACK SHEEP SCARVES PROBLEM

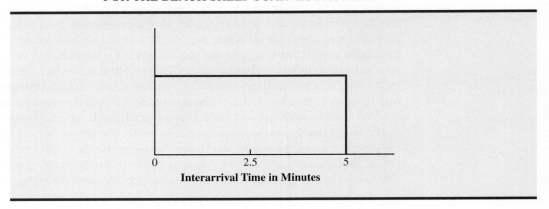

FIGURE 16.13 NORMAL PROBABILITY DISTRIBUTION OF SERVICE TIMES
FOR THE BLACK SHEEP SCARVES PROBLEM

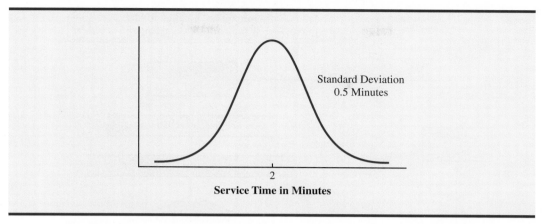

Standard Deviation
0.5 Minutes

2

Service Time in Minutes

1.4 minutes after the simulation run begins. A second random number of 0.2598 generates an interarrival time of 5(0.2598) = 1.3 minutes, indicating that scarf 2 arrives 1.3 minutes after scarf 1. Thus, scarf 2 arrives 1.4 + 1.3 = 2.7 minutes after the simulation begins. Continuing, a third random number of 0.9802 indicates that scarf 3 arrives 4.9 minutes after scarf 2, which is 7.6 minutes after the simulation begins.

Customer (Scarf) Service (Inspection) Times

Another random variable in the Black Sheep Scarves simulation model is service time, which is the time it takes a quality inspector to check a scarf. Past data from similar quality inspection departments indicate that a normal probability distribution with a mean of 2 minutes and a standard deviation of 0.5 minutes, as shown in Figure 16.13, can be used to describe service (inspection) times. As shown by equation (16.5) in Section 16.2, values from a normal probability distribution with mean 2 and standard deviation 0.5 can be generated using the Excel function =NORMINV(RAND(),2,0.5). For example, the random number of 0.7257 generates a scarf service time of 2.3 minutes.

Simulation Model

The random variables for the Black Sheep Scarves simulation model are the interarrival time and the service time. The controllable input is the number of quality inspectors. The output will consist of various operating characteristics such as the probability of waiting, the average waiting time, the maximum waiting time, and so on. Figure 16.14 shows a flow-chart that defines the sequence of logical and mathematical operations required to simulate the Black Sheep Scarves system. The flowchart uses the following notation:

$$IAT = \text{Interarrival time generated}$$
$$\text{Arrival time } (i) = \text{Time at which scarf } i \text{ arrives}$$
$$\text{Start time } (i) = \text{Time at which scarf } i \text{ starts service}$$
$$\text{Wait time } (i) = \text{Waiting time for scarf } i$$
$$ST = \text{Service time generated}$$
$$\text{Completion time } (i) = \text{Time at which scarf } i \text{ completes service}$$
$$\text{System time } (i) = \text{System time for scarf } i \text{ (completion time } - \text{ arrival time)}$$

FIGURE 16.14 FLOWCHART OF THE BLACK SHEEP SCARVES SIMULATION

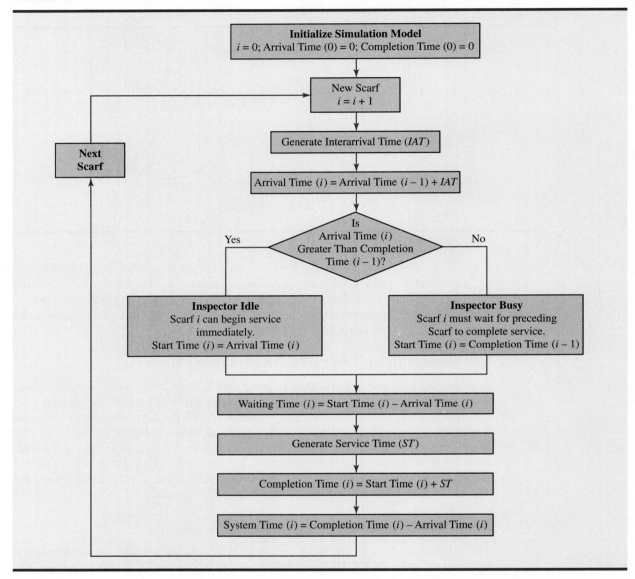

The decision rule for deciding whether the server (the quality inspector in the Black Sheep Scarves example) is idle or busy is the most difficult aspect of the logic in a waiting line simulation model.

Referring to Figure 16.14, we see that the simulation is initialized in the first block of the flowchart. A new scarf is then created. An interarrival time is generated to determine the time that has passed since the preceding scarf arrived.[4] The arrival time for the new scarf is then computed by adding the interarrival time to the arrival time of the preceding scarf.

The arrival time for the new scarf must be compared to the completion time of the preceding scarf to determine whether the quality inspector is idle or busy. If the arrival time of the new scarf is greater than the completion time of the preceding scarf, the preceding scarf will have finished service (been inspected) prior to the arrival of the new scarf. In this

---

[4]For the first scarf, the interarrival time determines how much time since the beginning of the simulation ($t = 0$) that the first scarf arrives.

case, the quality inspector will be idle, and the new scarf can begin service immediately. In such cases the service start time for the new scarf is equal to the arrival time of the new scarf. However, if the arrival time for the new scarf is not greater than the completion time of the preceding scarf, the new scarf arrived before the preceding scarf finished service. In this case, the quality inspector is busy, and inspection of the new scarf cannot begin until the quality inspector completes the inspection of the preceding scarf. The service start time for the new scarf is equal to the completion time of the preceding scarf.

Note that the time the new scarf has to wait to use the quality inspector is the difference between the scarf's service start time and the scarf's arrival time. At this point, the scarf is ready to use the quality inspector, and the simulation run continues with the generation of the scarf's service time. The time at which the scarf begins service plus the service time generated determine the scarf's completion time, which then becomes the earliest start time for inspection of the next scarf that arrives. Finally, the total time the scarf spends in the system is the difference between the scarf's service completion time and the scarf's arrival time. At this point, the computations are complete for the current scarf, and the simulation continues with the next scarf. The simulation is continued until a specified number of scarves have been served by the quality inspector.

Simulation results for a set of 10 scarves are shown in Table 16.4. We discuss the computations for the first three scarves to illustrate the logic of the simulation model and to show how the information in Table 16.4 was developed.

Scarf 1

- An interarrival time of $IAT = 1.4$ minutes is generated.
- Because the simulation run begins at time 0, the arrival time for scarf 1 is $0 + 1.4 = 1.4$ minutes.
- Scarf 1 may begin service immediately with a start time of 1.4 minutes.
- The waiting time for scarf 1 is the start time minus the arrival time: $1.4 - 1.4 = 0$ minutes.
- A service time of $ST = 2.3$ minutes is generated for scarf 1.
- The completion time for scarf 1 is the start time plus the service time: $1.4 + 2.3 = 3.7$ minutes.
- The time in the system for scarf 1 is the completion time minus the arrival time: $3.7 - 1.4 = 2.3$ minutes.

TABLE 16.4   SIMULATION RESULTS FOR 10 SCARVES

Scarf	Interarrival Time	Arrival Time	Service Start Time	Waiting Time	Service Time	Completion Time	Time in System
1	1.4	1.4	1.4	0.0	2.3	3.7	2.3
2	1.3	2.7	3.7	1.0	1.5	5.2	2.5
3	4.9	7.6	7.6	0.0	2.2	9.8	2.2
4	3.5	11.1	11.1	0.0	2.5	13.6	2.5
5	0.7	11.8	13.6	1.8	1.8	15.4	3.6
6	2.8	14.6	15.4	0.8	2.4	17.8	3.2
7	2.1	16.7	17.8	1.1	2.1	19.9	3.2
8	0.6	17.3	19.9	2.6	1.8	21.7	4.4
9	2.5	19.8	21.7	1.9	2.0	23.7	3.9
10	1.9	21.7	23.7	2.0	2.3	26.0	4.3
Totals	21.7			11.2	20.9		32.1
Averages	2.17			1.12	2.09		3.21

Scarf 2

- An interarrival time of $IAT = 1.3$ minutes is generated.
- Because the arrival time of scarf 1 is 1.4, the arrival time for scarf 2 is $1.4 + 1.3 = 2.7$ minutes.
- Because the completion time of scarf 1 is 3.7 minutes, the arrival time of scarf 2 is not greater than the completion time of scarf 1; thus, the quality inspector is busy when scarf 2 arrives.
- Scarf 2 must wait for scarf 1 to complete service before beginning service. Scarf 1 completes service at 3.7 minutes, which becomes the start time for scarf 2.
- The waiting time for scarf 2 is the start time minus the arrival time: $3.7 - 2.7 = 1$ minute.
- A service time of $ST = 1.5$ minutes is generated for scarf 2.
- The completion time for scarf 2 is the start time plus the service time: $3.7 + 1.5 = 5.2$ minutes.
- The time in the system for scarf 2 is the completion time minus the arrival time: $5.2 - 2.7 = 2.5$ minutes.

Scarf 3

- An interarrival time of $IAT = 4.9$ minutes is generated.
- Because the arrival time of scarf 2 was 2.7 minutes, the arrival time for scarf 3 is $2.7 + 4.9 = 7.6$ minutes.
- The completion time of scarf 2 is 5.2 minutes, so the arrival time for scarf 3 is greater than the completion time of scarf 2. Thus, the quality inspector is idle when scarf 3 arrives.
- Scarf 3 begins service immediately with a start time of 7.6 minutes.
- The waiting time for scarf 3 is the start time minus the arrival time: $7.6 - 7.6 = 0$ minutes.
- A service time of $ST = 2.2$ minutes is generated for scarf 3.
- The completion time for scarf 3 is the start time plus the service time: $7.6 + 2.2 = 9.8$ minutes.
- The time in the system for scarf 3 is the completion time minus the arrival time: $9.8 - 7.6 = 2.2$ minutes.

Using the totals in Table 16.4, we can compute an average waiting time for the 10 scarves of $11.2/10 = 1.12$ minutes, and an average time in the system of $32.1/10 = 3.21$ minutes. Table 16.4 shows that 7 of the 10 scarves had to wait. The total time for the 10-scarf simulation is given by the completion time of the 10th scarf: 26.0 minutes. However, at this point, we realize that a simulation for 10 scarves is much too short a period to draw any firm conclusions about the operation of the waiting line.

Simulation of Black Sheep Scarves

Using an Excel worksheet, we simulated the operation of the waiting line for the Black Sheep Scarves's quality inspection of 1000 scarves. The worksheet used to carry out the simulation is shown in Figure 16.15. Note that the simulation results for scarves 3 through 998 have been hidden so that the results can be shown in a reasonably sized figure. If desired, the rows for these scarves can be shown and the simulation results displayed for all 1000 scarves.

Before discussing the summary statistics, let us point out that many simulation studies of dynamic systems focus on the operation of the system during its long-run or steady-state operation. To ensure that the effects of start-up conditions are not included in the steady-state

FIGURE 16.15 OUTPUT FOR BLACK SHEEP SCARVES WITH ONE QUALITY INSPECTOR

	A	B	C	D	E	F	G	H
1	Black sheep Scarves with One Quality Inspector							
2								
3	Parameters							
4	Interarrival Times (Uniform Distribution)							
5	Smallest Value	0.0						
6	Largest Value	5.0						
7								
8	Service Times (Normal Distribution)							
9	Mean	2.0						
10	Standard Dev	0.5						
11								
12	Model							
13	Customer	Interarrival Time	Arrival Time	Service Start Time	Waiting Time	Service Time	Completion Time	Time in System
14	1	2.6	2.6	2.6	0.0	1.8	4.4	1.8
15	2	0.6	3.1	4.4	1.3	1.7	6.1	3.0
16	3	4.1	7.3	7.3	0.0	0.9	8.2	0.9
1012	999	2.9	2565.7	2565.9	0.3	1.9	2567.8	2.1
1013	1000	4.5	2570.1	2570.1	0.0	1.9	2572.0	1.9
1014								
1015	Summary Statistic			Wait Time Range	Bin	Frequency		
1016	Number Waiting	531		0–1	1	521.0		
1017	Number of Customers	900		1–2	2	164.0		
1018	Probability of Waiting	0.5900		2–3	3	89.0		
1019	Average Waiting Time	1.21		3–4	4	65.0		
1020	Maximum Waiting Time	8.6		4–5	5	29.0		
1021	Utilization of Quality Inspector	0.7829		5–6	6	15.0		
1022	Number Waiting > 1 Min	379		6–7	7	12.0		
1023	Probability Waiting > 1 Min	0.4211		7–8	8	3.0		
1024				8–9	9	2.0		
1025				9–10	10	0.0		

WEB file

**BlackSheep1
Inspector**

calculations, a dynamic simulation model is usually run for a specified period without collecting any data about the operation of the system. The length of the start-up period can vary depending on the application but can be determined by experimenting with the simulation model. Because the Black Sheep Scarves production facility operates 24 hours per day, we will avoid the transient effects by treating the results for the first 100 scarves as the startup period. Thus, the summary statistics shown in Figure 16.15 are for the 900 scarves arriving during the steady-state period.

The summary statistics show that 531 of the 900 scarves had to wait. This result provides a 531/900 = 0.59 probability that a scarf will have to wait for service. In other words, approximately 59% of the scarves will have to wait some amount of time because the quality inspector is in use when they arrive. The average waiting time is 1.21 minutes per scarf, with at least one scarf waiting the maximum time of 8.6 minutes. The utilization rate of 0.7829 indicates that the quality inspector is in use approximately 78% of the time. Finally, 379 of the 900 scarves had to wait more than 1 minute (approximately 42% of all scarves). From the wait time distribution, we observe 17 scarves (about 2% of all scarves) had a wait time greater than 6 minutes. Note that if we had used all 1000 simulated arrivals, these estimates could have been substantially different because the scarves that arrived early in the simulation had to wait less often and for less time.

The simulation supports the conclusion that the production facility will have a busy quality inspection department. With an average scarf wait time of 1.21 minutes, the system does not satisfy Black Sheep's service guideline of an average scarf wait time of less than one minute. This production facility is a good candidate for a second quality inspector or a more efficient inspection process.

Simulation with Two Quality Inspectors

In this section, we extend the logic of the Black Sheep simulation model to account for two quality inspectors. For the second quality inspector we also assume that the service time is normally distributed with a mean of 2 minutes and a standard deviation of 0.5 minutes. Table 16.5 shows the simulation results for the first 10 scarves. In comparing the two quality inspector system results in Table 16.5 with the single quality inspector simulation results shown in Table 16.4, we see that two additional columns are needed. These two columns show when each quality inspector becomes available for scarf service. We assume that, when a new scarf arrives, the scarf will be served by the quality inspector who is available first. When the simulation begins, the first scarf is arbitrarily assigned to quality inspector 1.

Table 16.5 shows that scarf 7 is the first scarf that has to wait to use a quality inspector. We describe how scarves 6, 7, and 8 are processed to show how the logic of the simulation run for two quality inspectors differs from that with a single quality inspector.

Scarf 6

- An interarrival time of 1.3 minutes is generated, and scarf 6 arrives 9.1 + 1.3 = 10.4 minutes into the simulation.
- From the scarf 5 row, we see that quality inspector 1 frees up at 5.8 minutes, and quality inspector 2 will free up at 11.3 minutes into the simulation. Because quality inspector 1 is free, scarf 6 does not wait and begins service on quality inspector 1 at the arrival time of 10.4 minutes.
- A service time of 1.6 minutes is generated for scarf 6. So scarf 6 has a completion time of 10.4 + 1.6 = 12.0 minutes.
- The time quality inspector 1 will next become available is set at 12.0 minutes; the time available for quality inspector 2 remains 11.3 minutes.

TABLE 16.5   SIMULATION RESULTS FOR 10 SCARVES FOR A TWO-QUALITY INSPECTOR SYSTEM

Scarf	Interarrival Time	Arrival Time	Service Start Time	Waiting Time	Service Time	Completion Time	Time in System	Time QI 1	Available QI 2
1	1.7	1.7	1.7	0.0	2.1	3.8	2.1	3.8	0.0
2	0.7	2.4	2.4	0.0	2.0	4.4	2.0	3.8	4.4
3	2.0	4.4	4.4	0.0	1.4	5.8	1.4	5.8	4.4
4	0.1	4.5	4.5	0.0	0.9	5.4	0.9	5.8	5.4
5	4.6	9.1	9.1	0.0	2.2	11.3	2.2	5.8	11.3
6	1.3	10.4	10.4	0.0	1.6	12.0	1.6	12.0	11.3
7	0.6	11.0	11.3	0.3	1.7	13.0	2.0	12.0	13.0
8	0.3	11.3	12.0	0.7	2.2	14.2	2.9	14.2	13.0
9	3.4	14.7	14.7	0.0	2.9	17.6	2.9	14.2	17.6
10	0.1	14.8	14.8	0.0	2.8	17.6	2.8	17.6	17.6
Totals	14.8			1.0	19.8		20.8		
Averages	1.48			0.1	1.98		2.08		

Scarf 7

- An interarrival time of 0.6 minute is generated, and scarf 7 arrives $10.4 + 0.6 = 11.0$ minutes into the simulation.
- From the previous row, we see that quality inspector 1 will not be available until 12.0 minutes, and quality inspector 2 will not be available until 11.3 minutes. So scarf 7 must wait to use a quality inspector. Because quality inspector 2 will free up first, scarf 7 begins service on that machine at a start time of 11.3 minutes. With an arrival time of 11.0 and a service start time of 11.3, scarf 7 experiences a waiting time of $11.3 - 11.0 = 0.3$ minute.
- A service time of 1.7 minutes is generated, leading to a completion time of $11.3 + 1.7 = 13.0$ minutes.
- The time available for quality inspector 2 is updated to 13.0 minutes, and the time available for quality inspector 1 remains at 12.0 minutes.

Scarf 8

- An interarrival time of 0.3 minute is generated, and scarf 8 arrives $11.0 + 0.3 = 11.3$ minutes into the simulation.
- From the previous row, we see that quality inspector 1 will be the first available. Thus, scarf 8 starts service on quality inspector 1 at 12.0 minutes, resulting in a waiting time of $12.0 - 11.3 = 0.7$ minute.
- A service time of 2.2 minutes is generated, resulting in a completion time of $12.0 + 2.2 = 14.2$ minutes and a system time of $0.7 + 2.2 = 2.9$ minutes.
- The time available for quality inspector 1 is updated to 14.2 minutes, and the time available for quality inspector 2 remains at 13.0 minutes.

From the totals in Table 16.5, we see that the average waiting time for these 10 scarves is only $1.0/10 = 0.1$ minute. Of course, a much longer simulation will be necessary before any reliable conclusions can be drawn.

Simulation Results with Two Quality Inspectors

The Excel worksheet that we used to conduct a simulation for 1000 scarves using two quality inspectors is shown in Figure 16.16. Results for the first 100 scarves were discarded to account for the startup period. With two quality inspectors, the number of scarves that had to wait was reduced from 531 to 87. This reduction results in a $87/900 = 0.0967$ probability that a scarf will have to wait for service when two quality inspectors are used. The two-quality inspector system also reduced the average waiting time to 0.07 minute (4.2 seconds) per scarf. The maximum waiting time was reduced from 8.6 to 2.8 minutes, and the quality inspectors were in use 39.61% of the time. Finally, only 24 of the 900 scarves had to wait more than 1 minute for a quality inspector to become available. Thus, only 2.67% of scarves had to wait more than 1 minute. The simulation results demonstrate the performance benefits of adding a second quality inspector, and in combination with cost information of this second quality inspector, Black Sheep Scarves can evaluate the decision to expand to two quality inspectors.

WEB file

BlackSheep2 Inspectors

The simulation models that we developed can now be used to study the quality inspection at other production facilities. In each case, assumptions must be made about the appropriate interarrival time and service time probability distributions. However, once appropriate assumptions have been made, the same simulation models can be used to determine the operating characteristics of the quality inspector waiting line system.

FIGURE 16.16   OUTPUT FOR BLACK SHEEP SCARVES WITH TWO QUALITY INSPECTORS

	A	B	C	D	E	F	G	H	I	J
1	Black Sheep Scarves with Two Quality Inspectors									
2										
3	Parameters									
4	Interarrival Times (Uniform Distribution									
5	Smallest value	0.0								
6	Largest Value	5.0								
7										
8	Service Times (Normal Diribution)									
9	Mean	2.0								
10	Standerd Dev	0.5								
11										
12	Model									
13	Customer	Interarrival Time	Arrival Time	Service Start Time	Waiting Time	Service Time	Completion Time	Time in System	Inspector 1 Available	Inspector 2 Available
14	1	4.4	4.4	4.4	0.0	1.6	6.0	1.6	6.0	0.0
15	2	0.8	5.2	5.2	0.0	2.0	7.2	2.0	6.0	7.2
16	3	2.1	7.3	7.3	0.0	1.8	9.1	1.8	9.1	7.2
1012	999	2.6	2507.0	2507.0	0.0	2.3	2509.3	2.3	2507.3	2509.3
1013	1000	3.0	2510.0	2510.0	0.0	3.0	2513.0	3.0	2513.0	2509.3
1014										
1015	Summary Statistics			Wait Time Range	Bin	Frequency				
1016	Number Waiting	87		0–1	1	876.0				
1017	Number of Customers	900		1–2	2	18.0				
1018	Probability of Waiting	0.0967		2–3	3	6.0				
1019	Average Waiting Time	0.07		3–4	4	0.0				
1020	Maximum Waiting Time	2.8		4–5	5	0.0				
1021	Utilization of Quality Inspectors	0.3961		5–6	6	0.0				
1022	Number Waiting > 1 Min	24		6–7	7	0.0				
1023	Probability of Waiting > 1 Min	0.0267		7–8	8	0.0				
1024				8–9	9	0.0				
1025				9–10	10	0.0				
1026				10–11	11	0.0				
1027				11–12	12	0.0				

The chart area (columns D–J, rows 2–11) shows a frequency plot with y-axis labeled "Frequency" ranging 0 to 1000 (in increments of 100), x-axis labeled "Wait Time (minutes)" with categories 0–1, 1–2, 2–3, 3–4, 4–5, 5–6, 6–7, 7–8, 8–9, 9–10, 10–11, 11–12, 12–13, 13–14, 14–15, 15–16, 16–17, 17–18, 18–19, 19–20, >20.

NOTES AND COMMENTS

1. The Black Sheep Scarves waiting line model was based on uniformly distributed interarrival times and normally distributed service times. One advantage of simulation is its flexibility in accommodating a variety of different probability distributions. For instance, if we believe an exponential distribution is more appropriate for interarrival times, this waiting line simulation could easily be repeated by simply changing the way the interarrival times are generated.

2. At the beginning of this section, we defined discrete-event simulation as involving a dynamic system that evolves over time. The simulation computations focus on the sequence of events as they occur at discrete points in time. In the Black Sheep Scarves waiting line example, scarf arrivals and the scarf service completions were the discrete events. Referring to the arrival times and completion times in the following table, we see that the first five discrete events for this waiting line simulation were as follows:

Event	Time
Scarf 1 arrives	1.4
Scarf 2 arrives	2.7
Scarf 1 finished	3.7
Scarf 2 finished	5.2
Scarf 3 arrives	7.6

3. We did not keep track of the number of scarves in the quality inspection waiting line as we carried out the quality inspection simulation computations on a scarf-by-scarf basis. However, we can determine the average number of scarves in the waiting line from other information in the simulation output. The following relationship is valid for any waiting line system:

$$\frac{\text{Average number}}{\text{in waiting line}} = \frac{\text{Total waiting time}}{\text{Total time of simulation}}$$

For the system with one quality inspector, suppose the 100th scarf completed service at 247.8 minutes into the simulation. Thus, the total time of the simulation for the next 900 scarves was 2572.0 − 247.8 = 2324.2 minutes. The average waiting time was 1.21 minutes. During the simulation, the 900 scarves had a total waiting time of 900(1.21) = 1089 minutes. Therefore, the average number of scarves in the waiting line is

$$
\begin{aligned}
\text{Average number} \\
\text{in waiting line} \quad &= 1089/2324.2 \\
&= 0.47 \text{ scarf}
\end{aligned}
$$

4. While it is possible to conduct small discrete-event simulations with native Excel functionality or with a Monte Carlo simulation package such as Analytic Solver Platform, discrete-event simulation modeling is best conducted with special-purpose software such as Arena®, ProModel®, and GPSS®. These packages have built-in simulation clocks, simplified methods for generating random variables, and procedures for collecting and summarizing the simulation output.

 # Simulation Considerations

Verification and Validation

An important step in any simulation study is confirmation that the simulation model accurately describes the real system. Inaccurate simulation models cannot be expected to provide worthwhile information. Thus, before using simulation results to draw conclusions about a real system, one must take steps to verify and validate the simulation model.

Verification is the process of determining that the computer procedure performing the simulation calculations is logically correct. Verification is largely a debugging task to ensure that there are no errors in the computer procedure that implements the simulation. In some cases, an analyst may compare computer results for a limited number of events with independent hand calculations. In other cases, tests may be performed to verify that the random variables are being generated correctly and that the output from the simulation model appears to be reasonable. The verification step is not complete until the user develops a high degree of confidence that the computer procedure is error free.

Validation is the process of ensuring that the simulation model provides an accurate representation of a real system. Validation requires an agreement among analysts and managers that the logic and the assumptions used in the design of the simulation model accurately reflect how the real system operates. The first phase of the validation process is done prior to, or in conjunction with, the development of the computer procedure for the simulation process. Validation continues after the computer program has been developed, with the analyst reviewing the simulation output to see whether the simulation results closely approximate the performance of the real system. If possible, the output of the simulation model is compared to the output of the existing real system to make sure that the simulation output closely approximates the performance of the real system. If this form of validation is not possible, an analyst can experiment with the simulation model, and one or more individuals experienced with the operation of the real system can review the simulation output to determine whether it is a reasonable approximation of what would be obtained with the real system under similar conditions.

Verification and validation are not tasks to be taken lightly. They are key steps in any simulation study and are necessary to ensure that decisions and conclusions based on the simulation results are appropriate for the real system.

Advantages and Disadvantages of Using Simulation

The primary advantages of simulation are that it is easy to understand and that the methodology can be used to model and learn about the behavior of complex systems that would be difficult, if not impossible, to deal with analytically. Simulation models are flexible; they can be used to describe systems without requiring the assumptions that are often required by mathematical models. In general, the larger the number of random variables a system has, the more likely that a simulation model will provide the most suitable approach for studying the system. Another advantage of simulation is that a simulation model provides a convenient experimental laboratory for the real system. Changing assumptions or operating policies in the simulation model and rerunning it can provide results that help us understand how such changes will affect the operation of the real system. Experimenting directly with a real system is often expensive or not feasible. Simulation models often warn against poor decision strategies by projecting disastrous outcomes such as system failures, large financial losses, and so on.

Simulation is not without disadvantages. For complex systems, the process of developing, verifying, and validating a simulation model can be time-consuming and expensive (however, the process of developing the model generally leads to a better understanding of the system, which is an important benefit). As with all mathematical models, the analyst must be mindful of the assumptions of the model in order to understand its limitations. In addition, each simulation run provides only a sample of how the real system will operate. As such, the summary of the simulation data provides only estimates or approximations about the real system. Nonetheless, the danger of obtaining poor solutions is greatly mitigated if the analyst exercises good judgment in developing the simulation model, follows proper verification and validation steps, and if the simulation process is run long enough under a wide variety of conditions so that the analyst has sufficient data to predict how the real system will operate.

Summary

Simulation is a method for learning about a real system by experimenting with a model that represents the system. Some of the reasons simulation is frequently used are

1. It can be used for a wide variety of practical problems.
2. The simulation approach is relatively easy to explain and understand. As a result, management confidence is increased, and acceptance of the results is more easily obtained.
3. Spreadsheet packages now provide another alternative for model implementation, and third-party vendors have developed add-ins that expand the capabilities of the spreadsheet packages.
4. Computer software developers have produced simulation packages that make it easier to develop and implement simulation models for more complex problems.

In this chapter, we first analyzed uncertainty by considering the base-case, best-case, and worst-case scenarios. Then, we showed how native Excel functions can be used to execute a simulation to evaluate risk involving the development of a new product, the Sanotronics device. Next we used the Butler Inventory problem to demonstrate another example of simulation modeling. Finally, we illustrated how to use Excel to create a discrete-event simulation for the Black Sheep problem. These examples represent a wide range of problems that can be addressed with simulation modeling.

Our approach throughout this chapter was to develop simulation models that contained both controllable inputs and random variables. Procedures were developed for randomly generating values for the random variables, the sequence of logical and mathematical operations that describe the steps of the simulation process were modeled, and simulation results were obtained by running the simulation for a suitable number of trials. Simulation results were obtained and conclusions were drawn about the operation of the real system.

Summary of Steps for Conducting a Simulation Analysis

1. **Construct a spreadsheet model that computes output measures for given values of inputs.** The foundation of a good simulation model is logic that correctly relates input values to outputs. Audit the spreadsheet to assure that the cell formulas correctly evaluate the outputs over the entire range of possible input values.

2. **Identify inputs that are uncertain and specify probability distributions for these cells** (rather than just static numbers). Note that not all inputs may have a large enough degree of uncertainty to require modeling with a probability distribution. Other inputs may actually be decision variables, which are values that the decision-maker can control and so are not random quantities to model with probability distributions.

3. **Select one or more outputs to record over the simulation trials.** Typical information recorded for an output include a histogram of output values and summary statistics such as the mean, standard deviation, maximum, minimum, percentile values, etc.

4. **Execute the simulation for a specified number of trials**. For most small- to moderate-sized simulation problems, we recommend the use of 10,000 trials. The amount of sampling error can be monitored by observing the degree by which simulation output measures fluctuate across multiple simulation runs.

5. **Analyze the outputs and interpret the implications on the decision-making process.** In addition to estimates of the mean output, simulation allows us to construct a distribution of possible output values.

Recall that for dynamic simulation models (discussed in Section 16.3), outputs are recorded for simulation trials occurring after an initial start-up period.

Glossary

Base-case scenario Determining output assuming the most likely values for the random variables of a model.

Best-case scenario Determining the output assuming the best values that can be expected for the random variables of a model.

Continuous probability distribution A probability distribution where the possible values for a random variable can take any value between two specified values. The specified values can include negative and positive infinity.

Controllable input Input to a simulation model that is selected by the decision maker.

Discrete-event simulation model A simulation model that describes how a system evolves over time by managing a discrete sequence of events (i.e., customer arrival or departure, over time).

Discrete probability distribution A probability distribution where the possible values for a random variable can take on only specified discrete values.

Dynamic simulation model A simulation model used in situations where the state of the system affects how the system changes or evolves over time.

Parameters Numerical values that appear in the mathematical relationships of a model.

Probability distribution A description of the range and relative likelihood of possible values of an uncertain variable.

Random variable or uncertain variable Input to a simulation model whose value is uncertain and described by a probability distribution.

Risk analysis The process of evaluating a decision in the face of uncertainty by quantifying the likelihood and magnitude of an undesirable outcome.

Simulation A method that uses repeated random sampling of values to represent uncertainty in a model representing a real system and computes the values of model outputs.

Static simulation model A simulation model in which each trial used in situations where the state of the system at one point in time does not affect the state of the system at future points in time. Each trial of the simulation is independent.

Validation The process of determining that a simulation model provides an accurate representation of a real system.

Verification The process of determining that a computer program implements a simulation model as it is intended.

What-if analysis A trial-and-error approach to learning about the range of possible outputs for a model. Trial values are chosen for the model inputs (these are the what-ifs) and the value of the output(s) is computed.

Worst-case scenario Determining the output assuming the worst values that can be expected for the random variables of a model.

Problems

1. The management of Brinkley Corporation is interested in using simulation to estimate the profit per unit for a new product. The selling price for the product will be $45 per unit. Probability distributions for the purchase cost, the labor cost, and the transportation cost are estimated as follows:

Procurement Cost ($)	Probability	Labor Cost ($)	Probability	Transportation Cost ($)	Probability
10	0.25	20	0.10	3	0.75
11	0.45	22	0.25	5	0.25
12	0.30	24	0.35		
		25	0.30		

a. Compute profit per unit for the base-case, worst-case, and best-case scenarios.
b. Construct a simulation model to estimate the mean profit per unit.
c. Why is the simulation approach to risk analysis preferable to generating a variety of what-if scenarios?
d. Management believes the project may not be sustainable if the profit per unit is less than $5. Use simulation to estimate the probability the profit per unit will be less than $5.

2. The management of Madeira Computing is considering the introduction of a wearable electronic device with the functionality of a laptop computer and phone. The fixed cost to launch this new product is $300,000. The variable cost for the product is expected to be between $160 and $240, with a most likely value of $200 per unit. The product will sell for $300 per unit. Demand estimates for the produce vary widely, ranging from 0 to 20,000 units, with an average of 4000 units.
a. Compute profit for the base-case, worst-case, and best-case scenarios.
b. Assume the variable cost is a uniform random variable between $16 and $24 and the product demand is an exponential random variable with a mean of 4000 units. Construct a simulation model to estimate the mean profit and the probability that the project will result in a loss.

3. Grear Tire Company has produced a new tire with an estimated mean lifetime mileage of 36,500 miles. Management also believes that the standard deviation is 5000 miles and that tire mileage is normally distributed. To promote the new tire, Grear has offered to refund a portion of the purchase price if the tire fails to reach 30,000 miles before the tire needs to be replaced. Specifically, for tires with a lifetime below 30,000 miles, Grear will refund a customer $1 per 100 miles short of 30,000.
   a. For each tire sold, what is the expected cost of the promotion?
   b. What is the probability that Grear will refund more than $50 for a tire?
   c. What mileage should Grear set the promotion claim if it wants the expected cost to be $2?

4. Construct a spreadsheet simulation in which each trial consists of rolling of four dice. That is, there are four random variables each with an outcome of 1, 2, 3, 4, 5, or 6. For each trial, record the value of the first dice, the sum of the first two dice, the sum of the first three dice, and the sum of the first four dice. Using the FREQUENCY command, create a frequency distribution for each of these four computations on a separate plot. What phenonemon do you observe?

5. To generate leads for new business, Gustin Investment Services offers free financial planning seminars at major hotels in Southwest Florida. Gustin conducts seminars for groups of 25 individuals. Each seminar costs Gustin $3500, and the average first-year commission for each new account opened is $5000. Gustin estimates that for each individual attending the seminar, there is a 0.01 probability that he/she will open a new account.
   a. Determine the equation for computing Gustin's profit per seminar, given values of the relevant parameters.
   b. What type of random variable is the number of new accounts opened? Hint: Review Appendix 16.1 for descriptions of various types of probability distributions.
   c. Construct a spreadsheet simulation model to analyze the profitability of Gustin's seminars. Would you recommend that Gustin continue running the seminars?
   d. How large of an audience does Gustin need before a seminar's expected profit is greater than zero?

6. The Statewide Auto Insurance Company developed the following probability distribution for automobile collision claims paid during the past year.
   a. Set up a table of intervals of random numbers that can be used with a VLOOKUP to generate automobile collision claim payments.
   b. Construct a simulation model to estimate the mean and standard deviation of claims payments. How accurate are these estimates? Compare them to the analytical calculation of the mean, $\mu = x_1 \times P(x = x_1) + x_2 \times P(x = x_2) + \cdots x_n \times P(x = x_n)$, and standard deviation, $\sqrt{\sigma} = \overline{(x_1 - \mu)^2 \times P(x = x_1) + (x_2 - \mu)^2 \times P(x = x_2) + \cdots (x_n - \mu)^2 \times P(x = x_n)(x_n - \mu)^2 \times P(x = x_n)}$. How can we improve the accuracy of the simulation estimates?

Payment($)	Probability
0	0.83
500	0.06
1,000	0.05
2,000	0.02
5,000	0.02
8,000	0.01
10,000	0.01

7. Baseball's World Series is a maximum of seven games, with the winner being the first team to win four games. Assume that the Atlanta Braves and the Minnesota Twins are playing in the World Series and that the first two games are to be played in Atlanta, the

next three games at the Twins' ballpark, and the last two games, if necessary, back in Atlanta. Taking into account the projected starting pitchers for each game and the home field advantage, the probabilities of Atlanta winning each game are as follows:

Game	1	2	3	4	5	6	7
Probability of Win	0.60	0.55	0.48	0.45	0.48	0.55	0.50

a.   Set up a spreadsheet simulation model for which whether Atlanta wins or loses each game is a random variable.
b.   What is the probability that the Atlanta Braves win the World Series?
c.   What is the average number of games played regardless of winner?

8.   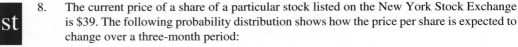 The current price of a share of a particular stock listed on the New York Stock Exchange is $39. The following probability distribution shows how the price per share is expected to change over a three-month period:

Stock Price Change ($)	Probability
−2	0.05
−1	0.10
0	0.25
+1	0.20
+2	0.20
+3	0.10
+4	0.10

a.   Construct a spreadsheet simulation model that computes the value of the stock price in 3 months, 6 months, 9 months, and 12 months under the assumption that the change in stock price over any 3-month period is independent of the change in stock price over any other 3-month period.
b.   With the current price of $39 per share, simulate the price per share for the next four 3-month periods. What is the average stock price per share in 12 months? What is the standard deviation of the stock price in 12 months?
c.   Based on the model assumptions, what are the lowest and highest possible prices for this stock in 12 months? Based on your knowledge of the stock market, how valid do you think these prices are? Propose an alternative to modeling how stock prices evolve over 3-month periods.

9.   The Iowa Energy of the National Basketball Association Developmental League (NBA-DL) are scheduled to play against the Maine Red Claws in an upcoming game. Because a player in the NBA-DL is still developing his skills, the number of points he scores in a game can vary dramatically. Assume that each player's point production can be represented as an integer uniform variable with the ranges provided in the table below.
a.   Develop a spreadsheet model that simulates the points scored by each team.
b.   What is the average and standard deviation of points scored by the Iowa Energy? What is the shape of the distribution of points scored by the Iowa Energy?
c.   What are the average and standard deviation of points scored by the Maine Red Claws? What is the shape of the distribution of points scored by the Maine Red Claws?
d.   Let Point Differential = Iowa Energy points − Maine Red Claw points. What is the average point differential between the Iowa Energy and Maine Red Claws? What is the standard deviation in the point differential? What is the shape of the point differential distribution?
e.   What is the probability of that the Iowa Energy scores more points than the Maine Red Claws?

f. The coach of the Iowa Energy feels that they are the underdog and is considering a "riskier" game strategy. The effect of the riskier game strategy is that the range of each Energy player's point production increases symmetrically so that the new range is [0, original upper bound + original lower bound]. For example, Energy player 1's range with the risky strategy is [0, 25]. How does the new strategy affect the average and standard deviation of the Energy point total? How is the probability of the Iowa Energy scoring more points that the Maine Red Claws affected?

Player	Iowa Energy	Maine Red Claws
1	[5, 20]	[7, 12]
2	[7, 20]	[15, 20]
3	[5, 10]	[10, 20]
4	[10, 40]	[15, 30]
5	[6, 20]	[5, 10]
6	[3, 10]	[1, 20]
7	[2, 5]	[1, 4]
8	[2, 4]	[2, 4]

10. A project has four activities (A, B, C, and D) that must be performed sequentially. The probability distributions for the time required to complete each of the activities are as follows:

Activity	Activity Time (weeks)	Probability
A	5	0.25
	6	0.35
	7	0.25
	8	0.15
B	3	0.20
	5	0.55
	7	0.25
C	10	0.10
	12	0.25
	14	0.40
	16	0.20
	18	0.05
D	8	0.60
	10	0.40

a. Construct a spreadsheet simulation model to estimate the average length of the project and the standard deviation of the project length.
b. What is the estimated probability that the project will be completed in 35 weeks or less?

11. In preparing for the upcoming holiday season, Fresh Toy Company (FTC) designed a new doll called The Dougie that teaches children how to dance. The fixed cost to produce the doll is $100,000. The variable cost, which includes material, labor, and shipping costs, is $34 per doll. During the holiday selling season, FTC will sell the dolls for $42 each. If FTC overproduces the dolls, the excess dolls will be sold in January through a distributor who has agreed to pay FTC $10 per doll. Demand for new toys during the holiday selling season is extremely uncertain. Forecasts are for expected sales of 60,000 dolls with a

standard deviation of 15,000. The normal probability distribution is assumed to be a good description of the demand. FTC has tentatively decided to produce 60,000 units (the same as average demand), but it wants to conduct an analysis regarding this production quantity before finalizing the decision.

a.   Create a what-if spreadsheet model using a formula that relate the values of production quantity, demand, sales, revenue from sales, amount of surplus, revenue from sales of surplus, total cost, and net profit. What is the profit corresponding to average demand (60,000 units)?

b.   Modeling demand as a normal random variable with a mean of 60,000 and a standard deviation of 15,000, simulate the sales of the Dougie doll using a production quantity of 60,000 units. What is the estimate of the average profit associated with the production quantity of 60,000 dolls? How does this compare to the profit corresponding to the average demand (as computed in part (a))?

c.   Before making a final decision on the production quantity, management wants an analysis of a more aggressive 70,000-unit production quantity and a more conservative 50,000-unit production quantity. Run your simulation with these two production quantities. What is the mean profit associated with each?

d.   In addition to mean profit, what other factors should FTC consider in determining a production quantity? Compare the three production quantities (50,000, 60,000, and 70,000) using all these factors. What trade-offs occur? What is your recommendation?

12.   South Central Airlines (SCA) operates a commuter flight between Atlanta and Charlotte. The regional jet holds 50 passengers, and currently SCA only books up to 50 reservations. Past data show that SCA always sells all 50 reservations, but on average, two passengers do not show up for the flight. As a result, with 50 reservations the flight is often being flown with empty seats. To capture additional profit, SCA is considering an overbooking strategy in which they would accept 52 reservations even though the airplane holds only 50 passengers. SCA believes that it will be able to always book all 52 reservations. The probability distribution for the number of passengers showing up when 52 reservations are accepted is estimated as follows:

Passengers Showing Up	Probability
48	0.05
49	0.25
50	0.50
51	0.15
52	0.05

SCA receives a marginal profit of $100 for each passenger who books a reservation (regardless whether they show up or not). The airline will also incur a cost for any passenger denied seating on the flight. This cost covers added expenses of rescheduling the passenger as well as loss of goodwill, estimated to be $150 per passenger. Develop a spreadsheet simulation model for this overbooking system and simulate the number of passengers that show up for a flight.

a.   What is the average net profit for each flight with the overbooking strategy?

b.   What is the probability that the net profit with the overbooking strategy will be less than the net profit without overbooking (50*$100 = $5000)?

c.   Explain how your simulation model could be used to evaluate other overbooking levels such as 51, 53, and 54 and for recommending a best overbooking strategy.

13.   The wedding date for a couple is quickly approaching, and the wedding planner must provide the caterer an estimate of how many people will attend the reception so that the appropriate quantity of food is prepared for the buffet. The following table contains

information on the number of RSVP guests for the 145 invitations. Unfortunately, the number of guests does not always correspond to the number of RSVPed guests.

Based on her experience, the wedding planner knows it is extremely rare for guests to attend a wedding if they notified that they will not be attending. Therefore, the wedding planner will assume that no one from these 50 invitations will attend. The wedding planner estimates that the each of the 25 guests planning to come solo has a 75% chance of attending alone, a 20% chance of not attending, and a 5% chance of bringing a companion. For each of the 60 RSVPs who plan to bring a companion, there is a 90% chance that she or he will attend with a companion, a 5% chance of attending solo, and a 5% chance of not attending at all. For the 10 people who have not responded, the wedding planner assumes that there is an 80% chance that each will not attend, a 15% chance each will attend alone, and a 5% chance each will attend with a companion.

RSVPed Guests	Number of Invitations
0	50
1	25
2	60
No response	10

a. Assist the wedding planner by constructing a spreadsheet simulation model to determine the expected number of guests who will attend the reception.

b. To be accommodating hosts, the couple has instructed the wedding planner to use the Monte Carlo simulation model to determine X, the minimum number of guests for which the caterer should prepare the meal, so that there is at least a 90% chance that the actual attendance is less than or equal to X. What is the best estimate for the value of X?

14. A building contractor is preparing a bid on a new construction project. Two other contractors will be submitting bids for the same project. Based on past bidding practices and the requirements of the project, the bid from Contractor A can be described with a uniform distribution between $600,000 and $800,000, while the bid from Contractor B can be described with a normal distribution with a mean of $700,000 and standard deviation of $50,000.

a. If the building contractor submits a bid of $750,000, what is the probability that the building contractor will obtain the bid?

b. The building contractor is also considering bids of $765,000 and $775,000. If the building contract would like to bid such that the probability of winning the bid is about 0.80, what bid would you recommend? Repeat the simulation with bids of $765,000 and $775,000 to justify your recommendation.

15. Strassel Investors buys real estate, develops it, and resells it for a profit. A new property is available, and Bud Strassel, the president and owner of Strassel Investors, believes if he purchases and develops this property it can then be sold for $160,000. The current property owner has asked for bids and stated that the property will be sold for the highest bid in excess of $100,000. Two competitors will be submitting bids for the property. Strassel does not know what the competitors will bid, but he assumes for planning purposes that the amount bid by each competitor will be uniformly distributed between $100,000 and $150,000.

a. Develop a worksheet that can be used to simulate the bids made by the two competitors. Strassel is considering a bid of $130,000 for the property. Using a simulation of 1000 trials, what is the estimate of the probability Strassel will be able to obtain the property using a bid of $130,000?

You will need to use native Excel functionality to solve Problems 13, 14, and 15 because the Educational version of ASP has a limit of 100 random variables.

b. How much does Strassel need to bid to be assured of obtaining the property? What is the profit associated with this bid?

c. Use the simulation model to compute the profit for each trial of the simulation run. With maximization of profit as Strassel's objective, use simulation to evaluate Strassel's bid alternatives of $130,000, $140,000, or $150,000. What is the recommended bid, and what is the expected profit?

BurgerDome

16. The Burger Dome is a fast-food restaurant that is currently appraising its customer service. In its current operation, an employee takes a customer's order, tabulates the cost, receives payment from the customer, and then fills the order. Once the customer's order is filled, the employee takes the order of the next customer waiting for service. Assume that time between each customer's arrival is an exponential random variable with a mean of 1.35 minutes. Assume also that the time for the employee to complete the customer's service is an exponential random variable with mean of 1 minute. Use the BurgerDome.xlsx template to complete a simulation model for the waiting line at Burger Dome for a 14-hour work day. Using the summary statistics gathered at the bottom of the spreadsheet model, answer the following questions.

a. What is the average wait time experienced by a customer?

b. What is the longest wait time experienced by a customer?

c. What is the probability that a customer waits more than 2 minutes?

d. Create a histogram depicting the wait time distribution.

e. By pressing the F9 key to generate a new set of simulation trials, one can observe the variability in the summary statistics from simulation to simulation. Typically, this variability can be reduced by increasing the number of trials. Why is this approach not appropriate for this problem?

17. One advantage of simulation is that a simulation model can be altered easily to reflect a change in the assumptions. Refer back to the Burger Dome analysis in Problem 16. Assume that the service time is more accurately described by a normal distribution with a mean of 1 minute and a standard deviation of 0.2 minutes. This distribution has less variability than the exponential distribution originally used. What is the impact of this change on the output measures?

BurgerDome TwoServers

18. Refer back to the Burger Dome analysis in Problem 16. Burger Dome wants to consider the effect of hiring a second employee to serve customers (in parallel with the first employee). Use the BurgerDomeTwoServers.xlsx template to complete a simulation model that accounts for the second employee. Hint: The time that a customer begins service will depend on the availability of employees. What is the impact of this change on the output measures?

19. Telephone calls come into an 24-hour airline call center (handling calls worldwide) randomly at the mean rate of 15 calls per hour. The time between calls follows an exponential distribution with a mean of 4 minutes. When the two reservation agents are busy, a telephone message tells the caller that the call is important and to please wait on the line until the next reservation agent becomes available. The service time for each reservation agent is normally distributed with a mean of 4 minutes and a standard deviation of 1 minute. Use a two-server waiting line simulation model to evaluate this waiting line system. Simulate the operation of the call center for 800 customers. Discard the first 100 customers, and collect data over the next 700 customers.

a. Compute the mean interarrival time and the mean service time. If your simulation model is operating correctly, both of these should have means of approximately 4 minutes.

b. What is the mean customer waiting time for this system?

c. Use the =COUNTIF function to determine the number of customers who have to wait for a reservation agent. What percentage of the customers have to wait?

20. Blackjack, or 21, is a popular casino game that begins with each player and the dealer being dealt two cards. The value of each hand is determined by the point total of the cards in the hand. Face cards and 10s count 10 points, aces can be counted as either 1 or 11 points, and all other cards count at their face value. For instance, the value of a hand consisting of a jack and an 8 is 18; the value of a hand consisting of an ace and a two is either 3 or 13, depending on whether player counts the ace as 1 or 11 points. The goal is to obtain a hand with a value as close as possible to 21 without exceeding 21. After the initial deal, each player and the dealer may draw additional cards (called "taking a hit") in order to improve her or his hand. If a player or the dealer takes a hit and the value of the hand exceeds 21, that person "goes broke" and loses. The dealer's advantage is that each player must decide whether to take a hit before the dealer decides whether to take a hit. If a player takes a hit and goes over 21, the player loses even if the dealer later takes a hit and goes over 21. For this reason, players will often decide not to take a hit when the value of their hand is 12 or greater.

The dealer's hand is dealt with one card up (face showing) and one card down (face hidden). The player then decides whether to take a hit based on knowledge of the dealer's up card.

a. A gambling professional determined that when the dealer's up card is a 6, the following probabilities describe the ending value of the dealer's hand:

Value of Hand	17	18	19	20	21	Broke
Probability	0.1654	0.1063	0.1063	0.1017	0.0972	0.4231

Set up intervals of random numbers that can be used to simulate the ending value of the dealer's hand when the dealer has a 6 as the up card.

b. Suppose you are playing blackjack and your hand has a value of 16 for the two cards initially dealt. If you decide to take a hit, the following cards will improve your hand: ace, 2, 3, 4, and 5. Any card with a point count greater than 5 will result in you going broke. Assume that if you have a hand with a value of 16 and decide to take a hit, the following probabilities describe the ending value of your hand:

Value of Hand	17	18	19	20	21	Broke
Probability	0.0769	0.0769	0.0769	0.0769	0.0769	0.6155

c. Set up intervals of random numbers that can be used to simulate the ending value of your hand after taking a hit with a value of 16.

d. Use the results of parts (a) and (b) to simulate the result of 20 blackjack hands when the dealer has a 6 up and the player chooses to take a hit with a hand that has a value of 16. What is the probability of the dealer winning, a push (a tie), and the player winning, respectively?

e. If the player has a hand with a value of 16 and doesn't take a hit, the only way the player can win is if the dealer goes broke. How many of the hands in part (b) result in the player winning without taking a hit? On the basis of this result and the results in part (d), would you recommend the player take a hit if the player has a hand with a value of 16 and the dealer has a 6 up?

Case Problem 1   Four Corners

What will your portfolio be worth in 10 years? In 20 years? When can you stop working? The Human Resources Department at Four Corners Corporation was asked to develop a financial planning model that would help employees address these questions. Tom Gifford was asked to lead this effort and decided to begin by developing a financial plan for himself. Tom is 40 years old, has a degree in business, and earns an annual salary of $85,000. Through contributions to his company's retirement program and the receipt of a small inheritance, Tom has accumulated a portfolio valued at $50,000. Tom plans to work 20 more years and hopes to accumulate a portfolio valued at $1,000,000. Can he do it?

Tom began with a few assumptions about his future salary, his new investment contributions, and his portfolio growth rate. He assumed a 5% annual salary growth rate and plans to make new investment contributions at 6% of his salary. After some research on historical stock market performance, Tom decided that a 10% annual portfolio growth rate was reasonable. Using these assumptions, Tom developed the Excel worksheet shown in the figure below. The worksheet provides a financial projection for the next five years. In computing the portfolio earnings for a given year, Tom assumed that his new investment contribution would occur evenly throughout the year, and thus half of the new investment could be included in the computation of the portfolio earnings for the year. From the figure below, we see that at age 45, Tom is projected to have a portfolio valued at $116,321.

Tom's plan was to use this worksheet as a template to develop financial plans for the company's employees. The data in the spreadsheet would be tailored for each employee, and rows would be added to the worksheet to reflect the employee's planning horizon. After adding another 15 rows to the worksheet, Tom found that he could expect to have a portfolio of $772,722 after 20 years. Tom then took his results to show his boss, Kate Krystkowiak.

Although Kate was pleased with Tom's progress, she voiced several criticisms. One of the criticisms was the assumption of a constant annual salary growth rate. She noted that most employees experience some variation in the annual salary growth rate from year to year. In addition, she pointed out that the constant annual portfolio growth rate was unrealistic and that the actual growth rate would vary considerably from year to year. She further suggested that a simulation model for the portfolio projection might allow Tom to account for the random variability in the salary growth rate and the portfolio growth rate.

After some research, Tom and Kate decided to assume that the annual salary growth rate would vary from 0% to 5% and that a uniform probability distribution would provide a realistic approximation. Four Corners's accountants suggested that the annual portfolio growth rate could be approximated by a normal probability distribution with a mean of 10% and a standard deviation of 5%. With this information, Tom set off to redesign his spreadsheet so that it could be used by the company's employees for financial planning.

WEB file

FourCorners

◢	A	B	C	D	E	F	G
1	Four Corners						
2							
3	Age	40					
4	Current Salary	$85,000					
5	Current Portfolio	$50,000					
6	Annual Investment Rate	6%					
7	Salary Growth Rate	5%					
8	Portfolio Growth Rate	10%					
9							
10	Year	Beginning Balance	Salary	New Investment	Earnings	Ending Balance	Age
11	1	$50,000	$85,000	$5,100	$5,255	$60,355	41
12	2	$60,355	$89,250	$5,355	$6,303	$72,013	42
13	3	$72,013	$93,713	$5,623	$7,482	$85,118	43
14	4	$85,118	$98,398	$5,904	$8,807	$99,829	44
15	5	$99,829	$103,318	$6,199	$10,293	$116,321	45
16							

Play the role of Tom Gifford and develop a simulation model for financial planning. Write a report for Tom's boss and, at a minimum, include the following:

For a review of Goal Seek, refer to Appendix A.

1. Without considering the random variability, extend the current worksheet to 20 years. Confirm that by using the constant annual salary growth rate and the constant annual portfolio growth rate, Tom can expect to have a 20-year portfolio of $772,722. What would Tom's annual investment rate have to increase to in order for his portfolio to reach a 20-year, $1,000,000 goal? Hint: Use Goal Seek.

2. Redesign the spreadsheet model to incorporate the random variability of the annual salary growth rate and the annual portfolio growth rate into a simulation model. Assume that Tom is willing to use the annual investment rate that predicted a 20-year, $1,000,000 portfolio in part 1. Show how to simulate Tom's 20-year financial plan. Use results from the simulation model to comment on the uncertainty associated with Tom reaching the 20-year, $1,000,000 goal.

3. What recommendations do you have for employees with a current profile similar to Tom's after seeing the impact of the uncertainty in the annual salary growth rate and the annual portfolio growth rate?

4. Assume that Tom is willing to consider working 25 more years instead of 20 years. What is your assessment of this strategy if Tom's goal is to have a portfolio worth $1,000,000?

5. Discuss how the financial planning model developed for Tom Gifford can be used as a template to develop a financial plan for any of the company's employees.

Case Problem 2   Harbor Dunes Golf Course

Harbor Dunes Golf Course was recently honored as one of the top public golf courses in South Carolina. The course, situated on land that was once a rice plantation, offers some of the best views of saltwater marshes available in the Carolinas. Harbor Dunes targets the upper end of the golf market, and in the peak spring golfing season it charges green fees of $160 per person and golf cart fees of $20 per person.

Harbor Dunes accepts reservations for tee times for groups of four players (foursomes) every nine minutes between 7:30 A.M. and 1:21 P.M. Two foursomes start at the same time: one on the front nine and one on the back nine of the course, with a new pair of foursomes teeing off every nine minutes. With the last tee time of the day set at 1:21 P.M. to ensure all players can complete 18 holes before dusk, Harbor Dunes can sell a maximum of 20 afternoon tee times.

Last year, Harbor Dunes was able to sell every morning tee time available for every day of the spring golf season. The same result is anticipated for the coming year. Afternoon tee times, however, are generally more difficult to sell. An analysis of the sales data for last year enabled Harbor Dunes to develop the probability distribution of sales for the afternoon tee times as shown in Table 16.6. For the season, Harbor Dunes averaged selling approximately 14 of the 20 available afternoon tee times. The average income from afternoon green fees and cart fees has been $10,240. However, the average of six unused tee times per day resulted in lost revenue.

In an effort to increase the sale of afternoon tee times, Harbor Dunes is considering an idea popular at other golf courses. These courses offer foursomes that play in the morning the option to play another round of golf in the afternoon by paying a reduced fee for the afternoon round. Harbor Dunes is considering two replay options: (1) a green fee of $25 per player plus a cart fee of $20 per player; (2) a green fee of $50 per player plus a

TABLE 16.6 PROBABILITY DISTRIBUTION OF SALES FOR THE AFTERNOON TEE TIMES

Number of Tee Times Sold	Probability
8	0.01
9	0.04
10	0.06
11	0.08
12	0.10
13	0.11
14	0.12
15	0.15
16	0.10
17	0.09
18	0.07
19	0.05
20	0.02

cart fee of $20 per player. For option 1, each foursome will generate additional revenues of $180; for option 2, each foursome will generate additional revenues of $280. The decision as to which option is best depends upon the number of groups that are induced to play a second round by each replay offer. Working with a consultant who has expertise in statistics and the golf industry, Harbor Dunes developed probability distributions for the number of foursomes requesting a replay for each of the two options. These probability distributions are shown in Table 16.7.

In offering these replay options, Harbor Dunes's first priority will be to sell full-price afternoon advance reservations. If the demand for replay tee times exceeds the number of afternoon tee times available, Harbor Dunes will post a notice that the course is full. In this case, any excess replay requests will not be accepted.

TABLE 16.7 PROBABILITY DISTRIBUTIONS FOR THE NUMBER OF GROUPS REQUESTING A REPLAY

Option 1: $25 per Person + Cart Fee		Option 2: $50 per Person + Cart Fee	
Number of Foursomes Requesting a Replay	Probability	Number of Foursomes Requesting a Replay	Probability
0	0.01	0	0.06
1	0.03	1	0.09
2	0.05	2	0.12
3	0.05	3	0.17
4	0.11	4	0.20
5	0.15	5	0.13
6	0.17	6	0.11
7	0.15	7	0.07
8	0.13	8	0.05
9	0.09		
10	0.06		

Managerial Report

Develop simulation models for both replay options using Analytic Solver Platform. Run each simulation for 10,000 trials. Prepare a report that will help management of Harbor Dunes Golf Course decide which replay option to implement for the upcoming spring golf season. In preparing your report, be sure to include the following:

1. Statistical summaries of the revenue expected under each replay option
2. Your recommendation as to the best replay option
3. Assuming a 90-day spring golf season, an estimate of the added revenue using your recommendation
4. Any other recommendations you have that might improve the income for Harbor Dunes

Case Problem 3 # County Beverage Drive-Thru

County Beverage Drive-Thru, Inc., operates a chain of beverage supply stores in northern Illinois. Each store has a single service lane; cars enter at one end of the store and exit at the other end. Customers pick up soft drinks, beer, snacks, and party supplies without getting out of their cars. When a new customer arrives at the store, the customer waits until the preceding customer's order is complete and then drives into the store for service.

Typically, three employees operate each store during peak periods; two clerks take and fill orders, and a third clerk serves as cashier and store supervisor. County Beverage is considering a revised store design in which computerized order-taking and payment are integrated with specialized warehousing equipment. Management hopes that the new design will permit operating each store with one clerk. To determine whether the new design is beneficial, management decided to build a new store using the revised design.

County Beverage's new store will be located near a major shopping center. Based on experience at other locations, management believes that during the peak late afternoon and evening hours, the time between arrivals will follow an exponential probability distribution with a mean of six minutes. These peak hours are the most critical time period for the company; most of their profit is generated during these peak hours.

An extensive study of times required to fill orders with a single clerk led to the following probability distribution of service times:

Service Time (minutes)	Probability
2	0.24
3	0.20
4	0.15
5	0.14
6	0.12
7	0.08
8	0.05
9	0.02
Total	1.00

In case customer waiting times prove to be too long with just a single clerk, County Beverage's management is considering two design alternatives: (1) adding a second clerk to assist the first clerk with bagging, taking orders, and related tasks (still serving one car at a time as a single-server system), or (2) enlarging the drive-through area so that two cars can be served at once (operating as a two-server system). With the two-server option, service times are expected to be the same for each server. With the second clerk teaming with the first clerk in the single server design, service times will be reduced and would be given by the probability distribution in the following table.

Service Time (minutes)	Probability
1	0.20
2	0.35
3	0.30
4	0.10
5	0.05
Total	1.00

County Beverage's management would like you to develop a spreadsheet simulation model of the new system and use it to compare the operation of the system using the following three designs:

Design	
A	Single-server system operated by one clerk
B	Single-server system operated by two clerks
C	Two-server system operated by two clerks

Management is especially concerned with how long customers have to wait for service. As a guideline, management requires the average waiting time to be less than 1.5 minutes.

Managerial Report

Prepare a report that discusses the general development of the spreadsheet simulation model, and make any recommendations that you have regarding the best store design and staffing plan for County Beverage. One additional consideration is that the design allowing for a two-server system will cost an additional $10,000 to build.

1. Construct a separate simulation model to evaluate the performance of each design alternative.
2. Execute the simulation for 360 minutes (representing the peak hours of 4 P.M. to 10 P.M). You may assume that the system begins empty at 4 P.M You may want to make more than one run with each alternative. Record relevant summary statistics over the simulation runs and use this information to support your final recommendation.

Appendix 16.1 # Probability Distributions for Random Variables

Selecting the appropriate probability distribution to characterize a random variable in a simulation model can be a critical modeling decision. In this appendix, we review several of the distributions from which one can easily generate values with native Excel functionality. For each distribution, the parameters are the values required to completely specify the distribution. The range provides the minimum and maximum values that can be taken by a random variable that follows the given distribution. We also provide a short description of the overall shape and/or common uses of the distribution.

Continuous Probability Distributions

Random variables which can be many possible values (even if these values are discrete) are often modeled with a continuous probability distribution.

Normal Distribution

> **Parameters:** mean (μ), stdev (σ)
> **Range:** $-\infty$ to $+\infty$
> **Excel command:** NORM.INV(RAND(), μ, σ)
> **Description:** The normal distribution is a bell-shaped, symmetric distribution centered at its mean μ. The normal distribution is often a good way to characterize a quantity that is the sum of many independent random variables.
> **Example:** In human resource management, employee performance is often well-represented by a normal distribution. Typically the performance of 68 percent of employees is within one standard deviation of the average performance and the performance of 95 percent of the employees is within two standard deviations. Employees with exceptionally low or high performance are rare.

Beta Distribution

> **Parameters:** shape1 (α), shape2 (β), min (A), max (B)
> **Range:** A to B
> **Excel command:** BETA.INV(RAND(), α, β, A, B)
> **Description:** The beta distribution has a very flexible shape (manipulated by adjusting α and β) over the range between values A and B. The beta distribution is useful in modeling an uncertain quantity that has a known minimum and maximum value.
> **Example:** Setting $A = 0$ and $B = 1$, the beta distribution can be used to describe the likelihood of values for the true proportion of drivers in an age group who would favor one model of car over another.

Exponential Distribution

> **Parameters:** mean (μ)
> **Range:** 0 to $+\infty$
> **Excel command:** LN(RAND())*($-\mu$)
> **Description:** The exponential distribution is characterized by a mean value that is equal to its standard deviation and a long right tail stretching from a mode value of 0.
> **Example:** The time between events, such as customer arrivals or customer defaults on bill payment, are commonly modeled with an exponential distribution. An exponential random variable possesses the "memoryless" property: the probability that there will be 25 or more minutes between customer arrivals if 10 minutes have passed since the last customer arrival is the same as the probability that there will be more than 15 minutes until the next arrival if a customer just arrived. That is, the probability of a customer arrival occurring in the next X minutes does not depend on how long it's been since the last arrival.

As the exponential distribution with mean μ is equivalent to the gamma distribution with parameters alpha = 1 and beta = (1/μ), an exponential random variable can also be generated by GAMMA. INV(RAND(), 1, 1/μ).

Uniform Distribution

Parameters: min (a), max (b)

Range: a to b

Excel command: RAND()*($b - a$) + a

Description: The uniform distribution is appropriate when a random variable is equally likely to be any value between a and b. In the case where little is known about a phenomenon besides its minimum and maximum possible values, the uniform distribution can be a safe choice to model an uncertain quantity.

Example: A service technician making a house call may quote a four-hour time window in which he will arrive. If the technician is equally likely to arrive any time during this time window, then the arrival time of the technician in this time window may be described with a uniform distribution.

Discrete Probability Distributions

Random variables which can be only a relatively small number of discrete values are often best modeled with a discrete distribution. The appropriate choice of discrete distribution relies on the specific situation. For discrete distributions, we provide the parameters required to specify the distribution, the possible values taken by a random variable that follows the distribution, and a short description of the distribution and an example of a possible application.

Bernoulli Distribution

As the Bernoulli distribution with probability of success p is equivalent to the binomial distribution with a single trial and probability of success p, a Bernoulli random variable can also be generated by BINOM. INV(1, p, RAND()).

Parameters: prob (p)

Possible values: 0 (event doesn't occur) or 1 (event occurs)

Excel command: IF(RAND() < p, 1, 0)

Description: A Bernoulli random variable corresponds to whether or not an event successfully occurs given a probability p of successfully occurring.

Example: Whether or not a particular stock increases in value over a defined length of time is a Bernoulli random variable.

Binomial Distribution

Parameters: trials (n), prob (p)

Possible values: 0, 1, 2, . . . , n

Excel command: BINOM.INV(n, p, RAND())

Description: A binomial random variable corresponds to the number of times an event successfully occurs in n trials, and the probability of a success at each trial is p and independent of whether a success occurs on other trials. Note that for $n = 1$, the binomial is equivalent to the Bernoulli distribution.

Example: In a portfolio of 20 similar stocks, each of which has the same probability of increasing in value of $p = 0.6$, the total number of stocks that increase in value can be described by a binomial distribution with parameters $n = 20$ and $p = 0.6$.

Integer Uniform Distribution

Parameters: lower (l), upper (u)

Possible values: $l, l + 1, l + 2, . . . , u - 2, u - 1, u$

Excel command: RANDBETWEEN(l, u)

Description: An integer uniform random variable assumes that the integer values between l and u are equally likely.

Example: The number of philanthropy volunteers from a class of 10 students may be an integer uniform variable with values 0, 1, 2, . . . , 10.

Discrete Uniform Distribution

Parameters: set of values $\{v_1, v_2, v_3, \ldots, v_k\}$

Possible values: $v_1, v_2, v_3, \ldots, v_k$

Excel command: CHOOSE(RANDBETWEEN(1, k), $v_1, v_2, \ldots, v_k$)

Description: A discrete uniform random variable is equally likely to be any of the specified set of values $\{v_1, v_2, v_3, \ldots, v_k\}$.

Example: Consider six envelopes containing \$1, \$5, \$10, \$20, \$50, \$100. If the game show reward that a contestant receives is randomly selected from one of these six, then the reward is a discrete uniform random variable with values {1, 5, 10, 20, 50, 100}.

Custom Discrete Distribution

Parameters: set of values $\{v_1, v_2, v_3, \ldots, v_k\}$ and corresponding weights $\{w_1, w_2, w_3, \ldots, w_k\}$ where $\sum_{j=1}^{k} w_j = 1$

Possible values: $v_1, v_2, v_3, \ldots, v_k$

Excel command: Use VLOOKUP with table of values and likelihoods (see direct labor cost in Figure 16.7).

Description: A custom discrete distribution can be used to create a tailored distribution to model a discrete, uncertain quantity. The value of a custom discrete random variable is equal to the value v_i with probability w_i.

Example: Analysis of daily sales for the past 50 days at a car dealership shows that on 2 days no cars were sold, on 5 days one car was sold, on 9 days two cars were sold, on 24 days three cars were sold, on 7 days four cars were sold, and on 3 days five cars were sold. We can estimate the probability distribution of daily sales using the relative frequencies. An estimate of the probability that no cars are sold on a given day is 2/50 = 0.04, an estimate of the probability the one car is sold is 5/50 = 0.10, and so on. Daily sales may then be described by a custom discrete distribution with values of {0, 1, 2, 3, 4, 5} with respective weights of {0.04, 0.10, 0.18, 0.48, 0.14, 0.06}.

Appendix 16.2   Simulation with Analytic Solver Platform

WEB file

ButlerASP

In Section 16.3 we constructed a spreadsheet simulation model to analyze the inventory policy for the Butler Internet Company. This simulation model was constructed using only native Excel functionality. The use of specialized simulation packages facilitates the construction and analysis of simulation models. In this appendix, we demonstrate how the Analytic Solver Platform (ASP) can be used to execute the Butler simulation model. We will run the simulation for 10,000 trials here.

Formulating a Model in Analytic Solver Platform

The first steps for building an Excel simulation model are very similar whether using native Excel functionality or ASP. As in Section 16.3, we begin by entering the problem data and cell formulas into the top portion of the worksheet. For the Butler model, we must enter the following parameters: gross profit per unit, holding cost per unit, shortage cost per unit, as well as the mean and standard deviation of the normally distributed demand. The controllable input (replenishment level) is entered and cell formula are entered to compute sales, gross profit, holding cost, shortage cost, and net profit.

Instead of constructing a table of simulation trials and manually collecting summary statistics, ASP provides functionality to ease the process of executing simulation trials and analyzing the output. Recall that monthly demand is a random variable in the Butler problem. ASP refers to random variables as uncertain variables. ASP allows you to characterize each cell containing an uncertain variable with a distribution that describes its possible values and the corresponding likelihood of these values.

Generating Values for Butler's Uncertain Demand

We are now ready to define the probability distribution for the demand for Butler's routers.

Step 1. Select cell B7
Step 2. Click the **ANALYTIC SOLVER PLATFORM** tab in the Ribbon
Step 3. Click **Distributions** in the **Simulation Model** group
Select **Common** and click **Normal**
Step 4. When the **$B$7** dialog box appears, in the **Parameters** area enter *E6* in the box to the right of **mean** and *E7* in the box to the right of **stdev** (see Figure 16.17)
Step 5. Click **Save**

Figure 16.18 summarizes the construction of the model at this stage. Observe that ASP has placed the formula =PsiNormal(100,20) in cell B7, and pressing the F9 key causes the spreadsheet to generate a new value for demand from a normal distribution with mean of 100 units and standard deviation of 20 units.

FIGURE 16.17   NORMAL DISTRIBUTION FOR ROUTER DEMAND

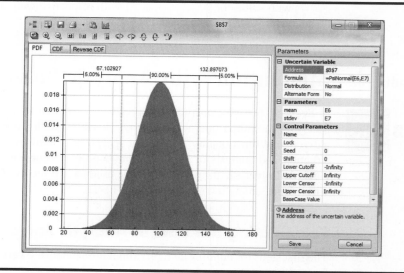

FIGURE 16.18   FORMULA VIEW OF BUTLER SIMULATION MODEL

	A	B	C	D	E
1	**Butler**				
2					
3	**Parameters**				
4	Gross Profit per Unit	50			
5	Holding Cost per Unit	15		**Demand (Normal Distribution)**	
6	Shortage Cost per Unit	30		Mean	100
7	Demand	=PsiNormal(100,20)		Standard Deviation	20
8					
9	**Model**				
10	Replenishment Level (Q)	140			
11	Sales	=MIN(B7,B10)			
12	Gross Profit	=B11*B4			
13	Holding Cost	=IF(B10>B7,(B10-B7)*B5,0)			
14	Shortage Cost	=IF(B7>B10,(B7-B10)*B6,0)			
15	Net Profit	=B12-B13-B14			

Tracking Output for Butler

After defining the distribution for demand, we are ready to track the simulation output. The following steps show this process for cell B16, which is the cell calculating Butler's monthly net profit:

Step 1. Select cell B16
Step 2. Click the **ANALYTIC SOLVER PLATFORM** tab in the Ribbon
Step 3. Click **Distributions** in the **Simulation Model** group
Select **Output**, and click **In Cell**

This procedure appends the formula in cell B15 with "+PsiOutput()" which triggers ASP to record the cell's value for each of the simulation trials. By collecting the value of net profit resulting from each simulation trial, ASP can then create a distribution of net profit.

Setting Simulation Options

Increasing the number of trials per simulation reduces the error in estimating the output. Unless the simulation model is extremely complex, it is recommended to use 10,000 trials (the maximum allowed in the educational version of ASP).

For the Butler simulation, we only need to specify the number of trials.

Step 1. Click the **ANALYTIC SOLVER PLATFORM** tab in the Ribbon
Step 2. Click the **Options** icon in the **Options** group
Step 3. Click the **Simulation** tab. In the **General** area, enter *10000* in the **Trials per Simulation:** box (see Figure 16.19)
Step 4. Click **OK**

FIGURE 16.19 SIMULATION OPTIONS MENU

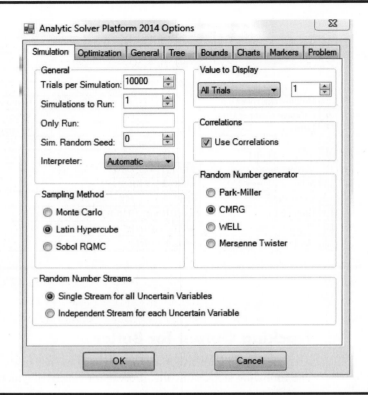

Running the Simulation

For each of the 10,000 simulation trials, ASP automatically repeats three tasks:

1. A value is generated for demand according to the defined probability distributions.
2. A new simulated net profit is computed based on the new value of demand.
3. The new simulated net profit is recorded.

The following steps describe how to execute the set of 10,000 simulation trials and to analyze simulation output.

When the interactive simulation in ASP is activated, the spreadsheet will automatically rerun the simulation whenever the spreadsheet is changed or the F9 key is pressed.

Step 1. Click the **ANALYTIC SOLVER PLATFORM** tab in the Ribbon
Step 2. Click the arrow under **Simulate** from the **Solve Action** group
From the drop-down menu that appears, select **Interactive**

When the run of 10,000 trials is complete, ASP displays the $B$15 dialog box, which shows a frequency distribution of the simulated net profit values obtained during the simulation run (see Figure 16.20). The chart for $B$15 in Figure 16.20 displays the distribution of Butler's monthly net profit over the 10,000 simulation trials (months). We see that the mean net profit in this simulation is $4,383.81. The worst result obtained in these 10,000 trials

Note that the minimum and maximum values of net profit will tend to be more extreme as the number of simulation trials increases.

is a loss of $1,134.60, and the best result is a profit of $6,999.96. These values are similar to the results obtained in Section 16.3. The differences result from the different random numbers used in the two simulations. If you perform another simulation, your results will differ slightly.

FIGURE 16.20   BUTLER SIMULATION OUTPUT

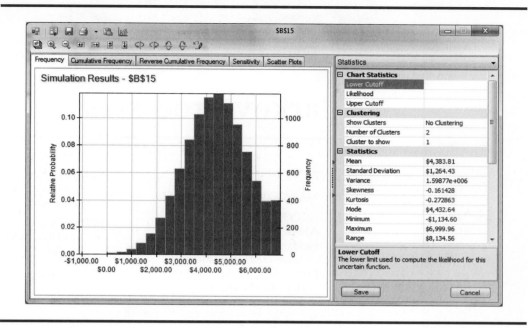

CHAPTER 17

Markov Processes

CONTENTS

Markov process models are useful in studying the evolution of systems over repeated trials. The repeated trials are often successive time periods in which the state of the system in any particular period cannot be determined with certainty. Rather, transition probabilities are used to describe the manner in which the system makes transitions from one period to the next. Hence, we are interested in the probability of the system being in a particular state at a given time period.

Markov process models can be used to describe the probability that a machine that is functioning in one period will continue to function or will break down in the next period. Models can also be used to describe the probability that a consumer purchasing brand A in one period will purchase brand B in the next period. The Q.M. in Action, Benefit of Health Care Services, describes how a Markov process model was used to determine the health status probabilities for persons age 65 and older. Such information was helpful in understanding the future need for health care services and the benefits of expanding current health care programs.

In this chapter we present a marketing application that involves an analysis of the store-switching behavior of supermarket customers. As a second illustration, we consider an accounting application that is concerned with the transitioning of accounts receivable dollars to different account-aging categories. Because an in-depth treatment of Markov processes is beyond the scope of this text, the analysis in both illustrations is restricted to situations consisting of a finite number of states, the transition probabilities remaining constant over time, and the probability of being in a particular state at any one time period depending only on the state in the immediately preceding time period. Such Markov processes are referred to as **Markov chains with stationary transition probabilities**.

Q.M. *in* ACTION

BENEFIT OF HEALTH CARE SERVICES*

The U.S. Government Accountability Office (GAO) is an independent, nonpolitical audit organization in the legislative branch of the federal government. GAO evaluators obtained data on the health conditions of individuals age 65 and older. The individuals were identified as being in three possible states:

Best: Able to perform daily activities without assistance

Next Best: Able to perform some daily activities without assistance

Worst: Unable to perform daily activities without assistance

Using a two-year period, the evaluators developed estimates of the transition probabilities among the three states. For example, a transition probability that a person in the Best state is still in the Best state one year later

was 0.80, while the transition probability that a person in the Best state moves to the Next Best state one year later is 0.10. The Markov analysis of the full set of transition probabilities determined the steady-state probabilities that individuals would be in each state. Thus, for a given population age 65 and older, the steady-state probabilities would indicate the percentage of the population that would be in each state in future years.

The GAO study further subdivided individuals into two groups: those receiving appropriate health care and those not receiving appropriate health care. For individuals not receiving appropriate health care, the kind of additional care and the cost of that care were estimated. The revised transition probabilities showed that with appropriate health care, the steady-state probabilities indicated the larger percentage of the population that would be in the Best and Next Best health states in future years. Using these results, the model provided evidence of the future benefits that would be achieved by expanding current health care programs.

*Based on information provided by Bill Ammann, U.S. Government Accountability Office.

17.1 Market Share Analysis

Suppose we are interested in analyzing the market share and customer loyalty for Murphy's Foodliner and Ashley's Supermarket, the only two grocery stores in a small town. We focus on the sequence of shopping trips of one customer and assume that the customer makes one shopping trip each week to either Murphy's Foodliner or Ashley's Supermarket, but not both.

Using the terminology of Markov processes, we refer to the weekly periods or shopping trips as the **trials of the process**. Thus, at each trial, the customer will shop at either Murphy's Foodliner or Ashley's Supermarket. The particular store selected in a given week is referred to as the **state of the system** in that period. Because the customer has two shopping alternatives at each trial, we say the system has two states. With a finite number of states, we identify the states as follows:

> **State 1.** The customer shops at Murphy's Foodliner
> **State 2.** The customer shops at Ashley's Supermarket

If we say the system is in state 1 at trial 3, we are simply saying that the customer shops at Murphy's during the third weekly shopping period.

As we continue the shopping trip process into the future, we cannot say for certain where the customer will shop during a given week or trial. In fact, we realize that during any given week, the customer may be either a Murphy's customer or an Ashley's customer. However, using a Markov process model, we will be able to compute the probability that the customer shops at each store during any period. For example, we may find a 0.6 probability that the customer will shop at Murphy's during a particular week and a 0.4 probability that the customer will shop at Ashley's.

To determine the probabilities of the various states occurring at successive trials of the Markov process, we need information on the probability that a customer remains with the same store or switches to the competing store as the process continues from trial to trial or week to week.

Suppose that, as part of a market research study, we collect data from 100 shoppers over a 10-week period. Suppose further that these data show each customer's weekly shopping trip pattern in terms of the sequence of visits to Murphy's and Ashley's. To develop a Markov process model for the sequence of weekly shopping trips, we need to express the probability of selecting each store (state) in a given period solely in terms of the store (state) that was selected during the previous period. In reviewing the data, suppose that we find that of all customers who shopped at Murphy's in a given week, 90% shopped at Murphy's the following week while 10% switched to Ashley's. Suppose that similar data for the customers who shopped at Ashley's in a given week show that 80% shopped at Ashley's the following week while 20% switched to Murphy's. Probabilities based on these data are shown in Table 17.1. Because these probabilities indicate that a customer moves, or makes a transition,

TABLE 17.1   TRANSITION PROBABILITIES FOR MURPHY'S AND ASHLEY'S GROCERY SALES

Current Weekly Shopping Period	Next Weekly Shopping Period	
	Murphy's Foodliner	**Ashley's Supermarket**
Murphy's Foodliner	0.9	0.1
Ashley's Supermarket	0.2	0.8

from a state in a given period to each state in the following period, these probabilities are called **transition probabilities**.

An important property of the table of transition probabilities is that the sum of the probabilities in each row is 1; each row of the table provides a conditional probability distribution. For example, a customer who shops at Murphy's one week must shop at either Murphy's or Ashley's the next week. The entries in row 1 give the probabilities associated with each of these events. The 0.9 and 0.8 probabilities in Table 17.1 can be interpreted as measures of store loyalty in that they indicate the probability of a repeat visit to the same store in consecutive weeks. Similarly, the 0.1 and 0.2 probabilities are measures of the store-switching characteristics of the customers. In developing a Markov process model for this problem, we are assuming that the transition probabilities will be the same for any customer and that the transition probabilities will not change over time.

Appendix 17.1 contains a review of matrix notation and operations.

Note that Table 17.1 has one row and one column for each state of the system. We will use the symbol p_{ij} to represent the transition probabilities and the symbol P to represent the matrix of transition probabilities; that is,

$$p_{ij} = \text{probability of making a transition from state } i \text{ in a given}$$
$$\text{period to state } j \text{ in the next period}$$

For the supermarket problem, we have

A quick check for a valid matrix of transition probabilities is to make sure the sum of the probabilities in each row equals 1.

$$P = \begin{bmatrix} p_{11} & p_{12} \\ p_{21} & p_{22} \end{bmatrix} = \begin{bmatrix} 0.9 & 0.1 \\ 0.2 & 0.8 \end{bmatrix}$$

Using the matrix of transition probabilities, we can now determine the probability that a customer will be a Murphy's customer or an Ashley's customer at some period in the future. Let us begin by assuming that we have a customer whose last weekly shopping trip was to Murphy's. What is the probability that this customer will shop at Murphy's on the next weekly shopping trip, period 1? In other words, what is the probability that the system will be in state 1 after the first transition? The matrix of transition probabilities indicates that this probability is $p_{11} = 0.9$.

Now let us consider the state of the system in period 2. A useful way of depicting what can happen on the second weekly shopping trip is to draw a tree diagram of the possible outcomes (see Figure 17.1). Using this tree diagram, we see that the probability that the customer shops at Murphy's during both the first and the second weeks is $(0.9)(0.9) = 0.81$. Also, note that the probability of the customer switching to Ashley's on the first trip and then switching back to Murphy's on the second trip is $(0.1)(0.2) = 0.02$. Because these options are the only two ways that the customer can be in state 1 (shopping at Murphy's) during the second period, the probability of the system being in state 1 during the second period is $0.81 + 0.02 = 0.83$. Similarly, the probability of the system being in state 2 during the second period is $(0.9)(0.1) + (0.1)(0.8) = 0.09 + 0.08 = 0.17$.

As desirable as the tree diagram approach may be from an intuitive point of view, it becomes cumbersome when we want to extend the analysis to three or more periods. Fortunately, we have an easier way to calculate the probabilities of the system being in state 1 or state 2 for any subsequent period. First, we introduce a notation that will allow us to represent these probabilities for any given period. Let

$$\pi_i(n) = \text{probability that the system is in state } i \text{ in period } n$$

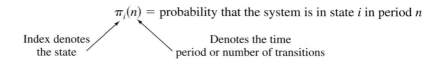

Index denotes the state   Denotes the time period or number of transitions

FIGURE 17.1   TREE DIAGRAM DEPICTING TWO WEEKLY SHOPPING TRIPS
OF A CUSTOMER WHO SHOPPED LAST AT MURPHY'S

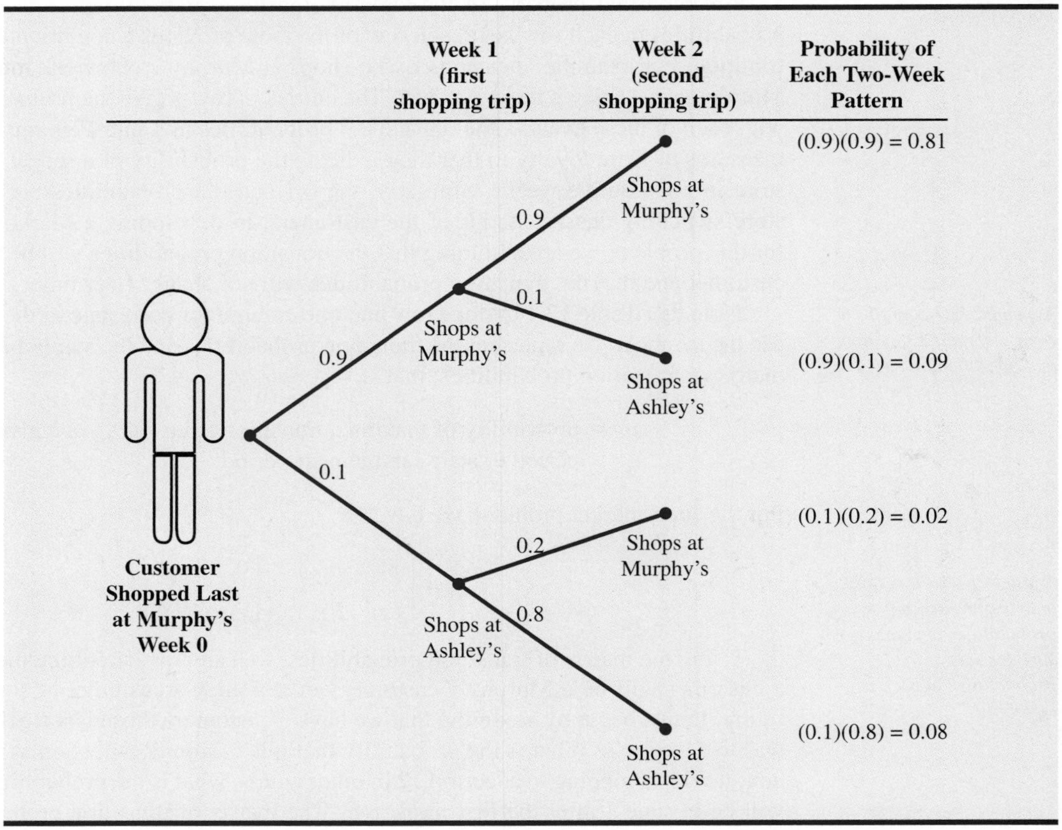

For example, $\pi_1(1)$ denotes the probability of the system being in state 1 in period 1, while $\pi_2(1)$ denotes the probability of the system being in state 2 in period 1. Because $\pi_i(n)$ is the probability that the system is in state i in period n, this probability is referred to as a **state probability**.

The terms $\pi_1(0)$ and $\pi_2(0)$ will denote the probability of the system being in state 1 or state 2 at some initial or starting period. Week 0 represents the most recent period, when we are beginning the analysis of a Markov process. If we set $\pi_1(0) = 1$ and $\pi_2(0) = 0$, we are saying that as an initial condition the customer shopped last week at Murphy's; alternatively, if we set $\pi_1(0) = 0$ and $\pi_2(0) = 1$, we would be starting the system with a customer who shopped last week at Ashley's. In the tree diagram of Figure 17.1, we consider the situation in which the customer shopped last at Murphy's. Thus,

$$[\pi_1(0) \quad \pi_2(0)] = [1 \quad 0]$$

is a vector that represents the initial state probabilities of the system. In general, we use the notation

$$\Pi(n) = [\pi_1(n) \quad \pi_2(n)]$$

to denote the vector of state probabilities for the system in period n. In the example, $\Pi(1)$ is a vector representing the state probabilities for the first week, $\Pi(2)$ is a vector representing the state probabilities for the second week, and so on.

*Appendix 17.1 provides
the step-by-step procedure
for vector and matrix
multiplication.*

Using this notation, we can find the state probabilities for period $n + 1$ by simply multiplying the known state probabilities for period n by the transition probability matrix.

Using the vector of state probabilities and the matrix of transition probabilities, the multiplication can be expressed as follows:

$$\Pi(\text{next period}) = \Pi(\text{current period})P$$

or

$$\Pi(n + 1) = \Pi(n)P \qquad \textbf{(17.1)}$$

Beginning with the system in state 1 at period 0, we have $\Pi(0) = [1 \quad 0]$. We can compute the state probabilities for period 1 as follows:

$$\Pi(1) = \Pi(0)P$$

or

$$[\pi_1(1) \quad \pi_2(1)] = [\pi_1(0) \quad \pi_2(0)]\begin{bmatrix} p_{11} & p_{12} \\ p_{21} & p_{22} \end{bmatrix}$$
$$= [1 \quad 0]\begin{bmatrix} 0.9 & 0.1 \\ 0.2 & 0.8 \end{bmatrix}$$
$$= [0.9 \quad 0.1]$$

The state probabilities $\pi_1(1) = 0.9$ and $\pi_2(1) = 0.1$ are the probabilities that a customer who shopped at Murphy's during week 0 will shop at Murphy's or at Ashley's during week 1.

Using equation (17.1), we can compute the state probabilities for the second week as follows:

$$\Pi(2) = \Pi(1)P$$

or

$$[\pi_1(2) \quad \pi_2(2)] = [\pi_1(1) \quad \pi_2(1)]\begin{bmatrix} p_{11} & p_{12} \\ p_{21} & p_{22} \end{bmatrix}$$
$$= [0.9 \quad 0.1]\begin{bmatrix} 0.9 & 0.1 \\ 0.2 & 0.8 \end{bmatrix}$$
$$= [0.83 \quad 0.17]$$

We see that the probability of shopping at Murphy's during the second week is 0.83, while the probability of shopping at Ashley's during the second week is 0.17. These same results were previously obtained using the tree diagram of Figure 17.1. By continuing to apply equation (17.1), we can compute the state probabilities for any future period; that is,

$$\Pi(3) = \Pi(2)P$$
$$\Pi(4) = \Pi(3)P$$
$$\vdots \qquad \vdots$$
$$\Pi(n + 1) = \Pi(n)P$$

Table 17.2 shows the result of carrying out these calculations for 10 periods.

TABLE 17.2 STATE PROBABILITIES FOR FUTURE PERIODS BEGINNING INITIALLY WITH A MURPHY'S CUSTOMER

State Probability	\ Period (n) 0	1	2	3	4	5	6	7	8	9	10
$\pi_1(n)$	1	0.9	0.83	0.781	0.747	0.723	0.706	0.694	0.686	0.680	0.676
$\pi_2(n)$	0	0.1	0.17	0.219	0.253	0.277	0.294	0.306	0.314	0.320	0.324

The vectors $\Pi(1), \Pi(2), \Pi(3), \dots$ contain the probabilities that a customer who started out as a Murphy customer will be in state 1 or state 2 in the first period, the second period, the third period, and so on. In Table 17.2 we see that after a few periods these probabilities do not change much from one period to the next.

If we had started with 1000 Murphy customers—that is, 1000 customers who last shopped at Murphy's—our analysis indicates that during the fifth weekly shopping period, on average, 723 would be customers of Murphy's, and 277 would be customers of Ashley's. Moreover, during the tenth weekly shopping period, 676 would be customers of Murphy's, and 324 would be customers of Ashley's.

Now let us repeat the analysis, but this time we will begin the process with a customer who shopped last at Ashley's. Thus,

$$\Pi(0) = [\pi_1(0) \quad \pi_2(0)] = [0 \quad 1]$$

Using equation (17.1), the probability of the system being in state 1 or state 2 in period 1 is given by

$$\Pi(1) = \Pi(0)P$$

or

$$[\pi_1(1) \quad \pi_2(1)] = [\pi_1(0) \quad \pi_2(0)]\begin{bmatrix} p_{11} & p_{12} \\ p_{21} & p_{22} \end{bmatrix}$$
$$= [0 \quad 1]\begin{bmatrix} 0.9 & 0.1 \\ 0.2 & 0.8 \end{bmatrix}$$
$$= [0.2 \quad 0.8]$$

Proceeding as before, we can calculate subsequent state probabilities. Doing so, we obtain the results shown in Table 17.3.

In the fifth shopping period, the probability that the customer will be shopping at Murphy's is 0.555, and the probability that the customer will be shopping at Ashley's is

TABLE 17.3 STATE PROBABILITIES FOR FUTURE PERIODS BEGINNING INITIALLY WITH AN ASHLEY'S CUSTOMER

State Probability	\ Period (n) 0	1	2	3	4	5	6	7	8	9	10
$\pi_1(n)$	0	0.2	0.34	0.438	0.507	0.555	0.589	0.612	0.628	0.640	0.648
$\pi_2(n)$	1	0.8	0.66	0.562	0.493	0.445	0.411	0.388	0.372	0.360	0.352

0.445. In the tenth period, the probability that a customer will be shopping at Murphy's is 0.648, and the probability that a customer will be shopping at Ashley's is 0.352.

As we continue the Markov process, we find that the probability of the system being in a particular state after a large number of periods is independent of the beginning state of the system. The probabilities that we approach after a large number of transitions are referred to as the **steady-state probabilities**. We shall denote the steady-state probability for state 1 with the symbol π_1 and the steady-state probability for state 2 with the symbol π_2. In other words, in the steady-state case, we simply omit the period designation from $\pi_i(n)$ because it is no longer necessary.

Analyses of Tables 17.2 and 17.3 indicate that as n gets larger, the difference between the state probabilities for period n and period $(n + 1)$ becomes increasingly smaller. This analysis leads us to the conclusion that as n gets large, the state probabilities for period $(n + 1)$ are very close to those for period n. This observation provides the basis of a simple method for computing the steady-state probabilities without having to actually carry out a large number of calculations.

In general, we know from equation (17.1) that

$$[\pi_1(n + 1) \quad \pi_2(n + 1)] = [\pi_1(n) \quad \pi_2(n)] \begin{bmatrix} p_{11} & p_{12} \\ p_{21} & p_{22} \end{bmatrix}$$

Because for sufficiently large n the difference between $\Pi(n + 1)$ and $\Pi(n)$ is negligible, we see that in the steady state $\pi_1(n + 1) = \pi_1(n) = \pi_1$ and $\pi_2(n + 1) = \pi_2(n) = \pi_2$. Thus, we have

$$[\pi_1 \quad \pi_2] = [\pi_1 \quad \pi_2] \begin{bmatrix} p_{11} & p_{12} \\ p_{21} & p_{22} \end{bmatrix}$$

$$= [\pi_1 \quad \pi_2] \begin{bmatrix} 0.9 & 0.1 \\ 0.2 & 0.8 \end{bmatrix}$$

After carrying out the multiplications, we obtain

$$\pi_1 = 0.9\pi_1 + 0.2\pi_2 \qquad \textbf{(17.2)}$$

and

$$\pi_2 = 0.1\pi_1 + 0.8\pi_2 \qquad \textbf{(17.3)}$$

However, we also know the steady-state probabilities must sum to 1 so

$$\pi_1 + \pi_2 = 1 \qquad \textbf{(17.4)}$$

Can you now compute the steady-state probabilities for Markov processes with two states? Problem 3 provides an application.

Using equation (17.4) to solve for π_2 and substituting the result in equation (17.2), we obtain

$$\pi_1 = 0.9\pi_1 + 0.2(1 - \pi_1)$$
$$\pi_1 = 0.9\pi_1 + 0.2 - 0.2\pi_1$$
$$\pi_1 - 0.7\pi_1 = 0.2$$
$$0.3\pi_1 = 0.2$$
$$\pi_1 = \tfrac{2}{3}$$

Then, using equation (17.4), we can conclude that $\pi_2 = 1 - \pi_1 = {}^1/_3$. Thus, using equations (17.2) and (17.4), we can solve for the steady-state probabilities directly. You can check for yourself that we could have obtained the same result using equations (17.3) and (17.4).[1]

Thus, if we have 1000 customers in the system, the Markov process model tells us that in the long run, with steady-state probabilities $\pi_1 = {}^2/_3$ and $\pi_2 = {}^1/_3$, ${}^2/_3(1000) = 667$ customers will be Murphy's and ${}^1/_3(1000) = 333$ customers will be Ashley's. The steady-state probabilities can be interpreted as the market shares for the two stores.

Market share information is often quite valuable in decision making. For example, suppose Ashley's Supermarket is contemplating an advertising campaign to attract more of Murphy's customers to its store. Let us suppose further that Ashley's believes this promotional strategy will increase the probability of a Murphy's customer switching to Ashley's from 0.10 to 0.15. The revised transition probabilities are given in Table 17.4.

With three states, the steady-state probabilities are found by solving three equations for the three unknown steady-state probabilities. Try Problem 8 as a slightly more difficult problem involving three states.

Given the new transition probabilities, we can modify equations (17.2) and (17.4) to solve for the new steady-state probabilities or market shares. Thus, we obtain

$$\pi_1 = 0.85\pi_1 + 0.20\pi_2$$

Substituting $\pi_2 = 1 - \pi_1$ from equation (17.4), we have

$$\pi_1 = 0.85\pi_1 + 0.20(1 - \pi_1)$$
$$\pi_1 = 0.85\pi_1 + 0.20 - 0.20\pi_1$$
$$\pi_1 - 0.65\pi_1 = 0.20$$
$$0.35\pi_1 = 0.20$$
$$\pi_1 = 0.57$$

and

$$\pi_2 = 1 - 0.57 = 0.43$$

We see that the proposed promotional strategy will increase Ashley's market share from $\pi_2 = 0.33$ to $\pi_2 = 0.43$. Suppose that the total market consists of 6000 customers per week. The new promotional strategy will increase the number of customers doing their weekly shopping at Ashley's from 2000 to 2580. If the average weekly profit per customer is \$10, the proposed promotional strategy can be expected to increase Ashley's profits by \$5800 per week. If the cost of the promotional campaign is less than \$5800 per week, Ashley's should consider implementing the strategy.

TABLE 17.4   REVISED TRANSITION PROBABILITIES FOR MURPHY'S AND ASHLEY'S GROCERY STORES

Current Weekly Shopping Period	Next Weekly Shopping Period	
	Murphy's Foodliner	**Ashley's Supermarket**
Murphy's Foodliner	0.85	0.15
Ashley's Supermarket	0.20	0.80

[1]Even though equations (17.2) and (17.3) provide two equations and two unknowns, we must include equation (17.4) when solving for π_1 and π_2 to ensure that the sum of steady-state probabilities will equal 1.

This example demonstrates how a Markov analysis of a firm's market share can be useful in decision making. Suppose that instead of trying to attract customers from Murphy's Foodliner, Ashley's directed a promotional effort at increasing the loyalty of its own customers. In this case, p_{22} would increase and p_{21} would decrease. Once we knew the amount of the change, we could calculate new steady-state probabilities and compute the impact on profits.

NOTES AND COMMENTS

1. The Markov processes presented in this section have what is called the memoryless property: the current state of the system together with the transition probabilities contain all the information necessary to predict the future behavior of the system. The prior states of the system do not have to be considered.

2. Analysis of a Markov process model is not intended to optimize any particular aspect of a system. Rather, the analysis predicts or describes the future and steady-state behavior of the system. For instance, in the grocery store example, the analysis of the steady-state behavior provided a forecast or prediction of the market shares for the two competitors. In other applications, quantitative analysts have extended the study of Markov processes to what are called *Markov decision processes*. In these models, decisions can be made at each period that affect the transition probabilities and hence influence the future behavior of the system. Markov decision processes have been used in analyzing machine breakdown and maintenance operations, determining drug treatment strategies for patients in hospitals, developing inspection strategies, evaluating managerial strategies in a baseball game, and analyzing financial investments.

Accounts Receivable Analysis

An accounting application in which Markov processes have produced useful results involves the estimation of the allowance for doubtful accounts receivable. This allowance is an estimate of the amount of accounts receivable that will ultimately prove to be uncollectible (i.e., bad debts).

Let us consider the accounts receivable situation for Heidman's Department Store. Heidman's uses two aging categories for its accounts receivable: (1) accounts that are classified as 0–30 days old, and (2) accounts that are classified as 31–90 days old. If any portion of an account balance exceeds 90 days, that portion is written off as a bad debt. Heidman's follows the procedure of aging the total balance in any customer's account according to the oldest unpaid bill. For example, suppose that one customer's account balance on September 30 is as follows:

Date of Purchase	Amount Charged
August 15	$25
September 18	10
September 28	50
Total	$85

An aging of the total balance of accounts receivable performed on September 30 would assign the total balance of $85 to the 31–90-day category because the oldest unpaid bill of

August 15 is 46 days old. Let us assume that one week later, October 7, the customer pays the August 15 bill of $25. The remaining total balance of $60 would now be placed in the 0–30-day category since the oldest unpaid amount, corresponding to the September 18 purchase, is less than 31 days old. This method of aging accounts receivable is called the *total balance method* because the total account balance is placed in the age category corresponding to the oldest unpaid amount.

Note that under the total balance method of aging accounts receivable, dollars appearing in a 31–90-day category at one point in time may appear in a 0–30-day category at a later point in time. In the preceding example, this movement between categories was true for $60 of September billings, which shifted from a 31–90-day to a 0–30-day category after the August bill had been paid.

Let us assume that on December 31 Heidman's shows a total of $3000 in its accounts receivable and that the firm's management would like an estimate of how much of the $3000 will eventually be collected and how much will eventually result in bad debts. The estimated amount of bad debts will appear as an allowance for doubtful accounts in the year-end financial statements.

Let us see how we can view the accounts receivable operation as a Markov process. First, concentrate on what happens to *one* dollar currently in accounts receivable. As the firm continues to operate into the future, we can consider each week as a trial of a Markov process with a dollar existing in one of the following states of the system:

State 1. Paid category
State 2. Bad debt category
State 3. 0–30-day category
State 4. 31–90-day category

Thus, we can track the week-by-week status of one dollar by using a Markov analysis to identify the state of the system at a particular week or period.

Using a Markov process model with the preceding states, we define the transition probabilities as follows:

p_{ij} = probability of a dollar in state i in one week moving to state j in the next week

Based on historical transitions of accounts receivable dollars, the following matrix of transition probabilities, P, has been developed for Heidman's Department Store:

$$P = \begin{bmatrix} p_{11} & p_{12} & p_{13} & p_{14} \\ p_{21} & p_{22} & p_{23} & p_{24} \\ p_{31} & p_{32} & p_{33} & p_{34} \\ p_{41} & p_{42} & p_{43} & p_{44} \end{bmatrix} = \begin{bmatrix} 1.0 & 0.0 & 0.0 & 0.0 \\ 0.0 & 1.0 & 0.0 & 0.0 \\ 0.4 & 0.0 & 0.3 & 0.3 \\ 0.4 & 0.2 & 0.3 & 0.1 \end{bmatrix}$$

Note that the probability of a dollar in the 0–30-day category (state 3) moving to the paid category (state 1) in the next period is 0.4. Also, this dollar has a 0.3 probability it will remain in the 0–30-day category (state 3) one week later, and a 0.3 probability that it will be in the 31–90-day category (state 4) one week later. Note also that a dollar in a 0–30-day account cannot make the transition to a bad debt (state 2) in one week.

When absorbing states are present, each row of the transition matrix corresponding to an absorbing state will have a single 1 and all other probabilities will be 0.

An important property of the Markov process model for Heidman's accounts receivable situation is the presence of *absorbing states*. For example, once a dollar makes a transition to state 1, the paid state, the probability of making a transition to any other state is zero. Similarly, once a dollar is in state 2, the bad debt state, the probability of a transition to any other state is zero. Thus, once a dollar reaches state 1 or state 2, the system will remain in this state forever. We can conclude that all accounts receivable dollars will eventually be absorbed into either the paid or the bad debt state, and hence the name **absorbing state**.

Fundamental Matrix and Associated Calculations

Whenever a Markov process has absorbing states, the probability of remaining forever in a nonabsorbing state is zero, so we are solely interested in knowing the probability that a unit will eventually end up in each of the absorbing states. Due to the presence of absorbing states, steady-state probabilities independent of the initial state vector do not exist. For example, in the Heidman's Department Store problem, a dollar currently in state 1 (paid) will never leave state 1, and a dollar currently in state 2 (bad debt) will never leave state 2. However, we may want to know the probability that a dollar currently in the 0–30-day age category will end up paid (absorbing state 1) as well as the probability that a dollar in this age category will end up a bad debt (absorbing state 2). We also want to know these absorbing-state probabilities for a dollar currently in the 31–90-day age category.

The algebraic computation of the absorbing-state probabilities requires the determination and use of what is called a **fundamental matrix**. The mathematical logic underlying the fundamental matrix is beyond the scope of this text. However, as we show, the fundamental matrix is derived from the matrix of transition probabilities and is relatively easy to compute for Markov processes with a small number of states. In the following example, we show the computation of the fundamental matrix and the determination of the absorbing-state probabilities for Heidman's Department Store.

Absorbing-state probabilities can also be numerically computed by repeatedly multiplying the vector of state probabilities and the matrix of transition probabilities similar to the calculation in Section 17.1.

We begin the computations by partitioning the matrix of transition probabilities into the following four parts:

$$
P = \begin{bmatrix} 1.0 & 0.0 & | & 0.0 & 0.0 \\ 0.0 & 1.0 & | & 0.0 & 0.0 \\ - & - & - & - & - \\ 0.4 & 0.0 & | & 0.3 & 0.3 \\ 0.4 & 0.2 & | & 0.3 & 0.1 \end{bmatrix} = \begin{bmatrix} 1.0 & 0.0 & | & 0.0 & 0.0 \\ 0.0 & 1.0 & | & 0.0 & 0.0 \\ - & - & - & - & - \\ & R & | & & Q \end{bmatrix}
$$

where

$$
R = \begin{bmatrix} 0.4 & 0.0 \\ 0.4 & 0.2 \end{bmatrix} \qquad Q = \begin{bmatrix} 0.3 & 0.3 \\ 0.3 & 0.1 \end{bmatrix}
$$

A matrix N, called a *fundamental matrix*, can be calculated using the following formula:

$$
N = (I - Q)^{-1} \tag{17.5}
$$

where I is an identity matrix with 1s on the main diagonal and 0s elsewhere. The superscript -1 is used to indicate the inverse of the matrix $(I - Q)$. In Appendix 17.1 we present formulas for finding the inverse of a matrix with two rows and two columns. In Appendix 17.2 we show how Excel's MINVERSE function can be used to compute an inverse.

Before proceeding, we note that to use equation (17.5), the identity matrix I must be chosen such that it has the *same size or dimensionality* as the matrix Q. In our example problem, Q has two rows and two columns, so we must choose

$$
I = \begin{bmatrix} 1.0 & 0.0 \\ 0.0 & 1.0 \end{bmatrix}
$$

Let us now continue with the example problem by computing the fundamental matrix:

$$
I - Q = \begin{bmatrix} 1.0 & 0.0 \\ 0.0 & 1.0 \end{bmatrix} - \begin{bmatrix} 0.3 & 0.3 \\ 0.3 & 0.1 \end{bmatrix}
$$

$$
= \begin{bmatrix} 0.7 & -0.3 \\ -0.3 & 0.9 \end{bmatrix}
$$

and (see Appendix 17.1)

$$N = (I - Q)^{-1} = \begin{bmatrix} 1.67 & 0.56 \\ 0.56 & 1.30 \end{bmatrix}$$

If we multiply the fundamental matrix N times the R portion of the P matrix, we obtain the probabilities that accounts receivable dollars initially in states 3 or 4 will eventually reach each of the absorbing states. The multiplication of N times R for the Heidman's Department Store problem provides the following results (again, see Appendix 17.1 for the steps of this matrix multiplication):

$$NR = \begin{bmatrix} 1.67 & 0.56 \\ 0.56 & 1.30 \end{bmatrix}\begin{bmatrix} 0.4 & 0.0 \\ 0.4 & 0.2 \end{bmatrix} = \begin{bmatrix} 0.89 & 0.11 \\ 0.74 & 0.26 \end{bmatrix}$$

The first row of the product NR is the probability that a dollar in the 0–30-day age category will end up in each absorbing state. Thus, we see a 0.89 probability that a dollar in the 0–30-day category will eventually be paid and a 0.11 probability that it will become a bad debt. Similarly, the second row shows the probabilities associated with a dollar in the 31–90-day category; that is, a dollar in the 31–90-day category has a 0.74 probability of eventually being paid and a 0.26 probability of proving to be uncollectible. Using this information, we can predict the amount of money that will be paid and the amount that will be lost as bad debts.

Establishing the Allowance for Doubtful Accounts

Let B represent a two-element vector that contains the current accounts receivable balances in the 0–30-day and the 31–90-day categories; that is,

$$B = [b_1 \quad b_2]$$

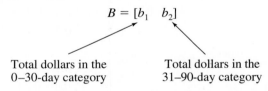

Total dollars in the   Total dollars in the
0–30-day category   31–90-day category

Suppose that the December 31 balance of accounts receivable for Heidman's shows $1000 in the 0–30-day category (state 3) and $2000 in the 31–90-day category (state 4).

$$B = [1000 \quad 2000]$$

We can multiply B times NR to determine how much of the $3000 will be collected and how much will be lost. For example,

$$BNR = [1000 \quad 2000]\begin{bmatrix} 0.89 & 0.11 \\ 0.74 & 0.26 \end{bmatrix}$$
$$= [2370 \quad 630]$$

Thus, we see that $2370 of the accounts receivable balances will be collected and $630 will be written off as a bad debt expense. Based on this analysis, the accounting department would set up an allowance for doubtful accounts of $630.

The matrix multiplication of BNR is simply a convenient way of computing the eventual collections and bad debts of the accounts receivable. Recall that the NR matrix showed a 0.89 probability of collecting dollars in the 0–30-day category and a 0.74 probability of collecting dollars in the 31–90-day category. Thus, as was shown by the BNR calculation, we expect to collect a total of $(1000)0.89 + (2000)0.74 = 890 + 1480 = \$2370$.

Suppose that on the basis of the previous analysis Heidman's would like to investigate the possibility of reducing the amount of bad debts. Recall that the analysis indicated that 11% of the amount in the 0–30-day age category and 26% of the amount in the 31–90-day age category will prove to be uncollectible. Let us assume that Heidman's is considering instituting a new credit policy involving a discount for prompt payment.

Management believes that the policy under consideration will increase the probability of a transition from the 0–30-day age category to the paid category and decrease the probability of a transition from the 0–30-day to the 31–90-day age category. Let us assume that a careful study of the effects of this new policy leads management to conclude that the following transition matrix would be applicable:

$$P = \begin{bmatrix} 1.0 & 0.0 & | & 0.0 & 0.0 \\ 0.0 & 1.0 & | & 0.0 & 0.0 \\ - & - & - & - & - & - \\ 0.6 & 0.0 & | & 0.3 & 0.1 \\ 0.4 & 0.2 & | & 0.3 & 0.1 \end{bmatrix}$$

We see that the probability of a dollar in the 0–30-day age category making a transition to the paid category in the next period has increased to 0.6, and that the probability of a dollar in the 0–30-day age category making a transition to the 31–90-day category has decreased to 0.1. To determine the effect of these changes on bad debt expense, we must calculate N, NR, and BNR. We begin by using equation (17.5) to calculate the fundamental matrix N:

$$N = (I - Q)^{-1} = \left\{ \begin{bmatrix} 1.0 & 0.0 \\ 0.0 & 1.0 \end{bmatrix} - \begin{bmatrix} 0.3 & 0.1 \\ 0.3 & 0.1 \end{bmatrix} \right\}^{-1}$$

$$= \begin{bmatrix} 0.7 & -0.1 \\ -0.3 & 0.9 \end{bmatrix}^{-1}$$

$$= \begin{bmatrix} 1.5 & 0.17 \\ 0.5 & 1.17 \end{bmatrix}$$

By multiplying N times R, we obtain the new probabilities that the dollars in each age category will end up in the two absorbing states:

$$NR = \begin{bmatrix} 1.5 & 0.17 \\ 0.5 & 1.17 \end{bmatrix} \begin{bmatrix} 0.6 & 0.0 \\ 0.4 & 0.2 \end{bmatrix}$$

$$= \begin{bmatrix} 0.97 & 0.03 \\ 0.77 & 0.23 \end{bmatrix}$$

We see that with the new credit policy we would expect only 3% of the funds in the 0–30-day age category and 23% of the funds in the 31–90-day age category to prove to be uncollectible. If, as before, we assume a current balance of $1000 in the 0–30-day age category and $2000 in the 31–90-day age category, we can calculate the total amount of accounts receivable that will end up in the two absorbing states by multiplying B times NR. We obtain

Problem 13, which provides a variation of Heidman's Department Store problem, will give you practice in analyzing Markov processes with absorbing states.

$$BNR = [1000 \quad 2000] \begin{bmatrix} 0.97 & 0.03 \\ 0.77 & 0.23 \end{bmatrix}$$

$$= [2510 \quad 490]$$

Thus, the new credit policy shows a bad debt expense of $490. Under the previous credit policy, we found the bad debt expense to be $630. Thus, a savings of $630 − $490 = $140 could be expected as a result of the new credit policy. Given the total accounts receivable balance of $3000, this savings represents a $140/$3000 = 4.7% reduction in bad debt expense. After considering the costs involved, management can evaluate the economics of adopting the new credit policy. If the cost, including discounts, is less than 4.7% of the accounts receivable balance, we would expect the new policy to lead to increased profits for Heidman's Department Store.

Summary

In this chapter we presented Markov process models as well as examples of their application. We saw that a Markov analysis could provide helpful decision-making information about a situation that involves a sequence of repeated trials with a finite number of possible states on each trial. A primary objective is obtaining information about the probability of each state after a large number of transitions or time periods.

A market share application showed the computational procedure for determining the steady-state probabilities that could be interpreted as market shares for two competing supermarkets. In an accounts receivable application, we introduced the notion of absorbing states; for the two absorbing states, referred to as the paid and bad debt categories, we showed how to determine the percentage of an accounts receivable balance that would be absorbed in each of these states.

Markov process models have also been used to model decision problems in sports. The Q.M. in Action, Markov Process Models and Fantasy Football Drafts, describes the use of a Markov process to model a fantasy football draft to maximize a fantasy team owner's chances of winning their fantasy league.

Q.M. *in* ACTION

MARKOV PROCESS MODELS AND FANTASY FOOTBALL DRAFTS

Fantasy sports are a billion-dollar-plus industry, with an estimated 30+ million people playing fantasy sports in the United States alone. In fantasy sports, a fantasy team owner picks players for their teams to compete against other fantasy teams. A fantasy team's score is determined by the statistics accumulated by the real players in their actual games. For instance, in fantasy football, a fantasy team owner earns points for the yards gained, touchdowns scored, and so forth by the players in their fantasy team's starting lineup.

The largest fantasy sport in the United States is fantasy football, wherein fantasy team owners select players for their teams from the National Football League (NFL). Most fantasy football leagues select their teams through a fantasy draft. A fantasy draft is similar to a professional sports draft in that each team takes a turn to select a player for their fantasy team. All current players in the NFL are eligible to be drafted, and each fantasy team must fill certain roster spots for their team (for example, a fantasy team may require one starting quarterback, two starting running backs, two starting wide receivers, etc.).

A fantasy draft can be modeled as a Markov process. The state space includes the number of quarterbacks, running backs, wide receivers, and so on that still need to be drafted by each team as well as all the players still available to be drafted. Transitions among states occur as each team selects players and fills their team needs and reduces the pool of available players. The choices of opposing teams are uncertain, but probabilistic estimates can be made about their selections based on other fantasy football drafts that have already been completed and based on expert opinions regarding the future performance of the NFL players. These estimates provide the transition probabilities for the Markov process. The goal is for the fantasy team owner to select the players that maximize their chances of beating their competitors.

The resulting number of states and possible actions in the Markov process model are very large, but there exist methods to reduce the computational complexity of solving this problem using various heuristics. DraftOpt is a software application that solves the Markov process model representing a fantasy football draft. DraftOpt automates the solving of the Markov process model and provides recommendations to the user for which player to select in the next round of their draft. As the fantasy draft unfolds, the user updates DraftOpt with the picks made by the opposing fantasy teams; DraftOpt then re-solves the Markov process model and provides updated drafting recommendations to the user. Comparisons with other common techniques for drafting fantasy teams have shown that DraftOpt performs very well and results in competitive fantasy teams for their owners.

Glossary

Absorbing state A state is said to be absorbing if the probability of making a transition out of that state is zero. Thus, once the system has made a transition into an absorbing state, it will remain there.

Fundamental matrix A matrix necessary for the computation of probabilities associated with absorbing states of a Markov process.

Markov chain with stationary transition probabilities A Markov process where the transition probabilities remain constant over time and the probability of being in a particular state at any one time period depends only on the state in the immediately preceding time period.

State of the system The condition of the system at any particular trial or time period.

State probability The probability that the system will be in any particular state. (That is, $\pi_i(n)$ is the probability of the system being in state i in period n.)

Steady-state probability The probability that the system will be in any particular state after a large number of transitions. Once steady state has been reached, the state probabilities do not change from period to period.

Transition probability Given that the system is in state i during one period, the transition probability p_{ij} is the probability that the system will be in state j during the next period.

Trials of the process The events that trigger transitions of the system from one state to another. In many applications, successive time periods represent the trials of the process.

Problems

1. In the market share analysis of Section 17.1, suppose that we are considering the Markov process associated with the shopping trips of one customer, but we do not know where the customer shopped during the last week. Thus, we might assume a 0.5 probability that the customer shopped at Murphy's and a 0.5 probability that the customer shopped at Ashley's at period 0; that is, $\pi_1(0) = 0.5$ and $\pi_2(0) = 0.5$. Given these initial state probabilities, develop a table similar to Table 17.2, showing the probability of each state in future periods. What do you observe about the long-run probabilities of each state?

2. Management of the New Fangled Softdrink Company believes that the probability of a customer purchasing Red Pop or the company's major competition, Super Cola, is based on the customer's most recent purchase. Suppose that the following transition probabilities are appropriate:

	To	
From	**Red Pop**	**Super Cola**
Red Pop	0.9	0.1
Super Cola	0.1	0.9

   a. Show the two-period tree diagram for a customer who last purchased Red Pop. What is the probability that this customer purchases Red Pop on the second purchase?
   b. What is the long-run market share for each of these two products?
   c. A Red Pop advertising campaign is being planned to increase the probability of attracting Super Cola customers. Management believes that the new campaign will increase to 0.15 the probability of a customer switching from Super Cola to Red Pop. What is the projected effect of the advertising campaign on the market shares?

3. The email server at Rockbottom University has been experiencing downtime. Let us assume that the trials of an associated Markov process are defined as one-hour periods and that the

probability of the system being in a running state or a down state is based on the state of the system in the previous period. Historical data show the following transition probabilities:

	To	
From	**Running**	**Down**
Running	0.90	0.10
Down	0.30	0.70

   a. If the system is initially running, what is the probability of the system being down in the next hour of operation?

   b. What are the steady-state probabilities of the system being in the running state and in the down state?

4. One cause of the downtime in Problem 3 was traced to a specific piece of computer hardware. Management believes that switching to a different hardware component will result in the following transition probabilities:

	To	
From	**Running**	**Down**
Running	0.95	0.05
Down	0.60	0.40

   a. What are the steady-state probabilities of the system being in the running and down states?

   b. If the cost of the system being down for any period is estimated to be $500 (including lost productivity and maintenance costs), what is the breakeven cost for the new hardware component on a time-period basis?

5. A major traffic problem in the Greater Cincinnati area involves traffic attempting to cross the Ohio River from Cincinnati to Kentucky using Interstate 75. Let us assume that the probability of no traffic delay in one period, given no traffic delay in the preceding period, is 0.85 and that the probability of finding a traffic delay in one period, given a delay in the preceding period, is 0.75. Traffic is classified as having either a delay or a no-delay state, and the period considered is 30 minutes.

   a. Assume that you are a motorist entering the traffic system and receive a radio report of a traffic delay. What is the probability that for the next 60 minutes (two time periods) the system will be in the delay state? Note that this result is the probability of being in the delay state for two consecutive periods.

   b. What is the probability that in the long run the traffic will not be in the delay state?

   c. An important assumption of the Markov process models presented in this chapter has been the constant or stationary transition probabilities as the system operates in the future. Do you believe this assumption should be questioned for this traffic problem? Explain.

6. Rock-Paper-Scissors is a simple game in which two players compete by simultaneously choosing rock, paper, or scissors. According to the classic rules of the game, paper beats rock, scissors beats paper, and rock beats scissors. After watching one particular player compete in this game for many rounds, you have observed that she chooses rock, paper, or scissors based on her previous choice according to the following transition probabilities:

	Next Choice		
Previous Choice	**Rock**	**Paper**	**Scissors**
Rock	0.27	0.42	0.31
Paper	0.36	0.15	0.49
Scissors	0.18	0.55	0.27

Assume you are competing against this player and that you must decide on all future choices now (before seeing any additional opponent choices).

a. Given the opposing player last chose Rock, what is your best choice in the next round as her opponent?

b. Given the opposing player last chose Rock, show the two-period tree diagram.

c. Given the opposing player last chose Rock, calculate $\pi(2)$ and use this to find the probability that the opposing player will choose Paper two rounds from now.

7. Data collected from selected major metropolitan areas in the eastern United States show that 2% of individuals living within the city limits move to the suburbs during a one-year period while 1% of individuals living in the suburbs move to the city during a one-year period. Answer the following questions, assuming that this process is modeled by a Markov process with two states: city and suburbs:

a. Prepare the matrix of transition probabilities.

b. Compute the steady-state probabilities.

c. In a particular metropolitan area, 40% of the population lives in the city, and 60% of the population lives in the suburbs. What population changes do your steady-state probabilities project for this metropolitan area?

8. Assume that a third grocery store, Quick Stop Groceries, enters the market share and customer loyalty situation described in Section 17.1. Quick Stop Groceries is smaller than either Murphy's Foodliner or Ashley's Supermarket. However, Quick Stop's convenience with faster service and gasoline for automobiles can be expected to attract some customers who currently make weekly shopping visits to either Murphy's or Ashley's. Assume that the transition probabilities are as follows:

	To		
From	**Murphy's**	**Ashley's**	**Quick Stop**
Murphy's Foodliner	0.85	0.10	0.05
Ashley's Supermarket	0.20	0.75	0.05
Quick Stop Groceries	0.15	0.10	0.75

a. Compute the steady-state probabilities for this three-state Markov process.

b. What market share will Quick Stop obtain?

c. With 1000 customers, the original two-state Markov process in Section 17.1 projected 667 weekly customer trips to Murphy's Foodliner and 333 weekly customer trips to Ashley's Supermarket. What impact will Quick Stop have on the customer visits at Murphy's and Ashley's? Explain.

9. The purchase patterns for two brands of toothpaste can be expressed as a Markov process with the following transition probabilities:

	To	
From	**Special B**	**MDA**
Special B	0.90	0.10
MDA	0.05	0.95

a. Which brand appears to have the most loyal customers? Explain.

b. What are the projected market shares for the two brands?

10. Suppose that in Problem 9 a new toothpaste brand enters the market such that the following transition probabilities exist:

	To		
From	**Special B**	**MDA**	**T-White**
Special B	0.80	0.10	0.10
MDA	0.05	0.75	0.20
T-White	0.40	0.30	0.30

What are the new long-run market shares? Which brand will suffer most from the introduction of the new brand of toothpaste?

11. In American football, touchdowns are worth 6 points. After scoring a touchdown, the scoring team may subsequently attempt to score one or two additional points. Going for one point is virtually an assured success, while going for two points is successful only with probability p. Consider the following game situation. The Temple Wildcats are losing by 14 points to the Killeen Tigers near the end of regulation time. The only way for Temple to win (or tie) this game is to score two touchdowns while not allowing Killeen to score again. The Temple coach must decide whether to attempt a 1-point or 2-point conversion after each touchdown. If the score is tied at the end of regulation time, the game goes into overtime. The Temple coach believes that there is a 50% chance that Temple will win if the game goes into overtime. The probability of successfully converting a 1-point conversion is 1.0. The probability of successfully converting a 2-point conversion is p.

   a. Assume Temple will score two touchdowns and Killeen will not score. Define the set of states to include states representing the score differential as well as states for the final outcome of the game (Win or Lose). Create a tree diagram for the situation in which Temple's coach attempts a 2-point conversion after the first touchdown. If the 2-point conversion is successful, Temple will go for 1 point after the second touchdown to win the game. If the 2-point conversion is unsuccessful, Temple will go for 2 points after the second touchdown in an attempt to tie the game and go to overtime.

   b. Create the transition probability matrix for the decision problem in part (a).

   c. If Temple's coach goes for a 1-point conversion after each touchdown, the game is assured of going to overtime and Temple will win with probability 0.5. For what values of p is the strategy defined in part (a) superior to going for 1 point after each touchdown?

12. Given the following transition matrix with states 1 and 2 as absorbing states, what is the probability that units in states 3 and 4 end up in each of the absorbing states?

$$P = \begin{bmatrix} 1.0 & 0.0 & 0.0 & 0.0 \\ 0.0 & 1.0 & 0.0 & 0.0 \\ 0.2 & 0.1 & 0.4 & 0.3 \\ 0.2 & 0.2 & 0.1 & 0.5 \end{bmatrix}$$

13. In the Heidman's Department Store problem of Section 17.2, suppose that the following transition matrix is appropriate:

$$P = \begin{bmatrix} 1.0 & 0.0 & 0.0 & 0.0 \\ 0.0 & 1.0 & 0.0 & 0.0 \\ 0.5 & 0.0 & 0.25 & 0.25 \\ 0.5 & 0.2 & 0.05 & 0.25 \end{bmatrix}$$

If Heidman's has $4000 in the 0–30-day category and $5000 in the 31–90-day category, what is your estimate of the amount of bad debts the company will experience?

14. The KLM Christmas Tree Farm owns a plot of land with 5000 evergreen trees. Each year KLM allows retailers of Christmas trees to select and cut trees for sale to individual customers. KLM protects small trees (usually less than 4 feet tall) so that they will be available for sale in future years. Currently, 1500 trees are classified as protected trees, while the remaining 3500 are available for cutting. However, even though a tree is available for cutting in a given year, it may not be selected for cutting until future years. Most trees not cut in a given year live until the next year, but some diseased trees are lost every year.

    In viewing the KLM Christmas Tree Farm operation as a Markov process with yearly periods, we define the following four states:

    State 1. Cut and sold

    State 2. Lost to disease

    State 3. Too small for cutting

    State 4. Available for cutting but not cut and sold

    The following transition matrix is appropriate:

    $$P = \begin{bmatrix} 1.0 & 0.0 & 0.0 & 0.0 \\ 0.0 & 1.0 & 0.0 & 0.0 \\ 0.1 & 0.2 & 0.5 & 0.2 \\ 0.4 & 0.1 & 0.0 & 0.5 \end{bmatrix}$$

    How many of the farm's 5000 trees will be sold eventually, and how many will be lost?

15. A large corporation collected data on the reasons both middle managers and senior managers leave the company. Some managers eventually retire, but others leave the company prior to retirement for personal reasons, including more attractive positions with other firms. Assume that the following matrix of one-year transition probabilities applies with the four states of the Markov process being retirement, leaves prior to retirement for personal reasons, stays as a middle manager, and stays as a senior manager.

	Retirement	Leaves—Personal	Middle Manager	Senior Manager
Retirement	1.00	0.00	0.00	0.00
Leaves—Personal	0.00	1.00	0.00	0.00
Middle Manager	0.03	0.07	0.80	0.10
Senior Manager	0.08	0.01	0.03	0.88

    a. What states are considered absorbing states? Why?
    b. Interpret the transition probabilities for the middle managers.
    c. Interpret the transition probabilities for the senior managers.
    d. What percentage of the current middle managers will eventually retire from the company? What percentage will leave the company for personal reasons?
    e. The company currently has 920 managers: 640 middle managers and 280 senior managers. How many of these managers will eventually retire from the company? How many will leave the company for personal reasons?

16. Players in a particular sports league are classified based on the amount of time they play as backups or starters. Players can also become seriously injured or they can retire from competition. Consider the following transition probability matrix.

	Backup	**Starter**	**Injured**	**Retired**
Backup	0.4	0.4	0.1	0.1
Starter	0.1	0.5	0.15	0.25
Injured	0	0	1	0
Retired	0	0	0	1

a. What state(s) are absorbing states?
b. What percentage of current starters will eventually be injured?
c. Currently a team called The Sharks has eight backups and five starters. How many of the players do you expect to end up injured? Retired?

Case Problem   Dealer's Absorbing State Probabilities in Blackjack

The game of blackjack (sometimes called "21") is a popular casino game. The goal is to have a hand with a value of 21 or as close to 21 as possible without exceeding 21. The player and the dealer are each dealt two cards initially. Both the player and dealer may draw additional cards (called "taking a hit") in order to improve their hand. If either the player or dealer takes a hit and the value of the hand exceeds 21, the player or dealer is said to have gone broke and loses. Face cards and tens count 10 points, aces can be counted as 1 or 11, and all other cards count at their face value. The dealer's advantage is that the player must decide on whether to take a hit first. The player who takes a hit and goes over 21 goes broke and loses, even if the dealer later goes broke. For instance, if the player has 16 and draws any card with a value higher than a 5, the player goes broke and loses. For this reason, players will often decide not to take a hit when the value of their hand is 12 or greater.

The dealer's hand is dealt with one card up and one card down. So, the player's decision of whether to take a hit is based on knowledge of the dealer's up card. A gambling professional asks you to help determine the probability of the ending value of the dealer's hand given different up cards. House rules at casinos require that the dealer continue to take a hit until the dealer's hand reaches a value of 17 or higher. Having just studied Markov processes, you suggest that the dealer's process of taking hits can be modeled as a Markov process with absorbing states.

Managerial Report

Prepare a report for the professional gambler that summarizes your findings. Include the following:

1. At some casinos, the dealer is required to stay (stop taking hits) when the dealer hand reaches soft or hard 17. A hand of soft 17 is one including an ace that may be counted as 1 or 11. In all casinos, the dealer is required to stay with soft 18, 19, 20, or 21. For each possible up card, determine the probability that the ending value of the dealer's hand is 17, 18, 19, 20, 21, or broke.
2. At other casinos, the dealer is required to take a hit on soft 17, but must stay on all other hands with a value of 17, 18, 19, 20, or 21. For this situation, determine the probability of the ending value of the dealer's hand.
3. Comment on whether the house rule of staying on soft 17 or hitting on soft 17 appears better for the player.

Appendix 17.1 Matrix Notation and Operations

Matrix Notation

A *matrix* is a rectangular arrangement of numbers. For example, consider the following matrix that we have named D:

$$D = \begin{bmatrix} 1 & 3 & 2 \\ 0 & 4 & 5 \end{bmatrix}$$

The matrix D is said to consist of six elements, where each element of D is a number. To identify a particular element of a matrix, we have to specify its location. Therefore, we introduce the concepts of rows and columns.

All elements across some horizontal line in a matrix are said to be in a row of the matrix. For example, elements 1, 3, and 2 in D are in the first row, and elements 0, 4, and 5 are in the second row. By convention, we refer to the top row as row 1, the second row from the top as row 2, and so on.

All elements along some vertical line are said to be in a column of the matrix. Elements 1 and 0 in D are elements in the first column, elements 3 and 4 are elements of the second column, and elements 2 and 5 are elements of the third column. By convention, we refer to the leftmost column as column 1, the next column to the right as column 2, and so on.

We can identify a particular element in a matrix by specifying its row and column position. For example, the element in row 1 and column 2 of D is the number 3. This position is written as

$$d_{12} = 3$$

In general, we use the following notation to refer to the specific elements of D:

$$d_{ij} = \text{element located in the } i\text{th row and } j\text{th column of } D$$

We always use capital letters for the names of matrixes and the corresponding lowercase letters with two subscripts to denote the elements.

The *size* of a matrix is the number of rows and columns in the matrix and is written as the number of rows $\times$ the number of columns. Thus, the size of D is 2×3.

Frequently we will encounter matrixes that have only one row or one column. For example,

$$G = \begin{bmatrix} 6 \\ 4 \\ 2 \\ 3 \end{bmatrix}$$

is a matrix that has only one column. Whenever a matrix has only one column, we call the matrix a *column vector*. In a similar manner, any matrix that has only one row is called a *row vector*. Using our previous notation for the elements of a matrix, we could refer to specific elements in G by writing g_{ij}. However, since G has only one column, the column position is unimportant, and we need only specify the row the element of interest is in. That is, instead of referring to elements in a vector using g_{ij}, we specify only one subscript, which denotes the position of the element in the vector. For example,

$$g_1 = 6 \qquad g_2 = 4 \qquad g_3 = 2 \qquad g_4 = 3$$

Matrix Operations

Matrix Transpose The transpose of a matrix is formed by making the rows in the original matrix the columns in the transpose matrix, and by making the columns in the original matrix the rows in the transpose matrix. For example, the transpose of the matrix

$$D = \begin{bmatrix} 1 & 3 & 2 \\ 0 & 4 & 5 \end{bmatrix}$$

is

$$D^t = \begin{bmatrix} 1 & 0 \\ 3 & 4 \\ 2 & 5 \end{bmatrix}$$

Note that we use the superscript t to denote the transpose of a matrix.

Matrix Multiplication We demonstrate how to perform two types of matrix multiplication: (1) multiplying two vectors, and (2) multiplying a matrix times a matrix.

The product of a row vector of size $1 \times n$ times a column vector of size $n \times 1$ is the number obtained by multiplying the first element in the row vector times the first element in the column vector, the second element in the row vector times the second element in the column vector, continuing on through the last element in the row vector times the last element in the column vector, and then summing the products. Suppose, for example, that we wanted to multiply the row vector H times the column vector G, where

$$H = [2 \quad 1 \quad 5 \quad 0] \text{ and } G = \begin{bmatrix} 6 \\ 4 \\ 2 \\ 3 \end{bmatrix}$$

The product HG, referred to as a vector product, is given by

$$HG = 2(6) + 1(4) + 5(2) + 0(3) = 26$$

The product of a matrix of size $p \times n$ and a matrix of size $n \times m$ is a new matrix of size $p \times m$. The element in the ith row and jth column of the new matrix is given by the vector product of the ith row of the $p \times n$ matrix times the jth column of the $n \times m$ matrix. Suppose, for example, that we want to multiply D times A, where

$$D = \begin{bmatrix} 1 & 3 & 2 \\ 0 & 4 & 5 \end{bmatrix} \quad A = \begin{bmatrix} 1 & 3 & 5 \\ 2 & 0 & 4 \\ 1 & 5 & 2 \end{bmatrix}$$

Let $C = DA$ denote the product of D times A. The element in row 1 and column 1 of C is given by the vector product of the first row of D times the first column of A. Thus,

$$c_{11} = [1 \quad 3 \quad 2] \begin{bmatrix} 1 \\ 2 \\ 1 \end{bmatrix} = 1(1) + 3(2) + 2(1) = 9$$

The element in row 2 and column 1 of C is given by the vector product of the second row of D times the first column of A. Thus,

$$c_{21} = [0 \quad 4 \quad 5] \begin{bmatrix} 1 \\ 2 \\ 1 \end{bmatrix} = 0(1) + 4(2) + 5(1) = 13$$

Calculating the remaining elements of C in a similar fashion, we obtain

$$C = \begin{bmatrix} 9 & 13 & 21 \\ 13 & 25 & 26 \end{bmatrix}$$

Clearly, the product of a matrix and a vector is just a special case of multiplying a matrix times a matrix. For example, the product of a matrix of size $m \times n$ and a vector of size $n \times 1$ is a new vector of size $m \times 1$. The element in the ith position of the new vector is given by the vector product of the ith row of the $m \times n$ matrix times the $n \times 1$ column vector. Suppose, for example, that we want to multiply D times K, where

$$D = \begin{bmatrix} 1 & 3 & 2 \\ 0 & 4 & 5 \end{bmatrix} \quad K = \begin{bmatrix} 1 \\ 4 \\ 2 \end{bmatrix}$$

The first element of DK is given by the vector product of the first row of D times K. Thus,

$$\begin{bmatrix} 1 & 3 & 2 \end{bmatrix} \begin{bmatrix} 1 \\ 4 \\ 2 \end{bmatrix} = 1(1) + 3(4) + 2(2) = 17$$

The second element of DK is given by the vector product of the second row of D and K. Thus,

$$\begin{bmatrix} 0 & 4 & 5 \end{bmatrix} \begin{bmatrix} 1 \\ 4 \\ 2 \end{bmatrix} = 0(1) + 4(4) + 5(2) = 26$$

Hence, we see that the product of the matrix D times the vector K is given by

$$DK = \begin{bmatrix} 1 & 3 & 2 \\ 0 & 4 & 5 \end{bmatrix} \begin{bmatrix} 1 \\ 4 \\ 2 \end{bmatrix} = \begin{bmatrix} 17 \\ 26 \end{bmatrix}$$

Can any two matrixes be multiplied? The answer is no. To multiply two matrixes, the number of the columns in the first matrix must equal the number of rows in the second. If this property is satisfied, the matrixes are said to *conform for multiplication.* Thus, in our example, D and K could be multiplied because D had three columns and K had three rows.

Matrix Inverse The inverse of a matrix A is another matrix, denoted A^{-1}, such that $A^{-1}A = I$ and $AA^{-1} = I$. The inverse of any square matrix A consisting of two rows and two columns is computed as follows:

$$A = \begin{bmatrix} a_{11} & a_{12} \\ a_{21} & a_{22} \end{bmatrix}$$

$$A^{-1} = \begin{bmatrix} a_{22}/d & -a_{12}/d \\ -a_{21}/d & a_{11}/d \end{bmatrix}$$

where $d = a_{11}a_{22} - a_{21}a_{12}$ is the determinant of the 2×2 matrix A. For example, if

$$A = \begin{bmatrix} 0.7 & -0.3 \\ -0.3 & 0.9 \end{bmatrix}$$

then

$$d = (0.7)(0.9) - (-0.3)(-0.3) = 0.54$$

and

$$A^{-1} = \begin{bmatrix} 0.9/0.54 & 0.3/0.54 \\ 0.3/0.54 & 0.7/0.54 \end{bmatrix} = \begin{bmatrix} 1.67 & 0.56 \\ 0.56 & 1.30 \end{bmatrix}$$

Appendix 17.2 Matrix Inversion with Excel

Excel provides a function called MINVERSE that can be used to compute the inverse of a matrix. This function is extremely useful when the inverse of a matrix of size 3 × 3 or larger is desired. To see how it is used, suppose we want to invert the following 3 × 3 matrix:

$$\begin{bmatrix} 3 & 5 & 0 \\ 0 & 1 & 1 \\ 8 & 5 & 0 \end{bmatrix}$$

Enter the matrix into cells B3:D5 of an Excel worksheet. The following steps will compute the inverse and place it in cells B7:D9:

Step 1. Select cells B7:D9
Step 2. Type =*MINVERSE(B3:D5)*
Step 3. Press **Ctrl + Shift + Enter**

Step 3 may appear strange. Excel's MINVERSE function returns an array (matrix) and must be used in what Excel calls an array formula. In step 3, we must press the Ctrl and Shift keys while we press Enter. The inverse matrix will then appear as follows in cells B7:D9:

$$\begin{bmatrix} -0.20 & 0 & 0.20 \\ 0.32 & 0 & -0.12 \\ -0.32 & 1 & 0.12 \end{bmatrix}$$

APPENDIXES

Appendix A   Building Spreadsheet Models

The purpose of this appendix is twofold. First, we provide an overview of Excel and discuss the basic operations needed to work with Excel workbooks and worksheets. Second, we provide an introduction to building mathematical models using Excel, including a discussion of how to find and use particular Excel functions, how to design and build good spreadsheet models, and how to ensure that these models are free of errors.

Overview of Microsoft Excel

A workbook is a file containing one or more worksheets.

When using Excel for modeling, the data and the model are displayed in workbooks, each of which contains a series of worksheets. Figure A.1 shows the layout of a blank workbook created each time Excel is opened. The workbook is named Book1 and contains a worksheet named Sheet1. Note that cell A1 is initially selected.

The wide bar located across the top of the workbook is referred to as the Ribbon. Tabs, located at the top of the Ribbon, provide quick access to groups of related commands. There are eight tabs: Home, Insert, Page Layout, Formulas, Data, Review, View, and Add-Ins. Each tab contains several groups of related commands. Note that the HOME tab is selected when Excel is opened. The seven groups associated with the HOME tab are displayed in Figure A.2. Under the HOME tab there are seven groups of related commands: Clipboard, Font, Alignment, Number, Styles, Cells, and Editing. Commands are arranged within each group. For example, to change selected text to boldface, click the HOME tab and click the Bold button **B** in the Font group.

FIGURE A.1   BLANK WORKBOOK CREATED WHEN EXCEL IS STARTED

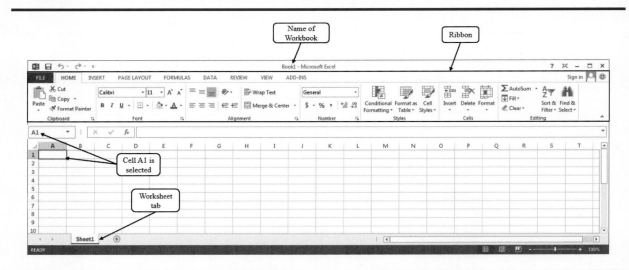

FIGURE A.2   PORTION OF THE HOME TAB

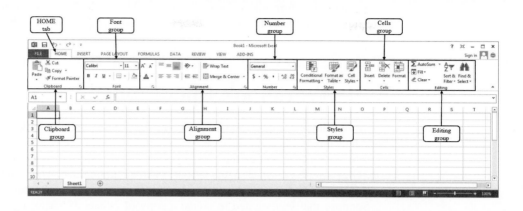

FIGURE A.3   EXCEL FILE TAB, QUICK ACCESS TOOLBAR, AND
FORMULA BAR

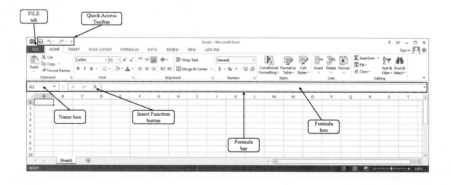

Figure A.3 illustrates the location of the FILE tab, the Quick Access Toolbar, and the Formula Bar. When you click the FILE tab, Excel provides a list of workbook options such as opening, saving, and printing (worksheets). The Quick Access Toolbar allows you to quickly access these workbook options. For instance, the Quick Access Toolbar shown in Figure A.3 includes a Save button 🖫 that can be used to save files without having to first click the FILE tab. To add or remove features on the Quick Access Toolbar click the Customize Quick Access Toolbar button ▾ on the Quick Access Toolbar.

The Formula Bar contains a Name box, the Insert Function button *fx*, and a Formula box. In Figure A.3, "A1" appears in the Name box because cell A1 is selected. You can select any other cell in the worksheet by using the mouse to move the cursor to another cell and clicking or by typing the new cell location in the name box and pressing the enter key. The Formula box is used to display the formula in the currently selected cell.

For instance, if you had entered $=A1+A2$ into cell A3, whenever you select cell A3, the formula $=A1+A2$ will be shown in the Formula box. This feature makes it very easy to see and edit a formula in a particular cell. The Insert Function button allows you to quickly access all of the functions available in Excel. Later, we show how to find and use a particular function.

Basic Workbook Operations

Figure A.4 illustrates the worksheet options that can be performed after right clicking on a worksheet tab. For instance, to change the name of the current worksheet from "Sheet1" to "NowlinModel," right click the worksheet tab named "Sheet1" and select the Rename option. The current worksheet name (Sheet1) will be highlighted. Then, simply type the new name (NowlinModel) and press the Enter key to rename the worksheet.

Suppose that you wanted to create a copy of "Sheet 1." After right clicking the tab named "Sheet1," select the Move or Copy option. When the Move or Copy dialog box appears, select Create a Copy and click OK. The name of the copied worksheet will appear as "Sheet1 (2)." You can then rename it, if desired.

To add a worksheet to the workbook, right click any worksheet tab and select the Insert option; when the Insert dialog box appears, select Worksheet and click OK. An additional blank worksheet titled Sheet2 will appear in the workbook. You can also insert a new worksheet by clicking the Insert Worksheet tab button ⊕ that appears to the right of the last worksheet tab displayed. Worksheets can be deleted by right clicking the worksheet tab and choosing Delete. After clicking Delete, a window will appear warning you that any data appearing in the worksheet will be lost. Click Delete to confirm that you do want to delete the worksheet. Worksheets can also be moved to other workbooks or a different position in the current workbook by using the Move or Copy option.

FIGURE A.4   WORKSHEET OPTIONS OBTAINED AFTER RIGHT CLICKING ON A WORKSHEET TAB

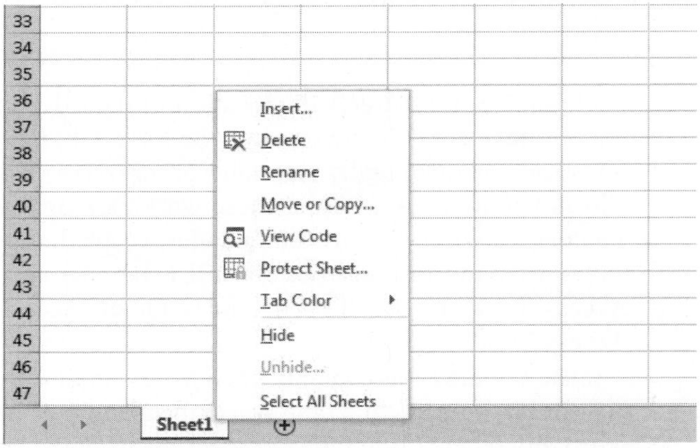

Creating, Saving, and Opening Files

As an illustration of manually entering, saving, and opening a file, we will use the Nowlin Plastics production example from Chapter 1. The objective is to compute the breakeven point for a product that has a fixed cost of $3000, a variable cost per unit of $2, and a selling price per unit of $5. We begin by creating a worksheet containing the problem data.

If you have just opened Excel, a blank workbook containing Sheet1 will be displayed. The Nowlin data can now be entered manually by simply typing the fixed cost of $3000, the variable cost of $2, and the selling price of $5 into one of the worksheets. If Excel is currently running and no blank workbook is displayed, you can create a new blank workbook using the following steps:

Step 1. Click the **FILE** tab
Step 2. Click **New** in the list of options
Step 3. Click **Blank Workbook**

A new workbook will appear.

We will place the data for the Nowlin example in the top portion of Sheet1 of the new workbook. First, we enter the label "Nowlin Plastics" into cell A1. To identify each of the three data values we enter the label "Fixed Cost" into cell A3, the label "Variable Cost Per Unit" into cell A5, and the label "Selling Price Per Unit" into cell A7. Next, we enter the actual cost and price data into the corresponding cells in column B: the value of $3000 in cell B3; the value of $2 in cell B5; and the value of $5 into cell B7. Finally, we will change the name of the worksheet from "Sheet1" to "NowlinModel" using the procedure described previously. Figure A.5 shows a portion of the worksheet we have just developed.

Before we begin the development of the model portion of the worksheet, we recommend that you first save the current file; this will prevent you from having to reenter the

FIGURE A.5   NOWLIN PLASTICS DATA

	A	B
1	**Nowlin Plastics**	
2		
3	**Fixed Cost**	$3,000
4		
5	**Variable Cost Per Unit**	$2
6		
7	**Selling Price Per Unit**	$5
8		
9		
10		
11		
12		
13		
14		
15		
16		
17		
18		

data in case something happens that causes Excel to close. To save the workbook using the filename "Nowlin," we perform the following steps:

Step 3 is only necessary for Excel 2013. In previous versions of Excel you may skip to Step 4.

Step 1. Click the **FILE** tab on the Ribbon
Step 2. Click **Save** in the list of options
Step 3. Select **Computer** under **Save As** and click **Browse**
Step 4. When the **Save As** dialog box appears:
Select the location where you want to save the file
Enter the file name *Nowlin* in the **File name** box
Click **Save**

Excel's Save command is designed to save the file as an Excel workbook. As you work with and build models in Excel, you should follow the practice of periodically saving the file so you will not lose any work. Simply follow the procedure described above, using the Save command.

*Keyboard shortcut: To save the file, press **CTRL S**.*

Sometimes you may want to create a copy of an existing file. For instance, suppose you change one or more of the data values and would like to save the modified file using the filename "NowlinMod." The following steps show how to save the modified workbook using filename "NowlinMod."

Step 1. Click the **FILE** tab in the Ribbon
Step 2. Click **Save As** in the list of options
Step 3. Select **Computer** under **Save As** and click **Browse**
Step 4. When the **Save As** dialog box appears:
Select the location where you want to save the file
Type the file name *NowlinMod* in the **File name** box
Click **Save**

Once the NowlinMod workbook has been saved, you can continue to work with the file to perform whatever type of analysis is appropriate. When you are finished working with the file, simply click the close window button ✖ located at the top right-hand corner of the Ribbon.

You can easily access a saved file at another point in time. For example, the following steps show how to open the previously saved Nowlin workbook.

Step 3 is only necessary in Excel 2013. The filename Nowlin *may also appear under the **Recent Workbooks** list in Excel to allow you to open it directly without navigating to where you saved the file.*

Step 1. Click the **FILE** tab in the Ribbon
Step 2. Click **Open** in the list of options
Step 3. Select **Computer** under **Open** and click **Browse**
Step 4. When the **Open** dialog box appears:
Find the location where you previously saved the *Nowlin* file
Click on the filename **Nowlin** so that it appears in the **File name** box
Click **Open**

The procedures we showed for saving or opening a workbook begin by clicking on the FILE tab to access the Save and Open commands. Once you have used Excel for a while, you will probably find it more convenient to add these commands to the Quick Access Toolbar.

Cells, References, and Formulas in Excel

Assume that the Nowlin workbook is open again and that we would like to develop a model that can be used to compute the profit or loss associated with a given production volume. We will use the bottom portion of the worksheet shown in Figure A.5 to develop the model. The model will contain formulas that *refer to the location of the data cells* in the upper section of the worksheet. By putting the location of the data cells in the formula, we will build a model that can be easily updated with new data. This will be discussed in more detail later in this appendix in the section Principles for Building Good Spreadsheet Models.

We enter the label "Model" into cell A10 to provide a visual reminder that the bottom portion of this worksheet will contain the model. Next, we enter the labels "Production Volume" into cell A12, "Total Cost" into cell A14, "Total Revenue" into cell A16, and "Total Profit (Loss)" into cell A18. Cell B12 is used to contain a value for the production volume. We will now enter formulas into cells B14, B16, and B18 that use the production volume in cell B12 to compute the values for total cost, total revenue, and total profit or loss.

*To display all formulas in the cells of a worksheet, hold down the **CTRL** key and then press the ` key.*

Total cost is the sum of the fixed cost (cell B3) and the total variable cost. The total variable cost is the product of the variable cost per unit (cell B5) and production volume (cell B12). Thus, the formula for total variable cost is B5*B12 and to compute the value of total cost, we enter the formula =B3+B5*B12 into cell B14. Next, assuming we are able to sell all that we produce, total revenue is the product of the selling price per unit (cell B7) and the number of units produced (cell B12), which we enter in cell B16 as the formula =B7*B12. Finally, the total profit or loss is the difference between the total revenue (cell B16) and the total cost (cell B14). Thus, in cell B18 we enter the formula =B16-B14. Figure A.6 shows a portion of the formula worksheet just described.

We can now compute the total profit or loss for a particular production volume by entering a value for the production volume into cell B12. Figure A.7 shows the results after entering a value of 800 into cell B12. We see that a production volume of 800 units results in a total cost of $4600, a total revenue of $4000, and a loss of $600.

FIGURE A.6   NOWLIN PLASTICS DATA AND MODEL

	A	B
1	**Nowlin Plastics**	
2		
3	**Fixed Cost**	3000
4		
5	**Variable Cost Per Unit**	2
6		
7	**Selling Price Per Unit**	5
8		
9		
10	**Model**	
11		
12	**Production Volume**	
13		
14	**Total Cost**	=B3+B5*B12
15		
16	**Total Revenue**	=B7*B12
17		
18	**Total Profit (Loss)**	=B16-B14

FIGURE A.7   NOWLIN PLASTICS RESULTS

	A	B
1	**Nowlin Plastics**	
2		
3	**Fixed Cost**	$3,000
4		
5	**Variable Cost Per Unit**	$2
6		
7	**Selling Price Per Unit**	$5
8		
9		
10	**Model**	
11		
12	**Production Volume**	800
13		
14	**Total Cost**	$4,600
15		
16	**Total Revenue**	$4,000
17		
18	**Total Profit (Loss)**	−$600

What–If Analysis

Excel offers a number of tools to facilitate what-if analysis. In this section we introduce two such tools, Data Tables and Goal Seek. Both of these tools are designed to rid the user of the tedious manual trial-and-error approach to analysis. Let us see how these two tools can help us analyze Nowlin's breakeven decision as discussed in Section 1.4.

Data Tables

An Excel **Data Table** quantifies the impact of changing the value of a specific input on an output of interest. Excel can generate either a **one-way data table**, which summarizes a single input's impact on the output, or a **two-way data table**, which summarizes two inputs' impact on the output.

Let us consider how profit changes as the quantity of Vipers produced changes. A one-way data table changing the production volume and reporting total profit (or loss) would be very useful. We will use the previously developed Nowlin spreadsheet for this analysis.

The first step in creating a one-way data table is to construct a sorted list of the values you would like to consider for the input. Let us investigate the production volume over a range from 0 to 1600 in increments of 100 units. Figure A.8 shows we have entered these data in cells D5 through D21, with a column label in D4. This column of data is the set of values that Excel will use as inputs for production volume. Since the output of interest is profit (or loss) (located in cell B18), we have entered the formula =B18 in cell E4. In general, set the cell to the right of the label to the cell location of the output

FIGURE A.8   THE INPUT FOR CONSTRUCTING A ONE-WAY DATA TABLE FOR NOWLIN PLASTICS

	A	B	C	D	E	F	G	H
1	**Nowlin Plastics**							
2								
3	**Fixed Cost**	$3,000						
4				Production Volume	-$600			
5	**Variable Cost Per Unit**	$2		0				
6				100				
7	**Selling Price Per Unit**	$5		200	Data Table		? X	
8				300	Row input cell:			
9				400	Column input cell:	$B$12		
10	**Model**			500	OK		Cancel	
11				600				
12	**Production Volume**	800		700				
13				800				
14	**Total Cost**	$4,600		900				
15				1000				
16	**Total Revenue**	$4,000		1100				
17				1200				
18	**Total Profit (Loss)**	-$600		1300				
19				1400				
20				1500				
21				1600				
22								

variable of interest. Once the basic structure is in place, we invoke the Data Table tool using the following steps:

*Entering B12 in the **Column input cell**: box indicates that the column of data corresponds to different values of the input located in cell B12.*

Step 1. Select cells D4:E21
Step 2. Click the **DATA** tab in the Ribbon
Step 3. Click **What-If Analysis** in the **Data Tools** group, and select **Data Table**
Step 4. When the **Data Table** dialog box appears, enter *B12* in the **Column input cell:** box
Click **OK**

As shown in Figure A.9, the table will be populated with profit (or loss) for each production volume in the table. For example, when production volume = 1200, profit = $600 and when production = 500, profit = −$1,500. We see that for a production volume of 1000 units, profit = 0. Hence, 1000 units is the breakeven volume. If Nowlin produces more than 1000 units, it will earn a profit; if Nowlin produces fewer than 1000 units, it will suffer a loss.

Suppose Nowlin would like to better understand how the breakeven production volume changes as selling price changes. A two-way data table with rows corresponding to production quantity and columns corresponding to various selling prices would be helpful.

In Figure A.10, we have entered various quantities in cells D5 through D21, as in the one-way table. These correspond to cell B12 in our model. In cells E4 through L4, we have entered selling prices from $3 to $10 in increments of $1. These correspond to B7, the selling price per unit. In cell D4, above the column input values and to the left of the row input values, we have entered the formula =B18, the location of the output of interest, in

FIGURE A.9   RESULTS OF ONE-WAY DATA TABLE FOR NOWLIN PLASTICS

	A	B	C	D	E	F
1	Nowlin Plastics					
2						
3	Fixed Cost	$3,000				
4				Production Volume	-$600	
5	Variable Cost Per Unit	$2		0	-$3,000	
6				100	-$2,700	
7	Selling Price Per Unit	$5		200	-$2,400	
8				300	-$2,100	
9				400	-$1,800	
10	Model			500	-$1,500	
11				600	-$1,200	
12	Production Volume	800		700	-$900	
13				800	-$600	
14	Total Cost	$4,600		900	-$300	
15				1000	$0	
16	Total Revenue	$4,000		1100	$300	
17				1200	$600	
18	Total Profit (Loss)	-$600		1300	$900	
19				1400	$1,200	
20				1500	$1,500	
21				1600	$1,800	

FIGURE A.10   THE INPUT FOR CONSTRUCTING A TWO-WAY DATA TABLE FOR NOWLIN PLASTICS

	A	B	C	D	E	F	G	H	I	J	K	L	M
1	Nowlin Plastics												
2													
3	Fixed Cost	$3,000											
4				-$600	$3	$4	$5	$6	$7	$8	$9	$10	
5	Variable Cost Per Unit	$2		0									
6				100									
7	Selling Price Per Unit	$5		200									
8				300									
9				400									
10	Model			500									
11				600									
12	Production Volume	800		700									
13				800									
14	Total Cost	$4,600		900									
15				1000									
16	Total Revenue	$4,000		1100									
17				1200									
18	Total Profit (Loss)	-$600		1300									
19				1400									
20				1500									
21				1600									
22													

Data Table
Row input cell: $B$7
Column input cell: $B$12
OK   Cancel

this case, profit (or loss). Once the table inputs have been entered into the spreadsheet, we perform the following steps to construct the two-way Data Table.

Step 1. Select cells D4:L21
Step 2. Click the **DATA** tab in the Ribbon
Step 3. Click **What-If Analysis** in the **Data Tools** group, and select **Data Table**
Step 4. When the **Data Table** dialog box appears:
Enter *B7* in the **Row input cell:** box
Enter *B12* in the **Column input cell:** box
Click **OK**

Figure A.10 shows the selected cells and the **Data Table** dialog box. The results are shown in Figure A.11.

From this two-way data table, we can make a number of observations about the breakeven production volume for various selling prices. For example, consider a selling price of $3; since losses are smaller at higher production volumes and there is a loss at 1600 units, we know that the breakeven production volume exceeds 1600 units. Likewise, we know the breakeven point for a selling price of $4 is 1500 units ($0 profit there). Similarly, we know the exact breakeven points for selling prices of $5, $7, and $8 are 1000, 600, and 500, respectively. Because of the change in sign from negative to positive (indicating a change from loss to profit), we see that the breakeven production volume for a selling price of $6 is between 700 and 800 units. For a selling price of $9, the breakeven is between 400 and 500 units, and for a selling price of $10 it is between 300 and 400 units. Next we show how to use Excel's Goal Seek tool to find the exact breakeven production volume for these selling prices.

FIGURE A.11   RESULTS OF TWO-WAY DATA TABLE FOR NOWLIN PLASTICS

	A	B	C	D	E	F	G	H	I	J	K	L	M
1	Nowlin Plastics												
2													
3	Fixed Cost	$3,000											
4				-$600	$3	$4	$5	$6	$7	$8	$9	$10	
5	Variable Cost Per Unit	$2		0	-$3,000	-$3,000	-$3,000	-$3,000	-$3,000	-$3,000	-$3,000	-$3,000	
6				100	-$2,900	-$2,800	-$2,700	-$2,600	-$2,500	-$2,400	-$2,300	-$2,200	
7	Selling Price Per Unit	$5		200	-$2,800	-$2,600	-$2,400	-$2,200	-$2,000	-$1,800	-$1,600	-$1,400	
8				300	-$2,700	-$2,400	-$2,100	-$1,800	-$1,500	-$1,200	-$900	-$600	
9				400	-$2,600	-$2,200	-$1,800	-$1,400	-$1,000	-$600	-$200	$200	
10	Model			500	-$2,500	-$2,000	-$1,500	-$1,000	-$500	$0	$500	$1,000	
11				600	-$2,400	-$1,800	-$1,200	-$600	$0	$600	$1,200	$1,800	
12	Production Volume	800		700	-$2,300	-$1,600	-$900	-$200	$500	$1,200	$1,900	$2,600	
13				800	-$2,200	-$1,400	-$600	$200	$1,000	$1,800	$2,600	$3,400	
14	Total Cost	$4,600		900	-$2,100	-$1,200	-$300	$600	$1,500	$2,400	$3,300	$4,200	
15				1000	-$2,000	-$1,000	$0	$1,000	$2,000	$3,000	$4,000	$5,000	
16	Total Revenue	$4,000		1100	-$1,900	-$800	$300	$1,400	$2,500	$3,600	$4,700	$5,800	
17				1200	-$1,800	-$600	$600	$1,800	$3,000	$4,200	$5,400	$6,600	
18	Total Profit (Loss)	-$600		1300	-$1,700	-$400	$900	$2,200	$3,500	$4,800	$6,100	$7,400	
19				1400	-$1,600	-$200	$1,200	$2,600	$4,000	$5,400	$6,800	$8,200	
20				1500	-$1,500	$0	$1,500	$3,000	$4,500	$6,000	$7,500	$9,000	
21				1600	-$1,400	$200	$1,800	$3,400	$5,000	$6,600	$8,200	$9,800	
22													

Goal Seek

Excel's **Goal Seek** tool allows the user to determine the value of an input cell that will cause the value of a related output cell to equal some specified value (the *goal*). In the case of Nowlin Plastics, suppose we want to know the exact breakeven production volume for a selling price of $6. We know from the two-way data table in Figure A.11 that the breakeven volume for a selling price of $6 is between 700 and 800 units (that is where the profit goes from negative to positive). Somewhere in this range of 700 to 800 units, the profit equals zero, and the production quantity where this occurs is the breakeven point. After setting cell B7 to $6, the following steps show how to use Goal Seek to find the breakeven point for this selling price.

Step 1. Click the **DATA** tab in the Ribbon
Step 2. Click **What-If Analysis** in the **Data Tools** group, and select **Goal Seek**
Step 3. When the **Goal Seek** dialog box appears (Figure A.12):
Enter *B18* in the **Set cell:** box
Enter *0* in the **To value:** box
Enter *B12* in the **By changing cell:** box
Click **OK**
Step 4. When the **Goal Seek Status** dialog box appears, click **OK**

The completed Goal Seek dialog box is shown in Figure A.12.
The results from Goal Seek are shown in Figure A.13. We see that the breakeven point for a selling price of $6 is 750 units.

FIGURE A.12   GOAL SEEK DIALOG BOX FOR NOWLIN PLASTICS

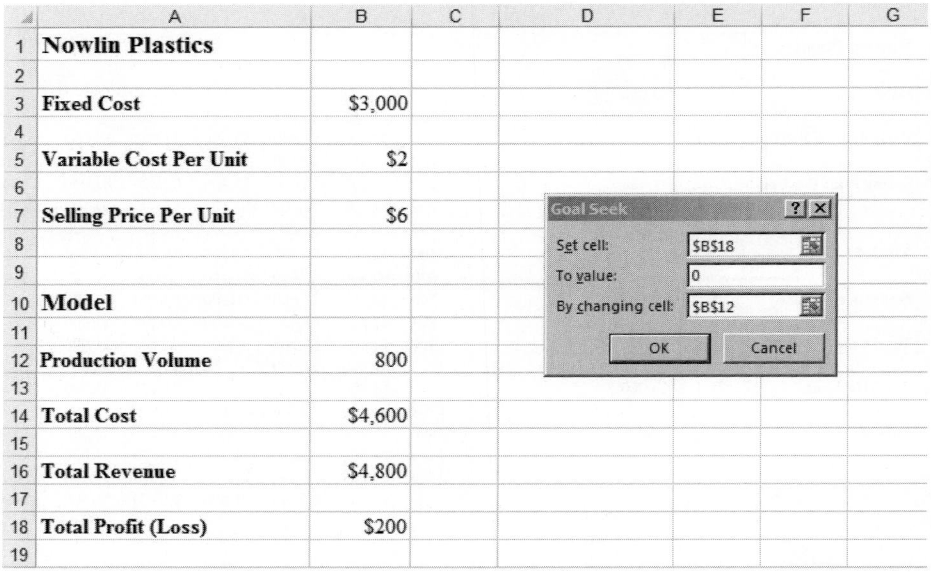

FIGURE A.13   RESULTS FROM GOAL SEEK FOR NOWLIN PLASTICS

	A	B	C	D	E	F	G
1	**Nowlin Plastics**						
2							
3	**Fixed Cost**	$3,000					
4							
5	**Variable Cost Per Unit**	$2					
6							
7	**Selling Price Per Unit**	$6					
8							
9							
10	**Model**						
11							
12	**Production Volume**	750					
13							
14	**Total Cost**	$4,500					
15							
16	**Total Revenue**	$4,500					
17							
18	**Total Profit (Loss)**	$0					
19							

Goal Seek Status dialog box overlay:

Goal Seek Status   ? X

Goal Seeking with Cell B18 found a solution.

Target value: 0
Current value: $0

Step   Pause

OK   Cancel

NOTES AND COMMENTS

1. We emphasize the location of the reference to the desired output in a one-way versus a two-way Data Table. For a one-way table, the reference to the output cell location is placed in the cell above and to the right of the column of input data so that it is in the cell just to the right of the label of the column of input data. For a two-way table, the reference to the output cell location is placed above the column of input data and to the left of the row input data.

2. Notice that in Figures A.9 and A.11, the tables are formatted as currency. This must be done manually after the table is constructed using the options in the **Number** group under the **HOME** tab in the Ribbon. It also a good idea to label the rows and the columns of the table.

3. For very complex functions, Goal Seek might not converge to a stable solution. Trying several different initial values (the actual value in the cell referenced in the **By changing cell:** box) when invoking Goal Seek may help.

Using Excel Functions

Excel provides a wealth of built-in formulas or functions for developing mathematical models. If we know which function is needed and how to use it, we can simply enter the function into the appropriate worksheet cell. However, if we are not sure which functions are available to accomplish a task or are not sure how to use a particular function, Excel can provide assistance.

Finding the Right Excel Function

To identify the functions available in Excel, click the FORMULAS tab on the Ribbon and then click the Insert Function button in the Function Library group. Alternatively, click the Insert Function button *fx* on the formula bar. Either approach provides the Insert Function dialog box shown in Figure A.14.

The Search for a function box at the top of the Insert Function dialog box enables us to type a brief description for what we want to do. After doing so and clicking Go, Excel will search for and display, in the Select a function box, the functions that may accomplish our task. In many situations, however, we may want to browse through an entire category of functions to see what is available. For this task, the Or select a category box is helpful. It contains a dropdown list of several categories of functions provided by Excel. Figure A.14 shows that we selected the Math & Trig category. As a result, Excel's Math & Trig functions appear in alphabetical order in the Select a function box. We see the ABS function listed first, followed by the ACOS function, and so on.

Colon Notation

Although many functions, such as the ABS function, have a single argument, some Excel functions depend on arrays. Colon notation provides an efficient way to convey arrays and matrices of cells to functions. The colon notation may be described as follows: B3:B5 means cell B1 "through" cell B5, namely the array of values stored in the locations

FIGURE A.14   INSERT FUNCTION DIALOG BOX

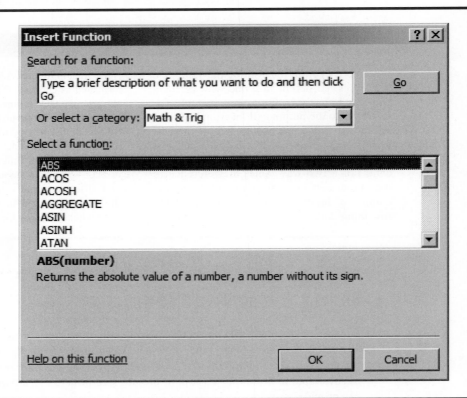

(B1,B2,B3,B4,B5). Consider, for example, the following function =SUM(B1:B5). The sum function adds up the elements contained in the function's argument. Hence, =SUM(B1:B5) evaluates the following formula:

$$=B1+B2+B3+B4+B5$$

Inserting a Function into a Worksheet Cell

Through the use of an example, we will now show how to use the Insert Function and Function Arguments dialog boxes to select a function, develop its arguments, and insert the function into a worksheet cell. We also illustrate the use of the SUMPRODUCT function, and how to use colon notation in the argument of a function.

The SUMPRODUCT function, as shown in Figure A.15, is used in many of the Solver examples in this textbook. Note that SUMPRODUCT is now highlighted, and that immediately below the Select a function box we see SUMPRODUCT(array1,array2,array3, . . .), which indicates that the SUMPRODUCT function contains the array arguments array1, array2, array3, ... In addition, we see that the description of the SUMPRODUCT function is "Returns the sum of the products of corresponding ranges or arrays." For example, the function =SUMPRODUCT(A1:A3, B1:B3) evaluates the formula A1*B1 + A2*B2 + A3*B3. As shown in the following example, this function can be very useful in calculations of cost, profit, and other such functions involving multiple arrays of numbers.

FIGURE A.15   DESCRIPTION OF THE SUMPRODUCT FUNCTION IN THE INSERT FUNCTION DIALOG BOX

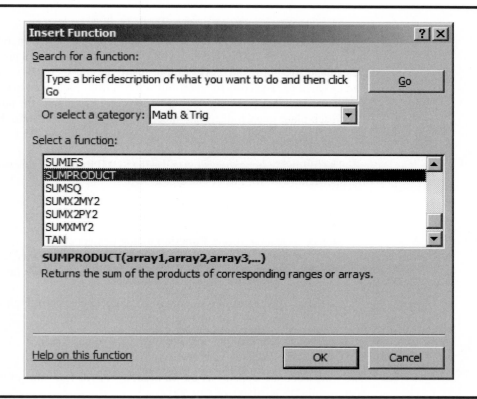

FIGURE A.16 EXCEL WORKSHEET USED TO CALCULATE TOTAL SHIPPING COSTS
FOR THE FOSTER GENERATORS TRANSPORTATION PROBLEM

FosterGenerators

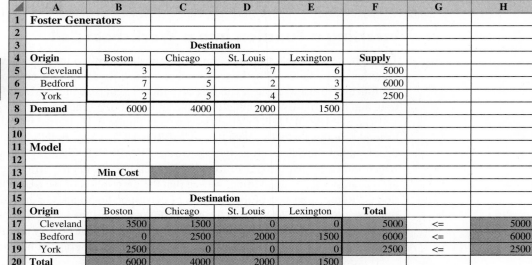

	A	B	C	D	E	F	G	H
1	**Foster Generators**							
2								
3			**Destination**					
4	**Origin**	Boston	Chicago	St. Louis	Lexington	**Supply**		
5	Cleveland	3	2	7	6	5000		
6	Bedford	7	5	2	3	6000		
7	York	2	5	4	5	2500		
8	**Demand**	6000	4000	2000	1500			
9								
10								
11	**Model**							
12								
13		**Min Cost**						
14								
15			**Destination**					
16	**Origin**	Boston	Chicago	St. Louis	Lexington	**Total**		
17	Cleveland	3500	1500	0	0	5000	<=	5000
18	Bedford	0	2500	2000	1500	6000	<=	6000
19	York	2500	0	0	0	2500	<=	2500
20	**Total**	6000	4000	2000	1500			
21		=	=	=	=			
22		6000	4000	2000	1500			

Figure A.16 displays an Excel worksheet for the Foster Generators Problem that appears in Chapter 10. This problem involves the transportation of a product from three plants (Cleveland, Bedford, and York) to four distribution centers (Boston, Chicago, St. Louis, and Lexington). The costs for each unit shipped from each plant to each distribution center are shown in cells B5:E7, and the values in cells B17:E19 are the number of units shipped from each plant to each distribution center. Cell B13 will contain the total transportation cost corresponding to the transportation cost values in cells B5:E7 and the values of the number of units shipped in cells B17:E19.

The following steps show how to use the SUMPRODUCT function to compute the total transportation cost for Foster Generators.

Step 1. Select **cell C13**
Step 2. Click *fx* on the formula bar
Step 3. When the **Insert Function** dialog box appears:
Select **Math & Trig** in the **Or select a category** box
Select **SUMPRODUCT** in the **Select a function** box (as shown in Figure A.15)
Click **OK**
Step 4. When the **Function Arguments** box appears (see Figure A.17):
Enter *B5:E7* in the **Array1** box
Enter *B17:E19* in the **Array2** box
Click **OK**

The worksheet then appears as shown in Figure A.18. The value of the total transportation cost in cell C13 is 39500, or $39,500.

FIGURE A.17   COMPLETED FUNCTION ARGUMENTS DIALOG BOX FOR THE
SUMPRODUCT FUNCTION

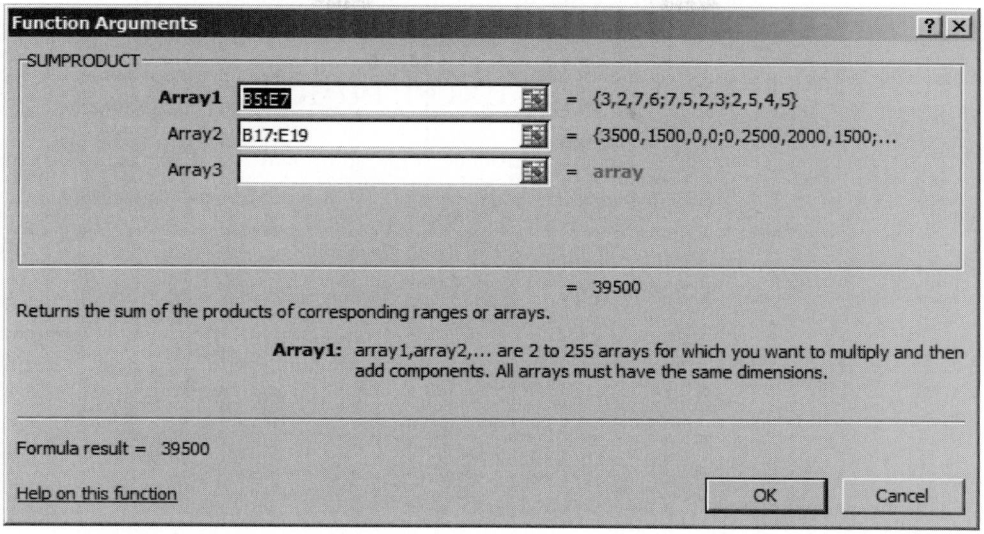

Function Arguments		? X
SUMPRODUCT		
Array1	B5:E7	= {3,2,7,6;7,5,2,3;2,5,4,5}
Array2	B17:E19	= {3500,1500,0,0;0,2500,2000,1500;...
Array3		= array

= 39500

Returns the sum of the products of corresponding ranges or arrays.

Array1: array1,array2,... are 2 to 255 arrays for which you want to multiply and then add components. All arrays must have the same dimensions.

Formula result = 39500

Help on this function   OK   Cancel

FIGURE A.18   EXCEL WORKSHEET SHOWING THE USE OF EXCEL'S SUMPRODUCT
FUNCTION TO CALCULATE TOTAL SHIPPING COSTS

	A	B	C	D	E	F	G	H
1	**Foster Generators**							
2								
3			**Destination**					
4	**Origin**	Boston	Chicago	St. Louis	Lexington	**Supply**		
5	Cleveland	3	2	7	6	5000		
6	Bedford	7	5	2	3	6000		
7	York	2	5	4	5	2500		
8	**Demand**	6000	4000	2000	1500			
9								
10								
11	**Model**							
12								
13		**Min Cost**	39500					
14								
15			**Destination**					
16	**Origin**	Boston	Chicago	St. Louis	Lexington	**Total**		
17	Cleveland	3500	1500	0	0	5000	<=	5000
18	Bedford	0	2500	2000	1500	6000	<=	6000
19	York	2500	0	0	0	2500	<=	2500
20	**Total**	6000	4000	2000	1500			
21		=	=	=	=			
22		6000	4000	2000	1500			

We illustrated the use of Excel's capability to provide assistance in using the SUM-PRODUCT function. The procedure is similar for all Excel functions. This capability is especially helpful if you do not know which function to use or forget the proper name and/or syntax for a function.

Additional Excel Functions for Modeling

In this section we introduce some additional Excel functions that have proven useful in modeling decision problems.

IF and COUNTIF Functions

Let us consider the case of Gambrell Manufacturing. Gambrell Manufacturing produces car stereos. Stereos are composed of a variety of components that the company must carry in inventory to keep production running smoothly. However, because inventory can be a costly investment, Gambrell generally likes to keep the amount of inventory of the components it uses in manufacturing to a minimum. To help monitor and control its inventory of components, Gambrell uses an inventory policy known as an "order up to" policy. This type of inventory policy and others are discussed in detail in Chapter 14.

The "order up to policy" is as follows. Whenever the inventory on hand drops below a certain level, enough units are ordered to return the inventory to that predetermined level. If the current number of units in inventory, denoted by H, drops below M units, we order enough to get the inventory level back up to M units. M is called the Order Up to Point. Stated mathematically, if Q is the amount we order, then

$$Q = M - H$$

An inventory model for Gambrell Manufacturing appears in Figure A.19. In this worksheet, labeled "OrderQuantity" in the upper half of the worksheet, the component ID number, inventory on hand (H), order up to point (M), and cost per unit are given for each of four components. Also given in this sheet is the fixed cost per order. The fixed cost is interpreted as follows: Each time a component is ordered, it costs Gambrell $120 to process the order. The fixed cost of $120 is incurred regardless of how many units are ordered.

The model portion of the worksheet calculates the order quantity for each component. For example, for component 570, $M = 100$ and $H = 5$, so $Q = M - H = 100 - 5 = 95$. For component 741, $M = 70$ and $H = 70$ and no units are ordered because the on-hand inventory of 70 units is equal to the up to order point of 70. The calculations are similar for the other two components.

Depending on the number of units ordered, Gambrell receives a discount on the cost per unit. If 50 or more units are ordered, there is a quantity discount of 10% on every unit purchased. For example, for component 741, the cost per unit is $4.50 and 95 units are ordered. Because 95 exceeds the 50-unit requirement, there is a 10% discount and the cost per unit is reduced to $4.50 - 0.1($4.50) = $4.50 - $0.45 = $4.05. Not including the fixed cost, the cost of goods purchased is then $4.05(95) = $384.75.

The Excel functions used to perform these calculations are shown in Figure A.20. The IF function is used to calculate the purchase cost of goods for each component in row 15. The general form of the IF function is

$$=IF(condition,\ result\ if\ condition\ is\ true,\ result\ if\ condition\ is\ false)$$

For example, in cell B15 we have =IF(B14>=50,0.9*B7,B7)*B14. This statement says if the order quantity (cell B14) is greater than or equal to 50, then the cost per unit is 0.9*B7 (there

FIGURE A.19 THE GAMBRELL MANUFACTURING COMPONENT ORDERING MODEL

	A	B	C	D	E	F
4	Component ID	570	578	741	755	
5	Inventory On-Hand	5	30	70	17	
6	Order Up to Point	100	55	70	45	
7	Cost per unit	$4.50	$12.50	$3.26	$4.15	
8						
9	Fixed Cost per Order	$120				
10						
11	**Model**					
12						
13	Component ID	570	578	741	755	
14	Order Quantity	95	25	0	28	
15	Cost of Goods	$384.75	$312.50	$0.00	$116.20	
16						
17	Total Number of Orders	3				
18						
19	Total Fixed costs	$360.00				
20	Total Cost of Goods	$813.45				
21	Total Cost	$1,173.45				
22						

WEB file

Gambrell

FIGURE A.20 FORMULAS AND FUNCTIONS FOR GAMBRELL MANUFACTURING

	A	B	C	D	E
1					
2	**Gambrell Manufacturing**				
3					
4	Component ID	570	578	741	755
5	Inventory On-Hand	5	30	70	17
6	Order Up to Point	100	55	70	45
7	Cost per unit	4.5	12.5	3.26	4.15
8					
9	Fixed Cost per Order	120			
10					
11	**Model**				
12					
13	Component ID	=B4	=C4	=D4	=E4
14	Order Quantity	=B6-B5	=C6-C5	=D6-D5	=E6-E5
15	Cost of Goods	=IF(B14>=50,0.9*B7,B7)*B14	=IF(C14>=50, 0.9*C7,C7)*C14	=IF(D14>=50, 0.9*D7,D7)*D14	=IF(E14>=50, 0.9*E7,E7)*E14
16					
17	Total Number of Orders	=COUNTIF(B14:E14,">0")			
18					
19	Total Fixed Costs	=B17*B9			
20	Total Cost of Goods	=SUM(B15:E15)			
21	Total Cost	=SUM(B19:B20)			
22					

is a 10% discount); otherwise, there is no discount and the cost per unit is the amount given in cell B7. The purchase cost of goods for the other components are computed in a like manner.

The total cost in cell B21 is the sum of the purchase cost of goods ordered in row 15 and the fixed ordering costs. Because we place three orders (one each for components 570, 578, and 755), the fixed cost of the orders is 3*120 = $360.

The COUNTIF function in cell B17 is used to count how many times we order. In particular, it counts the number of components having a positive order quantity. The general form of the COUNTIF function is

$$=\text{COUNTIF}(range, condition)$$

The *range* is the range to search for the *condition*. The condition is the test to be counted when satisfied. *Note that quotes are required for the condition with the COUNTIF function.* In the Gambrell model in Figure A.20, cell B17 counts the number of cells that are greater than zero in the range of cells B14:E14. In the model, because only cells B14, C14, and E14 are greater than zero, the COUNTIF function in cell B17 returns 3.

As we have seen, IF and COUNTIF are powerful functions that allow us to make calculations based on a condition holding (or not). There are other such conditional functions available in Excel. In the problems at the end of this appendix, we ask you to investigate one such function, the SUMIF function. Another conditional function that is extremely useful in modeling is the VLOOKUP function. We discuss the VLOOKUP function with an example in the next section.

VLOOKUP Function

Next, consider the workbook named *OM455* shown in Figure A.21. The worksheet named Grades is shown. This worksheet calculates the course grades for the course OM 455. There are 11 students in the course. Each student has a midterm exam score and a final exam score,

FIGURE A.21   OM455 GRADE SPREADSHEET

	A	B	C	D	E	F
1	OM455					
2	Section 001					
3	Course Grading Scale Based on Course Average:					
4		Lower	Upper	Course		
5		Limit	Limit	Grade		
6		0	59	F		
7		60	69	D		
8		70	79	C		
9		80	89	B		
10		90	100	A		
11						
12		Midterm	Final	Course	Course	
13	Lastname	Score	Score	Average	Grade	
14	Benson	70	56	63.0	D	
15	Chin	95	91	93.0	A	
16	Choi	82	80	81.0	B	
17	Cruz	45	78	61.5	D	
18	Doe	68	45	56.5	F	
19	Honda	91	98	94.5	A	
20	Hume	87	74	80.5	B	
21	Jones	60	80	70.0	C	
22	Miranda	80	93	86.5	B	
23	Murigami	97	98	97.5	A	
24	Ruebush	90	91	90.5	A	
25						

and these are averaged in column D to get the course average. The scale given in the upper portion of the worksheet is used to determine the course grade for each student. Consider, for example, the performance of student Choi in row 16. This student earned an 82 on the midterm, an 80 on the final, and a course average of 81. From the grading scale, this equates to a course grade of B.

The course average is simply the average of the midterm and final scores, but how do we get Excel to look in the grading scale table and automatically assign the correct course letter grade to each student? The VLOOKUP function allows us to do just that. The formulas and functions used in *OM455* are shown in Figure A.22.

The VLOOKUP function allows the user to pull a subset of data from a larger table of data based on some criterion. The general form of the VLOOKUP function is

$$=VLOOKUP(arg1,arg2,arg3,arg4)$$

where arg1 is the value to search for in the first column of the table, arg2 is the table location, arg3 is the column location in the table to be returned, and arg4 is TRUE if looking for the first partial match of arg1 and FALSE for looking for an exact match of arg1. We will explain the difference between a partial and exact match in a moment. VLOOKUP assumes that the first column of the table is sorted in ascending order.

The VLOOKUP function for student Choi in cell E16 is as follows:

$$=VLOOKUP(D16,B6:D10,3,TRUE)$$

FIGURE A.22   THE FORMULAS AND FUNCTIONS USED IN OM 455

	A	B	C	D	E
1	OM 455				
2	Section 001				
3	Course Grading Scale Based on Course Average:				
4		Lower	Upper	Course	
5		Limit	Limit	Grade	
6		0	59	F	
7		60	69	D	
8		70	79	C	
9		80	89	B	
10		90	100	A	
11					
12		Midterm	Final	Course	Course
13	Lastname	Score	Score	Average	Grade
14	Benson	70	56	=AVERAGE(B14:C14)	=VLOOKUP(D14,B6:D10,3,TRUE)
15	Chin	95	91	=AVERAGE(B15:C15)	=VLOOKUP(D15,B6:D10,3,TRUE)
16	Choi	82	80	=AVERAGE(B16:C16)	=VLOOKUP(D16,B6:D10,3,TRUE)
17	Cruz	45	78	=AVERAGE(B17:C17)	=VLOOKUP(D17,B6:D10,3,TRUE)
18	Doe	68	45	=AVERAGE(B18:C18)	=VLOOKUP(D18,B6:D10,3,TRUE)
19	Honda	91	98	=AVERAGE(B19:C19)	=VLOOKUP(D19,B6:D10,3,TRUE)
20	Hume	87	74	=AVERAGE(B20:C20)	=VLOOKUP(D20,B6:D10,3,TRUE)
21	Jones	60	80	=AVERAGE(B21:C21)	=VLOOKUP(D21,B6:D10,3,TRUE)
22	Miranda	80	93	=AVERAGE(B22:C22)	=VLOOKUP(D22,B6:D10,3,TRUE)
23	Murigami	97	98	=AVERAGE(B23:C23)	=VLOOKUP(D23,B6:D10,3,TRUE)
24	Ruebush	90	91	=AVERAGE(B24:C24)	=VLOOKUP(D24,B6:D10,3,TRUE)
25					

This function uses the course average from cell D16 and searches the first column of the table defined by B6:D10. In the first column of the table (column B), Excel searches from the top until it finds a number strictly greater than the value of D16 (81). It then backs up one row (to row 9). That is, it finds the last value in the first column less than or equal to 81. Because there is a 3 in the third argument of the VLOOKUP function, it takes the element in row 9 in the third column of the table, which is the letter "B." In summary, the VLOOKUP takes the first argument and searches the first column of the table for the last row that is less than or equal to the first argument. It then selects from that row the element in the column number of the third argument.

Note: If the last element of the VLOOKUP function is "False," the only change is that Excel searches for an exact match of the first argument in the first column of the data. VLOOKUP is very useful when you seek subsets of a table based on a condition.

Principles for Building Good Spreadsheet Models

We have covered some of the fundamentals of building spreadsheet models. There are some generally accepted guiding principles for how to build a spreadsheet so that it is more easily used by others and so that the risk of error is mitigated. In this section we discuss some of those principles.

Separate the Data from the Model

One of the first principles of good modeling is to separate the data from the model. This enables the user to update the model parameters without fear of mistakenly typing over a formula or function. For this reason, it is good practice to have a data section at the top of the spreadsheet. A separate model section should contain all calculations and in general should not be updated by a user. For a what-if model or an optimization model, there might also be a separate section for decision cells (values that are not data or calculations, but are the outputs we seek from the model).

The Nowlin model in Figure A.6 is a good example. The data section is in the upper part of the spreadsheet followed by the model section that contains the calculations. The Gambrell model in Figure A.19 does not totally employ the principle of data/model separation. A better model would have the 50-unit hurdle and the 90% cost (10% discount) as data in the upper section. Then the formulas in row 15 would simply refer to the cells in the upper section. This would allow the user to easily change the discount, for example, without having to change all four formulas in row 15.

Document the Model

A good spreadsheet model is well documented. Clear labels and proper formatting and alignment make the spreadsheet easier to navigate and understand. For example, if the values in a worksheet are cost, currency formatting should be used. No cells should be unlabeled. A new user should be able to easily understand the model and its calculations. Figure A.23 shows a better-documented version of the Foster Generators model previously discussed (Figure A.16). The tables are more explicitly labeled, and shading focuses the user on the objective and the decision cells (amount to ship). The per-unit shipping cost data and total (Min) cost have been properly formatted as currency.

FIGURE A.23   A BETTER-DOCUMENTED FOSTER GENERATORS MODEL

	A	B	C	D	E	F	G	H
1	**Foster Generators**							
2								
3	Origin to Destination—Cost per unit to ship							
4			**Destination**					
5	Origin	Boston	Chicago	St. Louis	Lexington	**Units Available**		
6	Cleveland	$3.00	$2.00	$7.00	$6.00	5000		
7	Bedford	$7.00	$5.00	$2.00	$3.00	6000		
8	York	$2.00	$5.00	$4.00	$5.00	2500		
9	**Units Demanded**	6000	4000	2000	1500			
10								
11								
12	**Model**							
13								
14		**Min Cost**	$39,500.00					
15								
16	Origin to Destination—Units Shipped							
17			**Destination**					
18	Origin	Boston	Chicago	St. Louis	Lexington	**Units Shipped**		
19	Cleveland	3500	1500	0	0	5000	<=	5000
20	Bedford	0	2500	2000	1500	6000	<=	6000
21	York	2500	0	0	0	2500	<=	2500
22	**Units Received**	6000	4000	2000	1500			
23		=	=	=	=			
24		6000	4000	2000	1500			

WEB file

FosterRev

Use Simple Formulas and Cell Names

Clear formulas can eliminate unnecessary calculations, reduce errors, and make it easier to maintain your spreadsheet. Long and complex calculations should be divided into several cells. This makes the formula easier to understand and easier to edit. Avoid using numbers in a formula. Instead, put the number in a cell in the data section of your worksheet and refer to the cell location of the data in the formula. Building the formula in this manner avoids having to edit the formula for a simple data change.

Using cell names can make a formula much easier to understand. To assign a name to a cell, use the following steps:

Step 1. Select the cell or range of cells you would like to name
Step 2. Select the **FORMULAS** tab from the Ribbon
Step 3. Choose **Define Name** from the Defined Names section
Step 4. The **New Name** dialog box will appear, as shown in Figure A.24
Enter the name you would like to use in the top portion of the dialog box and Click **OK**

Following this procedure and naming all cells in the *Nowlin Plastics* spreadsheet model leads to the model shown in Figure A.25. Compare this to Figure A.6 to easily understand the formulas in the model.

A name is also easily applied to range as follows. First, highlight the range of interest. Then click on the Name Box in the Formula Bar (refer back to Figure A.3) and type in the desired range name.

FIGURE A.24   THE DEFINE NAME DIALOG BOX

WEB file

NowlinPlastics

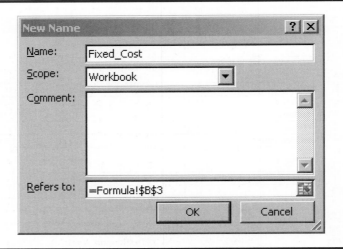

FIGURE A.25   THE NOWLIN PLASTIC MODEL FORMULAS WITH NAMED CELLS

	A	B
1	**Nowlin Plastics**	
2		
3	**Fixed Cost**	3000
4		
5	**Variable Cost Per Unit**	2
6		
7	**Selling Price Per Unit**	5
8		
9		
10	**Model**	
11		
12	**Production Volume**	800
13		
14	**Total Cost**	=Fixed_Cost+Variable_Cost*Production_Volume
15		
16	**Total Revenue**	=Selling_Price*Production_Volume
17		
18	**Total Profit (Loss)**	=Total_Revenue-Total_Cost

Use of Relative and Absolute Cell References

There are a number of ways to copy a formula from one cell to another in an Excel worksheet. One way to copy the a formula from one cell to another is presented here:

    Step 1. Select the cell you would like to copy
    Step 2. Right click on the mouse
    Step 3. Click **Copy**

Step 4. Select the cell where you would like to put the copy
Step 5. Right click on the mouse
Step 6. Click **Paste**

When copying in Excel, one can use a relative or an absolute address. When copied, a relative address adjusts with the move of the copy, whereas an absolute address stays in its original form. Relative addresses are of the form C7. Absolute addresses have $ in front of the column and row, for example, $C$7. How you use relative and absolute addresses can have an impact on the amount of effort it takes to build a model and the opportunity for error in constructing the model.

Let us reconsider the OM455 grading spreadsheet previously discussed in this appendix and shown in Figure A.22. Recall that we used the VLOOKUP function to retrieve the appropriate letter grade for each student. The following formula is in cell E14:

$$=VLOOKUP(D14,B6:D10,3,TRUE)$$

Note that this formula contains only relative addresses. If we copy this to cell E15, we get the following result:

$$=VLOOKUP(D15,B7:D11,3,TRUE)$$

Although the first argument has correctly changed to D15 (we want to calculate the letter grade for the student in row 15), the table in the function has also shifted to B7:D11. What we desired was for this table location to remain the same. A better approach would have been to use the following formula in cell E14:

$$=VLOOKUP(D14,\$B\$6:\$D\$10,3,TRUE)$$

Copying this formula to cell E15 results in the following formula:

$$=VLOOKUP(D15,\$B\$6:\$D\$10,3,TRUE)$$

This correctly changes the first argument to D15 and keeps the data table intact. Using absolute referencing is extremely useful if you have a function that has a reference that should not change when applied to another cell and you are copying the formula to other locations. In the case of the OM455 workbook, instead of typing the VLOOKUP for each student, we can use absolute referencing on the table and then copy from row 14 to rows 15 through 24.

In this section we have discussed guidelines for good spreadsheet model building. In the next section we discuss EXCEL tools available for checking and debugging spreadsheet models.

Auditing Excel Models

EXCEL contains a variety of tools to assist you in the development and debugging of spreadsheet models. These tools are found in the Formula Auditing group of the FORMULAS tab as shown in Figure A.26. Let us review each of the tools available in this group.

Trace Precedents and Dependents

The Trace Precedents button, ⊞ Trace Precedents, creates arrows pointing to the selected cell from cells that are part of the formula in that cell. The Trace Dependents button, ⊞ Trace Dependents, on the other hand, shows arrows pointing from the selected cell to

FIGURE A.26   THE FORMULA AUDITING GROUP OF THE FORMULAS TAB

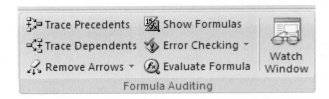

cells that depend on the selected cell. Both of these tools are excellent for quickly ascertaining how parts of a model are linked.

An example of Trace Precedents is shown in Figure A.27. Here we have opened the *Foster Rev* worksheet, selected cell C14, and clicked the Trace Precedents button in the Formula Auditing Group. Recall that the cost in cell C14 is calculated as the SUMPRODUCT of the per-unit shipping cost and units shipped. In Figure A.27, to show this relationship, arrows are drawn to these respective areas of the spreadsheet to cell C14. These arrows may be removed by clicking on the Remove Arrows button in the Auditing Tools Group.

An example of Trace Dependents is shown in Figure A.28. We have selected cell E20, the units shipped from Bedford to Lexington, and clicked on the Trace Dependents button

FIGURE A.27   TRACE PRECEDENTS FOR CELL C14 (COST) IN THE FOSTER
GENERATORS REV MODEL

	C14	▼	fx	=SUMPRODUCT(B6:E8,B19:E21)			
	A	**B**	**C**	**D**	**E**	**F**	**G**	**H**
1	**Foster Generators**							
2								
3	Origin to Destination—Cost per unit to ship							
4			**Destination**					
5	**Origin**	Boston	Chicago	St. Louis	Lexington	**Units Available**		
6	Cleveland	$3.00	$2.00	$7.00	$6.00	5000		
7	Bedford	$7.00	$5.00	$2.00	$3.00	6000		
8	York	$2.00	$5.00	$4.00	$5.00	2500		
9	**Units Demanded**	6000	4000	2000	1500			
10								
11								
12	**Model**							
13								
14		**Min Cost**	$39,500.00					
15								
16	Origin to Destination—Units Shipped							
17			**Destination**					
18	**Origin**	Boston	Chicago	St. Louis	Lexington	**Units Shipped**		
19	Cleveland	3500	1500	0	0	5000	<=	5000
20	Bedford	0	2500	2000	1500	6000	<=	6000
21	York	2500	0	0	0	2500	<=	2500
22	**Units Received**	6000	4000	2000	1500			
23		=	=	=	=			
24		6000	4000	2000	1500			

WEB file

FosterRev

FIGURE A.28   TRACE DEPENDENTS FOR CELL C14 (COST) IN THE FOSTER
GENERATORS REV MODEL

	E20		fx	1500				
	A	**B**	**C**	**D**	**E**	**F**	**G**	**H**
12	Model							
13								
14		Min Cost	$39,500.00					
15								
16	Origin to Destination—Units Shipped							
17				Destination				
18	**Origin**	Boston	Chicago	St. Louis	Lexington	**Units Shipped**		
19	Cleveland	3500	1500	0	0	5000	<=	5000
20	Bedford	0	2500	2000	1500	6000	<=	6000
21	York	2500	0	0	0	2500	<=	2500
22	**Units Received**	6000	4000	2000	1500			
23		=	=	=	=			
24		6000	4000	2000	1500			

in the Formula Auditing Group. As shown in Figure A.28, units shipped from Bedford to Lexington impacts the cost function in cell C14, the total units shipped from Bedford given in cell F20, and the total units shipped to Lexington in cell E22. These arrows may be removed by clicking on the Remove Arrows button in the Auditing Tools Group.

Trace Precedents and Trace Dependents can highlight errors in copying and formula construction by showing that incorrect sections of the worksheet are referenced.

Show Formulas

The Show Formulas button, 🔲 Show Formulas , does exactly that. To see the formulas in a worksheet, simply click on any cell in the worksheet and then click on Show Formulas. You will see the formulas that exist in that worksheet. To go back to hiding the formulas, click again on the Show Formulas button. Figure A.6 gives an example of the show formulas view. This allows you to inspect each formula in detail in its cell location.

Evaluate Formulas

The Evaluate Formula button, 🔘 Evaluate Formula , allows you to investigate the calculations of particular cell in great detail. To invoke this tool, we simply select a cell containing a formula and click on the Evaluate Formula button in the Formula Auditing Group. As an example, we select cell B15 of the Gambrell Manufacturing model (see Figures A.19 and A.20). Recall we are calculating cost of goods based upon whether or not there is a quantity discount. Clicking on the Evaluate button allows you to evaluate this formula explicitly. The Evaluate Formula dialog box appears in Figure A.29. Figure A.30 shows the result of one click of the Evaluate button. Cell B14 has changed to its value of 95. Further clicks would evaluate in order, from left to right, the remaining components of the formula. We ask the reader to further explore this tool in an exercise at the end of this appendix.

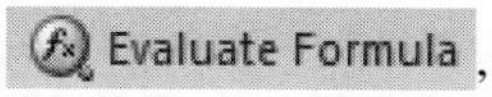

The Evaluate Formula tool provides an excellent means of identifying the exact location of an error in a formula.

FIGURE A.29   THE EVALUATE FORMULA DIALOG BOX FOR CELL B15 OF THE
GAMBRELL MANUFACTURING MODEL

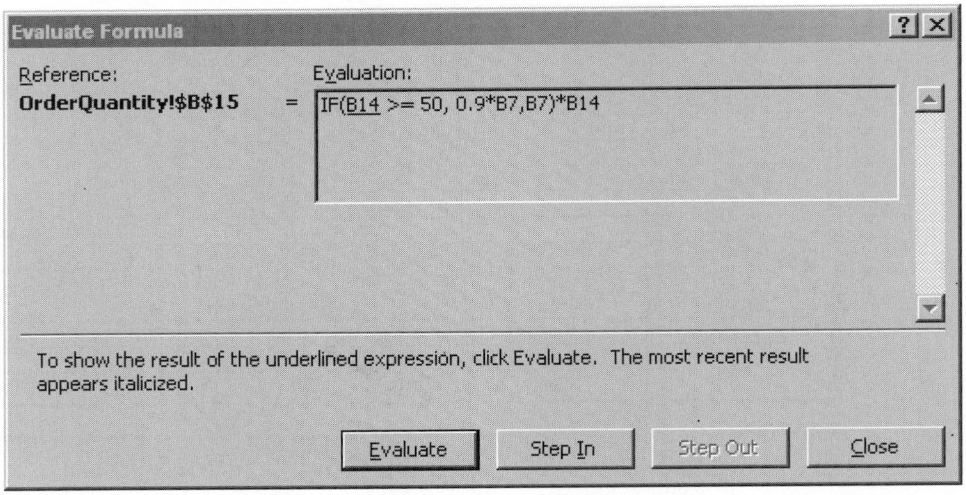

FIGURE A.30   THE EVALUATE FORMULA AFTER ONE CLICK OF THE EVALUATE
BUTTON FOR CELL B15 OF THE GAMBRELL MANUFACTURING
MODEL

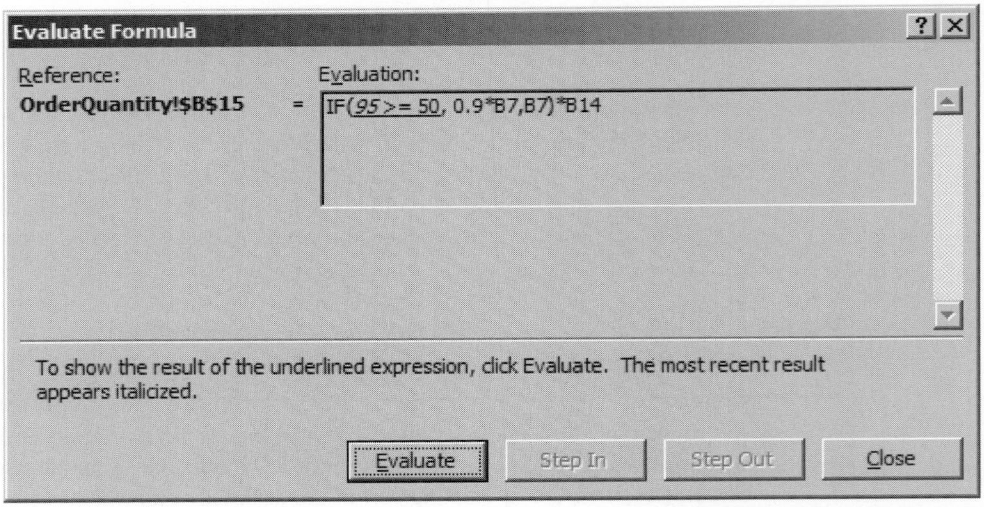

Error Checking

The Error Checking button,  , provides an automatic means of checking
for mathematical errors within formulas of a worksheet. Clicking on the Error Checking
button causes Excel to check every formula in the sheet for calculation errors. If an error is
found, the Error Checking dialog box appears. An example for a hypothetical division by

FIGURE A.31   THE ERROR CHECKING DIALOG BOX FOR A DIVISION
BY ZERO ERROR

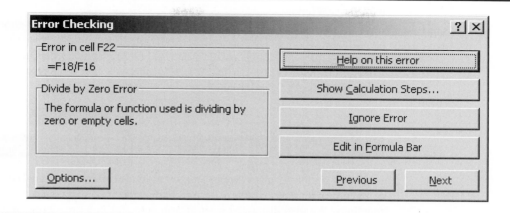

zero error is shown in Figure A.31. From this box, the formula can be edited or the calculation steps can be observed (as in the previous section on Evaluate Formulas).

Watch Window

The Watch Window, located in the Formula Auditing Group, allows the user to observe the values of cells included in the Watch Window box list. This is useful for large models when not all the model is observable on the screen or when multiple worksheets are used. The user can monitor how the listed cells change with a change in the model without searching through the worksheet or changing from one worksheet to another.

A Watch Window for the Gambrell Manufacturing model is shown in Figure A.32. The following steps were used from the OrderQuantity worksheet to add cell B15 of the OrderQuantity worksheet to the watch list:

Step 1. Select the **FORMULAS** tab
Step 2. Select **Watch Window** from the Formula Auditing Group
The Watch Window will appear
Step 3. Select **Add Watch**
Step 4. Click on the cell you would like to add to the watch list (in this case B15)

FIGURE A.32   THE WATCH WINDOW FOR THE GAMBRELL MANUFACTURING
MODEL

Book	Sheet	Name	Cell	Value	Formula
Gambr...	Order...		B15	$384.75	=IF(B14 >= 50, 0.9*B7,B7)*B14

As shown in Figure A.32, the list gives the workbook name, worksheet name, cell name (if used), cell location, cell value, and cell formula. To delete a cell from the watch list, select the entry from the list and then click on the Delete Watch button in the upper part of the Watch Window.

The Watch Window, as shown in Figure A.32, allows us to monitor the value of B15 as we make changes elsewhere in the worksheet. Furthermore, if we had other worksheets in this workbook, we could monitor changes to B15 of the OrderQuantity worksheet even from these other worksheets. The Watch Window is observable regardless of where we are in any worksheet of a workbook.

Summary

In this appendix we have discussed how to build effective spreadsheet models using Excel. We provided an overview of workbooks and worksheets and details on useful Excel functions. We also discussed a set of principles for good modeling and tools for auditing spreadsheet models.

Problems

NowlinPlastics

1. Open the file *NowlinPlastics*. Recall that we have modeled total profit for the product CD-50 in this spreadsheet. Suppose we have a second product called a CD-100, with the following characteristics:

$$\text{Fixed Cost} = \$2500$$
$$\text{Variable Cost per Unit} = \$1.67$$
$$\text{Selling Price per Unit} = \$4.40$$

Extend the model so that the profit is calculated for each product and then totaled to give an overall profit generated for the two products. Use a CD-100 production volume of 1200. Save this file as *NowlinPlastics2*. *Hint:* Place the data for CD-100 in column C and copy the formulas in rows 14, 16, and 18 to column C.

2. Assume that in an empty Excel worksheet in cell A1 you enter the formula =B1*$F$3. You now copy this formula into cell E6. What is the modified formula that appears in E6?

FosterRev

3. Open the file *FosterRev*. Select cells B6:E8 and name these cells Shipping_Cost. Select cells B19:E21 and name these cells Units_Shipped. Use these names in the SUMPRODUCT function in cell C14 to compute cost and verify that you obtain the same cost ($39,500).

4. Open the file *NowlinPlastics*. Recall that we have modeled total profit for the product CD-50 in this spreadsheet. Modify the spreadsheet to take into account production capacity and forecasted demand. If forecasted demand is less than or equal to capacity, Nowlin will produce only the forecasted demand; otherwise, they will produce the full capacity. For this example, use forecasted demand of 1200 and capacity of 1500. *Hint:* Enter demand and capacity into the data section of the model. Then use an IF statement to calculate production volume.

CoxElectric

5. Cox Electric, which makes electronic components, has estimated the following for a new design of one of its products:

$$\text{Fixed cost} = \$10,000$$
$$\text{Material cost per unit} = \$0.15$$
$$\text{Labor cost per unit} = \$0.10$$
$$\text{Revenue per unit} = \$0.65$$

These data are given in the file *CoxElectric*. Note that fixed cost is incurred regardless of the amount produced. Per-unit material and labor cost together make up the variable cost per unit.

Assuming Cox Electric sells all that it produces, profit is calculated by subtracting the fixed cost and total variable cost from total revenue.

a. Build a spreadsheet model that will calculate profit for Cox Electric using the principles of good spreadsheet design.

b. If Cox Electric produces 12,000 units of the new product, what is the resulting profit?

6. Use the Cox Electric spreadsheet model constructed for Problem 5 to answer the following:

a. Construct a one-way data table with production volume as the column input and profit as the output. Breakeven occurs when profit goes from a negative to a positive value; that is, breakeven is when total revenue = total cost, yielding a profit of zero. Vary production volume from 0 to 100,000 in increments of 10,000. In which interval of production volume does breakeven occur?

b. Use Goal Seek to find the exact breakeven point. Assign **Set cell:** equal to the location of profit, **To value:** = 0, and **By changing cell:** equal to the location of the production volume in your model.

7. Eastman Publishing Company is considering publishing an electronic textbook on spreadsheet applications for business. The fixed cost of manuscript preparation, textbook design, and website construction is estimated to be $160,000. Variable processing costs are estimated to be $6 per book. The publisher plans to sell access to the book for $46 each.

a. Build a spreadsheet model to calculate the profit/loss for a given demand. What profit can be anticipated with a demand of 3500 copies?

b. Use a data table to vary demand from 1000 to 6000 increments of 200 to assess the sensitivity of profit to demand.

c. Use Goal Seek to determine the access price per copy that the publisher must charge to break even with a demand of 3500 copies.

OM455

8. Open the workbook *OM455*. Save the file under a new name, *OM455COUNTIF*. Suppose we wish to automatically count the number of each letter grade.

a. Begin by putting the letters A, B, C, D, and F in cells C29:C33. Use the COUNTIF function in cells D29:D33 to count the number of each letter grade. *Hint:* Create the necessary COUNTIF function in cell D29. Use absolute referencing on the range ($E14:$E$24) and then copy the function to cells D30:D33 to count the number of each of the other letter grades.

b. We are considering a different grading scale as follows:

Lower	Upper	Grade
0	69	F
70	76	D
77	84	C
85	92	B
93	100	A

For the current list of students, use the COUNTIF function to determine the number of A, B, C, D, and F letter grades earned under this new system.

9. Open the workbook *OM455*. Save the file under a new name, *OM455Revised*. Suppose we wish to use a more refined grading system, as shown below:

Lower	Upper	Grade
0	59	F
60	69	D
70	72	C−
73	76	C−
77	79	C+
80	82	B−
83	86	B
87	89	B+
90	92	A−
93	100	A

Update the file to use this more refined grading system. How many of each letter grade are awarded under the new system? *Hint:* Build a new grading table and use VLOOKUP and an absolute reference to the table. Then use COUNTIF to count the number of each letter grade.

10. Richardson Ski Racing (RSR) sells equipment needed for downhill ski racing. One of RSR's products is fencing used on downhill courses. The fence product comes in 150-foot rolls and sells for $215 per roll. However, RSR offers quantity discounts. The following table shows the price per roll depending on order size:

Quantity Ordered		
From	To	Price per Roll
1	50	$215
51	100	$195
101	200	$175
201	and up	$155

The file RSR contains 172 orders that have arrived for the coming six weeks.
a. Use the VLOOKUP function with the preceding pricing table to determine the total revenue from these orders.
b. Use the COUNTIF function to determine the number of orders in each price bin.

11. Newton Manufacturing produces scientific calculators. The models are N350, N450, and the N900. Newton has planned its distribution of these products around eight customer zones: Brazil, China, France, Malaysia, U.S. Northeast, U.S. Southeast, U.S. Midwest, and U.S. West. Data for the current quarter (volume to be shipped in thousands of units) for each product and each customer zone are given in the file *NewtonData*.

Newton would like to know the total number of units going to each customer zone and also the total units of each product shipped. There are several ways to get this information from the data set. One way is to use the SUMIF function.

The SUMIF function extends the SUM function by allowing the user to add the values of cells meeting a logical condition. This general form of the function is

$$=SUMIF(test\ range,\ condition,\ range\ to\ be\ summed)$$

The *test range* is an area to search to test the *condition,* and the *range to be summed* is the position of the data to be summed. So, for example, using the *NewtonData* file, we would use the following function to get the total units sent to Malaysia:

$$=\text{SUMIF(A3:A26,A3,C3:C26)}$$

Here, A3 is Malaysia, A3:A26 is the range of customer zones, and C3:C26 are the volumes for each product for these customer zones. The SUMIF looks for matches of Malaysia in column A and, if a match is found, adds the volume to the total. Use the SUMIF function to get each total volume by zone and each total volume by product.

Williamson

12. Consider the transportation model given in the Excel file *Williamson*. It is a model that is very similar to the Foster Generators model. Williamson produces a single product and has plants in Atlanta, Lexington, Chicago, and Salt Lake City and warehouses in Portland, St. Paul, Las Vegas, Tuscon, and Cleveland. Each plant has a capacity and each warehouse has a demand. Williamson would like to find a low-cost shipping plan. Mr. Williamson has reviewed the results and notices right away that the total cost is way out of line. Use the Formula Auditing Tools under the FORMULAS tab in Excel to find any errors in this model. Correct the errors. *Hint:* There are two errors in this model. Be sure to check every formula.

Appendix B   Binomial Probabilities

Entries in the following table give the probability of x successes in n trials of a binomial experiment, where p is the probability of a success on one trial. For example, with $n = 6$ trials and $p = 0.40$, the probability of $x = 2$ successes is 0.3110.

						p					
n	x	0.05	0.10	0.15	0.20	0.25	0.30	0.35	0.40	0.45	0.50
1	0	0.9500	0.9000	0.8500	0.8000	0.7500	0.7000	0.6500	0.6000	0.5500	0.5000
	1	0.0500	0.1000	0.1500	0.2000	0.2500	0.3000	0.3500	0.4000	0.4500	0.5000
2	0	0.9025	0.8100	0.7225	0.6400	0.5625	0.4900	0.4225	0.3600	0.3025	0.2500
	1	0.0950	0.1800	0.2550	0.3200	0.3750	0.4200	0.4550	0.4800	0.4950	0.5000
	2	0.0025	0.0100	0.0225	0.0400	0.0625	0.0900	0.1225	0.1600	0.2025	0.2500
3	0	0.8574	0.7290	0.6141	0.5120	0.4219	0.3430	0.2746	0.2160	0.1664	0.1250
	1	0.1354	0.2430	0.3251	0.3840	0.4219	0.4410	0.4436	0.4320	0.4084	0.3750
	2	0.0071	0.0270	0.0574	0.0960	0.1406	0.1890	0.2389	0.2880	0.3341	0.3750
	3	0.0001	0.0010	0.0034	0.0080	0.0156	0.0270	0.0429	0.0640	0.0911	0.1250
4	0	0.8145	0.6561	0.5220	0.4096	0.3164	0.2401	0.1785	0.1296	0.0915	0.0625
	1	0.1715	0.2916	0.3685	0.4096	0.4219	0.4116	0.3845	0.3456	0.2995	0.2500
	2	0.0135	0.0486	0.0975	0.1536	0.2109	0.2646	0.3105	0.3456	0.3675	0.3750
	3	0.0005	0.0036	0.0115	0.0256	0.0469	0.0756	0.1115	0.1536	0.2005	0.2500
	4	0.0000	0.0001	0.0005	0.0016	0.0039	0.0081	0.0150	0.0256	0.0410	0.0625
5	0	0.7738	0.5905	0.4437	0.3277	0.2373	0.1681	0.1160	0.0778	0.0503	0.0312
	1	0.2036	0.3280	0.3915	0.4096	0.3955	0.3602	0.3124	0.2592	0.2059	0.1562
	2	0.0214	0.0729	0.1382	0.2048	0.2637	0.3087	0.3364	0.3456	0.3369	0.3125
	3	0.0011	0.0081	0.0244	0.0512	0.0879	0.1323	0.1811	0.2304	0.2757	0.3125
	4	0.0000	0.0004	0.0022	0.0064	0.0146	0.0284	0.0488	0.0768	0.1128	0.1562
	5	0.0000	0.0000	0.0001	0.0003	0.0010	0.0024	0.0053	0.0102	0.0185	0.0312
6	0	0.7351	0.5314	0.3771	0.2621	0.1780	0.1176	0.0754	0.0467	0.0277	0.0156
	1	0.2321	0.3543	0.3993	0.3932	0.3560	0.3025	0.2437	0.1866	0.1359	0.0938
	2	0.0305	0.0984	0.1762	0.2458	0.2966	0.3241	0.3280	0.3110	0.2780	0.2344
	3	0.0021	0.0146	0.0415	0.0819	0.1318	0.1852	0.2355	0.2765	0.3032	0.3125
	4	0.0001	0.0012	0.0055	0.0154	0.0330	0.0595	0.0951	0.1382	0.1861	0.2344
	5	0.0000	0.0001	0.0004	0.0015	0.0044	0.0102	0.0205	0.0369	0.0609	0.0938
	6	0.0000	0.0000	0.0000	0.0001	0.0002	0.0007	0.0018	0.0041	0.0083	0.0156
7	0	0.6983	0.4783	0.3206	0.2097	0.1335	0.0824	0.0490	0.0280	0.0152	0.0078
	1	0.2573	0.3720	0.3960	0.3670	0.3115	0.2471	0.1848	0.1306	0.0872	0.0547
	2	0.0406	0.1240	0.2097	0.2753	0.3115	0.3177	0.2985	0.2613	0.2140	0.1641
	3	0.0036	0.0230	0.0617	0.1147	0.1730	0.2269	0.2679	0.2903	0.2918	0.2734
	4	0.0002	0.0026	0.0109	0.0287	0.0577	0.0972	0.1442	0.1935	0.2388	0.2734
	5	0.0000	0.0002	0.0012	0.0043	0.0115	0.0250	0.0466	0.0774	0.1172	0.1641
	6	0.0000	0.0000	0.0001	0.0004	0.0013	0.0036	0.0084	0.0172	0.0320	0.0547
	7	0.0000	0.0000	0.0000	0.0000	0.0001	0.0002	0.0006	0.0016	0.0037	0.0078

Binomial Probabilities (*Continued*)

n	x	0.05	0.10	0.15	0.20	0.25	0.30	0.35	0.40	0.45	0.50
8	0	0.6634	0.4305	0.2725	0.1678	0.1001	0.0576	0.0319	0.0168	0.0084	0.0039
	1	0.2793	0.3826	0.3847	0.3355	0.2670	0.1977	0.1373	0.0896	0.0548	0.0312
	2	0.0515	0.1488	0.2376	0.2936	0.3115	0.2965	0.2587	0.2090	0.1569	0.1094
	3	0.0054	0.0331	0.0839	0.1468	0.2076	0.2541	0.2786	0.2787	0.2568	0.2188
	4	0.0004	0.0046	0.0185	0.0459	0.0865	0.1361	0.1875	0.2322	0.2627	0.2734
	5	0.0000	0.0004	0.0026	0.0092	0.0231	0.0467	0.0808	0.1239	0.1719	0.2188
	6	0.0000	0.0000	0.0002	0.0011	0.0038	0.0100	0.0217	0.0413	0.0703	0.1094
	7	0.0000	0.0000	0.0000	0.0001	0.0004	0.0012	0.0033	0.0079	0.0164	0.0312
	8	0.0000	0.0000	0.0000	0.0000	0.0000	0.0001	0.0002	0.0007	0.0017	0.0039
9	0	0.6302	0.3874	0.2316	0.1342	0.0751	0.0404	0.0207	0.0101	0.0046	0.0020
	1	0.2985	0.3874	0.3679	0.3020	0.2253	0.1556	0.1004	0.0605	0.0339	0.0176
	2	0.0629	0.1722	0.2597	0.3020	0.3003	0.2668	0.2162	0.1612	0.1110	0.0703
	3	0.0077	0.0446	0.1069	0.1762	0.2336	0.2668	0.2716	0.2508	0.2119	0.1641
	4	0.0006	0.0074	0.0283	0.0661	0.1168	0.1715	0.2194	0.2508	0.2600	0.2461
	5	0.0000	0.0008	0.0050	0.0165	0.0389	0.0735	0.1181	0.1672	0.2128	0.2461
	6	0.0000	0.0001	0.0006	0.0028	0.0087	0.0210	0.0424	0.0743	0.1160	0.1641
	7	0.0000	0.0000	0.0000	0.0003	0.0012	0.0039	0.0098	0.0212	0.0407	0.0703
	8	0.0000	0.0000	0.0000	0.0000	0.0001	0.0004	0.0013	0.0035	0.0083	0.0176
	9	0.0000	0.0000	0.0000	0.0000	0.0000	0.0000	0.0001	0.0003	0.0008	0.0020
10	0	0.5987	0.3487	0.1969	0.1074	0.0563	0.0282	0.0135	0.0060	0.0025	0.0010
	1	0.3151	0.3874	0.3474	0.2684	0.1877	0.1211	0.0725	0.0403	0.0207	0.0098
	2	0.0746	0.1937	0.2759	0.3020	0.2816	0.2335	0.1757	0.1209	0.0763	0.0439
	3	0.0105	0.0574	0.1298	0.2013	0.2503	0.2668	0.2522	0.2150	0.1665	0.1172
	4	0.0010	0.0112	0.0401	0.0881	0.1460	0.2001	0.2377	0.2508	0.2384	0.2051
	5	0.0001	0.0015	0.0085	0.0264	0.0584	0.1029	0.1536	0.2007	0.2340	0.2461
	6	0.0000	0.0001	0.0012	0.0055	0.0162	0.0368	0.0689	0.1115	0.1596	0.2051
	7	0.0000	0.0000	0.0001	0.0008	0.0031	0.0090	0.0212	0.0425	0.0746	0.1172
	8	0.0000	0.0000	0.0000	0.0001	0.0004	0.0014	0.0043	0.0106	0.0229	0.0439
	9	0.0000	0.0000	0.0000	0.0000	0.0000	0.0001	0.0005	0.0016	0.0042	0.0098
	10	0.0000	0.0000	0.0000	0.0000	0.0000	0.0000	0.0000	0.0001	0.0003	0.0010
12	0	0.5404	0.2824	0.1422	0.0687	0.0317	0.0138	0.0057	0.0022	0.0008	0.0002
	1	0.3413	0.3766	0.3012	0.2062	0.1267	0.0712	0.0368	0.0174	0.0075	0.0029
	2	0.0988	0.2301	0.2924	0.2835	0.2323	0.1678	0.1088	0.0639	0.0339	0.0161
	3	0.0173	0.0853	0.1720	0.2362	0.2581	0.2397	0.1954	0.1419	0.0923	0.0537
	4	0.0021	0.0213	0.0683	0.1329	0.1936	0.2311	0.2367	0.2128	0.1700	0.1208
	5	0.0002	0.0038	0.0193	0.0532	0.1032	0.1585	0.2039	0.2270	0.2225	0.1934
	6	0.0000	0.0005	0.0040	0.0155	0.0401	0.0792	0.1281	0.1766	0.2124	0.2256
	7	0.0000	0.0000	0.0006	0.0033	0.0115	0.0291	0.0591	0.1009	0.1489	0.1934
	8	0.0000	0.0000	0.0001	0.0005	0.0024	0.0078	0.0199	0.0420	0.0762	0.1208
	9	0.0000	0.0000	0.0000	0.0001	0.0004	0.0015	0.0048	0.0125	0.0277	0.0537
	10	0.0000	0.0000	0.0000	0.0000	0.0000	0.0002	0.0008	0.0025	0.0068	0.0161
	11	0.0000	0.0000	0.0000	0.0000	0.0000	0.0000	0.0001	0.0003	0.0010	0.0029
	12	0.0000	0.0000	0.0000	0.0000	0.0000	0.0000	0.0000	0.0000	0.0001	0.0002
15	0	0.4633	0.2059	0.0874	0.0352	0.0134	0.0047	0.0016	0.0005	0.0001	0.0000
	1	0.3658	0.3432	0.2312	0.1319	0.0668	0.0305	0.0126	0.0047	0.0016	0.0005
	2	0.1348	0.2669	0.2856	0.2309	0.1559	0.0916	0.0476	0.0219	0.0090	0.0032

Binomial Probabilities (*Continued*)

n	x	0.05	0.10	0.15	0.20	0.25	0.30	0.35	0.40	0.45	0.50
	3	0.0307	0.1285	0.2184	0.2501	0.2252	0.1700	0.1110	0.0634	0.0318	0.0139
	4	0.0049	0.0428	0.1156	0.1876	0.2252	0.2186	0.1792	0.1268	0.0780	0.0417
	5	0.0006	0.0105	0.0449	0.1032	0.1651	0.2061	0.2123	0.1859	0.1404	0.0916
	6	0.0000	0.0019	0.0132	0.0430	0.0917	0.1472	0.1906	0.2066	0.1914	0.1527
	7	0.0000	0.0003	0.0030	0.0138	0.0393	0.0811	0.1319	0.1771	0.2013	0.1964
	8	0.0000	0.0000	0.0005	0.0035	0.0131	0.0348	0.0710	0.1181	0.1647	0.1964
	9	0.0000	0.0000	0.0001	0.0007	0.0034	0.0116	0.0298	0.0612	0.1048	0.1527
	10	0.0000	0.0000	0.0000	0.0001	0.0007	0.0030	0.0096	0.0245	0.0515	0.0916
	11	0.0000	0.0000	0.0000	0.0000	0.0001	0.0006	0.0024	0.0074	0.0191	0.0417
	12	0.0000	0.0000	0.0000	0.0000	0.0000	0.0001	0.0004	0.0016	0.0052	0.0139
	13	0.0000	0.0000	0.0000	0.0000	0.0000	0.0000	0.0001	0.0003	0.0010	0.0032
	14	0.0000	0.0000	0.0000	0.0000	0.0000	0.0000	0.0000	0.0000	0.0001	0.0005
	15	0.0000	0.0000	0.0000	0.0000	0.0000	0.0000	0.0000	0.0000	0.0000	0.0000
18	0	0.3972	0.1501	0.0536	0.0180	0.0056	0.0016	0.0004	0.0001	0.0000	0.0000
	1	0.3763	0.3002	0.1704	0.0811	0.0338	0.0126	0.0042	0.0012	0.0003	0.0001
	2	0.1683	0.2835	0.2556	0.1723	0.0958	0.0458	0.0190	0.0069	0.0022	0.0006
	3	0.0473	0.1680	0.2406	0.2297	0.1704	0.1046	0.0547	0.0246	0.0095	0.0031
	4	0.0093	0.0700	0.1592	0.2153	0.2130	0.1681	0.1104	0.0614	0.0291	0.0117
	5	0.0014	0.0218	0.0787	0.1507	0.1988	0.2017	0.1664	0.1146	0.0666	0.0327
	6	0.0002	0.0052	0.0301	0.0816	0.1436	0.1873	0.1941	0.1655	0.1181	0.0708
	7	0.0000	0.0010	0.0091	0.0350	0.0820	0.1376	0.1792	0.1892	0.1657	0.1214
	8	0.0000	0.0002	0.0022	0.0120	0.0376	0.0811	0.1327	0.1734	0.1864	0.1669
	9	0.0000	0.0000	0.0004	0.0033	0.0139	0.0386	0.0794	0.1284	0.1694	0.1855
	10	0.0000	0.0000	0.0001	0.0008	0.0042	0.0149	0.0385	0.0771	0.1248	0.1669
	11	0.0000	0.0000	0.0000	0.0001	0.0010	0.0046	0.0151	0.0374	0.0742	0.1214
	12	0.0000	0.0000	0.0000	0.0000	0.0002	0.0012	0.0047	0.0145	0.0354	0.0708
	13	0.0000	0.0000	0.0000	0.0000	0.0000	0.0002	0.0012	0.0045	0.0134	0.0327
	14	0.0000	0.0000	0.0000	0.0000	0.0000	0.0000	0.0002	0.0011	0.0039	0.0117
	15	0.0000	0.0000	0.0000	0.0000	0.0000	0.0000	0.0000	0.0002	0.0009	0.0031
	16	0.0000	0.0000	0.0000	0.0000	0.0000	0.0000	0.0000	0.0000	0.0001	0.0006
	17	0.0000	0.0000	0.0000	0.0000	0.0000	0.0000	0.0000	0.0000	0.0000	0.0001
	18	0.0000	0.0000	0.0000	0.0000	0.0000	0.0000	0.0000	0.0000	0.0000	0.0000
20	0	0.3585	0.1216	0.0388	0.0115	0.0032	0.0008	0.0002	0.0000	0.0000	0.0000
	1	0.3774	0.2702	0.1368	0.0576	0.0211	0.0068	0.0020	0.0005	0.0001	0.0000
	2	0.1887	0.2852	0.2293	0.1369	0.0669	0.0278	0.0100	0.0031	0.0008	0.0002
	3	0.0596	0.1901	0.2428	0.2054	0.1339	0.0716	0.0323	0.0123	0.0040	0.0011
	4	0.0133	0.0898	0.1821	0.2182	0.1897	0.1304	0.0738	0.0350	0.0139	0.0046
	5	0.0022	0.0319	0.1028	0.1746	0.2023	0.1789	0.1272	0.0746	0.0365	0.0148
	6	0.0003	0.0089	0.0454	0.1091	0.1686	0.1916	0.1712	0.1244	0.0746	0.0370
	7	0.0000	0.0020	0.0160	0.0545	0.1124	0.1643	0.1844	0.1659	0.1221	0.0739
	8	0.0000	0.0004	0.0046	0.0222	0.0609	0.1144	0.1614	0.1797	0.1623	0.1201
	9	0.0000	0.0001	0.0011	0.0074	0.0271	0.0654	0.1158	0.1597	0.1771	0.1602
	10	0.0000	0.0000	0.0002	0.0020	0.0099	0.0308	0.0686	0.1171	0.1593	0.1762
	11	0.0000	0.0000	0.0000	0.0005	0.0030	0.0120	0.0336	0.0710	0.1185	0.1602
	12	0.0000	0.0000	0.0000	0.0001	0.0008	0.0039	0.0136	0.0355	0.0727	0.1201
	13	0.0000	0.0000	0.0000	0.0000	0.0002	0.0010	0.0045	0.0146	0.0366	0.0739
	14	0.0000	0.0000	0.0000	0.0000	0.0000	0.0002	0.0012	0.0049	0.0150	0.0370

Binomial Probabilities (*Continued*)

							p				
n	x	0.05	0.10	0.15	0.20	0.25	0.30	0.35	0.40	0.45	0.50
	15	0.0000	0.0000	0.0000	0.0000	0.0000	0.0000	0.0003	0.0013	0.0049	0.0148
	16	0.0000	0.0000	0.0000	0.0000	0.0000	0.0000	0.0000	0.0003	0.0013	0.0046
	17	0.0000	0.0000	0.0000	0.0000	0.0000	0.0000	0.0000	0.0000	0.0002	0.0011
	18	0.0000	0.0000	0.0000	0.0000	0.0000	0.0000	0.0000	0.0000	0.0000	0.0002
	19	0.0000	0.0000	0.0000	0.0000	0.0000	0.0000	0.0000	0.0000	0.0000	0.0000
	20	0.0000	0.0000	0.0000	0.0000	0.0000	0.0000	0.0000	0.0000	0.0000	0.0000

Binomial Probabilities (*Continued*)

						p				
n	x	0.55	0.60	0.65	0.70	0.75	0.80	0.85	0.90	0.95
2	0	0.2025	0.1600	0.1225	0.0900	0.0625	0.0400	0.0225	0.0100	0.0025
	1	0.4950	0.4800	0.4550	0.4200	0.3750	0.3200	0.2550	0.1800	0.0950
	2	0.3025	0.3600	0.4225	0.4900	0.5625	0.6400	0.7225	0.8100	0.9025
3	0	0.0911	0.0640	0.0429	0.0270	0.0156	0.0080	0.0034	0.0010	0.0001
	1	0.3341	0.2880	0.2389	0.1890	0.1406	0.0960	0.0574	0.0270	0.0071
	2	0.4084	0.4320	0.4436	0.4410	0.4219	0.3840	0.3251	0.2430	0.1354
	3	0.1664	0.2160	0.2746	0.3430	0.4219	0.5120	0.6141	0.7290	0.8574
4	0	0.0410	0.0256	0.0150	0.0081	0.0039	0.0016	0.0005	0.0001	0.0000
	1	0.2005	0.1536	0.1115	0.0756	0.0469	0.0256	0.0115	0.0036	0.0005
	2	0.3675	0.3456	0.3105	0.2646	0.2109	0.1536	0.0975	0.0486	0.0135
	3	0.2995	0.3456	0.3845	0.4116	0.4219	0.4096	0.3685	0.2916	0.1715
	4	0.0915	0.1296	0.1785	0.2401	0.3164	0.4096	0.5220	0.6561	0.8145
5	0	0.0185	0.0102	0.0053	0.0024	0.0010	0.0003	0.0001	0.0000	0.0000
	1	0.1128	0.0768	0.0488	0.0284	0.0146	0.0064	0.0022	0.0005	0.0000
	2	0.2757	0.2304	0.1811	0.1323	0.0879	0.0512	0.0244	0.0081	0.0011
	3	0.3369	0.3456	0.3364	0.3087	0.2637	0.2048	0.1382	0.0729	0.0214
	4	0.2059	0.2592	0.3124	0.3601	0.3955	0.4096	0.3915	0.3281	0.2036
	5	0.0503	0.0778	0.1160	0.1681	0.2373	0.3277	0.4437	0.5905	0.7738
6	0	0.0083	0.0041	0.0018	0.0007	0.0002	0.0001	0.0000	0.0000	0.0000
	1	0.0609	0.0369	0.0205	0.0102	0.0044	0.0015	0.0004	0.0001	0.0000
	2	0.1861	0.1382	0.0951	0.0595	0.0330	0.0154	0.0055	0.0012	0.0001
	3	0.3032	0.2765	0.2355	0.1852	0.1318	0.0819	0.0415	0.0146	0.0021
	4	0.2780	0.3110	0.3280	0.3241	0.2966	0.2458	0.1762	0.0984	0.0305
	5	0.1359	0.1866	0.2437	0.3025	0.3560	0.3932	0.3993	0.3543	0.2321
	6	0.0277	0.0467	0.0754	0.1176	0.1780	0.2621	0.3771	0.5314	0.7351
7	0	0.0037	0.0016	0.0006	0.0002	0.0001	0.0000	0.0000	0.0000	0.0000
	1	0.0320	0.0172	0.0084	0.0036	0.0013	0.0004	0.0001	0.0000	0.0000
	2	0.1172	0.0774	0.0466	0.0250	0.0115	0.0043	0.0012	0.0002	0.0000
	3	0.2388	0.1935	0.1442	0.0972	0.0577	0.0287	0.0109	0.0026	0.0002
	4	0.2918	0.2903	0.2679	0.2269	0.1730	0.1147	0.0617	0.0230	0.0036
	5	0.2140	0.2613	0.2985	0.3177	0.3115	0.2753	0.2097	0.1240	0.0406
	6	0.0872	0.1306	0.1848	0.2471	0.3115	0.3670	0.3960	0.3720	0.2573
	7	0.0152	0.0280	0.0490	0.0824	0.1335	0.2097	0.3206	0.4783	0.6983
8	0	0.0017	0.0007	0.0002	0.0001	0.0000	0.0000	0.0000	0.0000	0.0000
	1	0.0164	0.0079	0.0033	0.0012	0.0004	0.0001	0.0000	0.0000	0.0000
	2	0.0703	0.0413	0.0217	0.0100	0.0038	0.0011	0.0002	0.0000	0.0000
	3	0.1719	0.1239	0.0808	0.0467	0.0231	0.0092	0.0026	0.0004	0.0000
	4	0.2627	0.2322	0.1875	0.1361	0.0865	0.0459	0.0185	0.0046	0.0004
	5	0.2568	0.2787	0.2786	0.2541	0.2076	0.1468	0.0839	0.0331	0.0054
	6	0.1569	0.2090	0.2587	0.2965	0.3115	0.2936	0.2376	0.1488	0.0515
	7	0.0548	0.0896	0.1373	0.1977	0.2670	0.3355	0.3847	0.3826	0.2793
	8	0.0084	0.0168	0.0319	0.0576	0.1001	0.1678	0.2725	0.4305	0.6634

Binomial Probabilities (*Continued*)

						p				
n	x	0.55	0.60	0.65	0.70	0.75	0.80	0.85	0.90	0.95
9	0	0.0008	0.0003	0.0001	0.0000	0.0000	0.0000	0.0000	0.0000	0.0000
	1	0.0083	0.0035	0.0013	0.0004	0.0001	0.0000	0.0000	0.0000	0.0000
	2	0.0407	0.0212	0.0098	0.0039	0.0012	0.0003	0.0000	0.0000	0.0000
	3	0.1160	0.0743	0.0424	0.0210	0.0087	0.0028	0.0006	0.0001	0.0000
	4	0.2128	0.1672	0.1181	0.0735	0.0389	0.0165	0.0050	0.0008	0.0000
	5	0.2600	0.2508	0.2194	0.1715	0.1168	0.0661	0.0283	0.0074	0.0006
	6	0.2119	0.2508	0.2716	0.2668	0.2336	0.1762	0.1069	0.0446	0.0077
	7	0.1110	0.1612	0.2162	0.2668	0.3003	0.3020	0.2597	0.1722	0.0629
	8	0.0339	0.0605	0.1004	0.1556	0.2253	0.3020	0.3679	0.3874	0.2985
	9	0.0046	0.0101	0.0207	0.0404	0.0751	0.1342	0.2316	0.3874	0.6302
10	0	0.0003	0.0001	0.0000	0.0000	0.0000	0.0000	0.0000	0.0000	0.0000
	1	0.0042	0.0016	0.0005	0.0001	0.0000	0.0000	0.0000	0.0000	0.0000
	2	0.0229	0.0106	0.0043	0.0014	0.0004	0.0001	0.0000	0.0000	0.0000
	3	0.0746	0.0425	0.0212	0.0090	0.0031	0.0008	0.0001	0.0000	0.0000
	4	0.1596	0.1115	0.0689	0.0368	0.0162	0.0055	0.0012	0.0001	0.0000
	5	0.2340	0.2007	0.1536	0.1029	0.0584	0.0264	0.0085	0.0015	0.0001
	6	0.2384	0.2508	0.2377	0.2001	0.1460	0.0881	0.0401	0.0112	0.0010
	7	0.1665	0.2150	0.2522	0.2668	0.2503	0.2013	0.1298	0.0574	0.0105
	8	0.0763	0.1209	0.1757	0.2335	0.2816	0.3020	0.2759	0.1937	0.0746
	9	0.0207	0.0403	0.0725	0.1211	0.1877	0.2684	0.3474	0.3874	0.3151
	10	0.0025	0.0060	0.0135	0.0282	0.0563	0.1074	0.1969	0.3487	0.5987
12	0	0.0001	0.0000	0.0000	0.0000	0.0000	0.0000	0.0000	0.0000	0.0000
	1	0.0010	0.0003	0.0001	0.0000	0.0000	0.0000	0.0000	0.0000	0.0000
	2	0.0068	0.0025	0.0008	0.0002	0.0000	0.0000	0.0000	0.0000	0.0000
	3	0.0277	0.0125	0.0048	0.0015	0.0004	0.0001	0.0000	0.0000	0.0000
	4	0.0762	0.0420	0.0199	0.0078	0.0024	0.0005	0.0001	0.0000	0.0000
	5	0.1489	0.1009	0.0591	0.0291	0.0115	0.0033	0.0006	0.0000	0.0000
	6	0.2124	0.1766	0.1281	0.0792	0.0401	0.0155	0.0040	0.0005	0.0000
	7	0.2225	0.2270	0.2039	0.1585	0.1032	0.0532	0.0193	0.0038	0.0002
	8	0.1700	0.2128	0.2367	0.2311	0.1936	0.1329	0.0683	0.0213	0.0021
	9	0.0923	0.1419	0.1954	0.2397	0.2581	0.2362	0.1720	0.0852	0.0173
	10	0.0339	0.0639	0.1088	0.1678	0.2323	0.2835	0.2924	0.2301	0.0988
	11	0.0075	0.0174	0.0368	0.0712	0.1267	0.2062	0.3012	0.3766	0.3413
	12	0.0008	0.0022	0.0057	0.0138	0.0317	0.0687	0.1422	0.2824	0.5404
15	0	0.0000	0.0000	0.0000	0.0000	0.0000	0.0000	0.0000	0.0000	0.0000
	1	0.0001	0.0000	0.0000	0.0000	0.0000	0.0000	0.0000	0.0000	0.0000
	2	0.0010	0.0003	0.0001	0.0000	0.0000	0.0000	0.0000	0.0000	0.0000
	3	0.0052	0.0016	0.0004	0.0001	0.0000	0.0000	0.0000	0.0000	0.0000
	4	0.0191	0.0074	0.0024	0.0006	0.0001	0.0000	0.0000	0.0000	0.0000
	5	0.0515	0.0245	0.0096	0.0030	0.0007	0.0001	0.0000	0.0000	0.0000
	6	0.1048	0.0612	0.0298	0.0116	0.0034	0.0007	0.0001	0.0000	0.0000
	7	0.1647	0.1181	0.0710	0.0348	0.0131	0.0035	0.0005	0.0000	0.0000
	8	0.2013	0.1771	0.1319	0.0811	0.0393	0.0138	0.0030	0.0003	0.0000
	9	0.1914	0.2066	0.1906	0.1472	0.0917	0.0430	0.0132	0.0019	0.0000
	10	0.1404	0.1859	0.2123	0.2061	0.1651	0.1032	0.0449	0.0105	0.0006
	11	0.0780	0.1268	0.1792	0.2186	0.2252	0.1876	0.1156	0.0428	0.0049

Binomial Probabilities (*Continued*)

n	x	p								
		0.55	**0.60**	**0.65**	**0.70**	**0.75**	**0.80**	**0.85**	**0.90**	**0.95**
	12	0.0318	0.0634	0.1110	0.1700	0.2252	0.2501	0.2184	0.1285	0.0307
	13	0.0090	0.0219	0.0476	0.0916	0.1559	0.2309	0.2856	0.2669	0.1348
	14	0.0016	0.0047	0.0126	0.0305	0.0668	0.1319	0.2312	0.3432	0.3658
	15	0.0001	0.0005	0.0016	0.0047	0.0134	0.0352	0.0874	0.2059	0.4633
18	0	0.0000	0.0000	0.0000	0.0000	0.0000	0.0000	0.0000	0.0000	0.0000
	1	0.0000	0.0000	0.0000	0.0000	0.0000	0.0000	0.0000	0.0000	0.0000
	2	0.0001	0.0000	0.0000	0.0000	0.0000	0.0000	0.0000	0.0000	0.0000
	3	0.0009	0.0002	0.0000	0.0000	0.0000	0.0000	0.0000	0.0000	0.0000
	4	0.0039	0.0011	0.0002	0.0000	0.0000	0.0000	0.0000	0.0000	0.0000
	5	0.0134	0.0045	0.0012	0.0002	0.0000	0.0000	0.0000	0.0000	0.0000
	6	0.0354	0.0145	0.0047	0.0012	0.0002	0.0000	0.0000	0.0000	0.0000
	7	0.0742	0.0374	0.0151	0.0046	0.0010	0.0001	0.0000	0.0000	0.0000
	8	0.1248	0.0771	0.0385	0.0149	0.0042	0.0008	0.0001	0.0000	0.0000
	9	0.1694	0.1284	0.0794	0.0386	0.0139	0.0033	0.0004	0.0000	0.0000
	10	0.1864	0.1734	0.1327	0.0811	0.0376	0.0120	0.0022	0.0002	0.0000
	11	0.1657	0.1892	0.1792	0.1376	0.0820	0.0350	0.0091	0.0010	0.0000
	12	0.1181	0.1655	0.1941	0.1873	0.1436	0.0816	0.0301	0.0052	0.0002
	13	0.0666	0.1146	0.1664	0.2017	0.1988	0.1507	0.0787	0.0218	0.0014
	14	0.0291	0.0614	0.1104	0.1681	0.2130	0.2153	0.1592	0.0700	0.0093
	15	0.0095	0.0246	0.0547	0.1046	0.1704	0.2297	0.2406	0.1680	0.0473
	16	0.0022	0.0069	0.0190	0.0458	0.0958	0.1723	0.2556	0.2835	0.1683
	17	0.0003	0.0012	0.0042	0.0126	0.0338	0.0811	0.1704	0.3002	0.3763
	18	0.0000	0.0001	0.0004	0.0016	0.0056	0.0180	0.0536	0.1501	0.3972
20	0	0.0000	0.0000	0.0000	0.0000	0.0000	0.0000	0.0000	0.0000	0.0000
	1	0.0000	0.0000	0.0000	0.0000	0.0000	0.0000	0.0000	0.0000	0.0000
	2	0.0000	0.0000	0.0000	0.0000	0.0000	0.0000	0.0000	0.0000	0.0000
	3	0.0002	0.0000	0.0000	0.0000	0.0000	0.0000	0.0000	0.0000	0.0000
	4	0.0013	0.0003	0.0000	0.0000	0.0000	0.0000	0.0000	0.0000	0.0000
	5	0.0049	0.0013	0.0003	0.0000	0.0000	0.0000	0.0000	0.0000	0.0000
	6	0.0150	0.0049	0.0012	0.0002	0.0000	0.0000	0.0000	0.0000	0.0000
	7	0.0366	0.0146	0.0045	0.0010	0.0002	0.0000	0.0000	0.0000	0.0000
	8	0.0727	0.0355	0.0136	0.0039	0.0008	0.0001	0.0000	0.0000	0.0000
	9	0.1185	0.0710	0.0336	0.0120	0.0030	0.0005	0.0000	0.0000	0.0000
	10	0.1593	0.1171	0.0686	0.0308	0.0099	0.0020	0.0002	0.0000	0.0000
	11	0.1771	0.1597	0.1158	0.0654	0.0271	0.0074	0.0011	0.0001	0.0000
	12	0.1623	0.1797	0.1614	0.1144	0.0609	0.0222	0.0046	0.0004	0.0000
	13	0.1221	0.1659	0.1844	0.1643	0.1124	0.0545	0.0160	0.0020	0.0000
	14	0.0746	0.1244	0.1712	0.1916	0.1686	0.1091	0.0454	0.0089	0.0003
	15	0.0365	0.0746	0.1272	0.1789	0.2023	0.1746	0.1028	0.0319	0.0022
	16	0.0139	0.0350	0.0738	0.1304	0.1897	0.2182	0.1821	0.0898	0.0133
	17	0.0040	0.0123	0.0323	0.0716	0.1339	0.2054	0.2428	0.1901	0.0596
	18	0.0008	0.0031	0.0100	0.0278	0.0669	0.1369	0.2293	0.2852	0.1887
	19	0.0001	0.0005	0.0020	0.0068	0.0211	0.0576	0.1368	0.2702	0.3774
	20	0.0000	0.0000	0.0002	0.0008	0.0032	0.0115	0.0388	0.1216	0.3585

Appendix C   Poisson Probabilities

Entries in the following table give the probability of x occurrences for a Poisson process with a mean λ. For example, when $\lambda = 2.5$, the probability of $x = 4$ occurrences is 0.1336.

					λ					
x	0.1	0.2	0.3	0.4	0.5	0.6	0.7	0.8	0.9	1.0
0	0.9048	0.8187	0.7408	0.6703	0.6065	0.5488	0.4966	0.4493	0.4066	0.3679
1	0.0905	0.1637	0.2222	0.2681	0.3033	0.3293	0.3476	0.3595	0.3659	0.3679
2	0.0045	0.0164	0.0333	0.0536	0.0758	0.0988	0.1217	0.1438	0.1647	0.1839
3	0.0002	0.0011	0.0033	0.0072	0.0126	0.0198	0.0284	0.0383	0.0494	0.0613
4	0.0000	0.0001	0.0002	0.0007	0.0016	0.0030	0.0050	0.0077	0.0111	0.0153
5	0.0000	0.0000	0.0000	0.0001	0.0002	0.0004	0.0007	0.0012	0.0020	0.0031
6	0.0000	0.0000	0.0000	0.0000	0.0000	0.0000	0.0001	0.0002	0.0003	0.0005
7	0.0000	0.0000	0.0000	0.0000	0.0000	0.0000	0.0000	0.0000	0.0000	0.0001

					λ					
x	1.1	1.2	1.3	1.4	1.5	1.6	1.7	1.8	1.9	2.0
0	0.3329	0.3012	0.2725	0.2466	0.2231	0.2019	0.1827	0.1653	0.1496	0.1353
1	0.3662	0.3614	0.3543	0.3452	0.3347	0.3230	0.3106	0.2975	0.2842	0.2707
2	0.2014	0.2169	0.2303	0.2417	0.2510	0.2584	0.2640	0.2678	0.2700	0.2707
3	0.0738	0.0867	0.0998	0.1128	0.1255	0.1378	0.1496	0.1607	0.1710	0.1804
4	0.0203	0.0260	0.0324	0.0395	0.0471	0.0551	0.0636	0.0723	0.0812	0.0902
5	0.0045	0.0062	0.0084	0.0111	0.0141	0.0176	0.0216	0.0260	0.0309	0.0361
6	0.0008	0.0012	0.0018	0.0026	0.0035	0.0047	0.0061	0.0078	0.0098	0.0120
7	0.0001	0.0002	0.0003	0.0005	0.0008	0.0011	0.0015	0.0020	0.0027	0.0034
8	0.0000	0.0000	0.0001	0.0001	0.0001	0.0002	0.0003	0.0005	0.0006	0.0009
9	0.0000	0.0000	0.0000	0.0000	0.0000	0.0000	0.0001	0.0001	0.0001	0.0002

					λ					
x	2.1	2.2	2.3	2.4	2.5	2.6	2.7	2.8	2.9	3.0
0	0.1225	0.1108	0.1003	0.0907	0.0821	0.0743	0.0672	0.0608	0.0550	0.0498
1	0.2572	0.2438	0.2306	0.2177	0.2052	0.1931	0.1815	0.1703	0.1596	0.1494
2	0.2700	0.2681	0.2652	0.2613	0.2565	0.2510	0.2450	0.2384	0.2314	0.2240
3	0.1890	0.1966	0.2033	0.2090	0.2138	0.2176	0.2205	0.2225	0.2237	0.2240
4	0.0992	0.1082	0.1169	0.1254	0.1336	0.1414	0.1488	0.1557	0.1622	0.1680
5	0.0417	0.0476	0.0538	0.0602	0.0668	0.0735	0.0804	0.0872	0.0940	0.1008
6	0.0146	0.0174	0.0206	0.0241	0.0278	0.0319	0.0362	0.0407	0.0455	0.0540
7	0.0044	0.0055	0.0068	0.0083	0.0099	0.0118	0.0139	0.0163	0.0188	0.0216

Poisson Probabilities (*Continued*)

					λ					
x	2.1	2.2	2.3	2.4	2.5	2.6	2.7	2.8	2.9	3.0
8	0.0011	0.0015	0.0019	0.0025	0.0031	0.0038	0.0047	0.0057	0.0068	0.0081
9	0.0003	0.0004	0.0005	0.0007	0.0009	0.0011	0.0014	0.0018	0.0022	0.0027
10	0.0001	0.0001	0.0001	0.0002	0.0002	0.0003	0.0004	0.0005	0.0006	0.0008
11	0.0000	0.0000	0.0000	0.0000	0.0000	0.0001	0.0001	0.0001	0.0002	0.0002
12	0.0000	0.0000	0.0000	0.0000	0.0000	0.0000	0.0000	0.0000	0.0000	0.0001

					λ					
x	3.1	3.2	3.3	3.4	3.5	3.6	3.7	3.8	3.9	4.0
0	0.0450	0.0408	0.0369	0.0344	0.0302	0.0273	0.0247	0.0224	0.0202	0.0183
1	0.1397	0.1304	0.1217	0.1135	0.1057	0.0984	0.0915	0.0850	0.0789	0.0733
2	0.2165	0.2087	0.2008	0.1929	0.1850	0.1771	0.1692	0.1615	0.1539	0.1465
3	0.2237	0.2226	0.2209	0.2186	0.2158	0.2125	0.2087	0.2046	0.2001	0.1954
4	0.1734	0.1781	0.1823	0.1858	0.1888	0.1912	0.1931	0.1944	0.1951	0.1954
5	0.1075	0.1140	0.1203	0.1264	0.1322	0.1377	0.1429	0.1477	0.1522	0.1563
6	0.0555	0.0608	0.0662	0.0716	0.0771	0.0826	0.0881	0.0936	0.0989	0.1042
7	0.0246	0.0278	0.0312	0.0348	0.0385	0.0425	0.0466	0.0508	0.0551	0.0595
8	0.0095	0.0111	0.0129	0.0148	0.0169	0.0191	0.0215	0.0241	0.0269	0.0298
9	0.0033	0.0040	0.0047	0.0056	0.0066	0.0076	0.0089	0.0102	0.0116	0.0132
10	0.0010	0.0013	0.0016	0.0019	0.0023	0.0028	0.0033	0.0039	0.0045	0.0053
11	0.0003	0.0004	0.0005	0.0006	0.0007	0.0009	0.0011	0.0013	0.0016	0.0019
12	0.0001	0.0001	0.0001	0.0002	0.0002	0.0003	0.0003	0.0004	0.0005	0.0006
13	0.0000	0.0000	0.0000	0.0000	0.0001	0.0001	0.0001	0.0001	0.0002	0.0002
14	0.0000	0.0000	0.0000	0.0000	0.0000	0.0000	0.0000	0.0000	0.0000	0.0001

					λ					
x	4.1	4.2	4.3	4.4	4.5	4.6	4.7	4.8	4.9	5.0
0	0.0166	0.0150	0.0136	0.0123	0.0111	0.0101	0.0091	0.0082	0.0074	0.0067
1	0.0679	0.0630	0.0583	0.0540	0.0500	0.0462	0.0427	0.0395	0.0365	0.0337
2	0.1393	0.1323	0.1254	0.1188	0.1125	0.1063	0.1005	0.0948	0.0894	0.0842
3	0.1904	0.1852	0.1798	0.1743	0.1687	0.1631	0.1574	0.1517	0.1460	0.1404
4	0.1951	0.1944	0.1933	0.1917	0.1898	0.1875	0.1849	0.1820	0.1789	0.1755
5	0.1600	0.1633	0.1662	0.1687	0.1708	0.1725	0.1738	0.1747	0.1753	0.1755
6	0.1093	0.1143	0.1191	0.1237	0.1281	0.1323	0.1362	0.1398	0.1432	0.1462
7	0.0640	0.0686	0.0732	0.0778	0.0824	0.0869	0.0914	0.0959	0.1002	0.1044
8	0.0328	0.0360	0.0393	0.0428	0.0463	0.0500	0.0537	0.0575	0.0614	0.0653
9	0.0150	0.0168	0.0188	0.0209	0.0232	0.0255	0.0280	0.0307	0.0334	0.0363
10	0.0061	0.0071	0.0081	0.0092	0.0104	0.0118	0.0132	0.0147	0.0164	0.0181
11	0.0023	0.0027	0.0032	0.0037	0.0043	0.0049	0.0056	0.0064	0.0073	0.0082
12	0.0008	0.0009	0.0011	0.0014	0.0016	0.0019	0.0022	0.0026	0.0030	0.0034
13	0.0002	0.0003	0.0004	0.0005	0.0006	0.0007	0.0008	0.0009	0.0011	0.0013
14	0.0001	0.0001	0.0001	0.0001	0.0002	0.0002	0.0003	0.0003	0.0004	0.0005
15	0.0000	0.0000	0.0000	0.0000	0.0001	0.0001	0.0001	0.0001	0.0001	0.0002

Poisson Probabilities (*Continued*)

					λ					
x	5.1	5.2	5.3	5.4	5.5	5.6	5.7	5.8	5.9	6.0
0	0.0061	0.0055	0.0050	0.0045	0.0041	0.0037	0.0033	0.0030	0.0027	0.0025
1	0.0311	0.0287	0.0265	0.0244	0.0225	0.0207	0.0191	0.0176	0.0162	0.0149
2	0.0793	0.0746	0.0701	0.0659	0.0618	0.0580	0.0544	0.0509	0.0477	0.0446
3	0.1348	0.1293	0.1239	0.1185	0.1133	0.1082	0.1033	0.0985	0.0938	0.0892
4	0.1719	0.1681	0.1641	0.1600	0.1558	0.1515	0.1472	0.1428	0.1383	0.1339
5	0.1753	0.1748	0.1740	0.1728	0.1714	0.1697	0.1678	0.1656	0.1632	0.1606
6	0.1490	0.1515	0.1537	0.1555	0.1571	0.1587	0.1594	0.1601	0.1605	0.1606
7	0.1086	0.1125	0.1163	0.1200	0.1234	0.1267	0.1298	0.1326	0.1353	0.1377
8	0.0692	0.0731	0.0771	0.0810	0.0849	0.0887	0.0925	0.0962	0.0998	0.1033
9	0.0392	0.0423	0.0454	0.0486	0.0519	0.0552	0.0586	0.0620	0.0654	0.0688
10	0.0200	0.0220	0.0241	0.0262	0.0285	0.0309	0.0334	0.0359	0.0386	0.0413
11	0.0093	0.0104	0.0116	0.0129	0.0143	0.0157	0.0173	0.0190	0.0207	0.0225
12	0.0039	0.0045	0.0051	0.0058	0.0065	0.0073	0.0082	0.0092	0.0102	0.0113
13	0.0015	0.0018	0.0021	0.0024	0.0028	0.0032	0.0036	0.0041	0.0046	0.0052
14	0.0006	0.0007	0.0008	0.0009	0.0011	0.0013	0.0015	0.0017	0.0019	0.0022
15	0.0002	0.0002	0.0003	0.0003	0.0004	0.0005	0.0006	0.0007	0.0008	0.0009
16	0.0001	0.0001	0.0001	0.0001	0.0001	0.0002	0.0002	0.0002	0.0003	0.0003
17	0.0000	0.0000	0.0000	0.0000	0.0000	0.0001	0.0001	0.0001	0.0001	0.0001

					λ					
x	6.1	6.2	6.3	6.4	6.5	6.6	6.7	6.8	6.9	7.0
0	0.0022	0.0020	0.0018	0.0017	0.0015	0.0014	0.0012	0.0011	0.0010	0.0009
1	0.0137	0.0126	0.0116	0.0106	0.0098	0.0090	0.0082	0.0076	0.0070	0.0064
2	0.0417	0.0390	0.0364	0.0340	0.0318	0.0296	0.0276	0.0258	0.0240	0.0223
3	0.0848	0.0806	0.0765	0.0726	0.0688	0.0652	0.0617	0.0584	0.0552	0.0521
4	0.1294	0.1249	0.1205	0.1162	0.1118	0.1076	0.1034	0.0992	0.0952	0.0912
5	0.1579	0.1549	0.1519	0.1487	0.1454	0.1420	0.1385	0.1349	0.1314	0.1277
6	0.1605	0.1601	0.1595	0.1586	0.1575	0.1562	0.1546	0.1529	0.1511	0.1490
7	0.1399	0.1418	0.1435	0.1450	0.1462	0.1472	0.1480	0.1486	0.1489	0.1490
8	0.1066	0.1099	0.1130	0.1160	0.1188	0.1215	0.1240	0.1263	0.1284	0.1304
9	0.0723	0.0757	0.0791	0.0825	0.0858	0.0891	0.0923	0.0954	0.0985	0.1014
10	0.0441	0.0469	0.0498	0.0528	0.0558	0.0588	0.0618	0.0649	0.0679	0.0710
11	0.0245	0.0265	0.0285	0.0307	0.0330	0.0353	0.0377	0.0401	0.0426	0.0452
12	0.0124	0.0137	0.0150	0.0164	0.0179	0.0194	0.0210	0.0227	0.0245	0.0264
13	0.0058	0.0065	0.0073	0.0081	0.0089	0.0098	0.0108	0.0119	0.0130	0.0142
14	0.0025	0.0029	0.0033	0.0037	0.0041	0.0046	0.0052	0.0058	0.0064	0.0071
15	0.0010	0.0012	0.0014	0.0016	0.0018	0.0020	0.0023	0.0025	0.0029	0.0033
16	0.0004	0.0005	0.0005	0.0006	0.0007	0.0008	0.0010	0.0011	0.0013	0.0014
17	0.0001	0.0002	0.0002	0.0002	0.0003	0.0003	0.0004	0.0004	0.0005	0.0006
18	0.0000	0.0001	0.0001	0.0001	0.0001	0.0001	0.0001	0.0002	0.0002	0.0002
19	0.0000	0.0000	0.0000	0.0000	0.0000	0.0000	0.0000	0.0001	0.0001	0.0001

Poisson Probabilities (*Continued*)

					λ					
x	7.1	7.2	7.3	7.4	7.5	7.6	7.7	7.8	7.9	8.0
0	0.0008	0.0007	0.0007	0.0006	0.0006	0.0005	0.0005	0.0004	0.0004	0.0003
1	0.0059	0.0054	0.0049	0.0045	0.0041	0.0038	0.0035	0.0032	0.0029	0.0027
2	0.0208	0.0194	0.0180	0.0167	0.0156	0.0145	0.0134	0.0125	0.0116	0.0107
3	0.0492	0.0464	0.0438	0.0413	0.0389	0.0366	0.0345	0.0324	0.0305	0.0286
4	0.0874	0.0836	0.0799	0.0764	0.0729	0.0696	0.0663	0.0632	0.0602	0.0573
5	0.1241	0.1204	0.1167	0.1130	0.1094	0.1057	0.1021	0.0986	0.0951	0.0916
6	0.1468	0.1445	0.1420	0.1394	0.1367	0.1339	0.1311	0.1282	0.1252	0.1221
7	0.1489	0.1486	0.1481	0.1474	0.1465	0.1454	0.1442	0.1428	0.1413	0.1396
8	0.1321	0.1337	0.1351	0.1363	0.1373	0.1382	0.1388	0.1392	0.1395	0.1396
9	0.1042	0.1070	0.1096	0.1121	0.1144	0.1167	0.1187	0.1207	0.1224	0.1241
10	0.0740	0.0770	0.0800	0.0829	0.0858	0.0887	0.0914	0.0941	0.0967	0.0993
11	0.0478	0.0504	0.0531	0.0558	0.0585	0.0613	0.0640	0.0667	0.0695	0.0722
12	0.0283	0.0303	0.0323	0.0344	0.0366	0.0388	0.0411	0.0434	0.0457	0.0481
13	0.0154	0.0168	0.0181	0.0196	0.0211	0.0227	0.0243	0.0260	0.0278	0.0296
14	0.0078	0.0086	0.0095	0.0104	0.0113	0.0123	0.0134	0.0145	0.0157	0.0169
15	0.0037	0.0041	0.0046	0.0051	0.0057	0.0062	0.0069	0.0075	0.0083	0.0090
16	0.0016	0.0019	0.0021	0.0024	0.0026	0.0030	0.0033	0.0037	0.0041	0.0045
17	0.0007	0.0008	0.0009	0.0010	0.0012	0.0013	0.0015	0.0017	0.0019	0.0021
18	0.0003	0.0003	0.0004	0.0004	0.0005	0.0006	0.0006	0.0007	0.0008	0.0009
19	0.0001	0.0001	0.0001	0.0002	0.0002	0.0002	0.0003	0.0003	0.0003	0.0004
20	0.0000	0.0000	0.0001	0.0001	0.0001	0.0001	0.0001	0.0001	0.0001	0.0002
21	0.0000	0.0000	0.0000	0.0000	0.0000	0.0000	0.0000	0.0000	0.0001	0.0001

					λ					
x	8.1	8.2	8.3	8.4	8.5	8.6	8.7	8.8	8.9	9.0
0	0.0003	0.0003	0.0002	0.0002	0.0002	0.0002	0.0002	0.0002	0.0001	0.0001
1	0.0025	0.0023	0.0021	0.0019	0.0017	0.0016	0.0014	0.0013	0.0012	0.0011
2	0.0100	0.0092	0.0086	0.0079	0.0074	0.0068	0.0063	0.0058	0.0054	0.0050
3	0.0269	0.0252	0.0237	0.0222	0.0208	0.0195	0.0183	0.0171	0.0160	0.0150
4	0.0544	0.0517	0.0491	0.0466	0.0443	0.0420	0.0398	0.0377	0.0357	0.0337
5	0.0882	0.0849	0.0816	0.0784	0.0752	0.0722	0.0692	0.0663	0.0635	0.0607
6	0.1191	0.1160	0.1128	0.1097	0.1066	0.1034	0.1003	0.0972	0.0941	0.0911
7	0.1378	0.1358	0.1338	0.1317	0.1294	0.1271	0.1247	0.1222	0.1197	0.1171
8	0.1395	0.1392	0.1388	0.1382	0.1375	0.1366	0.1356	0.1344	0.1332	0.1318
9	0.1256	0.1269	0.1280	0.1290	0.1299	0.1306	0.1311	0.1315	0.1317	0.1318
10	0.1017	0.1040	0.1063	0.1084	0.1104	0.1123	0.1140	0.1157	0.1172	0.1186
11	0.0749	0.0776	0.0802	0.0828	0.0853	0.0878	0.0902	0.0925	0.0948	0.0970
12	0.0505	0.0530	0.0555	0.0579	0.0604	0.0629	0.0654	0.0679	0.0703	0.0728
13	0.0315	0.0334	0.0354	0.0374	0.0395	0.0416	0.0438	0.0459	0.0481	0.0504
14	0.0182	0.0196	0.0210	0.0225	0.0240	0.0256	0.0272	0.0289	0.0306	0.0324

Poisson Probabilities (*Continued*)

x	λ									
	8.1	**8.2**	**8.3**	**8.4**	**8.5**	**8.6**	**8.7**	**8.8**	**8.9**	**9.0**
15	0.0098	0.0107	0.0116	0.0126	0.0136	0.0147	0.0158	0.0169	0.0182	0.1094
16	0.0050	0.0055	0.0060	0.0066	0.0072	0.0079	0.0086	0.0093	0.0101	0.0109
17	0.0024	0.0026	0.0029	0.0033	0.0036	0.0040	0.0044	0.0048	0.0053	0.0058
18	0.0011	0.0012	0.0014	0.0015	0.0017	0.0019	0.0021	0.0024	0.0026	0.0029
19	0.0005	0.0005	0.0006	0.0007	0.0008	0.0009	0.0010	0.0011	0.0012	0.0014
20	0.0002	0.0002	0.0002	0.0003	0.0003	0.0004	0.0004	0.0005	0.0005	0.0006
21	0.0001	0.0001	0.0001	0.0001	0.0001	0.0002	0.0002	0.0002	0.0002	0.0003
22	0.0000	0.0000	0.0000	0.0000	0.0001	0.0001	0.0001	0.0001	0.0001	0.0001

x	λ									
	9.1	**9.2**	**9.3**	**9.4**	**9.5**	**9.6**	**9.7**	**9.8**	**9.9**	**10**
0	0.0001	0.0001	0.0001	0.0001	0.0001	0.0001	0.0001	0.0001	0.0001	0.0000
1	0.0010	0.0009	0.0009	0.0008	0.0007	0.0007	0.0006	0.0005	0.0005	0.0005
2	0.0046	0.0043	0.0040	0.0037	0.0034	0.0031	0.0029	0.0027	0.0025	0.0023
3	0.0140	0.0131	0.0123	0.0115	0.0107	0.0100	0.0093	0.0087	0.0081	0.0076
4	0.0319	0.0302	0.0285	0.0269	0.0254	0.0240	0.0226	0.0213	0.0201	0.0189
5	0.0581	0.0555	0.0530	0.0506	0.0483	0.0460	0.0439	0.0418	0.0398	0.0378
6	0.0881	0.0851	0.0822	0.0793	0.0764	0.0736	0.0709	0.0682	0.0656	0.0631
7	0.1145	0.1118	0.1091	0.1064	0.1037	0.1010	0.0982	0.0955	0.0928	0.0901
8	0.1302	0.1286	0.1269	0.1251	0.1232	0.1212	0.1191	0.1170	0.1148	0.1126
9	0.1317	0.1315	0.1311	0.1306	0.1300	0.1293	0.1284	0.1274	0.1263	0.1251
10	0.1198	0.1210	0.1219	0.1228	0.1235	0.1241	0.1245	0.1249	0.1250	0.1251
11	0.0991	0.1012	0.1031	0.1049	0.1067	0.1083	0.1098	0.1112	0.1125	0.1137
12	0.0752	0.0776	0.0799	0.0822	0.0844	0.0866	0.0888	0.0908	0.0928	0.0948
13	0.0526	0.0549	0.0572	0.0594	0.0617	0.0640	0.0662	0.0685	0.0707	0.0729
14	0.0342	0.0361	0.0380	0.0399	0.0419	0.0439	0.0459	0.0479	0.0500	0.0521
15	0.0208	0.0221	0.0235	0.0250	0.0265	0.0281	0.0297	0.0313	0.0330	0.0347
16	0.0118	0.0127	0.0137	0.0147	0.0157	0.0168	0.0180	0.0192	0.0204	0.0217
17	0.0063	0.0069	0.0075	0.0081	0.0088	0.0095	0.0103	0.0111	0.0119	0.0128
18	0.0032	0.0035	0.0039	0.0042	0.0046	0.0051	0.0055	0.0060	0.0065	0.0071
19	0.0015	0.0017	0.0019	0.0021	0.0023	0.0026	0.0028	0.0031	0.0034	0.0027
20	0.0007	0.0008	0.0009	0.0010	0.0011	0.0012	0.0014	0.0015	0.0017	0.0019
21	0.0003	0.0003	0.0004	0.0004	0.0005	0.0006	0.0006	0.0007	0.0008	0.0009
22	0.0001	0.0001	0.0002	0.0002	0.0002	0.0002	0.0003	0.0003	0.0004	0.0004
23	0.0000	0.0001	0.0001	0.0001	0.0001	0.0001	0.0001	0.0001	0.0002	0.0002
24	0.0000	0.0000	0.0000	0.0000	0.0000	0.0000	0.0000	0.0001	0.0001	0.0001

Poisson Probabilities (*Continued*)

					λ					
x	11	12	13	14	15	16	17	18	19	20
0	0.0000	0.0000	0.0000	0.0000	0.0000	0.0000	0.0000	0.0000	0.0000	0.0000
1	0.0002	0.0001	0.0000	0.0000	0.0000	0.0000	0.0000	0.0000	0.0000	0.0000
2	0.0010	0.0004	0.0002	0.0001	0.0000	0.0000	0.0000	0.0000	0.0000	0.0000
3	0.0037	0.0018	0.0008	0.0004	0.0002	0.0001	0.0000	0.0000	0.0000	0.0000
4	0.0102	0.0053	0.0027	0.0013	0.0006	0.0003	0.0001	0.0001	0.0000	0.0000
5	0.0224	0.0127	0.0070	0.0037	0.0019	0.0010	0.0005	0.0002	0.0001	0.0001
6	0.0411	0.0255	0.0152	0.0087	0.0048	0.0026	0.0014	0.0007	0.0004	0.0002
7	0.0646	0.0437	0.0281	0.0174	0.0104	0.0060	0.0034	0.0018	0.0010	0.0005
8	0.0888	0.0655	0.0457	0.0304	0.0194	0.0120	0.0072	0.0042	0.0024	0.0013
9	0.1085	0.0874	0.0661	0.0473	0.0324	0.0213	0.0135	0.0083	0.0050	0.0029
10	0.1194	0.1048	0.0859	0.0663	0.0486	0.0341	0.0230	0.0150	0.0095	0.0058
11	0.1194	0.1144	0.1015	0.0844	0.0663	0.0496	0.0355	0.0245	0.0164	0.0106
12	0.1094	0.1144	0.1099	0.0984	0.0829	0.0661	0.0504	0.0368	0.0259	0.0176
13	0.0926	0.1056	0.1099	0.1060	0.0956	0.0814	0.0658	0.0509	0.0378	0.0271
14	0.0728	0.0905	0.1021	0.1060	0.1024	0.0930	0.0800	0.0655	0.0514	0.0387
15	0.0534	0.0724	0.0885	0.0989	0.1024	0.0992	0.0906	0.0786	0.0650	0.0516
16	0.0367	0.0543	0.0719	0.0866	0.0960	0.0992	0.0963	0.0884	0.0772	0.0646
17	0.0237	0.0383	0.0550	0.0713	0.0847	0.0934	0.0963	0.0936	0.0863	0.0760
18	0.0145	0.0256	0.0397	0.0554	0.0706	0.0830	0.0909	0.0936	0.0911	0.0844
19	0.0084	0.0161	0.0272	0.0409	0.0557	0.0699	0.0814	0.0887	0.0911	0.0888
20	0.0046	0.0097	0.0177	0.0286	0.0418	0.0559	0.0692	0.0798	0.0866	0.0888
21	0.0024	0.0055	0.0109	0.0191	0.0299	0.0426	0.0560	0.0684	0.0783	0.0846
22	0.0012	0.0030	0.0065	0.0121	0.0204	0.0310	0.0433	0.0560	0.0676	0.0769
23	0.0006	0.0016	0.0037	0.0074	0.0133	0.0216	0.0320	0.0438	0.0559	0.0669
24	0.0003	0.0008	0.0020	0.0043	0.0083	0.0144	0.0226	0.0328	0.0442	0.0557
25	0.0001	0.0004	0.0010	0.0024	0.0050	0.0092	0.0154	0.0237	0.0336	0.0446
26	0.0000	0.0002	0.0005	0.0013	0.0029	0.0057	0.0101	0.0164	0.0246	0.0343
27	0.0000	0.0001	0.0002	0.0007	0.0016	0.0034	0.0063	0.0109	0.0173	0.0254
28	0.0000	0.0000	0.0001	0.0003	0.0009	0.0019	0.0038	0.0070	0.0117	0.0181
29	0.0000	0.0000	0.0001	0.0002	0.0004	0.0011	0.0023	0.0044	0.0077	0.0125
30	0.0000	0.0000	0.0000	0.0001	0.0002	0.0006	0.0013	0.0026	0.0049	0.0083
31	0.0000	0.0000	0.0000	0.0000	0.0001	0.0003	0.0007	0.0015	0.0030	0.0054
32	0.0000	0.0000	0.0000	0.0000	0.0001	0.0001	0.0004	0.0009	0.0018	0.0034
33	0.0000	0.0000	0.0000	0.0000	0.0000	0.0001	0.0002	0.0005	0.0010	0.0020
34	0.0000	0.0000	0.0000	0.0000	0.0000	0.0000	0.0001	0.0002	0.0006	0.0012
35	0.0000	0.0000	0.0000	0.0000	0.0000	0.0000	0.0000	0.0001	0.0003	0.0007
36	0.0000	0.0000	0.0000	0.0000	0.0000	0.0000	0.0000	0.0001	0.0002	0.0004
37	0.0000	0.0000	0.0000	0.0000	0.0000	0.0000	0.0000	0.0000	0.0001	0.0002
38	0.0000	0.0000	0.0000	0.0000	0.0000	0.0000	0.0000	0.0000	0.0000	0.0001
39	0.0000	0.0000	0.0000	0.0000	0.0000	0.0000	0.0000	0.0000	0.0000	0.0001

Appendix D   Areas for the Standard Normal Distribution

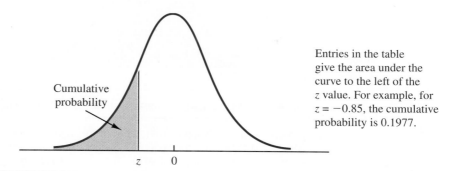

Cumulative probability

Entries in the table give the area under the curve to the left of the z value. For example, for $z = -0.85$, the cumulative probability is 0.1977.

z	0.00	0.01	0.02	0.03	0.04	0.05	0.06	0.07	0.08	0.09
−3.0	0.0013	0.0013	0.0013	0.0012	0.0012	0.0011	0.0011	0.0011	0.0010	0.0010
−2.9	0.0019	0.0018	0.0018	0.0017	0.0016	0.0016	0.0015	0.0015	0.0014	0.0014
−2.8	0.0026	0.0025	0.0024	0.0023	0.0023	0.0022	0.0021	0.0021	0.0020	0.0019
−2.7	0.0035	0.0034	0.0033	0.0032	0.0031	0.0030	0.0029	0.0028	0.0027	0.0026
−2.6	0.0047	0.0045	0.0044	0.0043	0.0041	0.0040	0.0039	0.0038	0.0037	0.0036
−2.5	0.0062	0.0060	0.0059	0.0057	0.0055	0.0054	0.0052	0.0051	0.0049	0.0048
−2.4	0.0082	0.0080	0.0078	0.0075	0.0073	0.0071	0.0069	0.0068	0.0066	0.0064
−2.3	0.0107	0.0104	0.0102	0.0099	0.0096	0.0094	0.0091	0.0089	0.0087	0.0084
−2.2	0.0139	0.0136	0.0132	0.0129	0.0125	0.0122	0.0119	0.0116	0.0113	0.0110
−2.1	0.0179	0.0174	0.0170	0.0166	0.0162	0.0158	0.0154	0.0150	0.0146	0.0143
−2.0	0.0228	0.0222	0.0217	0.0212	0.0207	0.0202	0.0197	0.0192	0.0188	0.0183
−1.9	0.0287	0.0281	0.0274	0.0268	0.0262	0.0256	0.0250	0.0244	0.0239	0.0233
−1.8	0.0359	0.0351	0.0344	0.0336	0.0329	0.0322	0.0314	0.0307	0.0301	0.0294
−1.7	0.0446	0.0436	0.0427	0.0418	0.0409	0.0401	0.0392	0.0384	0.0375	0.0367
−1.6	0.0548	0.0537	0.0526	0.0516	0.0505	0.0495	0.0485	0.0475	0.0465	0.0455
−1.5	0.0668	0.0655	0.0643	0.0630	0.0618	0.0606	0.0594	0.0582	0.0571	0.0559
−1.4	0.0808	0.0793	0.0778	0.0764	0.0749	0.0735	0.0721	0.0708	0.0694	0.0681
−1.3	0.0968	0.0951	0.0934	0.0918	0.0901	0.0885	0.0869	0.0853	0.0838	0.0823
−1.2	0.1151	0.1131	0.1112	0.1093	0.1075	0.1056	0.1038	0.1020	0.1003	0.0985
−1.1	0.1357	0.1335	0.1314	0.1292	0.1271	0.1251	0.1230	0.1210	0.1190	0.1170
−1.0	0.1587	0.1562	0.1539	0.1515	0.1492	0.1469	0.1446	0.1423	0.1401	0.1379
−0.9	0.1841	0.1814	0.1788	0.1762	0.1736	0.1711	0.1685	0.1660	0.1635	0.1611
−0.8	0.2119	0.2090	0.2061	0.2033	0.2005	0.1977	0.1949	0.1922	0.1894	0.1867
−0.7	0.2420	0.2389	0.2358	0.2327	0.2296	0.2266	0.2236	0.2206	0.2177	0.2148
−0.6	0.2743	0.2709	0.2676	0.2643	0.2611	0.2578	0.2546	0.2514	0.2483	0.2451
−0.5	0.3085	0.3050	0.3015	0.2981	0.2946	0.2912	0.2877	0.2843	0.2810	0.2776
−0.4	0.3446	0.3409	0.3372	0.3336	0.3300	0.3264	0.3228	0.3192	0.3156	0.3121
−0.3	0.3821	0.3783	0.3745	0.3707	0.3669	0.3632	0.3594	0.3557	0.3520	0.3483
−0.2	0.4207	0.4168	0.4129	0.4090	0.4052	0.4013	0.3974	0.3936	0.3897	0.3859
−0.1	0.4602	0.4562	0.4522	0.4483	0.4443	0.4404	0.4364	0.4325	0.4286	0.4247
−0.0	0.5000	0.4960	0.4920	0.4880	0.4840	0.4801	0.4761	0.4721	0.4681	0.4641

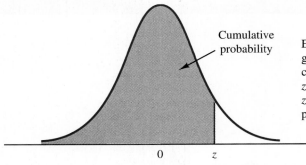

Cumulative probability

Entries in the table give the area under the curve to the left of the z value. For example, for $z = 1.25$, the cumulative probability is 0.8944.

z	0.00	0.01	0.02	0.03	0.04	0.05	0.06	0.07	0.08	0.09
0.0	0.5000	0.5040	0.5080	0.5120	0.5160	0.5199	0.5239	0.5279	0.5319	0.5359
0.1	0.5398	0.5438	0.5478	0.5517	0.5557	0.5596	0.5636	0.5675	0.5714	0.5753
0.2	0.5793	0.5832	0.5871	0.5910	0.5948	0.5987	0.6026	0.6064	0.6103	0.6141
0.3	0.6179	0.6217	0.6255	0.6293	0.6331	0.6368	0.6406	0.6443	0.6480	0.6517
0.4	0.6554	0.6591	0.6628	0.6664	0.6700	0.6736	0.6772	0.6808	0.6844	0.6879
0.5	0.6915	0.6950	0.6985	0.7019	0.7054	0.7088	0.7123	0.7157	0.7190	0.7224
0.6	0.7257	0.7291	0.7324	0.7357	0.7389	0.7422	0.7454	0.7486	0.7517	0.7549
0.7	0.7580	0.7611	0.7642	0.7673	0.7704	0.7734	0.7764	0.7794	0.7823	0.7852
0.8	0.7881	0.7910	0.7939	0.7967	0.7995	0.8023	0.8051	0.8078	0.8106	0.8133
0.9	0.8159	0.8186	0.8212	0.8238	0.8264	0.8289	0.8315	0.8340	0.8365	0.8389
1.0	0.8413	0.8438	0.8461	0.8485	0.8508	0.8531	0.8554	0.8577	0.8599	0.8621
1.1	0.8643	0.8665	0.8686	0.8708	0.8729	0.8749	0.8770	0.8790	0.8810	0.8830
1.2	0.8849	0.8869	0.8888	0.8907	0.8925	0.8944	0.8962	0.8980	0.8997	0.9015
1.3	0.9032	0.9049	0.9066	0.9082	0.9099	0.9115	0.9131	0.9147	0.9162	0.9177
1.4	0.9192	0.9207	0.9222	0.9236	0.9251	0.9265	0.9279	0.9292	0.9306	0.9319
1.5	0.9332	0.9345	0.9357	0.9370	0.9382	0.9394	0.9406	0.9418	0.9429	0.9441
1.6	0.9452	0.9463	0.9474	0.9484	0.9495	0.9505	0.9515	0.9525	0.9535	0.9545
1.7	0.9554	0.9564	0.9573	0.9582	0.9591	0.9599	0.9608	0.9616	0.9625	0.9633
1.8	0.9641	0.9649	0.9656	0.9664	0.9671	0.9678	0.9686	0.9693	0.9699	0.9706
1.9	0.9713	0.9719	0.9726	0.9732	0.9738	0.9744	0.9750	0.9756	0.9761	0.9767
2.0	0.9772	0.9778	0.9783	0.9788	0.9793	0.9798	0.9803	0.9808	0.9812	0.9817
2.1	0.9821	0.9826	0.9830	0.9834	0.9838	0.9842	0.9846	0.9850	0.9854	0.9857
2.2	0.9861	0.9864	0.9868	0.9871	0.9875	0.9878	0.9881	0.9884	0.9887	0.9890
2.3	0.9893	0.9896	0.9898	0.9901	0.9904	0.9906	0.9909	0.9911	0.9913	0.9916
2.4	0.9918	0.9920	0.9922	0.9925	0.9927	0.9929	0.9931	0.9932	0.9934	0.9936
2.5	0.9938	0.9940	0.9941	0.9943	0.9945	0.9946	0.9948	0.9949	0.9951	0.9952
2.6	0.9953	0.9955	0.9956	0.9957	0.9959	0.9960	0.9961	0.9962	0.9963	0.9964
2.7	0.9965	0.9966	0.9967	0.9968	0.9969	0.9970	0.9971	0.9972	0.9973	0.9974
2.8	0.9974	0.9975	0.9976	0.9977	0.9977	0.9978	0.9979	0.9979	0.9980	0.9981
2.9	0.9981	0.9982	0.9982	0.9983	0.9984	0.9984	0.9985	0.9985	0.9986	0.9986
3.0	0.9987	0.9987	0.9987	0.9988	0.9988	0.9989	0.9989	0.9989	0.9990	0.9990

Appendix E   Values of $e^{-\lambda}$

λ	$e^{-\lambda}$	λ	$e^{-\lambda}$	λ	$e^{-\lambda}$
0.05	0.9512	2.05	0.1287	4.05	0.0174
0.10	0.9048	2.10	0.1225	4.10	0.0166
0.15	0.8607	2.15	0.1165	4.15	0.0158
0.20	0.8187	2.20	0.1108	4.20	0.0150
0.25	0.7788	2.25	0.1054	4.25	0.0143
0.30	0.7408	2.30	0.1003	4.30	0.0136
0.35	0.7047	2.35	0.0954	4.35	0.0129
0.40	0.6703	2.40	0.0907	4.40	0.0123
0.45	0.6376	2.45	0.0863	4.45	0.0117
0.50	0.6065	2.50	0.0821	4.50	0.0111
0.55	0.5769	2.55	0.0781	4.55	0.0106
0.60	0.5488	2.60	0.0743	4.60	0.0101
0.65	0.5220	2.65	0.0707	4.65	0.0096
0.70	0.4966	2.70	0.0672	4.70	0.0091
0.75	0.4724	2.75	0.0639	4.75	0.0087
0.80	0.4493	2.80	0.0608	4.80	0.0082
0.85	0.4274	2.85	0.0578	4.85	0.0078
0.90	0.4066	2.90	0.0550	4.90	0.0074
0.95	0.3867	2.95	0.0523	4.95	0.0071
1.00	0.3679	3.00	0.0498	5.00	0.0067
1.05	0.3499	3.05	0.0474	5.05	0.0064
1.10	0.3329	3.10	0.0450	5.10	0.0061
1.15	0.3166	3.15	0.0429	5.15	0.0058
1.20	0.3012	3.20	0.0408	5.20	0.0055
1.25	0.2865	3.25	0.0388	5.25	0.0052
1.30	0.2725	3.30	0.0369	5.30	0.0050
1.35	0.2592	3.35	0.0351	5.35	0.0047
1.40	0.2466	3.40	0.0334	5.40	0.0045
1.45	0.2346	3.45	0.0317	5.45	0.0043
1.50	0.2231	3.50	0.0302	5.50	0.0041
1.55	0.2122	3.55	0.0287	5.55	0.0039
1.60	0.2019	3.60	0.0273	5.60	0.0037
1.65	0.1920	3.65	0.0260	5.65	0.0035
1.70	0.1827	3.70	0.0247	5.70	0.0033
1.75	0.1738	3.75	0.0235	5.75	0.0032
1.80	0.1653	3.80	0.0224	5.80	0.0030
1.85	0.1572	3.85	0.0213	5.85	0.0029
1.90	0.1496	3.90	0.0202	5.90	0.0027
1.95	0.1423	3.95	0.0193	5.95	0.0026
2.00	0.1353	4.00	0.0183	6.00	0.0025
				7.00	0.0009
				8.00	0.000335
				9.00	0.000123
				10.00	0.000045

Chapter 1 Introduction

Churchman, C. W., R. L. Ackoff, and E. L. Arnoff. *Introduction to Operations Research.* Wiley, 1957.

Horner, P. "The Sabre Story." *OR/MS Today* (June 2000).

Leon, L., Z. Przasnyski, and K. C. Seal. "Spreadsheets and OR/MS Models: An End-User Perspective." *Interfaces* (March/April 1996).

Powell, S. G. "Innovative Approaches to Management Science." *OR/MS Today* (October 1996).

Savage, S. "Weighing the Pros and Cons of Decision Technology and Spreadsheets." *OR/MS Today* (February 1997).

Winston, W. L. "The Teachers' Forum: Management Science with Spreadsheets for MBAs at Indiana University." *Interfaces* (March/April 1996).

Chapters 2 and 3 Probability

Anderson, D. R., D. J. Sweeney, and T. A. Williams. *Statistics for Business and Economics,* 10th ed. South-Western, 2008.

Hogg, R. V., and E. A. Tanis. *Probability and Statistical Inference,* 6th ed. Prentice Hall, 2001.

Ross, S. M. *Introduction to Probability Models,* 7th ed. Academic Press, 1993.

Wackerly, D. D., W. Mendenhall, and R. L. Scheaffer. *Mathematical Statistics with Applications,* 6th ed. Duxbury Press, 2002.

Chapters 4 and 5 Decision Analysis and Game Theory

Clemen, R. T., and T. Reilly. *Making Hard Decisions with Decision Tools.* Duxbury Press, 2001.

Davis, M. D. *Game Theory: A Nontechnical Introduction.* Dover, 1997.

Goodwin, P., and G. Wright. *Decision Analysis for Management Judgment,* 2nd ed. Wiley, 1999.

McMillian, J. *Games, Strategies, and Managers.* Oxford University Press, 1992.

Myerson, R. B. *Game Theory: Analysis of Conflict.* Harvard University Press, 1997.

Osborne, M. J. *An Introduction to Game Theory.* Oxford University Press, 2004.

Pratt, J. W., H. Raiffa, and R. Schlaiter. *Introduction to Statistical Decision Theory.* MIT Press, 1995.

Raiffa, H. *Decision Analysis.* McGraw-Hill, 1997.

Schlaiter, R. *Analysis of Decisions Under Uncertainty.* Krieger, 1978.

Chapter 6 Forecasting

Bowerman, B. L., and R. T. O'Connell. *Forecasting and Time Series: An Applied Approach,* 3rd ed. Duxbury Press, 1993.

Box, G. E. P., G. M. Jenkins, and G. C. Reinsel. *Time Series Analysis: Forecasting and Control,* 3rd ed. Prentice Hall, 1994.

Hanke, J. E., and A. G. Reitsch. *Business Forecasting,* 6th ed. Prentice Hall, 1998.

Makridakis, S. G., S. C. Wheelwright, and R. J. Hyndman. *Forecasting: Methods and Applications,* 3rd ed. Wiley, 1997.

Wilson, J. H., and B. Keating. *Business Forecasting,* 3rd ed. Irwin, 1998.

Chapters 7 to 11 Linear Programming, Distribution and Network Models, Integer Programming Problems

Ahuja, R. K., T. L. Magnanti, and J. B. Orlin. *Network Flows, Theory, Algorithms, and Applications.* Prentice-Hall 1993.

Bazarra, M. S., J. J. Jarvis, and H. D. Sherali. *Linear Programming and Network Flows,* 2nd ed. Wiley, 1990.

Dantzig, G. B. *Linear Programming and Extensions.* Princeton University Press, 1963.

Greenberg, H. J. "How to Analyze the Results of Linear Programs—Part 1: Preliminaries." *Interfaces* 23, no. 4 (July/August 1993): 56–67.

Greenberg, H. J. "How to Analyze the Results of Linear Programs—Part 2: Price Interpretation." *Interfaces* 23, no. 5 (September/October 1993): 97–114.

Greenberg, H. J. "How to Analyze the Results of Linear Programs—Part 3: Infeasibility Diagnosis." *Interfaces* 23, no. 6 (November/December 1993): 120–139.

Lillien, G., and A. Rangaswamy. *Marketing Engineering: Computer-Assisted Marketing Analysis and Planning.* Addison-Wesley, 1998.

Nemhauser, G. L., and L. A. Wolsey. *Integer and Combinatorial Optimization.* Wiley, 1988.

Schrage, L. *Optimization Modeling with LINGO,* 4th ed. LINDO Systems Inc., 2000.

Winston, W. L., and S. C. Albright. *Practical Management Science,* 2nd ed. Duxbury Press, 2001.

Chapter 12 Advanced Optimization Applications

Bazarra, M. S., H. D. Sherali, and C. M. Shetty. *Nonlinear Programming Theory and Applications*. Wiley, 1993.

Benninga, S. *Financial Modeling*. The MIT Press, 2000.

Luenberger, D. *Linear and Nonlinear Programming*, 2nd ed. Addison-Wesley Publishing Company, 1984.

Rardin, R. L. *Optimization in Operations Research*. Prentice-Hall, 1998.

Chapter 13 Project Scheduling: PERT/CPM

Moder, J. J., C. R. Phillips, and E. W. Davis. *Project Management with CPM, PERT and Precedence Diagramming*, 3rd ed. Blitz, 1995.

Wiest, J., and F. Levy. *Management Guide to PERT-CPM*, 2nd ed. Prentice Hall, 1977.

Chapter 14 Inventory Models

Fogarty, D. W., J. H. Blackstone, and T. R. Hoffman. *Production and Inventory Management,* 2nd ed. South-Western, 1990.

Hillier, F., and G. J. Lieberman. *Introduction to Operations Research,* 7th ed. McGraw-Hill, 2000.

Narasimhan, S. L., D. W. McLeavey, and P. B. Lington. *Production Planning and Inventory Control,* 2nd ed. Prentice Hall, 1995.

Orlicky, J., and G. W. Plossi. *Orlicky's Material Requirements Planning*. McGraw-Hill, 1994.

Vollmann, T. E., W. L. Berry, and D. C. Whybark. *Manufacturing Planning and Control Systems,* 4th ed. McGraw-Hill, 1997.

Zipkin, P. H. *Foundations of Inventory Management*. McGraw-Hill/Irwin, 2000.

Chapter 15 Waiting Line Models

Bunday, B. D. *An Introduction to Queueing Theory*. Wiley, 1996.

Gross, D., and C. M. Harris. *Fundamentals of Queueing Theory,* 3rd ed. Wiley, 1997.

Hall, R. W. *Queueing Methods: For Service and Manufacturing*. Prentice Hall, 1991.

Hillier, F., and G. J. Lieberman. *Introduction to Operations Research,* 7th ed. McGraw-Hill, 2000.

Kao, E. P. C. *An Introduction to Stochastic Processes*. Duxbury Press, 1996.

Chapter 16 Simulation

Banks, J., J. S. Carson, and B. L. Nelson. *Discrete-Event System Simulation,* 2nd ed. Prentice Hall, 1995.

Fishwick, P. A. *Simulation Model Design and Execution: Building Digital Worlds*. Prentice Hall, 1995.

Harrell, C. R., and K. Tumau. *Simulation Made Easy: A Manager's Guide*. Institute of Industrial Engineers, 1996.

Kelton, W. D., R. P. Sadowski, and D. T. Sturrock. *Simulation with Arena,* 4th ed. McGraw-Hill, 2007.

Law, A. M., and W. D. Kelton. *Simulation Modeling and Analysis,* 3rd ed. McGraw-Hill, 1999.

Pidd, M. *Computer Simulation in Management Science,* 4th ed. Wiley, 1998.

Savage, S. *The Flaw of Averages: Why We Underestimate Risk in the Face of Uncertainty*. Wiley, 2012.

Thesen, A., and L. E. Travis. *Simulation for Decision Making*. Wadsworth, 1992.

Chapter 17 Markov Processes

Bharucha-Reid, A. T. *Elements of the Theory of Markov Processes and Their Applications*. Dover, 1997.

Filar, J. A., and K. Vrieze. *Competitive Markov Decision Processes*. Springer-Verlag, 1996.

Norris, J. *Markov Chains*. Cambridge, 1997.

Chapter 1

2. Define the problem; identify the alternatives; determine the criteria; evaluate the alternatives; choose an alternative.

4. A quantitative approach should be considered because the problem is large, complex, important, new, and repetitive.

6. Quicker to formulate, easier to solve, and/or more easily understood

8. a. Max $10x + 5y$
s.t.
$$5x + 2y \le 40$$
$$x \ge 0, y \ge 0$$

b. Controllable inputs: x and y
Uncontrollable inputs: profit (10, 5), labor-hours (5, 2), and labor-hour availability (40)

c. See Figure G1.8c.

d. $x = 0, y = 20$; Profit = \$100 (solution by trial and error)

e. Deterministic

10. a. Total units received $= x + y$

b. Total cost $= 0.20x + 0.25y$

c. $x + y = 5000$

d. $x \le 4000$ Kansas City
$y \le 3000$ Minneapolis

e. Min $0.20x + 0.25y$
s.t.
$$x + \quad y = 5000$$
$$x \qquad \le 4000$$
$$y \le 3000$$
$$x, y \ge 0$$

FIGURE G1.8c

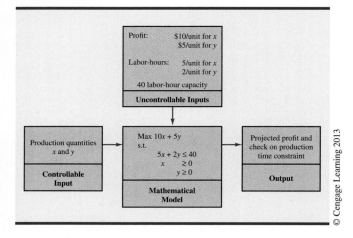

© Cengage Learning 2013

12. a. If x represents the number of pairs of shoes produced, a mathematical model for the total cost of producing x pairs of shoes is $TC = 2000 + 60x$. The two components of total cost in this model are fixed cost (\$2,000) and variable cost ($60x$).

b. If P represents the total profit, the total revenue (TR) is $80x$ and a mathematical model for the total profit realized from an order for x pairs of shoes is $P = TR - TC = 80x - (2000 + 60x) = 20x - 2000$.

c. The breakeven point is the number of shoes produced (x) at the point of no profit ($P = 0$).
Thus the breakeven point is the value of x when $P = 20x - 2000 = 0$. This occurs when $20x = 2000$ or $x = 100$ (i.e., the breakeven point is 100 pairs of shoes).

14. a. If x represents the number of copies of the book that are sold, total revenue (TR) $= 46x$ and total cost (TC) $= 160,000 + 6x$, so Profit $= TR - TC = 46x - (160,000 + 6x) = 40x - 160,000$. The breakeven point is the number of books produced (x) at the point of no profit ($P = 0$). Thus the breakeven point is the value of x when $P = 40x - 160,000 = 0$. This occurs when $40x = 160,00$ or $x = 4000$ (i.e., the breakeven point is 4000 copies of the book).

b. At a demand of 3800 copies, the publisher can expect a profit of $40(3800) - 160,000 = 152,000 - 160,000 = -8000$ (i.e., a loss of \$8,000).

c. Here we know demand ($d = 3800$) and want to determine the price p at which we will breakeven (the point at which profit is 0). The minimum price per copy that the publisher must charge to break even is Profit $= p(3800) - (160,000 + 6(3800)) = 3800p - 182,800$. This occurs where $3800p = 182,800$ or $p = 48.10526316$ or a price of approximately \$48.

d. If the publisher believes demand will remain at 4000 copies if the price per copy is increased to \$50.95, then the publisher could anticipate a profit of $TR - TC = 50.95(4000) - (160,000 + 6(4000)) = 203,800 - 184,000 = 19,800$ or a profit of \$19,800. This is a return of $p/TC = 10.8\%$ on the total cost of \$184,000, and the publisher should proceed if this return is sufficient.

16. a. The annual return per share of Oil Alaska is \$6.00 and the annual return per share of Southwest Petroleum is \$4.00, so the objective function that maximizes the total annual return is Max $6x + 4y$.

b. The price per share of Oil Alaska is $50.00 and the price per share of Southwest Petroleum is $30.00, so (1) the mathematical expression for the constraint that limits total investment funds to $800,000 is $50x + 30y \leq 800000$, (2) the mathematical expression for the constraint that limits investment in Oil Alaska to $500,000 is $50x \leq 500000$, and (3) the mathematical expression for the constraint that limits investment in Southwest Petroleum to $450,000 is $30x \leq 450000$.

Chapter 2

1. a. Record the number of persons waiting at the X-ray department at 9:00 A.M.
b. The experimental outcomes (sample points) are the number of people waiting: 0, 1, 2, 3, and 4. (*Note:* Although it is theoretically possible for more than four people to be waiting, we use what has actually been observed to define the experimental outcomes.)
c.

Number Waiting	Probability
0	0.10
1	0.25
2	0.30
3	0.20
4	0.15
Total	1.00

d. The relative frequency method

2. a. Choose a person at random, and have him/her taste the four blends of coffee and state a preference.
b. Assign a probability of $1/4$ to each blend, using the classical method of equally likely outcomes.
c.

Blend	Probability
1	0.20
2	0.30
3	0.35
4	0.15
Total	1.00

The relative frequency method was used.

4. a. $31,675,935/132,275,830 = 0.239$.
b. $122,742,594/132,275,830 = 0.928$.
c. $(12,893,802 + 2,288,550 + 265,612)/132,275,830 = 15,447,964/132,275,830 = 0.117$.
d. $0.01(26,463,973) = 264,639.73$ (or 264,640).
e. $0.0173(\$13,045,221,000.00) = \$225,699,891.81$.

6. a. $P(A) = P(150 - 199) + P(200 \text{ and over})$
$$= \frac{26}{100} + \frac{5}{100}$$
$$= 0.31$$
b. $P(B) = P(\text{less than } 50) + P(50 - 99) + P(100 - 149)$
$$= 0.13 + 0.22 + 0.34$$
$$= 0.69$$

7. a. $P(A) = 0.40, P(B) = 0.40, P(C) = 0.60$
b. $P(A < B) = P(E_1, E_2, E_3, E_4) = 0.80$.
Yes, $P(A < B) = P(A) + P(B)$
c. $A^c = \{E_3, E_4, E_5\}; C^c = \{E_1, E_4\}; P(A^c) = 0.60; P(C^c) = 0.40$
d. $A < B^c = \{E_1, E_2, E_5\}; P(A < B^c) = 0.60$
e. $P(B < C) = P(E_2, E_3, E_4, E_5) = 0.80$

8. a. Let $P(A)$ be the probability a hospital had a daily inpatient volume of at least 200 and $P(B)$ be the probability a hospital had a nurse to patient ratio of at least 3.0. From the list of 30 hospitals, 16 had a daily inpatient volume of at least 200, so by the relative frequency approach the probability one of these hospitals had a daily inpatient volume of at least 200 is $P(A) = 16/30 = 0.533$, Similarly, since 10 (one-third) of the hospitals had a nurse-to-patient ratio of at least 3.0, the probability of a hospital having a nurse-to-patient ratio of at least 3.0 is $P(B) = 10/30 = 0.333$. Finally, since seven of the hospitals had both a daily inpatient volume of at least 200 and a nurse-to-patient ratio of at least 3.0, the probability of a hospital having both a daily inpatient volume of at least 200 and a nurse-to-patient ratio of at least 3.0 is $P(A \cap B) = 7/30 = 0.233$.
b. The probability that a hospital had a daily inpatient volume of at least 200 or a nurse-to-patient ratio of at least 3.0 or both is $P(A \cup B) = P(A) + P(B) - P(A \cap B) = 16/30 + 10/30 - 7/30 = (16 + 10 - 7)/30 = 19/30 = 0.633$.
c. The probability that a hospital had neither a daily inpatient volume of at least 200 nor a nurse-to-patient ratio of at least 3.0 is $1 - P(A \cup B) = 1 - 19/30 = 11/30 = 0.367$.

10. $P(\text{Defective and Minor}) = 4/25$
$P(\text{Defective and Major}) = 2/25$
$P(\text{Defective}) = (4/25) + (2/25) = 6/25$
$P(\text{Major Defect I Defective}) = P(\text{Defective and Major})/P(\text{Defective}) = (2/25)/(6/25) = 2/6 = 1/3$.

12. a. $P(A \mid B) = \dfrac{P(A \cap B)}{P(B)} = \dfrac{0.40}{0.60} = 0.6667$
b. $P(B \mid A) = \dfrac{P(A \cap B)}{P(A)} = \dfrac{0.40}{0.50} = 0.80$
c. No, because $P(A \mid B) \neq P(A)$

13. a.

	Quality	Cost/ Convenience	Other	Total
		Reason for Applying		
Full Time	0.218	0.204	0.039	0.461
Part Time	0.208	0.307	0.024	0.539
Total	0.426	0.511	0.063	1.000

b. A student will most likely cite cost or convenience as the first reason: probability = 0.511; school quality is the first reason cited by the second largest number of students: probability = 0.426.

c. P(Quality I Full Time) = 0.218/0.461 = 0.473

d. P(Quality I Part Time) = 0.208/0.539 = 0.386

e. $P(B)$ = 0.426 and $P(B \mid A)$ = 0.473

Because $P(B) \neq P(B \mid A)$, the events are dependent.

14.

	$0–$499	$500–$999	≥$1000	
<2 yrs	120	240	90	450
≥2 yrs	75	275	200	550
	195	515	290	1000
<2 yrs	0.12	0.24	0.09	0.45
≥2 yrs	0.075	0.275	0.2	0.55
	0.195	0.515	0.29	1.00

a. P(< 2 yrs) = 0.45

b. P(≥ $1000) = 0.29

c. P(2 accounts have ≥ $1000) = (0.29)(0.29) = 0.0841

d. P($500 − $999 I ≥ 2 yrs) = P($500 − $999 and ≥ 2 yrs)/$P$(≥ 2yrs) = 0.275/0.55 = 0.5

e. P(< 2 yrs and ≥ $1000) = 0.09

f. P(≥ 2 yrs I $500 − $999) = 0.275/0.515 = 0.5340

16. a. 0.19
b. 0.71
c. 0.29

18. a. 0.25, 0.40, 0.10
b. 0.25
c. Independent; program does not help

20. a. $P(B \cap A_1) = P(A_1)P(B \mid A_1)$ = (0.20)(0.50) = 0.10
$P(B \cap A_2) = P(A_2)P(B \mid A_2)$ = (0.50)(0.40) = 0.20
$P(B \cap A_3) = P(A_3)P(B \mid A_3)$ = (0.30)(0.30) = 0.09

b. $P(A_2 \mid B) = \dfrac{0.20}{0.10 + 0.20 + 0.09} = 0.51$

c.

Events	$P(A_i)$	$P(B \mid A_i)$	$P(A_i \cap B)$	$P(A_i \mid B)$
A_1	0.20	0.50	0.10	0.26
A_2	0.50	0.40	0.20	0.51
A_3	0.30	0.30	0.09	0.23
	1.00		0.39	1.00

22. a. 0.40
b. 0.67

24. Let S = speeding is reported
S^C = speeding is not reported
F = Accident results in fatality for vehicle occupant
We have $P(S)$ = 0.129, so $P(S^C)$ = 0.871. Also $P(F \mid S)$ = 0.196 and $P(F \mid S^C)$ = 0.05. Using the tabular form of Bayes' theorem provides:

Events	Prior Proba- bilities	Conditional Proba- bilities	Joint Proba- bilities	Posterior Proba- bilities
S	0.129	0.196	0.0384	0.939
S^C	0.871	0.050	0.0025	0.061
	1.000		0.0409	1.000

25. a. P(defective part) = 0.0065 (see below)

Events	$P(A_i)$	$P(D \mid A_i)$	$P(A_i \cap D)$	$P(A_i \cap D)$
Supplier A	0.60	0.0025	0.0015	0.23
Supplier B	0.30	0.0100	0.0030	0.46
Supplier C	0.10	0.020	0.0020	0.31
	1.00		$P(D)$ = 0.0065	1.00

b. Supplier B (prob. = 0.46) is the most likely source.

26. a. $P(D_1 \mid S_1)$ = 0.2195, $P(D_2 \mid S_1)$ = 0.7805
b. $P(D_1 \mid S_2)$ = 0.5000, $P(D_2 \mid S_2)$ = 0.5000
c. $P(D_1 \mid S_3)$ = 0.8824, $P(D_2 \mid S_3)$ = 0.1176
d. 0.1582 and 0.8418

28. a. $P(A_1)$ = .095
$P(A_2)$ = .905
$P(W \mid A_1)$ = .60
$P(W \mid A_2)$ = .49
b. $P(A_1 \mid W)$ = .1139
c. $P(A_1 \mid M)$ = .0761
d. $P(W)$ = .50045
$P(M)$ = .49965

30. a.

	Male Applicants	Female Applicants
Accept	70	40
Deny	90	80

After combining these two crosstabulations into a single crosstabulation with Accept and Deny as the row labels and Male and Female as the column labels, we see that the rate of acceptance for males across the university is $70/(70 + 90) = 0.4375$ or approximately 44%, while the rate of acceptance for females across the university is $40/(40 + 80) = 0.33$ or 33%.

b. If we focus solely on the overall data, we would conclude that the university's admission process is biased in favor of male applicant. However, this occurs because most females apply to the College of Business (which has a far lower rate of acceptance that the College of Engineering). When we look at each college's acceptance rate by gender, we see that the acceptance rate of males and females are equal in the College of Engineering (75%) and the acceptance rate of males and females are equal in the College of Business (33%). The data do not support the accusation that the university favors male applicants in its admissions process.

Chapter 3

1. a. Values: 0, 1, 2, . . . , 20 discrete
   b. Values: 0, 1, 2, . . . discrete
   c. Values: 0, 1, 2, . . . , 50 discrete
   d. Values: $0 \leq x \leq 8$ continuous
   e. Values: $x \geq 0$ continuous

2. a. 0.05; probability of a $200,000 profit
   b. 0.70
   c. 0.40

3. a.

x	$f(x)$
1	$3/20 = 0.15$
2	$5/20 = 0.25$
3	$8/20 = 0.40$
4	$4/20 = 0.20$
	Total 1.00

b.

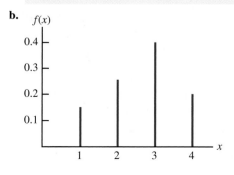

c. $f(x) \geq 0$ for $x = 1, 2, 3, 4$
   $\Sigma f(x) = 1$

4. a. $E(x) = \mu = 6.00$
   b. $Var(x) = \sigma^2 = 4.50$
   c. $\sigma = \sqrt{4.50} = 2.12$

6. a.

x	$f(x)$
1	0.97176
2	0.026675
3	0.00140
4	0.00014
5	0.00002

If we let $x = 5$ represent quintuplets or more, the probability distribution of the number children born per pregnancy in 1996 is provided in the first two columns of the preceding table.

b. $E[x] = 1.030$ and $Var[x] = \sigma^2 = 0.03305$.

c.

y	$f(y)$
1	0.965964
2	0.0333143
3	0.0014868
4	0.0000863
5	0.0000163

If we let $y = 5$ represent quintuplets or more, the probability distribution of the number children born per pregnancy in 2006 is provided in the first two columns of the preceding table.

d. $E[y] = 1.030$ and $Var[y] = \sigma^2 = 0.0390$.

e. The number of children born per pregnancy is greater in 2006 than in 1996, and the variation in the number of children born per pregnancy is also greater in 2006 than in 1996. However, these data provide no information on which we could base a determination of causes of this upward trend.

8. a. Medium 145; large 140; prefer medium
   b. Medium 2725; large 12,400; prefer medium

9. a. $f(1) = \binom{2}{1}(0.4)^1(0.6)^1 = \dfrac{2!}{1!1!}(0.4)(0.6) = 0.48$

   b. $f(0) = \binom{2}{0}(0.4)^0(0.6)^2 = \dfrac{2!}{0!2!}(1)(0.36) = 0.36$

   c. $f(2) = \binom{2}{2}(0.4)^2(0.6)^0 = \dfrac{2!}{2!0!}(0.16)(1) = 0.16$

   d. $P(x \geq 1) = f(1) + f(2) = 0.48 + 0.16 = 0.64$

   e. $E(x) = np = 2(0.4) = 0.8$
   $Var(x) = np(1 - p) = 2(0.4)(0.6) = 0.48$
   $\sigma = \sqrt{0.48} = 0.6928$

10. a. $f(0) = 0.3487$
   b. $f(2) = 0.1937$
   c. 0.9298

d. 0.6513

e. 1

f. $\sigma_2 = 0.9000$, $\sigma = 0.9487$

12. a. Probability of a defective part being produced must be 0.03 for each trial; trials must be independent.

b. Two outcomes result in exactly one defect.

c. $P(\text{no defects}) = (0.97)(0.97) = 0.9409$

$P(1 \text{ defect}) = 2(0.03)(0.97) = 0.0582$

$P(2 \text{ defects}) = (0.03)(0.03) = 0.0009$

14. a. $f(x) = \dfrac{2^x e^{-2}}{x!}$

b. $\mu = 6$ for 3 time periods

c. $f(x) = \dfrac{6^x e^{-6}}{x!}$

d. $f(2) = \dfrac{2^2 e^{-2}}{2!} = \dfrac{4(0.1353)}{2} = 0.2706$

e. $f(6) = \dfrac{6^6 e^{-6}}{6!} = 0.1606$

f. $f(5) = \dfrac{4^5 e^{-4}}{5!} = 0.1563$

16. a. 0.0009

b. 0.9927

c. 0.0302

d. 0.8271

18. a.

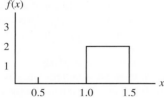

b. $P(x = 1.25) = 0$; the probability of any single point is zero because the area under the curve above any single point is zero.

c. $P(1.0 \le x \le 1.25) = 2(0.25) = 0.50$

d. $P(1.2 < x < 1.5) = 2(0.30) = 0.60$

20. a.

b. 0.50

c. 0.30

d. 0.40

21. a. $P(0 \le z \le 0.83) = 0.7967 - 0.5000 = 0.2967$

b. $P(-1.57 \le z \le 0) = 0.5000 - 0.0582 = 0.4418$

c. $P(z > 0.44) = 1.0000 - 0.6700 = 0.2300$

d. $P(z \ge -0.23) = 1.0000 - 0.4090 = 0.5910$

e. $P(z < 1.20) = 0.8849$

f. $P(z < -0.71) = 0.2389$

22. a. 1.96

b. 1.96

c. 0.61

d. 1.12

e. 0.44

f. 0.44

23. a. Area $= 0.2119$ $z = -0.80$

b. Area outside the interval 0.0970 must be split between the two tails.

Cumulative probability $= 0.5(0.0970) + 0.9030 = 0.9515$ $z = 1.66$

c. Area outside the interval 0.7948 must be split between the two tails.

Cumulative probability $= 0.5(0.7948) + 0.2052 = 0.6026$ $z = 0.26$

d. Area $= 0.9948$ $z = 2.56$

e. Area $= 1.0000 - 0.6915 = 0.3085$ $z = -0.50$

24. a. 0.3830

b. 0.1056

c. 0.0062

d. 0.1603

26. a. 0.7745

b. 36.32 days

c. 19%

28. $\mu = 19.23$

29. a. $P(x \le x_0) = 1 - e^{-x_0/3}$

b. $P(x \le 2) = 1 - e^{-2/3} = 1 - 0.5134 = 0.4866$

c. $P(x \ge 3) = 1 - P(x \le 3) = 1 - (1 - e^{-3/3}) = e^{-1} = 0.3679$

d. $P(x \le 5) = 1 - e^{-5/3} = 1 - 0.1889 = 0.8111$

e. $P(2 \le x \le 5) = P(x \le 5) - P(x \le 2) = 0.8111 - 0.4866 = 0.3245$

30. a. 0.5809

b. 0.2713

c. 0.1478

31. a.

b. $P(x \le 12) = 1 - e^{-12/12} = 0.6321$

c. $P(x \le 6) = 1 - e^{-6/12} = 0.3935$

d. $P(x \ge 30) = 1 - P(x < 30) = 1 - (1 - e^{-30/12}) = 0.0821$

32. a. 50 hours
  b. 0.3935
  c. 0.1353

34. a. 0.5130
  b. 0.1655
  c. 0.3679

Chapter 4

1. a.

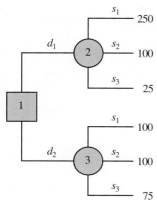

b.

Decision	Maximum Profit	Minimum Profit
d_1	250	25
d_2	100	75

Optimistic approach: Select d_1
Conservative approach: Select d_2
Regret or opportunity loss table:

Decision	s_1	s_2	s_3
d_1	0	0	50
d_2	150	0	0

Maximum regret: select d_1

2. a. Optimistic: d_1
  Conservative: d_3
  Minimax regret: d_3
  b. The choice of which approach to use is up to the decision maker.
  c. Optimistic: d_1
  Conservative: d_2 or d_3
  Minimax regret: d_2

3. a. Decision: Choose the best plant size from the two alternatives—a small plant and a large plant.
  Chance event: Market demand for the new product line with three possible outcomes (states of nature): low, medium, and high

b. Influence Diagram:

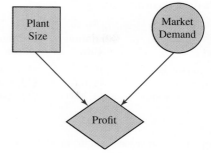

c.

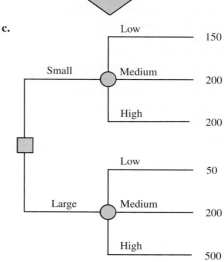

d.

Decision	Maximum Profit	Minimum Profit	Maximum Regret
Small	200	150	300
Large	500	50	100

Optimistic Approach: Large plant
Conservative Approach: Small plant
Minimax Regret: Large plant

4. a. The decision faced by Amy is to select the best lease option from three alternatives (Hepburn Honda, Midtown Motors, and Hopkins Automotive). The chance event is the number of miles Amy will drive.
  b. The payoff table for Amy's problem is:

Dealer	Actual Miles Driven Annually		
	12,000	15,000	18,000
Hepburn Honda	$10,764	$12,114	$13,464
Midtown Motors	$11,160	$11,160	$12,960
Hopkins Automotive	$11,700	$11,700	$11,700

c. The minimum and maximum payoffs for each of Amy's three alternatives are:

Dealer	Minimum Cost	Maximum Cost
Hepburn Honda	$10,764	$13,464
Midtown Motors	$11,160	$12,960
Hopkins Automotive	$11,700	$11,700

Thus:

The optimistic approach results in selection of the Hepburn Automotive lease option.

The conservative approach results in selection of the Hopkins Automotive lease option.

The minimax regret approach results in selection of the Hopkins Automotive lease option (which has the smallest regret of the three alternatives: $936).

d. The expected value approach results in selection of the Midtown Motors lease option (which has the minimum expected value of the three alternatives—$11,340).

e. The risk profile for the decision to lease from Midtown Motors is as follows:

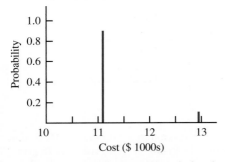

f. The expected value approach results in selection of either the Midtown Motors lease option or the Hopkins Automotive lease option (both of which have the minimum expected value of the three alternatives—$11,700).

6. a. Pharmaceuticals; 3.4%

    b. Financial; 4.6%

7. a. EV(own staff) = 0.2(650) + 0.5(650) + 0.3(600) = 635

    EV(outside vendor) = 0.2(900) + 0.5(600)
                           + 0.3(300) = 570

    EV(combination) = 0.2(800) + 0.5(650) + 0.3(500)
                          = 635

    Optimal decision: Hire an outside vendor with an expected cost of $570,000

    b.

	Cost	Probability
Own staff	300	0.3
Outside vendor	600	0.5
Combination	900	0.2
		1.0

8. a. $EV(d_1) = p(10) + (1 - p)(1) = 9p + 1$

    $EV(d_2) = p(4) + (1 - p)(3) = 1p + 3$

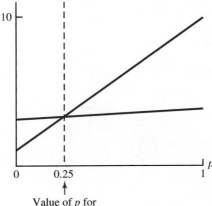

Value of p for which EVs are equal

$9p + 1 = 1p + 3$ and hence $p = 0.25$

d_2 is optimal for $p \geq 0.25$, d_1 is optimal for $p \geq 0.25$

    b. d_2

    c. As long as the payoff for $s_1 \geq 2$, then d_2 is optimal.

10. a.

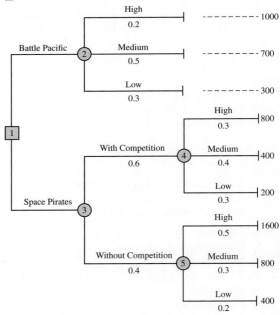

    b. Space Pirates

    c.

$200	0.18
$400	0.32
$800	0.30
$1600	0.20

    d. $P(\text{Competition}) > 0.7273$

12. a. Decision: Whether to lengthen the runway
Chance event: The location decisions of Air Express and DRI
Consequence: Annual revenue
b. $255,000
c. $270,000
d. No
e. Lengthen the runway.

14. a. If s_1, then d_1; if s_2, then d_1 or d_2; if s_3, then d_2
b. EVwPI = 0.65(250) + 0.15(100) + 0.20(75) = 192.5
c. From the solution to Problem 5, we know that EV(d_1) = 182.5 and EV(d_2) = 95; thus, recommended decision is d_1; hence, EVwoPI = 182.5.
d. EVPI = EVwPI − EVwoPI = 192.5 − 182.5 = 10

16. a.

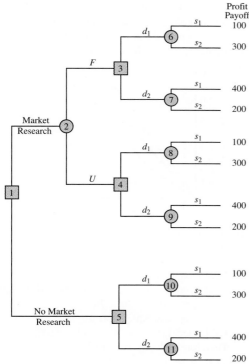

b. EV (node 6) = 0.57(100) + 0.43(300) = 186
EV (node 7) = 0.57(400) + 0.43(200) = 314
EV (node 8) = 0.18(100) + 0.82(300) = 264
EV (node 9) = 0.18(400) + 0.82(200) = 236
EV (node 10) = 0.40(100) + 0.60(300) = 220
EV (node 11) = 0.40(400) + 0.60(200) = 280
EV (node 3) = Max(186,314) = 314d_2
EV (node 4) = Max(264,236) = 264d_1
EV (node 5) = Max(220,280) = 280d_2
EV (node 2) = 0.56(314) + 0.44(264) = 292
EV (node 1) = Max(292,280) = 292
∴ Market Research
  If favorable, decision d_2
  If unfavorable, decision d_1

18. a. Outcome 1: 2650
Outcome 2: 650
b. Bid on the contract; do not do the market research; build the complex
c. Cost would have to decrease by at least $130,000.
d.

Payoff (in millions)	Probability
−$200	0.20
800	0.32
2800	0.48
	1.00

20. a.

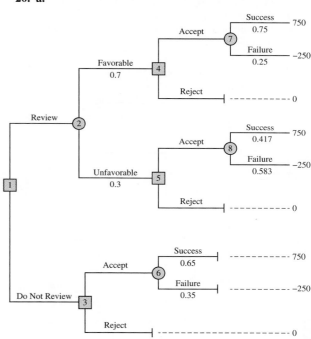

b. Always Accept
c. Do not review; EVSI = $0
d. EVPI = $87,500; a better procedure for assessing market potential for the textbook may be worthwhile

22. a. Order two lots; $60,000
b. If E, order two lots
  If V, order one lot
  EV = $60,500
c. EVPI = $14,000
  EVSI = $500
  Efficiency = 3.6%
  Yes, use consultant.

23.

State of Nature	$P(s_j)$	$P(I\|s_j)$	$P(I \cap s_j)$	$P(s_j\|I)$
s_1	0.2	0.10	0.020	0.1905
s_2	0.5	0.05	0.025	0.2381
s_3	0.3	0.20	0.060	0.5714
	1.0		$P(I) = 0.105$	1.0000

24. a. $P(C) = 0.695$, $P(O) = 0.215$, $P(R) = 0.090$

$P(s_1 \mid C) = 0.98$, $P(s_2 \mid C) = 0.02$

$P(s_1 \mid O) = 0.79$, $P(s_2 \mid O) = 0.21$

$P(s_1 \mid R) = 0.00$, $P(s_2 \mid R) = 1.00$

b.

c. Check the weather. If C, Expressway

If O, Expressway

If R, Queen City

26.6 minutes

Chapter 5

1. a. $EV(d_1) = 0.40(100) + 0.30(25) + 0.30(0) = 47.5$

$EV(d_2) = 0.40(75) + 0.30(50) + 0.30(25) = 52.5$

$EV(d_3) = 0.40(50) + 0.30(50) + 0.30(50) = 50.0$

The optimal solution is d_2.

b. Using utilities

Decision Maker A	Decision Maker B
$EU(d_1) = 4.9$	$EU(d_1) = 4.45$ Best
$EU(d_2) = 5.9$	$EU(d_2) = 3.75$
$EU(d_1) = 6.0$ Best	$EU(d_1) = 3.00$

c. Difference in attitude toward risk; decision maker A tends to avoid risk, whereas decision maker B tends to take a risk for the opportunity of a large payoff.

2. a. d_2; $EV(d_2) = \$5000$

b. p = probability of a $0 cost

$1 - p$ = probability of a $200,000 cost

c. d_1; $EV(d_1) = 9.9$

d. Expected utility approach; it avoids risk of large loss.

4. a. Route B; EV = 58.5

b. p = probability of a 45-minute travel time

$1 - p$ = probability of a 90-minute travel time

c. Route A; EV = 7.6; risk avoider

5. a.

b. A—risk avoider

B—risk taker

C—risk neutral

c. Risk avoider A, at $20 payoff $p = 0.70$

EV(Lottery) = $0.70(100) + 0.30(-100) = \$40$

Therefore, will pay $40 - 20 = \$20$

Risk taker B, at $20 payoff $p = 0.45$

EV(Lottery) = $0.45(100) + 0.55(-100) = -\$10$

Therefore, will pay $20 - (-10) = \$30$

6. A: d_1; B: d_2; C: d_2

8. a.

	Win	Lose
Bet	350	−10
Do not bet	0	0

b. d_2

c. Risk takers

d. Between 0 and 0.26

10. a. EV(Comedy) = $0.30(30\%) + 0.60(25\%)$

$+ 0.10(20\%) = 26.0\%$

and

EV(Reality Show) = $0.30(40\%) + 0.40(20\%)$

$+ 0.30(15\%) = 24.5\%$

Using the expected value approach, the manager should choose the Comedy.

b. p = probability of a 40% percentage of viewing audience

$1 - p$ = probability of a 15% percentage of viewing audience

c. Arbitrarily using a utility of 10 for the best payoff and a utility of 0 for the worst payoff, the utility table is as follows:

Percentage of Viewing Audience	Indifference Value of p	Utility Value
40%	Does not apply	10
30%	0.40	4
25%	0.30	3
20%	0.10	1
15%	Does not apply	0

and so the expected payoffs in terms of utilities are as follows:

$$EV(\text{Comedy}) = 0.30(4) + 0.60(3) + 0.10(1) = 3.1$$

and

$$EV(\text{Reality Show}) = 0.30(10) + 0.40(1) + 0.30(0) = 3.4$$

Using the expected utility approach, the manager should choose the Reality Show.

Although the Comedy has the higher expected payoff in terms of percentage of viewing audience, the Reality Show has the higher expected utility. This suggests the manager is a risk taker.

11.

		Player B			
		b_1	b_2	b_3	Minimum
	a_1	8	5	7	⑤
Player A	a_2	2	4	10	2
	Maximum	8	⑤	10	

The maximum of the row minimums is 5 and the minimum of the column maximums is 5. The game has a pure strategy. Player A should take strategy a_1 and Player B should take strategy b_2. The value of the game is 5.

12. a. The payoff table is as follows:

		Blue Army		
		Attack	Defend	Minimum
	Attack	30	50	30
Red Army	Defend	40	0	0
	Maximum	40	50	

The maximum of the row minimums is 30 and the minimum of the column maximums is 40. Because these values are not equal, a mixed strategy is optimal. Therefore, we must determine the best probability, p, for which the Red Army should choose the Attack strategy. Assume the Red Army chooses Attack with probability p and Defend with probability $1 - p$. If the Blue Army chooses Attack, the expected payoff is $30p + 40(1 - p)$. If the Blue Army chooses Defend, the expected payoff is $50p + 0(1 - p)$.

Setting these equations equal to each other and solving for p, we get $p = 2/3$.

Red Army should choose to Attack with probability $2/3$ and Defend with probability $1/3$.

b. Assume the Blue Army chooses Attack with probability q and Defend with probability $1 - q$. If the Red Army chooses Attack, the expected payoff for the Blue Army is $30q + 50(1 - q)$. If the Red Army chooses Defend, the expected payoff for the Blue Army is $40q + 0(1 - q)$. Setting these equations equal to each other and solving for q, we get $q = 0.833$. Therefore, the Blue Army should choose to Attack with probability 0.833 and Defend with probability $1 - 0.833 = 0.167$.

14. a. Strategy a_3 dominated by a_2

Strategy b_1 dominated by b_2

		Player B	
		b_2	b_3
Player A	a_1	-1	2
	a_2	4	-3

b. Let p = probability of a_1 and $(1 - p)$ = probability of a_2

If b_1, EV $= -1p + 4(1 - p)$

If b_2, EV $= 2p - 3(1 - p)$

$$-1p + 4(1 - p) = 2p - 3(1 - p)$$
$$-1p + 4 - 4p = 2p - 3 + 3p$$
$$10p = 7$$
$$p = 0.70$$

$p(a_1) = p = 0.70$

$p(a_2) = 1 - 0.70 = 0.30$

Let q = probability of b_2 and $(1 - q)$ = probability of b_3

If a_1, EV $= -1q + 2(1 - q)$

If a_2, EV $= 4q - 3(1 - q)$

$$-1q + 2(1 - q) = 4q - 3(1 - q)$$
$$-1q + 2 - 2q = 4q - 3 + 3q$$
$$10q = 5$$
$$q = 0.50$$

$P(b_2) = q = 0.50$

$P(b_3) = 1 - 0.50 = 0.50$

c. $-1p + 4(1 - p) = -(0.70) + 4(0.30) = +0.50$

16. A: $P(a_3) = 0.80$, $P(a_4) = 0.20$

B: $P(b_1) = 0.40$, $P(b_2) = 0.60$

Value $= 2.8$

Chapter 6

1. The following table shows the calculations for parts (a), (b), and (c).

Week	Time Series Value	Forecast	Forecast Error	Absolute Value of Forecast Error	Squared Forecast Error	Percent-age Error	Absolute Value of Percentage Error
1	18						
2	13	18	−5	5	25	−38.46	38.46
3	16	13	3	3	9	18.75	18.75
4	11	16	−5	5	25	−45.45	45.45
5	17	11	6	6	36	35.29	35.29
6	14	17	−3	3	9	−21.43	21.43
			Totals	22	104	−51.30	159.38

   a. MAE = 22/5 = 4.4
   b. MSE = 104/5 = 20.8
   c. MAPE = 159.38/5 = 31.88
   d. The forecast for week 7 is $F_7 = Y_7 = 14$.

2. The following table shows the calculations for parts (a), (b), and (c).

Week	Time Series Value	Forecast	Forecast Error	Absolute Value of Forecast Error	Squared Forecast Error	Percent-age Error	Absolute Value of Percentage Error
1	18						
2	13	18.00	−5.00	5.00	25.00	−38.46	38.46
3	16	15.50	0.50	0.50	0.25	3.13	3.13
4	11	15.67	−4.67	4.67	21.81	−42.45	42.45
5	17	14.50	2.50	2.50	6.25	14.71	14.71
6	14	15.00	−1.00	1.00	1.00	−7.14	7.14
			Totals	13.67	54.31	−70.21	105.86

   a. MAE = 13.67/5 = 2.73
   b. MSE = 54.31/5 = 10.86
   c. MAPE = 105.89/5 = 21.18
   d. The forecast for week 7 is $F_7 = (Y_1 + Y_2 + Y_3 + Y_4 + Y_5 + Y_6)/6 = (18 + 13 + 16 + 11 + 17 + 14)/6 = 14.83$.

3. The following table shows the measures of forecast error for both methods.

	Exercise 1	Exercise 2
MAE	4.40	2.73
MSE	20.80	10.86
MAPE	31.88	21.18

For each measure of forecast accuracy, the average of all the historical data provided more accurate forecasts than simply using the most recent value.

4. a.

Month	Time Series Value	Forecast	Forecast Error	Squared Forecast Error
1	24			
2	13	24	−11	121
3	20	13	7	49
4	12	20	−8	64
5	19	12	7	49
6	23	19	4	16
7	15	23	−8	64
			Total	363

   MSE = 363/6 = 60.5

   The forecast for month 8 is $F_8 = Y_8 = 15$.

   b.

Week	Time Series Value	Forecast	Forecast Error	Squared Forecast Error
1	24			
2	13	24.00	−11.00	121.00
3	20	18.50	1.50	2.25
4	12	19.00	−7.00	49.00
5	19	17.25	1.75	3.06
6	23	17.60	5.40	29.16
7	15	18.50	−3.50	12.25
			Total	216.72

   MSE = 216.72/6 = 36.12

   Forecast for month 8 is $F_8 = (Y_1 + Y_2 + Y_3 + Y_4 + Y_5 + Y_6 + Y_7)/7 = (24 + 13 + 20 + 12 + 19 + 23 + 15)/7 = 18$.

   c. The average of all the previous values is better because MSE is smaller.

5. a.

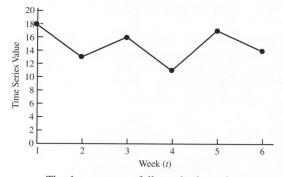

The data appear to follow a horizontal pattern.

b. Three-week moving average

Week	Time Series Value	Forecast	Forecast Error	Squared Forecast Error
1	18			
2	13			
3	16			
4	11	15.67	−4.67	21.78
5	17	13.33	3.67	13.44
6	14	14.67	−0.67	0.44
			Total	35.67

MSE = 35.67/3 = 11.89.

The forecast for week 7 is $F_7 = (Y_4 + Y_5 + Y_6)/3 = (11 + 17 + 14)/3 = 14$.

c. Smoothing constant $\alpha = 0.2$

Week	Time Series Value	Forecast	Forecast Error	Squared Forecast Error
1	18			
2	13	18.00	−5.00	25.00
3	16	17.00	−1.00	1.00
4	11	16.80	−5.80	33.64
5	17	15.64	1.36	1.85
6	14	15.91	−1.91	3.66
			Total	65.15

MSE = 65.15/5 = 13.03

The forecast for week 7 is $F_7 = \alpha Y_6 + (1 - \alpha)F_6 = 0.2(14) + (1 - 0.2)15.91 = 15.53$.

d. The three-week moving average provides a better forecast since it has a smaller MSE.

e. Several values of α will yield an MSE smaller than the MSE associated with $\alpha = 0.2$. The value of α that yields the minimum MSE is $\alpha = 0.367694922$, which yields an MSE of 12.060999.

$$\alpha = 0.367694922$$

Week	Time Series Value	Forecast	Forecast Error	Squared Forecast Error
1	18			
2	13	18	−5.00	25.00
3	16	16.16	−0.16	0.03
4	11	16.10	−5.10	26.03
5	17	14.23	2.77	7.69
6	14	15.25	−1.25	1.55
			Total	60.30

MSE = 60.30/5 = 12.060999

6. a.

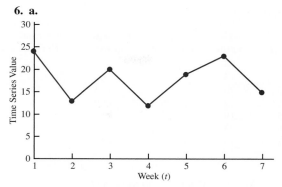

The data appear to follow a horizontal pattern.

b. Three-week moving average

Week	Time Series Value	Forecast	Forecast Error	Squared Forecast Error
1	24			
2	13			
3	20			
4	12	19.00	−7.00	49.00
5	19	15.00	4.00	16.00
6	23	17.00	6.00	36.00
7	15	18.00	−3.00	9.00
			Total	110.00

MSE = 110/4 = 27.5.

The forecast for week 8 is $F_8 = (Y_5 + Y_6 + Y_7)/3 = (19 + 23 + 15)/3 = 19$.

c. Smoothing constant $\alpha = 0.2$

Week	Time Series Value	Forecast	Forecast Error	Squared Forecast Error
1	24			
2	13	24.00	−11.00	121.00
3	20	21.80	−1.80	3.24
4	12	21.44	−9.44	89.11
5	19	19.55	−0.55	0.30
6	23	19.44	3.56	12.66
7	15	20.15	−5.15	26.56
			Total	252.87

MSE = 252.87/6 = 42.15

The forecast for week 8 is $F_8 = \alpha Y_7 + (1 - \alpha)F_7 = 0.2(15) + (1 - 0.2)20.15 = 19.12$.

d. The three-week moving average provides a better forecast since it has a smaller MSE.

e. Several values of α will yield an MSE smaller than the MSE associated with $\alpha = 0.2$. The value of α that yields the minimum MSE is $\alpha = 0.351404848$, which yields an MSE of 39.61428577.

$$\alpha = 0.351404848$$

Week	Time Series Value	Forecast	Forecast Error	Squared Forecast Error
1	24			
2	13	24.00	−11.00	121.00
3	20	20.13	−0.13	0.02
4	12	20.09	−8.09	65.40
5	19	17.25	1.75	3.08
6	23	17.86	5.14	26.40
7	15	19.67	−4.67	21.79
			Total	237.69

$$\text{MSE} = 237.69/6 = 39.61428577$$

8. a.

Week	Time Series Value	Weighted Moving Average Forecast	Forecast Error	Squared Forecast Error
1	17			
2	21			
3	19			
4	23	19.33	3.67	13.47
5	18	21.33	−3.33	11.09
6	16	19.83	−3.83	14.67
7	20	17.83	2.17	4.71
8	18	18.33	−0.33	0.11
9	22	18.33	3.67	13.47
10	20	20.33	−0.33	0.11
11	15	20.33	−5.33	28.41
12	22	17.83	4.17	17.39
			Total	103.43

  b. MSE = 103.43/9 = 11.49
  Prefer the unweighted moving average here; it has a smaller MSE.

  c. You could always find a weighted moving average at least as good as the unweighted moving average. Actually, the unweighted moving average is a special case of the weighted average for which the weights are equal.

9. a. Exponential smoothing forecasts using $\alpha = .1$:

Week	Time Series Value	Forecast
1	17	17.00
2	21	17.00
3	19	17.40
4	23	17.56
5	18	18.10
6	16	18.09
7	20	17.88
8	18	18.10
9	22	18.09
10	20	18.48
11	15	18.63
12	22	18.27

For a smoothing constant of $\alpha = .2$:

Week	Time Series Value	Forecast	Forecast Error	Squared Forecast Error
1	17	17.00		
2	21	17.00	4.00	16.00
3	19	17.40	1.60	2.56
4	23	17.56	5.44	29.59
5	18	18.10	−0.10	0.01
6	16	18.09	−2.09	4.38
7	20	17.88	2.12	4.48
8	18	18.10	−0.10	0.01
9	22	18.09	3.91	15.32
10	20	18.48	1.52	2.32
11	15	18.63	−3.63	13.18
12	22	18.27	3.73	13.94
			Total	101.78

$$\text{MSE} = 101.78/11 = 9.253$$

For a smoothing constant of $\alpha = .2$:

Week	Time Series Value	Forecast	Forecast Error	Squared Forecast Error
1	17	17.00		
2	21	17.00	4.00	16.00
3	19	17.80	1.20	1.44
4	23	18.04	4.96	24.60
5	18	19.03	−1.03	1.07
6	16	18.83	−2.83	7.98
7	20	18.26	1.74	3.03
8	18	18.61	−0.61	0.37
9	22	18.49	3.51	12.34
10	20	19.19	0.81	0.66
11	15	19.35	−4.35	18.94
12	22	18.48	3.52	12.38
			Total	98.80

$$\text{MSE} = 98.80/11 = 8.982$$

Applying the MSE measure of forecast accuracy, a smoothing constant of $\alpha = .2$ produces a smaller MSE and so is preferred.

  b. For a smoothing constant of $\alpha = .1$:

Week	Time Series Value	Forecast	Forecast Error	Absolute Forecast Error
1	17	17.00		
2	21	17.00	4.00	4.00
3	19	17.40	1.60	1.60
4	23	17.56	5.44	5.44
5	18	18.10	−0.10	0.10
6	16	18.09	−2.09	2.09
7	20	17.88	2.12	2.12
8	18	18.10	−0.10	0.10

Week	Time Series Value	Forecast	Forecast Error	Absolute Forecast Error
9	22	18.09	3.91	3.91
10	20	18.48	1.52	1.52
11	15	18.63	−3.63	3.63
12	22	18.27	3.73	3.73
			Total	28.25

MAE = 28.25/11 = 2.568

For a smoothing constant of $\alpha = .2$:

Week	Time Series Value	Forecast	Forecast Error	Absolute Forecast Error
1	17	17.00		
2	21	17.00	4.00	4.00
3	19	17.80	1.20	1.20
4	23	18.04	4.96	4.96
5	18	19.03	−1.03	1.03
6	16	18.83	−2.83	2.83
7	20	18.26	1.74	1.74
8	18	18.61	−0.61	0.61
9	22	18.49	3.51	3.51
10	20	19.19	0.81	0.81
11	15	19.35	−4.35	4.35
12	22	18.48	3.52	3.52
			Total	28.56

MAE = 28.56/11 = 2.596

Applying the MAE measure of forecast accuracy, a smoothing constant of $\alpha = .1$ produces a slightly smaller MAE and so is preferred.

c. For a smoothing constant of $\alpha = .1$:

Week	Time Series Value	Forecast	Forecast Error	100*(Forecast Error/Time Series Value)	Absolute Value of 100*(Forecast Error/Time Series Value)
1	17	17.00			
2	21	17.00	4.00	19.05	19.05
3	19	17.40	1.60	8.42	8.42
4	23	17.56	5.44	23.65	23.65
5	18	18.10	−0.10	−0.58	0.58
6	16	18.09	−2.09	−13.09	13.09
7	20	17.88	2.12	10.58	10.58
8	18	18.10	−0.10	−0.53	0.53
9	22	18.09	3.91	17.79	17.79
10	20	18.48	1.52	7.61	7.61
11	15	18.63	−3.63	−24.20	24.20
12	22	18.27	3.73	16.97	16.97
				Total	142.46

MAPE = 142.46/11 = 12.95

For a smoothing constant of $\alpha = .2$:

Week	Time Series Value	Forecast	Forecast Error	100*(Forecast Error/ Time Series Value)	Absolute Value of 100*(Forecast Error/ Time Series Value)
1	17	17.00			
2	21	17.00	4.00	19.05	19.05
3	19	17.80	1.20	6.32	6.32
4	23	18.04	4.96	21.57	21.57
5	18	19.03	−1.03	−5.73	5.73
6	16	18.83	−2.83	−17.66	17.66
7	20	18.26	1.74	8.70	8.70
8	18	18.61	−0.61	−3.38	3.38
9	22	18.49	3.51	15.97	15.97
10	20	19.19	0.81	4.05	4.05
11	15	19.35	−4.35	−29.01	29.01
12	22	18.48	3.52	15.99	15.99
				Total	147.43

MAPE = 147.43/11 = 13.40

Applying the MAPE measure of forecast accuracy, a smoothing constant of $\alpha = .1$ produces a smaller MAPE and so is preferred.

10. a. $F_{13} = 0.2Y_{12} + 0.16Y_{11} + 0.64(0.2Y_{10} + 0.8F_{10}) = 0.2Y_{12} + 0.16Y_{11} + 0.128Y_{10} + 0.512F_{10}$

$F_{13} = 0.2Y_{12} + 0.16Y_{11} + 0.128Y_{10} + 0.512(0.2Y_9 + 0.8F_9) = 0.2Y_{12} + 0.16Y_{11} + 0.128Y_{10} + 0.1024Y_9 + 0.4096F_9$

$F_{13} = 0.2Y_{12} + 0.16Y_{11} + 0.128Y_{10} + 0.1024Y_9 + 0.4096(0.2Y_8 + 0.8F_8) = 0.2Y_{12} + 0.16Y_{11} + 0.128Y_{10} + 0.1024Y_9 + 0.08192Y_8 + 0.32768F_8$

b. The more recent data receive the greater weight or importance in determining the forecast. The moving averages method weights the last n data values equally in determining the forecast.

12. a.

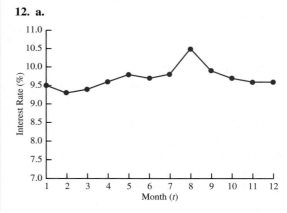

The data appear to follow a horizontal pattern.

b.

Month	Time Series Value	3-Month Moving Average Forecast	(Error)^2	4-Month Moving Average Forecast	(Error)^2
1	9.5				
2	9.3				
3	9.4				
4	9.6	9.40	0.04		
5	9.8	9.43	0.14	9.45	0.12
6	9.7	9.60	0.01	9.53	0.03
7	9.8	9.70	0.01	9.63	0.03
8	10.5	9.77	0.53	9.73	0.59
9	9.9	10.00	0.01	9.95	0.00
10	9.7	10.07	0.14	9.98	0.08
11	9.6	10.03	0.18	9.97	0.14
12	9.6	9.73	0.02	9.92	0.10
			1.08		1.09

$$\text{MSE(3-Month)} = 1.08/9 = 0.12$$
$$\text{MSE(4-Month)} = 1.09/8 = 0.14$$

The MSE for the 3-month moving average is smaller, so use the 3-month moving average.

c. The forecast for month 13 is $F_{13} = (Y_{10} + Y_{11} + Y_{12})/3 = (9.7 + 9.6 + 9.6)/3 = 9.63$.

13. a.

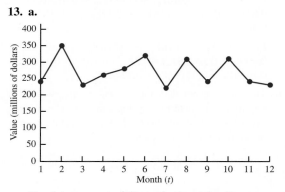

The data appear to follow a horizontal pattern.

b.

$$\alpha = 0.2$$

Month	Time Series Value	3-Month Moving Average Forecast	(Error)^2	Average Forecast	(Error)^2
1	240				
2	350			240.00	12100.00
3	230			262.00	1024.00
4	260	273.33	177.69	255.60	19.36
5	280	280.00	0.00	256.48	553.19
6	320	256.67	4010.69	261.18	3459.79
7	220	286.67	4444.89	272.95	2803.70

Month	Time Series Value	3-Month Moving Average Forecast	(Error)^2	Average Forecast	(Error)^2
8	310	273.33	1344.69	262.36	2269.57
9	240	283.33	1877.49	271.89	1016.97
10	310	256.67	2844.09	265.51	1979.36
11	240	286.67	2178.09	274.41	1184.05
12	230	263.33	1110.89	267.53	1408.50
			17,988.52		27,818.49

$$\text{MSE(3-Month)} = 17,988.52/9 = 1998.72$$
$$\text{MSE}(\alpha = 0.2) = 27,818.49/11 = 2528.95$$

Based on the above MSE values, the 3-month moving average appears better. However, exponential smoothing was penalized by including month 2, which was difficult for any method to forecast. Using only the errors for months 4 to 12, the MSE for exponential smoothing is as follows:

$$\text{MSE}(\alpha = 0.2) = 14,694.49/9 = 1632.72$$

Thus, exponential smoothing was better considering months 4 to 12.

c. Using exponential smoothing,

$$F_{13} = \alpha Y_{12} + (1 - \alpha)F_{12} = 0.20(230) + 0.80(267.53) = 260.$$

14. a.

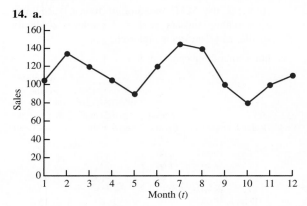

The data appear to follow a horizontal pattern.

b. Smoothing constant $\alpha = 0.3$.

Month t	Time Series Value Y_t	Forecast F_t	Forecast Error $Y_t - F_t$	Squared Error $(Y_t - F_t)^2$
1	105			
2	135	105.00	30.00	900.00
3	120	114.00	6.00	36.00
4	105	115.80	−10.80	116.64

Month t	Time Series Value Y_t	Forecast F_t	Forecast Error $Y_t - F_t$	Squared Error $(Y_t - F_t)^2$
5	90	112.56	−22.56	508.95
6	120	105.79	14.21	201.92
7	145	110.05	34.95	1221.50
8	140	120.54	19.46	378.69
9	100	126.38	−26.38	695.90
10	80	118.46	−38.46	1479.17
11	100	106.92	−6.92	47.89
12	110	104.85	5.15	26.52
			Total	5613.18

$$MSE = 5613.18/11 = 510.29$$

The forecast for month 13 is $F_{13} = \alpha Y_{12} + (1 - \alpha)F_{12} = 0.3(110) + 0.7(104.85) = 106.4$.

c. The value of α that yields the smallest possible MSE is $\alpha = 0.032564518$, which yields an MSE of 459.6929489.

$$\alpha = 0.032564518$$

Month	Time Series Value	Forecast	Forecast Error	Squared Error
1	105			
2	135	105	30.00	900.00
3	120	105.98	14.02	196.65
4	105	106.43	−1.43	2.06
5	90	106.39	−16.39	268.53
6	120	105.85	14.15	200.13
7	145	106.31	38.69	1496.61
8	140	107.57	32.43	1051.46
9	100	108.63	−8.63	74.47
10	80	108.35	−28.35	803.65
11	100	107.43	−7.43	55.14
12	110	107.18	2.82	7.93
			Total	5056.62

$$MSE = 5056.62/11 = 459.6929489$$

16. a.

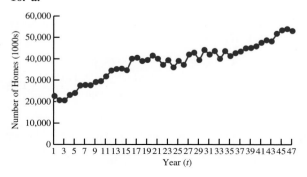

b. This time series plot indicates a possible linear trend in the data, so forecasting methods discussed in this chapter are appropriate to develop forecasts for this time series.

c. The following values are needed to compute the slope and intercept:

$$\Sigma t = 1128 \quad \Sigma t^2 = 35720 \quad \Sigma Y_t = 1808715 \quad \Sigma tY_t = 48566536$$

Computation of slope:

$$b_1 = \frac{\Sigma tY_t - \left(\Sigma t \, \Sigma Y_t\right)/n}{\Sigma t^2 - \left(\Sigma t\right)^2/n} = \frac{48566536 - (1128)(1808715)/47}{35720 - (1128)^2/47}$$

$$= 596.3663$$

Computation of intercept:

$$b_0 = \bar{Y} - b_1\bar{t} = (38483.30/47) - (596.366)(1128/47) = 24170.506$$

Equation for linear trend: $\hat{y}_t = 24170.506 + 596.366t$

The annual increase in households viewing the Super Bowl is approximately 596,366.

17. a.

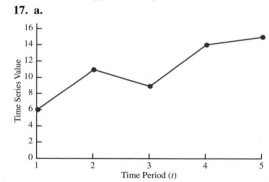

The time series plot shows a linear trend.

b. The regression estimates for the slope and y-intercept are as follows:

$$b_1 = \frac{\sum_{t=1}^{n} tY_t - \sum_{t=1}^{n} t \sum_{t=1}^{n} Y_t / n}{\sum_{t=1}^{n} t^2 - \left(\sum_{t=1}^{n} t\right)^2 / n} = \frac{186 - (15)(55)/5}{55 - (15)^2/5} = 2.10$$

$$b_0 = \bar{Y} - b_1\bar{t} = \frac{55}{5} - 2.10\left(\frac{15}{3}\right) = 4.70$$

which results in the following forecasts, errors, and MSE:

Year	Sales	Forecast	Forecast Error	Squared Forecast Error
1	6.00	6.80	−0.80	0.64
2	11.00	8.90	2.10	4.41
3	9.00	11.00	−2.00	4.00
4	14.00	13.10	0.90	0.81
5	15.00	15.20	−0.20	0.04
6		17.30	Total	9.9

$$MSE = 9.9/5 = 1.982.475$$

c. $F_6 = b_0 + b_1 t = 4.7 + 2.1(6) = 17.3$

18. a.

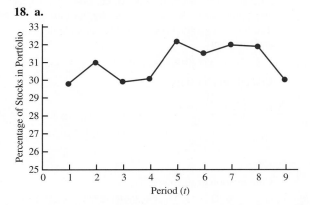

b. The value of the MSE will vary depending on the ultimate value of α that you select. The value of α that yields the smallest possible MSE is $\alpha = 0.467307293$, which yields an MSE of 1.222838367.

$\alpha = 0.467307293$

Period	Stock%	Forecast	Forecast Error	Squared Forecast Error
1st-2007	29.8			
2nd-2007	31.0	29.80	1.20	1.44
3rd-2007	29.9	30.36	−0.46	0.21
4th-2007	30.1	30.15	−0.05	0.00
1st-2008	32.2	30.12	2.08	4.31
2nd-2008	31.5	31.09	0.41	0.16
3rd-2008	32.0	31.28	0.72	0.51
4th-2008	31.9	31.62	0.28	0.08
1st-2009	30.0	31.75	−1.75	3.06
2nd-2009		30.93	Total	9.78

MSE = 1.222838367

c. The forecast for the next period will vary depending on the ultimate value of α that you selected in part (b). Using an exponential smoothing model with $\alpha = 0.467307293$, the forecast is 30.93.

20. a.

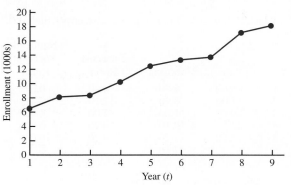

The time series plot shows a linear trend.

b. The regression estimates for the slope and y-intercept are as follows:

$$b_1 = \frac{\sum_{t=1}^{n} tY_t - \sum_{t=1}^{n} t \sum_{t=1}^{n} Y_t / n}{\sum_{t=1}^{n} t^2 - \left(\sum_{t=1}^{n} t\right)^2 / n} = \frac{627.4 - (45)(108)/9}{285 - (45)^2/9} = 4.7167$$

$$b_0 = \bar{Y} - b_1 \bar{t} = \frac{108}{9} - 4.7167\left(\frac{45}{9}\right) = 1.4567$$

which results in the following forecasts, errors, and MSE:

Period	Year	Enroll-ment	Forecast	Forecast Error	Squared Forecast Error
1	2001	6.50	6.17	0.33	0.11
2	2002	8.10	7.63	0.47	0.22
3	2003	8.40	9.09	−0.69	0.47
4	2004	10.20	10.54	−0.34	0.12
5	2005	12.50	12.00	0.50	0.25
6	2006	13.30	13.46	−0.16	0.02
7	2007	13.70	14.91	−1.21	1.47
8	2008	17.20	16.37	0.83	0.69
9	2009	18.10	17.83	0.27	0.07
10	2010		19.28	Total	3.427

MSE = 0.3808

c. $F_{10} = b_0 + b_1 t = 4.7167 + 1.4567(10) = 19.28$

22. a.

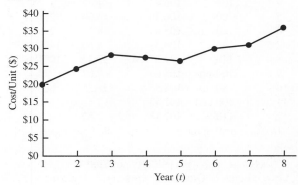

The time series plot shows an upward linear trend.

b. The regression estimates for the slope and y-intercept are as follows:

$$b_1 = \frac{\sum_{t=1}^{n} tY_t - \sum_{t=1}^{n} t \sum_{t=1}^{n} Y_t / n}{\sum_{t=1}^{n} t^2 - \left(\sum_{t=1}^{n} t\right)^2 / n} = \frac{1081.6 - (36)(223.8)/8}{204 - (36)^2/8} = 1.7738$$

$$b_0 = \bar{Y} - b_1 \bar{t} = \frac{223.8}{8} - 1.774\left(\frac{36}{8}\right) = 19.9928$$

which results in the following forecasts, errors, and MSE:

Year	Cost/ Unit($)	Forecast	Forecast Error	Squared Forecast Error
1	20.00	21.77	−1.77	3.12
2	24.50	23.54	0.96	0.92
3	28.20	25.31	2.89	8.33
4	27.50	27.09	0.41	0.17
5	26.60	28.86	−2.26	5.12
6	30.00	30.64	−0.64	0.40
7	31.00	32.41	−1.41	1.99
8	36.00	34.18	1.82	3.30
9		35.96	**Total**	23.34619

MSE = 2.9183

c. The average cost/unit has been increasing by approximately $1.77 per year.

d. $F_9 = b_0 + b_1 t = 19.9928 + 1.7738(9) = 35.96$

24. a.

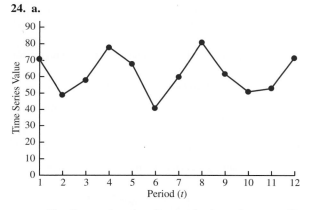

The time series plot shows a horizontal pattern. But there is a seasonal pattern in the data. For instance, in each year the lowest value occurs in quarter 2 and the highest value occurs in quarter 4.

b. After putting the data into the following format:

		Dummy Variables			
Year	Quarter	Quarter 1	Quarter 2	Quarter 3	Y_t
1	1	1	0	0	71
1	2	0	1	0	48
1	3	0	0	1	58
1	4	0	0	0	78
2	1	1	0	0	68
2	2	0	1	0	41
2	3	0	0	1	60
2	4	0	0	0	81
3	1	1	0	0	62
3	2	0	1	0	51
3	3	0	0	1	53
3	4	0	0	0	72

we can use the LINEST function to find the regression model:

Value = 77.00 − 10.00 Qtr1 − 30.33 Qtr2 − 20.00 Qtr3

c. The quarterly forecasts for next year are as follows:

Quarter 1 forecast = 77.0 − 10.0(1) − 30.33(0) − 20.0(0)
= 67.00

Quarter 2 forecast = 77.0 − 10.0(0) − 30.33(1) − 20.0(0)
= 46.67

Quarter 3 forecast = 77.0 − 10.0(0) − 30.33(0) − 20.0(1)
= 57.00

Quarter 4 forecast = 77.0 − 10.0(0) − 30.33(0) − 20.0(0)
= 77.00

26. a.

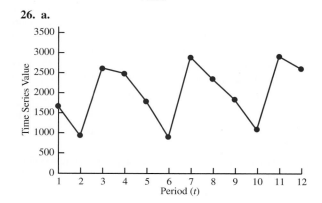

There appears to be a seasonal pattern in the data and perhaps a moderate upward linear trend.

b. After putting the data into the following format:

		Dummy Variables			
Year	Quarter	Quarter 1	Quarter 2	Quarter 3	Y_t
1	1	1	0	0	1690
1	2	0	1	0	940
1	3	0	0	1	2625
1	4	0	0	0	2500
2	1	1	0	0	1800
2	2	0	1	0	900
2	3	0	0	1	2900
2	4	0	0	0	2360
3	1	1	0	0	1850
3	2	0	1	0	1100
3	3	0	0	1	2930
3	4	0	0	0	2615

we can use the LINEST function to find the regression model:

Value = 2491.67 − 711.67 Qtr1 − 1511.67 Qtr2 + 326.67 Qtr3

c. The quarterly forecasts for next year are as follows:

Quarter 1 forecast = 2491.67 − 711.67(1) − 1511.67(0) + 326.67(0) = 1780.00

Quarter 2 forecast = 2491.67 − 711.67(0) − 1511.67(1)
  + 326.67(0) = 980.00

Quarter 3 forecast = 2491.67 − 711.67(0) − 1511.67(0)
  + 326.67(1) = 2818.33

Quarter 4 forecast = 2491.67 − 711.67(0) − 1511.67(0)
  + 326.67(0) = 2491.67

d. After putting the data into the following format:

			Dummy Variables			
Year	Quarter	Quarter 1	Quarter 2	Quarter 3	t	Y_t
1	1	1	0	0	1	1690
1	2	0	1	0	2	940
1	3	0	0	1	3	2625
1	4	0	0	0	4	2500
2	1	1	0	0	5	1800
2	2	0	1	0	6	900
2	3	0	0	1	7	2900
2	4	0	0	0	8	2360
3	1	1	0	0	9	1850
3	2	0	1	0	10	1100
3	3	0	0	1	11	2930
3	4	0	0	0	12	2615

we can use the LINEST function to find the regression model:

Value = 2306.67 − 642.29 Qtr1 − 1465.42 Qtr2
  + 349.79 Qtr3 + 23.13t

The quarterly forecasts for next year are as follows:

Quarter 1 forecast = 2306.67 − 642.29(1) − 1465.42(0)
  + 349.79(0) + 23.13(13) = 1965.00

Quarter 2 forecast = 2306.67 − 642.29(0) − 1465.42(1)
  + 349.79(0) + 23.13(14) = 1165.00

Quarter 3 forecast = 2306.67 − 642.29(0) − 1465.42(0)
  + 349.79(1) + 23.13(15) = 2011.33

Quarter 4 forecast = 2306.67 − 642.29(0) − 1465.42(0)
  + 349.79(0) + 23.13(16) = 2676.67

28. a.

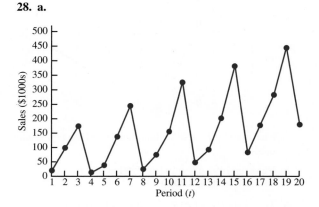

The time series plot shows both a linear trend and seasonal effects.

b. After putting the data into the following format:

			Dummy Variables		
Year	Quarter	Quarter 1	Quarter 2	Quarter 3	Y_t
1	1	1	0	0	20
1	2	0	1	0	100
1	3	0	0	1	175
1	4	0	0	0	13
2	1	1	0	0	37
2	2	0	1	0	136
2	3	0	0	1	245
2	4	0	0	0	26
3	1	1	0	0	75
3	2	0	1	0	155
3	3	0	0	1	326
3	4	0	0	0	48
4	1	1	0	0	92
4	2	0	1	0	202
4	3	0	0	1	384
4	4	0	0	0	82
5	1	1	0	0	176
5	2	0	1	0	282
5	3	0	0	1	445
5	4	0	0	0	181

we can use the LINEST function to find the regression model:

Revenue = 70.0 + 10.0 Qtr1 + 105 Qtr2 + 245 Qtr3

Quarter 1 forecast = 70.0 + 10.0(1) + 105(0) + 245(0) = 80
Quarter 2 forecast = 70.0 + 10.0(0) + 105(1) + 245(0) = 175
Quarter 3 forecast = 70.0 + 10.0(0) + 105(0) + 245(1) = 315
Quarter 4 forecast = 70.0 + 10.0(0) + 105(0) + 245(0) = 70

c. After putting the data into the following format:

			Dummy Variables			
Year	Quarter	Quarter 1	Quarter 2	Quarter 3	t	Y_t
1	1	1	0	0	1	20
1	2	0	1	0	2	100
1	3	0	0	1	3	175
1	4	0	0	0	4	13
2	1	1	0	0	5	37
2	2	0	1	0	6	136
2	3	0	0	1	7	245
2	4	0	0	0	8	26
3	1	1	0	0	9	75
3	2	0	1	0	10	155
3	3	0	0	1	11	326
3	4	0	0	0	12	48
4	1	1	0	0	13	92
4	2	0	1	0	14	202
4	3	0	0	1	15	384
4	4	0	0	0	16	82
5	1	1	0	0	17	176
5	2	0	1	0	18	282
5	3	0	0	1	19	445
5	4	0	0	0	20	181

we can use the LINEST function to find the regression model:

Revenue $= -70.10 + 45.03$ Qtr1 $+ 128.35$ Qtr2
$\qquad + 256.68$ Qtr3 $+ 11.68t$

Quarter 1 forecast $= -70.10 + 45.03(1) + 128.35(0)$
$\qquad\qquad + 256.68(0) + 11.68(21) = 221$

Quarter 2 forecast $= -70.10 + 45.03(0) + 128.35(1)$
$\qquad\qquad + 256.68(0) + 11.68(22) = 315$

Quarter 3 forecast $= -70.10 + 45.03(0) + 128.35(0)$
$\qquad\qquad + 256.68(1) + 11.68(23) = 456$

Quarter 4 forecast $= -70.10 + 45.03(0) + 128.35(0)$
$\qquad\qquad + 256.68(0) + 11.68(24) = 211$

Chapter 7

1. Parts (a), (b), and (e) are acceptable linear programming relationships.

Part (c) is not acceptable because of $-2x_2^2$.

Part (d) is not acceptable because of $3\sqrt{x_1}$.

Part (f) is not acceptable because of $1x_1x_2$.

Parts (c), (d), and (f) could not be found in a linear programming model because they contain nonlinear terms.

2. a.

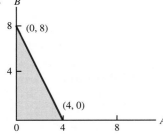

b.

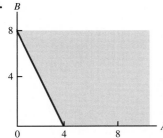

c.

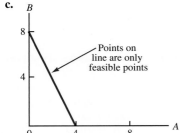

4. a.

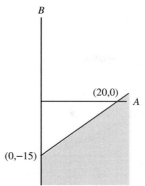

b.

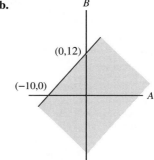

c.

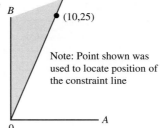

Note: Point shown was used to locate position of the constraint line

6. $7A + 10B = 420$
$\quad 6A + 4B = 420$
$\quad 4A + 7B = 420$

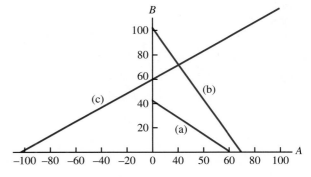

7.

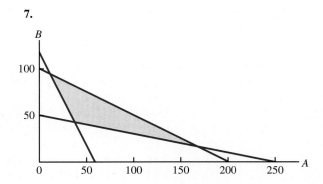

10.

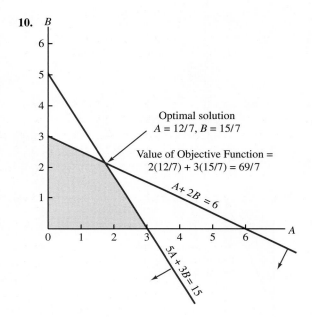

$$
\begin{array}{lrcll}
 & A + 2B & = & 6 & (1) \\
 & 5A + 3B & = & 15 & (2) \\
\text{Equation (1) times 5:} & 5A + 10B & = & 30 & (3) \\
\text{Equation (2) minus equation (3):} & -7B & = & -15 & \\
 & B & = & 15/7 & \\
\text{From equation (1):} & A & = & 6 - 2(15/7) & \\
 & & = & 6 - 30/7 = 12/7 &
\end{array}
$$

12. a. $A = 3, B = 1.5$; Value of optimal solution $= 13.5$

b. $A = 0, B = 3$; Value of optimal solution $= 18$

c. Four: (0, 0), (4, 0), (3, 1.5), and (0.3)

13. a.

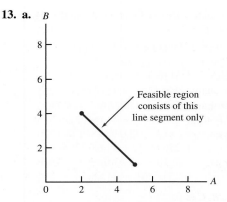

b. The extreme points are (5, 1) and (2, 4).

c.

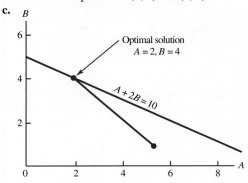

14. a. 540 standard bags, 252 deluxe bags

b. 7668

c. 630, 480, 708, 117

d. 0, 120, 0, 18

16. a. $3S + 9D$

b. (0,540)

c. 90, 150, 348, 0

17. Max $5A + 2B + 0s_1 + 0s_2 + 0s_3$

s.t.

$$
\begin{array}{rcl}
1A - 2B + 1s_1 & = & 420 \\
2A + 3B - \ \ \ + 1s_2 & = & 610 \\
6A - 1B + \ \ \ \ \ \ \ + 1s_3 & = & 125 \\
A, B, s_1, s_2, s_3 & \geq & 0
\end{array}
$$

18. b. $A = 18/7, B = 15/7$

c. 0, 0, 4/7

20. b. $A = 3.43, B = 3.43$

c. 2.86, 0, 1.43, 0

22. b.

Extreme Point	Coordinates	Profit ($)
1	(0, 0)	0
2	(1700, 0)	8500
3	(1400, 600)	9400
4	(800, 1200)	8800
5	(0, 1680)	6720

Extreme point 3 generates the highest profit.

c. $A = 1400, C = 600$

d. Cutting and dyeing constraint and the packaging constraint

e. $A = 800, C = 1200$; profit = $9200

24. a. Let R = number of units of regular model

C = number of units of catcher's model

Max $5R + 8C$

$1R + C + \frac{3}{2}C \le 900$ Cutting and sewing

$\frac{1}{2}R + \frac{1}{3}C \le 300$ Finishing

$\frac{1}{8}R + \frac{1}{4}C \le 100$ Packaging and shipping

$R, C \ge 0$

b.

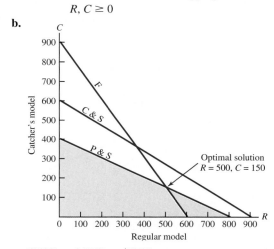

c. $5(500) + 8(150) = \$3700$

d. C & S $1(500) + \frac{3}{2}(150) = 725$

F $\frac{1}{2}(500) + \frac{1}{3}(150) = 300$

P & S $\frac{1}{8}(500) + \frac{1}{4}(150) = 100$

e.

Department	Capacity	Usage	Slack
Cutting and sewing	900	725	175 hours
Finishing	300	300	0 hours
Packaging and shipping	100	100	0 hours

26. a. Max $50N + 80R$

s.t.

$N + R = 1000$

$N \ge 250$

$R \ge 250$

$N - 2R \ge 0$

$N, R \ge 0$

b. $N = 666.67, R = 333.33$; Audience exposure = 60,000

28. a. Max $1W + 1.25M$

s.t.

$5W + 7M \le 4480$

$3W + 1M \le 2080$

$2W + 2M \le 1600$

$W, M \ge 0$

b. $W = 560, M = 240$; Profit = 860

30. a. Max $15E + 18C$

s.t.

$40E + 25C \le 50,000$

$40E \ge 15,000$

$25C \ge 10,000$

$25C \le 25,000$

$E, C \ge 0$

c. (375, 400); (1000, 400); (625, 1000); (375, 1000)

d. $E = 625, C = 1000$

Total return = $27,375

31.

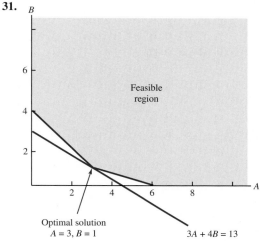

Objective function value = 13

32.

Objective Extreme Points	Function Value	Surplus Demand	Stock Total Production	Processing Time
(250, 100)	800	125	—	—
(125, 225)	925	—	—	125
(125, 350)	1300	—	125	—

34. a.

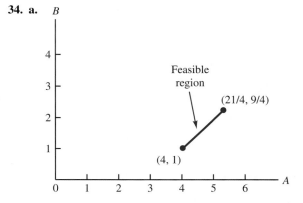

b. There are two extreme points:

$(A = 4, B = 1)$ and $(A = 21/4, B = 9/4)$

c. The optimal solution [see part (a)] is $A = 4, B = 1$.

35. a. Min $6A + 4B + 0s_1 + 0s_2 + 0s_3$

s.t.

$$
\begin{aligned}
2A + 1B - s_1 &= 12 \\
1A + 1B \quad\quad - s_2 &= 10 \\
1B \quad\quad\quad + s_3 &= 4 \\
A, B, s_1, s_2, s_3 &\geq 0
\end{aligned}
$$

b. The optimal solution is $A = 6, B = 4$

c. $s_1 = 4, s_2 = 0, s_3 = 0$

36. a. Min $10{,}000T + 8000P$

s.t.

$$
\begin{aligned}
T \quad\quad &\geq 8 \\
P &\geq 10 \\
T + \quad P &\geq 25 \\
3T + \quad 2P &\leq 84
\end{aligned}
$$

c. $(15, 10); (21.33, 10); (8, 30); (8, 17)$

d. $T = 8, P = 17$

Total cost $= \$216{,}000$

38. a. Min $7.50S + 9.00P$

s.t.

$$
\begin{aligned}
0.10S + 0.30P &\geq 6 \\
0.06S + 0.12P &\leq 3 \\
S + \quad P &= 30 \\
S, P &\geq 0
\end{aligned}
$$

c. The optimal solution is $S = 15, P = 15$.

d. No

e. Yes

40. $P_1 = 30, P_2 = 25$, Cost $= \$55$

42.

B

![Graph for problem 42](B axis labeled at 2, 4, 6, 8, 10; A axis labeled at 2, 4, 6, 8, 10. Line labeled "Satisfies constraint #2", region labeled "Infeasibility", line labeled "Satisfies constraint #1".)

43.

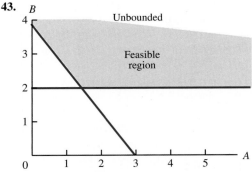

44. a. $A = 30/16, B = 30/16$; Value of optimal solution $= {}^{60}\!/_{16}$

    b. $A = 0, B = 3$; Value of optimal solution $= 6$

46. a. $180, 20$

    b. Alternative optimal solutions

    c. $120, 80$

48. No feasible solution

50. $M = 65.45, R = 261.82$; Profit $= \$45{,}818$

52. $S = 384, O = 80$

54. a. Max $160M_1 + 345M_2$

s.t.

$$
\begin{aligned}
M_1 \quad\quad &\leq 15 \\
M_2 &\leq 10 \\
M_1 \quad\quad &\geq 5 \\
M_2 &\geq 5 \\
40M_1 + 50M_2 &\leq 1000 \\
M_1, M_2 &\geq 0
\end{aligned}
$$

    b. $M_1 = 12.5, M_2 = 10$

Chapter 8

1. a.

B $A = 4, B = 6$

![Graph for Chapter 8, problem 1a](B axis labeled 2, 4, 6, 8, 10; A axis labeled 2, 4, 6, 8, 10. Dashed line labeled $3(7) + 2(3) = 27$. Optimal Solution $A = 7, B = 3$.)

b. The same extreme point, $A = 7$ and $B = 3$, remains optimal; Value of the objective function becomes $5(7) + 2(3) = 41$.

c. A new extreme point, $A = 4$ and $B = 6$, becomes optimal; Value of the objective function becomes $3(4) + 4(6) = 36$.

d. The objective coefficient range for variable A is 2 to 6; the optimal solution, $A = 7$ and $B = 3$, does not change. The objective coefficient range for variable B is 1 to 3; resolve the problem to find the new optimal solution.

2. a. The feasible region becomes larger with the new optimal solution of $A = 6.5$ and $B = 4.5$.

b. Value of the optimal solution to the revised problem is $3(6.5) + 2(4.5) = 28.5$; the one-unit increase in the right-hand side of constraint 1 increases the value of the optimal solution by $28.5 - 27 = 1.5$; therefore, the shadow price for constraint 1 is 1.5.

c. The right-hand-side range for constraint 1 is 8 to 11.2; as long as the right-hand side stays within this range, the shadow price of 1.5 is applicable.

d. The value of the optimal solution will increase by 0.5 for every unit increase in the right-hand side of constraint 2 as long as the right-hand side is between 18 and 30.

4. a. $X = 2.5$, $Y = 2.5$

b. -2

c. 5 to 11

d. The value of the optimal solution will increase by 3 for every unit increase in the right-hand side of constraint 2 as long as the right-hand side is between 9 and 18.

5. a. Regular glove $= 500$; Catcher's mitt $= 150$; Value $= 3700$

b. The finishing, packaging, and shipping constraints are binding; there is no slack.

c. Cutting and sewing $= 0$
Finishing $= 3$
Packaging and shipping $= 28$
Additional finishing time is worth \$3 per unit, and additional packaging and shipping time is worth \$28 per unit.

d. In the packaging and shipping department, each additional hour is worth \$28.

6. a. The optimal value for the Regular Glove variable is 5, the Allowable Decrease is 1, and the Allowable Increase is 7. The optimal value for the Catcher's Mitt variable is 8, the Allowable Decrease is 4.667, and the Allowable Increase is 2. Therefore, we can express the Objective Coefficient Ranges as follows:

Variable	Objective Coefficient Range
Regular Glove	$5 - 1 = 4$ to $5 + 7 = 12$
Catcher's Mitt	$8 - 4.667 = 3.333$ to $8 + 2 = 10$

b. As long as the profit contribution for the regular glove is between \$4.00 and \$12.00, the current solution is optimal; as long as the profit contribution for the catcher's mitt stays between \$3.33 and \$10.00, the current solution is optimal; the optimal solution is not sensitive to small changes in the profit contributions for the gloves.

c. The shadow prices for the resources are applicable over the following ranges:

Constraint	Right-Hand-Side Range
Cutting and sewing	$900 - 175 = 725$ to No Upper Limit
Finishing	$300 - 166.667 = 133.333$ to $300 + 100 = 400$
Packaging	$100 - 25 = 75$ to $100 + 35 = 135$

d. The shadow price of packaging and shipping constraint is 28, so the amount of increase $= (28)(20) = \$560$.

8. a. More than \$7.00

b. More than \$3.50

c. None

10. a. $S = 4000$
$M = 10{,}000$
Total risk $= 8(4000) + 3(10{,}000) = 62{,}000$

b.

Variable	Objective Coefficient Range
S	$8.000 - 4.250 = 3.750$ to No Upper Limit
M	No Upper Limit to $3.000 + 3.400 = 6.400$

c. $5(4000) + 4(10{,}000) = \$60{,}000$

d. $60{,}000/1{,}200{,}000 = 0.05$ or 5%

e. 0.057 risk units

f. $0.057(100) = 5.7\%$

12. a. $E = 80$, $S = 120$, $D = 0$
Profit $= 63(80) + 95(120) + 135(0) = \$16{,}440$

b. Fan motors and cooling coils

c. The manufacturing time constraint has slack; $2400 - 2080 = 320$ hours are available.

d. This represents an increase in the objective function coefficient for D of $\$150 - \$135 = \$15$. Because this is less than the allowable increase of \$24 for the objective function coefficient for D, there is no change in the optimal solution.

13. a. The range of optimality for each objective function coefficient is as follows:

E $63.000 - 15.5000 = 47.500$ to $63.000 + 12.000 = 75$
S $95.000 - 8.000 = 87.000$ to $95.000 + 31.000 = 126$
D No lower limit to $135.000 + 24.000 = 159.000$

b. Because more than one objective function coefficient value is changing at the same time here, we must resolve the problem to answer this question. Re-solving the problem with the new profit values shows that the optimal solution will not change. However, the change in total profit will be $69(80) + 93(120) + 135(0) = \$16,680$.

c. The range of feasibility for the right-hand side values for each constraint is as follows:

Fan motors constraint $200.000 - 40.000 = 160.000$ to $200.000 + 80.000 = 280.000$

Cooling coils constraint $320.000 - 120.000 = 200.000$ to $320.000 + 80.000 = 400.000$

Manufacturing time constraint $2400.000 - 320.000 = 2080.000$ to No Upper Limit

d. Yes, 100 is greater than the allowable increase for the fan motors constraint (80.000).

The shadow price will change.

14. a. The optimal solution is to manufacture 100 cases of model A and 60 cases of model B and purchase 90 cases of model B.

Total Cost $= 10(100) + 6(60) + 14(0) + 9(90) = \$2170$

b. Demand for A, demand for B, assembly time

c.

Constraint	Shadow Price
1	12.25
2	9.0
3	0
4	−0.375

If demand for model A increases by 1 unit, total cost will increase by $12.25.
If demand for model B increases by 1 unit, total cost will increase by $9.00.
If an additional minute of assembly time is available, total cost will decrease by $.375.

d. Assembly time constraint

16. a. 100 suits, 150 sport coats
Profit $= \$40,900$
40 hours of cutting overtime

b. Optimal solution will not change.

c. Consider ordering additional material.
$34.50 is the maximum price.

d. Profit will improve by $875.

18. a. The linear programming model is as follows:

Min $30AN + 50AO + 25BN + 40BO$

$$AN + AO \geq 50,000$$
$$BN + BO \geq 70,000$$
$$AN + BN \leq 80,000$$
$$AO + BO \leq 60,000$$
$$AN, AO, BN, BO \geq 0$$

b. Optimal solution

	New Line	Old Line
Model A	50,000	0
Model B	30,000	40,000

Total cost: $3,850,000

c. The first three constraints are binding.

d. The shadow price for the new production line capacity constraint is -15. Because the shadow price is negative, increasing the right-hand side of constraint 3 will cause the objective function to decrease. Thus, every 1-unit increase in the right hand side of this constraint will actually reduce the total production cost by $15. In other words, an increase in capacity for the new production line is desirable.

e. Because constraint 4 is not a binding constraint, any increase in the production line capacity of the old production line will have no effect on the optimal solution; thus, increasing the capacity of the old production line results in no benefit.

f. The reduced cost for model A made on the old production line is 5; thus, the cost would have to decrease by at least $5 before any units of model A would be produced on the old production line.

g. The right-hand-side range for constraint 2 shows an allowable decrease of 40,000. Thus, if the minimum production requirement is reduced 10,000 units to 60,000, the shadow price of 40 is applicable. Thus, total cost would decrease by $10,000(40) = \$400,000$.

20. a. Max $0.07H + 0.12P + 0.09A$

$$H + P + A = 1,000,000$$
$$0.6H - 0.4P - 0.4A \geq 0$$
$$P - 0.6A \leq 0$$
$$H, P, A \geq 0$$

b. $H = \$400,000, P = \$225,000, A = \$375,000$
Total annual return $= \$88,750$
Annual percentage return $= 8.875\%$

c. No change

d. Increase of $890

e. Increase of $312.50, or 0.031%

22. a. Min $30L + 25D + 18S$

$$L + D + S = 100$$
$$0.6L - 0.4D \geq 0$$
$$-0.15L - 0.15D + 0.85S \geq 0$$
$$-0.25L - 0.25D + S \leq 0$$
$$L \leq 50$$
$$L, D, S \geq 0$$

b. $L = 48, D = 72, S = 30$
Total cost $= \$3780$

c. No change
d. No change

24. a. Solution: $A = 333.3$, $B = 0$, $C = 833.3$, $D = 2500$

Risk: 14,666.7

Return: 18,000 (or 9%)

b.

Variable	Objective Coefficient Range
A	9.5 to 11
B	3.33 to No Upper Limit
C	3.2 to 4.4
D	No Lower Limit to 3.33

Individual changes in the risk measure coefficients within these ranges will not cause a change in the optimal investment decisions.

c. The shadow price associated with the rate of return constraint is 0.833. If the firm requires a 10% rate of return, this will increase the right-hand side of this constraint to $0.1*200,000 = 20,000$, which is an increase of 2000 units. Because this increase is within the right-hand-side range, this means that we would expect the objective function to increase by $2000*0.833 = 1666$ units. In other words, the increased rate of return would result in an increase in risk of 1660 units.

26. a. Let M_1 = units of component 1 manufactured
M_2 = units of component 2 manufactured
M_3 = units of component 3 manufactured
P_1 = units of component 1 purchased
P_2 = units of component 2 purchased
P_3 = units of component 3 purchased

$$\text{Min} \quad 4.50M_1 + 5.00M_2 + 2.75M_3 + 6.50P_1 + 8.80P_2 + 7.00P_3$$

$2M_1 + 3M_2 + 4M_3$	$\leq 21,600$	Production
$1M_1 + 1.5M_2 + 3M_3$	$\leq 15,000$	Assembly
$1.5M_1 + 2M_2 + 5M_3$	$\leq 18,000$	Testing/Packaging
$1M_1 \qquad\qquad + 1P_1$	$= 6,000$	Component 1
$1M_2 \qquad + 1P_2$	$= 4,000$	Component 2
$1M_3 + 1P_3$	$= 3,500$	Component 3

$$M_1, M_2, M_3, P_1, P_2, P_3 \geq 0$$

b.

Source	Component 1	Component 2	Component 3
Manufacture	2000	4000	1400
Purchase	4000		2100

Total Cost $73,550

c. Production: $54.36 per hour
Testing & Packaging: $7.50 per hour
d. Shadow prices = $7.969; it would cost Benson $7.969 to add a unit of component 2.

28. a. Let G = amount invested in growth stock fund
S = amount invested in income stock fund
M = amount invested in money market fund

$$\text{Max} \quad 0.20G + 0.10S + 0.06M$$
s.t.

$$0.10G + 0.05S + 0.01M \leq (0.05)(300,000)$$
$$G \geq (0.10)(300,000)$$
$$S \geq (0.10)(300,000)$$
$$M \geq (0.20)(300,000)$$
$$G + S + M \leq 300,000$$
$$G, S, M \geq 0$$

b. $G = 120,000$; $S = 30,000$; $M = 150,000$
c. 0.15 to 0.60; No Lower Limit to 0.122; 0.02 to 0.20
d. 4668
e. $G = 48,000$; $S = 192,000$; $M = 60,000$
f. The client's risk index and the amount of funds available

30. a. $L = 3$, $N = 7$, $W = 5$, $S = 5$
b. Each additional minute of broadcast time increases cost by $100.
c. If local coverage is increased by 1 minute, total cost will increase by $100.
d. If the time devoted to local and national news is increased by 1 minute, total cost will increase by $100.
e. Increasing the sports by 1 minute will have no effect because the shadow price is 0.

32. a. Let P_1 = number of PT-100 battery packs produced at the Philippines plant
P_2 = number of PT-200 battery packs produced at the Philippines plant
P_3 = number of PT-300 battery packs produced at the Philippines plant
M_1 = number of PT-100 battery packs produced at the Mexico plant
M_2 = number of PT-200 battery packs produced at the Mexico plant
M_3 = number of PT-300 battery packs produced at the Mexico plant

$$\text{Min} \quad 1.13P_1 + 1.16P_2 + 1.52P_3 + 1.08M_1 + 1.16M_2 + 1.25M_3$$

$P_1 + M_1$	$= 200,000$
$P_2 + M_2$	$= 100,000$
$P_3 + M_3$	$= 150,000$
$P_1 + P_2$	$\leq 175,000$
$M_1 + M_2$	$\leq 160,000$
P_3	$\leq 75,000$
M_3	$\leq 100,000$

$$P_1, P_2, P_3, M_1, M_2, M_3 \geq 0$$

b. The optimal solution is as follows:

	Philippines	Mexico
PT-100	40,000	160,000
PT-200	100,000	0
PT-300	50,000	100,000

Total production and transportation cost is $535,000.

c. The range of optimality for the objective function coefficient for P_1 shows a lower limit of $1.08; thus, the production and/or shipping cost would have to decrease by at least 5 cents per unit.

d. The range of optimality for the objective function coefficient for M_1 shows a lower limit of $1.11; thus, the production and/or shipping cost would have to decrease by at least 5 cents per unit.

Chapter 9

1. a. Let
T = number of television spot advertisements
R = number of radio advertisements
N = number of online advertisements

Max $100,000T + 18,000R + 40,000N$
s.t.

$2,000T + 300R + 600N \leq 18,200$ Budget
$T \qquad\qquad\qquad \leq 10$ Max TV
$\qquad R \qquad\qquad \leq 20$ Max Radio
$\qquad\qquad N \leq 10$ Max Online
$-0.5T + 0.5R - 0.5N \leq 0$ Max 50% Radio
$0.9T - 0.1R - 0.1N \geq 0$ Min 10% TV
$T, R, N, \geq 0$

	Budget \$
Solution: $T = 4$	\$ 8000
$R = 14$	4200
$N = 10$	6000
	\$18,200

Audience = 1,052,000

b. The shadow price for the budget constraint is 51.30. Thus, a $100 increase in budget should provide an increase in audience coverage of approximately 5130. The right-hand-side range for the budget constraint will show this interpretation is correct.

2. a. Let
x_1 = units of product 1 produced
x_2 = units of product 2 produced

Max $30x_1 + 15x_2$
s.t.

$x_1 + 0.35x_2 \leq 100$ Dept. A
$0.30x_1 + 0.20x_2 \leq 36$ Dept. B
$0.20x_1 + 0.50x_2 \leq 50$ Dept. C
$x_1, x_2 \leq 0$

Solution: $x_1 = 77.89$, $x_2 = 63.16$; Profit = \$3284.21

b. The shadow price for Department A is $15.79; for Department B it is $47.37; and for Department C it is $0.00. Therefore, we would attempt to schedule overtime in Departments A and B. Assuming the current labor available is a sunk cost, we should be willing to pay up to $15.79 per hour in Department A and up to $47.37 in Department B.

c. Let
x_A = hours of overtime in Department A
x_B = hours of overtime in Department B
x_C = hours of overtime in Department C

Max $30x_1 + 15x_2 - 18x_A - 22.5x_B - 12x_C$
s.t.

$x_1 + 0.35x_2 - x_A \qquad\qquad \leq 100$
$0.30x_1 + 0.20x_2 \qquad - x_B \qquad \leq 36$
$0.20x_1 + 0.50x_2 \qquad\qquad - x_C \leq 50$
$\qquad\qquad x_A \qquad\qquad \leq 10$
$\qquad\qquad\qquad x_B \qquad \leq 6$
$\qquad\qquad\qquad\qquad x_C \leq 8$

$x_1, x_2, x_A, x_B, x_C \leq 0$

$x_1 = 87.21$
$x_2 = 65.12$
Profit = \$3341.34

Overtime

Department A	10 hours
Department B	3.186 hours
Department C	0 hours

Increase in profit from overtime = $3341.34 - 3284.21 = $57.13

4. Let X_1 = the number of pounds of Party Nuts to produce
X_2 = the number of pounds of Mixed Nuts to produce
X_3 = the number of pounds of Premium Nuts to produce

Max $2(1.00)X_1 + 2(2.10)X_2 + 2(3.63)X_3 - 1.5(X_1 + 0.55X_2) - 5.35(0.25X_2 + 0.40X_3) - 6.25(0.1X_2 + 0.2X_3)$
s.t.

$X_1 + 0.55X_2 \qquad \leq 500$ (Peanuts)
$0.25X_2 + 0.40X_2 \leq 180$ (Cashews)
$0.1X_2 + 0.2X_2 \qquad \leq 100$ (Brazil Nuts)
$0.1X_2 + 0.4X_2 \qquad \leq 80$ (Hazelnuts)
$X_1, X_2, X_2 \qquad\qquad \geq 0$

The optimal solution is as follows:
$133 \frac{1}{3}$ pounds of Party Nuts (or $266 \frac{2}{3}$ bags)
$666 \frac{2}{3}$ pounds of Mixed Nuts (or $1333 \frac{1}{3}$ bags)
$33 \frac{1}{3}$ pounds of Premium Nuts (or $66 \frac{2}{3}$ bags)
Profit of \$537.33
The binding constraints are Peanuts, Cashews, and Hazelnuts.
Brazil Nuts are not binding (only $73 \frac{1}{3}$ pounds are used, resulting in slack of $26 \frac{2}{3}$ pounds).

6. Let
x_1 = units of product 1
x_2 = units of product 2
b_1 = labor-hours Department A
b_2 = labor-hours Department B

Max $25x_1 + 20x_2 + 0b_1 + 0b_2$
s.t.

$6x_1 + 8x_2 - 1b_1 \qquad\qquad = 0$
$12x_1 + 10x_2 - \qquad 1b_2 = 0$
$\qquad\qquad 1b_1 + 1b_2 \leq 900$
$x_1, x_2, b_1, b_2 \geq 0$

Solution: $x_1 = 50$, $x_2 = 0$, $b_1 = 300$, $b_2 = 600$; Profit: \$1250

8. Let x_1 = the number of officers scheduled to begin at
8:00 A.M.

x_2 = the number of officers scheduled to begin at noon

x_3 = the number of officers scheduled to begin at
4:00 P.M.

x_4 = the number of officers scheduled to begin at
8:00 P.M.

x_5 = the number of officers scheduled to begin at
midnight

x_6 = the number of officers scheduled to begin at
4:00 A.M.

The objective function to minimize the number of officers
required is as follows:

Min $x_1 + x_2 + x_3 + x_4 + x_5 + x_6$

The constraints require the total number of officers on
duty each of the six 4-hour periods to be at least equal to
the minimum officer requirements. The constraints for the
six 4-hour periods are as follows:

Time of Day

8:00 A.M.–Noon	$x_1 \qquad\qquad\qquad + x_6 \geq 5$
Noon-4:00 P.M.	$x_1 + x_2 \qquad\qquad\qquad \geq 6$
4:00 P.M.–8:00 P.M.	$x_2 + x_3 \qquad\qquad \geq 10$
8:00 P.M.–Midnight	$x_3 + x_4 \qquad\quad \geq 7$
Midnight–4:00 A.M.	$x_4 + x_5 \qquad \geq 4$
4:00 A.M.–8:00 A.M.	$x_5 + x_6 \geq 6$

$$x_1, x_2, x_3, x_4, x_5, x_6 \geq 0$$

Schedule 19 officers as follows:

x_1 = 3 begin at 8:00 A.M.

x_2 = 3 begin at noon

x_3 = 7 begin at 4:00 P.M.

x_4 = 0 begin at 8:00 P.M.

x_5 = 4 begin at midnight

x_6 = 2 begin at 4:00 A.M.

9. Let X_i = the number of call center employees who start
work on day i.

$(i = 1 = \text{Monday}, i = 2 = \text{Tuesday} \ldots)$

Min $X_1 + X_2 + X_3 + X_4 + X_5 + X_6 + X_7$
s.t.

$$
\begin{aligned}
X_1 + \qquad\qquad X_4 + X_5 + X_6 + X_7 &\geq 75 \\
X_1 + X_2 + \qquad\qquad X_5 + X_6 + X_7 &\geq 50 \\
X_1 + X_2 + X_3 + \qquad X_6 + X_7 &\geq 45 \\
X_1 + X_2 + X_3 + X_4 + \qquad X_7 &\geq 60 \\
X_1 + X_2 + X_3 + X_4 + X_5 &\geq 90 \\
X_2 + X_3 + X_4 + X_5 + X_6 &\geq 75 \\
X_3 + X_4 + X_5 + X_6 + X_7 &\geq 45
\end{aligned}
$$

$$X_1, X_2, X_3, X_4, X_5, X_6, X_7 \geq 0$$

Solution: $X_1 = 20$, $X_2 = 20$, $X_3 = 0$, $X_4 = 45$, $X_5 = 5$,
$X_6 = 5$, $X_7 = 0$

Total Number of Employees = 95

Excess employees: Thursday = 25, Sunday = 10, all
others = 0

Note: There are alternative optima to this problem (number of employees may differ from above, but will have
objective function value = 95).

10. a. Let S = the proportion of funds invested in stocks

B = the proportion of funds invested in bonds

M = the proportion of funds invested in mutual
funds

C = the proportion of funds invested in cash

The linear program and optimal solution are as follows:

Max $0.1S + 0.03B + 0.04M + 0.01C$
s.t.

(1) $1S + 1B + 1M + 1C = 1$

(2) $0.8S + 0.2B + 0.3M < 0.4$

(3) $1S < (0.75$

(4) $-1B + 1M > 0$

(5) $1C > 0.1$

(6) $1C < 0.3$

The optimal allocation among the four investment alternatives:

Stocks	40.9%
Bonds	14.5%
Mutual Funds	14.5%
Cash	30.0%

The annual return associated with the optimal portfolio is 5.4%.

Total risk = 0.409(0.8) + 0.145(0.2) + 0.145(0.3) +
0.300(0.0) = 0.4

b. Changing the right-hand-side value for constraint 2 to
0.18 and re-solving, we obtain the following optimal
solution:

Stocks	0.0%
Bonds	36.0%
Mutual Funds	36.0%
Cash	28.0%

The annual return associated with the optimal portfolio is 2.52%.

Total risk = 0.0(0.8) + 0.36(0.2) + 0.36(0.3) +
0.28(0.0) = 0.18

c. Changing the right-hand-side value for constraint 2
to 0.7 and re-solving, we obtain the following optimal
allocation among the four investment alternatives:

Stocks	75.0%
Bonds	0.0%
Mutual Funds	15.0%
Cash	10.0%

The annual return associated with the optimal
portfolio is 8.2%.

Total risk = 0.75(0.8) + 0.0(0.2) + 0.15(0.3) +
0.10(0.0) = 0.65

d. Note that a maximum risk of 0.7 was specified for this aggressive investor, but that the risk index for the portfolio is only 0.65. Thus, this investor is willing to take more risk than the solution shown above provides. There are only two ways the investor can become even more aggressive: by increasing the proportion invested in stocks to more than 75% or reducing the cash requirement of at least 10% so that additional cash could be put into stocks. For the data given here, the investor should ask the investment advisor to relax either or both of these constraints.

e. Defining the decision variables as proportions means the investment advisor can use the linear programming model for any investor, regardless of the amount of the investment. All the investor advisor must do is to establish the maximum total risk for the investor and resolve the problem using the new value for maximum total risk.

12. Let B_i = pounds of shrimp bought in week i, $i = 1, 2, 3, 4$
S_i = pounds of shrimp sold in week i, $i = 1, 2, 3, 4$
I_i = pounds of shrimp held in storage (inventory) in week i

Total purchase cost = $6.00B_1 + 6.20B_2 + 6.65B_3 + 5.55B_4$
Total sales revenue = $6.00S_1 + 6.20S_2 + 6.65S_3 + 5.55S_4$
Total storage cost = $0.15I_1 + 0.15I_2 + 0.15I_3 + 0.15I_4$
Total profit contribution = (Total sales revenue) − (Total purchase cost) − (Total storage cost)
Objective: Maximize total profit contribution subject to balance equations for each week, storage capacity for each week, and ending inventory requirement for week 4.

Max $6.00S_1 + 6.20S_2 + 6.65S_3 + 5.55S_4 - 6.00B_1 - 6.20B_2 - 6.65B_3 - 5.55B_4 - 0.15I_1 - 0.15I_2 - 0.15I_3 - 0.15I_4$

s.t.

$20{,}000 + B_1 - S_1 = I_1$		Balance equation—week 1
$I_1 + B_2 - S_2 = I_2$		Balance equation—week 2
$I_2 + B_3 - S_3 = I_3$		Balance equation—week 3
$I_3 + B_4 - S_4 = I_4$		Balance equation—week 4
$I_1 \leq 100{,}000$		Storage capacity—week 1
$I_2 \leq 100{,}000$		Storage capacity—week 2
$I_3 \leq 100{,}000$		Storage capacity—week 3
$I_4 \leq 100{,}000$		Storage capacity—week 4
$I_4 \leq 25{,}000$		Required inventory—week 4
all variables ≥ 0		

Note that the first four constraints can be written as follows:
$$I_1 - B_1 + S_1 = 20{,}000$$
$$I_1 - I_2 + B_2 - S_2 = 0$$
$$I_2 - I_3 + B_3 - S_3 = 0$$
$$I_3 - I_4 + B_4 - S_4 = 0$$

The optimal solution follows:

Week (i)	B_i	S_i	I_i
1	80,000	0	100,000
2	0	0	100,000
3	0	100,000	0
4	25,000	0	25,000

Total profit contribution = $12,500
Note, however, that ASC started week 1 with 20,000 pounds of shrimp and ended week 4 with 25,000 pounds of shrimp. During the 4-week period, ASC has taken profits to reinvest and build inventory by 5000 pounds in anticipation of future higher prices. The amount of profit reinvested in inventory is ($5.55 + $0.15)(5000) = $28,500. Thus, total profit for the 4-week period including reinvested profit is $12,500 + $28,500 = $41,000.

14. a. Let x_i = number of Classic 21 boats produced in Quarter i; $i = 1, 2, 3, 4$
s_i = ending inventory of Classic 21 boats in Quarter i; $i = 1, 2, 3, 4$

Min $10{,}000x_1 + 11{,}000x_2 + 12{,}100x_3 + 13{,}310x_4 + 250s_1 + 250s_2 + 300s_3 + 300s_4$

s.t.

$x_1 - s_1 = 1900$		Quarter 1 demand
$s_1 + x_2 - s_2 = 4000$		Quarter 2 demand
$s_2 + x_3 - s_3 = 3000$		Quarter 3 demand
$s_3 + x_4 - s_4 = 1500$		Quarter 4 demand
$s_4 \geq 500$		Ending Inventory
$x_1 \leq 4000$		Quarter 1 capacity
$x_2 \leq 3000$		Quarter 2 capacity
$x_3 \leq 2000$		Quarter 3 capacity
$x_4 \leq 4000$		Quarter 4 capacity

b.

Quarter	Production	Ending Inventory	Cost ($)
1	4000	2100	40,525,000
2	3000	1100	33,275,000
3	2000	100	24,230,000
4	1900	500	25,439,000
			$123,469,000

c. The shadow prices tell us how much it would cost if demand were to increase by one additional unit. For example, in Quarter 2 the shadow price is $12,760; thus, demand for one more boat in Quarter 2 will increase costs by $12,760.

d. The shadow price of 0 for Quarter 4 tells us we have excess capacity in Quarter 4. The negative shadow prices in Quarters 1–3 tell us how much increasing the production capacity will decrease costs. For example, the shadow price of −$2510 for Quarter 1 tells us that if capacity were increased by 1 unit for this quarter, costs would go down $2510.

15. Let R_i = the number of barrels of input i to use to produce Regular, $i = 1, 2, 3$

S_i = the number of barrels of input i to use to produce Super, $i = 1, 2, 3$

Max $\{18.5\ (R_1 + R_2 + R_3) + 20(R_1 + R_2 + R_3)$
$- 16.5(R_1 + S_1) - 14(R_2 + S_2) - 17.5(R_3 + S_3)\}$

s.t.

$$
\begin{aligned}
R_1 + S_1 &\leq 110000 \quad \text{Input 1 Capacity} \\
R_2 + S_2 &\leq 350000 \quad \text{Input 2 Capacity} \\
R_3 + S_3 &\leq 300000 \quad \text{Input 3 Capacity} \\
R_1 + R_2 + R_3 &\leq 350000 \quad \text{Max Demand for Regular} \\
S_1 + S_2 + S_3 &\leq 500000 \quad \text{Max Demand for Super}
\end{aligned}
$$

$100R_1 + 87R_2 + 110R_3 \geq 90 \ (R_1 + R_2 + R_3)$
Required Octane Level, Regular

$100S_1 + 87S_2 + 110S_3 \geq 100 \ (S_1 + S_2 + S_3)$
Required Octane Level, Super

$R_1, R_2, R_3, S_1, S_2, S_3 \geq 0$

Maximum Profit = \$2,845,000 by making 260,000 barrels of Regular and 500,000 barrels of Super. All available inputs are used (binding). The limit on maximum amount of Super we can sell is binding, as is the Octane Requirement for Super.

16. Let x_i = number of 10-inch rolls of paper processed by cutting alternative i; $i = 1, 2, \ldots, 7$

Min $x_1 + x_2 + x_3 + x_4 + x_5 + x_6 + x_7$

s.t.

$$
\begin{aligned}
6x_1 \quad\quad + 2x_3 \quad\quad + x_5 + x_6 + 4x_7 &\geq 1000 \quad 1\tfrac{1}{2}\text{" production} \\
4x_2 \quad\quad + x_4 + 3x_5 + 2x_6 \quad\quad &\geq 2000 \quad 2\tfrac{1}{2}\text{" production} \\
2x_3 + 2x_4 \quad\quad + x_6 + x_7 &\geq 4000 \quad 3\tfrac{1}{2}\text{" production}
\end{aligned}
$$

$x_1, x_2, x_3, x_4, x_5, x_6, x_7 \geq 0$

$$
\begin{aligned}
x_1 &= 0 \\
x_2 &= 125 \\
x_3 &= 500 \\
x_4 &= 1500 \\
x_5 &= 0 \\
x_6 &= 0 \\
x_7 &= 0
\end{aligned}
$$

Total Rolls = 125 + 500 + 1500 = 2125 Rolls

Production:

$1\tfrac{1}{2}$" 1000
$2\tfrac{1}{2}$" 2000
$3\tfrac{1}{2}$" 4000

Waste: Cut alternative 4 ($\tfrac{1}{2}$" per roll)

Therefore, waste = $\tfrac{1}{2}$(1500) = 750 inches

b. Only the objective function needs to be changed. An objective function minimizing waste production and the new optimal solution are given.

Min $x_1 + 0x_2 + 0x_3 + 0.5x_4 + x_5 + 0x_6 + 0.5x_7$

$$
\begin{aligned}
x_1 &= 0 \\
x_2 &= 500 \\
x_3 &= 2000
\end{aligned}
$$

$$
\begin{aligned}
x_4 &= 0 \\
x_5 &= 0 \\
x_6 &= 0 \\
x_7 &= 0
\end{aligned}
$$

Total Rolls = 2500 Rolls

Production:

$1\tfrac{1}{2}$" 4000
$2\tfrac{1}{2}$" 2000
$3\tfrac{1}{2}$" 4000

Waste is 0; however, we have overproduced the $1\tfrac{1}{2}$" size by 3000 units. Perhaps these can be inventoried for future use.

c. Minimizing waste may cause you to overproduce. In this case, we used 375 more rolls to generate a 3000 surplus of the $1\tfrac{1}{2}$" product. Alternative b might be preferred on the basis that the 3000 surplus could be held in inventory for later demand. However, in some trim problems, excess production cannot be used and must be scrapped. If this were the case, the 3000 unit $1\tfrac{1}{2}$" size would result in 4500 inches of waste, and thus alternative 1 would be the preferred solution.

18. a. Let x_1 = number of Super Tankers purchased

x_2 = number of Regular Line Tankers purchased

x_3 = number of Econo-Tankers purchased

Min $550x_1 + 425x_2 + 350x_3$

s.t.

$6700x_1 + 55000x_2 + 4600x_3 \leq 600,000$ Budget
$15(5000)x_1 + 20(2500)x_2 + 25(1000)x_3 \geq 550,000$

or

$75000x_1 + 50000x_2 + 25000x_3 \geq 550,000$ Meet Demand
$x_1 + x_2 + x_3 \leq 15$ Max. Total Vehicles
$x_3 \geq 3$ Min. Econo-Tankers

$x_1 \leq \tfrac{1}{2} (x_1 + x_2 + x_3)$

or

$\tfrac{1}{2}x_1 - \tfrac{1}{2}x_2 - \tfrac{1}{2}x_3 \leq 0$ No more than 50% Super Tankers
$x_1, x_2, x_3 \geq 0$

Solution: 5 Super Tankers, 2 Regular Tankers, 3 Econo-Tankers

Total Cost: \$583,000
Monthly Operating Cost: \$4650

b. The last two constraints in the preceding formulation must be deleted and the problem re-solved.

The optimal solution calls for $7\tfrac{1}{3}$ Super Tankers at an annual operating cost of \$4033. However, because a partial Super Tanker can't be purchased, we must round up to find a feasible solution of 8 Super Tankers with a monthly operating cost of \$4400.

Actually, this is an integer programming problem, because partial tankers can't be purchased. We were fortunate in part (a) that the optimal solution turned out integer.

The true optimal integer solution to part (b) is $x_1 = 6$ and $x_2 = 2$, with a monthly operating cost of \$4150. This is 6 Super Tankers and 2 Regular Line Tankers.

19. a. Let x_{11} = amount of men's model in month 1
x_{21} = amount of women's model in month 1
x_{12} = amount of men's model in month 2
x_{22} = amount of women's model in month 2
s_{11} = inventory of men's model at end of month 1
s_{21} = inventory of women's model at end of month 1
s_{12} = inventory of men's model at end of month 2
s_{22} = inventory of women's model at end of month 2

The model formulation for part (a) is given.

Min $120x_{11} + 90x_{21} + 120x_{12} + 90x_{22} + 2.4s_{11} + 1.8s_{21} + 2.4s_{12} + 1.8s_{22}$
s.t.

$20 + x_{11} - s_{11} = 150$

or

$x_{11} - s_{11} = 130$ Satisfy Demand   (1)
$30 + x_{21} - s_{21} = 125$

or

$x_{21} - s_{21} = 95$ Satisfy Demand   (2)
$s_{11} + x_{12} - s_{12} = 200$ Satisfy Demand   (3)
$s_{21} + x_{22} - s_{22} = 150$ Satisfy Demand   (4)
$s_{12} \geq 25$ Ending Inventory   (5)
$s_{22} \geq 25$ Ending Inventory   (6)
Labor-hours: Men's   = 2.0 + 1.5 = 3.5
           Women's = 1.6 + 1.0 = 2.6
$3.5 x_{11} + 2.6 x_{21} \geq 900$ Labor Smoothing for (7)
$3.5 x_{11} + 2.6 x_{21} \leq 1100$ Month 1   (8)
$3.5 x_{11} + 2.6 x_{21} - 3.5 x_{12} - 2.6 x_{22} \leq 100$ Labor Smoothing for (9)
$3.5 x_{11} + 2.6 x_{21} + 3.5 x_{12} + 2.6 x_{22} \leq 100$ Month 2   (10)
$x_{11}, x_{12}, x_{21}, x_{22}, s_{11}, s_{12}, s_{21}, s_{22} \geq 0$

The optimal solution is to produce 193 of the men's model in month 1, 162 of the men's model in month 2, 95 units of the women's model in month 1, and 175 of the women's model in month 2. Total Cost = $67,156.

Inventory Schedule

Month 1	63 Men's	0 Women's
Month 2	25 Men's	25 Women's

Labor Levels

Previous month	1000.00 hours
Month 1	922.25 hours
Month 2	1022.25 hours

b. To accommodate this new policy, the right-hand sides of constraints 7–10 must be changed to 950, 1050, 50, and 50, respectively. The revised optimal solution is given.

$x_{11} = 201$
$x_{21} = 95$
$x_{12} = 154$
$x_{22} = 175$ Total Cost = $67,175

We produce more men's models in the first month and carry a larger men's model inventory; the added cost, however, is only $19. This seems to be a small expense to have less drastic labor force fluctuations. The new labor levels are 1000, 950, and 994.5 hours each

month. Because the added cost is only $19, management might want to experiment with the labor force smoothing restrictions to enforce even less fluctuations. You may want to experiment yourself to see what happens.

20. Let x_m = number of units produced in month m
I_m = increase in the total production level in month m
D_m = decrease in the total production level in month m
s_m = inventory level at the end of month m

where

$m = 1$ refers to March
$m = 2$ refers to April
$m = 3$ refers to May

Min $1.25 I_1 + 1.25 I_2 + 1.25 I_3 + 1.00 D_1 + 1.00 D_2 + 1.00 D_3$
s.t.
Change in production level in March:

$x_1 - 10,000 = I_1 - D_1$

or

$x_1 - I_1 + D_1 = 10,000$

Change in production level in April:

$x_2 - x_1 = I_2 - D_2$

or

$x_2 - x_1 - I_2 + D_2 = 0$

Change in production level in May:

$x_3 - x_2 = I_3 - D_3$

or

$x_3 - x_2 - I_3 + D_3 = 0$

Demand in March:

$2500 + x_1 - s_1 = 12,000$

or

$x_1 - s_1 = 9500$

Demand in April:

$s_1 + x_2 - s_2 = 8000$

Demand in May:

$s_2 + x_3 = 15,000$

Inventory capacity in March:

$s_1 \leq 3000$

Inventory capacity in April:

$s_2 \leq 3000$

Optimal Solution:

Total cost of monthly production increases and decreases
= $2500

$x_1 = 10,250$	$I_1 = 250$	$D_1 = 0$
$x_2 = 10,250$	$I_2 = 0$	$D_2 = 0$
$x_3 = 12,000$	$I_3 = 1750$	$D_3 = 0$
$s_1 = 750$		
$s_2 = 3000$		

22. Let SM_1 = No. of small on machine M_1
SM_2 = No. of small on machine M_2

SM_3 = No. of small on machine M_3
LM_1 = No. of large on machine M_1
LM_2 = No. of large on machine M_2
LM_3 = No. of large on machine M_3
MM_2 = No. of meal on machine M_2
MM_3 = No. of meal on machine M_3

The formulation and solution follows. Note that constraints 1–3 guarantee that next week's schedule will be met and constraints 4–6 enforce machine capacities.

```
MIN
20SM1+24SM2+32SM3+15LM1+28LM2+35LM3+18MM2+36MM3

    S.T.

    1)   1SM1+1SM2+1SM3≤80000
    2)   +1LM1+1LM2+1LM3≥80000
    3)   +1MM2+1MM3≥65000
    4)   0.03333SM1+0.04LM1≤2100
    5)   +0.02222SM2+0.025LM2+0.03333MM2≤2100
    6)   +0.01667SM3+0.01923LM3+0.02273MM3≤2400


Optimal Solution

Objective Function Value =      5515886.58866

    Variable            Value
    --------       -------------     SM1   0.00000
      SM2            0.00000
      SM3        80000.00000
      LM1        52500.00000
      LM2            0.00000
      LM3        27500.00000
      MM2        63006.30063
      MM3         1993.69937


    Constraint          Slack/Surplus
    ----------         -------------
        1                  0.00000
        2                  0.00000
        3                  0.00000
        4                  0.00000
        5                  0.00000
        6                492.25821
```

Note that 5,515,887 square inches of waste are generated. Machine 3 has 492 minutes of idle capacity.

24. Let x_1 = proportion of investment A undertaken
x_2 = proportion of investment B undertaken
s_1 = funds placed in savings for period 1
s_2 = funds placed in savings for period 2
s_3 = funds placed in savings for period 3
s_4 = funds placed in savings for period 4
L_1 = funds received from loan in period 1

L_2 = funds received from loan in period 2
L_3 = funds received from loan in period 3
L_4 = funds received from loan in period 4

Objective Function:
In order to maximize the cash value at the end of the four periods, we must consider the value of investment A, the value of investment B, savings income from period 4, and loan expenses for period 4.

$$\text{Max}\quad 3200x_1 + 2500x_2 + 1.1s_4 - 1.18L_4$$

Constraints require the *use* of funds to equal the *source* of funds for each period.

Period 1:

$$1000x_1 + 800x_2 + s_1 = 1500 + L_1$$

or

$$1000x_1 + 800x_2 + s_1 - L_1 = 1500$$

Period 2:

$$800x_1 + 500x_2 + s_2 + 1.18L_1 = 400 + 1.1s_1 + L_2$$

or

$$800x_1 + 500x_2 - 1.1s_1 + s_2 + 1.18L_1 - L_2 = 400$$

Period 3:

$$200x_1 + 300x_2 + s_3 + 1.18L_2 = 500 + 1.1s_2 + L_3$$

or

$$200x_1 + 300x_2 - 1.1s_2 + s_3 + 1.18L_2 - L_3 = 500$$

Period 4:

$$s_4 + 1.18L_3 = 100 + 200x_1 + 300x_2 + 1.1s_3 + L_4$$

or

$$-200x_1 - 300x_2 - 1.1s_3 + s_4 + 1.18L_3 - L_4 = 100$$

Limits on Loan Funds Available:

$L_1 \le 200$
$L_2 \le 200$
$L_3 \le 200$
$L_4 \le 200$

Proportion of Investment Undertaken:

$x_1 \le 1$
$x_2 \le 1$

Optimal Solution: $4340.40

Investment A	$x_1 = 0.458$	or	45.8%
Investment B	$x_2 = 1.0$	or	100.0%

Savings/Loan Schedule:

	Period 1	Period 2	Period 3	Period 4
Savings	242.11	—	—	341.04
Loan	—	200.00	127.58	—

Chapter 10

1. The network model is shown:

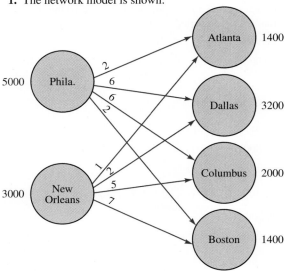

2. a. Let x_{11} = amount shipped from Jefferson City to Des Moines

x_{12} = amount shipped from Jefferson City to Kansas City

$\cdot$
$\cdot$
$\cdot$

Min $14x_{11} + 9x_{12} + 7x_{13} + 8x_{21} + 10x_{22} + 5x_{23}$
s.t.

$$x_{11} + x_{12} + x_{13} \leq 30$$
$$x_{21} + x_{22} + x_{23} \leq 20$$
$$x_{11} + x_{21} = 25$$
$$x_{12} + x_{22} = 15$$
$$x_{13} + x_{23} = 10$$
$$x_{11}, x_{12}, x_{13}, x_{21}, x_{22}, x_{23} \geq 0$$

b. Optimal Solution:

	Amount	Cost
Jefferson City–Des Moines	5	70
Jefferson City–Kansas City	15	135
Jefferson City–St. Louis	10	70
Omaha–Des Moines	20	160
Total		435

4. The optimization model can be written as

x_{ij} = Red GloFish shipped from i to j $i = M$ for Michigan, T for Texas; $j = 1, 2, 3$.

y_{ij} = Blue GloFish shipped from i to j, $i = M$ for Michigan, T for Texas; $j = 1, 2, 3$.

$$\text{Min} \, x_{M1} + 2.50x_{M2} + 0.50x_{M3} + y_{M1} + 2.50y_{M2} + 0.50y_{M3} + 2.00y_{T1} + 1.50y_{T2} + 2.80y_{T3}$$

subject to

$$x_{M1} + x_{M2} + x_{M3} \leq 1{,}000{,}000$$
$$y_{M1} + y_{M2} + y_{M3} \leq 1{,}000{,}000$$
$$y_{T1} + y_{T2} + y_{T3} \leq 600{,}000$$
$$x_{M1} \geq 320{,}000$$
$$x_{M2} \geq 300{,}000$$
$$x_{M3} \geq 160{,}000$$
$$y_{M1} + y_{T1} \geq 380{,}000$$
$$y_{M2} + y_{T2} \geq 450{,}000$$
$$y_{M3} + y_{T3} \geq 290{,}000$$
$$x_{ij} \geq 0$$

a. Solving this linear program using Solver, we find that we should produce 780,000 red GloFish in Michigan, 670,000 blue GloFish in Michigan, and 450,000 blue GloFish in Texas.

Using the notation in the model, the number of GloFish shipped from each farm to each retailer can be expressed as follows:

$x_{M1} = 320{,}000$
$x_{M2} = 300{,}000$
$x_{M3} = 160{,}000$
$y_{M1} = 380{,}000$
$y_{M2} = 0$
$y_{M3} = 290{,}000$
$y_{T1} = 0$
$y_{T2} = 450{,}000$
$y_{T3} = 0$

b. From Solver, the minimum transportation cost is $2.35 million.

c. We have to add variables x_{T1}, x_{T2}, and x_{T3} for Red GloFish shipped between Texas and Retailers 1, 2 and 3. The revised objective function is

Minimize $x_{M1} + 2.50x_{M2} + 0.50x_{M3} + y_{M1} + 2.50y_{M2} + 0.50y_{M3} + 2.00y_{T1} + 1.50y_{T2} + 2.80y_{T3} + x_{T1} + 2.50x_{T2} + 0.50x_{T3}$

We replace the third constraint above with

$x_{T1} + x_{T2} + x_{T3} + y_{T1} + y_{T2} + y_{T3} \leq 600{,}000$

And we change the constraints

$$x_{M1} \geq 320{,}000$$
$$x_{M2} \geq 300{,}000$$
$$x_{M3} \geq 160{,}000$$

to

$$x_{M1} + x_{T1} \geq 320{,}000$$
$$x_{M2} + x_{T2} \geq 300{,}000$$
$$x_{M3} + x_{T3} \geq 160{,}000$$

Using this new objective function and constraint the optimal solution is $2.2 million, so the savings are $150,000.

6. The network model, the linear programming formulation, and the optimal solution are shown. Note that the third constraint corresponds to the dummy origin. The variables x_{31}, x_{32}, x_{33}, and x_{34} are the amounts shipped out of the dummy origin; they do not appear in the objective function because they are given a coefficient of zero.

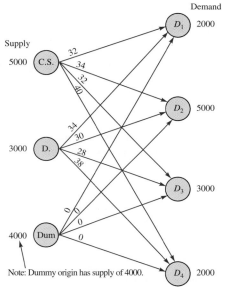

Note: Dummy origin has supply of 4000.

Max $32x_{11} + 34x_{12} + 32x_{13} + 40x_{14} + 34x_{21} + 30x_{22} + 28x_{23} + 38x_{24}$
s.t.

$$
\begin{array}{llllll}
x_{11} + x_{12} + x_{13} + x_{14} & & & \leq 5000 \\
& x_{21} + x_{22} + x_{23} + x_{24} & & \leq 3000 \\
& & x_{31} + x_{32} + x_{33} + x_{34} & \leq 4000 & \text{Dummy} \\
x_{11} & + x_{21} & + x_{31} & = 2000 \\
x_{12} & + x_{22} & + x_{32} & = 5000 \\
x_{13} & + x_{23} & + x_{33} & = 3000 \\
x_{14} & + x_{24} & + x_{34} & = 2000 \\
\end{array}
$$

$x_{ij} \geq 0$ for all i, j

Optimal Solution	Units	Cost
Clifton Springs–D_2	4000	$136,000
Clifton Springs–D_4	1000	40,000
Danville–D_1	2000	68,000
Danville–D_4	1000	38,000
	Total Cost	$282,000

Customer 2 demand has a shortfall of 1000.

Customer 3 demand of 3000 is not satisfied.

8. a.

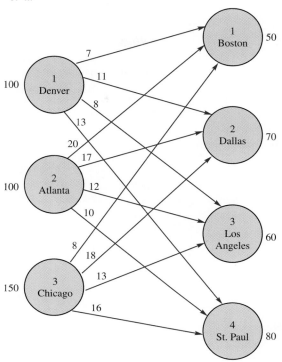

b. There are alternative optimal solutions.

Solution 1		Solution 2	
Denver to St. Paul:	10	Denver to St. Paul:	10
Atlanta to Boston:	50	Atlanta to Boston:	50
Atlanta to Dallas:	50	Atlanta to Los Angeles:	50
Chicago to Dallas:	20	Chicago to Dallas:	70
Chicago to Los Angeles:	60	Chicago to Los Angeles:	10
Chicago to St. Paul:	70	Chicago to St. Paul:	70
Total Profit: $4240			

If solution 1 is used, Forbelt should produce 10 motors at Denver, 100 motors at Atlanta, and 150 motors at Chicago. There will be idle capacity for 90 motors at Denver.

If solution 2 is used, Forbelt should adopt the same production schedule but a modified shipping schedule.

10. a. The total cost is the sum of the purchase cost and the transportation cost. We show the calculation for Division 1–Supplier 1 and present the result for the other Division-Supplier combinations.

Division 1–Supplier 1

Purchase cost (40,000 × $12.60)	$504,000
Transportation Cost (40,000 × $2.75)	110,000
Total Cost:	$614,000

Cost Matrix ($1000s)

	Supplier					
Division	1	2	3	4	5	6
1	614	660	534	680	590	630
2	603	639	702	693	693	630
3	865	830	775	850	900	930
4	532	553	511	581	595	553
5	720	648	684	693	657	747

b. Optimal Solution:

Supplier 1–Division 2	$ 603
Supplier 2–Division 5	648
Supplier 3–Division 3	775
Supplier 5–Division 1	590
Supplier 6–Division 4	553
Total	$3169

11. a. Network Model

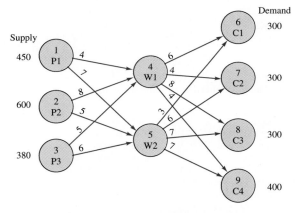

b. & c. The linear programming formulation and solution
are shown below:

```
LINEAR PROGRAMMING PROBLEM

MIN 4X14 + 7X15 + 8X24 + 5X25 + 5X34 +
6X35 + 6X46 + 4X47 + 8X48 + 4X49 + 3X56
+ 6X57 + 7X58 + 7X59

S.T.

(1) X14 + X15 < 450
(2) X24 + X25 < 600
(3) X34 + X35 < 380
(4) X46 + X47 + X48 + X49 − X14 − X24
    − X34 = 0
(5) X56 + X57 + X58 + X59 − X15 − X25
    − X35 = 0
(6) X46 + X56 = 300
(7) X47 + X57 = 300
(8) X48 + X58 = 300
(9) X49 + X59 = 400
```

```
OPTIMAL SOLUTION

Objective Function Value =     11850.000

   Variable          Value      Reduced Costs
   --------        ---------    -------------
     X14           450.000          0.000
     X15             0.000          3.000
     X24             0.000          3.000
     X25           600.000          0.000
     X34           250.000          0.000
     X35             0.000          1.000
     X46             0.000          3.000
     X47           300.000          0.000
     X48             0.000          1.000
     X49           400.000          0.000
     X56           300.000          0.000
     X57             0.000          2.000
     X58           300.000          0.000
     X59             0.000          3.000
```

There is an excess capacity of 130 units at plant 3.

12. a. Three arcs must be added to the network model in
Problem 11a. The new network is shown:

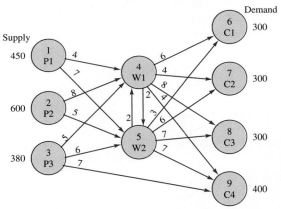

b. & c. The linear programming formulation and optimal
solution are shown below:

```
LINEAR PROGRAMMING PROBLEM

MIN 4X14 + 7X15 + 8X24 + 5X25 + 5X34 +
6X35 + 6X46 + 4X47 + 8X48 + 4X49 + 3X56 +
6X57 + 7X58 + 7X59 + 7X39 + 2X45 + 2X54

S.T.

(1) X14 + X15 < 450
(2) X24 + X25 < 600
(3) X34 + X35 + X39 < 380
(4) X45 + X46 + X47 + X48 + X49 − X14 −
    X24 − X34 − X54 = 0
(5) X54 + X56 + X57 + X58 + X59 − X15 −
    X25 − X35 − X45 = 0
(6) X46 + X56 = 300
(7) X47 + X57 = 300
(8) X48 + X58 = 300
(9) X39 + X49 + X59 = 400
```

```
OPTIMAL SOLUTION

Objective Function Value =  11220.000

    Variable          Value        Reduced Costs
 -----------       -----------     -------------
    X14            320.000            0.000
    X15              0.000            2.000
    X24              0.000            4.000
    X25            600.000            0.000
    X34              0.000            2.000
    X35              0.000            2.000
    X46              0.000            2.000
    X47            300.000            0.000
    X48              0.000            0.000
    X49             20.000            0.000
    X56            300.000            0.000
    X57              0.000            3.000
    X58            300.000            0.000
    X59              0.000            4.000
    X39            380.000            0.000
    X45              0.000            1.000
    X54              0.000            3.000
```

The value of the solution here is $630 less than the value of the solution for Problem 23. The new shipping route from plant 3 to customer 4 has helped ($x_{39} = 380$). There is now excess capacity of 130 units at plant 1.

14.

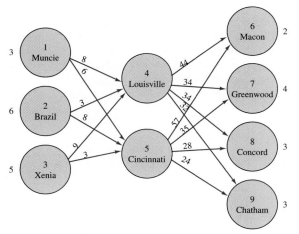

A linear programming model is

Min $8x_{14}+6x_{15}+3x_{24}+8x_{25}+9x_{34}+3x_{35}+44x_{46}+34x_{47}+34x_{48}+32x_{49}+57x_{56}+35x_{57}+28x_{58}+24x_{59}$
s.t.

$$
\begin{array}{rl}
x_{14}+ x_{15} & \le 3 \\
x_{24}+ x_{25} & \le 6 \\
x_{34}+ x_{35} & \le 5 \\
-x_{14} - x_{24} - x_{34} + x_{46}+ x_{47}+ x_{48}+ x_{49} & = 0 \\
- x_{15} - x_{25} - x_{35} + x_{56}+ x_{57}+ x_{58}+ x_{59} & = 0 \\
x_{46} + x_{56} & = 2 \\
x_{47} + x_{57} & = 4 \\
x_{48} + x_{58} & = 3 \\
x_{49} + x_{59} & = 3 \\
\end{array}
$$

$x_{ij} \ge 0$ for all i, j

Optimal Solution	Units Shipped	Cost
Muncie–Cincinnati	1	6
Cincinnati–Concord	3	84
Brazil–Louisville	6	18
Louisville–Macon	2	88
Louisville–Greenwood	4	136
Xenia–Cincinnati	5	15
Cincinnati–Chatham	3	72
		419

Two rail cars must be held at Muncie until a buyer is found.

16. a.

Min $20x_{12} + 25x_{15} + 30x_{25} + 45x_{27} + 20x_{31} + 35x_{36}$
$\quad\quad + 30x_{42} + 25x_{53} + 15x_{54} + 28x_{56} + 12x_{67} + 27x_{74}$

s.t.

$$
\begin{array}{rl}
x_{31} - x_{12} - x_{15} & = 8 \\
x_{25} + x_{27} - x_{12} - x_{42} & = 5 \\
x_{31} + x_{36} - x_{53} & = 3 \\
x_{54} + x_{74} - x_{42} & = 3 \\
x_{53} + x_{54} + x_{56} - x_{15} - x_{25} & = 2 \\
x_{36} + x_{56} - x_{67} & = 5 \\
x_{74} - x_{27} - x_{67} & = 6 \\
\end{array}
$$

$x_{ij} \ge 0$ for all i, j

b.

$x_{12} = 0$	$x_{53} = 5$
$x_{15} = 0$	$x_{54} = 0$
$x_{25} = 8$	$x_{56} = 5$
$x_{27} = 0$	$x_{67} = 0$
$x_{31} = 8$	$x_{74} = 6$
$x_{36} = 0$	$x_{56} = 5$
$x_{42} = 3$	

Total cost of redistributing cars = $917

17. a.

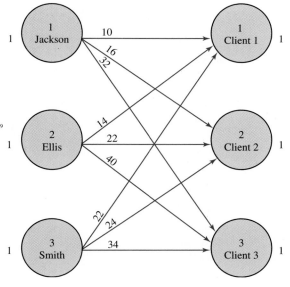

b.

Min $10x_{11} + 16x_{12} + 32x_{13} + 14x_{21} + 22x_{22} + 40x_{23} + 22x_{31} + 24x_{32} + 34x_{33}$
s.t.

$$
\begin{aligned}
x_{11} + x_{12} + x_{13} && \leq 1 \\
x_{21} + x_{22} + x_{23} && \leq 1 \\
x_{31} + x_{32} + x_{33} && \leq 1 \\
x_{11} \quad\quad + x_{21} \quad\quad + x_{31} && = 1 \\
x_{12} \quad\quad + x_{22} \quad\quad + x_{32} && = 1 \\
x_{13} \quad\quad + x_{23} \quad\quad + x_{33} && = 1 \\
\end{aligned}
$$
$x_{ij} \geq 0 \quad \text{for all } i, j$

Solution: $x_{12} = 1, x_{21} = 1, x_{33} = 1$
Total completion time = 64

18. a.

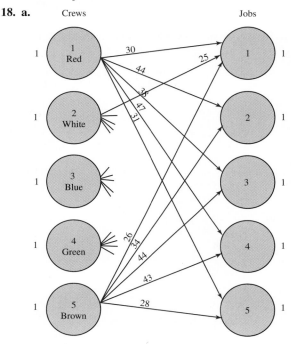

Crews   Jobs

b.

Min $30x_{11} + 44x_{12} + 38x_{13} + 47x_{14} + 31x_{15} + 25x_{21} + \cdots + 28x_{55}$
s.t.

$$
\begin{aligned}
x_{11} + x_{12} + x_{13} + x_{14} + x_{15} && \leq 1 \\
x_{21} + x_{22} + x_{23} + x_{24} + x_{25} && \leq 1 \\
x_{31} + x_{32} + x_{33} + x_{34} + x_{35} && \leq 1 \\
x_{41} + x_{42} + x_{43} + x_{44} + x_{45} && \leq 1 \\
x_{51} + x_{52} + x_{53} + x_{54} + x_{55} && \leq 1 \\
x_{11} + x_{21} + x_{31} + x_{41} + x_{51} && = 1 \\
x_{12} + x_{22} + x_{32} + x_{42} + x_{52} && = 1 \\
x_{13} + x_{23} + x_{33} + x_{43} + x_{53} && = 1 \\
x_{14} + x_{24} + x_{34} + x_{44} + x_{54} && = 1 \\
x_{15} + x_{25} + x_{35} + x_{45} + x_{55} && = 1 \\
\end{aligned}
$$
$x_{ij} \geq 0, \ i = 1, 2, \ldots, 5; \ j = 1, 2, \ldots, 5$

Optimal Solution:

Green to Job 1	$ 26
Brown to Job 2	34
Red to Job 3	38
Blue to Job 4	39
White to Job 5	25
	$162

Because the data are in hundreds of dollars, the total installation cost for the five contracts is $16,200.

20. a. This is the variation of the assignment problem in which multiple assignments are possible. Each distribution center may be assigned up to three customer zones.

The linear programming model of this problem has 40 variables (one for each combination of distribution center and customer zone). It has 13 constraints. There are 5 supply (≤ 3) constraints and 8 demand ($= 1$) constraints.

The optimal solution is as follows:

	Assignments	Cost ($1000s)
Plano	Kansas City, Dallas	34
Flagstaff	Los Angeles	15
Springfield	Chicago, Columbus, Atlanta	70
Boulder	Newark, Denver	97
	Total Cost	$216

b. The Nashville distribution center is not used.
c. All the distribution centers are used. Columbus is switched from Springfield to Nashville. Total cost increases by $11,000 to $227,000.

22. A linear programming formulation of this problem can be developed as follows. Let the first letter of each variable name represent the professor and the second two the course. Note that a *DPH* variable is not created because the assignment is unacceptable.

Max $2.8AUG + 2.2AMB + 3.3AMS + 3.0APH + 3.2BUG + \cdots + 2.5DMS$
s.t.

$$
\begin{aligned}
AUG + AMB + AMS + APH && \leq 1 \\
BUG + BMB + BMS + BPH && \leq 1 \\
CUG + CMB + CMS + CPH && \leq 1 \\
DUG + DMB + DMS && \leq 1 \\
AUG + BUG + CUG + DUG && = 1 \\
AMB + BMB + CMB + DMB && = 1 \\
AMS + BMS + CMS + DMS && = 1 \\
APH + BPH + CPH && = 1 \\
\end{aligned}
$$
All Variables ≥ 0

Optimal Solution	Rating
A to MS course	3.3
B to Ph.D. course	3.6
C to MBA course	3.2
D to Undergraduate course	3.2
Max Total Rating	13.3

23. Origin—Node 1
Transshipment—Nodes 2–5
Destination—Node 7

The linear program will have 14 variables for the arcs and 7 constraints for the nodes.

Let

$$x_{ij} = \begin{cases} 1 & \text{if the arc from node } i \text{ to node } j \text{ is on the shortest route} \\ 0 & \text{otherwise} \end{cases}$$

$$\text{Min } 7x_{12} + 9x_{13} + 18x_{14} + 3x_{23} + 5x_{25} + 3x_{32} + 4x_{35} \\ + 3x_{46} + 5x_{52} + 4x_{53} + 2x_{56} + 6x_{57} + 2x_{65} + 3x_{67}$$

s.t.

	Flow Out	Flow In	
Node 1	$x_{12} + x_{13} + x_{14}$		$= 1$
Node 2	$x_{23} + x_{25}$	$-x_{12} - x_{32} - x_{52}$	$= 0$
Node 3	$x_{32} + x_{35}$	$-x_{13} - x_{23} - x_{53}$	$= 0$
Node 4	x_{46}	$-x_{14}$	$= 0$
Node 5	$x_{52} + x_{53} + x_{56} + x_{57}$	$-x_{25} - x_{35} - x_{65}$	$= 0$
Node 6	$x_{65} + x_{67}$	$-x_{46} - x_{56}$	$= 0$
Node 7		$+x_{57} + x_{67}$	$= 1$

$$x_{ij} \geq 0 \text{ for all } i \text{ and } j$$

Optimal Solution: $x_{12} = 1$, $x_{25} = 1$, $x_{56} = 1$, and $x_{67} = 1$

Shortest Route: 1–2–5–6–7

Length = 17

24. The linear program has 13 variables for the arcs and 6 constraints for the nodes. Use the same 6 constraints for the Gorman shortest route problem, as shown in the text. The objective function changes to travel time as follows:

$$\text{Min } 40x_{12} + 36x_{13} + 6x_{23} + 6x_{32} + 12x_{24} + 12x_{42} + 25x_{26} \\ + 15x_{35} + 15x_{53} + 8x_{45} + 8x_{54} + 11x_{46} + 23x_{56}$$

Optimal Solution: $x_{12} = 1$, $x_{24} = 1$, and $x_{46} = 1$

Shortest Route: 1–2–4–6

Total Time = 63 minutes

26. Origin—Node 1

Transshipment—Nodes 2–5 and node 7

Destination—Node 6

The linear program will have 18 variables for the arcs and 7 constraints for the nodes.

Let

$$x_{ij} = \begin{cases} 1 & \text{if the arc from node } i \text{ to node } j \text{ is on the shortest route} \\ 0 & \text{otherwise} \end{cases}$$

$$\text{Min } 35x_{12} + 30x_{13} + 20x_{14} + 8x_{23} + 12x_{25} + 8x_{32} + 9x_{34} + 10x_{35} \\ + 20x_{36} + 9x_{43} + 15x_{47} + 12x_{52} + 10x_{53} + 5x_{56} + 20x_{57} + 15x_{74} \\ + 20x_{75} + 5x_{76}$$

s.t.

	Flow Out	Flow In	
Node 1	$x_{12} + x_{13} + x_{14}$		$= 1$
Node 2	$x_{23} + x_{25}$	$-x_{12} - x_{32} - x_{52}$	$= 0$
Node 3	$x_{32} + x_{34} + x_{35} + x_{36}$	$-x_{13} - x_{23} - x_{43} - x_{53}$	$= 0$
Node 4	$x_{43} + x_{47}$	$-x_{14} - x_{34} - x_{74}$	$= 0$
Node 5	$x_{52} + x_{53} + x_{56} + x_{57}$	$-x_{25} - x_{35} - x_{75}$	$= 0$
Node 6		$+x_{36} + x_{56} + x_{76}$	$= 1$
Node 7	$x_{74} + x_{75} + x_{76}$	$-x_{47} - x_{57}$	$= 0$

$$x_{ij} \geq 0 \quad \text{for all } i \text{ and } j$$

Optimal Solution: $x_{14} = 1$, $x_{47} = 1$, and $x_{76} = 1$

Shortest Route: 1–4–7–6

Total Distance = 40 miles

28. Origin—Node 0

Transshipment—Nodes 1 to 3

Destination—Node 4

The linear program will have 10 variables for the arcs and 5 constraints for the nodes.

Let

$$x_{ij} = \begin{cases} 1 & \text{if the arc from node } i \text{ to node } j \text{ is on the minimum cost route} \\ 0 & \text{otherwise} \end{cases}$$

$$\text{Min } 600x_{01} + 1000x_{02} + 2000x_{03} + 2800x_{04} + 500x_{12} + \\ 1400x_{13} + 2100x_{14} + 800x_{23} + 1600x_{24} + 700x_{34}$$

s.t.

	Flow Out	Flow In	
Node 0	$x_{01} + x_{02} + x_{03} + x_{04}$		$= 1$
Node 1	$x_{12} + x_{13} + x_{14}$	$-x_{01}$	$= 0$
Node 2	$x_{23} + x_{24}$	$-x_{02} - x_{12}$	$= 0$
Node 3	x_{34}	$-x_{03} - x_{13} - x_{23}$	$= 0$
Node 4		$-x_{04} - x_{14} - x_{24} - x_{34}$	$= 1$

$$x_{ij} \geq 0 \quad \text{for all } i \text{ and } j$$

Optimal Solution: $x_{02} = 1$, $x_{23} = 1$, and $x_{34} = 1$

Shortest Route: 0–2–3–4

Total Cost = $2500

29. The capacitated transshipment problem to solve is given:

Max x_{61}

s.t.

$$\begin{aligned}
x_{12} + x_{13} + x_{14} - x_{61} &= 0 \\
x_{24} + x_{25} - x_{12} - x_{42} &= 0 \\
x_{34} + x_{36} - x_{13} - x_{43} &= 0 \\
x_{42} + x_{43} + x_{45} + x_{46} - x_{14} - x_{24} - x_{34} - x_{54} &= 0 \\
x_{54} + x_{56} - x_{25} - x_{45} &= 0 \\
x_{61} - x_{36} + x_{46} - x_{56} &= 0
\end{aligned}$$

$$\begin{array}{lll}
x_{12} \leq 2 & x_{13} \leq 6 & x_{14} \leq 3 \\
x_{24} \leq 1 & x_{25} \leq 4 & \\
x_{34} \leq 3 & x_{36} \leq 2 & \\
x_{42} \leq 1 & x_{43} \leq 3 & x_{45} \leq 1 \qquad x_{46} \leq 3 \\
x_{54} \leq 1 & x_{56} \leq 6 &
\end{array}$$

$$x_{ij} \geq 0 \text{ for all } i, j$$

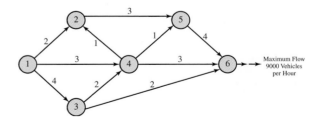

The system cannot accommodate a flow of 10,000 vehicles per hour.

30.

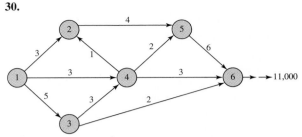

32. a. 10,000 gallons per hour or 10 hours
   b. Flow reduced to 9000 gallons per hour; 11.1 hours.

34. Maximal Flow = 23 gallons/minute. Five gallons will flow from node 3 to node 5.

36. a. Let R_1, R_2, R_3 represent regular time production in months 1, 2, 3

O_1, O_2, O_3 represent overtime production in months 1, 2, 3

D_1, D_2, D_3 represent demand in months 1, 2, 3

Using these nine nodes, a network model is shown:

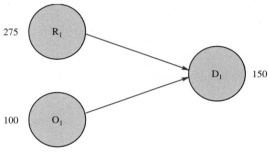

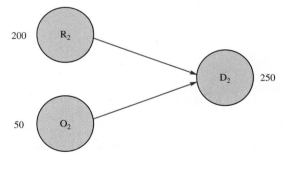

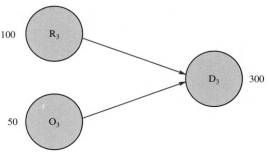

b. Use the following notation to define the variables: The first two characters designate the "from node" and the second two characters designate the "to node" of the arc. For instance, R_1D_1 is amount of regular time production available to satisfy demand in month 1; O_1D_1 is amount of overtime production in month 1 available to satisfy demand in month 1; D_1D_2 is the amount of inventory carried over from month 1 to month 2; and so on.

$$\text{Min } 50R_1D_1 + 800_1D_1 + 20D_1D_2 + 50R_2D_2 + 800_2D_2$$
$$+ 20D_2D_3 + 60R_3D_3 + 100O_3D_3$$

S.T.

(1)	R_1D_1	≤ 275
(2)	O_1D_1	≤ 100
(3)	R_2D_2	≤ 200
(4)	O_2D_2	≤ 50
(5)	R_3D_3	≤ 100
(6)	O_3D_3	≤ 50
(7)	$R_1D_1 + O_1D_1 - D_1D_2$	$= 150$
(8)	$R_2D_2 + O_2D_2 + D_1D_2 - D_2D_3$	$= 250$
(9)	$R_3D_3 + O_3D_3 + D_2D_3$	$= 300$

c. Optimal Solution:

Variable	Value
R_1D_1	275.000
O_1D_1	25.000
D_1D_2	150.000
R_2D_2	200.000
O_2D_2	50.000
D_2D_3	150.000
R_3D_3	100.000
O_3D_3	50.000

Value = $46,750
Note: Slack variable for constraint 2 = 75

d. The values of the slack variables for constraints 1 through 6 represent unused capacity. The only nonzero slack variable is for constraint 2; its value is 75. Thus, there are 75 units of unused overtime capacity in month 1.

Chapter 11

2. a.

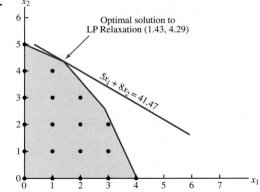

b. The optimal solution to the LP Relaxation is given by $x_1 = 1.43$, $x_2 = 4.29$ with an objective function value of 41.47. Rounding down gives the feasible integer solution $x_1 = 1$, $x_2 = 4$; its value is 37.

c.

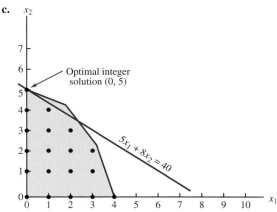

The optimal solution is given by $x_1 = 0$, $x_2 = 5$; its value is 40. It is not the same solution as found by rounding down; it provides a 3-unit increase in the value of the objective function.

4. a. $x_1 = 3.67$, $x_2 = 0$; Value = 36.7
Rounded: $x_1 = 3$, $x_2 = 0$; Value = 30
Lower bound = 30; Upper bound = 36.7
b. $x_1 = 3$, $x_2 = 2$; Value = 36
c. Alternative optimal solutions: $-x_1 = 0$, $x_2 = 5$
$\qquad\qquad\qquad\qquad\qquad\quad x_1 = 2$, $x_2 = 4$

5. a. The feasible mixed-integer solutions are indicated by the boldface vertical lines in the graph.

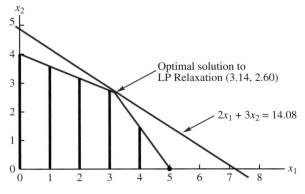

b. The optimal solution to the LP Relaxation is given by $x_1 = 3.14$, $x_2 = 2.60$; its value is 14.08.
   Rounding down the value of x_1 to find a feasible mixed-integer solution yields $x_1 = 3$, $x_2 = 2.60$ with a value of 13.8; this solution is clearly not optimal; with $x_1 = 3$, x_2 can be made larger without violating the constraints.

c. The optimal solution to the MILP is given by $x_1 = 3$, $x_2 = 2.67$; its value is 14, as shown in the following figure:

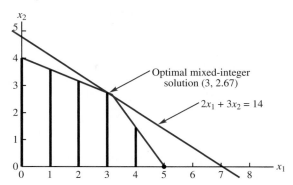

6. b. $x_1 = 1.96$, $x_2 = 5.48$; Value = 7.44
Rounded: $x_1 = 1.96$, $x_2 = 5$; Value = 6.96
Lower bound = 6.96; Upper bound = 7.44
c. $x_1 = 1.29$, $x_2 = 6$; Value = 7.29

7. a. $x_1 + x_3 + x_5 + x_6 = 2$
b. $x_3 - x_5 = 0$
c. $x_1 + x_4 = 1$
d. $x_4 \leq x_1$
$\quad x_4 \leq x_3$
e. $x_4 \leq x_1$
$\quad x_4 \leq x_3$
$\quad x_4 \leq x_1 + x_3 - 1$

8. a. $x_3 = 1$, $x_4 = 1$, $x_6 = 1$; Value = 17,500
b. Add $x_1 + x_2 \leq 1$.
c. Add $x_3 - x_4 = 0$.

10. b. Choose locations B and E.

12. a. We use the following data:

b_{ij} = the bid for city i from carrier j,
$i = 1, 2, \ldots 20 \quad j = 1, 2, \ldots 7$
dem_i = the demand in truckload for city i
$i = 1, 2, \ldots 20$
c_{ij} = the cost of assigning city i to carrier j
$i = 1, 2, \ldots 20 \quad j = 1, 2, \ldots 7$

Note: $c_{ij} = (dem_i)(b_{ij})$ used in the objective function.

Let $y[j] = 1$ if carrier j is selected, 0 if not $j = 1, 2, \ldots 7$

$x[i, j] = 1$ if city i is assigned to carrier j, 0 if not
$i = 1, 2, \ldots 20 \quad j = 1, 2, \ldots 7$

Minimize the cost of city-carrier assignments (note: for brevity, zeros are not shown).

Minimize

65640*x[1, 5] + 49980*x[1, 6] + 53700*x[1, 7] + 14530*x[2, 2] + 26020*x[2, 5] + 17670*x[2, 6] + 30680*x[3, 2] + 45660*x[3, 5] + 37140*x[3, 6] + 37400*x[3, 7] + 67480*x[4, 2] + 104680*x[4, 5] + 69520*x[4, 6] + 15230*x[5, 2] + 22390*x[5, 5] + 17710*x[5, 6] +

18550*x[5, 7] + 15210*x[6, 2] + 15710*x[6, 5] + 15450*x[6, 7] +
25200*x[7, 2] + 23064*x[7, 4] + 23256*x[7, 5] + 24600*x[7, 7] +
45000*x[8, 2] + 35800*x[8, 4] + 35400*x[8, 5] + 43475*x[8, 7] +
28350*x[9, 2] + 30825*x[9, 4] + 29525*x[9, 5] + 28750*x[9, 7] +
22176*x[10, 2] + 20130*x[10, 4] + 22077*x[10, 5] + 22374*x[10, 7] +
7964*x[11, 1] + 7953*x[11, 3] + 6897*x[11, 4] + 7227*x[11, 5] +
7766*x[11, 7] + 22214*x[12, 1] + 22214*x[12, 3] + 20909*x[12, 4] +
19778*x[12, 5] + 21257*x[12, 7] + 8892*x[13, 1] + 8940*x[13, 3] +
8184*x[13, 5] + 8796*x[13, 7] + 19560*x[14, 1] + 19200*x[14, 2] +
19872*x[14, 3] + 17880*x[14, 5] + 19968*x[14, 7] + 9040*x[15, 1] +
8800*x[15, 3] + 8910*x[15, 5] + 9140*x[15, 7] + 9580*x[16, 1] +
9330*x[16, 3] + 8910*x[16, 5] + 9140*x[16, 7] + 21275*x[17, 1] +
21367*x[17, 3] + 21551*x[17, 5] + 22632*x[17, 7] + 22300*x[18, 1] +
21725*x[18, 3] + 20550*x[18, 4] + 20725*x[18, 5] + 21600*x[18, 7] +
11124*x[19, 1] + 11628*x[19, 3] + 11604*x[19, 5] + 12096*x[19, 7] +
9630*x[20, 1] + 9380*x[20, 3] + 9550*x[20, 5] + 9950*x[20, 7]]

subject to

Every city is assigned to exactly one carrier:

x[1, 1] + x[1, 2] + x[1, 3] + x[1, 4] + x[1, 5] + x[1, 6] + x[1, 7] = 1
x[2, 1] + x[2, 2] + x[2, 3] + x[2, 4] + x[2, 5] + x[2, 6] + x[2, 7] = 1
x[3, 1] + x[3, 2] + x[3, 3] + x[3, 4] + x[3, 5] + x[3, 6] + x[3, 7] = 1
x[4, 1] + x[4, 2] + x[4, 3] + x[4, 4] + x[4, 5] + x[4, 6] + x[4, 7] = 1
x[5, 1] + x[5, 2] + x[5, 3] + x[5, 4] + x[5, 5] + x[5, 6] + x[5, 7] = 1
x[6, 1] + x[6, 2] + x[6, 3] + x[6, 4] + x[6, 5] + x[6, 6] + x[6, 7] = 1
x[7, 1] + x[7, 2] + x[7, 3] + x[7, 4] + x[7, 5] + x[7, 6] + x[7, 7] = 1
x[8, 1] + x[8, 2] + x[8, 3] + x[8, 4] + x[8, 5] + x[8, 6] + x[8, 7] = 1
x[9, 1] + x[9, 2] + x[9, 3] + x[9, 4] + x[9, 5] + x[9, 6] + x[9, 7] = 1
x[10, 1] + x[10, 2] + x[10, 3] + x[10, 4] + x[10, 5] + x[10, 6] + x[10, 7] = 1
x[11, 1] + x[11, 2] + x[11, 3] + x[11, 4] + x[11, 5] + x[11, 6] + x[11, 7] = 1
x[12, 1] + x[12, 2] + x[12, 3] + x[12, 4] + x[12, 5] + x[12, 6] + x[12, 7] = 1
x[13, 1] + x[13, 2] + x[13, 3] + x[13, 4] + x[13, 5] + x[13, 6] + x[13, 7] = 1
x[14, 1] + x[14, 2] + x[14, 3] + x[14, 4] + x[14, 5] + x[14, 6] + x[14, 7] = 1
x[15, 1] + x[15, 2] + x[15, 3] + x[15, 4] + x[15, 5] + x[15, 6] + x[15, 7] = 1
x[16, 1] + x[16, 2] + x[16, 3] + x[16, 4] + x[16, 5] + x[16, 6] + x[16, 7] = 1
x[17, 1] + x[17, 2] + x[17, 3] + x[17, 4] + x[17, 5] + x[17, 6] + x[17, 7] = 1
x[18, 1] + x[18, 2] + x[18, 3] + x[18, 4] + x[18, 5] + x[18, 6] + x[18, 7] = 1
x[19, 1] + x[19, 2] + x[19, 3] + x[19, 4] + x[19, 5] + x[19, 6] + x[19, 7] = 1
x[20, 1] + x[20, 2] + x[20, 3] + x[20, 4] + x[20, 5] + x[20, 6] + x[20, 7] = 1

If a carrier is selected, it can be assigned only the number
of bids made:

Note:

The idea here is that if carrier j is not chosen, then no
cities can be assigned to that carrier. Hence if $y[j] = 0$,
the sum must be less than or equal to zero and hence all
the associated x's must be zero. If $y[j] = 1$, then the constraint becomes redundant. It could also be modeled as
$x[i,j] <= y[j]$, but this would generate more constraints:

x[1, 1] + x[2, 1] + x[3, 1] + x[4, 1] + x[5, 1] + x[6, 1] + x[7, 1]+
x[8, 1] + x[9, 1] + x[10, 1] + x[11, 1] + x[12, 1] + x[13, 1] +
x[14, 1] + x[15, 1] + x[16, 1] + x[17, 1] + x[18, 1] + x[19, 1] +
x[20, 1] <= 10*y[1]

x[1, 2] + x[2, 2] + x[3, 2] + x[4, 2] + x[5, 2] + x[6, 2] + x[7, 2] +
x[8, 2] + x[9, 2] + x[10, 2] + x[11, 2] + x[12, 2] + x[13, 2] +
x[14, 2] + x[15, 2] + x[16, 2] + x[17, 2] + x[18, 2] + x[19, 2] +
x[20, 2] <= 10*y[2]

x[1, 3] + x[2, 3] + x[3, 3] + x[4, 3] + x[5, 3] + x[6, 3] + x[7, 3] +
x[8, 3] + x[9, 3] + x[10, 3] + x[11, 3] + x[12, 3] + x[13, 3] +
x[14, 3] + x[15, 3] + x[16, 3] + x[17, 3] + x[18, 3] + x[19, 3] +
x[20, 3] <= 10*y[3]

x[1, 4] + x[2, 4] + x[3, 4] + x[4, 4] + x[5, 4] + x[6, 4] + x[7, 4]+
x[8, 4] + x[9, 4] + x[10, 4] + x[11, 4] + x[12, 4] + x[13, 4] +
x[14, 4] + x[15, 4] + x[16, 4] + x[17, 4] + x[18, 4] + x[19, 4] +
x[20, 4] <= 7*y[4]

x[1, 5] + x[2, 5] + x[3, 5] + x[4, 5] + x[5, 5] + x[6, 5] + x[7, 5] +
x[8, 5] + x[9, 5] + x[10, 5] + x[11, 5] + x[12, 5] + x[13, 5] +
x[14, 5] + x[15, 5] + x[16, 5] + x[17, 5] + x[18, 5] + x[19, 5] +
x[20, 5] <= 20*y[5]

x[1, 6] + x[2, 6] + x[3, 6] + x[4, 6] + x[5, 6] + x[6, 6] + x[7, 6]+
x[8, 6] + x[9, 6] + x[10, 6] + x[11, 6] + x[12, 6] + x[13, 6] +
x[14, 6] + x[15, 6] + x[16, 6] + x[17, 6] + x[18, 6] + x[19, 6] +
x[20, 6] <= 5*y[6]

x[1, 7] + x[2, 7] + x[3, 7] + x[4, 7] + x[5, 7] + x[6, 7] + x[7, 7] +
x[8, 7] + x[9, 7] + x[10, 7] + x[11, 7] + x[12, 7] + x[13, 7] +
x[14, 7] + x[15, 7] + x[16, 7] + x[17, 7] + x[18, 7] + x[19, 7] +
x[20, 7] <= 18*y[7]

Nonbids must be set to 0:

x[1, 1] + x[2, 1] + x[3, 1] + x[4, 1] + x[5, 1] + x[6, 1] + x[7, 1] +
x[8, 1] + x[9, 1] + x[10, 1] = 0

x[1, 2] + x[11, 2] + x[12, 2] + x[13, 2] + x[15, 2] + x[16, 2] +
x[17, 2] + x[18, 2] + x[19, 2] + x[20, 2] = 0

x[1, 3] + x[2, 3] + x[3, 3] + x[4, 3] + x[5, 3] + x[6, 3] + x[7, 3] +
x[8, 3] + x[9, 3] + x[10, 3] = 0

x[1, 4] + x[2, 4] + x[3, 4] + x[4, 4] + x[5, 4] + x[6, 4] + x[13, 4] +
x[14, 4] + x[15, 4] + x[16, 4] + x[17, 4] + x[19, 4] + x[20, 4] = 0

x[6, 6] + x[7, 6] + x[8, 6] + x[9, 6] + x[10, 6] + x[11, 6] +
x[12, 6] + x[13, 6] + x[14, 6] + x[15, 6] + x[16, 6] + x[17, 6] +
x[18, 6] + x[19, 6] + x[20, 6] = 0

x[2, 7] + x[4, 7] = 0

No more than three carriers

y[1] + y[2] + y[3] + y[4] + y[5] + y[6] + y[7] <= 3

Solution:	Total Cost = $436,512
Carrier 2:	assigned cities 2, 3, 4, 5, 6, and 9
Carrier 5:	assigned cities 7, 8, and 10–20
Carrier 6:	assigned city 1

b.

# Carriers	Cost	Carriers Chosen
1	$524,677	5
2	$452,172	2,5
3	$436,512	2,5,6
4	$433,868	2,4,5,6
5	$433,112	1,2,4,5,6
6	$432,832	1,2,3,4,5,6
7	$432,832	1,2,3,4,5,6,7

Shipping Cost

Given the incremental drop in cost, three seems like the correct number of carriers (the curve flattens considerably after three carriers). Notice that when seven carriers are allowed, only six carriers are actually assigned a city. That is, allowing a seventh carrier provides no benefit.

13. a. Add the following multiple-choice constraint to the problem:

$y_1 + y_2 = 1$

New optimal solution: $y_1 = 1, y_3 = 1, x_{12} = 10, x_{31} = 30,$
$x_{52} = 10, x_{53} = 20$
Value = 940

b. Because one plant is already located in St. Louis, it is only necessary to add the following constraint to the model:

$y_3 + y_4 \le 1$

New optimal solution: $y_4 = 1, x_{42} = 20, x_{43} = 20, x_{51} = 30$
Value = 860

14. a. Let   1 denote the Michigan plant
2 denote the first New York plant
3 denote the second New York plant
4 denote the Ohio plant
5 denote the California plant

It is not possible to meet needs by modernizing only one plant.

The following table shows the options which involve modernizing two plants.

Plant					Transmission Capacity	Engine Block Capacity	Feasible?	Cost
1	2	3	4	5				
✓	✓				700	1300	No	
✓		✓			1100	900	Yes	60
✓			✓		900	1400	Yes	65
✓				✓	600	700	No	
	✓	✓			1200	1200	Yes	70
	✓		✓		1000	1700	Yes	75
	✓			✓	700	1000	No	
		✓	✓		1400	1300	Yes	75
		✓		✓	1100	600	No	
			✓	✓	900	1100	Yes	60

b. Modernize plants 1 and 3 or plants 4 and 5.

c. Let $x_i = \begin{cases} 1 & \text{if plant } i \text{ is modernized} \\ 0 & \text{if plant } i \text{ is not modernized} \end{cases}$

Min $25x_1 + 35x_2 + 35x_3 + 40x_4 + 25x_5$
s.t.

$300x_1 + 400x_2 + 800x_3 + 600x_4 + 300x_5 \ge 900$ Transmissions
$500x_1 + 800x_2 + 400x_3 + 900x_4 + 200x_5 \ge 900$ Engine Blocks
$x_1, x_2, x_3, x_4, x_5 \ge 0$

d. Modernize plants 1 and 3.

16. a.
Min $105x_9 + 105x_{10} + 105x_{11} + 32y_9 + 32y_{10} + 32y_{11} + 32y_{12} + 32y_1 + 32y_2 + 32y_3$

$\begin{array}{llll}
x_9 & + y_9 & & \ge 6 \\
x_9 + x_{10} & + y_9 + y_{10} & & \ge 4 \\
x_9 + x_{10} + x_{11} & + y_9 + y_{10} + y_{11} & & \ge 8 \\
x_9 + x_{10} + x_{11} & + y_9 + y_{10} + y_{11} + y_{12} & & \ge 10 \\
x_{10} + x_{11} & + y_{10} + y_{11} + y_{12} + y_1 & & \ge 9 \\
x_9 & + y_{11} + y_{12} + y_1 + y_2 & & \ge 6 \\
x_9 + x_{10} & + y_{12} + y_1 + y_2 + y_3 & & \ge 4 \\
x_9 + x_{10} + x_{11} & + y_1 + y_2 + y_3 & & \ge 7 \\
x_{10} + x_{11} & + y_2 + y_3 & & \ge 6 \\
x_{11} & + y_3 & & \ge 6 \\
\end{array}$

$x_i, y_j \ge 0$ and integer for $i = 9, 10, 11$ and $j = 9, 10, 11, 12, 1, 2, 3$

b. Use all part-time employees.
Bring on as follows: 9:00 A.M.–6, 11:00 A.M.–2, 12:00 noon–6, 1:00 P.M.–1, 3:00 P.M.–6
Cost = $672

c. Same as in part (b)

d. New solution is to bring on one full-time employee at 9:00 A.M., four more at 11:00 A.M., and part-time employees as follows:
9:00 A.M.–5, 12:00 noon–5, and 3:00 P.M.–2

18. a. 52, 49, 36, 83, 39, 70, 79, 59

b. Thick crust, cheese blend, chunky sauce, medium sausage. Six of eight consumers will prefer this pizza (75%).

20. a. New objective function: Min $25x_1 + 40x_2 + 40x_3 + 40x_4 + 25x_5$

b. $x_4 = x_5 = 1$; modernize the Ohio and California plants

c. Add the constraint $x_2 + x_3 = 1$.

d. $x_1 = x_3 = 1$

22. $x_1 + x_2 + x_3 = 3y_1 + 5y_2 + 7y_3$
$y_1 + y_2 + y_3 = 1$

24. a. $x_{111}, x_{112}, x_{121}$

b. $x_{111} + x_{112} + x_{121} \leq 1$

c. $x_{531} + x_{532} + x_{533} + x_{541} + x_{542} + x_{543} + x_{551} + x_{552} + x_{561} \leq 1$

d. Only two screens are available.

e. $x_{222} + x_{231} + x_{422} + x_{431} + x_{531} + x_{532} + x_{533} + x_{631} + x_{632} + x_{633} \leq 2$

26. Let X_i = the amount (dollars) to invest in alternative i
$i = 1, 2, \ldots 10$

$Y_i = 1$ if Dave invests in alternative i, 0 if not
$i = 1, 2 \ldots 10$

Max $0.067X_1 + 0.0765X_2 + 0.0755X_3 + 0.0745X_4 + 0.075X_5 + 0.0645X_6 + 0.0705X_7 + 0.069X_8 + 0.052X_9 + 0.059X_{10}$

Subject to

$X_1 + X_2 + X_3 + X_4 + X_5 + X_6 + X_7 + X_8 + X_9 + X_{10} = 100,000$

Invest $100,000

$X_i \leq 25,000Y_i \quad i = 1, 2, \ldots 10$

Invest no more than $25,000 in any one fund

$X_i \geq 10,000Y_i \quad i = 1, 2, \ldots 10$

If invest in a fund, invest at least $10,000 in a fund

$Y_1 + Y_2 + Y_3 + Y_4 \leq 2$

No more than 2 pure growth funds

$Y_9 + Y_{10} \geq 1$

At least 1 must be a pure bond fund

$X_9 + X_{10} \geq X_1 + X_2 + X_3 + X_4$

Amount in pure bonds must be at least that invested in pure growth funds

$X_i \geq 0 \qquad i = 1, 2, \ldots 10$

The optimal solution:

Fund	Amount Invested	Exp Return
1	$ 0	$ 0.00
2	$ 12,500	$ 956.25
3	$ 0	$ 0.00
4	$ 0	$ 0.00
5	$ 25,000	$ 1,875.00
6	$ 0	$ 0.00
7	$ 25,000	$ 1,762.50
8	$ 25,000	$ 1,725.50
9	$0	$0.00
10	$ 12,500	$ 737.50
	$100,000	$7,056.25

Chapter 12

2. a.

Min E

s.t.

$wa + wb + wc + wd + we + wf + wg = 1$
$55.31wa + 37.64wb + 32.91wc + 33.53wd + 32.48we + 48.78wf + 58.41wg \geq 33.53$
$49.52wa + 55.63wb + 25.77wc + 41.99wd + 55.30we + 81.92wf + 119.70wg \geq 41.99$
$281wa + 156wb + 141wc + 160wd + 157we + 285wf + 111wg \geq 160$
$47wa + 3wb + 26wc + 21wd + 82we + 92wf + 89wg \geq 21$

$-250E + 310wa + 278.5wb + 165.6wc + 250wd + 206.4we + 384wf + 530.1wg \leq 0$
$-316E + 134.6wa + 114.3wb + 131.3wc + 316wd + 151.2we + 217wf + 770.8wg \leq 0$
$-94.4E + 116wa + 106.8wb + 65.52wc + 94.4wd + 102.1we + 153.7wf + 215wg \leq 0$
$wa, wb, wc, wd, we, wf, wg \geq 0$

b. $E = 0.924$
$wa = 0.074$
$wc = 0.436$
$we = 0.489$

All other weights are zero.

c. D is relatively inefficient.
Composite requires 92.4 of D's resources.

d. 34.37 patient days (65 or older)
41.99 patient days (under 65)

e. Hospitals A, C, and E

4. a.

Min E

s.t.

$wb + wc + wj + wn + ws = 1$
$3800wb + 4600wc + 4400wj + 6500wn + 6000ws \geq 4600$
$25wb + 32wc + 35wj + 30wn + 28ws \geq 32$
$8wb + 8.5wc + 8wj + 10wn + 9ws \geq 8.5$
$-110E + 96wb + 110wc + 100wj + 125wn + 120ws \leq 0$
$-22E + 16wb + 22wc + 18wj + 25wn + 24ws \leq 0$
$-1400E + 850wb + 1400wc + 1200wj + 1500wn + 1600ws \leq 0$
$wb, wc, wj, wn, ws \geq 0$

b.

```
OPTIMAL SOLUTION

Objective Function Value = 0.960

    Variable        Value        Reduced Costs
    --------        -----        -------------
       E            0.960           0.000
      wb            0.175           0.000
      wc            0.000           0.040
      wj            0.575           0.000
      wn            0.250           0.000
      ws            0.000           0.085
```

c. Yes; $E = 0.960$ indicates a composite restaurant can produce Clarksville's output with 96% of Clarksville's available resources.

d. More Output (Constraint 2 Surplus) $220 more profit per week.

Less Input

Hours of Operation $110E = 105.6$ hours
FTE Staff $22 - 1.71$ (Constraint 6 Slack) $= 19.41$
Supply Expense $1400E - 129.614$ (Constraint 7
Slack) $= \$1214.39$

The composite restaurant uses 4.4 hours less operation time, 2.6 less employees, and $185.61 less supplies expense when compared to the Clarksville restaurant.

e. $wb = 0.175$, $wj = 0.575$, and $wn = 0.250$. Consider the Bardstown, Jeffersonville, and New Albany restaurants.

6. a. Flight Leg 1: $8 + 0 + 4 + 4 + 1 + 2 = 19$
Flight Leg 2: $6 + 3 + 2 + 4 + 2 + 1 = 18$
Flight Leg 3: $0 + 1 + 3 + 2 + 4 + 2 = 12$
Flight Leg 4: $4 + 2 + 2 + 1 + 6 + 3 = 18$

b. The calculation of the remaining demand for each ODIF is as follows:

ODIF	ODIF Code	Original Allocation	Seats Sold	Seats Available
1	PCQ	33	25	8
2	PMQ	44	44	0
3	POQ	45	18	27
4	PCY	16	12	4
5	PMY	6	5	1
6	POY	11	9	2
7	NCQ	26	20	6
8	NMQ	56	33	23
9	NOQ	39	37	2
10	NCY	15	11	4
11	NMY	7	5	2
12	NOY	9	8	1
13	CMQ	64	27	37
14	CMY	8	6	2
15	COQ	46	35	11
16	COY	10	7	3

c.

```
OPTIMAL SOLUTION

Objective Function Value = 15730.000

    Variable        Value        Reduced Costs
    --------      ---------      --------------
       PCQ         8.000             0.000
       PMQ         1.000             0.000
       POQ         3.000             0.000
       PCY         4.000             0.000
       PMY         1.000             0.000
       POY         2.000             0.000
       NCQ         6.000             0.000
       NMQ         3.000             0.000
       NOQ         2.000             0.000
       NCY         4.000             0.000
       NMY         2.000             0.000
       NOY         1.000             0.000
       CMQ         3.000             0.000
       CMY         2.000             0.000
       COQ         7.000             0.000
       COY         3.000             0.000
```

8. b. 65.7% small-cap growth fund
34.3% of the portfolio in a small-cap value
Expected return $= 18.5\%$

c. 10% foreign stock
50.8% small-cap fund
39.2% of the portfolio in small-cap value
Expected return $= 17.178\%$

10. Using LINGO or Excel Solver, the optimal solution is $X = 2$, $Y = -4$, for an optimal solution value of 0.

12. a. With $1000 being spent on radio and $1000 being spent on direct mail we can simply substitute those values into the sales function.

$$\begin{aligned} S &= -2R^2 - 10M^2 - 8RM + 18R + 34M \\ &= -2(2^2) - 10(1^2) - 8(2)(1) + 18(2) + 34(1) \\ &= -8 - 10 - 16 + 36 + 34 \\ &= 36 \end{aligned}$$

Sales of $36,000 will be realized with this allocation of the media budget.

b. Add a budget constraint to the sales function that is to be maximized.

$$\text{Max} \quad -2R^2 - 10M^2 - 8RM + 18R + 34M$$
s.t.
$$R + M \leq 3$$
$$R, M \geq 0$$

c. The optimal solution is to invest $2500 in radio advertising and $500 in direct mail advertising. The total sales generated will be $37,000.

14. a. The optimization model is

$$\text{Max} \quad 5L^{.25}C^{.75}$$
s.t.
$$25L + 75C \leq 75000$$
$$L, C \geq 0$$

b. The optimal solution to this is $L = 750$ and $C = 750$ for an optimal objective function value of 3750. If Excel Solver is used for this problem, we recommend starting with an initial solution that has $L > 0$ and $C > 0$.

16. a. Let OT be the number of overtime hours scheduled. Then the optimization model is

$$\text{Max} \quad -3x_1^2 + 42x_1 - 3x_2^2 + 48x_2 + 700 - 5OT$$
s.t.
$$4x_1 + 6x_2 \leq 24 + OT$$
$$x_1, x_2, OT \geq 0$$

b. The optimal solution is to schedule $OT = 8.66667$ overtime hours and produce $x_1 = 3.66667$ units of product 1 and $x_2 = 3.00000$ units of product 2 for a profit of 887.3333.

17. a. If X is the weekly production volume in thousands of units at the Dayton plant and Y is the weekly production volume in thousands of units at the Hamilton plant, then the optimization model is

Min $X^2 - X + 5 + Y^2 + 2Y + 3$

s.t.

$$X + Y = 8$$
$$X, Y \geq 0$$

b. Using LINGO or Excel Solver, the optimal solution is $X = 4.75$ and $Y = 3.25$ for an optimal objective value of 42.875.

18. Define the variables to be the dollars invested in the mutual fund. For example, IB $= 500$ means that $500 is invested in the Intermediate-Term Bond fund. The LINGO formulation is

```
MIN = (1/5)*((R1 - RBAR)^2 + (R2 - RBAR)^2 +
      (R3 - RBAR)^2 + (R4 - RBAR)^2 + (R5 -
      RBAR)^2);

0.1006*FS + 0.1764*IB + 0.3241*LG
+ 0.3236*LV + 0.3344*SG + 0.2456*SV = R1;
0.1312*FS + 0.0325*IB + 0.1871*LG
+ 0.2061*LV + 0.1940*SG + 0.2532*SV = R2;
0.1347*FS + 0.0751*IB + 0.3328*LG
+ 0.1293*LV + 0.0385*SG - 0.0670*SV = R3;
0.4542*FS - 0.0133*IB + 0.4146*LG
+ 0.0706*LV + 0.5868*SG + 0.0543*SV = R4;
-0.2193*FS + 0.0736*IB - 0.2326*LG
- 0.0537*LV - 0.0902*SG + 0.1731*SV = R5;
FS + IB + LG + LV + SG + SV = 50000;
(1/5)*(R1 + R2 + R3 + R4 + R5) = RBAR;
RBAR > RMIN;
RMIN = 5000;

@FREE(R1);
@FREE(R2);
@FREE(R3);
@FREE(R4);
@FREE(R5);
```

The optimal solution to this model using LINGO is

```
Local optimal solution found.
  Objective value:            6,784,038
  Total solver iterations:           19

  Model Title: MARKOWITZ

  Variable          Value      Reduced Cost
  --------      ------------   ------------
      R1         9478.492       0.000000
    RBAR         5000.000       0.000000
      R2         5756.023       0.000000
      R3         2821.951       0.000000
      R4         4864.037       0.000000
```

Variable	Value	Reduced Cost
R5	2079.496	0.000000
FS	7920.372	0.000000
IB	26273.98	0.000000
LG	2103.251	0.000000
LV	0.000000	208.2068
SG	0.000000	78.04764
SV	13702.40	0.000000
RMIN	5000.000	0.000000

Excel Solver will also produce the same optimal solution.

20. The optimal solution is $Q_1 = 52.223$, $Q_2 = 70.065$, $Q_3 = 37.689$, with a total cost of $25,830.

22.

Model Title: MATCHING S&P INFO TECH RETURNS

Variable	Value	Reduced Cost
R1	−0.1526620	0.000000
R2	0.7916129	0.000000
R3	0.9403282	0.000000
R4	0.1694353	0.000000
R5	−0.5132641	0.000000
R6	−0.4379140	0.000000
R7	0.2329556	0.000000
R8	0.3760108E-03	0.000000
R9	0.1671686E-01	0.000000
AAPL	0.000000	1.624161
AMD	0.1014161	0.000000
ORCL	0.8985839	0.000000

24. a. Let:

$FS =$ proportion of portfolio invested in the foreign stock mutual fund

$IB =$ proportion of portfolio invested in the intermediate-term bond fund

$LG =$ proportion of portfolio invested in the large-cap growth fund

$LV =$ proportion of portfolio invested in the large-cap value fund

$SG =$ proportion of portfolio invested in the small-cap growth fund

$SV =$ proportion of portfolio invested in the small-cap value fund

$\overline{R} =$ the expected return of the portfolio

$R_s =$ the return of the portfolio in years

Max $\bar{R}$

s.t.

$10.06FS + 17.64IB + 32.41LG + 32.36LV + 33.44SG + 24.56SV = R_1$
$13.12FS + 3.25IB + 18.71LG + 20.61LV + 19.40SG + 25.32SV = R_2$
$13.47FS + 7.51IB + 33.28LG + 12.93LV + 3.85SG - 6.70SV = R_3$
$45.42FS - 1.33IB + 41.46LG + 7.06LV + 58.68SG - 5.43SV = R_4$
$-21.93FS + 7.36IB - 23.26LG - 5.37LV - 9.02SG + 17.31SV = R_5$
$FS + IB + LG + LV + SG + SV = 1$

$$\frac{1}{5}\sum_{s=1}^{5} R_s = \bar{R}$$

$$\frac{1}{5}\sum_{s=1}^{5} (R_s - \bar{R})^2 \leq 30$$

$$FS, IB, LG, LV, SG, SV \geq 0$$

b. The optimal solution is (% are rounded to one place):

Foreign Stock	13.3%
Intermediate-Term Bond	49.6%
Large-Cap Growth	7.4%
Large-Cap Value	0.0%
Small-Cap Growth	0.0%
Small-Cap Value	29.8%
Maximum expected return = 10.45%	

26. This is a nonlinear 0-1 integer programming problem. Let $X_{ij} = 1$ if tanker 1 is assigned loading dock j and 0 if not. The optimal solution to this model is 10000.00. Tanker 1 should be assigned to dock 2, tanker 2 to dock 1, and tanker 3 to dock 3. Depending on the starting point, Excel Solver will likely get stuck at a local optimum and not find the optimal solution that LINGO finds.

28. a.

Let X = the x coordinate of the tool bin
Y = the y coordinate of the tool bin

Minimize $-(X - 1)^2 + (Y - 4)^2$
$+ \sqrt{(X - 1)^2 + (Y - 2)^2} + \sqrt{(X - 2.5)^2 + (Y - 2)^2}$
$+ \sqrt{(X - 3)^2 + (Y - 5)^2} + \sqrt{(X - 4)^2 + (Y - 4)^2}$

Solution: $X = 2.23$, $Y = 3.35$

b.

Minimize $12\sqrt{(X - 1)^2 + (Y - 4)^2}$
$+ 24\sqrt{(X - 1)^2 + (Y - 2)^2} + 13\sqrt{(X - 2.5)^2 + (Y - 2)^2}$
$+ 7\sqrt{(X - 3)^2 + (Y - 5)^2} + 17\sqrt{(X - 4)^2 + (Y - 4)^2}$

Solution: $X = 1.91$, $Y = 2.72$

c.

Distance:

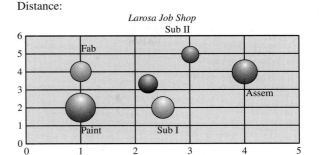

Demand-Weighted Distance

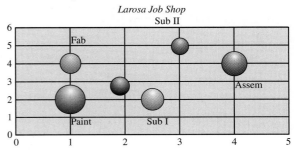

Using demand shifts the optimal location toward the paint cell (it has heavy demand).

30. Let X = the latitude of the optimal wedding location
Y = the longitude of the optimal wedding location

$$\text{Min} \sum_{i=1}^{15} R_i \left(69\sqrt{(X - lat_i)^2 + (Y - long_i)^2}\right)$$

where R_i = the number of relatives who are from the $(lat_i, long_i)$ location. The optimal solution is $X = 40.204$, $Y = -75.214$, with an objective function value of 67,444.286.

Chapter 13

2.

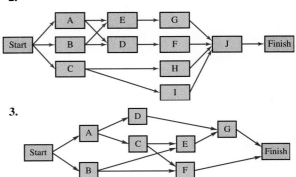

3.

4. a. A–D–G
  b. No; Time = 15 months

6. a. Critical path: A–D–F–H
  b. 22 weeks
  c. No, it is a critical activity.
  d. Yes, 2 weeks
  e. Schedule for activity E:

Earliest start	3
Latest start	4
Earliest finish	10
Latest finish	11

8. a.

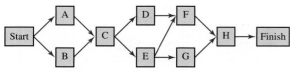

  b. B–C–E–F–H
  c.

Activity	Earliest Start	Latest Start	Earliest Finish	Latest Finish	Slack	Critical Activity
A	0	2	6	8	2	
B	0	0	8	8	0	Yes
C	8	8	20	20	0	Yes
D	20	22	24	26	2	
E	20	20	26	26	0	Yes
F	26	26	41	41	0	Yes
G	26	29	38	41	3	
H	41	41	49	49	0	Yes

  d. Yes, time = 49 weeks

10. a.

Activity	Optimistic	Most Probable	Pessimistic	Expected Times	Variance
A	4	5.0	6	5.00	0.11
B	8	9.0	10	9.00	0.11
C	7	7.5	11	8.00	0.44
D	7	9.0	10	8.83	0.25
E	6	7.0	9	7.17	0.25
F	5	6.0	7	6.00	0.11

  b. Critical activities: B–D–F
    Expected project completion time: $9.00 + 8.83 + 6.00 = 23.83$
    Variance of projection completion time: $0.11 + 0.25 + 0.11 = 0.47$

12. a. A–D–H–I
  b. 25.66 days
  c. 0.2578

13.

Activity	Expected Time	Variance
A	5	0.11
B	3	0.03
C	7	0.11
D	6	0.44
E	7	0.44
F	3	0.11
G	10	0.44
H	8	1.78

From Problem 6, A–D–F–H is the critical path, so $E(T) = 5 + 6 + 3 + 8 = 22$.
$\sigma^2 = 0.11 + 0.44 + 0.11 + 1.78 = 2.44$.

$$z = \frac{\text{Time} - E(T)}{\sigma} = \frac{\text{Time} - 22}{\sqrt{2.44}}$$

  a. Time = 21: $z = -0.64$
    Cumulative Probability = 0.2611
    $P(21 \text{ weeks}) = 0.2611$
  b. Time = 22: $z = 0.00$
    Cumulative Probability = 0.5000
    $P(22 \text{ weeks}) = 0.5000$
  c. Time = 25: $z = +1.92$
    Cumulative Probability = 0.9726
    $P(25 \text{ weeks}) = 0.9726$

14. a. A–C–E–G–H
  b. 52 weeks (1 year)
  c. 0.0174
  d. 0.0934
  e. 10 months—doubtful
    13 months—very likely
    Estimate 12 months (1 year)

16. a.

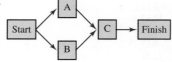

  b. B–C

Activity	Expected Time	Variance
A	6.67	2.78
B	7.50	1.36
C	1.00	0.00

Expected Time $= 7.5 + 1 = 8.5$ weeks
$\sigma^2 = 1.36 + 0 = 1.36$
$z = \dfrac{10 - 8.5}{\sqrt{1.36}} = 1.29$

Cumulative probability = 0.90

  c. A–C
    Expected Time $= 6.67 + 1 = 7.67$ weeks
    $\sigma^2 = 2.78 + 0 = 2.78$

$$z = \frac{10 - 7.67}{\sqrt{2.78}} = 1.40$$

Cumulative Probability = 0.92

P(Entire project completed) = 0.90 × 0.92 = 0.828

d. The probability estimate from (c) based on both paths is more accurate. Both paths must be completed for the entire project to be completed. These two paths only share one activity (C), which has no variability, and thus are effectively independent.

18. a.

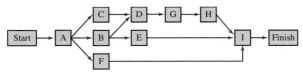

b.

Activity	Expected Time	Variance
A	1.17	0.03
B	6.00	0.44
C	4.00	0.44
D	2.00	0.11
E	3.00	0.11
F	2.00	0.11
G	2.00	0.11
H	2.00	0.11
I	1.00	0.00

Activity	Earliest Start	Latest Start	Earliest Finish	Latest Finish	Slack	Critical Activity
A	0.00	0.00	1.17	1.17	0.00	Yes
B	1.17	1.17	7.17	7.17	0.00	Yes
C	1.17	3.17	5.17	7.17	2.00	
D	7.17	7.17	9.17	9.17	0.00	Yes
E	7.17	10.17	10.17	13.17	3.00	
F	1.17	11.17	3.17	13.17	10.00	
G	9.17	9.17	11.17	11.17	0.00	Yes
H	11.17	11.17	13.17	13.17	0.00	Yes
I	13.17	13.17	14.17	14.17	0.00	Yes

c. A–B–D–G–H–I, 14.17 weeks

d. 0.0951, yes

20. a.

Activity	Maximum Crash	Crash Cost/Week
A	2	400
B	3	667
C	1	500
D	2	300
E	1	350
F	2	450
G	5	360
H	1	1000

Min $400Y_A + 667Y_B + 500Y_C + 300Y_D + 350Y_E + 450Y_F + 360Y_G + 1000Y_H$

s.t.

$$x_A + y_A \geq 3 \qquad x_E + y_E - x_D \geq 4 \qquad x_H + y_H - x_G \geq 3$$
$$x_B + y_B \geq 6 \qquad x_F + y_F - x_E \geq 3 \qquad x_H \leq 16$$
$$x_C + y_C - x_A \geq 2 \qquad x_G + y_G - x_C \geq 9$$
$$x_D + y_D - x_C \geq 5 \qquad x_G + y_G - x_B \geq 9$$
$$x_D + y_D - x_B \geq 5 \qquad x_H + y_H - x_F \geq 3$$

Maximum Crashing:

$$y_A \leq 2$$
$$y_B \leq 3$$
$$y_C \leq 1$$
$$y_D \leq 2$$
$$y_E \leq 1$$
$$y_F \leq 2$$
$$y_G \leq 5$$
$$y_H \leq 1$$

All $x, y \geq 0$

b. Crash B(1 week), D(2 weeks), E(1 week), F(1 week), G(1 week)

Total cost = $2427

c. All activities are critical.

21. a.

Activity	Earliest Start	Latest Start	Earliest Finish	Latest Finish	Slack	Critical Activity
A	0	0	3	3	0	Yes
B	0	1	2	3	1	
C	3	3	8	8	0	Yes
D	2	3	7	8	1	
E	8	8	14	14	0	Yes
F	8	10	10	12	2	
G	10	12	12	14	2	

Critical Path: A–C–E

Project completion time = $t_A + t_C + t_E = 3 + 5 + 6 = 14$ days

b. Total cost = $8400

22. a.

Activity	Max. Crash Days	Crash Cost/Day
A	1	600
B	1	700
C	2	400
D	2	400
E	2	500
F	1	400
G	1	500

Min $600Y_A + 700Y_B + 400Y_C + 400Y_D + 500Y_E + 400Y_F + 400Y_G$

s.t.

$$X_A + Y_A \geq 3$$
$$X_B + Y_B \geq 2$$
$$-X_A + X_C + Y_C \geq 5$$

$$-X_B + X_D + Y_D \geq 5$$
$$-X_C + X_E + Y_E \geq 6$$
$$-X_D + X_E + Y_E \geq 6$$
$$-X_C + X_F + Y_F \geq 2$$
$$-X_D + X_F + Y_F \geq 2$$
$$-X_F + X_G + Y_G \geq 2$$
$$-X_E + X_{FIN} \geq 0$$
$$-X_G + X_{FIN} \geq 0$$
$$X_{FIN} \leq 12$$
$$Y_A \leq 1$$
$$Y_B \leq 1$$
$$Y_C \leq 2$$
$$Y_D \leq 2$$
$$Y_E \leq 2$$
$$Y_F \leq 1$$
$$Y_G \leq 1$$
All $X, Y \geq 0$

b. Solution of the linear programming model in part (a) shows the following:

Activity	Crash	Crashing Cost
C	1 day	$400
E	1 day	500
	Total	$900

c. Total cost = Normal cost + Crashing cost
= $8400 + $900 = $9300

24. a.

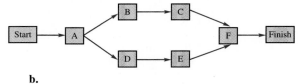

b.

Activity	Earliest Start	Latest Start	Earliest Finish	Latest Finish	Slack
A	0	0	10	10	0
B	10	10	18	18	0
C	18	18	28	28	0
D	10	11	17	18	1
E	17	18	27	28	1
F	28	28	31	31	0

c. A–B–C–F, 31 weeks
d. Crash A(2 weeks), B(2 weeks), C(1 week), D(1 week), E(1 week)
e. All activities are critical.
f. $112,500

Chapter 14

1. a. $Q^* = \sqrt{\dfrac{2DC_0}{C_h}} = \sqrt{\dfrac{2(3600)(20)}{0.25(3)}} = 438.18$

b. $r = dm = \dfrac{3600}{250}(5) = 72$

c. $T = \dfrac{250Q^*}{D} = \dfrac{250(438.18)}{3600} = 30.43$ days

d. $TC = \dfrac{1}{2}QC_h + \dfrac{D}{Q}C_0$

$= \dfrac{1}{2}(438.18)(0.25)(3) + \dfrac{3600}{438.18}(20) = \$328.63$

2. $164.32 for each; Total cost = $328.64

4. a. 1095.45
b. 240
c. 22.82 days
d. $273.86 for each; Total cost = $547.72

6. a. $Q^*_{pens} = \sqrt{\dfrac{2DC_0}{C_h}} = \sqrt{\dfrac{2(1500)(20)}{(1.50)(.10)}} = 632$ pens,

$T_{pens} = \dfrac{240Q^*}{D} = \dfrac{240(632)}{1500} = 101$ days

$Q^*_{pencils} = \sqrt{\dfrac{2DC_0}{C_h}} = \sqrt{\dfrac{2(400)(20)}{(4)(.10)}} = 200$ pencils,

$T_{pencils} = \dfrac{240Q^*}{D} = \dfrac{240(224)}{400} = 120$ days

$TC_{pens} = \dfrac{1}{2}Q_{pens}C_h + \dfrac{D}{Q_{pens}}C_0 = \dfrac{1}{2}(632)(.1)(1.5)$

$+ \dfrac{1500}{632}20 = \$94.87$

$TC_{pencils} = \dfrac{1}{2}Q_{pencils}C_h + \dfrac{D}{Q_{pencils}}C_0 = \dfrac{1}{2}(200)(.1)(4)$

$+ \dfrac{400}{200}20 = \$80$

Thus, the total cost is $94.87 + $80 = $174.87.

b. Setting the cycle times of pens and pencils equal:

$$\dfrac{240Q_{pens}}{D_{pens}} = \dfrac{240Q_{pencils}}{D_{pencils}}$$

which implies $Q_{pens} = 3.75Q_{pencils}$.

The total cost (for both pens and pencils) is:

$$TC = \dfrac{1}{2}Q_{pens}C_{h, pens} + \dfrac{D_{pens}}{Q_{pens}}C_{0, pens}$$

$$+ \dfrac{1}{2}Q_{pencils}C_{h, pencil} + \dfrac{D}{Q_{pencils}}C_{0, pencils}$$

Substituting $Q_{pens} = 3.75Q_{pencils}$ and combining like terms, we obtain

$$TC = \frac{1}{2} Q_{pencils} (3.75 C_{h,\,pens} + C_{h,\,pencils})$$

$$+ \frac{\dfrac{D_{pens} C_{0,\,pens}}{3.75} + D_{pencils} C_{0,\,pencils}}{Q_{pencils}}$$

We can solve for $Q_{pencils}$ by observing that this total cost equation is the same as

$$TC = \frac{1}{2} Q_{pencils} C_h' + \frac{(DC_0)'}{Q_{pencils}}$$

where $C_h' = 3.75 C_{h,\,pens} + C_{h,\,pencils}$ and $(DC_0)' =$
$\dfrac{D_{pens} C_{0,\,pens}}{3.75} + D_{pencils} C_{0,\,pencils}.$

Thus,

$$Q_{pencils} = \sqrt{\frac{2(DC_0)'}{C_h'}} = \sqrt{\frac{2\left(\dfrac{(1500)(15)}{3.75} + (400)(15)\right)}{3.75(.1)(1.5) + (.1)(4)}}$$

$$= 158 \text{ pencils}$$

$$Q_{pens} = 3.75(158) = 593 \text{ pens}$$

These quantities are ordered every T = (240)(593)/ 1500 = (240)(158)/400 = 95 days. The total cost (for both pens and pencils) is:

$$TC = \frac{1}{2}(593)(.1)(1.5) + \frac{1500}{593}(15) + \frac{1}{2}(158)(.1)(4)$$

$$+ \frac{400}{158}(15) = \$151.99.$$

Thus, the consolidated shipments result in annual savings of $174.87 - $151.99 = $22.88.

8. $Q^* = 11.73$, use 12
   5 classes per year
   $225,200

10. $Q^* = 1414.21$
   $T = 28.28$ days
   Production runs of 7.07 days

12. a. $Q^* = \sqrt{\dfrac{2(6000)(2345)}{\left(1 - \dfrac{6000}{16000}\right)20}} = 1500$

b. $D/Q^* = 6000/1500 = 4$ production runs
   12 months/4 = 3-month cycle time

c. Current total cost using $Q = 500$ is as follows:

$$TC = \frac{1}{2}\left(1 - \frac{D}{P}\right) Q C_h + \left(\frac{D}{C}\right) C_0 = \frac{1}{2}\left(1 - \frac{6000}{16000}\right) 500(20)$$

$$+ \frac{6000}{500}(2345) = 3125 + 28140 = \$31,265$$

Proposed Total Cost using $Q^* = 1500$ is as follows:

$$TC = \frac{1}{2}\left(1 - \frac{6000}{16000}\right) 1500(20) + \frac{6000}{1500}(2345)$$

$$= 9375 + 9380 = \$18,755$$

Change to $Q^* = 1500$
Savings = $31,265 - $18,755 = $12,510
12,510/31,265 = 40% savings over current policy

13. a. $Q^* = \sqrt{\dfrac{2DC_0}{(1 - D/P)C_h}}$

$$= \sqrt{\frac{2(7200)(150)}{(1 - 7200/25,000)(0.18)(14.50)}} = 1078.12$$

b. Number of production runs $= \dfrac{D}{Q^*} = \dfrac{7200}{1078.12} = 6.68$

c. $T = \dfrac{250Q}{D} = \dfrac{250(1078.12)}{7200} = 37.43$ days

d. Production run length $= \dfrac{Q}{P/250}$

$$= \frac{1078.12}{25,000/250} = 10.78 \text{ days}$$

e. Maximum inventory $= \left(1 - \dfrac{D}{P}\right)Q$

$$= \left(1 - \frac{7200}{25,000}\right)(1078.12)$$

$$= 767.62$$

f. Holding cost $= \dfrac{1}{2}\left(1 - \dfrac{D}{P}\right)Q C_h$

$$= \frac{1}{2}\left(1 - \frac{7200}{25,000}\right)(1078.12)(0.18)(14.50)$$

$$= \$1001.74$$

Ordering cost $= \dfrac{D}{Q} C_0 = \dfrac{7200}{1078.12}(150) = \$1001.74$

Total cost = $2003.48

g. $r = dm = \left(\dfrac{D}{250}\right)m = \dfrac{7200}{250}(15) = 432$

14. New $Q^* = 4509$

15. a. $Q^* = \sqrt{\dfrac{2DC_0}{C_h}\left(\dfrac{C_h + C_b}{C_b}\right)}$

$$= \sqrt{\frac{2(12,000)(25)}{0.50}\left(\frac{0.50 + 5}{0.50}\right)} = 1148.91$$

b. $S^* = Q^*\left(\dfrac{C_h}{C_h + C_b}\right) = 1148.91\left(\dfrac{0.50}{0.50 + 5}\right) = 104.45$

c. Max inventory $= Q^* - S^* = 1044.46$

d. $T = \dfrac{250Q^*}{D} = \dfrac{250(1148.91)}{12,000} = 23.94$ days

e. Holding $= \dfrac{(Q - S)^2}{2Q} C_h = \$237.38$

Ordering $= \dfrac{D}{Q} C_0 = \$261.12$

Backorder $= \dfrac{S^2}{2Q} C_b = \$23.74$

Total cost $= \$522.24$
The total cost for the EOQ model in Problem 4 was $547.72; allowing backorders reduces the total cost.

16. $135.55; r = dm - S;$ less than

18. $64, 24.44$

20. $Q^* = 100;$ Total cost $= \$3,601.50$

21. $Q = \sqrt{\dfrac{2DC_0}{C_h}}$

$Q_1 = \sqrt{\dfrac{2(500)(40)}{0.20(10)}} = 141.42$

$Q_2 = \sqrt{\dfrac{2(500)(40)}{0.20(9.7)}} = 143.59$

Because Q_1 is over its limit of 99 units, Q_1 cannot be optimal (see Problem 23); use $Q_2 = 143.59$ as the optimal order quantity.

Total cost $= \dfrac{1}{2}QC_h + \dfrac{D}{Q}C_0 + DC$

$= 139.28 + 139.28 + 4850.00 = \$5128.56$

22. $Q^* = 300;$ Savings $= \$480$

24. a. Cost of overestimation, $c_0 = \$9$

Cost of underestimation, $c_u = \$10 - \$9 - \$0.50 = \$0.50$

$P(\text{demand} \le Q^*) = \dfrac{c_u}{c_u + c_0} = \dfrac{0.5}{9.5} = 0.0526$

From the normal table, a cumulative probability of 0.0526 corresponds to $z = -1.62$.

Thus,

$Q^* = \mu - 1.62\sigma = 9000 - (1.62)(400) = 8352$ magazines

b. Cost of overestimation, $c_0 = \$9 - \$8 = \$1$
Cost of underestimation, $c_u = \$10 - \$9 - \$0.50 = \$0.50$

$P(\text{demand} \le Q^*) = \dfrac{c_u}{c_u + c_0} = \dfrac{0.5}{1.5} = 0.3333$

From the normal table, a cumulative probability of 0.3333 corresponds to $z = -0.43$.

Thus,

$Q^* = \mu - 0.43\sigma = 9000 - (0.43)(400) = 8828$ magazines

25. a. $c_0 = 80 - 50 = 30$
$c_u = 125 - 80 = 45$

$P(D \le Q^*) = \dfrac{c_u}{c_u + c_0} = \dfrac{45}{45 + 30} = 0.60$

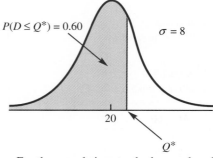

For the cumulative standard normal probability 0.60, $z = 0.25;$
$Q^* = 20 + 0.25(8) = 22$

b. $P(\text{Sell all}) = P(D \ge Q^*) = 1 - 0.60 = 0.40$

26. a. $150
b. $240 - \$150 = \$90
c. 47
d. 0.625

28. a. 440
b. 0.60
c. 710
d. $c_u = \$17$

29. a. $r = dm = (200/250)15 = 12$

b. $\dfrac{D}{Q} = \dfrac{200}{25} = 8$ orders/year

The limit of 1 stock-out per year means that $P(\text{Stock-out/cycle}) = 1/8 = 0.125.$

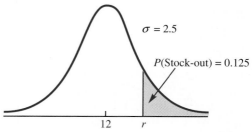

$P(\text{No stock-out/cycle}) = 1 - 0.125 = 0.875$
For cumulative probability 0.875, $z = 1.15$

Thus, $z = \dfrac{r - 12}{2.5} = 1.15$

$r = 12 + 1.15(2.5) = 14.875$ Use 15.

c. Safety stock $= 3$ units
Added cost $= 3(\$5) = \$15$/year

30. a. $Q^* = \sqrt{\dfrac{2DC_o}{C_h}} = \sqrt{\dfrac{2(52)\left(\dfrac{300}{100}\right)(15)}{(10)(.15)}} = 55.86$
≈ 56 boxes

b. $r = \mu + z\sigma = 300 + (2.33)(75) = 474.75 \approx 475$ cups.

32. a. 31.62

b. 19.8 (20); 0.2108

c. 5, $15

33. a. $1/52 = 0.0192$

b. P(No stock-out) $= 1 - 0.0192 = 0.9808$
For cumulative probability 0.9808, $z = 2.07$.

Thus, $z = \dfrac{M - 60}{12} = 2.07$

$M = \mu + z\sigma = 60 + 2.07(12) = 85$
c. $M = 35 + (0.9808)(85 - 35) = 84$

34. a. 243

b. 93, $54.87

c. 613

d. 163, $96.17

e. Yes, added cost would be only $41.30 per year.

f. Yes, added cost would be $4130 per year.

36. a. 40

b. 62.25; 7.9

c. 54

d. 36

Chapter 15

2. a. 0.4512

b. 0.6988

c. 0.3012

4.

n	P_n
0	0.3333
1	0.2222
2	0.1481
3	0.0988

$P(n > 3) = 1 - P(n <= 3) = 1 - 0.8024 = 0.1976$

5. a. $P_0 = 1 - \dfrac{\lambda}{\mu} = 1 - \dfrac{10}{12} = 0.1667$

b. $L_q = \dfrac{\lambda^2}{\mu(\mu - \lambda)} = \dfrac{10^2}{12(12 - 10)} = 4.1667$

c. $W_q = \dfrac{L_q}{\lambda} = 0.4167$ hour (25 minutes)

d. $W = W_q + \dfrac{1}{\mu} = 0.5$ hour (30 minutes)

e. $P_w = \dfrac{\lambda}{\mu} = \dfrac{10}{12} = 0.8333$

6. a. 0.3750

b. 1.0417

c. 0.8333 minutes (50 seconds)

d. 0.6250

e. Yes

8.   0.20, 3.2, 4, 3.2, 4, 0.80
Slightly poorer service

10. a. New: 1.3333, 2, 0.6667, 1, 0.6667
Experienced: 0.50, 1, 0.25, 0.50, 0.50

b. New $74; experienced $50; hire experienced

11. a. $\lambda = 2.5$; $\mu = \dfrac{60}{10} = 6$ customers per hour

$L_q = \dfrac{\lambda^2}{\mu(\mu - \lambda)} = \dfrac{(2.5)^2}{6(6 - 2.5)} = 0.2976$

$L = L_q + \dfrac{\lambda}{\mu} = 0.7143$

$W_q = \dfrac{L_q}{\lambda} = 0.1190$ hours (7.14 minutes)

$W = W_q + \dfrac{1}{\mu} = 0.2857$ hours

$P_w = \dfrac{\lambda}{\mu} = \dfrac{2.5}{6} = 0.4167$

b. No; $W_q = 7.14$ minutes; firm should increase the service rate (μ) for the consultant or hire a second consultant.

c. $\mu = \dfrac{60}{8} = 7.5$ customers per hour

$L_q = \dfrac{\lambda^2}{\mu(\mu - \lambda)} = \dfrac{(2.5)^2}{7.5(7.5 - 2.5)} = 0.1667$

$W_q = \dfrac{L_q}{\lambda} = 0.0667$ hour (4 minutes)

The service goal is being met.

12. a. 0.25, 2.25, 3, 0.15 hours, 0.20 hours, 0.75

b. The service needs improvement.

14. a. 8

b. 0.3750

c. 1.0417

d. 12.5 minutes

e. 0.6250

f. Add a second consultant.

16. a. 0.50

b. 0.50

c. 0.10 hours (6 minutes)

d. 0.20 hours (12 minutes)

e. Yes, $W_q = 6$ minutes is most likely acceptable for a marina.

18. a. $L_q = \dfrac{(\lambda/\mu)^2\lambda\mu}{(k-1)!(2\mu-\lambda)^2}P_0$

$= \dfrac{(1.8)^2(5.4)(3)}{(2-1)!(6-5.4)^2}(0.0526) = 7.67$

$L = L_q + \lambda/\mu = 7.67 + 1.8 = 9.47$

$W_q = \dfrac{L_q}{\lambda} = \dfrac{7.67}{5.4} = 1.42$ minutes

$W = W_q + 1/\mu = 1.42 + 0.33 = 1.75$ minutes

$P_W = \dfrac{1}{k!}\left(\dfrac{\lambda}{\mu}\right)^k\left(\dfrac{k\mu}{k\mu-\lambda}\right)P_0$

$= \dfrac{1}{2!}(1.8)^2\left(\dfrac{6}{6-5.4}\right)0.0526 = 0.8526$

b. $L_q = 7.67$; Yes
c. $W = 1.75$ minutes

20. a. Use $k = 2$.

$W = 3.7037$ minutes

$L = 4.4444$

$P_w = 0.7111$

b. For $k = 3$

$W = 7.1778$ minutes

$L = 15.0735$ customers

$P_N = 0.8767$

Expand post office.

21. $L_q = \dfrac{\lambda^2}{\mu(\mu-\lambda)} = \dfrac{(2.5)^2}{7.5(7.5-2.5)} = 0.1667$

$L = L_q + \dfrac{\lambda}{\mu} = 0.50$

Total cost $= \$25L + \$16$

$= 25(0.50) + 16 = \$28.50$

Two channels: $\lambda = 2.5$; $\mu = 60/10 = 6$

With $P_0 = 0.6552$,

$L_q = \dfrac{(\lambda/\mu)^2\lambda\mu}{1!(2\mu-\lambda)^2}P_0 = 0.0189$

$L = L_q + \dfrac{\lambda}{\mu} = 0.4356$

Total cost $= 25(0.4356) + 2(16) = \$42.89$

Use one consultant with an 8-minute service time.

22.

Characteristic	A	B	C
a. P_0	0.2000	0.5000	0.4286
b. L_q	3.2000	0.5000	0.1524
c. L	4.0000	1.0000	0.9524
d. W_q	0.1333	0.0208	0.0063
e. W	0.1667	0.0417	0.0397
f. P_w	0.8000	0.5000	0.2286

The two-channel System C provides the best service.

24. a. $\mu = {}^1\!/_2 = 0.5$
b. $W_q = W - 1/\mu = 10 - 1/0.5 = 8$ minutes
c. $L = \lambda W = 4(10) = 40$

26. a. 0.2668, 10 minutes, 0.6667
b. 0.0667, 7 minutes, 0.4669
c. \$25.33; \$33.34; one-channel is more economical

27. a. ${}^2\!/_8$ hours $= 0.25$ per hour
b. $1/3.2$ hours $= 0.3125$ per hour
c. $L_q = \dfrac{\lambda^2\sigma^2 + (\lambda/\mu)^2}{2(1-\lambda/\mu)}$

$= \dfrac{(0.25)^2(2)^2 + (0.25/0.3125)^2}{2(1-0.25/0.3125)} = 2.225$

d. $W_q = \dfrac{L_q}{\lambda} = \dfrac{2.225}{0.25} = 8.9$ hours

e. $W = W_q + \dfrac{1}{\mu} = 8.9 + \dfrac{1}{0.3125} = 12.1$ hours

f. Same as $P_w = \dfrac{\lambda}{\mu} = \dfrac{0.25}{0.3125} = 0.80$

80% of the time the welder is busy.

28. a. 10, 9.6
b. Design A with $\mu = 10$
c. 0.05, 0.01
d.

Characteristic	Design A	Design B
P_0	0.5000	0.4792
L_q	0.3125	0.2857
L	0.8125	0.8065
W_q	0.0625	0.0571
W	0.1625	0.1613
P_w	0.5000	0.5208

e. Design B has slightly less waiting time.

30. a. $\lambda = 42$; $\mu = 20$

i	$(\lambda/\mu)^i/i!$
0	1.0000
1	2.1000
2	2.2050
3	1.5435
Total	6.8485

j	P_j	
0	$1/6.8485$	$= -0.1460$
1	$2.1/6.8485$	$= -0.3066$
2	$2.2050/6.8485$	$= -0.3220$
3	$1.5435/6.8485$	$= -0.2254$
		1.0000

b. 0.2254

c. $L = \lambda/\mu(1 - P_k) = 42/20(1 - 0.2254) = 1.6267$

d. Four lines will be necessary; the probability of denied access is 0.1499.

32. a. 31.04%

   b. 27.58%

   c. 0.2758, 0.1092, 0.0351

   d. 3, 10.92%

34. $N = 5; \lambda = 0.025; \mu = 0.20; \lambda/\mu = 0.125$

a.

n	$\dfrac{N!}{(N-n)}\left(\dfrac{\lambda}{\mu}\right)^n$
0	1.0000
1	0.6250
2	0.3125
3	0.1172
4	0.0293
5	0.0037
Total	2.0877

$$P_0 = 1/2.0877 = 0.4790$$

b. $L_q = N - \left(\dfrac{\lambda + \mu}{\lambda}\right)(1 - P_0)$

$$= 5 - \left(\dfrac{0.225}{0.025}\right)(1 - 0.4790) = 0.3110$$

c. $L = L_q + (1 - P_0) = 0.3110 + (1 - 0.4790) = 0.8321$

d. $W_q = \dfrac{L_q}{(N - L)\lambda} = \dfrac{0.3110}{(5 - 0.8321)(0.025)}$

$$= 2.9854 \text{ minutes}$$

e. $W = W_q + \dfrac{1}{\mu} = 2.9854 + \dfrac{1}{0.20} = 7.9854$ minutes

f. Trips/day = (8 hours)(60 minutes/hour)(λ)

$$= (8)(60)(0.025) = 12 \text{ trips}$$

Time at copier: $12 \times 7.9854 = 95.8$ minutes/day

Wait time at copier: $12 \times 2.9854 = 35.8$ minutes/day

g. Yes, five assistants $\times$ 35.8 = 179 minutes (3 hours/day), so 3 hours per day are lost to waiting.

$(35.8/480)(100) = 7.5\%$ of each assistant's day is spent waiting for the copier.

Chapter 16

Simulation results will vary. These results provide general guidance on the approximate output values.

2. a. Base case: Profit = $(300 - 200) \times 4000 - 300,000 = 100,000$

Worst case: Profit = $(300 - 240) \times 0 - 300,000 = -300,000$

Best case: Profit = $(300 - 160) \times 20,000 - 300,000 = 2,500,000$

b. See Figure G16.2b. Average profit is approximately $108,681 with a probability of 0.54 of a loss. This project appears to be risky.

FIGURE G16.2b

	A	B	C	D	E	F	G
1	Madeira Manufacturing Company						
2							
3	Parameters						
4	Unit Selling Price	300					
5	Fixed Cost	300000					
6	Variable Cost	=RANDBETWEEN(B10,B11)					
7	Demand	=LN(RAND())*(−1*E10)					
8							
9	Variable Cost (Uniform Distribution)			Demand (Exponential Distribution)			
10	Smallest Value	160		Mean	4000		
11	Largest Value	240					
12							
13	Model						
14	Profit	=((B4−B6)*B7) − B5					
15							
16							
17	Simulation Trial	Unit Variable Cost	Demand		Profit	Summary Statistics	
18	1	=B6	=B7	=B14		Mean Profit	=AVERAGE(D18:D1017)
19	2	=TABLE(,D2)	=TABLE(,D2)	=TABLE(,D2)		Probability of Loss	=COUNTIF(D18:D1017,"<0")/COUNT(D18:D1017)
20	3	=TABLE(,D2)	=TABLE(,D2)	=TABLE(,D2)			
21	4	=TABLE(,D2)	=TABLE(,D2)	=TABLE(,D2)			
22	5	=TABLE(,D2)	=TABLE(,D2)	=TABLE(,D2)			
23	6	=TABLE(,D2)	=TABLE(,D2)	=TABLE(,D2)			
24	7	=TABLE(,D2)	=TABLE(,D2)	=TABLE(,D2)			
25	8	=TABLE(,D2)	=TABLE(,D2)	=TABLE(,D2)			
26	9	=TABLE(,D2)	=TABLE(,D2)	=TABLE(,D2)			
27	10	=TABLE(,D2)	=TABLE(,D2)	=TABLE(,D2)			

4. As the number of dice in the sum increases, the distribution becomes more bell-shaped. This demonstrates the central limit theorem.

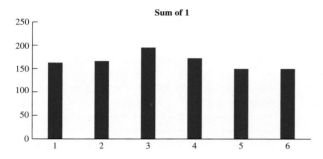

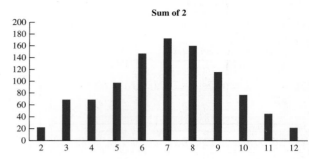

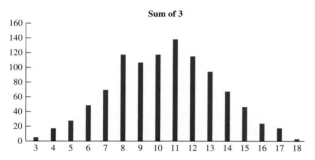

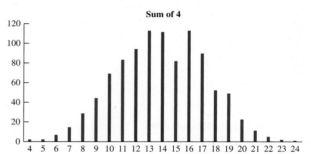

6. a.

	A	B	C	D	E	F
1	Statewide					
2						
3	Parameters					
4	Claims Payment	=VLOOKUP(RAND(),A8:C14,3,TRUE)				
5						
6	Claims Payment					
7	Lower End of Interval	Upper End of Interval	Payment	Probability		Squared Deviation From Mean
8	0	=D8+A8	0	0.83		=(C8-$F$17)^2
9	=B8	=D9+A9	500	0.06		=(C9-$F$17)^2
10	=B9	=D10+A10	1000	0.05		=(C10-$F$17)^2
11	=B10	=D11+A11	2000	0.02		=(C11-$F$17)^2
12	=B11	=D12+A12	5000	0.02		=(C12-$F$17)^2
13	=B12	=D13+A13	8000	0.01		=(C13-$F$17)^2
14	=B13	=D14+A14	10000	0.01		=(C14-$F$17)^2
15						
16	Simulation Trial	Claims Payment		Summary Statistic	Simulation Estimate	Formulaic Computation
17	1	=B4		Mean Payment	=AVERAGE(B17:B1016)	=SUMPRODUCT(C8:C14,D8:D14)
18	2	=TABLE(,H10)		Payment Standard Deviation	=STDEV.S(B17:B1016)	=SQRT(SUMPRODUCT(D8:D14,F8:F14))
19	3	=TABLE(,H10)				
20	4	=TABLE(,H10)				
21	5	=TABLE(,H10)				
22	6	=TABLE(,H10)				
23	7	=TABLE(,H10)				
24	8	=TABLE(,H10)				
25	9	=TABLE(,H10)				
26	10	=TABLE(,H10)				

b. The simulation-based estimates of the payment mean and standard deviation are $513 and $1736, respectively. Computing the mean and standard deviation directly from the distribution using the respective formulas, we obtain $400 and $1458, respectively. To reduce the discrepancy between the simulation-based estimates and the analytical computation, we can increase the number of simulation trials.

8. a.

	A	B	C	D	E	F	G	H
1	New York Stock Exchange							
2								
3	Parameters							
4	3-Month Stock Price Change	=VLOOKUP(RAND(),$A$11:$C$17,3,TRUE)						
5	3-Month Stock Price Change	=VLOOKUP(RAND(),$A$11:$C$17,3,TRUE)						
6	3-Month Stock Price Change	=VLOOKUP(RAND(),$A$11:$C$17,3,TRUE)						
7	3-Month Stock Price Change	=VLOOKUP(RAND(),$A$11:$C$17,3,TRUE)						
8								
9	3-Month Stock Price Change							
10	Lower End of Interval	Upper End of Interval	Change	Probability				
11	0	=D11+A11	−2	0.05				
12	=B11	=D12+A12	−1	0.1				
13	=B12	=D13+A13	0	0.25				
14	=B13	=D14+A14	1	0.2				
15	=B14	=D15+A15	2	0.2				
16	=B15	=D16+A16	3	0.1				
17	=B16	=D17+A17	4	0.1				
18	Model							
19	Current Stock Price	39						
20	Stock Price in 3 Months	=B19+B4						
21	Stock Price in 6 Months	=B20+B5						
22	Stock Price in 9 Months	=B21+B6						
23	Stock Price in 12 Months	=B22+B7						
24								
25	Simulation Trial	Stock Price in 3 Months	Stock Price in 6 Months	Stock Price in 9 Months	Stock Price in 12 Months		Summary Statistics	
26	1	=B20	=B21	=B22	=B23		Mean Stock Price in 12 Months	=AVERAGE(E26:E1025)
27	2	=TABLE(,G35)	=TABLE(,G35)	=TABLE(,G35)	=TABLE(,G35)		St. Dev. Stock Price in 12 Months	=STDEV.S(E26:E1025)
28	3	=TABLE(,G35)	=TABLE(,G35)	=TABLE(,G35)	=TABLE(,G35)			
29	4	=TABLE(,G35)	=TABLE(,G35)	=TABLE(,G35)	=TABLE(,G35)			
30	5	=TABLE(,G35)	=TABLE(,G35)	=TABLE(,G35)	=TABLE(,G35)			
31	6	=TABLE(,G35)	=TABLE(,G35)	=TABLE(,G35)	=TABLE(,G35)			
32	7	=TABLE(,G35)	=TABLE(,G35)	=TABLE(,G35)	=TABLE(,G35)			
33	8	=TABLE(,G35)	=TABLE(,G35)	=TABLE(,G35)	=TABLE(,G35)			
34	9	=TABLE(,G35)	=TABLE(,G35)	=TABLE(,G35)	=TABLE(,G35)			
35	10	=TABLE(,G35)	=TABLE(,G35)	=TABLE(,G35)	=TABLE(,G35)			

b. The mean stock price after 12 months is $43.51, and the standard deviation is $3.27.

c. The lowest stock price that is possible after 12 months is $31, resulting from four consecutive three-month changes of −$2. The highest stock price that is possible after 12 months is $55, resulting from four consecutive three-month changes of +$4. To model a wider range of outcomes, an unbounded distribution for the three-month change could be used. The normal distribution or skewed normal distribution may be two choices.

10. See Figure G16.10.

a. Expected project length is 33.91 weeks with a standard deviation of 2.81 weeks.

b. Probability of completing project in 35 weeks or less is 0.729.

FIGURE G16.10

	A	B	C	D	E	F	G	H	I
1	Project								
2									
3	Parameters								
4	Activity A Duration	=VLOOKUP(RAND(),A11:C14,3,TRUE)							
5	Activity B Duration	=VLOOKUP(RAND(),F11:H13,3,TRUE)							
6	Activity C Duration	=VLOOKUP(RAND(),A18:C22,3,TRUE)							
7	Activity D Duration	=VLOOKUP(RAND(),F18:H19,3,TRUE)							
8									
9	Activity A					Activity B			
10	Lower End of Interval	Upper End of Interval	Duration	Probability		Lower End of Interval	Upper End of Interval	Duration	Probability
11	0	−D11+A11	5	0.25		0	=I11+F11	3	0.2
12	=B11	=D12+A12	6	0.35		=G11	=I12+F12	5	0.55
13	=B12	=D13+A13	7	0.25		=G12	=I13+F13	7	0.25
14	=B13	=D14+A14	8	0.15					
15									
16	Activity C					Activity D			
17	Lower End of Interval	Upper End of Interval	Duration	Probability		Lower End of Interval	Upper End of Interval	Duration	Probability
18	0	=D18+A18	10	0.1		0	=I18+F18	8	0.6
19	=B18	=D19+A19	12	0.25		=G18	=I19+F19	10	0.4
20	=B19	=D20+A20	14	0.4					
21	=B20	=D21+A21	16	0.2					
22	=B21	=D22+A22	18	0.05					
23									
24	Model								
25	Project Length	=SUM(B4:B7)							
26									
27	Simulation Trial		Activity A	Activity B	Activity C	Activity D	Project Length		Summary Statistics	
28	1	=B4	=B5	=B6	=B7	=B25		Mean Project Length	=AVERAGE(F28:F1027)
29	2	=TABLE(,H33)	=TABLE(,H33)	=TABLE(,H33)	=TABLE(,H33)	=TABLE(,H33)		St. Dev. Project Length	=STDEV.S(F28:F1027)
30	3	=TABLE(,H33)	=TABLE(,H33)	=TABLE(,H33)	=TABLE(,H33)	=TABLE(,H33)		P(Project Length <36)	=COUNTIF(F28:F1027,"<36")/COUNT(F28:F1027)
31	4	=TABLE(,H33)	=TABLE(,H33)	=TABLE(,H33)	=TABLE(,H33)	=TABLE(,H33)			
32	5	=TABLE(,H33)	=TABLE(,H33)	=TABLE(,H33)	=TABLE(,H33)	=TABLE(,H33)			
33	6	=TABLE(,H33)	=TABLE(,H33)	=TABLE(,H33)	=TABLE(,H33)	=TABLE(,H33)			
34	7	=TABLE(,H33)	=TABLE(,H33)	=TABLE(,H33)	=TABLE(,H33)	=TABLE(,H33)			
35	8	=TABLE(,H33)	=TABLE(,H33)	=TABLE(,H33)	=TABLE(,H33)	=TABLE(,H33)			
36	9	=TABLE(,H33)	=TABLE(,H33)	=TABLE(,H33)	=TABLE(,H33)	=TABLE(,H33)			
37	10	=TABLE(,H33)	=TABLE(,H33)	=TABLE(,H33)	=TABLE(,H33)	=TABLE(,H33)			

12. a. Average net profit is $5,165.
   b. There is a .039 probability that the overbooking strategy will result in less than $5000 net profit (the net profit resulting from no overbooking).

	A	B	C	D	E	F
1	**South Central Airlines**					
2						
3	**Parameters**					
4	Capacity	50				
5	Number of Reservations	52				
6	Passengers Showing Up	=VLOOKUP(RAND(),A10:C14,3,TRUE)				
7						
8	**Passengers Showing Up**					
9	Lower End of Interval	Upper End of Interval	Cost	Probability		
10	0	=D10+A10	48	0.05		
11	=B10	=D11+A11	49	0.25		
12	=B11	=D12+A12	50	0.5		
13	=B12	=D13+A13	51	0.15		
14	=B13	=D14+A14	52	0.05		
15						
16	Marginal Profit	100				
17	Marginal Overbooking Cost	150				
18						
19	**Model**					
20	Profit from Reservations	=B5*B16				
21	Overbooked Passengers	=IF(B6>B4,B6–B4,0)				
22	Total Overbooking Cost	=B17*B21				
23	Net Profit	=B20–B22				
24						
25	**Simulation Trial**	**Passengers Showing Up**	**Net Profit**		**Summary Statistics**	
26	1	=B6	=B23		Mean Profit per Unit	=AVERAGE(C26:C1025)
27	2	=TABLE(,J26)	=TABLE(,J26)		P(Profit < $5000)	=COUNTIF(C26:C1025,"<5000")/COUNT(C26:C1025)
28	3	=TABLE(,J26)	=TABLE(,J26)			
29	4	=TABLE(,J26)	=TABLE(,J26)			
30	5	=TABLE(,J26)	=TABLE(,J26)			
31	6	=TABLE(,J26)	=TABLE(,J26)			
32	7	=TABLE(,J26)	=TABLE(,J26)			
33	8	=TABLE(,J26)	=TABLE(,J26)			
34	9	=TABLE(,J26)	=TABLE(,J26)			
35	10	=TABLE(,J26)	=TABLE(,J26)			

c. The same spreadsheet design can be used to simulate other overbooking strategies, including accepting 51, 53, and 54 passenger reservations. In each case, South Central would need to estimate the distribution of the number of passengers showing up and rerun the simulation model. This would enable South Central to evaluate the other overbooking alternatives and determine the most beneficial overbooking policy.

Alternatively, the distribution of passengers showing up for the flight could be modeled as a binomial random variable in which n = the reservation limit and p = probability of an individual passenger showing up for a flight.

14. See Figure G16.14.
   a. We win the bid about 64% of the time with a bid of $750,000.

FIGURE G16.14

	A	B	C	D	E	F	G	H
1	**Contractor Bidding**							
2								
3	**Parameters**							
4	Contractor A Bid	=B8+(B9–B8)*RAND()						
5	Contractor B Bid	=NORM.INV(RAND(),E8,E9)						
6								
7	**Contractor A (Uniform Distribution)**			**Contractor A (Normal Distribution)**				
8	Minimum Value	600000		Mean	700000			
9	Maximum Value	800000		Standard Deviation	50000			
10								
11	**Model**							
12	Our Bid	750000						
13	Winning Bid	=MAX(B4,B5,B12)						
14	Winning Contractor	=IF(B12>MAX(B4:B5),"US",IF(B4>B5,"A","B"))						
15								
16	**Simulation Trial**	Contractor A's Bid	Contractor B's Bid		Winning Bid	Winning Contractor	**Summary Statistics**	
17	1	=B4	=B5	=B13		=B14	P(We Win Bid)	=COUNTIF(E17:E1016,"=US")/COUNTA(E17:E1016)
18	2	=TABLE(,I8)	=TABLE(,I8)	=TABLE(,I8)		=TABLE(,I8)		
19	3	=TABLE(,I8)	=TABLE(,I8)	=TABLE(,I8)		=TABLE(,I8)		
20	4	=TABLE(,I8)	=TABLE(,I8)	=TABLE(,I8)		=TABLE(,I8)		
21	5	=TABLE(,I8)	=TABLE(,I8)	=TABLE(,I8)		=TABLE(,I8)		
22	6	=TABLE(,I8)	=TABLE(,I8)	=TABLE(,I8)		=TABLE(,I8)		
23	7	=TABLE(,I8)	=TABLE(,I8)	=TABLE(,I8)		=TABLE(,I8)		
24	8	=TABLE(,I8)	=TABLE(,I8)	=TABLE(,I8)		=TABLE(,I8)		
25	9	=TABLE(,I8)	=TABLE(,I8)	=TABLE(,I8)		=TABLE(,I8)		
26	10	=TABLE(,I8)	=TABLE(,I8)	=TABLE(,I8)		=TABLE(,I8)		

b. Bidding $765,000 results in winning approximately 75% of the time. Bidding $775,000 results in winning approximately 82% of the time. Thus, to ensure at least an 80% chance of winning the bid, we must bid $775,000.

16. See Figure G16.16. Estimates possess non-negligible variability.

FIGURE G16.16

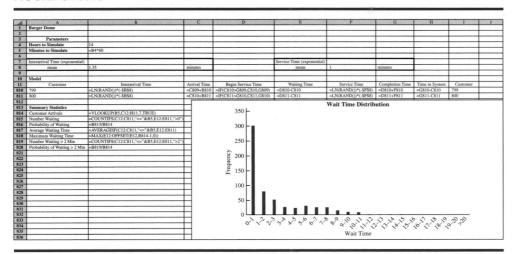

e. It is not appropriate to increase the number of trials because Burger Dome is trying to model the waiting line behavior during its 14-hour work day (and each day begins with no customers in the system from the previous day).

a. Average wait time is approximately 2.29 minutes.

b. The longest wait time varies, but 15.0 is a representative value.

c. There is an estimated probability of 0.4037 of a customer waiting more than 2 minutes.

d. See Figure G16.16.

18. Estimates possess considerable variability, but adding a second employee results in a reduced average wait time (0.16 minutes), decreased maximum wait time (5.1 minutes), and decreased probability of waiting more than 2 minutes (0.0180). Burger Dome needs to evaluate whether these improvements are worth the cost of the second employee.

20. See Figure G16.20.

FIGURE G16.20

	A	B	C	D	E
1	Blackjack				
2					
3	**Parameters**				
4	End Value of Dealer's Hand	=VLOOKUP(RAND(),A9:C14,3,TRUE)			
5	End Value of Your Hand	=VLOOKUP(RAND(),A18:C23,3,TRUE)			
6					
7	**End Value of Dealer's Hand**				
8	Lower End of Interval	Upper End of Interval	Value	Probability	
9	0	=D9+A9	17	0.1654	
10	=B9	=D10+A10	18	0.1063	
11	=B10	=D11+A11	19	0.1063	
12	=B11	=D12+A12	20	0.1017	
13	=B12	=D13+A13	21	0.0972	
14	=B13	=D14+A14	0	0.4231	
15					
16	**End Value of Your Hand**				
17	Lower End of Interval	Upper End of Interval	Value	Probability	
18	0	=D18+A18	17	0.0769	
19	=B18	=D19+A19	18	0.0769	
20	=B19	=D20+A20	19	0.0769	
21	=B20	=D21+A21	20	0.0769	
22	=B21	=D22+A22	21	0.0769	
23	=B22	=D23+A23	0	0.6155	
24					
25	**Model**				
26	Winner	=IF(B5=0,"Dealer",IF(B4>B5,"Dealer",IF(B4=B5,"Push","You")))			
27					
28	**Simulation Trial**		**Winner**	**Summary Statistics**	
29	1	=B26		P(Dealer Win)	=COUNTIF(B29:B1028,"=Dealer")/COUNTA(B29:B1028)
30	2	=TABLE(,G20)		P(Push)	=COUNTIF(B29:B1028,"=Push")/COUNTA(B29:B1028)
31	3	=TABLE(,G20)		P(You Win)	=COUNTIF(B29:B1028,"=You")/COUNTA(B29:B1028)
32	4	=TABLE(,G20)			
33	5	=TABLE(,G20)			
34	6	=TABLE(,G20)			
35	7	=TABLE(,G20)			
36	8	=TABLE(,G20)			
37	9	=TABLE(,G20)			

c. When the dealer has a 6 and you have a 16 and you decide to hit, you have about a 24.8% chance of winning, 3.9% chance of tying, and 71.3% chance of losing to the dealer.
d. When the dealer has a 6 and you have a 16 and you stay on 16, you have about a 43.5% chance of winning, 0% chance of tying, and 56.5% chance of losing to the dealer.

Chapter 17

2. a. 0.81
  b. $\pi_1 = 0.5$, $\pi_2 = 0.5$
  c. $\pi_1 = 0.6$, $\pi_2 = 0.4$

3. a. 0.10 as given by the transition probability
  b.
$$\pi_1 = 0.90\pi_1 + 0.30\pi_2 \quad (1)$$
$$\pi_2 = 0.10\pi_1 + 0.70\pi_2 \quad (2)$$
$$\pi_1 + \pi_2 = 1 \quad (3)$$
  Using (1) and (3),
$$0.10\pi_1 - 0.30\pi_2 = 0$$
$$0.10\pi_1 - 0.30(1 - \pi_1) = 0$$
$$0.10\pi_1 - 0.30 + 0.30\pi_1 = 0$$
$$0.40\pi_1 = 0.30$$
$$\pi_1 = 0.75$$
$$\pi_2 = (1 - \pi_1) = 0.25$$

4. a. $\pi_1 = 0.92$, $\pi_2 = 0.08$
  b. \$85

6. a. Given the opposing player last chose Rock, the transition matrix shows that she is most likely to choose Paper next (with probability 0.42). Therefore, you should choose Scissors (because Scissors beats Paper).
  b.

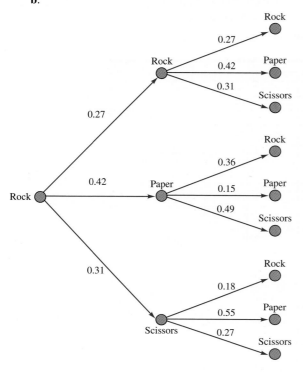

c. The one step probability matrix is
$$P = \begin{bmatrix} 0.27 & 0.42 & 0.31 \\ 0.36 & 0.15 & 0.49 \\ 0.18 & 0.55 & 0.27 \end{bmatrix}$$

The probability your opponent will choose Paper two rounds from now given she chose Rock last round is given by $\pi_2(2)$. This can be found from $\Pi(2)$ by first finding $\Pi(1)$ as follows:

$$\Pi(1) = \begin{bmatrix} 1 & 0 & 0 \end{bmatrix} \begin{bmatrix} 0.27 & 0.42 & 0.31 \\ 0.36 & 0.15 & 0.49 \\ 0.18 & 0.55 & 0.27 \end{bmatrix}$$
$$= \begin{bmatrix} 0.27 & 0.42 & 0.31 \end{bmatrix}$$

$$\Pi(2) = \begin{bmatrix} 0.27 & 0.42 & 0.31 \end{bmatrix} \begin{bmatrix} 0.27 & 0.42 & 0.31 \\ 0.36 & 0.15 & 0.49 \\ 0.18 & 0.55 & 0.27 \end{bmatrix}$$
$$= \begin{bmatrix} 0.28 & 0.35 & 0.37 \end{bmatrix}$$

So, $\pi_2(2)$ is 0.35.

8. a.
$$\pi_1 = 0.85\pi_1 + 0.20\pi_2 + 0.15\pi_3 \quad (1)$$
$$\pi_2 = 0.10\pi_1 + 0.75\pi_2 + 0.10\pi_3 \quad (2)$$
$$\pi_3 = 0.05\pi_1 + 0.05\pi_2 + 0.75\pi_3 \quad (3)$$
$$\pi_1 + \pi_2 + \pi_3 = 1 \quad (4)$$

Using (1), (2), and (4) provides three equations with three unknowns; solving provides $\pi_1 = 0.548$, $\pi_2 = 0.286$, and $\pi_3 = 0.166$.
  b. 16.6% as given by π_3
  c. Quick Stop should take
$$667 - 0.548(1000) = 119 \text{ Murphy's customers}$$
$$\text{and } 333 - 0.286(1000) = \underline{47} \text{ Ashley's customers}$$
$$\text{Total } \quad 166 \text{ Quick Stop customers}$$

10.
$$\pi_1 = 0.80\pi_1 + 0.05\pi_2 + 0.40\pi_3 \quad (1)$$
$$\pi_2 = 0.10\pi_1 + 0.75\pi_2 + 0.30\pi_3 \quad (2)$$
$$\pi_3 = 0.10\pi_1 + 0.20\pi_2 + 0.30\pi_3 \quad (3)$$
also
$$\pi_1 + \pi_2 + \pi_3 = 1 \quad (4)$$

Using equations 1, 2, and 4, we have $\pi_1 = 0.442$, $\pi_2 = 0.385$, and $\pi_3 = 0.173$.

The Markov analysis shows that Special B now has the largest market share. In fact, its market share has increased by almost 11%. The MDA brand will be hurt most by the introduction of the new brand, T-White. People who switch from MDA to T-White are more likely to make a second switch back to MDA.

12. $(I - Q) = \begin{bmatrix} 1 & 0 \\ 0 & 1 \end{bmatrix} - \begin{bmatrix} 0.4 & 0.3 \\ 0.1 & 0.5 \end{bmatrix} = \begin{bmatrix} 0.6 & -0.3 \\ -0.1 & 0.5 \end{bmatrix}$

$N = (I - Q)^{-1} = \begin{bmatrix} 1.85 & 1.11 \\ 0.37 & 2.22 \end{bmatrix}$

$$NR = \begin{bmatrix} 1.85 & 1.11 \\ 0.37 & 2.22 \end{bmatrix} \begin{bmatrix} 0.2 & 0.1 \\ 0.2 & 0.2 \end{bmatrix} = \begin{bmatrix} 0.59 & 0.41 \\ 0.52 & 0.48 \end{bmatrix}$$

0.59 probability state 3 units end up in state 1;
0.52 probability state 4 units end up in state 1.

13. $I = \begin{bmatrix} 1 & 0 \\ 0 & 1 \end{bmatrix}$ $Q = \begin{bmatrix} 0.25 & 0.25 \\ 0.05 & 0.25 \end{bmatrix}$

$$(I - Q) = \begin{bmatrix} 0.75 & -0.25 \\ -0.05 & 0.75 \end{bmatrix}$$

$$N = (I - Q)^{-1} = \begin{bmatrix} 1.3636 & 0.4545 \\ 0.0909 & 1.3636 \end{bmatrix}$$

$$NR = \begin{bmatrix} 1.3636 & 0.4545 \\ 0.0909 & 1.3636 \end{bmatrix} \begin{bmatrix} 0.5 & 0.01 \\ 0.5 & 0.5 \end{bmatrix} = \begin{bmatrix} 0.909 & 0.091 \\ 0.727 & 0.273 \end{bmatrix}$$

$$BNR = \begin{bmatrix} 4000 & 5000 \end{bmatrix} \begin{bmatrix} 0.909 & 0.091 \\ 0.727 & 0.273 \end{bmatrix} = \begin{bmatrix} 7271 & 1729 \end{bmatrix}$$

Estimate $1729 in bad debts.

14. 3580 will be sold eventually; 1420 will be lost.

16. a. The Injured and Retired states are absorbing states.
   b. Rearrange the transition probability matrix to the following:

	Injured	Retired	Backup	Starter
Injured	1	0	0	0
Retired	0	1	0	0
Backup	0.1	0.1	0.4	0.4
Starter	0.15	0.25	0.1	0.5

$$(I - Q) = \begin{bmatrix} 0.6 & -0.4 \\ -0.1 & 0.5 \end{bmatrix}$$

$$N = (I - Q)^{-1} = \begin{bmatrix} 1.923 & 1.538 \\ 0.385 & 2.308 \end{bmatrix}$$

$$NR = \begin{bmatrix} 0.423 & 0.577 \\ 0.385 & 0.615 \end{bmatrix}$$

38.5% of Starters will eventually be Injured and 61.5% will be Retired.

c. $BNR = \begin{bmatrix} 8 & 5 \end{bmatrix} \begin{bmatrix} 0.423 & 0.577 \\ 0.385 & 0.615 \end{bmatrix}$

$= \begin{bmatrix} 5.308 & 7.691 \end{bmatrix}$

We expect that 5.308 players will end up injured and 7.691 will retire.

Appendix A

2. =F6*$F$3

4.

	A	B	C	D
1	**Nowlin Plastics**			
2				
3	**Fixed Cost**	$3,000.00		
4				
5	**Variable Cost Per Unit**	$2.00		
6				
7	**Selling Price Per Unit**	$5.00		
8				
9	**Capacity**	1500		
10				
11	**Forecasted Demand**	1200		
12				
13	**Model**			
14				
15	**Production Volume**	1200		
16				
17	**Total Cost**	$5,400.00		
18				
19	**Total Revenue**	$6,000.00		
20				
21	**Total Profit (Loss)**	$600.00		
22				
23				

	A	B	C
1	**Nowlin Plastics**		
2			
3	**Fixed Cost**	3000	
4			
5	**Variable Cost Per Unit**	2	
6			
7	**Selling Price Per Unit**	5	
8			
9	**Capacity**	1500	
10			
11	**Forecasted Demand**	1200	
12			
13	**Model**		
14			
15	**Production Volume**	=IF(B11<B9,B11,B9)	
16			
17	**Total Cost**	=B3+B5*B15	
18			
19	**Total Revenue**	=B7*B15	
20			
21	**Total Profit (Loss)**	=B19-B17	
22			
23			

6. a.

	A	B	C	D	E
1	Cox Electric Breakeven Analysis				
2	Parameters				
3	Revenue per Unit	$0.65			
4				–$5,200.00	
5	Fixed Costs	$10,000.00	0	0	
6			10,000	–$6,000.00	
7	Material Cost per Unit	$0.15	20,000	–$2,000.00	
8			30,000	$2,000.00	
9	Labor Cost per Unit	$0.10	40,000	$6,000.00	
10			50,000	$10,000.00	
11			60,000	$14,000.00	
12	Model		70,000	$18,000.00	
13			80,000	$22,000.00	
14	Production Volume	12,000	90,000	$26,000.00	
15			100,000	$30,000.00	
16	Total Revenue	$7,800.00			
17			Data Table		
18	Material Cost	$1,800.00			
19	Labor Cost	$1,200.00	Row input cell:		
20	Fixed Cost	$10,000.00	Column input cell: $B$14		
21	Total Cost	$13,000.00			
22					
23	Profit	–$5,200.00	OK Cancel		
24					

Breakeven appears in the interval of 20,000 to 30,000 units.

b.

	A	B	C	D	E
1	Cox Electric Breakeven Analysis				
2					
3	Revenue per Unit	$0.65			
4					
5	Fixed Costs	$10,000.00			
6					
7	Material Cost per Unit	$0.15			
8					
9	Labor Cost per Unit	$0.10			
10					
11			Goal Seek		
12	Model				
13			Set cell: $B$23		
14	Production Volume	25,000	To value: 0		
15			By changing cell: $B$14		
16	Total Revenue	$16,250.00			
17			OK Cancel		
18	Material Cost	$3,750.00			
19	Labor Cost	$2,500.00			
20	Fixed Cost	$10,000.00			
21	Total Cost	$16,250.00			
22					
23	Profit	$0.00			
24					

8. a.

	A	B	C	D	E
1	OM 455				
2	Section 001				
3	Course Grading Scale Based on Course Average:				
4		Lower	Upper	Course	
5		Limit	Limit	Grade	
6		0	59	F	
7		60	69	D	
8		70	79	C	
9		80	89	B	
10		90	100	A	
11					
12		Midterm	Final	Course	Course
13	Lastname	Score	Score	Average	Grade
14	Benson	70	56	63.0	D
15	Chin	95	91	93.0	A
16	Choi	82	80	81.0	B
17	Cruz	45	78	61.5	D
18	Doe	68	45	56.5	F
19	Honda	91	98	94.5	A
20	Hume	87	74	80.5	B
21	Jones	60	80	70.0	C
22	Miranda	80	93	86.5	B
23	Murigami	97	98	97.5	A
24	Ruebush	90	91	90.5	A
25					
26					
27					
28			Grade	Count	
29			A	4	
30			B	3	
31			C	1	
32			D	2	
33			F	1	

	C	D
28	Grade	Count
29	A	=COUNTIF ($E$14:$E$24,C29)
30	B	=COUNTIF ($E$14:$E$24,C30)
31	C	=COUNTIF ($E$14:$E$24,C31)
32	D	=COUNTIF ($E$14:$E$24,C32)
33	F	=COUNTIF ($E$14:$E$24,C33)

b.

A	3
B	2
C	2
D	1
F	3

10. a. A portion of the spreadsheet is shown below.
   b. See column I below.

	A	B	C	D	E	F	G	H	I	J
1	Order	Quantity	Price per Roll	Revenue						
2	1	86	$195	$16,770		Quantity Ordered				
3	2	452	$155	$70,060		From	To	Price per Roll		
4	3	492	$155	$76,260		1	50	$215		
5	4	191	$175	$33,425		51	100	$195		
6	5	356	$155	$55,180		101	200	$175		
7	6	148	$175	$25,900		201	and up	$155		
8	7	342	$155	$53,010						
9	8	382	$155	$59,210						
10	9	276	$155	$42,780						
11	10	118	$175	$20,650		Total Revenue	$7,107,505			
12	11	464	$155	$71,920						
13	12	188	$175	$32,900						
14	13	25	$215	$5,375		From	To	Price per Roll	Number Orders	% of Orders
15	14	427	$155	$66,185		1	50	$215	13	7.6%
16	15	30	$215	$6,450		51	100	$195	15	8.7%
17	16	111	$175	$19,425		101	200	$175	37	21.5%
18	17	161	$175	$28,175		201	and up	$155	107	62.2%
19	18	314	$155	$48,670				Total:	172	100.0%
20	19	442	$155	$68,510						

	A	B	C	D	E	F	G	H	I	J
1	Order	Quantity	Price per Roll	Revenue						
2	1	86	=VLOOKUP(B2,$F$4:$H$7,3)	=B2*C2		Quantity Ordered				
3	2	452	=VLOOKUP(B3,$F$4:$H$7,3)	=B3*C3		From	To	Price per Roll		
4	3	492	=VLOOKUP(B4,$F$4:$H$7,3)	=B4*C4		1	50	215		
5	4	191	=VLOOKUP(B5,$F$4:$H$7,3)	=B5*C5		51	100	195		
6	5	356	=VLOOKUP(B6,$F$4:$H$7,3)	=B6*C6		101	200	175		
7	6	148	=VLOOKUP(B7,$F$4:$H$7,3)	=B7*C7		201	and up	155		
8	7	342	=VLOOKUP(B8,$F$4:$H$7,3)	=B8*C8						
9	8	382	=VLOOKUP(B9,$F$4:$H$7,3)	=B9*C9						
10	9	276	=VLOOKUP(B10,$F$4:$H$7,3)	=B10*C10						
11	10	118	=VLOOKUP(B11,$F$4:$H$7,3)	=B11*C11		Total Revenue	=SUM(D2:D173)			
12	11	464	=VLOOKUP(B12,$F$4:$H$7,3)	=B12*C12						
13	12	188	=VLOOKUP(B13,$F$4:$H$7,3)	=B13*C13						
14	13	25	=VLOOKUP(B14,$F$4:$H$7,3)	=B14*C14		=F3	=G3	=H3	Number Orders	% of Orders
15	14	427	=VLOOKUP(B15,$F$4:$H$7,3)	=B15*C15		=F4	=G4	=H4	=COUNTIF($C$2:$C$173,H15)	=I15/$I$19
16	15	30	=VLOOKUP(B16,$F$4:$H$7,3)	=B16*C16		=F5	=G5	=H5	=COUNTIF($C$2:$C$173,H16)	=I16/$I$19
17	16	111	=VLOOKUP(B17,$F$4:$H$7,3)	=B17*C17		=F6	=G6	=H6	=COUNTIF($C$2:$C$173,H17)	=I17/$I$19
18	17	161	=VLOOKUP(B18,$F$4:$H$7,3)	=B18*C18		=F7	=G7	=H7	=COUNTIF($C$2:$C$173,H18)	=I18/$I$19
19	18	314	=VLOOKUP(B19,$F$4:$H$7,3)	=B19*C19				Total:	=SUM(I15:I18)	=SUM(J15:J18)
20	19	442	=VLOOKUP(B20,$F$4:$H$7,3)	=B20*C20						

12. Error #1: The formula in cell C17
   is =SUMPRODUCT(C8:G11,B22:F25)
   but should be =SUMPRODUCT
   (C8:F11,B22:F25)

   Error #2: The formula in cell G22 is =SUM(B22:E22)
   but should be =SUM(B22:F22)

Analytic Solver Platform for Education

www.solver.com/aspe

Your new textbook, **Quantitative Methods for Business, 13e,** uses this software throughout. Here's how to get it for your course.

For Instructors:
Setting Up the Course Code

To set up a course code for your course, please email Frontline Systems at **academic@solver.com**, or call **775-831-0300**, press 0, and ask for the Academic Coordinator. Course codes MUST be renewed each year.

The course code is free, and it can usually be issued within 24 to 48 hours (often the same day). It will enable your students to download and install Analytic Solver Platform for Education with a semester-long (140 day) license, and will enable Frontline Systems to assist students with installation, and provide technical support to you during the course.

Please give the course code, plus the instructions on the reverse side, to your students. If you're evaluating the book for adoption, you can use the course code yourself to download and install the software as described on the reverse.

Instructions for Students: See reverse.
Installing Analytic Solver Platform for Education

FRONTLINE solvers

For Students:
Installing Analytic Solver Platform for Education

1) To download and install Analytic Solver Platform for Education from Frontline Systems to work with Microsoft® Excel® for Windows®, please visit:

www.solver.com/student

2) **Fill out the registration form on this page,** supplying your name, school, email address (key information will be sent to this address), course code (obtain this from your instructor), and textbook code (enter **AWMB13**).

3) On the download page, change 32-bit to 64-bit ONLY if you've confirmed that you have 64-bit Excel® (see below). **Click the Download Now** button, and save the downloaded file (**SolverSetup.exe** or **SolverSetup64.exe**).

4) **Close any Excel® windows** you have open.

5) **Run SolverSetup/SolverSetup64 to install the software.** When prompted, enter the installation password and the license activation code contained in the email sent to the address you entered on the form above.

If you have problems downloading or installing, please email **support@solver.com** or call **775-831-0300** and press 4 (tech support). Say that you have Analytic Solver Platform for Education, and have your course code and textbook code available.

If you have problems setting up or solving your model, or interpreting the results, please ask your instructor for assistance. Frontline Systems cannot help you with homework problems.

*If you have this textbook but you aren't enrolled in a course, call **775-831-0300** and press 0 for assistance with the software.*

*If you have a Mac, you'll need to install "dual-boot" or VM software, Microsoft Windows®, and Office or Excel® for Windows® first. **Excel® for Mac will NOT work.***

DO YOU HAVE 64-BIT EXCEL®?
*For Excel® 2007, always download **SolverSetup**.*
*In Excel® 2010, choose **File > Help** and look in the lower right.*
*In Excel® 2013, choose **File > Account > About Excel®** and look at the top of the dialog.*
*Download **SolverSetup64 ONLY** if you see "64-bit" displayed.*